# America Votes™ 26

# America Votes 26

## ELECTION RETURNS BY STATE

RICHARD M. SCAMMON
ALICE V. McGILLIVRAY
RHODES COOK

2003–2004

CQ PRESS

A Division of Congressional Quarterly Inc.
Washington, D.C.

CQ Press
1255 22nd Street, NW, Suite 400
Washington, DC 20037

Phone: 202-729-1900; toll-free, 1-866-427-7737 (1-866-4CQ-PRESS)

Web: www.cqpress.com

⊗ The paper used in this publication exceeds the requirements of the American National Standard for Information Sciences—Permanence of Paper for Printed Library Materials, ANSI Z39.48-1992.

Printed and bound in the United States of America

09  08  07  06  05      1  2  3  4  5

ISBN: 1-56802-974-8
ISSN: 0065-678X

# Contents

# List of Maps

# Introduction

Everyone knew the election of 2004 was for high stakes. It was the first presidential contest to be held after the al-Qaida attacks of 9/11; the first after the start of the bloody war in Iraq; the first after a state court in Massachusetts approved gay marriage; and the first since George W. Bush initially won the White House in 2000 on a split decision—winning the electoral vote but losing the popular vote.

To his critics, virtually everything about Bush was controversial—from the furor over his initial election to the president's embrace of an ideologically conservative agenda driven by an assertive leadership style. And the campaign of 2004 was waged against the backdrop of an uncertain economy, with both parties evenly matched—unified and well-financed for their rendezvous with the electorate.

Taken together, all these factors created a volatile political cocktail, which for the first time in decades produced an election in which nearly everyone agreed that it made a difference who won. In the end, there was little doubt that the election of 2004 was a victory for Bush and his Republican Party, but how great a victory is in the eye of the beholder.

Viewed from one angle, Republicans scored a decisive triumph that they claimed gave President Bush a mandate, which he quickly moved to assert after the November 2 balloting. From another perspective, the president's victory over Democrat John Kerry appeared tepid at best.

The twenty-sixth volume of *America Votes* details in numerical form the sweep of the 2004 election cycle, from the four gubernatorial elections in 2003, through the 2004 primary season, to the focus of this book—the November 2004 general election for president, Congress, and nearly a dozen governorships.

Looking at the results from the GOP vantage point, the election of 2004 was a remarkable success. Republicans fashioned a clear message that combined support for traditional family values and Bush's decisive leadership at home and abroad, while sharply questioning the suitability of Kerry to lead in troubled times. The GOP buttressed its effort with a focused advertising campaign and a quietly effective voter-targeting

## 2004: An Affirmation of Republican Rule

The Republicans tightened their grip on both ends of Pennsylvania Avenue in the 2004 election and maintained a majority of the nation's governorships. President George W. Bush was reelected with popular and electoral vote majorities, unlike in the 2000 election, when he lost the nationwide popular vote. Meanwhile, Republicans padded their majorities in both the Senate and the House of Representatives in 2004.

The chart below reflects partisan totals immediately before and after the 2004 general election. The preelection House totals include two Republican vacancies—in Florida and Nebraska—that are credited to the Republicans in the preelection count.

|  | Preelection | | | Postelection | | |
|---|---|---|---|---|---|---|
|  | Rep. | Dem. | Other | Rep. | Dem. | Other |
| Governor | 28 | 22 | 0 | 28 | 22 | 0 |
| Senate | 51 | 48 | 1 | 55 | 44 | 1 |
| House | 229 | 205 | 1 | 232 | 202 | 1 |

operation that in the end the Democrats could not match.

The result: Republicans strengthened their grip on both ends of Pennsylvania Avenue and maintained a clear majority of the nation's governorships in a history-making election that produced the nation's highest voter turnout ever.

For the first time since 1988, a presidential candidate captured a majority of the popular vote: Bush took 51 percent. For the first time since 1924, the GOP both reelected a president and won control of both the Senate and the House of Representatives. For the first time ever, a presidential candidate won more than 60 million votes, as Bush easily surpassed the previous record of nearly 54.5 million set by Ronald Reagan in 1984.

## Counting the 2004 Vote

The votes for president and the House of Representatives closely tracked each other in 2004, as Republicans won a majority of the vote at each level by roughly 3 million votes over the Democrats. The GOP also captured a majority of the Senate seats at stake, although Democrats won more votes, due in large part to their landslide Senate wins in California, Illinois, and New York. No blank and void ballots are included in the totals below. They are based on official returns for the presidential election, 15 gubernatorial contests (11 held in 2004, 4 in 2003), and 34 Senate races, as well as two versions of the House vote. "All Races" feature the results from every district in which a vote was taken. "Contested Races" are those in which both the Democrats and the Republicans fielded candidates.

| Office | Total Vote | Republican | Democratic | Other | Rep.-Dem. Plurality | Percentage of Total Vote | | |
| --- | --- | --- | --- | --- | --- | --- | --- | --- |
| | | | | | | Rep. | Dem. | Other |
| President | 122,295,345 | 62,040,610 | 59,028,439 | 1,226,296 | 3,012,171 R | 50.7% | 48.3% | 1.0% |
| Governor | 27,270,255 | 13,388,113 | 11,887,358 | 1,994,784 | 1,500,755 R | 49.1% | 43.6% | 7.3% |
| Senate | 86,225,383 | 39,920,857 | 44,010,885 | 2,293,641 | 4,090,028 D | 46.3% | 51.0% | 2.7% |
| House | | | | | | | | |
| All Races | 111,910,944 | 56,112,991 | 53,102,422 | 2,695,531 | 3,010,569 R | 50.1% | 47.5% | 2.4% |
| Contested Races | 99,458,935 | 49,370,747 | 48,453,450 | 1,634,738 | 917,297 R | 49.6% | 48.7% | 1.6% |

The incumbent prevailed in the face of a record high turnout of 122 million voters, almost 17 million more than turned out four years earlier. On the eve of the election, it was widely believed that a large turnout would benefit the challenger, but rather than fueling a vote for change, the additional ballots benefited Bush the most.

Although Kerry won 59 million votes, fully 8 million more than Democratic nominee Al Gore received in 2000,

## 2004: Close House Races

A total of 11 House members, only three of them incumbents, were elected to a seat in the 109th Congress in November 2004 with less than 52 percent of the total vote. The number of such close races was less than half the total in 2002, when there were 25 sub-52 percent House winners. An asterisk (*) indicates a member who won his or her first election to the House in November 2004. A pound sign (#) indicates that the percentage reflects the result of a runoff election.

| Republicans (5) | 2004 Winning Percentage | Democrats (6) | 2004 Winning Percentage |
| --- | --- | --- | --- |
| Mike Sodrel, Ind. 9* | 49.5% | Charlie Melancon, La. 3* | 50.2%# |
| John R. "Randy" Kuhl Jr., N.Y. 29* | 50.7% | John Salazar, Colo. 3* | 50.6% |
| Jim Gerlach, Pa. 6 | 51.0% | Brian Higgins, N.Y. 27* | 50.7% |
| Marilyn Musgrave, Colo. 4 | 51.0% | Chet Edwards, Texas 17 | 51.2% |
| Dave Reichert, Wash. 8* | 51.5% | Melissa Bean, Ill. 8* | 51.7% |
| | | John Barrow, Ga. 12* | 51.8% |

Bush increased his total from four years earlier by more than 11.5 million votes—the largest jump in a president's tally since Richard Nixon increased his 1968 total by more than 15 million votes in 1972.

The power of the moral values issue no doubt played a hand in the Bush upsurge. In the 11 primarily small states in the Republican heartland, where a ban on gay marriage was also on the November ballot, Bush gained more than two and a quarter million votes more than he did in 2000.

The trauma of 9/11 was also very much a driving force in the three states within a close radius of ground zero—New York, New Jersey, and Connecticut. In those three states alone, Bush gained an additional one million votes compared to the 2000 election. The increase was not enough for him to even come close to carrying any of the three, but the huge gain in his vote total spoke to the power of terrorism, and the president's handling of it, in the 2004 election.

The increase in Bush's vote from four years earlier was broad based, as his share went up in all but three states: North Carolina, South Dakota, and Vermont. Nationwide exit polls showed the president running better than in 2000 among Hispanics, Jews, Catholics, women, and suburbanites—all groups that some observers had predicted would form the pillars of an emerging Democratic majority.

It may be too soon to talk of a Republican realignment, but there is little doubt that the election of 2004 provided

# The House since 1990: From Democratic to Republican

The House of Representatives went from Democratic (D) to Republican (R) control in 1994, fueled in large part by the GOP upsurge in the South. Republican dominance in the region has since enabled the party to maintain their House majority even though the size of that majority has tended to contract and expand like an accordion. An "I" indicates Independent.

| | South | | | | West | | | Midwest | | | East | | | | Total House | | | |
|---|---|---|---|---|---|---|---|---|---|---|---|---|---|---|---|---|---|---|
| | R | D | I | | R | D | | R | D | | R | D | I | | R | D | I | |
| 1990 | 44 | 85 | 0 | D | 37 | 48 | D | 45 | 68 | D | 41 | 66 | 1 | D | 167 | 267 | 1 | D |
| 1992 | 52 | 85 | 0 | D | 38 | 55 | D | 44 | 61 | D | 42 | 57 | 1 | D | 176 | 258 | 1 | D |
| 1994 | 73 | 64 | 0 | R | 53 | 40 | R | 59 | 46 | R | 45 | 54 | 1 | D | 230 | 204 | 1 | R |
| 1996 | 82 | 55 | 0 | R | 51 | 42 | R | 55 | 50 | R | 39 | 60 | 1 | D | 227 | 207 | 1 | R |
| 1998 | 82 | 55 | 0 | R | 49 | 44 | R | 54 | 51 | R | 38 | 61 | 1 | D | 223 | 211 | 1 | R |
| 2000 | 81 | 55 | 1 | R | 43 | 50 | D | 57 | 48 | R | 40 | 59 | 1 | D | 221 | 212 | 2 | R |
| 2002 | 85 | 57 | 0 | R | 46 | 52 | D | 61 | 39 | R | 37 | 57 | 1 | D | 229 | 205 | 1 | R |
| 2004 | 91 | 51 | 0 | R | 45 | 53 | D | 60 | 40 | R | 36 | 58 | 1 | D | 232 | 202 | 1 | R |
| Net Change in GOP Seats, 1990–2004 | +47 | | | | +8 | | | +15 | | | −5 | | | | +65 | | | |

EAST—Connecticut, Delaware, Maine, Maryland, Massachusetts, New Hampshire, New Jersey, New York, Pennsylvania, Rhode Island, Vermont, West Virginia.
MIDWEST—Illinois, Indiana, Iowa, Kansas, Michigan, Minnesota, Missouri, Nebraska, North Dakota, Ohio, South Dakota, Wisconsin.
SOUTH—Alabama, Arkansas, Florida, Georgia, Kentucky, Louisiana, Mississippi, North Carolina, Oklahoma, South Carolina, Tennessee, Texas, Virginia.
WEST—Alaska, Arizona, California, Colorado, Hawaii, Idaho, Montana, Nevada, New Mexico, Oregon, Utah, Washington, Wyoming.

new evidence that the pendulum of American politics continues to swing steadily in the Republicans' direction since "the perfect tie" of 2000.

Yet the outcome of the 2004 election could be argued round or argued flat. In short, there is also a compelling set of data that points to a more hopeful scenario for the Democrats.

Bush's margin of victory in the popular vote—barely 3 million—was the smallest for any reelected president since Harry Truman scored his fabled come-from-behind victory in 1948. Then, less than half as many votes were cast as in 2004.

Bush's 35-vote margin of victory in the electoral college was the smallest for any reelected president since Woodrow Wilson won by 23 in 1916. Other than Wilson's, there has been no other successful presidential reelection in the electoral college as narrow as Bush's since the founding of the Republic.

To boot, Bush won the popular vote by only 2.4 percentage points—the smallest margin of victory for a reelected president in the nation's history.

The scope of Bush's victory in 2004 looked impressive when compared to his father's 1992 reelection defeat or "W's" own win on a split decision in 2000, when he won the electoral vote by five but lost the popular vote by more than a half million.

His victory looked a lot less gaudy when compared to recent incumbents Lyndon Johnson, Richard Nixon, and Ronald Reagan, who parlayed their popularity (and their opponents' weakness) into reelection landslides that exceeded 15 million votes, or for that matter, Bush's predecessor, Bill Clinton, who won a second term in 1996 by a margin of more than 8 million votes.

Neither Bush nor Kerry came close to running a 50-state campaign in 2004, operating instead on the closely divided electoral map from 2000 with its sharply defined red and blue shadings. Both candidates conceded huge chunks of the country to the other, to the extent that it could be argued that Bush's triumph in 2004 was less a rousing nationwide vote of approval than a more limited triumph based largely in one region, the South.

# 2004: Defeated Incumbents

The election of 2004 was the latest in a string of favorable ones for congressional incumbents. Only one sitting senator, Democrat Tom Daschle of South Dakota, was defeated. Only nine House members were defeated in the primaries and general election, six of whom were in Texas, where a Republican-orchestrated redistricting plan altered the congressional district lines before the election.

The chart below lists the gubernatorial, Senate, and House incumbents defeated in the 2004 primaries and general election, the number of terms they had served in that office before their loss in 2004, the percentage of the total vote they had received in the previous general election (1998 for senators, 2000 or 2002 for governors, and 2002 for House members), and their percentage of the total vote in the 2004 general election (for those who were not beaten in the primaries). The symbol "@" indicates a candidate who was not elected to the position he or she held at the time of the 2004 election. A pound sign (#) indicates that Republican governor Olene Walker of Utah was denied nomination at a preprimary convention.

| | Number of Terms | Previous Election Percentage | 2004 Election Percentage |
|---|---|---|---|
| GOVERNORS (4) | | | |
| Primaries | | | |
| *(1 Democrat, 1 Republican)* | | | |
| Bob Holden, D-Mo. | 1 | 49.1% | — |
| Olene Walker, R-Utah# | @ | — | — |
| | | | |
| General Election | | | |
| *(1 Democrat, 1 Republican)* | | | |
| Craig Benson, R-N.H. | 1 | 58.6% | 48.9% |
| Joseph E. Kernan, D-Ind. | @ | — | 45.5% |
| | | | |
| SENATOR (1) | | | |
| Primaries | | | |
| *(None)* | | | |
| | | | |
| General Election | | | |
| *(1 Democrat)* | | | |
| Tom Daschle, D-S.D. | 3 | 62.1% | 49.4% |
| | | | |
| REPRESENTATIVES (9) | | | |
| Primaries | | | |
| *(2 Democrats)* | | | |
| Chris Bell, D-Texas 9 | 1 | 54.8% | — |
| Ciro D. Rodriguez, D-Texas 28 | 3 | 71.1% | — |
| | | | |
| General Election | | | |
| *(5 Democrats, 2 Republicans)* | | | |
| Max Burns, R-Ga. 12 | 1 | 55.2% | 48.2% |
| Philip M. Crane, R-Ill. 8 | 17 | 57.4% | 48.3% |
| Martin Frost, D-Texas 32 | 13 | 64.7% | 44.0% |
| Baron P. Hill, D-Ind. 9 | 3 | 51.2% | 49.0% |
| Nick Lampson, D-Texas 2 | 4 | 58.6% | 42.9% |
| Max Sandlin, D-Texas 1 | 4 | 56.4% | 37.7% |
| Charles W. Stenholm, D-Texas 19 | 13 | 51.4% | 40.1% |

President Bush swept the 13 states of the South (the 11 of the old Confederacy plus Kentucky and Oklahoma) by nearly 6 million votes, but was beaten by Kerry in the rest of the country by almost 3 million. In electoral votes, Bush won 168 to 0 in the South, while Kerry won 251 to 118 outside the South. If Democrats have problems in rural America, Republicans have concerns almost as troubling in the large metropolitan areas of the Northeast, Midwest, and West.

The Republican showing in the election of 2004 was truly impressive when one moves beyond the presidential race to consider the totality of the GOP victory. In short, it was a notable victory for "Team Republican" as a whole.

Republicans in 2004 continued to strengthen their majorities on Capitol Hill. Since the election of 2000, GOP numbers in the Senate have swelled to 55 seats, from 50, and in the House to 232 seats from 221. The Republican Senate total after this election tied the party's highest number since the eve of the New Deal; the number of Republican House members was the highest postelection total for the party since 1946. In the process, Republicans have gone from razor-thin majorities in both houses of Congress to a more clear-cut advantage.

The 2004 election produced an unusual congruency in the nationwide voting for president and the House of Representatives—with the GOP majorities 3 million votes at both levels. This congruency was literally a generation in the making. Through much of the latter half of the twentieth century, Republicans dominated the balloting for president, Democrats for Congress. In 2000, the popular vote for president leaned slightly Democratic, the aggregate House vote leaned slightly Republican—each by roughly a half million votes.

In 2004, however, Republicans enjoyed a similar advantage in both the presidential and the congressional balloting. Bush defeated Kerry in the presidential vote by 2.4 percentage points—50.7 percent to 48.3 percent—and took 53 percent of the electoral vote. Republicans outpolled the Democrats in the nationwide House vote by 2.6 points—50.1 percent to 47.5 percent—and took 53 percent of all House seats.

Yet the election of 2004 was arguably as much about incumbency as anything else. Only one Senate incumbent, Democratic Senate minority leader Tom Daschle of South Dakota, was defeated in the November balloting. He was ousted by the margin of one percentage point.

Only seven incumbents lost in the House of Representatives, with most of the carnage concentrated in the president's home state of Texas. There, a controversial GOP-orchestrated redistricting in 2003 led to the defeat of four veteran Democratic House members in November 2004.

Two of the passel of governors up this year lost their bids for another term, but only one, Craig Benson of New Hampshire, had been elected to the post. The other,

Joseph E. Kernan of Indiana, ascended to the governorship in 2003 upon the death of his predecessor, Frank O'Bannon.

In the presidential race, Bush effectively underscored the value of incumbency in 2004 as he made an updated version of "don't change horses in the middle of the stream" a major theme that played particularly well in a campaign where fear of terrorism was a driving concern.

After all the effort and all the money spent, neither the presidential nor the congressional map changed that much in 2004. Republican Senate gains were concentrated in the GOP's strongest region, the South, where they picked up five open Democratic seats. Republican House gains were mainly in Texas, where the party picked up four seats. In the presidential election, only three states switched from one party to another: New Hampshire to Kerry, Iowa and New Mexico to Bush. All were states decided by less than 10,000 votes in 2000 and all were close again in 2004.

Undeniably, the election of 2004 was a Republican victory, but by historical standards, it was a tenuous one, in which the lines between the Democratic and Republican parts of the country so evident in 2000 continued to be deeply etched.

## The Methodology

The twenty-sixth volume of *America Votes* follows the general pattern used in previous editions of this series. The introduction, with text and tables, ties together various aspects of the 2004 election cycle. The section that follows contains tables with state-by-state voter turnout and vote for presidential, gubernatorial, Senate, and House elections in the 2004 election cycle. There are also a summary of special election results held between the general elections of 2002 and 2004 to fill vacancies in the 108th Congress and a listing of changes in congressional membership in the 109th Congress that occurred between the 2004 general election and the middle of September 2005.

Following this introductory material is the heart of the volume, 50 chapters—one for each state—plus an abbreviated chapter for the District of Columbia. Each state chapter begins with a profile sheet listing the current governor, senators, and representatives followed by tables of the statewide vote for president, governor, and senator from 1946 or 1948 to the present. Following this information is a map of the state showing its counties, major population centers, and congressional districts for members of the House in the 109th Congress. (For several states, additional maps of large metropolitan areas are also provided.) Following the map(s) are the county-by-county tables of presidential, gubernatorial, and Senate elections. These tables cover the 2004 general election, as well as the gubernatorial contests in California, Kentucky, Louisiana, and Mississippi, which were held in 2003.

The county tables for presidential, gubernatorial, and Senate elections feature a three-column format (Republican, Democratic, Other). The only exceptions are for elections where another candidate received at least 10 percent of the vote, in which case a column for his or her vote is also included. All the county tables include 2000 population figures from the Census Bureau.

The county tables are followed by a listing of votes cast for candidates for the House of Representatives, arranged by congressional district. The 2000 Census results led to redistricting changes in all multimember states before the 2002 election, with the exception of Maine, which drew new congressional district lines after 2002. There were also post-2002 district line changes in Pennsylvania and Texas, although only those in Texas had major political ramifications. Votes for House members are for the districts as defined for the 109th Congress. Results for elections before 2002 (and in the case of Texas before 2004) are not included except for states with a single member in the House.

The conclusion of each state chapter consists of two parts. The first is the notes section containing a breakdown of votes cast in the general election for third-party, independent, and write-in candidates. For those major party candidates who also ran on a third-party ballot line, votes are aggregated as Democratic or Republican. Blank spaces by a contest indicate that there were no votes cast in these categories. The second part provides primary election results for president, governor, Senate, and House held in the 2004 election cycle.

In the chapters for New England states, tables list the votes for president, governor, and senator by larger cities and towns as well as by counties. In Rhode Island, the results are listed for all cities and towns.

*America Votes* is compiled from official results obtained from election authorities in each state. Although complete accuracy is always the goal, it can sometimes prove elusive in a work such as this. On occasion, states may belatedly report changes in their vote totals after publication of this volume, and human nature being what it is, there is always an example or two of self-inflicted errors. The goal is always to keep these to a minimum.

There is the desire to make these reference volumes as useful as possible to readers and researchers. Suggestions concerning new materials and corrections of data are welcome.

As in the preparation of *America Votes 23, 24,* and *25,* heartfelt thanks are in order to the Federal Election Commission's Eileen J. Canavan, with whom I consulted in an effort to reconcile discrepancies in vote totals.

Thanks also to David Arthur and his colleagues at CQ Press, particularly Gwenda Larsen, who once again helped edit and shepherd the day-to-day movement of copy with skill and good humor. Her work, as well as that of others at the Press, enabled this project to be completed in the time frame that it was.

Rhodes Cook
September 2005

# ERRATA
## America Votes 25

The following corrections should be made in the previous edition of *America Votes,* covering the 2001–2002 election cycle.

Page 7. In the summary of 2001–2002 special House elections, the contests were to fill vacancies in the 107th Congress.

Page 23. The winner of the 1980 presidential vote in Alaska was Republican Ronald Reagan.

Page 99. The Democratic candidate for governor in Georgia in 1946 was Eugene Talmadge.

Page 327. The winner of the 2000 presidential vote in New York was Democrat Al Gore.

# America Votes™ 26

# UNITED STATES

## VOTER TURNOUT 2004

| State | 2004 Voting Age Population | Registration: 2004 General Election | Percentage Voting Age Registered | Presidential Vote | Presidential Vote as Percentage of | | U.S. House Vote | Senate Vote | Governor Vote |
|---|---|---|---|---|---|---|---|---|---|
| | | | | | Voting Age Population | Registered Voters | | | |
| Alabama | 3,419,000 | 2,842,985 | 83.2% | 1,883,449 | 55.1% | 66.2% | 1,792,759 | 1,839,066 | — |
| Alaska | 447,000 | 473,927 | 106.0% | 312,598 | 69.9% | 66.0% | 299,996 | 308,315 | — |
| Arizona | 3,768,000 | 2,643,331 | 70.2% | 2,012,585 | 53.4% | 76.1% | 1,871,445 | 1,961,677 | — |
| Arkansas | 2,057,000 | 1,684,684 | 81.9% | 1,054,945 | 51.3% | 62.6% | 791,240 | 1,039,349 | — |
| California | 20,754,000 | 16,557,273 | 79.8% | 12,421,852 | 59.9% | 75.0% | 11,623,753 | 12,053,295 | 8,657,915 |
| Colorado | 3,275,000 | 3,114,566 | 95.1% | 2,130,330 | 65.0% | 68.4% | 2,039,011 | 2,107,554 | — |
| Connecticut | 2,390,000 | 2,044,181 | 85.5% | 1,578,769 | 66.1% | 77.2% | 1,428,738 | 1,424,726 | — |
| Delaware | 601,000 | 553,885 | 92.2% | 375,190 | 62.4% | 67.7% | 356,045 | — | 365,008 |
| Florida | 11,904,000 | 10,301,290 | 86.5% | 7,609,810 | 63.9% | 73.9% | 5,627,494 | 7,429,894 | — |
| Georgia | 6,135,000 | 4,951,955 | 80.7% | 3,301,875 | 53.8% | 66.7% | 2,960,763 | 3,220,981 | — |
| Hawaii | 877,000 | 647,238 | 73.8% | 429,013 | 48.9% | 66.3% | 416,570 | 415,347 | — |
| Idaho | 985,000 | 798,015 | 81.0% | 598,447 | 60.8% | 75.0% | 572,426 | 503,932 | — |
| Illinois | 8,544,000 | 7,499,488 | 87.8% | 5,274,322 | 61.7% | 70.3% | 4,988,665 | 5,141,520 | — |
| Indiana | 4,572,000 | 4,296,602 | 94.0% | 2,468,002 | 54.0% | 57.4% | 2,416,251 | 2,428,233 | 2,448,498 |
| Iowa | 2,190,000 | 2,106,658 | 96.2% | 1,506,908 | 68.8% | 71.5% | 1,458,161 | 1,479,228 | — |
| Kansas | 1,954,000 | 1,591,428 | 81.4% | 1,187,756 | 60.8% | 74.6% | 1,156,383 | 1,129,022 | — |
| Kentucky | 3,134,000 | 2,794,286 | 89.2% | 1,795,882 | 57.3% | 64.3% | 1,635,243 | 1,724,362 | 1,083,443 |
| Louisiana | 3,310,000 | 2,923,395 | 88.3% | 1,943,106 | 58.7% | 66.5% | 1,545,982 | 1,848,056 | 1,407,842 |
| Maine | 984,000 | 1,023,956 | 104.1% | 740,752 | 75.3% | 72.3% | 710,176 | — | — |
| Maryland | 3,804,000 | 3,074,889 | 80.8% | 2,386,678 | 62.7% | 77.6% | 2,255,955 | 2,323,183 | — |
| Massachusetts | 4,501,000 | 4,098,634 | 91.1% | 2,912,388 | 64.7% | 71.1% | 2,580,955 | — | — |
| Michigan | 7,289,000 | 7,164,047 | 98.3% | 4,839,252 | 66.4% | 67.5% | 4,631,058 | — | — |
| Minnesota | 3,658,000 | 3,559,400 | 97.3% | 2,828,387 | 77.3% | 79.5% | 2,721,681 | — | — |
| Mississippi | 2,155,000 | 1,791,666 | 83.1% | 1,152,145 | 53.5% | 64.3% | 1,116,203 | — | 894,487 |
| Missouri | 4,242,000 | 4,194,146 | 98.9% | 2,731,364 | 64.4% | 65.1% | 2,667,023 | 2,706,402 | 2,719,599 |
| Montana | 709,000 | 638,474 | 90.1% | 450,445 | 63.5% | 70.6% | 444,230 | — | 446,146 |
| Nebraska | 1,256,000 | 1,160,199 | 92.4% | 778,186 | 62.0% | 67.1% | 764,972 | — | — |
| Nevada | 1,528,000 | 1,071,101 | 70.1% | 829,587 | 54.3% | 77.5% | 791,433 | 810,068 | — |
| New Hampshire | 942,000 | 855,861 | 90.9% | 677,738 | 71.9% | 79.2% | 651,566 | 657,086 | 667,020 |
| New Jersey | 5,702,000 | 5,005,959 | 87.8% | 3,611,691 | 63.3% | 72.1% | 3,284,595 | — | — |
| New Mexico | 1,322,000 | 1,105,372 | 83.6% | 756,304 | 57.2% | 68.4% | 742,899 | — | — |
| New York | 12,496,000 | 11,837,068 | 94.7% | 7,391,036 | 59.1% | 62.4% | 6,222,418 | 6,702,875 | — |
| North Carolina | 6,208,000 | 5,519,992 | 88.9% | 3,501,007 | 56.4% | 63.4% | 3,413,071 | 3,472,082 | 3,486,688 |
| North Dakota | 483,000 | — | | 312,833 | 64.8% | — | 310,814 | 310,696 | 309,873 |
| Ohio | 8,486,000 | 7,972,826 | 94.0% | 5,627,908 | 66.3% | 70.6% | 5,183,508 | 5,426,196 | — |
| Oklahoma | 2,581,000 | 2,143,978 | 83.1% | 1,463,758 | 56.7% | 68.3% | 1,374,610 | 1,446,846 | — |
| Oregon | 2,581,000 | 2,141,243 | 83.0% | 1,836,782 | 71.2% | 85.8% | 1,772,306 | 1,780,550 | — |
| Pennsylvania | 9,230,000 | 8,366,663 | 90.6% | 5,769,590 | 62.5% | 69.0% | 5,152,274 | 5,559,105 | — |
| Rhode Island | 752,000 | 651,950 | 86.7% | 437,134 | 58.1% | 67.1% | 402,175 | — | — |
| South Carolina | 3,120,000 | 2,315,462 | 74.2% | 1,617,730 | 51.9% | 69.9% | 1,439,118 | 1,597,221 | — |
| South Dakota | 569,000 | 552,441 | 97.1% | 388,215 | 68.2% | 70.3% | 389,468 | 391,188 | — |
| Tennessee | 4,462,000 | 3,742,829 | 83.9% | 2,437,319 | 54.6% | 65.1% | 2,218,738 | — | — |
| Texas | 14,197,000 | 13,098,329 | 92.3% | 7,410,765 | 52.2% | 56.6% | 6,958,603 | — | — |
| Utah | 1,587,000 | 1,278,251 | 80.5% | 927,844 | 58.5% | 72.6% | 908,857 | 911,726 | 919,960 |
| Vermont | 470,000 | 444,077 | 94.5% | 312,309 | 66.4% | 70.3% | 305,008 | 307,208 | 309,285 |
| Virginia | 5,290,000 | 4,517,980 | 85.4% | 3,198,367 | 60.5% | 70.8% | 3,004,007 | — | — |
| Washington | 4,370,000 | 3,508,208 | 80.3% | 2,859,084 | 65.4% | 81.5% | 2,729,995 | 2,818,651 | 2,810,058 |
| West Virginia | 1,423,000 | 1,168,694 | 82.1% | 755,887 | 53.1% | 64.7% | 721,656 | — | 744,433 |
| Wisconsin | 4,057,000 | — | | 2,997,007 | 73.9% | — | 2,821,613 | 2,949,743 | — |
| Wyoming | 380,000 | 232,396 | 61.2% | 243,428 | 64.1% | 104.7% | 239,034 | — | — |
| District of Columbia | 391,000 | 383,919 | 98.2% | 227,586 | 58.2% | 59.3% | — | — | — |
| Total | 201,541,000 | 172,445,197 | 85.6% | 122,295,345 | 60.7% | 70.9% | 111,910,944 | 86,225,383 | 27,270,255 |

Source: Voting age population figures were compiled by the Committee for the Study of the American Electorate (CSAE) and represent the estimated citizen voting age population in each state (and nationally) at the time of the November 2004 general election. CSAE employs a more conservative methodology than does the Census Bureau, which no longer provides election-year voting age population estimates. Registration figures are as of the November 2004 general election and were obtained from state election officials. In some cases, the registration totals are suspect as a number of states include inactive voters in their totals. In Alaska and Wyoming, for instance, the number of registered voters was more than 100 percent of the voting age population. The Minnesota total includes election-day registrations. The Mississippi total was as of April 2004. North Dakota and Wisconsin did not compile statewide registration figures.

Notes: Votes are from the November 2004 general election, with the exception of gubernatorial elections in California, Kentucky, Louisiana, and Mississippi, which were held in 2003. The California gubernatorial contest was a special recall election.

# GUBERNATORIAL ELECTIONS 2003 AND 2004

| State | Total Vote | Republican Vote | Republican Candidate | Democratic Vote | Democratic Candidate | Other Vote | Rep.-Dem. Plurality | Total Vote Rep. | Total Vote Dem. | Major Vote Rep. | Major Vote Dem. |
|---|---|---|---|---|---|---|---|---|---|---|---|
| California | 8,657,915 | 4,206,284 | Schwarzenegger, Arnold | 2,724,874 | Bustamante, Cruz | 1,726,757 | 1,481,410 R | 48.6% | 31.5% | — | — |
| Delaware | 365,008 | 167,115 | Lee, William Swain | 185,687 | Minner, Ruth Ann | 12,206 | 18,572 D | 45.8% | 50.9% | 47.4% | 52.6% |
| Indiana | 2,448,498 | 1,302,912 | Daniels, Mitch | 1,113,900 | Kernan, Joseph E. | 31,686 | 189,012 R | 53.2% | 45.5% | 53.9% | 46.1% |
| Kentucky | 1,083,443 | 596,284 | Fletcher, Ernie | 487,159 | Chandler, Ben | | 109,125 R | 55.0% | 45.0% | 55.0% | 45.0% |
| Louisiana | 1,407,842 | 676,484 | Jindal, Bobby | 731,358 | Blanco, Kathleen Babineaux | | 54,874 D | 48.1% | 51.9% | 48.1% | 51.9% |
| Mississippi | 894,487 | 470,404 | Barbour, Haley | 409,787 | Musgrove, Ronnie | 14,296 | 60,617 R | 52.6% | 45.8% | 53.4% | 46.6% |
| Missouri | 2,719,599 | 1,382,419 | Blunt, Matt | 1,301,442 | McCaskill, Claire | 35,738 | 80,977 R | 50.8% | 47.9% | 51.5% | 48.5% |
| Montana | 446,146 | 205,313 | Brown, Bob | 225,016 | Schweitzer, Brian | 15,817 | 19,703 D | 46.0% | 50.4% | 47.7% | 52.3% |
| New Hampshire | 667,020 | 325,981 | Benson, Craig | 340,299 | Lynch, John | 740 | 14,318 D | 48.9% | 51.0% | 48.9% | 51.1% |
| North Carolina | 3,486,688 | 1,495,021 | Ballantine, Patrick J. | 1,939,154 | Easley, Michael F. | 52,513 | 444,133 D | 42.9% | 55.6% | 43.5% | 56.5% |
| North Dakota | 309,873 | 220,803 | Hoeven, John | 84,877 | Satrom, Joseph A. | 4,193 | 135,926 R | 71.3% | 27.4% | 72.2% | 27.8% |
| Utah | 919,960 | 531,190 | Huntsman, Jon Jr. | 380,359 | Matheson, Scott M. Jr. | 8,411 | 150,831 R | 57.7% | 41.3% | 58.3% | 41.7% |
| Vermont | 309,285 | 181,540 | Douglas, Jim | 117,327 | Clavelle, Peter | 10,418 | 64,213 R | 58.7% | 37.9% | 60.7% | 39.3% |
| Washington | 2,810,058 | 1,373,232 | Rossi, Dino | 1,373,361 | Gregoire, Christine | 63,465 | 129 D | 48.9% | 48.9% | 50.0% | 50.0% |
| West Virginia | 744,433 | 253,131 | Warner, Monty | 472,758 | Manchin, Joe III | 18,544 | 219,627 D | 34.0% | 63.5% | 34.9% | 65.1% |
| Total | 27,270,255 | 13,388,113 | | 11,887,358 | | 1,994,784 | 1,500,755 R | 49.1% | 43.6% | 53.0% | 47.0% |

Note: California held a special 2003 recall election. There were two parts to the California ballot. A total of 8,984,057 votes were cast on the first part, on the question of whether Democratic governor Gray Davis should be recalled. The vote was Yes 4,976,274 (55.4 percent); No 4,007,783 (44.6 percent), a plurality of 968,491 votes for Davis' recall. The second part of the ballot chose his successor. All candidates, regardless of party, ran together. The leading Republican and Democratic candidates are listed in the table, with the vote for all other candidates, regardless of party, aggregated in the other vote column. The gubernatorial elections in Kentucky, Louisiana, and Mississippi were regularly scheduled elections, held in 2003. The Louisiana vote reflects the result of a runoff.

# SENATE ELECTIONS 2004

| State | Total Vote | Republican | | Democratic | | Other Vote | Rep.-Dem. Plurality | Percentage | | | |
|---|---|---|---|---|---|---|---|---|---|---|---|
| | | | | | | | | Total Vote | | Major Vote | |
| | | Vote | Candidate | Vote | Candidate | | | Rep. | Dem. | Rep. | Dem. |
| Alabama | 1,839,066 | 1,242,200 | Shelby, Richard C. | 595,018 | Sowell, Wayne | 1,848 | 647,182 R | 67.5% | 32.4% | 67.6% | 32.4% |
| Alaska | 308,315 | 149,773 | Murkowski, Lisa | 140,424 | Knowles, Tony | 18,118 | 9,349 R | 48.6% | 45.5% | 51.6% | 48.4% |
| Arizona | 1,961,677 | 1,505,372 | McCain, John | 404,507 | Starky, Stuart | 51,798 | 1,100,865 R | 76.7% | 20.6% | 78.8% | 21.2% |
| Arkansas | 1,039,349 | 458,036 | Holt, Jim | 580,973 | Lincoln, Blanche | 340 | 122,937 D | 44.1% | 55.9% | 44.1% | 55.9% |
| California | 12,053,295 | 4,555,922 | Jones, Bill | 6,955,728 | Boxer, Barbara | 541,645 | 2,399,806 D | 37.8% | 57.7% | 39.6% | 60.4% |
| Colorado | 2,107,554 | 980,668 | Coors, Pete | 1,081,188 | Salazar, Ken | 45,698 | 100,520 D | 46.5% | 51.3% | 47.6% | 52.4% |
| Connecticut | 1,424,726 | 457,749 | Orchulli, Jack | 945,347 | Dodd, Christopher J. | 21,630 | 487,598 D | 32.1% | 66.4% | 32.6% | 67.4% |
| Florida | 7,429,894 | 3,672,864 | Martinez, Mel | 3,590,201 | Castor, Betty | 166,829 | 82,663 R | 49.4% | 48.3% | 50.6% | 49.4% |
| Georgia | 3,220,981 | 1,864,202 | Isakson, Johnny | 1,287,690 | Majette, Denise L. | 69,089 | 576,512 R | 57.9% | 40.0% | 59.1% | 40.9% |
| Hawaii | 415,347 | 87,172 | Cavasso, Cam | 313,629 | Inouye, Daniel K. | 14,546 | 226,457 D | 21.0% | 75.5% | 21.7% | 78.3% |
| Idaho | 503,932 | 499,796 | Crapo, Michael D. | | — | 4,136 | 499,796 R | 99.2% | | 100.0% | |
| Illinois | 5,141,520 | 1,390,690 | Keyes, Alan | 3,597,456 | Obama, Barack | 153,374 | 2,206,766 D | 27.0% | 70.0% | 27.9% | 72.1% |
| Indiana | 2,428,233 | 903,913 | Scott, Marvin | 1,496,976 | Bayh, Evan | 27,344 | 593,063 D | 37.2% | 61.6% | 37.6% | 62.4% |
| Iowa | 1,479,228 | 1,038,175 | Grassley, Charles E. | 412,365 | Small, Arthur | 28,688 | 625,810 R | 70.2% | 27.9% | 71.6% | 28.4% |
| Kansas | 1,129,022 | 780,863 | Brownback, Sam | 310,337 | Jones, Lee | 37,822 | 470,526 R | 69.2% | 27.5% | 71.6% | 28.4% |
| Kentucky | 1,724,362 | 873,507 | Bunning, Jim | 850,855 | Mongiardo, Daniel | | 22,652 R | 50.7% | 49.3% | 50.7% | 49.3% |
| Louisiana | 1,848,056 | 943,014 | Vitter, David | 877,482 | John, Chris/Kennedy, John | 27,560 | 400,864 R | 51.0% | 47.5% | 51.8% | 48.2% |
| Maryland | 2,323,183 | 783,055 | Pipkin, E.J. | 1,504,691 | Mikulski, Barbara A. | 35,437 | 721,636 D | 33.7% | 64.8% | 34.2% | 65.8% |
| Missouri | 2,706,402 | 1,518,089 | Bond, Christopher S. | 1,158,261 | Farmer, Nancy | 30,052 | 359,828 R | 56.1% | 42.8% | 56.7% | 43.3% |
| Nevada | 810,068 | 284,640 | Ziser, Richard | 494,805 | Reid, Harry | 30,623 | 210,165 D | 35.1% | 61.1% | 36.5% | 63.5% |
| New Hampshire | 657,086 | 434,847 | Gregg, Judd | 221,549 | Haddock, Doris Granny D. | 690 | 213,298 R | 66.2% | 33.7% | 66.2% | 33.8% |
| New York | 6,702,875 | 1,625,069 | Mills, Howard | 4,769,824 | Schumer, Charles E. | 307,982 | 3,144,755 D | 24.2% | 71.2% | 25.4% | 74.6% |
| North Carolina | 3,472,082 | 1,791,450 | Burr, Richard M. | 1,632,527 | Bowles, Erskine | 48,105 | 158,923 R | 51.6% | 47.0% | 52.3% | 47.7% |
| North Dakota | 310,696 | 98,553 | Liffrig, Mike | 212,143 | Dorgan, Byron L. | | 113,590 D | 31.7% | 68.3% | 31.7% | 68.3% |
| Ohio | 5,426,196 | 3,464,651 | Voinovich, George V. | 1,961,249 | Fingerhut, Eric D. | 296 | 1,503,402 R | 63.9% | 36.1% | 63.9% | 36.1% |
| Oklahoma | 1,446,846 | 763,433 | Coburn, Tom | 596,750 | Carson, Brad | 86,663 | 166,683 R | 52.8% | 41.2% | 56.1% | 43.9% |
| Oregon | 1,780,550 | 565,254 | King, Al | 1,128,728 | Wyden, Ron | 86,568 | 563,474 D | 31.7% | 63.4% | 33.4% | 66.6% |
| Pennsylvania | 5,559,105 | 2,925,080 | Specter, Arlen | 2,334,126 | Hoeffel, Joseph M. | 299,899 | 590,954 R | 52.6% | 42.0% | 55.6% | 44.4% |
| South Carolina | 1,597,221 | 857,167 | DeMint, Jim | 704,384 | Tenenbaum, Inez | 35,670 | 152,783 R | 53.7% | 44.1% | 54.9% | 45.1% |
| South Dakota | 391,188 | 197,848 | Thune, John | 193,340 | Daschle, Tom | | 4,508 R | 50.6% | 49.4% | 50.6% | 49.4% |
| Utah | 911,726 | 626,640 | Bennett, Robert F. | 258,955 | Van Dam, R. Paul | 26,131 | 367,685 R | 68.7% | 28.4% | 70.8% | 29.2% |
| Vermont | 307,208 | 75,398 | McMullen, Jack | 216,972 | Leahy, Patrick J. | 14,838 | 141,574 D | 24.5% | 70.6% | 25.8% | 74.2% |
| Washington | 2,818,651 | 1,204,584 | Nethercutt, George | 1,549,708 | Murray, Patty | 64,359 | 345,124 D | 42.7% | 55.0% | 43.7% | 56.3% |
| Wisconsin | 2,949,743 | 1,301,183 | Michels, Tim | 1,632,697 | Feingold, Russell D. | 15,863 | 331,514 D | 44.1% | 55.4% | 44.4% | 55.6% |
| Total | 86,225,383 | 39,920,857 | | 44,010,885 | | 2,293,641 | 4,090,028 D | 46.3% | 51.0% | 47.6% | 52.4% |

Note: Louisiana has a unique electoral system. All candidates, regardless of party, ran together on the November ballot, and since Republican David Vitter won a majority of the vote, he was elected. Vitter was the only Republican candidate on the ballot, while there were four Democrats who together collected 877,482 votes (47.5 percent of the total vote). The bulk of these votes were garnered by the top two vote-getters, who are listed in the Democratic column. Vitter's plurality is measured over the runner-up, Chris John, who received 542,150 votes (29.3 percent of the total). The nationwide Democratic Senate total reflects the combined vote of the four Senate candidates in Louisiana who ran as Democrats. In Idaho, Democrats had a write-in candidate whose total is listed in the other vote column.

# HOUSE OF REPRESENTATIVES ELECTIONS 2004

| | Seats Won | | | | | | | | Percentage | | | |
| | | | | | | | | | Total Vote | | Major Vote | |
| State | Republican | Democratic | Independent | Total Vote | Republican | Democratic | Other | Rep.-Dem. Plurality | Rep. | Dem. | Rep. | Dem. |
|---|---|---|---|---|---|---|---|---|---|---|---|---|
| Alabama | 5 | 2 | | 1,792,759 | 1,079,657 | 708,425 | 4,677 | 371,232 R | 60.2% | 39.5% | 60.4% | 39.6% |
| Alaska | 1 | | | 299,996 | 213,216 | 67,074 | 19,706 | 146,142 R | 71.1% | 22.4% | 76.1% | 23.9% |
| Arizona | 6 | 2 | | 1,871,445 | 1,127,591 | 597,526 | 146,328 | 530,065 R | 60.3% | 31.9% | 65.4% | 34.6% |
| Arkansas | 1 | 3 | | 791,240 | 357,840 | 426,380 | 7,020 | 68,540 D | 45.2% | 53.9% | 45.6% | 54.4% |
| California | 20 | 33 | | 11,623,753 | 5,030,821 | 6,223,698 | 369,234 | 1,192,877 D | 43.3% | 53.5% | 44.7% | 55.3% |
| Colorado | 4 | 3 | | 2,039,011 | 991,835 | 995,283 | 51,893 | 3,448 D | 48.6% | 48.8% | 49.9% | 50.1% |
| Connecticut | 3 | 2 | | 1,428,738 | 629,934 | 785,747 | 13,057 | 155,813 D | 44.1% | 55.0% | 44.5% | 55.5% |
| Delaware | 1 | | | 356,045 | 245,978 | 105,716 | 4,351 | 140,262 R | 69.1% | 29.7% | 69.9% | 30.1% |
| Florida | 18 | 7 | | 5,627,494 | 3,319,296 | 2,212,324 | 95,874 | 1,106,972 R | 59.0% | 39.3% | 60.0% | 40.0% |
| Georgia | 7 | 6 | | 2,960,763 | 1,819,817 | 1,140,869 | 77 | 678,948 R | 61.5% | 38.5% | 61.5% | 38.5% |
| Hawaii | | 2 | | 416,570 | 148,443 | 261,884 | 6,243 | 113,441 D | 35.6% | 62.9% | 36.2% | 63.8% |
| Idaho | 2 | | | 572,426 | 401,366 | 171,060 | | 230,306 R | 70.1% | 29.9% | 70.1% | 29.9% |
| Illinois | 9 | 10 | | 4,988,665 | 2,271,676 | 2,675,273 | 41,716 | 403,597 D | 45.5% | 53.6% | 45.9% | 54.1% |
| Indiana | 7 | 2 | | 2,416,251 | 1,381,699 | 999,082 | 35,470 | 382,617 R | 57.2% | 41.3% | 58.0% | 42.0% |
| Iowa | 4 | 1 | | 1,458,161 | 822,653 | 624,620 | 10,888 | 198,033 R | 56.4% | 42.8% | 56.8% | 43.2% |
| Kansas | 3 | 1 | | 1,156,383 | 723,794 | 386,970 | 45,619 | 336,824 R | 62.6% | 33.5% | 65.2% | 34.8% |
| Kentucky | 5 | 1 | | 1,635,243 | 1,017,379 | 602,085 | 15,779 | 415,294 R | 62.2% | 36.8% | 62.8% | 37.2% |
| Louisiana | 5 | 2 | | 1,545,982 | 936,801 | 609,181 | | 327,620 R | 60.6% | 39.4% | 60.6% | 39.4% |
| Maine | | 2 | | 710,176 | 283,210 | 418,380 | 8,586 | 135,170 D | 39.9% | 58.9% | 40.4% | 59.6% |
| Maryland | 2 | 6 | | 2,255,955 | 896,232 | 1,310,791 | 48,932 | 414,559 D | 39.7% | 58.1% | 40.6% | 59.4% |
| Massachusetts | | 10 | | 2,580,955 | 435,239 | 2,059,984 | 85,732 | 1,624,745 D | 16.9% | 79.8% | 17.4% | 82.6% |
| Michigan | 9 | 6 | | 4,631,058 | 2,288,594 | 2,242,435 | 100,029 | 46,159 R | 49.4% | 48.4% | 50.5% | 49.5% |
| Minnesota | 4 | 4 | | 2,721,681 | 1,236,094 | 1,399,624 | 85,963 | 163,530 D | 45.4% | 51.4% | 46.9% | 53.1% |
| Mississippi | 2 | 2 | | 1,116,203 | 658,589 | 336,240 | 121,374 | 322,349 R | 59.0% | 30.1% | 66.2% | 33.8% |
| Missouri | 5 | 4 | | 2,667,023 | 1,429,767 | 1,192,674 | 44,582 | 237,093 R | 53.6% | 44.7% | 54.5% | 45.5% |
| Montana | 1 | | | 444,230 | 286,076 | 145,606 | 12,548 | 140,470 R | 64.4% | 32.8% | 66.3% | 33.7% |
| Nebraska | 3 | | | 764,972 | 515,115 | 230,697 | 19,160 | 284,418 R | 67.3% | 30.2% | 69.1% | 30.9% |
| Nevada | 2 | 1 | | 791,433 | 420,711 | 333,912 | 36,810 | 86,799 R | 53.2% | 42.2% | 55.8% | 44.2% |
| New Hampshire | 2 | | | 651,566 | 396,024 | 243,506 | 12,036 | 152,518 R | 60.8% | 37.4% | 61.9% | 38.1% |
| New Jersey | 6 | 7 | | 3,284,595 | 1,514,784 | 1,721,392 | 48,419 | 206,608 D | 46.1% | 52.4% | 46.8% | 53.2% |
| New Mexico | 2 | 1 | | 742,899 | 357,805 | 384,900 | 194 | 27,095 D | 48.2% | 51.8% | 48.2% | 51.8% |
| New York | 9 | 20 | | 6,222,418 | 2,448,345 | 3,681,789 | 92,284 | 1,233,444 D | 39.3% | 59.2% | 39.9% | 60.1% |
| North Carolina | 7 | 6 | | 3,413,071 | 1,743,131 | 1,669,864 | 76 | 73,267 R | 51.1% | 48.9% | 51.1% | 48.9% |
| North Dakota | | 1 | | 310,814 | 125,684 | 185,130 | | 59,446 D | 40.4% | 59.6% | 40.4% | 59.6% |
| Ohio | 12 | 6 | | 5,183,508 | 2,650,122 | 2,514,615 | 18,771 | 135,507 R | 51.1% | 48.5% | 51.3% | 48.7% |
| Oklahoma | 4 | 1 | | 1,374,610 | 875,033 | 389,029 | 110,548 | 486,004 R | 63.7% | 28.3% | 69.2% | 30.8% |
| Oregon | 1 | 4 | | 1,772,306 | 761,545 | 951,688 | 59,073 | 190,143 D | 43.0% | 53.7% | 44.5% | 55.5% |
| Pennsylvania | 12 | 7 | | 5,152,274 | 2,565,077 | 2,478,239 | 108,958 | 86,838 R | 49.8% | 48.1% | 50.9% | 49.1% |
| Rhode Island | | 2 | | 402,175 | 112,958 | 279,315 | 9,902 | 166,357 D | 28.1% | 69.5% | 28.8% | 71.2% |
| South Carolina | 4 | 2 | | 1,439,118 | 917,325 | 486,479 | 35,314 | 430,846 R | 63.7% | 33.8% | 65.3% | 34.7% |
| South Dakota | | 1 | | 389,468 | 178,823 | 207,837 | 2,808 | 29,014 D | 45.9% | 53.4% | 46.2% | 53.8% |
| Tennessee | 4 | 5 | | 2,218,738 | 1,160,821 | 1,031,959 | 25,958 | 128,862 R | 52.3% | 46.5% | 52.9% | 47.1% |
| Texas | 21 | 11 | | 6,958,603 | 4,012,534 | 2,713,968 | 232,101 | 1,298,566 R | 57.7% | 39.0% | 59.7% | 40.3% |
| Utah | 2 | 1 | | 908,857 | 520,403 | 361,628 | 26,826 | 158,775 R | 57.3% | 39.8% | 59.0% | 41.0% |
| Vermont | | | 1 | 305,008 | 74,271 | 21,684 | 209,053 | 131,503 I | 24.4% | 7.1% | 77.4% | 22.6% |
| Virginia | 8 | 3 | | 3,004,007 | 1,817,422 | 1,023,187 | 163,398 | 794,235 R | 60.5% | 34.1% | 64.0% | 36.0% |
| Washington | 3 | 6 | | 2,729,995 | 1,095,493 | 1,608,751 | 25,751 | 513,258 D | 40.1% | 58.9% | 40.5% | 59.5% |
| West Virginia | 1 | 2 | | 721,656 | 303,042 | 415,396 | 3,218 | 112,354 D | 42.0% | 57.6% | 42.2% | 57.8% |
| Wisconsin | 4 | 4 | | 2,821,613 | 1,380,819 | 1,368,537 | 72,257 | 12,282 R | 48.9% | 48.5% | 50.2% | 49.8% |
| Wyoming | 1 | | | 239,034 | 132,107 | 99,989 | 6,938 | 32,118 R | 55.3% | 41.8% | 56.9% | 43.1% |
| Total | 232 | 202 | 1 | 111,910,944 | 56,112,991 | 53,102,422 | 2,695,531 | 3,010,569 R | 50.1% | 47.5% | 51.4% | 48.6% |

Note: In Louisiana, all candidates ran together on the November ballot regardless of party. The Democratic and Republican vote represents the aggregate total for all House candidates of each party in Louisiana, not just the leading contenders. In Vermont, the winner was Independent Bernard Sanders with 67.5 percent of the vote.

# UNITED STATES

## PARTY SWITCHES, SPECIAL ELECTIONS, AND POSTELECTION CHANGES 2003–2004

### PARTY SWITCHES

Between the general elections of 2002 and 2004, there were two party switches in Congress—both in the House of Representatives.

### REPRESENTATIVES

Ralph M. Hall of the Texas 4th District switched from Democrat to Republican on January 5, 2004.

Rodney Alexander of the Louisiana 5th District switched from Democrat to Republican on August 6, 2004.

### SPECIAL ELECTIONS TO THE 108th CONGRESS

Between the beginning of 2003 and the general election of 2004, five special elections were held to fill vacancies in the House of Representatives. In addition, Republican Doug Bereuter of the Nebraska 1st District resigned his seat on August 31, 2004, to become president of the Asia Foundation, and Republican Porter Goss of the Florida 14th District resigned his seat on September 23, 2004, to become head of the Central Intelligence Agency (CIA). In neither case was there a special election. The House special elections held to fill vacancies in the 108th Congress are listed below.

### REPRESENTATIVES

#### HAWAII 2nd District

Patsy T. Mink (D) died September 28, 2002, but was elected posthumously in November 2002 to a seat in the 108th Congress. Ed Case (D) was elected January 4, 2003, to fill her term. Case had won a special election November 30, 2002, to fill the remaining weeks of her term in the 107th Congress. (For the results of that special election, see *America Votes 25*, p. 6).

#### January 4, 2003 Special Election

33,002 Ed Case (D); 23,050 Matt Matsunaga (D); 6,046 Colleen Hanabusa (D); 4,497 Barbara C. Marumoto (R); 4,298 Bob McDermott (R); 728 Chris Halford (R); 642 Kimo Kaloi (R); 521 John "Mahina" Carroll (R); 483 Frank F. Fasi (R); 449 Mark McNett (Nonpartisan); 414 Jim Rath (R); 212 Richard H. Haake (R); 208 Nelson J. Secretario (R); 201 Whitney T. Anderson (R); 91 Moana Keaulana-Dyball (Nonpartisan); 75 Nick Nikhilananda (Green); 69 Brian G. Cole (D); 68 Kekoa D. Kaapu (D); 58 Jeff Mallan (Libertarian); 52 Sophie Mataafa (Nonpartisan); 38 Doug Fairhurst (R); 35 Mike Gagne (D); 29 Carolyn Mart Golojuch (R); 27 G. "Iimz" Goodwin (Green); 25 Richard "Rich" Payne (R); 25 Clarence H. Weatherwax (R); 24 Kabba Anand (Nonpartisan); 22 Dan Vierra (Nonpartisan); 20 John L. Sabey (R); 19 Pat Rocco (D); 18 Bill Russell (Nonpartisan); 17 Steve Sparks (Nonpartisan); 16 Solomon Wong (Nonpartisan); 15 Art P. Reyes (D); 13 Paul Britos (D); 11 S. J. Harlan (Nonpartisan); 10 Charles Collins (D); 9 John "Jack" Randall (Nonpartisan); 9 Steve Tataii (D); 8 Mike Rethman (R); 8 Marshall Turner (Nonpartisan); 6 Herbert L. Jensen (D); 3 Alan R. Gano (Nonpartisan); 3 Bartle Lee Rowland (Nonpartisan).

#### KENTUCKY 6th District

Ernie Fletcher (R) resigned December 8, 2003, to become governor of Kentucky. Ben Chandler (D) was elected February 17, 2004, to fill the remainder of his term in the 108th Congress.

#### February 17, 2004 Special Election

84,168 Ben Chandler (D); 65,474 Alice Forgy Kerr (R); 2,952 Mark Gailey (Libertarian).

#### NORTH CAROLINA 1st District

Frank W. Ballance Jr. (D) resigned June 11, 2004, for health reasons. G. K. Butterfield (D) was elected July 20, 2004, to fill the remainder of his term in the 108th Congress.

# UNITED STATES

## SPECIAL ELECTIONS TO THE 108th CONGRESS

**July 20, 2004 Special Election**

48,567 G. K. Butterfield (D); 18,491 Greg Dority (R); 1,201 Thomas I. Eisenmenger (Libertarian).

### SOUTH DAKOTA At Large District

Bill Janklow (R) resigned January 20, 2004, to begin serving a prison sentence for vehicular manslaughter. Stephanie Herseth (D) was elected June 1, 2004, to fill the remainder of his term in the 108th Congress.

**June 1, 2004 Special Election**

132,420 Stephanie Herseth (D); 129,415 Larry Diedrich (R).

### TEXAS 19th District

Larry Combest (R) resigned May 31, 2003. Randy Neugebauer (R) was elected June 3, 2003, to fill the remainder of his term in the 108th Congress.

**May 3, 2003 Special Election**

13,091 Randy Neugebauer (R); 12,270 Mike Conaway (R); 11,015 Carl H. Isett (R); 8,053 David R. Langston (R); 2,609 Stace Williams (R); 1,987 Vickie Sutton (R); 1,907 Jamie Berryhill (R); 1,883 John D. Bell (R); 1,396 Kaye Gaddy (D); 1,046 Richard Bartlett (R); 1,029 William M. "Bill" Christian (R); 898 Jerri Simmons-Asmussen (D); 629 Donald May (R); 223 Julia Penelope (Green); 159 Richard "Chip" Peterson (Libertarian); 93 Thomas Flournoy (Constitution); 81 E. L. "Ed" Hicks (Independent).

**June 3, 2003 Special Runoff Election**

28,546 Randy Neugebauer (R); 27,959 Mike Conaway (R).

## HOUSE SPECIAL ELECTIONS 2003 TO 2004: A SUMMARY

Five special House elections were held to fill vacancies in the 108th Congress. Two special elections resulted in partisan change, with the Kentucky 6th District and South Dakota at large seats switching from Republican to Democratic hands. The results below are based on the decisive round of voting in each special election when the new member was elected to Congress. The special elections are listed in the chronological order in which they were held.

| District | Former Member | New Member | Date Elected | Winning Percentage | Voter Turnout |
|---|---|---|---|---|---|
| Hawaii 2nd | Patsy T. Mink (D) | Ed Case (D) | January 4, 2003 | 43.7% | 75,574 |
| Texas 19th | Larry Combest (R) | Randy Neugebauer (R) | June 3, 2003 | 50.5% | 56,505 |
| Kentucky 6th | Ernie Fletcher (R) | Ben Chandler (D) | February 17, 2004 | 55.2% | 152,594 |
| South Dakota AL | Bill Janklow (R) | Stephanie Herseth (D) | June 1, 2004 | 50.6% | 261,835 |
| North Carolina 1st | Frank W. Ballance Jr. (D) | G. K. Butterfield (D) | July 20, 2004 | 71.2% | 68,259 |

# UNITED STATES

## CHANGES FOLLOWING THE 2004 ELECTION

Following the 2004 general election, and through September 15, 2005, the following changes took place in the membership of the 109th Congress.

### REPRESENTATIVES

California 5th District—Robert T. Matsui (D) died January 1, 2005. Doris Matsui (D) was elected March 8, 2005, to succeed him.

California 48th District—Christopher Cox (R) resigned August 2, 2005, to become chairman of the Securities and Exchange Commission (SEC). A special election was scheduled for October 4, 2005, to fill the seat.

Ohio 2nd District—Rob Portman (R) resigned April 29, 2005, to become U.S. trade representative. Jean Schmidt (R) was elected August 2, 2005, to succeed him.

# PRESIDENT 2004

In New York the Republican total includes votes for their candidate on the Conservative line and the Democratic total includes votes for their candidate on the Working Families line.

In Minnesota the Democratic candidate appears on the ballot as Democratic-Farmer-Labor; in North Dakota as Democratic-Nonpartisan League. In many states various third party candidates appeared on the ballot with variations of the party designations, were carried with entirely different party labels, or were listed as "Independent." The state notes sections list the party labels used by the third party candidates.

The candidates listed below include all who appeared on the ballot in at least one state. Write-in votes for third party candidates are credited to their total below. See the third party chart on page 10 for details.

| | | |
|---|---|---|
| 62,040,610 | George W. Bush and Richard B. Cheney | Republican |
| 59,028,439 | John Kerry and John Edwards | Democratic |
| 465,650 | Ralph Nader and Peter Miguel Camejo | Independent |
| 397,265 | Michael Badnarik and Richard V. Campagna | Libertarian |
| 143,630 | Michael Peroutka and Chuck Baldwin | Constitution |
| 119,859 | David Cobb and Patricia LaMarche | Green |
| 27,607 | Leonard Peltier and Janice Jordan | Peace and Freedom |
| 10,837 | Walter F. Brown and Mary Alice Herbert | Socialist |
| 7,102 | James Harris and Margaret Trowe | Socialist Workers |
| 3,689 | Roger Calero and Arrin Hawkins | Socialist Workers |
| 2,387 | Thomas J. Harens and Jennifer A. Ryan | Christian Freedom |
| 1,944 | Gene Amondson and Leroy Pletten | Concerns of People |
| 1,861 | Bill Van Auken and Jim Lawrence | Socialist Equality |
| 1,646 | John Parker and Teresa Gutierrez | Workers World |
| 946 | Charles Jay and Marilyn Chambers Taylor | Personal Choice |
| 804 | Stanford E. "Andy" Andress and Irene M. Deasy | Unaffiliated |
| 140 | Earl F. Dodge and Howard F. Lydick | Prohibition |

In addition to the votes listed above, 37,241 scattered write-in votes were reported from various states, and 3,688 votes were cast for "None of these Candidates" in Nevada.

# UNITED STATES

## PRESIDENT 2004

| State | Electoral Vote Rep. | Electoral Vote Dem. | Electoral Vote Other | Total Vote | Republican | Democratic | Other | Rep.-Dem. Plurality | Percentage Total Vote Rep. | Percentage Total Vote Dem. | Percentage Major Vote Rep. | Percentage Major Vote Dem. |
|---|---|---|---|---|---|---|---|---|---|---|---|---|
| Alabama | 9 | | | 1,883,449 | 1,176,394 | 693,933 | 13,122 | 482,461 R | 62.5% | 36.8% | 62.9% | 37.1% |
| Alaska | 3 | | | 312,598 | 190,889 | 111,025 | 10,684 | 79,864 R | 61.1% | 35.5% | 63.2% | 36.8% |
| Arizona | 10 | | | 2,012,585 | 1,104,294 | 893,524 | 14,767 | 210,770 R | 54.9% | 44.4% | 55.3% | 44.7% |
| Arkansas | 6 | | | 1,054,945 | 572,898 | 469,953 | 12,094 | 102,945 R | 54.3% | 44.5% | 54.9% | 45.1% |
| California | | 55 | | 12,421,852 | 5,509,826 | 6,745,485 | 166,541 | 1,235,659 D | 44.4% | 54.3% | 45.0% | 55.0% |
| Colorado | 9 | | | 2,130,330 | 1,101,255 | 1,001,732 | 27,343 | 99,523 R | 51.7% | 47.0% | 52.4% | 47.6% |
| Connecticut | | 7 | | 1,578,769 | 693,826 | 857,488 | 27,455 | 163,662 D | 43.9% | 54.3% | 44.7% | 55.3% |
| Delaware | | 3 | | 375,190 | 171,660 | 200,152 | 3,378 | 28,492 D | 45.8% | 53.3% | 46.2% | 53.8% |
| Florida | 27 | | | 7,609,810 | 3,964,522 | 3,583,544 | 61,744 | 380,978 R | 52.1% | 47.1% | 52.5% | 47.5% |
| Georgia | 15 | | | 3,301,875 | 1,914,254 | 1,366,149 | 21,472 | 548,105 R | 58.0% | 41.4% | 58.4% | 41.6% |
| Hawaii | | 4 | | 429,013 | 194,191 | 231,708 | 3,114 | 37,517 D | 45.3% | 54.0% | 45.6% | 54.4% |
| Idaho | 4 | | | 598,447 | 409,235 | 181,098 | 8,114 | 228,137 R | 68.4% | 30.3% | 69.3% | 30.7% |
| Illinois | | 21 | | 5,274,322 | 2,345,946 | 2,891,550 | 36,826 | 545,604 D | 44.5% | 54.8% | 44.8% | 55.2% |
| Indiana | 11 | | | 2,468,002 | 1,479,438 | 969,011 | 19,553 | 510,427 R | 59.9% | 39.3% | 60.4% | 39.6% |
| Iowa | 7 | | | 1,506,908 | 751,957 | 741,898 | 13,053 | 10,059 R | 49.9% | 49.2% | 50.3% | 49.7% |
| Kansas | 6 | | | 1,187,756 | 736,456 | 434,993 | 16,307 | 301,463 R | 62.0% | 36.6% | 62.9% | 37.1% |
| Kentucky | 8 | | | 1,795,882 | 1,069,439 | 712,733 | 13,710 | 356,706 R | 59.5% | 39.7% | 60.0% | 40.0% |
| Louisiana | 9 | | | 1,943,106 | 1,102,169 | 820,299 | 20,638 | 281,870 R | 56.7% | 42.2% | 57.3% | 42.7% |
| Maine | | 4 | | 740,752 | 330,201 | 396,842 | 13,709 | 66,641 D | 44.6% | 53.6% | 45.4% | 54.6% |
| Maryland | | 10 | | 2,386,678 | 1,024,703 | 1,334,493 | 27,482 | 309,790 D | 42.9% | 55.9% | 43.4% | 56.6% |
| Massachusetts | | 12 | | 2,912,388 | 1,071,109 | 1,803,800 | 37,479 | 732,691 D | 36.8% | 61.9% | 37.3% | 62.7% |
| Michigan | | 17 | | 4,839,252 | 2,313,746 | 2,479,183 | 46,323 | 165,437 D | 47.8% | 51.2% | 48.3% | 51.7% |
| Minnesota | | 9 | 1 | 2,828,387 | 1,346,695 | 1,445,014 | 36,678 | 98,319 D | 47.6% | 51.1% | 48.2% | 51.8% |
| Mississippi | 6 | | | 1,152,145 | 684,981 | 458,094 | 9,070 | 226,887 R | 59.5% | 39.8% | 59.9% | 40.1% |
| Missouri | 11 | | | 2,731,364 | 1,455,713 | 1,259,171 | 16,480 | 196,542 R | 53.3% | 46.1% | 53.6% | 46.4% |
| Montana | 3 | | | 450,445 | 266,063 | 173,710 | 10,672 | 92,353 R | 59.1% | 38.6% | 60.5% | 39.5% |
| Nebraska | 5 | | | 778,186 | 512,814 | 254,328 | 11,044 | 258,486 R | 65.9% | 32.7% | 66.8% | 33.2% |
| Nevada | 5 | | | 829,587 | 418,690 | 397,190 | 13,707 | 21,500 R | 50.5% | 47.9% | 51.3% | 48.7% |
| New Hampshire | | 4 | | 677,738 | 331,237 | 340,511 | 5,990 | 9,274 D | 48.9% | 50.2% | 49.3% | 50.7% |
| New Jersey | | 15 | | 3,611,691 | 1,670,003 | 1,911,430 | 30,258 | 241,427 D | 46.2% | 52.9% | 46.6% | 53.4% |
| New Mexico | 5 | | | 756,304 | 376,930 | 370,942 | 8,432 | 5,988 R | 49.8% | 49.0% | 50.4% | 49.6% |
| New York | | 31 | | 7,391,036 | 2,962,567 | 4,314,280 | 114,189 | 1,351,713 D | 40.1% | 58.4% | 40.7% | 59.3% |
| North Carolina | 15 | | | 3,501,007 | 1,961,166 | 1,525,849 | 13,992 | 435,317 R | 56.0% | 43.6% | 56.2% | 43.8% |
| North Dakota | 3 | | | 312,833 | 196,651 | 111,052 | 5,130 | 85,599 R | 62.9% | 35.5% | 63.9% | 36.1% |
| Ohio | 20 | | | 5,627,908 | 2,859,768 | 2,741,167 | 26,973 | 118,601 R | 50.8% | 48.7% | 51.1% | 48.9% |
| Oklahoma | 7 | | | 1,463,758 | 959,792 | 503,966 | | 455,826 R | 65.6% | 34.4% | 65.6% | 34.4% |
| Oregon | | 7 | | 1,836,782 | 866,831 | 943,163 | 26,788 | 76,332 D | 47.2% | 51.3% | 47.9% | 52.1% |
| Pennsylvania | | 21 | | 5,769,590 | 2,793,847 | 2,938,095 | 37,648 | 144,248 D | 48.4% | 50.9% | 48.7% | 51.3% |
| Rhode Island | | 4 | | 437,134 | 169,046 | 259,760 | 8,328 | 90,714 D | 38.7% | 59.4% | 39.4% | 60.6% |
| South Carolina | 8 | | | 1,617,730 | 937,974 | 661,699 | 18,057 | 276,275 R | 58.0% | 40.9% | 58.6% | 41.4% |
| South Dakota | 3 | | | 388,215 | 232,584 | 149,244 | 6,387 | 83,340 R | 59.9% | 38.4% | 60.9% | 39.1% |
| Tennessee | 11 | | | 2,437,319 | 1,384,375 | 1,036,477 | 16,467 | 347,898 R | 56.8% | 42.5% | 57.2% | 42.8% |
| Texas | 34 | | | 7,410,765 | 4,526,917 | 2,832,704 | 51,144 | 1,694,213 R | 61.1% | 38.2% | 61.5% | 38.5% |
| Utah | 5 | | | 927,844 | 663,742 | 241,199 | 22,903 | 422,543 R | 71.5% | 26.0% | 73.3% | 26.7% |
| Vermont | | 3 | | 312,309 | 121,180 | 184,067 | 7,062 | 62,887 D | 38.8% | 58.9% | 39.7% | 60.3% |
| Virginia | 13 | | | 3,198,367 | 1,716,959 | 1,454,742 | 26,666 | 262,217 R | 53.7% | 45.5% | 54.1% | 45.9% |
| Washington | | 11 | | 2,859,084 | 1,304,894 | 1,510,201 | 43,989 | 205,307 D | 45.6% | 52.8% | 46.4% | 53.6% |
| West Virginia | 5 | | | 755,887 | 423,778 | 326,541 | 5,568 | 97,237 R | 56.1% | 43.2% | 56.5% | 43.5% |
| Wisconsin | | 10 | | 2,997,007 | 1,478,120 | 1,489,504 | 29,383 | 11,384 D | 49.3% | 49.7% | 49.8% | 50.2% |
| Wyoming | 3 | | | 243,428 | 167,629 | 70,776 | 5,023 | 96,853 R | 68.9% | 29.1% | 70.3% | 29.7% |
| District of Columbia | | 3 | | 227,586 | 21,256 | 202,970 | 3,360 | 181,714 D | 9.3% | 89.2% | 9.5% | 90.5% |
| Total | 286 | 251 | 1 | 122,295,345 | 62,040,610 | 59,028,439 | 1,226,296 | 3,012,171 R | 50.7% | 48.3% | 51.2% | 48.8% |

Note: A Democratic elector in Minnesota cast a vote for Edwards rather than Kerry.

# UNITED STATES
## PRESIDENT 2004 MINOR PARTIES

| State | Total | Nader | Badnarik | Peroutka | Cobb | Other Candidates and Scattered Write-ins |
|---|---|---|---|---|---|---|
| Alabama | 13,122 | 6,701 | 3,529 | 1,994 | | 898 |
| Alaska | 10,684 | 5,069 | 1,675 | 2,092 | 1,058 | 790 |
| Arizona | 14,767 | 2,773* | 11,856 | | 138* | |
| Arkansas | 12,094 | 6,171 | 2,352 | 2,083 | 1,488 | |
| California | 166,541 | 21,213* | 50,165 | 26,645 | 40,771 | 27,747 |
| Colorado | 27,343 | 12,718 | 7,664 | 2,562 | 1,591 | 2,808 |
| Connecticut | 27,455 | 12,969 | 3,367 | 1,543 | 9,564 | 12 |
| Delaware | 3,378 | 2,153 | 586 | 289 | 250 | 100 |
| Florida | 61,744 | 32,971 | 11,996 | 6,626 | 3,917 | 6,234 |
| Georgia | 21,472 | 2,231* | 18,387 | 580* | 228* | 46 |
| Hawaii | 3,114 | | 1,377 | | 1,737 | |
| Idaho | 8,114 | 1,115* | 3,844 | 3,084 | 58* | 13 |
| Illinois | 36,826 | 3,571* | 32,442 | 440* | 241* | 132 |
| Indiana | 19,553 | 1,328* | 18,058 | | 102* | 65 |
| Iowa | 13,053 | 5,973 | 2,992 | 1,304 | 1,141 | 1,643 |
| Kansas | 16,307 | 9,348 | 4,013 | 2,899 | 33* | 14 |
| Kentucky | 13,710 | 8,856 | 2,619 | 2,213 | | 22 |
| Louisiana | 20,638 | 7,032 | 2,781 | 5,203 | 1,276 | 4,346 |
| Maine | 13,709 | 8,069 | 1,965 | 735 | 2,936 | 4 |
| Maryland | 27,482 | 11,854 | 6,094 | 3,421 | 3,632 | 2,481 |
| Massachusetts | 37,479 | 4,806* | 15,022 | | 10,623 | 7,028 |
| Michigan | 46,323 | 24,035 | 10,552 | 4,980 | 5,325 | 1,431 |
| Minnesota | 36,678 | 18,683 | 4,639 | 3,074 | 4,408 | 5,874 |
| Mississippi | 9,070 | 3,177 | 1,793 | 1,759 | 1,073 | 1,268 |
| Missouri | 16,480 | 1,294* | 9,831 | 5,355 | | |
| Montana | 10,672 | 6,168 | 1,733 | 1,764 | 996 | 11 |
| Nebraska | 11,044 | 5,698 | 2,041 | 1,314 | 978 | 1,013 |
| Nevada | 13,707 | 4,838 | 3,176 | 1,152 | 853 | 3,688 |
| New Hampshire | 5,990 | 4,479 | 372* | 161* | | 978 |
| New Jersey | 30,258 | 19,418 | 4,514 | 2,750 | 1,807 | 1,769 |
| New Mexico | 8,432 | 4,053 | 2,382 | 771 | 1,226 | |
| New York | 114,189 | 99,873 | 11,607 | 207* | 87* | 2,415 |
| North Carolina | 13,992 | 1,805* | 11,731 | | 108* | 348 |
| North Dakota | 5,130 | 3,756 | 851 | 514 | | 9 |
| Ohio | 26,973 | | 14,676 | 11,939 | 192* | 166 |
| Oklahoma | | | | | | |
| Oregon | 26,788 | | 7,260 | 5,257 | 5,315 | 8,956 |
| Pennsylvania | 37,648 | 2,656* | 21,185 | 6,318 | 6,319 | 1,170 |
| Rhode Island | 8,328 | 4,651 | 907 | 339 | 1,333 | 1,098 |
| South Carolina | 18,057 | 5,520 | 3,608 | 5,317 | 1,488 | 2,124 |
| South Dakota | 6,387 | 4,320 | 964 | 1,103 | | |
| Tennessee | 16,467 | 8,992 | 4,866 | 2,570 | 33* | 6 |
| Texas | 51,144 | 9,159* | 38,787 | 1,636* | 1,014* | 548 |
| Utah | 22,903 | 11,305 | 3,375 | 6,841 | 39* | 1,343 |
| Vermont | 7,062 | 4,494 | 1,102 | | | 1,466 |
| Virginia | 26,666 | 2,393* | 11,032 | 10,161 | 104* | 2,976 |
| Washington | 43,989 | 23,283 | 11,955 | 3,922 | 2,974 | 1,855 |
| West Virginia | 5,568 | 4,063 | 1,405 | 82* | 5* | 13 |
| Wisconsin | 29,383 | 16,390 | 6,464 | | 2,661 | 3,868 |
| Wyoming | 5,023 | 2,741 | 1,171 | 631 | | 480 |
| District of Columbia | 3,360 | 1,485 | 502 | | 737 | 636 |
| Total | 1,226,296 | 465,650 | 397,265 | 143,630 | 119,859 | 99,892 |

Note: An asterisk (*) indicates write-in votes.

# UNITED STATES

## POPULAR VOTE FOR PRESIDENT 1920 TO 2004

| Year | Total Vote | Republican Vote | Republican Candidate | Democratic Vote | Democratic Candidate | Other Vote | Plurality | | Percentage Total Vote Rep. | Dem. | Major Vote Rep. | Dem. |
|---|---|---|---|---|---|---|---|---|---|---|---|---|
| 2004 | 122,295,345 | 62,040,610 | Bush, George W. | 59,028,439 | Kerry, John | 1,226,296 | 3,012,171 | R | 50.7% | 48.3% | 51.2% | 48.8% |
| 2000 | 105,396,627 | 50,455,156 | Bush, George W. | 50,992,335 | Gore, Al | 3,949,136 | 537,179 | D | 47.9% | 48.4% | 49.7% | 50.3% |
| 1996 | 96,277,872 | 39,198,755 | Dole, Bob | 47,402,357 | Clinton, Bill | 9,676,760 | 8,203,602 | D | 40.7% | 49.2% | 45.3% | 54.7% |
| 1992 | 104,425,014 | 39,103,882 | Bush, George | 44,909,326 | Clinton, Bill | 20,411,806 | 5,805,444 | D | 37.4% | 43.0% | 46.5% | 53.5% |
| 1988 | 91,594,809 | 48,886,097 | Bush, George | 41,809,074 | Dukakis, Michael S. | 899,638 | 7,077,023 | R | 53.4% | 45.6% | 53.9% | 46.1% |
| 1984 | 92,652,842 | 54,455,075 | Reagan, Ronald | 37,577,185 | Mondale, Walter F. | 620,582 | 16,877,890 | R | 58.8% | 40.6% | 59.2% | 40.8% |
| 1980 | 86,515,221 | 43,904,153 | Reagan, Ronald | 35,483,883 | Carter, Jimmy | 7,127,185 | 8,420,270 | R | 50.7% | 41.0% | 55.3% | 44.7% |
| 1976 | 81,555,889 | 39,147,793 | Ford, Gerald R. | 40,830,763 | Carter, Jimmy | 1,577,333 | 1,682,970 | D | 48.0% | 50.1% | 48.9% | 51.1% |
| 1972 | 77,718,554 | 47,169,911 | Nixon, Richard M. | 29,170,383 | McGovern, George S. | 1,378,260 | 17,999,528 | R | 60.7% | 37.5% | 61.8% | 38.2% |
| 1968 | 73,211,875 | 31,785,480 | Nixon, Richard M. | 31,275,166 | Humphrey, Hubert H. | 10,151,229 | 510,314 | R | 43.4% | 42.7% | 50.4% | 49.6% |
| 1964 | 70,644,592 | 27,178,188 | Goldwater, Barry M. | 43,129,566 | Johnson, Lyndon B. | 336,838 | 15,951,378 | D | 38.5% | 61.1% | 38.7% | 61.3% |
| 1960 | 68,838,219 | 34,108,157 | Nixon, Richard M. | 34,226,731 | Kennedy, John F. | 503,331 | 118,574 | D | 49.5% | 49.7% | 49.9% | 50.1% |
| 1956 | 62,026,908 | 35,590,472 | Eisenhower, Dwight D. | 26,022,752 | Stevenson, Adlai E. | 413,684 | 9,567,720 | R | 57.4% | 42.0% | 57.8% | 42.2% |
| 1952 | 61,550,918 | 33,936,234 | Eisenhower, Dwight D. | 27,314,992 | Stevenson, Adlai E. | 299,692 | 6,621,242 | R | 55.1% | 44.4% | 55.4% | 44.6% |
| 1948 | 48,793,826 | 21,991,291 | Dewey, Thomas E. | 24,179,345 | Truman, Harry S. | 2,623,190 | 2,188,054 | D | 45.1% | 49.6% | 47.6% | 52.4% |
| 1944 | 47,976,670 | 22,017,617 | Dewey, Thomas E. | 25,612,610 | Roosevelt, Franklin D. | 346,443 | 3,594,993 | D | 45.9% | 53.4% | 46.2% | 53.8% |
| 1940 | 49,900,418 | 22,348,480 | Willkie, Wendell | 27,313,041 | Roosevelt, Franklin D. | 238,897 | 4,964,561 | D | 44.8% | 54.7% | 45.0% | 55.0% |
| 1936 | 45,654,763 | 16,684,231 | Landon, Alfred M. | 27,757,333 | Roosevelt, Franklin D. | 1,213,199 | 11,073,102 | D | 36.5% | 60.8% | 37.5% | 62.5% |
| 1932 | 39,758,759 | 15,760,684 | Hoover, Herbert C. | 22,829,501 | Roosevelt, Franklin D. | 1,168,574 | 7,068,817 | D | 39.6% | 57.4% | 40.8% | 59.2% |
| 1928 | 36,805,951 | 21,437,277 | Hoover, Herbert C. | 15,007,698 | Smith, Alfred E. | 360,976 | 6,429,579 | R | 58.2% | 40.8% | 58.8% | 41.2% |
| 1924 | 29,095,023 | 15,719,921 | Coolidge, Calvin | 8,386,704 | Davis, John W. | 4,988,398 | 7,333,217 | R | 54.0% | 28.8% | 65.2% | 34.8% |
| 1920 | 26,768,613 | 16,153,115 | Harding, Warren G. | 9,133,092 | Cox, James M. | 1,482,406 | 7,020,023 | R | 60.3% | 34.1% | 63.9% | 36.1% |

Note: For detail of other vote see note section included with each U.S. summary table that follows.

## ELECTORAL COLLEGE VOTE 1920 TO 2004

| Year | Total | Republican | Democratic | Other | |
|---|---|---|---|---|---|
| 2004 | 538 | 286 | 251 | 1 | EDWARDS |
| 2000 | 538 | 271 | 266 | 1 | (Blank) |
| 1996 | 538 | 159 | 379 | — | |
| 1992 | 538 | 168 | 370 | — | |
| 1988 | 538 | 426 | 111 | 1 | BENTSEN |
| 1984 | 538 | 525 | 13 | — | |
| 1980 | 538 | 489 | 49 | — | |
| 1976 | 538 | 240 | 297 | 1 | REAGAN |
| 1972 | 538 | 520 | 17 | 1 | LIBERTARIAN |
| 1968 | 538 | 301 | 191 | 46 | AIP |
| 1964 | 538 | 52 | 486 | — | |
| 1960 | 537 | 219 | 303 | 15 | BYRD |
| 1956 | 531 | 457 | 73 | 1 | JONES |
| 1952 | 531 | 442 | 89 | — | |
| 1948 | 531 | 189 | 303 | 39 | SR |
| 1944 | 531 | 99 | 432 | — | |
| 1940 | 531 | 82 | 449 | — | |
| 1936 | 531 | 8 | 523 | — | |
| 1932 | 531 | 59 | 472 | — | |
| 1928 | 531 | 444 | 87 | — | |
| 1924 | 531 | 382 | 136 | 13 | PROGRESSIVE |
| 1920 | 531 | 404 | 127 | — | |

12

# PRESIDENT 2000

In New York the Republican figures include Conservative and the Democratic figures include Liberal and Working Families.

In Minnesota the Democratic candidate appears on the ballot as Democratic-Farmer-Labor. In many states various non-major party candidates appeared on the ballot with variations of the party designations, were carried with entirely different party labels, or were listed as "Independent."

The candidates listed below include all who appeared on the ballot in at least one state. Write-in votes for minor party candidates are credited to their total below. See the minor party chart on page 14 for details.

| | | |
|---|---|---|
| 50,455,156 | George W. Bush and Richard B. Cheney | Republican |
| 50,992,335 | Al Gore and Joseph I. Lieberman | Democratic |
| 2,882,738 | Ralph Nader and Winona LaDuke | Green |
| 449,077 | Pat Buchanan and Ezola Foster | Reform |
| 384,429 | Harry Browne and Art Olivier | Libertarian |
| 98,020 | Howard Phillips and J. Curtis Frazier | Constitution |
| 83,525 | John Hagelin and Nat Goldhaber | Natural Law |
| 7,378 | James E. Harris Jr. and Margaret Trowe | Socialist Worker |
| 5,775 | L. Neil Smith and Vin Suprynowicz | Arizona Libertarian |
| 5,602 | David McReynolds and Mary Cal Hollis | Socialist |
| 4,795 | Monica Moorehead and Gloria La Riva | Workers World |
| 1,606 | Cathy Gordon Brown and Sabrina R. Allen | Independent |
| 1,044 | Denny Lane and Dale Wilkinson | Vermont Grassroots |
| 535 | Randall Venson and Gene Kelly | Independent |
| 208 | Earl F. Dodge and W. Dean Watkins | Prohibition |
| 161 | Louie G. Youngkeit and Robert Leo Beck | Unaffiliated |

In addition to the votes listed above, 20,928 scattered write-in votes were reported from various states, and 3,315 votes were cast for "None of these Candidates" in Nevada.

# UNITED STATES

## PRESIDENT 2000

| State | Electoral Vote Rep. | Electoral Vote Dem. | Electoral Vote Other | Total Vote | Republican | Democratic | Green (Nader) | Other | Rep.-Dem. Plurality | Percentage Rep. | Percentage Dem. | Percentage Green |
|---|---|---|---|---|---|---|---|---|---|---|---|---|
| Alabama | 9 | | | 1,666,272 | 941,173 | 692,611 | 18,323 | 14,165 | 248,562 R | 56.5% | 41.6% | 1.1% |
| Alaska | 3 | | | 285,560 | 167,398 | 79,004 | 28,747 | 10,411 | 88,394 R | 58.6% | 27.7% | 10.1% |
| Arizona | 8 | | | 1,532,016 | 781,652 | 685,341 | 45,645 | 19,378 | 96,311 R | 51.0% | 44.7% | 3.0% |
| Arkansas | 6 | | | 921,781 | 472,940 | 422,768 | 13,421 | 12,652 | 50,172 R | 51.3% | 45.9% | 1.5% |
| California | | 54 | | 10,965,856 | 4,567,429 | 5,861,203 | 418,707 | 118,517 | 1,293,774 D | 41.7% | 53.4% | 3.8% |
| Colorado | 8 | | | 1,741,368 | 883,748 | 738,227 | 91,434 | 27,959 | 145,521 R | 50.8% | 42.4% | 5.3% |
| Connecticut | | 8 | | 1,459,525 | 561,094 | 816,015 | 64,452 | 17,964 | 254,921 D | 38.4% | 55.9% | 4.4% |
| Delaware | | 3 | | 327,622 | 137,288 | 180,068 | 8,307 | 1,959 | 42,780 D | 41.9% | 55.0% | 2.5% |
| Florida | 25 | | | 5,963,110 | 2,912,790 | 2,912,253 | 97,488 | 40,579 | 537 R | 48.8% | 48.8% | 1.6% |
| Georgia | 13 | | | 2,596,645 | 1,419,720 | 1,116,230 | 13,273 | 47,422 | 303,490 R | 54.7% | 43.0% | 0.5% |
| Hawaii | | 4 | | 367,951 | 137,845 | 205,286 | 21,623 | 3,197 | 67,441 D | 37.5% | 55.8% | 5.9% |
| Idaho | 4 | | | 501,621 | 336,937 | 138,637 | 12,292 | 13,755 | 198,300 R | 67.2% | 27.6% | 2.5% |
| Illinois | | 22 | | 4,742,123 | 2,019,421 | 2,589,026 | 103,759 | 29,917 | 569,605 D | 42.6% | 54.6% | 2.2% |
| Indiana | 12 | | | 2,199,302 | 1,245,836 | 901,980 | 18,531 | 32,955 | 343,856 R | 56.6% | 41.0% | 0.8% |
| Iowa | | 7 | | 1,315,563 | 634,373 | 638,517 | 29,374 | 13,299 | 4,144 D | 48.2% | 48.5% | 2.2% |
| Kansas | 6 | | | 1,072,218 | 622,332 | 399,276 | 36,086 | 14,524 | 223,056 R | 58.0% | 37.2% | 3.4% |
| Kentucky | 8 | | | 1,544,187 | 872,492 | 638,898 | 23,192 | 9,605 | 233,594 R | 56.5% | 41.4% | 1.5% |
| Louisiana | 9 | | | 1,765,656 | 927,871 | 792,344 | 20,473 | 24,968 | 135,527 R | 52.6% | 44.9% | 1.2% |
| Maine | | 4 | | 651,817 | 286,616 | 319,951 | 37,127 | 8,123 | 33,335 D | 44.0% | 49.1% | 5.7% |
| Maryland | | 10 | | 2,020,480 | 813,797 | 1,140,782 | 53,768 | 12,133 | 326,985 D | 40.3% | 56.5% | 2.7% |
| Massachusetts | | 12 | | 2,702,984 | 878,502 | 1,616,487 | 173,564 | 34,431 | 737,985 D | 32.5% | 59.8% | 6.4% |
| Michigan | | 18 | | 4,232,711 | 1,953,139 | 2,170,418 | 84,165 | 24,989 | 217,279 D | 46.1% | 51.3% | 2.0% |
| Minnesota | | 10 | | 2,438,685 | 1,109,659 | 1,168,266 | 126,696 | 34,064 | 58,607 D | 45.5% | 47.9% | 5.2% |
| Mississippi | 7 | | | 994,184 | 572,844 | 404,614 | 8,122 | 8,604 | 168,230 R | 57.6% | 40.7% | 0.8% |
| Missouri | 11 | | | 2,359,892 | 1,189,924 | 1,111,138 | 38,515 | 20,315 | 78,786 R | 50.4% | 47.1% | 1.6% |
| Montana | 3 | | | 410,997 | 240,178 | 137,126 | 24,437 | 9,256 | 103,052 R | 58.4% | 33.4% | 5.9% |
| Nebraska | 5 | | | 697,019 | 433,862 | 231,780 | 24,540 | 6,837 | 202,082 R | 62.2% | 33.3% | 3.5% |
| Nevada | 4 | | | 608,970 | 301,575 | 279,978 | 15,008 | 12,409 | 21,597 R | 49.5% | 46.0% | 2.5% |
| New Hampshire | 4 | | | 569,081 | 273,559 | 266,348 | 22,198 | 6,976 | 7,211 R | 48.1% | 46.8% | 3.9% |
| New Jersey | | 15 | | 3,187,226 | 1,284,173 | 1,788,850 | 94,554 | 19,649 | 504,677 D | 40.3% | 56.1% | 3.0% |
| New Mexico | | 5 | | 598,605 | 286,417 | 286,783 | 21,251 | 4,154 | 366 D | 47.8% | 47.9% | 3.6% |
| New York | | 33 | | 6,821,999 | 2,403,374 | 4,107,697 | 244,030 | 66,898 | 1,704,323 D | 35.2% | 60.2% | 3.6% |
| North Carolina | 14 | | | 2,911,262 | 1,631,163 | 1,257,692 | — | 22,407 | 373,471 R | 56.0% | 43.2% | — |
| North Dakota | 3 | | | 288,256 | 174,852 | 95,284 | 9,486 | 8,634 | 79,568 R | 60.7% | 33.1% | 3.3% |
| Ohio | 21 | | | 4,701,998 | 2,350,363 | 2,183,628 | 117,799 | 50,208 | 166,735 R | 50.0% | 46.4% | 2.5% |
| Oklahoma | 8 | | | 1,234,229 | 744,337 | 474,276 | | 15,616 | 270,061 R | 60.3% | 38.4% | — |
| Oregon | | 7 | | 1,533,968 | 713,577 | 720,342 | 77,357 | 22,692 | 6,765 D | 46.5% | 47.0% | 5.0% |
| Pennsylvania | | 23 | | 4,913,119 | 2,281,127 | 2,485,967 | 103,392 | 42,633 | 204,840 D | 46.4% | 50.6% | 2.1% |
| Rhode Island | | 4 | | 409,047 | 130,555 | 249,508 | 25,052 | 3,932 | 118,953 D | 31.9% | 61.0% | 6.1% |
| South Carolina | 8 | | | 1,382,717 | 785,937 | 565,561 | 20,200 | 11,019 | 220,376 R | 56.8% | 40.9% | 1.5% |
| South Dakota | 3 | | | 316,269 | 190,700 | 118,804 | — | 6,765 | 71,896 R | 60.3% | 37.6% | — |
| Tennessee | 11 | | | 2,076,181 | 1,061,949 | 981,720 | 19,781 | 12,731 | 80,229 R | 51.1% | 47.3% | 1.0% |
| Texas | 32 | | | 6,407,637 | 3,799,639 | 2,433,746 | 137,994 | 36,258 | 1,365,893 R | 59.3% | 38.0% | 2.2% |
| Utah | 5 | | | 770,754 | 515,096 | 203,053 | 35,850 | 16,755 | 312,043 R | 66.8% | 26.3% | 4.7% |
| Vermont | | 3 | | 294,308 | 119,775 | 149,022 | 20,374 | 5,137 | 29,247 D | 40.7% | 50.6% | 6.9% |
| Virginia | 13 | | | 2,739,447 | 1,437,490 | 1,217,290 | 59,398 | 25,269 | 220,200 R | 52.5% | 44.4% | 2.2% |
| Washington | | 11 | | 2,487,433 | 1,108,864 | 1,247,652 | 103,002 | 27,915 | 138,788 D | 44.6% | 50.2% | 4.1% |
| West Virginia | 5 | | | 648,124 | 336,475 | 295,497 | 10,680 | 5,472 | 40,978 R | 51.9% | 45.6% | 1.6% |
| Wisconsin | | 11 | | 2,598,607 | 1,237,279 | 1,242,987 | 94,070 | 24,271 | 5,708 D | 47.6% | 47.8% | 3.6% |
| Wyoming | 3 | | | 218,351 | 147,947 | 60,481 | 4,625 | 5,298 | 87,466 R | 67.8% | 27.7% | 2.1% |
| District of Columbia | | 2 | 1 | 201,894 | 18,073 | 171,923 | 10,576 | 1,322 | 153,850 D | 9.0% | 85.2% | 5.2% |
| Total | 271 | 266 | 1 | 105,396,627 | 50,455,156 | 50,992,335 | 2,882,738 | 1,066,398 | 537,179 D | 47.9% | 48.4% | 2.7% |

# UNITED STATES

## PRESIDENT 2000 MINOR PARTIES

| State | Total | Buchanan | Browne | Phillips | Hagelin | Other Candidates and Scattered Write-ins |
|---|---|---|---|---|---|---|
| Alabama | 14,165 | 6,351 | 5,893 | 775 | 447 | 699 |
| Alaska | 10,411 | 5,192 | 2,636 | 596 | 919 | 1,068 |
| Arizona | 19,378 | 12,373 | | 110 | 1,120 | 5,775 |
| Arkansas | 12,652 | 7,358 | 2,781 | 1,415 | 1,098 | — |
| California | 118,517 | 44,987 | 45,520 | 17,042 | 10,934 | 34 |
| Colorado | 27,959 | 10,465 | 12,799 | 1,319 | 2,240 | 1,136 |
| Connecticut | 17,964 | 4,731 | 3,484 | 9,695 | 40 | 14 |
| Delaware | 1,959 | 777 | 774 | 208 | 107 | 93 |
| Florida | 40,579 | 17,484 | 16,415 | 1,371 | 2,281 | 3,028 |
| Georgia | 47,422 | 10,926 | 36,332 | 140 | | 24 |
| Hawaii | 3,197 | 1,071 | 1,477 | 343 | 306 | — |
| Idaho | 13,755 | 7,615 | 3,488 | 1,469 | 1,177 | 6 |
| Illinois | 29,917 | 16,106 | 11,623 | 57 | 2,127 | 4 |
| Indiana | 32,955 | 16,959 | 15,530 | 200 | 167 | 99 |
| Iowa | 13,299 | 5,731 | 3,209 | 613 | 2,281 | 1,465 |
| Kansas | 14,524 | 7,370 | 4,525 | 1,254 | 1,375 | — |
| Kentucky | 9,605 | 4,173 | 2,896 | 923 | 1,533 | 80 |
| Louisiana | 24,968 | 14,356 | 2,951 | 5,483 | 1,075 | 1,103 |
| Maine | 8,123 | 4,443 | 3,074 | 579 | | 27 |
| Maryland | 12,133 | 4,248 | 5,310 | 919 | 176 | 1,480 |
| Massachusetts | 34,431 | 11,149 | 16,366 | | 2,884 | 4,032 |
| Michigan | 24,989 | 2,061 | 16,711 | 3,791 | 2,426 | — |
| Minnesota | 34,064 | 22,166 | 5,282 | 3,272 | 2,294 | 1,050 |
| Mississippi | 8,604 | 2,265 | 2,009 | 3,267 | 450 | 613 |
| Missouri | 20,315 | 9,818 | 7,436 | 1,957 | 1,104 | — |
| Montana | 9,256 | 5,697 | 1,718 | 1,155 | 675 | 11 |
| Nebraska | 6,837 | 3,646 | 2,245 | 468 | 478 | — |
| Nevada | 12,409 | 4,747 | 3,311 | 621 | 415 | 3,315 |
| New Hampshire | 6,976 | 2,615 | 2,757 | 328 | | 1,276 |
| New Jersey | 19,649 | 6,989 | 6,312 | 1,409 | 2,215 | 2,724 |
| New Mexico | 4,154 | 1,392 | 2,058 | 343 | 361 | — |
| New York | 66,898 | 31,599 | 7,649 | 1,498 | 24,361 | 1,791 |
| North Carolina | 22,407 | 8,874 | 12,307 | | | 1,226 |
| North Dakota | 8,634 | 7,288 | 660 | 373 | 313 | — |
| Ohio | 50,208 | 26,721 | 13,473 | 3,823 | 6,181 | 10 |
| Oklahoma | 15,616 | 9,014 | 6,602 | | | — |
| Oregon | 22,692 | 7,063 | 7,447 | 2,189 | 2,574 | 3,419 |
| Pennsylvania | 42,633 | 16,023 | 11,248 | 14,428 | | 934 |
| Rhode Island | 3,932 | 2,273 | 742 | 97 | 271 | 549 |
| South Carolina | 11,019 | 3,519 | 4,876 | 1,682 | 942 | — |
| South Dakota | 6,765 | 3,322 | 1,662 | 1,781 | | — |
| Tennessee | 12,731 | 4,250 | 4,284 | 1,015 | 613 | 2,569 |
| Texas | 36,258 | 12,394 | 23,160 | 567 | | 137 |
| Utah | 16,755 | 9,319 | 3,616 | 2,709 | 763 | 348 |
| Vermont | 5,137 | 2,192 | 784 | 153 | 219 | 1,789 |
| Virginia | 25,269 | 5,455 | 15,198 | 1,809 | | 2,807 |
| Washington | 27,915 | 7,171 | 13,135 | 1,989 | 2,927 | 2,693 |
| West Virginia | 5,472 | 3,169 | 1,912 | 23 | 367 | 1 |
| Wisconsin | 24,271 | 11,446 | 6,640 | 2,042 | 878 | 3,265 |
| Wyoming | 5,298 | 2,724 | 1,443 | 720 | 411 | — |
| District of Columbia | 1,322 | | 669 | | | 653 |
| Total | 1,066,398 | 449,077 | 384,429 | 98,020 | 83,525 | 51,347 |

# UNITED STATES

## VOTER TURNOUT 2000

| State | 2000 Voting Age Population Est. | November 2000 Registration | Percentage Voting Age Registered | Presidential Vote | Presidential Vote as Percentage of | | U.S. House Vote | Senate Vote | Governor Vote |
|---|---|---|---|---|---|---|---|---|---|
| | | | | | Voting Age Population | Registered Voters | | | |
| Alabama | 3,333,000 | 2,528,963 | 75.9% | 1,666,272 | 50.0% | 65.9% | 1,438,994 | | |
| Alaska | 430,000 | 473,648 | 110.2% | 285,560 | 66.4% | 60.3% | 274,393 | | |
| Arizona | 3,625,000 | 2,654,700 | 73.2% | 1,532,016 | 42.3% | 57.7% | 1,465,656 | 1,397,076 | |
| Arkansas | 1,929,000 | 1,555,809 | 80.7% | 921,781 | 47.8% | 59.2% | 632,765 | | |
| California | 24,873,000 | 15,707,307 | 63.2% | 10,965,856 | 44.1% | 69.8% | 10,437,665 | 10,623,614 | |
| Colorado | 3,067,000 | 2,858,239 | 93.2% | 1,741,368 | 56.8% | 60.9% | 1,623,882 | | |
| Connecticut | 2,499,000 | 2,031,626 | 81.3% | 1,459,525 | 58.4% | 71.8% | 1,313,490 | 1,311,261 | |
| Delaware | 582,000 | 503,672 | 86.5% | 327,622 | 56.3% | 65.0% | 313,171 | 327,017 | 323,688 |
| Florida | 11,774,000 | 8,752,717 | 74.3% | 5,963,110 | 50.6% | 68.1% | 5,011,372 | 5,856,731 | |
| Georgia | 5,893,000 | 4,648,205 | 78.9% | 2,596,645 | 44.1% | 55.9% | 2,416,622 | 2,428,510 | |
| Hawaii | 909,000 | 637,349 | 70.1% | 367,951 | 40.5% | 57.7% | 340,424 | 345,623 | |
| Idaho | 921,000 | 728,085 | 79.1% | 501,621 | 54.5% | 68.9% | 492,835 | | |
| Illinois | 8,983,000 | 7,117,449 | 79.2% | 4,742,123 | 52.8% | 66.6% | 4,393,352 | | |
| Indiana | 4,448,000 | 4,000,809 | 89.9% | 2,199,302 | 49.4% | 55.0% | 2,156,744 | 2,145,209 | 2,179,413 |
| Iowa | 2,165,000 | 1,969,199 | 91.0% | 1,315,563 | 60.8% | 66.8% | 1,275,934 | | |
| Kansas | 1,983,000 | 1,623,623 | 81.9% | 1,072,218 | 54.1% | 66.0% | 1,038,379 | | |
| Kentucky | 2,993,000 | 2,556,815 | 85.4% | 1,544,187 | 51.6% | 60.4% | 1,435,409 | | 580,074 |
| Louisiana | 3,255,000 | 2,782,929 | 85.5% | 1,765,656 | 54.2% | 63.4% | 1,202,171 | | 1,295,205 |
| Maine | 968,000 | 947,189 | 97.9% | 651,817 | 67.3% | 68.8% | 638,399 | 634,872 | |
| Maryland | 3,925,000 | 2,715,366 | 69.2% | 2,020,480 | 51.5% | 74.4% | 1,926,764 | 1,946,898 | |
| Massachusetts | 4,749,000 | 4,000,218 | 84.2% | 2,702,984 | 56.9% | 67.6% | 2,347,375 | 2,599,420 | |
| Michigan | 7,358,000 | 6,861,342 | 93.3% | 4,232,711 | 56.6% | 60.7% | 4,069,736 | 4,167,685 | |
| Minnesota | 3,547,000 | 2,801,077 | 79.0% | 2,438,685 | 68.8% | 87.1% | 2,363,738 | 2,419,520 | |
| Mississippi | 2,047,000 | | | 994,184 | 48.6% | | 986,139 | 994,144 | 763,938 |
| Missouri | 4,105,000 | 3,676,664 | 89.6% | 2,359,892 | 57.5% | 64.2% | 2,325,788 | 2,361,586 | 2,346,830 |
| Montana | 668,000 | 698,260 | 104.5% | 410,997 | 61.5% | 58.9% | 410,523 | 411,601 | 410,192 |
| Nebraska | 1,234,000 | 1,085,272 | 87.9% | 697,019 | 56.5% | 64.2% | 683,071 | 692,344 | |
| Nevada | 1,390,000 | 878,970 | 63.2% | 608,970 | 43.8% | 69.3% | 585,204 | 600,250 | |
| New Hampshire | 911,000 | 856,519 | 94.0% | 569,081 | 62.5% | 66.4% | 556,417 | | 564,953 |
| New Jersey | 6,245,000 | 4,710,768 | 75.4% | 3,187,226 | 51.0% | 67.7% | 2,988,233 | 3,015,662 | |
| New Mexico | 1,263,000 | 928,931 | 73.5% | 598,605 | 47.4% | 64.4% | 587,514 | 589,526 | |
| New York | 13,805,000 | 11,262,816 | 81.6% | 6,821,999 | 49.4% | 60.6% | 5,823,850 | 6,779,839 | |
| North Carolina | 5,797,000 | 5,186,094 | 89.5% | 2,911,262 | 50.2% | 56.1% | 2,779,800 | | 2,942,062 |
| North Dakota | 477,000 | | | 288,256 | 60.4% | | 285,658 | 287,539 | 289,412 |
| Ohio | 8,433,000 | 7,537,822 | 89.4% | 4,701,998 | 55.8% | 62.4% | 4,517,838 | 4,448,801 | |
| Oklahoma | 2,531,000 | 2,233,602 | 88.2% | 1,234,229 | 48.8% | 55.3% | 1,087,515 | | |
| Oregon | 2,530,000 | 1,950,902 | 77.1% | 1,533,968 | 60.6% | 78.6% | 1,440,002 | | |
| Pennsylvania | 9,155,000 | 7,781,997 | 85.0% | 4,913,119 | 53.7% | 63.1% | 4,554,347 | 4,735,504 | |
| Rhode Island | 753,000 | 655,107 | 87.0% | 409,047 | 54.3% | 62.4% | 384,127 | 391,537 | |
| South Carolina | 2,977,000 | 2,266,200 | 76.1% | 1,382,717 | 46.4% | 61.0% | 1,321,312 | | |
| South Dakota | 542,000 | 520,881 | 96.1% | 316,269 | 58.4% | 60.7% | 314,761 | | |
| Tennessee | 4,221,000 | 3,400,487 | 80.6% | 2,076,181 | 49.2% | 61.1% | 1,854,378 | 1,928,613 | |
| Texas | 14,850,000 | 12,365,235 | 83.3% | 6,407,637 | 43.1% | 51.8% | 5,985,763 | 6,276,652 | |
| Utah | 1,465,000 | 1,120,129 | 76.5% | 770,754 | 52.6% | 68.8% | 758,754 | 769,704 | 761,806 |
| Vermont | 460,000 | 427,354 | 92.9% | 294,308 | 64.0% | 68.9% | 283,366 | 288,500 | 293,473 |
| Virginia | 5,263,000 | 4,071,471 | 77.4% | 2,739,447 | 52.1% | 67.3% | 2,421,729 | 2,718,301 | |
| Washington | 4,368,000 | 3,335,714 | 76.4% | 2,487,433 | 56.9% | 74.6% | 2,382,411 | 2,461,379 | 2,469,852 |
| West Virginia | 1,416,000 | 1,067,822 | 75.4% | 648,124 | 45.8% | 60.7% | 579,872 | 603,477 | 648,047 |
| Wisconsin | 3,930,000 | | | 2,598,607 | 66.1% | | 2,506,314 | 2,540,083 | |
| Wyoming | 358,000 | 220,012 | 61.5% | 218,351 | 61.0% | 99.2% | 212,312 | 213,659 | |
| District of Columbia | 411,000 | 354,410 | | 201,894 | 49.1% | 57.0% | | | |
| Total | 205,814,000 | 159,049,775 | 77.3% | 105,396,627 | 51.2% | 66.3% | 97,226,268 | 79,312,137 | 15,868,945 |

Sources: Registration figures—Committee for the Study of the American Electorate; Voting Age Population—U.S. Census Bureau.

Notes: Voting age population excluding states without registration: 199,360,000. Wisconsin and North Dakota do not maintain registration systems. Figures for Mississippi were unavailable. Excluding these three states, the percentage of voting age population that was registered was 79.8 percent. The presidential vote as a percentage of voting age population was 50.9 percent and as a percentage of registered voters was 63.8 percent.

# PRESIDENT 1996

In New York the Republican figures include Conservative, Freedom, and Right to Life votes and the Democratic figures include Liberal votes.

In Minnesota the Democratic candidate appears on the ballot as Democratic-Farmer-Labor. In many states various non-major party candidates appeared on the ballot with variations of the party designations, were carried with entirely different party labels, or were listed as "Independent."

The candidates listed below include all those who appeared on the ballot in at least one state. Write-in votes for minor party candidates are credited to their total below. See the minor party vote chart on page 18 for details.

| | | |
|---|---|---|
| 47,402,357 | Bill Clinton and Al Gore | Democratic |
| 39,198,755 | Bob Dole and Jack Kemp | Republican |
| 8,085,402 | Ross Perot and Pat Choate | Reform |
| 685,040 | Ralph Nader and Winona LaDuke | Green |
| 485,798 | Harry Browne and Jo Jorgensen | Libertarian |
| 184,658 | Howard Phillips and Herbert W. Titus | U.S. Taxpayers |
| 113,668 | John Hagelin and Mike Tompkins | Natural Law |
| 29,083 | Monica Moorehead and Gloria La Riva | Workers World |
| 25,332 | Marsha Feinland and Kate McClatchy | Peace and Freedom |
| 8,930 | Charles Collins and Rosemary Giumarra | Independent |
| 8,476 | James Harris and Laura Garza | Socialist Workers |
| 5,378 | Dennis Peron and Arlin D. Troutt Jr. | Grassroots |
| 4,706 | Mary Cal Hollis and Eric Chester | Socialist |
| 2,438 | Jerome White and Fred Mazelis | Socialist Equality |
| 1,847 | Diane Beall Templin and Gary Van Horn | American |
| 1,298 | Earl F. Dodge and Rachel B. Kelly | Prohibition |
| 1,101 | A. Peter Crane and Connie Chandler | Independent |
| 932 | Ralph Forbes and "Pro-Life" Anderson | America First |
| 787 | John Birrenbach and George McMahon | Independent Grassroots |
| 752 | Isabell Masters and Shirley Jean Masters | Looking Back |
| 408 | Steve Michael and Ann Northrop | Independent |

In addition to the votes listed above, 25,118 scattered write-in votes were reported from various states, and 5,608 votes were cast for "None of these Candidates" in Nevada.

# UNITED STATES

## PRESIDENT 1996

| State | Electoral Vote Rep. | Dem. | Other | Total Vote | Republican | Democratic | Reform | Other | Plurality | Rep. | Dem. | Reform |
|---|---|---|---|---|---|---|---|---|---|---|---|---|
| Alabama | 9 | | | 1,534,349 | 769,044 | 662,165 | 92,149 | 10,991 | 106,879 R | 50.1% | 43.2% | 6.0% |
| Alaska | 3 | | | 241,620 | 122,746 | 80,380 | 26,333 | 12,161 | 42,366 R | 50.8% | 33.3% | 10.9% |
| Arizona | | 8 | | 1,404,105 | 622,073 | 653,288 | 112,072 | 16,972 | 31,215 D | 44.3% | 46.5% | 8.0% |
| Arkansas | | 6 | | 884,262 | 325,416 | 475,171 | 69,884 | 13,791 | 149,755 D | 36.8% | 53.7% | 7.9% |
| California | | 54 | | 10,019,484 | 3,828,380 | 5,119,835 | 697,847 | 373,422 | 1,291,455 D | 38.2% | 51.1% | 7.0% |
| Colorado | 8 | | | 1,510,704 | 691,848 | 671,152 | 99,629 | 48,075 | 20,696 R | 45.8% | 44.4% | 6.6% |
| Connecticut | | 8 | | 1,392,614 | 483,109 | 735,740 | 139,523 | 34,242 | 252,631 D | 34.7% | 52.8% | 10.0% |
| Delaware | | 3 | | 271,084 | 99,062 | 140,355 | 28,719 | 2,948 | 41,293 D | 36.5% | 51.8% | 10.6% |
| Florida | | 25 | | 5,303,794 | 2,244,536 | 2,546,870 | 483,870 | 28,518 | 302,334 D | 42.3% | 48.0% | 9.1% |
| Georgia | 13 | | | 2,299,071 | 1,080,843 | 1,053,849 | 146,337 | 18,042 | 26,994 R | 47.0% | 45.8% | 6.4% |
| Hawaii | | 4 | | 360,120 | 113,943 | 205,012 | 27,358 | 13,807 | 91,069 D | 31.6% | 56.9% | 7.6% |
| Idaho | 4 | | | 491,719 | 256,595 | 165,443 | 62,518 | 7,163 | 91,152 R | 52.2% | 33.6% | 12.7% |
| Illinois | | 22 | | 4,311,391 | 1,587,021 | 2,341,744 | 346,408 | 36,218 | 754,723 D | 36.8% | 54.3% | 8.0% |
| Indiana | 12 | | | 2,135,842 | 1,006,693 | 887,424 | 224,299 | 17,426 | 119,269 R | 47.1% | 41.5% | 10.5% |
| Iowa | | 7 | | 1,234,075 | 492,644 | 620,258 | 105,159 | 16,014 | 127,614 D | 39.9% | 50.3% | 8.5% |
| Kansas | 6 | | | 1,074,300 | 583,245 | 387,659 | 92,639 | 10,757 | 195,586 R | 54.3% | 36.1% | 8.6% |
| Kentucky | | 8 | | 1,388,708 | 623,283 | 636,614 | 120,396 | 8,415 | 13,331 D | 44.9% | 45.8% | 8.7% |
| Louisiana | | 9 | | 1,783,959 | 712,586 | 927,837 | 123,293 | 20,243 | 215,251 D | 39.9% | 52.0% | 6.9% |
| Maine | | 4 | | 605,897 | 186,378 | 312,788 | 85,970 | 20,761 | 126,410 D | 30.8% | 51.6% | 14.2% |
| Maryland | | 10 | | 1,780,870 | 681,530 | 966,207 | 115,812 | 17,321 | 284,677 D | 38.3% | 54.3% | 6.5% |
| Massachusetts | | 12 | | 2,556,785 | 718,107 | 1,571,763 | 227,217 | 39,698 | 853,656 D | 28.1% | 61.5% | 8.9% |
| Michigan | | 18 | | 3,848,844 | 1,481,212 | 1,989,653 | 336,670 | 41,309 | 508,441 D | 38.5% | 51.7% | 8.7% |
| Minnesota | | 10 | | 2,192,640 | 766,476 | 1,120,438 | 257,704 | 48,022 | 353,962 D | 35.0% | 51.1% | 11.8% |
| Mississippi | 7 | | | 893,857 | 439,838 | 394,022 | 52,222 | 7,775 | 45,816 R | 49.2% | 44.1% | 5.8% |
| Missouri | | 11 | | 2,158,065 | 890,016 | 1,025,935 | 217,188 | 24,926 | 135,919 D | 41.2% | 47.5% | 10.1% |
| Montana | 3 | | | 407,261 | 179,652 | 167,922 | 55,229 | 4,458 | 11,730 R | 44.1% | 41.2% | 13.6% |
| Nebraska | 5 | | | 677,415 | 363,467 | 236,761 | 71,278 | 5,909 | 126,706 R | 53.7% | 35.0% | 10.5% |
| Nevada | | 4 | | 464,279 | 199,244 | 203,974 | 43,986 | 17,075 | 4,730 D | 42.9% | 43.9% | 9.5% |
| New Hampshire | | 4 | | 499,175 | 196,532 | 246,214 | 48,390 | 8,039 | 49,682 D | 39.4% | 49.3% | 9.7% |
| New Jersey | | 15 | | 3,075,807 | 1,103,078 | 1,652,329 | 262,134 | 58,266 | 549,251 D | 35.9% | 53.7% | 8.5% |
| New Mexico | | 5 | | 556,074 | 232,751 | 273,495 | 32,257 | 17,571 | 40,744 D | 41.9% | 49.2% | 5.8% |
| New York | | 33 | | 6,316,129 | 1,933,492 | 3,756,177 | 503,458 | 123,002 | 1,822,685 D | 30.6% | 59.5% | 8.0% |
| North Carolina | 14 | | | 2,515,807 | 1,225,938 | 1,107,849 | 168,059 | 13,961 | 118,089 R | 48.7% | 44.0% | 6.7% |
| North Dakota | 3 | | | 266,411 | 125,050 | 106,905 | 32,515 | 1,941 | 18,145 R | 46.9% | 40.1% | 12.2% |
| Ohio | | 21 | | 4,534,434 | 1,859,883 | 2,148,222 | 483,207 | 43,122 | 288,339 D | 41.0% | 47.4% | 10.7% |
| Oklahoma | 8 | | | 1,206,713 | 582,315 | 488,105 | 130,788 | 5,505 | 94,210 R | 48.3% | 40.4% | 10.8% |
| Oregon | | 7 | | 1,377,760 | 538,152 | 649,641 | 121,221 | 68,746 | 111,489 D | 39.1% | 47.2% | 8.8% |
| Pennsylvania | | 23 | | 4,506,118 | 1,801,169 | 2,215,819 | 430,984 | 58,146 | 414,650 D | 40.0% | 49.2% | 9.6% |
| Rhode Island | | 4 | | 390,284 | 104,683 | 233,050 | 43,723 | 8,828 | 128,367 D | 26.8% | 59.7% | 11.2% |
| South Carolina | 8 | | | 1,151,689 | 573,458 | 506,283 | 64,386 | 7,562 | 67,175 R | 49.8% | 44.0% | 5.6% |
| South Dakota | 3 | | | 323,826 | 150,543 | 139,333 | 31,250 | 2,700 | 11,210 R | 46.5% | 43.0% | 9.7% |
| Tennessee | | 11 | | 1,894,105 | 863,530 | 909,146 | 105,918 | 15,511 | 45,616 D | 45.6% | 48.0% | 5.6% |
| Texas | 32 | | | 5,611,644 | 2,736,167 | 2,459,683 | 378,537 | 37,257 | 276,484 R | 48.8% | 43.8% | 6.7% |
| Utah | 5 | | | 665,629 | 361,911 | 221,633 | 66,461 | 15,624 | 140,278 R | 54.4% | 33.3% | 10.0% |
| Vermont | | 3 | | 258,449 | 80,352 | 137,894 | 31,024 | 9,179 | 57,542 D | 31.1% | 53.4% | 12.0% |
| Virginia | 13 | | | 2,416,642 | 1,138,350 | 1,091,060 | 159,861 | 27,371 | 47,290 R | 47.1% | 45.1% | 6.6% |
| Washington | | 11 | | 2,253,837 | 840,712 | 1,123,323 | 201,003 | 88,799 | 282,611 D | 37.3% | 49.8% | 8.9% |
| West Virginia | | 5 | | 636,459 | 233,946 | 327,812 | 71,639 | 3,062 | 93,866 D | 36.8% | 51.5% | 11.3% |
| Wisconsin | | 11 | | 2,196,169 | 845,029 | 1,071,971 | 227,339 | 51,830 | 226,942 D | 38.5% | 48.8% | 10.4% |
| Wyoming | 3 | | | 211,571 | 105,388 | 77,934 | 25,928 | 2,321 | 27,454 R | 49.8% | 36.8% | 12.3% |
| District of Columbia | | 3 | | 185,726 | 17,339 | 158,220 | 3,611 | 6,556 | 140,881 D | 9.3% | 85.2% | 1.9% |
| Total | 159 | 379 | | 96,277,872 | 39,198,755 | 47,402,357 | 8,085,402 | 1,591,358 | 8,203,602 D | 40.7% | 49.2% | 8.4% |

# UNITED STATES

## PRESIDENT 1996 MINOR PARTIES

| State | Total | Nader | Browne | Phillips | Hagelin | Moorehead | Feinland | Other Candidates and Scattered Write-ins |
|---|---|---|---|---|---|---|---|---|
| Alabama | 10,991 | | 5,290 | 2,365 | 1,697 | | | 1,639 |
| Alaska | 12,161 | 7,597 | 2,276 | 925 | 729 | | | 634 |
| Arizona | 16,972 | 2,062* | 14,358 | 347* | 153* | | | 52 |
| Arkansas | 13,791 | 3,649 | 3,076 | 2,065 | 729 | 747 | | 3,525 |
| California | 373,422 | 237,016 | 73,600 | 21,202 | 15,403 | | 25,332 | 869 |
| Colorado | 48,075 | 25,070 | 12,392 | 2,813 | 2,547 | 599 | | 4,654 |
| Connecticut | 34,242 | 24,321 | 5,788 | 2,425 | 1,703 | | | 5 |
| Delaware | 2,948 | 156* | 2,052 | 348 | 274 | | | 118 |
| Florida | 28,518 | 4,101* | 23,965 | | 418* | | | 34 |
| Georgia | 18,042 | | 17,870 | 145* | | | | 27 |
| Hawaii | 13,807 | 10,386 | 2,493 | 358 | 570 | | | |
| Idaho | 7,163 | | 3,325 | 2,230 | 1,600 | | | 8 |
| Illinois | 36,218 | 1,447* | 22,548 | 7,606 | 4,606 | | | 11 |
| Indiana | 17,426 | 895* | 15,632 | 291* | 118* | | | 490 |
| Iowa | 16,014 | 6,550 | 2,315 | 2,229 | 3,349 | | | 1,571 |
| Kansas | 10,757 | 914* | 4,557 | 3,519 | 1,655 | | | 112 |
| Kentucky | 8,415 | 701* | 4,009 | 2,204 | 1,493 | | | 8 |
| Louisiana | 20,243 | 4,719 | 7,499 | 3,366 | 2,981 | 1,678 | | |
| Maine | 20,761 | 15,279 | 2,996 | 1,517 | 825 | | | 144 |
| Maryland | 17,321 | 2,606* | 8,765 | 3,402 | 2,517 | | | 31 |
| Massachusetts | 39,698 | 4,565* | 20,426 | | 5,184 | 3,277 | | 6,246 |
| Michigan | 41,309 | 2,322* | 27,670 | 539* | 4,254 | 3,153 | | 3,371 |
| Minnesota | 48,022 | 24,908 | 8,271 | 3,416 | 1,808 | | | 9,619 |
| Mississippi | 7,775 | | 2,809 | 2,314 | 1,447 | | | 1,205 |
| Missouri | 24,926 | 534* | 10,522 | 11,521 | 2,287 | | | 62 |
| Montana | 4,458 | | 2,526 | 152* | 1,754 | | | 26 |
| Nebraska | 5,909 | | 2,792 | 1,928 | 1,189 | | | |
| Nevada | 17,075 | 4,730 | 4,460 | 1,732 | 545 | | | 5,608 |
| New Hampshire | 8,039 | | 4,237 | 1,346 | | | | 2,456 |
| New Jersey | 58,266 | 32,465 | 14,763 | 3,440 | 3,887 | 1,337 | | 2,374 |
| New Mexico | 17,571 | 13,218 | 2,996 | 713 | 644 | | | |
| New York | 123,002 | 75,956 | 12,220 | 23,580 | 5,011 | 3,473 | | 2,762 |
| North Carolina | 13,961 | 2,108* | 8,740 | 258* | 2,771 | | | 84 |
| North Dakota | 1,941 | | 847 | 745 | 349 | | | |
| Ohio | 43,122 | 2,962* | 12,851 | 7,361 | 9,120 | 10,813 | | 15 |
| Oklahoma | 5,505 | | 5,505 | | | | | |
| Oregon | 68,746 | 49,415 | 8,903 | 3,379 | 2,798 | | | 4,251 |
| Pennsylvania | 58,146 | 3,086* | 28,000 | 19,552 | 5,783 | | | 1,725 |
| Rhode Island | 8,828 | 6,040 | 1,109 | 1,021 | 435 | 186 | | 37 |
| South Carolina | 7,562 | | 4,271 | 2,043 | 1,248 | | | |
| South Dakota | 2,700 | | 1,472 | 912 | 316 | | | |
| Tennessee | 15,511 | 6,427 | 5,020 | 1,818 | 636 | | | 1,610 |
| Texas | 37,257 | 4,810* | 20,256 | 7,472 | 4,422 | | | 297 |
| Utah | 15,624 | 4,615 | 4,129 | 2,601 | 1,085 | 298 | | 2,896 |
| Vermont | 9,179 | 5,585 | 1,183 | 382 | 498 | | | 1,531 |
| Virginia | 27,371 | | 9,174 | 13,687 | 4,510 | | | |
| Washington | 88,799 | 60,322 | 12,522 | 4,578 | 6,076 | 2,189 | | 3,112 |
| West Virginia | 3,062 | | 3,062 | | | | | |
| Wisconsin | 51,830 | 28,723 | 7,929 | 8,811 | 1,379 | 1,333 | | 3,655 |
| Wyoming | 2,321 | | 1,739 | | 582 | | | |
| District of Columbia | 6,556 | 4,780 | 588 | | 283 | | | 905 |
| Total | 1,591,358 | 685,040 | 485,798 | 184,658 | 113,668 | 29,083 | 25,332 | 67,779 |

An asterisk (*) indicates write-in votes.

Notes: The vote, including write-ins, for other minor party candidates who were listed on the ballot in at least one state: 8,930 Collins (Arizona, Arkansas, California, Colorado, Georgia, Idaho, Kansas, Maryland, Mississippi, Missouri, Montana, Tennessee, Utah, Washington); 8,476 Harris (Alabama, California, Colorado, Connecticut, Florida, Georgia, Iowa, Minnesota, New Jersey, New York, North Carolina, Utah, Vermont, Washington, Wisconsin, District of Columbia); 5,378 Peron (Minnesota, Vermont); 4,706 Holllis (Arkansas, Colorado, Florida, Maryland, Massachusetts, Montana, Oregon, Texas, Utah, Vermont, Wisconsin); 2,438 White (Michigan, Minnesota, New Jersey); 1,847 Templin (Colorado, Utah); 1,298 Dodge (Arkansas, Colorado, Illinois, Massachusetts, Tennessee, Utah); 1,101 Crane (Utah); 932 Forbes (Arkansas); 787 Birrenbach (Minnesota); 752 Masters (Arkansas, California, Maryland); 408 Michael (Tennessee). The other candidates and scattered write-ins column includes 5,608 votes cast in Nevada for "None of these Candidates" and 25,118 scattered write-ins.

# UNITED STATES

## VOTER TURNOUT 1996

| State | 1996 Census Voting Age Pop. Est. | November 1996 Registration | Percentage Voting Age Registered | Total Valid Vote President | Percentage Voting Age Voted | Percentage Registered Voted |
|---|---|---|---|---|---|---|
| Alabama | 3,218,000 | 2,470,766 | 76.8% | 1,534,349 | 47.7% | 62.1% |
| Alaska | 425,000 | 414,817 | 97.6% | 241,620 | 56.9% | 58.2% |
| Arizona | 3,094,000 | 2,244,672 | 72.5% | 1,404,405 | 45.4% | 62.6% |
| Arkansas | 1,860,000 | 1,396,459 | 75.1% | 884,262 | 47.5% | 63.3% |
| California | 23,133,000 | 15,662,075 | 67.7% | 10,019,484 | 43.3% | 64.0% |
| Colorado | 2,843,000 | 2,285,503 | 80.4% | 1,510,704 | 53.1% | 66.1% |
| Connecticut | 2,468,000 | 1,975,000 | 80.0% | 1,392,614 | 56.4% | 70.5% |
| Delaware | 547,000 | 419,695 | 76.7% | 271,084 | 49.6% | 64.6% |
| Florida | 11,043,000 | 8,077,877 | 73.1% | 5,303,794 | 48.0% | 65.7% |
| Georgia | 5,396,000 | 3,811,284 | 70.6% | 2,299,071 | 42.6% | 60.3% |
| Hawaii | 882,000 | 544,916 | 61.8% | 360,120 | 40.8% | 66.1% |
| Idaho | 845,000 | 700,430 | 82.9% | 491,719 | 58.2% | 70.2% |
| Illinois | 8,764,000 | 6,663,301 | 76.0% | 4,311,391 | 49.2% | 64.7% |
| Indiana | 4,369,000 | 3,484,033 | 79.7% | 2,135,842 | 48.9% | 61.3% |
| Iowa | 2,138,000 | 1,776,433 | 83.1% | 1,234,075 | 57.7% | 69.5% |
| Kansas | 1,898,000 | 1,436,418 | 75.7% | 1,074,300 | 56.6% | 74.8% |
| Kentucky | 2,924,000 | 2,396,086 | 81.9% | 1,388,708 | 47.5% | 58.0% |
| Louisiana | 3,137,000 | 2,539,240 | 80.9% | 1,783,959 | 56.9% | 70.3% |
| Maine | 939,000 | 1,001,292 | 106.6% | 605,897 | 64.5% | 60.5% |
| Maryland | 3,811,000 | 2,587,977 | 67.9% | 1,780,870 | 46.7% | 68.8% |
| Massachusetts | 4,623,000 | 3,459,193 | 74.8% | 2,556,785 | 55.3% | 73.9% |
| Michigan | 7,067,000 | 6,688,893 | 94.6% | 3,848,844 | 54.5% | 57.5% |
| Minnesota | 3,412,000 | 2,730,505 | 80.0% | 2,192,640 | 64.3% | 80.3% |
| Mississippi | 1,961,000 | | | 893,857 | 45.6% | |
| Missouri | 3,980,000 | 3,339,852 | 83.9% | 2,158,065 | 54.2% | 64.6% |
| Montana | 647,000 | 590,749 | 91.3% | 407,261 | 62.9% | 68.9% |
| Nebraska | 1,208,000 | 1,015,056 | 84.0% | 677,415 | 56.1% | 66.7% |
| Nevada | 1,180,000 | 778,298 | 66.0% | 464,279 | 39.3% | 59.7% |
| New Hampshire | 860,000 | 713,236 | 82.9% | 499,175 | 58.0% | 70.0% |
| New Jersey | 6,005,000 | 4,320,866 | 72.0% | 3,075,807 | 51.2% | 71.2% |
| New Mexico | 1,210,000 | 837,794 | 69.2% | 556,074 | 46.0% | 66.4% |
| New York | 13,579,000 | 10,162,156 | 74.8% | 6,316,129 | 46.5% | 62.2% |
| North Carolina | 5,499,000 | 4,315,723 | 78.5% | 2,515,807 | 45.8% | 58.3% |
| North Dakota | 473,000 | | | 266,411 | 56.3% | |
| Ohio | 8,358,000 | 6,879,687 | 82.3% | 4,534,434 | 54.3% | 65.9% |
| Oklahoma | 2,419,000 | 1,979,017 | 81.8% | 1,206,713 | 49.9% | 61.0% |
| Oregon | 2,396,000 | 1,962,155 | 81.9% | 1,377,760 | 57.5% | 70.2% |
| Pennsylvania | 9,196,000 | 6,799,637 | 73.9% | 4,506,118 | 49.0% | 66.3% |
| Rhode Island | 750,000 | 602,692 | 80.4% | 390,284 | 52.0% | 64.8% |
| South Carolina | 2,777,000 | 1,814,777 | 65.4% | 1,151,689 | 41.5% | 63.5% |
| South Dakota | 530,000 | 476,422 | 89.9% | 323,826 | 61.1% | 68.0% |
| Tennessee | 4,021,000 | 3,097,336 | 77.0% | 1,894,105 | 47.1% | 61.2% |
| Texas | 13,622,000 | 10,520,379 | 77.2% | 5,611,644 | 41.2% | 53.3% |
| Utah | 1,323,000 | 1,050,452 | 79.4% | 665,629 | 50.3% | 63.4% |
| Vermont | 441,000 | 385,328 | 87.4% | 258,449 | 58.6% | 67.1% |
| Virginia | 5,089,000 | 3,322,740 | 65.3% | 2,416,642 | 47.5% | 72.7% |
| Washington | 4,122,000 | 3,081,971 | 74.8% | 2,253,837 | 54.7% | 73.1% |
| West Virginia | 1,414,000 | 970,745 | 68.7% | 636,459 | 45.0% | 65.6% |
| Wisconsin | 3,824,000 | | | 2,196,169 | 57.4% | |
| Wyoming | 352,000 | | | 211,571 | 60.1% | |
| District of Columbia | 435,000 | 361,419 | 83.1% | 185,726 | 42.7% | 51.4% |
| Total | 196,507,000 | 144,145,352 | 73.4% | 96,277,872 | 49.0% | 66.8% |

Source: Registration figures—Committee for the Study of the American Electorate.

Notes: Mississippi, North Dakota, Wisconsin, and Wyoming do not maintain formal voter registration systems or had no figures readily available. Excluding these four states, the percentage of the voting age population registered in the remaining states was 75.9 percent, and the percentage of registered that voted was 64.3 percent.

20

## PRESIDENT 1992

In New York the Republican figures include Conservative and Right to Life votes and the Democratic figures include Liberal votes.

In Minnesota the Republican candidates appear on the ballot as Independent-Republican, the Democratic as Democratic-Farmer-Labor. In many states various non-major party candidates appeared on the ballot with variations of the party designations, were carried with entirely different party labels, or were listed as "Independent." In several states minor party vice-presidential candidates were different from those listed below.

The candidates listed below include all those who appeared on the ballot in at least one state. Where identified by state authorities, write-in votes for minor party candidates are credited to their total below. See page 22 for details.

| 44,909,326 | Bill Clinton and Al Gore | Democratic |
| 39,103,882 | George Bush and J. Danforth Quayle | Republican |
| 19,741,657 | Ross Perot and James Stockdale | Independent |
| 291,627 | Andre V. Marrou and Nancy Lord | Libertarian |
| 107,014 | James Gritz and Cyril Minett | America First |
| 73,714 | Lenora B. Fulani and Maria E. Munoz | New Alliance |
| 43,434 | Howard Phillips and Albion W. Knight | Taxpayers |
| 39,179 | John Hagelin and Mike Tompkins | Natural Law |
| 27,961 | Ron Daniels and Asiba Tupahache | Peace and Freedom |
| 26,333 | Lyndon H. LaRouche Jr. and James L. Bevel | Economic Recovery |
| 23,096 | James Warren and Willie Mae Reid | Socialist Workers |
| 4,749 | Drew Bradford and no vice-presidential candidate | Independent |
| 3,875 | Jack Herer and Derrick P. Grimmer | Grassroots |
| 3,057 | J. Quinn Brisben and Barbara Garson | Socialist |
| 3,050 | Helen Halyard and Fred Mazelis | Workers League |
| 2,199 | John Yiamouyiannis and Allen C. McCone | Take Back America |
| 1,149 | Delbert L. Ehlers and Rick Wendt | Independent |
| 961 | Earl F. Dodge and George Ormsby | Prohibition |
| 956 | Jim Boren and Will Weidman | Apathy |
| 405 | Eugene A. Hem and Joanne Roland | Third Party |
| 339 | Isabell Masters and Walter Masters | Looking Back |
| 292 | Robert J. Smith and Doris Feimer | American |
| 181 | Gloria La Riva and Larry Holmes | Workers World |

In addition to the votes listed above, 14,041 scattered write-in votes were reported from various states, and 2,537 votes were cast for "None of these Candidates" in Nevada.

# UNITED STATES

## PRESIDENT 1992

| State | Electoral Vote Rep. | Electoral Vote Dem. | Electoral Vote Other | Total Vote | Republican | Democratic | Perot | Other | Plurality | | Percentage Rep. | Percentage Dem. | Percentage Perot |
|---|---|---|---|---|---|---|---|---|---|---|---|---|---|
| Alabama | 9 | | | 1,688,060 | 804,283 | 690,080 | 183,109 | 10,588 | 114,203 | R | 47.6% | 40.9% | 10.8% |
| Alaska | 3 | | | 258,506 | 102,000 | 78,294 | 73,481 | 4,731 | 23,706 | R | 39.5% | 30.3% | 28.4% |
| Arizona | 8 | | | 1,486,975 | 572,086 | 543,050 | 353,741 | 18,098 | 29,036 | R | 38.5% | 36.5% | 23.8% |
| Arkansas | | 6 | | 950,653 | 337,324 | 505,823 | 99,132 | 8,374 | 168,499 | D | 35.5% | 53.2% | 10.4% |
| California | | 54 | | 11,131,721 | 3,630,574 | 5,121,325 | 2,296,006 | 83,816 | 1,490,751 | D | 32.6% | 46.0% | 20.6% |
| Colorado | | 8 | | 1,569,180 | 562,850 | 629,681 | 366,010 | 10,639 | 66,831 | D | 35.9% | 40.1% | 23.3% |
| Connecticut | | 8 | | 1,616,332 | 578,313 | 682,318 | 348,771 | 6,930 | 104,005 | D | 35.8% | 42.2% | 21.6% |
| Delaware | | 3 | | 289,735 | 102,313 | 126,054 | 59,213 | 2,155 | 23,741 | D | 35.3% | 43.5% | 20.4% |
| Florida | 25 | | | 5,314,392 | 2,173,310 | 2,072,698 | 1,053,067 | 15,317 | 100,612 | R | 40.9% | 39.0% | 19.8% |
| Georgia | | 13 | | 2,321,125 | 995,252 | 1,008,966 | 309,657 | 7,250 | 13,714 | D | 42.9% | 43.5% | 13.3% |
| Hawaii | | 4 | | 372,842 | 136,822 | 179,310 | 53,003 | 3,707 | 42,488 | D | 36.7% | 48.1% | 14.2% |
| Idaho | 4 | | | 482,142 | 202,645 | 137,013 | 130,395 | 12,089 | 65,632 | R | 42.0% | 28.4% | 27.0% |
| Illinois | | 22 | | 5,050,157 | 1,734,096 | 2,453,350 | 840,515 | 22,196 | 719,254 | D | 34.3% | 48.6% | 16.6% |
| Indiana | 12 | | | 2,305,871 | 989,375 | 848,420 | 455,934 | 12,142 | 140,955 | R | 42.9% | 36.8% | 19.8% |
| Iowa | | 7 | | 1,354,607 | 504,891 | 586,353 | 253,468 | 9,895 | 81,462 | D | 37.3% | 43.3% | 18.7% |
| Kansas | 6 | | | 1,157,335 | 449,951 | 390,434 | 312,358 | 4,592 | 59,517 | R | 38.9% | 33.7% | 27.0% |
| Kentucky | | 8 | | 1,492,900 | 617,178 | 665,104 | 203,944 | 6,674 | 47,926 | D | 41.3% | 44.6% | 13.7% |
| Louisiana | | 9 | | 1,790,017 | 733,386 | 815,971 | 211,478 | 29,182 | 82,585 | D | 41.0% | 45.6% | 11.8% |
| Maine | | 4 | | 679,499 | 206,504 | 263,420 | 206,820 | 2,755 | 56,600 | D | 30.4% | 38.8% | 30.4% |
| Maryland | | 10 | | 1,985,046 | 707,094 | 988,571 | 281,414 | 7,967 | 281,477 | D | 35.6% | 49.8% | 14.2% |
| Massachusetts | | 12 | | 2,773,700 | 805,049 | 1,318,662 | 630,731 | 19,258 | 513,613 | D | 29.0% | 47.5% | 22.7% |
| Michigan | | 18 | | 4,274,673 | 1,554,940 | 1,871,182 | 824,813 | 23,738 | 316,242 | D | 36.4% | 43.8% | 19.3% |
| Minnesota | | 10 | | 2,347,948 | 747,841 | 1,020,997 | 562,506 | 16,604 | 273,156 | D | 31.9% | 43.5% | 24.0% |
| Mississippi | 7 | | | 981,793 | 487,793 | 400,258 | 85,626 | 8,116 | 87,535 | R | 49.7% | 40.8% | 8.7% |
| Missouri | | 11 | | 2,391,565 | 811,159 | 1,053,873 | 518,741 | 7,792 | 242,714 | D | 33.9% | 44.1% | 21.7% |
| Montana | | 3 | | 410,611 | 144,207 | 154,507 | 107,225 | 4,672 | 10,300 | D | 35.1% | 37.6% | 26.1% |
| Nebraska | 5 | | | 737,546 | 343,678 | 216,864 | 174,104 | 2,900 | 126,814 | R | 46.6% | 29.4% | 23.6% |
| Nevada | | 4 | | 506,318 | 175,828 | 189,148 | 132,580 | 8,762 | 13,320 | D | 34.7% | 37.4% | 26.2% |
| New Hampshire | | 4 | | 537,943 | 202,484 | 209,040 | 121,337 | 5,082 | 6,556 | D | 37.6% | 38.9% | 22.6% |
| New Jersey | | 15 | | 3,343,594 | 1,356,865 | 1,436,206 | 521,829 | 28,694 | 79,341 | D | 40.6% | 43.0% | 15.6% |
| New Mexico | | 5 | | 569,986 | 212,824 | 261,617 | 91,895 | 3,650 | 48,793 | D | 37.3% | 45.9% | 16.1% |
| New York | | 33 | | 6,926,925 | 2,346,649 | 3,444,450 | 1,090,721 | 45,105 | 1,097,801 | D | 33.9% | 49.7% | 15.7% |
| North Carolina | 14 | | | 2,611,850 | 1,134,661 | 1,114,042 | 357,864 | 5,283 | 20,619 | R | 43.4% | 42.7% | 13.7% |
| North Dakota | 3 | | | 308,133 | 136,244 | 99,168 | 71,084 | 1,637 | 37,076 | R | 44.2% | 32.2% | 23.1% |
| Ohio | | 21 | | 4,939,967 | 1,894,310 | 1,984,942 | 1,036,426 | 24,289 | 90,632 | D | 38.3% | 40.2% | 21.0% |
| Oklahoma | 8 | | | 1,390,359 | 592,929 | 473,066 | 319,878 | 4,486 | 119,863 | R | 42.6% | 34.0% | 23.0% |
| Oregon | | 7 | | 1,462,643 | 475,757 | 621,314 | 354,091 | 11,481 | 145,557 | D | 32.5% | 42.5% | 24.2% |
| Pennsylvania | | 23 | | 4,959,810 | 1,791,841 | 2,239,164 | 902,667 | 26,138 | 447,323 | D | 36.1% | 45.1% | 18.2% |
| Rhode Island | | 4 | | 453,477 | 131,601 | 213,299 | 105,045 | 3,532 | 81,698 | D | 29.0% | 47.0% | 23.2% |
| South Carolina | 8 | | | 1,202,527 | 577,507 | 479,514 | 138,872 | 6,634 | 97,993 | R | 48.0% | 39.9% | 11.5% |
| South Dakota | 3 | | | 336,254 | 136,718 | 124,888 | 73,295 | 1,353 | 11,830 | R | 40.7% | 37.1% | 21.8% |
| Tennessee | | 11 | | 1,982,638 | 841,300 | 933,521 | 199,968 | 7,849 | 92,221 | D | 42.4% | 47.1% | 10.1% |
| Texas | 32 | | | 6,154,018 | 2,496,071 | 2,281,815 | 1,354,781 | 21,351 | 214,256 | R | 40.6% | 37.1% | 22.0% |
| Utah | 5 | | | 743,999 | 322,632 | 183,429 | 203,400 | 34,538 | 119,232 | R | 43.4% | 24.7% | 27.3% |
| Vermont | | 3 | | 289,701 | 88,122 | 133,592 | 65,991 | 1,996 | 45,470 | D | 30.4% | 46.1% | 22.8% |
| Virginia | 13 | | | 2,558,665 | 1,150,517 | 1,038,650 | 348,639 | 20,859 | 111,867 | R | 45.0% | 40.6% | 13.6% |
| Washington | | 11 | | 2,288,230 | 731,234 | 993,037 | 541,780 | 22,179 | 261,803 | D | 32.0% | 43.4% | 23.7% |
| West Virginia | | 5 | | 683,762 | 241,974 | 331,001 | 108,829 | 1,958 | 89,027 | D | 35.4% | 48.4% | 15.9% |
| Wisconsin | | 11 | | 2,531,114 | 930,855 | 1,041,066 | 544,479 | 14,714 | 110,211 | D | 36.8% | 41.1% | 21.5% |
| Wyoming | 3 | | | 200,598 | 79,347 | 68,160 | 51,263 | 1,828 | 11,187 | R | 39.6% | 34.0% | 25.6% |
| District of Columbia | | 3 | | 227,572 | 20,698 | 192,619 | 9,681 | 4,574 | 171,921 | D | 9.1% | 84.6% | 4.3% |
| Total | 168 | 370 | | 104,425,014 | 39,103,882 | 44,909,326 | 19,741,657 | 670,149 | 5,805,444 | D | 37.4% | 43.0% | 18.9% |

# UNITED STATES

## PRESIDENT 1992 MINOR PARTIES

| State | Total | Marrou | Gritz | Fulani | Phillips | Hagelin | Daniels | LaRouche | Warren | Other Candidates and Scattered Write-ins |
|---|---|---|---|---|---|---|---|---|---|---|
| Alabama | 10,588 | 5,737 | | 2,161 | | 495 | | 641 | 831 | 723 |
| Alaska | 4,731 | 1,378 | 1,379 | 330 | 377 | 433 | | 469 | | 365 |
| Arizona | 18,098 | 6,759 | 8,141 | 923 | | 2,267 | | 8* | | |
| Arkansas | 8,374 | 1,261 | 819 | 1,022 | 1,437 | 764 | | 762 | | 2,309 |
| California | 83,816 | 48,139 | 3,077* | | 12,711 | 836* | 18,597 | 180* | 115* | 161 |
| Colorado | 10,639 | 8,669 | 274* | 1,608 | | 47* | | 20* | | 21 |
| Connecticut | 6,930 | 5,391 | 72* | 1,363 | 20* | 75* | | 4* | 5* | |
| Delaware | 2,155 | 935 | 9* | 1,105 | 2* | 6* | | 9* | 3* | 86 |
| Florida | 15,317 | 15,079 | | | | 214* | | | | 24 |
| Georgia | 7,250 | 7,110 | 78* | 44* | 7* | | | | 9* | 2 |
| Hawaii | 3,707 | 1,119 | 1,452 | 720 | | 416 | | | | |
| Idaho | 12,089 | 1,167 | 10,281 | 613 | | 24* | | 1* | | 3 |
| Illinois | 22,196 | 9,218 | 3,577 | 5,267 | | 2,751 | | | 1,361 | 22 |
| Indiana | 12,142 | 7,936 | 1,467* | 2,583 | | 126* | | 14* | | 16 |
| Iowa | 9,895 | 1,076 | 1,177 | 197 | 480 | 3,079 | 212 | 238 | 273 | 3,163 |
| Kansas | 4,592 | 4,314 | 79* | 10* | 55* | 77* | | | | 57 |
| Kentucky | 6,674 | 4,513 | 47* | 430 | 989 | 695 | | | | |
| Louisiana | 29,182 | 3,155 | 18,545 | 1,434 | 1,552 | 889 | 1,663 | 1,136 | | 808 |
| Maine | 2,755 | 1,681 | | 519 | 464 | | | | | 91 |
| Maryland | 7,967 | 4,715 | 41* | 2,786 | 22* | 191* | 167* | 18* | 25* | 2 |
| Massachusetts | 19,258 | 9,024 | | 3,172 | 2,218 | 1,812 | | 1,027 | | 2,005 |
| Michigan | 23,738 | 10,175 | 168* | 21* | 8,263 | 2,954 | | 14* | | 2,143 |
| Minnesota | 16,604 | 3,374 | 3,363 | 958 | 733 | 1,406 | | 622 | 990 | 5,158 |
| Mississippi | 8,116 | 2,154 | 545 | 2,625 | 1,652 | 1,140 | | | | |
| Missouri | 7,792 | 7,497 | 180* | 17* | | 64* | 12* | 13* | 6* | 3 |
| Montana | 4,672 | 986 | 3,658 | 8* | | 20* | | | | |
| Nebraska | 2,900 | 1,340 | | 846 | | 714 | | | | |
| Nevada | 8,762 | 1,835 | 2,892 | 483 | 677 | 338 | | | | 2,537 |
| New Hampshire | 5,082 | 3,548 | | 512 | | 292 | | | | 730 |
| New Jersey | 28,694 | 6,822 | 1,867 | 3,513 | 2,670 | 1,353 | 1,996 | 2,095 | 2,011 | 6,367 |
| New Mexico | 3,650 | 1,615 | | 369 | 620 | 562 | | | 183 | 301 |
| New York | 45,105 | 13,451 | 23* | 11,318 | | 4,420 | 385* | 20* | 15,472 | 16 |
| North Carolina | 5,283 | 5,171 | | 59* | | 41* | | | 12* | |
| North Dakota | 1,637 | 416 | | 143 | | 240 | | 642 | 193 | 3 |
| Ohio | 24,289 | 7,252 | 4,699 | 6,413 | | 3,437 | | 2,446 | 32* | 10 |
| Oklahoma | 4,486 | 4,486 | | | | | | | | |
| Oregon | 11,481 | 4,277 | 1,470* | 3,030 | | 91* | | | | 2,613 |
| Pennsylvania | 26,138 | 21,477 | | 4,661 | | | | | | |
| Rhode Island | 3,532 | 571 | 3* | 1,878 | 215 | 262 | 1* | 494 | | 108 |
| South Carolina | 6,634 | 2,719 | | 1,235 | 2,680 | | | | | |
| South Dakota | 1,353 | 814 | | 110 | | 429 | | | | |
| Tennessee | 7,849 | 1,847 | 756 | 727 | 579 | 599 | 511 | 460 | 277 | 2,093 |
| Texas | 21,351 | 19,699 | 505* | 301* | 359* | 217* | | 169* | | 101 |
| Utah | 34,538 | 1,900 | 28,602 | 414 | 393 | 1,319 | 177 | 1,089 | 200 | 444 |
| Vermont | 1,996 | 501 | | 429 | 124 | 315 | | 57 | 82 | 488 |
| Virginia | 20,859 | 5,730 | | 3,192 | | | | 11,937 | | |
| Washington | 22,179 | 7,533 | 4,854 | 1,776 | 2,354 | 2,456 | 1,171 | 855 | 515 | 665 |
| West Virginia | 1,958 | 1,873 | 34* | 6* | 2* | 2* | | | 6* | 35 |
| Wisconsin | 14,714 | 2,877 | 2,311 | 654 | 1,772 | 1,070 | 1,883 | 633 | 390 | 3,124 |
| Wyoming | 1,828 | 844 | 569* | 270 | 7* | 11* | | | | 127 |
| District of Columbia | 4,574 | 467 | | 1,459 | | 230 | 1,186 | 260 | 105 | 867 |
| Total | 670,149 | 291,627 | 107,014 | 73,714 | 43,434 | 39,179 | 27,961 | 26,333 | 23,096 | 37,791 |

An asterisk (*) indicates write-in votes.

Notes: The vote, including write-ins, for minor party candidates who received less than 5,000 votes is as follows: 4,749 Bradford (on the ballot in New Jersey); 3,875 Herer (on the ballot in Iowa, Minnesota, Wisconsin); 3,057 Brisben (on the ballot in Tennessee, Utah, Wisconsin, District of Columbia); 3,050 Halyard (on the ballot in Michigan and New Jersey); 2,199 Yiamouyiannis (on the ballot in Arkansas, Iowa, Louisiana, Tennessee); 1,149 Ehlers (on the ballot in Iowa); 961 Dodge (on the ballot in Arkansas, New Mexico, Tennessee); 956 Boren (on the ballot in Arkansas); 405 Hem (on the ballot in Wisconsin); 339 Masters (on the ballot in Arkansas); 292 Smith (on the ballot in Utah); 181 La Riva (on the ballot in New Mexico). The other candidates and scattered write-ins column also includes 2,537 votes cast in Nevada for "None of these Candidates" and 14,041 scattered write-ins.

# UNITED STATES

## VOTER TURNOUT 1992

| State | 1992 Census Voting Age Population Est. | November 1992 Registration | Percentage Voting Age Registered | Total Valid Vote President | Percentage Voting Age Voted | Percentage Registered Voted |
|---|---|---|---|---|---|---|
| Alabama | 3,056,000 | 2,367,972 | 77.5% | 1,688,060 | 55.2% | 71.3% |
| Alaska | 395,000 | 315,058 | 79.8% | 258,506 | 65.4% | 82.1% |
| Arizona | 2,749,000 | 1,964,949 | 71.5% | 1,486,975 | 54.1% | 75.7% |
| Arkansas | 1,768,000 | 1,317,944 | 74.5% | 950,653 | 53.8% | 72.1% |
| California | 22,668,000 | 15,101,473 | 66.6% | 11,131,721 | 49.1% | 73.7% |
| Colorado | 2,501,000 | 2,003,375 | 80.1% | 1,569,180 | 62.7% | 78.3% |
| Connecticut | 2,535,000 | 1,955,268 | 77.1% | 1,616,332 | 63.8% | 82.7% |
| Delaware | 525,000 | 342,088 | 65.2% | 289,735 | 55.2% | 84.7% |
| Florida | 10,586,000 | 6,541,825 | 61.8% | 5,314,392 | 50.2% | 81.2% |
| Georgia | 4,950,000 | 3,177,061 | 64.2% | 2,321,125 | 46.9% | 73.1% |
| Hawaii | 889,000 | 464,495 | 52.2% | 372,842 | 41.9% | 80.3% |
| Idaho | 740,000 | 611,121 | 82.6% | 482,142 | 65.2% | 78.9% |
| Illinois | 8,568,000 | 6,600,358 | 77.0% | 5,050,157 | 58.9% | 76.5% |
| Indiana | 4,176,000 | 3,180,157 | 76.2% | 2,305,871 | 55.2% | 72.5% |
| Iowa | 2,075,000 | 1,703,532 | 82.1% | 1,354,607 | 65.3% | 79.5% |
| Kansas | 1,836,000 | 1,365,849 | 74.4% | 1,157,335 | 63.0% | 84.7% |
| Kentucky | 2,779,000 | 2,076,263 | 74.7% | 1,492,900 | 53.7% | 71.9% |
| Louisiana | 2,992,000 | 2,292,129 | 76.6% | 1,790,017 | 59.8% | 78.1% |
| Maine | 944,000 | | | 679,499 | 72.0% | |
| Maryland | 3,719,000 | 2,463,010 | 66.2% | 1,985,046 | 53.4% | 80.6% |
| Massachusetts | 4,607,000 | 3,351,918 | 72.8% | 2,773,700 | 60.2% | 82.7% |
| Michigan | 6,923,000 | 6,147,083 | 88.8% | 4,274,673 | 61.7% | 69.5% |
| Minnesota | 3,278,000 | 3,138,901 | 95.8% | 2,347,948 | 71.6% | 74.8% |
| Mississippi | 1,861,000 | 1,640,150 | 88.1% | 981,793 | 52.8% | 59.9% |
| Missouri | 3,858,000 | 3,067,955 | 79.5% | 2,391,565 | 62.0% | 78.0% |
| Montana | 586,000 | 529,822 | 90.4% | 410,611 | 70.1% | 77.5% |
| Nebraska | 1,167,000 | 951,395 | 81.5% | 737,546 | 63.2% | 77.5% |
| Nevada | 1,013,000 | 649,913 | 64.2% | 506,318 | 50.0% | 77.9% |
| New Hampshire | 852,000 | 660,985 | 77.6% | 537,943 | 63.1% | 81.4% |
| New Jersey | 5,943,000 | 4,059,472 | 68.3% | 3,343,594 | 56.3% | 82.4% |
| New Mexico | 1,104,000 | 706,966 | 64.0% | 569,986 | 51.6% | 80.6% |
| New York | 13,609,000 | 9,193,391 | 67.6% | 6,926,925 | 50.9% | 75.3% |
| North Carolina | 5,217,000 | 3,817,380 | 73.2% | 2,611,850 | 50.1% | 68.4% |
| North Dakota | 458,000 | | | 308,133 | 67.3% | |
| Ohio | 8,146,000 | 6,542,931 | 80.3% | 4,939,967 | 60.6% | 75.5% |
| Oklahoma | 2,328,000 | 2,302,279 | 98.9% | 1,390,359 | 59.7% | 60.4% |
| Oregon | 2,226,000 | 1,774,449 | 79.7% | 1,462,643 | 65.7% | 82.4% |
| Pennsylvania | 9,129,000 | 5,993,002 | 65.6% | 4,959,810 | 54.3% | 82.8% |
| Rhode Island | 776,000 | 554,664 | 71.5% | 453,477 | 58.4% | 81.8% |
| South Carolina | 2,672,000 | 1,537,140 | 57.5% | 1,202,527 | 45.0% | 78.2% |
| South Dakota | 502,000 | 448,292 | 89.3% | 336,254 | 67.0% | 75.0% |
| Tennessee | 3,783,000 | 2,726,449 | 72.1% | 1,982,638 | 52.4% | 72.7% |
| Texas | 12,524,000 | 8,440,143 | 67.4% | 6,154,018 | 49.1% | 72.9% |
| Utah | 1,142,000 | 965,211 | 84.5% | 743,999 | 65.1% | 77.1% |
| Vermont | 429,000 | 383,371 | 89.4% | 289,701 | 67.5% | 75.6% |
| Virginia | 4,842,000 | 3,054,662 | 63.1% | 2,558,665 | 52.8% | 83.8% |
| Washington | 3,818,000 | 2,814,680 | 73.7% | 2,288,230 | 59.9% | 81.3% |
| West Virginia | 1,350,000 | 956,172 | 70.8% | 683,762 | 50.6% | 71.5% |
| Wisconsin | 3,669,000 | | | 2,531,114 | 69.0% | |
| Wyoming | 322,000 | 234,260 | 72.8% | 200,598 | 62.3% | 85.6% |
| District of Columbia | 459,000 | 340,953 | 74.3% | 227,572 | 49.6% | 66.7% |
| Total | 189,044,000 | 132,827,916 | 70.3% | 104,425,014 | 55.2% | 78.6% |

Notes: Maine registration figures not available; North Dakota has no formal registration system; Wisconsin has no statewide registration system.

# PRESIDENT 1988

In West Virginia one Democratic elector voted in the electoral college for Lloyd Bentsen for president and Michael S. Dukakis for vice president.

In New York the Republican figures include Conservative votes and the Democratic figures include Liberal votes.

In Minnesota the Republican candidates appear on the ballot as Independent-Republican, the Democratic as Democratic-Farmer-Labor. In many states various non-major party candidates appeared on the ballot with variations of the party designations given here, were listed as "Independent," or were carried with entirely different party labels.

In several states minor party vice-presidential candidates were different from those listed below. The full list of candidates for president and vice president was:

| | | |
|---:|---|---|
| 48,886,097 | George Bush and J. Danforth Quayle | Republican |
| 41,809,074 | Michael S. Dukakis and Lloyd Bentsen | Democratic |
| 432,179 | Ron Paul and Andre V. Marrou | Libertarian |
| 217,219 | Lenora B. Fulani and Joyce Dattner | New Alliance |
| 47,047 | David E. Duke and Floyd C. Parker | Populist |
| 30,905 | Eugene J. McCarthy and Florence Rice | Consumer |
| 27,818 | James C. Griffin and Charles J. Morsa | American Independent |
| 25,562 | Lyndon H. LaRouche Jr. and Debra H. Freeman | National Economic Recovery |
| 20,504 | William A. Matra and Joan Andrews | Right to Life |
| 18,693 | Ed Winn and Barry Porster | Workers League |
| 15,604 | James Warren and Kathleen Mickells | Socialist Workers |
| 10,370 | Herbert Lewin and Vikki Murdock | Peace and Freedom |
| 8,002 | Earl F. Dodge and George Ormsby | Prohibition |
| 7,846 | Larry Holmes and Gloria LaRiva | Workers World |
| 3,882 | Willa Kenoyer and Ron Ehrenreich | Socialist |
| 3,475 | Delmar Dennis and Earl Jeppson | American |
| 1,949 | Jack Herer and Dana Beal | Grassroots |
| 372 | Louie G. Youngkeit with no vice presidential candidate | Independent |
| 236 | John G. Martin and Cleveland Sparrow | Third World Assembly |

The candidates listed above include all those who appeared on the ballot in at least one state. Republican, Democratic, and New Alliance candidates appeared on the ballot in all fifty-one jurisdictions. The Libertarian nominees were on the ballot in all save four. Where identified by state authorities, write-in votes for minor party candidates are credited to their total above. In addition to the votes listed, 21,041 scattered write-in votes were reported from various states, and 6,934 votes were cast for "None of these Candidates" in Nevada.

# UNITED STATES

## PRESIDENT 1988

| State | Electoral Vote Rep. | Electoral Vote Dem. | Electoral Vote Other | Total Vote | Republican | Democratic | Other | Plurality | Total Vote Rep. | Total Vote Dem. | Major Vote Rep. | Major Vote Dem. |
|---|---|---|---|---|---|---|---|---|---|---|---|---|
| Alabama | 9 | | | 1,378,476 | 815,576 | 549,506 | 13,394 | 266,070 R | 59.2% | 39.9% | 59.7% | 40.3% |
| Alaska | 3 | | | 200,116 | 119,251 | 72,584 | 8,281 | 46,667 R | 59.6% | 36.3% | 62.2% | 37.8% |
| Arizona | 7 | | | 1,171,873 | 702,541 | 454,029 | 15,303 | 248,512 R | 60.0% | 38.7% | 60.7% | 39.3% |
| Arkansas | 6 | | | 827,738 | 466,578 | 349,237 | 11,923 | 117,341 R | 56.4% | 42.2% | 57.2% | 42.8% |
| California | 47 | | | 9,887,065 | 5,054,917 | 4,702,233 | 129,915 | 352,684 R | 51.1% | 47.6% | 51.8% | 48.2% |
| Colorado | 8 | | | 1,372,394 | 728,177 | 621,453 | 22,764 | 106,724 R | 53.1% | 45.3% | 54.0% | 46.0% |
| Connecticut | 8 | | | 1,443,394 | 750,241 | 676,584 | 16,569 | 73,657 R | 52.0% | 46.9% | 52.6% | 47.4% |
| Delaware | 3 | | | 249,891 | 139,639 | 108,647 | 1,605 | 30,992 R | 55.9% | 43.5% | 56.2% | 43.8% |
| Florida | 21 | | | 4,302,313 | 2,618,885 | 1,656,701 | 26,727 | 962,184 R | 60.9% | 38.5% | 61.3% | 38.7% |
| Georgia | 12 | | | 1,809,672 | 1,081,331 | 714,792 | 13,549 | 366,539 R | 59.8% | 39.5% | 60.2% | 39.8% |
| Hawaii | | 4 | | 354,461 | 158,625 | 192,364 | 3,472 | 33,739 D | 44.8% | 54.3% | 45.2% | 54.8% |
| Idaho | 4 | | | 408,968 | 253,881 | 147,272 | 7,815 | 106,609 R | 62.1% | 36.0% | 63.3% | 36.7% |
| Illinois | 24 | | | 4,559,120 | 2,310,939 | 2,215,940 | 32,241 | 94,999 R | 50.7% | 48.6% | 51.0% | 49.0% |
| Indiana | 12 | | | 2,168,621 | 1,297,763 | 860,643 | 10,215 | 437,120 R | 59.8% | 39.7% | 60.1% | 39.9% |
| Iowa | | 8 | | 1,225,614 | 545,355 | 670,557 | 9,702 | 125,202 D | 44.5% | 54.7% | 44.9% | 55.1% |
| Kansas | 7 | | | 993,044 | 554,049 | 422,636 | 16,359 | 131,413 R | 55.8% | 42.6% | 56.7% | 43.3% |
| Kentucky | 9 | | | 1,322,517 | 734,281 | 580,368 | 7,868 | 153,913 R | 55.5% | 43.9% | 55.9% | 44.1% |
| Louisiana | 10 | | | 1,628,202 | 883,702 | 717,460 | 27,040 | 166,242 R | 54.3% | 44.1% | 55.2% | 44.8% |
| Maine | 4 | | | 555,035 | 307,131 | 243,569 | 4,335 | 63,562 R | 55.3% | 43.9% | 55.8% | 44.2% |
| Maryland | 10 | | | 1,714,358 | 876,167 | 826,304 | 11,887 | 49,863 R | 51.1% | 48.2% | 51.5% | 48.5% |
| Massachusetts | | 13 | | 2,632,805 | 1,194,635 | 1,401,415 | 36,755 | 206,780 D | 45.4% | 53.2% | 46.0% | 54.0% |
| Michigan | 20 | | | 3,669,163 | 1,965,486 | 1,675,783 | 27,894 | 289,703 R | 53.6% | 45.7% | 54.0% | 46.0% |
| Minnesota | | 10 | | 2,096,790 | 962,337 | 1,109,471 | 24,982 | 147,134 D | 45.9% | 52.9% | 46.4% | 53.6% |
| Mississippi | 7 | | | 931,527 | 557,890 | 363,921 | 9,716 | 193,969 R | 59.9% | 39.1% | 60.5% | 39.5% |
| Missouri | 11 | | | 2,093,713 | 1,084,953 | 1,001,619 | 7,141 | 83,334 R | 51.8% | 47.8% | 52.0% | 48.0% |
| Montana | 4 | | | 365,674 | 190,412 | 168,936 | 6,326 | 21,476 R | 52.1% | 46.2% | 53.0% | 47.0% |
| Nebraska | 5 | | | 661,465 | 397,956 | 259,235 | 4,274 | 138,721 R | 60.2% | 39.2% | 60.6% | 39.4% |
| Nevada | 4 | | | 350,067 | 206,040 | 132,738 | 11,289 | 73,302 R | 58.9% | 37.9% | 60.8% | 39.2% |
| New Hampshire | 4 | | | 451,074 | 281,537 | 163,696 | 5,841 | 117,841 R | 62.4% | 36.3% | 63.2% | 36.8% |
| New Jersey | 16 | | | 3,099,553 | 1,743,192 | 1,320,352 | 36,009 | 422,840 R | 56.2% | 42.6% | 56.9% | 43.1% |
| New Mexico | 5 | | | 521,287 | 270,341 | 244,497 | 6,449 | 25,844 R | 51.9% | 46.9% | 52.5% | 47.5% |
| New York | | 36 | | 6,485,683 | 3,081,871 | 3,347,882 | 55,930 | 266,011 D | 47.5% | 51.6% | 47.9% | 52.1% |
| North Carolina | 13 | | | 2,134,370 | 1,237,258 | 890,167 | 6,945 | 347,091 R | 58.0% | 41.7% | 58.2% | 41.8% |
| North Dakota | 3 | | | 297,261 | 166,559 | 127,739 | 2,963 | 38,820 R | 56.0% | 43.0% | 56.6% | 43.4% |
| Ohio | 23 | | | 4,393,699 | 2,416,549 | 1,939,629 | 37,521 | 476,920 R | 55.0% | 44.1% | 55.5% | 44.5% |
| Oklahoma | 8 | | | 1,171,036 | 678,367 | 483,423 | 9,246 | 194,944 R | 57.9% | 41.3% | 58.4% | 41.6% |
| Oregon | | 7 | | 1,201,694 | 560,126 | 616,206 | 25,362 | 56,080 D | 46.6% | 51.3% | 47.6% | 52.4% |
| Pennsylvania | 25 | | | 4,536,251 | 2,300,087 | 2,194,944 | 41,220 | 105,143 R | 50.7% | 48.4% | 51.2% | 48.8% |
| Rhode Island | | 4 | | 404,620 | 177,761 | 225,123 | 1,736 | 47,362 D | 43.9% | 55.6% | 44.1% | 55.9% |
| South Carolina | 8 | | | 986,009 | 606,443 | 370,554 | 9,012 | 235,889 R | 61.5% | 37.6% | 62.1% | 37.9% |
| South Dakota | 3 | | | 312,991 | 165,415 | 145,560 | 2,016 | 19,855 R | 52.8% | 46.5% | 53.2% | 46.8% |
| Tennessee | 11 | | | 1,636,250 | 947,233 | 679,794 | 9,223 | 267,439 R | 57.9% | 41.5% | 58.2% | 41.8% |
| Texas | 29 | | | 5,427,410 | 3,036,829 | 2,352,748 | 37,833 | 684,081 R | 56.0% | 43.3% | 56.3% | 43.7% |
| Utah | 5 | | | 647,008 | 428,442 | 207,343 | 11,223 | 221,099 R | 66.2% | 32.0% | 67.4% | 32.6% |
| Vermont | 3 | | | 243,328 | 124,331 | 115,775 | 3,222 | 8,556 R | 51.1% | 47.6% | 51.8% | 48.2% |
| Virginia | 12 | | | 2,191,609 | 1,309,162 | 859,799 | 22,648 | 449,363 R | 59.7% | 39.2% | 60.4% | 39.6% |
| Washington | | 10 | | 1,865,253 | 903,835 | 933,516 | 27,902 | 29,681 D | 48.5% | 50.0% | 49.2% | 50.8% |
| West Virginia | | 5 | 1 | 653,311 | 310,065 | 341,016 | 2,230 | 30,951 D | 47.5% | 52.2% | 47.6% | 52.4% |
| Wisconsin | | 11 | | 2,191,608 | 1,047,499 | 1,126,794 | 17,315 | 79,295 D | 47.8% | 51.4% | 48.2% | 51.8% |
| Wyoming | 3 | | | 176,551 | 106,867 | 67,113 | 2,571 | 39,754 R | 60.5% | 38.0% | 61.4% | 38.6% |
| District of Columbia | | 3 | | 192,877 | 27,590 | 159,407 | 5,880 | 131,817 D | 14.3% | 82.6% | 14.8% | 85.2% |
| Total | 426 | 111 | 1 | 91,594,809 | 48,886,097 | 41,809,074 | 899,638 | 7,077,023 R | 53.4% | 45.6% | 53.9% | 46.1% |

## PRESIDENT 1984

In New York the Republican figures include Conservative votes and the Democratic figures include Liberal votes.

In Minnesota the Republican candidates appear on the ballot as Independent-Republican, the Democratic as Democratic-Farmer-Labor. In many states various non-major party candidates appeared on the ballot with variations of the party designations given here, were listed as "Independent" or "Non-Party," or were carried with entirely different party labels.

The Workers World candidate for president was Gavrielle Holmes in Ohio and Rhode Island; in several states minor party vice-presidential candidates were different from those listed below.

The full list of candidates for president and vice president was:

| | | |
|---:|---|---|
| 54,455,075 | Ronald Reagan and George Bush | Republican |
| 37,577,185 | Walter F. Mondale and Geraldine A. Ferraro | Democratic |
| 228,314 | David Bergland and James A. Lewis | Libertarian |
| 78,807 | Lyndon H. LaRouche Jr. and Billy M. Davis | Independent |
| 72,200 | Sonia Johnson and Richard Walton | Citizens |
| 66,336 | Bob Richards and Maureen Salaman | Populist |
| 46,868 | Dennis L. Serrette and Nancy Ross | Alliance |
| 36,386 | Gus Hall and Angela Davis | Communist |
| 24,706 | Mel Mason and Matilde Zimmermann | Socialist Workers |
| 17,985 | Larry Holmes and Gloria La Riva | Workers World |
| 13,161 | Delmar Dennis and Traves Brownlee | American |
| 10,801 | Ed Winn and Helen Halyard | Workers League |
| 4,242 | Earl F. Dodge and Warren C. Martin | Prohibition |
| 1,486 | John B. Anderson and Grace Pierce | National Unity |
| 892 | Gerald Baker and Ferris Alger | Big Deal |
| 825 | Arthur J. Lowery and Raymond L. Garland | United Sovereign Citizens |

The candidates listed above are those who appeared on the ballot in at least one state. Where identified by state authorities, write-in votes for minor party candidates are credited to their total above. In addition to the votes listed, 13,623 scattered write-in votes were reported from various states, and 3,950 votes were cast for "None of these Candidates" in Nevada.

# UNITED STATES
## PRESIDENT 1984

| State | Electoral Vote Rep. | Dem. | Other | Total Vote | Republican | Democratic | Other | Plurality | Percentage Total Vote Rep. | Dem. | Major Vote Rep. | Dem. |
|---|---|---|---|---|---|---|---|---|---|---|---|---|
| Alabama | 9 | | | 1,441,713 | 872,849 | 551,899 | 16,965 | 320,950 R | 60.5% | 38.3% | 61.3% | 38.7% |
| Alaska | 3 | | | 207,605 | 138,377 | 62,007 | 7,221 | 76,370 R | 66.7% | 29.9% | 69.1% | 30.9% |
| Arizona | 7 | | | 1,025,897 | 681,416 | 333,854 | 10,627 | 347,562 R | 66.4% | 32.5% | 67.1% | 32.9% |
| Arkansas | 6 | | | 884,406 | 534,774 | 338,646 | 10,986 | 196,128 R | 60.5% | 38.3% | 61.2% | 38.8% |
| California | 47 | | | 9,505,423 | 5,467,009 | 3,922,519 | 115,895 | 1,544,490 R | 57.5% | 41.3% | 58.2% | 41.8% |
| Colorado | 8 | | | 1,295,380 | 821,817 | 454,975 | 18,588 | 366,842 R | 63.4% | 35.1% | 64.4% | 35.6% |
| Connecticut | 8 | | | 1,466,900 | 890,877 | 569,597 | 6,426 | 321,280 R | 60.7% | 38.8% | 61.0% | 39.0% |
| Delaware | 3 | | | 254,572 | 152,190 | 101,656 | 726 | 50,534 R | 59.8% | 39.9% | 60.0% | 40.0% |
| Florida | 21 | | | 4,180,051 | 2,730,350 | 1,448,816 | 885 | 1,281,534 R | 65.3% | 34.7% | 65.3% | 34.7% |
| Georgia | 12 | | | 1,776,120 | 1,068,722 | 706,628 | 770 | 362,094 R | 60.2% | 39.8% | 60.2% | 39.8% |
| Hawaii | 4 | | | 335,846 | 185,050 | 147,154 | 3,642 | 37,896 R | 55.1% | 43.8% | 55.7% | 44.3% |
| Idaho | 4 | | | 411,144 | 297,523 | 108,510 | 5,111 | 189,013 R | 72.4% | 26.4% | 73.3% | 26.7% |
| Illinois | 24 | | | 4,819,088 | 2,707,103 | 2,086,499 | 25,486 | 620,604 R | 56.2% | 43.3% | 56.5% | 43.5% |
| Indiana | 12 | | | 2,233,069 | 1,377,230 | 841,481 | 14,358 | 535,749 R | 61.7% | 37.7% | 62.1% | 37.9% |
| Iowa | 8 | | | 1,319,805 | 703,088 | 605,620 | 11,097 | 97,468 R | 53.3% | 45.9% | 53.7% | 46.3% |
| Kansas | 7 | | | 1,021,991 | 677,296 | 333,149 | 11,546 | 344,147 R | 66.3% | 32.6% | 67.0% | 33.0% |
| Kentucky | 9 | | | 1,369,345 | 821,702 | 539,539 | 8,104 | 282,163 R | 60.0% | 39.4% | 60.4% | 39.6% |
| Louisiana | 10 | | | 1,706,822 | 1,037,299 | 651,586 | 17,937 | 385,713 R | 60.8% | 38.2% | 61.4% | 38.6% |
| Maine | 4 | | | 553,144 | 336,500 | 214,515 | 2,129 | 121,985 R | 60.8% | 38.8% | 61.1% | 38.9% |
| Maryland | 10 | | | 1,675,873 | 879,918 | 787,935 | 8,020 | 91,983 R | 52.5% | 47.0% | 52.8% | 47.2% |
| Massachusetts | 13 | | | 2,559,453 | 1,310,936 | 1,239,606 | 8,911 | 71,330 R | 51.2% | 48.4% | 51.4% | 48.6% |
| Michigan | 20 | | | 3,801,658 | 2,251,571 | 1,529,638 | 20,449 | 721,933 R | 59.2% | 40.2% | 59.5% | 40.5% |
| Minnesota | | 10 | | 2,084,449 | 1,032,603 | 1,036,364 | 15,482 | 3,761 D | 49.5% | 49.7% | 49.9% | 50.1% |
| Mississippi | 7 | | | 941,104 | 582,377 | 352,192 | 6,535 | 230,185 R | 61.9% | 37.4% | 62.3% | 37.7% |
| Missouri | 11 | | | 2,122,783 | 1,274,188 | 848,583 | 12 | 425,605 R | 60.0% | 40.0% | 60.0% | 40.0% |
| Montana | 4 | | | 384,377 | 232,450 | 146,742 | 5,185 | 85,708 R | 60.5% | 38.2% | 61.3% | 38.7% |
| Nebraska | 5 | | | 652,090 | 460,054 | 187,866 | 4,170 | 272,188 R | 70.6% | 28.8% | 71.0% | 29.0% |
| Nevada | 4 | | | 286,667 | 188,770 | 91,655 | 6,242 | 97,115 R | 65.8% | 32.0% | 67.3% | 32.7% |
| New Hampshire | 4 | | | 389,066 | 267,051 | 120,395 | 1,620 | 146,656 R | 68.6% | 30.9% | 68.9% | 31.1% |
| New Jersey | 16 | | | 3,217,862 | 1,933,630 | 1,261,323 | 22,909 | 672,307 R | 60.1% | 39.2% | 60.5% | 39.5% |
| New Mexico | 5 | | | 514,370 | 307,101 | 201,769 | 5,500 | 105,332 R | 59.7% | 39.2% | 60.3% | 39.7% |
| New York | 36 | | | 6,806,810 | 3,664,763 | 3,119,609 | 22,438 | 545,154 R | 53.8% | 45.8% | 54.0% | 46.0% |
| North Carolina | 13 | | | 2,175,361 | 1,346,481 | 824,287 | 4,593 | 522,194 R | 61.9% | 37.9% | 62.0% | 38.0% |
| North Dakota | 3 | | | 308,971 | 200,336 | 104,429 | 4,206 | 95,907 R | 64.8% | 33.8% | 65.7% | 34.3% |
| Ohio | 23 | | | 4,547,619 | 2,678,560 | 1,825,440 | 43,619 | 853,120 R | 58.9% | 40.1% | 59.5% | 40.5% |
| Oklahoma | 8 | | | 1,255,676 | 861,530 | 385,080 | 9,066 | 476,450 R | 68.6% | 30.7% | 69.1% | 30.9% |
| Oregon | 7 | | | 1,226,527 | 685,700 | 536,479 | 4,348 | 149,221 R | 55.9% | 43.7% | 56.1% | 43.9% |
| Pennsylvania | 25 | | | 4,844,903 | 2,584,323 | 2,228,131 | 32,449 | 356,192 R | 53.3% | 46.0% | 53.7% | 46.3% |
| Rhode Island | 4 | | | 410,492 | 212,080 | 197,106 | 1,306 | 14,974 R | 51.7% | 48.0% | 51.8% | 48.2% |
| South Carolina | 8 | | | 968,529 | 615,539 | 344,459 | 8,531 | 271,080 R | 63.6% | 35.6% | 64.1% | 35.9% |
| South Dakota | 3 | | | 317,867 | 200,267 | 116,113 | 1,487 | 84,154 R | 63.0% | 36.5% | 63.3% | 36.7% |
| Tennessee | 11 | | | 1,711,994 | 990,212 | 711,714 | 10,068 | 278,498 R | 57.8% | 41.6% | 58.2% | 41.8% |
| Texas | 29 | | | 5,397,571 | 3,433,428 | 1,949,276 | 14,867 | 1,484,152 R | 63.6% | 36.1% | 63.8% | 36.2% |
| Utah | 5 | | | 629,656 | 469,105 | 155,369 | 5,182 | 313,736 R | 74.5% | 24.7% | 75.1% | 24.9% |
| Vermont | 3 | | | 234,561 | 135,865 | 95,730 | 2,966 | 40,135 R | 57.9% | 40.8% | 58.7% | 41.3% |
| Virginia | 12 | | | 2,146,635 | 1,337,078 | 796,250 | 13,307 | 540,828 R | 62.3% | 37.1% | 62.7% | 37.3% |
| Washington | 10 | | | 1,883,910 | 1,051,670 | 807,352 | 24,888 | 244,318 R | 55.8% | 42.9% | 56.6% | 43.4% |
| West Virginia | 6 | | | 735,742 | 405,483 | 328,125 | 2,134 | 77,358 R | 55.1% | 44.6% | 55.3% | 44.7% |
| Wisconsin | 11 | | | 2,211,689 | 1,198,584 | 995,740 | 17,365 | 202,844 R | 54.2% | 45.0% | 54.6% | 45.4% |
| Wyoming | 3 | | | 188,968 | 133,241 | 53,370 | 2,357 | 79,871 R | 70.5% | 28.2% | 71.4% | 28.6% |
| District of Columbia | | 3 | | 211,288 | 29,009 | 180,408 | 1,871 | 151,399 D | 13.7% | 85.4% | 13.9% | 86.1% |
| Total | 525 | 13 | | 92,652,842 | 54,455,075 | 37,577,185 | 620,582 | 16,877,890 R | 58.8% | 40.6% | 59.2% | 40.8% |

# PRESIDENT 1980

In New York the Republican figures include Conservative votes. In a number of states candidates appeared on the ballot with variants of the party designations listed below, without any party designation, or with entirely different party names.

In several cases vice-presidential nominees were different from those listed for most states. The Socialist Workers Party nominee for president varied from state to state.

| | | |
|---|---|---|
| 43,904,153 | Ronald Reagan and George Bush | Republican |
| 35,483,883 | Jimmy Carter and Walter F. Mondale | Democratic |
| 5,720,060 | John B. Anderson and Patrick J. Lucey | Independent |
| 921,299 | Edward E. Clark and David Koch | Libertarian |
| 234,294 | Barry Commoner and LaDonna Harris | Citizens |
| 45,023 | Gus Hall and Angela Davis | Communist |
| 41,268 | John R. Rarick and Eileen M. Shearer | American Independent |
| 38,737 | Clifton DeBerry and Matilde Zimmermann | Socialist Workers |
| 32,327 | Ellen McCormack and Carroll Driscoll | Right to Life |
| 18,116 | Maureen Smith and Elizabeth Barron | Peace and Freedom |
| 13,300 | Deirdre Griswold and Larry Holmes | Workers World |
| 7,212 | Benjamin C. Bubar and Earl F. Dodge | Statesman |
| 6,898 | David McReynolds and Diane Drufenbrock | Socialist |
| 6,647 | Percy L. Greaves and Frank L. Varnum | American |
| 6,272 | Andrew Pulley and Matilde Zimmermann | Socialist Workers |
| 4,029 | Richard Congress and Matilde Zimmermann | Socialist Workers |
| 3,694 | Kurt Lynen and Harry Kieve | Middle Class |
| 1,718 | Bill Gahres and J. F. Loughlin | Down With Lawyers |
| 1,555 | Frank W. Shelton and George E. Jackson | American |
| 923 | Martin E. Wendelken with no vice-presidential candidate | Independent |
| 296 | Harley McLain and Jewelie Goeller | Natural Peoples |

In addition to these votes, 13,185 scattered write-in votes were reported from various states, 6,139 votes were cast in Minnesota for American Party electors without designated national nominees, and 4,193 votes were cast for "None of these Candidates" in Nevada.

# UNITED STATES

## PRESIDENT 1980

| State | Electoral Vote Rep. | Electoral Vote Dem. | Electoral Vote Other | Total Vote | Republican | Democratic | Other | Plurality | Percentage Total Vote Rep. | Percentage Total Vote Dem. | Percentage Major Vote Rep. | Percentage Major Vote Dem. |
|---|---|---|---|---|---|---|---|---|---|---|---|---|
| Alabama | 9 | | | 1,341,929 | 654,192 | 636,730 | 51,007 | 17,462 R | 48.8% | 47.4% | 50.7% | 49.3% |
| Alaska | 3 | | | 158,445 | 86,112 | 41,842 | 30,491 | 44,270 R | 54.3% | 26.4% | 67.3% | 32.7% |
| Arizona | 6 | | | 873,945 | 529,688 | 246,843 | 97,414 | 282,845 R | 60.6% | 28.2% | 68.2% | 31.8% |
| Arkansas | 6 | | | 837,582 | 403,164 | 398,041 | 36,377 | 5,123 R | 48.1% | 47.5% | 50.3% | 49.7% |
| California | 45 | | | 8,587,063 | 4,524,858 | 3,083,661 | 978,544 | 1,441,197 R | 52.7% | 35.9% | 59.5% | 40.5% |
| Colorado | 7 | | | 1,184,415 | 652,264 | 367,973 | 164,178 | 284,291 R | 55.1% | 31.1% | 63.9% | 36.1% |
| Connecticut | 8 | | | 1,406,285 | 677,210 | 541,732 | 187,343 | 135,478 R | 48.2% | 38.5% | 55.6% | 44.4% |
| Delaware | 3 | | | 235,900 | 111,252 | 105,754 | 18,894 | 5,498 R | 47.2% | 44.8% | 51.3% | 48.7% |
| Florida | 17 | | | 3,686,930 | 2,046,951 | 1,419,475 | 220,504 | 627,476 R | 55.5% | 38.5% | 59.1% | 40.9% |
| Georgia | | 12 | | 1,596,695 | 654,168 | 890,733 | 51,794 | 236,565 D | 41.0% | 55.8% | 42.3% | 57.7% |
| Hawaii | | 4 | | 303,287 | 130,112 | 135,879 | 37,296 | 5,767 D | 42.9% | 44.8% | 48.9% | 51.1% |
| Idaho | 4 | | | 437,431 | 290,699 | 110,192 | 36,540 | 180,507 R | 66.5% | 25.2% | 72.5% | 27.5% |
| Illinois | 26 | | | 4,749,721 | 2,358,049 | 1,981,413 | 410,259 | 376,636 R | 49.6% | 41.7% | 54.3% | 45.7% |
| Indiana | 13 | | | 2,242,033 | 1,255,656 | 844,197 | 142,180 | 411,459 R | 56.0% | 37.7% | 59.8% | 40.2% |
| Iowa | 8 | | | 1,317,661 | 676,026 | 508,672 | 132,963 | 167,354 R | 51.3% | 38.6% | 57.1% | 42.9% |
| Kansas | 7 | | | 979,795 | 566,812 | 326,150 | 86,833 | 240,662 R | 57.9% | 33.3% | 63.5% | 36.5% |
| Kentucky | 9 | | | 1,294,627 | 635,274 | 616,417 | 42,936 | 18,857 R | 49.1% | 47.6% | 50.8% | 49.2% |
| Louisiana | 10 | | | 1,548,591 | 792,853 | 708,453 | 47,285 | 84,400 R | 51.2% | 45.7% | 52.8% | 47.2% |
| Maine | 4 | | | 523,011 | 238,522 | 220,974 | 63,515 | 17,548 R | 45.6% | 42.3% | 51.9% | 48.1% |
| Maryland | | 10 | | 1,540,496 | 680,606 | 726,161 | 133,729 | 45,555 D | 44.2% | 47.1% | 48.4% | 51.6% |
| Massachusetts | 14 | | | 2,524,298 | 1,057,631 | 1,053,802 | 412,865 | 3,829 R | 41.9% | 41.7% | 50.1% | 49.9% |
| Michigan | 21 | | | 3,909,725 | 1,915,225 | 1,661,532 | 332,968 | 253,693 R | 49.0% | 42.5% | 53.5% | 46.5% |
| Minnesota | | 10 | | 2,051,980 | 873,268 | 954,174 | 224,538 | 80,906 D | 42.6% | 46.5% | 47.8% | 52.2% |
| Mississippi | 7 | | | 892,620 | 441,089 | 429,281 | 22,250 | 11,808 R | 49.4% | 48.1% | 50.7% | 49.3% |
| Missouri | 12 | | | 2,099,824 | 1,074,181 | 931,182 | 94,461 | 142,999 R | 51.2% | 44.3% | 53.6% | 46.4% |
| Montana | 4 | | | 363,952 | 206,814 | 118,032 | 39,106 | 88,782 R | 56.8% | 32.4% | 63.7% | 36.3% |
| Nebraska | 5 | | | 640,854 | 419,937 | 166,851 | 54,066 | 253,086 R | 65.5% | 26.0% | 71.6% | 28.4% |
| Nevada | 3 | | | 247,885 | 155,017 | 66,666 | 26,202 | 88,351 R | 62.5% | 26.9% | 69.9% | 30.1% |
| New Hampshire | 4 | | | 383,990 | 221,705 | 108,864 | 53,421 | 112,841 R | 57.7% | 28.4% | 67.1% | 32.9% |
| New Jersey | 17 | | | 2,975,684 | 1,546,557 | 1,147,364 | 281,763 | 399,193 R | 52.0% | 38.6% | 57.4% | 42.6% |
| New Mexico | 4 | | | 456,971 | 250,779 | 167,826 | 38,366 | 82,953 R | 54.9% | 36.7% | 59.9% | 40.1% |
| New York | 41 | | | 6,201,959 | 2,893,831 | 2,728,372 | 579,756 | 165,459 R | 46.7% | 44.0% | 51.5% | 48.5% |
| North Carolina | 13 | | | 1,855,833 | 915,018 | 875,635 | 65,180 | 39,383 R | 49.3% | 47.2% | 51.1% | 48.9% |
| North Dakota | 3 | | | 301,545 | 193,695 | 79,189 | 28,661 | 114,506 R | 64.2% | 26.3% | 71.0% | 29.0% |
| Ohio | 25 | | | 4,283,603 | 2,206,545 | 1,752,414 | 324,644 | 454,131 R | 51.5% | 40.9% | 55.7% | 44.3% |
| Oklahoma | 8 | | | 1,149,708 | 695,570 | 402,026 | 52,112 | 293,544 R | 60.5% | 35.0% | 63.4% | 36.6% |
| Oregon | 6 | | | 1,181,516 | 571,044 | 456,890 | 153,582 | 114,154 R | 48.3% | 38.7% | 55.6% | 44.4% |
| Pennsylvania | 27 | | | 4,561,501 | 2,261,872 | 1,937,540 | 362,089 | 324,332 R | 49.6% | 42.5% | 53.9% | 46.1% |
| Rhode Island | | 4 | | 416,072 | 154,793 | 198,342 | 62,937 | 43,549 D | 37.2% | 47.7% | 43.8% | 56.2% |
| South Carolina | 8 | | | 894,071 | 441,841 | 430,385 | 21,845 | 11,456 R | 49.4% | 48.1% | 50.7% | 49.3% |
| South Dakota | 4 | | | 327,703 | 198,343 | 103,855 | 25,505 | 94,488 R | 60.5% | 31.7% | 65.6% | 34.4% |
| Tennessee | 10 | | | 1,617,616 | 787,761 | 783,051 | 46,804 | 4,710 R | 48.7% | 48.4% | 50.1% | 49.9% |
| Texas | 26 | | | 4,541,636 | 2,510,705 | 1,881,147 | 149,784 | 629,558 R | 55.3% | 41.4% | 57.2% | 42.8% |
| Utah | 4 | | | 604,222 | 439,687 | 124,266 | 40,269 | 315,421 R | 72.8% | 20.6% | 78.0% | 22.0% |
| Vermont | 3 | | | 213,299 | 94,628 | 81,952 | 36,719 | 12,676 R | 44.4% | 38.4% | 53.6% | 46.4% |
| Virginia | 12 | | | 1,866,032 | 989,609 | 752,174 | 124,249 | 237,435 R | 53.0% | 40.3% | 56.8% | 43.2% |
| Washington | 9 | | | 1,742,394 | 865,244 | 650,193 | 226,957 | 215,051 R | 49.7% | 37.3% | 57.1% | 42.9% |
| West Virginia | | 6 | | 737,715 | 334,206 | 367,462 | 36,047 | 33,256 D | 45.3% | 49.8% | 47.6% | 52.4% |
| Wisconsin | 11 | | | 2,273,221 | 1,088,845 | 981,584 | 202,792 | 107,261 R | 47.9% | 43.2% | 52.6% | 47.4% |
| Wyoming | 3 | | | 176,713 | 110,700 | 49,427 | 16,586 | 61,273 R | 62.6% | 28.0% | 69.1% | 30.9% |
| District of Columbia | | 3 | | 175,237 | 23,545 | 131,113 | 20,579 | 107,568 D | 13.4% | 74.8% | 15.2% | 84.8% |
| Total | 489 | 49 | | 86,515,221 | 43,904,153 | 35,483,883 | 7,127,185 | 8,420,270 R | 50.7% | 41.0% | 55.3% | 44.7% |

# PRESIDENT 1976

In Washington one Republican elector voted in the electoral college for Ronald Reagan for president and Robert Dole for vice president.

In New York the Republican figures include Conservative votes, and the Democratic figures include Liberal votes; in Vermont the Democratic figures include votes cast on the Independent Vermonters Party ticket.

In a number of states candidates appeared on the ballot with variants of the party designations listed below and in several cases with entirely different party names.

The ballot designations for electors for Eugene J. McCarthy for president varied from state to state, as did the names of vice-presidential candidates running with him. In New Jersey the Maddox vice-presidential candidate was Edmund O. Matzal.

The full list of candidates for president and vice president was:

| | | |
|---|---|---|
| 40,830,763 | Jimmy Carter and Walter F. Mondale | Democratic |
| 39,147,793 | Gerald R. Ford and Robert Dole | Republican |
| 756,691 | Eugene J. McCarthy with various vice-presidential candidates | Independent |
| 173,011 | Roger L. MacBride and David D. Bergland | Libertarian |
| 170,531 | Lester G. Maddox and William D. Dyke | American Independent |
| 160,773 | Thomas J. Anderson and Rufus Shackelford | American |
| 91,314 | Peter Camejo and Willie Mae Reid | Socialist Workers |
| 58,992 | Gus Hall and Jarvis Tyner | Communist |
| 49,024 | Margaret Wright and Benjamin Spock | People's |
| 40,043 | Lyndon H. LaRouche Jr. and R. W. Evans | United States Labor |
| 15,934 | Benjamin C. Bubar and Earl F. Dodge | Prohibition |
| 9,616 | Julius Levin and Constance Blomen | Socialist Labor |
| 6,038 | Frank P. Zeidler and J. Q. Brisben | Socialist |
| 361 | Ernest L. Miller and Roy N. Eddy | Restoration |
| 36 | Frank Taylor and Henry Swan | United American |

In addition to these votes, 39,861 scattered write-in votes were reported from various states, and 5,108 votes were cast for "None of these Candidates" in Nevada.

# UNITED STATES

## PRESIDENT 1976

| State | Electoral Vote Rep. | Dem. | Other | Total Vote | Republican | Democratic | Other | Plurality | Percentage Total Vote Rep. | Dem. | Major Vote Rep. | Dem. |
|---|---|---|---|---|---|---|---|---|---|---|---|---|
| Alabama | | 9 | | 1,182,850 | 504,070 | 659,170 | 19,610 | 155,100 D | 42.6% | 55.7% | 43.3% | 56.7% |
| Alaska | 3 | | | 123,574 | 71,555 | 44,058 | 7,961 | 27,497 R | 57.9% | 35.7% | 61.9% | 38.1% |
| Arizona | 6 | | | 742,719 | 418,642 | 295,602 | 28,475 | 123,040 R | 56.4% | 39.8% | 58.6% | 41.4% |
| Arkansas | | 6 | | 767,535 | 267,903 | 498,604 | 1,028 | 230,701 D | 34.9% | 65.0% | 35.0% | 65.0% |
| California | 45 | | | 7,867,117 | 3,882,244 | 3,742,284 | 242,589 | 139,960 R | 49.3% | 47.6% | 50.9% | 49.1% |
| Colorado | 7 | | | 1,081,554 | 584,367 | 460,353 | 36,834 | 124,014 R | 54.0% | 42.6% | 55.9% | 44.1% |
| Connecticut | 8 | | | 1,381,526 | 719,261 | 647,895 | 14,370 | 71,366 R | 52.1% | 46.9% | 52.6% | 47.4% |
| Delaware | | 3 | | 235,834 | 109,831 | 122,596 | 3,407 | 12,765 D | 46.6% | 52.0% | 47.3% | 52.7% |
| Florida | | 17 | | 3,150,631 | 1,469,531 | 1,636,000 | 45,100 | 166,469 D | 46.6% | 51.9% | 47.3% | 52.7% |
| Georgia | | 12 | | 1,467,458 | 483,743 | 979,409 | 4,306 | 495,666 D | 33.0% | 66.7% | 33.1% | 66.9% |
| Hawaii | | 4 | | 291,301 | 140,003 | 147,375 | 3,923 | 7,372 D | 48.1% | 50.6% | 48.7% | 51.3% |
| Idaho | 4 | | | 344,071 | 204,151 | 126,549 | 13,371 | 77,602 R | 59.3% | 36.8% | 61.7% | 38.3% |
| Illinois | 26 | | | 4,718,914 | 2,364,269 | 2,271,295 | 83,350 | 92,974 R | 50.1% | 48.1% | 51.0% | 49.0% |
| Indiana | 13 | | | 2,220,362 | 1,183,958 | 1,014,714 | 21,690 | 169,244 R | 53.3% | 45.7% | 53.8% | 46.2% |
| Iowa | 8 | | | 1,279,306 | 632,863 | 619,931 | 26,512 | 12,932 R | 49.5% | 48.5% | 50.5% | 49.5% |
| Kansas | 7 | | | 957,845 | 502,752 | 430,421 | 24,672 | 72,331 R | 52.5% | 44.9% | 53.9% | 46.1% |
| Kentucky | | 9 | | 1,167,142 | 531,852 | 615,717 | 19,573 | 83,865 D | 45.6% | 52.8% | 46.3% | 53.7% |
| Louisiana | | 10 | | 1,278,439 | 587,446 | 661,365 | 29,628 | 73,919 D | 46.0% | 51.7% | 47.0% | 53.0% |
| Maine | 4 | | | 483,216 | 236,320 | 232,279 | 14,617 | 4,041 R | 48.9% | 48.1% | 50.4% | 49.6% |
| Maryland | | 10 | | 1,439,897 | 672,661 | 759,612 | 7,624 | 86,951 D | 46.7% | 52.8% | 47.0% | 53.0% |
| Massachusetts | | 14 | | 2,547,558 | 1,030,276 | 1,429,475 | 87,807 | 399,199 D | 40.4% | 56.1% | 41.9% | 58.1% |
| Michigan | 21 | | | 3,653,749 | 1,893,742 | 1,696,714 | 63,293 | 197,028 R | 51.8% | 46.4% | 52.7% | 47.3% |
| Minnesota | | 10 | | 1,949,931 | 819,395 | 1,070,440 | 60,096 | 251,045 D | 42.0% | 54.9% | 43.4% | 56.6% |
| Mississippi | | 7 | | 769,361 | 366,846 | 381,309 | 21,206 | 14,463 D | 47.7% | 49.6% | 49.0% | 51.0% |
| Missouri | | 12 | | 1,953,600 | 927,443 | 998,387 | 27,770 | 70,944 D | 47.5% | 51.1% | 48.2% | 51.8% |
| Montana | 4 | | | 328,734 | 173,703 | 149,259 | 5,772 | 24,444 R | 52.8% | 45.4% | 53.8% | 46.2% |
| Nebraska | 5 | | | 607,668 | 359,705 | 233,692 | 14,271 | 126,013 R | 59.2% | 38.5% | 60.6% | 39.4% |
| Nevada | 3 | | | 201,876 | 101,273 | 92,479 | 8,124 | 8,794 R | 50.2% | 45.8% | 52.3% | 47.7% |
| New Hampshire | 4 | | | 339,618 | 185,935 | 147,635 | 6,048 | 38,300 R | 54.7% | 43.5% | 55.7% | 44.3% |
| New Jersey | 17 | | | 3,014,472 | 1,509,688 | 1,444,653 | 60,131 | 65,035 R | 50.1% | 47.9% | 51.1% | 48.9% |
| New Mexico | 4 | | | 418,409 | 211,419 | 201,148 | 5,842 | 10,271 R | 50.5% | 48.1% | 51.2% | 48.8% |
| New York | | 41 | | 6,534,170 | 3,100,791 | 3,389,558 | 43,821 | 288,767 D | 47.5% | 51.9% | 47.8% | 52.2% |
| North Carolina | | 13 | | 1,678,914 | 741,960 | 927,365 | 9,589 | 185,405 D | 44.2% | 55.2% | 44.4% | 55.6% |
| North Dakota | 3 | | | 297,188 | 153,470 | 136,078 | 7,640 | 17,392 R | 51.6% | 45.8% | 53.0% | 47.0% |
| Ohio | | 25 | | 4,111,873 | 2,000,505 | 2,011,621 | 99,747 | 11,116 D | 48.7% | 48.9% | 49.9% | 50.1% |
| Oklahoma | 8 | | | 1,092,251 | 545,708 | 532,442 | 14,101 | 13,266 R | 50.0% | 48.7% | 50.6% | 49.4% |
| Oregon | 6 | | | 1,029,876 | 492,120 | 490,407 | 47,349 | 1,713 R | 47.8% | 47.6% | 50.1% | 49.9% |
| Pennsylvania | | 27 | | 4,620,787 | 2,205,604 | 2,328,677 | 86,506 | 123,073 D | 47.7% | 50.4% | 48.6% | 51.4% |
| Rhode Island | | 4 | | 411,170 | 181,249 | 227,636 | 2,285 | 46,387 D | 44.1% | 55.4% | 44.3% | 55.7% |
| South Carolina | | 8 | | 802,583 | 346,149 | 450,807 | 5,627 | 104,658 D | 43.1% | 56.2% | 43.4% | 56.6% |
| South Dakota | 4 | | | 300,678 | 151,505 | 147,068 | 2,105 | 4,437 R | 50.4% | 48.9% | 50.7% | 49.3% |
| Tennessee | | 10 | | 1,476,345 | 633,969 | 825,879 | 16,497 | 191,910 D | 42.9% | 55.9% | 43.4% | 56.6% |
| Texas | | 26 | | 4,071,884 | 1,953,300 | 2,082,319 | 36,265 | 129,019 D | 48.0% | 51.1% | 48.4% | 51.6% |
| Utah | 4 | | | 541,198 | 337,908 | 182,110 | 21,180 | 155,798 R | 62.4% | 33.6% | 65.0% | 35.0% |
| Vermont | 3 | | | 187,765 | 102,085 | 80,954 | 4,726 | 21,131 R | 54.4% | 43.1% | 55.8% | 44.2% |
| Virginia | 12 | | | 1,697,094 | 836,554 | 813,896 | 46,644 | 22,658 R | 49.3% | 48.0% | 50.7% | 49.3% |
| Washington | 8 | | 1 | 1,555,534 | 777,732 | 717,323 | 60,479 | 60,409 R | 50.0% | 46.1% | 52.0% | 48.0% |
| West Virginia | | 6 | | 750,964 | 314,760 | 435,914 | 290 | 121,154 D | 41.9% | 58.0% | 41.9% | 58.1% |
| Wisconsin | | 11 | | 2,104,175 | 1,004,987 | 1,040,232 | 58,956 | 35,245 D | 47.8% | 49.4% | 49.1% | 50.9% |
| Wyoming | 3 | | | 156,343 | 92,717 | 62,239 | 1,387 | 30,478 R | 59.3% | 39.8% | 59.8% | 40.2% |
| District of Columbia | | 3 | | 168,830 | 27,873 | 137,818 | 3,139 | 109,945 D | 16.5% | 81.6% | 16.8% | 83.2% |
| Total | 240 | 297 | 1 | 81,555,889 | 39,147,793 | 40,830,763 | 1,577,333 | 1,682,970 D | 48.0% | 50.1% | 48.9% | 51.1% |

# PRESIDENT 1972

In Virginia one Republican elector voted in the electoral college for the Libertarian candidates for president and vice president.

In New York the Republican figures include Conservative votes, and the Democratic figures include Liberal votes. In Alabama the Democratic figures include votes cast on the National Democratic Party of Alabama ticket, and in South Carolina they include United Citizens Party votes.

In certain states candidates appeared on the ballot under party names other than those used below; for the Socialist Workers Party the votes listed for Jenness and Pulley were actually cast for substitute candidates (Reed and DeBerry) or without named candidates in several states.

The Democratic vice-presidential candidate originally was Senator Thomas F. Eagleton; upon his withdrawal shortly after the party convention, R. Sargent Shriver was named by the Democratic National Committee as the candidate.

The full list of candidates for president and vice president was:

| | | |
|---|---|---|
| 47,169,911 | Richard M. Nixon and Spiro T. Agnew | Republican |
| 29,170,383 | George S. McGovern and R. Sargent Shriver | Democratic |
| 1,099,482 | John G. Schmitz and Thomas J. Anderson | American |
| 78,756 | Benjamin Spock and Julius Hobson | People's |
| 66,677 | Linda Jenness and Andrew Pulley | Socialist Workers |
| 53,814 | Louis Fisher and Genevieve Gunderson | Socialist Labor |
| 25,595 | Gus Hail and Jarvis Tyner | Communist |
| 13,505 | E. Harold Munn and Marshall E. Uncapher | Prohibition |
| 3,673 | John Hospers and Theodora Nathan | Libertarian |
| 1,743 | John V. Mahalchik and Irving Homer | America First |
| 220 | Gabriel Green and Daniel Fry | Universal |

In addition to the above, 34,795 scattered write-in votes were reported from various states.

Vice President Agnew resigned in October 1973 and Representative Gerald R. Ford of Michigan was nominated by President Nixon to fill the vacancy. In November (Senate) and December (House of Representatives) this action was approved by Congress.

In August 1974 President Nixon resigned and was succeeded by Vice President Ford. In the same month Nelson A. Rockefeller, former governor of New York, was nominated to be vice president and was confirmed by Congress in December 1974.

# UNITED STATES

## PRESIDENT 1972

| State | Electoral Vote Rep. | Electoral Vote Dem. | Electoral Vote Other | Total Vote | Republican | Democratic | Other | Plurality | Percentage Total Vote Rep. | Percentage Total Vote Dem. | Percentage Major Vote Rep. | Percentage Major Vote Dem. |
|---|---|---|---|---|---|---|---|---|---|---|---|---|
| Alabama | 9 | | | 1,006,111 | 728,701 | 256,923 | 20,487 | 471,778 R | 72.4% | 25.5% | 73.9% | 26.1% |
| Alaska | 3 | | | 95,219 | 55,349 | 32,967 | 6,903 | 22,382 R | 58.1% | 34.6% | 62.7% | 37.3% |
| Arizona | 6 | | | 622,926 | 402,812 | 198,540 | 21,574 | 204,272 R | 64.7% | 31.9% | 67.0% | 33.0% |
| Arkansas | 6 | | | 651,320 | 448,541 | 199,892 | 2,887 | 248,649 R | 68.9% | 30.7% | 69.2% | 30.8% |
| California | 45 | | | 8,367,862 | 4,602,096 | 3,475,847 | 289,919 | 1,126,249 R | 55.0% | 41.5% | 57.0% | 43.0% |
| Colorado | 7 | | | 953,884 | 597,189 | 329,980 | 26,715 | 267,209 R | 62.6% | 34.6% | 64.4% | 35.6% |
| Connecticut | 8 | | | 1,384,277 | 810,763 | 555,498 | 18,016 | 255,265 R | 58.6% | 40.1% | 59.3% | 40.7% |
| Delaware | 3 | | | 235,516 | 140,357 | 92,283 | 2,876 | 48,074 R | 59.6% | 39.2% | 60.3% | 39.7% |
| Florida | 17 | | | 2,583,283 | 1,857,759 | 718,117 | 7,407 | 1,139,642 R | 71.9% | 27.8% | 72.1% | 27.9% |
| Georgia | 12 | | | 1,174,772 | 881,496 | 289,529 | 3,747 | 591,967 R | 75.0% | 24.6% | 75.3% | 24.7% |
| Hawaii | 4 | | | 270,274 | 168,865 | 101,409 | | 67,456 R | 62.5% | 37.5% | 62.5% | 37.5% |
| Idaho | 4 | | | 310,379 | 199,384 | 80,826 | 30,169 | 118,558 R | 64.2% | 26.0% | 71.2% | 28.8% |
| Illinois | 26 | | | 4,723,236 | 2,788,179 | 1,913,472 | 21,585 | 874,707 R | 59.0% | 40.5% | 59.3% | 40.7% |
| Indiana | 13 | | | 2,125,529 | 1,405,154 | 708,568 | 11,807 | 696,586 R | 66.1% | 33.3% | 66.5% | 33.5% |
| Iowa | 8 | | | 1,225,944 | 706,207 | 496,206 | 23,531 | 210,001 R | 57.6% | 40.5% | 58.7% | 41.3% |
| Kansas | 7 | | | 916,095 | 619,812 | 270,287 | 25,996 | 349,525 R | 67.7% | 29.5% | 69.6% | 30.4% |
| Kentucky | 9 | | | 1,067,499 | 676,446 | 371,159 | 19,894 | 305,287 R | 63.4% | 34.8% | 64.6% | 35.4% |
| Louisiana | 10 | | | 1,051,491 | 686,852 | 298,142 | 66,497 | 388,710 R | 65.3% | 28.4% | 69.7% | 30.3% |
| Maine | 4 | | | 417,042 | 256,458 | 160,584 | | 95,874 R | 61.5% | 38.5% | 61.5% | 38.5% |
| Maryland | 10 | | | 1,353,812 | 829,305 | 505,781 | 18,726 | 323,524 R | 61.3% | 37.4% | 62.1% | 37.9% |
| Massachusetts | | 14 | | 2,458,756 | 1,112,078 | 1,332,540 | 14,138 | 220,462 D | 45.2% | 54.2% | 45.5% | 54.5% |
| Michigan | 21 | | | 3,489,727 | 1,961,721 | 1,459,435 | 68,571 | 502,286 R | 56.2% | 41.8% | 57.3% | 42.7% |
| Minnesota | 10 | | | 1,741,652 | 898,269 | 802,346 | 41,037 | 95,923 R | 51.6% | 46.1% | 52.8% | 47.2% |
| Mississippi | 7 | | | 645,963 | 505,125 | 126,782 | 14,056 | 378,343 R | 78.2% | 19.6% | 79.9% | 20.1% |
| Missouri | 12 | | | 1,855,803 | 1,153,852 | 697,147 | 4,804 | 456,705 R | 62.2% | 37.6% | 62.3% | 37.7% |
| Montana | 4 | | | 317,603 | 183,976 | 120,197 | 13,430 | 63,779 R | 57.9% | 37.8% | 60.5% | 39.5% |
| Nebraska | 5 | | | 576,289 | 406,298 | 169,991 | | 236,307 R | 70.5% | 29.5% | 70.5% | 29.5% |
| Nevada | 3 | | | 181,766 | 115,750 | 66,016 | | 49,734 R | 63.7% | 36.3% | 63.7% | 36.3% |
| New Hampshire | 4 | | | 334,055 | 213,724 | 116,435 | 3,896 | 97,289 R | 64.0% | 34.9% | 64.7% | 35.3% |
| New Jersey | 17 | | | 2,997,229 | 1,845,502 | 1,102,211 | 49,516 | 743,291 R | 61.6% | 36.8% | 62.6% | 37.4% |
| New Mexico | 4 | | | 386,241 | 235,606 | 141,084 | 9,551 | 94,522 R | 61.0% | 36.5% | 62.5% | 37.5% |
| New York | 41 | | | 7,165,919 | 4,192,778 | 2,951,084 | 22,057 | 1,241,694 R | 58.5% | 41.2% | 58.7% | 41.3% |
| North Carolina | 13 | | | 1,518,612 | 1,054,889 | 438,705 | 25,018 | 616,184 R | 69.5% | 28.9% | 70.6% | 29.4% |
| North Dakota | 3 | | | 280,514 | 174,109 | 100,384 | 6,021 | 73,725 R | 62.1% | 35.8% | 63.4% | 36.6% |
| Ohio | 25 | | | 4,094,787 | 2,441,827 | 1,558,889 | 94,071 | 882,938 R | 59.6% | 38.1% | 61.0% | 39.0% |
| Oklahoma | 8 | | | 1,029,900 | 759,025 | 247,147 | 23,728 | 511,878 R | 73.7% | 24.0% | 75.4% | 24.6% |
| Oregon | 6 | | | 927,946 | 486,686 | 392,760 | 48,500 | 93,926 R | 52.4% | 42.3% | 55.3% | 44.7% |
| Pennsylvania | 27 | | | 4,592,106 | 2,714,521 | 1,796,951 | 80,634 | 917,570 R | 59.1% | 39.1% | 60.2% | 39.8% |
| Rhode Island | 4 | | | 415,808 | 220,383 | 194,645 | 780 | 25,738 R | 53.0% | 46.8% | 53.1% | 46.9% |
| South Carolina | 8 | | | 673,960 | 477,044 | 186,824 | 10,092 | 290,220 R | 70.8% | 27.7% | 71.9% | 28.1% |
| South Dakota | 4 | | | 307,415 | 166,476 | 139,945 | 994 | 26,531 R | 54.2% | 45.5% | 54.3% | 45.7% |
| Tennessee | 10 | | | 1,201,182 | 813,147 | 357,293 | 30,742 | 455,854 R | 67.7% | 29.7% | 69.5% | 30.5% |
| Texas | 26 | | | 3,471,281 | 2,298,896 | 1,154,289 | 18,096 | 1,144,607 R | 66.2% | 33.3% | 66.6% | 33.4% |
| Utah | 4 | | | 478,476 | 323,643 | 126,284 | 28,549 | 197,359 R | 67.6% | 26.4% | 71.9% | 28.1% |
| Vermont | 3 | | | 186,947 | 117,149 | 68,174 | 1,624 | 48,975 R | 62.7% | 36.5% | 63.2% | 36.8% |
| Virginia | 11 | | 1 | 1,457,019 | 988,493 | 438,887 | 29,639 | 549,606 R | 67.8% | 30.1% | 69.3% | 30.7% |
| Washington | 9 | | | 1,470,847 | 837,135 | 568,334 | 65,378 | 268,801 R | 56.9% | 38.6% | 59.6% | 40.4% |
| West Virginia | 6 | | | 762,399 | 484,964 | 277,435 | | 207,529 R | 63.6% | 36.4% | 63.6% | 36.4% |
| Wisconsin | 11 | | | 1,852,890 | 989,430 | 810,174 | 53,286 | 179,256 R | 53.4% | 43.7% | 55.0% | 45.0% |
| Wyoming | 3 | | | 145,570 | 100,464 | 44,358 | 748 | 56,106 R | 69.0% | 30.5% | 69.4% | 30.6% |
| District of Columbia | | 3 | | 163,421 | 35,226 | 127,627 | 568 | 92,401 D | 21.6% | 78.1% | 21.6% | 78.4% |
| Total | 520 | 17 | 1 | 77,718,554 | 47,169,911 | 29,170,383 | 1,378,260 | 17,999,528 R | 60.7% | 37.5% | 61.8% | 38.2% |

## PRESIDENT 1968

In North Carolina one Republican elector voted in the electoral college for the American Independent candidates for president and vice president.

In New York the Democratic figure includes Liberal votes, and in Alabama the Democratic vote is the total of the Alabama Independent Democratic and National Democratic Party of Alabama votes. In certain states candidates appeared under variants of the party name used below, and in most states the vice-presidential candidate of the American Independent party was listed as Marvin Griffin rather than Curtis E. LeMay.

The full list of candidates for president and vice president was:

| | | |
|---|---|---|
| 31,785,480 | Richard M. Nixon and Spiro T. Agnew | Republican |
| 31,275,166 | Hubert H. Humphrey and Edmund S. Muskie | Democratic |
| 9,906,473 | George C. Wallace and Curtis E. LeMay | American Independent |
| 52,588 | Henning A. Blomen and George S. Taylor | Socialist Labor |
| 47,133 | Dick Gregory | Peace and Freedom, with various vice-presidential candidates |
| 41,388 | Fred Halstead and Paul Boutelle | Socialist Workers |
| 36,563 | Eldridge Cleaver | Peace and Freedom, with various vice-presidential candidates |
| 25,552 | Eugene J. McCarthy | Under various titles and written in, but without indication of vice-presidential candidates |
| 15,123 | E. Harold Munn and Rolland E. Fisher | Prohibition |
| 1,519 | Ventura Chavez and Adelicio Moya | People's Constitutional |
| 1,075 | Charlene Mitchell and Michael Zagarell | Communist |
| 142 | James Hensley and Roscoe B. MacKenna | Universal |
| 34 | Richard K. Troxell and Merle Thayer | Constitution |
| 7 | Kent M. Soeters and James P. Powers | Berkeley Defense Group |

In the vote listed above for Eldridge Cleaver, two states are included (California and Utah) in which only the party vice-presidential candidate appeared on the ballot.

In addition to these votes, 12,430 were cast for elector tickets for which there were no formal presidential or vice-presidential candidates, and 11,192 scattered votes were reported from various states.

# UNITED STATES

## PRESIDENT 1968

| State | Electoral Vote Rep. | Dem. | Other | Total Vote | Republican | Democratic | AIP | Other | Plurality | Percentage Rep. | Dem. | AIP |
|---|---|---|---|---|---|---|---|---|---|---|---|---|
| Alabama | | | 10 | 1,049,922 | 146,923 | 196,579 | 691,425 | 14,995 | 494,846 A | 14.0% | 18.7% | 65.9% |
| Alaska | 3 | | | 83,035 | 37,600 | 35,411 | 10,024 | | 2,189 R | 45.3% | 42.6% | 12.1% |
| Arizona | 5 | | | 486,936 | 266,721 | 170,514 | 46,573 | 3,128 | 96,207 R | 54.8% | 35.0% | 9.6% |
| Arkansas | | | 6 | 619,969 | 190,759 | 188,228 | 240,982 | | 50,223 A | 30.8% | 30.4% | 38.9% |
| California | 40 | | | 7,251,587 | 3,467,664 | 3,244,318 | 487,270 | 52,335 | 223,346 R | 47.8% | 44.7% | 6.7% |
| Colorado | 6 | | | 811,199 | 409,345 | 335,174 | 60,813 | 5,867 | 74,171 R | 50.5% | 41.3% | 7.5% |
| Connecticut | | 8 | | 1,256,232 | 556,721 | 621,561 | 76,650 | 1,300 | 64,840 D | 44.3% | 49.5% | 6.1% |
| Delaware | 3 | | | 214,367 | 96,714 | 89,194 | 28,459 | | 7,520 R | 45.1% | 41.6% | 13.3% |
| Florida | 14 | | | 2,187,805 | 886,804 | 676,794 | 624,207 | | 210,010 R | 40.5% | 30.9% | 28.5% |
| Georgia | | | 12 | 1,250,266 | 380,111 | 334,440 | 535,550 | 165 | 155,439 A | 30.4% | 26.7% | 42.8% |
| Hawaii | | | | 236,218 | 91,425 | 141,324 | 3,469 | | 49,899 D | 38.7% | 59.8% | 1.5% |
| Idaho | 4 | 4 | | 291,183 | 165,369 | 89,273 | 36,541 | | 76,096 R | 56.8% | 30.7% | 12.5% |
| Illinois | 26 | | | 4,619,749 | 2,174,774 | 2,039,814 | 390,958 | 14,203 | 134,960 R | 47.1% | 44.2% | 8.5% |
| Indiana | 13 | | | 2,123,597 | 1,067,885 | 806,659 | 243,108 | 5,945 | 261,226 R | 50.3% | 38.0% | 11.4% |
| Iowa | 9 | | | 1,167,931 | 619,106 | 476,699 | 66,422 | 5,704 | 142,407 R | 53.0% | 40.8% | 5.7% |
| Kansas | 7 | | | 872,783 | 478,674 | 302,996 | 88,921 | 2,192 | 175,678 R | 54.8% | 34.7% | 10.2% |
| Kentucky | 9 | | | 1,055,893 | 462,411 | 397,541 | 193,098 | 2,843 | 64,870 R | 43.8% | 37.6% | 18.3% |
| Louisiana | | | 10 | 1,097,450 | 257,535 | 309,615 | 530,300 | | 220,685 A | 23.5% | 28.2% | 48.3% |
| Maine | | 4 | | 392,936 | 169,254 | 217,312 | 6,370 | | 48,058 D | 43.1% | 55.3% | 1.6% |
| Maryland | | 10 | | 1,235,039 | 517,995 | 538,310 | 178,734 | | 20,315 D | 41.9% | 43.6% | 14.5% |
| Massachusetts | | 14 | | 2,331,752 | 766,844 | 1,469,218 | 87,088 | 8,602 | 702,374 D | 32.9% | 63.0% | 3.7% |
| Michigan | | 21 | | 3,306,250 | 1,370,665 | 1,593,082 | 331,968 | 10,535 | 222,417 D | 41.5% | 48.2% | 10.0% |
| Minnesota | | 10 | | 1,588,506 | 658,643 | 857,738 | 68,931 | 3,194 | 199,095 D | 41.5% | 54.0% | 4.3% |
| Mississippi | | | 7 | 654,509 | 88,516 | 150,644 | 415,349 | | 264,705 A | 13.5% | 23.0% | 63.5% |
| Missouri | 12 | | | 1,809,502 | 811,932 | 791,444 | 206,126 | | 20,488 R | 44.9% | 43.7% | 11.4% |
| Montana | 4 | | | 274,404 | 138,835 | 114,117 | 20,015 | 1,437 | 24,718 R | 50.6% | 41.6% | 7.3% |
| Nebraska | 5 | | | 536,851 | 321,163 | 170,784 | 44,904 | | 150,379 R | 59.8% | 31.8% | 8.4% |
| Nevada | 3 | | | 154,218 | 73,188 | 60,598 | 20,432 | | 12,590 R | 47.5% | 39.3% | 13.2% |
| New Hampshire | 4 | | | 297,298 | 154,903 | 130,589 | 11,173 | 633 | 24,314 R | 52.1% | 43.9% | 3.8% |
| New Jersey | 17 | | | 2,875,395 | 1,325,467 | 1,264,206 | 262,187 | 23,535 | 61,261 R | 46.1% | 44.0% | 9.1% |
| New Mexico | 4 | | | 327,350 | 169,692 | 130,081 | 25,737 | 1,840 | 39,611 R | 51.8% | 39.7% | 7.9% |
| New York | | 43 | | 6,791,688 | 3,007,932 | 3,378,470 | 358,864 | 46,422 | 370,538 D | 44.3% | 49.7% | 5.3% |
| North Carolina | 12 | | 1 | 1,587,493 | 627,192 | 464,113 | 496,188 | | 131,004 R | 39.5% | 29.2% | 31.3% |
| North Dakota | 4 | | | 247,882 | 138,669 | 94,769 | 14,244 | 200 | 43,900 R | 55.9% | 38.2% | 5.7% |
| Ohio | 26 | | | 3,959,698 | 1,791,014 | 1,700,586 | 467,495 | 603 | 90,428 R | 45.2% | 42.9% | 11.8% |
| Oklahoma | 8 | | | 943,086 | 449,697 | 301,658 | 191,731 | | 148,039 R | 47.7% | 32.0% | 20.3% |
| Oregon | 6 | | | 819,622 | 408,433 | 358,866 | 49,683 | 2,640 | 49,567 R | 49.8% | 43.8% | 6.1% |
| Pennsylvania | | 29 | | 4,747,928 | 2,090,017 | 2,259,405 | 378,582 | 19,924 | 169,388 D | 44.0% | 47.6% | 8.0% |
| Rhode Island | | 4 | | 385,000 | 122,359 | 246,518 | 15,678 | 445 | 124,159 D | 31.8% | 64.0% | 4.1% |
| South Carolina | 8 | | | 666,978 | 254,062 | 197,486 | 215,430 | | 38,632 R | 38.1% | 29.6% | 32.3% |
| South Dakota | 4 | | | 281,264 | 149,841 | 118,023 | 13,400 | | 31,818 R | 53.3% | 42.0% | 4.8% |
| Tennessee | 11 | | | 1,248,617 | 472,592 | 351,233 | 424,792 | | 47,800 R | 37.8% | 28.1% | 34.0% |
| Texas | | 25 | | 3,079,216 | 1,227,844 | 1,266,804 | 584,269 | 299 | 38,960 D | 39.9% | 41.1% | 19.0% |
| Utah | 4 | | | 422,568 | 238,728 | 156,665 | 26,906 | 269 | 82,063 R | 56.5% | 37.1% | 6.4% |
| Vermont | 3 | | | 161,404 | 85,142 | 70,255 | 5,104 | 903 | 14,887 R | 52.8% | 43.5% | 3.2% |
| Virginia | 12 | | | 1,361,491 | 590,319 | 442,387 | 321,833 | 6,952 | 147,932 R | 43.4% | 32.5% | 23.6% |
| Washington | | 9 | | 1,304,281 | 588,510 | 616,037 | 96,990 | 2,744 | 27,527 D | 45.1% | 47.2% | 7.4% |
| West Virginia | | 7 | | 754,206 | 307,555 | 374,091 | 72,560 | | 66,536 D | 40.8% | 49.6% | 9.6% |
| Wisconsin | 12 | | | 1,691,538 | 809,997 | 748,804 | 127,835 | 4,902 | 61,193 R | 47.9% | 44.3% | 7.6% |
| Wyoming | 3 | | | 127,205 | 70,927 | 45,173 | 11,105 | | 25,754 R | 55.8% | 35.5% | 8.7% |
| District of Columbia | | 3 | | 170,578 | 31,012 | 139,566 | | | 108,554 D | 18.2% | 81.8% | |
| Total | 301 | 191 | 46 | 73,211,875 | 31,785,480 | 31,275,166 | 9,906,473 | 244,756 | 510,314 R | 43.4% | 42.7% | 13.5% |

# PRESIDENT 1964

In New York the Democratic figure includes Liberal votes.

The full list of candidates for president and vice president was:

| | | |
|---|---|---|
| 43,129,566 | Lyndon B. Johnson and Hubert H. Humphrey | Democratic |
| 27,178,188 | Barry M. Goldwater and William E. Miller | Republican |
| 45,219 | Eric Hass and Henning A. Blomen | Socialist Labor |
| 32,720 | Clifton DeBerry and Edward Shaw | Socialist Workers |
| 23,267 | E. Harold Munn and Mark R. Shaw | Prohibition |
| 6,953 | John Kasper and J. B. Stoner | National States Rights |
| 5,060 | Joseph B. Lightburn and T. C. Billings | Constitution |
| 19 | James Hensley and John O. Hopkins | Universal |

In addition, 210,732 votes were cast in Alabama for an unpledged Democratic elector ticket, and 12,868 scattered write-in votes were reported from various states.

# UNITED STATES

## PRESIDENT 1964

| State | Electoral Vote Rep. | Dem. | Other | Total Vote | Republican | Democratic | Other | Plurality | Percentage Total Vote Rep. | Dem. | Major Vote Rep. | Dem. |
|---|---|---|---|---|---|---|---|---|---|---|---|---|
| Alabama | 10 | | | 689,818 | 479,085 | | 210,733 | 479,085 R | 69.5% | | 100.0% | |
| Alaska | | 3 | | 67,259 | 22,930 | 44,329 | | 21,399 D | 34.1% | 65.9% | 34.1% | 65.9% |
| Arizona | 5 | | | 480,770 | 242,535 | 237,753 | 482 | 4,782 R | 50.4% | 49.5% | 50.5% | 49.5% |
| Arkansas | | 6 | | 560,426 | 243,264 | 314,197 | 2,965 | 70,933 D | 43.4% | 56.1% | 43.6% | 56.4% |
| California | | 40 | | 7,057,586 | 2,879,108 | 4,171,877 | 6,601 | 1,292,769 D | 40.8% | 59.1% | 40.8% | 59.2% |
| Colorado | | 6 | | 776,986 | 296,767 | 476,024 | 4,195 | 179,257 D | 38.2% | 61.3% | 38.4% | 61.6% |
| Connecticut | | 8 | | 1,218,578 | 390,996 | 826,269 | 1,313 | 435,273 D | 32.1% | 67.8% | 32.1% | 67.9% |
| Delaware | | 3 | | 201,320 | 78,078 | 122,704 | 538 | 44,626 D | 38.8% | 60.9% | 38.9% | 61.1% |
| Florida | | 14 | | 1,854,481 | 905,941 | 948,540 | | 42,599 D | 48.9% | 51.1% | 48.9% | 51.1% |
| Georgia | 12 | | | 1,139,335 | 616,584 | 522,556 | 195 | 94,028 R | 54.1% | 45.9% | 54.1% | 45.9% |
| Hawaii | | 4 | | 207,271 | 44,022 | 163,249 | | 119,227 D | 21.2% | 78.8% | 21.2% | 78.8% |
| Idaho | | 4 | | 292,477 | 143,557 | 148,920 | | 5,363 D | 49.1% | 50.9% | 49.1% | 50.9% |
| Illinois | | 26 | | 4,702,841 | 1,905,946 | 2,796,833 | 62 | 890,887 D | 40.5% | 59.5% | 40.5% | 59.5% |
| Indiana | | 13 | | 2,091,606 | 911,118 | 1,170,848 | 9,640 | 259,730 D | 43.6% | 56.0% | 43.8% | 56.2% |
| Iowa | | 9 | | 1,184,539 | 449,148 | 733,030 | 2,361 | 283,882 D | 37.9% | 61.9% | 38.0% | 62.0% |
| Kansas | | 7 | | 857,901 | 386,579 | 464,028 | 7,294 | 77,449 D | 45.1% | 54.1% | 45.4% | 54.6% |
| Kentucky | | 9 | | 1,046,105 | 372,977 | 669,659 | 3,469 | 296,682 D | 35.7% | 64.0% | 35.8% | 64.2% |
| Louisiana | 10 | | | 896,293 | 509,225 | 387,068 | | 122,157 R | 56.8% | 43.2% | 56.8% | 43.2% |
| Maine | | 4 | | 380,965 | 118,701 | 262,264 | | 143,563 D | 31.2% | 68.8% | 31.2% | 68.8% |
| Maryland | | 10 | | 1,116,457 | 385,495 | 730,912 | 50 | 345,417 D | 34.5% | 65.5% | 34.5% | 65.5% |
| Massachusetts | | 14 | | 2,344,798 | 549,727 | 1,786,422 | 8,649 | 1,236,695 D | 23.4% | 76.2% | 23.5% | 76.5% |
| Michigan | | 21 | | 3,203,102 | 1,060,152 | 2,136,615 | 6,335 | 1,076,463 D | 33.1% | 66.7% | 33.2% | 66.8% |
| Minnesota | | 10 | | 1,554,462 | 559,624 | 991,117 | 3,721 | 431,493 D | 36.0% | 63.8% | 36.1% | 63.9% |
| Mississippi | 7 | | | 409,146 | 356,528 | 52,618 | | 303,910 R | 87.1% | 12.9% | 87.1% | 12.9% |
| Missouri | | 12 | | 1,817,879 | 653,535 | 1,164,344 | | 510,809 D | 36.0% | 64.0% | 36.0% | 64.0% |
| Montana | | 4 | | 278,628 | 113,032 | 164,246 | 1,350 | 51,214 D | 40.6% | 58.9% | 40.8% | 59.2% |
| Nebraska | | 5 | | 584,154 | 276,847 | 307,307 | | 30,460 D | 47.4% | 52.6% | 47.4% | 52.6% |
| Nevada | | 3 | | 135,433 | 56,094 | 79,339 | | 23,245 D | 41.4% | 58.6% | 41.4% | 58.6% |
| New Hampshire | | 4 | | 288,093 | 104,029 | 184,064 | | 80,035 D | 36.1% | 63.9% | 36.1% | 63.9% |
| New Jersey | | 17 | | 2,847,663 | 964,174 | 1,868,231 | 15,258 | 904,057 D | 33.9% | 65.6% | 34.0% | 66.0% |
| New Mexico | | 4 | | 328,645 | 132,838 | 194,015 | 1,792 | 61,177 D | 40.4% | 59.0% | 40.6% | 59.4% |
| New York | | 43 | | 7,166,275 | 2,243,559 | 4,913,102 | 9,614 | 2,669,543 D | 31.3% | 68.6% | 31.3% | 68.7% |
| North Carolina | | 13 | | 1,424,983 | 624,844 | 800,139 | | 175,295 D | 43.8% | 56.2% | 43.8% | 56.2% |
| North Dakota | | 4 | | 258,389 | 108,207 | 149,784 | 398 | 41,577 D | 41.9% | 58.0% | 41.9% | 58.1% |
| Ohio | | 26 | | 3,969,196 | 1,470,865 | 2,498,331 | | 1,027,466 D | 37.1% | 62.9% | 37.1% | 62.9% |
| Oklahoma | | 8 | | 932,499 | 412,665 | 519,834 | | 107,169 D | 44.3% | 55.7% | 44.3% | 55.7% |
| Oregon | | 6 | | 786,305 | 282,779 | 501,017 | 2,509 | 218,238 D | 36.0% | 63.7% | 36.1% | 63.9% |
| Pennsylvania | | 29 | | 4,822,690 | 1,673,657 | 3,130,954 | 18,079 | 1,457,297 D | 34.7% | 64.9% | 34.8% | 65.2% |
| Rhode Island | | 4 | | 390,091 | 74,615 | 315,463 | 13 | 240,848 D | 19.1% | 80.9% | 19.1% | 80.9% |
| South Carolina | 8 | | | 524,779 | 309,048 | 215,723 | 8 | 93,325 R | 58.9% | 41.1% | 58.9% | 41.1% |
| South Dakota | | 4 | | 293,118 | 130,108 | 163,010 | | 32,902 D | 44.4% | 55.6% | 44.4% | 55.6% |
| Tennessee | | 11 | | 1,143,946 | 508,965 | 634,947 | 34 | 125,982 D | 44.5% | 55.5% | 44.5% | 55.5% |
| Texas | | 25 | | 2,626,811 | 958,566 | 1,663,185 | 5,060 | 704,619 D | 36.5% | 63.3% | 36.6% | 63.4% |
| Utah | | 4 | | 401,413 | 181,785 | 219,628 | | 37,843 D | 45.3% | 54.7% | 45.3% | 54.7% |
| Vermont | | 3 | | 163,089 | 54,942 | 108,127 | 20 | 53,185 D | 33.7% | 66.3% | 33.7% | 66.3% |
| Virginia | | 12 | | 1,042,267 | 481,334 | 558,038 | 2,895 | 76,704 D | 46.2% | 53.5% | 46.3% | 53.7% |
| Washington | | 9 | | 1,258,556 | 470,366 | 779,881 | 8,309 | 309,515 D | 37.4% | 62.0% | 37.6% | 62.4% |
| West Virginia | | 7 | | 792,040 | 253,953 | 538,087 | | 284,134 D | 32.1% | 67.9% | 32.1% | 67.9% |
| Wisconsin | | 12 | | 1,691,815 | 638,495 | 1,050,424 | 2,896 | 411,929 D | 37.7% | 62.1% | 37.8% | 62.2% |
| Wyoming | | 3 | | 142,716 | 61,998 | 80,718 | | 18,720 D | 43.4% | 56.6% | 43.4% | 56.6% |
| District of Columbia | | 3 | | 198,597 | 28,801 | 169,796 | | 140,995 D | 14.5% | 85.5% | 14.5% | 85.5% |
| Total | 52 | 486 | | 70,644,592 | 27,178,188 | 43,129,566 | 336,838 | 15,951,378 D | 38.5% | 61.1% | 38.7% | 61.3% |

# PRESIDENT 1960

Senator Harry Flood Byrd received 15 votes for president in the electoral college; these were the votes of 6 of the 11 Democratic electors in Alabama, all 8 unpledged Democratic electors in Mississippi, and 1 of the 8 Republican electors in Oklahoma. The Alabama and Mississippi electors also cast 14 votes for Senator Strom Thurmond for vice president; the single Oklahoma elector voted for Senator Barry M. Goldwater for vice president.

In New York the Democratic figure includes Liberal votes.

The full list of candidates for president and vice president was:

| | | |
|---|---|---|
| 34,226,731 | John F. Kennedy and Lyndon B. Johnson | Democratic |
| 34,108,157 | Richard M. Nixon and Henry Cabot Lodge | Republican |
| 47,522 | Eric Hass and Georgia Cozzini | Socialist Labor |
| 46,203 | Rutherford L. Decker and E. Harold Munn | Prohibition |
| 44,977 | Orval E. Faubus and John G. Crommelin | National States Rights |
| 40,165 | Farrell Dobbs and Myra Tanner Weiss | Socialist Workers |
| 18,162 | Charles L. Sullivan and Merritt B. Curtis | Constitution |
| 8,708 | J. Bracken Lee and Kent H. Courtney | Conservative |
| 4,204 | C. Benton Coiner and Edward J. Silverman | Conservative |
| 1,767 | Lar Daly and B. M. Miller | Tax Cut |
| 1,485 | Clennon King and Reginald Carter | Independent Afro-American |
| 1,401 | Merritt B. Curtis and B. M. Miller | Constitution |

In addition, 169,572 votes were cast in Louisiana for Independent electors and 116,248 in Mississippi for an unpledged Democratic elector ticket. Another 539 votes were cast in Michigan for an Independent American ticket, and 2,378 scattered votes were reported from various states.

# UNITED STATES

## PRESIDENT 1960

| State | Electoral Vote Rep. | Electoral Vote Dem. | Electoral Vote Other | Total Vote | Republican | Democratic | Other | Plurality | Percentage Total Vote Rep. | Percentage Total Vote Dem. | Percentage Major Vote Rep. | Percentage Major Vote Dem. |
|---|---|---|---|---|---|---|---|---|---|---|---|---|
| Alabama | | 5 | 6 | 570,225 | 237,981 | 324,050 | 8,194 | 86,069 D | 41.7% | 56.8% | 42.3% | 57.7% |
| Alaska | 3 | | | 60,762 | 30,953 | 29,809 | | 1,144 R | 50.9% | 49.1% | 50.9% | 49.1% |
| Arizona | 4 | | | 398,491 | 221,241 | 176,781 | 469 | 44,460 R | 55.5% | 44.4% | 55.6% | 44.4% |
| Arkansas | | 8 | | 428,509 | 184,508 | 215,049 | 28,952 | 30,541 D | 43.1% | 50.2% | 46.2% | 53.8% |
| California | 32 | | | 6,506,578 | 3,259,722 | 3,224,099 | 22,757 | 35,623 R | 50.1% | 49.6% | 50.3% | 49.7% |
| Colorado | 6 | | | 736,236 | 402,242 | 330,629 | 3,365 | 71,613 R | 54.6% | 44.9% | 54.9% | 45.1% |
| Connecticut | | 8 | | 1,222,883 | 565,813 | 657,055 | 15 | 91,242 D | 46.3% | 53.7% | 46.3% | 53.7% |
| Delaware | | 3 | | 196,683 | 96,373 | 99,590 | 720 | 3,217 D | 49.0% | 50.6% | 49.2% | 50.8% |
| Florida | 10 | | | 1,544,176 | 795,476 | 748,700 | | 46,776 R | 51.5% | 48.5% | 51.5% | 48.5% |
| Georgia | | 12 | | 733,349 | 274,472 | 458,638 | 239 | 184,166 D | 37.4% | 62.5% | 37.4% | 62.6% |
| Hawaii | | 3 | | 184,705 | 92,295 | 92,410 | | 115 D | 50.0% | 50.0% | 50.0% | 50.0% |
| Idaho | 4 | | | 300,450 | 161,597 | 138,853 | | 22,744 R | 53.8% | 46.2% | 53.8% | 46.2% |
| Illinois | | 27 | | 4,757,409 | 2,368,988 | 2,377,846 | 10,575 | 8,858 D | 49.8% | 50.0% | 49.9% | 50.1% |
| Indiana | 13 | | | 2,135,360 | 1,175,120 | 952,358 | 7,882 | 222,762 R | 55.0% | 44.6% | 55.2% | 44.8% |
| Iowa | 10 | | | 1,273,810 | 722,381 | 550,565 | 864 | 171,816 R | 56.7% | 43.2% | 56.7% | 43.3% |
| Kansas | 8 | | | 928,825 | 561,474 | 363,213 | 4,138 | 198,261 R | 60.4% | 39.1% | 60.7% | 39.3% |
| Kentucky | 10 | | | 1,124,462 | 602,607 | 521,855 | | 80,752 R | 53.6% | 46.4% | 53.6% | 46.4% |
| Louisiana | | 10 | | 807,891 | 230,980 | 407,339 | 169,572 | 176,359 D | 28.6% | 50.4% | 36.2% | 63.8% |
| Maine | 5 | | | 421,767 | 240,608 | 181,159 | | 59,449 R | 57.0% | 43.0% | 57.0% | 43.0% |
| Maryland | | 9 | | 1,055,349 | 489,538 | 565,808 | 3 | 76,270 D | 46.4% | 53.6% | 46.4% | 53.6% |
| Massachusetts | | 16 | | 2,469,480 | 976,750 | 1,487,174 | 5,556 | 510,424 D | 39.6% | 60.2% | 39.6% | 60.4% |
| Michigan | | 20 | | 3,318,097 | 1,620,428 | 1,687,269 | 10,400 | 66,841 D | 48.8% | 50.9% | 49.0% | 51.0% |
| Minnesota | | 11 | | 1,541,887 | 757,915 | 779,933 | 4,039 | 22,018 D | 49.2% | 50.6% | 49.3% | 50.7% |
| Mississippi | | | 8 | 298,171 | 73,561 | 108,362 | 116,248 | 7,886 U | 24.7% | 36.3% | 40.4% | 59.6% |
| Missouri | | 13 | | 1,934,422 | 962,221 | 972,201 | | 9,980 D | 49.7% | 50.3% | 49.7% | 50.3% |
| Montana | 4 | | | 277,579 | 141,841 | 134,891 | 847 | 6,950 R | 51.1% | 48.6% | 51.3% | 48.7% |
| Nebraska | 6 | | | 613,095 | 380,553 | 232,542 | | 148,011 R | 62.1% | 37.9% | 62.1% | 37.9% |
| Nevada | | 3 | | 107,267 | 52,387 | 54,880 | | 2,493 D | 48.8% | 51.2% | 48.8% | 51.2% |
| New Hampshire | 4 | | | 295,761 | 157,989 | 137,772 | | 20,217 R | 53.4% | 46.6% | 53.4% | 46.6% |
| New Jersey | | 16 | | 2,773,111 | 1,363,324 | 1,385,415 | 24,372 | 22,091 D | 49.2% | 50.0% | 49.6% | 50.4% |
| New Mexico | | 4 | | 311,107 | 153,733 | 156,027 | 1,347 | 2,294 D | 49.4% | 50.2% | 49.6% | 50.4% |
| New York | | 45 | | 7,291,079 | 3,446,419 | 3,830,085 | 14,575 | 383,666 D | 47.3% | 52.5% | 47.4% | 52.6% |
| North Carolina | | 14 | | 1,368,556 | 655,420 | 713,136 | | 57,716 D | 47.9% | 52.1% | 47.9% | 52.1% |
| North Dakota | 4 | | | 278,431 | 154,310 | 123,963 | 158 | 30,347 R | 55.4% | 44.5% | 55.5% | 44.5% |
| Ohio | 25 | | | 4,161,859 | 2,217,611 | 1,944,248 | | 273,363 R | 53.3% | 46.7% | 53.3% | 46.7% |
| Oklahoma | 7 | | 1 | 903,150 | 533,039 | 370,111 | | 162,928 R | 59.0% | 41.0% | 59.0% | 41.0% |
| Oregon | 6 | | | 776,421 | 408,060 | 367,402 | 959 | 40,658 R | 52.6% | 47.3% | 52.6% | 47.4% |
| Pennsylvania | | 32 | | 5,006,541 | 2,439,956 | 2,556,282 | 10,303 | 116,326 D | 48.7% | 51.1% | 48.8% | 51.2% |
| Rhode Island | | 4 | | 405,535 | 147,502 | 258,032 | 1 | 110,530 D | 36.4% | 63.6% | 36.4% | 63.6% |
| South Carolina | | 8 | | 386,688 | 188,558 | 198,129 | 1 | 9,571 D | 48.8% | 51.2% | 48.8% | 51.2% |
| South Dakota | 4 | | | 306,487 | 178,417 | 128,070 | | 50,347 R | 58.2% | 41.8% | 58.2% | 41.8% |
| Tennessee | 11 | | | 1,051,792 | 556,577 | 481,453 | 13,762 | 75,124 R | 52.9% | 45.8% | 53.6% | 46.4% |
| Texas | | 24 | | 2,311,084 | 1,121,310 | 1,167,567 | 22,207 | 46,257 D | 48.5% | 50.5% | 49.0% | 51.0% |
| Utah | 4 | | | 374,709 | 205,361 | 169,248 | 100 | 36,113 R | 54.8% | 45.2% | 54.8% | 45.2% |
| Vermont | 3 | | | 167,324 | 98,131 | 69,186 | 7 | 28,945 R | 58.6% | 41.3% | 58.6% | 41.4% |
| Virginia | 12 | | | 771,449 | 404,521 | 362,327 | 4,601 | 42,194 R | 52.4% | 47.0% | 52.8% | 47.2% |
| Washington | 9 | | | 1,241,572 | 629,273 | 599,298 | 13,001 | 29,975 R | 50.7% | 48.3% | 51.2% | 48.8% |
| West Virginia | | 8 | | 837,781 | 395,995 | 441,786 | | 45,791 D | 47.3% | 52.7% | 47.3% | 52.7% |
| Wisconsin | 12 | | | 1,729,082 | 895,175 | 830,805 | 3,102 | 64,370 R | 51.8% | 48.0% | 51.9% | 48.1% |
| Wyoming | 3 | | | 140,782 | 77,451 | 63,331 | | 14,120 R | 55.0% | 45.0% | 55.0% | 45.0% |
| District of Columbia | | | | | | | | | | | | |
| Total | 219 | 303 | 15 | 68,838,219 | 34,108,157 | 34,226,731 | 503,331 | 118,574 D | 49.5% | 49.7% | 49.9% | 50.1% |

# PRESIDENTIAL PRIMARIES 2004

In 2004, 37 states and the District of Columbia held presidential primaries, in which at least one of the parties held contests where voters balloted directly for candidates or for a statewide slate of delegates that was pledged to a candidate. The total of primaries includes Democratic party-run contests in South Carolina and Utah, but does not include similar events in Michigan and New Mexico that were designated as caucuses by the Democratic state parties. The Democratic presidential primary in the District of Columbia that kicked off the 2004 primary season was a nonbinding event and was not involved in the selection of delegates. States that are not listed did not hold a presidential primary of any kind in 2004.

The list below, alphabetical by state, gives primary vote totals for all candidates that were listed on the ballot in at least one primary. The tables on pages 46 to 48 give a chronological summary of the primary votes for those candidates in the Republican and Democratic parties who received at least 200,000 votes nationwide.

Republican candidates on the ballot in at least one primary were: Blake Ashby, Richard P. Bosa, John Buchanan, George W. Bush, Michael Callis, George Gostigian, Robert Edward Haines, Mark "Dick" Harnes, Millie Howard, "Tom" Laughlin, Cornelius E. O'Connor, John Donald Rigazio, "Jim" Taylor, and Bill Wyatt.

Democratic candidates on the ballot in at least one primary were: George H. Ballard III, William Barchilon, Dianne Barker, Katherine Bateman, Keith Brand, Carol Moseley Braun, Harry W. Braun III, Ray Caplette, Willie Felix Carter, Jeanne Chebib, Wesley Clark, Randy Crow, Howard Dean, Gerry Dokka, John Edwards, Richard A. Gephardt, Mildred Glover, Vincent S. Hamm, Arthur H. Jackson Jr., John Kerry, Caroline Pettinato Killeen, Dennis J. Kucinich, Lyndon H. LaRouche Jr., R. Randy Lee, Joseph I. Lieberman, Robert H. Linnell, "Bill" McGaughey, Huda Muhammad, Edward Thomas O'Donnell Jr., Fern Penna, Al Sharpton, Vermin Supreme, Leonard Dennis Talbow, Evelyn Vitullo, Florence Walker, Lucian Wojciechowski, and Bill Wyatt.

## ALABAMA JUNE 1

Republican    187,038 Bush; 14,449 Uncommitted.

Democratic    164,021 Kerry; 38,223 Uncommitted; 9,076 Kucinich; 7,254 LaRouche.

## ARIZONA FEBRUARY 3

Republican    No presidential primary.

Democratic    101,809 Kerry; 63,256 Clark; 33,555 Dean; 16,596 Edwards; 15,906 Lieberman; 3,896 Kucinich; 1,177 Sharpton; 755 Gephardt; 325 Moseley Braun; 295 LaRouche; 257 Barker; 233 Wyatt; 225 Brand; 208 Penna; 136 Barchilon; 119 Muhammad; 117 Vitullo; 77 Caplette.

## ARKANSAS MAY 18

Republican    37,234 Bush; 1,129 Uncommitted.

Democratic    177,754 Kerry; 61,800 Uncommitted; 13,766 Kucinich; 13,528 LaRouche.

## CALIFORNIA MARCH 2

Republican    2,216,047 Bush; 95 Warrick (write-in); 90 Wyatt (write-in); 56 Ashby (write-in); 22 Barton (write-in); 17 Holtz (write-in); 12 Bosa (write-in); 12 Castellano (write-in).

Democratic    2,002,539 Kerry; 614,441 Edwards; 144,954 Kucinich; 130,892 Dean; 59,326 Sharpton; 52,780 Lieberman; 51,084 Clark; 24,501 Moseley Braun; 19,139 Gephardt; 7,953 LaRouche; 6 Dunmar (write-in); 4 Alexander-Pace (write-in); 4 Nigro (write-in); 3 Giacomuzzi (write-in); 3 Penna (write-in). A total of 3,107,629 votes were cast in the Democratic primary, 2,900,256 by registered Democratic voters and 207,353 votes by registered Unaffiliated voters. The two categories were tallied separately but combined into an overall vote, which also includes 20 write-in votes.

# PRESIDENTIAL PRIMARIES 2004

## CONNECTICUT MARCH 2

Republican      No presidential primary. Bush unopposed.

Democratic      75,860 Kerry; 30,844 Edwards; 6,705 Lieberman; 5,166 Dean; 4,133 Kucinich; 3,312 Sharpton; 1,546 Clark; 1,467 LaRouche; 990 Uncommitted.

## DELAWARE FEBRUARY 3

Republican      No presidential primary.

Democratic      16,787 Kerry; 3,706 Lieberman; 3,674 Edwards; 3,462 Dean; 3,165 Clark; 1,888 Sharpton; 344 Kucinich; 187 Gephardt; 78 LaRouche.

## DISTRICT OF COLUMBIA JANUARY 13

Republican      No presidential primary.

Democratic      18,132 Dean; 14,639 Sharpton; 4,924 Moseley Braun; 3,481 Kucinich; 522 LaRouche; 257 Walker; 241 Jackson; 149 Supreme; 85 Braun; 46 Chebib; 40 Wojciechowski.

## FLORIDA MARCH 9

Republican      No presidential primary. Bush unopposed.

Democratic      581,672 Kerry; 75,703 Edwards; 21,031 Sharpton; 20,834 Dean; 17,198 Kucinich; 14,287 Lieberman; 10,226 Clark; 6,789 Moseley Braun; 6,022 Gephardt.

## GEORGIA MARCH 2

Republican      161,374 Bush.

Democratic      293,265 Kerry; 259,386 Edwards; 39,129 Sharpton; 11,322 Dean; 7,701 Kucinich; 5,666 Lieberman; 4,247 Clark; 3,747 Moseley Braun; 2,350 Gephardt.

## IDAHO MAY 25

Republican      110,800 Bush; 12,993 None of the Names Shown; 15 Warrick (write-in).

Democratic      25,921 Kerry; 2,479 None of the Names Shown; 1,568 Kucinich; 927 Sharpton; 590 LaRouche.

## ILLINOIS MARCH 16

Republican      583,575 Bush.

Democratic      873,230 Kerry; 131,966 Edwards; 53,249 Moseley Braun; 47,343 Dean; 36,123 Sharpton; 28,083 Kucinich; 24,354 Lieberman; 19,304 Clark; 3,863 LaRouche.

## INDIANA MAY 4

Republican      469,528 Bush.

Democratic      231,047 Kerry; 35,651 Edwards; 21,482 Dean; 17,437 Clark; 7,003 Kucinich; 4,591 LaRouche.

# PRESIDENTIAL PRIMARIES 2004

## KENTUCKY MAY 18

Republican    108,603 Bush; 8,776 Uncommitted.

Democratic    138,175 Kerry; 33,403 Edwards; 21,199 Uncommitted; 11,062 Lieberman; 8,222 Dean; 6,519 Clark; 5,022 Sharpton; 4,508 Kucinich; 1,806 LaRouche.

## LOUISIANA MARCH 9

Republican    69,205 Bush; 2,805 Wyatt.

Democratic    112,639 Kerry; 26,074 Edwards; 7,948 Dean; 7,091 Clark; 3,161 McGaughey; 2,411 Kucinich; 2,329 LaRouche.

## MARYLAND MARCH 2

Republican    151,943 Bush.

Democratic    286,955 Kerry; 123,006 Edwards; 21,810 Sharpton; 12,461 Dean; 8,693 Kucinich; 8,527 Uncommitted; 5,245 Lieberman; 4,230 Clark; 4,039 Glover; 2,809 Moseley Braun; 2,146 Gephardt; 1,555 LaRouche.

## MASSACHUSETTS MARCH 2

Republican    62,773 Bush; 6,050 No Preference; 267 Kerry (write-in); 75 McCain (write-in); 63 Nader (write-in); 50 Edwards (write-in); 1,376 scattered write-in.

Democratic    440,964 Kerry; 108,051 Edwards; 25,198 Kucinich; 17,076 Dean; 6,123 Sharpton; 5,432 Lieberman; 4,451 No Preference; 3,109 Clark; 1,455 Gephardt; 1,019 Moseley Braun; 970 LaRouche; 168 Nader (write-in); 155 Robinson-Leon; 91 Bush (write-in); 34 H.R. Clinton (write-in); 892 scattered write-in.

## MISSISSIPPI MARCH 9

Republican    No presidential primary.

Democratic    59,815 Kerry; 5,582 Edwards; 3,933 Sharpton; 1,997 Dean; 1,878 Clark; 1,370 Uncommitted; 768 Kucinich; 716 Lieberman; 239 LaRouche.

## MISSOURI FEBRUARY 3

Republican    117,007 Bush; 3,830 Uncommitted; 1,268 Wyatt; 981 Ashby.

Democratic    211,745 Kerry; 103,088 Edwards; 36,288 Dean; 18,340 Clark; 14,727 Lieberman; 14,308 Sharpton; 8,281 Gephardt; 4,875 Kucinich; 4,311 Uncommitted; 1,088 Moseley Braun; 953 LaRouche; 335 Penna.

## MONTANA JUNE 8

Republican    106,407 Bush; 6,340 No Preference; 1 Warrick (write-in).

Democratic    63,611 Kerry; 9,686 Kucinich; 8,516 Edwards; 6,899 No Preference; 4,081 Clark; 750 LaRouche.

## NEBRASKA MAY 11

Republican    121,355 Bush.

Democratic    52,479 Kerry; 10,031 Edwards; 5,400 Dean; 1,490 Kucinich; 1,367 Sharpton; 805 LaRouche.

# PRESIDENTIAL PRIMARIES 2004

### NEW HAMPSHIRE JANUARY 27

Republican     53,962 Bush; 2,819 Kerry (write-in); 1,789 Dean (write-in); 1,407 Clark (write-in); 1,088 Edwards (write-in); 914 Lieberman (write-in); 841 Bosa; 836 Buchanan; 803 Rigazio; 579 Haines; 388 Callis; 264 Ashby; 239 Howard; 154 Laughlin; 153 Wyatt; 124 Taylor; 87 Harnes; 77 O'Connor; 52 Gostigian; 38 Kucinich (write-in); 15 Sharpton (write-in); 6 Moseley Braun (write-in); 5 LaRouche (write-in); 4 Gephardt (write-in); 3 Bateman (write-in); 1 Carter (write-in); 1 Linnell (write-in); 1 O'Donnell (write-in); 1 Penna (write-in); 973 scattered write-in.

Democratic     84,377 Kerry; 57,761 Dean; 27,314 Clark; 26,487 Edwards; 18,911 Lieberman; 3,114 Kucinich; 419 Gephardt; 347 Sharpton; 257 Bush (write-in); 90 LaRouche; 86 Carter; 81 Moseley Braun; 79 O'Donnell; 68 Bateman; 60 Crow; 58 Hamm; 49 Linnell; 42 Dokka; 31 Killeen; 15 Lee; 13 Braun; 11 Glover; 8 Penna; 8 Talbow; 5 Rigazio (write-in); 2 Ashby (write-in); 2 Buchanan (write-in); 92 scattered write-in.

### NEW JERSEY JUNE 8

Republican     141,752 Bush.

Democratic     198,213 Kerry; 9,251 Kucinich; 4,514 LaRouche; 2,826 Ballard.

### NEW MEXICO JUNE 6

Republican     49,165 Bush.

Democratic     No presidential primary.

### NEW YORK MARCH 2

Republican     No presidential primary. Bush unopposed.

Democratic     437,754 Kerry; 143,960 Edwards; 57,456 Sharpton; 36,680 Kucinich; 20,471 Dean; 9,314 Lieberman; 3,954 Gephardt; 3,517 Clark; 2,527 LaRouche.

### OHIO MARCH 2

Republican     793,833 Bush.

Democratic     632,599 Kerry; 416,106 Edwards; 110,067 Kucinich; 30,983 Dean; 14,676 Lieberman; 12,577 Clark; 4,018 LaRouche. The Democratic presidential vote was compiled by the Ohio secretary of state by congressional district. *America Votes* aggregated the results into statewide totals for each candidate.

### OKLAHOMA FEBRUARY 3

Republican     59,577 Bush; 6,621 Wyatt.

Democratic     90,526 Clark; 89,310 Edwards; 81,073 Kerry; 19,680 Lieberman; 12,734 Dean; 3,939 Sharpton; 2,544 Kucinich; 1,890 Gephardt; 689 LaRouche.

### OREGON MAY 18

Republican     293,806 Bush; 15,700 scattered write-in.

Democratic     289,804 Kerry; 60,019 Kucinich; 8,571 LaRouche; 10,150 scattered write-in.

# PRESIDENTIAL PRIMARIES 2004

## PENNSYLVANIA APRIL 27

Republican   861,555 Bush.

Democratic   585,683 Kerry; 79,799 Dean; 76,762 Edwards; 30,110 Kucinich; 17,528 LaRouche.

## RHODE ISLAND MARCH 2

Republican   2,152 Bush; 314 Uncommitted; 15 Kerry (write-in); 12 McCain (write-in); 6 Nader (write-in); 5 Edwards (write-in); 31 scattered write-in.

Democratic   25,466 Kerry; 6,635 Edwards; 1,425 Dean; 1,054 Kucinich; 415 Uncommitted; 303 Lieberman; 237 Clark; 63 LaRouche; 52 H.R. Clinton (write-in); 38 Sharpton (write-in); 10 Bush (write-in); 9 Nader (write-in); 52 scattered write-in.

## SOUTH CAROLINA FEBRUARY 3

Republican   No presidential primary.

Democratic   132,660 Edwards; 87,620 Kerry; 28,495 Sharpton; 21,218 Clark; 13,984 Dean; 7,101 Lieberman; 1,344 Kucinich; 828 Gephardt; 593 Moseley Braun.

## SOUTH DAKOTA JUNE 1

Republican   No presidential primary. Bush unopposed.

Democratic   69,473 Kerry; 5,105 Uncommitted; 4,838 Dean; 2,943 LaRouche; 2,046 Kucinich.

## TENNESSEE FEBRUARY 10

Republican   94,557 Bush; 4,504 Uncommitted.

Democratic   151,527 Kerry; 97,914 Edwards; 85,315 Clark; 16,128 Dean; 6,107 Sharpton; 3,213 Lieberman; 2,727 Uncommitted; 2,490 Moseley Braun; 2,279 Kucinich; 1,402 Gephardt; 283 LaRouche.

## TEXAS MARCH 9

Republican   635,948 Bush; 51,667 Uncommitted.

Democratic   563,237 Kerry; 120,413 Edwards; 40,035 Dean; 31,020 Sharpton; 25,245 Lieberman; 18,437 Clark; 15,475 Kucinich; 12,160 Gephardt; 6,871 LaRouche; 6,338 Crow.

## UTAH FEBRUARY 24

Republican   No presidential primary.

Democratic   19,232 Kerry; 10,384 Edwards; 2,590 Kucinich; 1,335 Dean; 489 Clark; 402 Lieberman; 298 Uncommitted; 124 Gephardt.

## VERMONT MARCH 2

Republican   25,415 Bush; 874 scattered write-in.

Democratic   44,393 Dean; 26,171 Kerry; 5,113 Edwards (write-in); 3,396 Kucinich; 2,749 Clark; 386 LaRouche; 673 scattered write-in.

# PRESIDENTIAL PRIMARIES 2004

## VIRGINIA FEBRUARY 10

Republican    No presidential primary.

Democratic    204,142 Kerry; 105,504 Edwards; 36,572 Clark; 27,637 Dean; 12,864 Sharpton; 5,016 Kucinich; 2,866 Lieberman; 1,042 LaRouche; 580 Gephardt.

## WEST VIRGINIA MAY 11

Republican    111,109 Bush.

Democratic    175,065 Kerry; 33,950 Edwards; 13,881 Lieberman; 10,576 Dean; 9,170 Clark; 6,114 Kucinich; 4,083 LaRouche.

## WISCONSIN FEBRUARY 17

Republican    158,933 Bush; 1,184 Uninstructed Delegation; 311 scattered write-in.

Democratic    328,358 Kerry; 284,163 Edwards; 150,845 Dean; 27,353 Kucinich; 14,701 Sharpton; 12,713 Clark; 3,929 Lieberman; 1,637 LaRouche; 1,590 Moseley Braun; 1,263 Gephardt; 1,146 Uninstructed Delegation; 666 scattered write-in.

# REPUBLICAN PRESIDENTIAL PRIMARIES 2004

| Date | State | Total Vote | Bush | Other |
|---|---|---|---|---|
| Jan. 27 | New Hampshire | 67,624 | 53,962<br>**79.8%** | 13,662<br>**20.2%** |
| Feb. 3 | Missouri | 123,086 | 117,007<br>**95.1%** | 6,079<br>**4.9%** |
| Feb. 3 | Oklahoma | 66,198 | 59,577<br>**90.0%** | 6,621<br>**10.0%** |
| Feb. 10 | Tennessee | 99,061 | 94,557<br>**95.5%** | 4,504<br>**4.5%** |
| Feb. 17 | Wisconsin | 160,428 | 158,933<br>**99.1%** | 1,495<br>**0.9%** |
| March 2 | California | 2,216,351 | 2,216,047<br>**100.0%** | 304 |
| March 2 | Georgia | 161,374 | 161,374<br>**100.0%** | |
| March 2 | Maryland | 151,943 | 151,943<br>**100.0%** | |
| March 2 | Massachusetts | 70,654 | 62,773<br>**88.8%** | 7,881<br>**11.2%** |
| March 2 | Ohio | 793,833 | 793,833<br>**100.0%** | |
| March 2 | Rhode Island | 2,535 | 2,152<br>**84.9%** | 383<br>**15.1%** |
| March 2 | Vermont | 26,289 | 25,415<br>**96.7%** | 874<br>**3.3%** |
| March 9 | Louisiana | 72,010 | 69,205<br>**96.1%** | 2,805<br>**3.9%** |
| March 9 | Texas | 687,615 | 635,948<br>**92.5%** | 51,667<br>**7.5%** |
| March 16 | Illinois | 583,575 | 583,575<br>**100.0%** | |
| April 27 | Pennsylvania | 861,555 | 861,555<br>**100.0%** | |
| May 4 | Indiana | 469,528 | 469,528<br>**100.0%** | |
| May 11 | Nebraska | 121,355 | 121,355<br>**100.0%** | |
| May 11 | West Virginia | 111,109 | 111,109<br>**100.0%** | |
| May 18 | Arkansas | 38,363 | 37,234<br>**97.1%** | 1,129<br>**2.9%** |
| May 18 | Kentucky | 117,379 | 108,603<br>**92.5%** | 8,776<br>**7.5%** |
| May 18 | Oregon | 309,506 | 293,806<br>**94.9%** | 15,700<br>**5.1%** |
| May 25 | Idaho | 123,808 | 110,800<br>**89.5%** | 13,008<br>**10.5%** |
| June 1 | Alabama | 201,487 | 187,038<br>**92.8%** | 14,449<br>**7.2%** |
| June 1 | New Mexico | 49,165 | 49,165<br>**100.0%** | |
| June 8 | Montana | 112,748 | 106,407<br>**94.4%** | 6,341<br>**5.6%** |
| June 8 | New Jersey | 141,752 | 141,752<br>**100.0%** | |
| | Total | 7,940,331 | 7,784,653<br>**98.0%** | 155,678<br>**2.0%** |

Notes: Other vote for entries that were on the ballot in at least one primary: 111,236 Uncommitted; 10,937 Wyatt; 1,301 Ashby; 853 Bosa; 836 Buchanan; 803 Rigazio; 579 Haines; 388 Callis; 239 Howard; 154 Laughlin; 124 Taylor; 87 Harnes; 77 O'Connor; 52 Gostigian; 28,012 scattered write-in.

The Uncommitted total includes votes cast on the following ballot lines: Uncommitted, None of the Names Shown, No Preference, and Uninstructed Delegation.

# DEMOCRATIC PRESIDENTIAL PRIMARIES 2004

| Date | State | Total Vote | Clark | Dean | Edwards | Kerry | Kucinich | Lieberman | Sharpton | Other |
|---|---|---|---|---|---|---|---|---|---|---|
| Jan. 13 | District of Columbia | 42,516 | | 18,132 | | | 3,481 | | 14,639 | 6,264 |
| | | | | 42.6% | | | 8.2% | | 34.4% | 14.7% |
| Jan. 27 | New Hampshire | 219,787 | 27,314 | 57,761 | 26,487 | 84,377 | 3,114 | 18,911 | 347 | 1,476 |
| | | | 12.4% | 26.3% | 12.1% | 38.4% | 1.4% | 8.6% | 0.2% | 0.7% |
| Feb. 3 | Arizona | 238,942 | 63,256 | 33,555 | 16,596 | 101,809 | 3,896 | 15,906 | 1,177 | 2,747 |
| | | | 26.5% | 14.0% | 6.9% | 42.6% | 1.6% | 6.7% | 0.5% | 1.1% |
| Feb. 3 | Delaware | 33,291 | 3,165 | 3,462 | 3,674 | 16,787 | 344 | 3,706 | 1,888 | 265 |
| | | | 9.5% | 10.4% | 11.0% | 50.4% | 1.0% | 11.1% | 5.7% | 0.8% |
| Feb. 3 | Missouri | 418,339 | 18,340 | 36,288 | 103,088 | 211,745 | 4,875 | 14,727 | 14,308 | 14,968 |
| | | | 4.4% | 8.7% | 24.6% | 50.6% | 1.2% | 3.5% | 3.4% | 3.6% |
| Feb. 3 | Oklahoma | 302,385 | 90,526 | 12,734 | 89,310 | 81,073 | 2,544 | 19,680 | 3,939 | 2,579 |
| | | | 29.9% | 4.2% | 29.5% | 26.8% | 0.8% | 6.5% | 1.3% | 0.9% |
| Feb. 3 | South Carolina | 293,843 | 21,218 | 13,984 | 132,660 | 87,620 | 1,344 | 7,101 | 28,495 | 1,421 |
| | | | 7.2% | 4.8% | 45.1% | 29.8% | 0.5% | 2.4% | 9.7% | 0.5% |
| Feb. 10 | Tennessee | 369,385 | 85,315 | 16,128 | 97,914 | 151,527 | 2,279 | 3,213 | 6,107 | 6,902 |
| | | | 23.1% | 4.4% | 26.5% | 41.0% | 0.6% | 0.9% | 1.7% | 1.9% |
| Feb. 10 | Virginia | 396,223 | 36,572 | 27,637 | 105,504 | 204,142 | 5,016 | 2,866 | 12,864 | 1,622 |
| | | | 9.2% | 7.0% | 26.6% | 51.5% | 1.3% | 0.7% | 3.2% | 0.4% |
| Feb. 17 | Wisconsin | 828,364 | 12,713 | 150,845 | 284,163 | 328,358 | 27,353 | 3,929 | 14,701 | 6,302 |
| | | | 1.5% | 18.2% | 34.3% | 39.6% | 3.3% | 0.5% | 1.8% | 0.8% |
| Feb. 24 | Utah | 34,854 | 489 | 1,335 | 10,384 | 19,232 | 2,590 | 402 | | 422 |
| | | | 1.4% | 3.8% | 29.8% | 55.2% | 7.4% | 1.2% | | 1.2% |
| March 2 | California | 3,107,629 | 51,084 | 130,892 | 614,441 | 2,002,539 | 144,954 | 52,780 | 59,326 | 51,613 |
| | | | 1.6% | 4.2% | 19.8% | 64.4% | 4.7% | 1.7% | 1.9% | 1.7% |
| March 2 | Connecticut | 130,023 | 1,546 | 5,166 | 30,844 | 75,860 | 4,133 | 6,705 | 3,312 | 2,457 |
| | | | 1.2% | 4.0% | 23.7% | 58.3% | 3.2% | 5.2% | 2.5% | 1.9% |
| March 2 | Georgia | 626,813 | 4,247 | 11,322 | 259,386 | 293,265 | 7,701 | 5,666 | 39,129 | 6,097 |
| | | | 0.7% | 1.8% | 41.4% | 46.8% | 1.2% | 0.9% | 6.2% | 1.0% |
| March 2 | Maryland | 481,476 | 4,230 | 12,461 | 123,006 | 286,955 | 8,693 | 5,245 | 21,810 | 19,076 |
| | | | 0.9% | 2.6% | 25.5% | 59.6% | 1.8% | 1.1% | 4.5% | 4.0% |
| March 2 | Massachusetts | 615,188 | 3,109 | 17,076 | 108,051 | 440,964 | 25,198 | 5,432 | 6,123 | 9,235 |
| | | | 0.5% | 2.8% | 17.6% | 71.7% | 4.1% | 0.9% | 1.0% | 1.5% |
| March 2 | New York | 715,633 | 3,517 | 20,471 | 143,960 | 437,754 | 36,680 | 9,314 | 57,456 | 6,481 |
| | | | 0.5% | 2.9% | 20.1% | 61.2% | 5.1% | 1.3% | 8.0% | 0.9% |
| March 2 | Ohio | 1,221,026 | 12,577 | 30,983 | 416,106 | 632,599 | 110,067 | 14,676 | | 4,018 |
| | | | 1.0% | 2.5% | 34.1% | 51.8% | 9.0% | 1.2% | | 0.3% |
| March 2 | Rhode Island | 35,759 | 237 | 1,425 | 6,635 | 25,466 | 1,054 | 303 | 38 | 601 |
| | | | 0.7% | 4.0% | 18.6% | 71.2% | 2.9% | 0.8% | 0.1% | 1.7% |
| March 2 | Vermont | 82,881 | 2,749 | 44,393 | 5,113 | 26,171 | 3,396 | | | 1,059 |
| | | | 3.3% | 53.6% | 6.2% | 31.6% | 4.1% | | | 1.3% |
| March 9 | Florida | 753,762 | 10,226 | 20,834 | 75,703 | 581,672 | 17,198 | 14,287 | 21,031 | 12,811 |
| | | | 1.4% | 2.8% | 10.0% | 77.2% | 2.3% | 1.9% | 2.8% | 1.7% |
| March 9 | Louisiana | 161,653 | 7,091 | 7,948 | 26,074 | 112,639 | 2,411 | | | 5,490 |
| | | | 4.4% | 4.9% | 16.1% | 69.7% | 1.5% | | | 3.4% |
| March 9 | Mississippi | 76,298 | 1,878 | 1,997 | 5,582 | 59,815 | 768 | 716 | 3,933 | 1,609 |
| | | | 2.5% | 2.6% | 7.3% | 78.4% | 1.0% | 0.9% | 5.2% | 2.1% |
| March 9 | Texas | 839,231 | 18,437 | 40,035 | 120,413 | 563,237 | 15,475 | 25,245 | 31,020 | 25,369 |
| | | | 2.2% | 4.8% | 14.3% | 67.1% | 1.8% | 3.0% | 3.7% | 3.0% |
| March 16 | Illinois | 1,217,515 | 19,304 | 47,343 | 131,966 | 873,230 | 28,083 | 24,354 | 36,123 | 57,112 |
| | | | 1.6% | 3.9% | 10.8% | 71.7% | 2.3% | 2.0% | 3.0% | 4.7% |
| April 27 | Pennsylvania | 789,882 | | 79,799 | 76,762 | 585,683 | 30,110 | | | 17,528 |
| | | | | 10.1% | 9.7% | 74.1% | 3.8% | | | 2.2% |
| May 4 | Indiana | 317,211 | 17,437 | 21,482 | 35,651 | 231,047 | 7,003 | | | 4,591 |
| | | | 5.5% | 6.8% | 11.2% | 72.8% | 2.2% | | | 1.4% |
| May 11 | Nebraska | 71,572 | | 5,400 | 10,031 | 52,479 | 1,490 | | 1,367 | 805 |
| | | | | 7.5% | 14.0% | 73.3% | 2.1% | | 1.9% | 1.1% |
| May 11 | West Virginia | 252,839 | 9,170 | 10,576 | 33,950 | 175,065 | 6,114 | 13,881 | | 4,083 |
| | | | 3.6% | 4.2% | 13.4% | 69.2% | 2.4% | 5.5% | | 1.6% |
| May 18 | Arkansas | 266,848 | | | | 177,754 | 13,766 | | | 75,328 |
| | | | | | | 66.6% | 5.2% | | | 28.2% |

# DEMOCRATIC PRESIDENTIAL PRIMARIES 2004

| Date | | State | Total Vote | Clark | Dean | Edwards | Kerry | Kucinich | Lieberman | Sharpton | Other |
|------|----|-------|-----------|-------|------|---------|-------|----------|-----------|----------|-------|
| May | 18 | Kentucky | 229,916 | 6,519 | 8,222 | 33,403 | 138,175 | 4,508 | 11,062 | 5,022 | 23,005 |
| | | | | 2.8% | 3.6% | 14.5% | 60.1% | 2.0% | 4.8% | 2.2% | 10.0% |
| May | 18 | Oregon | 368,544 | | | | 289,804 | 60,019 | | | 18,721 |
| | | | | | | | 78.6% | 16.3% | | | 5.1% |
| May | 25 | Idaho | 31,485 | | | | 25,921 | 1,568 | | 927 | 3,069 |
| | | | | | | | 82.3% | 5.0% | | 2.9% | 9.7% |
| June | 1 | Alabama | 218,574 | | | | 164,021 | 9,076 | | | 45,477 |
| | | | | | | | 75.0% | 4.2% | | | 20.8% |
| June | 1 | South Dakota | 84,405 | | 4,838 | | 69,473 | 2,046 | | | 8,048 |
| | | | | | 5.7% | | 82.3% | 2.4% | | | 9.5% |
| June | 8 | Montana | 93,543 | 4,081 | | 8,516 | 63,611 | 9,686 | | | 7,649 |
| | | | | 4.4% | | 9.1% | 68.0% | 10.4% | | | 8.2% |
| June | 8 | New Jersey | 214,804 | | | | 198,213 | 9,251 | | | 7,340 |
| | | | | | | | 92.3% | 4.3% | | | 3.4% |
| | | TOTAL | 16,182,439 | 536,347 | 894,524 | 3,135,373 | 9,870,082 | 617,284 | 280,107 | 385,082 | 463,640 |
| | | | | 3.3% | 5.5% | 19.4% | 61.0% | 3.8% | 1.7% | 2.4% | 2.9% |

Notes: The votes cast for Edwards in Vermont and Sharpton in Rhode Island were write-ins.

Candidates that received at least 200,000 votes in the Democratic primaries are included in the table above. Other vote for entries that were on the ballot in at least one primary: 159,940 Uncommitted; 104,793 LaRouche; 103,205 Moseley Braun; 62,955 Gephardt; 6,398 Crow; 4,050 Glover; 3,161 McGaughey; 2,826 Ballard; 554 Penna; 257 Barker; 257 Walker; 241 Jackson; 233 Wyatt; 225 Brand; 149 Supreme; 136 Barchilon; 119 Muhammad; 117 Vitullo; 98 Braun; 86 Carter; 79 O'Donnell; 77 Caplette; 68 Bateman; 58 Hamm; 49 Linnell; 46 Chebib; 42 Dokka; 40 Wojciechowski; 31 Killeen; 15 Lee; 8 Talbow; 13,327 scattered write-in.

The Uncommitted total includes votes cast on the following ballot lines: Uncommitted, None of the Names Shown, No Preference, and Uninstructed Delegation.

# ALABAMA

## GOVERNOR
Bob Riley (R). Elected 2002 to a four-year term.

## SENATORS (2 Republicans)
Jeff Sessions (R). Reelected 2002 to a six-year term. Previously elected 1996.

Richard C. Shelby (R). Reelected 2004 to a six-year term. Previously elected 1998, 1992, 1986. Changed party affiliation from Democratic to Republican in November 1994.

## REPRESENTATIVES (5 Republicans, 2 Democrats)
1. Jo Bonner (R)
2. Terry Everett (R)
3. Mike D. Rogers (R)
4. Robert B. Aderholt (R)
5. Robert E. "Bud" Cramer (D)
6. Spencer Bachus (R)
7. Artur Davis (D)

## POSTWAR VOTE FOR PRESIDENT

| Year | Total Vote | Republican Vote | Candidate | Democratic Vote | Candidate | Other Vote | Plurality | Total Vote Rep. | Dem. | Major Vote Rep. | Dem. |
|---|---|---|---|---|---|---|---|---|---|---|---|
| 2004 | 1,883,449 | 1,176,394 | Bush, George W. | 693,933 | Kerry, John | 13,122 | 482,461 R | 62.5% | 36.8% | 62.9% | 37.1% |
| 2000** | 1,666,272 | 941,173 | Bush, George W. | 692,611 | Gore, Al | 32,488 | 248,562 R | 56.5% | 41.6% | 57.6% | 42.4% |
| 1996** | 1,534,349 | 769,044 | Dole, Bob | 662,165 | Clinton, Bill | 103,140 | 106,879 R | 50.1% | 43.2% | 53.7% | 46.3% |
| 1992** | 1,688,060 | 804,283 | Bush, George | 690,080 | Clinton, Bill | 193,697 | 114,203 R | 47.6% | 40.9% | 53.8% | 46.2% |
| 1988 | 1,378,476 | 815,576 | Bush, George | 549,506 | Dukakis, Michael S. | 13,394 | 266,070 R | 59.2% | 39.9% | 59.7% | 40.3% |
| 1984 | 1,441,713 | 872,849 | Reagan, Ronald | 551,899 | Mondale, Walter F. | 16,965 | 320,950 R | 60.5% | 38.3% | 61.3% | 38.7% |
| 1980** | 1,341,929 | 654,192 | Reagan, Ronald | 636,730 | Carter, Jimmy | 51,007 | 17,462 R | 48.8% | 47.4% | 50.7% | 49.3% |
| 1976 | 1,182,850 | 504,070 | Ford, Gerald R. | 659,170 | Carter, Jimmy | 19,610 | 155,100 D | 42.6% | 55.7% | 43.3% | 56.7% |
| 1972 | 1,006,111 | 728,701 | Nixon, Richard M. | 256,923 | McGovern, George S. | 20,487 | 471,778 R | 72.4% | 25.5% | 73.9% | 26.1% |
| 1968** | 1,049,922 | 146,923 | Nixon, Richard M. | 196,579 | Humphrey, Hubert H. | 706,420 | 494,846 A | 14.0% | 18.7% | 42.8% | 57.2% |
| 1964** | 689,818 | 479,085 | Goldwater, Barry M. | | Johnson, Lyndon B. | 210,733 | 268,353 R | 69.5% | | 100.0% | |
| 1960 | 570,225 | 237,981 | Nixon, Richard M. | 324,050 | Kennedy, John F. | 8,194 | 86,069 D | 41.7% | 56.8% | 42.3% | 57.7% |
| 1956 | 496,861 | 195,694 | Eisenhower, Dwight D. | 280,844 | Stevenson, Adlai E. | 20,323 | 85,150 D | 39.4% | 56.5% | 41.1% | 58.9% |
| 1952 | 426,120 | 149,231 | Eisenhower, Dwight D. | 275,075 | Stevenson, Adlai E. | 1,814 | 125,844 D | 35.0% | 64.6% | 35.2% | 64.8% |
| 1948** | 214,980 | 40,930 | Dewey, Thomas E. | | Truman, Harry S. | 174,050 | 130,513 SR | 19.0% | | 100.0% | |

In past elections, the other vote included: 2000 - 18,323 Green (Ralph Nader); 1996 - 92,149 Reform (Ross Perot); 1992 - 183,109 Independent (Perot); 1980 - 16,481 Independent (John Anderson); 1968 - 691,425 American Independent (George Wallace); 1964 - 210,732 Unpledged Democratic; 1948 -171,443 States' Rights (Strom Thurmond). In 1948 and 1964 the national Democratic candidates were not listed on the ballot.

# ALABAMA

## POSTWAR VOTE FOR GOVERNOR

| Year | Total Vote | Republican Vote | Republican Candidate | Democratic Vote | Democratic Candidate | Other Vote | Rep.-Dem. Plurality | Percentage Total Vote Rep. | Dem. | Major Vote Rep. | Dem. |
|------|-----------|-----------------|---------------------|-----------------|---------------------|-----------|---------------------|-----------|------|-----------|------|
| 2002 | 1,367,053 | 672,225 | Riley, Bob | 669,105 | Siegelman, Don | 25,723 | 3,120 R | 49.2% | 48.9% | 50.1% | 49.9% |
| 1998 | 1,317,842 | 554,746 | James, Forrest H. | 760,155 | Siegelman, Don | 2,941 | 205,409 D | 42.1% | 57.7% | 42.2% | 57.8% |
| 1994 | 1,201,969 | 604,926 | James, Forrest H. | 594,169 | Folsom, James E. | 2,874 | 10,757 R | 50.3% | 49.4% | 50.4% | 49.6% |
| 1990 | 1,216,250 | 633,519 | Hunt, Guy | 582,106 | Hubbert, Paul R. | 625 | 51,413 R | 52.1% | 47.9% | 52.1% | 47.9% |
| 1986 | 1,236,230 | 696,203 | Hunt, Guy | 537,163 | Baxley, Bill | 2,864 | 159,040 R | 56.3% | 43.5% | 56.4% | 43.6% |
| 1982 | 1,128,725 | 440,815 | Folmar, Emory | 650,538 | Wallace, George C. | 37,372 | 209,723 D | 39.1% | 57.6% | 40.4% | 59.6% |
| 1978 | 760,474 | 196,963 | Hunt, Guy | 551,886 | James, Forrest H. | 11,625 | 354,923 D | 25.9% | 72.6% | 26.3% | 73.7% |
| 1974 | 598,305 | 88,381 | McCary, Elvin | 497,574 | Wallace, George C. | 12,350 | 409,193 D | 14.8% | 83.2% | 15.1% | 84.9% |
| 1970** | 854,952 | | — | 637,046 | Wallace, George C. | 217,906 | 637,046 D | | 74.5% | | 100.0% |
| 1966 | 848,101 | 262,943 | Martin, James D. | 537,505 | Wallace, Mrs. George C. | 47,653 | 274,562 D | 31.0% | 63.4% | 32.8% | 67.2% |
| 1962 | 315,776 | | — | 303,987 | Wallace, George C. | 11,789 | 303,987 D | | 96.3% | | 100.0% |
| 1958 | 270,952 | 30,415 | Longshore, W. L. | 239,633 | Patterson, John | 904 | 209,218 D | 11.2% | 88.4% | 11.3% | 88.7% |
| 1954 | 333,090 | 88,688 | Amernethy, Tom | 244,401 | Folsom, James E. | 1 | 155,713 D | 26.6% | 73.4% | 26.6% | 73.4% |
| 1950 | 170,541 | 15,127 | Crowder, John S. | 155,414 | Persons, Gordon | | 140,287 D | 8.9% | 91.1% | 8.9% | 91.1% |
| 1946 | 197,324 | 22,362 | Ward, Lyman | 174,962 | Folsom, James E. | | 152,600 D | 11.3% | 88.7% | 11.3% | 88.7% |

In past elections, the other vote included: 1970 - 125,491 National Democratic Party of Alabama (John Logan Cashin); 75,679 Independent (A. C. Shelton).

## POSTWAR VOTE FOR SENATOR

| Year | Total Vote | Republican Vote | Republican Candidate | Democratic Vote | Democratic Candidate | Other Vote | Rep.-Dem. Plurality | Percentage Total Vote Rep. | Dem. | Major Vote Rep. | Dem. |
|------|-----------|-----------------|---------------------|-----------------|---------------------|-----------|---------------------|-----------|------|-----------|------|
| 2004 | 1,839,066 | 1,242,200 | Shelby, Richard C. | 595,018 | Sowell, Wayne | 1,848 | 647,182 R | 67.5% | 32.4% | 67.6% | 32.4% |
| 2002 | 1,353,023 | 792,561 | Sessions, Jeff | 538,878 | Parker, Susan | 21,584 | 253,683 R | 58.6% | 39.8% | 59.5% | 40.5% |
| 1998 | 1,293,405 | 817,973 | Shelby, Richard C. | 474,568 | Suddith, Clayton | 864 | 343,405 R | 63.2% | 36.7% | 63.3% | 36.7% |
| 1996 | 1,499,393 | 786,436 | Sessions, Jeff | 681,651 | Bedford, Roger | 31,306 | 104,785 R | 52.5% | 45.5% | 53.6% | 46.4% |
| 1992 | 1,577,799 | 522,015 | Sellers, Richard | 1,022,698 | Shelby, Richard C. | 33,086 | 500,683 D | 33.1% | 64.8% | 33.8% | 66.2% |
| 1990 | 1,185,563 | 467,190 | Cabaniss, Bill | 717,814 | Heflin, Howell | 559 | 250,624 D | 39.4% | 60.5% | 39.4% | 60.6% |
| 1986 | 1,211,953 | 602,537 | Denton, Jeremiah | 609,360 | Shelby, Richard C. | 56 | 6,823 D | 49.7% | 50.3% | 49.7% | 50.3% |
| 1984 | 1,371,238 | 498,508 | Smith, Albert L. | 860,535 | Heflin, Howell | 12,195 | 362,027 D | 36.4% | 62.8% | 36.7% | 63.3% |
| 1980 | 1,296,757 | 650,362 | Denton, Jeremiah | 610,175 | Folsom, James E., Jr. | 36,220 | 40,187 R | 50.2% | 47.1% | 51.6% | 48.4% |
| 1978 | 582,025 | | — | 547,054 | Heflin, Howell | 34,971 | 547,054 D | | 94.0% | | 100.0% |
| 1978S | 731,614 | 316,170 | Martin, James D. | 401,852 | Stewart, Donald W. | 13,592 | 85,682 D | 43.2% | 54.9% | 44.0% | 56.0% |
| 1974 | 523,290 | | — | 501,541 | Allen, James B. | 21,749 | 501,541 D | | 95.8% | | 100.0% |
| 1972 | 1,051,099 | 347,523 | Blount, Winston M. | 654,491 | Sparkman, John J. | 49,085 | 306,968 D | 33.1% | 62.3% | 34.7% | 65.3% |
| 1968 | 912,708 | 201,227 | Hooper, Perry | 638,774 | Allen, James B. | 72,707 | 437,547 D | 22.0% | 70.0% | 24.0% | 76.0% |
| 1966 | 802,608 | 313,018 | Grenier, John | 482,138 | Sparkman, John J. | 7,452 | 169,120 D | 39.0% | 60.1% | 39.4% | 60.6% |
| 1962 | 397,079 | 195,134 | Martin, James D. | 201,937 | Hill, Lister | 8 | 6,803 D | 49.1% | 50.9% | 49.1% | 50.9% |
| 1960 | 554,081 | 164,868 | Elgin, Julian | 389,196 | Sparkman, John J. | 17 | 224,328 D | 29.8% | 70.2% | 29.8% | 70.2% |
| 1956 | 330,191 | | — | 330,182 | Hill, Lister | 9 | 330,182 D | | 100.0% | | 100.0% |
| 1954 | 314,459 | 55,110 | Guin, J. Foy | 259,348 | Sparkman, John J. | 1 | 204,238 D | 17.5% | 82.5% | 17.5% | 82.5% |
| 1950 | 164,011 | | — | 125,534 | Hill, Lister | 38,477 | 125,534 D | | 76.5% | | 100.0% |
| 1948 | 220,875 | 35,341 | Parsons, Paul G. | 185,534 | Sparkman, John J. | | 150,193 D | 16.0% | 84.0% | 16.0% | 84.0% |
| 1946S | 163,217 | | — | 163,217 | Sparkman, John J. | | 163,217 D | | 100.0% | | 100.0% |

The 1946 election and one of the 1978 elections were for short terms to fill vacancies.

# ALABAMA

Congressional districts first established for elections held in 2002
7 members

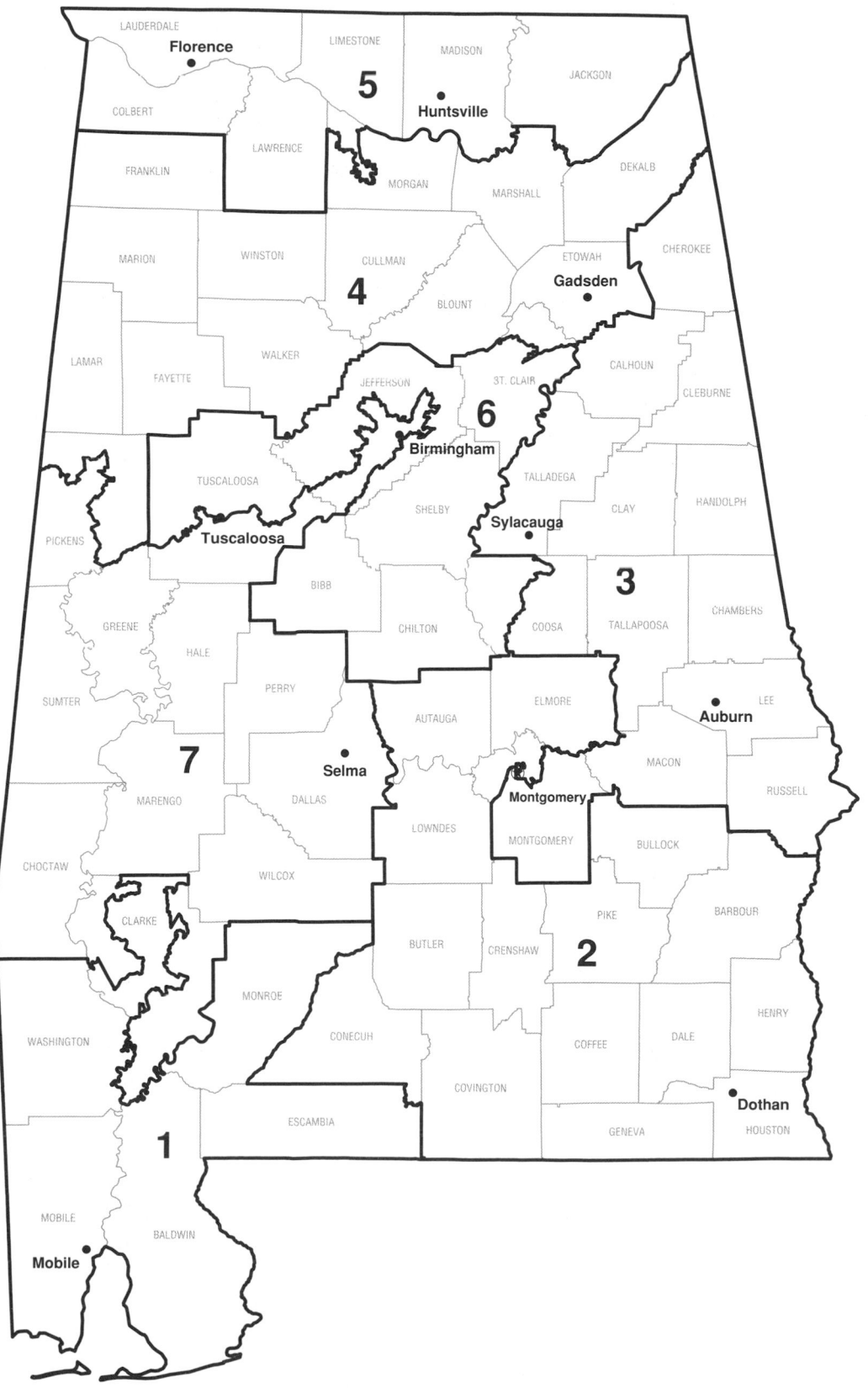

# ALABAMA

## PRESIDENT 2004

| 2000 Census Population | County | Total Vote | Republican | Democratic | Other | Rep.-Dem. Plurality | Percentage Total Vote Rep. | Dem. | Major Vote Rep. | Dem. |
|---|---|---|---|---|---|---|---|---|---|---|
| 43,671 | AUTAUGA | 20,081 | 15,196 | 4,758 | 127 | 10,438 R | 75.7% | 23.7% | 76.2% | 23.8% |
| 140,415 | BALDWIN | 69,320 | 52,971 | 15,599 | 750 | 37,372 R | 76.4% | 22.5% | 77.3% | 22.7% |
| 29,038 | BARBOUR | 10,777 | 5,899 | 4,832 | 46 | 1,067 R | 54.7% | 44.8% | 55.0% | 45.0% |
| 20,826 | BIBB | 7,600 | 5,472 | 2,089 | 39 | 3,383 R | 72.0% | 27.5% | 72.4% | 27.6% |
| 51,024 | BLOUNT | 21,504 | 17,386 | 3,938 | 180 | 13,448 R | 80.9% | 18.3% | 81.5% | 18.5% |
| 11,714 | BULLOCK | 4,717 | 1,494 | 3,210 | 13 | 1,716 D | 31.7% | 68.1% | 31.8% | 68.2% |
| 21,399 | BUTLER | 8,416 | 4,979 | 3,413 | 24 | 1,566 R | 59.2% | 40.6% | 59.3% | 40.7% |
| 112,249 | CALHOUN | 45,249 | 29,814 | 15,083 | 352 | 14,731 R | 65.9% | 33.3% | 66.4% | 33.6% |
| 36,583 | CHAMBERS | 13,032 | 7,622 | 5,347 | 63 | 2,275 R | 58.5% | 41.0% | 58.8% | 41.2% |
| 23,988 | CHEROKEE | 9,049 | 5,923 | 3,040 | 86 | 2,883 R | 65.5% | 33.6% | 66.1% | 33.9% |
| 39,593 | CHILTON | 16,693 | 12,829 | 3,778 | 86 | 9,051 R | 76.9% | 22.6% | 77.3% | 22.7% |
| 15,922 | CHOCTAW | 7,227 | 3,897 | 3,303 | 27 | 594 R | 53.9% | 45.7% | 54.1% | 45.9% |
| 27,867 | CLARKE | 11,394 | 6,730 | 4,627 | 37 | 2,103 R | 59.1% | 40.6% | 59.3% | 40.7% |
| 14,254 | CLAY | 6,576 | 4,624 | 1,893 | 59 | 2,731 R | 70.3% | 28.8% | 71.0% | 29.0% |
| 14,123 | CLEBURNE | 5,798 | 4,370 | 1,391 | 37 | 2,979 R | 75.4% | 24.0% | 75.9% | 24.1% |
| 43,615 | COFFEE | 17,616 | 13,019 | 4,480 | 117 | 8,539 R | 73.9% | 25.4% | 74.4% | 25.6% |
| 54,984 | COLBERT | 23,935 | 13,188 | 10,598 | 149 | 2,590 R | 55.1% | 44.3% | 55.4% | 44.6% |
| 14,089 | CONECUH | 6,021 | 3,271 | 2,719 | 31 | 552 R | 54.3% | 45.2% | 54.6% | 45.4% |
| 12,202 | COOSA | 5,001 | 2,905 | 2,055 | 41 | 850 R | 58.1% | 41.1% | 58.6% | 41.4% |
| 37,631 | COVINGTON | 14,627 | 11,119 | 3,423 | 85 | 7,696 R | 76.0% | 23.4% | 76.5% | 23.5% |
| 13,665 | CRENSHAW | 5,500 | 3,777 | 1,698 | 25 | 2,079 R | 68.7% | 30.9% | 69.0% | 31.0% |
| 77,483 | CULLMAN | 35,191 | 26,818 | 8,045 | 328 | 18,773 R | 76.2% | 22.9% | 76.9% | 23.1% |
| 49,129 | DALE | 18,231 | 13,621 | 4,484 | 126 | 9,137 R | 74.7% | 24.6% | 75.2% | 24.8% |
| 46,365 | DALLAS | 18,573 | 7,335 | 11,175 | 63 | 3,840 D | 39.5% | 60.2% | 39.6% | 60.4% |
| 64,452 | DE KALB | 24,169 | 16,904 | 7,092 | 173 | 9,812 R | 69.9% | 29.3% | 70.4% | 29.6% |
| 65,874 | ELMORE | 28,680 | 22,056 | 6,471 | 153 | 15,585 R | 76.9% | 22.6% | 77.3% | 22.7% |
| 38,440 | ESCAMBIA | 12,395 | 8,513 | 3,814 | 68 | 4,699 R | 68.7% | 30.8% | 69.1% | 30.9% |
| 103,459 | ETOWAH | 42,680 | 26,999 | 15,328 | 353 | 11,671 R | 63.3% | 35.9% | 63.8% | 36.2% |
| 18,495 | FAYETTE | 8,002 | 5,534 | 2,408 | 60 | 3,126 R | 69.2% | 30.1% | 69.7% | 30.3% |
| 31,223 | FRANKLIN | 12,269 | 7,690 | 4,514 | 65 | 3,176 R | 62.7% | 36.8% | 63.0% | 37.0% |
| 25,764 | GENEVA | 10,520 | 8,342 | 2,113 | 65 | 6,229 R | 79.3% | 20.1% | 79.8% | 20.2% |
| 9,974 | GREENE | 4,748 | 958 | 3,764 | 26 | 2,806 D | 20.2% | 79.3% | 20.3% | 79.7% |
| 17,185 | HALE | 7,945 | 3,281 | 4,631 | 33 | 1,350 D | 41.3% | 58.3% | 41.5% | 58.5% |
| 16,310 | HENRY | 7,361 | 4,881 | 2,452 | 28 | 2,429 R | 66.3% | 33.3% | 66.6% | 33.4% |
| 88,787 | HOUSTON | 36,201 | 26,874 | 9,144 | 183 | 17,730 R | 74.2% | 25.3% | 74.6% | 25.4% |
| 53,926 | JACKSON | 20,321 | 11,534 | 8,635 | 152 | 2,899 R | 56.8% | 42.5% | 57.2% | 42.8% |
| 662,047 | JEFFERSON | 292,967 | 158,680 | 132,286 | 2,001 | 26,394 R | 54.2% | 45.2% | 54.5% | 45.5% |
| 15,904 | LAMAR | 6,885 | 4,894 | 1,956 | 35 | 2,938 R | 71.1% | 28.4% | 71.4% | 28.6% |
| 87,966 | LAUDERDALE | 37,107 | 22,161 | 14,628 | 318 | 7,533 R | 59.7% | 39.4% | 60.2% | 39.8% |
| 34,803 | LAWRENCE | 14,001 | 7,730 | 6,155 | 116 | 1,575 R | 55.2% | 44.0% | 55.7% | 44.3% |
| 115,092 | LEE | 44,610 | 27,972 | 16,227 | 411 | 11,745 R | 62.7% | 36.4% | 63.3% | 36.7% |
| 65,676 | LIMESTONE | 29,073 | 19,702 | 9,126 | 245 | 10,576 R | 67.8% | 31.4% | 68.3% | 31.7% |
| 13,473 | LOWNDES | 6,021 | 1,786 | 4,233 | 2 | 2,447 D | 29.7% | 70.3% | 29.7% | 70.3% |
| 24,105 | MACON | 9,407 | 1,570 | 7,800 | 37 | 6,230 D | 16.7% | 82.9% | 16.8% | 83.2% |
| 276,700 | MADISON | 131,062 | 77,173 | 52,644 | 1,245 | 24,529 R | 58.9% | 40.2% | 59.4% | 40.6% |
| 22,539 | MARENGO | 10,322 | 5,255 | 5,037 | 30 | 218 R | 50.9% | 48.8% | 51.1% | 48.9% |
| 31,214 | MARION | 12,875 | 8,983 | 3,808 | 84 | 5,175 R | 69.8% | 29.6% | 70.2% | 29.8% |
| 82,231 | MARSHALL | 31,491 | 22,783 | 8,452 | 256 | 14,331 R | 72.3% | 26.8% | 72.9% | 27.1% |
| 399,843 | MOBILE | 156,771 | 92,014 | 63,732 | 1,025 | 28,282 R | 58.7% | 40.7% | 59.1% | 40.9% |
| 24,324 | MONROE | 9,534 | 5,831 | 3,666 | 37 | 2,165 R | 61.2% | 38.5% | 61.4% | 38.6% |
| 223,510 | MONTGOMERY | 89,650 | 44,097 | 45,160 | 393 | 1,063 D | 49.2% | 50.4% | 49.4% | 50.6% |
| 111,064 | MORGAN | 47,007 | 32,477 | 14,131 | 399 | 18,346 R | 69.1% | 30.1% | 69.7% | 30.3% |
| 11,861 | PERRY | 5,523 | 1,738 | 3,767 | 18 | 2,029 D | 31.5% | 68.2% | 31.6% | 68.4% |
| 20,949 | PICKENS | 9,132 | 5,170 | 3,915 | 47 | 1,255 R | 56.6% | 42.9% | 56.9% | 43.1% |
| 29,605 | PIKE | 11,883 | 7,483 | 4,334 | 66 | 3,149 R | 63.0% | 36.5% | 63.3% | 36.7% |
| 22,380 | RANDOLPH | 9,001 | 6,127 | 2,817 | 57 | 3,310 R | 68.1% | 31.3% | 68.5% | 31.5% |
| 49,756 | RUSSELL | 16,809 | 8,337 | 8,375 | 97 | 38 D | 49.6% | 49.8% | 49.9% | 50.1% |
| 64,742 | ST. CLAIR | 29,161 | 23,500 | 5,456 | 205 | 18,044 R | 80.6% | 18.7% | 81.2% | 18.8% |
| 143,293 | SHELBY | 78,906 | 63,435 | 14,850 | 621 | 48,585 R | 80.4% | 18.8% | 81.0% | 19.0% |
| 14,798 | SUMTER | 6,433 | 1,880 | 4,527 | 26 | 2,647 D | 29.2% | 70.4% | 29.3% | 70.7% |

# ALABAMA

## PRESIDENT 2004

| 2000 Census Population | County | Total Vote | Republican | Democratic | Other | Rep.-Dem. Plurality | Percentage Total Vote Rep. | Dem. | Major Vote Rep. | Dem. |
|---|---|---|---|---|---|---|---|---|---|---|
| 80,321 | TALLADEGA | 29,898 | 18,331 | 11,374 | 193 | 6,957 R | 61.3% | 38.0% | 61.7% | 38.3% |
| 41,475 | TALLAPOOSA | 17,952 | 12,392 | 5,451 | 109 | 6,941 R | 69.0% | 30.4% | 69.5% | 30.5% |
| 164,875 | TUSCALOOSA | 69,830 | 42,877 | 26,447 | 506 | 16,430 R | 61.4% | 37.9% | 61.9% | 38.1% |
| 70,713 | WALKER | 28,367 | 19,167 | 9,016 | 184 | 10,151 R | 67.6% | 31.8% | 68.0% | 32.0% |
| 18,097 | WASHINGTON | 8,247 | 5,060 | 3,145 | 42 | 1,915 R | 61.4% | 38.1% | 61.7% | 38.3% |
| 13,183 | WILCOX | 5,682 | 1,834 | 3,838 | 10 | 2,004 D | 32.3% | 67.5% | 32.3% | 67.7% |
| 24,843 | WINSTON | 10,423 | 8,130 | 2,236 | 57 | 5,894 R | 78.0% | 21.5% | 78.4% | 21.6% |
| 4,447,100 | TOTAL | 1,883,449 | 1,176,394 | 693,933 | 13,122 | 482,461 R | 62.5% | 36.8% | 62.9% | 37.1% |

# ALABAMA

## SENATOR 2004

| 2000 Census Population | County | Total Vote | Republican | Democratic | Other | Rep.-Dem. Plurality | Percentage Total Vote Rep. | Dem. | Major Vote Rep. | Dem. |
|---|---|---|---|---|---|---|---|---|---|---|
| 43,671 | AUTAUGA | 19,718 | 15,728 | 3,960 | 30 | 11,768 R | 79.8% | 20.1% | 79.9% | 20.1% |
| 140,415 | BALDWIN | 68,131 | 54,503 | 13,509 | 119 | 40,994 R | 80.0% | 19.8% | 80.1% | 19.9% |
| 29,038 | BARBOUR | 10,327 | 6,323 | 3,989 | 15 | 2,334 R | 61.2% | 38.6% | 61.3% | 38.7% |
| 20,826 | BIBB | 7,598 | 5,763 | 1,828 | 7 | 3,935 R | 75.8% | 24.1% | 75.9% | 24.1% |
| 51,024 | BLOUNT | 21,107 | 17,781 | 3,284 | 42 | 14,497 R | 84.2% | 15.6% | 84.4% | 15.6% |
| 11,714 | BULLOCK | 4,442 | 1,701 | 2,740 | 1 | 1,039 D | 38.3% | 61.7% | 38.3% | 61.7% |
| 21,399 | BUTLER | 8,202 | 5,223 | 2,969 | 10 | 2,254 R | 63.7% | 36.2% | 63.8% | 36.2% |
| 112,249 | CALHOUN | 44,409 | 32,273 | 12,077 | 59 | 20,196 R | 72.7% | 27.2% | 72.8% | 27.2% |
| 36,583 | CHAMBERS | 12,762 | 7,958 | 4,804 | | 3,154 R | 62.4% | 37.6% | 62.4% | 37.6% |
| 23,988 | CHEROKEE | 8,763 | 6,166 | 2,588 | 9 | 3,578 R | 70.4% | 29.5% | 70.4% | 29.6% |
| 39,593 | CHILTON | 16,297 | 13,168 | 3,103 | 26 | 10,065 R | 80.8% | 19.0% | 80.9% | 19.1% |
| 15,922 | CHOCTAW | 7,071 | 4,018 | 3,048 | 5 | 970 R | 56.8% | 43.1% | 56.9% | 43.1% |
| 27,867 | CLARKE | 11,076 | 6,925 | 4,141 | 10 | 2,784 R | 62.5% | 37.4% | 62.6% | 37.4% |
| 14,254 | CLAY | 6,484 | 4,928 | 1,552 | 4 | 3,376 R | 76.0% | 23.9% | 76.0% | 24.0% |
| 14,123 | CLEBURNE | 5,549 | 4,389 | 1,151 | 9 | 3,238 R | 79.1% | 20.7% | 79.2% | 20.8% |
| 43,615 | COFFEE | 17,300 | 13,731 | 3,552 | 17 | 10,179 R | 79.4% | 20.5% | 79.4% | 20.6% |
| 54,984 | COLBERT | 23,375 | 13,969 | 9,390 | 16 | 4,579 R | 59.8% | 40.2% | 59.8% | 40.2% |
| 14,089 | CONECUH | 5,782 | 3,357 | 2,418 | 7 | 939 R | 58.1% | 41.8% | 58.1% | 41.9% |
| 12,202 | COOSA | 4,883 | 3,112 | 1,768 | 3 | 1,344 R | 63.7% | 36.2% | 63.8% | 36.2% |
| 37,631 | COVINGTON | 14,252 | 11,500 | 2,734 | 18 | 8,766 R | 80.7% | 19.2% | 80.8% | 19.2% |
| 13,665 | CRENSHAW | 5,369 | 3,934 | 1,424 | 11 | 2,510 R | 73.3% | 26.5% | 73.4% | 26.6% |
| 77,483 | CULLMAN | 34,644 | 27,495 | 7,094 | 55 | 20,401 R | 79.4% | 20.5% | 79.5% | 20.5% |
| 49,129 | DALE | 17,822 | 13,994 | 3,796 | 32 | 10,198 R | 78.5% | 21.3% | 78.7% | 21.3% |
| 46,365 | DALLAS | 18,152 | 8,642 | 9,494 | 16 | 852 D | 47.6% | 52.3% | 47.7% | 52.3% |
| 64,452 | DE KALB | 22,592 | 16,839 | 5,753 | | 11,086 R | 74.5% | 25.5% | 74.5% | 25.5% |
| 65,874 | ELMORE | 28,186 | 22,724 | 5,419 | 43 | 17,305 R | 80.6% | 19.2% | 80.7% | 19.3% |
| 38,440 | ESCAMBIA | 11,919 | 8,424 | 3,482 | 13 | 4,942 R | 70.7% | 29.2% | 70.8% | 29.2% |
| 103,459 | ETOWAH | 42,123 | 28,496 | 13,544 | 83 | 14,952 R | 67.6% | 32.2% | 67.8% | 32.2% |
| 18,495 | FAYETTE | 7,832 | 5,785 | 2,034 | 13 | 3,751 R | 73.9% | 26.0% | 74.0% | 26.0% |
| 31,223 | FRANKLIN | 11,838 | 8,024 | 3,803 | 11 | 4,221 R | 67.8% | 32.1% | 67.8% | 32.2% |
| 25,764 | GENEVA | 10,323 | 8,595 | 1,708 | 20 | 6,887 R | 83.3% | 16.5% | 83.4% | 16.6% |
| 9,974 | GREENE | 4,547 | 1,283 | 3,263 | 1 | 1,980 D | 28.2% | 71.8% | 28.2% | 71.8% |
| 17,185 | HALE | 7,580 | 3,758 | 3,813 | 9 | 55 D | 49.6% | 50.3% | 49.6% | 50.4% |
| 16,310 | HENRY | 7,155 | 5,059 | 2,093 | 3 | 2,966 R | 70.7% | 29.3% | 70.7% | 29.3% |
| 88,787 | HOUSTON | 35,627 | 27,576 | 8,009 | 42 | 19,567 R | 77.4% | 22.5% | 77.5% | 22.5% |
| 53,926 | JACKSON | 19,601 | 12,283 | 7,292 | 26 | 4,991 R | 62.7% | 37.2% | 62.7% | 37.3% |
| 662,047 | JEFFERSON | 288,964 | 168,194 | 120,519 | 251 | 47,675 R | 58.2% | 41.7% | 58.3% | 41.7% |
| 15,904 | LAMAR | 6,718 | 4,919 | 1,799 | | 3,120 R | 73.2% | 26.8% | 73.2% | 26.8% |
| 87,966 | LAUDERDALE | 36,196 | 24,111 | 12,042 | 43 | 12,069 R | 66.6% | 33.3% | 66.7% | 33.3% |
| 34,803 | LAWRENCE | 13,634 | 8,372 | 5,254 | 8 | 3,118 R | 61.4% | 38.5% | 61.4% | 38.6% |

# ALABAMA

## SENATOR 2004

| 2000 Census Population | County | Total Vote | Republican | Democratic | Other | Rep.-Dem. Plurality | Total Vote Rep. | Dem. | Major Vote Rep. | Dem. |
|---|---|---|---|---|---|---|---|---|---|---|
| 115,092 | LEE | 43,561 | 29,393 | 14,168 | | 15,225 R | 67.5% | 32.5% | 67.5% | 32.5% |
| 65,676 | LIMESTONE | 28,412 | 21,060 | 7,324 | 28 | 13,736 R | 74.1% | 25.8% | 74.2% | 25.8% |
| 13,473 | LOWNDES | 5,715 | 2,177 | 3,534 | 4 | 1,357 D | 38.1% | 61.8% | 38.1% | 61.9% |
| 24,105 | MACON | 9,132 | 2,315 | 6,811 | 6 | 4,496 D | 25.4% | 74.6% | 25.4% | 74.6% |
| 276,700 | MADISON | 128,398 | 87,454 | 40,768 | 176 | 46,686 R | 68.1% | 31.8% | 68.2% | 31.8% |
| 22,539 | MARENGO | 10,078 | 5,808 | 4,265 | 5 | 1,543 R | 57.6% | 42.3% | 57.7% | 42.3% |
| 31,214 | MARION | 12,633 | 9,355 | 3,250 | 28 | 6,105 R | 74.1% | 25.7% | 74.2% | 25.8% |
| 82,231 | MARSHALL | 30,745 | 23,940 | 6,771 | 34 | 17,169 R | 77.9% | 22.0% | 78.0% | 22.0% |
| 399,843 | MOBILE | 149,129 | 93,892 | 55,222 | 15 | 38,670 R | 63.0% | 37.0% | 63.0% | 37.0% |
| 24,324 | MONROE | 9,366 | 6,029 | 3,327 | 10 | 2,702 R | 64.4% | 35.5% | 64.4% | 35.6% |
| 223,510 | MONTGOMERY | 86,232 | 47,044 | 39,181 | 7 | 7,863 R | 54.6% | 45.4% | 54.6% | 45.4% |
| 111,064 | MORGAN | 46,088 | 34,687 | 11,330 | 71 | 23,357 R | 75.3% | 24.6% | 75.4% | 24.6% |
| 11,861 | PERRY | 5,406 | 2,012 | 3,388 | 6 | 1,376 D | 37.2% | 62.7% | 37.3% | 62.7% |
| 20,949 | PICKENS | 9,088 | 5,600 | 3,488 | | 2,112 R | 61.6% | 38.4% | 61.6% | 38.4% |
| 29,605 | PIKE | 11,515 | 7,885 | 3,615 | 15 | 4,270 R | 68.5% | 31.4% | 68.6% | 31.4% |
| 22,380 | RANDOLPH | 8,670 | 6,150 | 2,517 | 3 | 3,633 R | 70.9% | 29.0% | 71.0% | 29.0% |
| 49,756 | RUSSELL | 16,254 | 8,500 | 7,723 | 31 | 777 R | 52.3% | 47.5% | 52.4% | 47.6% |
| 64,742 | ST. CLAIR | 28,762 | 24,021 | 4,692 | 49 | 19,329 R | 83.5% | 16.3% | 83.7% | 16.3% |
| 143,293 | SHELBY | 77,911 | 66,315 | 11,478 | 118 | 54,837 R | 85.1% | 14.7% | 85.2% | 14.8% |
| 14,798 | SUMTER | 6,330 | 2,145 | 4,183 | 2 | 2,038 D | 33.9% | 66.1% | 33.9% | 66.1% |
| 80,321 | TALLADEGA | 29,448 | 19,488 | 9,924 | 36 | 9,564 R | 66.2% | 33.7% | 66.3% | 33.7% |
| 41,475 | TALLAPOOSA | 17,527 | 12,875 | 4,627 | 25 | 8,248 R | 73.5% | 26.4% | 73.6% | 26.4% |
| 164,875 | TUSCALOOSA | 68,580 | 47,338 | 21,197 | 45 | 26,141 R | 69.0% | 30.9% | 69.1% | 30.9% |
| 70,713 | WALKER | 28,235 | 20,075 | 8,139 | 21 | 11,936 R | 71.1% | 28.8% | 71.2% | 28.8% |
| 18,097 | WASHINGTON | 7,968 | 5,254 | 2,703 | 11 | 2,551 R | 65.9% | 33.9% | 66.0% | 34.0% |
| 13,183 | WILCOX | 5,396 | 2,013 | 3,383 | | 1,370 D | 37.3% | 62.7% | 37.3% | 62.7% |
| 24,843 | WINSTON | 10,137 | 8,352 | 1,770 | 15 | 6,582 R | 82.4% | 17.5% | 82.5% | 17.5% |
| 4,447,100 | TOTAL | 1,839,066 | 1,242,200 | 595,018 | 1,848 | 647,182 R | 67.5% | 32.4% | 67.6% | 32.4% |

# ALABAMA

## HOUSE OF REPRESENTATIVES

| CD | Year | Total Vote | Republican Vote | Republican Candidate | Democratic Vote | Democratic Candidate | Other Vote | Rep.-Dem. Plurality | Total Vote Rep. | Dem. | Major Vote Rep. | Dem. |
|---|---|---|---|---|---|---|---|---|---|---|---|---|
| 1 | 2004 | 255,164 | 161,067 | Bonner, Jo* | 93,938 | Belk, Judy McCain | 159 | 67,129 R | 63.1% | 36.8% | 63.2% | 36.8% |
| 1 | 2002 | 178,687 | 108,102 | Bonner, Jo | 67,507 | Belk, Judy McCain | 3,078 | 40,595 R | 60.5% | 37.8% | 61.6% | 38.4% |
| 2 | 2004 | 247,947 | 177,086 | Everett, Terry* | 70,562 | James, Charles D. "Chuck" | 299 | 106,524 R | 71.4% | 28.5% | 71.5% | 28.5% |
| 2 | 2002 | 187,965 | 129,233 | Everett, Terry* | 55,495 | Woods, Charles | 3,237 | 73,738 R | 68.8% | 29.5% | 70.0% | 30.0% |
| 3 | 2004 | 245,784 | 150,411 | Rogers, Mike D.* | 95,240 | Fuller, Bill | 133 | 55,171 R | 61.2% | 38.7% | 61.2% | 38.8% |
| 3 | 2002 | 181,223 | 91,169 | Rogers, Mike D. | 87,351 | Turnham, Joe | 2,703 | 3,818 R | 50.3% | 48.2% | 51.1% | 48.9% |
| 4 | 2004 | 255,724 | 191,110 | Aderholt, Robert B.* | 64,278 | Cole, Carl | 336 | 126,832 R | 74.7% | 25.1% | 74.8% | 25.2% |
| 4 | 2002 | 161,101 | 139,705 | Aderholt, Robert B.* | | | 21,396 | 139,705 R | 86.7% | | 100.0% | |
| 5 | 2004 | 275,459 | 74,145 | Wallace, Gerald "Gerry" | 200,999 | Cramer, Robert E. "Bud"* | 315 | 126,854 D | 26.9% | 73.0% | 26.9% | 73.1% |
| 5 | 2002 | 195,171 | 48,226 | Engel, Stephen P. | 143,029 | Cramer, Robert E. "Bud"* | 3,916 | 94,803 D | 24.7% | 73.3% | 25.2% | 74.8% |

# ALABAMA

## HOUSE OF REPRESENTATIVES

| CD | Year | Total Vote | Republican Vote | Republican Candidate | Democratic Vote | Democratic Candidate | Other Vote | Rep.-Dem. Plurality | Percentage Total Vote Rep. | Percentage Total Vote Dem. | Percentage Major Vote Rep. | Percentage Major Vote Dem. |
|----|------|-----------|-----------------|----------------------|-----------------|----------------------|------------|---------------------|------|------|------|------|
| 6 | 2004 | 268,043 | 264,819 | Bachus, Spencer* | | | 3,224 | 264,819 R | 98.8% | | 100.0% | |
| 6 | 2002 | 198,346 | 178,171 | Bachus, Spencer* | | | 20,175 | 178,171 R | 89.8% | | 100.0% | |
| 7 | 2004 | 244,638 | 61,019 | Cameron, Steve F. | 183,408 | Davis, Artur* | 211 | 122,389 D | 24.9% | 75.0% | 25.0% | 75.0% |
| 7 | 2002 | 166,309 | | | 153,735 | Davis, Artur | 12,574 | 153,735 D | | 92.4% | | 100.0% |
| Total | 2004 | 1,792,759 | 1,079,657 | | 708,425 | | 4,677 | 371,232 R | 60.2% | 39.5% | 60.4% | 39.6% |
| Total | 2002 | 1,268,802 | 694,606 | | 507,117 | | 67,079 | 187,489 R | 54.7% | 40.0% | 57.8% | 42.2% |

An asterisk (*) denotes incumbent.

# ALABAMA

## GENERAL AND PRIMARY ELECTIONS

## 2004 GENERAL ELECTIONS

**President**   Other vote was 6,701 Independent (Ralph Nader); 3,529 Independent (Michael Badnarik); 1,994 Independent (Michael Peroutka); 898 scattered write-in.

**Senator**   Other vote was 1,848 scattered write-in.

**House**   Other vote was:

CD 1   159 scattered write-in.
CD 2   299 scattered write-in.
CD 3   133 scattered write-in.
CD 4   336 scattered write-in.
CD 5   315 scattered write-in.
CD 6   3,224 scattered write-in.
CD 7   211 scattered write-in.

## 2004 PRIMARY ELECTIONS

**Primary**   June 1, 2004

**Registration** (as of May 31, 2004)   2,502,082   No Party Registration

**Primary Runoff**   June 29, 2004

**Primary Type**   Open—Any registered voter could vote in either the Democratic or Republican primary, although any voter that participated in the Republican primary could not vote in the Democratic runoff. There was no such restriction on participation in the Republican runoff.

# ALABAMA

## GENERAL AND PRIMARY ELECTIONS

Note:  An asterisk (*) denotes incumbent. The names of unopposed candidates did not appear on the ballot; therefore, no votes were cast for these candidates.

| | REPUBLICAN PRIMARIES | | | DEMOCRATIC PRIMARIES | | |
|---|---|---|---|---|---|---|
| President | George W. Bush* | 187,038 | 92.8% | John Kerry | 164,021 | 75.0% |
| | Uncommitted | 14,449 | 7.2% | Uncommitted | 38,223 | 17.5% |
| | | | | Dennis J. Kucinich | 9,076 | 4.2% |
| | | | | Lyndon H. LaRouche Jr. | 7,254 | 3.3% |
| | TOTAL | 201,487 | | TOTAL | 218,574 | |
| Senator | Richard C. Shelby* | Unopposed | | Wayne Sowell | Unopposed | |
| Congressional District 1 | Jo Bonner* | Unopposed | | Judy McCain Belk | Unopposed | |
| Congressional District 2 | Terry Everett* | Unopposed | | Charles D. "Chuck" James | Unopposed | |
| Congressional District 3 | Mike D. Rogers* | Unopposed | | Bill Fuller | Unopposed | |
| Congressional District 4 | Robert B. Aderholt* | Unopposed | | Carl Cole | Unopposed | |
| Congressional District 5 | Gerald "Gerry" Wallace | 6,742 | 45.2% | Robert E. "Bud" Cramer* | 37,573 | 89.5% |
| | Steve Engel | 6,007 | 40.3% | Michael "People First" Williams | 4,393 | 10.5% |
| | Nate Bailie | 2,175 | 14.6% | | | |
| | TOTAL | 14,924 | | TOTAL | 41,966 | |
| | PRIMARY RUNOFF | | | | | |
| | Gerald "Gerry" Wallace | 2,371 | 52.7% | | | |
| | Steve Engel | 2,130 | 47.3% | | | |
| | TOTAL | 4,501 | | | | |
| Congressional District 6 | Spencer Bachus* | 45,448 | 86.7% | No Democratic candidate | | |
| | Phillip Jauregui | 7,000 | 13.3% | | | |
| | TOTAL | 52,448 | | | | |
| Congressional District 7 | Steve F. Cameron | Unopposed | | Artur Davis* | 58,193 | 87.8% |
| | | | | Albert Turner | 8,061 | 12.2% |
| | | | | TOTAL | 66,254 | |

# ALASKA

## GOVERNOR
Frank H. Murkowski (R). Elected 2002 to a four-year term.

## SENATORS (2 Republicans)
Lisa Murkowski (R). Elected 2004 to a six-year term. Had been appointed in December 2002 to fill the vacancy created by the resignation of her father, Frank H. Murkowski, to become governor of Alaska.

Ted Stevens (R). Reelected 2002 to a six-year term. Previously elected 1996, 1990, 1984, 1978, 1972, and in 1970 to fill out the term vacated by the death of Senator E. L. Bartlett; had been appointed in December 1968 to fill this vacancy.

## REPRESENTATIVE (1 Republican)
At Large. Don Young (R)

## POSTWAR VOTE FOR PRESIDENT

| Year | Total Vote | Republican Vote | Republican Candidate | Democratic Vote | Democratic Candidate | Other Vote | Plurality | Total Vote Rep. | Total Vote Dem. | Major Vote Rep. | Major Vote Dem. |
|---|---|---|---|---|---|---|---|---|---|---|---|
| 2004 | 312,598 | 190,889 | Bush, George W. | 111,025 | Kerry, John | 10,684 | 79,864 R | 61.1% | 35.5% | 63.2% | 36.8% |
| 2000** | 285,560 | 167,398 | Bush, George W. | 79,004 | Gore, Al | 39,158 | 88,394 R | 58.6% | 27.7% | 67.9% | 32.1% |
| 1996** | 241,620 | 122,746 | Dole, Bob | 80,380 | Clinton, Bill | 38,494 | 42,366 R | 50.8% | 33.3% | 60.4% | 39.6% |
| 1992** | 258,506 | 102,000 | Bush, George | 78,294 | Clinton, Bill | 78,212 | 23,706 R | 39.5% | 30.3% | 56.6% | 43.4% |
| 1988 | 200,116 | 119,251 | Bush, George | 72,584 | Dukakis, Michael S. | 8,281 | 46,667 R | 59.6% | 36.3% | 62.2% | 37.8% |
| 1984 | 207,605 | 138,377 | Reagan, Ronald | 62,007 | Mondale, Walter F. | 7,221 | 76,370 R | 66.7% | 29.9% | 69.1% | 30.9% |
| 1980** | 158,445 | 86,112 | Reagan, Ronald | 41,842 | Carter, Jimmy | 30,491 | 44,270 R | 54.3% | 26.4% | 67.3% | 32.7% |
| 1976 | 123,574 | 71,555 | Ford, Gerald R. | 44,058 | Carter, Jimmy | 7,961 | 27,497 R | 57.9% | 35.7% | 61.9% | 38.1% |
| 1972 | 95,219 | 55,349 | Nixon, Richard M. | 32,967 | McGovern, George S. | 6,903 | 22,382 R | 58.1% | 34.6% | 62.7% | 37.3% |
| 1968** | 83,035 | 37,600 | Nixon, Richard M. | 35,411 | Humphrey, Hubert H. | 10,024 | 2,189 R | 45.3% | 42.6% | 51.5% | 48.5% |
| 1964 | 67,259 | 22,930 | Goldwater, Barry M. | 44,329 | Johnson, Lyndon B. | | 21,399 D | 34.1% | 65.9% | 34.1% | 65.9% |
| 1960 | 60,762 | 30,953 | Nixon, Richard M. | 29,809 | Kennedy, John F. | | 1,144 R | 50.9% | 49.1% | 50.9% | 49.1% |

In past elections, the other vote included: 2000 - 28,747 Green (Ralph Nader); 1996 - 26,333 Reform (Ross Perot); 1992 - 73,481 Independent (Perot); 1980 - 18,479 Libertarian (Ed Clark) and 11,155 Independent (John Anderson); 1968 - 10,024 American Independent (George Wallace). Alaska was formally admitted as a state in January 1959.

## POSTWAR VOTE FOR GOVERNOR

| Year | Total Vote | Republican Vote | Republican Candidate | Democratic Vote | Democratic Candidate | Other Vote | Plurality | Total Vote Rep. | Total Vote Dem. | Major Vote Rep. | Major Vote Dem. |
|---|---|---|---|---|---|---|---|---|---|---|---|
| 2002 | 231,484 | 129,279 | Murkowski, Frank H. | 94,216 | Ulmer, Fran | 7,989 | 35,063 R | 55.8% | 40.7% | 57.8% | 42.2% |
| 1998** | 220,177 | 39,331 | Lindauer, John | 112,879 | Knowles, Tony | 67,967 | 73,548 D | 17.9% | 51.3% | 25.8% | 74.2% |
| 1994 | 213,435 | 87,157 | Campbell, James O. | 87,693 | Knowles, Tony | 38,585 | 536 D | 40.8% | 41.1% | 49.8% | 50.2% |
| 1990** | 194,750 | 50,991 | Sturgulewski, Arliss | 60,201 | Knowles, Tony | 83,558 | 15,520 I | 26.2% | 30.9% | 45.9% | 54.1% |
| 1986 | 179,555 | 76,515 | Sturgulewski, Arliss | 84,943 | Cowper, Steve | 18,097 | 8,428 D | 42.6% | 47.3% | 47.4% | 52.6% |
| 1982 | 194,885 | 72,291 | Fink, Tom | 89,918 | Sheffield, Bill | 32,676 | 17,627 D | 37.1% | 46.1% | 44.6% | 55.4% |
| 1978** | 126,910 | 49,580 | Hammond, Jay S. | 25,656 | Croft, Chancy | 51,674 | 16,025 R | 39.1% | 20.2% | 65.9% | 34.1% |
| 1974 | 96,163 | 45,840 | Hammond, Jay S. | 45,553 | Egan, William A. | 4,770 | 287 R | 47.7% | 47.4% | 50.2% | 49.8% |
| 1970 | 80,779 | 37,264 | Miller, Keith | 42,309 | Egan, William A. | 1,206 | 5,045 D | 46.1% | 52.4% | 46.8% | 53.2% |
| 1966 | 66,294 | 33,145 | Hickel, Walter J. | 32,065 | Egan, William A. | 1,084 | 1,080 R | 50.0% | 48.4% | 50.8% | 49.2% |
| 1962 | 56,681 | 27,054 | Stepovich, Mike | 29,627 | Egan, William A. | | 2,573 D | 47.7% | 52.3% | 47.7% | 52.3% |
| 1958 | 48,968 | 19,299 | Butrovich, John | 29,189 | Egan, William A. | 480 | 9,890 D | 39.4% | 59.6% | 39.8% | 60.2% |

In past elections, the other vote included: 1998 - 43,571 scattered write-in (most for Republican Robin Taylor); 1990 - 75,721 Alaskan Independence (Walter J. Hickel); 1978 - 33,555 write-in (Hickel) and 15,656 Alaskans for Kelly (Tom Kelly). Hickel won the 1990 election with 38.9 percent of the total vote.

# ALASKA

## POSTWAR VOTE FOR SENATOR

| Year | Total Vote | Republican Vote | Republican Candidate | Democratic Vote | Democratic Candidate | Other Vote | Plurality | | Percentage Total Vote Rep. | Dem. | Percentage Major Vote Rep. | Dem. |
|------|-----------|-----------------|---------------------|-----------------|---------------------|-----------|-----------|---|------|------|------|------|
| 2004 | 308,315 | 149,773 | Murkowski, Lisa | 140,424 | Knowles, Tony | 18,118 | 9,349 | R | 48.6% | 45.5% | 51.6% | 48.4% |
| 2002 | 229,548 | 179,438 | Stevens, Ted | 24,133 | Vondersaar, Frank | 25,977 | 155,305 | R | 78.2% | 10.5% | 88.1% | 11.9% |
| 1998 | 221,807 | 165,227 | Murkowski, Frank H. | 43,743 | Sonneman, Joseph | 12,837 | 121,484 | R | 74.5% | 19.7% | 79.1% | 20.9% |
| 1996** | 231,916 | 177,893 | Stevens, Ted | 23,977 | Obermeyer, Theresa | 30,046 | 148,856 | R | 76.7% | 10.3% | 88.1% | 11.9% |
| 1992 | 239,714 | 127,163 | Murkowski, Frank H. | 92,065 | Smith, Tony | 20,486 | 35,098 | R | 53.0% | 38.4% | 58.0% | 42.0% |
| 1990 | 189,957 | 125,806 | Stevens, Ted | 61,152 | Beasley, Michael | 2,999 | 64,654 | R | 66.2% | 32.2% | 67.3% | 32.7% |
| 1986 | 180,801 | 97,674 | Murkowski, Frank H. | 79,727 | Olds, Glenn | 3,400 | 17,947 | R | 54.0% | 44.1% | 55.1% | 44.9% |
| 1984 | 206,438 | 146,919 | Stevens, Ted | 58,804 | Havelock, John E. | 715 | 88,115 | R | 71.2% | 28.5% | 71.4% | 28.6% |
| 1980 | 156,762 | 84,159 | Murkowski, Frank H. | 72,007 | Gruening, Clark S. | 596 | 12,152 | R | 53.7% | 45.9% | 53.9% | 46.1% |
| 1978 | 122,741 | 92,783 | Stevens, Ted | 29,574 | Hobbs, Donald W. | 384 | 63,209 | R | 75.6% | 24.1% | 75.8% | 24.2% |
| 1974 | 93,275 | 38,914 | Lewis, C. R. | 54,361 | Gravel, Mike | | 15,447 | D | 41.7% | 58.3% | 41.7% | 58.3% |
| 1972 | 96,007 | 74,216 | Stevens, Ted | 21,791 | Guess, Gene | | 52,425 | R | 77.3% | 22.7% | 77.3% | 22.7% |
| 1970S | 80,364 | 47,908 | Stevens, Ted | 32,456 | Kay, Wendell P. | | 15,452 | R | 59.6% | 40.4% | 59.6% | 40.4% |
| 1968 | 80,931 | 30,286 | Rasmuson, Elmer | 36,527 | Gravel, Mike | 14,118 | 6,241 | D | 37.4% | 45.1% | 45.3% | 54.7% |
| 1966 | 65,250 | 15,961 | McKinley, Lee L. | 49,289 | Bartlett, E. L. | | 33,328 | D | 24.5% | 75.5% | 24.5% | 75.5% |
| 1962 | 58,181 | 24,354 | Stevens, Ted | 33,827 | Gruening, Ernest | | 9,473 | D | 41.9% | 58.1% | 41.9% | 58.1% |
| 1960 | 59,978 | 21,937 | McKinley, Lee L. | 38,041 | Bartlett, E. L. | | 16,104 | D | 36.6% | 63.4% | 36.6% | 63.4% |
| 1958S | 49,525 | 23,462 | Stepovich, Mike | 26,063 | Gruening, Ernest | | 2,601 | D | 47.4% | 52.6% | 47.4% | 52.6% |
| 1958S | 48,837 | 7,299 | Robertson, R. E. | 40,939 | Bartlett, E. L. | 599 | 33,640 | D | 14.9% | 83.8% | 15.1% | 84.9% |

In past elections, the other vote included: 1996 - 29,037 Green (Jed Whittaker). Whittaker finished second, 148,856 votes behind Republican Ted Stevens. The 1970 election was for a short term to fill a vacancy. The two 1958 elections were held to indeterminate terms, and the Senate later determined by lot that Senator Gruening would serve four years, Senator Bartlett two.

# ALASKA

One member At Large

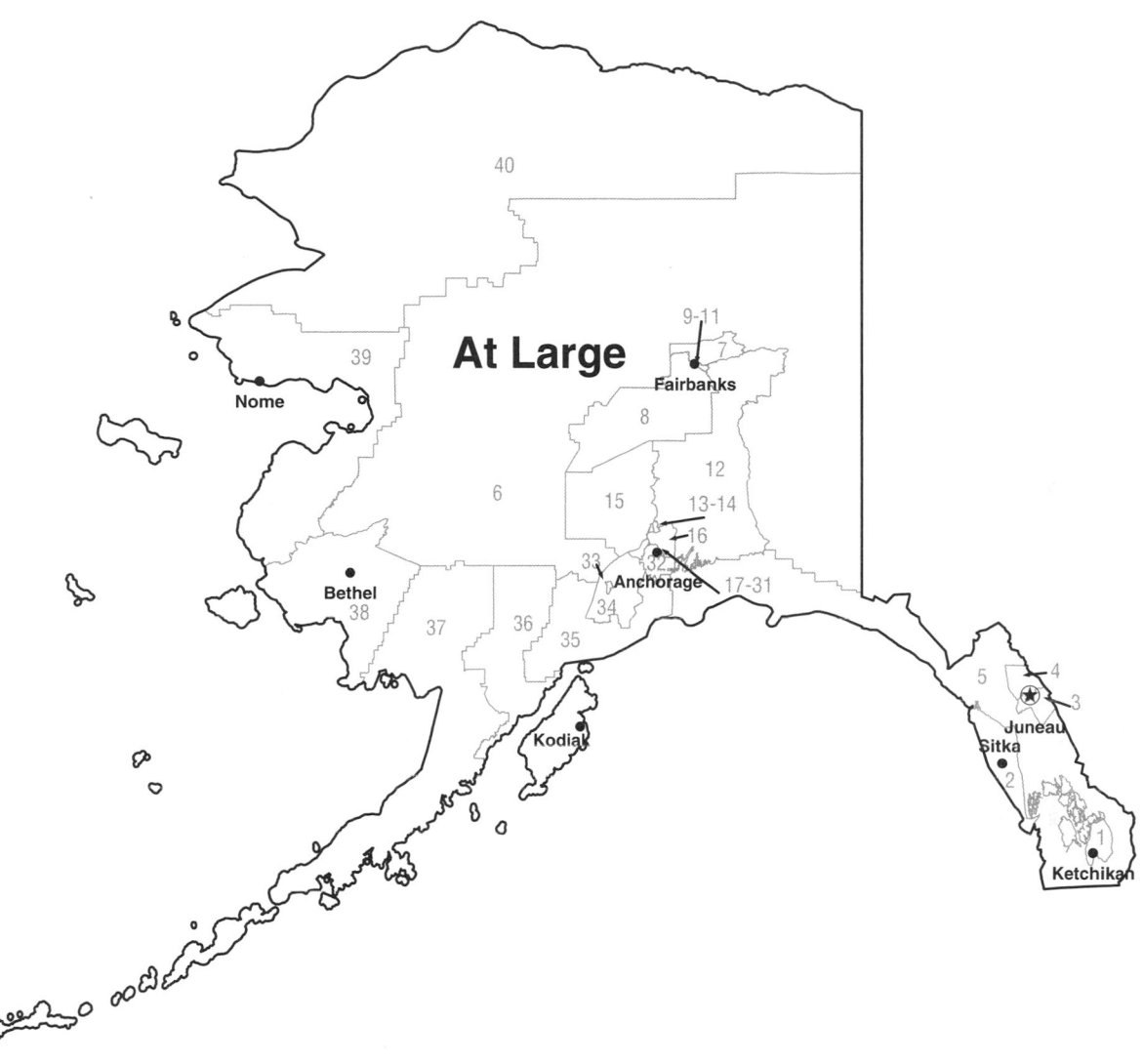

# ALASKA

## PRESIDENT 2004

| 2000 Census Population | District | Total Vote | Republican | Democratic | Other | Rep.-Dem. Plurality | Percentage | | | |
|---|---|---|---|---|---|---|---|---|---|---|
| | | | | | | | Total Vote | | Major Vote | |
| | | | | | | | Rep. | Dem. | Rep. | Dem. |
| 15,031 | DISTRICT 1 | 4,988 | 3,389 | 1,399 | 200 | 1,990 R | 67.9% | 28.0% | 70.8% | 29.2% |
| 14,991 | DISTRICT 2 | 5,878 | 3,214 | 2,403 | 261 | 811 R | 54.7% | 40.9% | 57.2% | 42.8% |
| 15,203 | DISTRICT 3 | 5,874 | 2,258 | 3,429 | 187 | 1,171 D | 38.4% | 58.4% | 39.7% | 60.3% |
| 15,508 | DISTRICT 4 | 5,811 | 3,263 | 2,353 | 195 | 910 R | 56.2% | 40.5% | 58.1% | 41.9% |
| 15,048 | DISTRICT 5 | 5,162 | 2,782 | 2,138 | 242 | 644 R | 53.9% | 41.4% | 56.5% | 43.5% |
| 14,905 | DISTRICT 6 | 4,792 | 2,892 | 1,685 | 215 | 1,207 R | 60.4% | 35.2% | 63.2% | 36.8% |
| 15,494 | DISTRICT 7 | 7,526 | 4,536 | 2,697 | 293 | 1,839 R | 60.3% | 35.8% | 62.7% | 37.3% |
| 15,552 | DISTRICT 8 | 7,116 | 3,547 | 3,251 | 318 | 296 R | 49.8% | 45.7% | 52.2% | 47.8% |
| 15,723 | DISTRICT 9 | 5,148 | 3,243 | 1,739 | 166 | 1,504 R | 63.0% | 33.8% | 65.1% | 34.9% |
| 15,599 | DISTRICT 10 | 4,045 | 2,693 | 1,236 | 116 | 1,457 R | 66.6% | 30.6% | 68.5% | 31.5% |
| 15,904 | DISTRICT 11 | 6,744 | 5,325 | 1,229 | 190 | 4,096 R | 79.0% | 18.2% | 81.2% | 18.8% |
| 16,303 | DISTRICT 12 | 5,352 | 3,926 | 1,262 | 164 | 2,664 R | 73.4% | 23.6% | 75.7% | 24.3% |
| 16,231 | DISTRICT 13 | 6,617 | 4,756 | 1,647 | 214 | 3,109 R | 71.9% | 24.9% | 74.3% | 25.7% |
| 16,119 | DISTRICT 14 | 6,240 | 4,734 | 1,338 | 168 | 3,396 R | 75.9% | 21.4% | 78.0% | 22.0% |
| 16,137 | DISTRICT 15 | 6,401 | 4,455 | 1,670 | 276 | 2,785 R | 69.6% | 26.1% | 72.7% | 27.3% |
| 16,104 | DISTRICT 16 | 7,125 | 5,133 | 1,779 | 213 | 3,354 R | 72.0% | 25.0% | 74.3% | 25.7% |
| 15,819 | DISTRICT 17 | 6,392 | 4,618 | 1,633 | 141 | 2,985 R | 72.2% | 25.5% | 73.9% | 26.1% |
| 15,639 | DISTRICT 18 | 3,189 | 2,231 | 902 | 56 | 1,329 R | 70.0% | 28.3% | 71.2% | 28.8% |
| 15,841 | DISTRICT 19 | 5,197 | 3,148 | 1,893 | 156 | 1,255 R | 60.6% | 36.4% | 62.4% | 37.6% |
| 15,837 | DISTRICT 20 | 3,540 | 1,999 | 1,377 | 164 | 622 R | 56.5% | 38.9% | 59.2% | 40.8% |
| 15,850 | DISTRICT 21 | 5,976 | 3,697 | 2,145 | 134 | 1,552 R | 61.9% | 35.9% | 63.3% | 36.7% |
| 15,831 | DISTRICT 22 | 4,533 | 2,369 | 2,003 | 161 | 366 R | 52.3% | 44.2% | 54.2% | 45.8% |
| 15,847 | DISTRICT 23 | 4,524 | 2,008 | 2,361 | 155 | 353 D | 44.4% | 52.2% | 46.0% | 54.0% |
| 15,812 | DISTRICT 24 | 4,884 | 2,847 | 1,886 | 151 | 961 R | 58.3% | 38.6% | 60.2% | 39.8% |
| 15,836 | DISTRICT 25 | 4,485 | 2,323 | 1,965 | 197 | 358 R | 51.8% | 43.8% | 54.2% | 45.8% |
| 15,823 | DISTRICT 26 | 6,023 | 2,981 | 2,864 | 178 | 117 R | 49.5% | 47.6% | 51.0% | 49.0% |
| 15,820 | DISTRICT 27 | 5,677 | 3,592 | 1,918 | 167 | 1,674 R | 63.3% | 33.8% | 65.2% | 34.8% |
| 15,839 | DISTRICT 28 | 6,358 | 4,183 | 2,019 | 156 | 2,164 R | 65.8% | 31.8% | 67.4% | 32.6% |
| 15,846 | DISTRICT 29 | 4,623 | 2,970 | 1,516 | 137 | 1,454 R | 64.2% | 32.8% | 66.2% | 33.8% |
| 15,839 | DISTRICT 30 | 6,113 | 3,945 | 2,031 | 137 | 1,914 R | 64.5% | 33.2% | 66.0% | 34.0% |
| 15,811 | DISTRICT 31 | 7,073 | 4,726 | 2,214 | 133 | 2,512 R | 66.8% | 31.3% | 68.1% | 31.9% |
| 15,329 | DISTRICT 32 | 7,832 | 4,560 | 3,063 | 209 | 1,497 R | 58.2% | 39.1% | 59.8% | 40.2% |
| 16,466 | DISTRICT 33 | 5,432 | 3,958 | 1,283 | 191 | 2,675 R | 72.9% | 23.6% | 75.5% | 24.5% |
| 16,409 | DISTRICT 34 | 5,680 | 4,304 | 1,164 | 212 | 3,140 R | 75.8% | 20.5% | 78.7% | 21.3% |
| 16,436 | DISTRICT 35 | 5,734 | 3,086 | 2,373 | 275 | 713 R | 53.8% | 41.4% | 56.5% | 43.5% |
| 14,928 | DISTRICT 36 | 4,460 | 2,840 | 1,452 | 168 | 1,388 R | 63.7% | 32.6% | 66.2% | 33.8% |
| 15,150 | DISTRICT 37 | 3,296 | 1,986 | 1,208 | 102 | 778 R | 60.3% | 36.7% | 62.2% | 37.8% |
| 14,921 | DISTRICT 38 | 3,688 | 1,792 | 1,723 | 173 | 69 R | 48.6% | 46.7% | 51.0% | 49.0% |
| 14,996 | DISTRICT 39 | 4,150 | 2,160 | 1,746 | 244 | 414 R | 52.0% | 42.1% | 55.3% | 44.7% |
| 15,155 | DISTRICT 40 | 4,243 | 2,391 | 1,680 | 172 | 711 R | 56.4% | 39.6% | 58.7% | 41.3% |
| 626,932 | Subtotal | 217,921 | 134,860 | 75,674 | 7,387 | 59,186 R | 61.9% | 34.7% | 64.1% | 35.9% |
| | Other Votes | 94,677 | 56,029 | 35,351 | 3,297 | 20,678 R | 59.2% | 37.3% | 61.3% | 38.7% |
| 626,932 | TOTAL | 312,598 | 190,889 | 111,025 | 10,684 | 79,864 R | 61.1% | 35.5% | 63.2% | 36.8% |

Note: There was not a complete presidential vote by state House district in 2004. The votes listed for each district were those cast by voters at the polls on election day. The line for "Other Votes" includes those cast in early voting or by absentee ballot.

# ALASKA

## SENATOR 2004

| 2000 Census Population | District | Total Vote | Republican | Democratic | Other | Rep.-Dem. Plurality | Percentage | | | |
|---|---|---|---|---|---|---|---|---|---|---|
| | | | | | | | Total Vote | | Major Vote | |
| | | | | | | | Rep. | Dem. | Rep. | Dem. |
| 15,031 | DISTRICT 1 | 5,000 | 3,063 | 1,699 | 238 | 1,364 R | 61.3% | 34.0% | 64.3% | 35.7% |
| 14,991 | DISTRICT 2 | 5,857 | 2,668 | 2,913 | 276 | 245 D | 45.6% | 49.7% | 47.8% | 52.2% |
| 15,203 | DISTRICT 3 | 5,875 | 1,700 | 3,994 | 181 | 2,294 D | 28.9% | 68.0% | 29.9% | 70.1% |
| 15,508 | DISTRICT 4 | 5,803 | 2,470 | 3,092 | 241 | 622 D | 42.6% | 53.3% | 44.4% | 55.6% |
| 15,048 | DISTRICT 5 | 5,171 | 2,166 | 2,651 | 354 | 485 D | 41.9% | 51.3% | 45.0% | 55.0% |
| 14,905 | DISTRICT 6 | 4,802 | 2,010 | 2,474 | 318 | 464 D | 41.9% | 51.5% | 44.8% | 55.2% |
| 15,494 | DISTRICT 7 | 7,520 | 3,961 | 3,126 | 433 | 835 R | 52.7% | 41.6% | 55.9% | 44.1% |
| 15,552 | DISTRICT 8 | 7,111 | 3,053 | 3,682 | 376 | 629 D | 42.9% | 51.8% | 45.3% | 54.7% |
| 15,723 | DISTRICT 9 | 5,148 | 2,565 | 2,336 | 247 | 229 R | 49.8% | 45.4% | 52.3% | 47.7% |
| 15,599 | DISTRICT 10 | 4,028 | 2,134 | 1,683 | 211 | 451 R | 53.0% | 41.8% | 55.9% | 44.1% |
| 15,904 | DISTRICT 11 | 6,727 | 1,829 | 4,451 | 447 | 2,622 D | 27.2% | 66.2% | 29.1% | 70.9% |
| 16,303 | DISTRICT 12 | 5,319 | 3,240 | 1,670 | 409 | 1,570 R | 60.9% | 31.4% | 66.0% | 34.0% |
| 16,231 | DISTRICT 13 | 6,625 | 3,818 | 2,268 | 539 | 1,550 R | 57.6% | 34.2% | 62.7% | 37.3% |
| 16,119 | DISTRICT 14 | 6,234 | 3,815 | 1,895 | 524 | 1,920 R | 61.2% | 30.4% | 66.8% | 33.2% |
| 16,137 | DISTRICT 15 | 6,387 | 3,504 | 2,135 | 748 | 1,369 R | 54.9% | 33.4% | 62.1% | 37.9% |
| 16,104 | DISTRICT 16 | 7,122 | 4,255 | 2,315 | 552 | 1,940 R | 59.7% | 32.5% | 64.8% | 35.2% |
| 15,819 | DISTRICT 17 | 6,396 | 3,715 | 2,297 | 384 | 1,418 R | 58.1% | 35.9% | 61.8% | 38.2% |
| 15,639 | DISTRICT 18 | 3,176 | 1,720 | 1,198 | 258 | 522 R | 54.2% | 37.7% | 58.9% | 41.1% |
| 15,841 | DISTRICT 19 | 5,197 | 2,387 | 2,487 | 323 | 100 D | 45.9% | 47.9% | 49.0% | 51.0% |
| 15,837 | DISTRICT 20 | 3,534 | 1,355 | 1,913 | 266 | 558 D | 38.3% | 54.1% | 41.5% | 58.5% |
| 15,850 | DISTRICT 21 | 5,973 | 2,870 | 2,808 | 295 | 62 R | 48.0% | 47.0% | 50.5% | 49.5% |
| 15,831 | DISTRICT 22 | 4,530 | 1,737 | 2,558 | 235 | 821 D | 38.3% | 56.5% | 40.4% | 59.6% |
| 15,847 | DISTRICT 23 | 4,529 | 1,518 | 2,790 | 221 | 1,272 D | 33.5% | 61.6% | 35.2% | 64.8% |
| 15,812 | DISTRICT 24 | 4,890 | 2,264 | 2,367 | 259 | 103 D | 46.3% | 48.4% | 48.9% | 51.1% |
| 15,836 | DISTRICT 25 | 4,494 | 1,793 | 2,426 | 275 | 633 D | 39.9% | 54.0% | 42.5% | 57.5% |
| 15,823 | DISTRICT 26 | 6,032 | 2,478 | 3,327 | 227 | 849 D | 41.1% | 55.2% | 42.7% | 57.3% |
| 15,820 | DISTRICT 27 | 5,672 | 2,916 | 2,465 | 291 | 451 R | 51.4% | 43.5% | 54.2% | 45.8% |
| 15,839 | DISTRICT 28 | 6,356 | 3,498 | 2,581 | 277 | 917 R | 55.0% | 40.6% | 57.5% | 42.5% |
| 15,846 | DISTRICT 29 | 4,623 | 2,276 | 2,073 | 274 | 203 R | 49.2% | 44.8% | 52.3% | 47.7% |
| 15,839 | DISTRICT 30 | 6,117 | 3,174 | 2,640 | 303 | 534 R | 51.9% | 43.2% | 54.6% | 45.4% |
| 15,811 | DISTRICT 31 | 7,069 | 4,033 | 2,777 | 259 | 1,256 R | 57.1% | 39.3% | 59.2% | 40.8% |
| 15,329 | DISTRICT 32 | 7,823 | 3,872 | 3,545 | 406 | 327 R | 49.5% | 45.3% | 52.2% | 47.8% |
| 16,466 | DISTRICT 33 | 5,430 | 3,202 | 1,779 | 449 | 1,423 R | 59.0% | 32.8% | 64.3% | 35.7% |
| 16,409 | DISTRICT 34 | 5,670 | 3,560 | 1,571 | 539 | 1,989 R | 62.8% | 27.7% | 69.4% | 30.6% |
| 16,436 | DISTRICT 35 | 5,723 | 2,495 | 2,768 | 460 | 273 D | 43.6% | 48.4% | 47.4% | 52.6% |
| 14,928 | DISTRICT 36 | 4,441 | 2,214 | 1,960 | 267 | 254 R | 49.9% | 44.1% | 53.0% | 47.0% |
| 15,150 | DISTRICT 37 | 3,293 | 1,390 | 1,735 | 168 | 345 D | 42.2% | 52.7% | 44.5% | 55.5% |
| 14,921 | DISTRICT 38 | 3,714 | 794 | 2,811 | 109 | 2,017 D | 21.4% | 75.7% | 22.0% | 78.0% |
| 14,996 | DISTRICT 39 | 4,163 | 1,132 | 2,848 | 183 | 1,716 D | 27.2% | 68.4% | 28.4% | 71.6% |
| 15,155 | DISTRICT 40 | 4,303 | 1,179 | 2,902 | 222 | 1,723 D | 27.4% | 67.4% | 28.9% | 71.1% |
| | Subtotal | 217,877 | 103,823 | 101,010 | 13,044 | 2,813 R | 47.7% | 46.4% | 50.7% | 49.3% |
| | Other Votes | 89,494 | 45,623 | 38,868 | 5,003 | 6,755 R | 51.0% | 43.4% | 54.0% | 46.0% |
| | Original Total | 307,371 | 149,446 | 139,878 | 18,047 | 9,568 R | 48.6% | 45.5% | 51.7% | 48.3% |
| 626,932 | RECOUNT | 308,315 | 149,773 | 140,424 | 18,118 | 9,349 R | 48.6% | 45.5% | 51.6% | 48.4% |

Note:   There was not a complete Senate vote by state House district in 2004. The votes listed for each district were those cast by voters at the polls on election day. The line for "Other Votes" includes those cast in early voting or by absentee ballot. The votes listed within the table are from the original official tally. They do not reflect the result of a recount for which only the statewide summary totals were released.

# ALASKA

## HOUSE OF REPRESENTATIVES

| | | | Republican | | Democratic | | Other | Rep.-Dem. | Percentage | | | |
| | | | | | | | | | Total Vote | | Major Vote | |
| CD | Year | Total Vote | Vote | Candidate | Vote | Candidate | Vote | Plurality | Rep. | Dem. | Rep. | Dem. |
|---|---|---|---|---|---|---|---|---|---|---|---|---|
| AL | 2004 | 299,996 | 213,216 | Young, Don* | 67,074 | Higgins, Thomas M. | 19,706 | 146,142 R | 71.1% | 22.4% | 76.1% | 23.9% |
| AL | 2002 | 227,725 | 169,685 | Young, Don* | 39,357 | Greene, Clifford | 18,683 | 130,328 R | 74.5% | 17.3% | 81.2% | 18.8% |
| AL | 2000 | 274,393 | 190,862 | Young, Don* | 45,372 | Greene, Clifford | 38,159 | 145,490 R | 69.6% | 16.5% | 80.8% | 19.2% |
| AL | 1998 | 223,300 | 139,676 | Young, Don* | 77,232 | Duncan, Jim | 6,392 | 62,444 R | 62.6% | 34.6% | 64.4% | 35.6% |
| AL | 1996 | 233,700 | 138,834 | Young, Don* | 85,114 | Lincoln, Georgianna | 9,752 | 53,720 R | 59.4% | 36.4% | 62.0% | 38.0% |
| AL | 1994 | 208,240 | 118,537 | Young, Don* | 68,172 | Smith, Tony | 21,531 | 50,365 R | 56.9% | 32.7% | 63.5% | 36.5% |
| AL | 1992 | 239,116 | 111,849 | Young, Don* | 102,378 | Devens, John S. | 24,889 | 9,471 R | 46.8% | 42.8% | 52.2% | 47.8% |
| AL | 1990 | 191,647 | 99,003 | Young, Don* | 91,677 | Devens, John S. | 967 | 7,326 R | 51.7% | 47.8% | 51.9% | 48.1% |
| AL | 1988 | 192,955 | 120,595 | Young, Don* | 71,881 | Gruenstein, Peter | 479 | 48,714 R | 62.5% | 37.3% | 62.7% | 37.3% |
| AL | 1986 | 180,277 | 101,799 | Young, Don* | 74,053 | Begich, Pegge | 4,425 | 27,746 R | 56.5% | 41.1% | 57.9% | 42.1% |
| AL | 1984 | 206,437 | 113,582 | Young, Don* | 86,052 | Begich, Pegge | 6,803 | 27,530 R | 55.0% | 41.7% | 56.9% | 43.1% |
| AL | 1982 | 181,084 | 128,274 | Young, Don* | 52,011 | Carlson, Dave | 799 | 76,263 R | 70.8% | 28.7% | 71.2% | 28.8% |
| AL | 1980 | 154,618 | 114,089 | Young, Don* | 39,922 | Parnell, Kevin | 607 | 74,167 R | 73.8% | 25.8% | 74.1% | 25.9% |
| AL | 1978 | 124,187 | 68,811 | Young, Don* | 55,176 | Rodney, Patrick | 200 | 13,635 R | 55.4% | 44.4% | 55.5% | 44.5% |
| AL | 1976 | 118,208 | 83,722 | Young, Don* | 34,194 | Hopson, Eben | 292 | 49,528 R | 70.8% | 28.9% | 71.0% | 29.0% |
| AL | 1974 | 95,921 | 51,641 | Young, Don* | 44,280 | Hensley, William L. | | 7,361 R | 53.8% | 46.2% | 53.8% | 46.2% |
| AL | 1972 | 95,401 | 41,750 | Young, Don | 53,651 | Begich, Nick* | | 11,901 D | 43.8% | 56.2% | 43.8% | 56.2% |
| AL | 1970 | 80,084 | 35,947 | Murkowski, Frank H. | 44,137 | Begich, Nick | | 8,190 D | 44.9% | 55.1% | 44.9% | 55.1% |
| AL | 1968 | 80,362 | 43,577 | Pollock, Howard W.* | 36,785 | Begich, Nick | | 6,792 R | 54.2% | 45.8% | 54.2% | 45.8% |
| AL | 1966 | 65,907 | 34,040 | Pollock, Howard W. | 31,867 | Rivers, Ralph J.* | | 2,173 R | 51.6% | 48.4% | 51.6% | 48.4% |
| AL | 1964 | 67,146 | 32,556 | Thomas, Lowell | 34,590 | Rivers, Ralph J.* | | 2,034 D | 48.5% | 51.5% | 48.5% | 51.5% |
| AL | 1962 | 58,591 | 26,638 | Thomas, Lowell | 31,953 | Rivers, Ralph J.* | | 5,315 D | 45.5% | 54.5% | 45.5% | 54.5% |
| AL | 1960 | 59,063 | 25,517 | Rettig, R. L. | 33,546 | Rivers, Ralph J.* | | 8,029 D | 43.2% | 56.8% | 43.2% | 56.8% |
| AL | 1958 | 48,647 | 20,699 | Benson, Henry A. | 27,948 | Rivers, Ralph J.* | | 7,249 D | 42.5% | 57.5% | 42.5% | 57.5% |

An asterisk (*) denotes incumbent.

# ALASKA

## GENERAL AND PRIMARY ELECTIONS

## 2004 GENERAL ELECTIONS

**President**  Other vote was 5,069 Populist (Ralph Nader); 2,092 Alaskan Independence (Michael Perotuka); 1,675 Alaska Libertarian (Michael Badnarik); 1,058 Green (David Cobb); 790 scattered write-in.

**Senator**  Other vote was 8,885 Nonpartisan (Marc J. Millican); 3,785 Alaskan Independence (Jerry Sanders); 3,053 Green (Jim Sykes); 1,240 Libertarian (Scott A. Kohlhaas); 732 Nonpartisan (Ted Gianoutsos); 423 scattered write-in.

**House**  Other vote was:

At Large  11,434 Green (Timothy A. Feller); 7,157 Libertarian (Alvin A. Anders); 1,115 scattered write-in.

## 2004 PRIMARY ELECTIONS

**Primary**  August 24, 2004

| **Registration** (as of Aug. 4, 2004) | | |
|---|---|---|
| | Republican | 115,104 |
| | Democratic | 69,182 |
| | Alaskan Independence | 16,066 |
| | Alaska Libertarian | 7,335 |
| | Green Party of Alaska | 4,528 |
| | Republican Moderate | 4,304 |
| | Other | 2,963 |
| | Nonpartisan | 67,024 |
| | Undeclared | 171,521 |
| | TOTAL | 458,027 |

# ALASKA

## GENERAL AND PRIMARY ELECTIONS

## 2004 PRIMARY ELECTIONS

**Primary Type**  Voters registered as Democrats or Republicans could participate only in their party's primary. Undeclared and nonpartisan voters could participate in either party's primary. (Undeclared voters may be associated with a party but do not wish to declare which one. Nonpartisan voters are not associated with any party.) In addition, any other registered voter (except those registered as Republican) could cast a separate ballot in the Democratic primary that was included in the overall tally.

Note:  An asterisk (*) denotes incumbent.

| | REPUBLICAN PRIMARIES | | | DEMOCRATIC PRIMARIES | | |
|---|---|---|---|---|---|---|
| **Senator** | Lisa Murkowski* | 45,710 | 58.1% | Tony Knowles | 40,881 | 95.1% |
| | Mike Miller | 29,313 | 37.3% | Don R. Wright | 1,080 | 2.5% |
| | Wev Shea | 2,857 | 3.6% | Theresa N. Obermeyer | 1,045 | 2.4% |
| | Jim Dore | 748 | 1.0% | | | |
| | TOTAL | 78,628 | | TOTAL | 43,006 | |
| **House At Large** | Don Young* | 70,142 | 100.0% | Thomas M. Higgins | 14,109 | 47.6% |
| | | | | Frank Vondersaar | 9,025 | 30.5% |
| | | | | Dae Miles | 6,479 | 21.9% |
| | | | | TOTAL | 29,613 | |

# ARIZONA

## GOVERNOR
Janet Napolitano (D). Elected 2002 to a four-year term.

## SENATORS (2 Republicans)
Jon Kyl (R). Reelected 2000 to a six-year term. Previously elected 1994.

John McCain (R). Reelected 2004 to a six-year term. Previously elected 1998, 1992, 1986.

## REPRESENTATIVES (6 Republicans, 2 Democrats)
1. Rick Renzi (R)
2. Trent Franks (R)
3. John Shadegg (R)
4. Ed Pastor (D)
5. J. D. Hayworth (R)
6. Jeff Flake (R)
7. Raul M. Grijalva (D)
8. Jim Kolbe (R)

## POSTWAR VOTE FOR PRESIDENT

| Year | Total Vote | Republican Vote | Republican Candidate | Democratic Vote | Democratic Candidate | Other Vote | Plurality | Percentage Total Vote Rep. | Dem. | Major Vote Rep. | Dem. |
|------|-----------|------|-----------|------|-----------|------|-----------|------|------|------|------|
| 2004 | 2,012,585 | 1,104,294 | Bush, George W. | 893,524 | Kerry, John | 14,767 | 210,770 R | 54.9% | 44.4% | 55.3% | 44.7% |
| 2000** | 1,532,016 | 781,652 | Bush, George W. | 685,341 | Gore, Al | 65,023 | 96,311 R | 51.0% | 44.7% | 53.3% | 46.7% |
| 1996** | 1,404,405 | 622,073 | Dole, Bob | 653,288 | Clinton, Bill | 129,044 | 31,215 D | 44.3% | 46.5% | 48.8% | 51.2% |
| 1992** | 1,486,975 | 572,086 | Bush, George | 543,050 | Clinton, Bill | 371,839 | 29,036 R | 38.5% | 36.5% | 51.3% | 48.7% |
| 1988 | 1,171,873 | 702,541 | Bush, George | 454,029 | Dukakis, Michael S. | 15,303 | 248,512 R | 60.0% | 38.7% | 60.7% | 39.3% |
| 1984 | 1,025,897 | 681,416 | Reagan, Ronald | 333,854 | Mondale, Walter F. | 10,627 | 347,562 R | 66.4% | 32.5% | 67.1% | 32.9% |
| 1980** | 873,945 | 529,688 | Reagan, Ronald | 246,843 | Carter, Jimmy | 97,414 | 282,845 R | 60.6% | 28.2% | 68.2% | 31.8% |
| 1976 | 742,719 | 418,642 | Ford, Gerald R. | 295,602 | Carter, Jimmy | 28,475 | 123,040 R | 56.4% | 39.8% | 58.6% | 41.4% |
| 1972 | 622,926 | 402,812 | Nixon, Richard M. | 198,540 | McGovern, George S. | 21,574 | 204,272 R | 64.7% | 31.9% | 67.0% | 33.0% |
| 1968** | 486,936 | 266,721 | Nixon, Richard M. | 170,514 | Humphrey, Hubert H. | 49,701 | 96,207 R | 54.8% | 35.0% | 61.0% | 39.0% |
| 1964 | 480,770 | 242,535 | Goldwater, Barry M. | 237,753 | Johnson, Lyndon B. | 482 | 4,782 R | 50.4% | 49.5% | 50.5% | 49.5% |
| 1960 | 398,491 | 221,241 | Nixon, Richard M. | 176,781 | Kennedy, John F. | 469 | 44,460 R | 55.5% | 44.4% | 55.6% | 44.4% |
| 1956 | 290,173 | 176,990 | Eisenhower, Dwight D. | 112,880 | Stevenson, Adlai E. | 303 | 64,110 R | 61.0% | 38.9% | 61.1% | 38.9% |
| 1952 | 260,570 | 152,042 | Eisenhower, Dwight D. | 108,528 | Stevenson, Adlai E. | | 43,514 R | 58.3% | 41.7% | 58.3% | 41.7% |
| 1948 | 177,065 | 77,597 | Dewey, Thomas E. | 95,251 | Truman, Harry S. | 4,217 | 17,654 D | 43.8% | 53.8% | 44.9% | 55.1% |

In past elections, the other vote included: 2000 - 45,645 Green (Ralph Nader); 1996 - 112,072 Reform (Ross Perot); 1992 - 353,741 Independent (Perot); 1980 - 76,952 Independent (John Anderson); 1968 - 46,573 American Independent (George Wallace).

# ARIZONA

## POSTWAR VOTE FOR GOVERNOR

| Year | Total Vote | Republican | | Democratic | | Other Vote | Rep.-Dem. Plurality | Percentage | | | |
|---|---|---|---|---|---|---|---|---|---|---|---|
| | | | | | | | | Total Vote | | Major Vote | |
| | | Vote | Candidate | Vote | Candidate | | | Rep. | Dem. | Rep. | Dem. |
| 2002 | 1,226,111 | 554,465 | Salmon, Matt | 566,284 | Napolitano, Janet | 105,362 | 11,819 D | 45.2% | 46.2% | 49.5% | 50.5% |
| 1998 | 1,017,616 | 620,188 | Hull, Jane Dee | 361,552 | Johnson, Paul | 35,876 | 258,636 R | 60.9% | 35.5% | 63.2% | 36.8% |
| 1994 | 1,129,607 | 593,492 | Symington, Fife | 500,702 | Basha, Eddie | 35,413 | 92,790 R | 52.5% | 44.3% | 54.2% | 45.8% |
| 1990** | 940,737 | 492,569 | Symington, Fife | 448,168 | Goddard, Terry | | 44,401 R | 52.4% | 47.6% | 52.4% | 47.6% |
| 1986** | 866,984 | 343,913 | Mecham, Evan | 298,986 | Warner, Carolyn | 224,085 | 44,927 R | 39.7% | 34.5% | 53.5% | 46.5% |
| 1982 | 726,364 | 235,877 | Corbet, Leo | 453,795 | Babbitt, Bruce | 36,692 | 217,918 D | 32.5% | 62.5% | 34.2% | 65.8% |
| 1978 | 538,556 | 241,093 | Mecham, Evan | 282,605 | Babbitt, Bruce | 14,858 | 41,512 D | 44.8% | 52.5% | 46.0% | 54.0% |
| 1974 | 552,202 | 273,674 | Williams, Russell | 278,375 | Castro, Raul H. | 153 | 4,701 D | 49.6% | 50.4% | 49.6% | 50.4% |
| 1970** | 411,409 | 209,522 | Williams, John R. | 201,887 | Castro, Raul H. | | 7,635 R | 50.9% | 49.1% | 50.9% | 49.1% |
| 1968 | 483,998 | 279,923 | Williams, John R. | 204,075 | Goddard, Sam | | 75,848 R | 57.8% | 42.2% | 57.8% | 42.2% |
| 1966 | 378,342 | 203,438 | Williams, John R. | 174,904 | Goddard, Sam | | 28,534 R | 53.8% | 46.2% | 53.8% | 46.2% |
| 1964 | 473,502 | 221,404 | Kleindienst, Richard | 252,098 | Goddard, Sam | | 30,694 D | 46.8% | 53.2% | 46.8% | 53.2% |
| 1962 | 365,841 | 200,578 | Fannin, Paul | 165,263 | Goddard, Sam | | 35,315 R | 54.8% | 45.2% | 54.8% | 45.2% |
| 1960 | 397,107 | 235,502 | Fannin, Paul | 161,605 | Ackerman, Lee | | 73,897 R | 59.3% | 40.7% | 59.3% | 40.7% |
| 1958 | 290,465 | 160,136 | Fannin, Paul | 130,329 | Morrison, Robert | | 29,807 R | 55.1% | 44.9% | 55.1% | 44.9% |
| 1956 | 288,592 | 116,744 | Griffen, Horace B. | 171,848 | McFarland, Ernest W. | | 55,104 D | 40.5% | 59.5% | 40.5% | 59.5% |
| 1954 | 243,970 | 115,866 | Pyle, Howard | 128,104 | McFarland, Ernest W. | | 12,238 D | 47.5% | 52.5% | 47.5% | 52.5% |
| 1952 | 260,285 | 156,592 | Pyle, Howard | 103,693 | Haldiman, Joe C. | | 52,899 R | 60.2% | 39.8% | 60.2% | 39.8% |
| 1950 | 195,227 | 99,109 | Pyle, Howard | 96,118 | Frohmiller, Ana | | 2,991 R | 50.8% | 49.2% | 50.8% | 49.2% |
| 1948 | 175,767 | 70,419 | Brockett, Bruce | 104,008 | Garvey, Dan E. | 1,340 | 33,589 D | 40.1% | 59.2% | 40.4% | 59.6% |
| 1946 | 122,462 | 48,867 | Brockett, Bruce | 73,595 | Osborn, Sidney P. | | 24,728 D | 39.9% | 60.1% | 39.9% | 60.1% |

In 1990 neither major party candidate won an absolute majority, therefore a runoff election was held February 26, 1991; the vote above is for the February runoff. In 1986 other vote was Independent (Bill Schulz). The term of office for Arizona's governor was increased from two to four years effective with the 1970 election.

## POSTWAR VOTE FOR SENATOR

| Year | Total Vote | Republican | | Democratic | | Other Vote | Rep.-Dem. Plurality | Percentage | | | |
|---|---|---|---|---|---|---|---|---|---|---|---|
| | | | | | | | | Total Vote | | Major Vote | |
| | | Vote | Candidate | Vote | Candidate | | | Rep. | Dem. | Rep. | Dem. |
| 2004 | 1,961,677 | 1,505,372 | McCain, John | 404,507 | Starky, Stuart | 51,798 | 1,100,865 R | 76.7% | 20.6% | 78.8% | 21.2% |
| 2000** | 1,397,076 | 1,108,196 | Kyl, Jon | — | | 288,880 | 1,108,196 R | 79.3% | | 100.0% | |
| 1998 | 1,013,280 | 696,577 | McCain, John | 275,224 | Ranger, Ed | 41,479 | 421,353 R | 68.7% | 27.2% | 71.7% | 28.3% |
| 1994 | 1,119,060 | 600,999 | Kyl, Jon | 442,510 | Coppersmith, Sam | 75,551 | 158,489 R | 53.7% | 39.5% | 57.6% | 42.4% |
| 1992 | 1,382,051 | 771,395 | McCain, John | 436,321 | Sargent, Claire | 174,335 | 335,074 R | 55.8% | 31.6% | 63.9% | 36.1% |
| 1988 | 1,164,539 | 478,060 | DeGreen, Keith | 660,403 | DeConcini, Dennis | 26,076 | 182,343 D | 41.1% | 56.7% | 42.0% | 58.0% |
| 1986 | 862,921 | 521,850 | McCain, John | 340,965 | Kimball, Richard | 106 | 180,885 R | 60.5% | 39.5% | 60.5% | 39.5% |
| 1982 | 723,885 | 291,749 | Dunn, Pete | 411,970 | DeConcini, Dennis | 20,166 | 120,221 D | 40.3% | 56.9% | 41.5% | 58.5% |
| 1980 | 874,238 | 432,371 | Goldwater, Barry M. | 422,972 | Schulz, Bill | 18,895 | 9,399 R | 49.5% | 48.4% | 50.5% | 49.5% |
| 1976 | 741,210 | 321,236 | Steiger, Sam | 400,334 | DeConcini, Dennis | 19,640 | 79,098 D | 43.3% | 54.0% | 44.5% | 55.5% |
| 1974 | 549,919 | 320,396 | Goldwater, Barry M. | 229,523 | Marshall, Jonathan | | 90,873 R | 58.3% | 41.7% | 58.3% | 41.7% |
| 1970 | 407,796 | 228,284 | Fannin, Paul | 179,512 | Grossman, Sam | | 48,772 R | 56.0% | 44.0% | 56.0% | 44.0% |
| 1968 | 479,945 | 274,607 | Goldwater, Barry M. | 205,338 | Elson, Roy L. | | 69,269 R | 57.2% | 42.8% | 57.2% | 42.8% |
| 1964 | 468,801 | 241,089 | Fannin, Paul | 227,712 | Elson, Roy L. | | 13,377 R | 51.4% | 48.6% | 51.4% | 48.6% |
| 1962 | 362,605 | 163,388 | Mecham, Evan | 199,217 | Hayden, Carl | | 35,829 D | 45.1% | 54.9% | 45.1% | 54.9% |
| 1958 | 293,623 | 164,593 | Goldwater, Barry M. | 129,030 | McFarland, Ernest W. | | 35,563 R | 56.1% | 43.9% | 56.1% | 43.9% |
| 1956 | 278,263 | 107,447 | Jones, Ross F. | 170,816 | Hayden, Carl | | 63,369 D | 38.6% | 61.4% | 38.6% | 61.4% |
| 1952 | 257,401 | 132,063 | Goldwater, Barry M. | 125,338 | McFarland, Ernest W. | | 6,725 R | 51.3% | 48.7% | 51.3% | 48.7% |
| 1950 | 185,092 | 68,846 | Brockett, Bruce | 116,246 | Hayden, Carl | | 47,400 D | 37.2% | 62.8% | 37.2% | 62.8% |
| 1946 | 116,239 | 35,022 | Powers, Ward S. | 80,415 | McFarland, Ernest W. | 802 | 45,393 D | 30.1% | 69.2% | 30.3% | 69.7% |

The Democratic Party did not run a candidate in the 2000 Senate election.

# ARIZONA

Congressional districts first established for elections held in 2002
8 members

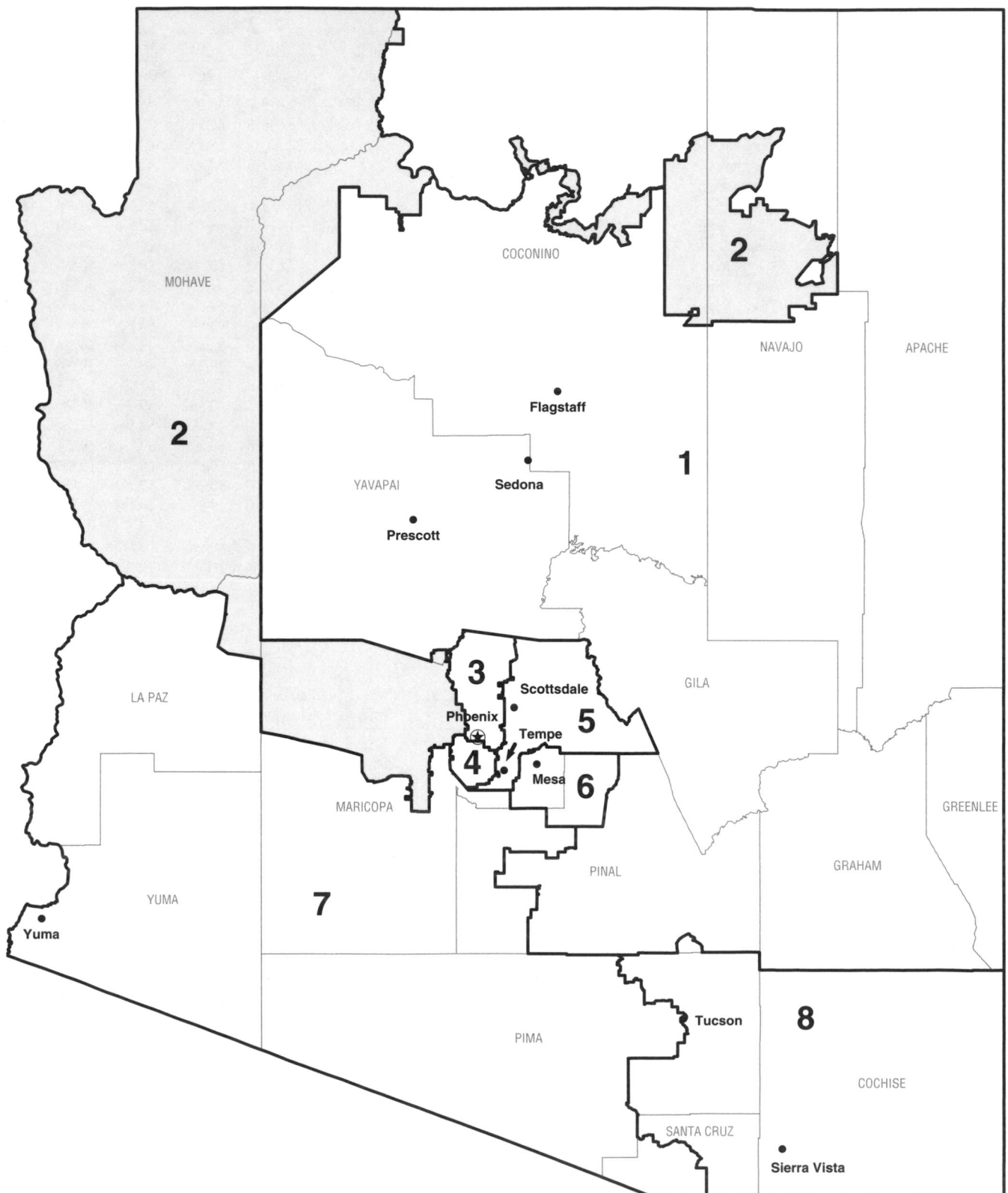

MOHAVE

COCONINO

NAVAJO

APACHE

2

• Flagstaff

YAVAPAI

• Sedona

1

• Prescott

GILA

LA PAZ

3

Scottsdale

Phoenix

5

Tempe

4

Mesa

6

GREENLEE

MARICOPA

GRAHAM

PINAL

YUMA

7

• Yuma

PIMA

• Tucson

8

COCHISE

SANTA CRUZ

• Sierra Vista

# ARIZONA

## PRESIDENT 2004

| 2000 Census Population | County | Total Vote | Republican | Democratic | Other | Rep.-Dem. Plurality | Percentage | | | |
|---|---|---|---|---|---|---|---|---|---|---|
| | | | | | | | Total Vote | | Major Vote | |
| | | | | | | | Rep. | Dem. | Rep. | Dem. |
| 69,423 | APACHE | 24,198 | 8,384 | 15,658 | 156 | 7,274 D | 34.6% | 64.7% | 34.9% | 65.1% |
| 117,755 | COCHISE | 44,483 | 26,556 | 17,514 | 413 | 9,042 R | 59.7% | 39.4% | 60.3% | 39.7% |
| 116,320 | COCONINO | 52,267 | 22,526 | 29,243 | 498 | 6,717 D | 43.1% | 55.9% | 43.5% | 56.5% |
| 51,335 | GILA | 20,843 | 12,343 | 8,314 | 186 | 4,029 R | 59.2% | 39.9% | 59.8% | 40.2% |
| 33,489 | GRAHAM | 10,720 | 7,467 | 3,185 | 68 | 4,282 R | 69.7% | 29.7% | 70.1% | 29.9% |
| 8,547 | GREENLEE | 3,067 | 1,899 | 1,146 | 22 | 753 R | 61.9% | 37.4% | 62.4% | 37.6% |
| 19,715 | LA PAZ | 5,055 | 3,158 | 1,849 | 48 | 1,309 R | 62.5% | 36.6% | 63.1% | 36.9% |
| 3,072,149 | MARICOPA | 1,192,751 | 679,455 | 504,849 | 8,447 | 174,606 R | 57.0% | 42.3% | 57.4% | 42.6% |
| 155,032 | MOHAVE | 57,807 | 36,794 | 20,503 | 510 | 16,291 R | 63.6% | 35.5% | 64.2% | 35.8% |
| 97,470 | NAVAJO | 32,343 | 17,277 | 14,815 | 251 | 2,462 R | 53.4% | 45.8% | 53.8% | 46.2% |
| 843,746 | PIMA | 366,907 | 171,109 | 193,128 | 2,670 | 22,019 D | 46.6% | 52.6% | 47.0% | 53.0% |
| 179,727 | PINAL | 64,622 | 37,006 | 27,252 | 364 | 9,754 R | 57.3% | 42.2% | 57.6% | 42.4% |
| 38,381 | SANTA CRUZ | 11,668 | 4,668 | 6,909 | 91 | 2,241 D | 40.0% | 59.2% | 40.3% | 59.7% |
| 167,517 | YAVAPAI | 87,389 | 53,468 | 33,127 | 794 | 20,341 R | 61.2% | 37.9% | 61.7% | 38.3% |
| 160,026 | YUMA | 38,465 | 22,184 | 16,032 | 249 | 6,152 R | 57.7% | 41.7% | 58.0% | 42.0% |
| 5,130,632 | TOTAL | 2,012,585 | 1,104,294 | 893,524 | 14,767 | 210,770 R | 54.9% | 44.4% | 55.3% | 44.7% |

# ARIZONA

## SENATOR 2004

| 2000 Census Population | County | Total Vote | Republican | Democratic | Other | Rep.-Dem. Plurality | Percentage | | | |
|---|---|---|---|---|---|---|---|---|---|---|
| | | | | | | | Total Vote | | Major Vote | |
| | | | | | | | Rep. | Dem. | Rep. | Dem. |
| 69,423 | APACHE | 23,416 | 12,923 | 9,588 | 905 | 3,335 R | 55.2% | 40.9% | 57.4% | 42.6% |
| 117,755 | COCHISE | 43,828 | 32,879 | 9,555 | 1,394 | 23,324 R | 75.0% | 21.8% | 77.5% | 22.5% |
| 116,320 | COCONINO | 50,873 | 35,849 | 13,520 | 1,504 | 22,329 R | 70.5% | 26.6% | 72.6% | 27.4% |
| 51,335 | GILA | 20,474 | 15,551 | 4,291 | 632 | 11,260 R | 76.0% | 21.0% | 78.4% | 21.6% |
| 33,489 | GRAHAM | 10,493 | 8,171 | 2,000 | 322 | 6,171 R | 77.9% | 19.1% | 80.3% | 19.7% |
| 8,547 | GREENLEE | 2,980 | 2,166 | 746 | 68 | 1,420 R | 72.7% | 25.0% | 74.4% | 25.6% |
| 19,715 | LA PAZ | 4,947 | 3,826 | 965 | 156 | 2,861 R | 77.3% | 19.5% | 79.9% | 20.1% |
| 3,072,149 | MARICOPA | 1,163,420 | 917,527 | 216,124 | 29,769 | 701,403 R | 78.9% | 18.6% | 80.9% | 19.1% |
| 155,032 | MOHAVE | 56,511 | 44,402 | 10,423 | 1,686 | 33,979 R | 78.6% | 18.4% | 81.0% | 19.0% |
| 97,470 | NAVAJO | 31,747 | 23,091 | 7,434 | 1,222 | 15,657 R | 72.7% | 23.4% | 75.6% | 24.4% |
| 843,746 | PIMA | 355,473 | 258,010 | 89,483 | 7,980 | 168,527 R | 72.6% | 25.2% | 74.2% | 25.8% |
| 179,727 | PINAL | 63,381 | 48,094 | 13,595 | 1,692 | 34,499 R | 75.9% | 21.4% | 78.0% | 22.0% |
| 38,381 | SANTA CRUZ | 11,337 | 7,502 | 3,583 | 252 | 3,919 R | 66.2% | 31.6% | 67.7% | 32.3% |
| 167,517 | YAVAPAI | 85,324 | 67,312 | 14,852 | 3,160 | 52,460 R | 78.9% | 17.4% | 81.9% | 18.1% |
| 160,026 | YUMA | 37,473 | 28,069 | 8,348 | 1,056 | 19,721 R | 74.9% | 22.3% | 77.1% | 22.9% |
| 5,130,632 | TOTAL | 1,961,677 | 1,505,372 | 404,507 | 51,798 | 1,100,865 R | 76.7% | 20.6% | 78.8% | 21.2% |

# ARIZONA

## HOUSE OF REPRESENTATIVES

| CD | Year | Total Vote | Republican Vote | Republican Candidate | Democratic Vote | Democratic Candidate | Other Vote | Rep.-Dem. Plurality | Total Vote Rep. | Total Vote Dem. | Major Vote Rep. | Major Vote Dem. |
|---|---|---|---|---|---|---|---|---|---|---|---|---|
| 1 | 2004 | 253,351 | 148,315 | Renzi, Rick* | 91,776 | Babbitt, Paul | 13,260 | 56,539 R | 58.5% | 36.2% | 61.8% | 38.2% |
| 1 | 2002 | 174,687 | 85,967 | Renzi, Rick | 79,730 | Cordova, George | 8,990 | 6,237 R | 49.2% | 45.6% | 51.9% | 48.1% |
| 2 | 2004 | 279,303 | 165,260 | Franks, Trent* | 107,406 | Camacho, Randy | 6,637 | 57,854 R | 59.2% | 38.5% | 60.6% | 39.4% |
| 2 | 2002 | 167,502 | 100,359 | Franks, Trent | 61,217 | Camacho, Randy | 5,926 | 39,142 R | 59.9% | 36.5% | 62.1% | 37.9% |
| 3 | 2004 | 225,974 | 181,012 | Shadegg, John* | | | 44,962 | 181,012 R | 80.1% | | 100.0% | |
| 3 | 2002 | 155,751 | 104,847 | Shadegg, John* | 47,173 | Hill, Charles | 3,731 | 57,674 R | 67.3% | 30.3% | 69.0% | 31.0% |
| 4 | 2004 | 110,027 | 28,238 | Karg, Don | 77,150 | Pastor, Ed* | 4,639 | 48,912 D | 25.7% | 70.1% | 26.8% | 73.2% |
| 4 | 2002 | 66,065 | 18,381 | Barnert, Jonathan | 44,517 | Pastor, Ed* | 3,167 | 26,136 D | 27.8% | 67.4% | 29.2% | 70.8% |
| 5 | 2004 | 268,007 | 159,455 | Hayworth, J.D.* | 102,363 | Rogers, Elizabeth | 6,189 | 57,092 R | 59.5% | 38.2% | 60.9% | 39.1% |
| 5 | 2002 | 169,812 | 103,870 | Hayworth, J.D.* | 61,559 | Columbus, Craig | 4,383 | 42,311 R | 61.2% | 36.3% | 62.8% | 37.2% |
| 6 | 2004 | 255,577 | 202,882 | Flake, Jeff* | | | 52,695 | 202,882 R | 79.4% | | 100.0% | |
| 6 | 2002 | 156,337 | 103,094 | Flake, Jeff* | 49,355 | Thomas, Deborah | 3,888 | 53,739 R | 65.9% | 31.6% | 67.6% | 32.4% |
| 7 | 2004 | 175,437 | 59,066 | Sweeney, Joseph | 108,868 | Grijalva, Raul M.* | 7,503 | 49,802 D | 33.7% | 62.1% | 35.2% | 64.8% |
| 7 | 2002 | 103,818 | 38,474 | Hieb, Ross | 61,256 | Grijalva, Raul M. | 4,088 | 22,782 D | 37.1% | 59.0% | 38.6% | 61.4% |
| 8 | 2004 | 303,769 | 183,363 | Kolbe, Jim* | 109,963 | Bacal, Eva | 10,443 | 73,400 R | 60.4% | 36.2% | 62.5% | 37.5% |
| 8 | 2002 | 200,428 | 126,930 | Kolbe, Jim* | 67,328 | Ryan, Mary Judge | 6,170 | 59,602 R | 63.3% | 33.6% | 65.3% | 34.7% |
| Total | 2004 | 1,871,445 | 1,127,591 | | 597,526 | | 146,328 | 530,065 R | 60.3% | 31.9% | 65.4% | 34.6% |
| Total | 2002 | 1,194,400 | 681,922 | | 472,135 | | 40,343 | 209,787 R | 57.1% | 39.5% | 59.1% | 40.9% |

An asterisk (*) denotes incumbent.

# ARIZONA

## GENERAL AND PRIMARY ELECTIONS

### 2004 GENERAL ELECTIONS

**President**  Other vote was 11,856 Libertarian (Michael Badnarik); 2,773 write-in (Ralph Nader); 138 write-in (David Cobb).

**Senator**  Other vote was 51,798 Libertarian (Ernest Hancock).

**House**  Other vote was:

CD 1  13,260 Libertarian (John Crockett).
CD 2  6,625 Libertarian (Powell Gammill); 12 write-in (William Crum).
CD 3  44,962 Libertarian (Mark Yannone).
CD 4  4,639 Libertarian (Gary Fallon).
CD 5  6,189 Libertarian (Michael Kielsky).
CD 6  52,695 Libertarian (Craig Stritar).
CD 7  7,503 Libertarian (Dave Kaplan).
CD 8  10,443 Libertarian (Robert Anderson).

### 2004 PRIMARY ELECTIONS

**Primary**  February 3, 2004 (Democratic President)
September 7, 2004 (Congress)

**Registration** (as of Sept. 1, 2004)

| Republican | 976,280 |
|---|---|
| Democratic | 856,075 |
| Libertarian | 17,429 |
| Other | 590,360 |
| TOTAL | 2,440,144 |

# ARIZONA

## GENERAL AND PRIMARY ELECTIONS

### 2004 PRIMARY ELECTIONS

**Primary Type**  The Democratic presidential primary in February was "closed"—only registered Democrats could participate. The congressional primary in September was "semi-open"—voters registered with a recognized party could participate only in their party's primary. Voters not registered with any political party could participate in the primary of their choice.

Note:  An asterisk (*) denotes incumbent.

| | REPUBLICAN PRIMARIES | | | DEMOCRATIC PRIMARIES | | |
|---|---|---|---|---|---|---|
| President | No Republican primary | | | John Kerry | 101,809 | 42.6% |
| | | | | Wesley Clark | 63,256 | 26.5% |
| | | | | Howard Dean | 33,555 | 14.0% |
| | | | | John Edwards | 16,596 | 6.9% |
| | | | | Joseph I. Lieberman | 15,906 | 6.7% |
| | | | | Dennis J. Kucinich | 3,896 | 1.6% |
| | | | | Al Sharpton | 1,177 | 0.5% |
| | | | | Richard A. Gephardt | 755 | 0.3% |
| | | | | Carol Moseley Braun | 325 | 0.1% |
| | | | | Lyndon H. LaRouche Jr. | 295 | 0.1% |
| | | | | Dianne Barker | 257 | 0.1% |
| | | | | Bill Wyatt | 233 | 0.1% |
| | | | | Keith Brand | 225 | 0.1% |
| | | | | Fern Penna | 208 | 0.1% |
| | | | | William Barchilon | 136 | 0.1% |
| | | | | Huda Muhammad | 119 | |
| | | | | Evelyn L. Vitullo | 117 | |
| | | | | Ray Caplette | 77 | |
| | | | | TOTAL | 238,942 | |
| Senator | John McCain* | 331,720 | 100.0% | Stuart Starky | 173,540 | 100.0% |
| Congressional District 1 | Rick Renzi* | 36,723 | 100.0% | Paul Babbitt | 35,422 | 73.7% |
| | | | | Bob Donahue | 12,629 | 26.3% |
| | | | | TOTAL | 48,051 | |
| Congressional District 2 | Trent Franks* | 45,261 | 63.6% | Randy Camacho | 12,833 | 52.7% |
| | Rick L. Murphy | 25,871 | 36.4% | Gene Scharer | 5,875 | 24.1% |
| | | | | Larry Coor | 5,652 | 23.2% |
| | TOTAL | 71,132 | | TOTAL | 24,360 | |
| Congressional District 3 | John Shadegg* | 43,552 | 100.0% | No Democratic candidate | | |
| Congressional District 4 | Don Karg | 8,854 | 100.0% | Ed Pastor* | 15,201 | 100.0% |
| Congressional District 5 | J.D. Hayworth* | 43,166 | 79.3% | Elizabeth Rogers | 11,362 | 69.5% |
| | Roselyn O'Connell | 11,296 | 20.7% | Ronald Maynard | 4,985 | 30.5% |
| | TOTAL | 54,462 | | TOTAL | 16,347 | |
| Congressional District 6 | Jeff Flake* | 33,784 | 59.3% | No Democratic candidate | | |
| | Stan Barnes | 23,186 | 40.7% | | | |
| | TOTAL | 56,970 | | | | |
| Congressional District 7 | Joseph Sweeney | 11,990 | 70.1% | Raul M. Grijalva* | 26,450 | 100.0% |
| | Lou Muñoz | 5,107 | 29.9% | | | |
| | TOTAL | 17,097 | | | | |
| Congressional District 8 | Jim Kolbe* | 36,039 | 57.5% | Eva Bacal | 20,216 | 58.6% |
| | Randy Graf | 26,686 | 42.5% | Tim Sultan | 9,177 | 26.6% |
| | | | | Jeffrey "Jeff" Chimene | 5,093 | 14.8% |
| | TOTAL | 62,725 | | TOTAL | 34,486 | |

# ARKANSAS

## GOVERNOR

Mike Huckabee (R). Reelected 2002 to a four-year term. Had become governor in July 1996 upon the resignation of Governor Jim Guy Tucker (D) who was convicted on fraud and conspiracy charges. Huckabee won his first full term in 1998.

## SENATORS (2 Democrats)

Blanche Lincoln (D). Reelected 2004 to a six-year term. Previously elected 1998.

Mark Pryor (D). Elected 2002 to a six-year term.

## REPRESENTATIVES (3 Democrats, 1 Republican)

1. Marion Berry (D)
2. Vic Snyder (D)
3. John Boozman (R)
4. Mike Ross (D)

## POSTWAR VOTE FOR PRESIDENT

| | | Republican | | Democratic | | Other | | Percentage | | | |
| | | | | | | | | Total Vote | | Major Vote | |
| Year | Total Vote | Vote | Candidate | Vote | Candidate | Vote | Plurality | Rep. | Dem. | Rep. | Dem. |
|---|---|---|---|---|---|---|---|---|---|---|---|
| 2004 | 1,054,945 | 572,898 | Bush, George W. | 469,953 | Kerry, John | 12,094 | 102,945 R | 54.3% | 44.5% | 54.9% | 45.1% |
| 2000** | 921,781 | 472,940 | Bush, George W. | 422,768 | Gore, Al | 26,073 | 50,172 R | 51.3% | 45.9% | 52.8% | 47.2% |
| 1996** | 884,262 | 325,416 | Dole, Bob | 475,171 | Clinton, Bill | 83,675 | 149,755 D | 36.8% | 53.7% | 40.6% | 59.4% |
| 1992** | 950,653 | 337,324 | Bush, George | 505,823 | Clinton, Bill | 107,506 | 168,499 D | 35.5% | 53.2% | 40.0% | 60.0% |
| 1988 | 827,738 | 466,578 | Bush, George | 349,237 | Dukakis, Michael S. | 11,923 | 117,341 R | 56.4% | 42.2% | 57.2% | 42.8% |
| 1984 | 884,406 | 534,774 | Reagan, Ronald | 338,646 | Mondale, Walter F. | 10,986 | 196,128 R | 60.5% | 38.3% | 61.2% | 38.8% |
| 1980** | 837,582 | 403,164 | Reagan, Ronald | 398,041 | Carter, Jimmy | 36,377 | 5,123 R | 48.1% | 47.5% | 50.3% | 49.7% |
| 1976 | 767,535 | 267,903 | Ford, Gerald R. | 498,604 | Carter, Jimmy | 1,028 | 230,701 D | 34.9% | 65.0% | 35.0% | 65.0% |
| 1972 | 651,320 | 448,541 | Nixon, Richard M. | 199,892 | McGovern, George S. | 2,887 | 248,649 R | 68.9% | 30.7% | 69.2% | 30.8% |
| 1968** | 619,969 | 190,759 | Nixon, Richard M. | 188,228 | Humphrey, Hubert H. | 240,982 | 50,223 A | 30.8% | 30.4% | 50.3% | 49.7% |
| 1964 | 560,426 | 243,264 | Goldwater, Barry M. | 314,197 | Johnson, Lyndon B. | 2,965 | 70,933 D | 43.4% | 56.1% | 43.6% | 56.4% |
| 1960 | 428,509 | 184,508 | Nixon, Richard M. | 215,049 | Kennedy, John F. | 28,952 | 30,541 D | 43.1% | 50.2% | 46.2% | 53.8% |
| 1956 | 406,572 | 186,287 | Eisenhower, Dwight D. | 213,277 | Stevenson, Adlai E. | 7,008 | 26,990 D | 45.8% | 52.5% | 46.6% | 53.4% |
| 1952 | 404,800 | 177,155 | Eisenhower, Dwight D. | 226,300 | Stevenson, Adlai E. | 1,345 | 49,145 D | 43.8% | 55.9% | 43.9% | 56.1% |
| 1948** | 242,475 | 50,959 | Dewey, Thomas E. | 149,659 | Truman, Harry S. | 41,857 | 98,700 D | 21.0% | 61.7% | 25.4% | 74.6% |

In past elections, the other vote included: 2000 - 13,421 Green (Ralph Nader); 1996 - 69,884 Reform (Ross Perot); 1992 - 99,132 Independent (Perot); 1980 - 22,468 Independent (John Anderson); 1968 - 240,982 American Independent (George Wallace); 1948 - 40,068 States' Rights (Strom Thurmond).

# ARKANSAS

## POSTWAR VOTE FOR GOVERNOR

| Year | Total Vote | Republican Vote | Republican Candidate | Democratic Vote | Democratic Candidate | Other Vote | Rep.-Dem. Plurality | Percentage Total Vote Rep. | Percentage Total Vote Dem. | Percentage Major Vote Rep. | Percentage Major Vote Dem. |
|---|---|---|---|---|---|---|---|---|---|---|---|
| 2002 | 805,696 | 427,082 | Huckabee, Mike | 378,250 | Fisher, Jimmie Lou | 364 | 48,832 R | 53.0% | 46.9% | 53.0% | 47.0% |
| 1998 | 706,011 | 421,989 | Huckabee, Mike | 272,923 | Bristow, Bill | 11,099 | 149,066 R | 59.8% | 38.7% | 60.7% | 39.3% |
| 1994 | 716,840 | 287,904 | Nelson, Sheffield | 428,936 | Tucker, Jim Guy | | 141,032 D | 40.2% | 59.8% | 40.2% | 59.8% |
| 1990 | 696,412 | 295,925 | Nelson, Sheffield | 400,386 | Clinton, Bill | 101 | 104,461 D | 42.5% | 57.5% | 42.5% | 57.5% |
| 1986** | 688,551 | 248,427 | White, Frank D. | 439,882 | Clinton, Bill | 242 | 191,455 D | 36.1% | 63.9% | 36.1% | 63.9% |
| 1984 | 886,548 | 331,987 | Freeman, Woody | 554,561 | Clinton, Bill | | 222,574 D | 37.4% | 62.6% | 37.4% | 62.6% |
| 1982 | 789,351 | 357,496 | White, Frank D. | 431,855 | Clinton, Bill | | 74,359 D | 45.3% | 54.7% | 45.3% | 54.7% |
| 1980 | 838,925 | 435,684 | White, Frank D. | 403,241 | Clinton, Bill | | 32,443 R | 51.9% | 48.1% | 51.9% | 48.1% |
| 1978 | 528,912 | 193,746 | Lowe, A. Lynn | 335,101 | Clinton, Bill | 65 | 141,355 D | 36.6% | 63.4% | 36.6% | 63.4% |
| 1976 | 726,949 | 121,716 | Griffith, Leon | 605,083 | Pryor, David H. | 150 | 483,367 D | 16.7% | 83.2% | 16.7% | 83.3% |
| 1974 | 545,974 | 187,872 | Coon, Ken | 358,018 | Pryor, David H. | 84 | 170,146 D | 34.4% | 65.6% | 34.4% | 65.6% |
| 1972 | 648,069 | 159,177 | Blaylock, Len E. | 488,892 | Bumpers, Dale | | 329,715 D | 24.6% | 75.4% | 24.6% | 75.4% |
| 1970 | 609,198 | 197,418 | Rockefeller, Winthrop | 375,648 | Bumpers, Dale | 36,132 | 178,230 D | 32.4% | 61.7% | 34.4% | 65.6% |
| 1968 | 615,595 | 322,782 | Rockefeller, Winthrop | 292,813 | Crank, Marion | | 29,969 R | 52.4% | 47.6% | 52.4% | 47.6% |
| 1966 | 563,527 | 306,324 | Rockefeller, Winthrop | 257,203 | Johnson, James D. | | 49,121 R | 54.4% | 45.6% | 54.4% | 45.6% |
| 1964 | 592,113 | 254,561 | Rockefeller, Winthrop | 337,489 | Faubus, Orval E. | 63 | 82,928 D | 43.0% | 57.0% | 43.0% | 57.0% |
| 1962 | 308,092 | 82,349 | Ricketts, Willis | 225,743 | Faubus, Orval E. | | 143,394 D | 26.7% | 73.3% | 26.7% | 73.3% |
| 1960 | 421,985 | 129,921 | Britt, Henry M. | 292,064 | Faubus, Orval E. | | 162,143 D | 30.8% | 69.2% | 30.8% | 69.2% |
| 1958 | 286,886 | 50,288 | Johnson, George W. | 236,598 | Faubus, Orval E. | | 186,310 D | 17.5% | 82.5% | 17.5% | 82.5% |
| 1956 | 399,012 | 77,215 | Mitchell, Roy | 321,797 | Faubus, Orval E. | | 244,582 D | 19.4% | 80.6% | 19.4% | 80.6% |
| 1954 | 335,176 | 127,004 | Remmel, Pratt C. | 208,121 | Faubus, Orval E. | 51 | 81,117 D | 37.9% | 62.1% | 37.9% | 62.1% |
| 1952 | 391,592 | 49,292 | Speck, Jefferson W. | 342,292 | Cherry, Francis | 8 | 293,000 D | 12.6% | 87.4% | 12.6% | 87.4% |
| 1950 | 317,087 | 50,309 | Speck, Jefferson W. | 266,778 | McMath, Sidney S. | | 216,469 D | 15.9% | 84.1% | 15.9% | 84.1% |
| 1948 | 249,301 | 26,500 | Black, Charles R. | 222,801 | McMath, Sidney S. | | 196,301 D | 10.6% | 89.4% | 10.6% | 89.4% |
| 1946 | 152,162 | 24,133 | Mills, W. T. | 128,029 | Laney, Ben T. | | 103,896 D | 15.9% | 84.1% | 15.9% | 84.1% |

The term of office for Arkansas' governor was increased from two to four years effective with the 1986 election.

## POSTWAR VOTE FOR SENATOR

| Year | Total Vote | Republican Vote | Republican Candidate | Democratic Vote | Democratic Candidate | Other Vote | Rep.-Dem. Plurality | Percentage Total Vote Rep. | Percentage Total Vote Dem. | Percentage Major Vote Rep. | Percentage Major Vote Dem. |
|---|---|---|---|---|---|---|---|---|---|---|---|
| 2004 | 1,039,349 | 458,036 | Holt, Jim | 580,973 | Lincoln, Blanche | 340 | 122,937 D | 44.1% | 55.9% | 44.1% | 55.9% |
| 2002 | 803,959 | 370,653 | Hutchinson, Tim | 433,306 | Pryor, Mark | | 62,653 D | 46.1% | 53.9% | 46.1% | 53.9% |
| 1998 | 700,644 | 295,870 | Boozman, Fay | 385,878 | Lincoln, Blanche | 18,896 | 90,008 D | 42.2% | 55.1% | 43.4% | 56.6% |
| 1996 | 846,183 | 445,942 | Hutchinson, Tim | 400,241 | Bryant, Winston | | 45,701 R | 52.7% | 47.3% | 52.7% | 47.3% |
| 1992 | 920,008 | 366,373 | Huckabee, Mike | 553,635 | Bumpers, Dale | | 187,262 D | 39.8% | 60.2% | 39.8% | 60.2% |
| 1990** | 494,735 | | — | 493,910 | Pryor, David H. | 825 | 493,910 D | | 99.8% | | 100.0% |
| 1986 | 695,487 | 262,313 | Hutchinson, Asa | 433,122 | Bumpers, Dale | 52 | 170,809 D | 37.7% | 62.3% | 37.7% | 62.3% |
| 1984 | 875,956 | 373,615 | Bethune, Ed | 502,341 | Pryor, David H. | | 128,726 D | 42.7% | 57.3% | 42.7% | 57.3% |
| 1980 | 808,812 | 330,576 | Clark, Bill | 477,905 | Bumpers, Dale | 331 | 147,329 D | 40.9% | 59.1% | 40.9% | 59.1% |
| 1978 | 522,239 | 84,722 | Kelly, Tom | 399,916 | Pryor, David H. | 37,601 | 315,194 D | 16.2% | 76.6% | 17.5% | 82.5% |
| 1974 | 543,082 | 82,026 | Jones, John H. | 461,056 | Bumpers, Dale | | 379,030 D | 15.1% | 84.9% | 15.1% | 84.9% |
| 1972 | 634,636 | 248,238 | Babbitt, Wayne H. | 386,398 | McClellan, John L. | | 138,160 D | 39.1% | 60.9% | 39.1% | 60.9% |
| 1968 | 591,704 | 241,739 | Bernard, Charles T. | 349,965 | Fulbright, J. W. | | 108,226 D | 40.9% | 59.1% | 40.9% | 59.1% |
| 1966** | | | — | | McClellan, John L. | | D | | | | |
| 1962 | 312,880 | 98,013 | Jones, Kenneth | 214,867 | Fulbright, J. W. | | 116,854 D | 31.3% | 68.7% | 31.3% | 68.7% |
| 1960** | | | — | | McClellan, John L. | | D | | | | |
| 1956 | 399,695 | 68,016 | Henley, Ben C. | 331,679 | Fulbright, J. W. | | 263,663 D | 17.0% | 83.0% | 17.0% | 83.0% |
| 1954 | 291,058 | | — | 291,058 | McClellan, John L. | | 291,058 D | | 100.0% | | 100.0% |
| 1950 | 302,582 | | — | 302,582 | Fulbright, J. W. | | 302,582 D | | 100.0% | | 100.0% |
| 1948 | 216,401 | | — | 216,401 | McClellan, John L. | | 216,401 D | | 100.0% | | 100.0% |

In 1990 Senator Pryor's vote was not canvassed in seven counties because he was unopposed. Senator McClellan was reelected in 1966 and in 1960, but his vote was not canvassed in many counties.

# ARKANSAS

Congressional districts first established for elections held in 2002
4 members

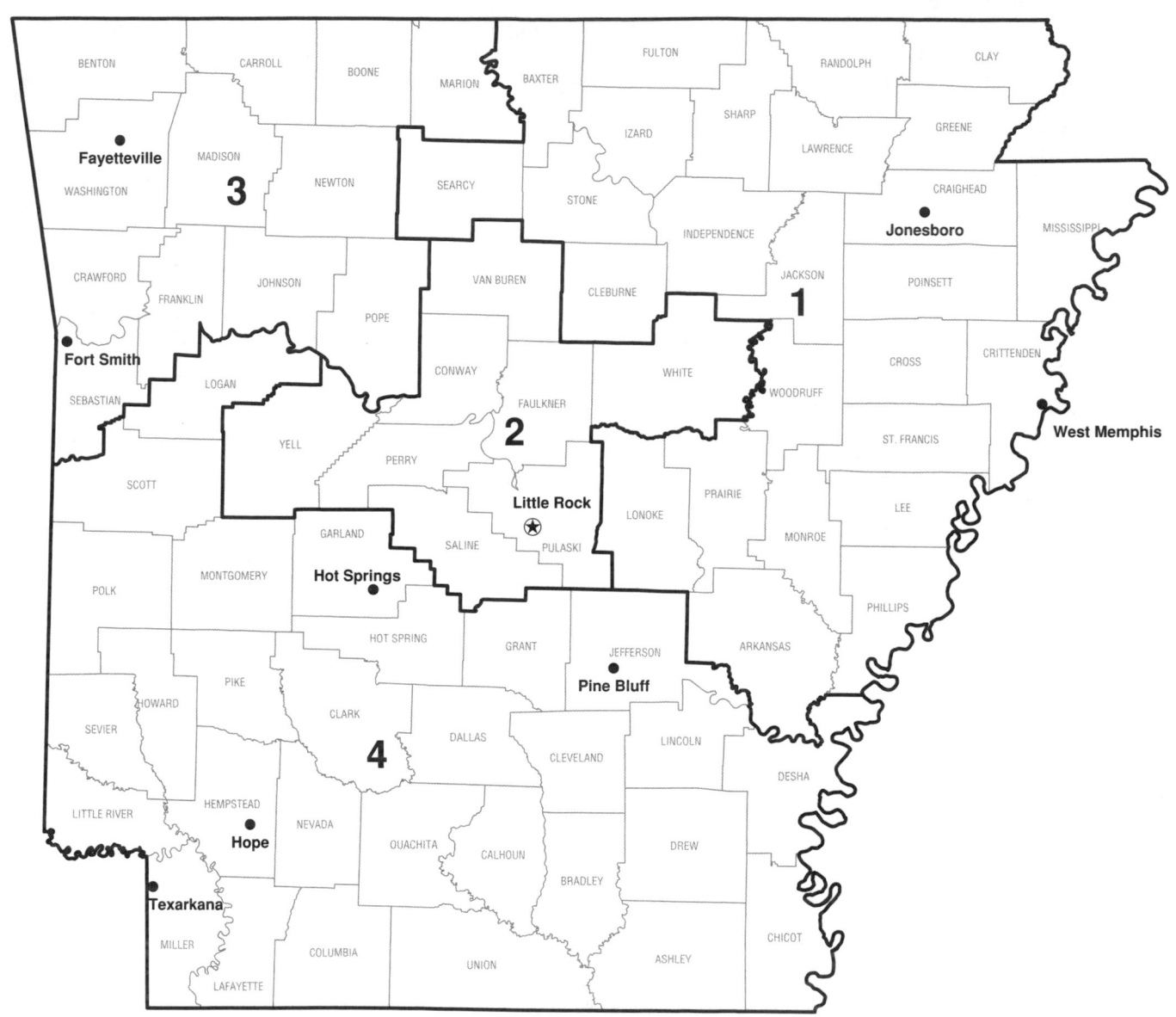

# ARKANSAS

## PRESIDENT 2004

| 2000 Census Population | County | Total Vote | Republican | Democratic | Other | Rep.-Dem. Plurality | | Percentage | | | |
|---|---|---|---|---|---|---|---|---|---|---|---|
| | | | | | | | | Total Vote | | Major Vote | |
| | | | | | | | | Rep. | Dem. | Rep. | Dem. |
| 20,749 | ARKANSAS | 6,946 | 3,789 | 3,110 | 47 | 679 | R | 54.5% | 44.8% | 54.9% | 45.1% |
| 24,209 | ASHLEY | 8,512 | 4,567 | 3,881 | 64 | 686 | R | 53.7% | 45.6% | 54.1% | 45.9% |
| 38,386 | BAXTER | 18,530 | 11,128 | 7,129 | 273 | 3,999 | R | 60.1% | 38.5% | 61.0% | 39.0% |
| 153,406 | BENTON | 68,121 | 46,571 | 20,756 | 794 | 25,815 | R | 68.4% | 30.5% | 69.2% | 30.8% |
| 33,948 | BOONE | 14,777 | 9,793 | 4,640 | 344 | 5,153 | R | 66.3% | 31.4% | 67.9% | 32.1% |
| 12,600 | BRADLEY | 4,249 | 2,011 | 2,206 | 32 | 195 | D | 47.3% | 51.9% | 47.7% | 52.3% |
| 5,744 | CALHOUN | 2,299 | 1,340 | 939 | 20 | 401 | R | 58.3% | 40.8% | 58.8% | 41.2% |
| 25,357 | CARROLL | 10,481 | 6,184 | 4,161 | 136 | 2,023 | R | 59.0% | 39.7% | 59.8% | 40.2% |
| 14,117 | CHICOT | 4,757 | 1,725 | 2,993 | 39 | 1,268 | D | 36.3% | 62.9% | 36.6% | 63.4% |
| 23,546 | CLARK | 9,211 | 4,144 | 4,990 | 77 | 846 | D | 45.0% | 54.2% | 45.4% | 54.6% |
| 17,609 | CLAY | 6,096 | 2,759 | 3,264 | 73 | 505 | D | 45.3% | 53.5% | 45.8% | 54.2% |
| 24,046 | CLEBURNE | 11,761 | 7,107 | 4,517 | 137 | 2,590 | R | 60.4% | 38.4% | 61.1% | 38.9% |
| 8,571 | CLEVELAND | 3,496 | 2,009 | 1,450 | 37 | 559 | R | 57.5% | 41.5% | 58.1% | 41.9% |
| 25,603 | COLUMBIA | 9,909 | 5,729 | 4,108 | 72 | 1,621 | R | 57.8% | 41.5% | 58.2% | 41.8% |
| 20,336 | CONWAY | 8,084 | 4,009 | 3,982 | 93 | 27 | R | 49.6% | 49.3% | 50.2% | 49.8% |
| 82,148 | CRAIGHEAD | 29,801 | 15,818 | 13,665 | 318 | 2,153 | R | 53.1% | 45.9% | 53.7% | 46.3% |
| 53,247 | CRAWFORD | 20,401 | 13,391 | 6,764 | 246 | 6,627 | R | 65.6% | 33.2% | 66.4% | 33.6% |
| 50,866 | CRITTENDEN | 15,300 | 6,930 | 8,277 | 93 | 1,347 | D | 45.3% | 54.1% | 45.6% | 54.4% |
| 19,526 | CROSS | 7,074 | 3,864 | 3,135 | 75 | 729 | R | 54.6% | 44.3% | 55.2% | 44.8% |
| 9,210 | DALLAS | 3,388 | 1,700 | 1,671 | 17 | 29 | R | 50.2% | 49.3% | 50.4% | 49.6% |
| 15,341 | DESHA | 4,647 | 1,729 | 2,851 | 67 | 1,122 | D | 37.2% | 61.4% | 37.8% | 62.2% |
| 18,723 | DREW | 6,249 | 3,262 | 2,952 | 35 | 310 | R | 52.2% | 47.2% | 52.5% | 47.5% |
| 86,014 | FAULKNER | 36,686 | 21,514 | 14,538 | 634 | 6,976 | R | 58.6% | 39.6% | 59.7% | 40.3% |
| 17,771 | FRANKLIN | 7,289 | 4,181 | 3,008 | 100 | 1,173 | R | 57.4% | 41.3% | 58.2% | 41.8% |
| 11,642 | FULTON | 4,955 | 2,522 | 2,370 | 63 | 152 | R | 50.9% | 47.8% | 51.6% | 48.4% |
| 88,068 | GARLAND | 40,154 | 21,734 | 18,040 | 380 | 3,694 | R | 54.1% | 44.9% | 54.6% | 45.4% |
| 16,464 | GRANT | 6,770 | 4,205 | 2,524 | 41 | 1,681 | R | 62.1% | 37.3% | 62.5% | 37.5% |
| 37,331 | GREENE | 13,955 | 7,237 | 6,564 | 154 | 673 | R | 51.9% | 47.0% | 52.4% | 47.6% |
| 23,587 | HEMPSTEAD | 7,452 | 3,580 | 3,817 | 55 | 237 | D | 48.0% | 51.2% | 48.4% | 51.6% |
| 30,353 | HOT SPRING | 12,065 | 5,960 | 5,901 | 204 | 59 | R | 49.4% | 48.9% | 50.2% | 49.8% |
| 14,300 | HOWARD | 4,943 | 2,736 | 2,166 | 41 | 570 | R | 55.4% | 43.8% | 55.8% | 44.2% |
| 34,233 | INDEPENDENCE | 13,011 | 7,430 | 5,443 | 138 | 1,987 | R | 57.1% | 41.8% | 57.7% | 42.3% |
| 13,249 | IZARD | 5,493 | 2,833 | 2,586 | 74 | 247 | R | 51.6% | 47.1% | 52.3% | 47.7% |
| 18,418 | JACKSON | 6,219 | 2,624 | 3,515 | 80 | 891 | D | 42.2% | 56.5% | 42.7% | 57.3% |
| 84,278 | JEFFERSON | 30,493 | 10,218 | 19,675 | 600 | 9,457 | D | 33.5% | 64.5% | 34.2% | 65.8% |
| 22,781 | JOHNSON | 8,044 | 4,311 | 3,622 | 111 | 689 | R | 53.6% | 45.0% | 54.3% | 45.7% |
| 8,559 | LAFAYETTE | 3,191 | 1,604 | 1,567 | 20 | 37 | R | 50.3% | 49.1% | 50.6% | 49.4% |
| 17,774 | LAWRENCE | 6,615 | 2,951 | 3,544 | 120 | 593 | D | 44.6% | 53.6% | 45.4% | 54.6% |
| 12,580 | LEE | 4,080 | 1,492 | 2,548 | 40 | 1,056 | D | 36.6% | 62.5% | 36.9% | 63.1% |
| 14,492 | LINCOLN | 4,109 | 1,921 | 2,149 | 39 | 228 | D | 46.8% | 52.3% | 47.2% | 52.8% |
| 13,628 | LITTLE RIVER | 5,294 | 2,575 | 2,677 | 42 | 102 | D | 48.6% | 50.6% | 49.0% | 51.0% |
| 22,486 | LOGAN | 8,551 | 5,076 | 3,361 | 114 | 1,715 | R | 59.4% | 39.3% | 60.2% | 39.8% |
| 52,828 | LONOKE | 22,030 | 14,398 | 7,454 | 178 | 6,944 | R | 65.4% | 33.8% | 65.9% | 34.1% |
| 14,243 | MADISON | 6,384 | 3,873 | 2,421 | 90 | 1,452 | R | 60.7% | 37.9% | 61.5% | 38.5% |
| 16,140 | MARION | 6,867 | 4,127 | 2,602 | 138 | 1,525 | R | 60.1% | 37.9% | 61.3% | 38.7% |
| 40,443 | MILLER | 14,678 | 8,448 | 6,139 | 91 | 2,309 | R | 57.6% | 41.8% | 57.9% | 42.1% |
| 51,979 | MISSISSIPPI | 14,153 | 6,121 | 7,593 | 439 | 1,472 | D | 43.2% | 53.6% | 44.6% | 55.4% |
| 10,254 | MONROE | 3,667 | 1,586 | 2,049 | 32 | 463 | D | 43.3% | 55.9% | 43.6% | 56.4% |
| 9,245 | MONTGOMERY | 3,958 | 2,367 | 1,524 | 67 | 843 | R | 59.8% | 38.5% | 60.8% | 39.2% |
| 9,955 | NEVADA | 3,477 | 1,752 | 1,694 | 31 | 58 | R | 50.4% | 48.7% | 50.8% | 49.2% |
| 8,608 | NEWTON | 4,378 | 2,779 | 1,506 | 93 | 1,273 | R | 63.5% | 34.4% | 64.9% | 35.1% |
| 28,790 | OUACHITA | 10,650 | 5,345 | 5,188 | 117 | 157 | R | 50.2% | 48.7% | 50.7% | 49.3% |
| 10,209 | PERRY | 4,431 | 2,435 | 1,921 | 75 | 514 | R | 55.0% | 43.4% | 55.9% | 44.1% |
| 26,445 | PHILLIPS | 8,868 | 3,161 | 5,642 | 65 | 2,481 | D | 35.6% | 63.6% | 35.9% | 64.1% |
| 11,303 | PIKE | 3,367 | 2,013 | 1,310 | 44 | 703 | R | 59.8% | 38.9% | 60.6% | 39.4% |
| 25,614 | POINSETT | 7,723 | 3,555 | 4,069 | 99 | 514 | D | 46.0% | 52.7% | 46.6% | 53.4% |
| 20,229 | POLK | 7,799 | 5,192 | 2,473 | 134 | 2,719 | R | 66.6% | 31.7% | 67.7% | 32.3% |
| 54,469 | POPE | 20,902 | 13,614 | 7,100 | 188 | 6,514 | R | 65.1% | 34.0% | 65.7% | 34.3% |
| 9,539 | PRAIRIE | 3,624 | 2,030 | 1,562 | 32 | 468 | R | 56.0% | 43.1% | 56.5% | 43.5% |
| 361,474 | PULASKI | 153,620 | 67,903 | 84,532 | 1,185 | 16,629 | D | 44.2% | 55.0% | 44.5% | 55.5% |

# ARKANSAS

## PRESIDENT 2004

| 2000 Census Population | County | Total Vote | Republican | Democratic | Other | Rep.-Dem. Plurality | Percentage | | | |
|---|---|---|---|---|---|---|---|---|---|---|
| | | | | | | | Total Vote | | Major Vote | |
| | | | | | | | Rep. | Dem. | Rep. | Dem. |
| 18,195 | RANDOLPH | 6,667 | 3,158 | 3,412 | 97 | 254 D | 47.4% | 51.2% | 48.1% | 51.9% |
| 29,329 | ST. FRANCIS | 9,588 | 3,815 | 5,684 | 89 | 1,869 D | 39.8% | 59.3% | 40.2% | 59.8% |
| 83,529 | SALINE | 39,376 | 24,864 | 14,153 | 359 | 10,711 R | 63.1% | 35.9% | 63.7% | 36.3% |
| 10,996 | SCOTT | 4,038 | 2,514 | 1,473 | 51 | 1,041 R | 62.3% | 36.5% | 63.1% | 36.9% |
| 8,261 | SEARCY | 3,992 | 2,565 | 1,370 | 57 | 1,195 R | 64.3% | 34.3% | 65.2% | 34.8% |
| 115,071 | SEBASTIAN | 44,211 | 27,303 | 16,479 | 429 | 10,824 R | 61.8% | 37.3% | 62.4% | 37.6% |
| 15,757 | SEVIER | 4,601 | 2,516 | 2,035 | 50 | 481 R | 54.7% | 44.2% | 55.3% | 44.7% |
| 17,119 | SHARP | 7,470 | 4,097 | 3,265 | 108 | 832 R | 54.8% | 43.7% | 55.7% | 44.3% |
| 11,499 | STONE | 5,549 | 3,188 | 2,255 | 106 | 933 R | 57.5% | 40.6% | 58.6% | 41.4% |
| 45,629 | UNION | 17,832 | 10,502 | 7,071 | 259 | 3,431 R | 58.9% | 39.7% | 59.8% | 40.2% |
| 16,192 | VAN BUREN | 7,374 | 3,988 | 3,310 | 76 | 678 R | 54.1% | 44.9% | 54.6% | 45.4% |
| 157,715 | WASHINGTON | 64,103 | 35,726 | 27,597 | 780 | 8,129 R | 55.7% | 43.1% | 56.4% | 43.6% |
| 67,165 | WHITE | 26,425 | 17,001 | 9,129 | 295 | 7,872 R | 64.3% | 34.5% | 65.1% | 34.9% |
| 8,741 | WOODRUFF | 3,026 | 1,021 | 1,972 | 33 | 951 D | 33.7% | 65.2% | 34.1% | 65.9% |
| 21,139 | YELL | 6,659 | 3,678 | 2,913 | 68 | 765 R | 55.2% | 43.7% | 55.8% | 44.2% |
| 2,673,400 | TOTAL | 1,054,945 | 572,898 | 469,953 | 12,094 | 102,945 R | 54.3% | 44.5% | 54.9% | 45.1% |

# ARKANSAS

## SENATOR 2004

| 2000 Census Population | County | Total Vote | Republican | Democratic | Other | Rep.-Dem. Plurality | Percentage | | | |
|---|---|---|---|---|---|---|---|---|---|---|
| | | | | | | | Total Vote | | Major Vote | |
| | | | | | | | Rep. | Dem. | Rep. | Dem. |
| 20,749 | ARKANSAS | 6,942 | 2,442 | 4,500 | | 2,058 D | 35.2% | 64.8% | 35.2% | 64.8% |
| 24,209 | ASHLEY | 8,615 | 3,691 | 4,909 | 15 | 1,218 D | 42.8% | 57.0% | 42.9% | 57.1% |
| 38,386 | BAXTER | 16,633 | 8,775 | 7,858 | | 917 R | 52.8% | 47.2% | 52.8% | 47.2% |
| 153,406 | BENTON | 66,904 | 39,010 | 27,894 | | 11,116 R | 58.3% | 41.7% | 58.3% | 41.7% |
| 33,948 | BOONE | 13,769 | 7,660 | 6,105 | 4 | 1,555 R | 55.6% | 44.3% | 55.6% | 44.4% |
| 12,600 | BRADLEY | 4,266 | 1,561 | 2,705 | | 1,144 D | 36.6% | 63.4% | 36.6% | 63.4% |
| 5,744 | CALHOUN | 2,282 | 1,026 | 1,230 | 26 | 204 D | 45.0% | 53.9% | 45.5% | 54.5% |
| 25,357 | CARROLL | 10,396 | 5,377 | 5,013 | 6 | 364 R | 51.7% | 48.2% | 51.8% | 48.2% |
| 14,117 | CHICOT | 4,628 | 1,299 | 3,329 | | 2,030 D | 28.1% | 71.9% | 28.1% | 71.9% |
| 23,546 | CLARK | 9,164 | 3,252 | 5,908 | 4 | 2,656 D | 35.5% | 64.5% | 35.5% | 64.5% |
| 17,609 | CLAY | 6,105 | 2,019 | 4,086 | | 2,067 D | 33.1% | 66.9% | 33.1% | 66.9% |
| 24,046 | CLEBURNE | 11,752 | 5,897 | 5,855 | | 42 R | 50.2% | 49.8% | 50.2% | 49.8% |
| 8,571 | CLEVELAND | 3,509 | 1,675 | 1,833 | 1 | 158 D | 47.7% | 52.2% | 47.7% | 52.3% |
| 25,603 | COLUMBIA | 9,380 | 4,142 | 5,238 | | 1,096 D | 44.2% | 55.8% | 44.2% | 55.8% |
| 20,336 | CONWAY | 7,998 | 3,124 | 4,874 | | 1,750 D | 39.1% | 60.9% | 39.1% | 60.9% |
| 82,148 | CRAIGHEAD | 29,699 | 12,496 | 17,167 | 36 | 4,671 D | 42.1% | 57.8% | 42.1% | 57.9% |
| 53,247 | CRAWFORD | 20,488 | 11,658 | 8,827 | 3 | 2,831 R | 56.9% | 43.1% | 56.9% | 43.1% |
| 50,866 | CRITTENDEN | 16,648 | 5,700 | 10,940 | 8 | 5,240 D | 34.2% | 65.7% | 34.3% | 65.7% |
| 19,526 | CROSS | 6,743 | 2,938 | 3,805 | | 867 D | 43.6% | 56.4% | 43.6% | 56.4% |
| 9,210 | DALLAS | 3,472 | 1,307 | 2,165 | | 858 D | 37.6% | 62.4% | 37.6% | 62.4% |
| 15,341 | DESHA | 4,227 | 1,097 | 3,130 | | 2,033 D | 26.0% | 74.0% | 26.0% | 74.0% |
| 18,723 | DREW | 6,291 | 2,482 | 3,809 | | 1,327 D | 39.5% | 60.5% | 39.5% | 60.5% |
| 86,014 | FAULKNER | 34,238 | 16,607 | 17,627 | 4 | 1,020 D | 48.5% | 51.5% | 48.5% | 51.5% |
| 17,771 | FRANKLIN | 7,216 | 3,479 | 3,737 | | 258 D | 48.2% | 51.8% | 48.2% | 51.8% |
| 11,642 | FULTON | 4,924 | 1,879 | 3,045 | | 1,166 D | 38.2% | 61.8% | 38.2% | 61.8% |
| 88,068 | GARLAND | 39,660 | 17,571 | 22,086 | 3 | 4,515 D | 44.3% | 55.7% | 44.3% | 55.7% |
| 16,464 | GRANT | 6,779 | 3,382 | 3,397 | | 15 D | 49.9% | 50.1% | 49.9% | 50.1% |
| 37,331 | GREENE | 14,085 | 5,914 | 8,154 | 17 | 2,240 D | 42.0% | 57.9% | 42.0% | 58.0% |
| 23,587 | HEMPSTEAD | 7,439 | 2,688 | 4,746 | 5 | 2,058 D | 36.1% | 63.8% | 36.2% | 63.8% |
| 30,353 | HOT SPRING | 11,543 | 4,861 | 6,682 | | 1,821 D | 42.1% | 57.9% | 42.1% | 57.9% |

# ARKANSAS
## SENATOR 2004

| 2000 Census Population | County | Total Vote | Republican | Democratic | Other | Rep.-Dem. Plurality | | Total Vote Rep. | Dem. | Major Vote Rep. | Dem. |
|---|---|---|---|---|---|---|---|---|---|---|---|
| 14,300 | HOWARD | 4,942 | 2,076 | 2,864 | 2 | 788 | D | 42.0% | 58.0% | 42.0% | 58.0% |
| 34,233 | INDEPENDENCE | 13,112 | 5,606 | 7,503 | 3 | 1,897 | D | 42.8% | 57.2% | 42.8% | 57.2% |
| 13,249 | IZARD | 5,354 | 2,195 | 3,158 | 1 | 963 | D | 41.0% | 59.0% | 41.0% | 59.0% |
| 18,418 | JACKSON | 6,250 | 2,004 | 4,246 | | 2,242 | D | 32.1% | 67.9% | 32.1% | 67.9% |
| 84,278 | JEFFERSON | 27,925 | 7,466 | 20,459 | | 12,993 | D | 26.7% | 73.3% | 26.7% | 73.3% |
| 22,781 | JOHNSON | 7,943 | 3,651 | 4,292 | | 641 | D | 46.0% | 54.0% | 46.0% | 54.0% |
| 8,559 | LAFAYETTE | 3,229 | 1,200 | 2,029 | | 829 | D | 37.2% | 62.8% | 37.2% | 62.8% |
| 17,774 | LAWRENCE | 6,640 | 2,422 | 4,139 | 79 | 1,717 | D | 36.5% | 62.3% | 36.9% | 63.1% |
| 12,580 | LEE | 4,145 | 861 | 3,284 | | 2,423 | D | 20.8% | 79.2% | 20.8% | 79.2% |
| 14,492 | LINCOLN | 4,147 | 1,325 | 2,815 | 7 | 1,490 | D | 32.0% | 67.9% | 32.0% | 68.0% |
| 13,628 | LITTLE RIVER | 5,328 | 1,980 | 3,348 | | 1,368 | D | 37.2% | 62.8% | 37.2% | 62.8% |
| 22,486 | LOGAN | 8,477 | 4,207 | 4,270 | | 63 | D | 49.6% | 50.4% | 49.6% | 50.4% |
| 52,828 | LONOKE | 21,900 | 11,254 | 10,628 | 18 | 626 | R | 51.4% | 48.5% | 51.4% | 48.6% |
| 14,243 | MADISON | 6,376 | 3,364 | 3,012 | | 352 | R | 52.8% | 47.2% | 52.8% | 47.2% |
| 16,140 | MARION | 6,148 | 3,262 | 2,886 | | 376 | R | 53.1% | 46.9% | 53.1% | 46.9% |
| 40,443 | MILLER | 14,548 | 6,438 | 8,110 | | 1,672 | D | 44.3% | 55.7% | 44.3% | 55.7% |
| 51,979 | MISSISSIPPI | 14,112 | 4,804 | 9,308 | | 4,504 | D | 34.0% | 66.0% | 34.0% | 66.0% |
| 10,254 | MONROE | 3,704 | 1,100 | 2,601 | 3 | 1,501 | D | 29.7% | 70.2% | 29.7% | 70.3% |
| 9,245 | MONTGOMERY | 3,953 | 2,022 | 1,930 | 1 | 92 | R | 51.2% | 48.8% | 51.2% | 48.8% |
| 9,955 | NEVADA | 3,638 | 1,273 | 2,365 | | 1,092 | D | 35.0% | 65.0% | 35.0% | 65.0% |
| 8,608 | NEWTON | 4,321 | 2,467 | 1,846 | 8 | 621 | R | 57.1% | 42.7% | 57.2% | 42.8% |
| 28,790 | OUACHITA | 10,313 | 3,747 | 6,566 | | 2,819 | D | 36.3% | 63.7% | 36.3% | 63.7% |
| 10,209 | PERRY | 4,315 | 2,013 | 2,302 | | 289 | D | 46.7% | 53.3% | 46.7% | 53.3% |
| 26,445 | PHILLIPS | 8,919 | 2,132 | 6,782 | 5 | 4,650 | D | 23.9% | 76.0% | 23.9% | 76.1% |
| 11,303 | PIKE | 3,592 | 1,890 | 1,702 | | 188 | R | 52.6% | 47.4% | 52.6% | 47.4% |
| 25,614 | POINSETT | 7,698 | 2,786 | 4,912 | | 2,126 | D | 36.2% | 63.8% | 36.2% | 63.8% |
| 20,229 | POLK | 7,729 | 4,419 | 3,310 | | 1,109 | R | 57.2% | 42.8% | 57.2% | 42.8% |
| 54,469 | POPE | 20,858 | 10,824 | 10,034 | | 790 | R | 51.9% | 48.1% | 51.9% | 48.1% |
| 9,539 | PRAIRIE | 3,651 | 1,485 | 2,166 | | 681 | D | 40.7% | 59.3% | 40.7% | 59.3% |
| 361,474 | PULASKI | 151,637 | 51,813 | 99,792 | 32 | 47,979 | D | 34.2% | 65.8% | 34.2% | 65.8% |
| 18,195 | RANDOLPH | 6,653 | 2,519 | 4,126 | 8 | 1,607 | D | 37.9% | 62.0% | 37.9% | 62.1% |
| 29,329 | ST. FRANCIS | 10,731 | 4,051 | 6,680 | | 2,629 | D | 37.8% | 62.2% | 37.8% | 62.2% |
| 83,529 | SALINE | 39,004 | 20,011 | 18,990 | 3 | 1,021 | R | 51.3% | 48.7% | 51.3% | 48.7% |
| 10,996 | SCOTT | 4,017 | 2,015 | 2,000 | 2 | 15 | R | 50.2% | 49.8% | 50.2% | 49.8% |
| 8,261 | SEARCY | 3,513 | 1,822 | 1,691 | | 131 | R | 51.9% | 48.1% | 51.9% | 48.1% |
| 115,071 | SEBASTIAN | 43,711 | 23,036 | 20,660 | 15 | 2,376 | R | 52.7% | 47.3% | 52.7% | 47.3% |
| 15,757 | SEVIER | 4,569 | 1,953 | 2,616 | | 663 | D | 42.7% | 57.3% | 42.7% | 57.3% |
| 17,119 | SHARP | 7,465 | 3,382 | 4,083 | | 701 | D | 45.3% | 54.7% | 45.3% | 54.7% |
| 11,499 | STONE | 5,556 | 2,841 | 2,701 | 14 | 140 | R | 51.1% | 48.6% | 51.3% | 48.7% |
| 45,629 | UNION | 16,971 | 7,762 | 9,209 | | 1,447 | D | 45.7% | 54.3% | 45.7% | 54.3% |
| 16,192 | VAN BUREN | 7,309 | 3,358 | 3,949 | 2 | 591 | D | 45.9% | 54.0% | 46.0% | 54.0% |
| 157,715 | WASHINGTON | 63,329 | 30,146 | 33,183 | | 3,037 | D | 47.6% | 52.4% | 47.6% | 52.4% |
| 67,165 | WHITE | 26,108 | 14,605 | 11,498 | 5 | 3,107 | R | 55.9% | 44.0% | 56.0% | 44.0% |
| 8,741 | WOODRUFF | 3,045 | 755 | 2,290 | | 1,535 | D | 24.8% | 75.2% | 24.8% | 75.2% |
| 21,139 | YELL | 6,669 | 2,685 | 3,984 | | 1,299 | D | 40.3% | 59.7% | 40.3% | 59.7% |
| 2,673,400 | TOTAL | 1,039,349 | 458,036 | 580,973 | 340 | 122,937 | D | 44.1% | 55.9% | 44.1% | 55.9% |

# ARKANSAS

## HOUSE OF REPRESENTATIVES

| CD | Year | Total Vote | Republican Vote | Republican Candidate | Democratic Vote | Democratic Candidate | Other Vote | Rep.-Dem. Plurality | Total Vote Rep. | Total Vote Dem. | Major Vote Rep. | Major Vote Dem. |
|---|---|---|---|---|---|---|---|---|---|---|---|---|
| 1 | 2004 | 243,944 | 81,556 | Humphrey, Vernon | 162,388 | Berry, Marion* | | 80,832 D | 33.4% | 66.6% | 33.4% | 66.6% |
| 1 | 2002 | 194,058 | 64,357 | Robinson, Tommy F. | 129,701 | Berry, Marion* | | 65,344 D | 33.2% | 66.8% | 33.2% | 66.8% |
| 2 | 2004 | 276,493 | 115,655 | Parks, Marvin | 160,834 | Snyder, Vic* | 4 | 45,179 D | 41.8% | 58.2% | 41.8% | 58.2% |
| 2 | 2002 | 153,626 | | | 142,752 | Snyder, Vic* | 10,874 | 142,752 D | | 92.9% | | 100.0% |
| 3 | 2004 | 270,803 | 160,629 | Boozman, John* | 103,158 | Judy, Jan | 7,016 | 57,471 R | 59.3% | 38.1% | 60.9% | 39.1% |
| 3 | 2002 | 143,055 | 141,478 | Boozman, John* | | | 1,577 | 141,478 R | 98.9% | | 100.0% | |
| 4 | 2004 | | | | | Ross, Mike* | | D | | | | |
| 4 | 2002 | 197,537 | 77,904 | Dickey, Jay | 119,633 | Ross, Mike* | | 41,729 D | 39.4% | 60.6% | 39.4% | 60.6% |
| Total | 2004 | 791,240 | 357,840 | | 426,380 | | 7,020 | 68,540 D | 45.2% | 53.9% | 45.6% | 54.4% |
| Total | 2002 | 688,276 | 283,739 | | 392,086 | | 12,451 | 108,347 D | 41.2% | 57.0% | 42.0% | 58.0% |

An asterisk (*) denotes incumbent.

# ARKANSAS

## GENERAL AND PRIMARY ELECTIONS

## 2004 GENERAL ELECTIONS

**President**    Other vote was 6,171 Populist Party of Arkansas (Ralph Nader); 2,352 Libertarian (Michael Badnarik); 2,083 Constitutional (Michael Peroutka); 1,488 Green Party of Arkansas (David Cobb).

**Senator**    Other vote was 212 write-in (Glen A. Schwarz); 128 write-in (Gene Mason).

**House**    Other vote was:

CD 1
CD 2    4 write-in (William Gabriel).
CD 3    7,016 Independent (Dale Morfey).
CD 4

## 2004 PRIMARY ELECTIONS

**Primary**    May 18, 2004        **Registration**        1,557,376    No Party Registration
(as of April 19, 2004)

**Primary Type**    Open—Any registered voter could vote in either the Democratic or Republican primary.

# ARKANSAS

## GENERAL AND PRIMARY ELECTIONS

Note:   An asterisk (*) denotes incumbent. No votes were tallied in contests where a candidate ran unopposed.

| | REPUBLICAN PRIMARIES | | | DEMOCRATIC PRIMARIES | | |
|---|---|---|---|---|---|---|
| **President** | George W. Bush* | 37,234 | 97.1% | John Kerry | 177,754 | 66.6% |
| | Uncommitted | 1,129 | 2.9% | Uncommitted | 61,800 | 23.2% |
| | | | | Dennis J. Kucinich | 13,766 | 5.2% |
| | | | | Lyndon H. LaRouche Jr. | 13,528 | 5.1% |
| | TOTAL | 38,363 | | TOTAL | 266,848 | |
| **Senator** | Jim Holt | 37,254 | 68.9% | Blanche Lincoln* | 231,037 | 83.1% |
| | Andy Lee | 10,709 | 19.8% | Lisa Burks | 47,010 | 16.9% |
| | Rosemarie Clampitt | 6,078 | 11.2% | | | |
| | TOTAL | 54,041 | | TOTAL | 278,047 | |
| **Congressional District 1** | Vernon Humphrey | Unopposed | | Marion Berry* | Unopposed | |
| **Congressional District 2** | Marvin Parks | 11,590 | 69.2% | Vic Snyder* | Unopposed | |
| | Ed Garner | 5,156 | 30.8% | | | |
| | TOTAL | 16,746 | | | | |
| **Congressional District 3** | John Boozman* | Unopposed | | Jan Judy | Unopposed | |
| **Congressional District 4** | No Republican candidate | | | Mike Ross* | Unopposed | |

# CALIFORNIA

## GOVERNOR

Arnold Schwarzenegger (R). Elected October 2003 to fill the remaining three years of the term vacated when Gray Davis (D) lost a recall vote in the same special election.

## SENATORS (2 Democrats)

Barbara Boxer (D). Reelected 2004 to a six-year term. Previously elected 1998, 1992.

Dianne Feinstein (D). Reelected 2000 to a six-year term. Previously elected 1994 and 1992 to fill the remaining two years of the term vacated when Senator Pete Wilson (R) was elected governor in November 1990.

## REPRESENTATIVES (33 Democrats, 19 Republicans, 1 Vacancy)

1. Mike Thompson (D)
2. Wally Herger (R)
3. Dan Lungren (R)
4. John T. Doolittle (R)
5. Doris Matsui (D)
6. Lynn Woolsey (D)
7. George Miller (D)
8. Nancy Pelosi (D)
9. Barbara Lee (D)
10. Ellen O. Tauscher (D)
11. Richard W. Pombo (R)
12. Tom Lantos (D)
13. Pete Stark (D)
14. Anna G. Eshoo (D)
15. Michael M. Honda (D)
16. Zoe Lofgren (D)
17. Sam Farr (D)
18. Dennis Cardoza (D)
19. George P. Radanovich (R)
20. Jim Costa (D)
21. Devin Nunes (R)
22. Bill Thomas (R)
23. Lois Capps (D)
24. Elton Gallegly (R)
25. Howard P. "Buck" McKeon (R)
26. David Dreier (R)
27. Brad Sherman (D)
28. Howard L. Berman (D)
29. Adam B. Schiff (D)
30. Henry A. Waxman (D)
31. Xavier Becerra (D)
32. Hilda L. Solis (D)
33. Diane Watson (D)
34. Lucille Roybal-Allard (D)
35. Maxine Waters (D)
36. Jane Harman (D)
37. Juanita Millender-McDonald (D)
38. Grace F. Napolitano (D)
39. Linda T. Sanchez (D)
40. Ed Royce (R)
41. Jerry Lewis (R)
42. Gary G. Miller (R)
43. Joe Baca (D)
44. Ken Calvert (R)
45. Mary Bono (R)
46. Dana Rohrabacher (R)
47. Loretta Sanchez (D)
48. Vacancy
49. Darrell Issa (R)
50. Randy "Duke" Cunningham (R)
51. Bob Filner (D)
52. Duncan Hunter (R)
53. Susan A. Davis (D)

## POSTWAR VOTE FOR PRESIDENT

| Year | Total Vote | Republican Vote | Republican Candidate | Democratic Vote | Democratic Candidate | Other Vote | Plurality | Total Vote Rep. | Total Vote Dem. | Major Vote Rep. | Major Vote Dem. |
|------|-----------|-----------------|----------------------|-----------------|----------------------|-----------|-----------|------|------|------|------|
| 2004 | 12,421,852 | 5,509,826 | Bush, George W. | 6,745,485 | Kerry, John | 166,541 | 1,235,659 D | 44.4% | 54.3% | 45.0% | 55.0% |
| 2000** | 10,965,856 | 4,567,429 | Bush, George W. | 5,861,203 | Gore, Al | 537,224 | 1,293,774 D | 41.7% | 53.4% | 43.8% | 56.2% |
| 1996** | 10,019,484 | 3,828,380 | Dole, Bob | 5,119,835 | Clinton, Bill | 1,071,269 | 1,291,455 D | 38.2% | 51.1% | 42.8% | 57.2% |
| 1992** | 11,131,721 | 3,630,574 | Bush, George | 5,121,325 | Clinton, Bill | 2,379,822 | 1,490,751 D | 32.6% | 46.0% | 41.5% | 58.5% |
| 1988 | 9,887,065 | 5,054,917 | Bush, George | 4,702,233 | Dukakis, Michael S. | 129,915 | 352,684 R | 51.1% | 47.6% | 51.8% | 48.2% |
| 1984 | 9,505,423 | 5,467,009 | Reagan, Ronald | 3,922,519 | Mondale, Walter F. | 115,895 | 1,544,490 R | 57.5% | 41.3% | 58.2% | 41.8% |
| 1980** | 8,587,063 | 4,524,858 | Reagan, Ronald | 3,083,661 | Carter, Jimmy | 978,544 | 1,441,197 R | 52.7% | 35.9% | 59.5% | 40.5% |
| 1976 | 7,867,117 | 3,882,244 | Ford, Gerald R. | 3,742,284 | Carter, Jimmy | 242,589 | 139,960 R | 49.3% | 47.6% | 50.9% | 49.1% |
| 1972 | 8,367,862 | 4,602,096 | Nixon, Richard M. | 3,475,847 | McGovern, George S. | 289,919 | 1,126,249 R | 55.0% | 41.5% | 57.0% | 43.0% |
| 1968** | 7,251,587 | 3,467,664 | Nixon, Richard M. | 3,244,318 | Humphrey, Hubert H. | 539,605 | 223,346 R | 47.8% | 44.7% | 51.7% | 48.3% |
| 1964 | 7,057,586 | 2,879,108 | Goldwater, Barry M. | 4,171,877 | Johnson, Lyndon B. | 6,601 | 1,292,769 D | 40.8% | 59.1% | 40.8% | 59.2% |
| 1960 | 6,506,578 | 3,259,722 | Nixon, Richard M. | 3,224,099 | Kennedy, John F. | 22,757 | 35,623 R | 50.1% | 49.6% | 50.3% | 49.7% |
| 1956 | 5,466,355 | 3,027,668 | Eisenhower, Dwight D. | 2,420,135 | Stevenson, Adlai E. | 18,552 | 607,533 R | 55.4% | 44.3% | 55.6% | 44.4% |
| 1952 | 5,141,849 | 2,897,310 | Eisenhower, Dwight D. | 2,197,548 | Stevenson, Adlai E. | 46,991 | 699,762 R | 56.3% | 42.7% | 56.9% | 43.1% |
| 1948 | 4,021,538 | 1,895,269 | Dewey, Thomas E. | 1,913,134 | Truman, Harry S. | 213,135 | 17,865 D | 47.1% | 47.6% | 49.8% | 50.2% |

In past elections, the other vote included: 2000 - 418,707 Green (Ralph Nader); 1996 - 697,847 Reform (Ross Perot); 1992 - 2,296,006 Independent (Perot); 1980 - 739,833 Independent (John Anderson); 1968 - 487,270 American Independent (George Wallace).

# CALIFORNIA

## POSTWAR VOTE FOR GOVERNOR

| Year | Total Vote | Republican Vote | Republican Candidate | Democratic Vote | Democratic Candidate | Other Vote | Rep.-Dem. Plurality | Percentage Total Vote Rep. | Dem. | Percentage Major Vote Rep. | Dem. |
|---|---|---|---|---|---|---|---|---|---|---|---|
| 2003S** | 8,657,915 | 4,206,284 | Schwarzenegger, Arnold | 2,724,874 | Bustamante, Cruz | 1,726,757 | 1,481,410 R | 48.6% | 31.5% | — | — |
| 2002 | 7,476,311 | 3,169,801 | Simon, Bill | 3,533,490 | Davis, Gray | 773,020 | 363,689 D | 42.4% | 47.3% | 47.3% | 52.7% |
| 1998 | 8,385,196 | 3,218,030 | Lungren, Dan | 4,860,702 | Davis, Gray | 306,464 | 1,642,672 D | 38.4% | 58.0% | 39.8% | 60.2% |
| 1994 | 8,665,375 | 4,781,766 | Wilson, Pete | 3,519,799 | Brown, Kathleen | 363,810 | 1,261,967 R | 55.2% | 40.6% | 57.6% | 42.4% |
| 1990 | 7,699,467 | 3,791,904 | Wilson, Pete | 3,525,197 | Feinstein, Dianne | 382,366 | 266,707 R | 49.2% | 45.8% | 51.8% | 48.2% |
| 1986 | 7,443,551 | 4,506,601 | Deukmejian, George | 2,781,714 | Bradley, Tom | 155,236 | 1,724,887 R | 60.5% | 37.4% | 61.8% | 38.2% |
| 1982 | 7,876,698 | 3,881,014 | Deukmejian, George | 3,787,669 | Bradley, Tom | 208,015 | 93,345 R | 49.3% | 48.1% | 50.6% | 49.4% |
| 1978 | 6,922,378 | 2,526,534 | Younger, Evelle J. | 3,878,812 | Brown, Edmund G. Jr. | 517,032 | 1,352,278 D | 36.5% | 56.0% | 39.4% | 60.6% |
| 1974 | 6,248,070 | 2,952,954 | Flournoy, Houston I. | 3,131,648 | Brown, Edmund G. Jr. | 163,468 | 178,694 D | 47.3% | 50.1% | 48.5% | 51.5% |
| 1970 | 6,510,072 | 3,439,664 | Reagan, Ronald | 2,938,607 | Unruh, Jess | 131,801 | 501,057 R | 52.8% | 45.1% | 53.9% | 46.1% |
| 1966 | 6,503,445 | 3,742,913 | Reagan, Ronald | 2,749,174 | Brown, Edmund G. | 11,358 | 993,739 R | 57.6% | 42.3% | 57.7% | 42.3% |
| 1962 | 5,853,270 | 2,740,351 | Nixon, Richard M. | 3,037,109 | Brown, Edmund G. | 75,810 | 296,758 D | 46.8% | 51.9% | 47.4% | 52.6% |
| 1958 | 5,255,777 | 2,110,911 | Knowland, William F. | 3,140,076 | Brown, Edmund G. | 4,790 | 1,029,165 D | 40.2% | 59.7% | 40.2% | 59.8% |
| 1954 | 4,030,368 | 2,290,519 | Knight, Goodwin J. | 1,739,368 | Graves, Richard P. | 481 | 551,151 R | 56.8% | 43.2% | 56.8% | 43.2% |
| 1950 | 3,796,090 | 2,461,754 | Warren, Earl | 1,333,856 | Roosevelt, James | 480 | 1,127,898 R | 64.8% | 35.1% | 64.9% | 35.1% |
| 1946** | 2,558,399 | 2,344,542 | Warren, Earl | — | | 213,857 | 2,344,542 R | 91.6% | | 100.0% | |

The 2003 election was for a short term to fill a vacancy created by voter approval of a measure to remove Governor Gray Davis (D) from office. The measure passed by a vote of 4,976,274 votes (55.4 percent) for recall to 4,007,783 (44.6 percent) against recall. In the same election, more than 100 candidates ran for the right to succeed Davis. No primary election was held to cull the field. All candidates, regardless of party, ran together on the same ballot. The winner, Republican Arnold Schwarzenegger, is listed as the Republican candidate. The leading Democratic vote-getter, Cruz Bustamante, is listed as the Democratic candidate. The percentages given are for Schwarzenegger and Bustamante. The leading other candidate was Republican Tom McClintock, who received 1,161,287 votes (13.4 percent of the total). In 1946 the Republican candidate won both major party nominations.

## POSTWAR VOTE FOR SENATOR

| Year | Total Vote | Republican Vote | Republican Candidate | Democratic Vote | Democratic Candidate | Other Vote | Rep.-Dem. Plurality | Percentage Total Vote Rep. | Dem. | Percentage Major Vote Rep. | Dem. |
|---|---|---|---|---|---|---|---|---|---|---|---|
| 2004 | 12,053,295 | 4,555,922 | Jones, Bill | 6,955,728 | Boxer, Barbara | 541,645 | 2,399,806 D | 37.8% | 57.7% | 39.6% | 60.4% |
| 2000 | 10,623,614 | 3,886,853 | Campbell, Tom | 5,932,522 | Feinstein, Dianne | 804,239 | 2,045,669 D | 36.6% | 55.8% | 39.6% | 60.4% |
| 1998 | 8,314,953 | 3,576,351 | Fong, Matt | 4,411,705 | Boxer, Barbara | 326,897 | 835,354 D | 43.0% | 53.1% | 44.8% | 55.2% |
| 1994 | 8,514,089 | 3,817,025 | Huffington, Michael | 3,979,152 | Feinstein, Dianne | 717,912 | 162,127 D | 44.8% | 46.7% | 49.0% | 51.0% |
| 1992 | 10,799,703 | 4,644,182 | Herschensohn, Bruce | 5,173,467 | Boxer, Barbara | 982,054 | 529,285 D | 43.0% | 47.9% | 47.3% | 52.7% |
| 1992S | 10,782,743 | 4,093,501 | Seymour, John | 5,853,651 | Feinstein, Dianne | 835,591 | 1,760,150 D | 38.0% | 54.3% | 41.2% | 58.8% |
| 1988 | 9,743,598 | 5,143,409 | Wilson, Pete | 4,287,253 | McCarthy, Leo | 312,936 | 856,156 R | 52.8% | 44.0% | 54.5% | 45.5% |
| 1986 | 7,398,549 | 3,541,804 | Zschau, Ed | 3,646,672 | Cranston, Alan | 210,073 | 104,868 D | 47.9% | 49.3% | 49.3% | 50.7% |
| 1982 | 7,805,538 | 4,022,565 | Wilson, Pete | 3,494,968 | Brown, Edmund G., Jr. | 288,005 | 527,597 R | 51.5% | 44.8% | 53.5% | 46.5% |
| 1980 | 8,327,481 | 3,093,426 | Gann, Paul | 4,705,399 | Cranston, Alan | 528,656 | 1,611,973 D | 37.1% | 56.5% | 39.7% | 60.3% |
| 1976 | 7,472,268 | 3,748,973 | Hayakawa, S. I. | 3,502,862 | Tunney, John V. | 220,433 | 246,111 R | 50.2% | 46.9% | 51.7% | 48.3% |
| 1974 | 6,102,432 | 2,210,267 | Richardson, H. L. | 3,693,160 | Cranston, Alan | 199,005 | 1,482,893 D | 36.2% | 60.5% | 37.4% | 62.6% |
| 1970 | 6,492,157 | 2,877,617 | Murphy, George | 3,496,558 | Tunney, John V. | 117,982 | 618,941 D | 44.3% | 53.9% | 45.1% | 54.9% |
| 1968 | 7,102,465 | 3,329,148 | Rafferty, Max | 3,680,352 | Cranston, Alan | 92,965 | 351,204 D | 46.9% | 51.8% | 47.5% | 52.5% |
| 1964 | 7,041,821 | 3,628,555 | Murphy, George | 3,411,912 | Salinger, Pierre | 1,354 | 216,643 R | 51.5% | 48.5% | 51.5% | 48.5% |
| 1962 | 5,647,952 | 3,180,483 | Kuchel, Thomas H. | 2,452,839 | Richards, Richard | 14,630 | 727,644 R | 56.3% | 43.4% | 56.5% | 43.5% |
| 1958 | 5,135,221 | 2,204,337 | Knight, Goodwin J. | 2,927,693 | Engle, Clair | 3,191 | 723,356 D | 42.9% | 57.0% | 43.0% | 57.0% |
| 1956 | 5,361,467 | 2,892,918 | Kuchel, Thomas H. | 2,445,816 | Richards, Richard | 22,733 | 447,102 R | 54.0% | 45.6% | 54.2% | 45.8% |
| 1954S | 3,929,668 | 2,090,836 | Kuchel, Thomas H. | 1,788,071 | Yorty, Samuel W. | 50,761 | 302,765 R | 53.2% | 45.5% | 53.9% | 46.1% |
| 1952** | 4,542,548 | 3,982,448 | Knowland, William F. | — | | 560,100 | 3,982,448 R | 87.7% | | 100.0% | |
| 1950 | 3,686,315 | 2,183,454 | Nixon, Richard M. | 1,502,507 | Douglas, Helen | 354 | 680,947 R | 59.2% | 40.8% | 59.2% | 40.8% |
| 1946 | 2,639,465 | 1,428,067 | Knowland, William F. | 1,167,161 | Rogers, Will | 44,237 | 260,906 R | 54.1% | 44.2% | 55.0% | 45.0% |

One of the 1992 elections was for a short term to fill a vacancy. The 1954 election was for a short term to fill a vacancy. In 1952 the Republican candidate won both major party nominations.

# CALIFORNIA

Congressional districts first established for elections held in 2002
53 members

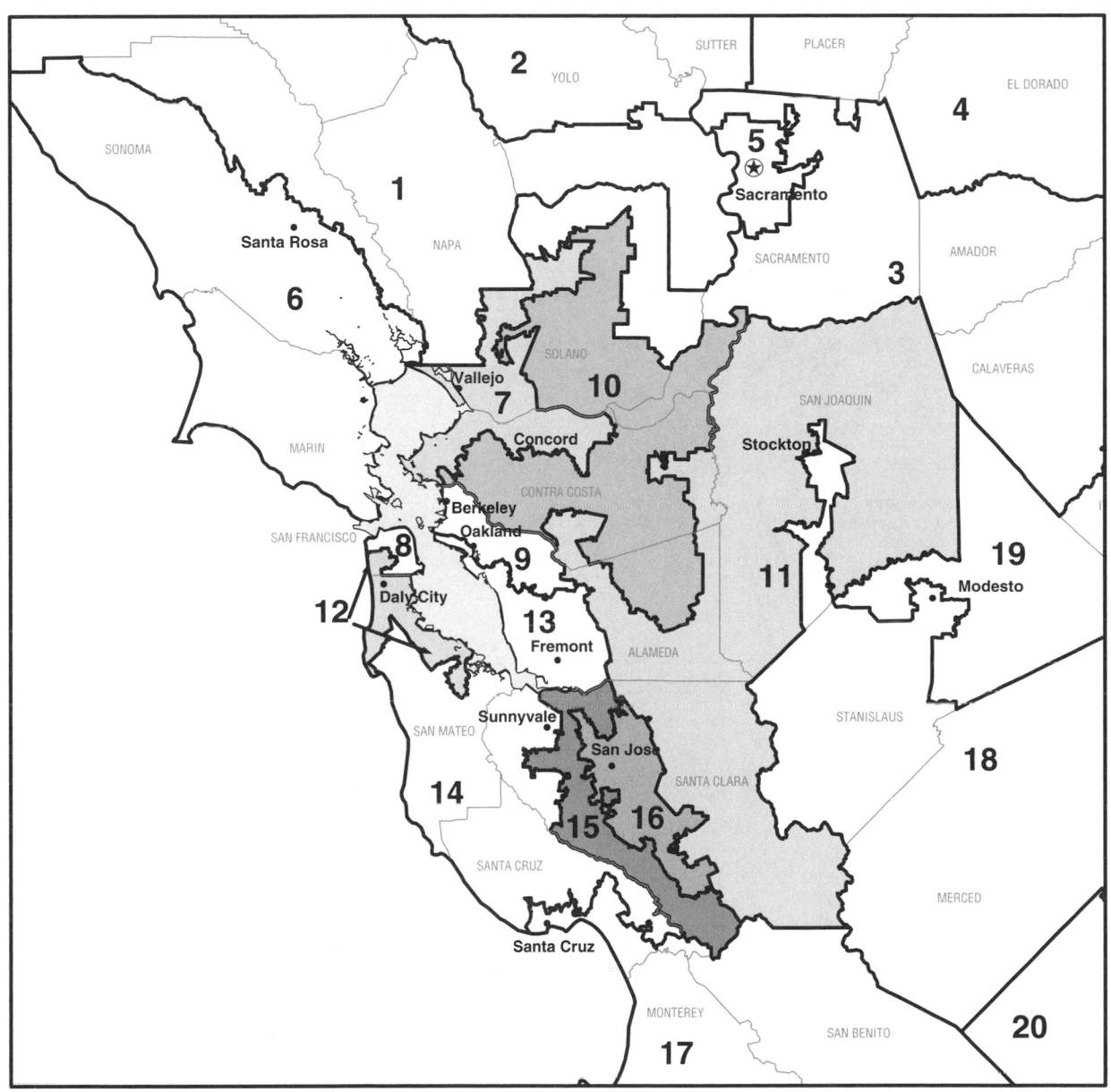

# CALIFORNIA

San Francisco Bay Area

82

# CALIFORNIA

Los Angeles, San Diego Areas

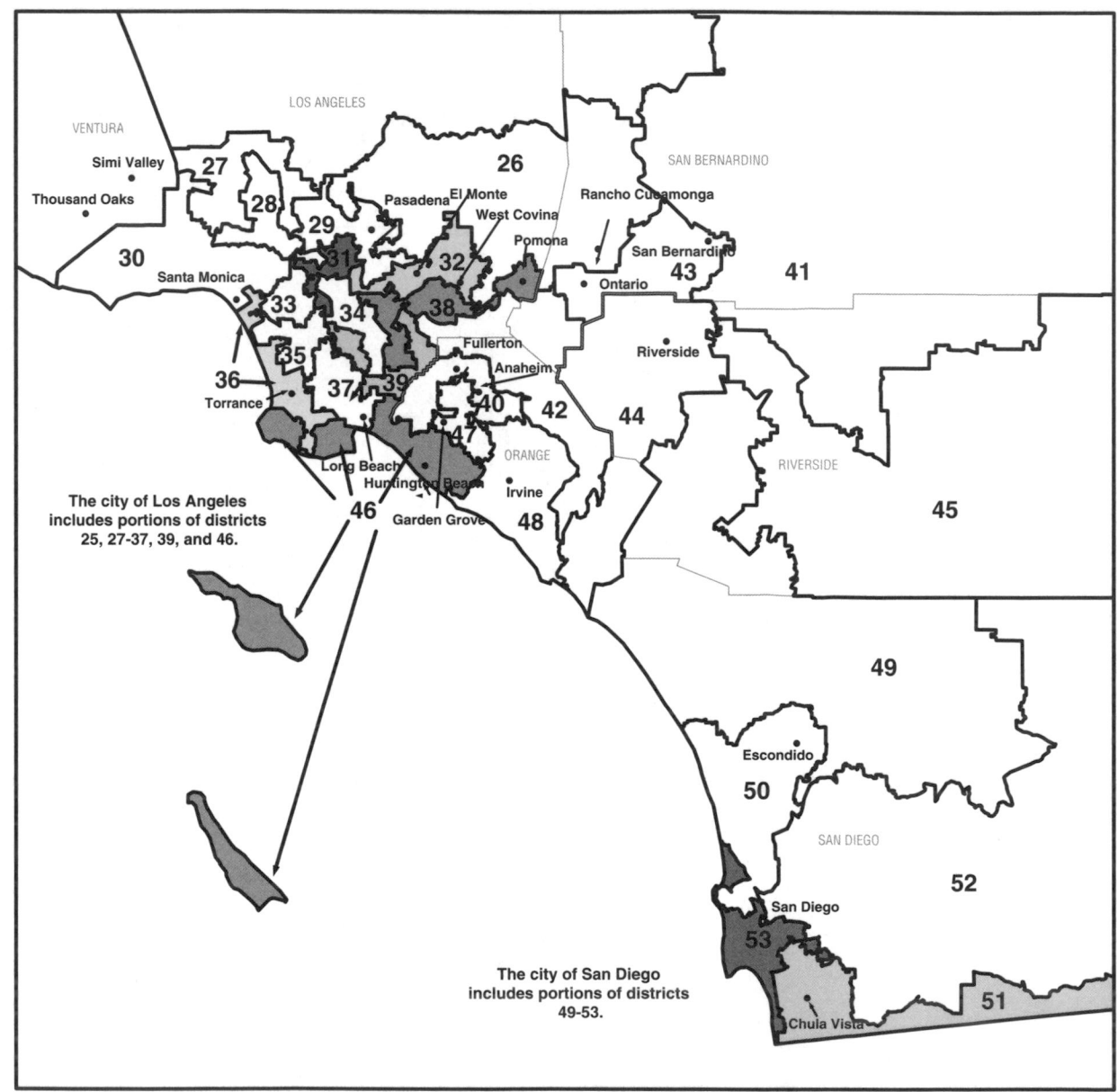

The city of Los Angeles
includes portions of districts
25, 27-37, 39, and 46.

The city of San Diego
includes portions of districts
49-53.

# CALIFORNIA

## PRESIDENT 2004

| 2000 Census Population | County | Total Vote | Republican | Democratic | Other | Rep.-Dem. Plurality | Percentage | | | |
|---|---|---|---|---|---|---|---|---|---|---|
| | | | | | | | Total Vote | | Major Vote | |
| | | | | | | | Rep. | Dem. | Rep. | Dem. |
| 1,443,741 | ALAMEDA | 562,090 | 130,911 | 422,585 | 8,594 | 291,674 D | 23.3% | 75.2% | 23.7% | 76.3% |
| 1,208 | ALPINE | 701 | 311 | 373 | 17 | 62 D | 44.4% | 53.2% | 45.5% | 54.5% |
| 35,100 | AMADOR | 17,891 | 11,107 | 6,541 | 243 | 4,566 R | 62.1% | 36.6% | 62.9% | 37.1% |
| 203,171 | BUTTE | 96,157 | 51,662 | 42,448 | 2,047 | 9,214 R | 53.7% | 44.1% | 54.9% | 45.1% |
| 40,554 | CALAVERAS | 22,343 | 13,601 | 8,286 | 456 | 5,315 R | 60.9% | 37.1% | 62.1% | 37.9% |
| 18,804 | COLUSA | 6,166 | 4,142 | 1,947 | 77 | 2,195 R | 67.2% | 31.6% | 68.0% | 32.0% |
| 948,816 | CONTRA COSTA | 413,028 | 150,608 | 257,254 | 5,166 | 106,646 D | 36.5% | 62.3% | 36.9% | 63.1% |
| 27,507 | DEL NORTE | 9,421 | 5,356 | 3,892 | 173 | 1,464 R | 56.9% | 41.3% | 57.9% | 42.1% |
| 156,299 | EL DORADO | 86,364 | 52,878 | 32,242 | 1,244 | 20,636 R | 61.2% | 37.3% | 62.1% | 37.9% |
| 799,407 | FRESNO | 247,463 | 141,988 | 103,154 | 2,321 | 38,834 R | 57.4% | 41.7% | 57.9% | 42.1% |
| 26,453 | GLENN | 9,454 | 6,308 | 2,995 | 151 | 3,313 R | 66.7% | 31.7% | 67.8% | 32.2% |
| 126,518 | HUMBOLDT | 65,886 | 25,714 | 37,988 | 2,184 | 12,274 D | 39.0% | 57.7% | 40.4% | 59.6% |
| 142,361 | IMPERIAL | 34,274 | 15,890 | 17,964 | 420 | 2,074 D | 46.4% | 52.4% | 46.9% | 53.1% |
| 17,945 | INYO | 8,616 | 5,091 | 3,350 | 175 | 1,741 R | 59.1% | 38.9% | 60.3% | 39.7% |
| 661,645 | KERN | 211,174 | 140,417 | 68,603 | 2,154 | 71,814 R | 66.5% | 32.5% | 67.2% | 32.8% |
| 129,461 | KINGS | 32,110 | 21,003 | 10,833 | 274 | 10,170 R | 65.4% | 33.7% | 66.0% | 34.0% |
| 58,309 | LAKE | 24,719 | 11,093 | 13,141 | 485 | 2,048 D | 44.9% | 53.2% | 45.8% | 54.2% |
| 33,828 | LASSEN | 11,450 | 8,126 | 3,158 | 166 | 4,968 R | 71.0% | 27.6% | 72.0% | 28.0% |
| 9,519,338 | LOS ANGELES | 3,023,280 | 1,076,225 | 1,907,736 | 39,319 | 831,511 D | 35.6% | 63.1% | 36.1% | 63.9% |
| 123,109 | MADERA | 38,850 | 24,871 | 13,481 | 498 | 11,390 R | 64.0% | 34.7% | 64.8% | 35.2% |
| 247,289 | MARIN | 135,325 | 34,378 | 99,070 | 1,877 | 64,692 D | 25.4% | 73.2% | 25.8% | 74.2% |
| 17,130 | MARIPOSA | 8,658 | 5,215 | 3,251 | 192 | 1,964 R | 60.2% | 37.5% | 61.6% | 38.4% |
| 86,265 | MENDOCINO | 38,429 | 12,955 | 24,385 | 1,089 | 11,430 D | 33.7% | 63.5% | 34.7% | 65.3% |
| 210,554 | MERCED | 57,960 | 32,773 | 24,491 | 696 | 8,282 R | 56.5% | 42.3% | 57.2% | 42.8% |
| 9,449 | MODOC | 4,467 | 3,235 | 1,149 | 83 | 2,086 R | 72.4% | 25.7% | 73.8% | 26.2% |
| 12,853 | MONO | 5,338 | 2,621 | 2,628 | 89 | 7 D | 49.1% | 49.2% | 49.9% | 50.1% |
| 401,762 | MONTEREY | 124,653 | 47,838 | 75,241 | 1,574 | 27,403 D | 38.4% | 60.4% | 38.9% | 61.1% |
| 124,279 | NAPA | 56,599 | 22,059 | 33,666 | 874 | 11,607 D | 39.0% | 59.5% | 39.6% | 60.4% |
| 92,033 | NEVADA | 53,920 | 28,790 | 24,220 | 910 | 4,570 R | 53.4% | 44.9% | 54.3% | 45.7% |
| 2,846,289 | ORANGE | 1,075,399 | 641,832 | 419,239 | 14,328 | 222,593 R | 59.7% | 39.0% | 60.5% | 39.5% |
| 248,399 | PLACER | 153,278 | 95,969 | 55,573 | 1,736 | 40,396 R | 62.6% | 36.3% | 63.3% | 36.7% |
| 20,824 | PLUMAS | 11,190 | 6,905 | 4,129 | 156 | 2,776 R | 61.7% | 36.9% | 62.6% | 37.4% |
| 1,545,387 | RIVERSIDE | 557,579 | 322,473 | 228,806 | 6,300 | 93,667 R | 57.8% | 41.0% | 58.5% | 41.5% |
| 1,223,499 | SACRAMENTO | 477,866 | 235,539 | 236,657 | 5,670 | 1,118 D | 49.3% | 49.5% | 49.9% | 50.1% |
| 53,234 | SAN BENITO | 18,725 | 8,698 | 9,851 | 176 | 1,153 D | 46.5% | 52.6% | 46.9% | 53.1% |
| 1,709,434 | SAN BERNARDINO | 523,276 | 289,306 | 227,789 | 6,181 | 61,517 R | 55.3% | 43.5% | 55.9% | 44.1% |
| 2,813,833 | SAN DIEGO | 1,136,344 | 596,033 | 526,437 | 13,874 | 69,596 R | 52.5% | 46.3% | 53.1% | 46.9% |
| 776,733 | SAN FRANCISCO | 357,465 | 54,355 | 296,772 | 6,338 | 242,417 D | 15.2% | 83.0% | 15.5% | 84.5% |
| 563,598 | SAN JOAQUIN | 189,864 | 100,978 | 87,012 | 1,874 | 13,966 R | 53.2% | 45.8% | 53.7% | 46.3% |
| 246,681 | SAN LUIS OBISPO | 129,050 | 67,995 | 58,742 | 2,313 | 9,253 R | 52.7% | 45.5% | 53.7% | 46.3% |
| 707,161 | SAN MATEO | 284,857 | 83,315 | 197,922 | 3,620 | 114,607 D | 29.2% | 69.5% | 29.6% | 70.4% |
| 399,347 | SANTA BARBARA | 169,861 | 76,806 | 90,314 | 2,741 | 13,508 D | 45.2% | 53.2% | 46.0% | 54.0% |
| 1,682,585 | SANTA CLARA | 603,816 | 209,094 | 386,100 | 8,622 | 177,006 D | 34.6% | 63.9% | 35.1% | 64.9% |
| 255,602 | SANTA CRUZ | 122,084 | 30,354 | 89,102 | 2,628 | 58,748 D | 24.9% | 73.0% | 25.4% | 74.6% |
| 163,256 | SHASTA | 77,731 | 52,249 | 24,339 | 1,143 | 27,910 R | 67.2% | 31.3% | 68.2% | 31.8% |
| 3,555 | SIERRA | 1,948 | 1,249 | 646 | 53 | 603 R | 64.1% | 33.2% | 65.9% | 34.1% |
| 44,301 | SISKIYOU | 20,899 | 12,673 | 7,880 | 346 | 4,793 R | 60.6% | 37.7% | 61.7% | 38.3% |
| 394,542 | SOLANO | 148,837 | 62,301 | 85,096 | 1,440 | 22,795 D | 41.9% | 57.2% | 42.3% | 57.7% |
| 458,614 | SONOMA | 220,690 | 68,204 | 148,261 | 4,225 | 80,057 D | 30.9% | 67.2% | 31.5% | 68.5% |
| 446,997 | STANISLAUS | 145,624 | 85,407 | 58,829 | 1,388 | 26,578 R | 58.6% | 40.4% | 59.2% | 40.8% |
| 78,930 | SUTTER | 30,145 | 20,254 | 9,602 | 289 | 10,652 R | 67.2% | 31.9% | 67.8% | 32.2% |
| 56,039 | TEHAMA | 23,444 | 15,572 | 7,504 | 368 | 8,068 R | 66.4% | 32.0% | 67.5% | 32.5% |
| 13,022 | TRINITY | 6,513 | 3,560 | 2,782 | 171 | 778 R | 54.7% | 42.7% | 56.1% | 43.9% |
| 368,021 | TULARE | 98,860 | 65,399 | 32,494 | 967 | 32,905 R | 66.2% | 32.9% | 66.8% | 33.2% |
| 54,501 | TUOLUMNE | 26,235 | 15,745 | 10,104 | 386 | 5,641 R | 60.0% | 38.5% | 60.9% | 39.1% |
| 753,197 | VENTURA | 313,193 | 160,314 | 148,859 | 4,020 | 11,455 R | 51.2% | 47.5% | 51.9% | 48.1% |
| 168,660 | YOLO | 72,269 | 28,005 | 42,885 | 1,379 | 14,880 D | 38.8% | 59.3% | 39.5% | 60.5% |
| 60,219 | YUBA | 18,024 | 12,076 | 5,687 | 261 | 6,389 R | 67.0% | 31.6% | 68.0% | 32.0% |
| 33,871,648 | TOTAL | 12,421,852 | 5,509,826 | 6,745,485 | 166,541 | 1,235,659 D | 44.4% | 54.3% | 45.0% | 55.0% |

# CALIFORNIA

## GOVERNOR 2003 (RECALL GOVERNOR ELECTION)

Question: Shall Gray Davis (D) be Recalled (Removed) from the Office of Governor?

| 2000 Census Population | County | Total Vote | Yes | No | Plurality | Percentage of Total Vote | |
|---|---|---|---|---|---|---|---|
| | | | | | | Yes | No |
| 1,443,741 | ALAMEDA | 422,269 | 126,713 | 295,556 | 168,843 N | 30.0% | 70.0% |
| 1,208 | ALPINE | 571 | 297 | 274 | 23 Y | 52.0% | 48.0% |
| 35,100 | AMADOR | 14,243 | 9,600 | 4,643 | 4,957 Y | 67.4% | 32.6% |
| 203,171 | BUTTE | 71,135 | 46,054 | 25,081 | 20,973 Y | 64.7% | 35.3% |
| 40,554 | CALAVERAS | 17,631 | 11,775 | 5,856 | 5,919 Y | 66.8% | 33.2% |
| 18,804 | COLUSA | 5,088 | 3,821 | 1,267 | 2,554 Y | 75.1% | 24.9% |
| 948,816 | CONTRA COSTA | 314,305 | 137,372 | 176,933 | 39,561 N | 43.7% | 56.3% |
| 27,507 | DEL NORTE | 6,918 | 4,315 | 2,603 | 1,712 Y | 62.4% | 37.6% |
| 156,299 | EL DORADO | 68,531 | 48,946 | 19,585 | 29,361 Y | 71.4% | 28.6% |
| 799,407 | FRESNO | 183,543 | 122,423 | 61,120 | 61,303 Y | 66.7% | 33.3% |
| 26,453 | GLENN | 7,480 | 5,706 | 1,774 | 3,932 Y | 76.3% | 23.7% |
| 126,518 | HUMBOLDT | 47,741 | 22,861 | 24,880 | 2,019 N | 47.9% | 52.1% |
| 142,361 | IMPERIAL | 23,286 | 14,759 | 8,527 | 6,232 Y | 63.4% | 36.6% |
| 17,945 | INYO | 7,009 | 4,689 | 2,320 | 2,369 Y | 66.9% | 33.1% |
| 661,645 | KERN | 160,345 | 121,431 | 38,914 | 82,517 Y | 75.7% | 24.3% |
| 129,461 | KINGS | 21,757 | 15,573 | 6,184 | 9,389 Y | 71.6% | 28.4% |
| 58,309 | LAKE | 17,948 | 9,799 | 8,149 | 1,650 Y | 54.6% | 45.4% |
| 33,828 | LASSEN | 8,849 | 6,671 | 2,178 | 4,493 Y | 75.4% | 24.6% |
| 9,519,338 | LOS ANGELES | 2,008,563 | 984,222 | 1,024,341 | 40,119 N | 49.0% | 51.0% |
| 123,109 | MADERA | 29,184 | 21,113 | 8,071 | 13,042 Y | 72.3% | 27.7% |
| 247,289 | MARIN | 107,856 | 35,050 | 72,806 | 37,756 N | 32.5% | 67.5% |
| 17,130 | MARIPOSA | 6,880 | 4,640 | 2,240 | 2,400 Y | 67.4% | 32.6% |
| 86,265 | MENDOCINO | 28,165 | 11,900 | 16,265 | 4,365 N | 42.3% | 57.7% |
| 210,554 | MERCED | 42,002 | 26,641 | 15,361 | 11,280 Y | 63.4% | 36.6% |
| 9,449 | MODOC | 3,429 | 2,544 | 885 | 1,659 Y | 74.2% | 25.8% |
| 12,853 | MONO | 3,394 | 2,174 | 1,220 | 954 Y | 64.1% | 35.9% |
| 401,762 | MONTEREY | 96,933 | 45,222 | 51,711 | 6,489 N | 46.7% | 53.3% |
| 124,279 | NAPA | 43,379 | 19,839 | 23,540 | 3,701 N | 45.7% | 54.3% |
| 92,033 | NEVADA | 43,279 | 27,201 | 16,078 | 11,123 Y | 62.9% | 37.1% |
| 2,846,289 | ORANGE | 804,418 | 589,700 | 214,718 | 374,982 Y | 73.3% | 26.7% |
| 248,399 | PLACER | 122,168 | 88,040 | 34,128 | 53,912 Y | 72.1% | 27.9% |
| 20,824 | PLUMAS | 8,825 | 6,049 | 2,776 | 3,273 Y | 68.5% | 31.5% |
| 1,545,387 | RIVERSIDE | 403,408 | 283,923 | 119,485 | 164,438 Y | 70.4% | 29.6% |
| 1,223,499 | SACRAMENTO | 380,042 | 226,567 | 153,475 | 73,092 Y | 59.6% | 40.4% |
| 53,234 | SAN BENITO | 14,504 | 7,978 | 6,526 | 1,452 Y | 55.0% | 45.0% |
| 1,709,434 | SAN BERNARDINO | 370,733 | 259,719 | 111,014 | 148,705 Y | 70.1% | 29.9% |
| 2,813,833 | SAN DIEGO | 805,420 | 530,269 | 275,151 | 255,118 Y | 65.8% | 34.2% |
| 776,733 | SAN FRANCISCO | 264,940 | 52,177 | 212,763 | 160,586 N | 19.7% | 80.3% |
| 563,598 | SAN JOAQUIN | 138,500 | 85,153 | 53,347 | 31,806 Y | 61.5% | 38.5% |
| 246,681 | SAN LUIS OBISPO | 92,815 | 58,668 | 34,147 | 24,521 Y | 63.2% | 36.8% |
| 707,161 | SAN MATEO | 215,319 | 80,109 | 135,210 | 55,101 N | 37.2% | 62.8% |
| 399,347 | SANTA BARBARA | 124,762 | 71,558 | 53,204 | 18,354 Y | 57.4% | 42.6% |
| 1,682,585 | SANTA CLARA | 432,911 | 182,332 | 250,579 | 68,247 N | 42.1% | 57.9% |
| 255,602 | SANTA CRUZ | 92,541 | 32,939 | 59,602 | 26,663 N | 35.6% | 64.4% |
| 163,256 | SHASTA | 56,707 | 40,874 | 15,833 | 25,041 Y | 72.1% | 27.9% |
| 3,555 | SIERRA | 1,464 | 1,007 | 457 | 550 Y | 68.8% | 31.2% |
| 44,301 | SISKIYOU | 16,026 | 11,378 | 4,648 | 6,730 Y | 71.0% | 29.0% |
| 394,542 | SOLANO | 105,811 | 52,151 | 53,660 | 1,509 N | 49.3% | 50.7% |
| 458,614 | SONOMA | 167,647 | 66,251 | 101,396 | 35,145 N | 39.5% | 60.5% |
| 446,997 | STANISLAUS | 106,743 | 66,938 | 39,805 | 27,133 Y | 62.7% | 37.3% |
| 78,930 | SUTTER | 23,202 | 17,958 | 5,244 | 12,714 Y | 77.4% | 22.6% |
| 56,039 | TEHAMA | 18,338 | 13,384 | 4,954 | 8,430 Y | 73.0% | 27.0% |
| 13,022 | TRINITY | 5,084 | 3,249 | 1,835 | 1,414 Y | 63.9% | 36.1% |
| 368,021 | TULARE | 74,711 | 53,893 | 20,818 | 33,075 Y | 72.1% | 27.9% |
| 54,501 | TUOLUMNE | 21,075 | 13,438 | 7,637 | 5,801 Y | 63.8% | 36.2% |
| 753,197 | VENTURA | 234,022 | 148,538 | 85,484 | 63,054 Y | 63.5% | 36.5% |
| 168,660 | YOLO | 55,714 | 27,778 | 27,936 | 158 N | 49.9% | 50.1% |
| 60,219 | YUBA | 14,494 | 10,905 | 3,589 | 7,316 Y | 75.2% | 24.8% |
| 33,871,648 | TOTAL | 8,984,057 | 4,976,274 | 4,007,783 | 968,491 Y | 55.4% | 44.6% |

# CALIFORNIA

## GOVERNOR 2003 (ELECTION OF NEW GOVERNOR)

| 2000 Census Population | County | Total Vote | Schwarzenegger (R) | Bustamante (D) | McClintock (R) | Other | Plurality | Percentage of Total Vote | | |
|---|---|---|---|---|---|---|---|---|---|---|
| | | | | | | | | Schwarzenegger (R) | Bustamante (D) | McClintock (R) |
| 1,443,741 | ALAMEDA | 385,025 | 98,461 | 205,643 | 39,776 | 41,145 | 107,182 B | 25.6% | 53.4% | 10.3% |
| 1,208 | ALPINE | 509 | 267 | 162 | 36 | 44 | 105 S | 52.5% | 31.8% | 7.1% |
| 35,100 | AMADOR | 14,297 | 8,281 | 2,658 | 2,592 | 766 | 5,623 S | 57.9% | 18.6% | 18.1% |
| 203,171 | BUTTE | 69,151 | 36,910 | 14,893 | 11,759 | 5,589 | 22,017 S | 53.4% | 21.5% | 17.0% |
| 40,554 | CALAVERAS | 17,500 | 9,410 | 3,587 | 3,431 | 1,072 | 5,823 S | 53.8% | 20.5% | 19.6% |
| 18,804 | COLUSA | 4,920 | 3,159 | 838 | 783 | 140 | 2,321 S | 64.2% | 17.0% | 15.9% |
| 948,816 | CONTRA COSTA | 288,784 | 114,187 | 110,824 | 42,152 | 21,621 | 3,363 S | 39.5% | 38.4% | 14.6% |
| 27,507 | DEL NORTE | 6,406 | 3,522 | 1,634 | 782 | 468 | 1,888 S | 55.0% | 25.5% | 12.2% |
| 156,299 | EL DORADO | 67,650 | 41,572 | 11,211 | 10,532 | 4,335 | 30,361 S | 61.5% | 16.6% | 15.6% |
| 799,407 | FRESNO | 180,096 | 93,375 | 50,888 | 29,393 | 6,440 | 42,487 S | 51.8% | 28.3% | 16.3% |
| 26,453 | GLENN | 7,070 | 4,429 | 1,035 | 1,285 | 321 | 3,144 S | 62.6% | 14.6% | 18.2% |
| 126,518 | HUMBOLDT | 45,281 | 18,756 | 16,088 | 3,992 | 6,445 | 2,668 S | 41.4% | 35.5% | 8.8% |
| 142,361 | IMPERIAL | 21,050 | 9,632 | 7,995 | 2,067 | 1,356 | 1,637 S | 45.8% | 38.0% | 9.8% |
| 17,945 | INYO | 6,665 | 3,610 | 1,482 | 1,067 | 506 | 2,128 S | 54.2% | 22.2% | 16.0% |
| 661,645 | KERN | 157,385 | 96,965 | 29,459 | 26,176 | 4,785 | 67,506 S | 61.6% | 18.7% | 16.6% |
| 129,461 | KINGS | 22,174 | 12,539 | 5,174 | 3,835 | 626 | 7,365 S | 56.5% | 23.3% | 17.3% |
| 58,309 | LAKE | 16,994 | 8,003 | 5,137 | 2,564 | 1,290 | 2,866 S | 47.1% | 30.2% | 15.1% |
| 33,828 | LASSEN | 8,491 | 5,167 | 1,306 | 1,505 | 513 | 3,662 S | 60.9% | 15.4% | 17.7% |
| 9,519,338 | LOS ANGELES | 1,960,605 | 878,747 | 735,066 | 217,404 | 129,388 | 143,681 S | 44.8% | 37.5% | 11.1% |
| 123,109 | MADERA | 29,194 | 16,034 | 6,216 | 5,923 | 1,021 | 9,818 S | 54.9% | 21.3% | 20.3% |
| 247,289 | MARIN | 97,823 | 31,321 | 46,784 | 9,955 | 9,763 | 15,463 B | 32.0% | 47.8% | 10.2% |
| 17,130 | MARIPOSA | 6,919 | 3,463 | 1,490 | 1,550 | 416 | 1,913 S | 50.1% | 21.5% | 22.4% |
| 86,265 | MENDOCINO | 26,751 | 9,949 | 10,510 | 2,909 | 3,383 | 561 B | 37.2% | 39.3% | 10.9% |
| 210,554 | MERCED | 39,891 | 20,267 | 11,191 | 7,128 | 1,305 | 9,076 S | 50.8% | 28.1% | 17.9% |
| 9,449 | MODOC | 3,156 | 1,909 | 453 | 636 | 158 | 1,273 S | 60.5% | 14.4% | 20.2% |
| 12,853 | MONO | 3,281 | 1,859 | 772 | 430 | 220 | 1,087 S | 56.7% | 23.5% | 13.1% |
| 401,762 | MONTEREY | 91,449 | 37,553 | 32,139 | 10,446 | 11,311 | 5,414 S | 41.1% | 35.1% | 11.4% |
| 124,279 | NAPA | 40,697 | 16,097 | 14,115 | 7,067 | 3,418 | 1,982 S | 39.6% | 34.7% | 17.4% |
| 92,033 | NEVADA | 41,950 | 22,607 | 9,534 | 6,610 | 3,199 | 13,073 S | 53.9% | 22.7% | 15.8% |
| 2,846,289 | ORANGE | 777,796 | 493,850 | 130,808 | 119,504 | 33,634 | 363,042 S | 63.5% | 16.8% | 15.4% |
| 248,399 | PLACER | 119,082 | 74,764 | 19,706 | 18,825 | 5,787 | 55,058 S | 62.8% | 16.5% | 15.8% |
| 20,824 | PLUMAS | 8,478 | 4,636 | 1,709 | 1,591 | 542 | 2,927 S | 54.7% | 20.2% | 18.8% |
| 1,545,387 | RIVERSIDE | 393,569 | 239,584 | 84,683 | 53,998 | 15,304 | 154,901 S | 60.9% | 21.5% | 13.7% |
| 1,223,499 | SACRAMENTO | 373,371 | 195,435 | 98,877 | 52,046 | 27,013 | 96,558 S | 52.3% | 26.5% | 13.9% |
| 53,234 | SAN BENITO | 13,269 | 6,452 | 4,213 | 1,836 | 768 | 2,239 S | 48.6% | 31.8% | 13.8% |
| 1,709,434 | SAN BERNARDINO | 364,305 | 218,989 | 78,718 | 52,636 | 13,962 | 140,271 S | 60.1% | 21.6% | 14.4% |
| 2,813,833 | SAN DIEGO | 816,114 | 485,563 | 192,605 | 97,198 | 40,748 | 292,958 S | 59.5% | 23.6% | 11.9% |
| 776,733 | SAN FRANCISCO | 236,226 | 44,665 | 149,237 | 13,694 | 28,630 | 104,572 B | 18.9% | 63.2% | 5.8% |
| 563,598 | SAN JOAQUIN | 131,739 | 63,905 | 35,868 | 25,699 | 6,267 | 28,037 S | 48.5% | 27.2% | 19.5% |
| 246,681 | SAN LUIS OBISPO | 90,176 | 44,665 | 23,177 | 16,630 | 5,704 | 21,488 S | 49.5% | 25.7% | 18.4% |
| 707,161 | SAN MATEO | 195,228 | 68,191 | 86,854 | 23,454 | 16,729 | 18,663 B | 34.9% | 44.5% | 12.0% |
| 399,347 | SANTA BARBARA | 118,815 | 55,473 | 36,171 | 19,559 | 7,612 | 19,302 S | 46.7% | 30.4% | 16.5% |
| 1,682,585 | SANTA CLARA | 410,548 | 160,807 | 163,768 | 51,069 | 34,904 | 2,961 B | 39.2% | 39.9% | 12.4% |
| 255,602 | SANTA CRUZ | 86,893 | 28,926 | 39,828 | 7,735 | 10,404 | 10,902 B | 33.3% | 45.8% | 8.9% |
| 163,256 | SHASTA | 55,218 | 31,949 | 9,441 | 11,177 | 2,651 | 20,772 S | 57.9% | 17.1% | 20.2% |
| 3,555 | SIERRA | 1,507 | 842 | 269 | 285 | 111 | 557 S | 55.9% | 17.9% | 18.9% |
| 44,301 | SISKIYOU | 15,322 | 8,974 | 3,070 | 2,403 | 875 | 5,904 S | 58.6% | 20.0% | 15.7% |
| 394,542 | SOLANO | 99,461 | 43,122 | 34,441 | 15,548 | 6,350 | 8,681 S | 43.4% | 34.6% | 15.6% |
| 458,614 | SONOMA | 156,258 | 54,651 | 63,588 | 21,202 | 16,817 | 8,937 B | 35.0% | 40.7% | 13.6% |
| 446,997 | STANISLAUS | 100,723 | 46,811 | 25,034 | 24,425 | 4,453 | 21,777 S | 46.5% | 24.9% | 24.2% |
| 78,930 | SUTTER | 23,121 | 14,919 | 3,459 | 3,957 | 786 | 10,962 S | 64.5% | 15.0% | 17.1% |
| 56,039 | TEHAMA | 17,290 | 10,038 | 2,772 | 3,586 | 894 | 6,452 S | 58.1% | 16.0% | 20.7% |
| 13,022 | TRINITY | 4,773 | 2,518 | 1,057 | 815 | 383 | 1,461 S | 52.8% | 22.1% | 17.1% |
| 368,021 | TULARE | 73,322 | 40,678 | 16,943 | 11,391 | 4,310 | 23,735 S | 55.5% | 23.1% | 15.5% |
| 54,501 | TUOLUMNE | 20,390 | 10,097 | 4,799 | 4,475 | 1,019 | 5,298 S | 49.5% | 23.5% | 21.9% |

# CALIFORNIA

## GOVERNOR 2003 (ELECTION OF NEW GOVERNOR)

| 2000 Census Population | County | Total Vote | Schwarzenegger (R) | Bustamante (D) | McClintock (R) | Other | Plurality | Percentage of Total Vote | | |
|---|---|---|---|---|---|---|---|---|---|---|
| | | | | | | | | Schwarzenegger (R) | Bustamante (D) | McClintock (R) |
| 753,197 | VENTURA | 226,707 | 116,722 | 53,705 | 44,408 | 11,872 | 63,017 S | 51.5% | 23.7% | 19.6% |
| 168,660 | YOLO | 53,097 | 22,375 | 19,489 | 6,061 | 5,172 | 2,886 S | 42.1% | 36.7% | 11.4% |
| 60,219 | YUBA | 13,953 | 8,632 | 2,301 | 2,295 | 725 | 6,331 S | 61.9% | 16.5% | 16.4% |
| 33,871,648 | TOTAL | 8,657,915 | 4,206,284 | 2,724,874 | 1,161,287 | 565,470 | 1,481,410 S | 48.6% | 31.5% | 13.4% |

Note: The vote to choose a successor to incumbent Gray Davis was held in conjunction with the recall vote. All candidates, regardless of party, ran together on the same ballot. Every county was won either by the winning candidate, Republican Arnold Schwarzenegger, or by the leading Democratic candidate, Cruz Bustamante. The plurality measures the difference between the vote for the winner and the runner-up, who in eight counties was Republican Tom McClintock.

# CALIFORNIA

## SENATOR 2004

| 2000 Census Population | County | Total Vote | Republican | Democratic | Other | Rep.-Dem. Plurality | Percentage | | | |
|---|---|---|---|---|---|---|---|---|---|---|
| | | | | | | | Total Vote | | Major Vote | |
| | | | | | | | Rep. | Dem. | Rep. | Dem. |
| 1,443,741 | ALAMEDA | 533,812 | 107,966 | 403,892 | 21,954 | 295,926 D | 20.2% | 75.7% | 21.1% | 78.9% |
| 1,208 | ALPINE | 692 | 289 | 373 | 30 | 84 D | 41.8% | 53.9% | 43.7% | 56.3% |
| 35,100 | AMADOR | 17,658 | 9,562 | 7,445 | 651 | 2,117 R | 54.2% | 42.2% | 56.2% | 43.8% |
| 203,171 | BUTTE | 94,547 | 46,446 | 42,512 | 5,589 | 3,934 R | 49.1% | 45.0% | 52.2% | 47.8% |
| 40,554 | CALAVERAS | 22,146 | 11,865 | 9,339 | 942 | 2,526 R | 53.6% | 42.2% | 56.0% | 44.0% |
| 18,804 | COLUSA | 6,085 | 3,657 | 2,228 | 200 | 1,429 R | 60.1% | 36.6% | 62.1% | 37.9% |
| 948,816 | CONTRA COSTA | 407,785 | 135,559 | 258,905 | 13,321 | 123,346 D | 33.2% | 63.5% | 34.4% | 65.6% |
| 27,507 | DEL NORTE | 9,264 | 4,513 | 4,264 | 487 | 249 R | 48.7% | 46.0% | 51.4% | 48.6% |
| 156,299 | EL DORADO | 85,183 | 47,775 | 33,715 | 3,693 | 14,060 R | 56.1% | 39.6% | 58.6% | 41.4% |
| 799,407 | FRESNO | 242,186 | 124,937 | 109,849 | 7,400 | 15,088 R | 51.6% | 45.4% | 53.2% | 46.8% |
| 26,453 | GLENN | 9,291 | 5,739 | 3,147 | 405 | 2,592 R | 61.8% | 33.9% | 64.6% | 35.4% |
| 126,518 | HUMBOLDT | 64,700 | 22,394 | 38,016 | 4,290 | 15,622 D | 34.6% | 58.8% | 37.1% | 62.9% |
| 142,361 | IMPERIAL | 33,823 | 12,195 | 19,498 | 2,130 | 7,303 D | 36.1% | 57.6% | 38.5% | 61.5% |
| 17,945 | INYO | 8,539 | 4,643 | 3,474 | 422 | 1,169 R | 54.4% | 40.7% | 57.2% | 42.8% |
| 661,645 | KERN | 209,220 | 118,882 | 79,769 | 10,569 | 39,113 R | 56.8% | 38.1% | 59.8% | 40.2% |
| 129,461 | KINGS | 31,577 | 17,075 | 13,485 | 1,017 | 3,590 R | 54.1% | 42.7% | 55.9% | 44.1% |
| 58,309 | LAKE | 24,525 | 9,619 | 13,812 | 1,094 | 4,193 D | 39.2% | 56.3% | 41.1% | 58.9% |
| 33,828 | LASSEN | 11,295 | 7,051 | 3,655 | 589 | 3,396 R | 62.4% | 32.4% | 65.9% | 34.1% |
| 9,519,338 | LOS ANGELES | 2,907,036 | 822,351 | 1,940,493 | 144,192 | 1,118,142 D | 28.3% | 66.8% | 29.8% | 70.2% |
| 123,109 | MADERA | 38,467 | 22,249 | 15,058 | 1,160 | 7,191 R | 57.8% | 39.1% | 59.6% | 40.4% |
| 247,289 | MARIN | 132,885 | 34,301 | 94,164 | 4,420 | 59,863 D | 25.8% | 70.9% | 26.7% | 73.3% |
| 17,130 | MARIPOSA | 8,511 | 4,751 | 3,437 | 323 | 1,314 R | 55.8% | 40.4% | 58.0% | 42.0% |
| 86,265 | MENDOCINO | 37,844 | 11,131 | 23,415 | 3,298 | 12,284 D | 29.4% | 61.9% | 32.2% | 67.8% |
| 210,554 | MERCED | 56,347 | 26,023 | 27,975 | 2,349 | 1,952 D | 46.2% | 49.6% | 48.2% | 51.8% |
| 9,449 | MODOC | 4,400 | 2,916 | 1,253 | 231 | 1,663 R | 66.3% | 28.5% | 69.9% | 30.1% |
| 12,853 | MONO | 5,189 | 2,314 | 2,592 | 283 | 278 D | 44.6% | 50.0% | 47.2% | 52.8% |
| 401,762 | MONTEREY | 123,017 | 40,547 | 76,647 | 5,823 | 36,100 D | 33.0% | 62.3% | 34.6% | 65.4% |
| 124,279 | NAPA | 55,681 | 20,012 | 33,577 | 2,092 | 13,565 D | 35.9% | 60.3% | 37.3% | 62.7% |
| 92,033 | NEVADA | 53,219 | 26,321 | 24,367 | 2,531 | 1,954 R | 49.5% | 45.8% | 51.9% | 48.1% |
| 2,846,289 | ORANGE | 1,048,778 | 533,406 | 458,604 | 56,768 | 74,802 R | 50.9% | 43.7% | 53.8% | 46.2% |
| 248,399 | PLACER | 150,000 | 85,163 | 59,554 | 5,283 | 25,609 R | 56.8% | 39.7% | 58.8% | 41.2% |
| 20,824 | PLUMAS | 10,980 | 6,019 | 4,347 | 614 | 1,672 R | 54.8% | 39.6% | 58.1% | 41.9% |
| 1,545,387 | RIVERSIDE | 546,928 | 266,197 | 259,169 | 21,562 | 7,028 R | 48.7% | 47.4% | 50.7% | 49.3% |
| 1,223,499 | SACRAMENTO | 465,278 | 196,984 | 252,016 | 16,278 | 55,032 D | 42.3% | 54.2% | 43.9% | 56.1% |
| 53,234 | SAN BENITO | 18,539 | 7,365 | 10,349 | 825 | 2,984 D | 39.7% | 55.8% | 41.6% | 58.4% |
| 1,709,434 | SAN BERNARDINO | 505,996 | 229,527 | 251,776 | 24,693 | 22,249 D | 45.4% | 49.8% | 47.7% | 52.3% |
| 2,813,833 | SAN DIEGO | 1,098,961 | 484,948 | 565,457 | 48,556 | 80,509 D | 44.1% | 51.5% | 46.2% | 53.8% |
| 776,733 | SAN FRANCISCO | 335,304 | 43,029 | 277,193 | 15,082 | 234,164 D | 12.8% | 82.7% | 13.4% | 86.6% |
| 563,598 | SAN JOAQUIN | 186,927 | 80,350 | 99,074 | 7,503 | 18,724 D | 43.0% | 53.0% | 44.8% | 55.2% |
| 246,681 | SAN LUIS OBISPO | 125,225 | 60,708 | 58,212 | 6,305 | 2,496 R | 48.5% | 46.5% | 51.0% | 49.0% |

# CALIFORNIA

## SENATOR 2004

| 2000 Census Population | County | Total Vote | Republican | Democratic | Other | Rep.-Dem. Plurality | Percentage | | | |
|---|---|---|---|---|---|---|---|---|---|---|
| | | | | | | | Total Vote | | Major Vote | |
| | | | | | | | Rep. | Dem. | Rep. | Dem. |
| 707,161 | SAN MATEO | 278,297 | 73,171 | 196,285 | 8,841 | 123,114 D | 26.3% | 70.5% | 27.2% | 72.8% |
| 399,347 | SANTA BARBARA | 165,265 | 66,146 | 91,055 | 8,064 | 24,909 D | 40.0% | 55.1% | 42.1% | 57.9% |
| 1,682,585 | SANTA CLARA | 576,596 | 172,008 | 380,551 | 24,037 | 208,543 D | 29.8% | 66.0% | 31.1% | 68.9% |
| 255,602 | SANTA CRUZ | 120,199 | 28,239 | 84,840 | 7,120 | 56,601 D | 23.5% | 70.6% | 25.0% | 75.0% |
| 163,256 | SHASTA | 76,109 | 45,667 | 26,795 | 3,647 | 18,872 R | 60.0% | 35.2% | 63.0% | 37.0% |
| 3,555 | SIERRA | 1,946 | 1,143 | 679 | 124 | 464 R | 58.7% | 34.9% | 62.7% | 37.3% |
| 44,301 | SISKIYOU | 20,577 | 11,308 | 8,215 | 1,054 | 3,093 R | 55.0% | 39.9% | 57.9% | 42.1% |
| 394,542 | SOLANO | 146,417 | 51,354 | 89,779 | 5,284 | 38,425 D | 35.1% | 61.3% | 36.4% | 63.6% |
| 458,614 | SONOMA | 217,943 | 64,438 | 143,124 | 10,381 | 78,686 D | 29.6% | 65.7% | 31.0% | 69.0% |
| 446,997 | STANISLAUS | 143,907 | 71,527 | 67,539 | 4,841 | 3,988 R | 49.7% | 46.9% | 51.4% | 48.6% |
| 78,930 | SUTTER | 29,677 | 17,824 | 10,864 | 989 | 6,960 R | 60.1% | 36.6% | 62.1% | 37.9% |
| 56,039 | TEHAMA | 22,902 | 13,488 | 8,285 | 1,129 | 5,203 R | 58.9% | 36.2% | 61.9% | 38.1% |
| 13,022 | TRINITY | 6,401 | 3,068 | 2,960 | 373 | 108 R | 47.9% | 46.2% | 50.9% | 49.1% |
| 368,021 | TULARE | 97,509 | 58,066 | 36,181 | 3,262 | 21,885 R | 59.5% | 37.1% | 61.6% | 38.4% |
| 54,501 | TUOLUMNE | 25,996 | 13,620 | 11,538 | 838 | 2,082 R | 52.4% | 44.4% | 54.1% | 45.9% |
| 753,197 | VENTURA | 306,751 | 133,917 | 159,920 | 12,914 | 26,003 D | 43.7% | 52.1% | 45.6% | 54.4% |
| 168,660 | YOLO | 71,177 | 24,234 | 44,085 | 2,858 | 19,851 D | 34.0% | 61.9% | 35.5% | 64.5% |
| 60,219 | YUBA | 17,786 | 9,925 | 6,926 | 935 | 2,999 R | 55.8% | 38.9% | 58.9% | 41.1% |
| 33,871,648 | TOTAL | 12,053,295 | 4,555,922 | 6,955,728 | 541,645 | 2,399,806 D | 37.8% | 57.7% | 39.6% | 60.4% |

# CALIFORNIA

## HOUSE OF REPRESENTATIVES

| CD | Year | Total Vote | Republican Vote | Republican Candidate | Democratic Vote | Democratic Candidate | Other Vote | Rep.-Dem. Plurality | Percentage | | | |
|---|---|---|---|---|---|---|---|---|---|---|---|---|
| | | | | | | | | | Total Vote | | Major Vote | |
| | | | | | | | | | Rep. | Dem. | Rep. | Dem. |
| 1 | 2004 | 282,971 | 79,970 | Wiesner, Lawrence R. | 189,366 | Thompson, Mike* | 13,635 | 109,396 D | 28.3% | 66.9% | 29.7% | 70.3% |
| 1 | 2002 | 185,216 | 60,013 | Wiesner, Lawrence R. | 118,669 | Thompson, Mike* | 6,534 | 58,656 D | 32.4% | 64.1% | 33.6% | 66.4% |
| 2 | 2004 | 272,429 | 182,119 | Herger, Wally* | 90,310 | Johnson, Mike | | 91,809 R | 66.9% | 33.1% | 66.9% | 33.1% |
| 2 | 2002 | 178,985 | 117,747 | Herger, Wally* | 52,455 | Johnson, Mike | 8,783 | 65,292 R | 65.8% | 29.3% | 69.2% | 30.8% |
| 3 | 2004 | 287,073 | 177,738 | Lungren, Dan | 100,025 | Castillo, Gabe | 9,310 | 77,713 R | 61.9% | 34.8% | 64.0% | 36.0% |
| 3 | 2002 | 194,918 | 121,732 | Ose, Doug* | 67,136 | Beeman, Howard | 6,050 | 54,596 R | 62.5% | 34.4% | 64.5% | 35.5% |
| 4 | 2004 | 339,369 | 221,926 | Doolittle, John T.* | 117,443 | Winters, David I. | | 104,483 R | 65.4% | 34.6% | 65.4% | 34.6% |
| 4 | 2002 | 228,506 | 147,997 | Doolittle, John T.* | 72,860 | Norberg, Mark A. | 7,649 | 75,137 R | 64.8% | 31.9% | 67.0% | 33.0% |
| 5 | 2004 | 193,387 | 45,120 | Dugas, Mike | 138,004 | Matsui, Robert T.* | 10,263 | 92,884 D | 23.3% | 71.4% | 24.6% | 75.4% |
| 5 | 2002 | 131,578 | 34,749 | Frankhuizen, Richard | 92,726 | Matsui, Robert T.* | 4,103 | 57,977 D | 26.4% | 70.5% | 27.3% | 72.7% |
| 6 | 2004 | 311,667 | 85,244 | Erickson, Paul L. | 226,423 | Woolsey, Lynn* | | 141,179 D | 27.4% | 72.6% | 27.4% | 72.6% |
| 6 | 2002 | 209,563 | 62,052 | Erickson, Paul L. | 139,750 | Woolsey, Lynn* | 7,761 | 77,698 D | 29.6% | 66.7% | 30.7% | 69.3% |
| 7 | 2004 | 219,277 | 52,446 | Hargrave, Charles | 166,831 | Miller, George* | | 114,385 D | 23.9% | 76.1% | 23.9% | 76.1% |
| 7 | 2002 | 138,376 | 36,584 | Hargrave, Charles | 97,849 | Miller, George* | 3,943 | 61,265 D | 26.4% | 70.7% | 27.2% | 72.8% |
| 8 | 2004 | 270,064 | 31,074 | Depalma, Jennifer | 224,017 | Pelosi, Nancy* | 14,973 | 192,943 D | 11.5% | 82.9% | 12.2% | 87.8% |
| 8 | 2002 | 160,441 | 20,063 | German, G. Michael | 127,684 | Pelosi, Nancy* | 12,694 | 107,621 D | 12.5% | 79.6% | 13.6% | 86.4% |
| 9 | 2004 | 255,039 | 31,278 | Bermudez, Claudia | 215,630 | Lee, Barbara* | 8,131 | 184,352 D | 12.3% | 84.5% | 12.7% | 87.3% |
| 9 | 2002 | 166,917 | 25,333 | Udinsky, Jerry | 135,893 | Lee, Barbara* | 5,691 | 110,560 D | 15.2% | 81.4% | 15.7% | 84.3% |
| 10 | 2004 | 278,099 | 95,349 | Ketelson, Jeff | 182,750 | Tauscher, Ellen O.* | | 87,401 D | 34.3% | 65.7% | 34.3% | 65.7% |
| 10 | 2002 | 167,197 | | | 126,390 | Tauscher, Ellen O.* | 40,807 | 126,390 D | | 75.6% | | 100.0% |
| 11 | 2004 | 267,169 | 163,582 | Pombo, Richard W.* | 103,587 | McNerney, Gerald "Jerry" M. | | 59,995 R | 61.2% | 38.8% | 61.2% | 38.8% |
| 11 | 2002 | 173,956 | 104,921 | Pombo, Richard W.* | 69,035 | Shaw, Elaine Dugger | | 35,886 R | 60.3% | 39.7% | 60.3% | 39.7% |

# CALIFORNIA

## HOUSE OF REPRESENTATIVES

| CD | Year | Total Vote | Republican | | Democratic | | Other Vote | Rep.-Dem. Plurality | Percentage | | | |
|---|---|---|---|---|---|---|---|---|---|---|---|---|
| | | | | | | | | | Total Vote | | Major Vote | |
| | | | Vote | Candidate | Vote | Candidate | | | Rep. | Dem. | Rep. | Dem. |
| 12 | 2004 | 252,599 | 52,593 | Garza, Mike | 171,852 | Lantos, Tom* | 28,154 | 119,259 D | 20.8% | 68.0% | 23.4% | 76.6% |
| 12 | 2002 | 154,984 | 38,381 | Moloney, Michael J. | 105,597 | Lantos, Tom* | 11,006 | 67,216 D | 24.8% | 68.1% | 26.7% | 73.3% |
| 13 | 2004 | 201,921 | 48,439 | Bruno, George I. | 144,605 | Stark, Pete* | 8,877 | 96,166 D | 24.0% | 71.6% | 25.1% | 74.9% |
| 13 | 2002 | 121,723 | 26,852 | Mahmood, Syed R. | 86,495 | Stark, Pete* | 8,376 | 59,643 D | 22.1% | 71.1% | 23.7% | 76.3% |
| 14 | 2004 | 261,888 | 69,564 | Haugen, Chris | 182,712 | Eshoo, Anna G.* | 9,612 | 113,148 D | 26.6% | 69.8% | 27.6% | 72.4% |
| 14 | 2002 | 171,678 | 48,346 | Nixon, Joseph H. | 117,055 | Eshoo, Anna G.* | 6,277 | 68,709 D | 28.2% | 68.2% | 29.2% | 70.8% |
| 15 | 2004 | 214,338 | 59,953 | Chukwu, Raymond L. | 154,385 | Honda, Michael M.* | | 94,432 D | 28.0% | 72.0% | 28.0% | 72.0% |
| 15 | 2002 | 133,022 | 41,251 | Hermann, Linda Rae | 87,482 | Honda, Michael M.* | 4,289 | 46,231 D | 31.0% | 65.8% | 32.0% | 68.0% |
| 16 | 2004 | 182,281 | 47,992 | McNea, Douglas Adams | 129,222 | Lofgren, Zoe* | 5,067 | 81,230 D | 26.3% | 70.9% | 27.1% | 72.9% |
| 16 | 2002 | 107,986 | 32,182 | McNea, Douglas Adams | 72,370 | Lofgren, Zoe* | 3,434 | 40,188 D | 29.8% | 67.0% | 30.8% | 69.2% |
| 17 | 2004 | 223,225 | 65,117 | Risley, Mark | 148,958 | Farr, Sam* | 9,150 | 83,841 D | 29.2% | 66.7% | 30.4% | 69.6% |
| 17 | 2002 | 149,296 | 40,334 | Engler, Clint C. | 101,632 | Farr, Sam* | 7,330 | 61,298 D | 27.0% | 68.1% | 28.4% | 71.6% |
| 18 | 2004 | 153,705 | 49,973 | Pringle, Charles F. | 103,732 | Cardoza, Dennis | | 53,759 D | 32.5% | 67.5% | 32.5% | 67.5% |
| 18 | 2002 | 109,593 | 47,528 | Monteith, Dick | 56,181 | Cardoza, Dennis | 5,884 | 8,653 D | 43.4% | 51.3% | 45.8% | 54.2% |
| 19 | 2004 | 235,264 | 155,354 | Radanovich, George P.* | 64,047 | Bufford, James Lex | 15,863 | 91,307 R | 66.0% | 27.2% | 70.8% | 29.2% |
| 19 | 2002 | 157,802 | 106,209 | Radanovich, George P.* | 47,403 | Veen, John | 4,190 | 58,806 R | 67.3% | 30.0% | 69.1% | 30.9% |
| 20 | 2004 | 114,236 | 53,231 | Ashburn, Roy | 61,005 | Costa, Jim | | 7,774 D | 46.6% | 53.4% | 46.6% | 53.4% |
| 20 | 2002 | 74,770 | 25,628 | Minuth, Andre | 47,627 | Dooley, Cal* | 1,515 | 21,999 D | 34.3% | 63.7% | 35.0% | 65.0% |
| 21 | 2004 | 192,315 | 140,721 | Nunes, Devin* | 51,594 | Davis, Fred B. | | 89,127 R | 73.2% | 26.8% | 73.2% | 26.8% |
| 21 | 2002 | 124,198 | 87,544 | Nunes, Devin | 32,584 | LaPere, David G. | 4,070 | 54,960 R | 70.5% | 26.2% | 72.9% | 27.1% |
| 22 | 2004 | 209,384 | 209,384 | Thomas, Bill* | | | | 209,384 R | 100.0% | | 100.0% | |
| 22 | 2002 | 164,285 | 120,473 | Thomas, Bill* | 38,988 | Corvera, Jaime A. | 4,824 | 81,485 R | 73.3% | 23.7% | 75.6% | 24.4% |
| 23 | 2004 | 244,297 | 83,926 | Regan, Don | 153,980 | Capps, Lois* | 6,391 | 70,054 D | 34.4% | 63.0% | 35.3% | 64.7% |
| 23 | 2002 | 162,222 | 62,604 | Rogers, Beth | 95,752 | Capps, Lois* | 3,866 | 33,148 D | 38.6% | 59.0% | 39.5% | 60.5% |
| 24 | 2004 | 284,378 | 178,660 | Gallegly, Elton* | 96,397 | Wagner, Brett | 9,321 | 82,263 R | 62.8% | 33.9% | 65.0% | 35.0% |
| 24 | 2002 | 185,006 | 120,585 | Gallegly, Elton* | 58,755 | Rudin, Fern | 5,666 | 61,830 R | 65.2% | 31.8% | 67.2% | 32.8% |
| 25 | 2004 | 225,970 | 145,575 | McKeon, Howard P. "Buck"* | 80,395 | Willoughby, Fred "Tim" | | 65,180 R | 64.4% | 35.6% | 64.4% | 35.6% |
| 25 | 2002 | 124,336 | 80,775 | McKeon, Howard P. "Buck"* | 38,674 | Conaway, Bob | 4,887 | 42,101 R | 65.0% | 31.1% | 67.6% | 32.4% |
| 26 | 2004 | 251,207 | 134,596 | Dreier, David* | 107,522 | Matthews, Cynthia M. | 9,089 | 27,074 R | 53.6% | 42.8% | 55.6% | 44.4% |
| 26 | 2002 | 149,530 | 95,360 | Dreier, David* | 50,081 | Mikels, Marjorie Musser | 4,089 | 45,279 R | 63.8% | 33.5% | 65.6% | 34.4% |
| 27 | 2004 | 201,198 | 66,946 | Levy, Robert M. | 125,296 | Sherman, Brad* | 8,956 | 58,350 D | 33.3% | 62.3% | 34.8% | 65.2% |
| 27 | 2002 | 128,811 | 48,996 | Levy, Robert M. | 79,815 | Sherman, Brad* | | 30,819 D | 38.0% | 62.0% | 38.0% | 62.0% |
| 28 | 2004 | 162,510 | 37,868 | Hernandez, David | 115,303 | Berman, Howard L.* | 9,339 | 77,435 D | 23.3% | 71.0% | 24.7% | 75.3% |
| 28 | 2002 | 103,326 | 23,926 | Hernandez, David | 73,771 | Berman, Howard L.* | 5,629 | 49,845 D | 23.2% | 71.4% | 24.5% | 75.5% |
| 29 | 2004 | 206,832 | 62,871 | Scolinos, Harry Frank | 133,670 | Schiff, Adam B.* | 10,291 | 70,799 D | 30.4% | 64.6% | 32.0% | 68.0% |
| 29 | 2002 | 121,541 | 40,616 | Scileppi, Jim | 76,036 | Schiff, Adam B.* | 4,889 | 35,420 D | 33.4% | 62.6% | 34.8% | 65.2% |
| 30 | 2004 | 304,147 | 87,465 | Elizalde, Victor | 216,682 | Waxman, Henry A.* | | 129,217 D | 28.8% | 71.2% | 28.8% | 71.2% |
| 30 | 2002 | 185,593 | 54,989 | Goss, Tony D. | 130,604 | Waxman, Henry A.* | | 75,615 D | 29.6% | 70.4% | 29.6% | 70.4% |
| 31 | 2004 | 111,411 | 22,048 | Vega, Luis | 89,363 | Becerra, Xavier* | | 67,315 D | 19.8% | 80.2% | 19.8% | 80.2% |
| 31 | 2002 | 67,243 | 12,674 | Vega, Luis | 54,569 | Becerra, Xavier* | | 41,895 D | 18.8% | 81.2% | 18.8% | 81.2% |
| 32 | 2004 | 140,146 | | | 119,144 | Solis, Hilda L.* | 21,002 | 119,144 D | | 85.0% | | 100.0% |
| 32 | 2002 | 85,079 | 23,366 | Fischbeck, Emma E. | 58,530 | Solis, Hilda L.* | 3,183 | 35,164 D | 27.5% | 68.8% | 28.5% | 71.5% |
| 33 | 2004 | 188,314 | | | 166,801 | Watson, Diane* | 21,513 | 166,801 D | | 88.6% | | 100.0% |
| 33 | 2002 | 118,449 | 16,699 | Kim, Andrew | 97,779 | Watson, Diane* | 3,971 | 81,080 D | 14.1% | 82.5% | 14.6% | 85.4% |

# CALIFORNIA

## HOUSE OF REPRESENTATIVES

| CD | Year | Total Vote | Republican Vote | Republican Candidate | Democratic Vote | Democratic Candidate | Other Vote | Rep.-Dem. Plurality | Total Vote Rep. | Total Vote Dem. | Major Vote Rep. | Major Vote Dem. |
|---|---|---|---|---|---|---|---|---|---|---|---|---|
| 34 | 2004 | 110,457 | 28,175 | Miller, Wayne | 82,282 | Roybal-Allard, Lucille* | | 54,107 D | 25.5% | 74.5% | 25.5% | 74.5% |
| 34 | 2002 | 65,824 | 17,090 | Miller, Wayne | 48,734 | Roybal-Allard, Lucille* | | 31,644 D | 26.0% | 74.0% | 26.0% | 74.0% |
| 35 | 2004 | 156,407 | 23,591 | Moen, Ross | 125,949 | Waters, Maxine* | 6,867 | 102,358 D | 15.1% | 80.5% | 15.8% | 84.2% |
| 35 | 2002 | 93,407 | 18,094 | Moen, Ross | 72,401 | Waters, Maxine* | 2,912 | 54,307 D | 19.4% | 77.5% | 20.0% | 80.0% |
| 36 | 2004 | 244,044 | 81,666 | Whitehead, Paul | 151,208 | Harman, Jane* | 11,170 | 69,542 D | 33.5% | 62.0% | 35.1% | 64.9% |
| 36 | 2002 | 143,751 | 50,328 | Johnson, Stuart | 88,198 | Harman, Jane* | 5,225 | 37,870 D | 35.0% | 61.4% | 36.3% | 63.7% |
| 37 | 2004 | 158,318 | 31,960 | Van, Vernon | 118,823 | Millender-McDonald, Juanita* | 7,535 | 86,863 D | 20.2% | 75.1% | 21.2% | 78.8% |
| 37 | 2002 | 87,012 | 20,154 | Velasco, Oscar A. | 63,445 | Millender-McDonald, Juanita* | 3,413 | 43,291 D | 23.2% | 72.9% | 24.1% | 75.9% |
| 38 | 2004 | 116,851 | | | 116,851 | Napolitano, Grace F.* | | 116,851 D | | 100.0% | | 100.0% |
| 38 | 2002 | 88,027 | 23,126 | Burrola, Alex A. | 62,600 | Napolitano, Grace F.* | 2,301 | 39,474 D | 26.3% | 71.1% | 27.0% | 73.0% |
| 39 | 2004 | 164,964 | 64,832 | Escobar, Tim | 100,132 | Sanchez, Linda T.* | | 35,300 D | 39.3% | 60.7% | 39.3% | 60.7% |
| 39 | 2002 | 95,346 | 38,925 | Escobar, Tim | 52,256 | Sanchez, Linda T. | 4,165 | 13,331 D | 40.8% | 54.8% | 42.7% | 57.3% |
| 40 | 2004 | 217,301 | 147,617 | Royce, Ed* | 69,684 | Williams, J. Tilman | | 77,933 R | 67.9% | 32.1% | 67.9% | 32.1% |
| 40 | 2002 | 136,642 | 92,422 | Royce, Ed* | 40,265 | Avalos, Christina | 3,955 | 52,157 R | 67.6% | 29.5% | 69.7% | 30.3% |
| 41 | 2004 | 218,937 | 181,605 | Lewis, Jerry* | | | 37,332 | 181,605 R | 82.9% | | 100.0% | |
| 41 | 2002 | 135,533 | 91,326 | Lewis, Jerry* | 40,155 | Johnson, Keith A. | 4,052 | 51,171 R | 67.4% | 29.6% | 69.5% | 30.5% |
| 42 | 2004 | 246,025 | 167,632 | Miller, Gary G.* | 78,393 | Myers, Lewis | | 89,239 R | 68.1% | 31.9% | 68.1% | 31.9% |
| 42 | 2002 | 145,246 | 98,476 | Miller, Gary G.* | 42,090 | Waldron, Richard | 4,680 | 56,386 R | 67.8% | 29.0% | 70.1% | 29.9% |
| 43 | 2004 | 130,834 | 44,004 | Laning, Ed | 86,830 | Baca, Joe* | | 42,826 D | 33.6% | 66.4% | 33.6% | 66.4% |
| 43 | 2002 | 68,340 | 20,821 | Neighbor, Wendy C. | 45,374 | Baca, Joe* | 2,145 | 24,553 D | 30.5% | 66.4% | 31.5% | 68.5% |
| 44 | 2004 | 225,123 | 138,768 | Calvert, Ken* | 78,796 | Vandenberg, Louis | 7,559 | 59,972 R | 61.6% | 35.0% | 63.8% | 36.2% |
| 44 | 2002 | 120,463 | 76,686 | Calvert, Ken* | 38,021 | Vandenberg, Louis | 5,756 | 38,665 R | 63.7% | 31.6% | 66.9% | 33.1% |
| 45 | 2004 | 230,490 | 153,523 | Bono, Mary* | 76,967 | Meyer, Richard J. | | 76,556 R | 66.6% | 33.4% | 66.6% | 33.4% |
| 45 | 2002 | 133,533 | 87,101 | Bono, Mary* | 43,692 | Kurpiewski, Elle K. | 2,740 | 43,409 R | 65.2% | 32.7% | 66.6% | 33.4% |
| 46 | 2004 | 276,690 | 171,318 | Rohrabacher, Dana* | 90,129 | Brandt, Jim | 15,243 | 81,189 R | 61.9% | 32.6% | 65.5% | 34.5% |
| 46 | 2002 | 176,265 | 108,807 | Rohrabacher, Dana* | 60,890 | Schipske, Gerrie | 6,568 | 47,917 R | 61.7% | 34.5% | 64.1% | 35.9% |
| 47 | 2004 | 108,783 | 43,099 | Coronado, Alexandria A. "Alex" | 65,684 | Sanchez, Loretta* | | 22,585 D | 39.6% | 60.4% | 39.6% | 60.4% |
| 47 | 2002 | 70,178 | 24,346 | Chavez, Jeff | 42,501 | Sanchez, Loretta* | 3,331 | 18,155 D | 34.7% | 60.6% | 36.4% | 63.6% |
| 48 | 2004 | 290,872 | 189,004 | Cox, Christopher* | 93,525 | Graham, John | 8,343 | 95,479 R | 65.0% | 32.2% | 66.9% | 33.1% |
| 48 | 2002 | 179,549 | 122,884 | Cox, Christopher* | 51,058 | Graham, John | 5,607 | 71,826 R | 68.4% | 28.4% | 70.6% | 29.4% |
| 49 | 2004 | 226,466 | 141,658 | Issa, Darrell* | 79,057 | Byron, Mike | 5,751 | 62,601 R | 62.6% | 34.9% | 64.2% | 35.8% |
| 49 | 2002 | 122,497 | 94,594 | Issa, Darrell* | | | 27,903 | 94,594 R | 77.2% | | 100.0% | |
| 50 | 2004 | 289,328 | 169,025 | Cunningham, Randy "Duke"* | 105,590 | Busby, Francine P. | 14,713 | 63,435 R | 58.4% | 36.5% | 61.5% | 38.5% |
| 50 | 2002 | 172,701 | 111,095 | Cunningham, Randy "Duke"* | 55,855 | Stewart, Del G. | 5,751 | 55,240 R | 64.3% | 32.3% | 66.5% | 33.5% |
| 51 | 2004 | 180,879 | 63,526 | Giorgino, Michael | 111,441 | Filner, Bob* | 5,912 | 47,915 D | 35.1% | 61.6% | 36.3% | 63.7% |
| 51 | 2002 | 102,787 | 40,430 | Garcia, Maria Guadalupe | 59,541 | Filner, Bob* | 2,816 | 19,111 D | 39.3% | 57.9% | 40.4% | 59.6% |
| 52 | 2004 | 271,438 | 187,799 | Hunter, Duncan* | 74,857 | Keliher, Brian S. | 8,782 | 112,942 R | 69.2% | 27.6% | 71.5% | 28.5% |
| 52 | 2002 | 169,010 | 118,561 | Hunter, Duncan* | 43,526 | Moore-Kochlacs, Peter | 6,923 | 75,035 R | 70.2% | 25.8% | 73.1% | 26.9% |
| 53 | 2004 | 221,436 | 63,897 | Hunzeker, Darin | 146,449 | Davis, Susan A.* | 11,090 | 82,552 D | 28.9% | 66.1% | 30.4% | 69.6% |
| 53 | 2002 | 116,180 | 43,891 | VanDeWeghe, Bill | 72,252 | Davis, Susan A.* | 37 | 28,361 D | 37.8% | 62.2% | 37.8% | 62.2% |
| Total | 2004 | 11,623,753 | 5,030,821 | | 6,223,698 | | 369,234 | 1,192,877 D | 43.3% | 53.5% | 44.7% | 55.3% |
| Total | 2002 | 7,258,417 | 3,225,666 | | 3,731,081 | | 301,670 | 505,415 D | 44.4% | 51.4% | 46.4% | 53.6% |

# CALIFORNIA

## GENERAL AND PRIMARY ELECTIONS

### 2003 GUBERNATORIAL RECALL ELECTION AND 2004 GENERAL ELECTIONS

**President**

Other vote was 50,165 Libertarian (Michael Badnarik); 40,771 Green (David Cobb); 27,607 Peace and Freedom (Leonard Peltier); 26,645 American Independent (Michael Peroutka); 21,213 write-in (Ralph Nader); 82 write-in (John Joseph Kennedy); 49 write-in (John Parker); 8 write-in (James Alexander-Pace); 1 write-in (Anthony Jabin).

**Governor (2003 Recall Election)**

Other vote was 242,247 Peter Miguel Camejo (Green); 47,505 Arianna Huffington (Independent); 25,134 Peter Ueberroth (R); 17,458 Larry Flynt (D); 14,242 Gary Coleman (Independent); 12,382 George B. Schwartzman (Independent); 11,179 Mary "Mary Carey" Cook (Independent); 9,188 Bruce Margolin (D); 8,913 Bill Simon (R); 7,226 Van Vo (R); 6,748 John Christopher Burton (Independent); 6,496 David Laughing Horse Robinson (D); 5,466 Leo Gallagher (Independent); 5,297 Cheryl Bly-Chester (R); 5,245 Lawrence Steven Strauss (D); 4,221 Ronald Jason Palmieri (D); 3,906 Calvin Y. Louie (D); 3,404 Badi Badiozamani (Independent); 3,358 Audie Bock (D); 3,199 Ralph A. Hernandez (D); 3,007 Edward "Ed" Kennedy (D); 2,927 Dan Feinstein (D); 2,857 Bob McClain (Independent); 2,848 James H. Green (D); 2,562 Garrett Gruener (D); 2,536 Angelyne (Independent); 2,455 Paul Mariano (D); 2,346 Ivan A. Hall (Green); 2,328 Jim Weir (D); 2,317 Jerry Kunzman (Independent); 2,250 Ned Roscoe (Libertarian); 2,216 Georgy Russell (D); 2,214 Jonathan Miller (D); 2,200 Jack Loyd Grisham (Independent); 2,039 Christopher Sproul (D); 2,021 Daniel Watts (Green); 1,948 Ken Hamidi (Libertarian); 1,840 Marc Valdez (D); 1,801 Frank A. Malcaluso Jr. (D); 1,778 Daniel C. "Danny" Ramirez (D); 1,771 Randall D. Sprague (R); 1,713 Brooke Adams (Independent); 1,709 Mohammad Arif (Independent); 1,697 Nathan Whitecloud Walton (Independent); 1,689 John J. "Jack" Hickey (Libertarian); 1,652 Mike Schmier (D); 1,626 C.T. Weber (Peace and Freedom); 1,577 Diana Foss (D); 1,562 Michael Wozniak (D); 1,545 B.E. Smith (Independent); 1,466 Lingel H. Winters (D); 1,422 Richard J. Simmons (Independent); 1,419 Joe Guzzardi (D); 1,351 Mike P. McCarthy (Independent); 1,344 Art Brown (D); 1,343 Leonard Padilla (Independent); 1,297 Iris Adam (Natural Law); 1,236 Maurice Walker (Green); 1,210 Trek Thunder Kelly (Independent); 1,168 Vik S. Bajwa (D); 1,166 David Ronald Sams (R); 1,152 Darin Price (Natural Law); 1,104 Charles "Chuck" Pineda Jr. (Ameican Independent); 1,078 John "Jack" Mortensen (D); 1,077 Sara Ann Hanlon (Independent); 1,067 Diane Beall Templin (American Independent); 1,065 Dick Lane (D); 1,046 Jim Hoffmann (R); 1,028 Bill Vaughn (D); 989 C. Stephen Henderson (Independent); 987 Robert C. Newman II (R); 943 Jamie Rosemary Safford (R); 914 Robert C. Mannheim (D); 907 Dorene Musilli (R); 903 Scott A. Mednick (D); 851 A. Lavar Taylor (D); 842 Brian Tracy (Independent); 837 Kurt E. "Tachikaze" Rightmyer (Independent); 823 Christopher Ranken (D); 821 Sharon Rushford (Independent); 814 Darrin H. Scheidle (D); 792 Patricia G. Tilley (Independent); 778 Darryl L. Mobley (Independent); 771 Alex-St. James (R); 758 Bob Lynn Edwards (D); 754 Douglas Anderson (R); 751 Joel Britton (Independent); 746 Michael Jackson (R); 727 Ed Beyer (R); 715 Paul "Chip" Mailander (D); 699 John W. Beard (R); 679 Paul Nave (D); 632 Robert Cullenbine (D); 626 Warren Farrell (D); 623 Chuck Walker (R); 610 William "Bill" S. Chambers (R); 607 Vip Bhola (R); 598 Gerold Lee Gorman (D); 591 Dennis Duggan McMahon (R); 588 James M. Vandeventer Jr. (R); 586 Eric Korevaar (D); 582 Kelly P. Kimball (D); 581 Mike McNeilly (R); 554 S. Issa (R); 532 Gino Martorana (R); 497 Rich Gosse (R); 489 Tim Sylvester (D); 474 Bill Prady (D); 474 Bryan Quinn (R); 455 Jeffrey L. Mock (R); 452 Paul W. Vann (R); 451 Michael Cheli (Independent); 444 Heather Peters (R); 425 Jeff Rainforth (Independent); 419 Ronald J. Friedman (Independent); 386 Todd Carson (R); 384 Scott Davis (Independent); 383 Daniel W. Richards (R); 376 Carl A. Mehr (R); 365 Lorraine "Abner Zurd" Fontanes (D); 359 Gary Leonard (D); 349 Gregory J. Pawlik (R); 346 Jon W. Zellhoefer (R); 333 Reva Renee Renz (R); 305 Kevin Richter (R); 298 Stephen L. Knapp (R); 281 William Tsangares (R); 274 D. "Logan Darrow" Clements (R); 273 Robert "Butch" Dole (R); 261 D.E. Kessinger (D); 235 Gene Forte (R); 192 Todd Richard Lewis (Independent); 16 Mathilda Karel Spak (Independent write-in); 11 Jason Alan Gastrich (R write-in); 11 Monty Manibog (D write-in); 7 Thomas "Tom" Benigno (Independent write-in); 7 R. Charlie Chadwick (Independent write-in); 5 Shirley Coly (Independent write-in); 5 Jane H. Dawson (D write-in); 4 Pauline Cooper (D write-in); 4 Paul Walton (Independent write-in); 3 Jim "Poorman" Trenton (R write-in); 3 Wignes K. Warren (D write-in); 2 Christy Cassel (Independent write-in); 2 Jacques Andre Istel (R write-in); 2 Christian F. Meister (D write-in); 2 Vincent Pallaver (Independent write-in); 2 Lincoln Pickard (D write-in); 2 Lynda L. Toth (D write-in); 2 Donald P. Wang (R write-in); 1 Robert D. Gibb (D write-in); 1 Ronald W. Spangler (Independent write-in); 1 Bill Thill (D write-in); 1 Jurlene Jeanne Kokoa White (D write-in); 1 Joel Wirth (R write-in).

# CALIFORNIA

## GENERAL AND PRIMARY ELECTIONS

**Senator**     Other vote was 243,846 Peace and Freedom (Marsha Feinland); 216,522 Libertarian (James P. "Jim" Gray); 81,224 American Independent (Don J. Grundmann); 43 write-in (Dennis Richter); 8 write-in (Howard Johnson); 2 write-in (John Emery Jones).

**House**     Other vote was:

CD 1     13,635 Green (Pamela Elizondo).
CD 2
CD 3     9,310 Libertarian (Douglas Arthur Tuma).
CD 4
CD 5     6,593 Green (Pat Driscoll); 3,670 Peace and Freedom (John C. Reiger).
CD 6
CD 7
CD 8     9,527 Peace and Freedom (Leilani Dowell); 5,446 write-in (Terry Baum).
CD 9     8,131 Libertarian (Jim Eyer).
CD 10
CD 11
CD 12     23,038 Green (Pat Gray); 5,116 Libertarian (Harland Harrison).
CD 13     8,877 Libertarian (Mark W. Stroberg).
CD 14     9,588 Libertarian (Brian Holtz); 24 write-in (Dennis Mitrzyk).
CD 15
CD 16     5,067 Libertarian (Markus Welch).
CD 17     3,645 Green (Ray Glock-Grueneich); 2,823 Peace and Freedom (Joe Williams); 2,607 Libertarian (Joel Smolen); 75 write-in (David Mauricio Munoz).
CD 18
CD 19     15,863 Green (Larry R. Mullen).
CD 20
CD 21
CD 22
CD 23     6,391 Libertarian (Michael Favorite).
CD 24     9,321 Green (Stuart A. Bechman).
CD 25
CD 26     9,089 Libertarian (Randall Weissbuch).
CD 27     8,956 Green (Eric J. Carter).
CD 28     9,339 Libertarian (Kelley L. Ross).
CD 29     5,715 Green (Philip Koebel); 4,570 Libertarian (Ted Brown); 6 write-in (John Christopher Burton).
CD 30
CD 31
CD 32     21,002 Libertarian (Leland Faegre).
CD 33     21,513 Libertarian (Robert G. Weber Jr.).
CD 34
CD 35     3,440 American Independent (Gordon Michael Mego); 3,427 Libertarian (Charles Tate).
CD 36     6,105 Peace and Freedom (Alice Stek); 5,065 Libertarian (Mike Binkley).
CD 37     7,535 Libertarian (Herb Peters).
CD 38
CD 39
CD 40
CD 41     37,332 Libertarian (Peymon Mottahedek).
CD 42
CD 43
CD 44     7,559 Peace and Freedom (Kevin Akin).
CD 45
CD 46     10,238 Green (Tom Lash); 5,005 Libertarian (Keith Gann).
CD 47
CD 48     8,343 Libertarian (Bruce Cohen).
CD 49     5,751 Libertarian (Lars R. Grossmith).

# CALIFORNIA

## GENERAL AND PRIMARY ELECTIONS

CD 50    6,504 Green (Gary M. Waayers); 4,723 American Independent (Diane Templin); 3,486 Libertarian (Brandon C. Osborne).

CD 51    5,912 Libertarian (Michael S. Metti).

CD 52    8,782 Libertarian (Michael Benoit).

CD 53    7,523 Green (Lawrence P. Rockwood); 3,567 Libertarian (Adam Van Sustern).

## 2004 PRIMARY ELECTIONS

**Primary**     March 2, 2004

**Registration** (as of Feb. 17, 2004)

| | |
|---|---|
| Republican | 5,364,832 |
| Democratic | 6,518,631 |
| American Independent | 291,055 |
| Green | 157,749 |
| Libertarian | 86,053 |
| Peace and Freedom | 70,475 |
| Natural Law | 30,597 |
| Miscellaneous | 91,729 |
| Declined to State | 2,480,039 |
| TOTAL | 15,091,160 |

**Primary Type**    Semi-open—Voters registered with a recognized party in California could vote only in their party's primary. Other voters not registered with a recognized party could participate in the primary of the Democratic or American Independent parties.

Note: An asterisk (*) denotes incumbent. There was no primary held before the special gubernatorial recall election on October 7, 2003. All candidates, regardless of party, ran together on the same ballot.

| | REPUBLICAN PRIMARIES | | | DEMOCRATIC PRIMARIES | | |
|---|---|---|---|---|---|---|
| President | George W. Bush* | 2,216,047 | 100.0% | John Kerry | 2,002,539 | 64.4% |
| | Nancy Warrick (write-in) | 95 | | John Edwards | 614,441 | 19.8% |
| | Bill Wyatt (write-in) | 90 | | Dennis J. Kucinich | 144,954 | 4.7% |
| | Blake Ashby (write-in) | 56 | | Howard Dean | 130,892 | 4.2% |
| | Bradley J. Barton (write-in) | 22 | | Al Sharpton | 59,326 | 1.9% |
| | Richard Allen Holtz (write-in) | 17 | | Joseph I. Lieberman | 52,780 | 1.7% |
| | Richard P. Bosa (write-in) | 12 | | Wesley Clark | 51,084 | 1.6% |
| | Doc Castellano (write-in) | 12 | | Carol Moseley Braun | 24,501 | 0.8% |
| | | | | Richard A. Gephardt | 19,139 | 0.6% |
| | | | | Lyndon H. LaRouche Jr. | 7,953 | 0.3% |
| | | | | Katarina Dunmar (write-in) | 6 | |
| | | | | James Alexander-Pace (write-in) | 4 | |
| | | | | John Nigro Jr. (write-in) | 4 | |
| | | | | David Giacomuzzi (write-in) | 3 | |
| | | | | Fern Penna (write-in) | 3 | |
| | TOTAL | 2,216,351 | | TOTAL | 3,107,629 | |
| Senator | Bill Jones | 1,015,747 | 44.8% | Barbara Boxer* | 2,566,198 | 100.0% |
| | Rosario Marin | 454,176 | 20.0% | | | |
| | Howard Kaloogian | 253,341 | 11.2% | | | |
| | Toni Casey | 142,080 | 6.3% | | | |
| | Tim Stoen | 124,938 | 5.5% | | | |
| | James Stewart | 78,264 | 3.5% | | | |
| | Barry L. Hatch | 71,241 | 3.1% | | | |
| | John M. Van Zandt | 56,925 | 2.5% | | | |
| | Danney Ball | 37,745 | 1.7% | | | |
| | Bill Quraishi | 32,515 | 1.4% | | | |
| | Louis E. Longoria (write-in) | 28 | | | | |
| | TOTAL | 2,267,000 | | | | |

# CALIFORNIA

## GENERAL AND PRIMARY ELECTIONS

| | REPUBLICAN PRIMARIES | | | DEMOCRATIC PRIMARIES | | |
|---|---|---|---|---|---|---|
| Congressional District 1 | Lawrence R. Wiesner | 48,710 | 100.0% | Mike Thompson* | 92,371 | 100.0% |
| Congressional District 2 | Wally Herger* | 79,923 | 100.0% | Mike Johnson | 20,760 | 44.3% |
| | | | | A.J. Sekhon | 14,246 | 30.4% |
| | | | | Jeffrey Vance | 11,897 | 25.4% |
| | | | | TOTAL | 46,903 | |
| Congressional District 3 | Dan Lungren | 35,595 | 38.9% | Gabe Castillo | 51,155 | 100.0% |
| | Rico Oller | 32,728 | 35.8% | | | |
| | Mary Ose | 21,469 | 23.5% | | | |
| | Richard Frankhuizen | 1,693 | 1.9% | | | |
| | TOTAL | 91,485 | | | | |
| Congressional District 4 | John T. Doolittle* | 105,015 | 100.0% | David I. Winters | 58,036 | 100.0% |
| Congressional District 5 | Mike Dugas | 26,674 | 100.0% | Robert T. Matsui* | 63,291 | 100.0% |
| | | | | Pat Driscoll (write-in) | 11 | |
| | | | | TOTAL | 63,302 | |
| Congressional District 6 | Paul L. Erickson | 43,248 | 100.0% | Lynn Woolsey* | 99,970 | 84.0% |
| | | | | Renn Vara | 19,039 | 16.0% |
| | | | | TOTAL | 119,009 | |
| Congressional District 7 | Charles Hargrave | 23,900 | 100.0% | George Miller* | 71,268 | 100.0% |
| Congressional District 8 | Jennifer Depalma | 8,814 | 100.0% | Nancy Pelosi* | 94,564 | 100.0% |
| Congressional District 9 | Claudia Bermudez | 11,813 | 100.0% | Barbara Lee* | 105,211 | 100.0% |
| Congressional District 10 | Jeff Ketelson | 45,615 | 100.0% | Ellen O. Tauscher* | 75,997 | 100.0% |
| Congressional District 11 | Richard W. Pombo* | 65,046 | 100.0% | Gerald "Jerry" M. McNerney (write-in) | 1,667 | 100.0% |
| Congressional District 12 | Mike Garza | 13,967 | 55.5% | Tom Lantos* | 63,323 | 73.5% |
| | Christopher Huskins | 11,214 | 44.5% | Ro Khanna | 17,107 | 19.9% |
| | | | | Maad Abu-Ghazalah | 5,678 | 6.6% |
| | | | | Norma Bureau Elias (write-in) | 5 | |
| | TOTAL | 25,181 | | TOTAL | 86,113 | |
| Congressional District 13 | George I. Bruno | 19,606 | 100.0% | Pete Stark* | 59,726 | 100.0% |
| Congressional District 14 | Chris Haugen | 33,732 | 100.0% | Anna G. Eshoo* | 81,911 | 100.0% |
| Congressional District 15 | Raymond L. Chukwu | 26,813 | 99.5% | Michael M. Honda* | 58,531 | 100.0% |
| | Peter Sundin Soule (write-in) | 143 | 0.5% | | | |
| | TOTAL | 26,956 | | | | |
| Congressional District 16 | Douglas Adams McNea | 20,411 | 100.0% | Zoe Lofgren* | 50,254 | 100.0% |
| Congressional District 17 | Mark Risley | 23,139 | 74.9% | Sam Farr* | 65,809 | 91.1% |
| | Connor Vlakancic | 7,751 | 25.1% | Art Dunn | 6,401 | 8.9% |
| | TOTAL | 30,890 | | TOTAL | 72,210 | |
| Congressional District 18 | Charles F. Pringle | 16,913 | 68.6% | Dennis Cardoza* | 39,565 | 100.0% |
| | Audrey Redmond | 7,756 | 31.4% | | | |
| | TOTAL | 24,669 | | | | |
| Congressional District 19 | George P. Radanovich* | 69,050 | 100.0% | James Lex Bufford | 39,637 | 100.0% |
| Congressional District 20 | Roy Ashburn | 15,394 | 79.6% | Jim Costa | 24,338 | 73.2% |
| | Gino L. Martorana | 3,934 | 20.4% | Lisa Quigley | 8,925 | 26.8% |
| | TOTAL | 19,328 | | TOTAL | 33,263 | |

# CALIFORNIA

## GENERAL AND PRIMARY ELECTIONS

| | REPUBLICAN PRIMARIES | | | DEMOCRATIC PRIMARIES | | |
|---|---|---|---|---|---|---|
| Congressional District 21 | Devin Nunes* | 59,510 | 100.0% | Fred B. Davis | 32,271 | 100.0% |
| Congressional District 22 | Bill Thomas* | 78,809 | 100.0% | No Democratic candidate | | |
| Congressional District 23 | Don Regan | 43,738 | 100.0% | Lois Capps* | 64,202 | 100.0% |
| Congressional District 24 | Elton Gallegly* | 78,839 | 100.0% | Brett Wagner | 47,259 | 100.0% |
| Congressional District 25 | Howard P. "Buck" McKeon* | 47,727 | 100.0% | Fred "Tim" Willoughby<br>Bob Conaway<br>TOTAL | 15,714<br>12,303<br>28,017 | 56.1%<br>43.9% |
| Congressional District 26 | David Dreier*<br>S. Sonny Sardo<br>TOTAL | 53,368<br>10,502<br>63,870 | 83.6%<br>16.4% | Cynthia M. Matthews<br>Vicki Lynn Johnson<br>TOTAL | 21,365<br>13,171<br>34,536 | 61.9%<br>38.1% |
| Congressional District 27 | Robert M. Levy | 24,883 | 100.0% | Brad Sherman* | 40,350 | 100.0% |
| Congressional District 28 | David Hernandez | 11,409 | 100.0% | Howard L. Berman*<br>Charles R. Coleman Jr.<br>TOTAL | 33,702<br>7,448<br>41,150 | 81.9%<br>18.1% |
| Congressional District 29 | Harry Frank Scolinos<br>William J. Bodell<br>Reza Torchizy<br>TOTAL | 17,077<br>8,238<br>3,864<br>29,179 | 58.5%<br>28.2%<br>13.2% | Adam B. Schiff* | 40,699 | 100.0% |
| Congressional District 30 | Victor Elizalde | 29,018 | 100.0% | Henry A. Waxman* | 78,362 | 100.0% |
| Congressional District 31 | Luis Vega | 5,634 | 100.0% | Xavier Becerra*<br>Marvin Leon Evans<br>TOTAL | 26,308<br>3,103<br>29,411 | 89.4%<br>10.6% |
| Congressional District 32 | No Republican candidate | | | Hilda L. Solis* | 28,948 | 100.0% |
| Congressional District 33 | No Republican candidate | | | Diane Watson* | 53,376 | 100.0% |
| Congressional District 34 | Wayne Miller | 7,683 | 100.0% | Lucille Roybal-Allard* | 22,593 | 100.0% |
| Congressional District 35 | Ross Moen | 7,573 | 100.0% | Maxine Waters* | 41,452 | 100.0% |
| Congressional District 36 | Paul Whitehead<br>Gloria E. Davis<br>Lee Leslie<br>TOTAL | 13,081<br>9,430<br>7,966<br>30,477 | 42.9%<br>30.9%<br>26.1% | Jane Harman* | 48,524 | 100.0% |
| Congressional District 37 | Vernon Van | 10,172 | 100.0% | Juanita Millender-McDonald*<br>Albert Robles<br>Peter Mathews<br>TOTAL | 27,047<br>7,800<br>6,802<br>41,649 | 64.9%<br>18.7%<br>16.3% |
| Congressional District 38 | No Republican candidate | | | Grace F. Napolitano*<br>Michael J. Manzo<br>TOTAL | 26,632<br>7,122<br>33,754 | 78.9%<br>21.1% |
| Congressional District 39 | Tim Escobar | 18,227 | 100.0% | Linda T. Sanchez* | 30,424 | 100.0% |
| Congressional District 40 | Ed Royce* | 61,464 | 100.0% | J. Tilman Williams<br>Christina Avalos<br>TOTAL | 17,294<br>16,144<br>33,438 | 51.7%<br>48.3% |
| Congressional District 41 | Jerry Lewis* | 63,453 | 100.0% | *Henry "Hank" F. Ramey Jr. received 30 write-in votes. But no Democratic candidate appeared on the general election ballot.* | | |

# CALIFORNIA

## GENERAL AND PRIMARY ELECTIONS

| | REPUBLICAN PRIMARIES | | | DEMOCRATIC PRIMARIES | | |
|---|---|---|---|---|---|---|
| **Congressional District 42** | Gary G. Miller* | 65,558 | 100.0% | Lewis Myers | 29,583 | 100.0% |
| **Congressional District 43** | Ed Laning | 13,599 | 100.0% | Joe Baca* | 27,769 | 100.0% |
| **Congressional District 44** | Ken Calvert*<br>David J. Rizzo<br>TOTAL | 49,107<br>8,132<br>57,239 | 85.8%<br>14.2% | Louis Vandenberg | 33,140 | 100.0% |
| **Congressional District 45** | Mary Bono*<br>John Barker<br><br>TOTAL | 51,429<br>8,422<br><br>59,851 | 85.9%<br>14.1% | Richard J. Meyer<br>Dennis Lockhart<br>John W. Thomas (write-in)<br>TOTAL | 27,117<br>11,168<br>12<br>38,297 | 70.8%<br>29.2% |
| **Congressional District 46** | Dana Rohrabacher*<br>Robert K. "Bob" Dornan<br><br>TOTAL | 69,132<br>13,630<br><br>82,762 | 83.5%<br>16.5% | Jim Brandt<br>Tan D. Nguyen<br>Paul C. Wilkins<br>TOTAL | 21,408<br>14,349<br>8,252<br>44,009 | 48.6%<br>32.6%<br>18.8% |
| **Congressional District 47** | Alexandria A. "Alex" Coronado<br>Virgel L. Nickell<br>TOTAL | 12,061<br>8,258<br>20,319 | 59.4%<br>40.6% | Loretta Sanchez* | 23,270 | 100.0% |
| **Congressional District 48** | Christopher Cox* | 85,697 | 100.0% | John Graham | 39,385 | 100.0% |
| **Congressional District 49** | Darrell Issa* | 66,710 | 100.0% | Mike Byron | 32,903 | 100.0% |
| **Congressional District 50** | Randy "Duke" Cunningham* | 81,854 | 100.0% | Francine P. Busby | 47,600 | 100.0% |
| **Congressional District 51** | Michael Giorgino<br>Ruben Ricardo Garcia<br>TOTAL | 19,948<br>8,662<br>28,610 | 69.7%<br>30.3% | Bob Filner*<br>Daniel C. "Danny" Ramirez<br>TOTAL | 33,046<br>10,074<br>43,120 | 76.6%<br>23.4% |
| **Congressional District 52** | Duncan Hunter* | 83,638 | 100.0% | Brian S. Keliher | 42,770 | 100.0% |
| **Congressional District 53** | Darin Hunzeker | 30,925 | 100.0% | Susan A. Davis* | 55,791 | 100.0% |

# COLORADO

## GOVERNOR
Bill Owens (R). Reelected 2002 to a four-year term. Previously elected 1998.

## SENATORS (1 Democrat, 1 Republican)
Wayne Allard (R). Reelected 2002 to a six-year term. Previously elected 1996.

Ken Salazar (D). Elected 2004 to a six-year term.

## REPRESENTATIVES (4 Republicans, 3 Democrats)
1. Diana DeGette (D)
2. Mark Udall (D)
3. John Salazar (D)
4. Marilyn Musgrave (R)
5. Joel Hefley (R)
6. Tom Tancredo (R)
7. Bob Beauprez (R)

## POSTWAR VOTE FOR PRESIDENT

| | | Republican | | Democratic | | Other | | Total Vote | | Major Vote | |
|---|---|---|---|---|---|---|---|---|---|---|---|
| Year | Total Vote | Vote | Candidate | Vote | Candidate | Vote | Plurality | Rep. | Dem. | Rep. | Dem. |
| 2004 | 2,130,330 | 1,101,255 | Bush, George W. | 1,001,732 | Kerry, John | 27,343 | 99,523 R | 51.7% | 47.0% | 52.4% | 47.6% |
| 2000** | 1,741,368 | 883,748 | Bush, George W. | 738,227 | Gore, Al | 119,393 | 145,521 R | 50.8% | 42.4% | 54.5% | 45.5% |
| 1996** | 1,510,704 | 691,848 | Dole, Bob | 671,152 | Clinton, Bill | 147,704 | 20,696 R | 45.8% | 44.4% | 50.8% | 49.2% |
| 1992** | 1,569,180 | 562,850 | Bush, George | 629,681 | Clinton, Bill | 376,649 | 66,831 D | 35.9% | 40.1% | 47.2% | 52.8% |
| 1988 | 1,372,394 | 728,177 | Bush, George | 621,453 | Dukakis, Michael S. | 22,764 | 106,724 R | 53.1% | 45.3% | 54.0% | 46.0% |
| 1984 | 1,295,380 | 821,817 | Reagan, Ronald | 454,975 | Mondale, Walter F. | 18,588 | 366,842 R | 63.4% | 35.1% | 64.4% | 35.6% |
| 1980** | 1,184,415 | 652,264 | Reagan, Ronald | 367,973 | Carter, Jimmy | 164,178 | 284,291 R | 55.1% | 31.1% | 63.9% | 36.1% |
| 1976 | 1,081,554 | 584,367 | Ford, Gerald R. | 460,353 | Carter, Jimmy | 36,834 | 124,014 R | 54.0% | 42.6% | 55.9% | 44.1% |
| 1972 | 953,884 | 597,189 | Nixon, Richard M. | 329,980 | McGovern, George S. | 26,715 | 267,209 R | 62.6% | 34.6% | 64.4% | 35.6% |
| 1968** | 811,199 | 409,345 | Nixon, Richard M. | 335,174 | Humphrey, Hubert H. | 66,680 | 74,171 R | 50.5% | 41.3% | 55.0% | 45.0% |
| 1964 | 776,986 | 296,767 | Goldwater, Barry M. | 476,024 | Johnson, Lyndon B. | 4,195 | 179,257 D | 38.2% | 61.3% | 38.4% | 61.6% |
| 1960 | 736,236 | 402,242 | Nixon, Richard M. | 330,629 | Kennedy, John F. | 3,365 | 71,613 R | 54.6% | 44.9% | 54.9% | 45.1% |
| 1956 | 657,074 | 394,479 | Eisenhower, Dwight D. | 257,997 | Stevenson, Adlai E. | 4,598 | 136,482 R | 60.0% | 39.3% | 60.5% | 39.5% |
| 1952 | 630,103 | 379,782 | Eisenhower, Dwight D. | 245,504 | Stevenson, Adlai E. | 4,817 | 134,278 R | 60.3% | 39.0% | 60.7% | 39.3% |
| 1948 | 515,237 | 239,714 | Dewey, Thomas E. | 267,288 | Truman, Harry S. | 8,235 | 27,574 D | 46.5% | 51.9% | 47.3% | 52.7% |

In past elections, the other vote included: 2000 - 91,434 Green (Ralph Nader); 1996 - 99,629 Reform (Ross Perot); 1992 - 366,010 Independent (Perot); 1980 - 130,633 Independent (John Anderson); 1968 - 60,813 American Independent (George Wallace).

# COLORADO

## POSTWAR VOTE FOR GOVERNOR

| Year | Total Vote | Republican | | Democratic | | Other Vote | Rep.-Dem. Plurality | Percentage | | | |
|------|-----------|------|-----------|------|-----------|------|-----------|------|------|------|------|
| | | Vote | Candidate | Vote | Candidate | | | Total Vote | | Major Vote | |
| | | | | | | | | Rep. | Dem. | Rep. | Dem. |
| 2002 | 1,412,602 | 884,583 | Owens, Bill | 475,373 | Heath, Rollie | 52,646 | 409,210 R | 62.6% | 33.7% | 65.0% | 35.0% |
| 1998 | 1,321,307 | 648,202 | Owens, Bill | 639,905 | Schoettler, Gail | 33,200 | 8,297 R | 49.1% | 48.4% | 50.3% | 49.7% |
| 1994 | 1,116,307 | 432,042 | Benson, Bruce | 619,205 | Romer, Roy | 65,060 | 187,163 D | 38.7% | 55.5% | 41.1% | 58.9% |
| 1990 | 1,011,272 | 358,403 | Andrews, John | 626,032 | Romer, Roy | 26,837 | 267,629 D | 35.4% | 61.9% | 36.4% | 63.6% |
| 1986 | 1,058,928 | 434,420 | Strickland, Ted | 616,325 | Romer, Roy | 8,183 | 181,905 D | 41.0% | 58.2% | 41.3% | 58.7% |
| 1982 | 956,021 | 302,740 | Fuhr, John D. | 627,960 | Lamm, Richard D. | 25,321 | 325,220 D | 31.7% | 65.7% | 32.5% | 67.5% |
| 1978 | 823,807 | 317,292 | Strickland, Ted | 483,985 | Lamm, Richard D. | 22,530 | 166,693 D | 38.5% | 58.7% | 39.6% | 60.4% |
| 1974 | 828,968 | 378,698 | Vanderhoof, John D. | 441,408 | Lamm, Richard D. | 8,862 | 62,710 D | 45.7% | 53.2% | 46.2% | 53.8% |
| 1970 | 668,496 | 350,690 | Love, John A. | 302,432 | Hogan, Mark | 15,374 | 48,258 R | 52.5% | 45.2% | 53.7% | 46.3% |
| 1966 | 660,063 | 356,730 | Love, John A. | 287,132 | Knous, Robert L. | 16,201 | 69,598 R | 54.0% | 43.5% | 55.4% | 44.6% |
| 1962 | 616,481 | 349,342 | Love, John A. | 262,890 | McNichols, Stephen | 4,249 | 86,452 R | 56.7% | 42.6% | 57.1% | 42.9% |
| 1958** | 549,808 | 228,643 | Burch, Palmer L. | 321,165 | McNichols, Stephen | | 92,522 D | 41.6% | 58.4% | 41.6% | 58.4% |
| 1956 | 645,233 | 313,950 | Brotzman, Donald G. | 331,283 | McNichols, Stephen | | 17,333 D | 48.7% | 51.3% | 48.7% | 51.3% |
| 1954 | 489,540 | 227,335 | Brotzman, Donald G. | 262,205 | Johnson, Ed C. | | 34,870 D | 46.4% | 53.6% | 46.4% | 53.6% |
| 1952 | 613,034 | 349,924 | Thornton, Dan | 260,044 | Metzger, John W. | 3,066 | 89,880 R | 57.1% | 42.4% | 57.4% | 42.6% |
| 1950 | 450,994 | 236,472 | Thornton, Dan | 212,976 | Johnson, Walter | 1,546 | 23,496 R | 52.4% | 47.2% | 52.6% | 47.4% |
| 1948 | 501,680 | 168,928 | Hamil, David A. | 332,752 | Knous, William Lee | | 163,824 D | 33.7% | 66.3% | 33.7% | 66.3% |
| 1946 | 335,087 | 160,483 | Lavington, Leon E. | 174,604 | Knous, William Lee | | 14,121 D | 47.9% | 52.1% | 47.9% | 52.1% |

The term of office of Colorado's governor was increased from two to four years effective with the 1958 election.

## POSTWAR VOTE FOR SENATOR

| Year | Total Vote | Republican | | Democratic | | Other Vote | Rep.-Dem. Plurality | Percentage | | | |
|------|-----------|------|-----------|------|-----------|------|-----------|------|------|------|------|
| | | Vote | Candidate | Vote | Candidate | | | Total Vote | | Major Vote | |
| | | | | | | | | Rep. | Dem. | Rep. | Dem. |
| 2004 | 2,107,554 | 980,668 | Coors, Pete | 1,081,188 | Salazar, Ken | 45,698 | 100,520 D | 46.5% | 51.3% | 47.6% | 52.4% |
| 2002 | 1,416,082 | 717,893 | Allard, Wayne | 648,130 | Strickland, Tom | 50,059 | 69,763 R | 50.7% | 45.8% | 52.6% | 47.4% |
| 1998 | 1,327,235 | 829,370 | Campbell, Ben Nighthorse | 464,754 | Lamm, Dottie | 33,111 | 364,616 R | 62.5% | 35.0% | 64.1% | 35.9% |
| 1996 | 1,469,611 | 750,325 | Allard, Wayne | 677,600 | Strickland, Tom | 41,686 | 72,725 R | 51.1% | 46.1% | 52.5% | 47.5% |
| 1992 | 1,552,289 | 662,893 | Considine, Terry | 803,725 | Campbell, Ben Nighthorse | 85,671 | 140,832 D | 42.7% | 51.8% | 45.2% | 54.8% |
| 1990 | 1,022,027 | 569,048 | Brown, Hank | 425,746 | Heath, Josie | 27,233 | 143,302 R | 55.7% | 41.7% | 57.2% | 42.8% |
| 1986 | 1,060,765 | 512,994 | Kramer, Ken | 529,449 | Wirth, Timothy E. | 18,322 | 16,455 D | 48.4% | 49.9% | 49.2% | 50.8% |
| 1984 | 1,297,809 | 833,821 | Armstrong, William L. | 449,327 | Dick, Nancy | 14,661 | 384,494 R | 64.2% | 34.6% | 65.0% | 35.0% |
| 1980 | 1,173,646 | 571,295 | Buchanan, Mary E. | 590,501 | Hart, Gary W. | 11,850 | 19,206 D | 48.7% | 50.3% | 49.2% | 50.8% |
| 1978 | 819,150 | 480,596 | Armstrong, William L. | 330,247 | Haskell, Floyd K. | 8,307 | 150,349 R | 58.7% | 40.3% | 59.3% | 40.7% |
| 1974 | 824,166 | 325,508 | Dominick, Peter H. | 471,691 | Hart, Gary W. | 26,967 | 146,183 D | 39.5% | 57.2% | 40.8% | 59.2% |
| 1972 | 926,093 | 447,957 | Allott, Gordon | 457,545 | Haskell, Floyd K. | 20,591 | 9,588 D | 48.4% | 49.4% | 49.5% | 50.5% |
| 1968 | 785,536 | 459,952 | Dominick, Peter H. | 325,584 | McNichols, Stephen | | 134,368 R | 58.6% | 41.4% | 58.6% | 41.4% |
| 1966 | 634,898 | 368,307 | Allott, Gordon | 266,259 | Romer, Roy | 332 | 102,048 R | 58.0% | 41.9% | 58.0% | 42.0% |
| 1962 | 613,444 | 328,655 | Dominick, Peter H. | 279,586 | Carroll, John A. | 5,203 | 49,069 R | 53.6% | 45.6% | 54.0% | 46.0% |
| 1960 | 727,633 | 389,428 | Allott, Gordon | 334,854 | Knous, Robert L. | 3,351 | 54,574 R | 53.5% | 46.0% | 53.8% | 46.2% |
| 1956 | 636,974 | 317,102 | Thornton, Dan | 319,872 | Carroll, John A. | | 2,770 D | 49.8% | 50.2% | 49.8% | 50.2% |
| 1954 | 484,188 | 248,502 | Allott, Gordon | 235,686 | Carroll, John A. | | 12,816 R | 51.3% | 48.7% | 51.3% | 48.7% |
| 1950 | 450,176 | 239,734 | Millikin, Eugene D. | 210,442 | Carroll, John A. | | 29,292 R | 53.3% | 46.7% | 53.3% | 46.7% |
| 1948 | 510,121 | 165,069 | Nicholson, W. F. | 340,719 | Johnson, Ed C. | 4,333 | 175,650 D | 32.4% | 66.8% | 32.6% | 67.4% |

# COLORADO

Congressional districts first established for elections held in 2002
7 members

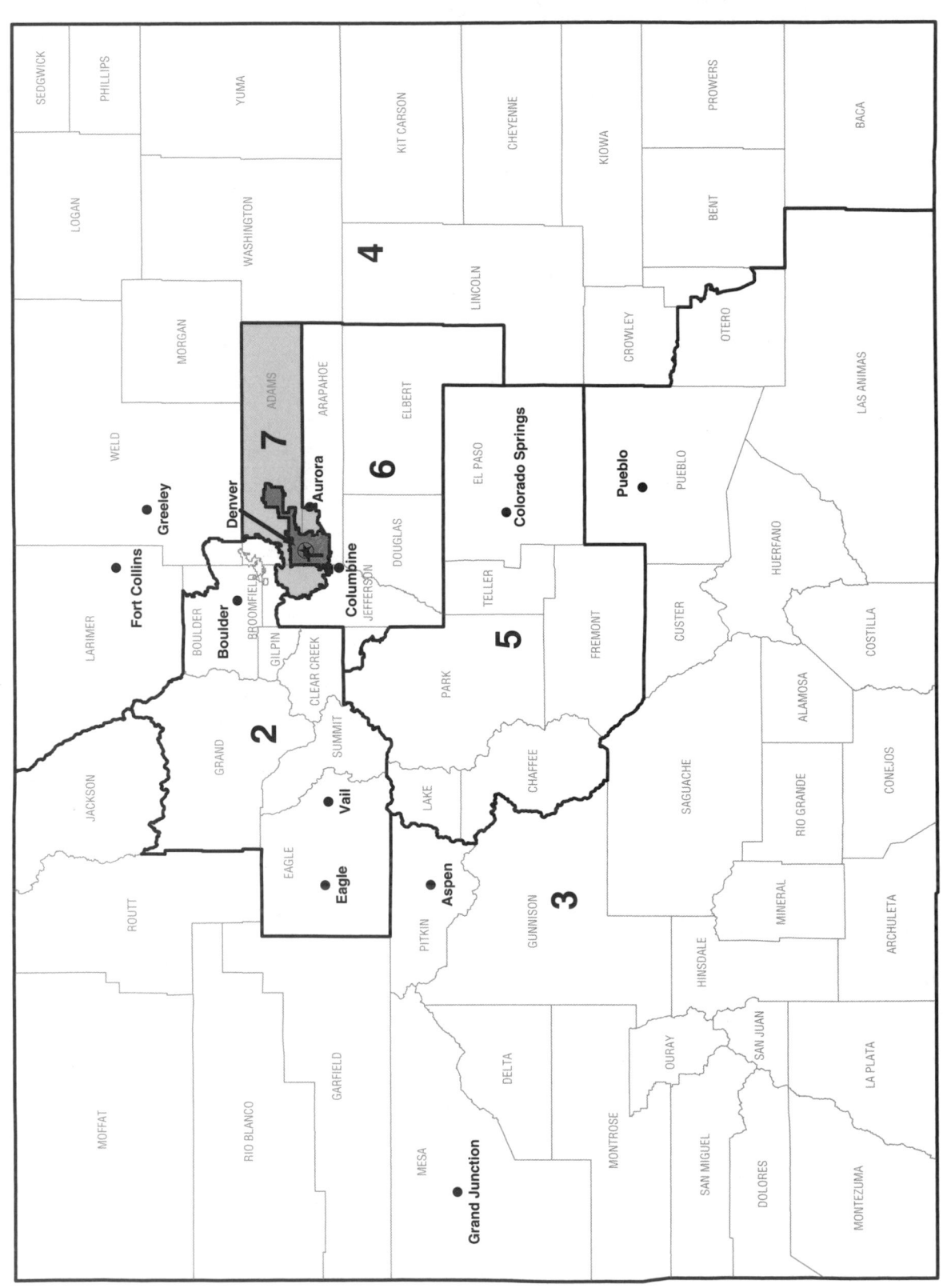

# COLORADO

## Denver Area

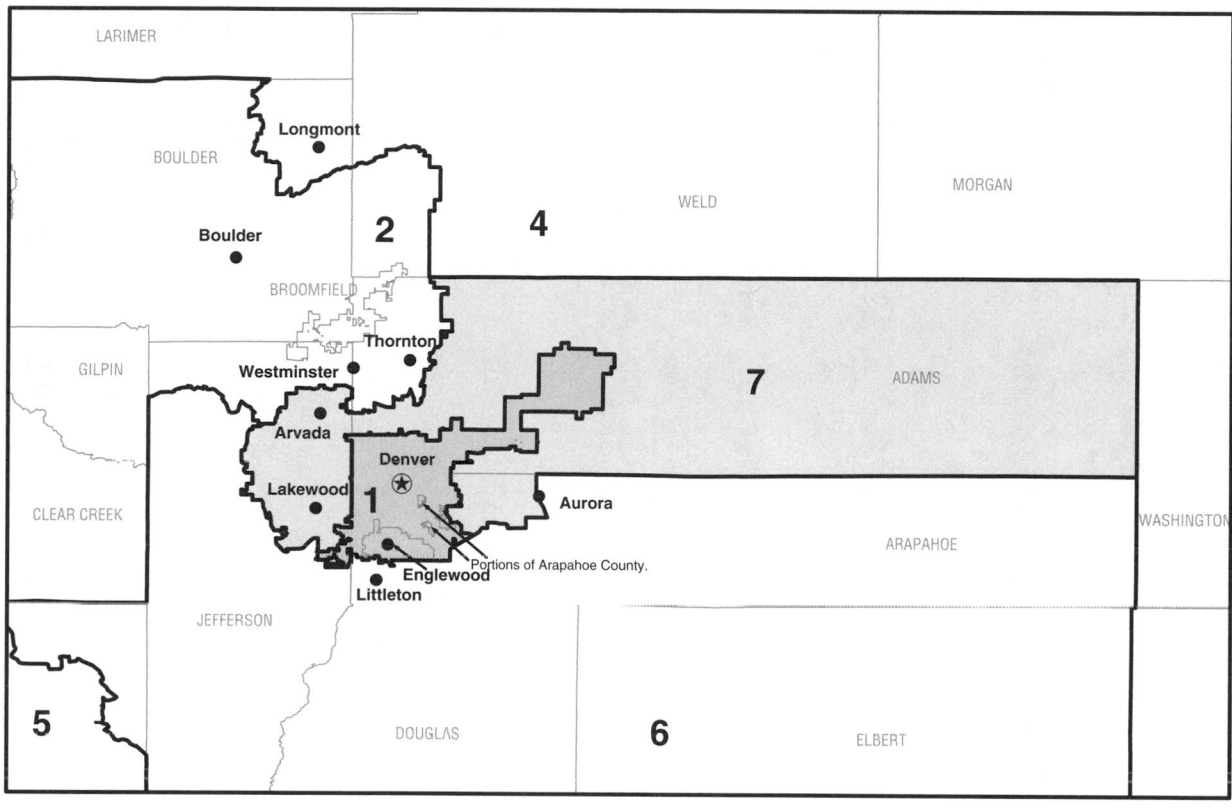

# COLORADO

## PRESIDENT 2004

| 2000 Census Population | County | Total Vote | Republican | Democratic | Other | Rep.-Dem. Plurality | Percentage | | | |
|---|---|---|---|---|---|---|---|---|---|---|
| | | | | | | | Total Vote | | Major Vote | |
| | | | | | | | Rep. | Dem. | Rep. | Dem. |
| 348,618 | ADAMS | 136,677 | 65,912 | 69,122 | 1,643 | 3,210 D | 48.2% | 50.6% | 48.8% | 51.2% |
| 14,966 | ALAMOSA | 6,279 | 3,179 | 3,017 | 83 | 162 R | 50.6% | 48.0% | 51.3% | 48.7% |
| 487,967 | ARAPAHOE | 232,365 | 119,475 | 110,262 | 2,628 | 9,213 R | 51.4% | 47.5% | 52.0% | 48.0% |
| 9,898 | ARCHULETA | 5,839 | 3,601 | 2,141 | 97 | 1,460 R | 61.7% | 36.7% | 62.7% | 37.3% |
| 4,517 | BACA | 2,186 | 1,680 | 483 | 23 | 1,197 R | 76.9% | 22.1% | 77.7% | 22.3% |
| 5,998 | BENT | 2,155 | 1,338 | 785 | 32 | 553 R | 62.1% | 36.4% | 63.0% | 37.0% |
| 269,814 | BOULDER | 159,259 | 51,586 | 105,564 | 2,109 | 53,978 D | 32.4% | 66.3% | 32.8% | 67.2% |
| 38,272 | BROOMFIELD* | 23,235 | 12,007 | 10,935 | 293 | 1,072 R | 51.7% | 47.1% | 52.3% | 47.7% |
| 16,242 | CHAFFEE | 8,770 | 4,875 | 3,766 | 129 | 1,109 R | 55.6% | 42.9% | 56.4% | 43.6% |
| 2,231 | CHEYENNE | 1,134 | 923 | 198 | 13 | 725 R | 81.4% | 17.5% | 82.3% | 17.7% |
| 9,322 | CLEAR CREEK | 5,613 | 2,522 | 2,989 | 102 | 467 D | 44.9% | 53.3% | 45.8% | 54.2% |
| 8,400 | CONEJOS | 3,803 | 1,864 | 1,894 | 45 | 30 D | 49.0% | 49.8% | 49.6% | 50.4% |
| 3,663 | COSTILLA | 1,760 | 566 | 1,170 | 24 | 604 D | 32.2% | 66.5% | 32.6% | 67.4% |
| 5,518 | CROWLEY | 1,493 | 1,006 | 478 | 9 | 528 R | 67.4% | 32.0% | 67.8% | 32.2% |
| 3,503 | CUSTER | 2,428 | 1,657 | 739 | 32 | 918 R | 68.2% | 30.4% | 69.2% | 30.8% |
| 27,834 | DELTA | 14,159 | 9,722 | 4,224 | 213 | 5,498 R | 68.7% | 29.8% | 69.7% | 30.3% |
| 554,636 | DENVER | 238,826 | 69,903 | 166,135 | 2,788 | 96,232 D | 29.3% | 69.6% | 29.6% | 70.4% |
| 1,844 | DOLORES | 1,146 | 785 | 333 | 28 | 452 R | 68.5% | 29.1% | 70.2% | 29.8% |
| 175,766 | DOUGLAS | 121,201 | 80,651 | 39,661 | 889 | 40,990 R | 66.5% | 32.7% | 67.0% | 33.0% |
| 41,659 | EAGLE | 18,511 | 8,533 | 9,744 | 234 | 1,211 D | 46.1% | 52.6% | 46.7% | 53.3% |
| 19,872 | ELBERT | 11,364 | 8,389 | 2,834 | 141 | 5,555 R | 73.8% | 24.9% | 74.7% | 25.3% |
| 516,929 | EL PASO | 241,788 | 161,361 | 77,648 | 2,779 | 83,713 R | 66.7% | 32.1% | 67.5% | 32.5% |
| 46,145 | FREMONT | 18,526 | 12,313 | 5,933 | 280 | 6,380 R | 66.5% | 32.0% | 67.5% | 32.5% |
| 43,791 | GARFIELD | 20,647 | 11,123 | 9,228 | 296 | 1,895 R | 53.9% | 44.7% | 54.7% | 45.3% |
| 4,757 | GILPIN | 3,196 | 1,329 | 1,807 | 60 | 478 D | 41.6% | 56.5% | 42.4% | 57.6% |
| 12,442 | GRAND | 7,609 | 4,260 | 3,243 | 106 | 1,017 R | 56.0% | 42.6% | 56.8% | 43.2% |
| 13,956 | GUNNISON | 8,420 | 3,479 | 4,782 | 159 | 1,303 D | 41.3% | 56.8% | 42.1% | 57.9% |
| 790 | HINSDALE | 602 | 355 | 236 | 11 | 119 R | 59.0% | 39.2% | 60.1% | 39.9% |
| 7,862 | HUERFANO | 3,402 | 1,700 | 1,663 | 39 | 37 R | 50.0% | 48.9% | 50.6% | 49.4% |
| 1,577 | JACKSON | 934 | 710 | 210 | 14 | 500 R | 76.0% | 22.5% | 77.2% | 22.8% |
| 525,507 | JEFFERSON | 271,568 | 140,644 | 126,558 | 4,366 | 14,086 R | 51.8% | 46.6% | 52.6% | 47.4% |
| 1,622 | KIOWA | 892 | 712 | 172 | 8 | 540 R | 79.8% | 19.3% | 80.5% | 19.5% |
| 8,011 | KIT CARSON | 3,502 | 2,721 | 729 | 52 | 1,992 R | 77.7% | 20.8% | 78.9% | 21.1% |
| 7,812 | LAKE | 2,949 | 1,261 | 1,623 | 65 | 362 D | 42.8% | 55.0% | 43.7% | 56.3% |
| 43,941 | LA PLATA | 25,513 | 11,704 | 13,409 | 400 | 1,705 D | 45.9% | 52.6% | 46.6% | 53.4% |
| 251,494 | LARIMER | 146,436 | 75,884 | 68,266 | 2,286 | 7,618 R | 51.8% | 46.6% | 52.6% | 47.4% |
| 15,207 | LAS ANIMAS | 6,592 | 3,196 | 3,300 | 96 | 104 D | 48.5% | 50.1% | 49.2% | 50.8% |
| 6,087 | LINCOLN | 2,337 | 1,819 | 503 | 15 | 1,316 R | 77.8% | 21.5% | 78.3% | 21.7% |
| 20,504 | LOGAN | 8,766 | 6,168 | 2,491 | 107 | 3,677 R | 70.4% | 28.4% | 71.2% | 28.8% |
| 116,255 | MESA | 61,885 | 41,539 | 19,564 | 782 | 21,975 R | 67.1% | 31.6% | 68.0% | 32.0% |
| 831 | MINERAL | 619 | 383 | 227 | 9 | 156 R | 61.9% | 36.7% | 62.8% | 37.2% |
| 13,184 | MOFFAT | 5,725 | 4,247 | 1,355 | 123 | 2,892 R | 74.2% | 23.7% | 75.8% | 24.2% |
| 23,830 | MONTEZUMA | 11,015 | 6,988 | 3,867 | 160 | 3,121 R | 63.4% | 35.1% | 64.4% | 35.6% |
| 33,432 | MONTROSE | 16,219 | 11,218 | 4,776 | 225 | 6,442 R | 69.2% | 29.4% | 70.1% | 29.9% |
| 27,171 | MORGAN | 9,936 | 6,787 | 3,039 | 110 | 3,748 R | 68.3% | 30.6% | 69.1% | 30.9% |
| 20,311 | OTERO | 8,180 | 4,947 | 3,164 | 69 | 1,783 R | 60.5% | 38.7% | 61.0% | 39.0% |
| 3,742 | OURAY | 2,721 | 1,402 | 1,278 | 41 | 124 R | 51.5% | 47.0% | 52.3% | 47.7% |
| 14,523 | PARK | 8,357 | 4,781 | 3,445 | 131 | 1,336 R | 57.2% | 41.2% | 58.1% | 41.9% |
| 4,480 | PHILLIPS | 2,325 | 1,717 | 582 | 26 | 1,135 R | 73.8% | 25.0% | 74.7% | 25.3% |
| 14,872 | PITKIN | 9,256 | 2,784 | 6,335 | 137 | 3,551 D | 30.1% | 68.4% | 30.5% | 69.5% |
| 14,483 | PROWERS | 4,745 | 3,392 | 1,308 | 45 | 2,084 R | 71.5% | 27.6% | 72.2% | 27.8% |
| 141,472 | PUEBLO | 67,187 | 31,117 | 35,369 | 701 | 4,252 D | 46.3% | 52.6% | 46.8% | 53.2% |
| 5,986 | RIO BLANCO | 3,003 | 2,403 | 566 | 34 | 1,837 R | 80.0% | 18.8% | 80.9% | 19.1% |
| 12,413 | RIO GRANDE | 5,526 | 3,448 | 2,006 | 72 | 1,442 R | 62.4% | 36.3% | 63.2% | 36.8% |
| 19,690 | ROUTT | 11,762 | 5,199 | 6,392 | 171 | 1,193 D | 44.2% | 54.3% | 44.9% | 55.1% |
| 5,917 | SAGUACHE | 2,803 | 1,163 | 1,594 | 46 | 431 D | 41.5% | 56.9% | 42.2% | 57.8% |
| 558 | SAN JUAN | 486 | 216 | 253 | 17 | 37 D | 44.4% | 52.1% | 46.1% | 53.9% |
| 6,594 | SAN MIGUEL | 4,019 | 1,079 | 2,876 | 64 | 1,797 D | 26.8% | 71.6% | 27.3% | 72.7% |
| 2,747 | SEDGWICK | 1,360 | 971 | 374 | 15 | 597 R | 71.4% | 27.5% | 72.2% | 27.8% |
| 23,548 | SUMMIT | 13,735 | 5,370 | 8,144 | 221 | 2,774 D | 39.1% | 59.3% | 39.7% | 60.3% |

# COLORADO

## PRESIDENT 2004

| 2000 Census Population | County | Total Vote | Republican | Democratic | Other | Rep.-Dem. Plurality | Percentage | | | |
|---|---|---|---|---|---|---|---|---|---|---|
| | | | | | | | Total Vote | | Major Vote | |
| | | | | | | | Rep. | Dem. | Rep. | Dem. |
| 20,555 | TELLER | 11,842 | 8,094 | 3,556 | 192 | 4,538 R | 68.3% | 30.0% | 69.5% | 30.5% |
| 4,926 | WASHINGTON | 2,530 | 2,050 | 455 | 25 | 1,595 R | 81.0% | 18.0% | 81.8% | 18.2% |
| 180,926 | WELD | 88,653 | 55,591 | 31,868 | 1,194 | 23,723 R | 62.7% | 35.9% | 63.6% | 36.4% |
| 9,841 | YUMA | 4,559 | 3,456 | 1,064 | 39 | 2,392 R | 75.8% | 23.3% | 76.5% | 23.5% |
| 4,301,261 | TOTAL | 2,130,330 | 1,101,255 | 1,001,732 | 27,343 | 99,523 R | 51.7% | 47.0% | 52.4% | 47.6% |

Note: Broomfield County was created effective 2001 out of portions of Adams, Boulder, Jefferson, and Weld counties. The population figures in this table have been adjusted for each county using 2000 census data.

# COLORADO

## SENATOR 2004

| 2000 Census Population | County | Total Vote | Republican | Democratic | Other | Rep.-Dem. Plurality | Percentage | | | |
|---|---|---|---|---|---|---|---|---|---|---|
| | | | | | | | Total Vote | | Major Vote | |
| | | | | | | | Rep. | Dem. | Rep. | Dem. |
| 348,618 | ADAMS | 134,982 | 55,438 | 76,101 | 3,443 | 20,663 D | 41.1% | 56.4% | 42.1% | 57.9% |
| 14,966 | ALAMOSA | 6,195 | 2,158 | 3,937 | 100 | 1,779 D | 34.8% | 63.6% | 35.4% | 64.6% |
| 487,967 | ARAPAHOE | 230,361 | 105,921 | 120,225 | 4,215 | 14,304 D | 46.0% | 52.2% | 46.8% | 53.2% |
| 9,898 | ARCHULETA | 5,777 | 3,051 | 2,531 | 195 | 520 R | 52.8% | 43.8% | 54.7% | 45.3% |
| 4,517 | BACA | 2,148 | 1,248 | 848 | 52 | 400 R | 58.1% | 39.5% | 59.5% | 40.5% |
| 5,998 | BENT | 2,145 | 962 | 1,124 | 59 | 162 D | 44.8% | 52.4% | 46.1% | 53.9% |
| 269,814 | BOULDER | 157,414 | 47,899 | 106,481 | 3,034 | 58,582 D | 30.4% | 67.6% | 31.0% | 69.0% |
| 38,272 | BROOMFIELD* | 22,985 | 10,588 | 11,940 | 457 | 1,352 D | 46.1% | 51.9% | 47.0% | 53.0% |
| 16,242 | CHAFFEE | 8,701 | 4,286 | 4,229 | 186 | 57 R | 49.3% | 48.6% | 50.3% | 49.7% |
| 2,231 | CHEYENNE | 1,128 | 762 | 330 | 36 | 432 R | 67.6% | 29.3% | 69.8% | 30.2% |
| 9,322 | CLEAR CREEK | 5,587 | 2,246 | 3,179 | 162 | 933 D | 40.2% | 56.9% | 41.4% | 58.6% |
| 8,400 | CONEJOS | 3,863 | 1,177 | 2,624 | 62 | 1,447 D | 30.5% | 67.9% | 31.0% | 69.0% |
| 3,663 | COSTILLA | 1,796 | 372 | 1,363 | 61 | 991 D | 20.7% | 75.9% | 21.4% | 78.6% |
| 5,518 | CROWLEY | 1,478 | 823 | 608 | 47 | 215 R | 55.7% | 41.1% | 57.5% | 42.5% |
| 3,503 | CUSTER | 2,404 | 1,449 | 902 | 53 | 547 R | 60.3% | 37.5% | 61.6% | 38.4% |
| 27,834 | DELTA | 14,087 | 8,598 | 5,060 | 429 | 3,538 R | 61.0% | 35.9% | 63.0% | 37.0% |
| 554,636 | DENVER | 233,788 | 60,387 | 169,580 | 3,821 | 109,193 D | 25.8% | 72.5% | 26.3% | 73.7% |
| 1,844 | DOLORES | 1,127 | 581 | 498 | 48 | 83 R | 51.6% | 44.2% | 53.8% | 46.2% |
| 175,766 | DOUGLAS | 119,995 | 72,911 | 45,425 | 1,659 | 27,486 R | 60.8% | 37.9% | 61.6% | 38.4% |
| 41,659 | EAGLE | 18,185 | 7,636 | 10,110 | 439 | 2,474 D | 42.0% | 55.6% | 43.0% | 57.0% |
| 19,872 | ELBERT | 11,228 | 7,475 | 3,497 | 256 | 3,978 R | 66.6% | 31.1% | 68.1% | 31.9% |
| 516,929 | EL PASO | 238,719 | 151,414 | 81,403 | 5,902 | 70,011 R | 63.4% | 34.1% | 65.0% | 35.0% |
| 46,145 | FREMONT | 18,557 | 10,942 | 7,053 | 562 | 3,889 R | 59.0% | 38.0% | 60.8% | 39.2% |
| 43,791 | GARFIELD | 20,455 | 9,840 | 9,959 | 656 | 119 D | 48.1% | 48.7% | 49.7% | 50.3% |
| 4,757 | GILPIN | 3,173 | 1,221 | 1,815 | 137 | 594 D | 38.5% | 57.2% | 40.2% | 59.8% |
| 12,442 | GRAND | 7,545 | 3,788 | 3,560 | 197 | 228 R | 50.2% | 47.2% | 51.6% | 48.4% |
| 13,956 | GUNNISON | 8,348 | 2,872 | 5,280 | 196 | 2,408 D | 34.4% | 63.2% | 35.2% | 64.8% |
| 790 | HINSDALE | 601 | 296 | 279 | 26 | 17 R | 49.3% | 46.4% | 51.5% | 48.5% |
| 7,862 | HUERFANO | 3,426 | 1,364 | 1,969 | 93 | 605 D | 39.8% | 57.5% | 40.9% | 59.1% |
| 1,577 | JACKSON | 931 | 547 | 352 | 32 | 195 R | 58.8% | 37.8% | 60.8% | 39.2% |
| 525,507 | JEFFERSON | 270,064 | 127,048 | 137,554 | 5,462 | 10,506 D | 47.0% | 50.9% | 48.0% | 52.0% |
| 1,622 | KIOWA | 890 | 574 | 295 | 21 | 279 R | 64.5% | 33.1% | 66.1% | 33.9% |
| 8,011 | KIT CARSON | 3,470 | 2,284 | 1,106 | 80 | 1,178 R | 65.8% | 31.9% | 67.4% | 32.6% |
| 7,812 | LAKE | 2,950 | 1,062 | 1,778 | 110 | 716 D | 36.0% | 60.3% | 37.4% | 62.6% |
| 43,941 | LA PLATA | 25,092 | 10,561 | 13,989 | 542 | 3,428 D | 42.1% | 55.8% | 43.0% | 57.0% |
| 251,494 | LARIMER | 144,539 | 67,597 | 73,204 | 3,738 | 5,607 D | 46.8% | 50.6% | 48.0% | 52.0% |
| 15,207 | LAS ANIMAS | 6,633 | 2,650 | 3,783 | 200 | 1,133 D | 40.0% | 57.0% | 41.2% | 58.8% |
| 6,087 | LINCOLN | 2,311 | 1,580 | 682 | 49 | 898 R | 68.4% | 29.5% | 69.8% | 30.2% |
| 20,504 | LOGAN | 8,710 | 5,415 | 3,114 | 181 | 2,301 R | 62.2% | 35.8% | 63.5% | 36.5% |
| 116,255 | MESA | 61,242 | 38,080 | 21,718 | 1,444 | 16,362 R | 62.2% | 35.5% | 63.7% | 36.3% |

# COLORADO

## SENATOR 2004

| 2000 Census Population | County | Total Vote | Republican | Democratic | Other | Rep.-Dem. Plurality | Total Vote Rep. | Total Vote Dem. | Major Vote Rep. | Major Vote Dem. |
|---|---|---|---|---|---|---|---|---|---|---|
| 831 | MINERAL | 613 | 267 | 338 | 8 | 71 D | 43.6% | 55.1% | 44.1% | 55.9% |
| 13,184 | MOFFAT | 5,694 | 3,494 | 1,966 | 234 | 1,528 R | 61.4% | 34.5% | 64.0% | 36.0% |
| 23,830 | MONTEZUMA | 10,851 | 5,724 | 4,773 | 354 | 951 R | 52.8% | 44.0% | 54.5% | 45.5% |
| 33,432 | MONTROSE | 16,481 | 10,433 | 5,603 | 445 | 4,830 R | 63.3% | 34.0% | 65.1% | 34.9% |
| 27,171 | MORGAN | 9,917 | 5,745 | 3,938 | 234 | 1,807 R | 57.9% | 39.7% | 59.3% | 40.7% |
| 20,311 | OTERO | 8,187 | 4,037 | 3,963 | 187 | 74 R | 49.3% | 48.4% | 50.5% | 49.5% |
| 3,742 | OURAY | 2,698 | 1,332 | 1,315 | 51 | 17 R | 49.4% | 48.7% | 50.3% | 49.7% |
| 14,523 | PARK | 8,307 | 4,330 | 3,696 | 281 | 634 R | 52.1% | 44.5% | 53.9% | 46.1% |
| 4,480 | PHILLIPS | 2,285 | 1,443 | 804 | 38 | 639 R | 63.2% | 35.2% | 64.2% | 35.8% |
| 14,872 | PITKIN | 9,101 | 2,783 | 6,135 | 183 | 3,352 D | 30.6% | 67.4% | 31.2% | 68.8% |
| 14,483 | PROWERS | 4,723 | 2,628 | 1,987 | 108 | 641 R | 55.6% | 42.1% | 56.9% | 43.1% |
| 141,472 | PUEBLO | 67,187 | 26,160 | 39,687 | 1,340 | 13,527 D | 38.9% | 59.1% | 39.7% | 60.3% |
| 5,986 | RIO BLANCO | 2,986 | 2,004 | 871 | 111 | 1,133 R | 67.1% | 29.2% | 69.7% | 30.3% |
| 12,413 | RIO GRANDE | 5,546 | 2,571 | 2,854 | 121 | 283 D | 46.4% | 51.5% | 47.4% | 52.6% |
| 19,690 | ROUTT | 11,604 | 4,522 | 6,771 | 311 | 2,249 D | 39.0% | 58.4% | 40.0% | 60.0% |
| 5,917 | SAGUACHE | 2,787 | 889 | 1,817 | 81 | 928 D | 31.9% | 65.2% | 32.9% | 67.1% |
| 558 | SAN JUAN | 488 | 150 | 320 | 18 | 170 D | 30.7% | 65.6% | 31.9% | 68.1% |
| 6,594 | SAN MIGUEL | 3,971 | 1,002 | 2,858 | 111 | 1,856 D | 25.2% | 72.0% | 26.0% | 74.0% |
| 2,747 | SEDGWICK | 1,343 | 800 | 512 | 31 | 288 R | 59.6% | 38.1% | 61.0% | 39.0% |
| 23,548 | SUMMIT | 13,565 | 5,022 | 8,205 | 338 | 3,183 D | 37.0% | 60.5% | 38.0% | 62.0% |
| 20,555 | TELLER | 11,725 | 7,617 | 3,740 | 368 | 3,877 R | 65.0% | 31.9% | 67.1% | 32.9% |
| 4,926 | WASHINGTON | 2,519 | 1,717 | 742 | 60 | 975 R | 68.2% | 29.5% | 69.8% | 30.2% |
| 180,926 | WELD | 87,446 | 47,986 | 37,320 | 2,140 | 10,666 R | 54.9% | 42.7% | 56.3% | 43.7% |
| 9,841 | YUMA | 4,500 | 2,909 | 1,488 | 103 | 1,421 R | 64.6% | 33.1% | 66.2% | 33.8% |
| 4,301,261 | TOTAL | 2,107,554 | 980,668 | 1,081,188 | 45,698 | 100,520 D | 46.5% | 51.3% | 47.6% | 52.4% |

Note: Broomfield County was created effective 2001 out of portions of Adams, Boulder, Jefferson, and Weld counties. The population figures in this table have been adjusted for each county using 2000 census data.

# COLORADO

## HOUSE OF REPRESENTATIVES

| CD | Year | Total Vote | Republican Vote | Republican Candidate | Democratic Vote | Democratic Candidate | Other Vote | Rep.-Dem. Plurality | Total Vote Rep. | Total Vote Dem. | Major Vote Rep. | Major Vote Dem. |
|---|---|---|---|---|---|---|---|---|---|---|---|---|
| 1 | 2004 | 240,929 | 58,659 | Chicas, Roland | 177,077 | DeGette, Diana* | 5,193 | 118,418 D | 24.3% | 73.5% | 24.9% | 75.1% |
| 1 | 2002 | 168,564 | 49,884 | Chlouber, Ken | 111,718 | DeGette, Diana* | 6,962 | 61,834 D | 29.6% | 66.3% | 30.9% | 69.1% |
| 2 | 2004 | 309,364 | 94,160 | Hackman, Stephen M. | 207,900 | Udall, Mark* | 7,304 | 113,740 D | 30.4% | 67.2% | 31.2% | 68.8% |
| 2 | 2002 | 205,522 | 75,564 | Hume, Sandy | 123,504 | Udall, Mark* | 6,454 | 47,940 D | 36.8% | 60.1% | 38.0% | 62.0% |
| 3 | 2004 | 303,646 | 141,376 | Walcher, Greg | 153,500 | Salazar, John | 8,770 | 12,124 D | 46.6% | 50.6% | 47.9% | 52.1% |
| 3 | 2002 | 217,972 | 143,433 | McInnis, Scott* | 68,160 | Berckefeldt, Denis | 6,379 | 75,273 R | 65.8% | 31.3% | 67.8% | 32.2% |
| 4 | 2004 | 305,509 | 155,958 | Musgrave, Marilyn* | 136,812 | Matsunaka, Stan | 12,739 | 19,146 R | 51.0% | 44.8% | 53.3% | 46.7% |
| 4 | 2002 | 209,955 | 115,359 | Musgrave, Marilyn | 87,499 | Matsunaka, Stan | 7,097 | 27,860 R | 54.9% | 41.7% | 56.9% | 43.1% |
| 5 | 2004 | 274,058 | 193,333 | Hefley, Joel* | 74,098 | Hardee, Fred | 6,627 | 119,235 R | 70.5% | 27.0% | 72.3% | 27.7% |
| 5 | 2002 | 184,677 | 128,118 | Hefley, Joel* | 45,587 | Imrie, Curtis | 10,972 | 82,531 R | 69.4% | 24.7% | 73.8% | 26.2% |

# COLORADO

## HOUSE OF REPRESENTATIVES

| CD | Year | Total Vote | Republican Vote | Republican Candidate | Democratic Vote | Democratic Candidate | Other Vote | Rep.-Dem. Plurality | Total Vote Rep. | Total Vote Dem. | Major Vote Rep. | Major Vote Dem. |
|----|------|-----------|-----------------|----------------------|-----------------|----------------------|------------|---------------------|-----------------|-----------------|-----------------|-----------------|
| 6 | 2004 | 357,741 | 212,778 | Tancredo, Tom* | 139,870 | Conti, Joanna L. | 5,093 | 72,908 R | 59.5% | 39.1% | 60.3% | 39.7% |
| 6 | 2002 | 237,501 | 158,851 | Tancredo, Tom* | 71,327 | Wright, Lance | 7,323 | 87,524 R | 66.9% | 30.0% | 69.0% | 31.0% |
| 7 | 2004 | 247,764 | 135,571 | Beauprez, Bob* | 106,026 | Thomas, Dave | 6,167 | 29,545 R | 54.7% | 42.8% | 56.1% | 43.9% |
| 7 | 2002 | 172,879 | 81,789 | Beauprez, Bob | 81,668 | Feeley, Mike | 9,422 | 121 R | 47.3% | 47.2% | 50.0% | 50.0% |
| Total | 2004 | 2,039,011 | 991,835 | | 995,283 | | 51,893 | 3,448 D | 48.6% | 48.8% | 49.9% | 50.1% |
| Total | 2002 | 1,397,070 | 752,998 | | 589,463 | | 54,609 | 163,535 R | 53.9% | 42.2% | 56.1% | 43.9% |

An asterisk (*) denotes incumbent.

# COLORADO

## GENERAL AND PRIMARY ELECTIONS

## 2004 GENERAL ELECTIONS

**President**    Other vote was 12,718 Colorado Reform (Ralph Nader); 7,664 Libertarian (Michael Badnarik); 2,562 American Constitution (Michael Peroutka); 1,591 Green (David Cobb); 804 Unaffiliated (Stanford E. "Andy" Andress); 700 write-in (John Joseph Kennedy); 378 Concerns of People (Gene Amondson); 329 Socialist Equality (Bill Van Auken); 241 Socialist Workers (James E. Harris); 216 Socialist (Walter F. Brown); 140 Prohibition (Earl F. Dodge).

**Senator**    Other vote was 18,783 American Constitution (Douglas "Dayhorse" Campbell); 10,160 Libertarian (Richard Randall); 8,442 Independent (John R. Harris); 6,481 Colorado Reform (Victor Good); 1,750 Unaffiliated (Finn Gotaas); 46 write-in (Raul Acosta); 17 write-in (Joyce Cumbie Broughton); 7 write-in (Daniel "Muh Sigh Uh" Masia-s); 5 write-in (George Walker); 3 write-in (Daniel James Barnett); 2 write-in (Robert "Doc" Greenheck); 1 write-in (Gary Cooper); 1 write-in (Dwight Henson).

**House**    Other vote was:

CD 1    5,193 American Constitution (George C. Lilly).
CD 2    7,304 Libertarian (Norm Olsen).
CD 3    8,770 Unaffiliated (Jim Krug).
CD 4    12,739 Green (Bob Kinsey).
CD 5    6,627 Libertarian (Arthur "Rob" Roberts).
CD 6    3,857 Libertarian (Jack J. Woehr); 1,236 American Constitution (Peter Shevchuk).
CD 7    6,167 American Constitution (Clyde J. Harkins).

# COLORADO

## GENERAL AND PRIMARY ELECTIONS

### 2004 PRIMARY ELECTIONS

| | | | | |
|---|---|---|---|---|
| Primary | August 10, 2004 | | Registration (as of July 16, 2004) | |

| | |
|---|---|
| Republican | 1,046,753 |
| Democratic | 858,703 |
| Libertarian | 5,713 |
| Green | 5,307 |
| Natural Law | 561 |
| Reform | 337 |
| American Constitution | 142 |
| Concerns of the People | 39 |
| Unaffiliated | 925,109 |
| TOTAL | 2,842,664 |

Primary Type    Semi-open—Registered Democrats and Republicans could vote only in their party's primary. "Unaffiliated" voters could vote in either primary but in the process had to declare their affiliation with that party.

Note:    An asterisk (*) denotes incumbent.

| | REPUBLICAN PRIMARIES | | | DEMOCRATIC PRIMARIES | | |
|---|---|---|---|---|---|---|
| Senator | Pete Coors | 203,157 | 60.6% | Ken Salazar | 173,167 | 73.0% |
| | Bob Schaffer | 132,274 | 39.4% | Mike Miles | 63,973 | 27.0% |
| | TOTAL | 335,431 | | TOTAL | 237,140 | |
| Congressional District 1 | Roland Chicas | 16,417 | 100.0% | Diana DeGette* | 47,579 | 100.0% |
| Congressional District 2 | Stephen M. Hackman | 12,538 | 52.1% | Mark Udall* | 32,679 | 100.0% |
| | Michael P. Kennedy | 11,518 | 47.9% | | | |
| | TOTAL | 24,056 | | | | |
| Congressional District 3 | Greg Walcher | 15,572 | 31.9% | John Salazar | 34,464 | 100.0% |
| | Matt Smith | 15,298 | 31.3% | | | |
| | Gregg P. Rippy | 7,968 | 16.3% | | | |
| | Dan Corsentino | 5,612 | 11.5% | | | |
| | Matt Aljanich | 4,408 | 9.0% | | | |
| | TOTAL | 48,858 | | | | |
| Congressional District 4 | Marilyn Musgrave* | 44,649 | 78.1% | Stan Matsunaka | 24,894 | 100.0% |
| | Bob Faust | 12,553 | 21.9% | | | |
| | TOTAL | 57,202 | | | | |
| Congressional District 5 | Joel Hefley* | 52,282 | 84.2% | Fred Hardee | 15,763 | 100.0% |
| | Mike Payton | 9,785 | 15.8% | | | |
| | TOTAL | 62,067 | | | | |
| Congressional District 6 | Tom Tancredo* | 58,446 | 100.0% | Joanna L. Conti | 23,111 | 100.0% |
| Congressional District 7 | Bob Beauprez* | 34,729 | 100.0% | Dave Thomas | 27,706 | 100.0% |

# CONNECTICUT

## GOVERNOR
M. Jodi Rell (R). Assumed office July 1, 2004, following the resignation of John G. Rowland (R), who was under threat of impeachment for accepting gifts from state employees and contractors.

## SENATORS (2 Democrats)
Christopher J. Dodd (D). Reelected 2004 to a six-year term. Previously elected 1998, 1992, 1986, 1980.

Joseph I. Lieberman (D). Reelected 2000 to a six-year term. Previously elected 1994, 1988.

## REPRESENTATIVES (3 Republicans, 2 Democrats)
1. John B. Larson (D)
2. Rob Simmons (R)
3. Rosa DeLauro (D)
4. Christopher Shays (R)
5. Nancy L. Johnson (R)

## POSTWAR VOTE FOR PRESIDENT

| | | Republican | | Democratic | | Other | | Percentage Total Vote | | Major Vote | |
| Year | Total Vote | Vote | Candidate | Vote | Candidate | Vote | Plurality | Rep. | Dem. | Rep. | Dem. |
|---|---|---|---|---|---|---|---|---|---|---|---|
| 2004 | 1,578,769 | 693,826 | Bush, George W. | 857,488 | Kerry, John | 27,455 | 163,662 D | 43.9% | 54.3% | 44.7% | 55.3% |
| 2000** | 1,459,525 | 561,094 | Bush, George W. | 816,015 | Gore, Al | 82,416 | 254,921 D | 38.4% | 55.9% | 40.7% | 59.3% |
| 1996** | 1,392,614 | 483,109 | Dole, Bob | 735,740 | Clinton, Bill | 173,765 | 252,631 D | 34.7% | 52.8% | 39.6% | 60.4% |
| 1992** | 1,616,332 | 578,313 | Bush, George | 682,318 | Clinton, Bill | 355,701 | 104,005 D | 35.8% | 42.2% | 45.9% | 54.1% |
| 1988 | 1,443,394 | 750,241 | Bush, George | 676,584 | Dukakis, Michael S. | 16,569 | 73,657 R | 52.0% | 46.9% | 52.6% | 47.4% |
| 1984 | 1,466,900 | 890,877 | Reagan, Ronald | 569,597 | Mondale, Walter F. | 6,426 | 321,280 R | 60.7% | 38.8% | 61.0% | 39.0% |
| 1980** | 1,406,285 | 677,210 | Reagan, Ronald | 541,732 | Carter, Jimmy | 187,343 | 135,478 R | 48.2% | 38.5% | 55.6% | 44.4% |
| 1976 | 1,381,526 | 719,261 | Ford, Gerald R. | 647,895 | Carter, Jimmy | 14,370 | 71,366 R | 52.1% | 46.9% | 52.6% | 47.4% |
| 1972 | 1,384,277 | 810,763 | Nixon, Richard M. | 555,498 | McGovern, George S. | 18,016 | 255,265 R | 58.6% | 40.1% | 59.3% | 40.7% |
| 1968** | 1,256,232 | 556,721 | Nixon, Richard M. | 621,561 | Humphrey, Hubert H. | 77,950 | 64,840 D | 44.3% | 49.5% | 47.2% | 52.8% |
| 1964 | 1,218,578 | 390,996 | Goldwater, Barry M. | 826,269 | Johnson, Lyndon B. | 1,313 | 435,273 D | 32.1% | 67.8% | 32.1% | 67.9% |
| 1960 | 1,222,883 | 565,813 | Nixon, Richard M. | 657,055 | Kennedy, John F. | 15 | 91,242 D | 46.3% | 53.7% | 46.3% | 53.7% |
| 1956 | 1,117,121 | 711,837 | Eisenhower, Dwight D. | 405,079 | Stevenson, Adlai E. | 205 | 306,758 R | 63.7% | 36.3% | 63.7% | 36.3% |
| 1952 | 1,096,911 | 611,012 | Eisenhower, Dwight D. | 481,649 | Stevenson, Adlai E. | 4,250 | 129,363 R | 55.7% | 43.9% | 55.9% | 44.1% |
| 1948 | 883,518 | 437,754 | Dewey, Thomas E. | 423,297 | Truman, Harry S. | 22,467 | 14,457 R | 49.5% | 47.9% | 50.8% | 49.2% |

In past elections, the other vote included: 2000 - 64,452 Green (Ralph Nader); 1996 - 139,523 Reform (Ross Perot); 1992 - 348,771 Independent (Perot); 1980 - 171,807 Independent (John Anderson); 1968 - 76,650 American Independent (George Wallace).

# CONNECTICUT

## POSTWAR VOTE FOR GOVERNOR

| Year | Total Vote | Republican | | Democratic | | Other Vote | Plurality | Percentage | | | |
|---|---|---|---|---|---|---|---|---|---|---|---|
| | | Vote | Candidate | Vote | Candidate | | | Total Vote | | Major Vote | |
| | | | | | | | | Rep. | Dem. | Rep. | Dem. |
| 2002 | 1,022,998 | 573,958 | Rowland, John G. | 448,984 | Curry, Bill | 56 | 124,974 R | 56.1% | 43.9% | 56.1% | 43.9% |
| 1998 | 999,537 | 628,707 | Rowland, John G. | 354,187 | Kennelly, Barbara B. | 16,643 | 274,520 R | 62.9% | 35.4% | 64.0% | 36.0% |
| 1994** | 1,147,084 | 415,201 | Rowland, John G. | 375,133 | Curry, Bill | 356,750 | 40,068 R | 36.2% | 32.7% | 52.5% | 47.5% |
| 1990** | 1,141,122 | 427,840 | Rowland, John G. | 236,641 | Morrison, Bruce A. | 476,641 | 32,736 C | 37.5% | 20.7% | 64.4% | 35.6% |
| 1986 | 993,692 | 408,489 | Belaga, Julie D. | 575,638 | O'Neill, William A. | 9,565 | 167,149 D | 41.1% | 57.9% | 41.5% | 58.5% |
| 1982 | 1,084,156 | 497,773 | Rome, Lewis B. | 578,264 | O'Neill, William A. | 8,119 | 80,491 D | 45.9% | 53.3% | 46.3% | 53.7% |
| 1978 | 1,036,608 | 422,316 | Sarasin, Ronald A. | 613,109 | Grasso, Ella T. | 1,183 | 190,793 D | 40.7% | 59.1% | 40.8% | 59.2% |
| 1974 | 1,102,773 | 440,169 | Steele, Robert H. | 643,490 | Grasso, Ella T. | 19,114 | 203,321 D | 39.9% | 58.4% | 40.6% | 59.4% |
| 1970 | 1,082,797 | 582,160 | Meskill, Thomas J. | 500,561 | Daddario, Emilio | 76 | 81,599 R | 53.8% | 46.2% | 53.8% | 46.2% |
| 1966 | 1,008,557 | 446,536 | Gengras, E. Clayton | 561,599 | Dempsey, John N. | 422 | 115,063 D | 44.3% | 55.7% | 44.3% | 55.7% |
| 1962 | 1,031,902 | 482,852 | Alsop, John | 549,027 | Dempsey, John N. | 23 | 66,175 D | 46.8% | 53.2% | 46.8% | 53.2% |
| 1958 | 974,509 | 360,644 | Zeller, Fred R. | 607,012 | Ribicoff, Abraham A. | 6,853 | 246,368 D | 37.0% | 62.3% | 37.3% | 62.7% |
| 1954 | 936,753 | 460,528 | Lodge, John D. | 463,643 | Ribicoff, Abraham A. | 12,582 | 3,115 D | 49.2% | 49.5% | 49.8% | 50.2% |
| 1950** | 878,735 | 436,418 | Lodge, John D. | 419,404 | Bowles, Chester | 22,913 | 17,014 R | 49.7% | 47.7% | 51.0% | 49.0% |
| 1948 | 875,170 | 429,071 | Shannon, James C. | 431,296 | Bowles, Chester | 14,803 | 2,225 D | 49.0% | 49.3% | 49.9% | 50.1% |
| 1946 | 683,831 | 371,852 | McConaughy, J. L. | 276,335 | Snow, Wilbert | 35,644 | 95,517 R | 54.4% | 40.4% | 57.4% | 42.6% |

In past elections, the other vote included: 1994 - 216,585 A Connecticut Party (Elaine Strong Groark); 130,128 Independent (Tom Scott); 1990 - 460,576 A Connecticut Party (Lowell P. Weicker Jr.). Weicker received 40.4 percent of the total vote and won the election with a 32,736-vote plurality. The term of office for Connecticut's governor was increased from two to four years effective with the 1950 election.

## POSTWAR VOTE FOR SENATOR

| Year | Total Vote | Republican | | Democratic | | Other Vote | Rep.-Dem. Plurality | Percentage | | | |
|---|---|---|---|---|---|---|---|---|---|---|---|
| | | Vote | Candidate | Vote | Candidate | | | Total Vote | | Major Vote | |
| | | | | | | | | Rep. | Dem. | Rep. | Dem. |
| 2004 | 1,424,726 | 457,749 | Orchulli, Jack | 945,347 | Dodd, Christopher J. | 21,630 | 487,598 D | 32.1% | 66.4% | 32.6% | 67.4% |
| 2000 | 1,311,261 | 448,077 | Giordano, Philip A. | 828,902 | Lieberman, Joseph I. | 34,282 | 380,825 D | 34.2% | 63.2% | 35.1% | 64.9% |
| 1998 | 964,457 | 312,177 | Franks, Gary A. | 628,306 | Dodd, Christopher J. | 23,974 | 316,129 D | 32.4% | 65.1% | 33.2% | 66.8% |
| 1994 | 1,079,767 | 334,833 | Labriola, Jerry | 723,842 | Lieberman, Joseph I. | 21,092 | 389,009 D | 31.0% | 67.0% | 31.6% | 68.4% |
| 1992 | 1,500,709 | 572,036 | Johnson, Brook | 882,569 | Dodd, Christopher J. | 46,104 | 310,533 D | 38.1% | 58.8% | 39.3% | 60.7% |
| 1988 | 1,383,526 | 678,454 | Weicker, Lowell P. | 688,499 | Lieberman, Joseph I. | 16,573 | 10,045 D | 49.0% | 49.8% | 49.6% | 50.4% |
| 1986 | 976,933 | 340,438 | Eddy, Roger W. | 632,695 | Dodd, Christopher J. | 3,800 | 292,257 D | 34.8% | 64.8% | 35.0% | 65.0% |
| 1982 | 1,083,613 | 545,987 | Weicker, Lowell P. | 499,146 | Moffett, Anthony T. | 38,480 | 46,841 R | 50.4% | 46.1% | 52.2% | 47.8% |
| 1980 | 1,356,075 | 581,884 | Buckley, James L. | 763,969 | Dodd, Christopher J. | 10,222 | 182,085 D | 42.9% | 56.3% | 43.2% | 56.8% |
| 1976 | 1,361,666 | 785,683 | Weicker, Lowell P. | 561,018 | Schaffer, Gloria | 14,965 | 224,665 R | 57.7% | 41.2% | 58.3% | 41.7% |
| 1974 | 1,084,918 | 372,055 | Brannen, James H. | 690,820 | Ribicoff, Abraham A. | 22,043 | 318,765 D | 34.3% | 63.7% | 35.0% | 65.0% |
| 1970 | 1,089,353 | 454,721 | Weicker, Lowell P. | 368,111 | Duffey, Joseph D. | 266,521 | 86,610 R | 41.7% | 33.8% | 55.3% | 44.7% |
| 1968 | 1,206,537 | 551,455 | May, Edwin H. | 655,043 | Ribicoff, Abraham A. | 39 | 103,588 D | 45.7% | 54.3% | 45.7% | 54.3% |
| 1964 | 1,208,163 | 426,939 | Lodge, John D. | 781,008 | Dodd, Thomas J. | 216 | 354,069 D | 35.3% | 64.6% | 35.3% | 64.7% |
| 1962 | 1,029,301 | 501,694 | Seely-Brown, Horace | 527,522 | Ribicoff, Abraham A. | 85 | 25,828 D | 48.7% | 51.3% | 48.7% | 51.3% |
| 1958 | 965,463 | 410,622 | Purtell, William A. | 554,841 | Dodd, Thomas J. | | 144,219 D | 42.5% | 57.5% | 42.5% | 57.5% |
| 1956 | 1,113,819 | 610,829 | Bush, Prescott | 479,460 | Dodd, Thomas J. | 23,530 | 131,369 R | 54.8% | 43.0% | 56.0% | 44.0% |
| 1952 | 1,093,467 | 573,854 | Purtell, William A. | 485,066 | Benton, William | 34,547 | 88,788 R | 52.5% | 44.4% | 54.2% | 45.8% |
| 1952S | 1,093,268 | 559,465 | Bush, Prescott | 530,505 | Ribicoff, Abraham A. | 3,298 | 28,960 R | 51.2% | 48.5% | 51.3% | 48.7% |
| 1950 | 877,827 | 409,053 | Talbot, Joseph E. | 453,646 | McMahon, Brien | 15,128 | 44,593 D | 46.6% | 51.7% | 47.4% | 52.6% |
| 1950S | 877,135 | 430,311 | Bush, Prescott | 431,413 | Benton, William | 15,411 | 1,102 D | 49.1% | 49.2% | 49.9% | 50.1% |
| 1946 | 682,921 | 381,328 | Baldwin, Raymond | 276,424 | Tone, Joseph M. | 25,169 | 104,904 R | 55.8% | 40.5% | 58.0% | 42.0% |

One each of the 1952 and 1950 elections was for a short term to fill a vacancy.

# CONNECTICUT

Congressional districts first established for elections held in 2002
5 members

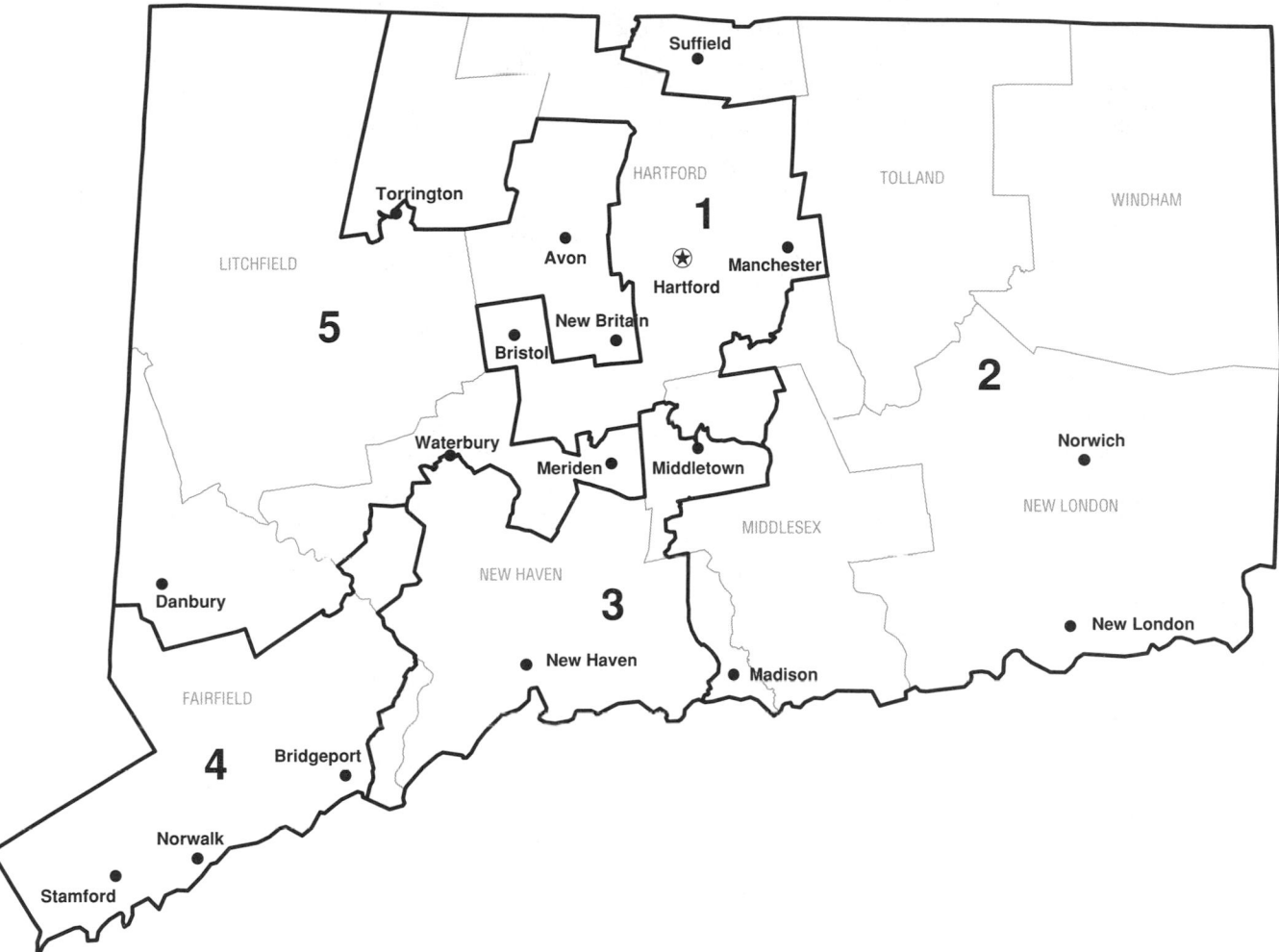

# CONNECTICUT

## PRESIDENT 2004

| 2000 Census Population | County | Total Vote | Republican | Democratic | Other | Rep.-Dem. Plurality | | Percentage | | | |
|---|---|---|---|---|---|---|---|---|---|---|---|
| | | | | | | | | Total Vote | | Major Vote | |
| | | | | | | | | Rep. | Dem. | Rep. | Dem. |
| 882,567 | FAIRFIELD | 400,967 | 189,605 | 205,902 | 5,460 | 16,297 | D | 47.3% | 51.4% | 47.9% | 52.1% |
| 857,183 | HARTFORD | 391,808 | 154,919 | 229,902 | 6,987 | 74,983 | D | 39.5% | 58.7% | 40.3% | 59.7% |
| 182,193 | LITCHFIELD | 96,668 | 50,160 | 44,647 | 1,861 | 5,513 | R | 51.9% | 46.2% | 52.9% | 47.1% |
| 155,071 | MIDDLESEX | 83,984 | 35,252 | 47,292 | 1,440 | 12,040 | D | 42.0% | 56.3% | 42.7% | 57.3% |
| 824,008 | NEW HAVEN | 366,392 | 160,390 | 199,060 | 6,942 | 38,670 | D | 43.8% | 54.3% | 44.6% | 55.4% |
| 259,088 | NEW LONDON | 118,360 | 49,931 | 66,062 | 2,367 | 16,131 | D | 42.2% | 55.8% | 43.0% | 57.0% |
| 136,364 | TOLLAND | 71,729 | 31,245 | 39,146 | 1,338 | 7,901 | D | 43.6% | 54.6% | 44.4% | 55.6% |
| 109,091 | WINDHAM | 48,861 | 22,324 | 25,477 | 1,060 | 3,153 | D | 45.7% | 52.1% | 46.7% | 53.3% |
| 3,405,565 | TOTAL | 1,578,769 | 693,826 | 857,488 | 27,455 | 163,662 | D | 43.9% | 54.3% | 44.7% | 55.3% |
| | City/Town | | | | | | | | | | |
| 18,554 | ANSONIA | 7,493 | 3,272 | 4,065 | 156 | 793 | D | 43.7% | 54.3% | 44.6% | 55.4% |
| 19,587 | BLOOMFIELD | 10,650 | 2,337 | 8,156 | 157 | 5,819 | D | 21.9% | 76.6% | 22.3% | 77.7% |
| 28,683 | BRANFORD | 14,851 | 6,286 | 8,338 | 227 | 2,052 | D | 42.3% | 56.1% | 43.0% | 57.0% |
| 139,529 | BRIDGEPORT | 37,191 | 10,326 | 26,280 | 585 | 15,954 | D | 27.8% | 70.7% | 28.2% | 71.8% |
| 60,062 | BRISTOL | 25,206 | 10,619 | 14,201 | 386 | 3,582 | D | 42.1% | 56.3% | 42.8% | 57.2% |
| 28,543 | CHESHIRE | 15,047 | 7,583 | 7,283 | 181 | 300 | R | 50.4% | 48.4% | 51.0% | 49.0% |
| 74,848 | DANBURY | 26,248 | 12,399 | 13,477 | 372 | 1,078 | D | 47.2% | 51.3% | 47.9% | 52.1% |
| 19,607 | DARIEN | 11,057 | 6,888 | 4,057 | 112 | 2,831 | R | 62.3% | 36.7% | 62.9% | 37.1% |
| 49,575 | EAST HARTFORD | 18,672 | 6,322 | 11,996 | 354 | 5,674 | D | 33.9% | 64.2% | 34.5% | 65.5% |
| 28,289 | EAST HAVEN | 11,866 | 5,427 | 6,196 | 243 | 769 | D | 45.7% | 52.2% | 46.7% | 53.3% |
| 45,212 | ENFIELD | 19,797 | 8,669 | 10,826 | 302 | 2,157 | D | 43.8% | 54.7% | 44.5% | 55.5% |
| 57,340 | FAIRFIELD | 30,222 | 14,706 | 15,068 | 448 | 362 | D | 48.7% | 49.9% | 49.4% | 50.6% |
| 23,641 | FARMINGTON | 13,700 | 6,298 | 7,209 | 193 | 911 | D | 46.0% | 52.6% | 46.6% | 53.4% |
| 31,876 | GLASTONBURY | 19,105 | 8,854 | 9,971 | 280 | 1,117 | D | 46.3% | 52.2% | 47.0% | 53.0% |
| 61,101 | GREENWICH | 30,500 | 15,830 | 14,334 | 336 | 1,496 | R | 51.9% | 47.0% | 52.5% | 47.5% |
| 39,907 | GROTON | 14,757 | 6,473 | 8,014 | 270 | 1,541 | D | 43.9% | 54.3% | 44.7% | 55.3% |
| 21,398 | GUILFORD | 12,990 | 5,554 | 7,294 | 142 | 1,740 | D | 42.8% | 56.2% | 43.2% | 56.8% |
| 56,913 | HAMDEN | 28,265 | 9,990 | 17,774 | 501 | 7,784 | D | 35.3% | 62.9% | 36.0% | 64.0% |
| 121,578 | HARTFORD | 28,372 | 4,623 | 22,595 | 1,154 | 17,972 | D | 16.3% | 79.6% | 17.0% | 83.0% |
| 54,740 | MANCHESTER | 25,626 | 9,949 | 15,269 | 408 | 5,320 | D | 38.8% | 59.6% | 39.5% | 60.5% |
| 20,720 | MANSFIELD | 8,596 | 2,171 | 6,169 | 256 | 3,998 | D | 25.3% | 71.8% | 26.0% | 74.0% |
| 58,244 | MERIDEN | 22,719 | 8,845 | 13,368 | 506 | 4,523 | D | 38.9% | 58.8% | 39.8% | 60.2% |
| 43,167 | MIDDLETOWN | 19,964 | 6,512 | 13,035 | 417 | 6,523 | D | 32.6% | 65.3% | 33.3% | 66.7% |
| 52,305 | MILFORD | 26,473 | 12,882 | 13,149 | 442 | 267 | D | 48.7% | 49.7% | 49.5% | 50.5% |
| 30,989 | NAUGATUCK | 12,853 | 6,838 | 5,745 | 270 | 1,093 | R | 53.2% | 44.7% | 54.3% | 45.7% |
| 71,538 | NEW BRITAIN | 21,074 | 6,560 | 14,122 | 392 | 7,562 | D | 31.1% | 67.0% | 31.7% | 68.3% |
| 123,626 | NEW HAVEN | 39,286 | 7,175 | 30,979 | 1,132 | 23,804 | D | 18.3% | 78.9% | 18.8% | 81.2% |
| 25,671 | NEW LONDON | 8,582 | 2,381 | 5,984 | 217 | 3,603 | D | 27.7% | 69.7% | 28.5% | 71.5% |
| 27,121 | NEW MILFORD | 13,237 | 7,174 | 5,854 | 209 | 1,320 | R | 54.2% | 44.2% | 55.1% | 44.9% |
| 29,306 | NEWINGTON | 15,852 | 6,252 | 9,365 | 235 | 3,113 | D | 39.4% | 59.1% | 40.0% | 60.0% |
| 25,031 | NEWTOWN | 14,466 | 7,740 | 6,540 | 186 | 1,200 | R | 53.5% | 45.2% | 54.2% | 45.8% |
| 23,035 | NORTH HAVEN | 13,056 | 6,471 | 6,359 | 226 | 112 | R | 49.6% | 48.7% | 50.4% | 49.6% |
| 82,951 | NORWALK | 35,449 | 14,201 | 20,615 | 633 | 6,414 | D | 40.1% | 58.2% | 40.8% | 59.2% |
| 36,117 | NORWICH | 13,382 | 4,841 | 8,223 | 318 | 3,382 | D | 36.2% | 61.4% | 37.1% | 62.9% |
| 23,643 | RIDGEFIELD | 14,119 | 7,408 | 6,554 | 157 | 854 | R | 52.5% | 46.4% | 53.1% | 46.9% |
| 38,101 | SHELTON | 19,663 | 11,137 | 8,247 | 279 | 2,890 | R | 56.6% | 41.9% | 57.5% | 42.5% |
| 23,234 | SIMSBURY | 13,824 | 6,767 | 6,825 | 232 | 58 | D | 49.0% | 49.4% | 49.8% | 50.2% |
| 24,412 | SOUTH WINDSOR | 14,025 | 6,174 | 7,643 | 208 | 1,469 | D | 44.0% | 54.5% | 44.7% | 55.3% |
| 39,728 | SOUTHINGTON | 21,561 | 10,179 | 11,044 | 338 | 865 | D | 47.2% | 51.2% | 48.0% | 52.0% |
| 117,083 | STAMFORD | 47,078 | 18,866 | 27,588 | 624 | 8,722 | D | 40.1% | 58.6% | 40.6% | 59.4% |
| 49,976 | STRATFORD | 24,395 | 11,945 | 12,057 | 393 | 112 | D | 49.0% | 49.4% | 49.8% | 50.2% |
| 35,202 | TORRINGTON | 15,881 | 8,175 | 7,362 | 344 | 813 | R | 51.5% | 46.4% | 52.6% | 47.4% |
| 34,243 | TRUMBULL | 19,666 | 10,789 | 8,656 | 221 | 2,133 | R | 54.9% | 44.0% | 55.5% | 44.5% |
| 28,063 | VERNON | 13,654 | 5,765 | 7,695 | 194 | 1,930 | D | 42.2% | 56.4% | 42.8% | 57.2% |
| 43,026 | WALLINGFORD | 21,986 | 9,956 | 11,644 | 386 | 1,688 | D | 45.3% | 53.0% | 46.1% | 53.9% |

# CONNECTICUT

## PRESIDENT 2004

| 2000 Census Population | City/Town | Total Vote | Republican | Democratic | Other | Rep.-Dem. Plurality | Percentage | | | |
|---|---|---|---|---|---|---|---|---|---|---|
| | | | | | | | Total Vote | | Major Vote | |
| | | | | | | | Rep. | Dem. | Rep. | Dem. |
| 107,271 | WATERBURY | 32,772 | 15,961 | 16,122 | 689 | 161 D | 48.7% | 49.2% | 49.7% | 50.3% |
| 21,661 | WATERTOWN | 11,322 | 6,954 | 4,146 | 222 | 2,808 R | 61.4% | 36.6% | 62.6% | 37.4% |
| 63,589 | WEST HARTFORD | 33,740 | 11,641 | 21,612 | 487 | 9,971 D | 34.5% | 64.1% | 35.0% | 65.0% |
| 52,360 | WEST HAVEN | 21,319 | 7,840 | 13,047 | 432 | 5,207 D | 36.8% | 61.2% | 37.5% | 62.5% |
| 25,749 | WESTPORT | 15,328 | 6,063 | 9,115 | 150 | 3,052 D | 39.6% | 59.5% | 39.9% | 60.1% |
| 26,271 | WETHERSFIELD | 14,971 | 6,517 | 8,227 | 227 | 1,710 D | 43.5% | 55.0% | 44.2% | 55.8% |
| 22,857 | WINDHAM | 8,092 | 2,770 | 5,135 | 187 | 2,365 D | 34.2% | 63.5% | 35.0% | 65.0% |
| 28,237 | WINDSOR | 14,868 | 5,253 | 9,297 | 318 | 4,044 D | 35.3% | 62.5% | 36.1% | 63.9% |

# CONNECTICUT

## SENATOR 2004

| 2000 Census Population | County | Total Vote | Republican | Democratic | Other | Rep.-Dem. Plurality | Percentage | | | |
|---|---|---|---|---|---|---|---|---|---|---|
| | | | | | | | Total Vote | | Major Vote | |
| | | | | | | | Rep. | Dem. | Rep. | Dem. |
| 882,567 | FAIRFIELD | 360,796 | 133,982 | 222,523 | 4,291 | 88,541 D | 37.1% | 61.7% | 37.6% | 62.4% |
| 857,183 | HARTFORD | 356,737 | 101,132 | 250,482 | 5,123 | 149,350 D | 28.3% | 70.2% | 28.8% | 71.2% |
| 182,193 | LITCHFIELD | 88,340 | 34,975 | 51,010 | 2,355 | 16,035 D | 39.6% | 57.7% | 40.7% | 59.3% |
| 155,071 | MIDDLESEX | 77,639 | 23,154 | 53,536 | 949 | 30,382 D | 29.8% | 69.0% | 30.2% | 69.8% |
| 824,008 | NEW HAVEN | 325,548 | 101,720 | 218,571 | 5,257 | 116,851 D | 31.2% | 67.1% | 31.8% | 68.2% |
| 259,088 | NEW LONDON | 107,257 | 29,683 | 75,762 | 1,812 | 46,079 D | 27.7% | 70.6% | 28.2% | 71.8% |
| 136,364 | TOLLAND | 65,156 | 20,049 | 44,101 | 1,006 | 24,052 D | 30.8% | 67.7% | 31.3% | 68.7% |
| 109,091 | WINDHAM | 43,253 | 13,054 | 29,362 | 837 | 16,308 D | 30.2% | 67.9% | 30.8% | 69.2% |
| 3,405,565 | TOTAL | 1,424,726 | 457,749 | 945,347 | 21,630 | 487,598 D | 32.1% | 66.4% | 32.6% | 67.4% |
| | City/Town | | | | | | | | | |
| 18,554 | ANSONIA | 6,688 | 1,934 | 4,646 | 108 | 2,712 D | 28.9% | 69.5% | 29.4% | 70.6% |
| 19,587 | BLOOMFIELD | 9,655 | 1,547 | 8,025 | 83 | 6,478 D | 16.0% | 83.1% | 16.2% | 83.8% |
| 28,683 | BRANFORD | 13,632 | 3,933 | 9,553 | 146 | 5,620 D | 28.9% | 70.1% | 29.2% | 70.8% |
| 139,529 | BRIDGEPORT | 32,207 | 6,505 | 25,077 | 625 | 18,572 D | 20.2% | 77.9% | 20.6% | 79.4% |
| 60,062 | BRISTOL | 22,907 | 6,616 | 15,978 | 313 | 9,362 D | 28.9% | 69.8% | 29.3% | 70.7% |
| 28,543 | CHESHIRE | 12,347 | 5,287 | 6,918 | 142 | 1,631 D | 42.8% | 56.0% | 43.3% | 56.7% |
| 74,848 | DANBURY | 23,476 | 8,669 | 14,468 | 339 | 5,799 D | 36.9% | 61.6% | 37.5% | 62.5% |
| 19,607 | DARIEN | 10,131 | 5,589 | 4,487 | 55 | 1,102 R | 55.2% | 44.3% | 55.5% | 44.5% |
| 49,575 | EAST HARTFORD | 16,726 | 3,877 | 12,518 | 331 | 8,641 D | 23.2% | 74.8% | 23.6% | 76.4% |
| 28,289 | EAST HAVEN | 10,289 | 3,085 | 6,978 | 226 | 3,893 D | 30.0% | 67.8% | 30.7% | 69.3% |
| 45,212 | ENFIELD | 17,685 | 5,263 | 12,146 | 276 | 6,883 D | 29.8% | 68.7% | 30.2% | 69.8% |
| 57,340 | FAIRFIELD | 27,714 | 10,224 | 17,250 | 240 | 7,026 D | 36.9% | 62.2% | 37.2% | 62.8% |
| 23,641 | FARMINGTON | 12,712 | 4,375 | 8,185 | 152 | 3,810 D | 34.4% | 64.4% | 34.8% | 65.2% |
| 31,876 | GLASTONBURY | 17,686 | 5,580 | 11,948 | 158 | 6,368 D | 31.6% | 67.6% | 31.8% | 68.2% |
| 61,101 | GREENWICH | 27,121 | 12,090 | 14,725 | 306 | 2,635 D | 44.6% | 54.3% | 45.1% | 54.9% |
| 39,907 | GROTON | 13,417 | 3,851 | 9,335 | 231 | 5,484 D | 28.7% | 69.6% | 29.2% | 70.8% |
| 21,398 | GUILFORD | 12,118 | 3,727 | 8,262 | 129 | 4,535 D | 30.8% | 68.2% | 31.1% | 68.9% |
| 56,913 | HAMDEN | 25,328 | 6,102 | 18,881 | 345 | 12,779 D | 24.1% | 74.5% | 24.4% | 75.6% |
| 121,578 | HARTFORD | 24,332 | 2,846 | 20,926 | 560 | 18,080 D | 11.7% | 86.0% | 12.0% | 88.0% |
| 54,740 | MANCHESTER | 23,510 | 6,614 | 16,547 | 349 | 9,933 D | 28.1% | 70.4% | 28.6% | 71.4% |
| 20,720 | MANSFIELD | 7,519 | 1,308 | 6,084 | 127 | 4,776 D | 17.4% | 80.9% | 17.7% | 82.3% |
| 58,244 | MERIDEN | 3,370 | 1,138 | 2,198 | 34 | 1,060 D | 33.8% | 65.2% | 34.1% | 65.9% |
| 43,167 | MIDDLETOWN | 18,137 | 4,290 | 13,510 | 337 | 9,220 D | 23.7% | 74.5% | 24.1% | 75.9% |
| 52,305 | MILFORD | 24,132 | 7,795 | 16,017 | 320 | 8,222 D | 32.3% | 66.4% | 32.7% | 67.3% |
| 30,989 | NAUGATUCK | 11,175 | 4,174 | 6,748 | 253 | 2,574 D | 37.4% | 60.4% | 38.2% | 61.8% |

# CONNECTICUT

## SENATOR 2004

| 2000 Census Population | City/Town | Total Vote | Republican | Democratic | Other | Rep.-Dem. Plurality | Percentage | | | |
|---|---|---|---|---|---|---|---|---|---|---|
| | | | | | | | Total Vote | | Major Vote | |
| | | | | | | | Rep. | Dem. | Rep. | Dem. |
| 71,538 | NEW BRITAIN | 17,774 | 3,982 | 13,383 | 409 | 9,401 D | 22.4% | 75.3% | 22.9% | 77.1% |
| 123,626 | NEW HAVEN | 33,566 | 4,110 | 28,631 | 825 | 24,521 D | 12.2% | 85.3% | 12.6% | 87.4% |
| 25,671 | NEW LONDON | 7,292 | 1,381 | 5,698 | 213 | 4,317 D | 18.9% | 78.1% | 19.5% | 80.5% |
| 27,121 | NEW MILFORD | 11,958 | 4,666 | 7,066 | 226 | 2,400 D | 39.0% | 59.1% | 39.8% | 60.2% |
| 29,306 | NEWINGTON | 14,582 | 3,901 | 10,502 | 179 | 6,601 D | 26.8% | 72.0% | 27.1% | 72.9% |
| 25,031 | NEWTOWN | 13,209 | 5,469 | 7,569 | 171 | 2,100 D | 41.4% | 57.3% | 41.9% | 58.1% |
| 23,035 | NORTH HAVEN | 11,776 | 4,200 | 7,424 | 152 | 3,224 D | 35.7% | 63.0% | 36.1% | 63.9% |
| 82,951 | NORWALK | 31,750 | 10,083 | 21,282 | 385 | 11,199 D | 31.8% | 67.0% | 32.1% | 67.9% |
| 36,117 | NORWICH | 11,585 | 2,634 | 8,693 | 258 | 6,059 D | 22.7% | 75.0% | 23.3% | 76.7% |
| 23,643 | RIDGEFIELD | 13,344 | 5,778 | 7,453 | 113 | 1,675 D | 43.3% | 55.9% | 43.7% | 56.3% |
| 38,101 | SHELTON | 17,525 | 7,260 | 9,976 | 289 | 2,716 D | 41.4% | 56.9% | 42.1% | 57.9% |
| 23,234 | SIMSBURY | 13,274 | 4,963 | 8,123 | 188 | 3,160 D | 37.4% | 61.2% | 37.9% | 62.1% |
| 24,412 | SOUTH WINDSOR | 12,758 | 3,694 | 8,884 | 180 | 5,190 D | 29.0% | 69.6% | 29.4% | 70.6% |
| 39,728 | SOUTHINGTON | 19,916 | 6,643 | 13,044 | 229 | 6,401 D | 33.4% | 65.5% | 33.7% | 66.3% |
| 117,083 | STAMFORD | 41,351 | 12,740 | 28,105 | 506 | 15,365 D | 30.8% | 68.0% | 31.2% | 68.8% |
| 49,976 | STRATFORD | 21,294 | 7,121 | 13,878 | 295 | 6,757 D | 33.4% | 65.2% | 33.9% | 66.1% |
| 35,202 | TORRINGTON | 14,502 | 5,538 | 8,741 | 223 | 3,203 D | 38.2% | 60.3% | 38.8% | 61.2% |
| 34,243 | TRUMBULL | 18,019 | 7,444 | 10,410 | 165 | 2,966 D | 41.3% | 57.8% | 41.7% | 58.3% |
| 28,063 | VERNON | 12,417 | 3,861 | 8,406 | 150 | 4,545 D | 31.1% | 67.7% | 31.5% | 68.5% |
| 43,026 | WALLINGFORD | 19,804 | 6,113 | 13,411 | 280 | 7,298 D | 30.9% | 67.7% | 31.3% | 68.7% |
| 107,271 | WATERBURY | 28,250 | 10,598 | 16,967 | 685 | 6,369 D | 37.5% | 60.1% | 38.4% | 61.6% |
| 21,661 | WATERTOWN | 9,961 | 4,776 | 5,054 | 131 | 278 D | 47.9% | 50.7% | 48.6% | 51.4% |
| 63,589 | WEST HARTFORD | 31,685 | 7,898 | 23,482 | 305 | 15,584 D | 24.9% | 74.1% | 25.2% | 74.8% |
| 52,360 | WEST HAVEN | 18,884 | 4,452 | 14,154 | 278 | 9,702 D | 23.6% | 75.0% | 23.9% | 76.1% |
| 25,749 | WESTPORT | 14,197 | 4,427 | 9,662 | 108 | 5,235 D | 31.2% | 68.1% | 31.4% | 68.6% |
| 26,271 | WETHERSFIELD | 13,616 | 4,170 | 9,280 | 166 | 5,110 D | 30.6% | 68.2% | 31.0% | 69.0% |
| 22,857 | WINDHAM | 6,999 | 1,499 | 5,306 | 194 | 3,807 D | 21.4% | 75.8% | 22.0% | 78.0% |
| 28,237 | WINDSOR | 13,473 | 3,368 | 9,876 | 229 | 6,508 D | 25.0% | 73.3% | 25.4% | 74.6% |

# CONNECTICUT

## HOUSE OF REPRESENTATIVES

| CD | Year | Total Vote | Republican | | Democratic | | Other Vote | Rep.-Dem. Plurality | Percentage | | | |
|---|---|---|---|---|---|---|---|---|---|---|---|---|
| | | | Vote | Candidate | Vote | Candidate | | | Total Vote | | Major Vote | |
| | | | | | | | | | Rep. | Dem. | Rep. | Dem. |
| 1 | 2004 | 272,403 | 73,601 | Halstead, John M. | 198,802 | Larson, John B.* | | 125,201 D | 27.0% | 73.0% | 27.0% | 73.0% |
| 1 | 2002 | 201,688 | 66,968 | Steele, Phil | 134,698 | Larson, John B.* | 22 | 67,730 D | 33.2% | 66.8% | 33.2% | 66.8% |
| 2 | 2004 | 307,078 | 166,412 | Simmons, Rob* | 140,536 | Sullivan, Jim | 130 | 25,876 R | 54.2% | 45.8% | 54.2% | 45.8% |
| 2 | 2002 | 217,108 | 117,434 | Simmons, Rob* | 99,674 | Courtney, Joe | | 17,760 R | 54.1% | 45.9% | 54.1% | 45.9% |
| 3 | 2004 | 276,980 | 69,160 | Elser, Richter | 200,638 | DeLauro, Rosa* | 7,182 | 131,478 D | 25.0% | 72.4% | 25.6% | 74.4% |
| 3 | 2002 | 185,364 | 54,757 | Elser, Richter | 121,557 | DeLauro, Rosa* | 9,050 | 66,800 D | 29.5% | 65.6% | 31.1% | 68.9% |
| 4 | 2004 | 290,830 | 152,493 | Shays, Christopher* | 138,333 | Farrell, Diane | 4 | 14,160 R | 52.4% | 47.6% | 52.4% | 47.6% |
| 4 | 2002 | 175,695 | 113,197 | Shays, Christopher* | 62,491 | Sanchez, Stephanie H. | 7 | 50,706 R | 64.4% | 35.6% | 64.4% | 35.6% |
| 5 | 2004 | 281,447 | 168,268 | Johnson, Nancy L.* | 107,438 | Gerratana, Theresa B. | 5,741 | 60,830 R | 59.8% | 38.2% | 61.0% | 39.0% |
| 5 | 2002 | 209,454 | 113,626 | Johnson, Nancy L.* | 90,616 | Maloney, Jim* | 5,212 | 23,010 R | 54.2% | 43.3% | 55.6% | 44.4% |
| Total | 2004 | 1,428,738 | 629,934 | | 785,747 | | 13,057 | 155,813 D | 44.1% | 55.0% | 44.5% | 55.5% |
| Total | 2002 | 989,309 | 465,982 | | 509,036 | | 14,291 | 43,054 D | 47.1% | 51.5% | 47.8% | 52.2% |

An asterisk (*) denotes incumbent.

# CONNECTICUT

## GENERAL AND PRIMARY ELECTIONS

### 2004 GENERAL ELECTIONS

| | |
|---|---|
| **President** | Other vote was 12,969 Petitioning Candidate (Ralph Nader); 9,564 Green (David Cobb); 3,367 Libertarian (Michael Badnarik); 1,543 Concerned Citizens (Michael Peroutka); 12 write-in (Roger Calero). |
| **Senator** | Other vote was 12,442 Concerned Citizens (Timothy A. Knibbs); 9,188 Libertarian (Leonard H. Rasch). |
| **House** | Other vote was: |

| | |
|---|---|
| CD 1 | |
| CD 2 | 130 write-in (David R. Lyon). |
| CD 3 | 7,182 Green (Ralph Anthony Ferrucci). |
| CD 4 | 4 write-in (Carl E. Vassar). |
| CD 5 | 3,196 Working Families (Fernando Ramirez); 2,545 Concerned Citizens (Wildey J. Moore). |

### 2004 PRIMARY ELECTIONS

| | | | | |
|---|---|---|---|---|
| **Primary** | March 2, 2004 (President)<br>August 10, 2004 (Congress) | **Registration**<br>(as of Oct. 21, 2003—<br>includes 142,399 inactive<br>registrants) | Republican<br>Democratic<br>Green<br>Libertarian<br>Concerned Citizens<br>Other Parties<br>Unaffiliated | 449,735<br>671,665<br>2,142<br>705<br>264<br>1,411<br>839,928 |
| | | | TOTAL | 1,965,850 |

**Primary Type**  Closed—Only registered Democrats and Republicans could vote in their party's primary.

Note:  An asterisk (*) denotes incumbent. A Senate or House candidate had to receive at least 15 percent of the vote in a pre-primary convention to force a primary or to petition to appear on the primary ballot.

| | REPUBLICAN PRIMARIES | | DEMOCRATIC PRIMARIES | | |
|---|---|---|---|---|---|
| **President** | No Republican primary | | John Kerry | 75,860 | 58.3% |
| | | | John Edwards | 30,844 | 23.7% |
| | | | Joseph I. Lieberman | 6,705 | 5.2% |
| | | | Howard Dean | 5,166 | 4.0% |
| | | | Dennis J. Kucinich | 4,133 | 3.2% |
| | | | Al Sharpton | 3,312 | 2.5% |
| | | | Wesley Clark | 1,546 | 1.2% |
| | | | Lyndon H. LaRouche Jr. | 1,467 | 1.1% |
| | | | Uncommitted | 990 | 0.8% |
| | | | TOTAL | 130,023 | |
| **Senator** | Jack Orchulli | Nominated by convention | Christopher J. Dodd* | Nominated by convention | |
| **Congressional District 1** | John M. Halstead | Nominated by convention | John B. Larson* | Nominated by convention | |
| **Congressional District 2** | Rob Simmons* | Nominated by convention | Jim Sullivan | 11,673 | 62.8% |
| | | | Shaun McNally | 6,911 | 37.2% |
| | | | TOTAL | 18,584 | |
| **Congressional District 3** | Richter Elser | Nominated by convention | Rosa DeLauro* | Nominated by convention | |
| **Congressional District 4** | Christopher Shays* | Nominated by convention | Diane Farrell | Nominated by convention | |
| **Congressional District 5** | Nancy L. Johnson* | Nominated by convention | *Robert Louis Marconi was nominated by convention but subsequently withdrew from the race. Theresa B. Gerratana was selected by party leaders to fill the vacancy on the general election ballot.* | | |

# DELAWARE

## GOVERNOR
Ruth Ann Minner (D). Reelected 2004 to a four-year term. Previously elected 2000.

## SENATORS (2 Democrats)
Thomas R. Carper (D). Elected 2000 to a six-year term.

Joseph R. Biden Jr. (D). Reelected 2002 to a six-year term. Previously elected 1996, 1990, 1984, 1978, 1972.

## REPRESENTATIVE (1 Republican)
At Large. Michael N. Castle (R)

## POSTWAR VOTE FOR PRESIDENT

| | | Republican | | Democratic | | Other | | Total Vote | | Major Vote | |
|---|---|---|---|---|---|---|---|---|---|---|---|
| Year | Total Vote | Vote | Candidate | Vote | Candidate | Vote | Plurality | Rep. | Dem. | Rep. | Dem. |
| 2004 | 375,190 | 171,660 | Bush, George W. | 200,152 | Kerry, John | 3,378 | 28,492 D | 45.8% | 53.3% | 46.2% | 53.8% |
| 2000** | 327,622 | 137,288 | Bush, George W. | 180,068 | Gore, Al | 10,266 | 42,780 D | 41.9% | 55.0% | 43.3% | 56.7% |
| 1996** | 271,084 | 99,062 | Dole, Bob | 140,355 | Clinton, Bill | 31,667 | 41,293 D | 36.5% | 51.8% | 41.4% | 58.6% |
| 1992** | 289,735 | 102,313 | Bush, George | 126,054 | Clinton, Bill | 61,368 | 23,741 D | 35.3% | 43.5% | 44.8% | 55.2% |
| 1988 | 249,891 | 139,639 | Bush, George | 108,647 | Dukakis, Michael S. | 1,605 | 30,992 R | 55.9% | 43.5% | 56.2% | 43.8% |
| 1984 | 254,572 | 152,190 | Reagan, Ronald | 101,656 | Mondale, Walter F. | 726 | 50,534 R | 59.8% | 39.9% | 60.0% | 40.0% |
| 1980** | 235,900 | 111,252 | Reagan, Ronald | 105,754 | Carter, Jimmy | 18,894 | 5,498 R | 47.2% | 44.8% | 51.3% | 48.7% |
| 1976 | 235,834 | 109,831 | Ford, Gerald R. | 122,596 | Carter, Jimmy | 3,407 | 12,765 D | 46.6% | 52.0% | 47.3% | 52.7% |
| 1972 | 235,516 | 140,357 | Nixon, Richard M. | 92,283 | McGovern, George S. | 2,876 | 48,074 R | 59.6% | 39.2% | 60.3% | 39.7% |
| 1968** | 214,367 | 96,714 | Nixon, Richard M. | 89,194 | Humphrey, Hubert H. | 28,459 | 7,520 R | 45.1% | 41.6% | 52.0% | 48.0% |
| 1964 | 201,320 | 78,078 | Goldwater, Barry M. | 122,704 | Johnson, Lyndon B. | 538 | 44,626 D | 38.8% | 60.9% | 38.9% | 61.1% |
| 1960 | 196,683 | 96,373 | Nixon, Richard M. | 99,590 | Kennedy, John F. | 720 | 3,217 D | 49.0% | 50.6% | 49.2% | 50.8% |
| 1956 | 177,988 | 98,057 | Eisenhower, Dwight D. | 79,421 | Stevenson, Adlai E. | 510 | 18,636 R | 55.1% | 44.6% | 55.3% | 44.7% |
| 1952 | 174,025 | 90,059 | Eisenhower, Dwight D. | 83,315 | Stevenson, Adlai E. | 651 | 6,744 R | 51.8% | 47.9% | 51.9% | 48.1% |
| 1948 | 139,073 | 69,588 | Dewey, Thomas E. | 67,813 | Truman, Harry S. | 1,672 | 1,775 R | 50.0% | 48.8% | 50.6% | 49.4% |

In past elections, the other vote included: 2000 - 8,307 Green (Ralph Nader); 1996 - 28,719 Reform (Ross Perot); 1992 - 59,213 Independent (Perot); 1980 - 16,288 Independent (John Anderson); 1968 - 28,459 American Independent (George Wallace).

## POSTWAR VOTE FOR GOVERNOR

| | | Republican | | Democratic | | Other | Rep.-Dem. | Total Vote | | Major Vote | |
|---|---|---|---|---|---|---|---|---|---|---|---|
| Year | Total Vote | Vote | Candidate | Vote | Candidate | Vote | Plurality | Rep. | Dem. | Rep. | Dem. |
| 2004 | 365,008 | 167,115 | Lee, William Swain | 185,687 | Minner, Ruth Ann | 12,206 | 18,572 D | 45.8% | 50.9% | 47.4% | 52.6% |
| 2000 | 323,688 | 128,603 | Burris, John M. | 191,695 | Minner, Ruth Ann | 3,390 | 63,092 D | 39.7% | 59.2% | 40.2% | 59.8% |
| 1996 | 271,122 | 82,654 | Rzewnicki, Janet | 188,300 | Carper, Thomas R. | 168 | 105,646 D | 30.5% | 69.5% | 30.5% | 69.5% |
| 1992 | 277,058 | 90,725 | Scott, B. Gary | 179,365 | Carper, Thomas R. | 6,968 | 88,640 D | 32.7% | 64.7% | 33.6% | 66.4% |
| 1988 | 239,969 | 169,733 | Castle, Michael N. | 70,236 | Kreshtoll, Jacob | | 99,497 R | 70.7% | 29.3% | 70.7% | 29.3% |
| 1984 | 243,565 | 135,250 | Castle, Michael N. | 108,315 | Quillen, William T. | | 26,935 R | 55.5% | 44.5% | 55.5% | 44.5% |
| 1980 | 225,081 | 159,004 | duPont, Pierre | 64,217 | Gordy, William J. | 1,860 | 94,787 R | 70.6% | 28.5% | 71.2% | 28.8% |
| 1976 | 229,563 | 130,531 | duPont, Pierre | 97,480 | Tribbitt, Sherman W. | 1,552 | 33,051 R | 56.9% | 42.5% | 57.2% | 42.8% |
| 1972 | 228,722 | 109,583 | Peterson, Russell W. | 117,274 | Tribbitt, Sherman W. | 1,865 | 7,691 D | 47.9% | 51.3% | 48.3% | 51.7% |
| 1968 | 206,834 | 104,474 | Peterson, Russell W. | 102,360 | Terry, Charles L. | | 2,114 R | 50.5% | 49.5% | 50.5% | 49.5% |
| 1964 | 200,171 | 97,374 | Buckson, David P. | 102,797 | Terry, Charles L. | | 5,423 D | 48.6% | 51.4% | 48.6% | 51.4% |
| 1960 | 194,835 | 94,043 | Rollins, John W. | 100,792 | Carvel, Elbert N. | | 6,749 D | 48.3% | 51.7% | 48.3% | 51.7% |
| 1956 | 177,012 | 91,965 | Boggs, J. Caleb | 85,047 | McConnell, J. H. T. | | 6,918 R | 52.0% | 48.0% | 52.0% | 48.0% |
| 1952 | 170,749 | 88,977 | Boggs, J. Caleb | 81,772 | Carvel, Elbert N. | | 7,205 R | 52.1% | 47.9% | 52.1% | 47.9% |
| 1948 | 140,335 | 64,996 | George, Hyland P. | 75,339 | Carvel, Elbert N. | | 10,343 D | 46.3% | 53.7% | 46.3% | 53.7% |

# DELAWARE

## POSTWAR VOTE FOR SENATOR

| Year | Total Vote | Republican | | Democratic | | Other Vote | Rep.-Dem. Plurality | Percentage | | | |
|---|---|---|---|---|---|---|---|---|---|---|---|
| | | Vote | Candidate | Vote | Candidate | | | Total Vote | | Major Vote | |
| | | | | | | | | Rep. | Dem. | Rep. | Dem. |
| 2002 | 232,314 | 94,793 | Clatworthy, Raymond J. | 135,253 | Biden, Joseph R. Jr. | 2,268 | 40,460 D | 40.8% | 58.2% | 41.2% | 58.8% |
| 2000 | 327,017 | 142,891 | Roth, William V. | 181,566 | Carper, Thomas R. | 2,560 | 38,675 D | 43.7% | 55.5% | 44.0% | 56.0% |
| 1996 | 275,605 | 105,088 | Clatworthy, Raymond J. | 165,465 | Biden, Joseph R. Jr. | 5,052 | 60,377 D | 38.1% | 60.0% | 38.8% | 61.2% |
| 1994 | 199,029 | 111,088 | Roth, William V. | 84,554 | Oberly, Charles M. | 3,387 | 26,534 R | 55.8% | 42.5% | 56.8% | 43.2% |
| 1990 | 180,152 | 64,554 | Brady, M. Jane | 112,918 | Biden, Joseph R. Jr. | 2,680 | 48,364 D | 35.8% | 62.7% | 36.4% | 63.6% |
| 1988 | 243,493 | 151,115 | Roth, William V. | 92,378 | Woo, S. B. | | 58,737 R | 62.1% | 37.9% | 62.1% | 37.9% |
| 1984 | 245,932 | 98,101 | Burris, John M. | 147,831 | Biden, Joseph R. Jr. | | 49,730 D | 39.9% | 60.1% | 39.9% | 60.1% |
| 1982 | 190,960 | 105,357 | Roth, William V. | 84,413 | Levinson, David N. | 1,190 | 20,944 R | 55.2% | 44.2% | 55.5% | 44.5% |
| 1978 | 162,072 | 66,479 | Baxter, James H. | 93,930 | Biden, Joseph R. Jr. | 1,663 | 27,451 D | 41.0% | 58.0% | 41.4% | 58.6% |
| 1976 | 224,859 | 125,502 | Roth, William V. | 98,055 | Maloney, Thomas C. | 1,302 | 27,447 R | 55.8% | 43.6% | 56.1% | 43.9% |
| 1972 | 229,828 | 112,844 | Boggs, J. Caleb | 116,006 | Biden, Joseph R. Jr. | 978 | 3,162 D | 49.1% | 50.5% | 49.3% | 50.7% |
| 1970 | 161,439 | 94,979 | Roth, William V. | 64,740 | Zimmerman, Jacob | 1,720 | 30,239 R | 58.8% | 40.1% | 59.5% | 40.5% |
| 1966 | 164,549 | 97,268 | Boggs, J. Caleb | 67,281 | Tunnell, James M., Jr. | | 29,987 R | 59.1% | 40.9% | 59.1% | 40.9% |
| 1964 | 200,703 | 103,782 | Williams, John J. | 96,850 | Carvel, Elbert N. | 71 | 6,932 R | 51.7% | 48.3% | 51.7% | 48.3% |
| 1960 | 194,964 | 98,874 | Boggs, J. Caleb | 96,090 | Frear, J. Allen | | 2,784 R | 50.7% | 49.3% | 50.7% | 49.3% |
| 1958 | 154,432 | 82,280 | Williams, John J. | 72,152 | Carvel, Elbert N. | | 10,128 R | 53.3% | 46.7% | 53.3% | 46.7% |
| 1954 | 144,900 | 62,389 | Warburton, H. B. | 82,511 | Frear, J. Allen | | 20,122 D | 43.1% | 56.9% | 43.1% | 56.9% |
| 1952 | 170,705 | 93,020 | Williams, John J. | 77,685 | Bayard, A. I. duP. | | 15,335 R | 54.5% | 45.5% | 54.5% | 45.5% |
| 1948 | 141,362 | 68,246 | Buck, C. Douglas | 71,888 | Frear, J. Allen | 1,228 | 3,642 D | 48.3% | 50.9% | 48.7% | 51.3% |
| 1946 | 113,513 | 62,603 | Williams, John J. | 50,910 | Tunnell, James M. | | 11,693 R | 55.2% | 44.8% | 55.2% | 44.8% |

# DELAWARE

One member At Large

Wilmington

Newark

NEW CASTLE

Dover

KENT

**At Large**

SUSSEX

Rehoboth Beach

Bethany Beach

# DELAWARE

## PRESIDENT 2004

| 2000 Census Population | County | Total Vote | Republican | Democratic | Other | Rep.-Dem. Plurality | Percentage | | | |
|---|---|---|---|---|---|---|---|---|---|---|
| | | | | | | | Total Vote | | Major Vote | |
| | | | | | | | Rep. | Dem. | Rep. | Dem. |
| 126,697 | KENT | 55,980 | 31,578 | 23,875 | 527 | 7,703 R | 56.4% | 42.6% | 56.9% | 43.1% |
| 500,265 | NEW CASTLE | 241,461 | 93,079 | 146,179 | 2,203 | 53,100 D | 38.5% | 60.5% | 38.9% | 61.1% |
| 156,638 | SUSSEX | 77,749 | 47,003 | 30,098 | 648 | 16,905 R | 60.5% | 38.7% | 61.0% | 39.0% |
| 783,600 | TOTAL | 375,190 | 171,660 | 200,152 | 3,378 | 28,492 D | 45.8% | 53.3% | 46.2% | 53.8% |

# DELAWARE

## GOVERNOR 2004

| 2000 Census Population | County | Total Vote | Republican | Democratic | Other | Rep.-Dem. Plurality | Percentage | | | |
|---|---|---|---|---|---|---|---|---|---|---|
| | | | | | | | Total Vote | | Major Vote | |
| | | | | | | | Rep. | Dem. | Rep. | Dem. |
| 126,697 | KENT | 54,892 | 28,562 | 22,324 | 4,006 | 6,238 R | 52.0% | 40.7% | 56.1% | 43.9% |
| 500,265 | NEW CASTLE | 233,623 | 99,586 | 129,092 | 4,945 | 29,506 D | 42.6% | 55.3% | 43.5% | 56.5% |
| 156,638 | SUSSEX | 76,493 | 38,967 | 34,271 | 3,255 | 4,696 R | 50.9% | 44.8% | 53.2% | 46.8% |
| 783,600 | TOTAL | 365,008 | 167,115 | 185,687 | 12,206 | 18,572 D | 45.8% | 50.9% | 47.4% | 52.6% |

# DELAWARE

## HOUSE OF REPRESENTATIVES

| CD | Year | Total Vote | Republican | | Democratic | | Other Vote | Rep.-Dem. Plurality | Percentage | | | |
|---|---|---|---|---|---|---|---|---|---|---|---|---|
| | | | Vote | Candidate | Vote | Candidate | | | Total Vote | | Major Vote | |
| | | | | | | | | | Rep. | Dem. | Rep. | Dem. |
| AL | 2004 | 356,045 | 245,978 | Castle, Michael N.* | 105,716 | Donnelly, Paul | 4,351 | 140,262 R | 69.1% | 29.7% | 69.9% | 30.1% |
| AL | 2002 | 228,405 | 164,605 | Castle, Michael N.* | 61,011 | Miller, Micheal C. | 2,789 | 103,594 R | 72.1% | 26.7% | 73.0% | 27.0% |
| AL | 2000 | 313,126 | 211,797 | Castle, Michael N.* | 96,488 | Miller, Micheal C. | 4,841 | 115,309 R | 67.6% | 30.8% | 68.7% | 31.3% |
| AL | 1998 | 180,527 | 119,811 | Castle, Michael N.* | 57,446 | Williams, Dennis E. | 3,270 | 62,365 R | 66.4% | 31.8% | 67.6% | 32.4% |
| AL | 1996 | 266,836 | 185,576 | Castle, Michael N.* | 73,253 | Williams, Dennis E. | 8,007 | 112,323 R | 69.5% | 27.5% | 71.7% | 28.3% |
| AL | 1994 | 195,037 | 137,960 | Castle, Michael N.* | 51,803 | Desantis, Carol Ann | 5,274 | 86,157 R | 70.7% | 26.6% | 72.7% | 27.3% |
| AL | 1992 | 276,157 | 153,037 | Castle, Michael N. | 117,426 | Woo, S. B. | 5,694 | 35,611 R | 55.4% | 42.5% | 56.6% | 43.4% |
| AL | 1990 | 177,432 | 58,037 | Williams, Ralph O. | 116,274 | Carper, Thomas R.* | 3,121 | 58,237 D | 32.7% | 65.5% | 33.3% | 66.7% |
| AL | 1988 | 234,517 | 76,179 | Krapf, James P. | 158,338 | Carper, Thomas R.* | | 82,159 D | 32.5% | 67.5% | 32.5% | 67.5% |
| AL | 1986 | 160,757 | 53,767 | Neubergr, Thomas S. | 106,351 | Carper, Thomas R.* | 639 | 52,584 D | 33.4% | 66.2% | 33.6% | 66.4% |
| AL | 1984 | 243,014 | 100,650 | DuPont, Pierre | 142,070 | Carper, Thomas R.* | 294 | 41,420 D | 41.4% | 58.5% | 41.5% | 58.5% |
| AL | 1982 | 188,064 | 87,153 | Evans, Thomas B.* | 98,533 | Carper, Thomas R. | 2,378 | 11,380 D | 46.3% | 52.4% | 46.9% | 53.1% |
| AL | 1980 | 216,629 | 133,842 | Evans, Thomas B.* | 81,227 | Maxwell, Robert L. | 1,560 | 52,615 R | 61.8% | 37.5% | 62.2% | 37.8% |
| AL | 1978 | 157,566 | 91,689 | Evans, Thomas B.* | 64,863 | Hindes, Gary E. | 1,014 | 26,826 R | 58.2% | 41.2% | 58.6% | 41.4% |
| AL | 1976 | 214,799 | 110,677 | Evans, Thomas B. | 102,431 | Shipley, Samuel L. | 1,691 | 8,246 R | 51.5% | 47.7% | 51.9% | 48.1% |
| AL | 1974 | 160,328 | 93,826 | DuPont, Pierre* | 63,490 | Soles, James | 3,012 | 30,336 R | 58.5% | 39.6% | 59.6% | 40.4% |
| AL | 1972 | 225,851 | 141,237 | DuPont, Pierre* | 83,230 | Handloff, Norma | 1,384 | 58,007 R | 62.5% | 36.9% | 62.9% | 37.1% |
| AL | 1970 | 160,313 | 86,125 | DuPont, Pierre | 71,429 | Daniello, John D. | 2,759 | 14,696 R | 53.7% | 44.6% | 54.7% | 45.3% |
| AL | 1968 | 200,820 | 117,827 | Roth, William V.* | 82,993 | McDowell, Harris B. | | 34,834 R | 58.7% | 41.3% | 58.7% | 41.3% |
| AL | 1966 | 163,103 | 90,961 | Roth, William V. | 72,142 | McDowell, Harris B.* | | 18,819 R | 55.8% | 44.2% | 55.8% | 44.2% |
| AL | 1964 | 198,691 | 86,254 | Snowden, James H. | 112,361 | McDowell, Harris B.* | 76 | 26,107 D | 43.4% | 56.6% | 43.4% | 56.6% |
| AL | 1962 | 153,356 | 71,934 | Williams, Wilmer F. | 81,166 | McDowell, Harris B.* | 256 | 9,232 D | 46.9% | 52.9% | 47.0% | 53.0% |
| AL | 1960 | 194,564 | 96,337 | McKinstry, James T. | 98,227 | McDowell, Harris B.* | | 1,890 D | 49.5% | 50.5% | 49.5% | 50.5% |
| AL | 1958 | 152,896 | 76,099 | Haskell, Harry G.* | 76,797 | McDowell, Harris B. | | 698 D | 49.8% | 50.2% | 49.8% | 50.2% |
| AL | 1956 | 176,182 | 91,538 | Haskell, Harry G. | 84,644 | McDowell, Harris B.* | | 6,894 R | 52.0% | 48.0% | 52.0% | 48.0% |
| AL | 1954 | 144,236 | 65,035 | Martin, Lilllian | 79,201 | McDowell, Harris B. | | 14,166 D | 45.1% | 54.9% | 45.1% | 54.9% |
| AL | 1952 | 170,015 | 88,285 | Warburton, H.B. | 81,730 | Scannell, Joseph S. | | 6,555 R | 51.9% | 48.1% | 51.9% | 48.1% |
| AL | 1950 | 129,404 | 73,313 | Boggs, J. Caleb* | 56,091 | Winchester, H.M. | | 17,222 R | 56.7% | 43.3% | 56.7% | 43.3% |
| AL | 1948 | 140,535 | 71,127 | Boggs, J. Caleb* | 68,909 | McGuigan, J. Carl | 499 | 2,218 R | 50.6% | 49.0% | 50.8% | 49.2% |
| AL | 1946 | 112,621 | 63,516 | Boggs, J. Caleb | 49,105 | Traynor, Philip A.* | | 14,411 R | 56.4% | 43.6% | 56.4% | 43.6% |

An asterisk (*) denotes incumbent.

# DELAWARE

## GENERAL AND PRIMARY ELECTIONS

## 2004 GENERAL ELECTIONS

**President**  Other vote was 2,153 Independent Party of Delaware (Ralph Nader); 586 Libertarian (Michael Badnarik); 289 Constitution (Michael Peroutka); 250 Green (David Cobb); 100 Natural Law (Walter F. Brown).

**Governor**  Other vote was 10,756 Independent Party of Delaware (Frank Infante); 1,450 Libertarian (Frank Infante). Infante received a total of 12,206 votes on the two ballot lines.

**House**  Other vote was:

At Large  2,337 Independent Party of Delaware (Maurice J. Barros); 2,014 Libertarian (William E. Morris).

## 2004 PRIMARY ELECTIONS

| **Primary** | February 3, 2004 (President)<br>September 11, 2004 (Congress) | **Registration**<br>(as of Sept. 1, 2004) | Republican | 177,399 |
|---|---|---|---|---|
| | | | Democratic | 234,045 |
| | | | Libertarian | 765 |
| | | | Green | 646 |
| | | | Independent Party<br>of Delaware | 419 |
| | | | Constitution | 312 |
| | | | Natural Law | 280 |
| | | | Reform | 224 |
| | | | Other Parties | 1,105 |
| | | | Independent | 121,096 |
| | | | TOTAL | 536,291 |

**Primary Type**  Closed—Only registered Democrats and Republicans could vote in their party's primary.

Note:  An asterisk (*) denotes incumbent. The names of unopposed candidates did not appear on the primary ballot; therefore, no votes were cast for these candidates.

| | REPUBLICAN PRIMARIES | | | DEMOCRATIC PRIMARIES | | |
|---|---|---|---|---|---|---|
| **President** | No Republican primary | | | John Kerry | 16,787 | 50.4% |
| | | | | Joseph I. Lieberman | 3,706 | 11.1% |
| | | | | John Edwards | 3,674 | 11.0% |
| | | | | Howard Dean | 3,462 | 10.4% |
| | | | | Wesley Clark | 3,165 | 9.5% |
| | | | | Al Sharpton | 1,888 | 5.7% |
| | | | | Dennis J. Kucinich | 344 | 1.0% |
| | | | | Richard A. Gephardt | 187 | 0.6% |
| | | | | Lyndon H. LaRouche Jr. | 78 | 0.2% |
| | | | | TOTAL | 33,291 | |
| **Governor** | William Swain Lee | 15,270 | 70.5% | Ruth Ann Minner* | Unopposed | |
| | Michael D. Protack | 5,108 | 23.6% | | | |
| | David Charles Graham | 1,292 | 6.0% | | | |
| | TOTAL | 21,670 | | | | |
| **House**<br>**At Large** | Michael N. Castle* | Unopposed | | Paul Donnelly | Unopposed | |

# FLORIDA

## GOVERNOR
Jeb Bush (R). Reelected 2002 to a four-year term. Previously elected 1998.

## SENATORS (1 Democrat, 1 Republican)
Mel Martinez (R). Elected 2004 to a six-year term.

Bill Nelson (D). Elected 2000 to a six-year term.

## REPRESENTATIVES (18 Republicans, 7 Democrats)

1. Jeff Miller (R)
2. Allen Boyd (D)
3. Corrine Brown (D)
4. Ander Crenshaw (R)
5. Ginny Brown-Waite (R)
6. Cliff Stearns (R)
7. John L. Mica (R)
8. Ric Keller (R)
9. Michael Bilirakis (R)
10. C.W. Bill Young (R)
11. Jim Davis (D)
12. Adam H. Putnam (R)
13. Katherine Harris (R)
14. Connie Mack (R)
15. Dave Weldon (R)
16. Mark Foley (R)
17. Kendrick B. Meek (D)
18. Ileana Ros-Lehtinen (R)
19. Robert Wexler (D)
20. Debbie Wasserman-Schultz (D)
21. Lincoln Diaz-Balart (R)
22. E. Clay Shaw Jr. (R)
23. Alcee L. Hastings (D)
24. Tom Feeney (R)
25. Mario Diaz-Balart (R)

## POSTWAR VOTE FOR PRESIDENT

| | | Republican | | Democratic | | Other | | Percentage | | | |
| | | | | | | | | Total Vote | | Major Vote | |
| Year | Total Vote | Vote | Candidate | Vote | Candidate | Vote | Plurality | Rep. | Dem. | Rep. | Dem. |
|---|---|---|---|---|---|---|---|---|---|---|---|
| 2004 | 7,609,810 | 3,964,522 | Bush, George W. | 3,583,544 | Kerry, John | 61,744 | 380,978 R | 52.1% | 47.1% | 52.5% | 47.5% |
| 2000** | 5,963,110 | 2,912,790 | Bush, George W. | 2,912,253 | Gore, Al | 138,067 | 537 R | 48.8% | 48.8% | 50.0% | 50.0% |
| 1996** | 5,303,794 | 2,244,536 | Dole, Bob | 2,546,870 | Clinton, Bill | 512,388 | 302,334 D | 42.3% | 48.0% | 46.8% | 53.2% |
| 1992** | 5,314,392 | 2,173,310 | Bush, George | 2,072,698 | Clinton, Bill | 1,068,384 | 100,612 R | 40.9% | 39.0% | 51.2% | 48.8% |
| 1988 | 4,302,313 | 2,618,885 | Bush, George | 1,656,701 | Dukakis, Michael S. | 26,727 | 962,184 R | 60.9% | 38.5% | 61.3% | 38.7% |
| 1984 | 4,180,051 | 2,730,350 | Reagan, Ronald | 1,448,816 | Mondale, Walter F. | 885 | 1,281,534 R | 65.3% | 34.7% | 65.3% | 34.7% |
| 1980** | 3,686,930 | 2,046,951 | Reagan, Ronald | 1,419,475 | Carter, Jimmy | 220,504 | 627,476 R | 55.5% | 38.5% | 59.1% | 40.9% |
| 1976 | 3,150,631 | 1,469,531 | Ford, Gerald R. | 1,636,000 | Carter, Jimmy | 45,100 | 166,469 D | 46.6% | 51.9% | 47.3% | 52.7% |
| 1972 | 2,583,283 | 1,857,759 | Nixon, Richard M. | 718,117 | McGovern, George S. | 7,407 | 1,139,642 R | 71.9% | 27.8% | 72.1% | 27.9% |
| 1968** | 2,187,805 | 886,804 | Nixon, Richard M. | 676,794 | Humphrey, Hubert H. | 624,207 | 210,010 R | 40.5% | 30.9% | 56.7% | 43.3% |
| 1964 | 1,854,481 | 905,941 | Goldwater, Barry M. | 948,540 | Johnson, Lyndon B. | | 42,599 D | 48.9% | 51.1% | 48.9% | 51.1% |
| 1960 | 1,544,176 | 795,476 | Nixon, Richard M. | 748,700 | Kennedy, John F. | | 46,776 R | 51.5% | 48.5% | 51.5% | 48.5% |
| 1956 | 1,125,762 | 643,849 | Eisenhower, Dwight D. | 480,371 | Stevenson, Adlai E. | 1,542 | 163,478 R | 57.2% | 42.7% | 57.3% | 42.7% |
| 1952 | 989,337 | 544,036 | Eisenhower, Dwight D. | 444,950 | Stevenson, Adlai E. | 351 | 99,086 R | 55.0% | 45.0% | 55.0% | 45.0% |
| 1948** | 577,643 | 194,280 | Dewey, Thomas E. | 281,988 | Truman, Harry S. | 101,375 | 87,708 D | 33.6% | 48.8% | 40.8% | 59.2% |

In past elections, the other vote included: 2000 - 97,488 Green (Ralph Nader); 1996 - 483,870 Reform (Ross Perot); 1992 - 1,053,067 Independent (Perot); 1980 - 189,692 Independent (John Anderson); 1968 - 624,207 American Independent (George Wallace); 1948 - 89,755 States' Rights (Strom Thurmond).

# FLORIDA

## POSTWAR VOTE FOR GOVERNOR

| Year | Total Vote | Republican Vote | Republican Candidate | Democratic Vote | Democratic Candidate | Other Vote | Rep.-Dem. Plurality | Total Vote Rep. | Total Vote Dem. | Major Vote Rep. | Major Vote Dem. |
|------|-----------|-----------------|----------------------|-----------------|----------------------|-----------|---------------------|-----------------|-----------------|-----------------|-----------------|
| 2002 | 5,100,581 | 2,856,845 | Bush, Jeb | 2,201,427 | McBride, Bill | 42,309 | 655,418 R | 56.0% | 43.2% | 56.5% | 43.5% |
| 1998 | 3,964,441 | 2,191,105 | Bush, Jeb | 1,773,054 | MacKay, Buddy | 282 | 418,051 R | 55.3% | 44.7% | 55.3% | 44.7% |
| 1994 | 4,206,659 | 2,071,068 | Bush, Jeb | 2,135,008 | Chiles, Lawton | 583 | 63,940 D | 49.2% | 50.8% | 49.2% | 50.8% |
| 1990 | 3,530,871 | 1,535,068 | Martinez, Bob | 1,995,206 | Chiles, Lawton | 597 | 460,138 D | 43.5% | 56.5% | 43.5% | 56.5% |
| 1986 | 3,386,171 | 1,847,525 | Martinez, Bob | 1,538,620 | Pajcic, Steve | 26 | 308,905 R | 54.6% | 45.4% | 54.6% | 45.4% |
| 1982 | 2,688,566 | 949,013 | Bafalis, L. A. | 1,739,553 | Graham, Bob | | 790,540 D | 35.3% | 64.7% | 35.3% | 64.7% |
| 1978 | 2,530,468 | 1,123,888 | Eckerd, Jack M. | 1,406,580 | Graham, Bob | | 282,692 D | 44.4% | 55.6% | 44.4% | 55.6% |
| 1974 | 1,828,392 | 709,438 | Thomas, Jerry | 1,118,954 | Askew, Reubin | | 409,516 D | 38.8% | 61.2% | 38.8% | 61.2% |
| 1970 | 1,730,813 | 746,243 | Kirk, Claude R. | 984,305 | Askew, Reubin | 265 | 238,062 D | 43.1% | 56.9% | 43.1% | 56.9% |
| 1966 | 1,489,661 | 821,190 | Kirk, Claude R. | 668,233 | High, Robert King | 238 | 152,957 R | 55.1% | 44.9% | 55.1% | 44.9% |
| 1964S | 1,663,481 | 686,297 | Holley, Charles R. | 933,554 | Burns, Haydon | 43,630 | 247,257 D | 41.3% | 56.1% | 42.4% | 57.6% |
| 1960 | 1,419,343 | 569,936 | Petersen, George C. | 849,407 | Bryant, Farris | | 279,471 D | 40.2% | 59.8% | 40.2% | 59.8% |
| 1956 | 1,014,733 | 266,980 | Washburne, W. A. | 747,753 | Collins, LeRoy | | 480,773 D | 26.3% | 73.7% | 26.3% | 73.7% |
| 1954S | 357,783 | 69,852 | Watson, J. Tom | 287,769 | Collins, LeRoy | 162 | 217,917 D | 19.5% | 80.4% | 19.5% | 80.5% |
| 1952 | 834,518 | 210,009 | Swan, Harry S. | 624,463 | McCarty, Dan | 46 | 414,454 D | 25.2% | 74.8% | 25.2% | 74.8% |
| 1948 | 457,638 | 76,153 | Acker, Bert Lee | 381,459 | Warren, Fuller | 26 | 305,306 D | 16.6% | 83.4% | 16.6% | 83.4% |

The 1964 election was for a two-year term to permit shifting the vote for governor to non-presidential years. The 1954 election was for a short term to fill a vacancy.

## POSTWAR VOTE FOR SENATOR

| Year | Total Vote | Republican Vote | Republican Candidate | Democratic Vote | Democratic Candidate | Other Vote | Rep.-Dem. Plurality | Total Vote Rep. | Total Vote Dem. | Major Vote Rep. | Major Vote Dem. |
|------|-----------|-----------------|----------------------|-----------------|----------------------|-----------|---------------------|-----------------|-----------------|-----------------|-----------------|
| 2004 | 7,429,894 | 3,672,864 | Martinez, Mel | 3,590,201 | Castor, Betty | 166,829 | 82,663 R | 49.4% | 48.3% | 50.6% | 49.4% |
| 2000 | 5,856,731 | 2,705,348 | McCollum, Bill | 2,989,487 | Nelson, Bill | 161,896 | 284,139 D | 46.2% | 51.0% | 47.5% | 52.5% |
| 1998 | 3,900,162 | 1,463,755 | Crist, Charlie | 2,436,407 | Graham, Bob | | 972,652 D | 37.5% | 62.5% | 37.5% | 62.5% |
| 1994 | 4,106,176 | 2,894,726 | Mack, Connie | 1,210,412 | Rodham, Hugh E. | 1,038 | 1,684,314 R | 70.5% | 29.5% | 70.5% | 29.5% |
| 1992 | 4,962,290 | 1,716,505 | Grant, Bill | 3,245,565 | Graham, Bob | 220 | 1,529,060 D | 34.6% | 65.4% | 34.6% | 65.4% |
| 1988 | 4,068,209 | 2,051,071 | Mack, Connie | 2,016,553 | MacKay, Buddy | 585 | 34,518 R | 50.4% | 49.6% | 50.4% | 49.6% |
| 1986 | 3,429,996 | 1,552,376 | Hawkins, Paula | 1,877,543 | Graham, Bob | 77 | 325,167 D | 45.3% | 54.7% | 45.3% | 54.7% |
| 1982 | 2,653,419 | 1,015,330 | Poole, Van B. | 1,637,667 | Chiles, Lawton | 422 | 622,337 D | 38.3% | 61.7% | 38.3% | 61.7% |
| 1980 | 3,528,028 | 1,822,460 | Hawkins, Paula | 1,705,409 | Gunter, Bill | 159 | 117,051 R | 51.7% | 48.3% | 51.7% | 48.3% |
| 1976 | 2,857,534 | 1,057,886 | Grady, John | 1,799,518 | Chiles, Lawton | 130 | 741,632 D | 37.0% | 63.0% | 37.0% | 63.0% |
| 1974 | 1,800,539 | 736,674 | Eckerd, Jack M. | 781,031 | Stone, Richard | 282,834 | 44,357 D | 40.9% | 43.4% | 48.5% | 51.5% |
| 1970 | 1,675,378 | 772,817 | Cramer, William C. | 902,438 | Chiles, Lawton | 123 | 129,621 D | 46.1% | 53.9% | 46.1% | 53.9% |
| 1968 | 2,024,136 | 1,131,499 | Gurney, Edward J. | 892,637 | Collins, LeRoy | | 238,862 R | 55.9% | 44.1% | 55.9% | 44.1% |
| 1964 | 1,560,337 | 562,212 | Kirk, Claude R. | 997,585 | Holland, Spessard L. | 540 | 435,373 D | 36.0% | 63.9% | 36.0% | 64.0% |
| 1962 | 939,207 | 281,381 | Rupert, Emerson H. | 657,633 | Smathers, George A. | 193 | 376,252 D | 30.0% | 70.0% | 30.0% | 70.0% |
| 1958 | 542,069 | 155,956 | Hyzer, Leland | 386,113 | Holland, Spessard L. | | 230,157 D | 28.8% | 71.2% | 28.8% | 71.2% |
| 1956 | 655,418 | | — | 655,418 | Smathers, George A. | | 655,418 D | | 100.0% | | 100.0% |
| 1952 | 617,800 | | — | 616,665 | Holland, Spessard L. | 1,135 | 616,665 D | | 99.8% | | 100.0% |
| 1950 | 313,487 | 74,228 | Booth, John P. | 238,987 | Smathers, George A. | 272 | 164,759 D | 23.7% | 76.2% | 23.7% | 76.3% |
| 1946 | 198,640 | 42,408 | Schad, J. Harry | 156,232 | Holland, Spessard L. | | 113,824 D | 21.3% | 78.7% | 21.3% | 78.7% |

# FLORIDA

Congressional districts first established for elections held in 2002
25 members

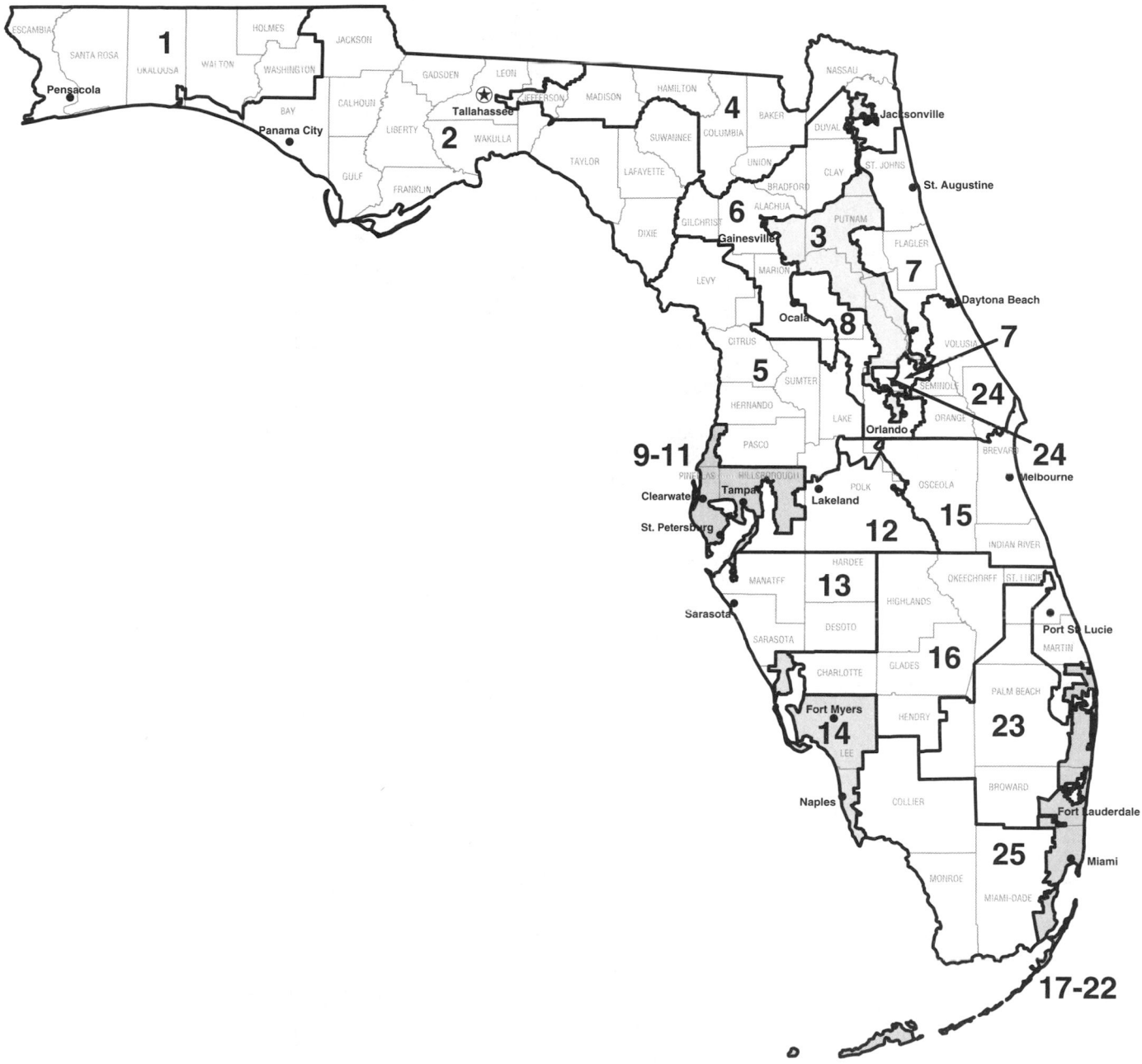

120

# FLORIDA

St. Petersburg, Tampa, Fort Myers Areas

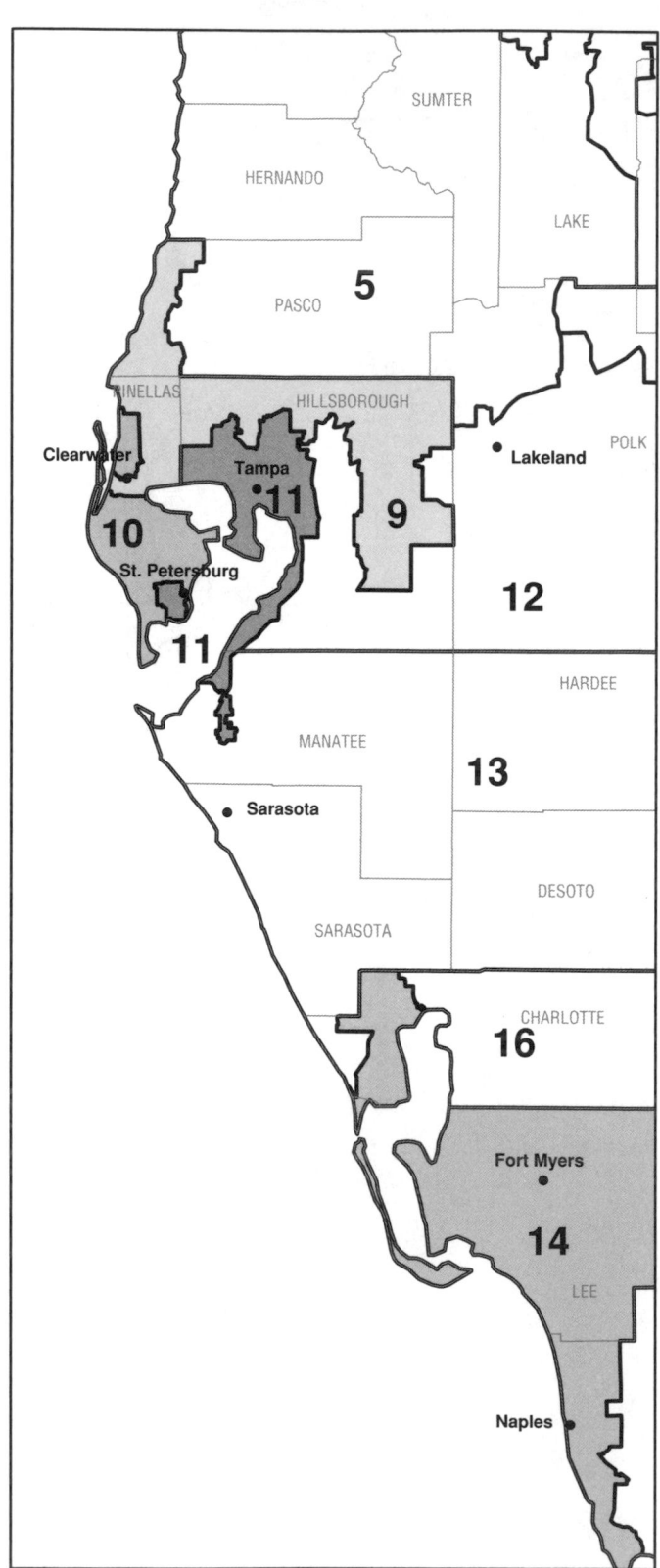

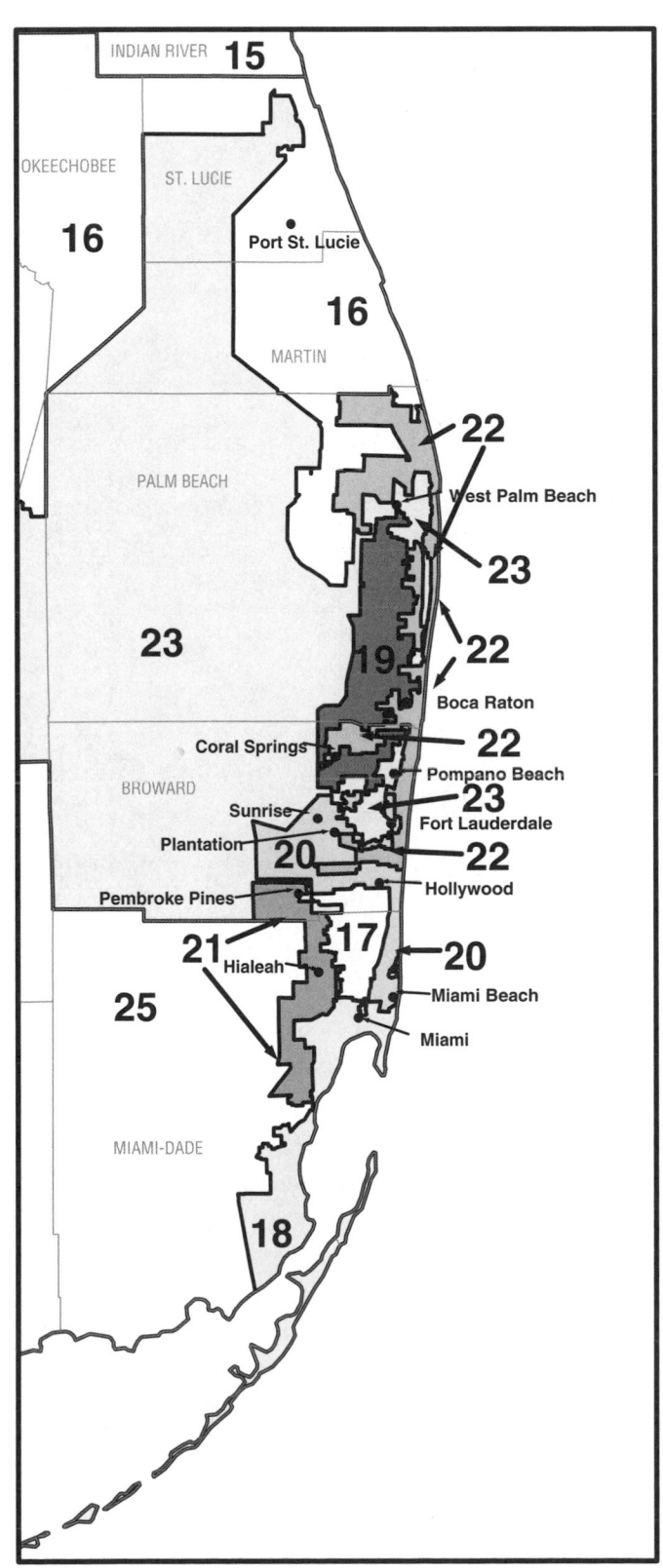

# FLORIDA

Miami, Fort Lauderdale Areas

# FLORIDA

## PRESIDENT 2004

| 2000 Census Population | County | Total Vote | Republican | Democratic | Other | Rep.-Dem. Plurality | Percentage Total Vote Rep. | Dem. | Major Vote Rep. | Dem. |
|---|---|---|---|---|---|---|---|---|---|---|
| 217,955 | ALACHUA | 111,328 | 47,762 | 62,504 | 1,062 | 14,742 D | 42.9% | 56.1% | 43.3% | 56.7% |
| 22,259 | BAKER | 9,955 | 7,738 | 2,180 | 37 | 5,558 R | 77.7% | 21.9% | 78.0% | 22.0% |
| 148,217 | BAY | 75,024 | 53,404 | 21,068 | 552 | 32,336 R | 71.2% | 28.1% | 71.7% | 28.3% |
| 26,088 | BRADFORD | 10,855 | 7,557 | 3,244 | 54 | 4,313 R | 69.6% | 29.9% | 70.0% | 30.0% |
| 476,230 | BREVARD | 265,462 | 153,068 | 110,309 | 2,085 | 42,759 R | 57.7% | 41.6% | 58.1% | 41.9% |
| 1,623,018 | BROWARD | 706,872 | 244,674 | 453,873 | 8,325 | 209,199 D | 34.6% | 64.2% | 35.0% | 65.0% |
| 13,017 | CALHOUN | 5,963 | 3,782 | 2,116 | 65 | 1,666 R | 63.4% | 35.5% | 64.1% | 35.9% |
| 141,627 | CHARLOTTE | 79,786 | 44,428 | 34,256 | 1,102 | 10,172 R | 55.7% | 42.9% | 56.5% | 43.5% |
| 118,085 | CITRUS | 69,467 | 39,500 | 29,277 | 690 | 10,223 R | 56.9% | 42.1% | 57.4% | 42.6% |
| 140,814 | CLAY | 81,495 | 62,078 | 18,971 | 446 | 43,107 R | 76.2% | 23.3% | 76.6% | 23.4% |
| 251,377 | COLLIER | 128,683 | 83,631 | 43,892 | 1,160 | 39,739 R | 65.0% | 34.1% | 65.6% | 34.4% |
| 56,513 | COLUMBIA | 24,991 | 16,758 | 8,031 | 202 | 8,727 R | 67.1% | 32.1% | 67.6% | 32.4% |
| 32,209 | DESOTO | 9,510 | 5,524 | 3,913 | 73 | 1,611 R | 58.1% | 41.1% | 58.5% | 41.5% |
| 13,827 | DIXIE | 6,442 | 4,434 | 1,960 | 48 | 2,474 R | 68.8% | 30.4% | 69.3% | 30.7% |
| 778,879 | DUVAL | 381,061 | 220,190 | 158,610 | 2,261 | 61,580 R | 57.8% | 41.6% | 58.1% | 41.9% |
| 294,410 | ESCAMBIA | 143,278 | 93,566 | 48,329 | 1,383 | 45,237 R | 65.3% | 33.7% | 65.9% | 34.1% |
| 49,832 | FLAGLER | 38,480 | 19,633 | 18,578 | 269 | 1,055 R | 51.0% | 48.3% | 51.4% | 48.6% |
| 11,057 | FRANKLIN | 5,931 | 3,472 | 2,401 | 58 | 1,071 R | 58.5% | 40.5% | 59.1% | 40.9% |
| 45,087 | GADSDEN | 20,984 | 6,253 | 14,629 | 102 | 8,376 D | 29.8% | 69.7% | 29.9% | 70.1% |
| 14,437 | GILCHRIST | 7,015 | 4,936 | 2,017 | 62 | 2,919 R | 70.4% | 28.8% | 71.0% | 29.0% |
| 10,576 | GLADES | 4,188 | 2,443 | 1,718 | 27 | 725 R | 58.3% | 41.0% | 58.7% | 41.3% |
| 13,332 | GULF | 7,277 | 4,805 | 2,407 | 65 | 2,398 R | 66.0% | 33.1% | 66.6% | 33.4% |
| 13,327 | HAMILTON | 5,079 | 2,792 | 2,260 | 27 | 532 R | 55.0% | 44.5% | 55.3% | 44.7% |
| 26,938 | HARDEE | 7,249 | 5,049 | 2,149 | 51 | 2,900 R | 69.7% | 29.6% | 70.1% | 29.9% |
| 36,210 | HENDRY | 9,775 | 5,757 | 3,960 | 58 | 1,797 R | 58.9% | 40.5% | 59.2% | 40.8% |
| 130,802 | HERNANDO | 80,547 | 42,635 | 37,187 | 725 | 5,448 R | 52.9% | 46.2% | 53.4% | 46.6% |
| 87,366 | HIGHLANDS | 41,496 | 25,878 | 15,347 | 271 | 10,531 R | 62.4% | 37.0% | 62.8% | 37.2% |
| 998,948 | HILLSBOROUGH | 463,222 | 245,576 | 214,132 | 3,514 | 31,444 R | 53.0% | 46.2% | 53.4% | 46.6% |
| 18,564 | HOLMES | 8,300 | 6,412 | 1,810 | 78 | 4,602 R | 77.3% | 21.8% | 78.0% | 22.0% |
| 112,947 | INDIAN RIVER | 61,414 | 36,938 | 23,956 | 520 | 12,982 R | 60.1% | 39.0% | 60.7% | 39.3% |
| 46,755 | JACKSON | 19,807 | 12,122 | 7,555 | 130 | 4,567 R | 61.2% | 38.1% | 61.6% | 38.4% |
| 12,902 | JEFFERSON | 7,478 | 3,298 | 4,135 | 45 | 837 D | 44.1% | 55.3% | 44.4% | 55.6% |
| 7,022 | LAFAYETTE | 3,325 | 2,460 | 845 | 20 | 1,615 R | 74.0% | 25.4% | 74.4% | 25.6% |
| 210,528 | LAKE | 123,950 | 74,389 | 48,221 | 1,340 | 26,168 R | 60.0% | 38.9% | 60.7% | 39.3% |
| 440,888 | LEE | 240,667 | 144,176 | 93,860 | 2,631 | 50,316 R | 59.9% | 39.0% | 60.6% | 39.4% |
| 239,452 | LEON | 136,379 | 51,615 | 83,873 | 891 | 32,258 D | 37.8% | 61.5% | 38.1% | 61.9% |
| 34,450 | LEVY | 16,652 | 10,410 | 6,074 | 168 | 4,336 R | 62.5% | 36.5% | 63.2% | 36.8% |
| 7,021 | LIBERTY | 3,021 | 1,927 | 1,070 | 24 | 857 R | 63.8% | 35.4% | 64.3% | 35.7% |
| 18,733 | MADISON | 8,304 | 4,191 | 4,050 | 63 | 141 R | 50.5% | 48.8% | 50.9% | 49.1% |
| 264,002 | MANATEE | 143,621 | 81,318 | 61,262 | 1,041 | 20,056 R | 56.6% | 42.7% | 57.0% | 43.0% |
| 258,916 | MARION | 139,677 | 81,283 | 57,271 | 1,123 | 24,012 R | 58.2% | 41.0% | 58.7% | 41.3% |
| 126,731 | MARTIN | 72,453 | 41,362 | 30,208 | 883 | 11,154 R | 57.1% | 41.7% | 57.8% | 42.2% |
| 2,253,362 | MIAMI-DADE | 774,726 | 361,095 | 409,732 | 3,899 | 48,637 D | 46.6% | 52.9% | 46.8% | 53.2% |
| 79,589 | MONROE | 39,535 | 19,467 | 19,654 | 414 | 187 D | 49.2% | 49.7% | 49.8% | 50.2% |
| 57,663 | NASSAU | 32,743 | 23,783 | 8,573 | 387 | 15,210 R | 72.6% | 26.2% | 73.5% | 26.5% |
| 170,498 | OKALOOSA | 89,756 | 69,693 | 19,368 | 695 | 50,325 R | 77.6% | 21.6% | 78.3% | 21.7% |
| 35,910 | OKEECHOBEE | 12,190 | 6,978 | 5,153 | 59 | 1,825 R | 57.2% | 42.3% | 57.5% | 42.5% |
| 896,344 | ORANGE | 388,044 | 192,539 | 193,354 | 2,151 | 815 D | 49.6% | 49.8% | 49.9% | 50.1% |
| 172,493 | OSCEOLA | 82,204 | 43,117 | 38,633 | 454 | 4,484 R | 52.5% | 47.0% | 52.7% | 47.3% |
| 1,131,184 | PALM BEACH | 544,622 | 212,688 | 328,687 | 3,247 | 115,999 D | 39.1% | 60.4% | 39.3% | 60.7% |
| 344,765 | PASCO | 190,916 | 103,230 | 84,749 | 2,937 | 18,481 R | 54.1% | 44.4% | 54.9% | 45.1% |
| 921,482 | PINELLAS | 455,357 | 225,686 | 225,460 | 4,211 | 226 R | 49.6% | 49.5% | 50.0% | 50.0% |
| 483,924 | POLK | 210,830 | 123,559 | 86,009 | 1,262 | 37,550 R | 58.6% | 40.8% | 59.0% | 41.0% |
| 70,423 | PUTNAM | 30,973 | 18,311 | 12,412 | 250 | 5,899 R | 59.1% | 40.1% | 59.6% | 40.4% |
| 123,135 | ST. JOHNS | 86,290 | 59,196 | 26,399 | 695 | 32,797 R | 68.6% | 30.6% | 69.2% | 30.8% |
| 192,695 | ST. LUCIE | 100,063 | 47,592 | 51,835 | 636 | 4,243 D | 47.6% | 51.8% | 47.9% | 52.1% |
| 117,743 | SANTA ROSA | 67,307 | 52,059 | 14,659 | 589 | 37,400 R | 77.3% | 21.8% | 78.0% | 22.0% |
| 325,957 | SARASOTA | 195,652 | 104,692 | 88,442 | 2,518 | 16,250 R | 53.5% | 45.2% | 54.2% | 45.8% |
| 365,196 | SEMINOLE | 186,195 | 108,172 | 76,971 | 1,052 | 31,201 R | 58.1% | 41.3% | 58.4% | 41.6% |
| 53,345 | SUMTER | 31,842 | 19,800 | 11,584 | 458 | 8,216 R | 62.2% | 36.4% | 63.1% | 36.9% |

# FLORIDA

## PRESIDENT 2004

| 2000 Census Population | County | Total Vote | Republican | Democratic | Other | Rep.-Dem. Plurality | Percentage | | | |
|---|---|---|---|---|---|---|---|---|---|---|
| | | | | | | | Total Vote | | Major Vote | |
| | | | | | | | Rep. | Dem. | Rep. | Dem. |
| 34,844 | SUWANNEE | 15,802 | 11,153 | 4,522 | 127 | 6,631 R | 70.6% | 28.6% | 71.2% | 28.8% |
| 19,256 | TAYLOR | 8,581 | 5,467 | 3,049 | 65 | 2,418 R | 63.7% | 35.5% | 64.2% | 35.8% |
| 13,442 | UNION | 4,675 | 3,396 | 1,251 | 28 | 2,145 R | 72.6% | 26.8% | 73.1% | 26.9% |
| 443,343 | VOLUSIA | 228,939 | 111,924 | 115,519 | 1,496 | 3,595 D | 48.9% | 50.5% | 49.2% | 50.8% |
| 22,863 | WAKULLA | 11,763 | 6,777 | 4,896 | 90 | 1,881 R | 57.6% | 41.6% | 58.1% | 41.9% |
| 40,601 | WALTON | 23,976 | 17,555 | 6,213 | 208 | 11,342 R | 73.2% | 25.9% | 73.9% | 26.1% |
| 20,973 | WASHINGTON | 10,366 | 7,369 | 2,912 | 85 | 4,457 R | 71.1% | 28.1% | 71.7% | 28.3% |
| 15,982,378 | TOTAL | 7,609,810 | 3,964,522 | 3,583,544 | 61,744 | 380,978 R | 52.1% | 47.1% | 52.5% | 47.5% |

# FLORIDA

## SENATOR 2004

| 2000 Census Population | County | Total Vote | Republican | Democratic | Other | Rep.-Dem. Plurality | Percentage | | | |
|---|---|---|---|---|---|---|---|---|---|---|
| | | | | | | | Total Vote | | Major Vote | |
| | | | | | | | Rep. | Dem. | Rep. | Dem. |
| 217,955 | ALACHUA | 108,685 | 43,074 | 63,809 | 1,802 | 20,735 D | 39.6% | 58.7% | 40.3% | 59.7% |
| 22,259 | BAKER | 9,854 | 6,815 | 2,853 | 186 | 3,962 R | 69.2% | 29.0% | 70.5% | 29.5% |
| 148,217 | BAY | 73,393 | 49,639 | 22,190 | 1,564 | 27,449 R | 67.6% | 30.2% | 69.1% | 30.9% |
| 26,088 | BRADFORD | 10,742 | 6,534 | 3,938 | 270 | 2,596 R | 60.8% | 36.7% | 62.4% | 37.6% |
| 476,230 | BREVARD | 261,553 | 142,394 | 111,477 | 7,682 | 30,917 R | 54.4% | 42.6% | 56.1% | 43.9% |
| 1,623,018 | BROWARD | 687,774 | 231,266 | 442,728 | 13,780 | 211,462 D | 33.6% | 64.4% | 34.3% | 65.7% |
| 13,017 | CALHOUN | 5,834 | 3,133 | 2,526 | 175 | 607 R | 53.7% | 43.3% | 55.4% | 44.6% |
| 141,627 | CHARLOTTE | 77,645 | 43,079 | 32,837 | 1,729 | 10,242 R | 55.5% | 42.3% | 56.7% | 43.3% |
| 118,085 | CITRUS | 68,439 | 33,998 | 31,699 | 2,742 | 2,299 R | 49.7% | 46.3% | 51.7% | 48.3% |
| 140,814 | CLAY | 80,465 | 58,131 | 20,831 | 1,503 | 37,300 R | 72.2% | 25.9% | 73.6% | 26.4% |
| 251,377 | COLLIER | 124,214 | 81,948 | 40,332 | 1,934 | 41,616 R | 66.0% | 32.5% | 67.0% | 33.0% |
| 56,513 | COLUMBIA | 24,520 | 14,014 | 9,780 | 726 | 4,234 R | 57.2% | 39.9% | 58.9% | 41.1% |
| 32,209 | DESOTO | 9,320 | 4,994 | 4,031 | 295 | 963 R | 53.6% | 43.3% | 55.3% | 44.7% |
| 13,827 | DIXIE | 6,307 | 3,322 | 2,735 | 250 | 587 R | 52.7% | 43.4% | 54.8% | 45.2% |
| 778,879 | DUVAL | 374,909 | 205,001 | 163,748 | 6,160 | 41,253 R | 54.7% | 43.7% | 55.6% | 44.4% |
| 294,410 | ESCAMBIA | 139,693 | 88,787 | 48,274 | 2,632 | 40,513 R | 63.6% | 34.6% | 64.8% | 35.2% |
| 49,832 | FLAGLER | 38,010 | 18,294 | 18,812 | 904 | 518 D | 48.1% | 49.5% | 49.3% | 50.7% |
| 11,057 | FRANKLIN | 5,742 | 2,706 | 2,886 | 150 | 180 D | 47.1% | 50.3% | 48.4% | 51.6% |
| 45,087 | GADSDEN | 20,792 | 5,230 | 15,246 | 316 | 10,016 D | 25.2% | 73.3% | 25.5% | 74.5% |
| 14,437 | GILCHRIST | 6,896 | 4,060 | 2,578 | 258 | 1,482 R | 58.9% | 37.4% | 61.2% | 38.8% |
| 10,576 | GLADES | 4,117 | 2,147 | 1,821 | 149 | 326 R | 52.1% | 44.2% | 54.1% | 45.9% |
| 13,332 | GULF | 7,124 | 4,086 | 2,858 | 180 | 1,228 R | 57.4% | 40.1% | 58.8% | 41.2% |
| 13,327 | HAMILTON | 4,930 | 2,206 | 2,597 | 127 | 391 D | 44.7% | 52.7% | 45.9% | 54.1% |
| 26,938 | HARDEE | 7,137 | 4,024 | 2,806 | 307 | 1,218 R | 56.4% | 39.3% | 58.9% | 41.1% |
| 36,210 | HENDRY | 9,596 | 5,350 | 4,027 | 219 | 1,323 R | 55.8% | 42.0% | 57.1% | 42.9% |
| 130,802 | HERNANDO | 79,334 | 36,557 | 39,634 | 3,143 | 3,077 D | 46.1% | 50.0% | 48.0% | 52.0% |
| 87,366 | HIGHLANDS | 40,800 | 22,326 | 17,196 | 1,278 | 5,130 R | 54.7% | 42.1% | 56.5% | 43.5% |
| 998,948 | HILLSBOROUGH | 447,890 | 207,331 | 230,298 | 10,261 | 22,967 D | 46.3% | 51.4% | 47.4% | 52.6% |
| 18,564 | HOLMES | 8,064 | 5,114 | 2,608 | 342 | 2,506 R | 63.4% | 32.3% | 66.2% | 33.8% |
| 112,947 | INDIAN RIVER | 59,392 | 34,338 | 23,511 | 1,543 | 10,827 R | 57.8% | 39.6% | 59.4% | 40.6% |
| 46,755 | JACKSON | 19,449 | 10,449 | 8,605 | 395 | 1,844 R | 53.7% | 44.2% | 54.8% | 45.2% |
| 12,902 | JEFFERSON | 7,371 | 2,722 | 4,504 | 145 | 1,782 D | 36.9% | 61.1% | 37.7% | 62.3% |
| 7,022 | LAFAYETTE | 3,240 | 1,768 | 1,390 | 82 | 378 R | 54.6% | 42.9% | 56.0% | 44.0% |
| 210,528 | LAKE | 121,379 | 68,425 | 49,635 | 3,319 | 18,790 R | 56.4% | 40.9% | 58.0% | 42.0% |
| 440,888 | LEE | 233,389 | 139,810 | 89,048 | 4,531 | 50,762 R | 59.9% | 38.2% | 61.1% | 38.9% |
| 239,452 | LEON | 133,324 | 45,453 | 86,180 | 1,691 | 40,727 D | 34.1% | 64.6% | 34.5% | 65.5% |
| 34,450 | LEVY | 16,361 | 8,735 | 7,129 | 497 | 1,606 R | 53.4% | 43.6% | 55.1% | 44.9% |
| 7,021 | LIBERTY | 2,970 | 1,448 | 1,459 | 63 | 11 D | 48.8% | 49.1% | 49.8% | 50.2% |
| 18,733 | MADISON | 8,177 | 3,318 | 4,640 | 219 | 1,322 D | 40.6% | 56.7% | 41.7% | 58.3% |
| 264,002 | MANATEE | 141,323 | 72,829 | 64,795 | 3,699 | 8,034 R | 51.5% | 45.8% | 52.9% | 47.1% |

# FLORIDA

## SENATOR 2004

| 2000 Census Population | County | Total Vote | Republican | Democratic | Other | Rep.-Dem. Plurality | Rep. | Dem. | Rep. | Dem. |
|---|---|---|---|---|---|---|---|---|---|---|
| 258,916 | MARION | 138,143 | 73,530 | 60,814 | 3,799 | 12,716 R | 53.2% | 44.0% | 54.7% | 45.3% |
| 126,731 | MARTIN | 70,523 | 39,076 | 29,868 | 1,579 | 9,208 R | 55.4% | 42.4% | 56.7% | 43.3% |
| 2,253,362 | MIAMI-DADE | 747,551 | 367,867 | 366,482 | 13,202 | 1,385 R | 49.2% | 49.0% | 50.1% | 49.9% |
| 79,589 | MONROE | 38,303 | 18,075 | 18,961 | 1,267 | 886 D | 47.2% | 49.5% | 48.8% | 51.2% |
| 57,663 | NASSAU | 32,007 | 21,893 | 9,519 | 595 | 12,374 R | 68.4% | 29.7% | 69.7% | 30.3% |
| 170,498 | OKALOOSA | 87,204 | 65,146 | 19,645 | 2,413 | 45,501 R | 74.7% | 22.5% | 76.8% | 23.2% |
| 35,910 | OKEECHOBEE | 11,919 | 5,959 | 5,464 | 496 | 495 R | 50.0% | 45.8% | 52.2% | 47.8% |
| 896,344 | ORANGE | 382,751 | 188,121 | 187,549 | 7,081 | 572 R | 49.1% | 49.0% | 50.1% | 49.9% |
| 172,493 | OSCEOLA | 80,968 | 42,103 | 36,569 | 2,296 | 5,534 R | 52.0% | 45.2% | 53.5% | 46.5% |
| 1,131,184 | PALM BEACH | 528,050 | 200,442 | 318,042 | 9,566 | 117,600 D | 38.0% | 60.2% | 38.7% | 61.3% |
| 344,765 | PASCO | 186,225 | 89,420 | 90,761 | 6,044 | 1,341 D | 48.0% | 48.7% | 49.6% | 50.4% |
| 921,482 | PINELLAS | 444,470 | 197,640 | 234,451 | 12,379 | 36,811 D | 44.5% | 52.7% | 45.7% | 54.3% |
| 483,924 | POLK | 208,056 | 108,774 | 93,231 | 6,051 | 15,543 R | 52.3% | 44.8% | 53.8% | 46.2% |
| 70,423 | PUTNAM | 30,518 | 15,941 | 13,701 | 876 | 2,240 R | 52.2% | 44.9% | 53.8% | 46.2% |
| 123,135 | ST. JOHNS | 84,990 | 56,251 | 27,319 | 1,420 | 28,932 R | 66.2% | 32.1% | 67.3% | 32.7% |
| 192,695 | ST. LUCIE | 98,001 | 44,436 | 50,660 | 2,905 | 6,224 D | 45.3% | 51.7% | 46.7% | 53.3% |
| 117,743 | SANTA ROSA | 65,838 | 49,149 | 15,165 | 1,524 | 33,984 R | 74.7% | 23.0% | 76.4% | 23.6% |
| 325,957 | SARASOTA | 190,531 | 95,425 | 91,651 | 3,455 | 3,774 R | 50.1% | 48.1% | 51.0% | 49.0% |
| 365,196 | SEMINOLE | 183,391 | 102,898 | 76,579 | 3,914 | 26,319 R | 56.1% | 41.8% | 57.3% | 42.7% |
| 53,345 | SUMTER | 31,429 | 17,929 | 12,844 | 656 | 5,085 R | 57.0% | 40.9% | 58.3% | 41.7% |
| 34,844 | SUWANNEE | 15,561 | 9,095 | 6,069 | 397 | 3,026 R | 58.4% | 39.0% | 60.0% | 40.0% |
| 19,256 | TAYLOR | 8,454 | 4,241 | 3,972 | 241 | 269 R | 50.2% | 47.0% | 51.6% | 48.4% |
| 13,442 | UNION | 4,599 | 2,874 | 1,632 | 93 | 1,242 R | 62.5% | 35.5% | 63.8% | 36.2% |
| 443,343 | VOLUSIA | 225,138 | 104,032 | 114,932 | 6,174 | 10,900 D | 46.2% | 51.0% | 47.5% | 52.5% |
| 22,863 | WAKULLA | 11,619 | 5,240 | 6,048 | 331 | 808 D | 45.1% | 52.1% | 46.4% | 53.6% |
| 40,601 | WALTON | 23,393 | 16,038 | 6,770 | 585 | 9,268 R | 68.6% | 28.9% | 70.3% | 29.7% |
| 20,973 | WASHINGTON | 10,108 | 6,414 | 3,452 | 242 | 2,962 R | 63.5% | 34.2% | 65.0% | 35.0% |
| 15,982,378 | TOTAL | 7,429,894 | 3,672,864 | 3,590,201 | 166,829 | 82,663 R | 49.4% | 48.3% | 50.6% | 49.4% |

# FLORIDA

## HOUSE OF REPRESENTATIVES

| CD | Year | Total Vote | Vote | Candidate | Vote | Candidate | Other Vote | Rep.-Dem. Plurality | Rep. | Dem. | Rep. | Dem. |
|---|---|---|---|---|---|---|---|---|---|---|---|---|
| 1 | 2004 | 309,110 | 236,604 | Miller, Jeff* | 72,506 | Coutu, Mark S. | | 164,098 R | 76.5% | 23.5% | 76.5% | 23.5% |
| 1 | 2002 | 204,626 | 152,635 | Miller, Jeff* | 51,972 | Oram, Bert | 19 | 100,663 R | 74.6% | 25.4% | 74.6% | 25.4% |
| 2 | 2004 | 326,987 | 125,399 | Kilmer, Bev | 201,577 | Boyd, Allen* | 11 | 76,178 D | 38.3% | 61.6% | 38.4% | 61.6% |
| 2 | 2002 | 227,439 | 75,275 | McGurk, Tom | 152,164 | Boyd, Allen* | | 76,889 D | 33.1% | 66.9% | 33.1% | 66.9% |
| 3 | 2004 | 174,156 | | | 172,833 | Brown, Corrine* | 1,323 | 172,833 D | | 99.2% | | 100.0% |
| 3 | 2002 | 149,213 | 60,747 | Carroll, Jennifer | 88,462 | Brown, Corrine* | 4 | 27,715 D | 40.7% | 59.3% | 40.7% | 59.3% |
| 4 | 2004 | 257,327 | 256,157 | Crenshaw, Ander* | | | 1,170 | 256,157 R | 99.5% | | 100.0% | |
| 4 | 2002 | 171,661 | 171,152 | Crenshaw, Ander* | | | 509 | 171,152 R | 99.7% | | 100.0% | |
| 5 | 2004 | 364,488 | 240,315 | Brown-Waite, Ginny* | 124,140 | Whittel, Robert G. | 33 | 116,175 R | 65.9% | 34.1% | 65.9% | 34.1% |
| 5 | 2002 | 254,671 | 121,998 | Brown-Waite, Ginny | 117,758 | Thurman, Karen L.* | 14,915 | 4,240 R | 47.9% | 46.2% | 50.9% | 49.1% |
| 6 | 2004 | 327,853 | 211,137 | Stearns, Cliff* | 116,680 | Bruderly, David E. | 36 | 94,457 R | 64.4% | 35.6% | 64.4% | 35.6% |
| 6 | 2002 | 216,616 | 141,570 | Stearns, Cliff* | 75,046 | Bruderly, David E. | | 66,524 R | 65.4% | 34.6% | 65.4% | 34.6% |
| 7 | 2004 | | | Mica, John L.* | | | | R | | | | |
| 7 | 2002 | 238,591 | 142,147 | Mica, John L.* | 96,444 | Hogan, Wayne | | 45,703 R | 59.6% | 40.4% | 59.6% | 40.4% |

# FLORIDA

## HOUSE OF REPRESENTATIVES

| CD | Year | Total Vote | Republican Vote | Republican Candidate | Democratic Vote | Democratic Candidate | Other Vote | Rep.-Dem. Plurality | Percentage Total Vote Rep. | Dem. | Major Vote Rep. | Dem. |
|----|------|-----------|-----------------|----------------------|-----------------|----------------------|------------|---------------------|------|------|------|------|
| 8 | 2004 | 284,575 | 172,232 | Keller, Ric* | 112,343 | Murray, Stephen | | 59,889 R | 60.5% | 39.5% | 60.5% | 39.5% |
| 8 | 2002 | 189,596 | 123,497 | Keller, Ric* | 66,099 | Diaz, Eddie | | 57,398 R | 65.1% | 34.9% | 65.1% | 34.9% |
| 9 | 2004 | 284,278 | 284,035 | Bilirakis, Michael * | | | 243 | 284,035 R | 99.9% | | 100.0% | |
| 9 | 2002 | 237,008 | 169,369 | Bilirakis, Michael * | 67,623 | Kalogianis, Chuck | 16 | 101,746 R | 71.5% | 28.5% | 71.5% | 28.5% |
| 10 | 2004 | 298,833 | 207,175 | Young, C.W. Bill* | 91,658 | Derry, Robert D. "Bob" | | 115,517 R | 69.3% | 30.7% | 69.3% | 30.7% |
| 10 | 2002 | | | Young, C.W. Bill* | | | | R | | | | |
| 11 | 2004 | 223,481 | | | 191,780 | Davis, Jim* | 31,701 | 191,780 D | | 85.8% | | 100.0% |
| 11 | 2002 | | | | | Davis, Jim* | | D | | | | |
| 12 | 2004 | 276,169 | 179,204 | Putnam, Adam H.* | 96,965 | Hagenmaier, Bob | | 82,239 R | 64.9% | 35.1% | 64.9% | 35.1% |
| 12 | 2002 | | | Putnam, Adam H.* | | | | R | | | | |
| 13 | 2004 | 344,438 | 190,477 | Harris, Katherine* | 153,961 | Schneider, Jan | | 36,516 R | 55.3% | 44.7% | 55.3% | 44.7% |
| 13 | 2002 | 253,809 | 139,048 | Harris, Katherine | 114,739 | Schneider, Jan | 22 | 24,309 R | 54.8% | 45.2% | 54.8% | 45.2% |
| 14 | 2004 | 335,334 | 226,662 | Mack, Connie | 108,672 | Neeld, Robert M. | | 117,990 R | 67.6% | 32.4% | 67.6% | 32.4% |
| 14 | 2002 | | | Goss, Porter J.* | | | | R | | | | |
| 15 | 2004 | 321,926 | 210,388 | Weldon, Dave* | 111,538 | Pristoop, Simon | | 98,850 R | 65.4% | 34.6% | 65.4% | 34.6% |
| 15 | 2002 | 231,857 | 146,414 | Weldon, Dave* | 85,433 | Tso, Jim | 10 | 60,981 R | 63.1% | 36.8% | 63.2% | 36.8% |
| 16 | 2004 | 316,810 | 215,563 | Foley, Mark* | 101,247 | Fisher, Jeff | | 114,316 R | 68.0% | 32.0% | 68.0% | 32.0% |
| 16 | 2002 | 223,340 | 176,171 | Foley, Mark* | | | 47,169 | 176,171 R | 78.9% | | 100.0% | |
| 17 | 2004 | 179,424 | | | 178,690 | Meek, Kendrick B.* | 734 | 178,690 D | | 99.6% | | 100.0% |
| 17 | 2002 | 113,822 | | | 113,749 | Meek, Kendrick B. | 73 | 113,749 D | | 99.9% | | 100.0% |
| 18 | 2004 | 221,928 | 143,647 | Ros-Lehtinen, Ileana* | 78,281 | Sheldon, Sam | | 65,366 R | 64.7% | 35.3% | 64.7% | 35.3% |
| 18 | 2002 | 149,787 | 103,512 | Ros-Lehtinen, Ileana* | 42,852 | Chote, Ray | 3,423 | 60,660 R | 69.1% | 28.6% | 70.7% | 29.3% |
| 19 | 2004 | | | | | Wexler, Robert* | | D | | | | |
| 19 | 2002 | 217,224 | 60,477 | Merkl, Jack | 156,747 | Wexler, Robert* | | 96,270 D | 27.8% | 72.2% | 27.8% | 72.2% |
| 20 | 2004 | 272,408 | 81,213 | Hostetter, Margaret | 191,195 | Wasserman-Schultz, Debbie | | 109,982 D | 29.8% | 70.2% | 29.8% | 70.2% |
| 20 | 2002 | | | | | Deutsch, Peter* | | D | | | | |
| 21 | 2004 | 201,243 | 146,507 | Diaz-Balart, Lincoln* | | | 54,736 | 146,507 R | 72.8% | | 100.0% | |
| 21 | 2002 | | | Diaz-Balart, Lincoln* | | | | R | | | | |
| 22 | 2004 | 306,726 | 192,581 | Shaw, E. Clay Jr.* | 108,258 | Rorapaugh, Robin | 5,887 | 84,323 R | 62.8% | 35.3% | 64.0% | 36.0% |
| 22 | 2002 | 217,115 | 131,930 | Shaw, E. Clay Jr.* | 83,265 | Roberts, Carol A. | 1,920 | 48,665 R | 60.8% | 38.4% | 61.3% | 38.7% |
| 23 | 2004 | | | | | Hastings, Alcee L.* | | D | | | | |
| 23 | 2002 | 124,338 | 27,986 | Laurie, Charles | 96,347 | Hastings, Alcee L.* | 5 | 68,361 D | 22.5% | 77.5% | 22.5% | 77.5% |
| 24 | 2004 | | | Feeney, Tom* | | | | R | | | | |
| 24 | 2002 | 219,243 | 135,576 | Feeney, Tom | 83,667 | Jacobs, Harry | | 51,909 R | 61.8% | 38.2% | 61.8% | 38.2% |
| 25 | 2004 | | | Diaz-Balart, Mario* | | | | R | | | | |
| 25 | 2002 | 126,602 | 81,845 | Diaz-Balart, Mario | 44,757 | Betancourt, Annie | | 37,088 R | 64.6% | 35.4% | 64.6% | 35.4% |
| Total | 2004 | 5,627,494 | 3,319,296 | | 2,212,324 | | 95,874 | 1,106,972 R | 59.0% | 39.3% | 60.0% | 40.0% |
| Total | 2002 | 3,766,558 | 2,161,349 | | 1,537,124 | | 68,085 | 624,225 R | 57.4% | 40.8% | 58.4% | 41.6% |

An asterisk (*) denotes incumbent. In Florida districts where a candidate had no opposition at all, including write-ins, no vote was taken.

# FLORIDA

## GENERAL AND PRIMARY ELECTIONS

## 2004 GENERAL ELECTIONS

**President**    Other vote was 32,971 Reform (Ralph Nader); 11,996 Libertarian Party of Florida (Michael Badnarik); 6,626 Constitution Party of Florida (Michael Peroutka); 3,917 Green Party of Florida (David Cobb); 3,502 Socialist Party of Florida (Walter F. Brown); 2,732 Florida Socialist Workers (James Harris).

**Senator**    Other vote was 166,642 Veterans Party of America (Dennis F. Bradley); 119 write-in (Mark Stufft); 27 write-in (Nancy Travis); 25 write-in (Rachele Fruit); 16 write-in (Peter Blass).

**House**    Other vote was:

| | |
|---|---|
| CD 1 | |
| CD 2 | 11 write-in (T.A. Frederick). |
| CD 3 | 1,323 write-in (Johnny M. Brown). |
| CD 4 | 1,170 write-in (Richard Grayson). |
| CD 5 | 33 write-in (Werder). |
| CD 6 | 36 write-in (N.W. O'Brien). |
| CD 7 | |
| CD 8 | |
| CD 9 | 243 write-in (Andrew Pasayan). |
| CD 10 | |
| CD 11 | 31,579 Libertarian Party of Florida (Robert Edward Johnson); 122 write-in (Karl M. Butts). |
| CD 12 | |
| CD 13 | |
| CD 14 | |
| CD 15 | |
| CD 16 | |
| CD 17 | 734 write-in (Omari Musa). |
| CD 18 | |
| CD 19 | |
| CD 20 | |
| CD 21 | 54,736 Libertarian Party of Florida (Frank J. Gonzalez). |
| CD 22 | 5,260 Constitution Party of Florida (Jack McLain); 627 write-in (Don Kennedy). |
| CD 23 | |
| CD 24 | |
| CD 25 | |

# FLORIDA

## GENERAL AND PRIMARY ELECTIONS

## 2004 PRIMARY ELECTIONS

| Primary | March 9, 2004 (President) | Registration | Republican | 3,705,081 |
|---|---|---|---|---|
| | August 31, 2004 (Congress) | (as of Aug. 2, 2004) | Democratic | 4,066,068 |
| | | | Independent Party | 205,058 |
| | | | Independence Party of Florida | 16,253 |
| | | | Libertarian Party of Florida | 13,197 |
| | | | Green Party of Florida | 6,369 |
| | | | Reform | 3,994 |
| | | | Other Parties | 7,037 |
| | | | No Party Affiliation | 1,731,254 |
| | | | TOTAL | 9,754,311 |

**Primary Type** Closed—Only registered Democrats and Republicans could vote in their party's primary, with the exception of races where there were to be no other candidates (including write-ins) on the general election ballot. Then, the contested primary would be open to all voters. That was the case in the Democratic primary in the 23rd District.

Note: An asterisk (*) denotes incumbent. The names of unopposed candidates did not appear on the primary ballot; therefore, no votes were cast for these candidates. The voter registration total at the time of the 2004 primary was listed by the state election division as 9,753,819, although it adds to 9,754,311.

| REPUBLICAN PRIMARIES | | | DEMOCRATIC PRIMARIES | | |
|---|---|---|---|---|---|
| **President** No Republican primary | | | John Kerry | 581,672 | 77.2% |
| | | | John Edwards | 75,703 | 10.0% |
| | | | Al Sharpton | 21,031 | 2.8% |
| | | | Howard Dean | 20,834 | 2.8% |
| | | | Dennis J. Kucinich | 17,198 | 2.3% |
| | | | Joseph I. Lieberman | 14,287 | 1.9% |
| | | | Wesley Clark | 10,226 | 1.4% |
| | | | Carol Moseley Braun | 6,789 | 0.9% |
| | | | Richard A. Gephardt | 6,022 | 0.8% |
| | | | TOTAL | 753,762 | |
| **Senator** Mel Martinez | 522,994 | 44.9% | Betty Castor | 669,346 | 58.1% |
| Bill McCollum | 360,474 | 30.9% | Peter Deutsch | 321,922 | 27.9% |
| Doug Gallagher | 158,360 | 13.6% | Alex Penelas | 115,898 | 10.1% |
| Johnnie Byrd | 68,982 | 5.9% | Bernard E. Klein | 45,347 | 3.9% |
| Karen Saull | 20,365 | 1.7% | | | |
| Sonya March | 17,804 | 1.5% | | | |
| Larry Klayman | 13,257 | 1.1% | | | |
| William Billy Kogut | 3,695 | 0.3% | | | |
| TOTAL | 1,165,931 | | TOTAL | 1,152,513 | |
| **Congressional District 1** Jeff Miller* | Unopposed | | Mark S. Coutu | Unopposed | |
| **Congressional District 2** Bev Kilmer | Unopposed | | Allen Boyd* | Unopposed | |
| **Congressional District 3** No Republican candidate | | | Corrine Brown* | 46,285 | 81.3% |
| | | | Prince Brown | 10,639 | 18.7% |
| | | | TOTAL | 56,924 | |
| **Congressional District 4** Ander Crenshaw* | 48,129 | 90.0% | No Democratic candidate | | |
| Deborah Katz Pueschel | 5,368 | 10.0% | | | |
| TOTAL | 53,497 | | | | |

# FLORIDA

## GENERAL AND PRIMARY ELECTIONS

| | REPUBLICAN PRIMARIES | | | DEMOCRATIC PRIMARIES | | |
|---|---|---|---|---|---|---|
| Congressional District 5 | Ginny Brown-Waite* | Unopposed | | Robert G. Whittel | 15,938 | 31.2% |
| | | | | John Russell | 13,388 | 26.2% |
| | | | | Brian Moore | 11,532 | 22.6% |
| | | | | Rick Penberthy | 10,211 | 20.0% |
| | | | | TOTAL | 51,069 | |
| Congressional District 6 | Cliff Stearns* | Unopposed | | David E. Bruderly | Unopposed | |
| Congressional District 7 | John L. Mica* | Unopposed | | No Democratic candidate | | |
| Congressional District 8 | Ric Keller* | Unopposed | | Stephen Murray | Unopposed | |
| Congressional District 9 | Michael Bilirakis* | 44,579 | 84.5% | No Democratic candidate | | |
| | Joseph H. Stanley | 8,189 | 15.5% | | | |
| | TOTAL | 52,768 | | | | |
| Congressional District 10 | C.W. Bill Young* | Unopposed | | Robert D. "Bob" Derry | Unopposed | |
| Congressional District 11 | No Republican candidate | | | Jim Davis* | Unopposed | |
| Congressional District 12 | Adam H. Putnam* | 42,605 | 92.3% | Bob Hagenmaier | 21,044 | 57.1% |
| | Robert Wirengard | 3,546 | 7.7% | Jeff Siemer | 15,781 | 42.9% |
| | TOTAL | 46,151 | | TOTAL | 36,825 | |
| Congressional District 13 | Katherine Harris* | Unopposed | | Jan Schneider | 20,573 | 46.8% |
| | | | | Christine Jennings | 16,581 | 37.7% |
| | | | | C.J. Czaia | 3,880 | 8.8% |
| | | | | Floyd Jay Winters | 2,966 | 6.7% |
| | | | | TOTAL | 44,000 | |
| Congressional District 14 | Connie Mack | 27,526 | 35.8% | Robert M. Neeld | Unopposed | |
| | Carole Green | 24,767 | 32.2% | | | |
| | Andy Coy | 17,089 | 22.2% | | | |
| | Frank Schwerin | 7,465 | 9.7% | | | |
| | TOTAL | 76,847 | | | | |
| Congressional District 15 | Dave Weldon* | Unopposed | | Simon Pristoop | Unopposed | |
| Congressional District 16 | Mark Foley* | Unopposed | | Jeff Fisher | Unopposed | |
| Congressional District 17 | No Republican candidate | | | Kendrick B. Meek* | Unopposed | |
| Congressional District 18 | Ileana Ros-Lehtinen* | Unopposed | | Sam Sheldon | 12,869 | 50.5% |
| | | | | David Y. Patlak | 12,591 | 49.5% |
| | | | | TOTAL | 25,460 | |
| Congressional District 19 | No Republican candidate | | | Robert Wexler* | Unopposed | |
| Congressional District 20 | Margaret Hostetter | Unopposed | | Debbie Wasserman-Schultz | Unopposed | |
| Congressional District 21 | Lincoln Diaz-Balart* | Unopposed | | No Democratic candidate | | |
| Congressional District 22 | E. Clay Shaw Jr.* | Unopposed | | *Jim Stork ran unopposed in the primary but subsequently withdrew from the race. Robin Rorapaugh was selected by party leaders to fill the vacancy on the general election ballot.* | | |
| Congressional District 23 | No Republican candidate | | | Alcee L. Hastings* | 49,284 | 74.2% |
| | | | | Keith A. Clayborne | 17,106 | 25.8% |
| | | | | TOTAL | 66,390 | |
| Congressional District 24 | Tom Feeney* | Unopposed | | No Democratic candidate | | |
| Congressional District 25 | Mario Diaz-Balart* | Unopposed | | No Democratic candidate | | |

# GEORGIA

## GOVERNOR
Sonny Perdue (R). Elected 2002 to a four-year term.

## SENATORS (2 Republicans)
Saxby Chambliss (R). Elected 2002 to a six-year term.

Johnny Isakson (R). Elected 2004 to a six-year term.

## REPRESENTATIVES (7 Republicans, 6 Democrats)
1. Jack Kingston (R)
2. Sanford D. Bishop Jr. (D)
3. Jim Marshall (D)
4. Cynthia A. McKinney (D)
5. John Lewis (D)
6. Tom Price (R)
7. John Linder (R)
8. Lynn Westmoreland (R)
9. Charlie Norwood (R)
10. Nathan Deal (R)
11. Phil Gingrey (R)
12. John Barrow (D)
13. David Scott (D)

## POSTWAR VOTE FOR PRESIDENT

| | | Republican | | Democratic | | | | Percentage | | | |
| | | | | | | | | Total Vote | | Major Vote | |
| Year | Total Vote | Vote | Candidate | Vote | Candidate | Other Vote | Plurality | Rep. | Dem. | Rep. | Dem. |
|---|---|---|---|---|---|---|---|---|---|---|---|
| 2004 | 3,301,875 | 1,914,254 | Bush, George W. | 1,366,149 | Kerry, John | 21,472 | 548,105 R | 58.0% | 41.4% | 58.4% | 41.6% |
| 2000** | 2,596,645 | 1,419,720 | Bush, George W. | 1,116,230 | Gore, Al | 60,695 | 303,490 R | 54.7% | 43.0% | 56.0% | 44.0% |
| 1996** | 2,299,071 | 1,080,843 | Dole, Bob | 1,053,849 | Clinton, Bill | 164,379 | 26,994 R | 47.0% | 45.8% | 50.6% | 49.4% |
| 1992** | 2,321,125 | 995,252 | Bush, George | 1,008,966 | Clinton, Bill | 316,907 | 13,714 D | 42.9% | 43.5% | 49.7% | 50.3% |
| 1988 | 1,809,672 | 1,081,331 | Bush, George | 714,792 | Dukakis, Michael S. | 13,549 | 366,539 R | 59.8% | 39.5% | 60.2% | 39.8% |
| 1984 | 1,776,120 | 1,068,722 | Reagan, Ronald | 706,628 | Mondale, Walter F. | 770 | 362,094 R | 60.2% | 39.8% | 60.2% | 39.8% |
| 1980** | 1,596,695 | 654,168 | Reagan, Ronald | 890,733 | Carter, Jimmy | 51,794 | 236,565 D | 41.0% | 55.8% | 42.3% | 57.7% |
| 1976 | 1,467,458 | 483,743 | Ford, Gerald R. | 979,409 | Carter, Jimmy | 4,306 | 495,666 D | 33.0% | 66.7% | 33.1% | 66.9% |
| 1972 | 1,174,772 | 881,496 | Nixon, Richard M. | 289,529 | McGovern, George S. | 3,747 | 591,967 R | 75.0% | 24.6% | 75.3% | 24.7% |
| 1968** | 1,250,266 | 380,111 | Nixon, Richard M. | 334,440 | Humphrey, Hubert H. | 535,715 | 155,439 A | 30.4% | 26.7% | 53.2% | 46.8% |
| 1964 | 1,139,335 | 616,584 | Goldwater, Barry M. | 522,556 | Johnson, Lyndon B. | 195 | 94,028 R | 54.1% | 45.9% | 54.1% | 45.9% |
| 1960 | 733,349 | 274,472 | Nixon, Richard M. | 458,638 | Kennedy, John F. | 239 | 184,166 D | 37.4% | 62.5% | 37.4% | 62.6% |
| 1956 | 669,655 | 222,778 | Eisenhower, Dwight D. | 444,688 | Stevenson, Adlai E. | 2,189 | 221,910 D | 33.3% | 66.4% | 33.4% | 66.6% |
| 1952 | 655,785 | 198,961 | Eisenhower, Dwight D. | 456,823 | Stevenson, Adlai E. | 1 | 257,862 D | 30.3% | 69.7% | 30.3% | 69.7% |
| 1948** | 418,844 | 76,691 | Dewey, Thomas E. | 254,646 | Truman, Harry S. | 87,507 | 169,511 D | 18.3% | 60.8% | 23.1% | 76.9% |

In past elections, the other vote included: 2000 - 13,273 Green (Ralph Nader); 1996 - 146,337 Reform (Ross Perot); 1992 - 309,657 Independent (Perot); 1980 - 36,055 Independent (John Anderson); 1968 - 535,550 American Independent (George Wallace); 1948 - 85,135 States' Rights (Strom Thurmond).

130

# GEORGIA

## POSTWAR VOTE FOR GOVERNOR

| Year | Total Vote | Republican Vote | Republican Candidate | Democratic Vote | Democratic Candidate | Other Vote | Rep.-Dem. Plurality | Total Vote Rep. | Total Vote Dem. | Major Vote Rep. | Major Vote Dem. |
|------|-----------|-----------------|---------------------|-----------------|---------------------|-----------|---------------------|-----------------|-----------------|-----------------|-----------------|
| 2002 | 2,027,177 | 1,041,700 | Perdue, Sonny | 937,070 | Barnes, Roy | 48,407 | 104,630 R | 51.4% | 46.2% | 52.6% | 47.4% |
| 1998 | 1,792,808 | 790,201 | Millner, Guy | 941,076 | Barnes, Roy | 61,531 | 150,875 D | 44.1% | 52.5% | 45.6% | 54.4% |
| 1994 | 1,545,328 | 756,371 | Millner, Guy | 788,926 | Miller, Zell | 31 | 32,555 D | 48.9% | 51.1% | 48.9% | 51.1% |
| 1990 | 1,449,682 | 645,625 | Isakson, Johnny | 766,662 | Miller, Zell | 37,395 | 121,037 D | 44.5% | 52.9% | 45.7% | 54.3% |
| 1986 | 1,175,114 | 346,512 | Davis, Guy | 828,465 | Harris, Joe Frank | 137 | 481,953 D | 29.5% | 70.5% | 29.5% | 70.5% |
| 1982 | 1,169,041 | 434,496 | Bell, Robert H. | 734,090 | Harris, Joe Frank | 455 | 299,594 D | 37.2% | 62.8% | 37.2% | 62.8% |
| 1978 | 662,862 | 128,139 | Cook, Rodney M. | 534,572 | Busbee, George | 151 | 406,433 D | 19.3% | 80.6% | 19.3% | 80.7% |
| 1974 | 936,438 | 289,113 | Thompson, Ronnie | 646,777 | Busbee, George | 548 | 357,664 D | 30.9% | 69.1% | 30.9% | 69.1% |
| 1970 | 1,046,663 | 424,983 | Suit, Hal | 620,419 | Carter, Jimmy | 1,261 | 195,436 D | 40.6% | 59.3% | 40.7% | 59.3% |
| 1966** | 975,019 | 453,665 | Callaway, Howard H. | 450,626 | Maddox, Lester | 70,728 | 3,039 R | 46.5% | 46.2% | 50.2% | 49.8% |
| 1962 | 311,691 | | — | 311,524 | Sanders, Carl E. | 167 | 311,524 D | | 99.9% | | 100.0% |
| 1958 | 168,497 | | — | 168,414 | Vandiver, Ernest | 83 | 168,414 D | | 100.0% | | 100.0% |
| 1954 | 331,966 | | — | 331,899 | Griffin, Marvin | 67 | 331,899 D | | 100.0% | | 100.0% |
| 1950 | 234,430 | | — | 230,771 | Talmadge, Herman | 3,659 | 230,771 D | | 98.4% | | 100.0% |
| 1948S | 363,763 | | — | 354,711 | Talmadge, Herman | 9,052 | 354,711 D | | 97.5% | | 100.0% |
| 1946 | 145,403 | | — | 143,279 | Talmadge, Eugene | 2,124 | 143,279 D | | 98.5% | | 100.0% |

In 1966 in the absence of a majority for any candidate, the state legislature elected Democrat Lester Maddox to a four-year term. The 1948 election was for a short term to fill a vacancy.

## POSTWAR VOTE FOR SENATOR

| Year | Total Vote | Republican Vote | Republican Candidate | Democratic Vote | Democratic Candidate | Other Vote | Rep.-Dem. Plurality | Total Vote Rep. | Total Vote Dem. | Major Vote Rep. | Major Vote Dem. |
|------|-----------|-----------------|---------------------|-----------------|---------------------|-----------|---------------------|-----------------|-----------------|-----------------|-----------------|
| 2004 | 3,220,981 | 1,864,202 | Isakson, Johnny | 1,287,690 | Majette, Denise L. | 69,089 | 576,512 R | 57.9% | 40.0% | 59.1% | 40.9% |
| 2002 | 2,030,608 | 1,071,464 | Chambliss, Saxby | 932,156 | Cleland, Max | 26,988 | 139,308 R | 52.8% | 45.9% | 53.5% | 46.5% |
| 2000S | 2,428,510 | 920,478 | Mattingly, Mack | 1,413,224 | Miller, Zell | 94,808 | 492,746 D | 37.9% | 58.2% | 39.4% | 60.6% |
| 1998 | 1,753,911 | 918,540 | Coverdell, Paul | 791,904 | Coles, Michael | 43,467 | 126,636 R | 52.4% | 45.2% | 53.7% | 46.3% |
| 1996 | 2,259,232 | 1,073,969 | Millner, Guy | 1,103,993 | Cleland, Max | 81,270 | 30,024 D | 47.5% | 48.9% | 49.3% | 50.7% |
| 1992** | 1,253,991 | 635,114 | Coverdell, Paul | 618,877 | Fowler, Wyche | | 16,237 R | 50.6% | 49.4% | 50.6% | 49.4% |
| 1990 | 1,033,517 | | — | 1,033,439 | Nunn, Sam | 78 | 1,033,439 D | | 100.0% | | 100.0% |
| 1986 | 1,225,008 | 601,241 | Mattingly, Mack | 623,707 | Fowler, Wyche | 60 | 22,466 D | 49.1% | 50.9% | 49.1% | 50.9% |
| 1984 | 1,681,344 | 337,196 | Hicks, Jon Michael | 1,344,104 | Nunn, Sam | 44 | 1,006,908 D | 20.1% | 79.9% | 20.1% | 79.9% |
| 1980 | 1,580,340 | 803,686 | Mattingly, Mack | 776,143 | Talmadge, Herman | 511 | 27,543 R | 50.9% | 49.1% | 50.9% | 49.1% |
| 1978 | 645,164 | 108,808 | Stokes, John W. | 536,320 | Nunn, Sam | 36 | 427,512 D | 16.9% | 83.1% | 16.9% | 83.1% |
| 1974 | 874,555 | 246,866 | Johnson, Jerry R. | 627,376 | Talmadge, Herman | 313 | 380,510 D | 28.2% | 71.7% | 28.2% | 71.8% |
| 1972 | 1,178,708 | 542,331 | Thompson, Fletcher | 635,970 | Nunn, Sam | 407 | 93,639 D | 46.0% | 54.0% | 46.0% | 54.0% |
| 1968 | 1,141,889 | 256,796 | Patton, E. Earl | 885,093 | Talmadge, Herman | | 628,297 D | 22.5% | 77.5% | 22.5% | 77.5% |
| 1966 | 622,371 | | — | 622,043 | Russell, Richard B. | 328 | 622,043 D | | 99.9% | | 100.0% |
| 1962 | 306,250 | | — | 306,250 | Talmadge, Herman | | 306,250 D | | 100.0% | | 100.0% |
| 1960 | 576,495 | | — | 576,140 | Russell, Richard B. | 355 | 576,140 D | | 99.9% | | 100.0% |
| 1956 | 541,267 | | — | 541,094 | Talmadge, Herman | 173 | 541,094 D | | 100.0% | | 100.0% |
| 1954 | 333,936 | | — | 333,917 | Russell, Richard B. | 19 | 333,917 D | | 100.0% | | 100.0% |
| 1950 | 261,293 | | — | 261,290 | George, Walter F. | 3 | 261,290 D | | 100.0% | | 100.0% |
| 1948 | 362,504 | | — | 362,104 | Russell, Richard B. | 400 | 362,104 D | | 99.9% | | 100.0% |

The 2000 election was for a short term to fill a vacancy. The 1992 figures in the table are for the runoff election held November 24 as no candidate received a majority of the vote in the November 3 general election. The vote in the November 3 election was 1,073,282 (47.7 percent) Republican (Paul Coverdell); 1,108,416 (49.2 percent) Democratic (Wyche Fowler); and 69,889 (3.1 percent) Other.

# GEORGIA

Congressional districts first established for elections held in 2002
13 members

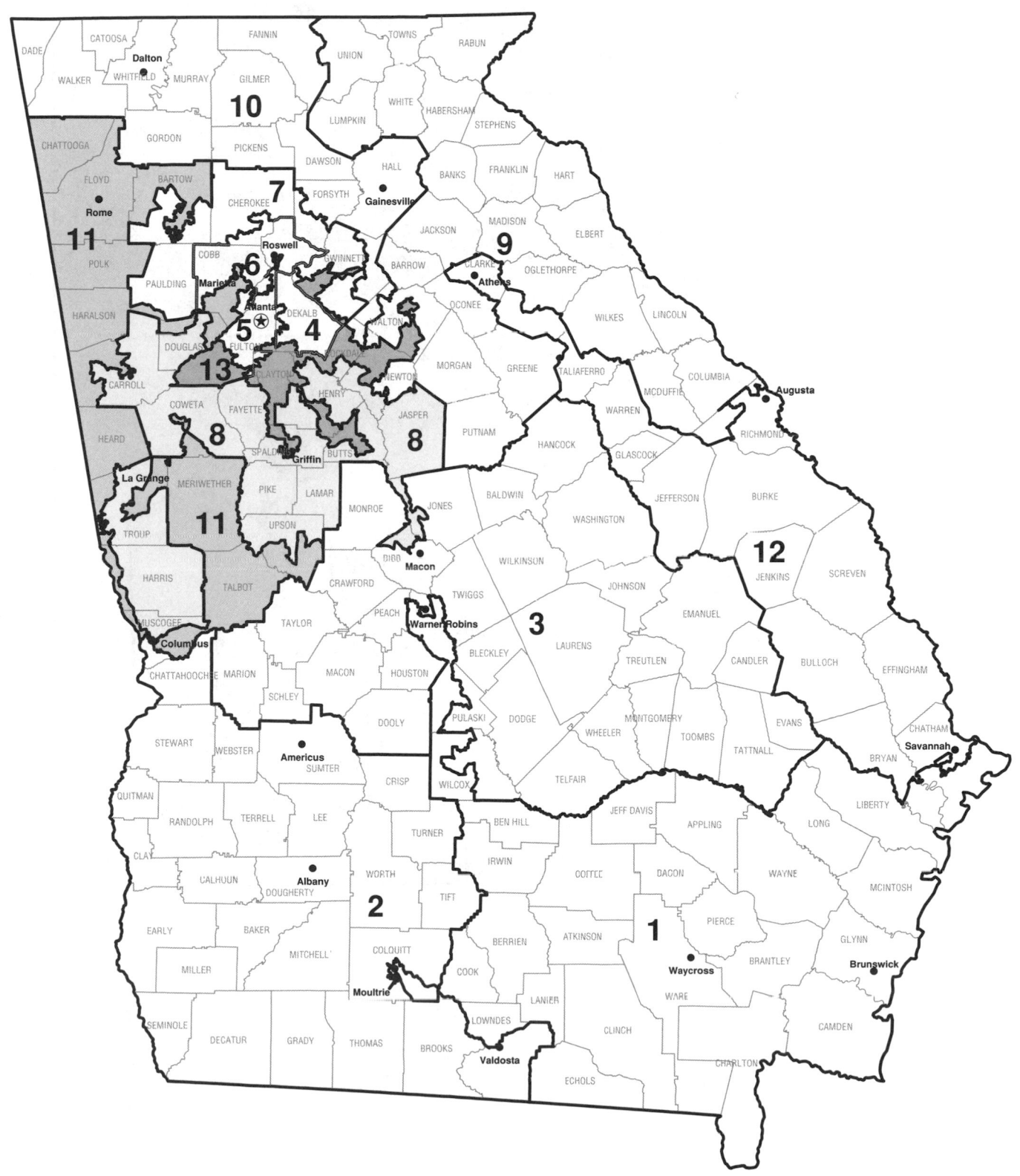

# GEORGIA

Atlanta Area

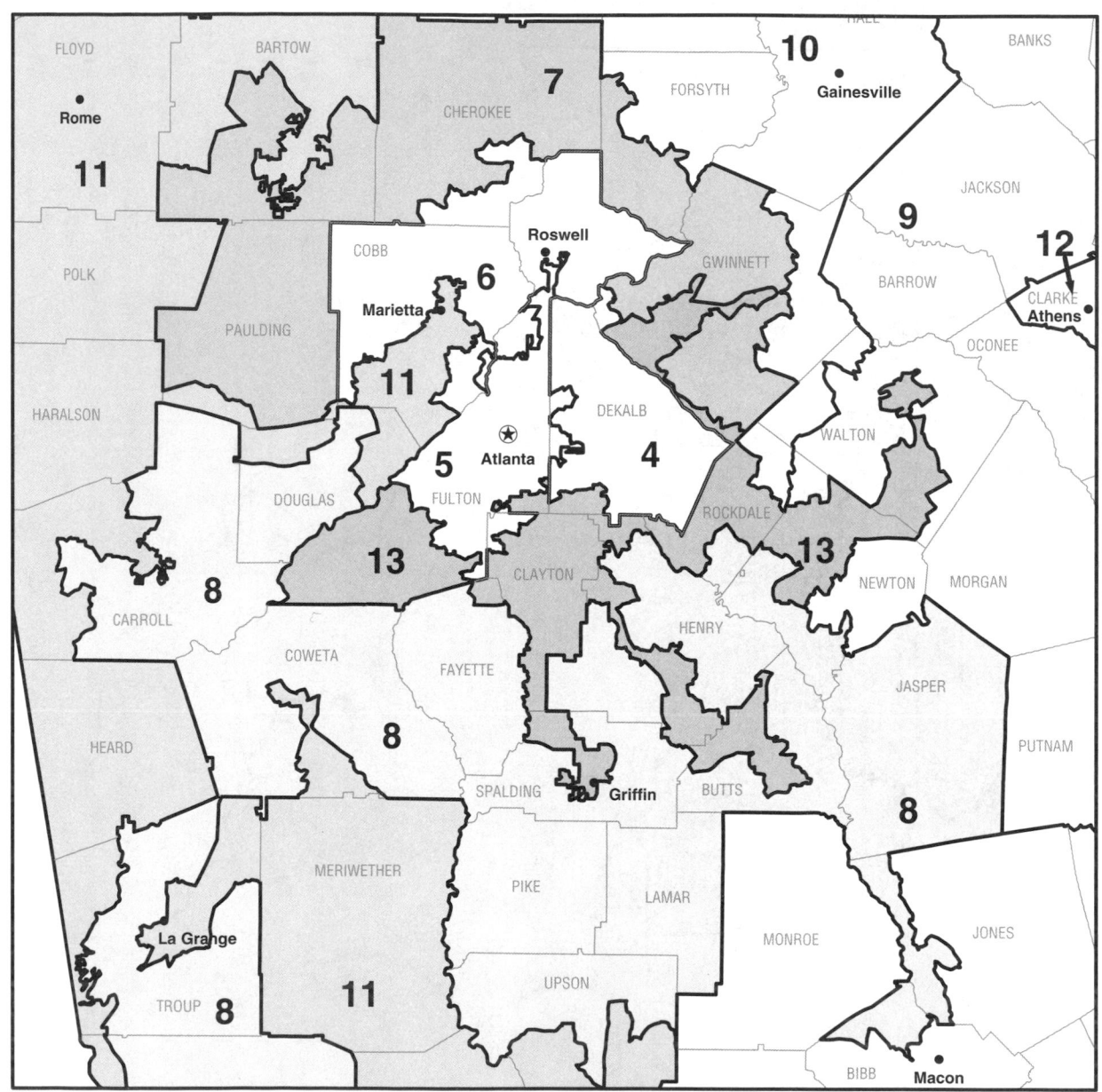

# GEORGIA

## PRESIDENT 2004

| 2000 Census Population | County | Total Vote | Republican | Democratic | Other | Rep.-Dem. Plurality | | Percentage Total Vote Rep. | Dem. | Major Vote Rep. | Dem. |
|---|---|---|---|---|---|---|---|---|---|---|---|
| 17,419 | APPLING | 6,370 | 4,494 | 1,848 | 28 | 2,646 | R | 70.5% | 29.0% | 70.9% | 29.1% |
| 7,609 | ATKINSON | 2,470 | 1,666 | 799 | 5 | 867 | R | 67.4% | 32.3% | 67.6% | 32.4% |
| 10,103 | BACON | 3,792 | 2,853 | 930 | 9 | 1,923 | R | 75.2% | 24.5% | 75.4% | 24.6% |
| 4,074 | BAKER | 1,764 | 821 | 936 | 7 | 115 | D | 46.5% | 53.1% | 46.7% | 53.3% |
| 44,700 | BALDWIN | 14,560 | 7,709 | 6,775 | 76 | 934 | R | 52.9% | 46.5% | 53.2% | 46.8% |
| 14,422 | BANKS | 5,592 | 4,410 | 1,149 | 33 | 3,261 | R | 78.9% | 20.5% | 79.3% | 20.7% |
| 46,144 | BARROW | 17,744 | 13,520 | 4,095 | 129 | 9,425 | R | 76.2% | 23.1% | 76.8% | 23.2% |
| 76,019 | BARTOW | 30,277 | 22,311 | 7,741 | 225 | 14,570 | R | 73.7% | 25.6% | 74.2% | 25.8% |
| 17,484 | BEN HILL | 5,540 | 3,331 | 2,180 | 29 | 1,151 | R | 60.1% | 39.4% | 60.4% | 39.6% |
| 16,235 | BERRIEN | 5,599 | 3,917 | 1,638 | 44 | 2,279 | R | 70.0% | 29.3% | 70.5% | 29.5% |
| 153,887 | BIBB | 57,754 | 28,107 | 29,322 | 325 | 1,215 | D | 48.7% | 50.8% | 48.9% | 51.1% |
| 11,666 | BLECKLEY | 4,468 | 3,167 | 1,281 | 20 | 1,886 | R | 70.9% | 28.7% | 71.2% | 28.8% |
| 14,629 | BRANTLEY | 5,621 | 4,333 | 1,258 | 30 | 3,075 | R | 77.1% | 22.4% | 77.5% | 22.5% |
| 16,450 | BROOKS | 5,116 | 2,912 | 2,193 | 11 | 719 | R | 56.9% | 42.9% | 57.0% | 43.0% |
| 23,417 | BRYAN | 9,983 | 7,363 | 2,590 | 30 | 4,773 | R | 73.8% | 25.9% | 74.0% | 26.0% |
| 55,983 | BULLOCH | 19,195 | 12,252 | 6,840 | 103 | 5,412 | R | 63.8% | 35.6% | 64.2% | 35.8% |
| 22,243 | BURKE | 8,482 | 4,232 | 4,213 | 37 | 19 | R | 49.9% | 49.7% | 50.1% | 49.9% |
| 19,522 | BUTTS | 7,735 | 5,119 | 2,572 | 44 | 2,547 | R | 66.2% | 33.3% | 66.6% | 33.4% |
| 6,320 | CALHOUN | 2,019 | 890 | 1,119 | 10 | 229 | D | 44.1% | 55.4% | 44.3% | 55.7% |
| 43,664 | CAMDEN | 14,175 | 9,488 | 4,637 | 50 | 4,851 | R | 66.9% | 32.7% | 67.2% | 32.8% |
| 9,577 | CANDLER | 3,151 | 2,048 | 1,096 | 7 | 952 | R | 65.0% | 34.8% | 65.1% | 34.9% |
| 87,268 | CARROLL | 35,317 | 24,837 | 10,224 | 256 | 14,613 | R | 70.3% | 28.9% | 70.8% | 29.2% |
| 53,282 | CATOOSA | 22,328 | 16,406 | 5,807 | 115 | 10,599 | R | 73.5% | 26.0% | 73.9% | 26.1% |
| 10,282 | CHARLTON | 3,387 | 2,311 | 1,064 | 12 | 1,247 | R | 68.2% | 31.4% | 68.5% | 31.5% |
| 232,048 | CHATHAM | 91,607 | 45,484 | 45,630 | 493 | 146 | D | 49.7% | 49.8% | 49.9% | 50.1% |
| 14,882 | CHATTAHOOCHEE | 1,689 | 905 | 773 | 11 | 132 | R | 53.6% | 45.8% | 53.9% | 46.1% |
| 25,470 | CHATTOOGA | 7,853 | 4,992 | 2,809 | 52 | 2,183 | R | 63.6% | 35.8% | 64.0% | 36.0% |
| 141,903 | CHEROKEE | 73,686 | 58,238 | 14,824 | 624 | 43,414 | R | 79.0% | 20.1% | 79.7% | 20.3% |
| 101,489 | CLARKE | 37,388 | 15,052 | 21,718 | 618 | 6,666 | D | 40.3% | 58.1% | 40.9% | 59.1% |
| 3,357 | CLAY | 1,309 | 509 | 798 | 2 | 289 | D | 38.9% | 61.0% | 38.9% | 61.1% |
| 236,517 | CLAYTON | 79,600 | 23,106 | 56,113 | 381 | 33,007 | D | 29.0% | 70.5% | 29.2% | 70.8% |
| 6,878 | CLINCH | 2,266 | 1,501 | 750 | 15 | 751 | R | 66.2% | 33.1% | 66.7% | 33.3% |
| 607,751 | COBB | 279,866 | 173,467 | 103,955 | 2,444 | 69,512 | R | 62.0% | 37.1% | 62.5% | 37.5% |
| 37,413 | COFFEE | 12,332 | 8,306 | 3,979 | 47 | 4,327 | R | 67.4% | 32.3% | 67.6% | 32.4% |
| 42,053 | COLQUITT | 11,745 | 8,296 | 3,378 | 71 | 4,918 | R | 70.6% | 28.8% | 71.1% | 28.9% |
| 89,288 | COLUMBIA | 47,170 | 35,549 | 11,442 | 179 | 24,107 | R | 75.4% | 24.3% | 75.7% | 24.3% |
| 15,771 | COOK | 4,820 | 3,065 | 1,733 | 22 | 1,332 | R | 63.6% | 36.0% | 63.9% | 36.1% |
| 89,215 | COWETA | 42,545 | 31,682 | 10,647 | 216 | 21,035 | R | 74.5% | 25.0% | 74.8% | 25.2% |
| 12,495 | CRAWFORD | 4,406 | 2,830 | 1,552 | 24 | 1,278 | R | 64.2% | 35.2% | 64.6% | 35.4% |
| 21,996 | CRISP | 6,251 | 3,865 | 2,357 | 29 | 1,508 | R | 61.8% | 37.7% | 62.1% | 37.9% |
| 15,154 | DADE | 6,247 | 4,368 | 1,823 | 56 | 2,545 | R | 69.9% | 29.2% | 70.6% | 29.4% |
| 15,999 | DAWSON | 8,117 | 6,649 | 1,407 | 61 | 5,242 | R | 81.9% | 17.3% | 82.5% | 17.5% |
| 28,240 | DECATUR | 8,951 | 5,348 | 3,577 | 26 | 1,771 | R | 59.7% | 40.0% | 59.9% | 40.1% |
| 665,865 | DEKALB | 276,509 | 73,570 | 200,787 | 2,152 | 127,217 | D | 26.6% | 72.6% | 26.8% | 73.2% |
| 19,171 | DODGE | 6,995 | 4,584 | 2,384 | 27 | 2,200 | R | 65.5% | 34.1% | 65.8% | 34.2% |
| 11,525 | DOOLY | 3,844 | 1,853 | 1,973 | 18 | 120 | D | 48.2% | 51.3% | 48.4% | 51.6% |
| 96,065 | DOUGHERTY | 33,662 | 13,711 | 19,805 | 146 | 6,094 | D | 40.7% | 58.8% | 40.9% | 59.1% |
| 92,174 | DOUGLAS | 42,104 | 25,846 | 15,997 | 261 | 9,849 | R | 61.4% | 38.0% | 61.8% | 38.2% |
| 12,354 | EARLY | 4,213 | 2,495 | 1,701 | 17 | 794 | R | 59.2% | 40.4% | 59.5% | 40.5% |
| 3,754 | ECHOLS | 991 | 757 | 231 | 3 | 526 | R | 76.4% | 23.3% | 76.6% | 23.4% |
| 37,535 | EFFINGHAM | 16,167 | 12,503 | 3,613 | 51 | 8,890 | R | 77.3% | 22.3% | 77.6% | 22.4% |
| 20,511 | ELBERT | 7,659 | 4,626 | 2,984 | 49 | 1,642 | R | 60.4% | 39.0% | 60.8% | 39.2% |
| 21,837 | EMANUEL | 7,470 | 4,666 | 2,774 | 30 | 1,892 | R | 62.5% | 37.1% | 62.7% | 37.3% |
| 10,495 | EVANS | 3,514 | 2,291 | 1,213 | 10 | 1,078 | R | 65.2% | 34.5% | 65.4% | 34.6% |
| 19,798 | FANNIN | 9,666 | 6,862 | 2,727 | 77 | 4,135 | R | 71.0% | 28.2% | 71.6% | 28.4% |
| 91,263 | FAYETTE | 52,587 | 37,346 | 14,887 | 354 | 22,459 | R | 71.0% | 28.3% | 71.5% | 28.5% |
| 90,565 | FLOYD | 31,625 | 21,400 | 10,038 | 187 | 11,362 | R | 67.7% | 31.7% | 68.1% | 31.9% |
| 98,407 | FORSYTH | 56,904 | 47,267 | 9,201 | 436 | 38,066 | R | 83.1% | 16.2% | 83.7% | 16.3% |
| 20,285 | FRANKLIN | 7,502 | 5,218 | 2,245 | 39 | 2,973 | R | 69.6% | 29.9% | 69.9% | 30.1% |
| 816,006 | FULTON | 336,407 | 134,372 | 199,436 | 2,599 | 65,064 | D | 39.9% | 59.3% | 40.3% | 59.7% |

# GEORGIA

## PRESIDENT 2004

| 2000 Census Population | County | Total Vote | Republican | Democratic | Other | Rep.-Dem. Plurality | Percentage | | | |
|---|---|---|---|---|---|---|---|---|---|---|
| | | | | | | | Total Vote | | Major Vote | |
| | | | | | | | Rep. | Dem. | Rep. | Dem. |
| 23,456 | GILMER | 10,014 | 7,414 | 2,510 | 90 | 4,904 R | 74.0% | 25.1% | 74.7% | 25.3% |
| 2,556 | GLASCOCK | 1,269 | 1,016 | 250 | 3 | 766 R | 80.1% | 19.7% | 80.3% | 19.7% |
| 67,568 | GLYNN | 27,696 | 18,608 | 8,962 | 126 | 9,646 R | 67.2% | 32.4% | 67.5% | 32.5% |
| 44,104 | GORDON | 15,792 | 11,671 | 4,028 | 93 | 7,643 R | 73.9% | 25.5% | 74.3% | 25.7% |
| 23,659 | GRADY | 8,194 | 5,068 | 3,092 | 34 | 1,976 R | 61.9% | 37.7% | 62.1% | 37.9% |
| 14,406 | GREENE | 6,874 | 4,069 | 2,774 | 31 | 1,295 R | 59.2% | 40.4% | 59.5% | 40.5% |
| 588,448 | GWINNETT | 244,179 | 160,445 | 81,708 | 2,026 | 78,737 R | 65.7% | 33.5% | 66.3% | 33.7% |
| 35,902 | HABERSHAM | 13,269 | 10,434 | 2,750 | 85 | 7,684 R | 78.6% | 20.7% | 79.1% | 20.9% |
| 139,277 | HALL | 49,744 | 38,883 | 10,514 | 347 | 28,369 R | 78.2% | 21.1% | 78.7% | 21.3% |
| 10,076 | HANCOCK | 3,550 | 822 | 2,715 | 13 | 1,893 D | 23.2% | 76.5% | 23.2% | 76.8% |
| 25,690 | HARALSON | 10,193 | 7,703 | 2,434 | 56 | 5,269 R | 75.6% | 23.9% | 76.0% | 24.0% |
| 23,695 | HARRIS | 12,350 | 8,878 | 3,400 | 72 | 5,478 R | 71.9% | 27.5% | 72.3% | 27.7% |
| 22,997 | HART | 9,029 | 5,500 | 3,479 | 50 | 2,021 R | 60.9% | 38.5% | 61.3% | 38.7% |
| 11,012 | HEARD | 3,956 | 2,788 | 1,148 | 20 | 1,640 R | 70.5% | 29.0% | 70.8% | 29.2% |
| 119,341 | HENRY | 64,153 | 42,759 | 21,096 | 298 | 21,663 R | 66.7% | 32.9% | 67.0% | 33.0% |
| 110,765 | HOUSTON | 45,198 | 29,862 | 15,054 | 282 | 14,808 R | 66.1% | 33.3% | 66.5% | 33.5% |
| 9,931 | IRWIN | 3,414 | 2,347 | 1,051 | 16 | 1,296 R | 68.7% | 30.8% | 69.1% | 30.9% |
| 41,589 | JACKSON | 16,173 | 12,611 | 3,468 | 94 | 9,143 R | 78.0% | 21.4% | 78.4% | 21.6% |
| 11,426 | JASPER | 4,742 | 3,157 | 1,558 | 27 | 1,599 R | 66.6% | 32.9% | 67.0% | 33.0% |
| 12,684 | JEFF DAVIS | 4,845 | 3,549 | 1,277 | 19 | 2,272 R | 73.3% | 26.4% | 73.5% | 26.5% |
| 17,266 | JEFFERSON | 6,537 | 3,066 | 3,447 | 24 | 381 D | 46.9% | 52.7% | 47.1% | 52.9% |
| 8,575 | JENKINS | 3,404 | 1,898 | 1,494 | 12 | 404 R | 55.8% | 43.9% | 56.0% | 44.0% |
| 8,560 | JOHNSON | 3,553 | 2,279 | 1,263 | 11 | 1,016 R | 64.1% | 35.5% | 64.3% | 35.7% |
| 23,639 | JONES | 10,853 | 6,939 | 3,855 | 59 | 3,084 R | 63.9% | 35.5% | 64.3% | 35.7% |
| 15,912 | LAMAR | 6,498 | 4,027 | 2,432 | 39 | 1,595 R | 62.0% | 37.4% | 62.3% | 37.7% |
| 7,241 | LANIER | 2,587 | 1,641 | 931 | 15 | 710 R | 63.4% | 36.0% | 63.8% | 36.2% |
| 44,874 | LAURENS | 17,237 | 10,883 | 6,281 | 73 | 4,602 R | 63.1% | 36.4% | 63.4% | 36.6% |
| 24,757 | LEE | 10,421 | 8,201 | 2,182 | 38 | 6,019 R | 78.7% | 20.9% | 79.0% | 21.0% |
| 61,610 | LIBERTY | 12,805 | 6,131 | 6,619 | 55 | 488 D | 47.9% | 51.7% | 48.1% | 51.9% |
| 8,348 | LINCOLN | 3,657 | 2,309 | 1,337 | 11 | 972 R | 63.1% | 36.6% | 63.3% | 36.7% |
| 10,304 | LONG | 3,039 | 1,994 | 1,033 | 12 | 961 R | 65.6% | 34.0% | 65.9% | 34.1% |
| 92,115 | LOWNDES | 31,654 | 18,981 | 12,516 | 157 | 6,465 R | 60.0% | 39.5% | 60.3% | 39.7% |
| 21,016 | LUMPKIN | 8,886 | 6,690 | 2,091 | 105 | 4,599 R | 75.3% | 23.5% | 76.2% | 23.8% |
| 21,231 | MCDUFFIE | 7,773 | 4,846 | 2,899 | 28 | 1,947 R | 62.3% | 37.3% | 62.6% | 37.4% |
| 10,847 | MCINTOSH | 5,379 | 2,837 | 2,523 | 19 | 314 R | 52.7% | 46.9% | 52.9% | 47.1% |
| 14,074 | MACON | 4,777 | 1,851 | 2,906 | 20 | 1,055 D | 38.7% | 60.8% | 38.9% | 61.1% |
| 25,730 | MADISON | 9,843 | 7,254 | 2,527 | 62 | 4,727 R | 73.7% | 25.7% | 74.2% | 25.8% |
| 7,144 | MARION | 2,955 | 1,670 | 1,275 | 10 | 395 R | 56.5% | 43.1% | 56.7% | 43.3% |
| 22,534 | MERIWETHER | 8,155 | 4,402 | 3,709 | 44 | 693 R | 54.0% | 45.5% | 54.3% | 45.7% |
| 6,383 | MILLER | 2,442 | 1,694 | 736 | 12 | 958 R | 69.4% | 30.1% | 69.7% | 30.3% |
| 23,932 | MITCHELL | 7,267 | 3,885 | 3,360 | 22 | 525 R | 53.5% | 46.2% | 53.6% | 46.4% |
| 21,757 | MONROE | 9,789 | 6,522 | 3,216 | 51 | 3,306 R | 66.6% | 32.9% | 67.0% | 33.0% |
| 8,270 | MONTGOMERY | 3,169 | 2,150 | 1,007 | 12 | 1,143 R | 67.8% | 31.8% | 68.1% | 31.9% |
| 15,457 | MORGAN | 7,243 | 4,902 | 2,304 | 37 | 2,598 R | 67.7% | 31.8% | 68.0% | 32.0% |
| 36,506 | MURRAY | 10,689 | 7,745 | 2,899 | 45 | 4,846 R | 72.5% | 27.1% | 72.8% | 27.2% |
| 186,291 | MUSCOGEE | 64,006 | 30,850 | 32,867 | 289 | 2,017 D | 48.2% | 51.3% | 48.4% | 51.6% |
| 62,001 | NEWTON | 29,179 | 18,095 | 10,939 | 145 | 7,156 R | 62.0% | 37.5% | 62.3% | 37.7% |
| 26,225 | OCONEE | 14,182 | 10,276 | 3,789 | 117 | 6,487 R | 72.5% | 26.7% | 73.1% | 26.9% |
| 12,635 | OGLETHORPE | 5,631 | 3,688 | 1,899 | 44 | 1,789 R | 65.5% | 33.7% | 66.0% | 34.0% |
| 81,678 | PAULDING | 40,496 | 30,843 | 9,420 | 233 | 21,423 R | 76.2% | 23.3% | 76.6% | 23.4% |
| 23,668 | PEACH | 8,549 | 4,554 | 3,961 | 34 | 593 R | 53.3% | 46.3% | 53.5% | 46.5% |
| 22,983 | PICKENS | 10,630 | 8,115 | 2,444 | 71 | 5,671 R | 76.3% | 23.0% | 76.9% | 23.1% |
| 15,636 | PIERCE | 5,924 | 4,680 | 1,234 | 10 | 3,446 R | 79.0% | 20.8% | 79.1% | 20.9% |
| 13,688 | PIKE | 6,745 | 5,193 | 1,506 | 46 | 3,687 R | 77.0% | 22.3% | 77.5% | 22.5% |
| 38,127 | POLK | 12,414 | 8,467 | 3,868 | 79 | 4,599 R | 68.2% | 31.2% | 68.6% | 31.4% |
| 9,588 | PULASKI | 3,516 | 2,202 | 1,294 | 20 | 908 R | 62.6% | 36.8% | 63.0% | 37.0% |
| 18,812 | PUTNAM | 8,111 | 5,188 | 2,880 | 43 | 2,308 R | 64.0% | 35.5% | 64.3% | 35.7% |
| 2,598 | QUITMAN | 965 | 409 | 543 | 13 | 134 D | 42.4% | 56.3% | 43.0% | 57.0% |
| 15,050 | RABUN | 6,638 | 4,650 | 1,918 | 70 | 2,732 R | 70.1% | 28.9% | 70.8% | 29.2% |
| 7,791 | RANDOLPH | 3,047 | 1,418 | 1,612 | 17 | 194 D | 46.5% | 52.9% | 46.8% | 53.2% |

# GEORGIA

## PRESIDENT 2004

| 2000 Census Population | County | Total Vote | Republican | Democratic | Other | Rep.-Dem. Plurality | Percentage | | | |
|---|---|---|---|---|---|---|---|---|---|---|
| | | | | | | | Total Vote | | Major Vote | |
| | | | | | | | Rep. | Dem. | Rep. | Dem. |
| 199,775 | RICHMOND | 69,349 | 29,764 | 39,262 | 323 | 9,498 D | 42.9% | 56.6% | 43.1% | 56.9% |
| 70,111 | ROCKDALE | 31,181 | 18,856 | 12,136 | 189 | 6,720 R | 60.5% | 38.9% | 60.8% | 39.2% |
| 3,766 | SCHLEY | 1,530 | 1,063 | 464 | 3 | 599 R | 69.5% | 30.3% | 69.6% | 30.4% |
| 15,374 | SCREVEN | 5,923 | 3,360 | 2,534 | 29 | 826 R | 56.7% | 42.8% | 57.0% | 43.0% |
| 9,369 | SEMINOLE | 3,275 | 1,977 | 1,278 | 20 | 699 R | 60.4% | 39.0% | 60.7% | 39.3% |
| 58,417 | SPALDING | 21,026 | 13,461 | 7,460 | 105 | 6,001 R | 64.0% | 35.5% | 64.3% | 35.7% |
| 25,435 | STEPHENS | 9,670 | 6,904 | 2,714 | 52 | 4,190 R | 71.4% | 28.1% | 71.8% | 28.2% |
| 5,252 | STEWART | 2,031 | 797 | 1,220 | 14 | 423 D | 39.2% | 60.1% | 39.5% | 60.5% |
| 33,200 | SUMTER | 11,291 | 5,688 | 5,562 | 41 | 126 R | 50.4% | 49.3% | 50.6% | 49.4% |
| 6,498 | TALBOT | 2,945 | 1,103 | 1,830 | 12 | 727 D | 37.5% | 62.1% | 37.6% | 62.4% |
| 2,077 | TALIAFERRO | 951 | 335 | 612 | 4 | 277 D | 35.2% | 64.4% | 35.4% | 64.6% |
| 22,305 | TATTNALL | 6,463 | 4,657 | 1,787 | 19 | 2,870 R | 72.1% | 27.6% | 72.3% | 27.7% |
| 8,815 | TAYLOR | 3,381 | 1,912 | 1,458 | 11 | 454 R | 56.6% | 43.1% | 56.7% | 43.3% |
| 11,794 | TELFAIR | 3,775 | 2,171 | 1,590 | 14 | 581 R | 57.5% | 42.1% | 57.7% | 42.3% |
| 10,970 | TERRELL | 3,824 | 1,859 | 1,951 | 14 | 92 D | 48.6% | 51.0% | 48.8% | 51.2% |
| 42,737 | THOMAS | 15,707 | 9,659 | 5,997 | 51 | 3,662 R | 61.5% | 38.2% | 61.7% | 38.3% |
| 38,407 | TIFT | 12,529 | 8,619 | 3,864 | 46 | 4,755 R | 68.8% | 30.8% | 69.0% | 31.0% |
| 26,067 | TOOMBS | 8,814 | 6,196 | 2,567 | 51 | 3,629 R | 70.3% | 29.1% | 70.7% | 29.3% |
| 9,319 | TOWNS | 5,280 | 3,823 | 1,430 | 27 | 2,393 R | 72.4% | 27.1% | 72.8% | 27.2% |
| 6,854 | TREUTLEN | 2,758 | 1,691 | 1,052 | 15 | 639 R | 61.3% | 38.1% | 61.6% | 38.4% |
| 58,779 | TROUP | 21,927 | 14,183 | 7,630 | 114 | 6,553 R | 64.7% | 34.8% | 65.0% | 35.0% |
| 9,504 | TURNER | 2,964 | 1,815 | 1,135 | 14 | 680 R | 61.2% | 38.3% | 61.5% | 38.5% |
| 10,590 | TWIGGS | 4,365 | 2,112 | 2,220 | 33 | 108 D | 48.4% | 50.9% | 48.8% | 51.2% |
| 17,289 | UNION | 9,228 | 6,847 | 2,327 | 54 | 4,520 R | 74.2% | 25.2% | 74.6% | 25.4% |
| 27,597 | UPSON | 10,091 | 6,634 | 3,424 | 33 | 3,210 R | 65.7% | 33.9% | 66.0% | 34.0% |
| 61,053 | WALKER | 21,453 | 15,340 | 5,986 | 127 | 9,354 R | 71.5% | 27.9% | 71.9% | 28.1% |
| 60,687 | WALTON | 27,624 | 21,594 | 5,887 | 143 | 15,707 R | 78.2% | 21.3% | 78.6% | 21.4% |
| 35,483 | WARE | 11,281 | 7,790 | 3,449 | 42 | 4,341 R | 69.1% | 30.6% | 69.3% | 30.7% |
| 6,336 | WARREN | 2,489 | 1,121 | 1,360 | 8 | 239 D | 45.0% | 54.6% | 45.2% | 54.8% |
| 21,176 | WASHINGTON | 7,847 | 4,081 | 3,733 | 33 | 348 R | 52.0% | 47.6% | 52.2% | 47.8% |
| 26,565 | WAYNE | 9,555 | 6,819 | 2,683 | 53 | 4,136 R | 71.4% | 28.1% | 71.8% | 28.2% |
| 2,390 | WEBSTER | 1,008 | 485 | 515 | 8 | 30 D | 48.1% | 51.1% | 48.5% | 51.5% |
| 6,179 | WHEELER | 2,049 | 1,192 | 847 | 10 | 345 R | 58.2% | 41.3% | 58.5% | 41.5% |
| 19,944 | WHITE | 9,498 | 7,403 | 2,016 | 79 | 5,387 R | 77.9% | 21.2% | 78.6% | 21.4% |
| 83,525 | WHITFIELD | 26,378 | 19,297 | 6,933 | 148 | 12,364 R | 73.2% | 26.3% | 73.6% | 26.4% |
| 8,577 | WILCOX | 2,619 | 1,705 | 902 | 12 | 803 R | 65.1% | 34.4% | 65.4% | 34.6% |
| 10,687 | WILKES | 4,544 | 2,490 | 2,028 | 26 | 462 R | 54.8% | 44.6% | 55.1% | 44.9% |
| 10,220 | WILKINSON | 4,514 | 2,261 | 2,235 | 18 | 26 R | 50.1% | 49.5% | 50.3% | 49.7% |
| 21,967 | WORTH | 7,353 | 5,105 | 2,219 | 29 | 2,886 R | 69.4% | 30.2% | 69.7% | 30.3% |
| 8,186,453 | TOTAL | 3,301,875 | 1,914,254 | 1,366,149 | 21,472 | 548,105 R | 58.0% | 41.4% | 58.4% | 41.6% |

# GEORGIA

## SENATOR 2004

| 2000 Census Population | County | Total Vote | Republican | Democratic | Other | Rep.-Dem. Plurality | | Percentage | | | |
|---|---|---|---|---|---|---|---|---|---|---|---|
| | | | | | | | | Total Vote | | Major Vote | |
| | | | | | | | | Rep. | Dem. | Rep. | Dem. |
| 17,419 | APPLING | 6,028 | 4,149 | 1,788 | 91 | 2,361 | R | 68.8% | 29.7% | 69.9% | 30.1% |
| 7,609 | ATKINSON | 2,311 | 1,468 | 798 | 45 | 670 | R | 63.5% | 34.5% | 64.8% | 35.2% |
| 10,103 | BACON | 3,448 | 2,501 | 888 | 59 | 1,613 | R | 72.5% | 25.8% | 73.8% | 26.2% |
| 4,074 | BAKER | 1,644 | 799 | 819 | 26 | 20 | D | 48.6% | 49.8% | 49.4% | 50.6% |
| 44,700 | BALDWIN | 14,194 | 7,483 | 6,468 | 243 | 1,015 | R | 52.7% | 45.6% | 53.6% | 46.4% |
| 14,422 | BANKS | 5,461 | 4,168 | 1,181 | 112 | 2,987 | R | 76.3% | 21.6% | 77.9% | 22.1% |
| 46,144 | BARROW | 17,458 | 12,845 | 4,156 | 457 | 8,689 | R | 73.6% | 23.8% | 75.6% | 24.4% |
| 76,019 | BARTOW | 29,712 | 21,392 | 7,596 | 724 | 13,796 | R | 72.0% | 25.6% | 73.8% | 26.2% |
| 17,484 | BEN HILL | 5,391 | 3,043 | 2,265 | 83 | 778 | R | 56.4% | 42.0% | 57.3% | 42.7% |
| 16,235 | BERRIEN | 5,437 | 3,754 | 1,574 | 109 | 2,180 | R | 69.0% | 28.9% | 70.5% | 29.5% |
| 153,887 | BIBB | 56,632 | 28,213 | 27,517 | 902 | 696 | R | 49.8% | 48.6% | 50.6% | 49.4% |
| 11,666 | BLECKLEY | 4,268 | 3,045 | 1,143 | 80 | 1,902 | R | 71.3% | 26.8% | 72.7% | 27.3% |
| 14,629 | BRANTLEY | 5,206 | 3,716 | 1,377 | 113 | 2,339 | R | 71.4% | 26.5% | 73.0% | 27.0% |
| 16,450 | BROOKS | 4,788 | 2,786 | 1,905 | 97 | 881 | R | 58.2% | 39.8% | 59.4% | 40.6% |
| 23,417 | BRYAN | 9,672 | 7,130 | 2,410 | 132 | 4,720 | R | 73.7% | 24.9% | 74.7% | 25.3% |
| 55,983 | BULLOCH | 18,778 | 12,409 | 6,103 | 266 | 6,306 | R | 66.1% | 32.5% | 67.0% | 33.0% |
| 22,243 | BURKE | 8,098 | 4,401 | 3,601 | 96 | 800 | R | 54.3% | 44.5% | 55.0% | 45.0% |
| 19,522 | BUTTS | 7,603 | 4,841 | 2,615 | 147 | 2,226 | R | 63.7% | 34.4% | 64.9% | 35.1% |
| 6,320 | CALHOUN | 1,951 | 904 | 1,018 | 29 | 114 | D | 46.3% | 52.2% | 47.0% | 53.0% |
| 43,664 | CAMDEN | 13,367 | 8,780 | 4,300 | 287 | 4,480 | R | 65.7% | 32.2% | 67.1% | 32.9% |
| 9,577 | CANDLER | 3,036 | 2,000 | 987 | 49 | 1,013 | R | 65.9% | 32.5% | 67.0% | 33.0% |
| 87,268 | CARROLL | 34,646 | 23,661 | 10,193 | 792 | 13,468 | R | 68.3% | 29.4% | 69.9% | 30.1% |
| 53,282 | CATOOSA | 20,887 | 15,362 | 5,160 | 365 | 10,202 | R | 73.5% | 24.7% | 74.9% | 25.1% |
| 10,282 | CHARLTON | 2,980 | 1,876 | 1,017 | 87 | 859 | R | 63.0% | 34.1% | 64.8% | 35.2% |
| 232,048 | CHATHAM | 89,280 | 45,108 | 42,691 | 1,481 | 2,417 | R | 50.5% | 47.8% | 51.4% | 48.6% |
| 14,882 | CHATTAHOOCHEE | 1,618 | 827 | 756 | 35 | 71 | R | 51.1% | 46.7% | 52.2% | 47.8% |
| 25,470 | CHATTOOGA | 7,394 | 4,499 | 2,731 | 164 | 1,768 | R | 60.8% | 36.9% | 62.2% | 37.8% |
| 141,903 | CHEROKEE | 72,575 | 56,657 | 13,983 | 1,935 | 42,674 | R | 78.1% | 19.3% | 80.2% | 19.8% |
| 101,489 | CLARKE | 36,617 | 15,312 | 20,020 | 1,285 | 4,708 | D | 41.8% | 54.7% | 43.3% | 56.7% |
| 3,357 | CLAY | 1,215 | 498 | 702 | 15 | 204 | D | 41.0% | 57.8% | 41.5% | 58.5% |
| 236,517 | CLAYTON | 77,881 | 20,939 | 55,591 | 1,351 | 34,652 | D | 26.9% | 71.4% | 27.4% | 72.6% |
| 6,878 | CLINCH | 2,034 | 1,319 | 662 | 53 | 657 | R | 64.8% | 32.5% | 66.6% | 33.4% |
| 607,751 | COBB | 275,406 | 174,434 | 93,909 | 7,063 | 80,525 | R | 63.3% | 34.1% | 65.0% | 35.0% |
| 37,413 | COFFEE | 11,638 | 7,647 | 3,807 | 184 | 3,840 | R | 65.7% | 32.7% | 66.8% | 33.2% |
| 42,053 | COLQUITT | 11,337 | 7,946 | 3,213 | 178 | 4,733 | R | 70.1% | 28.3% | 71.2% | 28.8% |
| 89,288 | COLUMBIA | 45,933 | 35,249 | 10,118 | 566 | 25,131 | R | 76.7% | 22.0% | 77.7% | 22.3% |
| 15,771 | COOK | 4,667 | 2,965 | 1,613 | 89 | 1,352 | R | 63.5% | 34.6% | 64.8% | 35.2% |
| 89,215 | COWETA | 41,883 | 30,618 | 10,389 | 876 | 20,229 | R | 73.1% | 24.8% | 74.7% | 25.3% |
| 12,495 | CRAWFORD | 4,278 | 2,723 | 1,458 | 97 | 1,265 | R | 63.7% | 34.1% | 65.1% | 34.9% |
| 21,996 | CRISP | 6,015 | 3,783 | 2,156 | 76 | 1,627 | R | 62.9% | 35.8% | 63.7% | 36.3% |
| 15,154 | DADE | 5,685 | 3,917 | 1,561 | 207 | 2,356 | R | 68.9% | 27.5% | 71.5% | 28.5% |
| 15,999 | DAWSON | 7,984 | 6,397 | 1,379 | 208 | 5,018 | R | 80.1% | 17.3% | 82.3% | 17.7% |
| 28,240 | DECATUR | 8,514 | 5,037 | 3,280 | 197 | 1,757 | R | 59.2% | 38.5% | 60.6% | 39.4% |
| 665,865 | DEKALB | 271,576 | 72,595 | 192,182 | 6,799 | 119,587 | D | 26.7% | 70.8% | 27.4% | 72.6% |
| 19,171 | DODGE | 6,675 | 4,236 | 2,320 | 119 | 1,916 | R | 63.5% | 34.8% | 64.6% | 35.4% |
| 11,525 | DOOLY | 3,692 | 1,897 | 1,749 | 46 | 148 | R | 51.4% | 47.4% | 52.0% | 48.0% |
| 96,065 | DOUGHERTY | 33,026 | 13,575 | 19,085 | 366 | 5,510 | D | 41.1% | 57.8% | 41.6% | 58.4% |
| 92,174 | DOUGLAS | 41,484 | 24,788 | 15,820 | 876 | 8,968 | R | 59.8% | 38.1% | 61.0% | 39.0% |
| 12,354 | EARLY | 3,984 | 2,320 | 1,583 | 81 | 737 | R | 58.2% | 39.7% | 59.4% | 40.6% |
| 3,754 | ECHOLS | 929 | 680 | 218 | 31 | 462 | R | 73.2% | 23.5% | 75.7% | 24.3% |
| 37,535 | EFFINGHAM | 15,816 | 12,083 | 3,536 | 197 | 8,547 | R | 76.4% | 22.4% | 77.4% | 22.6% |
| 20,511 | ELBERT | 7,295 | 4,354 | 2,775 | 166 | 1,579 | R | 59.7% | 38.0% | 61.1% | 38.9% |
| 21,837 | EMANUEL | 6,983 | 4,447 | 2,411 | 125 | 2,036 | R | 63.7% | 34.5% | 64.8% | 35.2% |
| 10,495 | EVANS | 3,385 | 2,213 | 1,143 | 29 | 1,070 | R | 65.4% | 33.8% | 65.9% | 34.1% |
| 19,798 | FANNIN | 9,319 | 6,597 | 2,520 | 202 | 4,077 | R | 70.8% | 27.0% | 72.4% | 27.6% |
| 91,263 | FAYETTE | 51,765 | 36,595 | 13,988 | 1,182 | 22,607 | R | 70.7% | 27.0% | 72.3% | 27.7% |
| 90,565 | FLOYD | 31,015 | 20,768 | 9,625 | 622 | 11,143 | R | 67.0% | 31.0% | 68.3% | 31.7% |
| 98,407 | FORSYTH | 55,999 | 46,118 | 8,394 | 1,487 | 37,724 | R | 82.4% | 15.0% | 84.6% | 15.4% |
| 20,285 | FRANKLIN | 7,224 | 4,773 | 2,289 | 162 | 2,484 | R | 66.1% | 31.7% | 67.6% | 32.4% |
| 816,006 | FULTON | 329,953 | 138,696 | 182,724 | 8,533 | 44,028 | D | 42.0% | 55.4% | 43.2% | 56.8% |

# GEORGIA
## SENATOR 2004

| 2000 Census Population | County | Total Vote | Republican | Democratic | Other | Rep.-Dem. Plurality | Percentage Total Vote Rep. | Dem. | Major Vote Rep. | Dem. |
|---|---|---|---|---|---|---|---|---|---|---|
| 23,456 | GILMER | 9,744 | 7,134 | 2,366 | 244 | 4,768 R | 73.2% | 24.3% | 75.1% | 24.9% |
| 2,556 | GLASCOCK | 1,150 | 931 | 204 | 15 | 727 R | 81.0% | 17.7% | 82.0% | 18.0% |
| 67,568 | GLYNN | 26,894 | 18,317 | 8,146 | 431 | 10,171 R | 68.1% | 30.3% | 69.2% | 30.8% |
| 44,104 | GORDON | 15,311 | 11,051 | 3,930 | 330 | 7,121 R | 72.2% | 25.7% | 73.8% | 26.2% |
| 23,659 | GRADY | 7,556 | 4,484 | 2,886 | 186 | 1,598 R | 59.3% | 38.2% | 60.8% | 39.2% |
| 14,406 | GREENE | 6,786 | 4,033 | 2,662 | 91 | 1,371 R | 59.4% | 39.2% | 60.2% | 39.8% |
| 588,448 | GWINNETT | 240,034 | 155,790 | 77,906 | 6,338 | 77,884 R | 64.9% | 32.5% | 66.7% | 33.3% |
| 35,902 | HABERSHAM | 12,989 | 10,056 | 2,695 | 238 | 7,361 R | 77.4% | 20.7% | 78.9% | 21.1% |
| 139,277 | HALL | 48,998 | 37,503 | 10,439 | 1,056 | 27,064 R | 76.5% | 21.3% | 78.2% | 21.8% |
| 10,076 | HANCOCK | 3,405 | 802 | 2,544 | 59 | 1,742 D | 23.6% | 74.7% | 24.0% | 76.0% |
| 25,690 | HARALSON | 10,005 | 7,259 | 2,501 | 245 | 4,758 R | 72.6% | 25.0% | 74.4% | 25.6% |
| 23,695 | HARRIS | 12,035 | 8,507 | 3,252 | 276 | 5,255 R | 70.7% | 27.0% | 72.3% | 27.7% |
| 22,997 | HART | 8,497 | 5,121 | 3,171 | 205 | 1,950 R | 60.3% | 37.3% | 61.8% | 38.2% |
| 11,012 | HEARD | 3,843 | 2,617 | 1,154 | 72 | 1,463 R | 68.1% | 30.0% | 69.4% | 30.6% |
| 119,341 | HENRY | 63,182 | 40,999 | 20,839 | 1,344 | 20,160 R | 64.9% | 33.0% | 66.3% | 33.7% |
| 110,765 | HOUSTON | 44,196 | 29,024 | 14,497 | 675 | 14,527 R | 65.7% | 32.8% | 66.7% | 33.3% |
| 9,931 | IRWIN | 3,305 | 2,219 | 1,028 | 58 | 1,191 R | 67.1% | 31.1% | 68.3% | 31.7% |
| 41,589 | JACKSON | 15,948 | 12,207 | 3,398 | 343 | 8,809 R | 76.5% | 21.3% | 78.2% | 21.8% |
| 11,426 | JASPER | 4,670 | 3,070 | 1,515 | 85 | 1,555 R | 65.7% | 32.4% | 67.0% | 33.0% |
| 12,684 | JEFF DAVIS | 4,520 | 3,149 | 1,291 | 80 | 1,858 R | 69.7% | 28.6% | 70.9% | 29.1% |
| 17,266 | JEFFERSON | 6,146 | 3,048 | 3,027 | 71 | 21 R | 49.6% | 49.3% | 50.2% | 49.8% |
| 8,575 | JENKINS | 3,214 | 1,925 | 1,234 | 55 | 691 R | 59.9% | 38.4% | 60.9% | 39.1% |
| 8,560 | JOHNSON | 3,317 | 2,142 | 1,105 | 70 | 1,037 R | 64.6% | 33.3% | 66.0% | 34.0% |
| 23,639 | JONES | 10,622 | 6,786 | 3,643 | 193 | 3,143 R | 63.9% | 34.3% | 65.1% | 34.9% |
| 15,912 | LAMAR | 6,413 | 3,953 | 2,367 | 93 | 1,586 R | 61.6% | 36.9% | 62.5% | 37.5% |
| 7,241 | LANIER | 2,352 | 1,418 | 871 | 63 | 547 R | 60.3% | 37.0% | 61.9% | 38.1% |
| 44,874 | LAURENS | 16,777 | 10,526 | 6,035 | 216 | 4,491 R | 62.7% | 36.0% | 63.6% | 36.4% |
| 24,757 | LEE | 10,197 | 7,932 | 2,157 | 108 | 5,775 R | 77.8% | 21.2% | 78.6% | 21.4% |
| 61,610 | LIBERTY | 12,309 | 5,557 | 6,568 | 184 | 1,011 D | 45.1% | 53.4% | 45.8% | 54.2% |
| 8,348 | LINCOLN | 3,500 | 2,272 | 1,188 | 40 | 1,084 R | 64.9% | 33.9% | 65.7% | 34.3% |
| 10,304 | LONG | 2,875 | 1,790 | 1,038 | 47 | 752 R | 62.3% | 36.1% | 63.3% | 36.7% |
| 92,115 | LOWNDES | 30,351 | 18,188 | 11,607 | 556 | 6,581 R | 59.9% | 38.2% | 61.0% | 39.0% |
| 21,016 | LUMPKIN | 8,727 | 6,391 | 2,127 | 209 | 4,264 R | 73.2% | 24.4% | 75.0% | 25.0% |
| 21,231 | MCDUFFIE | 7,504 | 4,889 | 2,536 | 79 | 2,353 R | 65.2% | 33.8% | 65.8% | 34.2% |
| 10,847 | MCINTOSH | 5,212 | 2,755 | 2,379 | 78 | 376 R | 52.9% | 45.6% | 53.7% | 46.3% |
| 14,074 | MACON | 4,558 | 1,847 | 2,647 | 64 | 800 D | 40.5% | 58.1% | 41.1% | 58.9% |
| 25,730 | MADISON | 9,576 | 6,864 | 2,515 | 197 | 4,349 R | 71.7% | 26.3% | 73.2% | 26.8% |
| 7,144 | MARION | 2,831 | 1,597 | 1,177 | 57 | 420 R | 56.4% | 41.6% | 57.6% | 42.4% |
| 22,534 | MERIWETHER | 7,827 | 4,221 | 3,480 | 126 | 741 R | 53.9% | 44.5% | 54.8% | 45.2% |
| 6,383 | MILLER | 2,239 | 1,479 | 696 | 64 | 783 R | 66.1% | 31.1% | 68.0% | 32.0% |
| 23,932 | MITCHELL | 7,063 | 3,844 | 3,130 | 89 | 714 R | 54.4% | 44.3% | 55.1% | 44.9% |
| 21,757 | MONROE | 9,385 | 6,293 | 2,928 | 164 | 3,365 R | 67.1% | 31.2% | 68.2% | 31.8% |
| 8,270 | MONTGOMERY | 3,024 | 2,031 | 945 | 48 | 1,086 R | 67.2% | 31.3% | 68.2% | 31.8% |
| 15,457 | MORGAN | 7,133 | 4,892 | 2,123 | 118 | 2,769 R | 68.6% | 29.8% | 69.7% | 30.3% |
| 36,506 | MURRAY | 10,084 | 7,020 | 2,783 | 281 | 4,237 R | 69.6% | 27.6% | 71.6% | 28.4% |
| 186,291 | MUSCOGEE | 62,338 | 30,034 | 31,106 | 1,198 | 1,072 D | 48.2% | 49.9% | 49.1% | 50.9% |
| 62,001 | NEWTON | 28,727 | 17,493 | 10,666 | 568 | 6,827 R | 60.9% | 37.1% | 62.1% | 37.9% |
| 26,225 | OCONEE | 13,989 | 10,252 | 3,430 | 307 | 6,822 R | 73.3% | 24.5% | 74.9% | 25.1% |
| 12,635 | OGLETHORPE | 5,482 | 3,561 | 1,808 | 113 | 1,753 R | 65.0% | 33.0% | 66.3% | 33.7% |
| 81,678 | PAULDING | 39,931 | 29,569 | 9,465 | 897 | 20,104 R | 74.1% | 23.7% | 75.8% | 24.2% |
| 23,668 | PEACH | 8,349 | 4,472 | 3,749 | 128 | 723 R | 53.6% | 44.9% | 54.4% | 45.6% |
| 22,983 | PICKENS | 10,436 | 7,883 | 2,304 | 249 | 5,579 R | 75.5% | 22.1% | 77.4% | 22.6% |
| 15,636 | PIERCE | 5,697 | 4,491 | 1,137 | 69 | 3,354 R | 78.8% | 20.0% | 79.8% | 20.2% |
| 13,688 | PIKE | 6,632 | 5,031 | 1,445 | 156 | 3,586 R | 75.9% | 21.8% | 77.7% | 22.3% |
| 38,127 | POLK | 12,114 | 7,998 | 3,866 | 250 | 4,132 R | 66.0% | 31.9% | 67.4% | 32.6% |
| 9,588 | PULASKI | 3,400 | 2,218 | 1,135 | 47 | 1,083 R | 65.2% | 33.4% | 66.1% | 33.9% |
| 18,812 | PUTNAM | 7,963 | 5,103 | 2,708 | 152 | 2,395 R | 64.1% | 34.0% | 65.3% | 34.7% |
| 2,598 | QUITMAN | 885 | 395 | 463 | 27 | 68 D | 44.6% | 52.3% | 46.0% | 54.0% |
| 15,050 | RABUN | 6,461 | 4,520 | 1,786 | 155 | 2,734 R | 70.0% | 27.6% | 71.7% | 28.3% |
| 7,791 | RANDOLPH | 2,933 | 1,404 | 1,495 | 34 | 91 D | 47.9% | 51.0% | 48.4% | 51.6% |

# GEORGIA

## SENATOR 2004

| 2000 Census Population | County | Total Vote | Republican | Democratic | Other | Rep.-Dem. Plurality | Percentage | | | |
|---|---|---|---|---|---|---|---|---|---|---|
| | | | | | | | Total Vote | | Major Vote | |
| | | | | | | | Rep. | Dem. | Rep. | Dem. |
| 199,775 | RICHMOND | 66,415 | 29,086 | 36,488 | 841 | 7,402 D | 43.8% | 54.9% | 44.4% | 55.6% |
| 70,111 | ROCKDALE | 30,709 | 18,227 | 11,845 | 637 | 6,382 R | 59.4% | 38.6% | 60.6% | 39.4% |
| 3,766 | SCHLEY | 1,457 | 1,032 | 406 | 19 | 626 R | 70.8% | 27.9% | 71.8% | 28.2% |
| 15,374 | SCREVEN | 5,645 | 3,305 | 2,237 | 103 | 1,068 R | 58.5% | 39.6% | 59.6% | 40.4% |
| 9,369 | SEMINOLE | 3,054 | 1,742 | 1,233 | 79 | 509 R | 57.0% | 40.4% | 58.6% | 41.4% |
| 58,417 | SPALDING | 20,663 | 13,004 | 7,319 | 340 | 5,685 R | 62.9% | 35.4% | 64.0% | 36.0% |
| 25,435 | STEPHENS | 9,199 | 6,436 | 2,593 | 170 | 3,843 R | 70.0% | 28.2% | 71.3% | 28.7% |
| 5,252 | STEWART | 1,815 | 775 | 1,011 | 29 | 236 D | 42.7% | 55.7% | 43.4% | 56.6% |
| 33,200 | SUMTER | 10,885 | 5,696 | 5,054 | 135 | 642 R | 52.3% | 46.4% | 53.0% | 47.0% |
| 6,498 | TALBOT | 2,806 | 1,075 | 1,677 | 54 | 602 D | 38.3% | 59.8% | 39.1% | 60.9% |
| 2,077 | TALIAFERRO | 900 | 338 | 548 | 14 | 210 D | 37.6% | 60.9% | 38.1% | 61.9% |
| 22,305 | TATTNALL | 6,111 | 4,342 | 1,685 | 84 | 2,657 R | 71.1% | 27.6% | 72.0% | 28.0% |
| 8,815 | TAYLOR | 3,277 | 1,890 | 1,346 | 41 | 544 R | 57.7% | 41.1% | 58.4% | 41.6% |
| 11,794 | TELFAIR | 3,600 | 2,030 | 1,501 | 69 | 529 R | 56.4% | 41.7% | 57.5% | 42.5% |
| 10,970 | TERRELL | 3,701 | 1,872 | 1,776 | 53 | 96 R | 50.6% | 48.0% | 51.3% | 48.7% |
| 42,737 | THOMAS | 15,040 | 9,260 | 5,476 | 304 | 3,784 R | 61.6% | 36.4% | 62.8% | 37.2% |
| 38,407 | TIFT | 12,179 | 8,344 | 3,660 | 175 | 4,684 R | 68.5% | 30.1% | 69.5% | 30.5% |
| 26,067 | TOOMBS | 8,416 | 5,877 | 2,397 | 142 | 3,480 R | 69.8% | 28.5% | 71.0% | 29.0% |
| 9,319 | TOWNS | 5,065 | 3,595 | 1,381 | 89 | 2,214 R | 71.0% | 27.3% | 72.2% | 27.8% |
| 6,854 | TREUTLEN | 2,613 | 1,571 | 996 | 46 | 575 R | 60.1% | 38.1% | 61.2% | 38.8% |
| 58,779 | TROUP | 21,409 | 13,604 | 7,483 | 322 | 6,121 R | 63.5% | 35.0% | 64.5% | 35.5% |
| 9,504 | TURNER | 2,865 | 1,775 | 1,042 | 48 | 733 R | 62.0% | 36.4% | 63.0% | 37.0% |
| 10,590 | TWIGGS | 4,196 | 2,016 | 2,067 | 113 | 51 D | 48.0% | 49.3% | 49.4% | 50.6% |
| 17,289 | UNION | 8,941 | 6,402 | 2,369 | 170 | 4,033 R | 71.6% | 26.5% | 73.0% | 27.0% |
| 27,597 | UPSON | 9,898 | 6,440 | 3,321 | 137 | 3,119 R | 65.1% | 33.6% | 66.0% | 34.0% |
| 61,053 | WALKER | 20,410 | 14,445 | 5,511 | 454 | 8,934 R | 70.8% | 27.0% | 72.4% | 27.6% |
| 60,687 | WALTON | 27,217 | 20,947 | 5,708 | 562 | 15,239 R | 77.0% | 21.0% | 78.6% | 21.4% |
| 35,483 | WARE | 10,709 | 7,233 | 3,297 | 179 | 3,936 R | 67.5% | 30.8% | 68.7% | 31.3% |
| 6,336 | WARREN | 2,336 | 1,157 | 1,147 | 32 | 10 R | 49.5% | 49.1% | 50.2% | 49.8% |
| 21,176 | WASHINGTON | 7,503 | 4,019 | 3,400 | 84 | 619 R | 53.6% | 45.3% | 54.2% | 45.8% |
| 26,565 | WAYNE | 9,260 | 6,372 | 2,761 | 127 | 3,611 R | 68.8% | 29.8% | 69.8% | 30.2% |
| 2,390 | WEBSTER | 971 | 497 | 457 | 17 | 40 R | 51.2% | 47.1% | 52.1% | 47.9% |
| 6,179 | WHEELER | 1,947 | 1,095 | 832 | 20 | 263 R | 56.2% | 42.7% | 56.8% | 43.2% |
| 19,944 | WHITE | 9,336 | 7,084 | 2,064 | 188 | 5,020 R | 75.9% | 22.1% | 77.4% | 22.6% |
| 83,525 | WHITFIELD | 25,343 | 18,568 | 6,257 | 518 | 12,311 R | 73.3% | 24.7% | 74.8% | 25.2% |
| 8,577 | WILCOX | 2,557 | 1,692 | 846 | 19 | 846 R | 66.2% | 33.1% | 66.7% | 33.3% |
| 10,687 | WILKES | 4,320 | 2,492 | 1,764 | 64 | 728 R | 57.7% | 40.8% | 58.6% | 41.4% |
| 10,220 | WILKINSON | 4,355 | 2,221 | 2,074 | 60 | 147 R | 51.0% | 47.6% | 51.7% | 48.3% |
| 21,967 | WORTH | 7,147 | 4,953 | 2,108 | 86 | 2,845 R | 69.3% | 29.5% | 70.1% | 29.9% |
| 8,186,453 | TOTAL | 3,220,981 | 1,864,202 | 1,287,690 | 69,089 | 576,512 R | 57.9% | 40.0% | 59.1% | 40.9% |

# GEORGIA

## HOUSE OF REPRESENTATIVES

| CD | Year | Total Vote | Republican Vote | Republican Candidate | Democratic Vote | Democratic Candidate | Other Vote | Rep.-Dem. Plurality | Total Vote Rep. | Total Vote Dem. | Major Vote Rep. | Major Vote Dem. |
|---|---|---|---|---|---|---|---|---|---|---|---|---|
| 1 | 2004 | 188,347 | 188,347 | Kingston, Jack* | | | | 188,347 R | 100.0% | | 100.0% | |
| 1 | 2002 | 143,700 | 103,661 | Kingston, Jack* | 40,026 | Smart, Don | 13 | 63,635 R | 72.1% | 27.9% | 72.1% | 27.9% |
| 2 | 2004 | 194,629 | 64,645 | Eversman, David | 129,984 | Bishop, Sanford D. Jr.* | | 65,339 D | 33.2% | 66.8% | 33.2% | 66.8% |
| 2 | 2002 | 102,925 | | | 102,925 | Bishop, Sanford D. Jr.* | | 102,925 D | | 100.0% | | 100.0% |
| 3 | 2004 | 216,708 | 80,435 | Clay, Calder | 136,273 | Marshall, Jim* | | 55,838 D | 37.1% | 62.9% | 37.1% | 62.9% |
| 3 | 2002 | 149,260 | 73,866 | Clay, Calder | 75,394 | Marshall, Jim | | 1,528 D | 49.5% | 50.5% | 49.5% | 50.5% |
| 4 | 2004 | 246,970 | 89,509 | Davis, Catherine | 157,461 | McKinney, Cynthia A. | | 67,952 D | 36.2% | 63.8% | 36.2% | 63.8% |
| 4 | 2002 | 153,247 | 35,202 | Van Auken, Cynthia | 118,045 | Majette, Denise L. | | 82,843 D | 23.0% | 77.0% | 23.0% | 77.0% |
| 5 | 2004 | 201,773 | | | 201,773 | Lewis, John* | | 201,773 D | | 100.0% | | 100.0% |
| 5 | 2002 | 116,230 | | | 116,230 | Lewis, John* | | 116,230 D | | 100.0% | | 100.0% |
| 6 | 2004 | 267,619 | 267,542 | Price, Tom | | | 77 | 267,542 R | 100.0% | | 100.0% | |
| 6 | 2002 | 204,252 | 163,209 | Isakson, Johnny* | 41,043 | Weisberger, Jeff | | 122,166 R | 79.9% | 20.1% | 79.9% | 20.1% |
| 7 | 2004 | 258,982 | 258,982 | Linder, John* | | | | 258,982 R | 100.0% | | 100.0% | |
| 7 | 2002 | 176,170 | 139,019 | Linder, John* | 37,127 | Berlon, Mike | 24 | 101,892 R | 78.9% | 21.1% | 78.9% | 21.1% |
| 8 | 2004 | 301,156 | 227,524 | Westmoreland, Lynn | 73,632 | Delamar, Silvia | | 153,892 R | 75.6% | 24.4% | 75.6% | 24.4% |
| 8 | 2002 | 181,927 | 142,505 | Collins, Mac* | 39,422 | Petrakopoulos, Angelos | | 103,083 R | 78.3% | 21.7% | 78.3% | 21.7% |
| 9 | 2004 | 266,331 | 197,869 | Norwood, Charlie* | 68,462 | Ellis, Bob | | 129,407 R | 74.3% | 25.7% | 74.3% | 25.7% |
| 9 | 2002 | 169,287 | 123,313 | Norwood, Charlie* | 45,974 | Irwin, Barry | | 77,339 R | 72.8% | 27.2% | 72.8% | 27.2% |
| 10 | 2004 | 219,136 | 219,136 | Deal, Nathan* | | | | 219,136 R | 100.0% | | 100.0% | |
| 10 | 2002 | 129,242 | 129,242 | Deal, Nathan* | | | | 129,242 R | 100.0% | | 100.0% | |
| 11 | 2004 | 210,287 | 120,696 | Gingrey, Phil* | 89,591 | Crawford, Rick | | 31,105 R | 57.4% | 42.6% | 57.4% | 42.6% |
| 11 | 2002 | 134,184 | 69,261 | Gingrey, Phil | 64,923 | Kahn, Roger | | 4,338 R | 51.6% | 48.4% | 51.6% | 48.4% |
| 12 | 2004 | 218,168 | 105,132 | Burns, Max* | 113,036 | Barrow, John | | 7,904 D | 48.2% | 51.8% | 48.2% | 51.8% |
| 12 | 2002 | 140,457 | 77,479 | Burns, Max | 62,904 | Walker, Champ | 74 | 14,575 R | 55.2% | 44.8% | 55.2% | 44.8% |
| 13 | 2004 | 170,657 | | | 170,657 | Scott, David* | | 170,657 D | | 100.0% | | 100.0% |
| 13 | 2002 | 117,416 | 47,405 | Cox, Clay | 70,011 | Scott, David | | 22,606 D | 40.4% | 59.6% | 40.4% | 59.6% |
| Total | 2004 | 2,960,763 | 1,819,817 | | 1,140,869 | | 77 | 678,948 R | 61.5% | 38.5% | 61.5% | 38.5% |
| Total | 2002 | 1,918,297 | 1,104,162 | | 814,024 | | 111 | 290,138 R | 57.6% | 42.4% | 57.6% | 42.4% |

An asterisk (*) denotes incumbent.

# GEORGIA

## GENERAL AND PRIMARY ELECTIONS

### 2004 GENERAL ELECTIONS

**President**    Other vote was 18,387 Libertarian (Michael Badnarik); 2,231 write-in (Ralph Nader); 580 write-in (Michael Peroutka); 228 write-in (David Cobb); 26 write-in (Tom Tancredo); 8 write-in (John J. Kennedy); 7 write-in (David Byrne); 5 write-in (James Pace).

**Senator**    Other vote was 69,051 Libertarian (Allen Buckley); 31 write-in (Al Bartell); 7 write-in (Matthew Jamison).

**House**    Other vote was:

CD 1
CD 2
CD 3
CD 4
CD 5
CD 6    77 write-in (Gary Pelphrey).
CD 7
CD 8
CD 9
CD 10
CD 11
CD 12
CD 13

### 2004 PRIMARY ELECTIONS

**Primary**    March 2, 2004 (President)    **Registration**    3,919,421    No Party Registration
July 20, 2004 (Congress)    (active registrants
as of July 20, 2004)

**Primary Runoff**  August 10, 2004

**Primary Type**    Open—Registered voters could participate in either the Democratic or Republican primary, although if they voted in one party's primary they could not participate in a primary runoff of the other party.

# GEORGIA

## GENERAL AND PRIMARY ELECTIONS

Note: An asterisk (*) denotes incumbent.

| | REPUBLICAN PRIMARIES | | | DEMOCRATIC PRIMARIES | | |
|---|---|---|---|---|---|---|
| President | George W. Bush* | 161,374 | 100.0% | John Kerry | 293,265 | 46.8% |
| | | | | John Edwards | 259,386 | 41.4% |
| | | | | Al Sharpton | 39,129 | 6.2% |
| | | | | Howard Dean | 11,322 | 1.8% |
| | | | | Dennis J. Kucinich | 7,701 | 1.2% |
| | | | | Joseph I. Lieberman | 5,666 | 0.9% |
| | | | | Wesley Clark | 4,247 | 0.7% |
| | | | | Carol Moseley Braun | 3,747 | 0.6% |
| | | | | Richard A. Gephardt | 2,350 | 0.4% |
| | | | | TOTAL | 626,813 | |
| Senator | Johnny Isakson | 346,670 | 53.3% | Denise L. Majette | 258,469 | 41.3% |
| | Herman Cain | 170,370 | 26.2% | Cliff Oxford | 128,531 | 20.6% |
| | Mac Collins | 133,952 | 20.6% | Jim Boyd | 87,694 | 14.0% |
| | | | | Mary Squires | 55,040 | 8.8% |
| | | | | Leigh Baier | 47,484 | 7.6% |
| | | | | Jim Finkelstein | 22,532 | 3.6% |
| | | | | Sid Cottingham | 16,200 | 2.6% |
| | | | | Govind Patel | 9,165 | 1.5% |
| | TOTAL | 650,992 | | TOTAL | 625,115 | |
| | | | | PRIMARY RUNOFF | | |
| | | | | Denise L. Majette | 161,733 | 59.4% |
| | | | | Cliff Oxford | 110,526 | 40.6% |
| | | | | TOTAL | 272,259 | |
| Congressional District 1 | Jack Kingston* | 43,942 | 100.0% | No Democratic candidate | | |
| Congressional District 2 | David Eversman | 18,033 | 100.0% | Sanford D. Bishop Jr.* | 67,126 | 100.0% |
| Congressional District 3 | Calder Clay | 19,039 | 100.0% | Jim Marshall* | 69,518 | 100.0% |
| Congressional District 4 | Catherine Davis | 14,612 | 100.0% | Cynthia A. McKinney | 48,512 | 50.8% |
| | | | | Liane Levetan | 19,723 | 20.6% |
| | | | | Cathy Woolard | 18,164 | 19.0% |
| | | | | Connie Stokes | 4,972 | 5.2% |
| | | | | Nadine Thomas | 2,938 | 3.1% |
| | | | | Chris Vaughn | 1,280 | 1.3% |
| | | | | TOTAL | 95,589 | |
| Congressional District 5 | No Republican candidate | | | John Lewis* | 62,114 | 100.0% |
| Congressional District 6 | Tom Price | 29,144 | 35.2% | No Democratic candidate | | |
| | Robert Lamutt | 23,176 | 28.0% | | | |
| | Chuck Clay | 17,705 | 21.4% | | | |
| | Roger Hines | 7,645 | 9.2% | | | |
| | Alfred Beverly | 3,187 | 3.8% | | | |
| | Chris Chatwood | 991 | 1.2% | | | |
| | Kevin Johns | 974 | 1.2% | | | |
| | TOTAL | 82,822 | | | | |
| | PRIMARY RUNOFF | | | | | |
| | Tom Price | 28,180 | 54.0% | | | |
| | Robert Lamutt | 23,959 | 46.0% | | | |
| | TOTAL | 52,139 | | | | |
| Congressional District 7 | John Linder* | 71,349 | 100.0% | No Democratic candidate | | |

# GEORGIA

## GENERAL AND PRIMARY ELECTIONS

| | REPUBLICAN PRIMARIES | | | DEMOCRATIC PRIMARIES | | |
|---|---|---|---|---|---|---|
| **Congressional District 8** | Lynn Westmoreland | 43,005 | 45.8% | Silvia Delamar | 21,934 | 100.0% |
| | Dylan Glenn | 35,276 | 37.6% | | | |
| | Mike Crotts | 10,596 | 11.3% | | | |
| | Tom Mills | 4,926 | 5.3% | | | |
| | TOTAL | 93,803 | | | | |
| | PRIMARY RUNOFF | | | | | |
| | Lynn Westmoreland | 34,250 | 55.5% | | | |
| | Dylan Glenn | 27,485 | 44.5% | | | |
| | TOTAL | 61,735 | | | | |
| **Congressional District 9** | Charlie Norwood* | 72,652 | 100.0% | Bob Ellis | 30,977 | 100.0% |
| **Congressional District 10** | Nathan Deal* | 65,148 | 100.0% | No Democratic candidate | | |
| **Congressional District 11** | Phil Gingrey* | 32,408 | 100.0% | Rick Crawford | 33,546 | 100.0% |
| **Congressional District 12** | Max Burns* | 29,962 | 100.0% | John Barrow | 28,110 | 51.5% |
| | | | | Doug Haines | 15,808 | 28.9% |
| | | | | Tony Center | 8,122 | 14.9% |
| | | | | Caine Cortellino | 2,585 | 4.7% |
| | | | | TOTAL | 54,625 | |
| **Congressional District 13** | No Republican candidate | | | David Scott* | 42,498 | 83.6% |
| | | | | William Ogletree | 8,340 | 16.4% |
| | | | | TOTAL | 50,838 | |

# HAWAII

## GOVERNOR
Linda Lingle (R). Elected 2002 to a four-year term.

## SENATORS (2 Democrats)
Daniel K. Akaka (D). Reelected 2000 to a six-year term. Previously elected 1994 and 1990 to fill out the remaining four years of the term vacated by the death of Senator Spark M. Matsunaga (D); had been appointed May 1990 to fill this vacancy.

Daniel K. Inouye (D). Reelected 2004 to a six-year term. Previously elected 1998, 1992, 1986, 1980, 1974, 1968, 1962.

## REPRESENTATIVES (2 Democrats)
1. Neil Abercrombie (D)          2. Ed Case (D)

## POSTWAR VOTE FOR PRESIDENT

| | | Republican | | Democratic | | | | Percentage | | | |
| | | | | | | | | Total Vote | | Major Vote | |
| Year | Total Vote | Vote | Candidate | Vote | Candidate | Other Vote | Plurality | Rep. | Dem. | Rep. | Dem. |
|---|---|---|---|---|---|---|---|---|---|---|---|
| 2004 | 429,013 | 194,191 | Bush, George W. | 231,708 | Kerry, John | 3,114 | 37,517 D | 45.3% | 54.0% | 45.6% | 54.4% |
| 2000** | 367,951 | 137,845 | Bush, George W. | 205,286 | Gore, Al | 24,820 | 67,441 D | 37.5% | 55.8% | 40.2% | 59.8% |
| 1996** | 360,120 | 113,943 | Dole, Bob | 205,012 | Clinton, Bill | 41,165 | 91,069 D | 31.6% | 56.9% | 35.7% | 64.3% |
| 1992** | 372,842 | 136,822 | Bush, George | 179,310 | Clinton, Bill | 56,710 | 42,488 D | 36.7% | 48.1% | 43.3% | 56.7% |
| 1988 | 354,461 | 158,625 | Bush, George | 192,364 | Dukakis, Michael S. | 3,472 | 33,739 D | 44.8% | 54.3% | 45.2% | 54.8% |
| 1984 | 335,846 | 185,050 | Reagan, Ronald | 147,154 | Mondale, Walter F. | 3,642 | 37,896 R | 55.1% | 43.8% | 55.7% | 44.3% |
| 1980** | 303,287 | 130,112 | Reagan, Ronald | 135,879 | Carter, Jimmy | 37,296 | 5,767 D | 42.9% | 44.8% | 48.9% | 51.1% |
| 1976 | 291,301 | 140,003 | Ford, Gerald R. | 147,375 | Carter, Jimmy | 3,923 | 7,372 D | 48.1% | 50.6% | 48.7% | 51.3% |
| 1972 | 270,274 | 168,865 | Nixon, Richard M. | 101,409 | McGovern, George S. | | 67,456 R | 62.5% | 37.5% | 62.5% | 37.5% |
| 1968** | 236,218 | 91,425 | Nixon, Richard M. | 141,324 | Humphrey, Hubert H. | 3,469 | 49,899 D | 38.7% | 59.8% | 39.3% | 60.7% |
| 1964 | 207,271 | 44,022 | Goldwater, Barry M. | 163,249 | Johnson, Lyndon B. | | 119,227 D | 21.2% | 78.8% | 21.2% | 78.8% |
| 1960 | 184,705 | 92,295 | Nixon, Richard M. | 92,410 | Kennedy, John F. | | 115 D | 50.0% | 50.0% | 50.0% | 50.0% |

In past elections, the other vote included: 2000 - 21,623 Green (Ralph Nader); 1996 - 27,358 Reform (Ross Perot); 1992 - 53,003 Independent (Perot); 1980 - 32,021 Independent (John Anderson); 1968 - 3,469 American Independent (George Wallace). Hawaii was formally admitted as a state in August 1959.

# HAWAII

## POSTWAR VOTE FOR GOVERNOR

| Year | Total Vote | Republican | | Democratic | | Other Vote | Plurality | Percentage | | | |
|---|---|---|---|---|---|---|---|---|---|---|---|
| | | Vote | Candidate | Vote | Candidate | | | Total Vote | | Major Vote | |
| | | | | | | | | Rep. | Dem. | Rep. | Dem. |
| 2002 | 382,110 | 197,009 | Lingle, Linda | 179,647 | Hirono, Mazie K. | 5,454 | 17,362 R | 51.6% | 47.0% | 52.3% | 47.7% |
| 1998 | 407,556 | 198,952 | Lingle, Linda | 204,206 | Cayetano, Benjamin J. | 4,398 | 5,254 D | 48.8% | 50.1% | 49.3% | 50.7% |
| 1994** | 369,013 | 107,908 | Saiki, Patricia | 134,978 | Cayetano, Benjamin J. | 126,127 | 21,820 D | 29.2% | 36.6% | 44.4% | 55.6% |
| 1990 | 340,132 | 131,310 | Hemmings, Fred | 203,491 | Waihee, John | 5,331 | 72,181 D | 38.6% | 59.8% | 39.2% | 60.8% |
| 1986 | 334,115 | 160,460 | Anderson, D. G. | 173,655 | Waihee, John | | 13,195 D | 48.0% | 52.0% | 48.0% | 52.0% |
| 1982** | 311,853 | 81,507 | Anderson, D. G. | 141,043 | Ariyoshi, George R. | 89,303 | 51,740 D | 26.1% | 45.2% | 36.6% | 63.4% |
| 1978 | 281,587 | 124,610 | Leopold, John | 153,394 | Ariyoshi, George R. | 3,583 | 28,784 D | 44.3% | 54.5% | 44.8% | 55.2% |
| 1974 | 249,650 | 113,388 | Crossley, Randolph | 136,262 | Ariyoshi, George R. | | 22,874 D | 45.4% | 54.6% | 45.4% | 54.6% |
| 1970 | 239,061 | 101,249 | King, Samuel P. | 137,812 | Burns, John A. | | 36,563 D | 42.4% | 57.6% | 42.4% | 57.6% |
| 1966 | 213,164 | 104,324 | Crossley, Randolph | 108,840 | Burns, John A. | | 4,516 D | 48.9% | 51.1% | 48.9% | 51.1% |
| 1962 | 196,015 | 81,707 | Quinn, William F. | 114,308 | Burns, John A. | | 32,601 D | 41.7% | 58.3% | 41.7% | 58.3% |
| 1959S | 168,662 | 86,213 | Quinn, William F. | 82,074 | Burns, John A. | 375 | 4,139 R | 51.1% | 48.7% | 51.2% | 48.8% |

In 1994 the Best Party candidate (Frank F. Fasi) ran second with 113,158 votes (30.7 percent of the total vote) and the Democratic plurality over the runner-up was 21,820. In 1982 Independent Democrat (Frank F. Fasi) ran second with 89,303 votes (28.6 percent of the total vote) and the Democratic plurality over the runner-up was 51,740. The 1959 election was for a short term pending the regular vote in 1962.

## POSTWAR VOTE FOR SENATOR

| Year | Total Vote | Republican | | Democratic | | Other Vote | Rep.-Dem. Plurality | Percentage | | | |
|---|---|---|---|---|---|---|---|---|---|---|---|
| | | Vote | Candidate | Vote | Candidate | | | Total Vote | | Major Vote | |
| | | | | | | | | Rep. | Dem. | Rep. | Dem. |
| 2004 | 415,347 | 87,172 | Cavasso, Cam | 313,629 | Inouye, Daniel K. | 14,546 | 226,457 D | 21.0% | 75.5% | 21.7% | 78.3% |
| 2000 | 345,623 | 84,701 | Carroll, John S. | 251,215 | Akaka, Daniel K. | 9,707 | 166,514 D | 24.5% | 72.7% | 25.2% | 74.8% |
| 1998 | 398,124 | 70,964 | Young, Crystal | 315,252 | Inouye, Daniel K. | 11,908 | 244,288 D | 17.8% | 79.2% | 18.4% | 81.6% |
| 1994 | 356,902 | 86,320 | Hustace, Maria M. | 256,189 | Akaka, Daniel K. | 14,393 | 169,869 D | 24.2% | 71.8% | 25.2% | 74.8% |
| 1992 | 363,662 | 97,928 | Reed, Rick | 208,266 | Inouye, Daniel K. | 57,468 | 110,338 D | 26.9% | 57.3% | 32.0% | 68.0% |
| 1990S | 349,666 | 155,978 | Saiki, Patricia | 188,901 | Akaka, Daniel K. | 4,787 | 32,923 D | 44.6% | 54.0% | 45.2% | 54.8% |
| 1988 | 323,876 | 66,987 | Hustace, Maria M. | 247,941 | Matsunaga, Spark M. | 8,948 | 180,954 D | 20.7% | 76.6% | 21.3% | 78.7% |
| 1986 | 328,797 | 86,910 | Hutchinson, Frank | 241,887 | Inouye, Daniel K. | | 154,977 D | 26.4% | 73.6% | 26.4% | 73.6% |
| 1982 | 306,410 | 52,071 | Brown, Clarence J. | 245,386 | Matsunaga, Spark M. | 8,953 | 193,315 D | 17.0% | 80.1% | 17.5% | 82.5% |
| 1980 | 288,006 | 53,068 | Brown, Cooper | 224,485 | Inouye, Daniel K. | 10,453 | 171,417 D | 18.4% | 77.9% | 19.1% | 80.9% |
| 1976 | 302,092 | 122,724 | Quinn, William F. | 162,305 | Matsunaga, Spark M. | 17,063 | 39,581 D | 40.6% | 53.7% | 43.1% | 56.9% |
| 1974 | 250,221 | | — | 207,454 | Inouye, Daniel K. | 42,767 | 207,454 D | | 82.9% | | 100.0% |
| 1970 | 240,760 | 124,163 | Fong, Hiram L. | 116,597 | Heftel, Cecil | | 7,566 R | 51.6% | 48.4% | 51.6% | 48.4% |
| 1968 | 226,927 | 34,008 | Thiessen, Wayne C. | 189,248 | Inouye, Daniel K. | 3,671 | 155,240 D | 15.0% | 83.4% | 15.2% | 84.8% |
| 1964 | 208,814 | 110,747 | Fong, Hiram L. | 96,789 | Gill, Thomas P. | 1,278 | 13,958 R | 53.0% | 46.4% | 53.4% | 46.6% |
| 1962 | 196,361 | 60,067 | Dillingham, Ben F. | 136,294 | Inouye, Daniel K. | | 76,227 D | 30.6% | 69.4% | 30.6% | 69.4% |
| 1959** | 164,808 | 87,161 | Fong, Hiram L. | 77,647 | Fasi, Frank F. | | 9,514 R | 52.9% | 47.1% | 52.9% | 47.1% |
| 1959S | 163,875 | 79,123 | Tsukiyama, W. C. | 83,700 | Long, Oren E. | 1,052 | 4,577 D | 48.3% | 51.1% | 48.6% | 51.4% |

The 1990 election was for a short term to fill a vacancy. The two 1959 elections were held to indeterminate terms, and the Senate later determined by lot that Senator Long would serve a short term, Senator Fong a long term.

# HAWAII

Congressional districts first established for elections held in 2002
2 members

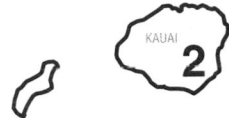

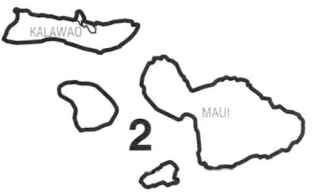

# HAWAII

## PRESIDENT 2004

| 2000 Census Population | County | Total Vote | Republican | Democratic | Other | Rep.-Dem. Plurality | Total Vote Rep. | Total Vote Dem. | Major Vote Rep. | Major Vote Dem. |
|---|---|---|---|---|---|---|---|---|---|---|
| 148,677 | HAWAII | 57,702 | 22,032 | 35,116 | 554 | 13,084 D | 38.2% | 60.9% | 38.6% | 61.4% |
| 876,156 | HONOLULU | 298,547 | 144,157 | 152,500 | 1,890 | 8,343 D | 48.3% | 51.1% | 48.6% | 51.4% |
| 58,463 | KAUAI | 24,876 | 9,740 | 14,916 | 220 | 5,176 D | 39.2% | 60.0% | 39.5% | 60.5% |
| 128,094 | MAUI | 47,430 | 18,187 | 28,803 | 440 | 10,616 D | 38.3% | 60.7% | 38.7% | 61.3% |
| | Overseas Ballots | 458 | 75 | 373 | 10 | 298 D | 16.4% | 81.4% | 16.7% | 83.3% |
| 1,211,537 | TOTAL | 429,013 | 194,191 | 231,708 | 3,114 | 37,517 D | 45.3% | 54.0% | 45.6% | 54.4% |

Note: The 2000 Census includes 147 people in Kalawao County; their votes are part of the Maui County returns.

# HAWAII

## SENATOR 2004

| 2000 Census Population | County | Total Vote | Republican | Democratic | Other | Rep.-Dem. Plurality | Total Vote Rep. | Total Vote Dem. | Major Vote Rep. | Major Vote Dem. |
|---|---|---|---|---|---|---|---|---|---|---|
| 148,677 | HAWAII | 55,945 | 11,583 | 41,840 | 2,522 | 30,257 D | 20.7% | 74.8% | 21.7% | 78.3% |
| 876,156 | HONOLULU | 289,758 | 62,027 | 218,464 | 9,267 | 156,437 D | 21.4% | 75.4% | 22.1% | 77.9% |
| 58,463 | KAUAI | 23,618 | 3,891 | 18,838 | 889 | 14,947 D | 16.5% | 79.8% | 17.1% | 82.9% |
| 128,094 | MAUI | 45,615 | 9,620 | 34,145 | 1,850 | 24,525 D | 21.1% | 74.9% | 22.0% | 78.0% |
| | Overseas Ballots | 411 | 51 | 342 | 18 | 291 D | 12.4% | 83.2% | 13.0% | 87.0% |
| 1,211,537 | TOTAL | 415,347 | 87,172 | 313,629 | 14,546 | 226,457 D | 21.0% | 75.5% | 21.7% | 78.3% |

Note: The 2000 Census includes 147 people in Kalawao County; their votes are part of the Maui County returns.

# HAWAII

## HOUSE OF REPRESENTATIVES

| CD | Year | Total Vote | Republican Vote | Republican Candidate | Democratic Vote | Democratic Candidate | Other Vote | Rep.-Dem. Plurality | Total Vote Rep. | Total Vote Dem. | Major Vote Rep. | Major Vote Dem. |
|---|---|---|---|---|---|---|---|---|---|---|---|---|
| 1 | 2004 | 204,181 | 69,371 | Tanonaka, Dalton | 128,567 | Abercrombie, Neil* | 6,243 | 59,196 D | 34.0% | 63.0% | 35.0% | 65.0% |
| 1 | 2002 | 180,733 | 45,032 | Terry, Mark | 131,673 | Abercrombie, Neil* | 4,028 | 86,641 D | 24.9% | 72.9% | 25.5% | 74.5% |
| 2 | 2004 | 212,389 | 79,072 | Gabbard, Mike | 133,317 | Case, Ed* | | 54,245 D | 37.2% | 62.8% | 37.2% | 62.8% |
| 2 | 2002 | 179,251 | 71,661 | McDermott, Bob | 100,671 | Mink, Patsy T.* | 6,919 | 29,010 D | 40.0% | 56.2% | 41.6% | 58.4% |
| Total | 2004 | 416,570 | 148,443 | | 261,884 | | 6,243 | 113,441 D | 35.6% | 62.9% | 36.2% | 63.8% |
| Total | 2002 | 359,984 | 116,693 | | 232,344 | | 10,947 | 115,651 D | 32.4% | 64.5% | 33.4% | 66.6% |

An asterisk (*) denotes incumbent.

# HAWAII

## GENERAL AND PRIMARY ELECTIONS

## 2004 GENERAL ELECTIONS

**President**     Other vote was 1,737 Green (David Cobb); 1,377 Libertarian (Michael Badnarik).

**Senator**     Other vote was 9,269 Nonpartisan (Jim Brewer); 5,277 Libertarian (Jeff Mallan).

**House**     Other vote was:

  CD 1     6,243 Libertarian (Elyssa "Erin O'Bryn" Young).
  CD 2

## 2004 PRIMARY ELECTIONS

**Primary**     September 18, 2004     **Registration**     626,120     No Party Registration
                                          (as of Sept. 18, 2004)

**Primary Type**     Open—Registered voters could participate in the party primary of their choice.

Note:   An asterisk (*) denotes incumbent.

| | REPUBLICAN PRIMARIES | | | DEMOCRATIC PRIMARIES | | |
|---|---|---|---|---|---|---|
| **Senator** | Cam Cavasso | 21,645 | 49.2% | Daniel K. Inouye* | 157,367 | 93.8% |
| | Rich Payne | 9,630 | 21.9% | Brian Evans | 8,051 | 4.8% |
| | Jay Friedheim | 7,028 | 16.0% | Eddie Yoon | 2,437 | 1.5% |
| | James R. DeLuze | 5,653 | 12.9% | | | |
| | TOTAL | 43,956 | | TOTAL | 167,855 | |
| **Congressional District 1** | Dalton Tanonaka | 26,475 | 100.0% | Neil Abercrombie* | 73,934 | 100.0% |
| **Congressional District 2** | Mike Gabbard | 21,698 | 83.3% | Ed Case* | 73,705 | 94.7% |
| | Inam Rahman | 2,102 | 8.1% | John Gentile | 4,121 | 5.3% |
| | Jonathan Treat | 1,134 | 4.4% | | | |
| | Miles Shiratori | 1,116 | 4.3% | | | |
| | TOTAL | 26,050 | | TOTAL | 77,826 | |

# IDAHO

## GOVERNOR
Dirk Kempthorne (R). Reelected 2002 to a four-year term. Previously elected 1998.

## SENATORS (2 Republicans)
Larry E. Craig (R). Reelected 2002 to a six-year term. Previously elected 1996, 1990.

Michael D. Crapo (R). Reelected 2004 to a six-year term. Previously elected 1998.

## REPRESENTATIVES (2 Republicans)
1. C. L. "Butch" Otter (R)        2. Mike Simpson (R)

## POSTWAR VOTE FOR PRESIDENT

| Year | Total Vote | Republican Vote | Republican Candidate | Democratic Vote | Democratic Candidate | Other Vote | Plurality | Total Vote Rep. | Total Vote Dem. | Major Vote Rep. | Major Vote Dem. |
|------|-----------|-----------------|---------------------|-----------------|---------------------|-----------|-----------|------|------|------|------|
| 2004 | 598,447 | 409,235 | Bush, George W. | 181,098 | Kerry, John | 8,114 | 228,137 R | 68.4% | 30.3% | 69.3% | 30.7% |
| 2000** | 501,621 | 336,937 | Bush, George W. | 138,637 | Gore, Al | 26,047 | 198,300 R | 67.2% | 27.6% | 70.8% | 29.2% |
| 1996** | 491,719 | 256,595 | Dole, Bob | 165,443 | Clinton, Bill | 69,681 | 91,152 R | 52.2% | 33.6% | 60.8% | 39.2% |
| 1992** | 482,142 | 202,645 | Bush, George | 137,013 | Clinton, Bill | 142,484 | 65,632 R | 42.0% | 28.4% | 59.7% | 40.3% |
| 1988 | 408,968 | 253,881 | Bush, George | 147,272 | Dukakis, Michael S. | 7,815 | 106,609 R | 62.1% | 36.0% | 63.3% | 36.7% |
| 1984 | 411,144 | 297,523 | Reagan, Ronald | 108,510 | Mondale, Walter F. | 5,111 | 189,013 R | 72.4% | 26.4% | 73.3% | 26.7% |
| 1980** | 437,431 | 290,699 | Reagan, Ronald | 110,192 | Carter, Jimmy | 36,540 | 180,507 R | 66.5% | 25.2% | 72.5% | 27.5% |
| 1976 | 344,071 | 204,151 | Ford, Gerald R. | 126,549 | Carter, Jimmy | 13,371 | 77,602 R | 59.3% | 36.8% | 61.7% | 38.3% |
| 1972** | 310,379 | 199,384 | Nixon, Richard M. | 80,826 | McGovern, George S. | 30,169 | 118,558 R | 64.2% | 26.0% | 71.2% | 28.8% |
| 1968** | 291,183 | 165,369 | Nixon, Richard M. | 89,273 | Humphrey, Hubert H. | 36,541 | 76,096 R | 56.8% | 30.7% | 64.9% | 35.1% |
| 1964 | 292,477 | 143,557 | Goldwater, Barry M. | 148,920 | Johnson, Lyndon B. | | 5,363 D | 49.1% | 50.9% | 49.1% | 50.9% |
| 1960 | 300,450 | 161,597 | Nixon, Richard M. | 138,853 | Kennedy, John F. | | 22,744 R | 53.8% | 46.2% | 53.8% | 46.2% |
| 1956 | 272,989 | 166,979 | Eisenhower, Dwight D. | 105,868 | Stevenson, Adlai E. | 142 | 61,111 R | 61.2% | 38.8% | 61.2% | 38.8% |
| 1952 | 276,254 | 180,707 | Eisenhower, Dwight D. | 95,081 | Stevenson, Adlai E. | 466 | 85,626 R | 65.4% | 34.4% | 65.5% | 34.5% |
| 1948 | 214,816 | 101,514 | Dewey, Thomas E. | 107,370 | Truman, Harry S. | 5,932 | 5,856 D | 47.3% | 50.0% | 48.6% | 51.4% |

In past elections, the other vote included: 2000 - 12,292 Green (Ralph Nader); 1996 - 62,518 Reform (Ross Perot); 1992 - 130,395 Independent (Perot); 1980 - 27,058 Independent (John Anderson); 1972 - 28,869 American (John Schmitz); 1968 - 36,541 American Independent (George Wallace).

# IDAHO

## POSTWAR VOTE FOR GOVERNOR

| Year | Total Vote | Republican Vote | Republican Candidate | Democratic Vote | Democratic Candidate | Other Vote | Rep.-Dem. Plurality | Total Vote Rep. | Total Vote Dem. | Major Vote Rep. | Major Vote Dem. |
|---|---|---|---|---|---|---|---|---|---|---|---|
| 2002 | 411,477 | 231,566 | Kempthorne, Dirk | 171,711 | Brady, Jerry M. | 8,200 | 59,855 R | 56.3% | 41.7% | 57.4% | 42.6% |
| 1998 | 381,248 | 258,095 | Kempthorne, Dirk | 110,815 | Huntley, Robert C. | 12,338 | 147,280 R | 67.7% | 29.1% | 70.0% | 30.0% |
| 1994 | 413,346 | 216,123 | Batt, Phil | 181,363 | EchoHawk, Larry | 15,860 | 34,760 R | 52.3% | 43.9% | 54.4% | 45.6% |
| 1990 | 320,610 | 101,937 | Fairchild, Roger | 218,673 | Andrus, Cecil D. | | 116,736 D | 31.8% | 68.2% | 31.8% | 68.2% |
| 1986 | 387,426 | 189,794 | Leroy, David H. | 193,429 | Andrus, Cecil D. | 4,203 | 3,635 D | 49.0% | 49.9% | 49.5% | 50.5% |
| 1982 | 326,522 | 161,157 | Batt, Philip | 165,365 | Evans, John V. | | 4,208 D | 49.4% | 50.6% | 49.4% | 50.6% |
| 1978 | 288,566 | 114,149 | Larsen, Allan | 169,540 | Evans, John V. | 4,877 | 55,391 D | 39.6% | 58.8% | 40.2% | 59.8% |
| 1974 | 259,632 | 68,731 | Murphy, Jack M. | 184,142 | Andrus, Cecil D. | 6,759 | 115,411 D | 26.5% | 70.9% | 27.2% | 72.8% |
| 1970 | 245,112 | 117,108 | Samuelson, Don | 128,004 | Andrus, Cecil D. | | 10,896 D | 47.8% | 52.2% | 47.8% | 52.2% |
| 1966 | 252,593 | 104,586 | Samuelson, Don | 93,744 | Andrus, Cecil D. | 54,263 | 10,842 R | 41.4% | 37.1% | 52.7% | 47.3% |
| 1962 | 255,454 | 139,578 | Smylie, Robert E. | 115,876 | Smith, Vernon K. | | 23,702 R | 54.6% | 45.4% | 54.6% | 45.4% |
| 1958 | 239,046 | 121,810 | Smylie, Robert E. | 117,236 | Derr, A. M. | | 4,574 R | 51.0% | 49.0% | 51.0% | 49.0% |
| 1954 | 228,685 | 124,038 | Smylie, Robert E. | 104,647 | Hamilton, Clark | | 19,391 R | 54.2% | 45.8% | 54.2% | 45.8% |
| 1950 | 204,792 | 107,642 | Jordan, Len B. | 97,150 | Wright, Calvin E. | | 10,492 R | 52.6% | 47.4% | 52.6% | 47.4% |
| 1946 | 181,364 | 102,233 | Robins, C. A. | 79,131 | Williams, Arnold | | 23,102 R | 56.4% | 43.6% | 56.4% | 43.6% |

## POSTWAR VOTE FOR SENATOR

| Year | Total Vote | Republican Vote | Republican Candidate | Democratic Vote | Democratic Candidate | Other Vote | Rep.-Dem. Plurality | Total Vote Rep. | Total Vote Dem. | Major Vote Rep. | Major Vote Dem. |
|---|---|---|---|---|---|---|---|---|---|---|---|
| 2004** | 503,932 | 499,796 | Crapo, Michael D. | - | | 4,136 | 499,796 R | 99.2% | | 100.0% | |
| 2002 | 408,544 | 266,215 | Craig, Larry E. | 132,975 | Blinken, Alan | 9,354 | 133,240 R | 65.2% | 32.5% | 66.7% | 33.3% |
| 1998 | 378,174 | 262,966 | Crapo, Michael D. | 107,375 | Mauk, Bill | 7,833 | 155,591 R | 69.5% | 28.4% | 71.0% | 29.0% |
| 1996 | 497,233 | 283,532 | Craig, Larry E. | 198,422 | Minnick, Walt | 15,279 | 85,110 R | 57.0% | 39.9% | 58.8% | 41.2% |
| 1992 | 478,522 | 270,468 | Kempthorne, Dirk | 208,036 | Stallings, Richard | 18 | 62,432 R | 56.5% | 43.5% | 56.5% | 43.5% |
| 1990 | 315,936 | 193,641 | Craig, Larry E. | 122,295 | Twilegar, Ron J. | | 71,346 R | 61.3% | 38.7% | 61.3% | 38.7% |
| 1986 | 382,024 | 196,958 | Symms, Steven D. | 185,066 | Evans, John V. | | 11,892 R | 51.6% | 48.4% | 51.6% | 48.4% |
| 1984 | 406,168 | 293,193 | McClure, James A. | 105,591 | Busch, Peter M. | 7,384 | 187,602 R | 72.2% | 26.0% | 73.5% | 26.5% |
| 1980 | 439,647 | 218,701 | Symms, Steven D. | 214,439 | Church, Frank | 6,507 | 4,262 R | 49.7% | 48.8% | 50.5% | 49.5% |
| 1978 | 284,047 | 194,412 | McClure, James A. | 89,635 | Jensen, Dwight | | 104,777 R | 68.4% | 31.6% | 68.4% | 31.6% |
| 1974 | 258,847 | 109,072 | Smith, Robert L. | 145,140 | Church, Frank | 4,635 | 36,068 D | 42.1% | 56.1% | 42.9% | 57.1% |
| 1972 | 309,602 | 161,804 | McClure, James A. | 140,913 | Davis, William E. | 6,885 | 20,891 R | 52.3% | 45.5% | 53.5% | 46.5% |
| 1968 | 287,876 | 114,394 | Hansen, George V. | 173,482 | Church, Frank | | 59,088 D | 39.7% | 60.3% | 39.7% | 60.3% |
| 1966 | 252,456 | 139,819 | Jordan, Len B. | 112,637 | Harding, Ralph R. | | 27,182 R | 55.4% | 44.6% | 55.4% | 44.6% |
| 1962 | 258,786 | 117,129 | Hawley, Jack | 141,657 | Church, Frank | | 24,528 D | 45.3% | 54.7% | 45.3% | 54.7% |
| 1962S | 257,677 | 131,279 | Jordan, Len B. | 126,398 | Pfost, Gracie | | 4,881 R | 50.9% | 49.1% | 50.9% | 49.1% |
| 1960 | 292,096 | 152,648 | Dworshak, Henry C. | 139,448 | McLaughlin, Bob | | 13,200 R | 52.3% | 47.7% | 52.3% | 47.7% |
| 1956 | 265,292 | 102,781 | Welker, Herman | 149,096 | Church, Frank | 13,415 | 46,315 D | 38.7% | 56.2% | 40.8% | 59.2% |
| 1954 | 226,408 | 142,269 | Dworshak, Henry C. | 84,139 | Taylor, Glen H. | | 58,130 R | 62.8% | 37.2% | 62.8% | 37.2% |
| 1950 | 201,417 | 124,237 | Welker, Herman | 77,180 | Clark, D. Worth | | 47,057 R | 61.7% | 38.3% | 61.7% | 38.3% |
| 1950S | 201,970 | 104,068 | Dworshak, Henry C. | 97,902 | Burtenshaw, Claude | | 6,166 R | 51.5% | 48.5% | 51.5% | 48.5% |
| 1948 | 214,188 | 103,868 | Dworshak, Henry C. | 107,000 | Miller, Bert H. | 3,320 | 3,132 D | 48.5% | 50.0% | 49.3% | 50.7% |
| 1946S | 180,152 | 105,523 | Dworshak, Henry C. | 74,629 | Donart, George E. | | 30,894 R | 58.6% | 41.4% | 58.6% | 41.4% |

In 2004 there was no candidate on the Democratic line. A write-in candidate, who was a Democrat, received 4,136 votes, which are listed in the other vote column. One each of the 1962 and 1950 elections and the 1946 election were for short terms to fill vacancies.

# IDAHO

Congressional districts first established for elections held in 2002
2 members

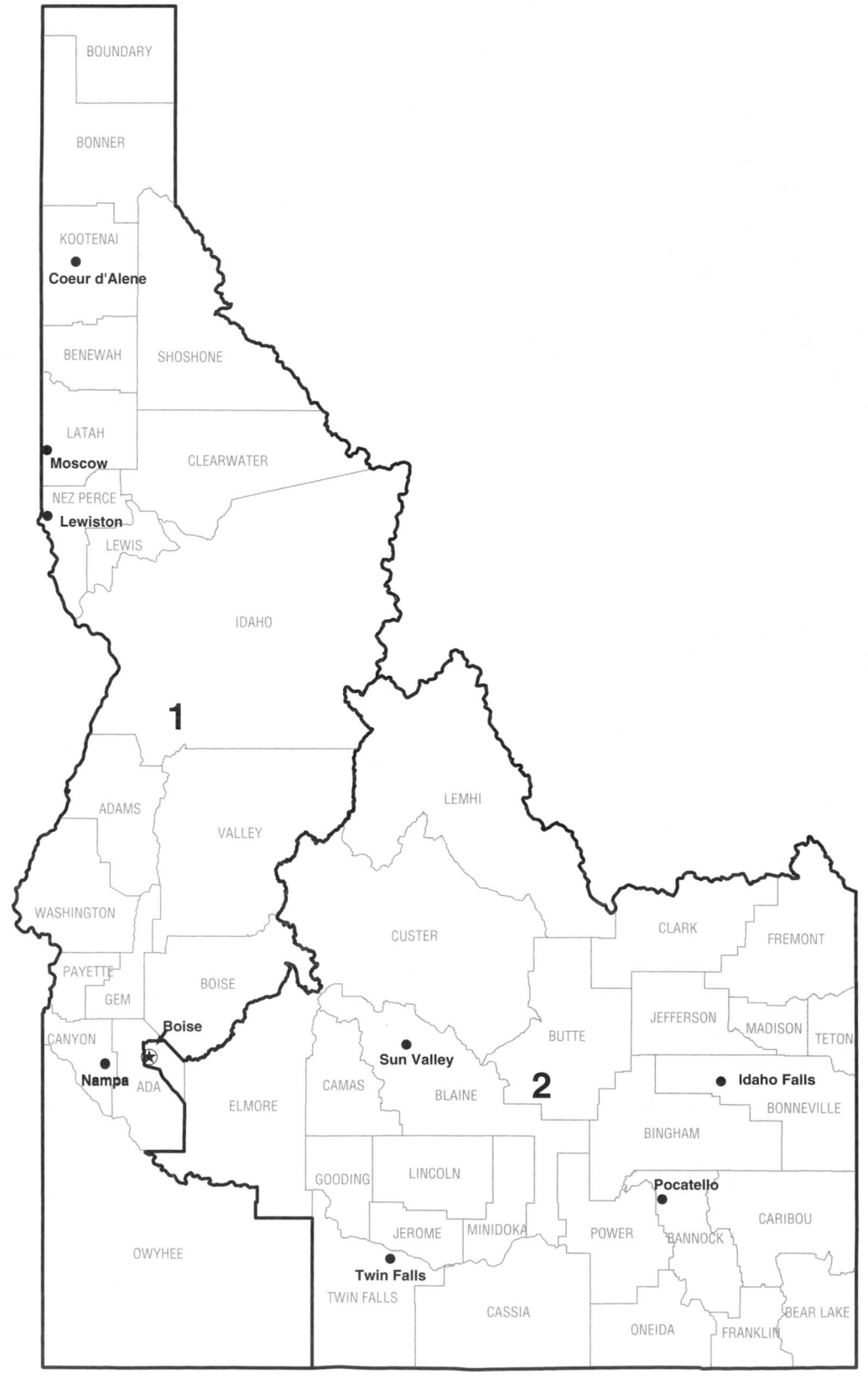

# IDAHO

## PRESIDENT 2004

| 2000 Census Population | County | Total Vote | Republican | Democratic | Other | Rep.-Dem. Plurality | | Percentage Total Vote | | Major Vote | |
|---|---|---|---|---|---|---|---|---|---|---|---|
| | | | | | | | | Rep. | Dem. | Rep. | Dem. |
| 300,904 | ADA | 155,030 | 94,641 | 58,523 | 1,866 | 36,118 | R | 61.0% | 37.7% | 61.8% | 38.2% |
| 3,476 | ADAMS | 2,063 | 1,468 | 555 | 40 | 913 | R | 71.2% | 26.9% | 72.6% | 27.4% |
| 75,565 | BANNOCK | 34,844 | 21,479 | 12,903 | 462 | 8,576 | R | 61.6% | 37.0% | 62.5% | 37.5% |
| 6,411 | BEAR LAKE | 3,040 | 2,506 | 494 | 40 | 2,012 | R | 82.4% | 16.3% | 83.5% | 16.5% |
| 9,171 | BENEWAH | 4,050 | 2,823 | 1,148 | 79 | 1,675 | R | 69.7% | 28.3% | 71.1% | 28.9% |
| 41,735 | BINGHAM | 16,565 | 12,734 | 3,605 | 226 | 9,129 | R | 76.9% | 21.8% | 77.9% | 22.1% |
| 18,991 | BLAINE | 10,147 | 4,034 | 5,992 | 121 | 1,958 | D | 39.8% | 59.1% | 40.2% | 59.8% |
| 6,670 | BOISE | 3,527 | 2,501 | 970 | 56 | 1,531 | R | 70.9% | 27.5% | 72.1% | 27.9% |
| 36,835 | BONNER | 17,684 | 10,697 | 6,649 | 338 | 4,048 | R | 60.5% | 37.6% | 61.7% | 38.3% |
| 82,522 | BONNEVILLE | 38,871 | 30,048 | 8,356 | 467 | 21,692 | R | 77.3% | 21.5% | 78.2% | 21.8% |
| 9,871 | BOUNDARY | 4,379 | 3,012 | 1,268 | 99 | 1,744 | R | 68.8% | 29.0% | 70.4% | 29.6% |
| 2,899 | BUTTE | 1,406 | 1,077 | 321 | 8 | 756 | R | 76.6% | 22.8% | 77.0% | 23.0% |
| 991 | CAMAS | 595 | 450 | 139 | 6 | 311 | R | 75.6% | 23.4% | 76.4% | 23.6% |
| 131,441 | CANYON | 55,698 | 41,599 | 13,415 | 684 | 28,184 | R | 74.7% | 24.1% | 75.6% | 24.4% |
| 7,304 | CARIBOU | 3,281 | 2,753 | 491 | 37 | 2,262 | R | 83.9% | 15.0% | 84.9% | 15.1% |
| 21,416 | CASSIA | 7,821 | 6,562 | 1,153 | 106 | 5,409 | R | 83.9% | 14.7% | 85.1% | 14.9% |
| 1,022 | CLARK | 353 | 302 | 46 | 5 | 256 | R | 85.6% | 13.0% | 86.8% | 13.2% |
| 8,930 | CLEARWATER | 4,034 | 2,839 | 1,117 | 78 | 1,722 | R | 70.4% | 27.7% | 71.8% | 28.2% |
| 4,342 | CUSTER | 2,358 | 1,762 | 559 | 37 | 1,203 | R | 74.7% | 23.7% | 75.9% | 24.1% |
| 29,130 | ELMORE | 8,061 | 6,011 | 1,959 | 91 | 4,052 | R | 74.6% | 24.3% | 75.4% | 24.6% |
| 11,329 | FRANKLIN | 5,054 | 4,527 | 456 | 71 | 4,071 | R | 89.6% | 9.0% | 90.8% | 9.2% |
| 11,819 | FREMONT | 5,769 | 4,965 | 741 | 63 | 4,224 | R | 86.1% | 12.8% | 87.0% | 13.0% |
| 15,181 | GEM | 7,134 | 5,416 | 1,628 | 90 | 3,788 | R | 75.9% | 22.8% | 76.9% | 23.1% |
| 14,155 | GOODING | 5,325 | 3,973 | 1,278 | 74 | 2,695 | R | 74.6% | 24.0% | 75.7% | 24.3% |
| 15,511 | IDAHO | 7,970 | 6,017 | 1,689 | 264 | 4,328 | R | 75.5% | 21.2% | 78.1% | 21.9% |
| 19,155 | JEFFERSON | 8,906 | 7,703 | 1,084 | 119 | 6,619 | R | 86.5% | 12.2% | 87.7% | 12.3% |
| 18,342 | JEROME | 6,580 | 5,177 | 1,344 | 59 | 3,833 | R | 78.7% | 20.4% | 79.4% | 20.6% |
| 108,685 | KOOTENAI | 54,603 | 36,173 | 17,584 | 846 | 18,589 | R | 66.2% | 32.2% | 67.3% | 32.7% |
| 34,935 | LATAH | 17,553 | 8,686 | 8,430 | 437 | 256 | R | 49.5% | 48.0% | 50.7% | 49.3% |
| 7,806 | LEMHI | 4,055 | 3,079 | 915 | 61 | 2,164 | R | 75.9% | 22.6% | 77.1% | 22.9% |
| 3,747 | LEWIS | 1,820 | 1,359 | 440 | 21 | 919 | R | 74.7% | 24.2% | 75.5% | 24.5% |
| 4,044 | LINCOLN | 1,876 | 1,388 | 466 | 22 | 922 | R | 74.0% | 24.8% | 74.9% | 25.1% |
| 27,467 | MADISON | 11,637 | 10,693 | 826 | 118 | 9,867 | R | 91.9% | 7.1% | 92.8% | 7.2% |
| 20,174 | MINIDOKA | 7,201 | 5,797 | 1,331 | 73 | 4,466 | R | 80.5% | 18.5% | 81.3% | 18.7% |
| 37,410 | NEZ PERCE | 17,700 | 11,009 | 6,476 | 215 | 4,533 | R | 62.2% | 36.6% | 63.0% | 37.0% |
| 4,125 | ONEIDA | 2,133 | 1,789 | 304 | 40 | 1,485 | R | 83.9% | 14.3% | 85.5% | 14.5% |
| 10,644 | OWYHEE | 3,590 | 2,859 | 685 | 46 | 2,174 | R | 79.6% | 19.1% | 80.7% | 19.3% |
| 20,578 | PAYETTE | 8,181 | 6,256 | 1,848 | 77 | 4,408 | R | 76.5% | 22.6% | 77.2% | 22.8% |
| 7,538 | POWER | 2,958 | 2,105 | 829 | 24 | 1,276 | R | 71.2% | 28.0% | 71.7% | 28.3% |
| 13,771 | SHOSHONE | 5,337 | 2,922 | 2,331 | 84 | 591 | R | 54.7% | 43.7% | 55.6% | 44.4% |
| 5,999 | TETON | 3,690 | 2,235 | 1,416 | 39 | 819 | R | 60.6% | 38.4% | 61.2% | 38.8% |
| 64,284 | TWIN FALLS | 26,435 | 19,672 | 6,458 | 305 | 13,214 | R | 74.4% | 24.4% | 75.3% | 24.7% |
| 7,651 | VALLEY | 4,774 | 2,863 | 1,843 | 68 | 1,020 | R | 60.0% | 38.6% | 60.8% | 39.2% |
| 9,977 | WASHINGTON | 4,359 | 3,274 | 1,033 | 52 | 2,241 | R | 75.1% | 23.7% | 76.0% | 24.0% |
| 1,293,953 | TOTAL | 598,447 | 409,235 | 181,098 | 8,114 | 228,137 | R | 68.4% | 30.3% | 69.3% | 30.7% |

# IDAHO

## SENATOR 2004

| 2000 Census Population | County | Total Vote | Republican | Democratic | Other | Rep.-Dem. Plurality | Percentage Total Vote Rep. | Dem. | Major Vote Rep. | Dem. |
|---|---|---|---|---|---|---|---|---|---|---|
| 300,904 | ADA | 127,793 | 127,353 | | 440 | 127,353 R | 99.7% | | 100.0% | |
| 3,476 | ADAMS | 1,634 | 1,633 | | 1 | 1,633 R | 99.9% | | 100.0% | |
| 75,565 | BANNOCK | 29,071 | 28,592 | | 479 | 28,592 R | 98.4% | | 100.0% | |
| 6,411 | BEAR LAKE | 2,711 | 2,706 | | 5 | 2,706 R | 99.8% | | 100.0% | |
| 9,171 | BENEWAH | 3,285 | 3,205 | | 80 | 3,205 R | 97.6% | | 100.0% | |
| 41,735 | BINGHAM | 14,851 | 14,804 | | 47 | 14,804 R | 99.7% | | 100.0% | |
| 18,991 | BLAINE | 7,235 | 7,196 | | 39 | 7,196 R | 99.5% | | 100.0% | |
| 6,670 | BOISE | 2,943 | 2,919 | | 24 | 2,919 R | 99.2% | | 100.0% | |
| 36,835 | BONNER | 13,374 | 13,137 | | 237 | 13,137 R | 98.2% | | 100.0% | |
| 82,522 | BONNEVILLE | 34,733 | 34,311 | | 422 | 34,311 R | 98.8% | | 100.0% | |
| 9,871 | BOUNDARY | 3,435 | 3,399 | | 36 | 3,399 R | 99.0% | | 100.0% | |
| 2,899 | BUTTE | 1,200 | 1,187 | | 13 | 1,187 R | 98.9% | | 100.0% | |
| 991 | CAMAS | 501 | 499 | | 2 | 499 R | 99.6% | | 100.0% | |
| 131,441 | CANYON | 48,335 | 48,271 | | 64 | 48,271 R | 99.9% | | 100.0% | |
| 7,304 | CARIBOU | 3,002 | 2,994 | | 8 | 2,994 R | 99.7% | | 100.0% | |
| 21,416 | CASSIA | 7,063 | 7,046 | | 17 | 7,046 R | 99.8% | | 100.0% | |
| 1,022 | CLARK | 324 | 324 | | | 324 R | 100.0% | | 100.0% | |
| 8,930 | CLEARWATER | 3,313 | 3,307 | | 6 | 3,307 R | 99.8% | | 100.0% | |
| 4,342 | CUSTER | 1,957 | 1,937 | | 20 | 1,937 R | 99.0% | | 100.0% | |
| 29,130 | ELMORE | 6,932 | 6,926 | | 6 | 6,926 R | 99.9% | | 100.0% | |
| 11,329 | FRANKLIN | 4,764 | 4,762 | | 2 | 4,762 R | 100.0% | | 100.0% | |
| 11,819 | FREMONT | 5,493 | 5,478 | | 15 | 5,478 R | 99.7% | | 100.0% | |
| 15,181 | GEM | 6,138 | 6,126 | | 12 | 6,126 R | 99.8% | | 100.0% | |
| 14,155 | GOODING | 4,744 | 4,708 | | 36 | 4,708 R | 99.2% | | 100.0% | |
| 15,511 | IDAHO | 6,603 | 6,550 | | 53 | 6,550 R | 99.2% | | 100.0% | |
| 19,155 | JEFFERSON | 8,376 | 8,352 | | 24 | 8,352 R | 99.7% | | 100.0% | |
| 18,342 | JEROME | 5,870 | 5,718 | | 152 | 5,718 R | 97.4% | | 100.0% | |
| 108,685 | KOOTENAI | 44,687 | 43,986 | | 701 | 43,986 R | 98.4% | | 100.0% | |
| 34,935 | LATAH | 13,503 | 12,913 | | 590 | 12,913 R | 95.6% | | 100.0% | |
| 7,806 | LEMHI | 3,392 | 3,333 | | 59 | 3,333 R | 98.3% | | 100.0% | |
| 3,747 | LEWIS | 1,514 | 1,506 | | 8 | 1,506 R | 99.5% | | 100.0% | |
| 4,044 | LINCOLN | 1,635 | 1,621 | | 14 | 1,621 R | 99.1% | | 100.0% | |
| 27,467 | MADISON | 11,028 | 11,004 | | 24 | 11,004 R | 99.8% | | 100.0% | |
| 20,174 | MINIDOKA | 6,542 | 6,529 | | 13 | 6,529 R | 99.8% | | 100.0% | |
| 37,410 | NEZ PERCE | 14,417 | 14,353 | | 64 | 14,353 R | 99.6% | | 100.0% | |
| 4,125 | ONEIDA | 1,824 | 1,824 | | | 1,824 R | 100.0% | | 100.0% | |
| 10,644 | OWYHEE | 3,070 | 3,067 | | 3 | 3,067 R | 99.9% | | 100.0% | |
| 20,578 | PAYETTE | 7,160 | 7,150 | | 10 | 7,150 R | 99.9% | | 100.0% | |
| 7,538 | POWER | 2,434 | 2,429 | | 5 | 2,429 R | 99.8% | | 100.0% | |
| 13,771 | SHOSHONE | 4,206 | 4,182 | | 24 | 4,182 R | 99.4% | | 100.0% | |
| 5,999 | TETON | 2,783 | 2,777 | | 6 | 2,777 R | 99.8% | | 100.0% | |
| 64,284 | TWIN FALLS | 22,590 | 22,219 | | 371 | 22,219 R | 98.4% | | 100.0% | |
| 7,651 | VALLEY | 3,739 | 3,735 | | 4 | 3,735 R | 99.9% | | 100.0% | |
| 9,977 | WASHINGTON | 3,728 | 3,728 | | | 3,728 R | 100.0% | | 100.0% | |
| 1,293,953 | TOTAL | 503,932 | 499,796 | | 4,136 | 499,796 R | 99.2% | | 100.0% | |

Note: The Democratic Party did not field a Senate candidate on the Democratic line on the ballot, although the lone write-in candidate was a Democrat. His vote is listed in the "Other" column.

# IDAHO

## HOUSE OF REPRESENTATIVES

| CD | Year | Total Vote | Republican Vote | Republican Candidate | Democratic Vote | Democratic Candidate | Other Vote | Rep.-Dem. Plurality | Percentage Total Vote Rep. | Percentage Total Vote Dem. | Percentage Major Vote Rep. | Percentage Major Vote Dem. |
|---|---|---|---|---|---|---|---|---|---|---|---|---|
| 1 | 2004 | 298,589 | 207,662 | Otter, C. L. "Butch"* | 90,927 | Preston, Naomi | | 116,735 R | 69.5% | 30.5% | 69.5% | 30.5% |
| 1 | 2002 | 206,141 | 120,743 | Otter, C. L. "Butch"* | 80,269 | Richardson, Betty | 5,129 | 40,474 R | 58.6% | 38.9% | 60.1% | 39.9% |
| 2 | 2004 | 273,837 | 193,704 | Simpson, Mike* | 80,133 | Whitworth, Lin | | 113,571 R | 70.7% | 29.3% | 70.7% | 29.3% |
| 2 | 2002 | 198,882 | 135,605 | Simpson, Mike* | 57,769 | Kinghorn, Edward | 5,508 | 77,836 R | 68.2% | 29.0% | 70.1% | 29.9% |
| Total | 2004 | 572,426 | 401,366 | | 171,060 | | | 230,306 R | 70.1% | 29.9% | 70.1% | 29.9% |
| Total | 2002 | 405,023 | 256,348 | | 138,038 | | 10,637 | 118,310 R | 63.3% | 34.1% | 65.0% | 35.0% |

An asterisk (*) denotes incumbent.

# IDAHO

## GENERAL AND PRIMARY ELECTIONS

### 2004 GENERAL ELECTIONS

**President**   Other vote was 3,844 Libertarian (Michael Badnarik); 3,084 Constitution (Michael Peroutka); 1,115 write-in (Ralph Nader); 58 write-in (David Cobb); 9 write-in (John Joseph Kennedy); 3 write-in (Walter F. Brown); 1 write-in (Reverend Merepeace-msmere).

**Senator**   Other vote was 4,136 Democratic write-in (Scott F. McClure).

**House**   Other vote was:

    CD 1
    CD 2

### 2004 PRIMARY ELECTIONS

**Primary**   May 25, 2004          **Registration** (as of May 25, 2004)   642,011   No Party Registration

**Primary Type**   Open—Any registered voter could participate in either the Democratic or Republican primary.

Note:   An asterisk (*) denotes incumbent.

| | REPUBLICAN PRIMARIES | | | DEMOCRATIC PRIMARIES | | |
|---|---|---|---|---|---|---|
| President | George W. Bush* | 110,800 | 89.5% | John Kerry | 25,921 | 82.3% |
| | None of the Names Shown | 12,993 | 10.5% | None of the Names Shown | 2,479 | 7.9% |
| | Nancy Warrick (write-in) | 15 | | Dennis J. Kucinich | 1,568 | 5.0% |
| | | | | Al Sharpton | 927 | 2.9% |
| | | | | Lyndon H. LaRouche Jr. | 590 | 1.9% |
| | TOTAL | 123,808 | | TOTAL | 31,485 | |
| Senator | Michael D. Crapo* | 118,286 | 100.0% | No Democratic primary | | |
| Congressional District 1 | C.L. "Butch" Otter* | 48,986 | 78.5% | Naomi Preston | 13,250 | 100.0% |
| | Jim Pratt | 13,433 | 21.5% | | | |
| | TOTAL | 62,419 | | | | |
| Congressional District 2 | Mike Simpson* | 57,124 | 100.0% | Lin Whitworth | 12,491 | 100.0% |

# ILLINOIS

## GOVERNOR
Rod R. Blagojevich (D). Elected 2002 to a four-year term.

## SENATORS (2 Democrats)
Richard J. Durbin (D). Reelected 2002 to a six-year term. Previously elected 1996.

Barack Obama (D). Elected 2004 to a six-year term.

## REPRESENTATIVES (10 Democrats, 9 Republicans)
1. Bobby L. Rush (D)
2. Jesse L. Jackson Jr. (D)
3. Daniel Lipinski (D)
4. Luis V. Gutierrez (D)
5. Rahm Emanuel (D)
6. Henry J. Hyde (R)
7. Danny K. Davis (D)
8. Melissa Bean (D)
9. Jan Schakowsky (D)
10. Mark Steven Kirk (R)
11. Jerry Weller (R)
12. Jerry F. Costello (D)
13. Judy Biggert (R)
14. J. Dennis Hastert (R)
15. Timothy V. Johnson (R)
16. Donald Manzullo (R)
17. Lane Evans (D)
18. Ray LaHood (R)
19. John Shimkus (R)

## POSTWAR VOTE FOR PRESIDENT

| | | Republican | | Democratic | | Other | | Total Vote | | Major Vote | |
|---|---|---|---|---|---|---|---|---|---|---|---|
| Year | Total Vote | Vote | Candidate | Vote | Candidate | Vote | Plurality | Rep. | Dem. | Rep. | Dem. |
| 2004 | 5,274,322 | 2,345,946 | Bush, George W. | 2,891,550 | Kerry, John | 36,826 | 545,604 D | 44.5% | 54.8% | 44.8% | 55.2% |
| 2000** | 4,742,123 | 2,019,421 | Bush, George W. | 2,589,026 | Gore, Al | 133,676 | 569,605 D | 42.6% | 54.6% | 43.8% | 56.2% |
| 1996** | 4,311,391 | 1,587,021 | Dole, Bob | 2,341,744 | Clinton, Bill | 382,626 | 754,723 D | 36.8% | 54.3% | 40.4% | 59.6% |
| 1992** | 5,050,157 | 1,734,096 | Bush, George | 2,453,350 | Clinton, Bill | 862,711 | 719,254 D | 34.3% | 48.6% | 41.4% | 58.6% |
| 1988 | 4,559,120 | 2,310,939 | Bush, George | 2,215,940 | Dukakis, Michael S. | 32,241 | 94,999 R | 50.7% | 48.6% | 51.0% | 49.0% |
| 1984 | 4,819,088 | 2,707,103 | Reagan, Ronald | 2,086,499 | Mondale, Walter F. | 25,486 | 620,604 R | 56.2% | 43.3% | 56.5% | 43.5% |
| 1980** | 4,749,721 | 2,358,049 | Reagan, Ronald | 1,981,413 | Carter, Jimmy | 410,259 | 376,636 R | 49.6% | 41.7% | 54.3% | 45.7% |
| 1976 | 4,718,914 | 2,364,269 | Ford, Gerald R. | 2,271,295 | Carter, Jimmy | 83,350 | 92,974 R | 50.1% | 48.1% | 51.0% | 49.0% |
| 1972 | 4,723,236 | 2,788,179 | Nixon, Richard M. | 1,913,472 | McGovern, George S. | 21,585 | 874,707 R | 59.0% | 40.5% | 59.3% | 40.7% |
| 1968** | 4,619,749 | 2,174,774 | Nixon, Richard M. | 2,039,814 | Humphrey, Hubert H. | 405,161 | 134,960 R | 47.1% | 44.2% | 51.6% | 48.4% |
| 1964 | 4,702,841 | 1,905,946 | Goldwater, Barry M. | 2,796,833 | Johnson, Lyndon B. | 62 | 890,887 D | 40.5% | 59.5% | 40.5% | 59.5% |
| 1960 | 4,757,409 | 2,368,988 | Nixon, Richard M. | 2,377,846 | Kennedy, John F. | 10,575 | 8,858 D | 49.8% | 50.0% | 49.9% | 50.1% |
| 1956 | 4,407,407 | 2,623,327 | Eisenhower, Dwight D. | 1,775,682 | Stevenson, Adlai E. | 8,398 | 847,645 R | 59.5% | 40.3% | 59.6% | 40.4% |
| 1952 | 4,481,058 | 2,457,327 | Eisenhower, Dwight D. | 2,013,920 | Stevenson, Adlai E. | 9,811 | 443,407 R | 54.8% | 44.9% | 55.0% | 45.0% |
| 1948 | 3,984,046 | 1,961,103 | Dewey, Thomas E. | 1,994,715 | Truman, Harry S. | 28,228 | 33,612 D | 49.2% | 50.1% | 49.6% | 50.4% |

In past elections, the other vote included: 2000 - 103,759 Green (Ralph Nader); 1996 - 346,408 Reform (Ross Perot); 1992 - 840,515 Independent (Perot); 1980 - 346,754 Independent (John Anderson); 1968 - 390,958 American Independent (George Wallace).

# ILLINOIS

## POSTWAR VOTE FOR GOVERNOR

| Year | Total Vote | Republican Vote | Republican Candidate | Democratic Vote | Democratic Candidate | Other Vote | Rep.-Dem. Plurality | Total Vote Rep. | Total Vote Dem. | Major Vote Rep. | Major Vote Dem. |
|------|-----------|-----------------|----------------------|-----------------|----------------------|------------|---------------------|------|------|------|------|
| 2002 | 3,538,891 | 1,594,960 | Ryan, Jim | 1,847,040 | Blagojevich, Rod R. | 96,891 | 252,080 D | 45.1% | 52.2% | 46.3% | 53.7% |
| 1998 | 3,358,705 | 1,714,094 | Ryan, George H. | 1,594,191 | Poshard, Glenn | 50,420 | 119,903 R | 51.0% | 47.5% | 51.8% | 48.2% |
| 1994 | 3,106,566 | 1,984,318 | Edgar, Jim | 1,069,850 | Netsch, Dawn C. | 52,398 | 914,468 R | 63.9% | 34.4% | 65.0% | 35.0% |
| 1990 | 3,257,410 | 1,653,126 | Edgar, Jim | 1,569,217 | Hartigan, Neil F. | 35,067 | 83,909 R | 50.7% | 48.2% | 51.3% | 48.7% |
| 1986** | 3,143,978 | 1,655,849 | Thompson, James R. | 208,830 | [See note below] | 1,279,299 | 1,447,019 R | 52.7% | 6.6% | 88.8% | 11.2% |
| 1982 | 3,673,681 | 1,816,101 | Thompson, James R. | 1,811,027 | Stevenson, Adlai E., III | 46,553 | 5,074 R | 49.4% | 49.3% | 50.1% | 49.9% |
| 1978 | 3,150,095 | 1,859,684 | Thompson, James R. | 1,263,134 | Bakalis, Michael | 27,277 | 596,550 R | 59.0% | 40.1% | 59.6% | 40.4% |
| 1976S | 4,638,997 | 3,000,395 | Thompson, James R. | 1,610,258 | Howlett, Michael J. | 28,344 | 1,390,137 R | 64.7% | 34.7% | 65.1% | 34.9% |
| 1972 | 4,678,804 | 2,293,809 | Ogilvie, Richard B. | 2,371,303 | Walker, Daniel | 13,692 | 77,494 D | 49.0% | 50.7% | 49.2% | 50.8% |
| 1968 | 4,506,000 | 2,307,295 | Ogilvie, Richard B. | 2,179,501 | Shapiro, Samuel H. | 19,204 | 127,794 R | 51.2% | 48.4% | 51.4% | 48.6% |
| 1964 | 4,657,500 | 2,239,095 | Percy, Charles H. | 2,418,394 | Kerner, Otto | 11 | 179,299 D | 48.1% | 51.9% | 48.1% | 51.9% |
| 1960 | 4,674,187 | 2,070,479 | Stratton, William G. | 2,594,731 | Kerner, Otto | 8,977 | 524,252 D | 44.3% | 55.5% | 44.4% | 55.6% |
| 1956 | 4,314,611 | 2,171,786 | Stratton, William G. | 2,134,909 | Austin, Richard B. | 7,916 | 36,877 R | 50.3% | 49.5% | 50.4% | 49.6% |
| 1952 | 4,415,864 | 2,317,363 | Stratton, William G. | 2,089,721 | Dixon, Sherwood | 8,780 | 227,642 R | 52.5% | 47.3% | 52.6% | 47.4% |
| 1948 | 3,940,257 | 1,678,007 | Green, Dwight H. | 2,250,074 | Stevenson, Adlai E. | 12,176 | 572,067 D | 42.6% | 57.1% | 42.7% | 57.3% |

In 1986 there was no Democratic candidate for governor on the ballot. Mark Fairchild, a supporter of Lyndon H. LaRouche Jr., was the "paired" Democratic candidate for lieutenant governor and the Democratic vote above was cast for this ticket of "no name" and Fairchild. The other vote in this election included: 1,256,626 Illinois Solidarity (Adlai E. Stevenson III), which received 40.0 percent of the total vote and came in second. The 1976 vote was for a two-year term to permit shifting the election for governor to non-presidential years.

## POSTWAR VOTE FOR SENATOR

| Year | Total Vote | Republican Vote | Republican Candidate | Democratic Vote | Democratic Candidate | Other Vote | Rep.-Dem. Plurality | Total Vote Rep. | Total Vote Dem. | Major Vote Rep. | Major Vote Dem. |
|------|-----------|-----------------|----------------------|-----------------|----------------------|------------|---------------------|------|------|------|------|
| 2004 | 5,141,520 | 1,390,690 | Keyes, Alan | 3,597,456 | Obama, Barack | 153,374 | 2,206,766 D | 27.0% | 70.0% | 27.9% | 72.1% |
| 2002 | 3,486,851 | 1,325,703 | Durkin, Jim | 2,103,766 | Durbin, Richard J. | 57,382 | 778,063 D | 38.0% | 60.3% | 38.7% | 61.3% |
| 1998 | 3,394,521 | 1,709,041 | Fitzgerald, Peter G. | 1,610,496 | Moseley-Braun, Carol | 74,984 | 98,545 R | 50.3% | 47.4% | 51.5% | 48.5% |
| 1996 | 4,250,722 | 1,728,824 | Salvi, Al | 2,384,028 | Durbin, Richard J. | 137,870 | 655,204 D | 40.7% | 56.1% | 42.0% | 58.0% |
| 1992 | 4,939,558 | 2,126,833 | Williamson, Richard S. | 2,631,229 | Moseley-Braun, Carol | 181,496 | 504,396 D | 43.1% | 53.3% | 44.7% | 55.3% |
| 1990 | 3,251,005 | 1,135,628 | Martin, Lynn | 2,115,377 | Simon, Paul | | 979,749 D | 34.9% | 65.1% | 34.9% | 65.1% |
| 1986 | 3,122,883 | 1,053,734 | Koehler, Judy | 2,033,783 | Dixon, Alan J. | 35,366 | 980,049 D | 33.7% | 65.1% | 34.1% | 65.9% |
| 1984 | 4,787,473 | 2,308,039 | Percy, Charles H. | 2,397,303 | Simon, Paul | 82,131 | 89,264 D | 48.2% | 50.1% | 49.1% | 50.9% |
| 1980 | 4,580,029 | 1,946,296 | O'Neal, David C. | 2,565,302 | Dixon, Alan J. | 68,431 | 619,006 D | 42.5% | 56.0% | 43.1% | 56.9% |
| 1978 | 3,184,764 | 1,698,711 | Percy, Charles H. | 1,448,187 | Seith, Alex | 37,866 | 250,524 R | 53.3% | 45.5% | 54.0% | 46.0% |
| 1974 | 2,914,666 | 1,084,884 | Burditt, George M. | 1,811,496 | Stevenson, Adlai E., III | 18,286 | 726,612 D | 37.2% | 62.2% | 37.5% | 62.5% |
| 1972 | 4,608,380 | 2,867,078 | Percy, Charles H. | 1,721,031 | Pucinski, Roman C. | 20,271 | 1,146,047 R | 62.2% | 37.3% | 62.5% | 37.5% |
| 1970S | 3,599,272 | 1,519,718 | Smith, Ralph T. | 2,065,054 | Stevenson, Adlai E., III | 14,500 | 545,336 D | 42.2% | 57.4% | 42.4% | 57.6% |
| 1968 | 4,449,757 | 2,358,947 | Dirksen, Everett M. | 2,073,242 | Clark, William G. | 17,568 | 285,705 R | 53.0% | 46.6% | 53.2% | 46.8% |
| 1966 | 3,822,725 | 2,100,449 | Percy, Charles H. | 1,678,147 | Douglas, Paul H. | 44,129 | 422,302 R | 54.9% | 43.9% | 55.6% | 44.4% |
| 1962 | 3,709,216 | 1,961,202 | Dirksen, Everett M. | 1,748,007 | Yates, Sidney R. | 7 | 213,195 R | 52.9% | 47.1% | 52.9% | 47.1% |
| 1960 | 4,632,796 | 2,093,846 | Witwer, Samuel W. | 2,530,943 | Douglas, Paul H. | 8,007 | 437,097 D | 45.2% | 54.6% | 45.3% | 54.7% |
| 1956 | 4,264,830 | 2,307,352 | Dirksen, Everett M. | 1,949,883 | Stengel, Richard | 7,595 | 357,469 R | 54.1% | 45.7% | 54.2% | 45.8% |
| 1954 | 3,368,025 | 1,563,683 | Meek, Joseph T. | 1,804,338 | Douglas, Paul H. | 4 | 240,655 D | 46.4% | 53.6% | 46.4% | 53.6% |
| 1950 | 3,622,673 | 1,951,984 | Dirksen, Everett M. | 1,657,630 | Lucas, Scott W. | 13,059 | 294,354 R | 53.9% | 45.8% | 54.1% | 45.9% |
| 1948 | 3,900,285 | 1,740,026 | Brooks, C. Wayland | 2,147,754 | Douglas, Paul H. | 12,505 | 407,728 D | 44.6% | 55.1% | 44.8% | 55.2% |

The 1970 election was for a short term to fill a vacancy.

156

# ILLINOIS

Congressional districts first established for elections held in 2002
19 members

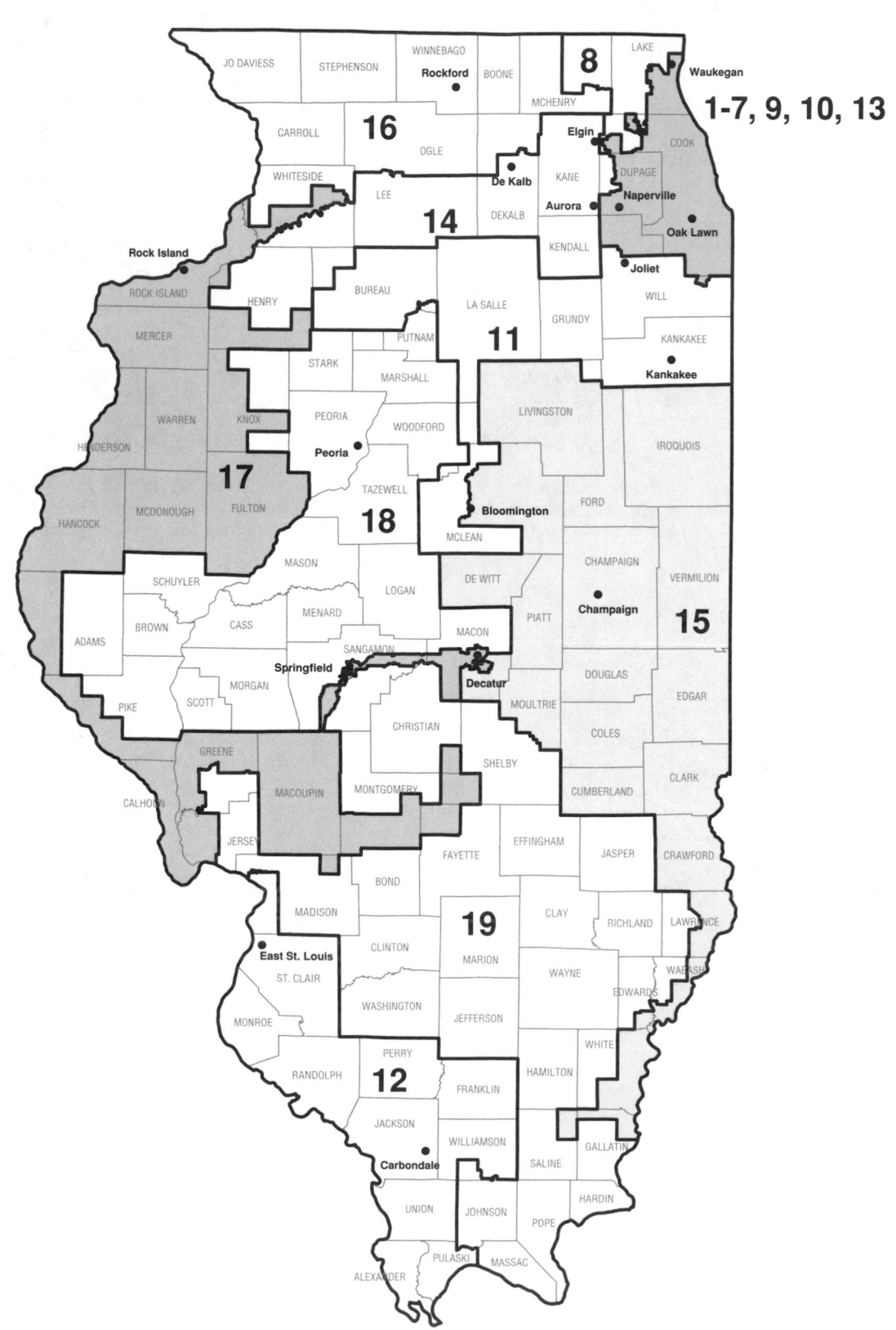

1-7, 9, 10, 13

# ILLINOIS

Chicago Area

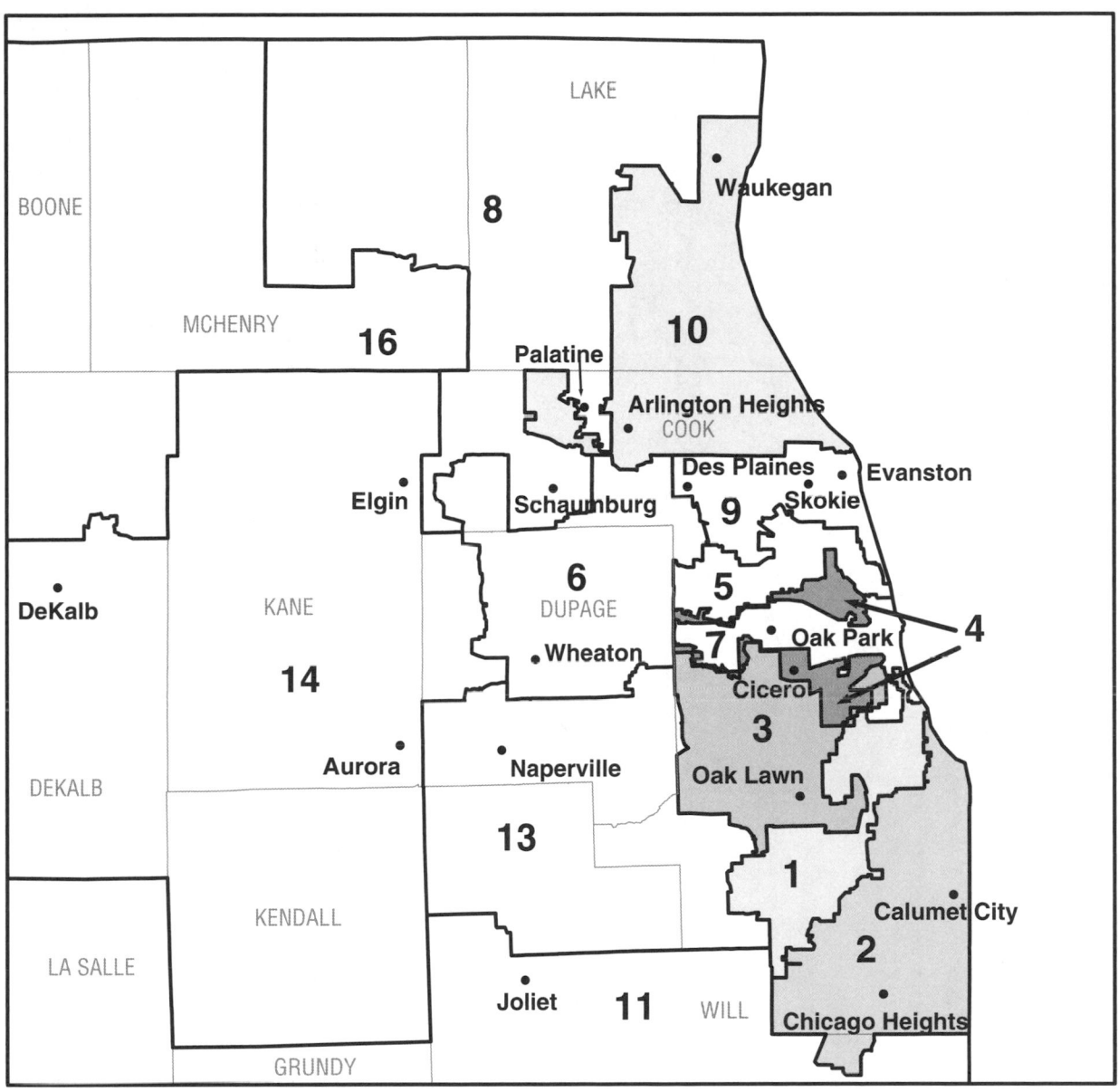

# ILLINOIS

## PRESIDENT 2004

| 2000 Census Population | County | Total Vote | Republican | Democratic | Other | Rep.-Dem. Plurality | Percentage | | | |
|---|---|---|---|---|---|---|---|---|---|---|
| | | | | | | | Total Vote | | Major Vote | |
| | | | | | | | Rep. | Dem. | Rep. | Dem. |
| 68,277 | ADAMS | 31,477 | 20,834 | 10,511 | 132 | 10,323 R | 66.2% | 33.4% | 66.5% | 33.5% |
| 9,590 | ALEXANDER | 3,873 | 1,831 | 2,016 | 26 | 185 D | 47.3% | 52.1% | 47.6% | 52.4% |
| 17,633 | BOND | 7,369 | 4,068 | 3,228 | 73 | 840 R | 55.2% | 43.8% | 55.8% | 44.2% |
| 41,786 | BOONE | 19,541 | 11,132 | 8,286 | 123 | 2,846 R | 57.0% | 42.4% | 57.3% | 42.7% |
| 6,950 | BROWN | 2,585 | 1,679 | 895 | 11 | 784 R | 65.0% | 34.6% | 65.2% | 34.8% |
| 35,503 | BUREAU | 17,902 | 9,822 | 7,961 | 119 | 1,861 R | 54.9% | 44.5% | 55.2% | 44.8% |
| 5,084 | CALHOUN | 2,706 | 1,317 | 1,367 | 22 | 50 D | 48.7% | 50.5% | 49.1% | 50.9% |
| 16,674 | CARROLL | 8,135 | 4,534 | 3,537 | 64 | 997 R | 55.7% | 43.5% | 56.2% | 43.8% |
| 13,695 | CASS | 5,700 | 3,163 | 2,492 | 45 | 671 R | 55.5% | 43.7% | 55.9% | 44.1% |
| 179,669 | CHAMPAIGN | 82,434 | 39,896 | 41,524 | 1,014 | 1,628 D | 48.4% | 50.4% | 49.0% | 51.0% |
| 35,372 | CHRISTIAN | 15,267 | 9,044 | 6,112 | 111 | 2,932 R | 59.2% | 40.0% | 59.7% | 40.3% |
| 17,008 | CLARK | 8,007 | 5,082 | 2,877 | 48 | 2,205 R | 63.5% | 35.9% | 63.9% | 36.1% |
| 14,560 | CLAY | 6,554 | 4,416 | 2,101 | 37 | 2,315 R | 67.4% | 32.1% | 67.8% | 32.2% |
| 35,535 | CLINTON | 17,131 | 10,219 | 6,797 | 115 | 3,422 R | 59.7% | 39.7% | 60.1% | 39.9% |
| 53,196 | COLES | 22,780 | 13,015 | 9,566 | 199 | 3,449 R | 57.1% | 42.0% | 57.6% | 42.4% |
| 5,376,741 | COOK | 2,049,434 | 597,405 | 1,439,724 | 12,305 | 842,319 D | 29.1% | 70.2% | 29.3% | 70.7% |
| 20,452 | CRAWFORD | 9,332 | 6,083 | 3,194 | 55 | 2,889 R | 65.2% | 34.2% | 65.6% | 34.4% |
| 11,253 | CUMBERLAND | 5,416 | 3,497 | 1,862 | 57 | 1,635 R | 64.6% | 34.4% | 65.3% | 34.7% |
| 88,969 | DE KALB | 40,768 | 21,095 | 19,263 | 410 | 1,832 R | 51.7% | 47.3% | 52.3% | 47.7% |
| 16,798 | DE WITT | 7,798 | 4,920 | 2,836 | 42 | 2,084 R | 63.1% | 36.4% | 63.4% | 36.6% |
| 19,922 | DOUGLAS | 8,540 | 5,702 | 2,767 | 71 | 2,935 R | 66.8% | 32.4% | 67.3% | 32.7% |
| 904,161 | DU PAGE | 402,446 | 218,902 | 180,097 | 3,447 | 38,805 R | 54.4% | 44.8% | 54.9% | 45.1% |
| 19,704 | EDGAR | 8,429 | 5,258 | 3,093 | 78 | 2,165 R | 62.4% | 36.7% | 63.0% | 37.0% |
| 6,971 | EDWARDS | 3,364 | 2,412 | 930 | 22 | 1,482 R | 71.7% | 27.6% | 72.2% | 27.8% |
| 34,264 | EFFINGHAM | 16,278 | 11,774 | 4,388 | 116 | 7,386 R | 72.3% | 27.0% | 72.8% | 27.2% |
| 21,802 | FAYETTE | 9,549 | 5,880 | 3,571 | 98 | 2,309 R | 61.6% | 37.4% | 62.2% | 37.8% |
| 14,241 | FORD | 6,479 | 4,511 | 1,912 | 56 | 2,599 R | 69.6% | 29.5% | 70.2% | 29.8% |
| 39,018 | FRANKLIN | 19,352 | 10,388 | 8,816 | 148 | 1,572 R | 53.7% | 45.6% | 54.1% | 45.9% |
| 38,250 | FULTON | 17,035 | 7,818 | 9,080 | 137 | 1,262 D | 45.9% | 53.3% | 46.3% | 53.7% |
| 6,445 | GALLATIN | 3,225 | 1,619 | 1,573 | 33 | 46 R | 50.2% | 48.8% | 50.7% | 49.3% |
| 14,761 | GREENE | 6,068 | 3,559 | 2,457 | 52 | 1,102 R | 58.7% | 40.5% | 59.2% | 40.8% |
| 37,535 | GRUNDY | 19,831 | 11,198 | 8,463 | 170 | 2,735 R | 56.5% | 42.7% | 57.0% | 43.0% |
| 8,621 | HAMILTON | 4,514 | 2,653 | 1,814 | 47 | 839 R | 58.8% | 40.2% | 59.4% | 40.6% |
| 20,121 | HANCOCK | 9,899 | 5,837 | 3,975 | 87 | 1,862 R | 59.0% | 40.2% | 59.5% | 40.5% |
| 4,800 | HARDIN | 2,437 | 1,501 | 923 | 13 | 578 R | 61.6% | 37.9% | 61.9% | 38.1% |
| 8,213 | HENDERSON | 4,153 | 1,857 | 2,269 | 27 | 412 D | 44.7% | 54.6% | 45.0% | 55.0% |
| 51,020 | HENRY | 25,241 | 13,212 | 11,877 | 152 | 1,335 R | 52.3% | 47.1% | 52.7% | 47.3% |
| 31,334 | IROQUOIS | 13,835 | 9,914 | 3,832 | 89 | 6,082 R | 71.7% | 27.7% | 72.1% | 27.9% |
| 59,612 | JACKSON | 25,826 | 11,190 | 14,300 | 336 | 3,110 D | 43.3% | 55.4% | 43.9% | 56.1% |
| 10,117 | JASPER | 5,336 | 3,529 | 1,781 | 26 | 1,748 R | 66.1% | 33.4% | 66.5% | 33.5% |
| 40,045 | JEFFERSON | 16,948 | 10,160 | 6,713 | 75 | 3,447 R | 59.9% | 39.6% | 60.2% | 39.8% |
| 21,668 | JERSEY | 10,137 | 5,435 | 4,597 | 105 | 838 R | 53.6% | 45.3% | 54.2% | 45.8% |
| 22,289 | JO DAVIESS | 11,584 | 6,174 | 5,311 | 99 | 863 R | 53.3% | 45.8% | 53.8% | 46.2% |
| 12,878 | JOHNSON | 5,865 | 3,997 | 1,813 | 55 | 2,184 R | 68.2% | 30.9% | 68.8% | 31.2% |
| 404,119 | KANE | 167,297 | 92,065 | 73,813 | 1,419 | 18,252 R | 55.0% | 44.1% | 55.5% | 44.5% |
| 103,833 | KANKAKEE | 45,036 | 24,739 | 20,003 | 294 | 4,736 R | 54.9% | 44.4% | 55.3% | 44.7% |
| 54,544 | KENDALL | 32,527 | 19,776 | 12,497 | 254 | 7,279 R | 60.8% | 38.4% | 61.3% | 38.7% |
| 55,836 | KNOX | 24,708 | 11,111 | 13,403 | 194 | 2,292 D | 45.0% | 54.2% | 45.3% | 54.7% |
| 644,356 | LAKE | 275,295 | 139,081 | 134,352 | 1,862 | 4,729 R | 50.5% | 48.8% | 50.9% | 49.1% |
| 111,509 | LA SALLE | 50,729 | 26,101 | 24,263 | 365 | 1,838 R | 51.5% | 47.8% | 51.8% | 48.2% |
| 15,452 | LAWRENCE | 6,729 | 4,162 | 2,518 | 49 | 1,644 R | 61.9% | 37.4% | 62.3% | 37.7% |
| 36,062 | LEE | 15,876 | 9,307 | 6,416 | 153 | 2,891 R | 58.6% | 40.4% | 59.2% | 40.8% |
| 39,678 | LIVINGSTON | 16,039 | 10,316 | 5,632 | 91 | 4,684 R | 64.3% | 35.1% | 64.7% | 35.3% |
| 31,183 | LOGAN | 13,467 | 9,112 | 4,273 | 82 | 4,839 R | 67.7% | 31.7% | 68.1% | 31.9% |
| 32,913 | MCDONOUGH | 14,929 | 7,656 | 7,119 | 154 | 537 R | 51.3% | 47.7% | 51.8% | 48.2% |
| 260,077 | MCHENRY | 127,948 | 76,412 | 50,330 | 1,206 | 26,082 R | 59.7% | 39.3% | 60.3% | 39.7% |
| 150,433 | MCLEAN | 71,620 | 41,276 | 29,877 | 467 | 11,399 R | 57.6% | 41.7% | 58.0% | 42.0% |
| 114,706 | MACON | 51,746 | 28,118 | 23,341 | 287 | 4,777 R | 54.3% | 45.1% | 54.6% | 45.4% |
| 49,019 | MACOUPIN | 22,785 | 11,413 | 11,193 | 179 | 220 R | 50.1% | 49.1% | 50.5% | 49.5% |
| 258,941 | MADISON | 123,678 | 59,384 | 63,399 | 895 | 4,015 D | 48.0% | 51.3% | 48.4% | 51.6% |

# ILLINOIS

## PRESIDENT 2004

| 2000 Census Population | County | Total Vote | Republican | Democratic | Other | Rep.-Dem. Plurality | Percentage | | | |
|---|---|---|---|---|---|---|---|---|---|---|
| | | | | | | | Total Vote | | Major Vote | |
| | | | | | | | Rep. | Dem. | Rep. | Dem. |
| 41,691 | MARION | 17,224 | 9,413 | 7,694 | 117 | 1,719 R | 54.7% | 44.7% | 55.0% | 45.0% |
| 13,180 | MARSHALL | 6,584 | 3,734 | 2,806 | 44 | 928 R | 56.7% | 42.6% | 57.1% | 42.9% |
| 16,038 | MASON | 7,183 | 3,907 | 3,215 | 61 | 692 R | 54.4% | 44.8% | 54.9% | 45.1% |
| 15,161 | MASSAC | 7,424 | 4,578 | 2,805 | 41 | 1,773 R | 61.7% | 37.8% | 62.0% | 38.0% |
| 12,486 | MENARD | 6,574 | 4,408 | 2,137 | 29 | 2,271 R | 67.1% | 32.5% | 67.3% | 32.7% |
| 16,957 | MERCER | 8,974 | 4,405 | 4,512 | 57 | 107 D | 49.1% | 50.3% | 49.4% | 50.6% |
| 27,619 | MONROE | 16,370 | 9,468 | 6,788 | 114 | 2,680 R | 57.8% | 41.5% | 58.2% | 41.8% |
| 30,652 | MONTGOMERY | 12,930 | 6,851 | 5,979 | 100 | 872 R | 53.0% | 46.2% | 53.4% | 46.6% |
| 36,616 | MORGAN | 15,180 | 9,392 | 5,650 | 138 | 3,742 R | 61.9% | 37.2% | 62.4% | 37.6% |
| 14,287 | MOULTRIE | 6,466 | 4,028 | 2,388 | 50 | 1,640 R | 62.3% | 36.9% | 62.8% | 37.2% |
| 51,032 | OGLE | 24,091 | 14,918 | 9,018 | 155 | 5,900 R | 61.9% | 37.4% | 62.3% | 37.7% |
| 183,433 | PEORIA | 82,771 | 41,051 | 41,121 | 599 | 70 D | 49.6% | 49.7% | 50.0% | 50.0% |
| 23,094 | PERRY | 10,425 | 5,589 | 4,770 | 66 | 819 R | 53.6% | 45.8% | 54.0% | 46.0% |
| 16,365 | PIATT | 8,586 | 5,392 | 3,124 | 70 | 2,268 R | 62.8% | 36.4% | 63.3% | 36.7% |
| 17,384 | PIKE | 7,980 | 5,032 | 2,849 | 99 | 2,183 R | 63.1% | 35.7% | 63.8% | 36.2% |
| 4,413 | POPE | 2,436 | 1,500 | 918 | 18 | 582 R | 61.6% | 37.7% | 62.0% | 38.0% |
| 7,348 | PULASKI | 3,108 | 1,720 | 1,372 | 16 | 348 R | 55.3% | 44.1% | 55.6% | 44.4% |
| 6,086 | PUTNAM | 3,352 | 1,623 | 1,704 | 25 | 81 D | 48.4% | 50.8% | 48.8% | 51.2% |
| 33,893 | RANDOLPH | 14,956 | 8,076 | 6,771 | 109 | 1,305 R | 54.0% | 45.3% | 54.4% | 45.6% |
| 16,149 | RICHLAND | 7,749 | 5,153 | 2,529 | 67 | 2,624 R | 66.5% | 32.6% | 67.1% | 32.9% |
| 149,374 | ROCK ISLAND | 69,972 | 29,663 | 39,880 | 429 | 10,217 D | 42.4% | 57.0% | 42.7% | 57.3% |
| 256,082 | ST. CLAIR | 113,189 | 50,203 | 62,410 | 576 | 12,207 D | 44.4% | 55.1% | 44.6% | 55.4% |
| 26,733 | SALINE | 11,814 | 7,057 | 4,697 | 60 | 2,360 R | 59.7% | 39.8% | 60.0% | 40.0% |
| 188,951 | SANGAMON | 95,375 | 55,904 | 38,630 | 841 | 17,274 R | 58.6% | 40.5% | 59.1% | 40.9% |
| 7,189 | SCHUYLER | 4,031 | 2,403 | 1,594 | 34 | 809 R | 59.6% | 39.5% | 60.1% | 39.9% |
| 5,537 | SCOTT | 2,636 | 1,696 | 927 | 13 | 769 R | 64.3% | 35.2% | 64.7% | 35.3% |
| 22,893 | SHELBY | 10,577 | 6,753 | 3,744 | 80 | 3,009 R | 63.8% | 35.4% | 64.3% | 35.7% |
| 6,332 | STARK | 3,061 | 1,841 | 1,189 | 31 | 652 R | 60.1% | 38.8% | 60.8% | 39.2% |
| 48,979 | STEPHENSON | 21,320 | 12,212 | 8,913 | 195 | 3,299 R | 57.3% | 41.8% | 57.8% | 42.2% |
| 128,485 | TAZEWELL | 62,338 | 36,058 | 25,814 | 466 | 10,244 R | 57.8% | 41.4% | 58.3% | 41.7% |
| 18,293 | UNION | 9,119 | 5,333 | 3,735 | 51 | 1,598 R | 58.5% | 41.0% | 58.8% | 41.2% |
| 83,919 | VERMILION | 33,714 | 18,731 | 14,726 | 257 | 4,005 R | 55.6% | 43.7% | 56.0% | 44.0% |
| 12,937 | WABASH | 6,006 | 4,212 | 1,752 | 42 | 2,460 R | 70.1% | 29.2% | 70.6% | 29.4% |
| 18,735 | WARREN | 8,457 | 4,474 | 3,938 | 45 | 536 R | 52.9% | 46.6% | 53.2% | 46.8% |
| 15,148 | WASHINGTON | 8,104 | 5,072 | 2,986 | 46 | 2,086 R | 62.6% | 36.8% | 62.9% | 37.1% |
| 17,151 | WAYNE | 8,287 | 6,102 | 2,139 | 46 | 3,963 R | 73.6% | 25.8% | 74.0% | 26.0% |
| 15,371 | WHITE | 8,301 | 5,180 | 3,071 | 50 | 2,109 R | 62.4% | 37.0% | 62.8% | 37.2% |
| 60,653 | WHITESIDE | 26,873 | 12,959 | 13,723 | 191 | 764 D | 48.2% | 51.1% | 48.6% | 51.4% |
| 502,266 | WILL | 249,609 | 130,728 | 117,172 | 1,709 | 13,556 R | 52.4% | 46.9% | 52.7% | 47.3% |
| 61,296 | WILLIAMSON | 29,960 | 18,086 | 11,685 | 189 | 6,401 R | 60.4% | 39.0% | 60.8% | 39.2% |
| 278,418 | WINNEBAGO | 121,425 | 60,782 | 59,740 | 903 | 1,042 R | 50.1% | 49.2% | 50.4% | 49.6% |
| 35,469 | WOODFORD | 18,802 | 12,698 | 6,005 | 99 | 6,693 R | 67.5% | 31.9% | 67.9% | 32.1% |
| 12,419,293 | TOTAL | 5,274,322 | 2,345,946 | 2,891,550 | 36,826 | 545,604 D | 44.5% | 54.8% | 44.8% | 55.2% |

# ILLINOIS
## SENATOR 2004

| 2000 Census Population | County | Total Vote | Republican | Democratic | Other | Rep.-Dem. Plurality | Percentage | | | |
|---|---|---|---|---|---|---|---|---|---|---|
| | | | | | | | Total Vote | | Major Vote | |
| | | | | | | | Rep. | Dem. | Rep. | Dem. |
| 68,277 | ADAMS | 30,613 | 13,857 | 16,036 | 720 | 2,179 D | 45.3% | 52.4% | 46.4% | 53.6% |
| 9,590 | ALEXANDER | 3,651 | 1,148 | 2,395 | 108 | 1,247 D | 31.4% | 65.6% | 32.4% | 67.6% |
| 17,633 | BOND | 7,191 | 2,717 | 4,227 | 247 | 1,510 D | 37.8% | 58.8% | 39.1% | 60.9% |
| 41,786 | BOONE | 19,115 | 7,317 | 11,206 | 592 | 3,889 D | 38.3% | 58.6% | 39.5% | 60.5% |
| 6,950 | BROWN | 2,456 | 1,073 | 1,308 | 75 | 235 D | 43.7% | 53.3% | 45.1% | 54.9% |
| 35,503 | BUREAU | 17,421 | 6,284 | 10,648 | 489 | 4,364 D | 36.1% | 61.1% | 37.1% | 62.9% |
| 5,084 | CALHOUN | 2,600 | 912 | 1,604 | 84 | 692 D | 35.1% | 61.7% | 36.2% | 63.8% |
| 16,674 | CARROLL | 7,941 | 2,730 | 4,961 | 250 | 2,231 D | 34.4% | 62.5% | 35.5% | 64.5% |
| 13,695 | CASS | 5,450 | 1,896 | 3,341 | 213 | 1,445 D | 34.8% | 61.3% | 36.2% | 63.8% |
| 179,669 | CHAMPAIGN | 80,297 | 25,548 | 51,813 | 2,936 | 26,265 D | 31.8% | 64.5% | 33.0% | 67.0% |
| 35,372 | CHRISTIAN | 14,913 | 5,101 | 9,323 | 489 | 4,222 D | 34.2% | 62.5% | 35.4% | 64.6% |
| 17,008 | CLARK | 7,665 | 3,833 | 3,566 | 266 | 267 R | 50.0% | 46.5% | 51.8% | 48.2% |
| 14,560 | CLAY | 6,299 | 3,614 | 2,505 | 180 | 1,109 R | 57.4% | 39.8% | 59.1% | 40.9% |
| 35,535 | CLINTON | 16,528 | 6,565 | 9,437 | 526 | 2,872 D | 39.7% | 57.1% | 41.0% | 59.0% |
| 53,196 | COLES | 22,083 | 8,625 | 12,758 | 700 | 4,133 D | 39.1% | 57.8% | 40.3% | 59.7% |
| 5,376,741 | COOK | 2,008,079 | 329,671 | 1,629,296 | 49,112 | 1,299,625 D | 16.4% | 81.1% | 16.8% | 83.2% |
| 20,452 | CRAWFORD | 8,948 | 4,261 | 4,302 | 385 | 41 D | 47.6% | 48.1% | 49.8% | 50.2% |
| 11,253 | CUMBERLAND | 5,266 | 2,492 | 2,598 | 176 | 106 D | 47.3% | 49.3% | 49.0% | 51.0% |
| 88,969 | DE KALB | 39,694 | 11,954 | 26,077 | 1,663 | 14,123 D | 30.1% | 65.7% | 31.4% | 68.6% |
| 16,798 | DE WITT | 7,547 | 2,973 | 4,340 | 234 | 1,367 D | 39.4% | 57.5% | 40.7% | 59.3% |
| 19,922 | DOUGLAS | 8,227 | 3,717 | 4,239 | 271 | 522 D | 45.2% | 51.5% | 46.7% | 53.3% |
| 904,161 | DU PAGE | 391,041 | 124,642 | 251,445 | 14,954 | 126,803 D | 31.9% | 64.3% | 33.1% | 66.9% |
| 19,704 | EDGAR | 8,152 | 3,858 | 4,014 | 280 | 156 D | 47.3% | 49.2% | 49.0% | 51.0% |
| 6,971 | EDWARDS | 3,129 | 1,876 | 1,155 | 98 | 721 R | 60.0% | 36.9% | 61.9% | 38.1% |
| 34,264 | EFFINGHAM | 15,642 | 8,930 | 6,264 | 448 | 2,666 R | 57.1% | 40.0% | 58.8% | 41.2% |
| 21,802 | FAYETTE | 9,242 | 4,127 | 4,826 | 289 | 699 D | 44.7% | 52.2% | 46.1% | 53.9% |
| 14,241 | FORD | 6,236 | 2,984 | 3,021 | 231 | 37 D | 47.9% | 48.4% | 49.7% | 50.3% |
| 39,018 | FRANKLIN | 18,698 | 6,221 | 11,949 | 528 | 5,728 D | 33.3% | 63.9% | 34.2% | 65.8% |
| 38,250 | FULTON | 16,725 | 4,556 | 11,729 | 440 | 7,173 D | 27.2% | 70.1% | 28.0% | 72.0% |
| 6,445 | GALLATIN | 2,986 | 786 | 2,109 | 91 | 1,323 D | 26.3% | 70.6% | 27.2% | 72.8% |
| 14,761 | GREENE | 5,828 | 2,281 | 3,343 | 204 | 1,062 D | 39.1% | 57.4% | 40.6% | 59.4% |
| 37,535 | GRUNDY | 19,258 | 6,308 | 12,285 | 665 | 5,977 D | 32.8% | 63.8% | 33.9% | 66.1% |
| 8,621 | HAMILTON | 4,274 | 1,680 | 2,458 | 136 | 778 D | 39.3% | 57.5% | 40.6% | 59.4% |
| 20,121 | HANCOCK | 9,552 | 4,125 | 5,143 | 284 | 1,018 D | 43.2% | 53.8% | 44.5% | 55.5% |
| 4,800 | HARDIN | 2,330 | 991 | 1,253 | 86 | 262 D | 42.5% | 53.8% | 44.2% | 55.8% |
| 8,213 | HENDERSON | 4,030 | 1,195 | 2,704 | 131 | 1,509 D | 29.7% | 67.1% | 30.6% | 69.4% |
| 51,020 | HENRY | 24,741 | 8,219 | 15,965 | 557 | 7,746 D | 33.2% | 64.5% | 34.0% | 66.0% |
| 31,334 | IROQUOIS | 13,333 | 6,736 | 6,177 | 420 | 559 R | 50.5% | 46.3% | 52.2% | 47.8% |
| 59,612 | JACKSON | 25,050 | 6,924 | 17,295 | 831 | 10,371 D | 27.6% | 69.0% | 28.6% | 71.4% |
| 10,117 | JASPER | 5,062 | 2,768 | 2,141 | 153 | 627 R | 54.7% | 42.3% | 56.4% | 43.6% |
| 40,045 | JEFFERSON | 16,332 | 6,778 | 9,111 | 443 | 2,333 D | 41.5% | 55.8% | 42.7% | 57.3% |
| 21,668 | JERSEY | 9,791 | 3,825 | 5,670 | 296 | 1,845 D | 39.1% | 57.9% | 40.3% | 59.7% |
| 22,289 | JO DAVIESS | 11,051 | 3,968 | 6,714 | 369 | 2,746 D | 35.9% | 60.8% | 37.1% | 62.9% |
| 12,878 | JOHNSON | 5,576 | 2,617 | 2,781 | 178 | 164 D | 46.9% | 49.9% | 48.5% | 51.5% |
| 404,119 | KANE | 159,676 | 52,319 | 101,105 | 6,252 | 48,786 D | 32.8% | 63.3% | 34.1% | 65.9% |
| 103,833 | KANKAKEE | 44,112 | 14,614 | 28,164 | 1,334 | 13,550 D | 33.1% | 63.8% | 34.2% | 65.8% |
| 54,544 | KENDALL | 31,353 | 11,522 | 18,450 | 1,381 | 6,928 D | 36.7% | 58.8% | 38.4% | 61.6% |
| 55,836 | KNOX | 24,332 | 6,703 | 17,098 | 531 | 10,395 D | 27.5% | 70.3% | 28.2% | 71.8% |
| 644,356 | LAKE | 267,841 | 75,199 | 183,717 | 8,925 | 108,518 D | 28.1% | 68.6% | 29.0% | 71.0% |
| 111,509 | LA SALLE | 49,509 | 15,676 | 32,193 | 1,640 | 16,517 D | 31.7% | 65.0% | 32.7% | 67.3% |
| 15,452 | LAWRENCE | 6,446 | 2,956 | 3,255 | 235 | 299 D | 45.9% | 50.5% | 47.6% | 52.4% |
| 36,062 | LEE | 15,547 | 6,186 | 8,873 | 488 | 2,687 D | 39.8% | 57.1% | 41.1% | 58.9% |
| 39,678 | LIVINGSTON | 15,476 | 6,513 | 8,474 | 489 | 1,961 D | 42.1% | 54.8% | 43.5% | 56.5% |
| 31,183 | LOGAN | 12,863 | 5,517 | 6,945 | 401 | 1,428 D | 42.9% | 54.0% | 44.3% | 55.7% |
| 32,913 | MCDONOUGH | 14,445 | 4,693 | 9,422 | 330 | 4,729 D | 32.5% | 65.2% | 33.2% | 66.8% |
| 260,077 | MCHENRY | 124,402 | 42,936 | 76,652 | 4,814 | 33,716 D | 34.5% | 61.6% | 35.9% | 64.1% |
| 150,433 | MCLEAN | 69,798 | 25,040 | 43,027 | 1,731 | 17,987 D | 35.9% | 61.6% | 36.8% | 63.2% |
| 114,706 | MACON | 50,505 | 18,511 | 30,729 | 1,265 | 12,218 D | 36.7% | 60.8% | 37.6% | 62.4% |
| 49,019 | MACOUPIN | 22,154 | 6,946 | 14,423 | 785 | 7,477 D | 31.4% | 65.1% | 32.5% | 67.5% |
| 258,941 | MADISON | 120,638 | 39,431 | 77,208 | 3,999 | 37,777 D | 32.7% | 64.0% | 33.8% | 66.2% |

# ILLINOIS

## SENATOR 2004

| 2000 Census Population | County | Total Vote | Republican | Democratic | Other | Rep.-Dem. Plurality | | Percentage | | | |
|---|---|---|---|---|---|---|---|---|---|---|---|
| | | | | | | | | Total Vote | | Major Vote | |
| | | | | | | | | Rep. | Dem. | Rep. | Dem. |
| 41,691 | MARION | 16,704 | 6,099 | 10,088 | 517 | 3,989 | D | 36.5% | 60.4% | 37.7% | 62.3% |
| 13,180 | MARSHALL | 6,420 | 2,354 | 3,909 | 157 | 1,555 | D | 36.7% | 60.9% | 37.6% | 62.4% |
| 16,038 | MASON | 6,937 | 2,230 | 4,498 | 209 | 2,268 | D | 32.1% | 64.8% | 33.1% | 66.9% |
| 15,161 | MASSAC | 7,151 | 3,689 | 3,309 | 153 | 380 | R | 51.6% | 46.3% | 52.7% | 47.3% |
| 12,486 | MENARD | 6,285 | 2,453 | 3,529 | 303 | 1,076 | D | 39.0% | 56.1% | 41.0% | 59.0% |
| 16,957 | MERCER | 8,645 | 2,685 | 5,729 | 231 | 3,044 | D | 31.1% | 66.3% | 31.9% | 68.1% |
| 27,619 | MONROE | 15,743 | 6,089 | 9,150 | 504 | 3,061 | D | 38.7% | 58.1% | 40.0% | 60.0% |
| 30,652 | MONTGOMERY | 12,442 | 4,078 | 7,903 | 461 | 3,825 | D | 32.8% | 63.5% | 34.0% | 66.0% |
| 36,616 | MORGAN | 14,696 | 5,478 | 8,578 | 640 | 3,100 | D | 37.3% | 58.4% | 39.0% | 61.0% |
| 14,287 | MOULTRIE | 6,224 | 2,622 | 3,449 | 153 | 827 | D | 42.1% | 55.4% | 43.2% | 56.8% |
| 51,032 | OGLE | 23,558 | 9,912 | 12,903 | 743 | 2,991 | D | 42.1% | 54.8% | 43.4% | 56.6% |
| 183,433 | PEORIA | 81,470 | 24,888 | 55,061 | 1,521 | 30,173 | D | 30.5% | 67.6% | 31.1% | 68.9% |
| 23,094 | PERRY | 10,048 | 3,285 | 6,464 | 299 | 3,179 | D | 32.7% | 64.3% | 33.7% | 66.3% |
| 16,365 | PIATT | 8,272 | 3,396 | 4,548 | 328 | 1,152 | D | 41.1% | 55.0% | 42.7% | 57.3% |
| 17,384 | PIKE | 7,742 | 3,573 | 3,887 | 282 | 314 | D | 46.2% | 50.2% | 47.9% | 52.1% |
| 4,413 | POPE | 2,305 | 1,020 | 1,211 | 74 | 191 | D | 44.3% | 52.5% | 45.7% | 54.3% |
| 7,348 | PULASKI | 2,966 | 1,137 | 1,749 | 80 | 612 | D | 38.3% | 59.0% | 39.4% | 60.6% |
| 6,086 | PUTNAM | 3,251 | 971 | 2,192 | 88 | 1,221 | D | 29.9% | 67.4% | 30.7% | 69.3% |
| 33,893 | RANDOLPH | 14,407 | 4,961 | 9,009 | 437 | 4,048 | D | 34.4% | 62.5% | 35.5% | 64.5% |
| 16,149 | RICHLAND | 7,448 | 4,185 | 3,048 | 215 | 1,137 | R | 56.2% | 40.9% | 57.9% | 42.1% |
| 149,374 | ROCK ISLAND | 69,072 | 18,620 | 49,096 | 1,356 | 30,476 | D | 27.0% | 71.1% | 27.5% | 72.5% |
| 256,082 | ST. CLAIR | 110,923 | 33,288 | 74,447 | 3,188 | 41,159 | D | 30.0% | 67.1% | 30.9% | 69.1% |
| 26,733 | SALINE | 11,260 | 4,133 | 6,851 | 276 | 2,718 | D | 36.7% | 60.8% | 37.6% | 62.4% |
| 188,951 | SANGAMON | 91,998 | 29,432 | 57,385 | 5,181 | 27,953 | D | 32.0% | 62.4% | 33.9% | 66.1% |
| 7,189 | SCHUYLER | 3,883 | 1,542 | 2,241 | 100 | 699 | D | 39.7% | 57.7% | 40.8% | 59.2% |
| 5,537 | SCOTT | 2,508 | 1,101 | 1,315 | 92 | 214 | D | 43.9% | 52.4% | 45.6% | 54.4% |
| 22,893 | SHELBY | 10,259 | 4,626 | 5,364 | 269 | 738 | D | 45.1% | 52.3% | 46.3% | 53.7% |
| 6,332 | STARK | 2,931 | 1,119 | 1,722 | 90 | 603 | D | 38.2% | 58.8% | 39.4% | 60.6% |
| 48,979 | STEPHENSON | 20,715 | 7,882 | 12,244 | 589 | 4,362 | D | 38.0% | 59.1% | 39.2% | 60.8% |
| 128,485 | TAZEWELL | 60,427 | 22,955 | 36,058 | 1,414 | 13,103 | D | 38.0% | 59.7% | 38.9% | 61.1% |
| 18,293 | UNION | 8,670 | 3,338 | 4,761 | 571 | 1,423 | D | 38.5% | 54.9% | 41.2% | 58.8% |
| 83,919 | VERMILION | 32,961 | 12,413 | 19,500 | 1,048 | 7,087 | D | 37.7% | 59.2% | 38.9% | 61.1% |
| 12,937 | WABASH | 5,732 | 3,110 | 2,404 | 218 | 706 | R | 54.3% | 41.9% | 56.4% | 43.6% |
| 18,735 | WARREN | 8,260 | 2,685 | 5,402 | 173 | 2,717 | D | 32.5% | 65.4% | 33.2% | 66.8% |
| 15,148 | WASHINGTON | 7,676 | 3,315 | 4,110 | 251 | 795 | D | 43.2% | 53.5% | 44.6% | 55.4% |
| 17,151 | WAYNE | 7,967 | 4,502 | 3,233 | 232 | 1,269 | R | 56.5% | 40.6% | 58.2% | 41.8% |
| 15,371 | WHITE | 7,831 | 3,492 | 4,038 | 301 | 546 | D | 44.6% | 51.6% | 46.4% | 53.6% |
| 60,653 | WHITESIDE | 26,157 | 7,879 | 17,585 | 693 | 9,706 | D | 30.1% | 67.2% | 30.9% | 69.1% |
| 502,266 | WILL | 244,003 | 72,786 | 162,891 | 8,326 | 90,105 | D | 29.8% | 66.8% | 30.9% | 69.1% |
| 61,296 | WILLIAMSON | 29,033 | 10,902 | 17,113 | 1,018 | 6,211 | D | 37.6% | 58.9% | 38.9% | 61.1% |
| 278,418 | WINNEBAGO | 119,108 | 40,470 | 74,911 | 3,727 | 34,441 | D | 34.0% | 62.9% | 35.1% | 64.9% |
| 35,469 | WOODFORD | 18,292 | 8,550 | 9,304 | 438 | 754 | D | 46.7% | 50.9% | 47.9% | 52.1% |
| 12,419,293 | TOTAL | 5,141,520 | 1,390,690 | 3,597,456 | 153,374 | 2,206,766 | D | 27.0% | 70.0% | 27.9% | 72.1% |

# ILLINOIS

## HOUSE OF REPRESENTATIVES

| CD | Year | Total Vote | Republican Vote | Republican Candidate | Democratic Vote | Democratic Candidate | Other Vote | Rep.-Dem. Plurality | Percentage Total Vote Rep. | Total Vote Dem. | Major Vote Rep. | Major Vote Dem. |
|----|------|-----------|-----------------|----------------------|-----------------|----------------------|-----------|--------------------|---------------------------|-----------------|-----------------|-----------------|
| 1 | 2004 | 249,949 | 37,840 | Wardingley, Raymond G. | 212,109 | Rush, Bobby L.* | | 174,269 D | 15.1% | 84.9% | 15.1% | 84.9% |
| 1 | 2002 | 183,656 | 29,776 | Wardingley, Raymond G. | 149,068 | Rush, Bobby L.* | 4,812 | 119,292 D | 16.2% | 81.2% | 16.6% | 83.4% |
| 2 | 2004 | 234,525 | | | 207,535 | Jackson, Jesse L. Jr.* | 26,990 | 207,535 D | | 88.5% | | 100.0% |
| 2 | 2002 | 184,010 | 32,567 | Nelson, Doug | 151,443 | Jackson, Jesse L. Jr.* | | 118,876 D | 17.7% | 82.3% | 17.7% | 82.3% |
| 3 | 2004 | 229,956 | 57,845 | Chlada, Ryan | 167,034 | Lipinski, Daniel | 5,077 | 109,189 D | 25.2% | 72.6% | 25.7% | 74.3% |
| 3 | 2002 | 156,042 | | | 156,042 | Lipinski, William O.* | | 156,042 D | | 100.0% | | 100.0% |
| 4 | 2004 | 125,142 | 15,536 | Cisneros, Tony | 104,761 | Gutierrez, Luis V.* | 4,845 | 89,225 D | 12.4% | 83.7% | 12.9% | 87.1% |
| 4 | 2002 | 84,513 | 12,778 | Lopez-Cisneros, Anthony J. "Tony" | 67,339 | Gutierrez, Luis V.* | 4,396 | 54,561 D | 15.1% | 79.7% | 15.9% | 84.1% |
| 5 | 2004 | 207,930 | 49,530 | Best, Bruce | 158,400 | Emanuel, Rahm* | | 108,870 D | 23.8% | 76.2% | 23.8% | 76.2% |
| 5 | 2002 | 159,435 | 46,008 | Augusti, Mark A. | 106,514 | Emanuel, Rahm | 6,913 | 60,506 D | 28.9% | 66.8% | 30.2% | 69.8% |
| 6 | 2004 | 250,097 | 139,627 | Hyde, Henry J.* | 110,470 | Cegelis, Christine | | 29,157 R | 55.8% | 44.2% | 55.8% | 44.2% |
| 6 | 2002 | 173,872 | 113,174 | Hyde, Henry J.* | 60,698 | Berry, Tom | | 52,476 R | 65.1% | 34.9% | 65.1% | 34.9% |
| 7 | 2004 | 256,736 | 35,603 | Davis-Fairman, Antonio | 221,133 | Davis, Danny K.* | | 185,530 D | 13.9% | 86.1% | 13.9% | 86.1% |
| 7 | 2002 | 165,756 | 25,280 | Tunney, Mark | 137,933 | Davis, Danny K.* | 2,543 | 112,653 D | 15.3% | 83.2% | 15.5% | 84.5% |
| 8 | 2004 | 270,393 | 130,601 | Crane, Philip M.* | 139,792 | Bean, Melissa | | 9,191 D | 48.3% | 51.7% | 48.3% | 51.7% |
| 8 | 2002 | 165,926 | 95,275 | Crane, Philip M.* | 70,626 | Bean, Melissa | 25 | 24,649 R | 57.4% | 42.6% | 57.4% | 42.6% |
| 9 | 2004 | 231,417 | 56,135 | Eckhardt, Kurt J. | 175,282 | Schakowsky, Jan* | | 119,147 D | 24.3% | 75.7% | 24.3% | 75.7% |
| 9 | 2002 | 168,836 | 45,307 | Duric, Nicholas M. | 118,642 | Schakowsky, Jan* | 4,887 | 73,335 D | 26.8% | 70.3% | 27.6% | 72.4% |
| 10 | 2004 | 276,711 | 177,493 | Kirk, Mark Steven* | 99,218 | Goodman, Lee | | 78,275 R | 64.1% | 35.9% | 64.1% | 35.9% |
| 10 | 2002 | 186,911 | 128,611 | Kirk, Mark Steven* | 58,300 | Perritt, Henry H. "Hank" | | 70,311 R | 68.8% | 31.2% | 68.8% | 31.2% |
| 11 | 2004 | 294,960 | 173,057 | Weller, Jerry* | 121,903 | Renner, Tari | | 51,154 R | 58.7% | 41.3% | 58.7% | 41.3% |
| 11 | 2002 | 193,085 | 124,192 | Weller, Jerry* | 68,893 | Van Duyne, Keith S. | | 55,299 R | 64.3% | 35.7% | 64.3% | 35.7% |
| 12 | 2004 | 286,435 | 82,677 | Zweigart, Erin R. | 198,962 | Costello, Jerry F.* | 4,796 | 116,285 D | 28.9% | 69.5% | 29.4% | 70.6% |
| 12 | 2002 | 190,020 | 58,440 | Sadler, David | 131,580 | Costello, Jerry F.* | | 73,140 D | 30.8% | 69.2% | 30.8% | 69.2% |
| 13 | 2004 | 308,312 | 200,472 | Biggert, Judy* | 107,836 | Andersen, Gloria Schor | 4 | 92,636 R | 65.0% | 35.0% | 65.0% | 35.0% |
| 13 | 2002 | 198,615 | 139,546 | Biggert, Judy* | 59,069 | Mason, Tom | | 80,477 R | 70.3% | 29.7% | 70.3% | 29.7% |
| 14 | 2004 | 279,208 | 191,618 | Hastert, J. Dennis* | 87,590 | Zamora, Ruben | | 104,028 R | 68.6% | 31.4% | 68.6% | 31.4% |
| 14 | 2002 | 182,363 | 135,198 | Hastert, J. Dennis* | 47,165 | Quick, Laurence J. | | 88,033 R | 74.1% | 25.9% | 74.1% | 25.9% |
| 15 | 2004 | 291,739 | 178,114 | Johnson, Timothy V.* | 113,625 | Gill, David | | 64,489 R | 61.1% | 38.9% | 61.1% | 38.9% |
| 15 | 2002 | 206,617 | 134,650 | Johnson, Timothy V.* | 64,131 | Hartke, Joshua T. | 7,836 | 70,519 R | 65.2% | 31.0% | 67.7% | 32.3% |
| 16 | 2004 | 295,806 | 204,350 | Manzullo, Donald* | 91,452 | Kutsch, John H. | 4 | 112,898 R | 69.1% | 30.9% | 69.1% | 30.9% |
| 16 | 2002 | 188,827 | 133,339 | Manzullo, Donald* | 55,488 | Kutsch, John H. | | 77,851 R | 70.6% | 29.4% | 70.6% | 29.4% |
| 17 | 2004 | 284,000 | 111,680 | Zinga, Andrea Lane | 172,320 | Evans, Lane* | | 60,640 D | 39.3% | 60.7% | 39.3% | 60.7% |
| 17 | 2002 | 203,612 | 76,519 | Calderone, Peter | 127,093 | Evans, Lane* | | 50,574 D | 37.6% | 62.4% | 37.6% | 62.4% |
| 18 | 2004 | 307,595 | 216,047 | LaHood, Ray* | 91,548 | Waterworth, Steve | | 124,499 R | 70.2% | 29.8% | 70.2% | 29.8% |
| 18 | 2002 | 192,567 | 192,567 | LaHood, Ray* | | | | 192,567 R | 100.0% | | 100.0% | |
| 19 | 2004 | 307,754 | 213,451 | Shimkus, John* | 94,303 | Bagwell, Tim | | 119,148 R | 69.4% | 30.6% | 69.4% | 30.6% |
| 19 | 2002 | 244,473 | 133,956 | Shimkus, John* | 110,517 | Phelps, David* | | 23,439 R | 54.8% | 45.2% | 54.8% | 45.2% |
| Total | 2004 | 4,988,665 | 2,271,676 | | 2,675,273 | | 41,716 | 403,597 D | 45.5% | 53.6% | 45.9% | 54.1% |
| Total | 2002 | 3,429,136 | 1,657,183 | | 1,740,541 | | 31,412 | 83,358 D | 48.3% | 50.8% | 48.8% | 51.2% |

An asterisk (*) denotes incumbent.

# ILLINOIS

## GENERAL AND PRIMARY ELECTIONS

## 2004 GENERAL ELECTIONS

**President**  Other vote was 32,442 Libertarian (Michael Badnarik); 3,571 write-in (Ralph Nader); 440 write-in (Michael Peroutka); 241 write-in (David Cobb); 115 write-in (Peter M. Camejo); 4 write-in (Lawson Bone); 4 write-in (Ernest Virag); 3 write-in (John Joseph Kennedy); 2 write-in (David Cook); 1 write-in (Margaret Trowe); 1 write-in (Joann Breivogel); 1 write-in (John Kennedy); 1 write-in (Robert M. Christensen). The Nader write-in vote included 2,357 votes cast for the Nader-Camejo ticket and 1,214 votes for Nader alone.

**Senator**  Other vote was 81,164 Independent (Albert J. Franzen); 69,253 Libertarian (Jerry Kohn); 2,268 write-in (Mark Kuhnke); 339 write-in (Scott Doody); 134 write-in (Donald McArthur-Self); 129 write-in (Kathy Campbell); 37 write-in (Shaun L. Bill); 23 write-in (Marcus Hester); 20 write-in (Tom Carlson); 5 write-in (Orlando McDowell); 1 write-in (Arthur C. Brumfield); 1 write-in (Lowell Seida).

**House**  Other vote was:

CD 1
CD 2  26,990 Libertarian (Stephanie Sailor).
CD 3  5,077 write-in (Krista Grimm).
CD 4  4,845 Libertarian (Jake Witmer).
CD 5
CD 6
CD 7
CD 8
CD 9
CD 10
CD 11
CD 12  4,794 Libertarian (Walter B. Steele); 2 write-in (Patricia Elaine Beard).
CD 13  4 write-in (Mark Alan Mastrogiovanni).
CD 14
CD 15
CD 16  4 write-in (Tom Carlson).
CD 17
CD 18
CD 19

## 2004 PRIMARY ELECTIONS

**Primary**  March 16, 2004  **Registration**  7,137,954  No Party Registration
(as of March 16, 2004)

**Primary Type**  Open—Any registered voter could participate in the party primary of their choice.

# ILLINOIS

## GENERAL AND PRIMARY ELECTIONS

Note:   An asterisk (*) denotes incumbent.

| | REPUBLICAN PRIMARIES | | | DEMOCRATIC PRIMARIES | | |
|---|---|---|---|---|---|---|
| President | George W. Bush* | 583,575 | 100.0% | John Kerry | 873,230 | 71.7% |
| | | | | John Edwards | 131,966 | 10.8% |
| | | | | Carol Moseley Braun | 53,249 | 4.4% |
| | | | | Howard Dean | 47,343 | 3.9% |
| | | | | Al Sharpton | 36,123 | 3.0% |
| | | | | Dennis J. Kucinich | 28,083 | 2.3% |
| | | | | Joseph I. Lieberman | 24,354 | 2.0% |
| | | | | Wesley Clark | 19,304 | 1.6% |
| | | | | Lyndon H. LaRouche Jr. | 3,863 | 0.3% |
| | | | | TOTAL | 1,217,515 | |
| Senator | Jack Ryan | 234,791 | 35.5% | Barack Obama | 655,923 | 52.8% |
| | Jim Oberweis | 155,794 | 23.5% | Daniel W. Hynes | 294,717 | 23.7% |
| | Steven J. Rauschenberger | 132,655 | 20.0% | M. Blair Hull | 134,453 | 10.8% |
| | Andy McKenna | 97,238 | 14.7% | Maria Pappas | 74,987 | 6.0% |
| | Jonathan C. Wright | 17,189 | 2.6% | Gery Chico | 53,433 | 4.3% |
| | John Borling | 13,390 | 2.0% | Nancy Skinner | 16,098 | 1.3% |
| | Norm Hill | 5,637 | 0.9% | Joyce Washington | 13,375 | 1.1% |
| | Chirinjeev Kathuria | 5,110 | 0.8% | Estella Johnson Hunt (write-in) | 10 | |
| | TOTAL | 661,804 | | TOTAL | 1,242,996 | |
| | Jack Ryan subsequently quit the race and was replaced on the general election ballot by Alan Keyes. | | | | | |
| Congressional District 1 | Raymond G. Wardingley | 7,190 | 100.0% | Bobby L. Rush* | 102,540 | 100.0% |
| Congressional District 2 | No Republican candidate | | | Jesse L. Jackson Jr.* | 106,506 | 88.5% |
| | | | | Melvin "Mel" J. Reynolds | 7,103 | 5.9% |
| | | | | Anthony W. Williams | 5,159 | 4.3% |
| | | | | Everett Drayden Shumpert | 1,516 | 1.3% |
| | | | | TOTAL | 120,284 | |
| Congressional District 3 | Ryan Chlada | 17,201 | 100.0% | William O. Lipinski* | 74,420 | 100.0% |
| | | | | William O. Lipinski subsequently quit the race and was replaced on the general election ballot by his son, Daniel Lipinski. | | |
| Congressional District 4 | Tony Cisneros | 3,296 | 100.0% | Luis V. Gutierrez* | 37,382 | 100.0% |
| Congressional District 5 | Bruce Best | 10,148 | 100.0% | Rahm Emanuel* | 60,821 | 83.2% |
| | | | | Mark Arnold Fredrickson | 12,255 | 16.8% |
| | | | | TOTAL | 73,076 | |
| Congressional District 6 | Henry J. Hyde* | 50,583 | 100.0% | Christine Cegelis | 23,253 | 64.3% |
| | | | | Tom Berry | 12,905 | 35.7% |
| | | | | TOTAL | 36,158 | |
| Congressional District 7 | Antonio Davis-Fairman | 6,780 | 100.0% | Danny K. Davis* | 84,950 | 82.2% |
| | | | | Anita Rivkin-Carothers | 15,190 | 14.7% |
| | | | | Robert Dallas | 3,191 | 3.1% |
| | | | | TOTAL | 103,331 | |
| Congressional District 8 | Philip M. Crane* | 35,412 | 68.7% | Melissa Bean | 26,740 | 78.1% |
| | David W. Phelps | 16,146 | 31.3% | William C. Scheurer | 7,518 | 21.9% |
| | TOTAL | 51,558 | | TOTAL | 34,258 | |
| Congressional District 9 | No Republican candidate filed for the primary. Kurt J. Eckhardt was subsequently named to fill the vacancy on the general election ballot. | | | Jan Schakowsky* | 70,736 | 100.0% |
| Congressional District 10 | Mark Steven Kirk* | 37,764 | 100.0% | Lee Goodman | 34,488 | 100.0% |
| Congressional District 11 | Jerry Weller* | 44,378 | 100.0% | Tari Renner | 36,745 | 100.0% |

# ILLINOIS

## GENERAL AND PRIMARY ELECTIONS

| | REPUBLICAN PRIMARIES | | | DEMOCRATIC PRIMARIES | | |
|---|---|---|---|---|---|---|
| **Congressional District 12** | Erin R. Zweigart | 18,714 | 100.0% | Jerry F. Costello*<br>Kenneth Charles Wiezer<br>TOTAL | 56,397<br>6,265<br>62,662 | 90.0%<br>10.0% |
| **Congressional District 13** | Judy Biggert*<br>Bob Hart (write-in)<br>TOTAL | 46,861<br>231<br>47,092 | 99.5%<br>0.5% | Gloria Schor Andersen | 37,636 | 100.0% |
| **Congressional District 14** | J. Dennis Hastert* | 54,168 | 100.0% | *No Democratic candidate filed for the primary. Ruben Zamora was subsequently named to fill the vacancy on the general election ballot.* | | |
| **Congressional District 15** | Timothy V. Johnson* | 53,150 | 100.0% | David Gill<br>Ralph L. Langenheim Jr.<br>TOTAL | 21,323<br>7,565<br>28,888 | 73.8%<br>26.2% |
| **Congressional District 16** | Donald Manzullo* | 59,507 | 100.0% | John H. Kutsch | 34,141 | 100.0% |
| **Congressional District 17** | Andrea Lane Zinga | 30,160 | 100.0% | Lane Evans* | 46,328 | 100.0% |
| **Congressional District 18** | Ray LaHood* | 52,026 | 100.0% | Steve Waterworth | 25,838 | 100.0% |
| **Congressional District 19** | John Shimkus* | 38,892 | 100.0% | Tim Bagwell | 32,795 | 100.0% |

# INDIANA

## GOVERNOR
Mitch Daniels (R). Elected 2004 to a four-year term.

## SENATORS (1 Democrat, 1 Republican)
Evan Bayh (D). Reelected 2004 to a six-year term. Previously elected 1998.

Richard G. Lugar (R). Reelected 2000 to a six-year term. Previously elected 1994, 1988, 1982, 1976.

## REPRESENTATIVES (7 Republicans, 2 Democrats)
1. Peter J. Visclosky (D)
2. Chris Chocola (R)
3. Mark Souder (R)
4. Steve Buyer (R)
5. Dan Burton (R)
6. Mike Pence (R)
7. Julia Carson (D)
8. John Hostettler (R)
9. Mike Sodrel (R)

## POSTWAR VOTE FOR PRESIDENT

| Year | Total Vote | Republican | | Democratic | | Other Vote | Plurality | Percentage | | | |
|------|-----------|------|-----------|------|-----------|------|-----------|------|------|------|------|
| | | | | | | | | Total Vote | | Major Vote | |
| | | Vote | Candidate | Vote | Candidate | | | Rep. | Dem. | Rep. | Dem. |
| 2004 | 2,468,002 | 1,479,438 | Bush, George W. | 969,011 | Kerry, John | 19,553 | 510,427 R | 59.9% | 39.3% | 60.4% | 39.6% |
| 2000** | 2,199,302 | 1,245,836 | Bush, George W. | 901,980 | Gore, Al | 51,486 | 343,856 R | 56.6% | 41.0% | 58.0% | 42.0% |
| 1996** | 2,135,842 | 1,006,693 | Dole, Bob | 887,424 | Clinton, Bill | 241,725 | 119,269 R | 47.1% | 41.5% | 53.1% | 46.9% |
| 1992** | 2,305,871 | 989,375 | Bush, George | 848,420 | Clinton, Bill | 468,076 | 140,955 R | 42.9% | 36.8% | 53.8% | 46.2% |
| 1988 | 2,168,621 | 1,297,763 | Bush, George | 860,643 | Dukakis, Michael S. | 10,215 | 437,120 R | 59.8% | 39.7% | 60.1% | 39.9% |
| 1984 | 2,233,069 | 1,377,230 | Reagan, Ronald | 841,481 | Mondale, Walter F. | 14,358 | 535,749 R | 61.7% | 37.7% | 62.1% | 37.9% |
| 1980** | 2,242,033 | 1,255,656 | Reagan, Ronald | 844,197 | Carter, Jimmy | 142,180 | 411,459 R | 56.0% | 37.7% | 59.8% | 40.2% |
| 1976 | 2,220,362 | 1,183,958 | Ford, Gerald R. | 1,014,714 | Carter, Jimmy | 21,690 | 169,244 R | 53.3% | 45.7% | 53.8% | 46.2% |
| 1972 | 2,125,529 | 1,405,154 | Nixon, Richard M. | 708,568 | McGovern, George S. | 11,807 | 696,586 R | 66.1% | 33.3% | 66.5% | 33.5% |
| 1968** | 2,123,597 | 1,067,885 | Nixon, Richard M. | 806,659 | Humphrey, Hubert H. | 249,053 | 261,226 R | 50.3% | 38.0% | 57.0% | 43.0% |
| 1964 | 2,091,606 | 911,118 | Goldwater, Barry M. | 1,170,848 | Johnson, Lyndon B. | 9,640 | 259,730 D | 43.6% | 56.0% | 43.8% | 56.2% |
| 1960 | 2,135,360 | 1,175,120 | Nixon, Richard M. | 952,358 | Kennedy, John F. | 7,882 | 222,762 R | 55.0% | 44.6% | 55.2% | 44.8% |
| 1956 | 1,974,607 | 1,182,811 | Eisenhower, Dwight D. | 783,908 | Stevenson, Adlai E. | 7,888 | 398,903 R | 59.9% | 39.7% | 60.1% | 39.9% |
| 1952 | 1,955,049 | 1,136,259 | Eisenhower, Dwight D. | 801,530 | Stevenson, Adlai E. | 17,260 | 334,729 R | 58.1% | 41.0% | 58.6% | 41.4% |
| 1948 | 1,656,212 | 821,079 | Dewey, Thomas E. | 807,831 | Truman, Harry S. | 27,302 | 13,248 R | 49.6% | 48.8% | 50.4% | 49.6% |

In past elections, the other vote included: 2000 - 18,531 Green (Ralph Nader); 1996 - 224,299 Reform (Ross Perot); 1992 - 455,934 Independent (Perot); 1980 - 111,639 Independent (John Anderson); 1968 - 243,108 American Independent (George Wallace).

# INDIANA

## POSTWAR VOTE FOR GOVERNOR

| Year | Total Vote | Republican Vote | Republican Candidate | Democratic Vote | Democratic Candidate | Other Vote | Rep.-Dem. Plurality | Percentage Total Vote Rep. | Percentage Total Vote Dem. | Percentage Major Vote Rep. | Percentage Major Vote Dem. |
|------|-----------|----------------|---------------------|----------------|---------------------|-----------|---------------------|------|------|------|------|
| 2004 | 2,448,498 | 1,302,912 | Daniels, Mitch | 1,113,900 | Kernan, Joseph E. | 31,686 | 189,012 R | 53.2% | 45.5% | 53.9% | 46.1% |
| 2000 | 2,179,413 | 908,285 | McIntosh, David M. | 1,232,525 | O'Bannon, Frank L. | 38,603 | 324,240 D | 41.7% | 56.6% | 42.4% | 57.6% |
| 1996 | 2,110,047 | 986,982 | Goldsmith, Stephen | 1,087,128 | O'Bannon, Frank L. | 35,937 | 100,146 D | 46.8% | 51.5% | 47.6% | 52.4% |
| 1992 | 2,229,116 | 822,533 | Pearson, Linley E. | 1,382,151 | Bayh, Evan | 24,432 | 559,618 D | 36.9% | 62.0% | 37.3% | 62.7% |
| 1988 | 2,140,781 | 1,002,207 | Mutz, John M. | 1,138,574 | Bayh, Evan | | 136,367 D | 46.8% | 53.2% | 46.8% | 53.2% |
| 1984 | 2,197,988 | 1,146,497 | Orr, Robert D. | 1,036,922 | Townsend, W. Wayne | 14,569 | 109,575 R | 52.2% | 47.2% | 52.5% | 47.5% |
| 1980 | 2,178,403 | 1,257,383 | Orr, Robert D. | 913,116 | Hillenbrand, John A. | 7,904 | 344,267 R | 57.7% | 41.9% | 57.9% | 42.1% |
| 1976 | 2,175,324 | 1,236,555 | Bowen, Otis R. | 927,243 | Conrad, Larry A. | 11,526 | 309,312 R | 56.8% | 42.6% | 57.1% | 42.9% |
| 1972 | 2,120,847 | 1,203,903 | Bowen, Otis R. | 900,489 | Welsh, Matthew E. | 16,455 | 303,414 R | 56.8% | 42.5% | 57.2% | 42.8% |
| 1968 | 2,049,072 | 1,080,271 | Whitcomb, Edgar D. | 965,816 | Rock, Robert L. | 2,985 | 114,455 R | 52.7% | 47.1% | 52.8% | 47.2% |
| 1964 | 2,072,915 | 901,342 | Ristine, Richard O. | 1,164,620 | Branigin, Roger D. | 6,953 | 263,278 D | 43.5% | 56.2% | 43.6% | 56.4% |
| 1960 | 2,128,965 | 1,049,540 | Parker, Crawford F. | 1,072,717 | Welsh, Matthew E. | 6,708 | 23,177 D | 49.3% | 50.4% | 49.5% | 50.5% |
| 1956 | 1,954,290 | 1,086,868 | Handley, Harold W. | 859,393 | Tucker, Ralph | 8,029 | 227,475 R | 55.6% | 44.0% | 55.8% | 44.2% |
| 1952 | 1,931,869 | 1,075,685 | Craig, George N. | 841,984 | Watkins, John A. | 14,200 | 233,701 R | 55.7% | 43.6% | 56.1% | 43.9% |
| 1948 | 1,652,321 | 745,892 | Creighton, Hobart | 884,995 | Schricker, Henry F. | 21,434 | 139,103 D | 45.1% | 53.6% | 45.7% | 54.3% |

## POSTWAR VOTE FOR SENATOR

| Year | Total Vote | Republican Vote | Republican Candidate | Democratic Vote | Democratic Candidate | Other Vote | Rep.-Dem. Plurality | Percentage Total Vote Rep. | Percentage Total Vote Dem. | Percentage Major Vote Rep. | Percentage Major Vote Dem. |
|------|-----------|----------------|---------------------|----------------|---------------------|-----------|---------------------|------|------|------|------|
| 2004 | 2,428,233 | 903,913 | Scott, Marvin | 1,496,976 | Bayh, Evan | 27,344 | 593,063 D | 37.2% | 61.6% | 37.6% | 62.4% |
| 2000 | 2,145,209 | 1,427,944 | Lugar, Richard G. | 683,273 | Johnson, David L. | 33,992 | 744,671 R | 66.6% | 31.9% | 67.6% | 32.4% |
| 1998 | 1,588,617 | 552,732 | Helmke, Paul | 1,012,244 | Bayh, Evan | 23,641 | 459,512 D | 34.8% | 63.7% | 35.3% | 64.7% |
| 1994 | 1,543,568 | 1,039,625 | Lugar, Richard G. | 470,799 | Jontz, Jim | 33,144 | 568,826 R | 67.4% | 30.5% | 68.8% | 31.2% |
| 1992 | 2,211,426 | 1,267,972 | Coats, Daniel R. | 900,148 | Hogsett, Joseph H. | 43,306 | 367,824 R | 57.3% | 40.7% | 58.5% | 41.5% |
| 1990S | 1,504,302 | 806,048 | Coats, Daniel R. | 696,639 | Hill, Baron P. | 1,615 | 109,409 R | 53.6% | 46.3% | 53.6% | 46.4% |
| 1988 | 2,099,303 | 1,430,525 | Lugar, Richard G. | 668,778 | Wickes, Jack | | 761,747 R | 68.1% | 31.9% | 68.1% | 31.9% |
| 1986 | 1,545,563 | 936,143 | Quayle, J. Danforth | 595,192 | Long, Jill L. | 14,228 | 340,951 R | 60.6% | 38.5% | 61.1% | 38.9% |
| 1982 | 1,817,287 | 978,301 | Lugar, Richard G. | 828,400 | Fithian, Floyd | 10,586 | 149,901 R | 53.8% | 45.6% | 54.1% | 45.9% |
| 1980 | 2,198,376 | 1,182,414 | Quayle, J. Danforth | 1,015,962 | Bayh, Birch | | 166,452 R | 53.8% | 46.2% | 53.8% | 46.2% |
| 1976 | 2,171,187 | 1,275,833 | Lugar, Richard G. | 878,522 | Hartke, R. Vance | 16,832 | 397,311 R | 58.8% | 40.5% | 59.2% | 40.8% |
| 1974 | 1,752,978 | 814,117 | Lugar, Richard G. | 889,269 | Bayh, Birch | 49,592 | 75,152 D | 46.4% | 50.7% | 47.8% | 52.2% |
| 1970 | 1,737,697 | 866,707 | Roudebush, Richard | 870,990 | Hartke, R. Vance | | 4,283 D | 49.9% | 50.1% | 49.9% | 50.1% |
| 1968 | 2,053,118 | 988,571 | Ruckelshaus, William | 1,060,456 | Bayh, Birch | 4,091 | 71,885 D | 48.1% | 51.7% | 48.2% | 51.8% |
| 1964 | 2,076,963 | 941,519 | Bontrager, D. Russell | 1,128,505 | Hartke, R. Vance | 6,939 | 186,986 D | 45.3% | 54.3% | 45.5% | 54.5% |
| 1962 | 1,800,038 | 894,547 | Capehart, Homer E. | 905,491 | Bayh, Birch | | 10,944 D | 49.7% | 50.3% | 49.7% | 50.3% |
| 1958 | 1,724,598 | 731,635 | Handley, Harold W. | 973,636 | Hartke, R. Vance | 19,327 | 242,001 D | 42.4% | 56.5% | 42.9% | 57.1% |
| 1956 | 1,963,986 | 1,084,262 | Capehart, Homer E. | 871,781 | Wickard, Claude | 7,943 | 212,481 R | 55.2% | 44.4% | 55.4% | 44.6% |
| 1952 | 1,946,118 | 1,020,605 | Jenner, William E. | 911,169 | Schricker, Henry F. | 14,344 | 109,436 R | 52.4% | 46.8% | 52.8% | 47.2% |
| 1950 | 1,598,724 | 844,303 | Capehart, Homer E. | 741,025 | Campbell, Alex M. | 13,396 | 103,278 R | 52.8% | 46.4% | 53.3% | 46.7% |
| 1946 | 1,347,434 | 739,809 | Jenner, William E. | 584,288 | Townsend, M. Clifford | 23,337 | 155,521 R | 54.9% | 43.4% | 55.9% | 44.1% |

The 1990 election was for a short term to fill a vacancy.

# INDIANA

### Congressional districts first established for elections held in 2002
### 9 members

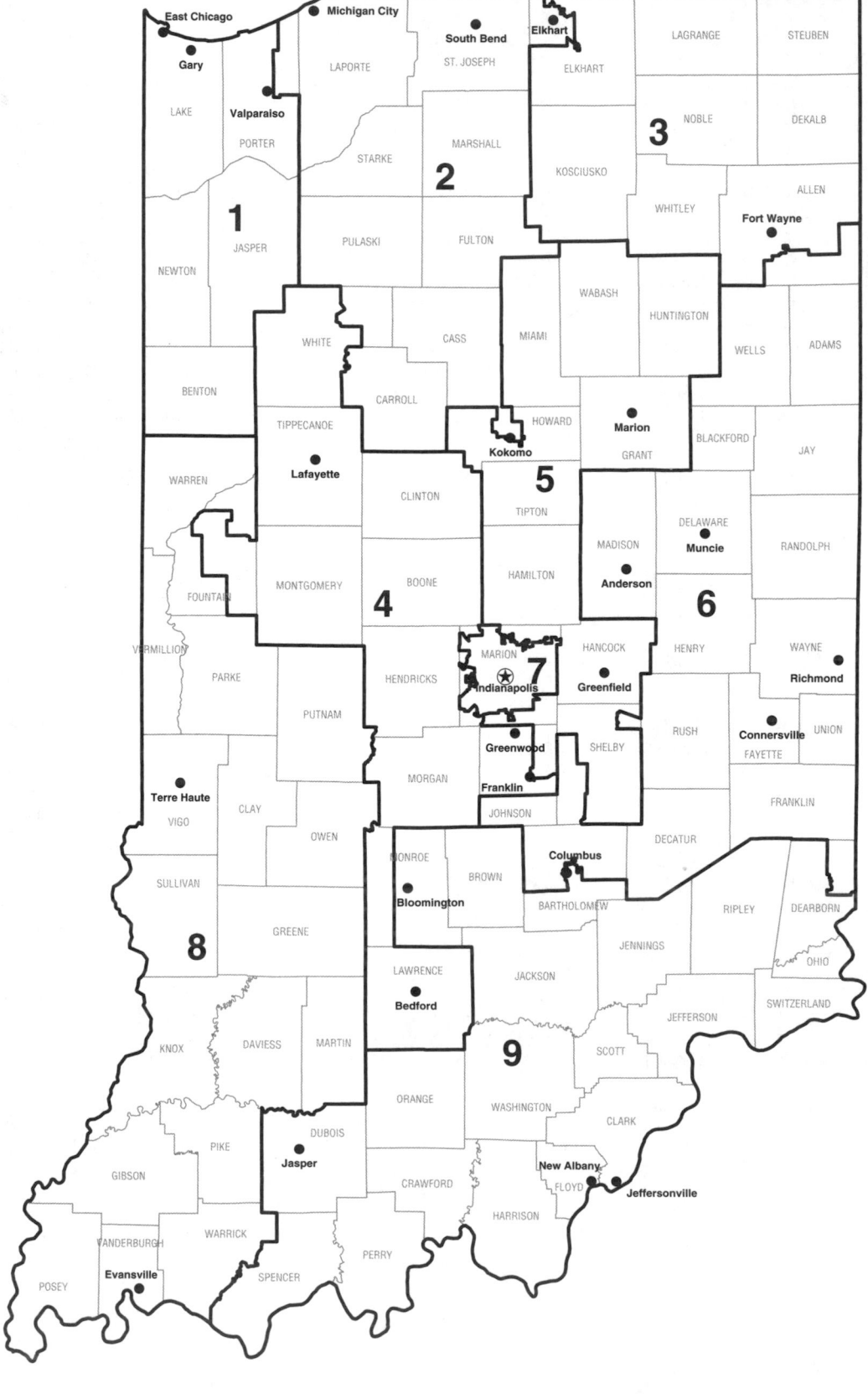

# INDIANA

## PRESIDENT 2004

| 2000 Census Population | County | Total Vote | Republican | Democratic | Other | Rep.-Dem. Plurality | | Percentage Total Vote Rep. | Dem. | Major Vote Rep. | Dem. |
|---|---|---|---|---|---|---|---|---|---|---|---|
| 33,625 | ADAMS | 13,340 | 9,734 | 3,512 | 94 | 6,222 | R | 73.0% | 26.3% | 73.5% | 26.5% |
| 331,849 | ALLEN | 129,609 | 82,013 | 46,710 | 886 | 35,303 | R | 63.3% | 36.0% | 63.7% | 36.3% |
| 71,435 | BARTHOLOMEW | 28,515 | 19,093 | 9,191 | 231 | 9,902 | R | 67.0% | 32.2% | 67.5% | 32.5% |
| 9,421 | BENTON | 3,992 | 2,797 | 1,135 | 60 | 1,662 | R | 70.1% | 28.4% | 71.1% | 28.9% |
| 14,048 | BLACKFORD | 5,380 | 3,447 | 1,903 | 30 | 1,544 | R | 64.1% | 35.4% | 64.4% | 35.6% |
| 46,107 | BOONE | 22,898 | 17,055 | 5,636 | 207 | 11,419 | R | 74.5% | 24.6% | 75.2% | 24.8% |
| 14,957 | BROWN | 7,330 | 4,512 | 2,730 | 88 | 1,782 | R | 61.6% | 37.2% | 62.3% | 37.7% |
| 20,165 | CARROLL | 8,638 | 5,868 | 2,689 | 81 | 3,179 | R | 67.9% | 31.1% | 68.6% | 31.4% |
| 40,930 | CASS | 13,931 | 9,480 | 4,315 | 136 | 5,165 | R | 68.0% | 31.0% | 68.7% | 31.3% |
| 96,472 | CLARK | 42,337 | 24,495 | 17,648 | 194 | 6,847 | R | 57.9% | 41.7% | 58.1% | 41.9% |
| 26,556 | CLAY | 10,783 | 7,361 | 3,333 | 89 | 4,028 | R | 68.3% | 30.9% | 68.8% | 31.2% |
| 33,866 | CLINTON | 11,877 | 8,471 | 3,335 | 71 | 5,136 | R | 71.3% | 28.1% | 71.8% | 28.2% |
| 10,743 | CRAWFORD | 4,574 | 2,609 | 1,932 | 33 | 677 | R | 57.0% | 42.2% | 57.5% | 42.5% |
| 29,820 | DAVIESS | 10,599 | 7,936 | 2,573 | 90 | 5,363 | R | 74.9% | 24.3% | 75.5% | 24.5% |
| 46,109 | DEARBORN | 20,969 | 14,231 | 6,596 | 142 | 7,635 | R | 67.9% | 31.5% | 68.3% | 31.7% |
| 24,555 | DECATUR | 10,199 | 7,499 | 2,621 | 79 | 4,878 | R | 73.5% | 25.7% | 74.1% | 25.9% |
| 40,285 | DE KALB | 15,403 | 10,468 | 4,810 | 125 | 5,658 | R | 68.0% | 31.2% | 68.5% | 31.5% |
| 118,769 | DELAWARE | 47,939 | 27,064 | 20,436 | 439 | 6,628 | R | 56.5% | 42.6% | 57.0% | 43.0% |
| 39,674 | DUBOIS | 17,066 | 11,726 | 5,210 | 130 | 6,516 | R | 68.7% | 30.5% | 69.2% | 30.8% |
| 182,791 | ELKHART | 61,380 | 42,967 | 17,966 | 447 | 25,001 | R | 70.0% | 29.3% | 70.5% | 29.5% |
| 25,588 | FAYETTE | 9,468 | 5,761 | 3,626 | 81 | 2,135 | R | 60.8% | 38.3% | 61.4% | 38.6% |
| 70,823 | FLOYD | 33,890 | 19,877 | 13,857 | 156 | 6,020 | R | 58.7% | 40.9% | 58.9% | 41.1% |
| 17,954 | FOUNTAIN | 7,804 | 5,260 | 2,477 | 67 | 2,783 | R | 67.4% | 31.7% | 68.0% | 32.0% |
| 22,151 | FRANKLIN | 9,992 | 6,977 | 2,925 | 90 | 4,052 | R | 69.8% | 29.3% | 70.5% | 29.5% |
| 20,511 | FULTON | 8,703 | 6,027 | 2,607 | 69 | 3,420 | R | 69.3% | 30.0% | 69.8% | 30.2% |
| 32,500 | GIBSON | 14,614 | 9,133 | 5,378 | 103 | 3,755 | R | 62.5% | 36.8% | 62.9% | 37.1% |
| 73,403 | GRANT | 27,460 | 18,769 | 8,509 | 182 | 10,260 | R | 68.4% | 31.0% | 68.8% | 31.2% |
| 33,157 | GREENE | 13,352 | 8,609 | 4,606 | 137 | 4,003 | R | 64.5% | 34.5% | 65.1% | 34.9% |
| 182,740 | HAMILTON | 104,906 | 77,887 | 26,388 | 631 | 51,499 | R | 74.2% | 25.2% | 74.7% | 25.3% |
| 55,391 | HANCOCK | 27,867 | 20,771 | 6,912 | 184 | 13,859 | R | 74.5% | 24.8% | 75.0% | 25.0% |
| 34,325 | HARRISON | 17,310 | 11,015 | 6,171 | 124 | 4,844 | R | 63.6% | 35.6% | 64.1% | 35.9% |
| 104,093 | HENDRICKS | 52,302 | 38,430 | 13,548 | 324 | 24,882 | R | 73.5% | 25.9% | 73.9% | 26.1% |
| 48,508 | HENRY | 20,504 | 13,137 | 7,176 | 191 | 5,961 | R | 64.1% | 35.0% | 64.7% | 35.3% |
| 84,964 | HOWARD | 37,021 | 23,714 | 12,998 | 309 | 10,716 | R | 64.1% | 35.1% | 64.6% | 35.4% |
| 38,075 | HUNTINGTON | 15,627 | 11,617 | 3,877 | 133 | 7,740 | R | 74.3% | 24.8% | 75.0% | 25.0% |
| 41,335 | JACKSON | 16,309 | 11,083 | 5,092 | 134 | 5,991 | R | 68.0% | 31.2% | 68.5% | 31.5% |
| 30,043 | JASPER | 11,844 | 8,056 | 3,678 | 110 | 4,378 | R | 68.0% | 31.1% | 68.7% | 31.3% |
| 21,806 | JAY | 8,232 | 5,427 | 2,740 | 65 | 2,687 | R | 65.9% | 33.3% | 66.5% | 33.5% |
| 31,705 | JEFFERSON | 12,971 | 7,763 | 5,117 | 91 | 2,646 | R | 59.8% | 39.4% | 60.3% | 39.7% |
| 27,554 | JENNINGS | 10,517 | 6,864 | 3,538 | 115 | 3,326 | R | 65.3% | 33.6% | 66.0% | 34.0% |
| 115,209 | JOHNSON | 51,255 | 37,765 | 13,109 | 381 | 24,656 | R | 73.7% | 25.6% | 74.2% | 25.8% |
| 39,256 | KNOX | 15,746 | 9,990 | 5,649 | 107 | 4,341 | R | 63.4% | 35.9% | 63.9% | 36.1% |
| 74,057 | KOSCIUSKO | 28,360 | 22,136 | 5,977 | 247 | 16,159 | R | 78.1% | 21.1% | 78.7% | 21.3% |
| 34,909 | LAGRANGE | 9,003 | 6,430 | 2,523 | 50 | 3,907 | R | 71.4% | 28.0% | 71.8% | 28.2% |
| 484,564 | LAKE | 188,022 | 71,903 | 114,743 | 1,376 | 42,840 | D | 38.2% | 61.0% | 38.5% | 61.5% |
| 110,106 | LA PORTE | 42,606 | 20,916 | 21,114 | 576 | 198 | D | 49.1% | 49.6% | 49.8% | 50.2% |
| 45,922 | LAWRENCE | 17,698 | 12,207 | 5,346 | 145 | 6,861 | R | 69.0% | 30.2% | 69.5% | 30.5% |
| 133,358 | MADISON | 54,855 | 32,526 | 21,882 | 447 | 10,644 | R | 59.3% | 39.9% | 59.8% | 40.2% |
| 860,454 | MARION | 320,838 | 156,072 | 162,249 | 2,517 | 6,177 | D | 48.6% | 50.6% | 49.0% | 51.0% |
| 45,128 | MARSHALL | 17,814 | 12,074 | 5,593 | 147 | 6,481 | R | 67.8% | 31.4% | 68.3% | 31.7% |
| 10,369 | MARTIN | 4,996 | 3,414 | 1,522 | 60 | 1,892 | R | 68.3% | 30.5% | 69.2% | 30.8% |
| 36,082 | MIAMI | 13,628 | 9,600 | 3,886 | 142 | 5,714 | R | 70.4% | 28.5% | 71.2% | 28.8% |
| 120,563 | MONROE | 50,467 | 22,834 | 26,965 | 668 | 4,131 | D | 45.2% | 53.4% | 45.9% | 54.1% |
| 37,629 | MONTGOMERY | 14,548 | 10,901 | 3,536 | 111 | 7,365 | R | 74.9% | 24.3% | 75.5% | 24.5% |
| 66,689 | MORGAN | 26,029 | 19,197 | 6,650 | 182 | 12,547 | R | 73.8% | 25.5% | 74.3% | 25.7% |
| 14,566 | NEWTON | 5,848 | 3,757 | 2,032 | 59 | 1,725 | R | 64.2% | 34.7% | 64.9% | 35.1% |
| 46,275 | NOBLE | 15,679 | 10,859 | 4,703 | 117 | 6,156 | R | 69.3% | 30.0% | 69.8% | 30.2% |
| 5,623 | OHIO | 2,958 | 1,796 | 1,139 | 23 | 657 | R | 60.7% | 38.5% | 61.2% | 38.8% |
| 19,306 | ORANGE | 8,652 | 5,683 | 2,885 | 84 | 2,798 | R | 65.7% | 33.3% | 66.3% | 33.7% |
| 21,786 | OWEN | 7,604 | 5,000 | 2,536 | 68 | 2,464 | R | 65.8% | 33.4% | 66.3% | 33.7% |

# INDIANA

## PRESIDENT 2004

| 2000 Census Population | County | Total Vote | Republican | Democratic | Other | Rep.-Dem. Plurality | | Percentage | | | |
|---|---|---|---|---|---|---|---|---|---|---|---|
| | | | | | | | | Total Vote | | Major Vote | |
| | | | | | | | | Rep. | Dem. | Rep. | Dem. |
| 17,241 | PARKE | 6,971 | 4,550 | 2,362 | 59 | 2,188 | R | 65.3% | 33.9% | 65.8% | 34.2% |
| 18,899 | PERRY | 8,315 | 4,137 | 4,131 | 47 | 6 | R | 49.8% | 49.7% | 50.0% | 50.0% |
| 12,837 | PIKE | 6,212 | 3,745 | 2,418 | 49 | 1,327 | R | 60.3% | 38.9% | 60.8% | 39.2% |
| 146,798 | PORTER | 64,873 | 34,794 | 29,388 | 691 | 5,406 | R | 53.6% | 45.3% | 54.2% | 45.8% |
| 27,061 | POSEY | 11,986 | 7,833 | 4,085 | 68 | 3,748 | R | 65.4% | 34.1% | 65.7% | 34.3% |
| 13,755 | PULASKI | 5,614 | 3,797 | 1,750 | 67 | 2,047 | R | 67.6% | 31.2% | 68.5% | 31.5% |
| 36,019 | PUTNAM | 13,136 | 8,908 | 4,103 | 125 | 4,805 | R | 67.8% | 31.2% | 68.5% | 31.5% |
| 27,401 | RANDOLPH | 11,092 | 7,172 | 3,812 | 108 | 3,360 | R | 64.7% | 34.4% | 65.3% | 34.7% |
| 26,523 | RIPLEY | 11,834 | 8,224 | 3,510 | 100 | 4,714 | R | 69.5% | 29.7% | 70.1% | 29.9% |
| 18,261 | RUSH | 7,421 | 5,363 | 2,000 | 58 | 3,363 | R | 72.3% | 27.0% | 72.8% | 27.2% |
| 265,559 | ST. JOSEPH | 108,619 | 55,254 | 52,637 | 728 | 2,617 | R | 50.9% | 48.5% | 51.2% | 48.8% |
| 22,960 | SCOTT | 8,677 | 4,793 | 3,822 | 62 | 971 | R | 55.2% | 44.0% | 55.6% | 44.4% |
| 43,445 | SHELBY | 16,027 | 11,397 | 4,519 | 111 | 6,878 | R | 71.1% | 28.2% | 71.6% | 28.4% |
| 20,391 | SPENCER | 9,924 | 5,934 | 3,920 | 70 | 2,014 | R | 59.8% | 39.5% | 60.2% | 39.8% |
| 23,556 | STARKE | 8,937 | 4,846 | 3,987 | 104 | 859 | R | 54.2% | 44.6% | 54.9% | 45.1% |
| 33,214 | STEUBEN | 12,905 | 8,433 | 4,345 | 127 | 4,088 | R | 65.3% | 33.7% | 66.0% | 34.0% |
| 21,751 | SULLIVAN | 8,394 | 4,999 | 3,341 | 54 | 1,658 | R | 59.6% | 39.8% | 59.9% | 40.1% |
| 9,065 | SWITZERLAND | 3,671 | 2,161 | 1,479 | 31 | 682 | R | 58.9% | 40.3% | 59.4% | 40.6% |
| 148,955 | TIPPECANOE | 52,360 | 30,897 | 20,818 | 645 | 10,079 | R | 59.0% | 39.8% | 59.7% | 40.3% |
| 16,577 | TIPTON | 7,892 | 5,628 | 2,203 | 61 | 3,425 | R | 71.3% | 27.9% | 71.9% | 28.1% |
| 7,349 | UNION | 3,344 | 2,266 | 1,045 | 33 | 1,221 | R | 67.8% | 31.3% | 68.4% | 31.6% |
| 171,922 | VANDERBURGH | 70,654 | 41,463 | 28,767 | 424 | 12,696 | R | 58.7% | 40.7% | 59.0% | 41.0% |
| 16,788 | VERMILLION | 7,017 | 3,536 | 3,424 | 57 | 112 | R | 50.4% | 48.8% | 50.8% | 49.2% |
| 105,848 | VIGO | 39,744 | 20,988 | 18,426 | 330 | 2,562 | R | 52.8% | 46.4% | 53.3% | 46.7% |
| 34,960 | WABASH | 13,602 | 9,607 | 3,920 | 75 | 5,687 | R | 70.6% | 28.8% | 71.0% | 29.0% |
| 8,419 | WARREN | 3,960 | 2,565 | 1,356 | 39 | 1,209 | R | 64.8% | 34.2% | 65.4% | 34.6% |
| 52,383 | WARRICK | 26,025 | 16,930 | 8,980 | 115 | 7,950 | R | 65.1% | 34.5% | 65.3% | 34.7% |
| 27,223 | WASHINGTON | 10,880 | 6,915 | 3,879 | 86 | 3,036 | R | 63.6% | 35.7% | 64.1% | 35.9% |
| 71,097 | WAYNE | 27,657 | 16,586 | 10,775 | 296 | 5,811 | R | 60.0% | 39.0% | 60.6% | 39.4% |
| 27,600 | WELLS | 12,354 | 9,168 | 3,112 | 74 | 6,056 | R | 74.2% | 25.2% | 74.7% | 25.3% |
| 25,267 | WHITE | 10,366 | 6,974 | 3,277 | 115 | 3,697 | R | 67.3% | 31.6% | 68.0% | 32.0% |
| 30,707 | WHITLEY | 13,481 | 9,512 | 3,880 | 89 | 5,632 | R | 70.6% | 28.8% | 71.0% | 29.0% |
| 6,080,485 | TOTAL | 2,468,002 | 1,479,438 | 969,011 | 19,553 | 510,427 | R | 59.9% | 39.3% | 60.4% | 39.6% |

# INDIANA

## GOVERNOR 2004

| 2000 Census Population | County | Total Vote | Republican | Democratic | Other | Rep.-Dem. Plurality | Percentage Total Vote Rep. | Dem. | Major Vote Rep. | Dem. |
|---|---|---|---|---|---|---|---|---|---|---|
| 33,625 | ADAMS | 13,265 | 8,350 | 4,816 | 99 | 3,534 R | 62.9% | 36.3% | 63.4% | 36.6% |
| 331,849 | ALLEN | 128,771 | 73,689 | 53,899 | 1,183 | 19,790 R | 57.2% | 41.9% | 57.8% | 42.2% |
| 71,435 | BARTHOLOMEW | 28,386 | 16,858 | 11,008 | 520 | 5,850 R | 59.4% | 38.8% | 60.5% | 39.5% |
| 9,421 | BENTON | 3,999 | 2,432 | 1,498 | 69 | 934 R | 60.8% | 37.5% | 61.9% | 38.1% |
| 14,048 | BLACKFORD | 5,354 | 2,741 | 2,567 | 46 | 174 R | 51.2% | 47.9% | 51.6% | 48.4% |
| 46,107 | BOONE | 22,820 | 16,189 | 6,326 | 305 | 9,863 R | 70.9% | 27.7% | 71.9% | 28.1% |
| 14,957 | BROWN | 7,292 | 4,010 | 3,118 | 164 | 892 R | 55.0% | 42.8% | 56.3% | 43.7% |
| 20,165 | CARROLL | 8,592 | 5,090 | 3,387 | 115 | 1,703 R | 59.2% | 39.4% | 60.0% | 40.0% |
| 40,930 | CASS | 13,975 | 7,946 | 5,808 | 221 | 2,138 R | 56.9% | 41.6% | 57.8% | 42.2% |
| 96,472 | CLARK | 41,795 | 20,471 | 20,964 | 360 | 493 D | 49.0% | 50.2% | 49.4% | 50.6% |
| 26,556 | CLAY | 10,549 | 5,724 | 4,677 | 148 | 1,047 R | 54.3% | 44.3% | 55.0% | 45.0% |
| 33,866 | CLINTON | 11,814 | 7,537 | 4,129 | 148 | 3,408 R | 63.8% | 35.0% | 64.6% | 35.4% |
| 10,743 | CRAWFORD | 4,522 | 2,231 | 2,231 | 60 |  | 49.3% | 49.3% | 50.0% | 50.0% |
| 29,820 | DAVIESS | 10,459 | 6,223 | 4,049 | 187 | 2,174 R | 59.5% | 38.7% | 60.6% | 39.4% |
| 46,109 | DEARBORN | 20,384 | 12,514 | 7,573 | 297 | 4,941 R | 61.4% | 37.2% | 62.3% | 37.7% |
| 24,555 | DECATUR | 10,019 | 6,355 | 3,524 | 140 | 2,831 R | 63.4% | 35.2% | 64.3% | 35.7% |
| 40,285 | DE KALB | 15,437 | 9,242 | 6,012 | 183 | 3,230 R | 59.9% | 38.9% | 60.6% | 39.4% |
| 118,769 | DELAWARE | 47,712 | 22,917 | 24,132 | 663 | 1,215 D | 48.0% | 50.6% | 48.7% | 51.3% |
| 39,674 | DUBOIS | 16,425 | 9,385 | 6,871 | 169 | 2,514 R | 57.1% | 41.8% | 57.7% | 42.3% |
| 182,791 | ELKHART | 61,339 | 38,430 | 22,406 | 503 | 16,024 R | 62.7% | 36.5% | 63.2% | 36.8% |
| 25,588 | FAYETTE | 9,326 | 4,981 | 4,224 | 121 | 757 R | 53.4% | 45.3% | 54.1% | 45.9% |
| 70,823 | FLOYD | 33,651 | 16,869 | 16,503 | 279 | 366 R | 50.1% | 49.0% | 50.5% | 49.5% |
| 17,954 | FOUNTAIN | 7,765 | 4,786 | 2,878 | 101 | 1,908 R | 61.6% | 37.1% | 62.4% | 37.6% |
| 22,151 | FRANKLIN | 9,798 | 5,822 | 3,862 | 114 | 1,960 R | 59.4% | 39.4% | 60.1% | 39.9% |
| 20,511 | FULTON | 8,726 | 5,103 | 3,513 | 110 | 1,590 R | 58.5% | 40.3% | 59.2% | 40.8% |
| 32,500 | GIBSON | 14,556 | 7,289 | 7,101 | 166 | 188 R | 50.1% | 48.8% | 50.7% | 49.3% |
| 73,403 | GRANT | 27,194 | 15,543 | 11,376 | 275 | 4,167 R | 57.2% | 41.8% | 57.7% | 42.3% |
| 33,157 | GREENE | 13,127 | 6,791 | 6,123 | 213 | 668 R | 51.7% | 46.6% | 52.6% | 47.4% |
| 182,740 | HAMILTON | 104,670 | 76,433 | 27,316 | 921 | 49,117 R | 73.0% | 26.1% | 73.7% | 26.3% |
| 55,391 | HANCOCK | 27,930 | 18,825 | 8,746 | 359 | 10,079 R | 67.4% | 31.3% | 68.3% | 31.7% |
| 34,325 | HARRISON | 17,222 | 9,242 | 7,809 | 171 | 1,433 R | 53.7% | 45.3% | 54.2% | 45.8% |
| 104,093 | HENDRICKS | 52,093 | 35,761 | 15,691 | 641 | 20,070 R | 68.6% | 30.1% | 69.5% | 30.5% |
| 48,508 | HENRY | 20,371 | 11,408 | 8,674 | 289 | 2,734 R | 56.0% | 42.6% | 56.8% | 43.2% |
| 84,964 | HOWARD | 37,042 | 19,885 | 16,742 | 415 | 3,143 R | 53.7% | 45.2% | 54.3% | 45.7% |
| 38,075 | HUNTINGTON | 15,620 | 10,484 | 4,953 | 183 | 5,531 R | 67.1% | 31.7% | 67.9% | 32.1% |
| 41,335 | JACKSON | 16,305 | 9,587 | 6,527 | 191 | 3,060 R | 58.8% | 40.0% | 59.5% | 40.5% |
| 30,043 | JASPER | 11,650 | 6,781 | 4,701 | 168 | 2,080 R | 58.2% | 40.4% | 59.1% | 40.9% |
| 21,806 | JAY | 8,070 | 4,537 | 3,453 | 80 | 1,084 R | 56.2% | 42.8% | 56.8% | 43.2% |
| 31,705 | JEFFERSON | 12,801 | 6,542 | 6,109 | 150 | 433 R | 51.1% | 47.7% | 51.7% | 48.3% |
| 27,554 | JENNINGS | 10,478 | 5,806 | 4,482 | 190 | 1,324 R | 55.4% | 42.8% | 56.4% | 43.6% |
| 115,209 | JOHNSON | 51,224 | 34,269 | 16,253 | 702 | 18,016 R | 66.9% | 31.7% | 67.8% | 32.2% |
| 39,256 | KNOX | 15,594 | 7,569 | 7,797 | 228 | 228 D | 48.5% | 50.0% | 49.3% | 50.7% |
| 74,057 | KOSCIUSKO | 28,248 | 20,047 | 7,885 | 316 | 12,162 R | 71.0% | 27.9% | 71.8% | 28.2% |
| 34,909 | LAGRANGE | 9,016 | 5,748 | 3,171 | 97 | 2,577 R | 63.8% | 35.2% | 64.4% | 35.6% |
| 484,564 | LAKE | 183,036 | 61,720 | 118,697 | 2,619 | 56,977 D | 33.7% | 64.8% | 34.2% | 65.8% |
| 110,106 | LA PORTE | 42,164 | 16,234 | 25,049 | 881 | 8,815 D | 38.5% | 59.4% | 39.3% | 60.7% |
| 45,922 | LAWRENCE | 17,641 | 11,480 | 5,904 | 257 | 5,576 R | 65.1% | 33.5% | 66.0% | 34.0% |
| 133,358 | MADISON | 54,737 | 28,142 | 25,972 | 623 | 2,170 R | 51.4% | 47.4% | 52.0% | 48.0% |
| 860,454 | MARION | 319,817 | 148,825 | 167,097 | 3,895 | 18,272 D | 46.5% | 52.2% | 47.1% | 52.9% |
| 45,128 | MARSHALL | 17,705 | 10,745 | 6,756 | 204 | 3,989 R | 60.7% | 38.2% | 61.4% | 38.6% |
| 10,369 | MARTIN | 4,963 | 2,664 | 2,205 | 94 | 459 R | 53.7% | 44.4% | 54.7% | 45.3% |
| 36,082 | MIAMI | 13,396 | 8,155 | 5,062 | 179 | 3,093 R | 60.9% | 37.8% | 61.7% | 38.3% |
| 120,563 | MONROE | 49,540 | 22,031 | 26,317 | 1,192 | 4,286 D | 44.5% | 53.1% | 45.6% | 54.4% |
| 37,629 | MONTGOMERY | 14,549 | 9,639 | 4,711 | 199 | 4,928 R | 66.3% | 32.4% | 67.2% | 32.8% |
| 66,689 | MORGAN | 25,880 | 16,716 | 8,740 | 424 | 7,976 R | 64.6% | 33.8% | 65.7% | 34.3% |
| 14,566 | NEWTON | 5,806 | 3,164 | 2,531 | 111 | 633 R | 54.5% | 43.6% | 55.6% | 44.4% |
| 46,275 | NOBLE | 15,609 | 9,570 | 5,863 | 176 | 3,707 R | 61.3% | 37.6% | 62.0% | 38.0% |
| 5,623 | OHIO | 2,881 | 1,512 | 1,328 | 41 | 184 R | 52.5% | 46.1% | 53.2% | 46.8% |
| 19,306 | ORANGE | 8,548 | 4,818 | 3,621 | 109 | 1,197 R | 56.4% | 42.4% | 57.1% | 42.9% |
| 21,786 | OWEN | 7,604 | 4,179 | 3,249 | 176 | 930 R | 55.0% | 42.7% | 56.3% | 43.7% |

# INDIANA

## GOVERNOR 2004

| 2000 Census Population | County | Total Vote | Republican | Democratic | Other | Rep.-Dem. Plurality | | Percentage | | | |
|---|---|---|---|---|---|---|---|---|---|---|---|
| | | | | | | | | Total Vote | | Major Vote | |
| | | | | | | | | Rep. | Dem. | Rep. | Dem. |
| 17,241 | PARKE | 6,954 | 3,745 | 3,101 | 108 | 644 | R | 53.9% | 44.6% | 54.7% | 45.3% |
| 18,899 | PERRY | 8,263 | 3,559 | 4,640 | 64 | 1,081 | D | 43.1% | 56.2% | 43.4% | 56.6% |
| 12,837 | PIKE | 6,126 | 2,517 | 3,510 | 99 | 993 | D | 41.1% | 57.3% | 41.8% | 58.2% |
| 146,798 | PORTER | 63,879 | 27,565 | 35,206 | 1,108 | 7,641 | D | 43.2% | 55.1% | 43.9% | 56.1% |
| 27,061 | POSEY | 11,886 | 6,252 | 5,525 | 109 | 727 | R | 52.6% | 46.5% | 53.1% | 46.9% |
| 13,755 | PULASKI | 5,514 | 3,185 | 2,267 | 62 | 918 | R | 57.8% | 41.1% | 58.4% | 41.6% |
| 36,019 | PUTNAM | 13,171 | 8,002 | 4,984 | 185 | 3,018 | R | 60.8% | 37.8% | 61.6% | 38.4% |
| 27,401 | RANDOLPH | 11,048 | 6,274 | 4,628 | 146 | 1,646 | R | 56.8% | 41.9% | 57.5% | 42.5% |
| 26,523 | RIPLEY | 11,711 | 6,925 | 4,635 | 151 | 2,290 | R | 59.1% | 39.6% | 59.9% | 40.1% |
| 18,261 | RUSH | 7,321 | 4,529 | 2,676 | 116 | 1,853 | R | 61.9% | 36.6% | 62.9% | 37.1% |
| 265,559 | ST. JOSEPH | 108,526 | 49,198 | 58,327 | 1,001 | 9,129 | D | 45.3% | 53.7% | 45.8% | 54.2% |
| 22,960 | SCOTT | 8,633 | 3,862 | 4,681 | 90 | 819 | D | 44.7% | 54.2% | 45.2% | 54.8% |
| 43,445 | SHELBY | 15,941 | 9,862 | 5,885 | 194 | 3,977 | R | 61.9% | 36.9% | 62.6% | 37.4% |
| 20,391 | SPENCER | 9,909 | 5,183 | 4,612 | 114 | 571 | R | 52.3% | 46.5% | 52.9% | 47.1% |
| 23,556 | STARKE | 8,694 | 4,024 | 4,539 | 131 | 515 | D | 46.3% | 52.2% | 47.0% | 53.0% |
| 33,214 | STEUBEN | 12,765 | 7,684 | 4,915 | 166 | 2,769 | R | 60.2% | 38.5% | 61.0% | 39.0% |
| 21,751 | SULLIVAN | 8,333 | 3,687 | 4,530 | 116 | 843 | D | 44.2% | 54.4% | 44.9% | 55.1% |
| 9,065 | SWITZERLAND | 3,608 | 1,780 | 1,780 | 48 | | | 49.3% | 49.3% | 50.0% | 50.0% |
| 148,955 | TIPPECANOE | 51,827 | 28,458 | 22,504 | 865 | 5,954 | R | 54.9% | 43.4% | 55.8% | 44.2% |
| 16,577 | TIPTON | 7,810 | 4,729 | 2,973 | 108 | 1,756 | R | 60.6% | 38.1% | 61.4% | 38.6% |
| 7,349 | UNION | 3,316 | 2,040 | 1,217 | 59 | 823 | R | 61.5% | 36.7% | 62.6% | 37.4% |
| 171,922 | VANDERBURGH | 69,817 | 34,129 | 34,819 | 869 | 690 | D | 48.9% | 49.9% | 49.5% | 50.5% |
| 16,788 | VERMILLION | 7,008 | 2,769 | 4,121 | 118 | 1,352 | D | 39.5% | 58.8% | 40.2% | 59.8% |
| 105,848 | VIGO | 39,664 | 16,804 | 22,054 | 806 | 5,250 | D | 42.4% | 55.6% | 43.2% | 56.8% |
| 34,960 | WABASH | 13,394 | 8,691 | 4,569 | 134 | 4,122 | R | 64.9% | 34.1% | 65.5% | 34.5% |
| 8,419 | WARREN | 3,951 | 2,214 | 1,679 | 58 | 535 | R | 56.0% | 42.5% | 56.9% | 43.1% |
| 52,383 | WARRICK | 25,817 | 13,877 | 11,678 | 262 | 2,199 | R | 53.8% | 45.2% | 54.3% | 45.7% |
| 27,223 | WASHINGTON | 10,850 | 6,419 | 4,297 | 134 | 2,122 | R | 59.2% | 39.6% | 59.9% | 40.1% |
| 71,097 | WAYNE | 27,690 | 14,530 | 12,565 | 595 | 1,965 | R | 52.5% | 45.4% | 53.6% | 46.4% |
| 27,600 | WELLS | 12,163 | 8,071 | 3,979 | 113 | 4,092 | R | 66.4% | 32.7% | 67.0% | 33.0% |
| 25,267 | WHITE | 10,408 | 5,980 | 4,260 | 168 | 1,720 | R | 57.5% | 40.9% | 58.4% | 41.6% |
| 30,707 | WHITLEY | 13,239 | 8,332 | 4,758 | 149 | 3,574 | R | 62.9% | 35.9% | 63.7% | 36.3% |
| 6,080,485 | TOTAL | 2,448,498 | 1,302,912 | 1,113,900 | 31,686 | 189,012 | R | 53.2% | 45.5% | 53.9% | 46.1% |

# INDIANA

## SENATOR 2004

| 2000 Census Population | County | Total Vote | Republican | Democratic | Other | Rep.-Dem. Plurality | Percentage Total Vote Rep. | Total Vote Dem. | Major Vote Rep. | Major Vote Dem. |
|---|---|---|---|---|---|---|---|---|---|---|
| 33,625 | ADAMS | 13,153 | 5,476 | 7,551 | 126 | 2,075 D | 41.6% | 57.4% | 42.0% | 58.0% |
| 331,849 | ALLEN | 127,982 | 52,845 | 74,011 | 1,126 | 21,166 D | 41.3% | 57.8% | 41.7% | 58.3% |
| 71,435 | BARTHOLOMEW | 28,245 | 11,422 | 16,507 | 316 | 5,085 D | 40.4% | 58.4% | 40.9% | 59.1% |
| 9,421 | BENTON | 3,970 | 1,400 | 2,501 | 69 | 1,101 D | 35.3% | 63.0% | 35.9% | 64.1% |
| 14,048 | BLACKFORD | 5,345 | 1,609 | 3,694 | 42 | 2,085 D | 30.1% | 69.1% | 30.3% | 69.7% |
| 46,107 | BOONE | 22,672 | 11,343 | 11,074 | 255 | 269 R | 50.0% | 48.8% | 50.6% | 49.4% |
| 14,957 | BROWN | 7,264 | 2,803 | 4,336 | 125 | 1,533 D | 38.6% | 59.7% | 39.3% | 60.7% |
| 20,165 | CARROLL | 8,483 | 3,331 | 5,067 | 85 | 1,736 D | 39.3% | 59.7% | 39.7% | 60.3% |
| 40,930 | CASS | 13,861 | 5,829 | 7,873 | 159 | 2,044 D | 42.1% | 56.8% | 42.5% | 57.5% |
| 96,472 | CLARK | 41,513 | 15,091 | 26,054 | 368 | 10,963 D | 36.4% | 62.8% | 36.7% | 63.3% |
| 26,556 | CLAY | 10,669 | 3,629 | 6,928 | 112 | 3,299 D | 34.0% | 64.9% | 34.4% | 65.6% |
| 33,866 | CLINTON | 11,719 | 5,011 | 6,600 | 108 | 1,589 D | 42.8% | 56.3% | 43.2% | 56.8% |
| 10,743 | CRAWFORD | 4,451 | 1,572 | 2,832 | 47 | 1,260 D | 35.3% | 63.6% | 35.7% | 64.3% |
| 29,820 | DAVIESS | 10,445 | 4,447 | 5,891 | 107 | 1,444 D | 42.6% | 56.4% | 43.0% | 57.0% |
| 46,109 | DEARBORN | 20,250 | 10,675 | 9,264 | 311 | 1,411 R | 52.7% | 45.7% | 53.5% | 46.5% |
| 24,555 | DECATUR | 10,069 | 3,808 | 6,173 | 88 | 2,365 D | 37.8% | 61.3% | 38.2% | 61.8% |
| 40,285 | DE KALB | 15,184 | 6,523 | 8,529 | 132 | 2,006 D | 43.0% | 56.2% | 43.3% | 56.7% |
| 118,769 | DELAWARE | 46,519 | 13,627 | 32,312 | 580 | 18,685 D | 29.3% | 69.5% | 29.7% | 70.3% |
| 39,674 | DUBOIS | 16,862 | 5,560 | 11,166 | 136 | 5,606 D | 33.0% | 66.2% | 33.2% | 66.8% |
| 182,791 | ELKHART | 60,900 | 29,168 | 31,186 | 546 | 2,018 D | 47.9% | 51.2% | 48.3% | 51.7% |
| 25,588 | FAYETTE | 9,307 | 3,212 | 5,961 | 134 | 2,749 D | 34.5% | 64.0% | 35.0% | 65.0% |
| 70,823 | FLOYD | 33,642 | 12,412 | 20,898 | 332 | 8,486 D | 36.9% | 62.1% | 37.3% | 62.7% |
| 17,954 | FOUNTAIN | 7,547 | 2,955 | 4,532 | 60 | 1,577 D | 39.2% | 60.1% | 39.5% | 60.5% |
| 22,151 | FRANKLIN | 9,813 | 4,395 | 5,247 | 171 | 852 D | 44.8% | 53.5% | 45.6% | 54.4% |
| 20,511 | FULTON | 8,679 | 3,324 | 5,264 | 91 | 1,940 D | 38.3% | 60.7% | 38.7% | 61.3% |
| 32,500 | GIBSON | 14,528 | 4,289 | 10,110 | 129 | 5,821 D | 29.5% | 69.6% | 29.8% | 70.2% |
| 73,403 | GRANT | 27,065 | 10,189 | 16,620 | 256 | 6,431 D | 37.6% | 61.4% | 38.0% | 62.0% |
| 33,157 | GREENE | 12,875 | 4,402 | 8,336 | 137 | 3,934 D | 34.2% | 64.7% | 34.6% | 65.4% |
| 182,740 | HAMILTON | 103,379 | 54,408 | 48,001 | 970 | 6,407 R | 52.6% | 46.4% | 53.1% | 46.9% |
| 55,391 | HANCOCK | 27,798 | 12,941 | 14,548 | 309 | 1,607 D | 46.6% | 52.3% | 47.1% | 52.9% |
| 34,325 | HARRISON | 17,098 | 6,824 | 10,094 | 180 | 3,270 D | 39.9% | 59.0% | 40.3% | 59.7% |
| 104,093 | HENDRICKS | 51,771 | 26,441 | 24,844 | 486 | 1,597 R | 51.1% | 48.0% | 51.6% | 48.4% |
| 48,508 | HENRY | 20,232 | 7,312 | 12,666 | 254 | 5,354 D | 36.1% | 62.6% | 36.6% | 63.4% |
| 84,964 | HOWARD | 36,876 | 14,776 | 21,732 | 368 | 6,956 D | 40.1% | 58.9% | 40.5% | 59.5% |
| 38,075 | HUNTINGTON | 15,388 | 7,103 | 8,125 | 160 | 1,022 D | 46.2% | 52.8% | 46.6% | 53.4% |
| 41,335 | JACKSON | 16,186 | 5,944 | 10,071 | 171 | 4,127 D | 36.7% | 62.2% | 37.1% | 62.9% |
| 30,043 | JASPER | 11,629 | 5,772 | 5,727 | 130 | 45 R | 49.6% | 49.2% | 50.2% | 49.8% |
| 21,806 | JAY | 8,056 | 2,845 | 5,117 | 94 | 2,272 D | 35.3% | 63.5% | 35.7% | 64.3% |
| 31,705 | JEFFERSON | 12,700 | 4,764 | 7,794 | 142 | 3,030 D | 37.5% | 61.4% | 37.9% | 62.1% |
| 27,554 | JENNINGS | 10,418 | 3,944 | 6,349 | 125 | 2,405 D | 37.9% | 60.9% | 38.3% | 61.7% |
| 115,209 | JOHNSON | 50,985 | 23,330 | 27,149 | 506 | 3,819 D | 45.8% | 53.2% | 46.2% | 53.8% |
| 39,256 | KNOX | 15,560 | 4,275 | 11,130 | 155 | 6,855 D | 27.5% | 71.5% | 27.8% | 72.2% |
| 74,057 | KOSCIUSKO | 27,497 | 14,574 | 12,554 | 369 | 2,020 R | 53.0% | 45.7% | 53.7% | 46.3% |
| 34,909 | LAGRANGE | 8,961 | 4,006 | 4,865 | 90 | 859 D | 44.7% | 54.3% | 45.2% | 54.8% |
| 484,564 | LAKE | 182,689 | 49,919 | 130,450 | 2,320 | 80,531 D | 27.3% | 71.4% | 27.7% | 72.3% |
| 110,106 | LA PORTE | 41,351 | 11,685 | 28,826 | 840 | 17,141 D | 28.3% | 69.7% | 28.8% | 71.2% |
| 45,922 | LAWRENCE | 17,438 | 8,064 | 9,132 | 242 | 1,068 D | 46.2% | 52.4% | 46.9% | 53.1% |
| 133,358 | MADISON | 53,444 | 18,541 | 34,379 | 524 | 15,838 D | 34.7% | 64.3% | 35.0% | 65.0% |
| 860,454 | MARION | 317,973 | 104,819 | 210,107 | 3,047 | 105,288 D | 33.0% | 66.1% | 33.3% | 66.7% |
| 45,128 | MARSHALL | 17,578 | 7,293 | 10,111 | 174 | 2,818 D | 41.5% | 57.5% | 41.9% | 58.1% |
| 10,369 | MARTIN | 4,942 | 1,587 | 3,297 | 58 | 1,710 D | 32.1% | 66.7% | 32.5% | 67.5% |
| 36,082 | MIAMI | 13,474 | 5,967 | 7,339 | 168 | 1,372 D | 44.3% | 54.5% | 44.8% | 55.2% |
| 120,563 | MONROE | 49,097 | 14,396 | 33,821 | 880 | 19,425 D | 29.3% | 68.9% | 29.9% | 70.1% |
| 37,629 | MONTGOMERY | 14,445 | 5,635 | 8,651 | 159 | 3,016 D | 39.0% | 59.9% | 39.4% | 60.6% |
| 66,689 | MORGAN | 25,689 | 12,498 | 12,878 | 313 | 380 D | 48.7% | 50.1% | 49.3% | 50.7% |
| 14,566 | NEWTON | 5,791 | 2,475 | 3,225 | 91 | 750 D | 42.7% | 55.7% | 43.4% | 56.6% |
| 46,275 | NOBLE | 15,540 | 6,527 | 8,853 | 160 | 2,326 D | 42.0% | 57.0% | 42.4% | 57.6% |
| 5,623 | OHIO | 2,891 | 1,282 | 1,572 | 37 | 290 D | 44.3% | 54.4% | 44.9% | 55.1% |
| 19,306 | ORANGE | 8,272 | 3,127 | 5,056 | 89 | 1,929 D | 37.8% | 61.1% | 38.2% | 61.8% |
| 21,786 | OWEN | 7,503 | 2,851 | 4,538 | 114 | 1,687 D | 38.0% | 60.5% | 38.6% | 61.4% |

# INDIANA
## SENATOR 2004

| 2000 Census Population | County | Total Vote | Republican | Democratic | Other | Rep.-Dem. Plurality | Percentage Total Vote Rep. | Dem. | Major Vote Rep. | Dem. |
|---|---|---|---|---|---|---|---|---|---|---|
| 17,241 | PARKE | 6,807 | 2,249 | 4,480 | 78 | 2,231 D | 33.0% | 65.8% | 33.4% | 66.6% |
| 18,899 | PERRY | 8,086 | 2,234 | 5,790 | 62 | 3,556 D | 27.6% | 71.6% | 27.8% | 72.2% |
| 12,837 | PIKE | 6,033 | 1,765 | 4,209 | 59 | 2,444 D | 29.3% | 69.8% | 29.5% | 70.5% |
| 146,798 | PORTER | 62,446 | 21,411 | 39,876 | 1,159 | 18,465 D | 34.3% | 63.9% | 34.9% | 65.1% |
| 27,061 | POSEY | 11,663 | 3,523 | 8,052 | 88 | 4,529 D | 30.2% | 69.0% | 30.4% | 69.6% |
| 13,755 | PULASKI | 5,629 | 2,236 | 3,328 | 65 | 1,092 D | 39.7% | 59.1% | 40.2% | 59.8% |
| 36,019 | PUTNAM | 13,002 | 5,185 | 7,683 | 134 | 2,498 D | 39.9% | 59.1% | 40.3% | 59.7% |
| 27,401 | RANDOLPH | 10,701 | 3,943 | 6,625 | 133 | 2,682 D | 36.8% | 61.9% | 37.3% | 62.7% |
| 26,523 | RIPLEY | 11,662 | 5,282 | 6,212 | 168 | 930 D | 45.3% | 53.3% | 46.0% | 54.0% |
| 18,261 | RUSH | 7,361 | 2,962 | 4,316 | 83 | 1,354 D | 40.2% | 58.6% | 40.7% | 59.3% |
| 265,559 | ST. JOSEPH | 107,598 | 31,372 | 75,340 | 886 | 43,968 D | 29.2% | 70.0% | 29.4% | 70.6% |
| 22,960 | SCOTT | 8,590 | 2,435 | 6,070 | 85 | 3,635 D | 28.3% | 70.7% | 28.6% | 71.4% |
| 43,445 | SHELBY | 15,839 | 6,717 | 8,986 | 136 | 2,269 D | 42.4% | 56.7% | 42.8% | 57.2% |
| 20,391 | SPENCER | 9,886 | 3,317 | 6,495 | 74 | 3,178 D | 33.6% | 65.7% | 33.8% | 66.2% |
| 23,556 | STARKE | 9,012 | 2,762 | 6,108 | 142 | 3,346 D | 30.6% | 67.8% | 31.1% | 68.9% |
| 33,214 | STEUBEN | 12,686 | 5,070 | 7,447 | 169 | 2,377 D | 40.0% | 58.7% | 40.5% | 59.5% |
| 21,751 | SULLIVAN | 8,250 | 2,099 | 6,072 | 79 | 3,973 D | 25.4% | 73.6% | 25.7% | 74.3% |
| 9,065 | SWITZERLAND | 3,605 | 1,404 | 2,148 | 53 | 744 D | 38.9% | 59.6% | 39.5% | 60.5% |
| 148,955 | TIPPECANOE | 51,605 | 18,002 | 32,766 | 837 | 14,764 D | 34.9% | 63.5% | 35.5% | 64.5% |
| 16,577 | TIPTON | 7,786 | 3,142 | 4,557 | 87 | 1,415 D | 40.4% | 58.5% | 40.8% | 59.2% |
| 7,349 | UNION | 3,252 | 1,417 | 1,777 | 58 | 360 D | 43.6% | 54.6% | 44.4% | 55.6% |
| 171,922 | VANDERBURGH | 68,147 | 21,242 | 46,088 | 817 | 24,846 D | 31.2% | 67.6% | 31.5% | 68.5% |
| 16,788 | VERMILLION | 7,014 | 1,480 | 5,468 | 66 | 3,988 D | 21.1% | 78.0% | 21.3% | 78.7% |
| 105,848 | VIGO | 39,627 | 9,307 | 29,828 | 492 | 20,521 D | 23.5% | 75.3% | 23.8% | 76.2% |
| 34,960 | WABASH | 13,277 | 6,313 | 6,853 | 111 | 540 D | 47.5% | 51.6% | 47.9% | 52.1% |
| 8,419 | WARREN | 3,859 | 1,454 | 2,357 | 48 | 903 D | 37.7% | 61.1% | 38.2% | 61.8% |
| 52,383 | WARRICK | 25,037 | 9,260 | 15,572 | 205 | 6,312 D | 37.0% | 62.2% | 37.3% | 62.7% |
| 27,223 | WASHINGTON | 10,730 | 4,304 | 6,270 | 156 | 1,966 D | 40.1% | 58.4% | 40.7% | 59.3% |
| 71,097 | WAYNE | 27,486 | 10,821 | 16,081 | 584 | 5,260 D | 39.4% | 58.5% | 40.2% | 59.8% |
| 27,600 | WELLS | 12,218 | 5,583 | 6,532 | 103 | 949 D | 45.7% | 53.5% | 46.1% | 53.9% |
| 25,267 | WHITE | 10,364 | 3,589 | 6,667 | 108 | 3,078 D | 34.6% | 64.3% | 35.0% | 65.0% |
| 30,707 | WHITLEY | 13,312 | 5,761 | 7,405 | 146 | 1,644 D | 43.3% | 55.6% | 43.8% | 56.2% |
| 6,080,485 | TOTAL | 2,428,233 | 903,913 | 1,496,976 | 27,344 | 593,063 D | 37.2% | 61.6% | 37.6% | 62.4% |

# INDIANA

## HOUSE OF REPRESENTATIVES

| CD | Year | Total Vote | Republican Vote | Republican Candidate | Democratic Vote | Democratic Candidate | Other Vote | Rep.-Dem. Plurality | Total Vote Rep. | Total Vote Dem. | Major Vote Rep. | Major Vote Dem. |
|---|---|---|---|---|---|---|---|---|---|---|---|---|
| 1 | 2004 | 261,264 | 82,858 | Leyva, Mark J. | 178,406 | Visclosky, Peter J.* | | 95,548 D | 31.7% | 68.3% | 31.7% | 68.3% |
| 1 | 2002 | 135,111 | 41,909 | Leyva, Mark J. | 90,443 | Visclosky, Peter J.* | 2,759 | 48,534 D | 31.0% | 66.9% | 31.7% | 68.3% |
| 2 | 2004 | 259,355 | 140,496 | Chocola, Chris* | 115,513 | Donnelly, Joseph S. | 3,346 | 24,983 R | 54.2% | 44.5% | 54.9% | 45.1% |
| 2 | 2002 | 188,458 | 95,081 | Chocola, Chris | 86,253 | Thompson, Jill Long | 7,124 | 8,828 R | 50.5% | 45.8% | 52.4% | 47.6% |
| 3 | 2004 | 247,621 | 171,389 | Souder, Mark* | 76,232 | Parra, Maria M. | | 95,157 R | 69.2% | 30.8% | 69.2% | 30.8% |
| 3 | 2002 | 146,606 | 92,566 | Souder, Mark* | 50,509 | Rigdon, Jay | 3,531 | 42,057 R | 63.1% | 34.5% | 64.7% | 35.3% |
| 4 | 2004 | 274,136 | 190,445 | Buyer, Steve* | 77,574 | Sanders, David Avram | 6,117 | 112,871 R | 69.5% | 28.3% | 71.1% | 28.9% |
| 4 | 2002 | 158,008 | 112,760 | Buyer, Steve* | 41,314 | Abbott, Bill | 3,934 | 71,446 R | 71.4% | 26.1% | 73.2% | 26.8% |
| 5 | 2004 | 318,363 | 228,718 | Burton, Dan* | 82,637 | Carr, Katherine Fox | 7,008 | 146,081 R | 71.8% | 26.0% | 73.5% | 26.5% |
| 5 | 2002 | 179,855 | 129,442 | Burton, Dan* | 45,283 | Carr, Katherine Fox | 5,130 | 84,159 R | 72.0% | 25.2% | 74.1% | 25.9% |
| 6 | 2004 | 272,049 | 182,529 | Pence, Mike* | 85,123 | Fox, Melina Ann | 4,397 | 97,406 R | 67.1% | 31.3% | 68.2% | 31.8% |
| 6 | 2002 | 185,653 | 118,436 | Pence, Mike* | 63,871 | Fox, Melina Ann | 3,346 | 54,565 R | 63.8% | 34.4% | 65.0% | 35.0% |
| 7 | 2004 | 223,175 | 97,491 | Horning, Andrew | 121,303 | Carson, Julia* | 4,381 | 23,812 D | 43.7% | 54.4% | 44.6% | 55.4% |
| 7 | 2002 | 145,840 | 64,379 | McVey, Brose A. | 77,478 | Carson, Julia* | 3,983 | 13,099 D | 44.1% | 53.1% | 45.4% | 54.6% |
| 8 | 2004 | 272,778 | 145,576 | Hostettler, John * | 121,522 | Jennings, Jon P. | 5,680 | 24,054 R | 53.4% | 44.5% | 54.5% | 45.5% |
| 8 | 2002 | 192,865 | 98,952 | Hostettler, John * | 88,763 | Hartke, Bryan L. | 5,150 | 10,189 R | 51.3% | 46.0% | 52.7% | 47.3% |
| 9 | 2004 | 287,510 | 142,197 | Sodrel, Mike | 140,772 | Hill, Baron P.* | 4,541 | 1,425 R | 49.5% | 49.0% | 50.3% | 49.7% |
| 9 | 2002 | 188,957 | 87,169 | Sodrel, Mike | 96,654 | Hill, Baron P.* | 5,134 | 9,485 D | 46.1% | 51.2% | 47.4% | 52.6% |
| Total | 2004 | 2,416,251 | 1,381,699 | | 999,082 | | 35,470 | 382,617 R | 57.2% | 41.3% | 58.0% | 42.0% |
| Total | 2002 | 1,521,353 | 840,694 | | 640,568 | | 40,091 | 200,126 R | 55.3% | 42.1% | 56.8% | 43.2% |

An asterisk (*) denotes incumbent.

# INDIANA

## GENERAL AND PRIMARY ELECTIONS

## 2004 GENERAL ELECTIONS

**President** Other vote was 18,058 Libertarian (Michael Badnarik); 1,328 write-in (Ralph Nader); 102 write-in (David Cobb); 37 write-in (John Joseph Kennedy); 22 write-in (Walter F. Brown); 6 write-in (Lawson Mitchell Bone).

**Governor** Other vote was 31,664 Libertarian (Kenn Gividen); 22 write-in (Velko Kapetanov).

**Senator** Other vote was 27,344 Libertarian (Albert Barger).

**House** Other vote was:

CD 1
CD 2 3,346 Libertarian (Douglas Barnes).
CD 3
CD 4 6,117 Libertarian (Kevin R. Fleming).
CD 5 7,008 Libertarian (Rick Hodgin).
CD 6 4,397 Libertarian (Chad "Wick" Roots).
CD 7 4,381 Libertarian (Barry Campbell).
CD 8 5,680 Libertarian (Mark Garvin).
CD 9 4,541 Libertarian (Al Cox).

# INDIANA

## GENERAL AND PRIMARY ELECTIONS

## 2004 PRIMARY ELECTIONS

| | | | | |
|---|---|---|---|---|
| **Primary** | May 4, 2004 | | **Registration** (as of May 4, 2004) | 4,162,606 No Party Registration |

**Primary Type** Open—Registered voters could participate in the primary of either party, although in doing so they were considered affiliated with that party and could be challenged if they subsequently sought to vote in the other party's primary.

Note: An asterisk (*) denotes incumbent.

| | **REPUBLICAN PRIMARIES** | | | **DEMOCRATIC PRIMARIES** | | |
|---|---|---|---|---|---|---|
| President | George W. Bush* | 469,528 | 100.0% | John Kerry | 231,047 | 72.8% |
| | | | | John Edwards | 35,651 | 11.2% |
| | | | | Howard Dean | 21,482 | 6.8% |
| | | | | Wesley Clark | 17,437 | 5.5% |
| | | | | Dennis J. Kucinich | 7,003 | 2.2% |
| | | | | Lyndon H. LaRouche Jr. | 4,591 | 1.4% |
| | | | | TOTAL | 317,211 | |
| Governor | Mitch Daniels | 335,828 | 66.4% | Joseph E. Kernan* | 283,924 | 100.0% |
| | Eric Miller | 169,930 | 33.6% | | | |
| | TOTAL | 505,758 | | | | |
| Senator | Marvin Scott | 335,215 | 100.0% | Evan Bayh* | 304,267 | 100.0% |
| Congressional District 1 | Mark J. Levya | 9,529 | 44.7% | Peter J. Visclosky* | 45,141 | 100.0% |
| | Frank E. Kendrick | 9,113 | 42.7% | | | |
| | Cyril B. "Cy" Huerter | 2,696 | 12.6% | | | |
| | TOTAL | 21,338 | | | | |
| Congressional District 2 | Chris Chocola* | 36,847 | 84.0% | Joseph S. Donnelly | 29,117 | 100.0% |
| | Tony Zirkle | 7,043 | 16.0% | | | |
| | TOTAL | 43,890 | | | | |
| Congressional District 3 | Mark Souder* | 46,583 | 79.2% | Maria M. Parra | 5,982 | 42.8% |
| | William Larsen | 12,210 | 20.8% | Mark A. Summers | 5,202 | 37.2% |
| | | | | Steve G. Hope | 2,790 | 20.0% |
| | TOTAL | 58,793 | | TOTAL | 13,974 | |
| Congressional District 4 | Steve Buyer* | 52,921 | 65.7% | David Avram Sanders | 9,320 | 62.4% |
| | Dennis Hardy | 10,862 | 13.5% | Bill Abbott | 5,604 | 37.6% |
| | Mike Campbell | 8,403 | 10.4% | | | |
| | Brian D. Paasch | 8,305 | 10.3% | | | |
| | TOTAL | 80,491 | | TOTAL | 14,924 | |
| Congressional District 5 | Dan Burton* | 83,136 | 86.4% | Katherine Fox Carr | 11,224 | 62.5% |
| | George Thomas Holland | 8,825 | 9.2% | Mike Brinegar | 6,732 | 37.5% |
| | Victor Dean Wakley | 4,287 | 4.5% | | | |
| | TOTAL | 96,248 | | TOTAL | 17,956 | |
| Congressional District 6 | Mike Pence* | 61,794 | 100.0% | Melina Ann Fox | 31,231 | 100.0% |
| Congressional District 7 | Andrew Horning | 23,152 | 72.5% | Julia Carson* | 30,915 | 89.4% |
| | Bob Croddy | 8,764 | 27.5% | Bob Hidalgo | 3,652 | 10.6% |
| | TOTAL | 31,916 | | TOTAL | 34,567 | |
| Congressional District 8 | John Hostettler* | 39,721 | 100.0% | Jon P. Jennings | 37,853 | 73.5% |
| | | | | Bill Pearman | 13,652 | 26.5% |
| | | | | TOTAL | 51,505 | |
| Congressional District 9 | Mike Sodrel | 35,293 | 100.0% | Baron P. Hill* | 47,514 | 88.2% |
| | | | | Lendall B. Terry | 6,335 | 11.8% |
| | | | | TOTAL | 53,849 | |

# IOWA

## GOVERNOR
Tom Vilsack (D). Reelected 2002 to a four-year term. Previously elected 1998.

## SENATORS (1 Democrat, 1 Republican)
Charles E. Grassley (R). Reelected 2004 to a six-year term. Previously elected 1998, 1992, 1986, 1980.

Tom Harkin (D). Reelected 2002 to a six-year term. Previously elected 1996, 1990, 1984.

## REPRESENTATIVES (4 Republicans, 1 Democrat)
1. Jim Nussle (R)
2. Jim Leach (R)
3. Leonard L. Boswell (D)
4. Tom Latham (R)
5. Steve King (R)

## POSTWAR VOTE FOR PRESIDENT

| Year | Total Vote | Republican Vote | Republican Candidate | Democratic Vote | Democratic Candidate | Other Vote | Plurality | Total Vote Rep. | Total Vote Dem. | Major Vote Rep. | Major Vote Dem. |
|------|-----------|------|-----------|------|-----------|------|-----------|------|------|------|------|
| 2004 | 1,506,908 | 751,957 | Bush, George W. | 741,898 | Kerry, John | 13,053 | 10,059 R | 49.9% | 49.2% | 50.3% | 49.7% |
| 2000** | 1,315,563 | 634,373 | Bush, George W. | 638,517 | Gore, Al | 42,673 | 4,144 D | 48.2% | 48.5% | 49.8% | 50.2% |
| 1996** | 1,234,075 | 492,644 | Dole, Bob | 620,258 | Clinton, Bill | 121,173 | 127,614 D | 39.9% | 50.3% | 44.3% | 55.7% |
| 1992** | 1,354,607 | 504,891 | Bush, George | 586,353 | Clinton, Bill | 263,363 | 81,462 D | 37.3% | 43.3% | 46.3% | 53.7% |
| 1988 | 1,225,614 | 545,355 | Bush, George | 670,557 | Dukakis, Michael S. | 9,702 | 125,202 D | 44.5% | 54.7% | 44.9% | 55.1% |
| 1984 | 1,319,805 | 703,088 | Reagan, Ronald | 605,620 | Mondale, Walter F. | 11,097 | 97,468 R | 53.3% | 45.9% | 53.7% | 46.3% |
| 1980** | 1,317,661 | 676,026 | Reagan, Ronald | 508,672 | Carter, Jimmy | 132,963 | 167,354 R | 51.3% | 38.6% | 57.1% | 42.9% |
| 1976 | 1,279,306 | 632,863 | Ford, Gerald R. | 619,931 | Carter, Jimmy | 26,512 | 12,932 R | 49.5% | 48.5% | 50.5% | 49.5% |
| 1972 | 1,225,944 | 706,207 | Nixon, Richard M. | 496,206 | McGovern, George S. | 23,531 | 210,001 R | 57.6% | 40.5% | 58.7% | 41.3% |
| 1968** | 1,167,931 | 619,106 | Nixon, Richard M. | 476,699 | Humphrey, Hubert H. | 72,126 | 142,407 R | 53.0% | 40.8% | 56.5% | 43.5% |
| 1964 | 1,184,539 | 449,148 | Goldwater, Barry M. | 733,030 | Johnson, Lyndon B. | 2,361 | 283,882 D | 37.9% | 61.9% | 38.0% | 62.0% |
| 1960 | 1,273,810 | 722,381 | Nixon, Richard M. | 550,565 | Kennedy, John F. | 864 | 171,816 R | 56.7% | 43.2% | 56.7% | 43.3% |
| 1956 | 1,234,564 | 729,187 | Eisenhower, Dwight D. | 501,858 | Stevenson, Adlai E. | 3,519 | 227,329 R | 59.1% | 40.7% | 59.2% | 40.8% |
| 1952 | 1,268,773 | 808,906 | Eisenhower, Dwight D. | 451,513 | Stevenson, Adlai E. | 8,354 | 357,393 R | 63.8% | 35.6% | 64.2% | 35.8% |
| 1948 | 1,038,264 | 494,018 | Dewey, Thomas E. | 522,380 | Truman, Harry S. | 21,866 | 28,362 D | 47.6% | 50.3% | 48.6% | 51.4% |

In past elections, the other vote included: 2000 - 29,374 Green (Ralph Nader); 1996 - 105,159 Reform (Ross Perot); 1992 - 253,468 Independent (Perot); 1980 - 115,633 Independent (John Anderson); 1968 - 66,422 American Independent (George Wallace).

# IOWA

## POSTWAR VOTE FOR GOVERNOR

| Year | Total Vote | Republican Vote | Candidate | Democratic Vote | Candidate | Other Vote | Rep.-Dem. Plurality | Total Vote Rep. | Dem. | Major Vote Rep. | Dem. |
|------|-----------|-----------------|-----------|-----------------|-----------|-----------|---------------------|-----------------|------|-----------------|------|
| 2002 | 1,025,802 | 456,612 | Gross, Doug | 540,449 | Vilsack, Tom | 28,741 | 83,837 D | 44.5% | 52.7% | 45.8% | 54.2% |
| 1998 | 956,418 | 444,787 | Lightfoot, Jim Ross | 500,231 | Vilsack, Tom | 11,400 | 55,444 D | 46.5% | 52.3% | 47.1% | 52.9% |
| 1994 | 997,248 | 566,395 | Branstad, Terry E. | 414,453 | Campbell, Bonnie J. | 16,400 | 151,942 R | 56.8% | 41.6% | 57.7% | 42.3% |
| 1990 | 976,483 | 591,852 | Branstad, Terry E. | 379,372 | Avenson, Donald D. | 5,259 | 212,480 R | 60.6% | 38.9% | 60.9% | 39.1% |
| 1986 | 910,623 | 472,712 | Branstad, Terry E. | 436,987 | Junkins, Lowell L. | 924 | 35,725 R | 51.9% | 48.0% | 52.0% | 48.0% |
| 1982 | 1,038,229 | 548,313 | Branstad, Terry E. | 483,291 | Conlin, Roxanne | 6,625 | 65,022 R | 52.8% | 46.5% | 53.2% | 46.8% |
| 1978 | 843,190 | 491,713 | Ray, Robert | 345,519 | Fitzgerald, Jerome D. | 5,958 | 146,194 R | 58.3% | 41.0% | 58.7% | 41.3% |
| 1974** | 920,458 | 534,518 | Ray, Robert | 377,553 | Schaben, James, F. | 8,387 | 156,965 R | 58.1% | 41.0% | 58.6% | 41.4% |
| 1972 | 1,210,222 | 707,177 | Ray, Robert | 487,282 | Franzenburg, Paul | 15,763 | 219,895 R | 58.4% | 40.3% | 59.2% | 40.8% |
| 1970 | 791,241 | 403,394 | Ray, Robert | 368,911 | Fulton, Robert | 18,936 | 34,483 R | 51.0% | 46.6% | 52.2% | 47.8% |
| 1968 | 1,136,489 | 614,328 | Ray, Robert | 521,216 | Franzenburg, Paul | 945 | 93,112 R | 54.1% | 45.9% | 54.1% | 45.9% |
| 1966 | 893,175 | 394,518 | Murray, William G. | 494,259 | Hughes, Harold E. | 4,398 | 99,741 D | 44.2% | 55.3% | 44.4% | 55.6% |
| 1964 | 1,167,734 | 365,131 | Hultman, Evan | 794,610 | Hughes, Harold E. | 7,993 | 429,479 D | 31.3% | 68.0% | 31.5% | 68.5% |
| 1962 | 819,854 | 388,955 | Erbe, Norman A. | 430,899 | Hughes, Harold E. | | 41,944 D | 47.4% | 52.6% | 47.4% | 52.6% |
| 1960 | 1,237,089 | 645,026 | Erbe, Norman A. | 592,063 | McManus, E. J. | | 52,963 R | 52.1% | 47.9% | 52.1% | 47.9% |
| 1958 | 859,095 | 394,071 | Murray, William G. | 465,024 | Loveless, Herschel C. | | 70,953 D | 45.9% | 54.1% | 45.9% | 54.1% |
| 1956 | 1,204,235 | 587,383 | Hoegh, Leo A. | 616,852 | Loveless, Herschel C. | | 29,469 D | 48.8% | 51.2% | 48.8% | 51.2% |
| 1954 | 848,592 | 435,944 | Hoegh, Leo A. | 410,255 | Herring, Clyde E. | 2,393 | 25,689 R | 51.4% | 48.3% | 51.5% | 48.5% |
| 1952 | 1,230,045 | 638,388 | Beardsley, William | 587,671 | Loveless, Herschel C. | 3,986 | 50,717 R | 51.9% | 47.8% | 52.1% | 47.9% |
| 1950 | 857,213 | 506,642 | Beardsley, William | 347,176 | Gillette, Lester S. | 3,395 | 159,466 R | 59.1% | 40.5% | 59.3% | 40.7% |
| 1948 | 994,833 | 553,900 | Beardsley, William | 434,432 | Switzer, Carroll O. | 6,501 | 119,468 R | 55.7% | 43.7% | 56.0% | 44.0% |
| 1946 | 631,681 | 362,592 | Blue, Robert D. | 266,190 | Miles, Frank | 2,899 | 96,402 R | 57.4% | 42.1% | 57.7% | 42.3% |

The term of office of Iowa's governor was increased from two to four years effective with the 1974 election.

## POSTWAR VOTE FOR SENATOR

| Year | Total Vote | Republican Vote | Candidate | Democratic Vote | Candidate | Other Vote | Rep.-Dem. Plurality | Total Vote Rep. | Dem. | Major Vote Rep. | Dem. |
|------|-----------|-----------------|-----------|-----------------|-----------|-----------|---------------------|-----------------|------|-----------------|------|
| 2004 | 1,479,228 | 1,038,175 | Grassley, Charles E. | 412,365 | Small, Arthur | 28,688 | 625,810 R | 70.2% | 27.9% | 71.6% | 28.4% |
| 2002 | 1,023,075 | 447,892 | Ganske, Greg | 554,278 | Harkin, Tom | 20,905 | 106,386 D | 43.8% | 54.2% | 44.7% | 55.3% |
| 1998 | 947,907 | 648,480 | Grassley, Charles E. | 289,049 | Osterberg, David | 10,378 | 359,431 R | 68.4% | 30.5% | 69.2% | 30.8% |
| 1996 | 1,224,054 | 571,807 | Lightfoot, Jim Ross | 634,166 | Harkin, Tom | 18,081 | 62,359 D | 46.7% | 51.8% | 47.4% | 52.6% |
| 1992 | 1,292,494 | 899,761 | Grassley, Charles E. | 351,561 | Lloyd-Jones, Jean | 41,172 | 548,200 R | 69.6% | 27.2% | 71.9% | 28.1% |
| 1990 | 983,933 | 446,869 | Tauke, Tom | 535,975 | Harkin, Tom | 1,089 | 89,106 D | 45.4% | 54.5% | 45.5% | 54.5% |
| 1986 | 891,762 | 588,880 | Grassley, Charles E. | 299,406 | Roehrick, John P. | 3,476 | 289,474 R | 66.0% | 33.6% | 66.3% | 33.7% |
| 1984 | 1,292,700 | 564,381 | Jepsen, Roger W. | 716,883 | Harkin, Tom | 11,436 | 152,502 D | 43.7% | 55.5% | 44.0% | 56.0% |
| 1980 | 1,277,034 | 683,014 | Grassley, Charles E. | 581,545 | Culver, John C. | 12,475 | 101,469 R | 53.5% | 45.5% | 54.0% | 46.0% |
| 1978 | 824,654 | 421,598 | Jepsen, Roger W. | 395,066 | Clark, Richard | 7,990 | 26,532 R | 51.1% | 47.9% | 51.6% | 48.4% |
| 1974 | 889,561 | 420,546 | Stanley, David M. | 462,947 | Culver, John C. | 6,068 | 42,401 D | 47.3% | 52.0% | 47.6% | 52.4% |
| 1972 | 1,203,333 | 530,525 | Miller, Jack | 662,637 | Clark, Richard | 10,171 | 132,112 D | 44.1% | 55.1% | 44.5% | 55.5% |
| 1968 | 1,144,086 | 568,469 | Stanley, David M. | 574,884 | Hughes, Harold E. | 733 | 6,415 D | 49.7% | 50.2% | 49.7% | 50.3% |
| 1966 | 857,496 | 522,339 | Miller, Jack | 324,114 | Smith, E. B. | 11,043 | 198,225 R | 60.9% | 37.8% | 61.7% | 38.3% |
| 1962 | 807,972 | 431,364 | Hickenlooper, Bourke B. | 376,602 | Smith, E. B. | 6 | 54,762 R | 53.4% | 46.6% | 53.4% | 46.6% |
| 1960 | 1,237,582 | 642,463 | Miller, Jack | 595,119 | Loveless, Herschel C. | | 47,344 R | 51.9% | 48.1% | 51.9% | 48.1% |
| 1956 | 1,178,655 | 635,499 | Hickenlooper, Bourke B. | 543,156 | Evans, R. M. | | 92,343 R | 53.9% | 46.1% | 53.9% | 46.1% |
| 1954 | 847,355 | 442,409 | Martin, Thomas E. | 402,712 | Gillette, Guy | 2,234 | 39,697 R | 52.2% | 47.5% | 52.3% | 47.7% |
| 1950 | 858,523 | 470,613 | Hickenlooper, Bourke B. | 383,766 | Loveland, A. J. | 4,144 | 86,847 R | 54.8% | 44.7% | 55.1% | 44.9% |
| 1948 | 1,000,412 | 415,778 | Wilson, George A. | 578,226 | Gillette, Guy | 6,408 | 162,448 D | 41.6% | 57.8% | 41.8% | 58.2% |

# IOWA

### Congressional districts first established for elections held in 2002
### 5 members

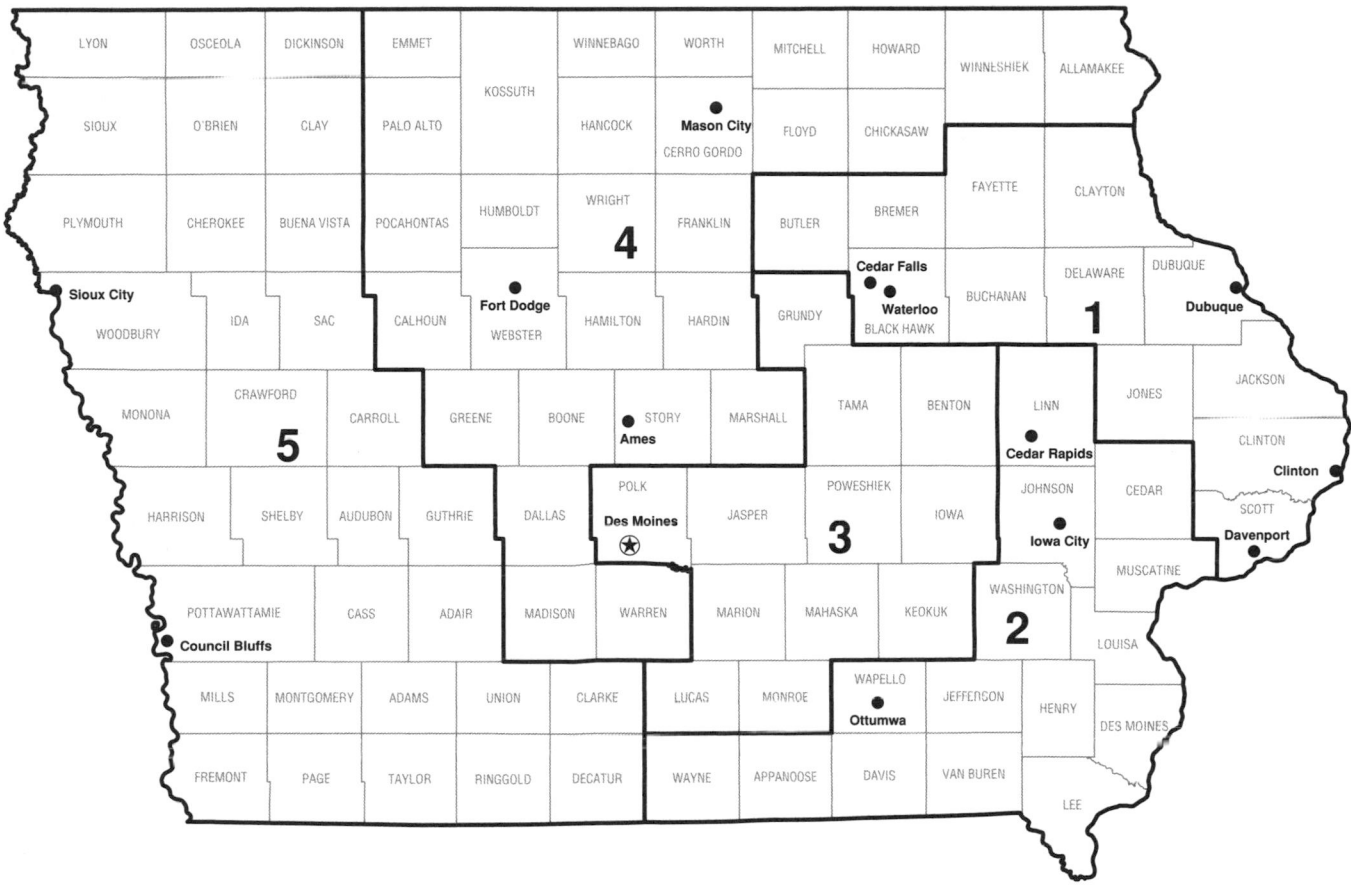

# IOWA
## PRESIDENT 2004

| 2000 Census Population | County | Total Vote | Republican | Democratic | Other | Rep.-Dem. Plurality | Percentage Total Vote Rep. | Total Vote Dem. | Major Vote Rep. | Major Vote Dem. |
|---|---|---|---|---|---|---|---|---|---|---|
| 8,243 | ADAIR | 4,278 | 2,402 | 1,844 | 32 | 558 R | 56.1% | 43.1% | 56.6% | 43.4% |
| 4,482 | ADAMS | 2,325 | 1,317 | 977 | 31 | 340 R | 56.6% | 42.0% | 57.4% | 42.6% |
| 14,675 | ALLAMAKEE | 7,062 | 3,530 | 3,449 | 83 | 81 R | 50.0% | 48.8% | 50.6% | 49.4% |
| 13,721 | APPANOOSE | 6,450 | 3,340 | 3,063 | 47 | 277 R | 51.8% | 47.5% | 52.2% | 47.8% |
| 6,830 | AUDUBON | 3,592 | 1,958 | 1,608 | 26 | 350 R | 54.5% | 44.8% | 54.9% | 45.1% |
| 25,308 | BENTON | 13,501 | 6,658 | 6,747 | 96 | 89 D | 49.3% | 50.0% | 49.7% | 50.3% |
| 128,012 | BLACK HAWK | 63,907 | 28,046 | 35,392 | 469 | 7,346 D | 43.9% | 55.4% | 44.2% | 55.8% |
| 26,224 | BOONE | 14,009 | 6,870 | 7,027 | 112 | 157 D | 49.0% | 50.2% | 49.4% | 50.6% |
| 23,325 | BREMER | 12,779 | 6,665 | 6,025 | 89 | 640 R | 52.2% | 47.1% | 52.5% | 47.5% |
| 21,093 | BUCHANAN | 10,475 | 4,797 | 5,608 | 70 | 811 D | 45.8% | 53.5% | 46.1% | 53.9% |
| 20,411 | BUENA VISTA | 8,490 | 4,887 | 3,520 | 83 | 1,367 R | 57.6% | 41.5% | 58.1% | 41.9% |
| 15,305 | BUTLER | 7,475 | 4,417 | 3,001 | 57 | 1,416 R | 59.1% | 40.1% | 59.5% | 40.5% |
| 11,115 | CALHOUN | 5,542 | 3,255 | 2,243 | 44 | 1,012 R | 58.7% | 40.5% | 59.2% | 40.8% |
| 21,421 | CARROLL | 10,524 | 5,762 | 4,689 | 73 | 1,073 R | 54.8% | 44.6% | 55.1% | 44.9% |
| 14,684 | CASS | 7,543 | 4,796 | 2,679 | 68 | 2,117 R | 63.6% | 35.5% | 64.2% | 35.8% |
| 18,187 | CEDAR | 9,694 | 4,869 | 4,747 | 78 | 122 R | 50.2% | 49.0% | 50.6% | 49.4% |
| 46,447 | CERRO GORDO | 24,516 | 10,960 | 13,372 | 184 | 2,412 D | 44.7% | 54.5% | 45.0% | 55.0% |
| 13,035 | CHEROKEE | 6,796 | 3,758 | 2,988 | 50 | 770 R | 55.3% | 44.0% | 55.7% | 44.3% |
| 13,095 | CHICKASAW | 6,806 | 3,040 | 3,708 | 58 | 668 D | 44.7% | 54.5% | 45.1% | 54.9% |
| 9,133 | CLARKE | 4,566 | 2,200 | 2,323 | 43 | 123 D | 48.2% | 50.9% | 48.6% | 51.4% |
| 17,372 | CLAY | 8,588 | 4,898 | 3,547 | 143 | 1,351 R | 57.0% | 41.3% | 58.0% | 42.0% |
| 18,678 | CLAYTON | 9,168 | 4,312 | 4,736 | 120 | 424 D | 47.0% | 51.7% | 47.7% | 52.3% |
| 50,149 | CLINTON | 24,684 | 10,666 | 13,813 | 205 | 3,147 D | 43.2% | 56.0% | 43.6% | 56.4% |
| 16,942 | CRAWFORD | 7,242 | 3,955 | 3,220 | 67 | 735 R | 54.6% | 44.5% | 55.1% | 44.9% |
| 40,750 | DALLAS | 26,293 | 15,183 | 10,917 | 193 | 4,266 R | 57.7% | 41.5% | 58.2% | 41.8% |
| 8,541 | DAVIS | 3,918 | 2,148 | 1,731 | 39 | 417 R | 54.8% | 44.2% | 55.4% | 44.6% |
| 8,689 | DECATUR | 4,011 | 2,088 | 1,859 | 64 | 229 R | 52.1% | 46.3% | 52.9% | 47.1% |
| 18,404 | DELAWARE | 9,200 | 4,908 | 4,227 | 65 | 681 R | 53.3% | 45.9% | 53.7% | 46.3% |
| 42,351 | DES MOINES | 20,874 | 8,221 | 12,456 | 197 | 4,235 D | 39.4% | 59.7% | 39.8% | 60.2% |
| 16,424 | DICKINSON | 9,553 | 5,337 | 4,140 | 76 | 1,197 R | 55.9% | 43.3% | 56.3% | 43.7% |
| 89,143 | DUBUQUE | 47,043 | 20,100 | 26,561 | 382 | 6,461 D | 42.7% | 56.5% | 43.1% | 56.9% |
| 11,027 | EMMET | 5,156 | 2,697 | 2,405 | 54 | 292 R | 52.3% | 46.6% | 52.9% | 47.1% |
| 22,008 | FAYETTE | 10,392 | 5,128 | 5,185 | 79 | 57 D | 49.3% | 49.9% | 49.7% | 50.3% |
| 16,900 | FLOYD | 8,167 | 3,745 | 4,349 | 73 | 604 D | 45.9% | 53.3% | 46.3% | 53.7% |
| 10,704 | FRANKLIN | 5,521 | 3,128 | 2,340 | 53 | 788 R | 56.7% | 42.4% | 57.2% | 42.8% |
| 8,010 | FREMONT | 3,911 | 2,362 | 1,510 | 39 | 852 R | 60.4% | 38.6% | 61.0% | 39.0% |
| 10,366 | GREENE | 5,113 | 2,618 | 2,459 | 36 | 159 R | 51.2% | 48.1% | 51.6% | 48.4% |
| 12,369 | GRUNDY | 6,849 | 4,429 | 2,386 | 34 | 2,043 R | 64.7% | 34.8% | 65.0% | 35.0% |
| 11,353 | GUTHRIE | 5,994 | 3,325 | 2,614 | 55 | 711 R | 55.5% | 43.6% | 56.0% | 44.0% |
| 16,438 | HAMILTON | 8,335 | 4,367 | 3,895 | 73 | 472 R | 52.4% | 46.7% | 52.9% | 47.1% |
| 12,100 | HANCOCK | 5,905 | 3,368 | 2,484 | 53 | 884 R | 57.0% | 42.1% | 57.6% | 42.4% |
| 18,812 | HARDIN | 8,949 | 4,875 | 4,015 | 59 | 860 R | 54.5% | 44.9% | 54.8% | 45.2% |
| 15,666 | HARRISON | 7,680 | 4,680 | 2,906 | 94 | 1,774 R | 60.9% | 37.8% | 61.7% | 38.3% |
| 20,336 | HENRY | 9,457 | 5,220 | 4,127 | 110 | 1,093 R | 55.2% | 43.6% | 55.8% | 44.2% |
| 9,932 | HOWARD | 4,697 | 2,028 | 2,614 | 55 | 586 D | 43.2% | 55.7% | 43.7% | 56.3% |
| 10,381 | HUMBOLDT | 5,350 | 3,162 | 2,146 | 42 | 1,016 R | 59.1% | 40.1% | 59.6% | 40.4% |
| 7,837 | IDA | 3,774 | 2,342 | 1,415 | 17 | 927 R | 62.1% | 37.5% | 62.3% | 37.7% |
| 15,671 | IOWA | 8,454 | 4,544 | 3,841 | 69 | 703 R | 53.7% | 45.4% | 54.2% | 45.8% |
| 20,296 | JACKSON | 10,011 | 4,242 | 5,656 | 113 | 1,414 D | 42.4% | 56.5% | 42.9% | 57.1% |
| 37,213 | JASPER | 20,062 | 9,462 | 10,430 | 170 | 968 D | 47.2% | 52.0% | 47.6% | 52.4% |
| 16,181 | JEFFERSON | 8,281 | 3,648 | 4,490 | 143 | 842 D | 44.1% | 54.2% | 44.8% | 55.2% |
| 111,006 | JOHNSON | 65,373 | 22,715 | 41,847 | 811 | 19,132 D | 34.7% | 64.0% | 35.2% | 64.8% |
| 20,221 | JONES | 9,978 | 4,834 | 5,054 | 90 | 220 D | 48.4% | 50.7% | 48.9% | 51.1% |
| 11,400 | KEOKUK | 5,480 | 3,119 | 2,294 | 67 | 825 R | 56.9% | 41.9% | 57.6% | 42.4% |
| 17,163 | KOSSUTH | 9,258 | 5,042 | 4,132 | 84 | 910 R | 54.5% | 44.6% | 55.0% | 45.0% |
| 38,052 | LEE | 17,858 | 7,472 | 10,152 | 234 | 2,680 D | 41.8% | 56.8% | 42.4% | 57.6% |
| 191,701 | LINN | 110,740 | 49,442 | 60,442 | 856 | 11,000 D | 44.6% | 54.6% | 45.0% | 55.0% |
| 12,183 | LOUISA | 4,916 | 2,572 | 2,297 | 47 | 275 R | 52.3% | 46.7% | 52.8% | 47.2% |
| 9,422 | LUCAS | 4,571 | 2,543 | 1,987 | 41 | 556 R | 55.6% | 43.5% | 56.1% | 43.9% |
| 11,763 | LYON | 6,101 | 4,751 | 1,303 | 47 | 3,448 R | 77.9% | 21.4% | 78.5% | 21.5% |

# IOWA

## PRESIDENT 2004

| 2000 Census Population | County | Total Vote | Republican | Democratic | Other | Rep.-Dem. Plurality | Percentage | | | |
|---|---|---|---|---|---|---|---|---|---|---|
| | | | | | | | Total Vote | | Major Vote | |
| | | | | | | | Rep. | Dem. | Rep. | Dem. |
| 14,019 | MADISON | 8,004 | 4,538 | 3,380 | 86 | 1,158 R | 56.7% | 42.2% | 57.3% | 42.7% |
| 22,335 | MAHASKA | 10,728 | 6,858 | 3,790 | 80 | 3,068 R | 63.9% | 35.3% | 64.4% | 35.6% |
| 32,052 | MARION | 16,696 | 9,990 | 6,574 | 132 | 3,416 R | 59.8% | 39.4% | 60.3% | 39.7% |
| 39,311 | MARSHALL | 19,164 | 9,557 | 9,443 | 164 | 114 R | 49.9% | 49.3% | 50.3% | 49.7% |
| 14,547 | MILLS | 6,940 | 4,556 | 2,308 | 76 | 2,248 R | 65.6% | 33.3% | 66.4% | 33.6% |
| 10,874 | MITCHELL | 5,480 | 2,646 | 2,785 | 49 | 139 D | 48.3% | 50.8% | 48.7% | 51.3% |
| 10,020 | MONONA | 5,018 | 2,575 | 2,397 | 46 | 178 R | 51.3% | 47.8% | 51.8% | 48.2% |
| 8,016 | MONROE | 3,963 | 2,067 | 1,855 | 41 | 212 R | 52.2% | 46.8% | 52.7% | 47.3% |
| 11,771 | MONTGOMERY | 5,556 | 3,601 | 1,899 | 56 | 1,702 R | 64.8% | 34.2% | 65.5% | 34.5% |
| 41,722 | MUSCATINE | 18,717 | 9,020 | 9,542 | 155 | 522 D | 48.2% | 51.0% | 48.6% | 51.4% |
| 15,102 | O'BRIEN | 7,731 | 5,328 | 2,330 | 73 | 2,998 R | 68.9% | 30.1% | 69.6% | 30.4% |
| 7,003 | OSCEOLA | 3,266 | 2,295 | 934 | 37 | 1,361 R | 70.3% | 28.6% | 71.1% | 28.9% |
| 16,976 | PAGE | 7,513 | 5,243 | 2,211 | 59 | 3,032 R | 69.8% | 29.4% | 70.3% | 29.7% |
| 10,147 | PALO ALTO | 5,191 | 2,674 | 2,482 | 35 | 192 R | 51.5% | 47.8% | 51.9% | 48.1% |
| 24,849 | PLYMOUTH | 12,222 | 7,810 | 4,278 | 134 | 3,532 R | 63.9% | 35.0% | 64.6% | 35.4% |
| 8,662 | POCAHONTAS | 4,313 | 2,441 | 1,822 | 50 | 619 R | 56.6% | 42.2% | 57.3% | 42.7% |
| 374,601 | POLK | 202,618 | 95,828 | 105,218 | 1,572 | 9,390 D | 47.3% | 51.9% | 47.7% | 52.3% |
| 87,704 | POTTAWATTAMIE | 41,820 | 24,558 | 16,906 | 356 | 7,652 R | 58.7% | 40.4% | 59.2% | 40.8% |
| 18,815 | POWESHIEK | 10,091 | 4,965 | 5,043 | 83 | 78 D | 49.2% | 50.0% | 49.6% | 50.4% |
| 5,469 | RINGGOLD | 2,778 | 1,466 | 1,286 | 26 | 180 R | 52.8% | 46.3% | 53.3% | 46.7% |
| 11,529 | SAC | 5,374 | 3,128 | 2,215 | 31 | 913 R | 58.2% | 41.2% | 58.5% | 41.5% |
| 158,668 | SCOTT | 82,722 | 39,958 | 42,122 | 642 | 2,164 D | 48.3% | 50.9% | 48.7% | 51.3% |
| 13,173 | SHELBY | 6,670 | 4,256 | 2,355 | 59 | 1,901 R | 63.8% | 35.3% | 64.4% | 35.6% |
| 31,589 | SIOUX | 16,570 | 14,229 | 2,259 | 82 | 11,970 R | 85.9% | 13.6% | 86.3% | 13.7% |
| 79,981 | STORY | 44,652 | 20,819 | 23,296 | 537 | 2,477 D | 46.6% | 52.2% | 47.2% | 52.8% |
| 18,103 | TAMA | 9,001 | 4,456 | 4,487 | 58 | 31 D | 49.5% | 49.9% | 49.8% | 50.2% |
| 6,958 | TAYLOR | 3,190 | 1,908 | 1,252 | 30 | 656 R | 59.8% | 39.2% | 60.4% | 39.6% |
| 12,309 | UNION | 5,978 | 3,165 | 2,747 | 66 | 418 R | 52.9% | 46.0% | 53.5% | 46.5% |
| 7,809 | VAN BUREN | 3,836 | 2,211 | 1,568 | 57 | 643 R | 57.6% | 40.9% | 58.5% | 41.5% |
| 36,051 | WAPELLO | 16,707 | 7,403 | 9,125 | 179 | 1,722 D | 44.3% | 54.6% | 44.8% | 55.2% |
| 40,671 | WARREN | 23,053 | 12,160 | 10,730 | 163 | 1,430 R | 52.7% | 46.5% | 53.1% | 46.9% |
| 20,670 | WASHINGTON | 10,688 | 5,977 | 4,595 | 116 | 1,382 R | 55.9% | 43.0% | 56.5% | 43.5% |
| 6,730 | WAYNE | 3,133 | 1,733 | 1,379 | 21 | 354 R | 55.3% | 44.0% | 55.7% | 44.3% |
| 40,235 | WEBSTER | 18,631 | 8,959 | 9,561 | 111 | 602 D | 48.1% | 51.3% | 48.4% | 51.6% |
| 11,723 | WINNEBAGO | 5,952 | 3,175 | 2,707 | 70 | 468 R | 53.3% | 45.5% | 54.0% | 46.0% |
| 21,310 | WINNESHIEK | 10,784 | 5,324 | 5,354 | 106 | 30 D | 49.4% | 49.6% | 49.9% | 50.1% |
| 103,877 | WOODBURY | 44,195 | 22,451 | 21,455 | 289 | 996 R | 50.8% | 48.5% | 51.1% | 48.9% |
| 7,909 | WORTH | 4,123 | 1,795 | 2,286 | 42 | 491 D | 43.5% | 55.4% | 44.0% | 56.0% |
| 14,334 | WRIGHT | 6,603 | 3,631 | 2,930 | 42 | 701 R | 55.0% | 44.4% | 55.3% | 44.7% |
| 2,926,324 | TOTAL | 1,506,908 | 751,957 | 741,898 | 13,053 | 10,059 R | 49.9% | 49.2% | 50.3% | 49.7% |

# IOWA

## SENATOR 2004

| 2000 Census Population | County | Total Vote | Republican | Democratic | Other | Rep.-Dem. Plurality | Percentage | | | |
|---|---|---|---|---|---|---|---|---|---|---|
| | | | | | | | Total Vote | | Major Vote | |
| | | | | | | | Rep. | Dem. | Rep. | Dem. |
| 8,243 | ADAIR | 4,239 | 3,359 | 816 | 64 | 2,543 R | 79.2% | 19.2% | 80.5% | 19.5% |
| 4,482 | ADAMS | 2,294 | 1,841 | 407 | 46 | 1,434 R | 80.3% | 17.7% | 81.9% | 18.1% |
| 14,675 | ALLAMAKEE | 6,968 | 4,971 | 1,835 | 162 | 3,136 R | 71.3% | 26.3% | 73.0% | 27.0% |
| 13,721 | APPANOOSE | 6,185 | 4,300 | 1,810 | 75 | 2,490 R | 69.5% | 29.3% | 70.4% | 29.6% |
| 6,830 | AUDUBON | 3,512 | 2,765 | 701 | 46 | 2,064 R | 78.7% | 20.0% | 79.8% | 20.2% |
| 25,308 | BENTON | 13,294 | 9,769 | 3,294 | 231 | 6,475 R | 73.5% | 24.8% | 74.8% | 25.2% |
| 128,012 | BLACK HAWK | 63,037 | 42,746 | 19,151 | 1,140 | 23,595 R | 67.8% | 30.4% | 69.1% | 30.9% |
| 26,224 | BOONE | 13,854 | 9,811 | 3,797 | 246 | 6,014 R | 70.8% | 27.4% | 72.1% | 27.9% |
| 23,325 | BREMER | 12,704 | 9,761 | 2,779 | 164 | 6,982 R | 76.8% | 21.9% | 77.8% | 22.2% |
| 21,093 | BUCHANAN | 10,450 | 7,463 | 2,839 | 148 | 4,624 R | 71.4% | 27.2% | 72.4% | 27.6% |
| 20,411 | BUENA VISTA | 8,310 | 6,529 | 1,682 | 99 | 4,847 R | 78.6% | 20.2% | 79.5% | 20.5% |
| 15,305 | BUTLER | 7,427 | 6,042 | 1,302 | 83 | 4,740 R | 81.4% | 17.5% | 82.3% | 17.7% |
| 11,115 | CALHOUN | 5,484 | 4,382 | 1,031 | 71 | 3,351 R | 79.9% | 18.8% | 81.0% | 19.0% |
| 21,421 | CARROLL | 10,278 | 7,761 | 2,375 | 142 | 5,386 R | 75.5% | 23.1% | 76.6% | 23.4% |
| 14,684 | CASS | 7,405 | 6,029 | 1,239 | 137 | 4,790 R | 81.4% | 16.7% | 83.0% | 17.0% |
| 18,187 | CEDAR | 9,577 | 6,951 | 2,433 | 193 | 4,518 R | 72.6% | 25.4% | 74.1% | 25.9% |
| 46,447 | CERRO GORDO | 24,269 | 16,872 | 6,980 | 417 | 9,892 R | 69.5% | 28.8% | 70.7% | 29.3% |
| 13,035 | CHEROKEE | 6,733 | 5,419 | 1,192 | 122 | 4,227 R | 80.5% | 17.7% | 82.0% | 18.0% |
| 13,095 | CHICKASAW | 6,731 | 5,053 | 1,577 | 101 | 3,476 R | 75.1% | 23.4% | 76.2% | 23.8% |
| 9,133 | CLARKE | 4,511 | 3,323 | 1,096 | 92 | 2,227 R | 73.7% | 24.3% | 75.2% | 24.8% |
| 17,372 | CLAY | 8,451 | 6,409 | 1,911 | 131 | 4,498 R | 75.8% | 22.6% | 77.0% | 23.0% |
| 18,678 | CLAYTON | 9,085 | 6,628 | 2,303 | 154 | 4,325 R | 73.0% | 25.3% | 74.2% | 25.8% |
| 50,149 | CLINTON | 23,441 | 14,612 | 8,485 | 344 | 6,127 R | 62.3% | 36.2% | 63.3% | 36.7% |
| 16,942 | CRAWFORD | 7,051 | 5,579 | 1,320 | 152 | 4,259 R | 79.1% | 18.7% | 80.9% | 19.1% |
| 40,750 | DALLAS | 25,943 | 19,819 | 5,714 | 410 | 14,105 R | 76.4% | 22.0% | 77.6% | 22.4% |
| 8,541 | DAVIS | 3,877 | 2,926 | 898 | 53 | 2,028 R | 75.5% | 23.2% | 76.5% | 23.5% |
| 8,689 | DECATUR | 3,959 | 2,959 | 897 | 103 | 2,062 R | 74.7% | 22.7% | 76.7% | 23.3% |
| 18,404 | DELAWARE | 9,077 | 6,965 | 1,987 | 125 | 4,978 R | 76.7% | 21.9% | 77.8% | 22.2% |
| 42,351 | DES MOINES | 20,476 | 11,990 | 8,101 | 385 | 3,889 R | 58.6% | 39.6% | 59.7% | 40.3% |
| 16,424 | DICKINSON | 9,427 | 7,386 | 1,860 | 181 | 5,526 R | 78.3% | 19.7% | 79.9% | 20.1% |
| 89,143 | DUBUQUE | 45,935 | 29,250 | 15,837 | 848 | 13,413 R | 63.7% | 34.5% | 64.9% | 35.1% |
| 11,027 | EMMET | 5,062 | 3,783 | 1,198 | 81 | 2,585 R | 74.7% | 23.7% | 75.9% | 24.1% |
| 22,008 | FAYETTE | 10,086 | 7,315 | 2,643 | 128 | 4,672 R | 72.5% | 26.2% | 73.5% | 26.5% |
| 16,900 | FLOYD | 8,132 | 6,066 | 1,928 | 138 | 4,138 R | 74.6% | 23.7% | 75.9% | 24.1% |
| 10,704 | FRANKLIN | 5,490 | 4,471 | 953 | 66 | 3,518 R | 81.4% | 17.4% | 82.4% | 17.6% |
| 8,010 | FREMONT | 3,877 | 3,048 | 743 | 86 | 2,305 R | 78.6% | 19.2% | 80.4% | 19.6% |
| 10,366 | GREENE | 5,050 | 3,837 | 1,143 | 70 | 2,694 R | 76.0% | 22.6% | 77.0% | 23.0% |
| 12,369 | GRUNDY | 6,798 | 5,747 | 994 | 57 | 4,753 R | 84.5% | 14.6% | 85.3% | 14.7% |
| 11,353 | GUTHRIE | 5,922 | 4,528 | 1,290 | 104 | 3,238 R | 76.5% | 21.8% | 77.8% | 22.2% |
| 16,438 | HAMILTON | 8,252 | 6,287 | 1,839 | 126 | 4,448 R | 76.2% | 22.3% | 77.4% | 22.6% |
| 12,100 | HANCOCK | 5,848 | 4,641 | 1,116 | 91 | 3,525 R | 79.4% | 19.1% | 80.6% | 19.4% |
| 18,812 | HARDIN | 8,847 | 6,704 | 2,029 | 114 | 4,675 R | 75.8% | 22.9% | 76.8% | 23.2% |
| 15,666 | HARRISON | 7,531 | 5,807 | 1,569 | 155 | 4,238 R | 77.1% | 20.8% | 78.7% | 21.3% |
| 20,336 | HENRY | 9,297 | 7,037 | 2,090 | 170 | 4,947 R | 75.7% | 22.5% | 77.1% | 22.9% |
| 9,932 | HOWARD | 4,657 | 3,466 | 1,121 | 70 | 2,345 R | 74.4% | 24.1% | 75.6% | 24.4% |
| 10,381 | HUMBOLDT | 5,300 | 4,274 | 959 | 67 | 3,315 R | 80.6% | 18.1% | 81.7% | 18.3% |
| 7,837 | IDA | 3,713 | 3,073 | 603 | 37 | 2,470 R | 82.8% | 16.2% | 83.6% | 16.4% |
| 15,671 | IOWA | 8,416 | 6,280 | 1,982 | 154 | 4,298 R | 74.6% | 23.6% | 76.0% | 24.0% |
| 20,296 | JACKSON | 9,640 | 6,592 | 2,890 | 158 | 3,702 R | 68.4% | 30.0% | 69.5% | 30.5% |
| 37,213 | JASPER | 19,842 | 13,391 | 6,173 | 278 | 7,218 R | 67.5% | 31.1% | 68.4% | 31.6% |
| 16,181 | JEFFERSON | 8,082 | 4,979 | 2,598 | 505 | 2,381 R | 61.6% | 32.1% | 65.7% | 34.3% |
| 111,006 | JOHNSON | 63,521 | 33,301 | 27,509 | 2,711 | 5,792 R | 52.4% | 43.3% | 54.8% | 45.2% |
| 20,221 | JONES | 9,863 | 7,173 | 2,504 | 186 | 4,669 R | 72.7% | 25.4% | 74.1% | 25.9% |
| 11,400 | KEOKUK | 5,407 | 4,340 | 990 | 77 | 3,350 R | 80.3% | 18.3% | 81.4% | 18.6% |
| 17,163 | KOSSUTH | 9,171 | 7,133 | 1,933 | 105 | 5,200 R | 77.8% | 21.1% | 78.7% | 21.3% |
| 38,052 | LEE | 17,632 | 10,604 | 6,442 | 586 | 4,162 R | 60.1% | 36.5% | 62.2% | 37.8% |
| 191,701 | LINN | 108,710 | 70,828 | 35,576 | 2,306 | 35,252 R | 65.2% | 32.7% | 66.6% | 33.4% |
| 12,183 | LOUISA | 4,941 | 3,588 | 1,259 | 94 | 2,329 R | 72.6% | 25.5% | 74.0% | 26.0% |
| 9,422 | LUCAS | 4,480 | 3,381 | 1,052 | 47 | 2,329 R | 75.5% | 23.5% | 76.3% | 23.7% |
| 11,763 | LYON | 5,975 | 5,202 | 717 | 56 | 4,485 R | 87.1% | 12.0% | 87.9% | 12.1% |

# IOWA

## SENATOR 2004

| 2000 Census Population | County | Total Vote | Republican | Democratic | Other | Rep.-Dem. Plurality | Percentage | | | |
|---|---|---|---|---|---|---|---|---|---|---|
| | | | | | | | Total Vote | | Major Vote | |
| | | | | | | | Rep. | Dem. | Rep. | Dem. |
| 14,019 | MADISON | 7,935 | 6,007 | 1,778 | 150 | 4,229 R | 75.7% | 22.4% | 77.2% | 22.8% |
| 22,335 | MAHASKA | 10,497 | 8,542 | 1,828 | 127 | 6,714 R | 81.4% | 17.4% | 82.4% | 17.6% |
| 32,052 | MARION | 16,357 | 12,592 | 3,574 | 191 | 9,018 R | 77.0% | 21.8% | 77.9% | 22.1% |
| 39,311 | MARSHALL | 18,905 | 13,343 | 5,259 | 303 | 8,084 R | 70.6% | 27.8% | 71.7% | 28.3% |
| 14,547 | MILLS | 6,802 | 5,392 | 1,218 | 192 | 4,174 R | 79.3% | 17.9% | 81.6% | 18.4% |
| 10,874 | MITCHELL | 5,547 | 4,159 | 1,325 | 63 | 2,834 R | 75.0% | 23.9% | 75.8% | 24.2% |
| 10,020 | MONONA | 4,951 | 3,711 | 1,142 | 98 | 2,569 R | 75.0% | 23.1% | 76.5% | 23.5% |
| 8,016 | MONROE | 3,911 | 3,008 | 847 | 56 | 2,161 R | 76.9% | 21.7% | 78.0% | 22.0% |
| 11,771 | MONTGOMERY | 5,443 | 4,561 | 764 | 118 | 3,797 R | 83.8% | 14.0% | 85.7% | 14.3% |
| 41,722 | MUSCATINE | 18,299 | 12,368 | 5,525 | 406 | 6,843 R | 67.6% | 30.2% | 69.1% | 30.9% |
| 15,102 | O'BRIEN | 7,575 | 6,363 | 1,110 | 102 | 5,253 R | 84.0% | 14.7% | 85.1% | 14.9% |
| 7,003 | OSCEOLA | 3,238 | 2,733 | 461 | 44 | 2,272 R | 84.4% | 14.2% | 85.6% | 14.4% |
| 16,976 | PAGE | 7,430 | 6,081 | 1,221 | 128 | 4,860 R | 81.8% | 16.4% | 83.3% | 16.7% |
| 10,147 | PALO ALTO | 5,101 | 3,909 | 1,126 | 66 | 2,783 R | 76.6% | 22.1% | 77.6% | 22.4% |
| 24,849 | PLYMOUTH | 11,975 | 9,588 | 2,229 | 158 | 7,359 R | 80.1% | 18.6% | 81.1% | 18.9% |
| 8,662 | POCAHONTAS | 4,257 | 3,432 | 763 | 62 | 2,669 R | 80.6% | 17.9% | 81.8% | 18.2% |
| 374,601 | POLK | 198,928 | 132,900 | 62,183 | 3,845 | 70,717 R | 66.8% | 31.3% | 68.1% | 31.9% |
| 87,704 | POTTAWATTAMIE | 41,140 | 29,649 | 10,449 | 1,042 | 19,200 R | 72.1% | 25.4% | 73.9% | 26.1% |
| 18,815 | POWESHIEK | 9,873 | 6,599 | 3,049 | 225 | 3,550 R | 66.8% | 30.9% | 68.4% | 31.6% |
| 5,469 | RINGGOLD | 2,724 | 2,218 | 477 | 29 | 1,741 R | 81.4% | 17.5% | 82.3% | 17.7% |
| 11,529 | SAC | 5,301 | 4,291 | 962 | 48 | 3,329 R | 80.9% | 18.1% | 81.7% | 18.3% |
| 158,668 | SCOTT | 80,638 | 54,320 | 24,847 | 1,471 | 29,473 R | 67.4% | 30.8% | 68.6% | 31.4% |
| 13,173 | SHELBY | 6,515 | 5,306 | 1,100 | 109 | 4,206 R | 81.4% | 16.9% | 82.8% | 17.2% |
| 31,589 | SIOUX | 15,662 | 14,437 | 1,166 | 59 | 13,271 R | 92.2% | 7.4% | 92.5% | 7.5% |
| 79,981 | STORY | 43,586 | 30,065 | 12,261 | 1,260 | 17,804 R | 69.0% | 28.1% | 71.0% | 29.0% |
| 18,103 | TAMA | 8,885 | 6,541 | 2,233 | 111 | 4,308 R | 73.6% | 25.1% | 74.5% | 25.5% |
| 6,958 | TAYLOR | 3,131 | 2,489 | 580 | 62 | 1,909 R | 79.5% | 18.5% | 81.1% | 18.9% |
| 12,309 | UNION | 5,836 | 4,347 | 1,402 | 87 | 2,945 R | 74.5% | 24.0% | 75.6% | 24.4% |
| 7,809 | VAN BUREN | 3,789 | 2,971 | 762 | 56 | 2,209 R | 78.4% | 20.1% | 79.6% | 20.4% |
| 36,051 | WAPELLO | 16,420 | 10,389 | 5,670 | 361 | 4,719 R | 63.3% | 34.5% | 64.7% | 35.3% |
| 40,671 | WARREN | 22,492 | 16,018 | 6,163 | 311 | 9,855 R | 71.2% | 27.4% | 72.2% | 27.8% |
| 20,670 | WASHINGTON | 10,492 | 8,082 | 2,190 | 220 | 5,892 R | 77.0% | 20.9% | 78.7% | 21.3% |
| 6,730 | WAYNE | 3,084 | 2,333 | 713 | 38 | 1,620 R | 75.6% | 23.1% | 76.6% | 23.4% |
| 40,235 | WEBSTER | 18,410 | 12,958 | 5,180 | 272 | 7,778 R | 70.4% | 28.1% | 71.4% | 28.6% |
| 11,723 | WINNEBAGO | 5,904 | 4,528 | 1,282 | 94 | 3,246 R | 76.7% | 21.7% | 77.9% | 22.1% |
| 21,310 | WINNESHIEK | 10,615 | 7,688 | 2,629 | 298 | 5,059 R | 72.4% | 24.8% | 74.5% | 25.5% |
| 103,877 | WOODBURY | 43,422 | 29,522 | 13,109 | 791 | 16,413 R | 68.0% | 30.2% | 69.3% | 30.7% |
| 7,909 | WORTH | 4,102 | 3,108 | 938 | 56 | 2,170 R | 75.8% | 22.9% | 76.8% | 23.2% |
| 14,334 | WRIGHT | 6,530 | 5,081 | 1,358 | 91 | 3,723 R | 77.8% | 20.8% | 78.9% | 21.1% |
| 2,926,324 | TOTAL | 1,479,228 | 1,038,175 | 412,365 | 28,688 | 625,810 R | 70.2% | 27.9% | 71.6% | 28.4% |

# IOWA

## HOUSE OF REPRESENTATIVES

| CD | Year | Total Vote | Republican Vote | Republican Candidate | Democratic Vote | Democratic Candidate | Other Vote | Rep.-Dem. Plurality | Percentage Total Vote Rep. | Dem. | Major Vote Rep. | Dem. |
|----|------|-----------|------|-----------|------|-----------|------|------|------|------|------|------|
| 1 | 2004 | 290,054 | 159,993 | Nussle, Jim* | 125,490 | Gluba, Bill | 4,571 | 34,503 R | 55.2% | 43.3% | 56.0% | 44.0% |
| 1 | 2002 | 196,455 | 112,280 | Nussle, Jim* | 83,779 | Hutchinson, Ann | 396 | 28,501 R | 57.2% | 42.6% | 57.3% | 42.7% |
| 2 | 2004 | 299,881 | 176,684 | Leach, Jim* | 117,405 | Franker, Dave | 5,792 | 59,279 R | 58.9% | 39.2% | 60.1% | 39.9% |
| 2 | 2002 | 207,171 | 108,130 | Leach, Jim* | 94,767 | Thomas, Julie | 4,274 | 13,363 R | 52.2% | 45.7% | 53.3% | 46.7% |
| 3 | 2004 | 304,319 | 136,099 | Thompson, Stan | 168,007 | Boswell, Leonard L.* | 213 | 31,908 D | 44.7% | 55.2% | 44.8% | 55.2% |
| 3 | 2002 | 15,985 | 97,285 | Thompson, Stan | 115,367 | Boswell, Leonard L.* | 3,333 | 18,082 D | 45.0% | 53.4% | 45.7% | 54.3% |
| 4 | 2004 | 297,566 | 181,294 | Latham, Tom* | 116,121 | Johnson, Paul W. | 151 | 65,173 R | 60.9% | 39.0% | 61.0% | 39.0% |
| 4 | 2002 | 210,774 | 115,430 | Latham, Tom* | 90,784 | Norris, John | 4,560 | 24,646 R | 54.8% | 43.1% | 56.0% | 44.0% |
| 5 | 2004 | 266,341 | 168,583 | King, Steve* | 97,597 | Schulte, E. Joyce | 161 | 70,986 R | 63.3% | 36.6% | 63.3% | 36.7% |
| 5 | 2002 | 182,237 | 113,257 | King, Steve | 68,853 | Shomshor, Paul | 127 | 44,404 R | 62.1% | 37.8% | 62.2% | 37.8% |
| Total | 2004 | 1,458,161 | 822,653 | | 624,620 | | 10,888 | 198,033 R | 56.4% | 42.8% | 56.8% | 43.2% |
| Total | 2002 | 1,012,622 | 546,382 | | 453,550 | | 12,690 | 92,832 R | 54.0% | 44.8% | 54.6% | 45.4% |

An asterisk (*) denotes incumbent.

# IOWA

## GENERAL AND PRIMARY ELECTIONS

### 2004 GENERAL ELECTIONS

**President**   Other vote was 5,973 Nominated by Petition (Ralph Nader); 2,992 Libertarian (Michael Badnarik); 1,304 Constitution (Michael Peroutka); 1,141 Iowa Green (David Cobb); 373 Socialist Workers (James Harris); 176 Nominated by Petition (Bill Van Auken); 1,094 scattered write-in.

**Senator**   Other vote was 15,218 Libertarian (Christy Ann Welty); 11,121 Iowa Green (Daryl A. Northrop); 1,874 Socialist Workers (Edwin Fruit); 475 scattered write-in.

**House**   Other vote was:

CD 1   2,727 Libertarian (Mark Nelson); 1,756 Nominated by Petition (Denny Heath); 88 scattered write-in.
CD 2   5,586 Libertarian (Kevin Litten); 206 scattered write-in.
CD 3   213 scattered write-in.
CD 4   151 scattered write-in.
CD 5   161 scattered write-in.

# IOWA

## GENERAL AND PRIMARY ELECTIONS

## 2004 PRIMARY ELECTIONS

| | | |
|---|---|---|
| **Primary** | June 8, 2004 | |

| **Registration** | Republican | 618,241 |
|---|---|---|
| (as of May 29, 2004— | Democratic | 606,743 |
| includes 174,898 | Green | 93 |
| inactive registrants) | No Party | 786,590 |
| | TOTAL | 2,011,667 |

**Primary Type**   Semi-open—Registered Democrats and Republicans could vote only in their party's primary, although registered voters could participate in either party's primary by changing their registration to that party on primary day.

Note:   An asterisk (*) denotes incumbent. The Iowa precinct caucuses held January 19, 2004, had considerable importance in the Democratic presidential nominating contest but did not involve a direct vote as does a primary.

| | REPUBLICAN PRIMARIES | | | DEMOCRATIC PRIMARIES | | |
|---|---|---|---|---|---|---|
| **Senator** | Charles E. Grassley* | 78,819 | 99.7% | Arthur Small | 52,318 | 99.2% |
| | Write-in | 218 | 0.3% | Write-in | 398 | 0.8% |
| | TOTAL | 79,037 | | TOTAL | 52,716 | |
| **Congressional District 1** | Jim Nussle* | 12,082 | 99.7% | Bill Gluba | 7,126 | 59.8% |
| | Write-in | 41 | 0.3% | Denny Heath | 4,741 | 39.8% |
| | | | | Write-in | 41 | 0.3% |
| | TOTAL | 12,123 | | TOTAL | 11,908 | |
| **Congressional District 2** | Jim Leach* | 11,419 | 99.4% | Dave Franker | 16,351 | 99.1% |
| | Write-in | 66 | 0.6% | Write-in | 146 | 0.9% |
| | TOTAL | 11,485 | | TOTAL | 16,497 | |
| **Congressional District 3** | Stan Thompson | 7,684 | 99.5% | Leonard L. Boswell* | 9,882 | 99.4% |
| | Write-in | 36 | 0.5% | Write-in | 57 | 0.6% |
| | TOTAL | 7,720 | | TOTAL | 9,939 | |
| **Congressional District 4** | Tom Latham* | 12,350 | 99.7% | Paul W. Johnson | 9,653 | 99.7% |
| | Write-in | 34 | 0.3% | Write-in | 31 | 0.3% |
| | TOTAL | 12,384 | | TOTAL | 9,684 | |
| **Congressional District 5** | Steve King* | 30,198 | 99.6% | E. Joyce Schulte | 4,902 | 51.3% |
| | Write-in | 129 | 0.4% | Gene Blanshan | 3,117 | 32.6% |
| | | | | Sal Mohamed | 1,513 | 15.8% |
| | | | | Write-in | 20 | 0.2% |
| | TOTAL | 30,327 | | TOTAL | 9,552 | |

# KANSAS

## GOVERNOR
Kathleen Sebelius (D). Elected 2002 to a four-year term.

## SENATORS (2 Republicans)
Sam Brownback (R). Reelected 2004 to a six-year term. Previously elected 1998 and 1996 to fill out the remaining two years of the term vacated when Senator Robert Dole (R) resigned to run for president.

Pat Roberts (R). Reelected 2002 to a six-year term. Previously elected 1996.

## REPRESENTATIVES (3 Republicans, 1 Democrat)
1. Jerry Moran (R)
2. Jim Ryun (R)
3. Dennis Moore (D)
4. Todd Tiahrt (R)

## POSTWAR VOTE FOR PRESIDENT

| | | Republican | | Democratic | | Other | | Total Vote | | Major Vote | |
|---|---|---|---|---|---|---|---|---|---|---|---|
| Year | Total Vote | Vote | Candidate | Vote | Candidate | Vote | Plurality | Rep. | Dem. | Rep. | Dem. |
| 2004 | 1,187,756 | 736,456 | Bush, George W. | 434,993 | Kerry, John | 16,307 | 301,463 R | 62.0% | 36.6% | 62.9% | 37.1% |
| 2000** | 1,072,218 | 622,332 | Bush, George W. | 399,276 | Gore, Al | 50,610 | 223,056 R | 58.0% | 37.2% | 60.9% | 39.1% |
| 1996** | 1,074,300 | 583,245 | Dole, Bob | 387,659 | Clinton, Bill | 103,396 | 195,586 R | 54.3% | 36.1% | 60.1% | 39.9% |
| 1992** | 1,157,335 | 449,951 | Bush, George | 390,434 | Clinton, Bill | 316,950 | 59,517 R | 38.9% | 33.7% | 53.5% | 46.5% |
| 1988 | 993,044 | 554,049 | Bush, George | 422,636 | Dukakis, Michael S. | 16,359 | 131,413 R | 55.8% | 42.6% | 56.7% | 43.3% |
| 1984 | 1,021,991 | 677,296 | Reagan, Ronald | 333,149 | Mondale, Walter F. | 11,546 | 344,147 R | 66.3% | 32.6% | 67.0% | 33.0% |
| 1980** | 979,795 | 566,812 | Reagan, Ronald | 326,150 | Carter, Jimmy | 86,833 | 240,662 R | 57.9% | 33.3% | 63.5% | 36.5% |
| 1976 | 957,845 | 502,752 | Ford, Gerald R. | 430,421 | Carter, Jimmy | 24,672 | 72,331 R | 52.5% | 44.9% | 53.9% | 46.1% |
| 1972 | 916,095 | 619,812 | Nixon, Richard M. | 270,287 | McGovern, George S. | 25,996 | 349,525 R | 67.7% | 29.5% | 69.6% | 30.4% |
| 1968** | 872,783 | 478,674 | Nixon, Richard M. | 302,996 | Humphrey, Hubert H. | 91,113 | 175,678 R | 54.8% | 34.7% | 61.2% | 38.8% |
| 1964 | 857,901 | 386,579 | Goldwater, Barry M. | 464,028 | Johnson, Lyndon B. | 7,294 | 77,449 D | 45.1% | 54.1% | 45.4% | 54.6% |
| 1960 | 928,825 | 561,474 | Nixon, Richard M. | 363,213 | Kennedy, John F. | 4,138 | 198,261 R | 60.4% | 39.1% | 60.7% | 39.3% |
| 1956 | 866,243 | 566,878 | Eisenhower, Dwight D. | 296,317 | Stevenson, Adlai E. | 3,048 | 270,561 R | 65.4% | 34.2% | 65.7% | 34.3% |
| 1952 | 896,166 | 616,302 | Eisenhower, Dwight D. | 273,296 | Stevenson, Adlai E. | 6,568 | 343,006 R | 68.8% | 30.5% | 69.3% | 30.7% |
| 1948 | 788,819 | 423,039 | Dewey, Thomas E. | 351,902 | Truman, Harry S. | 13,878 | 71,137 R | 53.6% | 44.6% | 54.6% | 45.4% |

In past elections, the other vote included: 2000 - 36,086 Green (Ralph Nader); 1996 - 92,639 Reform (Ross Perot); 1992 - 312,358 Independent (Perot); 1980 - 68,231 Independent (John Anderson); 1968 - 88,921 American Independent (George Wallace).

# KANSAS

## POSTWAR VOTE FOR GOVERNOR

| Year | Total Vote | Republican Vote | Republican Candidate | Democratic Vote | Democratic Candidate | Other Vote | Rep.-Dem. Plurality | Total Vote Rep. | Total Vote Dem. | Major Vote Rep. | Major Vote Dem. |
|---|---|---|---|---|---|---|---|---|---|---|---|
| 2002 | 835,692 | 376,830 | Shallenburger, Tim | 441,858 | Sebelius, Kathleen | 17,004 | 65,028 D | 45.1% | 52.9% | 46.0% | 54.0% |
| 1998 | 742,665 | 544,882 | Graves, Bill | 168,243 | Sawyer, Tom | 29,540 | 376,639 R | 73.4% | 22.7% | 76.4% | 23.6% |
| 1994 | 821,030 | 526,113 | Graves, Bill | 294,733 | Slattery, Jim | 184 | 231,380 R | 64.1% | 35.9% | 64.1% | 35.9% |
| 1990 | 783,325 | 333,589 | Hayden, Mike | 380,609 | Finney, Joan | 69,127 | 47,020 D | 42.6% | 48.6% | 46.7% | 53.3% |
| 1986 | 840,605 | 436,267 | Hayden, Mike | 404,338 | Docking, Thomas R. | | 31,929 R | 51.9% | 48.1% | 51.9% | 48.1% |
| 1982 | 763,263 | 339,356 | Hardage, Sam | 405,772 | Carlin, John | 18,135 | 66,416 D | 44.5% | 53.2% | 45.5% | 54.5% |
| 1978 | 736,246 | 348,015 | Bennett, Robert F. | 363,835 | Carlin, John | 24,396 | 15,820 D | 47.3% | 49.4% | 48.9% | 51.1% |
| 1974** | 783,875 | 387,792 | Bennett, Robert F. | 384,115 | Miller, Vern | 11,968 | 3,677 R | 49.5% | 49.0% | 50.2% | 49.8% |
| 1972 | 921,552 | 341,440 | Kay, Morris | 571,256 | Docking, Robert | 8,856 | 229,816 D | 37.1% | 62.0% | 37.4% | 62.6% |
| 1970 | 745,196 | 333,227 | Frizzell, Kent | 404,611 | Docking, Robert | 7,358 | 71,384 D | 44.7% | 54.3% | 45.2% | 54.8% |
| 1968 | 862,473 | 410,673 | Harman, Rick | 447,269 | Docking, Robert | 4,531 | 36,596 D | 47.6% | 51.9% | 47.9% | 52.1% |
| 1966 | 692,955 | 304,325 | Avery, William H. | 380,030 | Docking, Robert | 8,600 | 75,705 D | 43.9% | 54.8% | 44.5% | 55.5% |
| 1964 | 850,414 | 432,667 | Avery, William H. | 400,264 | Wiles, Harry G. | 17,483 | 32,403 R | 50.9% | 47.1% | 51.9% | 48.1% |
| 1962 | 638,798 | 341,257 | Anderson, John | 291,285 | Saffels, Dale E. | 6,256 | 49,972 R | 53.4% | 45.6% | 54.0% | 46.0% |
| 1960 | 922,522 | 511,534 | Anderson, John | 402,261 | Docking, George | 8,727 | 109,273 R | 55.4% | 43.6% | 56.0% | 44.0% |
| 1958 | 735,939 | 313,036 | Reed, Clyde M. | 415,506 | Docking, George | 7,397 | 102,470 D | 42.5% | 56.5% | 43.0% | 57.0% |
| 1956 | 864,935 | 364,340 | Shaw, Warren W. | 479,701 | Docking, George | 20,894 | 115,361 D | 42.1% | 55.5% | 43.2% | 56.8% |
| 1954 | 622,633 | 329,868 | Hall, Fred | 286,218 | Docking, George | 6,547 | 43,650 R | 53.0% | 46.0% | 53.5% | 46.5% |
| 1952 | 872,139 | 491,338 | Arn, Edward F. | 363,482 | Rooney, Charles | 17,319 | 127,856 R | 56.3% | 41.7% | 57.5% | 42.5% |
| 1950 | 619,310 | 333,001 | Arn, Edward F. | 275,494 | Anderson, Kenneth | 10,815 | 57,507 R | 53.8% | 44.5% | 54.7% | 45.3% |
| 1948 | 760,407 | 433,396 | Carlson, Frank | 307,485 | Carpenter, Randolph | 19,526 | 125,911 R | 57.0% | 40.4% | 58.5% | 41.5% |
| 1946 | 577,694 | 309,064 | Carlson, Frank | 254,283 | Woodring, Harry H. | 14,347 | 54,781 R | 53.5% | 44.0% | 54.9% | 45.1% |

The term of office of Kansas' governor was increased from two to four years effective with the 1974 election.

## POSTWAR VOTE FOR SENATOR

| Year | Total Vote | Republican Vote | Republican Candidate | Democratic Vote | Democratic Candidate | Other Vote | Rep.-Dem. Plurality | Total Vote Rep. | Total Vote Dem. | Major Vote Rep. | Major Vote Dem. |
|---|---|---|---|---|---|---|---|---|---|---|---|
| 2004 | 1,129,022 | 780,863 | Brownback, Sam | 310,337 | Jones, Lee | 37,822 | 470,526 R | 69.2% | 27.5% | 71.6% | 28.4% |
| 2002 | 776,850 | 641,075 | Roberts, Pat | — | | 135,775 | 641,075 R | 82.5% | | 100.0% | |
| 1998 | 727,236 | 474,639 | Brownback, Sam | 229,718 | Feleciano, Paul, Jr. | 22,879 | 244,921 R | 65.3% | 31.6% | 67.4% | 32.6% |
| 1996 | 1,052,300 | 652,677 | Roberts, Pat | 362,380 | Thompson, Sally | 37,243 | 290,297 R | 62.0% | 34.4% | 64.3% | 35.7% |
| 1996S | 1,064,716 | 574,021 | Brownback, Sam | 461,344 | Docking, Jill | 29,351 | 112,677 R | 53.9% | 43.3% | 55.4% | 44.6% |
| 1992 | 1,126,447 | 706,246 | Dole, Robert | 349,525 | O'Dell, Gloria | 70,676 | 356,721 R | 62.7% | 31.0% | 66.9% | 33.1% |
| 1990 | 786,235 | 578,605 | Kassebaum, Nancy Landon | 207,491 | Williams, Dick | 139 | 371,114 R | 73.6% | 26.4% | 73.6% | 26.4% |
| 1986 | 823,566 | 576,902 | Dole, Robert | 246,664 | MacDonald, Guy | | 330,238 R | 70.0% | 30.0% | 70.0% | 30.0% |
| 1984 | 996,729 | 757,402 | Kassebaum, Nancy Landon | 211,664 | Maher, James | 27,663 | 545,738 R | 76.0% | 21.2% | 78.2% | 21.8% |
| 1980 | 938,957 | 598,686 | Dole, Robert | 340,271 | Simpson, John | | 258,415 R | 63.8% | 36.2% | 63.8% | 36.2% |
| 1978 | 748,839 | 403,354 | Kassebaum, Nancy Landon | 317,602 | Roy, William R. | 27,883 | 85,752 R | 53.9% | 42.4% | 55.9% | 44.1% |
| 1974 | 794,437 | 403,983 | Dole, Robert | 390,451 | Roy, William R. | 3 | 13,532 R | 50.9% | 49.1% | 50.9% | 49.1% |
| 1972 | 871,722 | 622,591 | Pearson, James B. | 200,764 | Tetzlaff, Arch O. | 48,367 | 421,827 R | 71.4% | 23.0% | 75.6% | 24.4% |
| 1968 | 817,096 | 490,911 | Dole, Robert | 315,911 | Robinson, William I. | 10,274 | 175,000 R | 60.1% | 38.7% | 60.8% | 39.2% |
| 1966 | 671,345 | 350,077 | Pearson, James B. | 303,223 | Breeding, J. Floyd | 18,045 | 46,854 R | 52.1% | 45.2% | 53.6% | 46.4% |
| 1962 | 622,232 | 388,500 | Carlson, Frank | 223,630 | Smith, K. L. | 10,102 | 164,870 R | 62.4% | 35.9% | 63.5% | 36.5% |
| 1962S | 613,250 | 344,689 | Pearson, James B. | 260,756 | Aylward, Paul L. | 7,805 | 83,933 R | 56.2% | 42.5% | 56.9% | 43.1% |
| 1960 | 888,592 | 485,499 | Schoeppel, Andrew F. | 388,895 | Theis, Frank | 14,198 | 96,604 R | 54.6% | 43.8% | 55.5% | 44.5% |
| 1956 | 825,280 | 477,822 | Carlson, Frank | 333,939 | Hart, George | 13,519 | 143,883 R | 57.9% | 40.5% | 58.9% | 41.1% |
| 1954 | 618,063 | 348,144 | Schoeppel, Andrew F. | 258,575 | McGill, George | 11,344 | 89,569 R | 56.3% | 41.8% | 57.4% | 42.6% |
| 1950 | 619,104 | 335,880 | Carlson, Frank | 271,365 | Aiken, Paul | 11,859 | 64,515 R | 54.3% | 43.8% | 55.3% | 44.7% |
| 1948 | 716,342 | 393,412 | Schoeppel, Andrew F. | 305,987 | McGill, George | 16,943 | 87,425 R | 54.9% | 42.7% | 56.3% | 43.7% |

One of the 1996 and 1962 elections was for a short term to fill a vacancy.

# KANSAS

Congressional districts first established for elections held in 2002
4 members

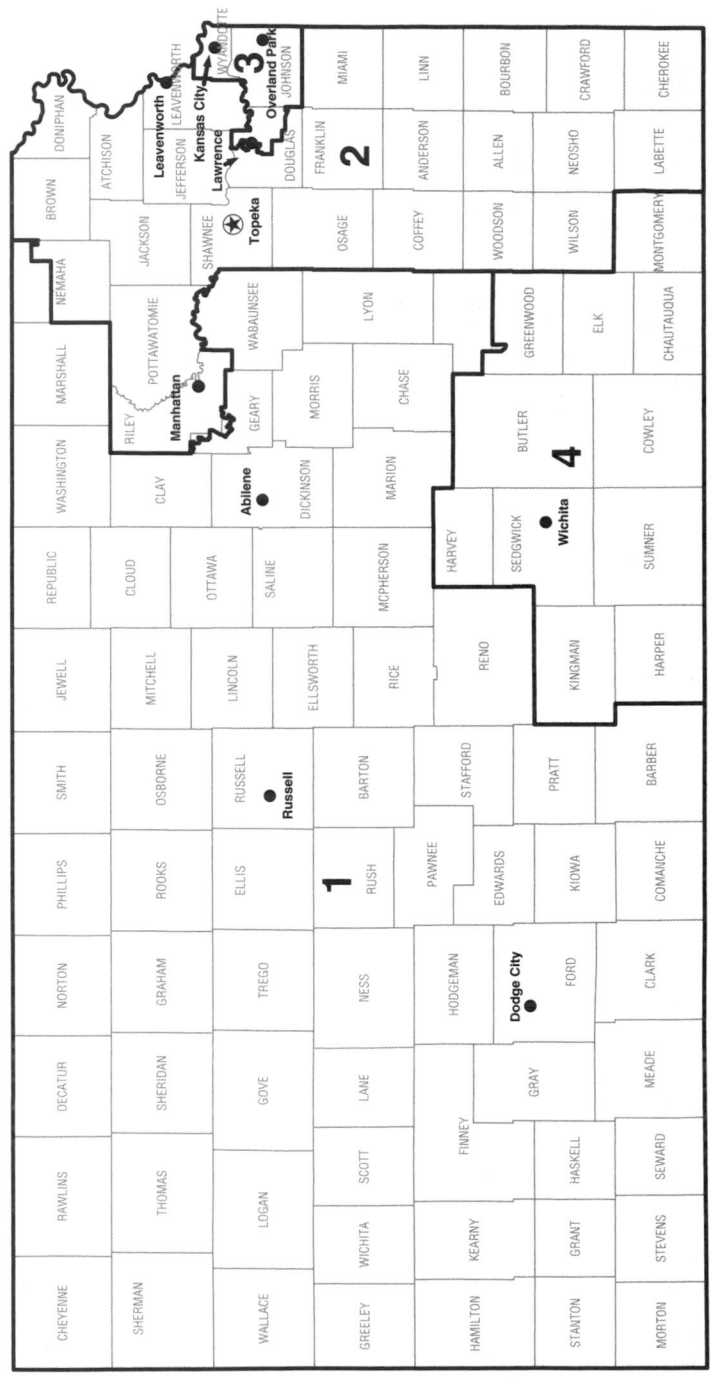

# KANSAS

## PRESIDENT 2004

| 2000 Census Population | County | Total Vote | Republican | Democratic | Other | Rep.-Dem. Plurality | Percentage | | | |
|---|---|---|---|---|---|---|---|---|---|---|
| | | | | | | | Total Vote | | Major Vote | |
| | | | | | | | Rep. | Dem. | Rep. | Dem. |
| 14,385 | ALLEN | 5,873 | 3,867 | 1,922 | 84 | 1,945 R | 65.8% | 32.7% | 66.8% | 33.2% |
| 8,110 | ANDERSON | 3,863 | 2,500 | 1,295 | 68 | 1,205 R | 64.7% | 33.5% | 65.9% | 34.1% |
| 16,774 | ATCHISON | 7,118 | 3,880 | 3,120 | 118 | 760 R | 54.5% | 43.8% | 55.4% | 44.6% |
| 5,307 | BARBER | 2,403 | 1,782 | 588 | 33 | 1,194 R | 74.2% | 24.5% | 75.2% | 24.8% |
| 28,205 | BARTON | 11,706 | 8,666 | 2,874 | 166 | 5,792 R | 74.0% | 24.6% | 75.1% | 24.9% |
| 15,379 | BOURBON | 6,686 | 4,372 | 2,216 | 98 | 2,156 R | 65.4% | 33.1% | 66.4% | 33.6% |
| 10,724 | BROWN | 4,418 | 3,092 | 1,268 | 58 | 1,824 R | 70.0% | 28.7% | 70.9% | 29.1% |
| 59,482 | BUTLER | 26,280 | 18,438 | 7,495 | 347 | 10,943 R | 70.2% | 28.5% | 71.1% | 28.9% |
| 3,030 | CHASE | 1,501 | 1,055 | 418 | 28 | 637 R | 70.3% | 27.8% | 71.6% | 28.4% |
| 4,359 | CHAUTAUQUA | 1,960 | 1,529 | 404 | 27 | 1,125 R | 78.0% | 20.6% | 79.1% | 20.9% |
| 22,605 | CHEROKEE | 9,913 | 6,083 | 3,726 | 104 | 2,357 R | 61.4% | 37.6% | 62.0% | 38.0% |
| 3,165 | CHEYENNE | 1,692 | 1,353 | 320 | 19 | 1,033 R | 80.0% | 18.9% | 80.9% | 19.1% |
| 2,390 | CLARK | 1,291 | 1,014 | 257 | 20 | 757 R | 78.5% | 19.9% | 79.8% | 20.2% |
| 8,822 | CLAY | 4,010 | 3,174 | 793 | 43 | 2,381 R | 79.2% | 19.8% | 80.0% | 20.0% |
| 10,268 | CLOUD | 4,503 | 3,221 | 1,210 | 72 | 2,011 R | 71.5% | 26.9% | 72.7% | 27.3% |
| 8,865 | COFFEY | 4,408 | 3,259 | 1,093 | 56 | 2,166 R | 73.9% | 24.8% | 74.9% | 25.1% |
| 1,967 | COMANCHE | 981 | 770 | 200 | 11 | 570 R | 78.5% | 20.4% | 79.4% | 20.6% |
| 36,291 | COWLEY | 14,447 | 9,407 | 4,818 | 222 | 4,589 R | 65.1% | 33.3% | 66.1% | 33.9% |
| 38,242 | CRAWFORD | 16,527 | 8,626 | 7,617 | 284 | 1,009 R | 52.2% | 46.1% | 53.1% | 46.9% |
| 3,472 | DECATUR | 1,740 | 1,355 | 355 | 30 | 1,000 R | 77.9% | 20.4% | 79.2% | 20.8% |
| 19,344 | DICKINSON | 8,791 | 6,295 | 2,364 | 132 | 3,931 R | 71.6% | 26.9% | 72.7% | 27.3% |
| 8,249 | DONIPHAN | 3,603 | 2,491 | 1,065 | 47 | 1,426 R | 69.1% | 29.6% | 70.1% | 29.9% |
| 99,962 | DOUGLAS | 50,111 | 20,544 | 28,634 | 933 | 8,090 D | 41.0% | 57.1% | 41.8% | 58.2% |
| 3,449 | EDWARDS | 1,496 | 1,084 | 386 | 26 | 698 R | 72.5% | 25.8% | 73.7% | 26.3% |
| 3,261 | ELK | 1,515 | 1,119 | 369 | 27 | 750 R | 73.9% | 24.4% | 75.2% | 24.8% |
| 27,507 | ELLIS | 12,187 | 7,891 | 4,033 | 263 | 3,858 R | 64.7% | 33.1% | 66.2% | 33.8% |
| 6,525 | ELLSWORTH | 3,102 | 2,259 | 801 | 42 | 1,458 R | 72.8% | 25.8% | 73.8% | 26.2% |
| 40,523 | FINNEY | 9,933 | 7,479 | 2,351 | 103 | 5,128 R | 75.3% | 23.7% | 76.1% | 23.9% |
| 32,458 | FORD | 9,016 | 6,632 | 2,286 | 98 | 4,346 R | 73.6% | 25.4% | 74.4% | 25.6% |
| 24,784 | FRANKLIN | 11,476 | 7,391 | 3,921 | 164 | 3,470 R | 64.4% | 34.2% | 65.3% | 34.7% |
| 27,947 | GEARY | 7,328 | 4,703 | 2,531 | 94 | 2,172 R | 64.2% | 34.5% | 65.0% | 35.0% |
| 3,068 | GOVE | 1,467 | 1,196 | 247 | 24 | 949 R | 81.5% | 16.8% | 82.9% | 17.1% |
| 2,946 | GRAHAM | 1,440 | 1,082 | 334 | 24 | 748 R | 75.1% | 23.2% | 76.4% | 23.6% |
| 7,909 | GRANT | 2,758 | 2,169 | 561 | 28 | 1,608 R | 78.6% | 20.3% | 79.5% | 20.5% |
| 5,904 | GRAY | 2,245 | 1,816 | 408 | 21 | 1,408 R | 80.9% | 18.2% | 81.7% | 18.3% |
| 1,534 | GREELEY | 735 | 584 | 138 | 13 | 446 R | 79.5% | 18.8% | 80.9% | 19.1% |
| 7,673 | GREENWOOD | 3,244 | 2,282 | 911 | 51 | 1,371 R | 70.3% | 28.1% | 71.5% | 28.5% |
| 2,670 | HAMILTON | 1,130 | 888 | 229 | 13 | 659 R | 78.6% | 20.3% | 79.5% | 20.5% |
| 6,536 | HARPER | 2,930 | 2,154 | 727 | 49 | 1,427 R | 73.5% | 24.8% | 74.8% | 25.2% |
| 32,869 | HARVEY | 15,110 | 9,534 | 5,331 | 245 | 4,203 R | 63.1% | 35.3% | 64.1% | 35.9% |
| 4,307 | HASKELL | 1,599 | 1,356 | 227 | 16 | 1,129 R | 84.8% | 14.2% | 85.7% | 14.3% |
| 2,085 | HODGEMAN | 1,183 | 953 | 223 | 7 | 730 R | 80.6% | 18.9% | 81.0% | 19.0% |
| 12,657 | JACKSON | 5,888 | 3,730 | 2,064 | 94 | 1,666 R | 63.3% | 35.1% | 64.4% | 35.6% |
| 18,426 | JEFFERSON | 8,793 | 5,408 | 3,253 | 132 | 2,155 R | 61.5% | 37.0% | 62.4% | 37.6% |
| 3,791 | JEWELL | 1,915 | 1,495 | 385 | 35 | 1,110 R | 78.1% | 20.1% | 79.5% | 20.5% |
| 451,086 | JOHNSON | 258,687 | 158,103 | 97,866 | 2,718 | 60,237 R | 61.1% | 37.8% | 61.8% | 38.2% |
| 4,531 | KEARNY | 1,455 | 1,177 | 272 | 6 | 905 R | 80.9% | 18.7% | 81.2% | 18.8% |
| 8,673 | KINGMAN | 3,764 | 2,801 | 904 | 59 | 1,897 R | 74.4% | 24.0% | 75.6% | 24.4% |
| 3,278 | KIOWA | 1,565 | 1,275 | 256 | 34 | 1,019 R | 81.5% | 16.4% | 83.3% | 16.7% |
| 22,835 | LABETTE | 9,139 | 5,400 | 3,615 | 124 | 1,785 R | 59.1% | 39.6% | 59.9% | 40.1% |
| 2,155 | LANE | 1,014 | 823 | 181 | 10 | 642 R | 81.2% | 17.9% | 82.0% | 18.0% |
| 68,691 | LEAVENWORTH | 27,331 | 15,949 | 11,039 | 343 | 4,910 R | 58.4% | 40.4% | 59.1% | 40.9% |
| 3,578 | LINCOLN | 1,800 | 1,368 | 391 | 41 | 977 R | 76.0% | 21.7% | 77.8% | 22.2% |
| 9,570 | LINN | 4,741 | 3,048 | 1,631 | 62 | 1,417 R | 64.3% | 34.4% | 65.1% | 34.9% |
| 3,046 | LOGAN | 1,523 | 1,255 | 248 | 20 | 1,007 R | 82.4% | 16.3% | 83.5% | 16.5% |
| 35,935 | LYON | 13,440 | 7,951 | 5,234 | 255 | 2,717 R | 59.2% | 38.9% | 60.3% | 39.7% |
| 29,554 | MCPHERSON | 13,367 | 9,595 | 3,589 | 183 | 6,006 R | 71.8% | 26.8% | 72.8% | 27.2% |
| 13,361 | MARION | 6,159 | 4,516 | 1,536 | 107 | 2,980 R | 73.3% | 24.9% | 74.6% | 25.4% |
| 10,965 | MARSHALL | 5,108 | 3,261 | 1,789 | 58 | 1,472 R | 63.8% | 35.0% | 64.6% | 35.4% |
| 4,631 | MEADE | 2,121 | 1,748 | 356 | 17 | 1,392 R | 82.4% | 16.8% | 83.1% | 16.9% |

# KANSAS

## PRESIDENT 2004

| 2000 Census Population | County | Total Vote | Republican | Democratic | Other | Rep.-Dem. Plurality | Percentage | | | |
|---|---|---|---|---|---|---|---|---|---|---|
| | | | | | | | Total Vote | | Major Vote | |
| | | | | | | | Rep. | Dem. | Rep. | Dem. |
| 28,351 | MIAMI | 14,016 | 9,013 | 4,838 | 165 | 4,175 R | 64.3% | 34.5% | 65.1% | 34.9% |
| 6,932 | MITCHELL | 3,349 | 2,609 | 693 | 47 | 1,916 R | 77.9% | 20.7% | 79.0% | 21.0% |
| 36,252 | MONTGOMERY | 14,116 | 9,598 | 4,338 | 180 | 5,260 R | 68.0% | 30.7% | 68.9% | 31.1% |
| 6,104 | MORRIS | 2,936 | 1,961 | 931 | 44 | 1,030 R | 66.8% | 31.7% | 67.8% | 32.2% |
| 3,496 | MORTON | 1,576 | 1,287 | 276 | 13 | 1,011 R | 81.7% | 17.5% | 82.3% | 17.7% |
| 10,717 | NEMAHA | 5,463 | 4,027 | 1,355 | 81 | 2,672 R | 73.7% | 24.8% | 74.8% | 25.2% |
| 16,997 | NEOSHO | 7,231 | 4,705 | 2,424 | 102 | 2,281 R | 65.1% | 33.5% | 66.0% | 34.0% |
| 3,454 | NESS | 1,818 | 1,407 | 382 | 29 | 1,025 R | 77.4% | 21.0% | 78.6% | 21.4% |
| 5,953 | NORTON | 2,599 | 2,092 | 473 | 34 | 1,619 R | 80.5% | 18.2% | 81.6% | 18.4% |
| 16,712 | OSAGE | 7,463 | 4,800 | 2,537 | 126 | 2,263 R | 64.3% | 34.0% | 65.4% | 34.6% |
| 4,452 | OSBORNE | 2,075 | 1,587 | 454 | 34 | 1,133 R | 76.5% | 21.9% | 77.8% | 22.2% |
| 6,163 | OTTAWA | 2,971 | 2,333 | 595 | 43 | 1,738 R | 78.5% | 20.0% | 79.7% | 20.3% |
| 7,233 | PAWNEE | 2,988 | 2,172 | 773 | 43 | 1,399 R | 72.7% | 25.9% | 73.8% | 26.2% |
| 6,001 | PHILLIPS | 2,847 | 2,256 | 557 | 34 | 1,699 R | 79.2% | 19.6% | 80.2% | 19.8% |
| 18,209 | POTTAWATOMIE | 8,823 | 6,326 | 2,176 | 321 | 4,150 R | 71.7% | 24.7% | 74.4% | 25.6% |
| 9,647 | PRATT | 4,384 | 3,121 | 1,200 | 63 | 1,921 R | 71.2% | 27.4% | 72.2% | 27.8% |
| 2,966 | RAWLINS | 1,720 | 1,414 | 289 | 17 | 1,125 R | 82.2% | 16.8% | 83.0% | 17.0% |
| 64,790 | RENO | 27,324 | 17,748 | 9,114 | 462 | 8,634 R | 65.0% | 33.4% | 66.1% | 33.9% |
| 5,835 | REPUBLIC | 2,889 | 2,238 | 607 | 44 | 1,631 R | 77.5% | 21.0% | 78.7% | 21.3% |
| 10,761 | RICE | 4,376 | 3,182 | 1,130 | 64 | 2,052 R | 72.7% | 25.8% | 73.8% | 26.2% |
| 62,843 | RILEY | 20,911 | 12,672 | 7,908 | 331 | 4,764 R | 60.6% | 37.8% | 61.6% | 38.4% |
| 5,685 | ROOKS | 2,710 | 2,121 | 534 | 55 | 1,587 R | 78.3% | 19.7% | 79.9% | 20.1% |
| 3,551 | RUSH | 1,789 | 1,226 | 517 | 46 | 709 R | 68.5% | 28.9% | 70.3% | 29.7% |
| 7,370 | RUSSELL | 3,525 | 2,671 | 810 | 44 | 1,861 R | 75.8% | 23.0% | 76.7% | 23.3% |
| 53,597 | SALINE | 23,041 | 15,111 | 7,524 | 406 | 7,587 R | 65.6% | 32.7% | 66.8% | 33.2% |
| 5,120 | SCOTT | 2,299 | 1,924 | 347 | 28 | 1,577 R | 83.7% | 15.1% | 84.7% | 15.3% |
| 452,869 | SEDGWICK | 177,679 | 110,381 | 64,839 | 2,459 | 45,542 R | 62.1% | 36.5% | 63.0% | 37.0% |
| 22,510 | SEWARD | 5,439 | 4,272 | 1,122 | 45 | 3,150 R | 78.5% | 20.6% | 79.2% | 20.8% |
| 169,871 | SHAWNEE | 81,577 | 44,188 | 36,264 | 1,125 | 7,924 R | 54.2% | 44.5% | 54.9% | 45.1% |
| 2,813 | SHERIDAN | 1,406 | 1,144 | 239 | 23 | 905 R | 81.4% | 17.0% | 82.7% | 17.3% |
| 6,760 | SHERMAN | 2,762 | 2,088 | 632 | 42 | 1,456 R | 75.6% | 22.9% | 76.8% | 23.2% |
| 4,536 | SMITH | 2,370 | 1,803 | 540 | 27 | 1,263 R | 76.1% | 22.8% | 77.0% | 23.0% |
| 4,789 | STAFFORD | 2,186 | 1,649 | 506 | 31 | 1,143 R | 75.4% | 23.1% | 76.5% | 23.5% |
| 2,406 | STANTON | 966 | 796 | 165 | 5 | 631 R | 82.4% | 17.1% | 82.8% | 17.2% |
| 5,463 | STEVENS | 2,265 | 1,936 | 310 | 19 | 1,626 R | 85.5% | 13.7% | 86.2% | 13.8% |
| 25,946 | SUMNER | 10,488 | 7,092 | 3,217 | 179 | 3,875 R | 67.6% | 30.7% | 68.8% | 31.2% |
| 8,180 | THOMAS | 3,870 | 3,007 | 816 | 47 | 2,191 R | 77.7% | 21.1% | 78.7% | 21.3% |
| 3,319 | TREGO | 1,686 | 1,225 | 434 | 27 | 791 R | 72.7% | 25.7% | 73.8% | 26.2% |
| 6,885 | WABAUNSEE | 3,604 | 2,531 | 1,001 | 72 | 1,530 R | 70.2% | 27.8% | 71.7% | 28.3% |
| 1,749 | WALLACE | 876 | 742 | 112 | 22 | 630 R | 84.7% | 12.8% | 86.9% | 13.1% |
| 6,483 | WASHINGTON | 3,190 | 2,498 | 643 | 49 | 1,855 R | 78.3% | 20.2% | 79.5% | 20.5% |
| 2,531 | WICHITA | 1,062 | 869 | 183 | 10 | 686 R | 81.8% | 17.2% | 82.6% | 17.4% |
| 10,332 | WILSON | 4,398 | 3,263 | 1,060 | 75 | 2,203 R | 74.2% | 24.1% | 75.5% | 24.5% |
| 3,788 | WOODSON | 1,763 | 1,204 | 530 | 29 | 674 R | 68.3% | 30.1% | 69.4% | 30.6% |
| 157,882 | WYANDOTTE | 53,401 | 17,919 | 34,923 | 559 | 17,004 D | 33.6% | 65.4% | 33.9% | 66.1% |
| 2,688,418 | TOTAL | 1,187,756 | 736,456 | 434,993 | 16,307 | 301,463 R | 62.0% | 36.6% | 62.9% | 37.1% |

# KANSAS

## SENATOR 2004

| 2000 Census Population | County | Total Vote | Republican | Democratic | Other | Rep.-Dem. Plurality | Total Vote Rep. | Total Vote Dem. | Major Vote Rep. | Major Vote Dem. |
|---|---|---|---|---|---|---|---|---|---|---|
| 14,385 | ALLEN | 5,778 | 4,312 | 1,334 | 132 | 2,978 R | 74.6% | 23.1% | 76.4% | 23.6% |
| 8,110 | ANDERSON | 3,805 | 2,828 | 872 | 105 | 1,956 R | 74.3% | 22.9% | 76.4% | 23.6% |
| 16,774 | ATCHISON | 6,982 | 4,611 | 2,161 | 210 | 2,450 R | 66.0% | 31.0% | 68.1% | 31.9% |
| 5,307 | BARBER | 2,358 | 1,916 | 362 | 80 | 1,554 R | 81.3% | 15.4% | 84.1% | 15.9% |
| 28,205 | BARTON | 11,604 | 9,520 | 1,810 | 274 | 7,710 R | 82.0% | 15.6% | 84.0% | 16.0% |
| 15,379 | BOURBON | 6,584 | 5,016 | 1,425 | 143 | 3,591 R | 76.2% | 21.6% | 77.9% | 22.1% |
| 10,724 | BROWN | 4,350 | 3,471 | 788 | 91 | 2,683 R | 79.8% | 18.1% | 81.5% | 18.5% |
| 59,482 | BUTLER | 25,771 | 19,527 | 5,287 | 957 | 14,240 R | 75.8% | 20.5% | 78.7% | 21.3% |
| 3,030 | CHASE | 1,455 | 1,100 | 302 | 53 | 798 R | 75.6% | 20.8% | 78.5% | 21.5% |
| 4,359 | CHAUTAUQUA | 1,895 | 1,525 | 309 | 61 | 1,216 R | 80.5% | 16.3% | 83.2% | 16.8% |
| 22,605 | CHEROKEE | 9,803 | 7,068 | 2,499 | 236 | 4,569 R | 72.1% | 25.5% | 73.9% | 26.1% |
| 3,165 | CHEYENNE | 1,650 | 1,409 | 197 | 44 | 1,212 R | 85.4% | 11.9% | 87.7% | 12.3% |
| 2,390 | CLARK | 1,256 | 1,065 | 147 | 44 | 918 R | 84.8% | 11.7% | 87.9% | 12.1% |
| 8,822 | CLAY | 4,053 | 3,505 | 455 | 93 | 3,050 R | 86.5% | 11.2% | 88.5% | 11.5% |
| 10,268 | CLOUD | 4,404 | 3,545 | 715 | 144 | 2,830 R | 80.5% | 16.2% | 83.2% | 16.8% |
| 8,865 | COFFEY | 4,352 | 3,566 | 702 | 84 | 2,864 R | 81.9% | 16.1% | 83.6% | 16.4% |
| 1,967 | COMANCHE | 968 | 830 | 106 | 32 | 724 R | 85.7% | 11.0% | 88.7% | 11.3% |
| 36,291 | COWLEY | 14,141 | 10,176 | 3,409 | 556 | 6,767 R | 72.0% | 24.1% | 74.9% | 25.1% |
| 38,242 | CRAWFORD | 16,255 | 10,659 | 5,219 | 377 | 5,440 R | 65.6% | 32.1% | 67.1% | 32.9% |
| 3,472 | DECATUR | 1,665 | 1,383 | 224 | 58 | 1,159 R | 83.1% | 13.5% | 86.1% | 13.9% |
| 19,344 | DICKINSON | 8,651 | 6,864 | 1,517 | 270 | 5,347 R | 79.3% | 17.5% | 81.9% | 18.1% |
| 8,249 | DONIPHAN | 3,523 | 2,752 | 681 | 90 | 2,071 R | 78.1% | 19.3% | 80.2% | 19.8% |
| 99,962 | DOUGLAS | 48,229 | 24,488 | 21,759 | 1,982 | 2,729 R | 50.8% | 45.1% | 53.0% | 47.0% |
| 3,449 | EDWARDS | 1,470 | 1,214 | 214 | 42 | 1,000 R | 82.6% | 14.6% | 85.0% | 15.0% |
| 3,261 | ELK | 1,481 | 1,130 | 290 | 61 | 840 R | 76.3% | 19.6% | 79.6% | 20.4% |
| 27,507 | ELLIS | 11,747 | 8,405 | 2,999 | 343 | 5,406 R | 71.6% | 25.5% | 73.7% | 26.3% |
| 6,525 | ELLSWORTH | 3,052 | 2,455 | 531 | 66 | 1,924 R | 80.4% | 17.4% | 82.2% | 17.8% |
| 40,523 | FINNEY | 9,666 | 7,777 | 1,578 | 311 | 6,199 R | 80.5% | 16.3% | 83.1% | 16.9% |
| 32,458 | FORD | 8,872 | 7,129 | 1,555 | 188 | 5,574 R | 80.4% | 17.5% | 82.1% | 17.9% |
| 24,784 | FRANKLIN | 11,240 | 7,898 | 2,978 | 364 | 4,920 R | 70.3% | 26.5% | 72.6% | 27.4% |
| 27,947 | GEARY | 7,166 | 5,076 | 1,867 | 223 | 3,209 R | 70.8% | 26.1% | 73.1% | 26.9% |
| 3,068 | GOVE | 1,433 | 1,238 | 172 | 23 | 1,066 R | 86.4% | 12.0% | 87.8% | 12.2% |
| 2,946 | GRAHAM | 1,389 | 1,118 | 229 | 42 | 889 R | 80.5% | 16.5% | 83.0% | 17.0% |
| 7,909 | GRANT | 2,705 | 2,219 | 388 | 98 | 1,831 R | 82.0% | 14.3% | 85.1% | 14.9% |
| 5,904 | GRAY | 2,200 | 1,929 | 229 | 42 | 1,700 R | 87.7% | 10.4% | 89.4% | 10.6% |
| 1,534 | GREELEY | 708 | 609 | 77 | 22 | 532 R | 86.0% | 10.9% | 88.8% | 11.2% |
| 7,673 | GREENWOOD | 3,172 | 2,407 | 646 | 119 | 1,761 R | 75.9% | 20.4% | 78.8% | 21.2% |
| 2,670 | HAMILTON | 1,097 | 944 | 123 | 30 | 821 R | 86.1% | 11.2% | 88.5% | 11.5% |
| 6,536 | HARPER | 2,842 | 2,326 | 442 | 74 | 1,884 R | 81.8% | 15.6% | 84.0% | 16.0% |
| 32,869 | HARVEY | 14,882 | 10,659 | 3,716 | 507 | 6,943 R | 71.6% | 25.0% | 74.1% | 25.9% |
| 4,307 | HASKELL | 1,570 | 1,406 | 129 | 35 | 1,277 R | 89.6% | 8.2% | 91.6% | 8.4% |
| 2,085 | HODGEMAN | 1,147 | 1,007 | 118 | 22 | 889 R | 87.8% | 10.3% | 89.5% | 10.5% |
| 12,657 | JACKSON | 5,794 | 4,319 | 1,300 | 175 | 3,019 R | 74.5% | 22.4% | 76.9% | 23.1% |
| 18,426 | JEFFERSON | 8,624 | 6,091 | 2,268 | 265 | 3,823 R | 70.6% | 26.3% | 72.9% | 27.1% |
| 3,791 | JEWELL | 1,850 | 1,535 | 264 | 51 | 1,271 R | 83.0% | 14.3% | 85.3% | 14.7% |
| 451,086 | JOHNSON | 250,332 | 162,385 | 79,501 | 8,446 | 82,884 R | 64.9% | 31.8% | 67.1% | 32.9% |
| 4,531 | KEARNY | 1,420 | 1,235 | 151 | 34 | 1,084 R | 87.0% | 10.6% | 89.1% | 10.9% |
| 8,673 | KINGMAN | 3,693 | 3,031 | 559 | 103 | 2,472 R | 82.1% | 15.1% | 84.4% | 15.6% |
| 3,278 | KIOWA | 1,484 | 1,263 | 156 | 65 | 1,107 R | 85.1% | 10.5% | 89.0% | 11.0% |
| 22,835 | LABETTE | 8,943 | 6,334 | 2,391 | 218 | 3,943 R | 70.8% | 26.7% | 72.6% | 27.4% |
| 2,155 | LANE | 984 | 863 | 104 | 17 | 759 R | 87.7% | 10.6% | 89.2% | 10.8% |
| 68,691 | LEAVENWORTH | 26,635 | 16,729 | 8,977 | 929 | 7,752 R | 62.8% | 33.7% | 65.1% | 34.9% |
| 3,578 | LINCOLN | 1,746 | 1,469 | 220 | 57 | 1,249 R | 84.1% | 12.6% | 87.0% | 13.0% |
| 9,570 | LINN | 4,690 | 3,423 | 1,159 | 108 | 2,264 R | 73.0% | 24.7% | 74.7% | 25.3% |
| 3,046 | LOGAN | 1,508 | 1,341 | 134 | 33 | 1,207 R | 88.9% | 8.9% | 90.9% | 9.1% |
| 35,935 | LYON | 13,176 | 9,013 | 3,747 | 416 | 5,266 R | 68.4% | 28.4% | 70.6% | 29.4% |
| 29,554 | MCPHERSON | 13,161 | 10,271 | 2,534 | 356 | 7,737 R | 78.0% | 19.3% | 80.2% | 19.8% |
| 13,361 | MARION | 5,959 | 4,789 | 1,014 | 156 | 3,775 R | 80.4% | 17.0% | 82.5% | 17.5% |
| 10,965 | MARSHALL | 5,008 | 3,875 | 1,034 | 99 | 2,841 R | 77.4% | 20.6% | 78.9% | 21.1% |
| 4,631 | MEADE | 2,092 | 1,839 | 225 | 28 | 1,614 R | 87.9% | 10.8% | 89.1% | 10.9% |

# KANSAS

## SENATOR 2004

| 2000 Census Population | County | Total Vote | Republican | Democratic | Other | Rep.-Dem. Plurality | Percentage Total Vote Rep. | Dem. | Major Vote Rep. | Dem. |
|---|---|---|---|---|---|---|---|---|---|---|
| 28,351 | MIAMI | 13,756 | 9,378 | 4,045 | 333 | 5,333 R | 68.2% | 29.4% | 69.9% | 30.1% |
| 6,932 | MITCHELL | 3,294 | 2,757 | 474 | 63 | 2,283 R | 83.7% | 14.4% | 85.3% | 14.7% |
| 36,252 | MONTGOMERY | 13,822 | 9,959 | 3,445 | 418 | 6,514 R | 72.1% | 24.9% | 74.3% | 25.7% |
| 6,104 | MORRIS | 2,848 | 2,220 | 551 | 77 | 1,669 R | 77.9% | 19.3% | 80.1% | 19.9% |
| 3,496 | MORTON | 1,512 | 1,280 | 195 | 37 | 1,085 R | 84.7% | 12.9% | 86.8% | 13.2% |
| 10,717 | NEMAHA | 5,364 | 4,460 | 819 | 85 | 3,641 R | 83.1% | 15.3% | 84.5% | 15.5% |
| 16,997 | NEOSHO | 7,094 | 5,250 | 1,679 | 165 | 3,571 R | 74.0% | 23.7% | 75.8% | 24.2% |
| 3,454 | NESS | 1,793 | 1,525 | 239 | 29 | 1,286 R | 85.1% | 13.3% | 86.5% | 13.5% |
| 5,953 | NORTON | 2,549 | 2,157 | 328 | 64 | 1,829 R | 84.6% | 12.9% | 86.8% | 13.2% |
| 16,712 | OSAGE | 7,401 | 5,549 | 1,649 | 203 | 3,900 R | 75.0% | 22.3% | 77.1% | 22.9% |
| 4,452 | OSBORNE | 2,049 | 1,689 | 303 | 57 | 1,386 R | 82.4% | 14.8% | 84.8% | 15.2% |
| 6,163 | OTTAWA | 2,927 | 2,441 | 402 | 84 | 2,039 R | 83.4% | 13.7% | 85.9% | 14.1% |
| 7,233 | PAWNEE | 2,970 | 2,398 | 512 | 60 | 1,886 R | 80.7% | 17.2% | 82.4% | 17.6% |
| 6,001 | PHILLIPS | 2,759 | 2,337 | 371 | 51 | 1,966 R | 84.7% | 13.4% | 86.3% | 13.7% |
| 18,209 | POTTAWATOMIE | 8,680 | 7,050 | 1,359 | 271 | 5,691 R | 81.2% | 15.7% | 83.8% | 16.2% |
| 9,647 | PRATT | 4,276 | 3,407 | 759 | 110 | 2,648 R | 79.7% | 17.8% | 81.8% | 18.2% |
| 2,966 | RAWLINS | 1,704 | 1,452 | 205 | 47 | 1,247 R | 85.2% | 12.0% | 87.6% | 12.4% |
| 64,790 | RENO | 26,808 | 19,926 | 5,934 | 948 | 13,992 R | 74.3% | 22.1% | 77.1% | 22.9% |
| 5,835 | REPUBLIC | 2,789 | 2,339 | 404 | 46 | 1,935 R | 83.9% | 14.5% | 85.3% | 14.7% |
| 10,761 | RICE | 4,315 | 3,497 | 704 | 114 | 2,793 R | 81.0% | 16.3% | 83.2% | 16.8% |
| 62,843 | RILEY | 20,353 | 14,240 | 5,589 | 524 | 8,651 R | 70.0% | 27.5% | 71.8% | 28.2% |
| 5,685 | ROOKS | 2,652 | 2,221 | 368 | 63 | 1,853 R | 83.7% | 13.9% | 85.8% | 14.2% |
| 3,551 | RUSH | 1,756 | 1,368 | 335 | 53 | 1,033 R | 77.9% | 19.1% | 80.3% | 19.7% |
| 7,370 | RUSSELL | 3,477 | 2,872 | 521 | 84 | 2,351 R | 82.6% | 15.0% | 84.6% | 15.4% |
| 53,597 | SALINE | 22,544 | 16,717 | 5,102 | 725 | 11,615 R | 74.2% | 22.6% | 76.6% | 23.4% |
| 5,120 | SCOTT | 2,259 | 2,008 | 207 | 44 | 1,801 R | 88.9% | 9.2% | 90.7% | 9.3% |
| 452,869 | SEDGWICK | 169,976 | 118,261 | 44,106 | 7,609 | 74,155 R | 69.6% | 25.9% | 72.8% | 27.2% |
| 22,510 | SEWARD | 5,266 | 4,284 | 768 | 214 | 3,516 R | 81.4% | 14.6% | 84.8% | 15.2% |
| 169,871 | SHAWNEE | 54,530 | 36,895 | 15,927 | 1,708 | 20,968 R | 67.7% | 29.2% | 69.8% | 30.2% |
| 2,813 | SHERIDAN | 1,381 | 1,181 | 176 | 24 | 1,005 R | 85.5% | 12.7% | 87.0% | 13.0% |
| 6,760 | SHERMAN | 2,679 | 2,222 | 393 | 64 | 1,829 R | 82.9% | 14.7% | 85.0% | 15.0% |
| 4,536 | SMITH | 2,303 | 1,914 | 340 | 49 | 1,574 R | 83.1% | 14.8% | 84.9% | 15.1% |
| 4,789 | STAFFORD | 2,147 | 1,785 | 324 | 38 | 1,461 R | 83.1% | 15.1% | 84.6% | 15.4% |
| 2,406 | STANTON | 900 | 835 | 40 | 25 | 795 R | 92.8% | 4.4% | 95.4% | 4.6% |
| 5,463 | STEVENS | 2,236 | 2,018 | 177 | 41 | 1,841 R | 90.3% | 7.9% | 91.9% | 8.1% |
| 25,946 | SUMNER | 10,361 | 7,666 | 2,302 | 393 | 5,364 R | 74.0% | 22.2% | 76.9% | 23.1% |
| 8,180 | THOMAS | 3,799 | 3,189 | 528 | 82 | 2,661 R | 83.9% | 13.9% | 85.8% | 14.2% |
| 3,319 | TREGO | 1,646 | 1,342 | 270 | 34 | 1,072 R | 81.5% | 16.4% | 83.3% | 16.7% |
| 6,885 | WABAUNSEE | 3,543 | 2,847 | 574 | 122 | 2,273 R | 80.4% | 16.2% | 83.2% | 16.8% |
| 1,749 | WALLACE | 852 | 775 | 54 | 23 | 721 R | 91.0% | 6.3% | 93.5% | 6.5% |
| 6,483 | WASHINGTON | 3,109 | 2,703 | 344 | 62 | 2,359 R | 86.9% | 11.1% | 88.7% | 11.3% |
| 2,531 | WICHITA | 1,036 | 901 | 117 | 18 | 784 R | 87.0% | 11.3% | 88.5% | 11.5% |
| 10,332 | WILSON | 4,289 | 3,429 | 725 | 135 | 2,704 R | 79.9% | 16.9% | 82.5% | 17.5% |
| 3,788 | WOODSON | 1,705 | 1,275 | 375 | 55 | 900 R | 74.8% | 22.0% | 77.3% | 22.7% |
| 157,882 | WYANDOTTE | 51,043 | 18,957 | 29,999 | 2,087 | 11,042 D | 37.1% | 58.8% | 38.7% | 61.3% |
| 2,688,418 | TOTAL | 1,129,022 | 780,863 | 310,337 | 37,822 | 470,526 R | 69.2% | 27.5% | 71.6% | 28.4% |

# KANSAS

## HOUSE OF REPRESENTATIVES

| | | Total | Republican | | Democratic | | Other | Rep.-Dem. | Percentage | | | |
|---|---|---|---|---|---|---|---|---|---|---|---|---|
| | | | | | | | | | Total Vote | | Major Vote | |
| CD | Year | Vote | Vote | Candidate | Vote | Candidate | Vote | Plurality | Rep. | Dem. | Rep. | Dem. |
| 1 | 2004 | 264,293 | 239,776 | Moran, Jerry* | | | 24,517 | 239,776 R | 90.7% | | 100.0% | |
| 1 | 2002 | 208,561 | 189,976 | Moran, Jerry* | | | 18,585 | 189,976 R | 91.1% | | 100.0% | |
| 2 | 2004 | 294,436 | 165,325 | Ryun, Jim* | 121,532 | Boyda, Nancy | 7,579 | 43,793 R | 56.1% | 41.3% | 57.6% | 42.4% |
| 2 | 2002 | 210,977 | 127,477 | Ryun, Jim* | 79,160 | Lykins, Dan | 4,340 | 48,317 R | 60.4% | 37.5% | 61.7% | 38.3% |
| 3 | 2004 | 335,739 | 145,542 | Kobach, Kris | 184,050 | Moore, Dennis* | 6,147 | 38,508 D | 43.3% | 54.8% | 44.2% | 55.8% |
| 3 | 2002 | 219,389 | 102,882 | Taff, Adam | 110,095 | Moore, Dennis* | 6,412 | 7,213 D | 46.9% | 50.2% | 48.3% | 51.7% |
| 4 | 2004 | 261,915 | 173,151 | Tiahrt, Todd* | 81,388 | Kinard, Michael | 7,376 | 91,763 R | 66.1% | 31.1% | 68.0% | 32.0% |
| 4 | 2002 | 190,963 | 115,691 | Tiahrt, Todd* | 70,656 | Nolla, Carlos | 4,616 | 45,035 R | 60.6% | 37.0% | 62.1% | 37.9% |
| Total | 2004 | 1,156,383 | 723,794 | | 386,970 | | 45,619 | 336,824 R | 62.6% | 33.5% | 65.2% | 34.8% |
| Total | 2002 | 829,890 | 536,026 | | 259,911 | | 33,953 | 276,115 R | 64.6% | 31.3% | 67.3% | 32.7% |

An asterisk (*) denotes incumbent.

# KANSAS

## GENERAL AND PRIMARY ELECTIONS

## 2004 GENERAL ELECTIONS

**President**      Other vote was 9,348 Reform (Ralph Nader); 4,013 Libertarian (Michael Badnarik); 2,899 Independent (Michael Peroutka); 33 write-in (David Cobb); 5 write-in (John Joseph Kennedy); 5 write-in (Bill Van Auken); 4 write-in (Walter F. Brown).

**Senator**      Other vote was 21,842 Libertarian (Steven A. Rosile); 15,980 Reform (George Cook).

**House**      Other vote was:

CD 1      24,517 Libertarian (Jack Warner).
CD 2      7,579 Libertarian (Dennis Hawver).
CD 3      3,191 Libertarian (Joe Bellis); 2,956 Reform (Richard Wells).
CD 4      7,376 Libertarian (David Loomis).

## 2002 PRIMARY ELECTIONS

**Primary**      August 3, 2004

| **Registration** (as of July 19, 2004) | | |
|---|---|---|
| | Republican | 730,049 |
| | Democratic | 428,728 |
| | Libertarian | 9,019 |
| | Reform | 1,686 |
| | Unaffiliated | 421,946 |
| | TOTAL | 1,591,428 |

**Primary Type**      Semi-open—Registered Democrats and Republicans could vote only in their party's primary. "Unaffiliated" voters could participate in either primary, although if they voted in the Republican primary they had to change their registration to Republican on primary day.

# KANSAS

## GENERAL AND PRIMARY ELECTIONS

Note:   An asterisk (*) denotes incumbent.

| | REPUBLICAN PRIMARIES | | | DEMOCRATIC PRIMARIES | | |
|---|---|---|---|---|---|---|
| Senator | Sam Brownback* | 286,839 | 87.0% | Robert A. Conroy | 61,052 | 55.9% |
| | Arch Naramore | 42,880 | 13.0% | Lee Jones | 48,133 | 44.1% |
| | TOTAL | 329,719 | | TOTAL | 109,185 | |
| | | | | *Robert A. Conroy subsequently quit the race and was replaced on the general election ballot by Lee Jones.* | | |
| Congressional District 1 | Jerry Moran* | 94,098 | 100.0% | No Democratic candidate | | |
| Congressional District 2 | Jim Ryun* | 69,368 | 100.0% | Nancy Boyda | 36,771 | 100.0% |
| Congressional District 3 | Kris Kobach | 39,129 | 44.0% | Dennis Moore* | 33,466 | 100.0% |
| | Adam Taff | 38,922 | 43.8% | | | |
| | Patricia Lightner | 10,836 | 12.2% | | | |
| | TOTAL | 88,887 | | | | |
| Congressional District 4 | Todd Tiahrt* | 53,202 | 100.0% | Michael Kinard | 14,308 | 73.0% |
| | | | | Marty Mork | 5,279 | 27.0% |
| | | | | TOTAL | 19,587 | |

# KENTUCKY

## GOVERNOR
Ernie Fletcher (R). Elected 2003 to a four-year term.

## SENATORS (2 Republicans)
Jim Bunning (R). Reelected 2004 to a six-year term. Previously elected 1998.

Mitch McConnell (R). Reelected 2002 to a six-year term. Previously elected 1996, 1990, 1984.

## REPRESENTATIVES (5 Republicans, 1 Democrat)
1. Edward Whitfield (R)
2. Ron Lewis (R)
3. Anne M. Northup (R)
4. Geoff Davis (R)
5. Harold Rogers (R)
6. Ben Chandler (D)

## POSTWAR VOTE FOR PRESIDENT

| | | Republican | | Democratic | | Other | | Percentage Total Vote | | Major Vote | |
|---|---|---|---|---|---|---|---|---|---|---|---|
| Year | Total Vote | Vote | Candidate | Vote | Candidate | Vote | Plurality | Rep. | Dem. | Rep. | Dem. |
| 2004 | 1,795,882 | 1,069,439 | Bush, George W. | 712,733 | Kerry, John | 13,710 | 356,706 R | 59.5% | 39.7% | 60.0% | 40.0% |
| 2000** | 1,544,187 | 872,492 | Bush, George W. | 638,898 | Gore, Al | 32,797 | 233,594 R | 56.5% | 41.4% | 57.7% | 42.3% |
| 1996** | 1,388,708 | 623,283 | Dole, Bob | 636,614 | Clinton, Bill | 128,811 | 13,331 D | 44.9% | 45.8% | 49.5% | 50.5% |
| 1992** | 1,492,900 | 617,178 | Bush, George | 665,104 | Clinton, Bill | 210,618 | 47,926 D | 41.3% | 44.6% | 48.1% | 51.9% |
| 1988 | 1,322,517 | 734,281 | Bush, George | 580,368 | Dukakis, Michael S. | 7,868 | 153,913 R | 55.5% | 43.9% | 55.9% | 44.1% |
| 1984 | 1,369,345 | 821,702 | Reagan, Ronald | 539,539 | Mondale, Walter F. | 8,104 | 282,163 R | 60.0% | 39.4% | 60.4% | 39.6% |
| 1980** | 1,294,627 | 635,274 | Reagan, Ronald | 616,417 | Carter, Jimmy | 42,936 | 18,857 R | 49.1% | 47.6% | 50.8% | 49.2% |
| 1976 | 1,167,142 | 531,852 | Ford, Gerald R. | 615,717 | Carter, Jimmy | 19,573 | 83,865 D | 45.6% | 52.8% | 46.3% | 53.7% |
| 1972 | 1,067,499 | 676,446 | Nixon, Richard M. | 371,159 | McGovern, George S. | 19,894 | 305,287 R | 63.4% | 34.8% | 64.6% | 35.4% |
| 1968** | 1,055,893 | 462,411 | Nixon, Richard M. | 397,541 | Humphrey, Hubert H. | 195,941 | 64,870 R | 43.8% | 37.6% | 53.8% | 46.2% |
| 1964 | 1,046,105 | 372,977 | Goldwater, Barry M. | 669,659 | Johnson, Lyndon B. | 3,469 | 296,682 D | 35.7% | 64.0% | 35.8% | 64.2% |
| 1960 | 1,124,462 | 602,607 | Nixon, Richard M. | 521,855 | Kennedy, John F. | | 80,752 R | 53.6% | 46.4% | 53.6% | 46.4% |
| 1956 | 1,053,805 | 572,192 | Eisenhower, Dwight D. | 476,453 | Stevenson, Adlai E. | 5,160 | 95,739 R | 54.3% | 45.2% | 54.6% | 45.4% |
| 1952 | 993,148 | 495,029 | Eisenhower, Dwight D. | 495,729 | Stevenson, Adlai E. | 2,390 | 700 D | 49.8% | 49.9% | 50.0% | 50.0% |
| 1948 | 822,658 | 341,210 | Dewey, Thomas E. | 466,756 | Truman, Harry S. | 14,692 | 125,546 D | 41.5% | 56.7% | 42.2% | 57.8% |

In past elections, the other vote included: 2000 - 23,192 Green (Ralph Nader); 1996 - 120,396 Reform (Ross Perot); 1992 - 203,944 Independent (Perot); 1980 - 31,127 Independent (John Anderson); 1968 - 193,098 American Independent (George Wallace).

# KENTUCKY

## POSTWAR VOTE FOR GOVERNOR

| Year | Total Vote | Republican Vote | Republican Candidate | Democratic Vote | Democratic Candidate | Other Vote | Rep.-Dem. Plurality | Total Vote Rep. | Total Vote Dem. | Major Vote Rep. | Major Vote Dem. |
|---|---|---|---|---|---|---|---|---|---|---|---|
| 2003 | 1,083,443 | 596,284 | Fletcher, Ernie | 487,159 | Chandler, Ben | | 109,125 R | 55.0% | 45.0% | 55.0% | 45.0% |
| 1999** | 580,074 | 128,788 | Martin, Peppy | 352,099 | Patton, Paul E. | 99,187 | 223,311 D | 22.2% | 60.7% | 26.8% | 73.2% |
| 1995 | 983,979 | 479,227 | Forgy, Larry | 500,787 | Patton, Paul E. | 3,965 | 21,560 D | 48.7% | 50.9% | 48.9% | 51.1% |
| 1991 | 834,920 | 294,452 | Hopkins, Larry J. | 540,468 | Jones, Brereton C. | | 246,016 D | 35.3% | 64.7% | 35.3% | 64.7% |
| 1987 | 777,815 | 273,141 | Harper, John | 504,674 | Wilkinson, Wallace G. | | 231,533 D | 35.1% | 64.9% | 35.1% | 64.9% |
| 1983 | 1,030,671 | 454,650 | Bunning, Jim | 561,674 | Collins, Martha Layne | 14,347 | 107,024 D | 44.1% | 54.5% | 44.7% | 55.3% |
| 1979 | 939,366 | 381,278 | Nunn, Louie B. | 558,088 | Brown, J. Y., Jr. | | 176,810 D | 40.6% | 59.4% | 40.6% | 59.4% |
| 1975 | 748,157 | 277,998 | Gable, Robert E. | 470,159 | Carroll, Julian | | 192,161 D | 37.2% | 62.8% | 37.2% | 62.8% |
| 1971 | 930,790 | 412,653 | Emberton, Thomas | 470,720 | Ford, Wendell H. | 47,417 | 58,067 D | 44.3% | 50.6% | 46.7% | 53.3% |
| 1967 | 886,946 | 454,123 | Nunn, Louie B. | 425,674 | Ward, Henry | 7,149 | 28,449 R | 51.2% | 48.0% | 51.6% | 48.4% |
| 1963 | 886,047 | 436,496 | Nunn, Louie B. | 449,551 | Breathitt, Edward T. | | 13,055 D | 49.3% | 50.7% | 49.3% | 50.7% |
| 1959 | 853,005 | 336,456 | Robsion, John M. | 516,549 | Combs, Bert T. | | 180,093 D | 39.4% | 60.6% | 39.4% | 60.6% |
| 1955 | 778,488 | 322,671 | Denney, Edwin R. | 451,647 | Chandler, Albert B. | 4,170 | 128,976 D | 41.4% | 58.0% | 41.7% | 58.3% |
| 1951 | 634,359 | 288,014 | Siler, Eugene | 346,345 | Wetherby, Lawrence | | 58,331 D | 45.4% | 54.6% | 45.4% | 54.6% |
| 1947 | 672,372 | 287,130 | Dummit, Eldon S. | 385,242 | Clements, Earle C. | | 98,112 D | 42.7% | 57.3% | 42.7% | 57.3% |

In past elections, the other vote included: 1999 - 88,930 Reform (Gatewood Galbraith).

## POSTWAR VOTE FOR SENATOR

| Year | Total Vote | Republican Vote | Republican Candidate | Democratic Vote | Democratic Candidate | Other Vote | Rep.-Dem. Plurality | Total Vote Rep. | Total Vote Dem. | Major Vote Rep. | Major Vote Dem. |
|---|---|---|---|---|---|---|---|---|---|---|---|
| 2004 | 1,724,362 | 873,507 | Bunning, Jim | 850,855 | Mongiardo, Daniel | | 22,652 R | 50.7% | 49.3% | 50.7% | 49.3% |
| 2002 | 1,131,475 | 731,679 | McConnell, Mitch | 399,634 | Weinberg, Lois Combs | 162 | 332,045 R | 64.7% | 35.3% | 64.7% | 35.3% |
| 1998 | 1,145,414 | 569,817 | Bunning, Jim | 563,051 | Baesler, Scotty | 12,546 | 6,766 R | 49.7% | 49.2% | 50.3% | 49.7% |
| 1996 | 1,307,046 | 724,794 | McConnell, Mitch | 560,012 | Beshear, Steven L. | 22,240 | 164,782 R | 55.5% | 42.8% | 56.4% | 43.6% |
| 1992 | 1,330,858 | 476,604 | Williams, David L. | 836,888 | Ford, Wendell H. | 17,366 | 360,284 D | 35.8% | 62.9% | 36.3% | 63.7% |
| 1990 | 916,010 | 478,034 | McConnell, Mitch | 437,976 | Sloane, Harvey | | 40,058 R | 52.2% | 47.8% | 52.2% | 47.8% |
| 1986 | 677,280 | 173,330 | Andrews, Jackson M. | 503,775 | Ford, Wendell H. | 175 | 330,445 D | 25.6% | 74.4% | 25.6% | 74.4% |
| 1984 | 1,292,407 | 644,990 | McConnell, Mitch | 639,721 | Huddleston, Walter | 7,696 | 5,269 R | 49.9% | 49.5% | 50.2% | 49.8% |
| 1980 | 1,106,890 | 386,029 | Foust, Mary Louise | 720,861 | Ford, Wendell H. | | 334,832 D | 34.9% | 65.1% | 34.9% | 65.1% |
| 1978 | 476,783 | 175,766 | Guenthner, Louie | 290,730 | Huddleston, Walter | 10,287 | 114,964 D | 36.9% | 61.0% | 37.7% | 62.3% |
| 1974 | 745,994 | 328,982 | Cook, Marlow W. | 399,406 | Ford, Wendell H. | 17,606 | 70,424 D | 44.1% | 53.5% | 45.2% | 54.8% |
| 1972 | 1,037,861 | 494,337 | Nunn, Louie B. | 528,550 | Huddleston, Walter | 14,974 | 34,213 D | 47.6% | 50.9% | 48.3% | 51.7% |
| 1968 | 942,865 | 484,260 | Cook, Marlow W. | 448,960 | Peden, Katherine | 9,645 | 35,300 R | 51.4% | 47.6% | 51.9% | 48.1% |
| 1966 | 749,884 | 483,805 | Cooper, John Sherman | 266,079 | Brown, J. Y. | | 217,726 R | 64.5% | 35.5% | 64.5% | 35.5% |
| 1962 | 820,088 | 432,648 | Morton, Thruston B. | 387,440 | Wyatt, Wilson W. | | 45,208 R | 52.8% | 47.2% | 52.8% | 47.2% |
| 1960 | 1,088,377 | 644,087 | Cooper, John Sherman | 444,290 | Johnson, Keen | | 199,797 R | 59.2% | 40.8% | 59.2% | 40.8% |
| 1956 | 1,006,825 | 506,903 | Morton, Thruston B. | 499,922 | Clements, Earle C. | | 6,981 R | 50.3% | 49.7% | 50.3% | 49.7% |
| 1956S | 1,011,645 | 538,505 | Cooper, John Sherman | 473,140 | Wetherby, Lawrence | | 65,365 R | 53.2% | 46.8% | 53.2% | 46.8% |
| 1954 | 797,057 | 362,948 | Cooper, John Sherman | 434,109 | Barkley, Alben W. | | 71,161 D | 45.5% | 54.5% | 45.5% | 54.5% |
| 1952S | 960,228 | 494,576 | Cooper, John Sherman | 465,652 | Underwood, Thomas R. | | 28,924 R | 51.5% | 48.5% | 51.5% | 48.5% |
| 1950 | 612,617 | 278,368 | Dawson, Charles L. | 334,249 | Clements, Earle C. | | 55,881 D | 45.4% | 54.6% | 45.4% | 54.6% |
| 1948 | 794,469 | 383,776 | Cooper, John Sherman | 408,256 | Chapman, Virgil | 2,437 | 24,480 D | 48.3% | 51.4% | 48.5% | 51.5% |
| 1946S | 615,119 | 327,652 | Cooper, John Sherman | 285,829 | Brown, J. Y. | 1,638 | 41,823 R | 53.3% | 46.5% | 53.4% | 46.6% |

One of the 1956 elections and those in 1952 and 1946 were for short terms to fill vacancies.

# KENTUCKY

Congressional districts first established for elections held in 2002
6 members

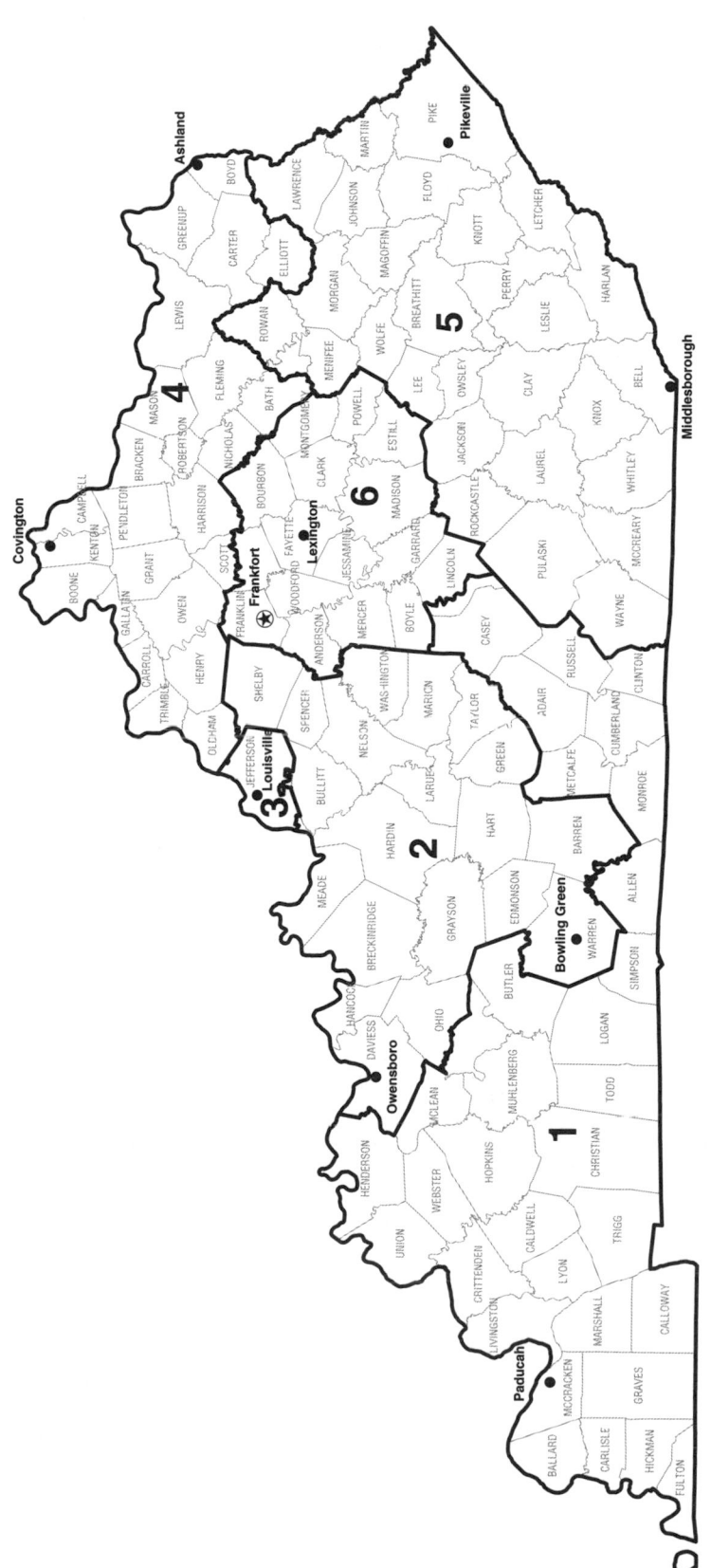

KENTUCKY

## KENTUCKY
### PRESIDENT 2004

| 2000 Census Population | County | Total Vote | Republican | Democratic | Other | Rep.-Dem. Plurality | Total Vote Rep. | Total Vote Dem. | Major Vote Rep. | Major Vote Dem. |
|---|---|---|---|---|---|---|---|---|---|---|
| 17,244 | ADAIR | 7,447 | 5,628 | 1,764 | 55 | 3,864 R | 75.6% | 23.7% | 76.1% | 23.9% |
| 17,800 | ALLEN | 7,163 | 5,202 | 1,923 | 38 | 3,279 R | 72.6% | 26.8% | 73.0% | 27.0% |
| 19,111 | ANDERSON | 9,591 | 6,363 | 3,141 | 87 | 3,222 R | 66.3% | 32.7% | 67.0% | 33.0% |
| 8,286 | BALLARD | 4,177 | 2,389 | 1,759 | 29 | 630 R | 57.2% | 42.1% | 57.6% | 42.4% |
| 38,033 | BARREN | 16,140 | 10,822 | 5,216 | 102 | 5,606 R | 67.1% | 32.3% | 67.5% | 32.5% |
| 11,085 | BATH | 4,919 | 2,269 | 2,608 | 42 | 339 D | 46.1% | 53.0% | 46.5% | 53.5% |
| 30,060 | BELL | 11,002 | 6,722 | 4,210 | 70 | 2,512 R | 61.1% | 38.3% | 61.5% | 38.5% |
| 85,991 | BOONE | 45,082 | 32,329 | 12,391 | 362 | 19,938 R | 71.7% | 27.5% | 72.3% | 27.7% |
| 19,360 | BOURBON | 8,217 | 4,953 | 3,198 | 66 | 1,755 R | 60.3% | 38.9% | 60.8% | 39.2% |
| 49,752 | BOYD | 21,780 | 11,501 | 10,132 | 147 | 1,369 R | 52.8% | 46.5% | 53.2% | 46.8% |
| 27,697 | BOYLE | 12,490 | 7,764 | 4,646 | 80 | 3,118 R | 62.2% | 37.2% | 62.6% | 37.4% |
| 8,279 | BRACKEN | 3,610 | 2,363 | 1,213 | 34 | 1,150 R | 65.5% | 33.6% | 66.1% | 33.9% |
| 16,100 | BREATHITT | 5,944 | 2,542 | 3,327 | 75 | 785 D | 42.8% | 56.0% | 43.3% | 56.7% |
| 18,648 | BRECKINRIDGE | 8,520 | 5,580 | 2,884 | 56 | 2,696 R | 65.5% | 33.8% | 65.9% | 34.1% |
| 61,236 | BULLITT | 28,627 | 19,433 | 9,043 | 151 | 10,390 R | 67.9% | 31.6% | 68.2% | 31.8% |
| 13,010 | BUTLER | 5,578 | 4,109 | 1,436 | 33 | 2,673 R | 73.7% | 25.7% | 74.1% | 25.9% |
| 13,060 | CALDWELL | 6,349 | 4,066 | 2,245 | 38 | 1,821 R | 64.0% | 35.4% | 64.4% | 35.6% |
| 34,177 | CALLOWAY | 15,145 | 9,293 | 5,728 | 124 | 3,565 R | 61.4% | 37.8% | 61.9% | 38.1% |
| 88,616 | CAMPBELL | 40,178 | 25,540 | 14,253 | 385 | 11,287 R | 63.6% | 35.5% | 64.2% | 35.8% |
| 5,351 | CARLISLE | 2,845 | 1,734 | 1,102 | 9 | 632 R | 60.9% | 38.7% | 61.1% | 38.9% |
| 10,155 | CARROLL | 3,897 | 2,175 | 1,688 | 34 | 487 R | 55.8% | 43.3% | 56.3% | 43.7% |
| 26,889 | CARTER | 11,117 | 5,422 | 5,577 | 118 | 155 D | 48.8% | 50.2% | 49.3% | 50.7% |
| 15,447 | CASEY | 6,321 | 5,109 | 1,174 | 38 | 3,935 R | 80.8% | 18.6% | 81.3% | 18.7% |
| 72,265 | CHRISTIAN | 21,015 | 13,935 | 6,970 | 110 | 6,965 R | 66.3% | 33.2% | 66.7% | 33.3% |
| 33,144 | CLARK | 15,317 | 9,540 | 5,661 | 116 | 3,879 R | 62.3% | 37.0% | 62.8% | 37.2% |
| 24,556 | CLAY | 7,687 | 5,726 | 1,901 | 60 | 3,825 R | 74.5% | 24.7% | 75.1% | 24.9% |
| 9,634 | CLINTON | 4,352 | 3,369 | 952 | 31 | 2,417 R | 77.4% | 21.9% | 78.0% | 22.0% |
| 9,384 | CRITTENDEN | 4,190 | 2,726 | 1,438 | 26 | 1,288 R | 65.1% | 34.3% | 65.5% | 34.5% |
| 7,147 | CUMBERLAND | 3,239 | 2,356 | 848 | 35 | 1,508 R | 72.7% | 26.2% | 73.5% | 26.5% |
| 91,545 | DAVIESS | 41,483 | 25,372 | 15,788 | 323 | 9,584 R | 61.2% | 38.1% | 61.6% | 38.4% |
| 11,644 | EDMONSON | 5,481 | 3,595 | 1,856 | 30 | 1,739 R | 65.6% | 33.9% | 66.0% | 34.0% |
| 6,748 | ELLIOTT | 2,957 | 871 | 2,064 | 22 | 1,193 D | 29.5% | 69.8% | 29.7% | 70.3% |
| 15,307 | ESTILL | 5,575 | 3,633 | 1,907 | 35 | 1,726 R | 65.2% | 34.2% | 65.6% | 34.4% |
| 260,512 | FAYETTE | 125,584 | 66,406 | 57,994 | 1,184 | 8,412 R | 52.9% | 46.2% | 53.4% | 46.6% |
| 13,792 | FLEMING | 6,203 | 3,749 | 2,406 | 48 | 1,343 R | 60.4% | 38.8% | 60.9% | 39.1% |
| 42,441 | FLOYD | 17,885 | 6,612 | 11,132 | 141 | 4,520 D | 37.0% | 62.2% | 37.3% | 62.7% |
| 47,687 | FRANKLIN | 24,134 | 12,281 | 11,620 | 233 | 661 R | 50.9% | 48.1% | 51.4% | 48.6% |
| 7,752 | FULTON | 2,890 | 1,527 | 1,340 | 23 | 187 R | 52.8% | 46.4% | 53.3% | 46.7% |
| 7,870 | GALLATIN | 3,073 | 1,869 | 1,188 | 16 | 681 R | 60.8% | 38.7% | 61.1% | 38.9% |
| 14,792 | GARRARD | 6,658 | 4,784 | 1,841 | 33 | 2,943 R | 71.9% | 27.7% | 72.2% | 27.8% |
| 22,384 | GRANT | 8,824 | 5,951 | 2,818 | 55 | 3,133 R | 67.4% | 31.9% | 67.9% | 32.1% |
| 37,028 | GRAVES | 16,231 | 9,903 | 6,206 | 122 | 3,697 R | 61.0% | 38.2% | 61.5% | 38.5% |
| 24,053 | GRAYSON | 10,143 | 7,170 | 2,905 | 68 | 4,265 R | 70.7% | 28.6% | 71.2% | 28.8% |
| 11,518 | GREEN | 5,206 | 3,866 | 1,312 | 28 | 2,554 R | 74.3% | 25.2% | 74.7% | 25.3% |
| 36,891 | GREENUP | 16,435 | 8,696 | 7,630 | 109 | 1,066 R | 52.9% | 46.4% | 53.3% | 46.7% |
| 8,392 | HANCOCK | 4,029 | 2,286 | 1,709 | 34 | 577 R | 56.7% | 42.4% | 57.2% | 42.8% |
| 94,174 | HARDIN | 36,441 | 24,627 | 11,507 | 307 | 13,120 R | 67.6% | 31.6% | 68.2% | 31.8% |
| 33,202 | HARLAN | 11,070 | 6,659 | 4,332 | 79 | 2,327 R | 60.2% | 39.1% | 60.6% | 39.4% |
| 17,983 | HARRISON | 7,731 | 4,855 | 2,807 | 69 | 2,048 R | 62.8% | 36.3% | 63.4% | 36.6% |
| 17,445 | HART | 6,784 | 4,269 | 2,470 | 45 | 1,799 R | 62.9% | 36.4% | 63.3% | 36.7% |
| 44,829 | HENDERSON | 18,701 | 10,467 | 8,101 | 133 | 2,366 R | 56.0% | 43.3% | 56.4% | 43.6% |
| 15,060 | HENRY | 6,499 | 4,094 | 2,366 | 39 | 1,728 R | 63.0% | 36.4% | 63.4% | 36.6% |
| 5,262 | HICKMAN | 2,342 | 1,395 | 926 | 21 | 469 R | 59.6% | 39.5% | 60.1% | 39.9% |
| 46,519 | HOPKINS | 18,843 | 12,314 | 6,420 | 109 | 5,894 R | 65.4% | 34.1% | 65.7% | 34.3% |
| 13,495 | JACKSON | 5,178 | 4,369 | 769 | 40 | 3,600 R | 84.4% | 14.9% | 85.0% | 15.0% |
| 693,604 | JEFFERSON | 337,351 | 164,566 | 170,158 | 2,627 | 5,592 D | 48.8% | 50.4% | 49.2% | 50.8% |
| 39,041 | JESSAMINE | 18,580 | 12,972 | 5,476 | 132 | 7,496 R | 69.8% | 29.5% | 70.3% | 29.7% |
| 23,445 | JOHNSON | 9,304 | 5,940 | 3,288 | 76 | 2,652 R | 63.8% | 35.3% | 64.4% | 35.6% |
| 151,464 | KENTON | 67,124 | 43,664 | 22,834 | 626 | 20,830 R | 65.0% | 34.0% | 65.7% | 34.3% |
| 17,649 | KNOTT | 7,394 | 2,648 | 4,685 | 61 | 2,037 D | 35.8% | 63.4% | 36.1% | 63.9% |

198

# KENTUCKY

## PRESIDENT 2004

| 2000 Census Population | County | Total Vote | Republican | Democratic | Other | Rep.-Dem. Plurality | Percentage Total Vote Rep. | Dem. | Major Vote Rep. | Dem. |
|---|---|---|---|---|---|---|---|---|---|---|
| 31,795 | KNOX | 12,028 | 8,108 | 3,822 | 98 | 4,286 R | 67.4% | 31.8% | 68.0% | 32.0% |
| 13,373 | LARUE | 5,968 | 4,111 | 1,823 | 34 | 2,288 R | 68.9% | 30.5% | 69.3% | 30.7% |
| 52,715 | LAUREL | 22,264 | 16,819 | 5,297 | 148 | 11,522 R | 75.5% | 23.8% | 76.0% | 24.0% |
| 15,569 | LAWRENCE | 6,513 | 3,755 | 2,705 | 53 | 1,050 R | 57.7% | 41.5% | 58.1% | 41.9% |
| 7,916 | LEE | 2,920 | 2,018 | 878 | 24 | 1,140 R | 69.1% | 30.1% | 69.7% | 30.3% |
| 12,401 | LESLIE | 4,964 | 3,661 | 1,266 | 37 | 2,395 R | 73.8% | 25.5% | 74.3% | 25.7% |
| 25,277 | LETCHER | 9,065 | 4,801 | 4,192 | 72 | 609 R | 53.0% | 46.2% | 53.4% | 46.6% |
| 14,092 | LEWIS | 5,484 | 3,778 | 1,667 | 39 | 2,111 R | 68.9% | 30.4% | 69.4% | 30.6% |
| 23,361 | LINCOLN | 8,863 | 5,996 | 2,796 | 71 | 3,200 R | 67.7% | 31.5% | 68.2% | 31.8% |
| 9,804 | LIVINGSTON | 4,706 | 2,675 | 2,007 | 24 | 668 R | 56.8% | 42.6% | 57.1% | 42.9% |
| 26,573 | LOGAN | 10,644 | 6,815 | 3,768 | 61 | 3,047 R | 64.0% | 35.4% | 64.4% | 35.6% |
| 8,080 | LYON | 3,925 | 2,132 | 1,769 | 24 | 363 R | 54.3% | 45.1% | 54.7% | 45.3% |
| 65,514 | MCCRACKEN | 29,797 | 18,218 | 11,361 | 218 | 6,857 R | 61.1% | 38.1% | 61.6% | 38.4% |
| 17,080 | MCCREARY | 5,693 | 4,121 | 1,530 | 42 | 2,591 R | 72.4% | 26.9% | 72.9% | 27.1% |
| 9,938 | MCLEAN | 4,435 | 2,584 | 1,823 | 28 | 761 R | 58.3% | 41.1% | 58.6% | 41.4% |
| 70,872 | MADISON | 30,707 | 18,922 | 11,525 | 260 | 7,397 R | 61.6% | 37.5% | 62.1% | 37.9% |
| 13,332 | MAGOFFIN | 5,718 | 2,836 | 2,843 | 39 | 7 D | 49.6% | 49.7% | 49.9% | 50.1% |
| 18,212 | MARION | 7,354 | 3,905 | 3,399 | 50 | 506 R | 53.1% | 46.2% | 53.5% | 46.5% |
| 30,125 | MARSHALL | 15,521 | 9,049 | 6,383 | 89 | 2,666 R | 58.3% | 41.1% | 58.6% | 41.4% |
| 12,578 | MARTIN | 4,539 | 2,996 | 1,504 | 39 | 1,492 R | 66.0% | 33.1% | 66.6% | 33.4% |
| 16,800 | MASON | 7,079 | 4,381 | 2,644 | 54 | 1,737 R | 61.9% | 37.3% | 62.4% | 37.6% |
| 26,349 | MEADE | 10,951 | 7,152 | 3,724 | 75 | 3,428 R | 65.3% | 34.0% | 65.8% | 34.2% |
| 6,556 | MENIFEE | 2,528 | 1,215 | 1,284 | 29 | 69 D | 48.1% | 50.8% | 48.6% | 51.4% |
| 20,817 | MERCER | 10,028 | 6,745 | 3,224 | 59 | 3,521 R | 67.3% | 32.1% | 67.7% | 32.3% |
| 10,037 | METCALFE | 4,157 | 2,645 | 1,472 | 40 | 1,173 R | 63.6% | 35.4% | 64.2% | 35.8% |
| 11,756 | MONROE | 5,843 | 4,657 | 1,158 | 28 | 3,499 R | 79.7% | 19.8% | 80.1% | 19.9% |
| 22,554 | MONTGOMERY | 10,230 | 5,647 | 4,506 | 77 | 1,141 R | 55.2% | 44.0% | 55.6% | 44.4% |
| 13,948 | MORGAN | 5,272 | 2,682 | 2,532 | 58 | 150 R | 50.9% | 48.0% | 51.4% | 48.6% |
| 31,839 | MUHLENBERG | 13,479 | 6,749 | 6,636 | 94 | 113 R | 50.1% | 49.2% | 50.4% | 49.6% |
| 37,477 | NELSON | 16,844 | 10,161 | 6,524 | 159 | 3,637 R | 60.3% | 38.7% | 60.9% | 39.1% |
| 6,813 | NICHOLAS | 3,059 | 1,700 | 1,332 | 27 | 368 R | 55.6% | 43.5% | 56.1% | 43.9% |
| 22,916 | OHIO | 10,028 | 6,311 | 3,627 | 90 | 2,684 R | 62.9% | 36.2% | 63.5% | 36.5% |
| 46,178 | OLDHAM | 27,132 | 18,801 | 8,080 | 251 | 10,721 R | 69.3% | 29.8% | 69.9% | 30.1% |
| 10,547 | OWEN | 4,741 | 3,084 | 1,615 | 42 | 1,469 R | 65.0% | 34.1% | 65.6% | 34.4% |
| 4,858 | OWSLEY | 1,999 | 1,558 | 430 | 11 | 1,128 R | 77.9% | 21.5% | 78.4% | 21.6% |
| 14,390 | PENDLETON | 6,025 | 4,045 | 1,940 | 40 | 2,105 R | 67.1% | 32.2% | 67.6% | 32.4% |
| 29,390 | PERRY | 11,655 | 6,187 | 5,400 | 68 | 787 R | 53.1% | 46.3% | 53.4% | 46.6% |
| 68,736 | PIKE | 26,770 | 12,611 | 14,002 | 157 | 1,391 D | 47.1% | 52.3% | 47.4% | 52.6% |
| 13,237 | POWELL | 4,960 | 2,687 | 2,249 | 24 | 438 R | 54.2% | 45.3% | 54.4% | 45.6% |
| 56,217 | PULASKI | 25,516 | 19,535 | 5,829 | 152 | 13,706 R | 76.6% | 22.8% | 77.0% | 23.0% |
| 2,266 | ROBERTSON | 1,090 | 670 | 413 | 7 | 257 R | 61.5% | 37.9% | 61.9% | 38.1% |
| 16,582 | ROCKCASTLE | 6,166 | 4,804 | 1,320 | 42 | 3,484 R | 77.9% | 21.4% | 78.4% | 21.6% |
| 22,094 | ROWAN | 8,706 | 4,063 | 4,556 | 87 | 493 D | 46.7% | 52.3% | 47.1% | 52.9% |
| 16,315 | RUSSELL | 7,821 | 6,009 | 1,772 | 40 | 4,237 R | 76.8% | 22.7% | 77.2% | 22.8% |
| 33,061 | SCOTT | 17,051 | 10,600 | 6,325 | 126 | 4,275 R | 62.2% | 37.1% | 62.6% | 37.4% |
| 33,337 | SHELBY | 16,314 | 10,909 | 5,277 | 128 | 5,632 R | 66.9% | 32.3% | 67.4% | 32.6% |
| 16,405 | SIMPSON | 7,043 | 4,273 | 2,730 | 40 | 1,543 R | 60.7% | 38.8% | 61.0% | 39.0% |
| 11,766 | SPENCER | 6,822 | 4,816 | 1,970 | 36 | 2,846 R | 70.6% | 28.9% | 71.0% | 29.0% |
| 22,927 | TAYLOR | 10,295 | 7,247 | 2,979 | 69 | 4,268 R | 70.4% | 28.9% | 70.9% | 29.1% |
| 11,971 | TODD | 4,754 | 3,242 | 1,491 | 21 | 1,751 R | 68.2% | 31.4% | 68.5% | 31.5% |
| 12,597 | TRIGG | 6,111 | 4,023 | 2,046 | 42 | 1,977 R | 65.8% | 33.5% | 66.3% | 33.7% |
| 8,125 | TRIMBLE | 3,790 | 2,332 | 1,428 | 30 | 904 R | 61.5% | 37.7% | 62.0% | 38.0% |
| 15,637 | UNION | 5,977 | 3,534 | 2,398 | 45 | 1,136 R | 59.1% | 40.1% | 59.6% | 40.4% |
| 92,522 | WARREN | 39,712 | 25,100 | 14,326 | 286 | 10,774 R | 63.2% | 36.1% | 63.7% | 36.3% |
| 10,916 | WASHINGTON | 5,236 | 3,479 | 1,724 | 33 | 1,755 R | 66.4% | 32.9% | 66.9% | 33.1% |
| 19,923 | WAYNE | 7,685 | 5,027 | 2,616 | 42 | 2,411 R | 65.4% | 34.0% | 65.8% | 34.2% |
| 14,120 | WEBSTER | 5,547 | 3,207 | 2,304 | 36 | 903 R | 57.8% | 41.5% | 58.2% | 41.8% |
| 35,865 | WHITLEY | 13,629 | 9,559 | 3,985 | 85 | 5,574 R | 70.1% | 29.2% | 70.6% | 29.4% |
| 7,065 | WOLFE | 3,155 | 1,385 | 1,744 | 26 | 359 D | 43.9% | 55.3% | 44.3% | 55.7% |
| 23,208 | WOODFORD | 11,502 | 6,937 | 4,480 | 85 | 2,457 R | 60.3% | 38.9% | 60.8% | 39.2% |
| 4,041,769 | TOTAL | 1,795,882 | 1,069,439 | 712,733 | 13,710 | 356,706 R | 59.5% | 39.7% | 60.0% | 40.0% |

# KENTUCKY

## GOVERNOR 2003

| 2000 Census Population | County | Total Vote | Republican | Democratic | Other | Rep.-Dem. Plurality | Percentage Total Vote Rep. | Dem. | Major Vote Rep. | Dem. |
|---|---|---|---|---|---|---|---|---|---|---|
| 17,244 | ADAIR | 4,659 | 3,085 | 1,574 | | 1,511 R | 66.2% | 33.8% | 66.2% | 33.8% |
| 17,800 | ALLEN | 3,388 | 2,202 | 1,186 | | 1,016 R | 65.0% | 35.0% | 65.0% | 35.0% |
| 19,111 | ANDERSON | 6,891 | 4,052 | 2,839 | | 1,213 R | 58.8% | 41.2% | 58.8% | 41.2% |
| 8,286 | BALLARD | 3,080 | 1,433 | 1,647 | | 214 D | 46.5% | 53.5% | 46.5% | 53.5% |
| 38,033 | BARREN | 8,960 | 5,065 | 3,895 | | 1,170 R | 56.5% | 43.5% | 56.5% | 43.5% |
| 11,085 | BATH | 3,285 | 1,398 | 1,887 | | 489 D | 42.6% | 57.4% | 42.6% | 57.4% |
| 30,060 | BELL | 5,264 | 2,885 | 2,379 | | 506 R | 54.8% | 45.2% | 54.8% | 45.2% |
| 85,991 | BOONE | 20,113 | 14,399 | 5,714 | | 8,685 R | 71.6% | 28.4% | 71.6% | 28.4% |
| 19,360 | BOURBON | 5,291 | 2,941 | 2,350 | | 591 R | 55.6% | 44.4% | 55.6% | 44.4% |
| 49,752 | BOYD | 11,470 | 4,874 | 6,596 | | 1,722 D | 42.5% | 57.5% | 42.5% | 57.5% |
| 27,697 | BOYLE | 8,337 | 4,929 | 3,408 | | 1,521 R | 59.1% | 40.9% | 59.1% | 40.9% |
| 8,279 | BRACKEN | 2,164 | 1,139 | 1,025 | | 114 R | 52.6% | 47.4% | 52.6% | 47.4% |
| 16,100 | BREATHITT | 3,819 | 1,236 | 2,583 | | 1,347 D | 32.4% | 67.6% | 32.4% | 67.6% |
| 18,648 | BRECKINRIDGE | 5,245 | 3,007 | 2,238 | | 769 R | 57.3% | 42.7% | 57.3% | 42.7% |
| 61,236 | BULLITT | 15,585 | 9,127 | 6,458 | | 2,669 R | 58.6% | 41.4% | 58.6% | 41.4% |
| 13,010 | BUTLER | 3,226 | 2,294 | 932 | | 1,362 R | 71.1% | 28.9% | 71.1% | 28.9% |
| 13,060 | CALDWELL | 3,993 | 2,181 | 1,812 | | 369 R | 54.6% | 45.4% | 54.6% | 45.4% |
| 34,177 | CALLOWAY | 8,922 | 4,792 | 4,130 | | 662 R | 53.7% | 46.3% | 53.7% | 46.3% |
| 88,616 | CAMPBELL | 20,715 | 13,154 | 7,561 | | 5,593 R | 63.5% | 36.5% | 63.5% | 36.5% |
| 5,351 | CARLISLE | 2,013 | 1,014 | 999 | | 15 R | 50.4% | 49.6% | 50.4% | 49.6% |
| 10,155 | CARROLL | 2,243 | 991 | 1,252 | | 261 D | 44.2% | 55.8% | 44.2% | 55.8% |
| 26,889 | CARTER | 5,606 | 2,219 | 3,387 | | 1,168 D | 39.6% | 60.4% | 39.6% | 60.4% |
| 15,447 | CASEY | 3,935 | 2,958 | 977 | | 1,981 R | 75.2% | 24.8% | 75.2% | 24.8% |
| 72,265 | CHRISTIAN | 10,753 | 5,921 | 4,832 | | 1,089 R | 55.1% | 44.9% | 55.1% | 44.9% |
| 33,144 | CLARK | 9,751 | 5,600 | 4,151 | | 1,449 R | 57.4% | 42.6% | 57.4% | 42.6% |
| 24,556 | CLAY | 5,125 | 3,092 | 2,033 | | 1,059 R | 60.3% | 39.7% | 60.3% | 39.7% |
| 9,634 | CLINTON | 2,543 | 1,935 | 608 | | 1,327 R | 76.1% | 23.9% | 76.1% | 23.9% |
| 9,384 | CRITTENDEN | 2,716 | 1,633 | 1,083 | | 550 R | 60.1% | 39.9% | 60.1% | 39.9% |
| 7,147 | CUMBERLAND | 1,857 | 1,250 | 607 | | 643 R | 67.3% | 32.7% | 67.3% | 32.7% |
| 91,545 | DAVIESS | 26,297 | 13,794 | 12,503 | | 1,291 R | 52.5% | 47.5% | 52.5% | 47.5% |
| 11,644 | EDMONSON | 3,204 | 1,927 | 1,277 | | 650 R | 60.1% | 39.9% | 60.1% | 39.9% |
| 6,748 | ELLIOTT | 1,630 | 354 | 1,276 | | 922 D | 21.7% | 78.3% | 21.7% | 78.3% |
| 15,307 | ESTILL | 3,682 | 2,176 | 1,506 | | 670 R | 59.1% | 40.9% | 59.1% | 40.9% |
| 260,512 | FAYETTE | 77,858 | 42,260 | 35,598 | | 6,662 R | 54.3% | 45.7% | 54.3% | 45.7% |
| 13,792 | FLEMING | 4,113 | 2,151 | 1,962 | | 189 R | 52.3% | 47.7% | 52.3% | 47.7% |
| 42,441 | FLOYD | 10,725 | 3,611 | 7,114 | | 3,503 D | 33.7% | 66.3% | 33.7% | 66.3% |
| 47,687 | FRANKLIN | 19,545 | 9,126 | 10,419 | | 1,293 D | 46.7% | 53.3% | 46.7% | 53.3% |
| 7,752 | FULTON | 1,825 | 880 | 945 | | 65 D | 48.2% | 51.8% | 48.2% | 51.8% |
| 7,870 | GALLATIN | 1,591 | 851 | 740 | | 111 R | 53.5% | 46.5% | 53.5% | 46.5% |
| 14,792 | GARRARD | 4,406 | 2,994 | 1,412 | | 1,582 R | 68.0% | 32.0% | 68.0% | 32.0% |
| 22,384 | GRANT | 4,386 | 2,575 | 1,811 | | 764 R | 58.7% | 41.3% | 58.7% | 41.3% |
| 37,028 | GRAVES | 11,968 | 6,180 | 5,788 | | 392 R | 51.6% | 48.4% | 51.6% | 48.4% |
| 24,053 | GRAYSON | 5,909 | 3,873 | 2,036 | | 1,837 R | 65.5% | 34.5% | 65.5% | 34.5% |
| 11,518 | GREEN | 3,328 | 2,236 | 1,092 | | 1,144 R | 67.2% | 32.8% | 67.2% | 32.8% |
| 36,891 | GREENUP | 8,471 | 3,720 | 4,751 | | 1,031 D | 43.9% | 56.1% | 43.9% | 56.1% |
| 8,392 | HANCOCK | 2,575 | 1,114 | 1,461 | | 347 D | 43.3% | 56.7% | 43.3% | 56.7% |
| 94,174 | HARDIN | 20,915 | 12,631 | 8,284 | | 4,347 R | 60.4% | 39.6% | 60.4% | 39.6% |
| 33,202 | HARLAN | 6,056 | 2,851 | 3,205 | | 354 D | 47.1% | 52.9% | 47.1% | 52.9% |
| 17,983 | HARRISON | 5,200 | 2,953 | 2,247 | | 706 R | 56.8% | 43.2% | 56.8% | 43.2% |
| 17,445 | HART | 4,183 | 2,187 | 1,996 | | 191 R | 52.3% | 47.7% | 52.3% | 47.7% |
| 44,829 | HENDERSON | 11,155 | 5,252 | 5,903 | | 651 D | 47.1% | 52.9% | 47.1% | 52.9% |
| 15,060 | HENRY | 4,441 | 2,376 | 2,065 | | 311 R | 53.5% | 46.5% | 53.5% | 46.5% |
| 5,262 | HICKMAN | 1,702 | 859 | 843 | | 16 R | 50.5% | 49.5% | 50.5% | 49.5% |
| 46,519 | HOPKINS | 10,722 | 6,074 | 4,648 | | 1,426 R | 56.6% | 43.4% | 56.6% | 43.4% |
| 13,495 | JACKSON | 3,196 | 2,590 | 606 | | 1,984 R | 81.0% | 19.0% | 81.0% | 19.0% |
| 693,604 | JEFFERSON | 210,502 | 102,716 | 107,786 | | 5,070 D | 48.8% | 51.2% | 48.8% | 51.2% |
| 39,041 | JESSAMINE | 11,512 | 7,520 | 3,992 | | 3,528 R | 65.3% | 34.7% | 65.3% | 34.7% |
| 23,445 | JOHNSON | 5,614 | 3,348 | 2,266 | | 1,082 R | 59.6% | 40.4% | 59.6% | 40.4% |
| 151,464 | KENTON | 33,733 | 21,935 | 11,798 | | 10,137 R | 65.0% | 35.0% | 65.0% | 35.0% |
| 17,649 | KNOTT | 4,263 | 1,572 | 2,691 | | 1,119 D | 36.9% | 63.1% | 36.9% | 63.1% |

# KENTUCKY

## GOVERNOR 2003

| 2000 Census Population | County | Total Vote | Republican | Democratic | Other | Rep.-Dem. Plurality | Percentage Total Vote Rep. | Dem. | Major Vote Rep. | Dem. |
|---:|---|---:|---:|---:|---|---:|---:|---:|---:|---:|
| 31,795 | KNOX | 7,339 | 4,845 | 2,494 | | 2,351 R | 66.0% | 34.0% | 66.0% | 34.0% |
| 13,373 | LARUE | 3,703 | 2,075 | 1,628 | | 447 R | 56.0% | 44.0% | 56.0% | 44.0% |
| 52,715 | LAUREL | 12,721 | 9,403 | 3,318 | | 6,085 R | 73.9% | 26.1% | 73.9% | 26.1% |
| 15,569 | LAWRENCE | 3,257 | 1,603 | 1,654 | | 51 D | 49.2% | 50.8% | 49.2% | 50.8% |
| 7,916 | LEE | 2,087 | 1,363 | 724 | | 639 R | 65.3% | 34.7% | 65.3% | 34.7% |
| 12,401 | LESLIE | 3,081 | 2,015 | 1,066 | | 949 R | 65.4% | 34.6% | 65.4% | 34.6% |
| 25,277 | LETCHER | 5,163 | 2,261 | 2,902 | | 641 D | 43.8% | 56.2% | 43.8% | 56.2% |
| 14,092 | LEWIS | 2,675 | 1,833 | 842 | | 991 R | 68.5% | 31.5% | 68.5% | 31.5% |
| 23,361 | LINCOLN | 5,405 | 3,230 | 2,175 | | 1,055 R | 59.8% | 40.2% | 59.8% | 40.2% |
| 9,804 | LIVINGSTON | 3,130 | 1,439 | 1,691 | | 252 D | 46.0% | 54.0% | 46.0% | 54.0% |
| 26,573 | LOGAN | 5,698 | 2,984 | 2,714 | | 270 R | 52.4% | 47.6% | 52.4% | 47.6% |
| 8,080 | LYON | 2,820 | 1,409 | 1,411 | | 2 D | 50.0% | 50.0% | 50.0% | 50.0% |
| 65,514 | MCCRACKEN | 20,488 | 12,075 | 8,413 | | 3,662 R | 58.9% | 41.1% | 58.9% | 41.1% |
| 17,080 | MCCREARY | 2,948 | 2,029 | 919 | | 1,110 R | 68.8% | 31.2% | 68.8% | 31.2% |
| 9,938 | MCLEAN | 2,745 | 1,356 | 1,389 | | 33 D | 49.4% | 50.6% | 49.4% | 50.6% |
| 70,872 | MADISON | 18,091 | 10,704 | 7,387 | | 3,317 R | 59.2% | 40.8% | 59.2% | 40.8% |
| 13,332 | MAGOFFIN | 3,775 | 1,481 | 2,294 | | 813 D | 39.2% | 60.8% | 39.2% | 60.8% |
| 18,212 | MARION | 5,140 | 2,200 | 2,940 | | 740 D | 42.8% | 57.2% | 42.8% | 57.2% |
| 30,125 | MARSHALL | 10,654 | 5,537 | 5,117 | | 420 R | 52.0% | 48.0% | 52.0% | 48.0% |
| 12,578 | MARTIN | 2,643 | 1,801 | 842 | | 959 R | 68.1% | 31.9% | 68.1% | 31.9% |
| 16,800 | MASON | 4,114 | 2,308 | 1,806 | | 502 R | 56.1% | 43.9% | 56.1% | 43.9% |
| 26,349 | MEADE | 6,279 | 3,379 | 2,900 | | 479 R | 53.8% | 46.2% | 53.8% | 46.2% |
| 6,556 | MENIFEE | 1,586 | 710 | 876 | | 166 D | 44.8% | 55.2% | 44.8% | 55.2% |
| 20,817 | MERCER | 7,723 | 4,525 | 3,198 | | 1,327 R | 58.6% | 41.4% | 58.6% | 41.4% |
| 10,037 | METCALFE | 2,625 | 1,450 | 1,175 | | 275 R | 55.2% | 44.8% | 55.2% | 44.8% |
| 11,756 | MONROE | 3,337 | 2,676 | 661 | | 2,015 R | 80.2% | 19.8% | 80.2% | 19.8% |
| 22,554 | MONTGOMERY | 6,482 | 3,420 | 3,062 | | 358 R | 52.8% | 47.2% | 52.8% | 47.2% |
| 13,948 | MORGAN | 3,208 | 1,366 | 1,842 | | 476 D | 42.6% | 57.4% | 42.6% | 57.4% |
| 31,839 | MUHLENBERG | 7,424 | 3,162 | 4,262 | | 1,100 D | 42.6% | 57.4% | 42.6% | 57.4% |
| 37,477 | NELSON | 9,876 | 5,014 | 4,862 | | 152 R | 50.8% | 49.2% | 50.8% | 49.2% |
| 6,813 | NICHOLAS | 1,975 | 1,026 | 949 | | 77 R | 51.9% | 48.1% | 51.9% | 48.1% |
| 22,916 | OHIO | 6,253 | 3,496 | 2,757 | | 739 R | 55.9% | 44.1% | 55.9% | 44.1% |
| 46,178 | OLDHAM | 18,611 | 12,565 | 6,046 | | 6,519 R | 67.5% | 32.5% | 67.5% | 32.5% |
| 10,547 | OWEN | 3,143 | 1,768 | 1,375 | | 393 R | 56.3% | 43.7% | 56.3% | 43.7% |
| 4,858 | OWSLEY | 1,281 | 872 | 409 | | 463 R | 68.1% | 31.9% | 68.1% | 31.9% |
| 14,390 | PENDLETON | 3,375 | 2,017 | 1,358 | | 659 R | 59.8% | 40.2% | 59.8% | 40.2% |
| 29,390 | PERRY | 6,714 | 2,902 | 3,812 | | 910 D | 43.2% | 56.8% | 43.2% | 56.8% |
| 68,736 | PIKE | 16,445 | 7,062 | 9,383 | | 2,321 D | 42.9% | 57.1% | 42.9% | 57.1% |
| 13,237 | POWELL | 3,179 | 1,601 | 1,578 | | 23 R | 50.4% | 49.6% | 50.4% | 49.6% |
| 56,217 | PULASKI | 16,168 | 11,847 | 4,321 | | 7,526 R | 73.3% | 26.7% | 73.3% | 26.7% |
| 2,266 | ROBERTSON | 722 | 409 | 313 | | 96 R | 56.6% | 43.4% | 56.6% | 43.4% |
| 16,582 | ROCKCASTLE | 3,883 | 2,974 | 909 | | 2,065 R | 76.6% | 23.4% | 76.6% | 23.4% |
| 22,094 | ROWAN | 5,268 | 2,262 | 3,006 | | 744 D | 42.9% | 57.1% | 42.9% | 57.1% |
| 16,315 | RUSSELL | 5,386 | 3,771 | 1,615 | | 2,156 R | 70.0% | 30.0% | 70.0% | 30.0% |
| 33,061 | SCOTT | 10,400 | 5,940 | 4,460 | | 1,480 R | 57.1% | 42.9% | 57.1% | 42.9% |
| 33,337 | SHELBY | 10,601 | 6,324 | 4,277 | | 2,047 R | 59.7% | 40.3% | 59.7% | 40.3% |
| 16,405 | SIMPSON | 3,207 | 1,715 | 1,492 | | 223 R | 53.5% | 46.5% | 53.5% | 46.5% |
| 11,766 | SPENCER | 3,844 | 2,314 | 1,530 | | 784 R | 60.2% | 39.8% | 60.2% | 39.8% |
| 22,927 | TAYLOR | 6,490 | 3,947 | 2,543 | | 1,404 R | 60.8% | 39.2% | 60.8% | 39.2% |
| 11,971 | TODD | 2,225 | 1,177 | 1,048 | | 129 R | 52.9% | 47.1% | 52.9% | 47.1% |
| 12,597 | TRIGG | 3,819 | 2,133 | 1,686 | | 447 R | 55.9% | 44.1% | 55.9% | 44.1% |
| 8,125 | TRIMBLE | 2,219 | 1,098 | 1,121 | | 23 D | 49.5% | 50.5% | 49.5% | 50.5% |
| 15,637 | UNION | 3,480 | 1,526 | 1,954 | | 428 D | 43.9% | 56.1% | 43.9% | 56.1% |
| 92,522 | WARREN | 22,844 | 13,846 | 8,998 | | 4,848 R | 60.6% | 39.4% | 60.6% | 39.4% |
| 10,916 | WASHINGTON | 3,523 | 1,908 | 1,615 | | 293 R | 54.2% | 45.8% | 54.2% | 45.8% |
| 19,923 | WAYNE | 4,567 | 2,680 | 1,887 | | 793 R | 58.7% | 41.3% | 58.7% | 41.3% |
| 14,120 | WEBSTER | 3,332 | 1,428 | 1,904 | | 476 D | 42.9% | 57.1% | 42.9% | 57.1% |
| 35,865 | WHITLEY | 8,192 | 5,618 | 2,574 | | 3,044 R | 68.6% | 31.4% | 68.6% | 31.4% |
| 7,065 | WOLFE | 1,985 | 826 | 1,159 | | 333 D | 41.6% | 58.4% | 41.6% | 58.4% |
| 23,208 | WOODFORD | 8,439 | 4,087 | 4,352 | | 265 D | 48.4% | 51.6% | 48.4% | 51.6% |
| 4,041,769 | TOTAL | 1,083,443 | 596,284 | 487,159 | | 109,125 R | 55.0% | 45.0% | 55.0% | 45.0% |

# KENTUCKY

## SENATOR 2004

| 2000 Census Population | County | Total Vote | Republican | Democratic | Other | Rep.-Dem. Plurality | Percentage | | | |
|---|---|---|---|---|---|---|---|---|---|---|
| | | | | | | | Total Vote | | Major Vote | |
| | | | | | | | Rep. | Dem. | Rep. | Dem. |
| 17,244 | ADAIR | 7,008 | 4,857 | 2,151 | | 2,706 R | 69.3% | 30.7% | 69.3% | 30.7% |
| 17,800 | ALLEN | 6,670 | 4,640 | 2,030 | | 2,610 R | 69.6% | 30.4% | 69.6% | 30.4% |
| 19,111 | ANDERSON | 9,216 | 4,676 | 4,540 | | 136 R | 50.7% | 49.3% | 50.7% | 49.3% |
| 8,286 | BALLARD | 4,083 | 1,752 | 2,331 | | 579 D | 42.9% | 57.1% | 42.9% | 57.1% |
| 38,033 | BARREN | 15,208 | 8,749 | 6,459 | | 2,290 R | 57.5% | 42.5% | 57.5% | 42.5% |
| 11,085 | BATH | 4,583 | 1,673 | 2,910 | | 1,237 D | 36.5% | 63.5% | 36.5% | 63.5% |
| 30,060 | BELL | 10,088 | 4,442 | 5,646 | | 1,204 D | 44.0% | 56.0% | 44.0% | 56.0% |
| 85,991 | BOONE | 43,705 | 31,162 | 12,543 | | 18,619 R | 71.3% | 28.7% | 71.3% | 28.7% |
| 19,360 | BOURBON | 7,864 | 3,614 | 4,250 | | 636 D | 46.0% | 54.0% | 46.0% | 54.0% |
| 49,752 | BOYD | 20,894 | 10,181 | 10,713 | | 532 D | 48.7% | 51.3% | 48.7% | 51.3% |
| 27,697 | BOYLE | 11,985 | 6,179 | 5,806 | | 373 R | 51.6% | 48.4% | 51.6% | 48.4% |
| 8,279 | BRACKEN | 3,432 | 2,249 | 1,183 | | 1,066 R | 65.5% | 34.5% | 65.5% | 34.5% |
| 16,100 | BREATHITT | 5,808 | 1,607 | 4,201 | | 2,594 D | 27.7% | 72.3% | 27.7% | 72.3% |
| 18,648 | BRECKINRIDGE | 8,183 | 4,633 | 3,550 | | 1,083 R | 56.6% | 43.4% | 56.6% | 43.4% |
| 61,236 | BULLITT | 27,588 | 15,675 | 11,913 | | 3,762 R | 56.8% | 43.2% | 56.8% | 43.2% |
| 13,010 | BUTLER | 5,266 | 3,665 | 1,601 | | 2,064 R | 69.6% | 30.4% | 69.6% | 30.4% |
| 13,060 | CALDWELL | 6,059 | 3,025 | 3,034 | | 9 D | 49.9% | 50.1% | 49.9% | 50.1% |
| 34,177 | CALLOWAY | 14,519 | 7,456 | 7,063 | | 393 R | 51.4% | 48.6% | 51.4% | 48.6% |
| 88,616 | CAMPBELL | 38,682 | 24,603 | 14,079 | | 10,524 R | 63.6% | 36.4% | 63.6% | 36.4% |
| 5,351 | CARLISLE | 2,739 | 1,327 | 1,412 | | 85 D | 48.4% | 51.6% | 48.4% | 51.6% |
| 10,155 | CARROLL | 3,759 | 1,788 | 1,971 | | 183 D | 47.6% | 52.4% | 47.6% | 52.4% |
| 26,889 | CARTER | 10,548 | 4,794 | 5,754 | | 960 D | 45.4% | 54.6% | 45.4% | 54.6% |
| 15,447 | CASEY | 5,959 | 4,483 | 1,476 | | 3,007 R | 75.2% | 24.8% | 75.2% | 24.8% |
| 72,265 | CHRISTIAN | 19,635 | 12,331 | 7,304 | | 5,027 R | 62.8% | 37.2% | 62.8% | 37.2% |
| 33,144 | CLARK | 14,606 | 7,047 | 7,559 | | 512 D | 48.2% | 51.8% | 48.2% | 51.8% |
| 24,556 | CLAY | 6,979 | 4,336 | 2,643 | | 1,693 R | 62.1% | 37.9% | 62.1% | 37.9% |
| 9,634 | CLINTON | 4,031 | 3,094 | 937 | | 2,157 R | 76.8% | 23.2% | 76.8% | 23.2% |
| 9,384 | CRITTENDEN | 4,027 | 2,214 | 1,813 | | 401 R | 55.0% | 45.0% | 55.0% | 45.0% |
| 7,147 | CUMBERLAND | 2,885 | 2,103 | 782 | | 1,321 R | 72.9% | 27.1% | 72.9% | 27.1% |
| 91,545 | DAVIESS | 39,887 | 20,148 | 19,739 | | 409 R | 50.5% | 49.5% | 50.5% | 49.5% |
| 11,644 | EDMONSON | 5,107 | 3,165 | 1,942 | | 1,223 R | 62.0% | 38.0% | 62.0% | 38.0% |
| 6,748 | ELLIOTT | 2,826 | 801 | 2,025 | | 1,224 D | 28.3% | 71.7% | 28.3% | 71.7% |
| 15,307 | ESTILL | 5,306 | 2,892 | 2,414 | | 478 R | 54.5% | 45.5% | 54.5% | 45.5% |
| 260,512 | FAYETTE | 121,007 | 50,209 | 70,798 | | 20,589 D | 41.5% | 58.5% | 41.5% | 58.5% |
| 13,792 | FLEMING | 5,895 | 3,080 | 2,815 | | 265 R | 52.2% | 47.8% | 52.2% | 47.8% |
| 42,441 | FLOYD | 17,107 | 5,015 | 12,092 | | 7,077 D | 29.3% | 70.7% | 29.3% | 70.7% |
| 47,687 | FRANKLIN | 23,322 | 7,998 | 15,324 | | 7,326 D | 34.3% | 65.7% | 34.3% | 65.7% |
| 7,752 | FULTON | 2,663 | 1,237 | 1,426 | | 189 D | 46.5% | 53.5% | 46.5% | 53.5% |
| 7,870 | GALLATIN | 2,920 | 1,736 | 1,184 | | 552 R | 59.5% | 40.5% | 59.5% | 40.5% |
| 14,792 | GARRARD | 6,323 | 3,767 | 2,556 | | 1,211 R | 59.6% | 40.4% | 59.6% | 40.4% |
| 22,384 | GRANT | 8,504 | 5,497 | 3,007 | | 2,490 R | 64.6% | 35.4% | 64.6% | 35.4% |
| 37,028 | GRAVES | 15,484 | 7,448 | 8,036 | | 588 D | 48.1% | 51.9% | 48.1% | 51.9% |
| 24,053 | GRAYSON | 9,512 | 5,894 | 3,618 | | 2,276 R | 62.0% | 38.0% | 62.0% | 38.0% |
| 11,518 | GREEN | 4,880 | 3,324 | 1,556 | | 1,768 R | 68.1% | 31.9% | 68.1% | 31.9% |
| 36,891 | GREENUP | 15,678 | 7,804 | 7,874 | | 70 D | 49.8% | 50.2% | 49.8% | 50.2% |
| 8,392 | HANCOCK | 3,844 | 1,834 | 2,010 | | 176 D | 47.7% | 52.3% | 47.7% | 52.3% |
| 94,174 | HARDIN | 34,826 | 19,916 | 14,910 | | 5,006 R | 57.2% | 42.8% | 57.2% | 42.8% |
| 33,202 | HARLAN | 10,605 | 3,340 | 7,265 | | 3,925 D | 31.5% | 68.5% | 31.5% | 68.5% |
| 17,983 | HARRISON | 7,440 | 3,738 | 3,702 | | 36 R | 50.2% | 49.8% | 50.2% | 49.8% |
| 17,445 | HART | 6,303 | 3,518 | 2,785 | | 733 R | 55.8% | 44.2% | 55.8% | 44.2% |
| 44,829 | HENDERSON | 17,909 | 8,419 | 9,490 | | 1,071 D | 47.0% | 53.0% | 47.0% | 53.0% |
| 15,060 | HENRY | 6,290 | 3,266 | 3,024 | | 242 R | 51.9% | 48.1% | 51.9% | 48.1% |
| 5,262 | HICKMAN | 2,252 | 1,093 | 1,159 | | 66 D | 48.5% | 51.5% | 48.5% | 51.5% |
| 46,519 | HOPKINS | 18,091 | 10,161 | 7,930 | | 2,231 R | 56.2% | 43.8% | 56.2% | 43.8% |
| 13,495 | JACKSON | 4,825 | 3,755 | 1,070 | | 2,685 R | 77.8% | 22.2% | 77.8% | 22.2% |
| 693,604 | JEFFERSON | 333,240 | 134,699 | 198,541 | | 63,842 D | 40.4% | 59.6% | 40.4% | 59.6% |
| 39,041 | JESSAMINE | 17,732 | 10,002 | 7,730 | | 2,272 R | 56.4% | 43.6% | 56.4% | 43.6% |
| 23,445 | JOHNSON | 8,953 | 5,242 | 3,711 | | 1,531 R | 58.6% | 41.4% | 58.6% | 41.4% |
| 151,464 | KENTON | 64,917 | 42,158 | 22,759 | | 19,399 R | 64.9% | 35.1% | 64.9% | 35.1% |
| 17,649 | KNOTT | 7,156 | 1,345 | 5,811 | | 4,466 D | 18.8% | 81.2% | 18.8% | 81.2% |

# KENTUCKY

## SENATOR 2004

| 2000 Census Population | County | Total Vote | Republican | Democratic | Other | Rep.-Dem. Plurality | Percentage | | | |
|---|---|---|---|---|---|---|---|---|---|---|
| | | | | | | | Total Vote | | Major Vote | |
| | | | | | | | Rep. | Dem. | Rep. | Dem. |
| 31,795 | KNOX | 11,276 | 6,685 | 4,591 | | 2,094 R | 59.3% | 40.7% | 59.3% | 40.7% |
| 13,373 | LARUE | 5,670 | 3,429 | 2,241 | | 1,188 R | 60.5% | 39.5% | 60.5% | 39.5% |
| 52,715 | LAUREL | 21,441 | 14,427 | 7,014 | | 7,413 R | 67.3% | 32.7% | 67.3% | 32.7% |
| 15,569 | LAWRENCE | 6,112 | 3,322 | 2,790 | | 532 R | 54.4% | 45.6% | 54.4% | 45.6% |
| 7,916 | LEE | 2,732 | 1,606 | 1,126 | | 480 R | 58.8% | 41.2% | 58.8% | 41.2% |
| 12,401 | LESLIE | 4,777 | 2,438 | 2,339 | | 99 R | 51.0% | 49.0% | 51.0% | 49.0% |
| 25,277 | LETCHER | 8,635 | 2,751 | 5,884 | | 3,133 D | 31.9% | 68.1% | 31.9% | 68.1% |
| 14,092 | LEWIS | 5,071 | 3,562 | 1,509 | | 2,053 R | 70.2% | 29.8% | 70.2% | 29.8% |
| 23,361 | LINCOLN | 8,565 | 4,870 | 3,695 | | 1,175 R | 56.9% | 43.1% | 56.9% | 43.1% |
| 9,804 | LIVINGSTON | 4,545 | 2,025 | 2,520 | | 495 D | 44.6% | 55.4% | 44.6% | 55.4% |
| 26,573 | LOGAN | 9,946 | 5,847 | 4,099 | | 1,748 R | 58.8% | 41.2% | 58.8% | 41.2% |
| 8,080 | LYON | 3,762 | 1,680 | 2,082 | | 402 D | 44.7% | 55.3% | 44.7% | 55.3% |
| 65,514 | MCCRACKEN | 28,874 | 14,934 | 13,940 | | 994 R | 51.7% | 48.3% | 51.7% | 48.3% |
| 17,080 | MCCREARY | 5,104 | 3,603 | 1,501 | | 2,102 R | 70.6% | 29.4% | 70.6% | 29.4% |
| 9,938 | MCLEAN | 4,257 | 2,078 | 2,179 | | 101 D | 48.8% | 51.2% | 48.8% | 51.2% |
| 70,872 | MADISON | 29,533 | 14,743 | 14,790 | | 47 D | 49.9% | 50.1% | 49.9% | 50.1% |
| 13,332 | MAGOFFIN | 4,916 | 2,100 | 2,816 | | 716 D | 42.7% | 57.3% | 42.7% | 57.3% |
| 18,212 | MARION | 6,993 | 2,881 | 4,112 | | 1,231 D | 41.2% | 58.8% | 41.2% | 58.8% |
| 30,125 | MARSHALL | 15,128 | 7,191 | 7,937 | | 746 D | 47.5% | 52.5% | 47.5% | 52.5% |
| 12,578 | MARTIN | 4,241 | 2,744 | 1,497 | | 1,247 R | 64.7% | 35.3% | 64.7% | 35.3% |
| 16,800 | MASON | 6,632 | 3,884 | 2,748 | | 1,136 R | 58.6% | 41.4% | 58.6% | 41.4% |
| 26,349 | MEADE | 10,574 | 5,574 | 5,000 | | 574 R | 52.7% | 47.3% | 52.7% | 47.3% |
| 6,556 | MENIFEE | 2,430 | 946 | 1,484 | | 538 D | 38.9% | 61.1% | 38.9% | 61.1% |
| 20,817 | MERCER | 9,553 | 5,019 | 4,534 | | 485 R | 52.5% | 47.5% | 52.5% | 47.5% |
| 10,037 | METCALFE | 3,868 | 2,260 | 1,608 | | 652 R | 58.4% | 41.6% | 58.4% | 41.6% |
| 11,756 | MONROE | 5,096 | 3,940 | 1,156 | | 2,784 R | 77.3% | 22.7% | 77.3% | 22.7% |
| 22,554 | MONTGOMERY | 9,688 | 4,130 | 5,558 | | 1,428 D | 42.6% | 57.4% | 42.6% | 57.4% |
| 13,948 | MORGAN | 4,558 | 1,800 | 2,758 | | 958 D | 39.5% | 60.5% | 39.5% | 60.5% |
| 31,839 | MUHLENBERG | 12,782 | 5,604 | 7,178 | | 1,574 D | 43.8% | 56.2% | 43.8% | 56.2% |
| 37,477 | NELSON | 16,054 | 7,754 | 8,300 | | 546 D | 48.3% | 51.7% | 48.3% | 51.7% |
| 6,813 | NICHOLAS | 2,874 | 1,236 | 1,638 | | 402 D | 43.0% | 57.0% | 43.0% | 57.0% |
| 22,916 | OHIO | 9,573 | 5,371 | 4,202 | | 1,169 R | 56.1% | 43.9% | 56.1% | 43.9% |
| 46,178 | OLDHAM | 26,482 | 15,751 | 10,731 | | 5,020 R | 59.5% | 40.5% | 59.5% | 40.5% |
| 10,547 | OWEN | 4,546 | 2,637 | 1,909 | | 728 R | 58.0% | 42.0% | 58.0% | 42.0% |
| 4,858 | OWSLEY | 1,802 | 1,142 | 660 | | 482 R | 63.4% | 36.6% | 63.4% | 36.6% |
| 14,390 | PENDLETON | 5,866 | 3,824 | 2,042 | | 1,782 R | 65.2% | 34.8% | 65.2% | 34.8% |
| 29,390 | PERRY | 11,279 | 2,620 | 8,659 | | 6,039 D | 23.2% | 76.8% | 23.2% | 76.8% |
| 68,736 | PIKE | 24,965 | 9,672 | 15,293 | | 5,621 D | 38.7% | 61.3% | 38.7% | 61.3% |
| 13,237 | POWELL | 4,767 | 1,961 | 2,806 | | 845 D | 41.1% | 58.9% | 41.1% | 58.9% |
| 56,217 | PULASKI | 23,901 | 16,053 | 7,848 | | 8,205 R | 67.2% | 32.8% | 67.2% | 32.8% |
| 2,266 | ROBERTSON | 1,027 | 559 | 468 | | 91 R | 54.4% | 45.6% | 54.4% | 45.6% |
| 16,582 | ROCKCASTLE | 5,768 | 3,956 | 1,812 | | 2,144 R | 68.6% | 31.4% | 68.6% | 31.4% |
| 22,094 | ROWAN | 8,420 | 3,388 | 5,032 | | 1,644 D | 40.2% | 59.8% | 40.2% | 59.8% |
| 16,315 | RUSSELL | 7,334 | 5,092 | 2,242 | | 2,850 R | 69.4% | 30.6% | 69.4% | 30.6% |
| 33,061 | SCOTT | 16,490 | 8,126 | 8,364 | | 238 D | 49.3% | 50.7% | 49.3% | 50.7% |
| 33,337 | SHELBY | 15,813 | 8,544 | 7,269 | | 1,275 R | 54.0% | 46.0% | 54.0% | 46.0% |
| 16,405 | SIMPSON | 6,603 | 3,665 | 2,938 | | 727 R | 55.5% | 44.5% | 55.5% | 44.5% |
| 11,766 | SPENCER | 6,620 | 3,799 | 2,821 | | 978 R | 57.4% | 42.6% | 57.4% | 42.6% |
| 22,927 | TAYLOR | 9,762 | 6,119 | 3,643 | | 2,476 R | 62.7% | 37.3% | 62.7% | 37.3% |
| 11,971 | TODD | 4,246 | 2,696 | 1,550 | | 1,146 R | 63.5% | 36.5% | 63.5% | 36.5% |
| 12,597 | TRIGG | 5,811 | 3,354 | 2,457 | | 897 R | 57.7% | 42.3% | 57.7% | 42.3% |
| 8,125 | TRIMBLE | 3,717 | 1,865 | 1,852 | | 13 R | 50.2% | 49.8% | 50.2% | 49.8% |
| 15,637 | UNION | 5,671 | 2,791 | 2,880 | | 89 D | 49.2% | 50.8% | 49.2% | 50.8% |
| 92,522 | WARREN | 37,715 | 21,258 | 16,457 | | 4,801 R | 56.4% | 43.6% | 56.4% | 43.6% |
| 10,916 | WASHINGTON | 4,907 | 2,761 | 2,146 | | 615 R | 56.3% | 43.7% | 56.3% | 43.7% |
| 19,923 | WAYNE | 6,997 | 4,214 | 2,783 | | 1,431 R | 60.2% | 39.8% | 60.2% | 39.8% |
| 14,120 | WEBSTER | 5,228 | 2,490 | 2,738 | | 248 D | 47.6% | 52.4% | 47.6% | 52.4% |
| 35,865 | WHITLEY | 12,702 | 8,082 | 4,620 | | 3,462 R | 63.6% | 36.4% | 63.6% | 36.4% |
| 7,065 | WOLFE | 2,767 | 911 | 1,856 | | 945 D | 32.9% | 67.1% | 32.9% | 67.1% |
| 23,208 | WOODFORD | 11,083 | 4,887 | 6,196 | | 1,309 D | 44.1% | 55.9% | 44.1% | 55.9% |
| 4,041,769 | TOTAL | 1,724,362 | 873,507 | 850,855 | | 22,652 R | 50.7% | 49.3% | 50.7% | 49.3% |

# KENTUCKY

## HOUSE OF REPRESENTATIVES

| CD | Year | Total Vote | Republican | | Democratic | | Other Vote | Rep.-Dem. Plurality | Percentage | | | |
| | | | Vote | Candidate | Vote | Candidate | | | Total Vote | | Major Vote | |
| | | | | | | | | | Rep. | Dem. | Rep. | Dem. |
|---|---|---|---|---|---|---|---|---|---|---|---|---|
| 1 | 2004 | 261,387 | 175,972 | Whitfield, Edward* | 85,229 | Cartwright, Billy R. | 186 | 90,743 R | 67.3% | 32.6% | 67.4% | 32.6% |
| 1 | 2002 | 180,217 | 117,600 | Whitfield, Edward* | 62,617 | Alexander, Klint | | 54,983 R | 65.3% | 34.7% | 65.3% | 34.7% |
| 2 | 2004 | 272,979 | 185,394 | Lewis, Ron* | 87,585 | Smith, Adam | | 97,809 R | 67.9% | 32.1% | 67.9% | 32.1% |
| 2 | 2002 | 176,288 | 122,773 | Lewis, Ron* | 51,431 | Williams, David L. | 2,084 | 71,342 R | 69.6% | 29.2% | 70.5% | 29.5% |
| 3 | 2004 | 328,154 | 197,736 | Northup, Anne M.* | 124,040 | Miller, Tony | 6,378 | 73,696 R | 60.3% | 37.8% | 61.5% | 38.5% |
| 3 | 2002 | 229,074 | 118,228 | Northup, Anne M.* | 110,846 | Conway, Jack | | 7,382 R | 51.6% | 48.4% | 51.6% | 48.4% |
| 4 | 2004 | 295,927 | 160,982 | Davis, Geoff | 129,876 | Clooney, Nick | 5,069 | 31,106 R | 54.4% | 43.9% | 55.3% | 44.7% |
| 4 | 2002 | 171,735 | 81,651 | Davis, Geoff | 87,776 | Lucas, Ken* | 2,308 | 6,125 D | 47.5% | 51.1% | 48.2% | 51.8% |
| 5 | 2004 | 177,579 | 177,579 | Rogers, Harold* | | | | 177,579 R | 100.0% | | 100.0% | |
| 5 | 2002 | 176,240 | 137,986 | Rogers, Harold* | 38,254 | Bailey, Sidney Jane | | 99,732 R | 78.3% | 21.7% | 78.3% | 21.7% |
| 6 | 2004 | 299,217 | 119,716 | Buford, Tom | 175,355 | Chandler, Ben* | 4,146 | 55,639 D | 40.0% | 58.6% | 40.6% | 59.4% |
| 6 | 2002 | 160,688 | 115,622 | Fletcher, Ernie* | | | 45,066 | 115,622 R | 72.0% | | 100.0% | |
| Total | 2004 | 1,635,243 | 1,017,379 | | 602,085 | | 15,779 | 415,294 R | 62.2% | 36.8% | 62.8% | 37.2% |
| Total | 2002 | 1,094,242 | 693,860 | | 350,924 | | 49,458 | 342,936 R | 63.4% | 32.1% | 66.4% | 33.6% |

An asterisk (*) denotes incumbent.

# KENTUCKY

## GENERAL AND PRIMARY ELECTIONS

### 2003–2004 GENERAL ELECTIONS

**President**     Other vote was 8,856 Independent (Ralph Nader); 2,619 Libertarian (Michael Badnarik); 2,213 Constitution (Michael Peroutka); 13 write-in (Walter F. Brown); 9 write-in (John Joseph Kennedy).

**Governor (2003)**

**Senator**

**House**     Other vote was:

CD 1     186 write-in (Tom Barlow).
CD 2
CD 3     6,363 Libertarian (George C. Dick); 15 write-in (Corley Everett).
CD 4     5,069 Independent (Michael E. Slider).
CD 5
CD 6     2,388 Constitution (Stacy Abner); 1,758 Libertarian (Mark Gailey).

# KENTUCKY

## GENERAL AND PRIMARY ELECTIONS

## 2003–2004 PRIMARY ELECTIONS

| | | | | |
|---|---|---|---|---|
| **Primary** | May 20, 2003 (Governor)<br>May 18, 2004 (Congress) | **Registration**<br>(as of May 18, 2004) | Republican<br>Democratic<br>Other | 951,255<br>1,580,524<br>174,813 |
| | | | TOTAL | 2,706,593 |

(The statewide registration total is reported as the number above but adds to 2,706,592.)

**Primary Type**   Closed—Only registered Democrats and Republicans could vote in their party's primary.

Note:   An asterisk (*) denotes incumbent. The names of unopposed candidates did not appear on the primary ballot; therefore, no votes were cast for these candidates.

| | REPUBLICAN PRIMARIES | | | DEMOCRATIC PRIMARIES | | |
|---|---|---|---|---|---|---|
| **President** | George W. Bush* | 108,603 | 92.5% | John Kerry | 138,175 | 60.1% |
| | Uncommitted | 8,776 | 7.5% | John Edwards | 33,403 | 14.5% |
| | | | | Uncommitted | 21,199 | 9.2% |
| | | | | Joseph I. Lieberman | 11,062 | 4.8% |
| | | | | Howard Dean | 8,222 | 3.6% |
| | | | | Wesley Clark | 6,519 | 2.8% |
| | | | | Al Sharpton | 5,022 | 2.2% |
| | | | | Dennis J. Kucinich | 4,508 | 2.0% |
| | | | | Lyndon H. LaRouche Jr. | 1,806 | 0.8% |
| | TOTAL | 117,379 | | TOTAL | 229,916 | |
| **Governor (2003)** | Ernie Fletcher | 90,912 | 57.3% | Ben Chandler | 143,150 | 50.2% |
| | Rebecca Jackson | 44,084 | 27.8% | Jody Richards | 132,627 | 46.5% |
| | Steve Nunn | 21,167 | 13.4% | Otis Hensley Jr. | 9,372 | 3.3% |
| | Virgil Moore | 2,365 | 1.5% | | | |
| | TOTAL | 158,528 | | TOTAL | 285,149 | |
| **Senator** | Jim Bunning* | 96,545 | 84.0% | Daniel Mongiardo | 142,162 | 64.9% |
| | Barry Metcalf | 18,395 | 16.0% | David L. Williams | 76,807 | 35.1% |
| | TOTAL | 114,940 | | TOTAL | 218,969 | |
| **Congressional District 1** | Edward Whitfield* | Unopposed | | Billy R. Cartwright | Unopposed | |
| **Congressional District 2** | Ron Lewis* | Unopposed | | Adam Smith | 14,565 | 44.3% |
| | | | | James E. Rice | 9,228 | 28.0% |
| | | | | Pete Tabb | 9,115 | 27.7% |
| | | | | TOTAL | 32,908 | |
| **Congressional District 3** | Anne M. Northup* | Unopposed | | Tony Miller | 39,883 | 81.8% |
| | | | | Burrel Charles Farnsley | 8,883 | 18.2% |
| | | | | TOTAL | 48,766 | |
| **Congressional District 4** | Geoff Davis | 13,957 | 58.0% | Nick Clooney | Unopposed | |
| | Kevin L. Murphy | 7,672 | 31.9% | | | |
| | John Kelly King | 2,434 | 10.1% | | | |
| | TOTAL | 24,063 | | | | |
| **Congressional District 5** | Harold Rogers* | 26,909 | 91.3% | No Democratic candidate | | |
| | Billy Ray Wilson | 2,566 | 8.7% | | | |
| | TOTAL | 29,475 | | | | |
| **Congressional District 6** | Tom Buford | 8,478 | 62.2% | Ben Chandler* | Unopposed | |
| | Bryan Samuel Coffman | 3,526 | 25.8% | | | |
| | Don Swarthout | 1,637 | 12.0% | | | |
| | TOTAL | 13,641 | | | | |

# LOUISIANA

## GOVERNOR
Kathleen Babineaux Blanco (D). Elected 2003 to a four-year term.

## SENATORS (1 Democrat, 1 Republican)
Mary L. Landrieu (D). Reelected 2002 to a six-year term. Previously elected 1996.

David Vitter (R). Elected 2004 to a six-year term.

## REPRESENTATIVES (5 Republicans, 2 Democrats)
1. Bobby Jindal (R)
2. William J. Jefferson (D)
3. Charlie Melancon (D)
4. Jim McCrery (R)
5. Rodney Alexander (R)
6. Richard H. Baker (R)
7. Charles Boustany Jr. (R)

## POSTWAR VOTE FOR PRESIDENT

| Year | Total Vote | Republican Vote | Republican Candidate | Democratic Vote | Democratic Candidate | Other Vote | Plurality | Total Vote Rep. | Total Vote Dem. | Major Vote Rep. | Major Vote Dem. |
|------|-----------|------|-----------|------|-----------|-------|-----------|------|------|------|------|
| 2004 | 1,943,106 | 1,102,169 | Bush, George W. | 820,299 | Kerry, John | 20,638 | 281,870 R | 56.7% | 42.2% | 57.3% | 42.7% |
| 2000** | 1,765,656 | 927,871 | Bush, George W. | 792,344 | Gore, Al | 45,441 | 135,527 R | 52.6% | 44.9% | 53.9% | 46.1% |
| 1996** | 1,783,959 | 712,586 | Dole, Bob | 927,837 | Clinton, Bill | 143,536 | 215,251 D | 39.9% | 52.0% | 43.4% | 56.6% |
| 1992** | 1,790,017 | 733,386 | Bush, George | 815,971 | Clinton, Bill | 240,660 | 82,585 D | 41.0% | 45.6% | 47.3% | 52.7% |
| 1988 | 1,628,202 | 883,702 | Bush, George | 717,460 | Dukakis, Michael S. | 27,040 | 166,242 R | 54.3% | 44.1% | 55.2% | 44.8% |
| 1984 | 1,706,822 | 1,037,299 | Reagan, Ronald | 651,586 | Mondale, Walter F. | 17,937 | 385,713 R | 60.8% | 38.2% | 61.4% | 38.6% |
| 1980** | 1,548,591 | 792,853 | Reagan, Ronald | 708,453 | Carter, Jimmy | 47,285 | 84,400 R | 51.2% | 45.7% | 52.8% | 47.2% |
| 1976 | 1,278,439 | 587,446 | Ford, Gerald R. | 661,365 | Carter, Jimmy | 29,628 | 73,919 D | 46.0% | 51.7% | 47.0% | 53.0% |
| 1972 | 1,051,491 | 686,852 | Nixon, Richard M. | 298,142 | McGovern, George S. | 66,497 | 388,710 R | 65.3% | 28.4% | 69.7% | 30.3% |
| 1968** | 1,097,450 | 257,535 | Nixon, Richard M. | 309,615 | Humphrey, Hubert H. | 530,300 | 220,685 A | 23.5% | 28.2% | 45.4% | 54.6% |
| 1964 | 896,293 | 509,225 | Goldwater, Barry M. | 387,068 | Johnson, Lyndon B. | | 122,157 R | 56.8% | 43.2% | 56.8% | 43.2% |
| 1960** | 807,891 | 230,980 | Nixon, Richard M. | 407,339 | Kennedy, John F. | 169,572 | 176,359 D | 28.6% | 50.4% | 36.2% | 63.8% |
| 1956 | 617,544 | 329,047 | Eisenhower, Dwight D. | 243,977 | Stevenson, Adlai E. | 44,520 | 85,070 R | 53.3% | 39.5% | 57.4% | 42.6% |
| 1952 | 651,952 | 306,925 | Eisenhower, Dwight D. | 345,027 | Stevenson, Adlai E. | | 38,102 D | 47.1% | 52.9% | 47.1% | 52.9% |
| 1948** | 416,336 | 72,657 | Dewey, Thomas E. | 136,344 | Truman, Harry S. | 207,335 | 67,946 SR | 17.5% | 32.7% | 34.8% | 65.2% |

In past elections, the other vote included: 2000 - 20,473 Green (Ralph Nader); 1996 - 123,293 Reform (Ross Perot); 1992 - 211,478 Independent (Perot); 1980 - 26,345 Independent (John Anderson); 1968 - 530,300 American Independent (George Wallace); 1960 - 169,572 Unpledged Independent Electors; 1948 - 204,290 States' Rights (Strom Thurmond).

# LOUISIANA

## POSTWAR VOTE FOR GOVERNOR

| Year | Total Vote | Republican Vote | Republican Candidate | Democratic Vote | Democratic Candidate | Other Vote | Plurality | Total Vote Rep. | Total Vote Dem. | Major Vote Rep. | Major Vote Dem. |
|---|---|---|---|---|---|---|---|---|---|---|---|
| 2003* | 1,407,842 | 676,484 | Jindal, Bobby | 731,358 | Blanco, Kathleen Babineaux | | 54,874 D | 48.1% | 51.9% | 48.1% | 51.9% |
| 1999 | 1,295,205 | 805,203 | Foster, Mike | 382,445 | Jefferson, William J. | 107,557 | 422,758 R | 62.2% | 29.5% | | |
| 1995* | 1,550,360 | 984,499 | Foster, Mike | 565,861 | Fields, Cleo | | 418,638 R | 63.5% | 36.5% | 63.5% | 36.5% |
| 1991* | 1,728,040 | 671,009 | Duke, David E. | 1,057,031 | Edwards, Edwin W. | | 386,022 D | 38.8% | 61.2% | 38.8% | 61.2% |
| 1987** | 1,558,730 | 287,780 | Livingston, Robert L. | 516,078 | Roemer, Charles | 754,872 | 78,277 D | 18.5% | 33.1% | | |
| 1983 | 1,615,905 | 588,508 | Treen, David C. | 1,006,561 | Edwards, Edwin W. | 20,836 | 418,053 D | 36.4% | 62.3% | | |
| 1979* | 1,371,825 | 690,691 | Treen, David C. | 681,134 | Lambert, Louis | | 9,557 R | 50.3% | 49.7% | 50.3% | 49.7% |
| 1975 | 430,095 | | — | 430,095 | Edwards, Edwin W. | | 430,095 D | | 100.0% | | 100.0% |
| 1972 | 1,121,570 | 480,424 | Treen, David C. | 641,146 | Edwards, Edwin W. | | 160,722 D | 42.8% | 57.2% | 42.8% | 57.2% |
| 1968 | 372,762 | | — | 372,762 | McKeithen, John J. | | 372,762 D | | 100.0% | | 100.0% |
| 1964 | 773,390 | 297,753 | Lyons, C. H. | 469,589 | McKeithen, John J. | 6,048 | 171,836 D | 38.5% | 60.7% | 38.8% | 61.2% |
| 1960 | 506,562 | 86,135 | Grevemberg, F. C. | 407,907 | Davis, Jimmie H. | 12,520 | 321,772 D | 17.0% | 80.5% | 17.4% | 82.6% |
| 1956 | 172,291 | | — | 172,291 | Long, Earl K. | | 172,291 D | | 100.0% | | 100.0% |
| 1952 | 123,681 | 4,958 | Bagwell, Harrison G. | 118,723 | Kennon, Robert F. | | 113,765 D | 4.0% | 96.0% | 4.0% | 96.0% |
| 1948 | 76,566 | | — | 76,566 | Long, Earl K. | | 76,566 D | | 100.0% | | 100.0% |

Since 1978 Louisiana has had a two-tier election system in which all candidates, regardless of party, run together in a first-round, open primary. A candidate that wins a majority of the vote in the first round is elected. If no candidate receives 50 percent, a runoff is held between the top two finishers. An asterisk (*) indicates gubernatorial elections that were decided in a runoff, with the runoff results listed. In elections that did not require a runoff, the leading Democratic and Republican candidates are listed with their first-round votes. The votes for other candidates are listed in the other vote column, regardless of whether they were Democratic, Republican, or independent. In 1987, Democrat Edwin W. Edwards withdrew after finishing second in the initial round of voting. Democrat Charles Roemer finished first with 33.1 percent, 78,277 votes ahead of Edwards. With Edwards' withdrawal, no runoff was held. The major party vote percentages are given for those elections where there was no more than one Democratic and one Republican candidate.

## POSTWAR VOTE FOR SENATOR

| Year | Total Vote | Republican Vote | Republican Candidate | Democratic Vote | Democratic Candidate | Other Vote | Plurality | Total Vote Rep. | Total Vote Dem. | Major Vote Rep. | Major Vote Dem. |
|---|---|---|---|---|---|---|---|---|---|---|---|
| 2004 | 1,848,056 | 943,014 | Vitter, David | 542,150 | John, Chris | 362,892 | 400,864 R | 51.0% | 29.3% | | |
| 2002* | 1,235,296 | 596,642 | Terrell, Suzanne Haik | 638,654 | Landrieu, Mary L. | | 42,012 D | 48.3% | 51.7% | 48.3% | 51.7% |
| 1998 | 969,165 | 306,616 | Donelon, Jim | 620,502 | Breaux, John B. | 42,047 | 313,886 D | 31.6% | 64.0% | | |
| 1996* | 1,700,102 | 847,157 | Jenkins, Louis | 852,945 | Landrieu, Mary L. | | 5,788 D | 49.8% | 50.2% | 49.8% | 50.2% |
| 1992 | 843,037 | 69,986 | Stockstill, Lyle | 616,021 | Breaux, John B. | 157,030 | 541,236 D | 8.3% | 73.1% | | |
| 1990 | 1,396,113 | 607,391 | Duke, David E. | 752,902 | Johnston, J. Bennett | 35,820 | 145,511 D | 43.5% | 53.9% | | |
| 1986* | 1,369,897 | 646,311 | Moore, W. Henson | 723,586 | Breaux, John B. | | 77,275 D | 47.2% | 52.8% | 47.2% | 52.8% |
| 1984 | 977,473 | 86,546 | Robert M. Ross | 838,181 | Johnston, J. Bennett | 52,746 | 751,635 D | 8.9% | 85.7% | | |
| 1980 | 841,013 | 13,739 | Bardwell, Jerry C. | 484,770 | Long, Russell B. | 342,504 | 158,848 D | 1.6% | 57.6% | | |
| 1978 | 839,669 | | — | 498,773 | Johnston, J. Bennett | 340,896 | 157,877 D | | 59.4% | | |
| 1974 | 434,643 | | — | 434,643 | Long, Russell B. | | 434,643 D | | 100.0% | | 100.0% |
| 1972** | 1,084,904 | 206,846 | Toledano, Ben C. | 598,987 | Johnston, J. Bennett | 279,071 | 348,826 D | 19.1% | 55.2% | 25.7% | 74.3% |
| 1968 | 518,586 | | — | 518,586 | Long, Russell B. | | 518,586 D | | 100.0% | | 100.0% |
| 1966 | 437,695 | | — | 437,695 | Ellender, Allen J. | | 437,695 D | | 100.0% | | 100.0% |
| 1962 | 421,904 | 103,066 | O'Hearn, Taylor W. | 318,838 | Long, Russell B. | | 215,772 D | 24.4% | 75.6% | 24.4% | 75.6% |
| 1960 | 541,928 | 109,698 | Reese, George W. | 432,228 | Ellender, Allen J. | 2 | 322,530 D | 20.2% | 79.8% | 20.2% | 79.8% |
| 1956 | 335,564 | | — | 335,564 | Long, Russell B. | | 335,564 D | | 100.0% | | 100.0% |
| 1954 | 207,115 | | — | 207,115 | Ellender, Allen J. | | 207,115 D | | 100.0% | | 100.0% |
| 1950 | 251,838 | 30,931 | Gerth, Charles S. | 220,907 | Long, Russell B. | | 189,976 D | 12.3% | 87.7% | 12.3% | 87.7% |
| 1948 | 330,124 | | — | 330,115 | Ellender, Allen J. | 9 | 330,115 D | | 100.0% | | 100.0% |
| 1948S | 408,667 | 102,331 | Clarke, Clem S. | 306,336 | Long, Russell B. | | 204,005 D | 25.0% | 75.0% | 25.0% | 75.0% |

An asterisk (*) indicates Senate elections since 1978 that have been decided in a runoff, with the runoff results listed. In elections that did not require a runoff, the leading Democratic and Republican candidates are listed with their first-round votes. The votes for other candidates are listed in the other vote column, regardless of whether they were Democratic, Republican, or independent. In 1972 the other vote included 250,161 votes for John J. McKeithen (Independent). One of the 1948 elections was for a short term to fill a vacancy. The major party vote percentages are given for those elections where there was no more than one Democratic and one Republican candidate.

# LOUISIANA

Congressional districts first established for elections held in 2002
7 members

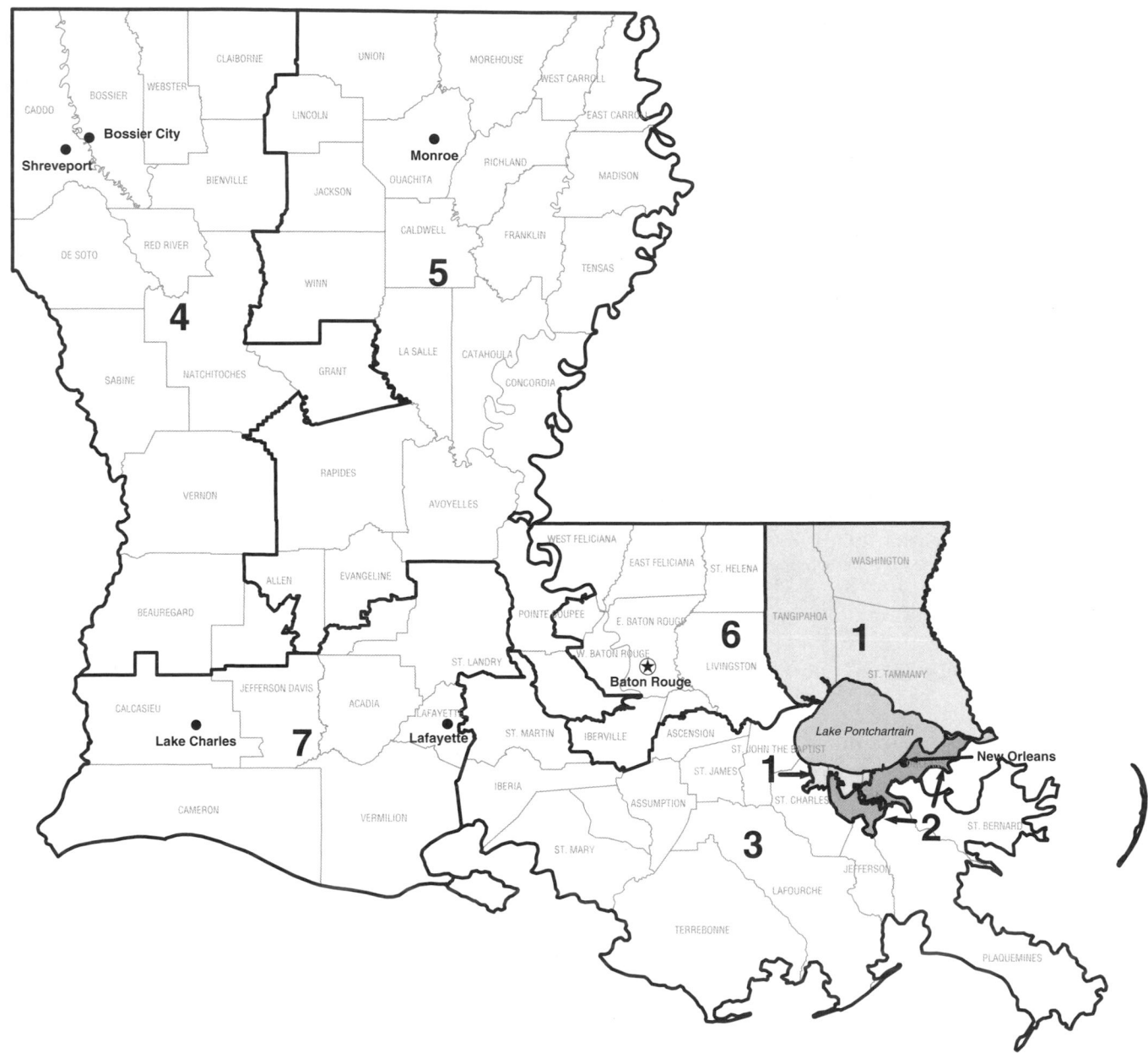

# LOUISIANA

## PRESIDENT 2004

| 2000 Census Population | Parish | Total Vote | Republican | Democratic | Other | Rep.-Dem. Plurality | Percentage | | | |
|---|---|---|---|---|---|---|---|---|---|---|
| | | | | | | | Total Vote | | Major Vote | |
| | | | | | | | Rep. | Dem. | Rep. | Dem. |
| 58,861 | ACADIA | 25,230 | 16,083 | 8,937 | 210 | 7,146 R | 63.7% | 35.4% | 64.3% | 35.7% |
| 25,440 | ALLEN | 9,124 | 5,140 | 3,791 | 193 | 1,349 R | 56.3% | 41.5% | 57.6% | 42.4% |
| 76,627 | ASCENSION | 39,100 | 24,661 | 13,955 | 484 | 10,706 R | 63.1% | 35.7% | 63.9% | 36.1% |
| 23,388 | ASSUMPTION | 10,735 | 4,966 | 5,585 | 184 | 619 D | 46.3% | 52.0% | 47.1% | 52.9% |
| 41,481 | AVOYELLES | 15,525 | 8,302 | 6,976 | 247 | 1,326 R | 53.5% | 44.9% | 54.3% | 45.7% |
| 32,986 | BEAUREGARD | 13,281 | 9,470 | 3,666 | 145 | 5,804 R | 71.3% | 27.6% | 72.1% | 27.9% |
| 15,752 | BIENVILLE | 7,157 | 3,612 | 3,399 | 146 | 213 R | 50.5% | 47.5% | 51.5% | 48.5% |
| 98,310 | BOSSIER | 42,705 | 30,040 | 12,317 | 348 | 17,723 R | 70.3% | 28.8% | 70.9% | 29.1% |
| 252,161 | CADDO | 106,595 | 54,292 | 51,739 | 564 | 2,553 R | 50.9% | 48.5% | 51.2% | 48.8% |
| 183,577 | CALCASIEU | 79,698 | 46,075 | 32,864 | 759 | 13,211 R | 57.8% | 41.2% | 58.4% | 41.6% |
| 10,560 | CALDWELL | 4,752 | 3,308 | 1,384 | 60 | 1,924 R | 69.6% | 29.1% | 70.5% | 29.5% |
| 9,991 | CAMERON | 4,640 | 3,190 | 1,367 | 83 | 1,823 R | 68.8% | 29.5% | 70.0% | 30.0% |
| 10,920 | CATAHOULA | 4,954 | 3,219 | 1,673 | 62 | 1,546 R | 65.0% | 33.8% | 65.8% | 34.2% |
| 16,851 | CLAIBORNE | 6,630 | 3,704 | 2,854 | 72 | 850 R | 55.9% | 43.0% | 56.5% | 43.5% |
| 20,247 | CONCORDIA | 8,980 | 5,427 | 3,446 | 107 | 1,981 R | 60.4% | 38.4% | 61.2% | 38.8% |
| 25,494 | DE SOTO | 11,336 | 6,211 | 5,026 | 99 | 1,185 R | 54.8% | 44.3% | 55.3% | 44.7% |
| 412,852 | EAST BATON ROUGE | 183,642 | 99,943 | 82,298 | 1,401 | 17,645 R | 54.4% | 44.8% | 54.8% | 45.2% |
| 9,421 | EAST CARROLL | 3,395 | 1,357 | 1,980 | 58 | 623 D | 40.0% | 58.3% | 40.7% | 59.3% |
| 21,360 | EAST FELICIANA | 9,201 | 5,021 | 4,091 | 89 | 930 R | 54.6% | 44.5% | 55.1% | 44.9% |
| 35,434 | EVANGELINE | 13,979 | 7,949 | 5,757 | 273 | 2,192 R | 56.9% | 41.2% | 58.0% | 42.0% |
| 21,263 | FRANKLIN | 9,103 | 6,141 | 2,828 | 134 | 3,313 R | 67.5% | 31.1% | 68.5% | 31.5% |
| 18,698 | GRANT | 7,991 | 5,911 | 1,977 | 103 | 3,934 R | 74.0% | 24.7% | 74.9% | 25.1% |
| 73,266 | IBERIA | 32,273 | 19,420 | 12,426 | 427 | 6,994 R | 60.2% | 38.5% | 61.0% | 39.0% |
| 33,320 | IBERVILLE | 14,827 | 6,333 | 8,259 | 235 | 1,926 D | 42.7% | 55.7% | 43.4% | 56.6% |
| 15,397 | JACKSON | 7,647 | 5,038 | 2,525 | 84 | 2,513 R | 65.9% | 33.0% | 66.6% | 33.4% |
| 455,466 | JEFFERSON | 191,663 | 117,882 | 72,136 | 1,645 | 45,746 R | 61.5% | 37.6% | 62.0% | 38.0% |
| 31,435 | JEFFERSON DAVIS | 13,007 | 8,055 | 4,745 | 207 | 3,310 R | 61.9% | 36.5% | 62.9% | 37.1% |
| 190,503 | LAFAYETTE | 89,923 | 57,732 | 31,210 | 981 | 26,522 R | 64.2% | 34.7% | 64.9% | 35.1% |
| 89,974 | LAFOURCHE | 37,864 | 22,734 | 14,417 | 713 | 8,317 R | 60.0% | 38.1% | 61.2% | 38.8% |
| 14,282 | LA SALLE | 6,238 | 5,015 | 1,155 | 68 | 3,860 R | 80.4% | 18.5% | 81.3% | 18.7% |
| 42,509 | LINCOLN | 18,218 | 10,791 | 7,242 | 185 | 3,549 R | 59.2% | 39.8% | 59.8% | 40.2% |
| 91,814 | LIVINGSTON | 44,253 | 33,976 | 9,895 | 382 | 24,081 R | 76.8% | 22.4% | 77.4% | 22.6% |
| 13,728 | MADISON | 4,673 | 2,291 | 2,334 | 48 | 43 D | 49.0% | 49.9% | 49.5% | 50.5% |
| 31,021 | MOREHOUSE | 12,971 | 7,471 | 5,336 | 164 | 2,135 R | 57.6% | 41.1% | 58.3% | 41.7% |
| 39,080 | NATCHITOCHES | 16,966 | 9,261 | 7,398 | 307 | 1,863 R | 54.6% | 43.6% | 55.6% | 44.4% |
| 484,674 | ORLEANS | 197,103 | 42,847 | 152,610 | 1,646 | 109,763 D | 21.7% | 77.4% | 21.9% | 78.1% |
| 147,250 | OUACHITA | 64,444 | 41,750 | 22,016 | 678 | 19,734 R | 64.8% | 34.2% | 65.5% | 34.5% |
| 26,757 | PLAQUEMINES | 12,153 | 7,866 | 4,181 | 106 | 3,685 R | 64.7% | 34.4% | 65.3% | 34.7% |
| 22,763 | POINTE COUPEE | 11,271 | 5,429 | 5,712 | 130 | 283 D | 48.2% | 50.7% | 48.7% | 51.3% |
| 126,337 | RAPIDES | 54,069 | 34,492 | 18,904 | 673 | 15,588 R | 63.8% | 35.0% | 64.6% | 35.4% |
| 9,622 | RED RIVER | 4,717 | 2,507 | 2,140 | 70 | 367 R | 53.1% | 45.4% | 53.9% | 46.1% |
| 20,981 | RICHLAND | 8,665 | 5,471 | 3,082 | 112 | 2,389 R | 63.1% | 35.6% | 64.0% | 36.0% |
| 23,459 | SABINE | 9,576 | 6,711 | 2,743 | 122 | 3,968 R | 70.1% | 28.6% | 71.0% | 29.0% |
| 67,229 | ST. BERNARD | 29,838 | 19,597 | 9,956 | 285 | 9,641 R | 65.7% | 33.4% | 66.3% | 33.7% |
| 48,072 | ST. CHARLES | 23,837 | 14,747 | 8,856 | 234 | 5,891 R | 61.9% | 37.2% | 62.5% | 37.5% |
| 10,525 | ST. HELENA | 5,508 | 2,235 | 3,173 | 100 | 938 D | 40.6% | 57.6% | 41.3% | 58.7% |
| 21,216 | ST. JAMES | 11,108 | 4,545 | 6,407 | 156 | 1,862 D | 40.9% | 57.7% | 41.5% | 58.5% |
| 43,044 | ST. JOHN THE BAPTIST | 19,617 | 9,039 | 10,305 | 273 | 1,266 D | 46.1% | 52.5% | 46.7% | 53.3% |
| 87,700 | ST. LANDRY | 36,760 | 18,315 | 18,166 | 279 | 149 R | 49.8% | 49.4% | 50.2% | 49.8% |
| 48,583 | ST. MARTIN | 22,824 | 12,095 | 10,321 | 408 | 1,774 R | 53.0% | 45.2% | 54.0% | 46.0% |
| 53,500 | ST. MARY | 22,694 | 12,877 | 9,547 | 270 | 3,330 R | 56.7% | 42.1% | 57.4% | 42.6% |
| 191,268 | ST. TAMMANY | 100,592 | 75,139 | 24,665 | 788 | 50,474 R | 74.7% | 24.5% | 75.3% | 24.7% |
| 100,588 | TANGIPAHOA | 42,135 | 26,181 | 15,345 | 609 | 10,836 R | 62.1% | 36.4% | 63.0% | 37.0% |
| 6,618 | TENSAS | 2,963 | 1,453 | 1,469 | 41 | 16 D | 49.0% | 49.6% | 49.7% | 50.3% |
| 104,503 | TERREBONNE | 40,574 | 26,358 | 13,684 | 532 | 12,674 R | 65.0% | 33.7% | 65.8% | 34.2% |
| 22,803 | UNION | 10,718 | 7,457 | 3,089 | 172 | 4,368 R | 69.6% | 28.8% | 70.7% | 29.3% |
| 53,807 | VERMILION | 24,552 | 15,069 | 9,085 | 398 | 5,984 R | 61.4% | 37.0% | 62.4% | 37.6% |
| 52,531 | VERNON | 15,229 | 11,032 | 4,035 | 162 | 6,997 R | 72.4% | 26.5% | 73.2% | 26.8% |
| 43,926 | WASHINGTON | 17,841 | 11,006 | 6,554 | 281 | 4,452 R | 61.7% | 36.7% | 62.7% | 37.3% |
| 41,831 | WEBSTER | 18,449 | 11,070 | 6,833 | 546 | 4,237 R | 60.0% | 37.0% | 61.8% | 38.2% |

# LOUISIANA

## PRESIDENT 2004

| 2000 Census Population | Parish | Total Vote | Republican | Democratic | Other | Rep.-Dem. Plurality | Percentage | | | |
|---|---|---|---|---|---|---|---|---|---|---|
| | | | | | | | Total Vote | | Major Vote | |
| | | | | | | | Rep. | Dem. | Rep. | Dem. |
| 21,601 | WEST BATON ROUGE | 10,835 | 5,822 | 4,932 | 81 | 890 R | 53.7% | 45.5% | 54.1% | 45.9% |
| 12,314 | WEST CARROLL | 5,033 | 3,740 | 1,231 | 62 | 2,509 R | 74.3% | 24.5% | 75.2% | 24.8% |
| 15,111 | WEST FELICIANA | 5,218 | 2,932 | 2,214 | 72 | 718 R | 56.2% | 42.4% | 57.0% | 43.0% |
| 16,894 | WINN | 6,507 | 4,366 | 2,056 | 85 | 2,310 R | 67.1% | 31.6% | 68.0% | 32.0% |
| 4,468,976 | TOTAL | 1,943,106 | 1,102,169 | 820,299 | 20,638 | 281,870 R | 56.7% | 42.2% | 57.3% | 42.7% |

# LOUISIANA

## GOVERNOR 2003 (RUNOFF)

| 2000 Census Population | Parish | Total Vote | Republican (Jindal) | Democratic (Blanco) | Other | Rep.-Dem. Plurality | Percentage | | | |
|---|---|---|---|---|---|---|---|---|---|---|
| | | | | | | | Total Vote | | Major Vote | |
| | | | | | | | Rep. | Dem. | Rep. | Dem. |
| 58,861 | ACADIA | 19,164 | 8,226 | 10,938 | | 2,712 D | 42.9% | 57.1% | 42.9% | 57.1% |
| 25,440 | ALLEN | 6,611 | 2,109 | 4,502 | | 2,393 D | 31.9% | 68.1% | 31.9% | 68.1% |
| 76,627 | ASCENSION | 30,005 | 16,272 | 13,733 | | 2,539 R | 54.2% | 45.8% | 54.2% | 45.8% |
| 23,388 | ASSUMPTION | 9,436 | 3,470 | 5,966 | | 2,496 D | 36.8% | 63.2% | 36.8% | 63.2% |
| 41,481 | AVOYELLES | 11,726 | 3,395 | 8,331 | | 4,936 D | 29.0% | 71.0% | 29.0% | 71.0% |
| 32,986 | BEAUREGARD | 8,421 | 4,165 | 4,256 | | 91 D | 49.5% | 50.5% | 49.5% | 50.5% |
| 15,752 | BIENVILLE | 5,213 | 1,953 | 3,260 | | 1,307 D | 37.5% | 62.5% | 37.5% | 62.5% |
| 98,310 | BOSSIER | 24,382 | 15,331 | 9,051 | | 6,280 R | 62.9% | 37.1% | 62.9% | 37.1% |
| 252,161 | CADDO | 67,296 | 33,004 | 34,292 | | 1,288 D | 49.0% | 51.0% | 49.0% | 51.0% |
| 183,577 | CALCASIEU | 52,518 | 24,835 | 27,683 | | 2,848 D | 47.3% | 52.7% | 47.3% | 52.7% |
| 10,560 | CALDWELL | 3,831 | 1,346 | 2,485 | | 1,139 D | 35.1% | 64.9% | 35.1% | 64.9% |
| 9,991 | CAMERON | 4,637 | 1,783 | 2,854 | | 1,071 D | 38.5% | 61.5% | 38.5% | 61.5% |
| 10,920 | CATAHOULA | 3,439 | 1,010 | 2,429 | | 1,419 D | 29.4% | 70.6% | 29.4% | 70.6% |
| 16,851 | CLAIBORNE | 4,424 | 2,074 | 2,350 | | 276 D | 46.9% | 53.1% | 46.9% | 53.1% |
| 20,247 | CONCORDIA | 8,673 | 3,119 | 5,554 | | 2,435 D | 36.0% | 64.0% | 36.0% | 64.0% |
| 25,494 | DE SOTO | 7,605 | 3,425 | 4,180 | | 755 D | 45.0% | 55.0% | 45.0% | 55.0% |
| 412,852 | EAST BATON ROUGE | 133,185 | 70,547 | 62,638 | | 7,909 R | 53.0% | 47.0% | 53.0% | 47.0% |
| 9,421 | EAST CARROLL | 2,269 | 696 | 1,573 | | 877 D | 30.7% | 69.3% | 30.7% | 69.3% |
| 21,360 | EAST FELICIANA | 7,167 | 2,735 | 4,432 | | 1,697 D | 38.2% | 61.8% | 38.2% | 61.8% |
| 35,434 | EVANGELINE | 11,391 | 3,442 | 7,949 | | 4,507 D | 30.2% | 69.8% | 30.2% | 69.8% |
| 21,263 | FRANKLIN | 6,579 | 2,541 | 4,038 | | 1,497 D | 38.6% | 61.4% | 38.6% | 61.4% |
| 18,698 | GRANT | 5,849 | 2,344 | 3,505 | | 1,161 D | 40.1% | 59.9% | 40.1% | 59.9% |
| 73,266 | IBERIA | 23,829 | 9,446 | 14,383 | | 4,937 D | 39.6% | 60.4% | 39.6% | 60.4% |
| 33,320 | IBERVILLE | 12,739 | 4,240 | 8,499 | | 4,259 D | 33.3% | 66.7% | 33.3% | 66.7% |
| 15,397 | JACKSON | 6,309 | 2,717 | 3,592 | | 875 D | 43.1% | 56.9% | 43.1% | 56.9% |
| 455,466 | JEFFERSON | 140,031 | 87,712 | 52,319 | | 35,393 R | 62.6% | 37.4% | 62.6% | 37.4% |
| 31,435 | JEFFERSON DAVIS | 9,088 | 3,886 | 5,202 | | 1,316 D | 42.8% | 57.2% | 42.8% | 57.2% |
| 190,503 | LAFAYETTE | 67,685 | 34,951 | 32,734 | | 2,217 R | 51.6% | 48.4% | 51.6% | 48.4% |
| 89,974 | LAFOURCHE | 29,124 | 13,429 | 15,695 | | 2,266 D | 46.1% | 53.9% | 46.1% | 53.9% |
| 14,282 | LA SALLE | 4,891 | 1,917 | 2,974 | | 1,057 D | 39.2% | 60.8% | 39.2% | 60.8% |
| 42,509 | LINCOLN | 10,874 | 5,194 | 5,680 | | 486 D | 47.8% | 52.2% | 47.8% | 52.2% |
| 91,814 | LIVINGSTON | 31,263 | 17,812 | 13,451 | | 4,361 R | 57.0% | 43.0% | 57.0% | 43.0% |
| 13,728 | MADISON | 3,695 | 948 | 2,747 | | 1,799 D | 25.7% | 74.3% | 25.7% | 74.3% |
| 31,021 | MOREHOUSE | 8,511 | 3,594 | 4,917 | | 1,323 D | 42.2% | 57.8% | 42.2% | 57.8% |
| 39,080 | NATCHITOCHES | 10,811 | 4,681 | 6,130 | | 1,449 D | 43.3% | 56.7% | 43.3% | 56.7% |
| 484,674 | ORLEANS | 135,751 | 43,005 | 92,746 | | 49,741 D | 31.7% | 68.3% | 31.7% | 68.3% |
| 147,250 | OUACHITA | 42,685 | 22,491 | 20,194 | | 2,297 R | 52.7% | 47.3% | 52.7% | 47.3% |
| 26,757 | PLAQUEMINES | 10,601 | 5,645 | 4,956 | | 689 R | 53.2% | 46.8% | 53.2% | 46.8% |
| 22,763 | POINTE COUPEE | 9,449 | 3,351 | 6,098 | | 2,747 D | 35.5% | 64.5% | 35.5% | 64.5% |
| 126,337 | RAPIDES | 37,067 | 16,192 | 20,875 | | 4,683 D | 43.7% | 56.3% | 43.7% | 56.3% |

# LOUISIANA

## GOVERNOR 2003 (RUNOFF)

| 2000 Census Population | Parish | Total Vote | Republican (Jindal) | Democratic (Blanco) | Other | Rep.-Dem. Plurality | | Percentage | | | |
|---|---|---|---|---|---|---|---|---|---|---|---|
| | | | | | | | | Total Vote | | Major Vote | |
| | | | | | | | | Rep. | Dem. | Rep. | Dem. |
| 9,622 | RED RIVER | 3,447 | 1,318 | 2,129 | | 811 | D | 38.2% | 61.8% | 38.2% | 61.8% |
| 20,981 | RICHLAND | 6,504 | 2,773 | 3,731 | | 958 | D | 42.6% | 57.4% | 42.6% | 57.4% |
| 23,459 | SABINE | 6,198 | 3,140 | 3,058 | | 82 | R | 50.7% | 49.3% | 50.7% | 49.3% |
| 67,229 | ST. BERNARD | 25,002 | 14,428 | 10,574 | | 3,854 | R | 57.7% | 42.3% | 57.7% | 42.3% |
| 48,072 | ST. CHARLES | 18,627 | 10,727 | 7,900 | | 2,827 | R | 57.6% | 42.4% | 57.6% | 42.4% |
| 10,525 | ST. HELENA | 5,240 | 1,322 | 3,918 | | 2,596 | D | 25.2% | 74.8% | 25.2% | 74.8% |
| 21,216 | ST. JAMES | 9,169 | 3,442 | 5,727 | | 2,285 | D | 37.5% | 62.5% | 37.5% | 62.5% |
| 43,044 | ST. JOHN THE BAPTIST | 17,617 | 8,135 | 9,482 | | 1,347 | D | 46.2% | 53.8% | 46.2% | 53.8% |
| 87,700 | ST. LANDRY | 28,549 | 9,049 | 19,500 | | 10,451 | D | 31.7% | 68.3% | 31.7% | 68.3% |
| 48,583 | ST. MARTIN | 17,666 | 6,259 | 11,407 | | 5,148 | D | 35.4% | 64.6% | 35.4% | 64.6% |
| 53,500 | ST. MARY | 16,855 | 7,088 | 9,767 | | 2,679 | D | 42.1% | 57.9% | 42.1% | 57.9% |
| 191,268 | ST. TAMMANY | 66,742 | 49,675 | 17,067 | | 32,608 | R | 74.4% | 25.6% | 74.4% | 25.6% |
| 100,588 | TANGIPAHOA | 34,625 | 16,711 | 17,914 | | 1,203 | D | 48.3% | 51.7% | 48.3% | 51.7% |
| 6,618 | TENSAS | 2,957 | 919 | 2,038 | | 1,119 | D | 31.1% | 68.9% | 31.1% | 68.9% |
| 104,503 | TERREBONNE | 30,723 | 14,626 | 16,097 | | 1,471 | D | 47.6% | 52.4% | 47.6% | 52.4% |
| 22,803 | UNION | 7,113 | 3,501 | 3,612 | | 111 | D | 49.2% | 50.8% | 49.2% | 50.8% |
| 53,807 | VERMILION | 22,168 | 7,863 | 14,305 | | 6,442 | D | 35.5% | 64.5% | 35.5% | 64.5% |
| 52,531 | VERNON | 9,574 | 4,133 | 5,441 | | 1,308 | D | 43.2% | 56.8% | 43.2% | 56.8% |
| 43,926 | WASHINGTON | 15,106 | 6,501 | 8,605 | | 2,104 | D | 43.0% | 57.0% | 43.0% | 57.0% |
| 41,831 | WEBSTER | 13,178 | 6,251 | 6,927 | | 676 | D | 47.4% | 52.6% | 47.4% | 52.6% |
| 21,601 | WEST BATON ROUGE | 9,043 | 4,120 | 4,923 | | 803 | D | 45.6% | 54.4% | 45.6% | 54.4% |
| 12,314 | WEST CARROLL | 4,379 | 1,950 | 2,429 | | 479 | D | 44.5% | 55.5% | 44.5% | 55.5% |
| 15,111 | WEST FELICIANA | 4,183 | 1,612 | 2,571 | | 959 | D | 38.5% | 61.5% | 38.5% | 61.5% |
| 16,894 | WINN | 4,953 | 1,908 | 3,045 | | 1,137 | D | 38.5% | 61.5% | 38.5% | 61.5% |
| 4,468,976 | TOTAL | 1,407,842 | 676,484 | 731,358 | | 54,874 | D | 48.1% | 51.9% | 48.1% | 51.9% |

# LOUISIANA

## SENATOR 2004 (FIRST ROUND)

| 2000 Census Population | Parish | Total Vote | Vitter (R) | John (D) | Kennedy (D) | Other | Plurality | Winner | Percentage of Total Vote | | |
|---|---|---|---|---|---|---|---|---|---|---|---|
| | | | | | | | | | Vitter (R) | John (D) | Kennedy (D) |
| 58,861 | ACADIA | 25,079 | 10,193 | 13,401 | 1,045 | 440 | 3,208 | John | 40.6% | 53.4% | 4.2% |
| 25,440 | ALLEN | 8,660 | 3,418 | 3,797 | 1,006 | 439 | 379 | John | 39.5% | 43.8% | 11.6% |
| 76,627 | ASCENSION | 38,368 | 21,641 | 9,753 | 5,848 | 1,126 | 11,888 | Vitter | 56.4% | 25.4% | 15.2% |
| 23,388 | ASSUMPTION | 9,991 | 3,803 | 3,612 | 1,996 | 580 | 191 | Vitter | 38.1% | 36.2% | 20.0% |
| 41,481 | AVOYELLES | 14,520 | 6,177 | 5,333 | 2,350 | 660 | 844 | Vitter | 42.5% | 36.7% | 16.2% |
| 32,986 | BEAUREGARD | 12,088 | 7,472 | 3,200 | 982 | 434 | 4,272 | Vitter | 61.8% | 26.5% | 8.1% |
| 15,752 | BIENVILLE | 6,550 | 3,131 | 1,977 | 1,147 | 295 | 1,154 | Vitter | 47.8% | 30.2% | 17.5% |
| 98,310 | BOSSIER | 38,049 | 25,000 | 8,051 | 4,114 | 884 | 16,949 | Vitter | 65.7% | 21.2% | 10.8% |
| 252,161 | CADDO | 100,636 | 48,571 | 28,931 | 19,933 | 3,201 | 19,640 | Vitter | 48.3% | 28.7% | 19.8% |
| 183,577 | CALCASIEU | 77,935 | 35,284 | 35,056 | 5,789 | 1,806 | 228 | Vitter | 45.3% | 45.0% | 7.4% |
| 10,560 | CALDWELL | 4,496 | 2,564 | 1,001 | 685 | 246 | 1,563 | Vitter | 57.0% | 22.3% | 15.2% |
| 9,991 | CAMERON | 4,368 | 1,967 | 1,904 | 353 | 144 | 63 | Vitter | 45.0% | 43.6% | 8.1% |
| 10,920 | CATAHOULA | 4,511 | 2,290 | 1,246 | 697 | 278 | 1,044 | Vitter | 50.8% | 27.6% | 15.5% |
| 16,851 | CLAIBORNE | 5,927 | 3,162 | 1,607 | 948 | 210 | 1,555 | Vitter | 53.3% | 27.1% | 16.0% |
| 20,247 | CONCORDIA | 8,282 | 4,307 | 2,449 | 1,051 | 475 | 1,858 | Vitter | 52.0% | 29.6% | 12.7% |
| 25,494 | DE SOTO | 10,373 | 5,064 | 3,214 | 1,805 | 290 | 1,850 | Vitter | 48.8% | 31.0% | 17.4% |
| 412,852 | EAST BATON ROUGE | 178,095 | 88,925 | 50,844 | 31,367 | 6,959 | 38,081 | Vitter | 49.9% | 28.5% | 17.6% |
| 9,421 | EAST CARROLL | 3,130 | 1,127 | 703 | 1,097 | 203 | 30 | Vitter | 36.0% | 22.5% | 35.0% |
| 21,360 | EAST FELICIANA | 8,866 | 4,185 | 2,453 | 1,746 | 482 | 1,732 | Vitter | 47.2% | 27.7% | 19.7% |
| 35,434 | EVANGELINE | 13,277 | 5,569 | 6,052 | 1,096 | 560 | 483 | John | 41.9% | 45.6% | 8.3% |

# LOUISIANA

## SENATOR 2004 (FIRST ROUND)

| 2000 Census Population | Parish | Total Vote | Vitter (R) | John (D) | Kennedy (D) | Other | Plurality | Winner | Percentage of Total Vote Vitter (R) | John (D) | Kennedy (D) |
|---|---|---|---|---|---|---|---|---|---|---|---|
| 21,263 | FRANKLIN | 8,554 | 5,033 | 1,739 | 1,390 | 392 | 3,294 | Vitter | 58.8% | 20.3% | 16.2% |
| 18,698 | GRANT | 7,235 | 4,558 | 1,537 | 840 | 300 | 3,021 | Vitter | 63.0% | 21.2% | 11.6% |
| 73,266 | IBERIA | 29,859 | 14,138 | 11,058 | 3,316 | 1,347 | 3,080 | Vitter | 47.3% | 37.0% | 11.1% |
| 33,320 | IBERVILLE | 13,756 | 4,828 | 4,992 | 3,143 | 793 | 164 | John | 35.1% | 36.3% | 22.8% |
| 15,397 | JACKSON | 7,021 | 4,120 | 1,630 | 966 | 305 | 2,490 | Vitter | 58.7% | 23.2% | 13.8% |
| 455,466 | JEFFERSON | 184,074 | 113,838 | 38,419 | 23,767 | 8,050 | 75,419 | Vitter | 61.8% | 20.9% | 12.9% |
| 31,435 | JEFFERSON DAVIS | 12,365 | 5,336 | 5,841 | 811 | 377 | 505 | John | 43.2% | 47.2% | 6.6% |
| 190,503 | LAFAYETTE | 86,328 | 44,433 | 33,959 | 5,428 | 2,508 | 10,474 | Vitter | 51.5% | 39.3% | 6.3% |
| 89,974 | LAFOURCHE | 35,092 | 18,818 | 9,816 | 4,840 | 1,618 | 9,002 | Vitter | 53.6% | 28.0% | 13.8% |
| 14,282 | LA SALLE | 5,918 | 4,065 | 949 | 607 | 297 | 3,116 | Vitter | 68.7% | 16.0% | 10.3% |
| 42,509 | LINCOLN | 17,055 | 9,412 | 4,885 | 2,116 | 642 | 4,527 | Vitter | 55.2% | 28.6% | 12.4% |
| 91,814 | LIVINGSTON | 42,132 | 28,218 | 6,785 | 5,694 | 1,435 | 21,433 | Vitter | 67.0% | 16.1% | 13.5% |
| 13,728 | MADISON | 4,551 | 1,824 | 1,639 | 795 | 293 | 185 | Vitter | 40.1% | 36.0% | 17.5% |
| 31,021 | MOREHOUSE | 11,914 | 6,143 | 3,179 | 2,003 | 589 | 2,964 | Vitter | 51.6% | 26.7% | 16.8% |
| 39,080 | NATCHITOCHES | 15,999 | 7,600 | 4,353 | 3,417 | 629 | 3,247 | Vitter | 47.5% | 27.2% | 21.4% |
| 484,674 | ORLEANS | 187,306 | 42,775 | 68,110 | 53,571 | 22,850 | 25,335 | John | 22.8% | 36.4% | 28.6% |
| 147,250 | OUACHITA | 60,981 | 36,889 | 12,470 | 9,448 | 2,174 | 24,419 | Vitter | 60.5% | 20.4% | 15.5% |
| 26,757 | PLAQUEMINES | 11,590 | 7,031 | 2,185 | 1,569 | 805 | 4,846 | Vitter | 60.7% | 18.9% | 13.5% |
| 22,763 | POINTE COUPEE | 10,575 | 4,372 | 3,862 | 1,815 | 526 | 510 | Vitter | 41.3% | 36.5% | 17.2% |
| 126,337 | RAPIDES | 50,587 | 27,367 | 14,456 | 6,367 | 2,397 | 12,911 | Vitter | 54.1% | 28.6% | 12.6% |
| 9,622 | RED RIVER | 4,348 | 1,989 | 1,341 | 816 | 202 | 648 | Vitter | 45.7% | 30.8% | 18.8% |
| 20,981 | RICHLAND | 8,238 | 4,707 | 1,675 | 1,519 | 337 | 3,032 | Vitter | 57.1% | 20.3% | 18.4% |
| 23,459 | SABINE | 8,730 | 5,368 | 2,013 | 1,070 | 279 | 3,355 | Vitter | 61.5% | 23.1% | 12.3% |
| 67,229 | ST. BERNARD | 28,866 | 18,091 | 6,052 | 3,603 | 1,120 | 12,039 | Vitter | 62.7% | 21.0% | 12.5% |
| 48,072 | ST. CHARLES | 22,347 | 13,223 | 4,628 | 3,403 | 1,093 | 8,595 | Vitter | 59.2% | 20.7% | 15.2% |
| 10,525 | ST. HELENA | 5,067 | 1,905 | 1,736 | 983 | 443 | 169 | Vitter | 37.6% | 34.3% | 19.4% |
| 21,216 | ST. JAMES | 10,377 | 3,735 | 3,231 | 2,880 | 531 | 504 | Vitter | 36.0% | 31.1% | 27.8% |
| 43,044 | ST. JOHN THE BAPTIST | 18,441 | 8,079 | 4,936 | 4,203 | 1,223 | 3,143 | Vitter | 43.8% | 26.8% | 22.8% |
| 87,700 | ST. LANDRY | 35,875 | 13,199 | 18,452 | 3,021 | 1,203 | 5,253 | John | 36.8% | 51.4% | 8.4% |
| 48,583 | ST. MARTIN | 22,351 | 8,638 | 10,725 | 2,074 | 914 | 2,087 | John | 38.6% | 48.0% | 9.3% |
| 53,500 | ST. MARY | 21,249 | 10,387 | 6,818 | 2,851 | 1,193 | 3,569 | Vitter | 48.9% | 32.1% | 13.4% |
| 191,268 | ST. TAMMANY | 97,604 | 73,466 | 13,012 | 8,525 | 2,601 | 60,454 | Vitter | 75.3% | 13.3% | 8.7% |
| 100,588 | TANGIPAHOA | 41,226 | 26,153 | 8,553 | 5,163 | 1,357 | 17,600 | Vitter | 63.4% | 20.7% | 12.5% |
| 6,618 | TENSAS | 2,765 | 1,145 | 881 | 554 | 185 | 264 | Vitter | 41.4% | 31.9% | 20.0% |
| 104,503 | TERREBONNE | 37,761 | 21,806 | 8,954 | 5,087 | 1,914 | 12,852 | Vitter | 57.7% | 23.7% | 13.5% |
| 22,803 | UNION | 10,047 | 6,378 | 1,948 | 1,383 | 338 | 4,430 | Vitter | 63.5% | 19.4% | 13.8% |
| 53,807 | VERMILION | 23,407 | 9,916 | 11,343 | 1,501 | 647 | 1,427 | John | 42.4% | 48.5% | 6.4% |
| 52,531 | VERNON | 13,707 | 7,977 | 3,903 | 1,235 | 592 | 4,074 | Vitter | 58.2% | 28.5% | 9.0% |
| 43,926 | WASHINGTON | 16,796 | 10,008 | 3,996 | 2,035 | 757 | 6,012 | Vitter | 59.6% | 23.8% | 12.1% |
| 41,831 | WEBSTER | 17,223 | 9,352 | 4,524 | 2,634 | 713 | 4,828 | Vitter | 54.3% | 26.3% | 15.3% |
| 21,601 | WEST BATON ROUGE | 10,528 | 4,806 | 3,257 | 1,969 | 496 | 1,549 | Vitter | 45.6% | 30.9% | 18.7% |
| 12,314 | WEST CARROLL | 4,241 | 2,517 | 853 | 646 | 225 | 1,664 | Vitter | 59.3% | 20.1% | 15.2% |
| 15,111 | WEST FELICIANA | 4,762 | 2,248 | 1,376 | 942 | 196 | 872 | Vitter | 47.2% | 28.9% | 19.8% |
| 16,894 | WINN | 6,007 | 3,273 | 1,495 | 766 | 473 | 1,778 | Vitter | 54.5% | 24.9% | 12.8% |
| 4,468,976 | TOTAL | 1,848,056 | 943,014 | 542,150 | 275,821 | 87,071 | 400,864 | Vitter | 51.0% | 29.3% | 14.9% |

# LOUISIANA

## HOUSE OF REPRESENTATIVES

| CD | Year | Total Vote | Republican Vote | Republican Candidate | Democratic Vote | Democratic Candidate | Other Vote | Rep.-Dem. Plurality | Total Vote Rep. | Total Vote Dem. | Major Vote Rep. | Major Vote Dem. |
|---|---|---|---|---|---|---|---|---|---|---|---|---|
| 1 | 2004 | 287,897 | 225,708 | Jindal, Bobby | 19,266 | Armstrong, Roy | 42,923 | 206,442 R | 78.4% | 6.7% | | |
| 1 | 2002 | 180,570 | 147,117 | Vitter, David* | | | 33,453 | 147,117 R | 81.5% | | | |
| 2 | 2004 | 219,607 | 46,097 | Schwertz, Arthur L. "Art" | 173,510 | Jefferson, William J.* | | 127,413 D | 21.0% | 79.0% | 21.0% | 79.0% |
| 2 | 2002 | 142,156 | 15,440 | Sullivan, "Silky" | 90,310 | Jefferson, William J.* | 36,406 | 74,870 D | 10.9% | 63.5% | | |
| 3 | 2004# | 114,653 | 57,042 | Tauzin, W.J. "Billy" III | 57,611 | Melancon, Charlie | | 569 D | 49.8% | 50.2% | 49.8% | 50.2% |
| 3 | 2002 | 150,342 | 130,323 | Tauzin, Billy* | | | 20,019 | 130,323 R | 86.7% | | 100.0% | |
| 4 | 2004 | | | McCrery, Jim* | | | | R | | | | |
| 4 | 2002 | 160,093 | 114,649 | McCrery, Jim* | 42,340 | Milkovich, John | 3,104 | 72,309 R | 71.6% | 26.4% | 73.0% | 27.0% |
| 5 | 2004 | 238,057 | 141,495 | Alexander, Rodney* | 58,591 | Blakes, Zelma "Tisa" | 37,971 | 82,904 R | 59.4% | 24.6% | | |
| 5 | 2002# | 172,462 | 85,744 | Fletcher, Lee | 86,718 | Alexander, Rodney | | 974 D | 49.7% | 50.3% | 49.7% | 50.3% |
| 6 | 2004 | 261,869 | 189,106 | Baker, Richard H.* | 50,732 | Craig, Rufus Holt Jr. | 22,031 | 138,374 R | 72.2% | 19.4% | | |
| 6 | 2002 | 174,830 | 146,932 | Baker, Richard H.* | | | 27,898 | 146,932 R | 84.0% | | 100.0% | |
| 7 | 2004# | 136,532 | 75,039 | Boustany, Charles Jr. | 61,493 | Mount, Willie Landry | | 13,546 R | 55.0% | 45.0% | 55.0% | 45.0% |
| 7 | 2002 | 159,710 | | | 138,659 | John, Chris* | 21,051 | 138,659 D | | 86.8% | | 100.0% |
| Total | 2004 | 1,545,982 | 936,801 | | 609,181 | | | 327,620 R | 60.6% | 39.4% | 60.6% | 39.4% |
| Total | 2002 | 1,152,358 | 707,923 | | 361,473 | | 82,962 | 346,450 R | 61.4% | 31.4% | 66.2% | 33.8% |

An asterisk (*) denotes incumbent.

Note: Louisiana has a unique two-tier electoral system, with a first round of voting that features candidates from all parties running together on the same ballot. A candidate that wins a majority of the vote in the first round is elected. Otherwise, the top two finishers meet in a runoff. In 2002, one runoff for the House of Representatives was required; in 2004 there were two. In these three cases, the runoff results are listed and indicated by a pound sign (#). In elections that did not require a runoff, the leading Democratic and Republican candidates are listed with their first-round votes. The votes for other candidates are listed in the other vote column, regardless of whether they were Democratic, Republican, or unaffiliated with either party. However, the statewide vote total represents the aggregate vote for all House candidates of each party in the November balloting, not just the top contenders. The major party vote percentages are given for those elections where there was no more than one Democratic and one Republican candidate.

# LOUISIANA

## GENERAL AND PRIMARY ELECTIONS

## 2003–2004 GENERAL ELECTIONS

**President**     Other vote was 7,032 The Better Life (Ralph Nader); 5,203 Constitution (Michael Peroutka); 2,781 Libertarian (Michael Badnarik); 1,795 Protecting Working Families (Walter Brown); 1,566 Prohibition (Gene Amondson); 1,276 Louisiana Green (David Cobb); 985 Socialist Workers (James Harris).

Note:     Louisiana has a unique two-tier election system that governs contests for governor and other federal offices besides president. Listed below are candidates who did not finish among the top two vote-getters in races that were decided in the first round of voting. The complete first-round results for contests that were eventually decided in runoffs are presented in the primary elections section on p. 215.

**Governor (2003)**

**Senator**     Other vote was 275,821 Democrat (John Kennedy); 47,222 Democrat (Arthur A. Morrell); 15,097 Other (Richard M. Fontanesi); 12,463 Other (R.A. "Skip" Galan); 12,289 Democrat (Sam Houston Melton Jr.).

**House**     Other vote was:

  CD 1     12,779 Democrat (M.V. "Vinny" Mendoza); 12,135 Democrat (Daniel Zimmerman); 10,034 Democrat ("Jerry" Watts); 7,975 Republican ("Mike" Rogers).

  CD 2
  CD 3
  CD 4
  CD 5     37,971 Republican (John W. "Jock" Scott).
  CD 6     22,031 Democrat (Edward Anthony "Scott" Galmon).
  CD 7

## 2003–2004 PRIMARY ELECTIONS

| | | | | |
|---|---|---|---|---|
| **Primary** | March 9, 2004 (President) | **Registration** (as of Nov. 2, 2004) | Republican | 700,691 |
| | | | Democratic | 1,618,431 |
| **Open Election** | October 4, 2003 (Governor) November 2, 2004 | | Other | 604,273 |
| | | | TOTAL | 2,923,395 |
| **Runoff Election** | November 15, 2003 (Governor) December 4, 2004 (Congress) | | | |

**Primary Type**     Louisiana had a closed presidential primary. Only registered Democrats and Republicans could participate. For governor and other federal offices, Louisiana has a two-tier electoral system open to all voters, with a first round of voting (sometimes called an open primary) that features candidates from all parties running together on the same ballot. A candidate that wins a majority of the vote in the first round is elected. Otherwise, there is a runoff held several weeks later between the top two finishers, regardless of party. Runoffs were necessary for governor in 2003 and two House seats in 2004.

# LOUISIANA

## GENERAL AND PRIMARY ELECTIONS

Note:   An asterisk (*) denotes incumbent. An "O" indicates "Other," the designation for a candidate in Louisiana who did not file as a Democrat or Republican. A pound sign (#) indicates the candidate qualified for a runoff. Listed below are the results from the Democratic and Republican presidential primaries, as well as first-round results for contests that were eventually decided in a runoff. The names of unopposed candidates did not appear on the first-round ballot; therefore, no votes were cast for these candidates.

| | REPUBLICAN PRIMARIES | | | DEMOCRATIC PRIMARIES | | |
|---|---|---|---|---|---|---|
| President | George W. Bush* | 69,205 | 96.1% | John Kerry | 112,639 | 69.7% |
| | "Bill" Wyatt | 2,805 | 3.9% | John Edwards | 26,074 | 16.1% |
| | | | | Howard Dean | 7,948 | 4.9% |
| | | | | Wesley Clark | 7,091 | 4.4% |
| | | | | "Bill" McGaughey | 3,161 | 2.0% |
| | | | | Dennis J. Kucinich | 2,411 | 1.5% |
| | | | | Lyndon H. LaRouche Jr. | 2,329 | 1.4% |
| | TOTAL | 72,010 | | TOTAL | 161,653 | |

## FIRST-ROUND VOTE (2003–2004)

| | | | | |
|---|---|---|---|---|
| Governor (2003) | Bobby Jindal (R)# | 443,389 | 32.5% | |
| | Kathleen Babineaux Blanco (D)# | 250,136 | 18.4% | |
| | Richard Leyoub (D) | 223,513 | 16.4% | |
| | Claude "Buddy" Leach (D) | 187,872 | 13.8% | |
| | Randy Ewing (D) | 123,936 | 9.1% | |
| | "Hunt" Downer (R) | 84,718 | 6.2% | |
| | Alan Allgood (R) | 7,866 | 0.6% | |
| | Patrick Henry "Dat" Barthel (D) | 7,338 | 0.5% | |
| | Patrick "Live Wire" Landry (O) | 7,195 | 0.5% | |
| | Edward "Eddie" Mangin (O) | 6,745 | 0.5% | |
| | J.D. "Boudreaux" Estilette (O) | 6,439 | 0.5% | |
| | J.E. Jumonville Jr. (D) | 3,410 | 0.3% | |
| | John M. "Doc" Simoneaux Jr. (O) | 3,280 | 0.2% | |
| | Quentin R. Brown Jr. (O) | 2,414 | 0.2% | |
| | "Mike" Stagg (D) | 1,667 | 0.1% | |
| | Richard McCoy (D) | 1,513 | 0.1% | |
| | Fred Robertson (D) | 1,093 | 0.1% | |
| | TOTAL | 1,362,524 | | |
| Congressional District 3 | W.J. "Billy" Tauzin III (R)# | 84,680 | 32.0% | |
| | Charlie Melancon (D)# | 63,328 | 23.9% | |
| | Craig Romero (R) | 61,132 | 23.1% | |
| | Damon J. Baldone (D) | 25,783 | 9.7% | |
| | Charmaine Degruise Caccioppi (D) | 19,347 | 7.3% | |
| | Kevin D. Chiasson (R) | 10,350 | 3.9% | |
| | TOTAL | 264,620 | | |
| Congressional District 7 | Charles Boustany Jr. (R)# | 105,761 | 38.6% | |
| | Willie Landry Mount (D)# | 69,079 | 25.2% | |
| | "Don" Cravins (D) | 67,389 | 24.6% | |
| | David Thibodaux (R) | 26,526 | 9.7% | |
| | Malcolm R. Carriere (D) | 5,177 | 1.9% | |
| | TOTAL | 273,932 | | |

# MAINE

## GOVERNOR
John Baldacci (D). Elected 2002 to a four-year term.

## SENATORS (2 Republicans)
Susan Collins (R). Reelected 2002 to a six-year term. Previously elected 1996.

Olympia J. Snowe (R). Reelected 2000 to a six-year term. Previously elected 1994.

## REPRESENTATIVES (2 Democrats)
1. Tom Allen (D)        2. Michael H. Michaud (D)

## POSTWAR VOTE FOR PRESIDENT

| Year | Total Vote | Republican Vote | Candidate | Democratic Vote | Candidate | Other Vote | Plurality | Total Vote Rep. | Total Vote Dem. | Major Vote Rep. | Major Vote Dem. |
|------|-----------|------|-----------|------|-----------|------|-----------|------|------|------|------|
| 2004 | 740,752 | 330,201 | Bush, George W. | 396,842 | Kerry, John | 13,709 | 66,641 D | 44.6% | 53.6% | 45.4% | 54.6% |
| 2000** | 651,817 | 286,616 | Bush, George W. | 319,951 | Gore, Al | 45,250 | 33,335 D | 44.0% | 49.1% | 47.3% | 52.7% |
| 1996** | 605,897 | 186,378 | Dole, Bob | 312,788 | Clinton, Bill | 106,731 | 126,410 D | 30.8% | 51.6% | 37.3% | 62.7% |
| 1992** | 679,499 | 206,504 | Bush, George | 263,420 | Clinton, Bill | 209,575 | 56,600 D | 30.4% | 38.8% | 43.9% | 56.1% |
| 1988 | 555,035 | 307,131 | Bush, George | 243,569 | Dukakis, Michael S. | 4,335 | 63,562 R | 55.3% | 43.9% | 55.8% | 44.2% |
| 1984 | 553,144 | 336,500 | Reagan, Ronald | 214,515 | Mondale, Walter F. | 2,129 | 121,985 R | 60.8% | 38.8% | 61.1% | 38.9% |
| 1980** | 523,011 | 238,522 | Reagan, Ronald | 220,974 | Carter, Jimmy | 63,515 | 17,548 R | 45.6% | 42.3% | 51.9% | 48.1% |
| 1976 | 483,216 | 236,320 | Ford, Gerald R. | 232,279 | Carter, Jimmy | 14,617 | 4,041 R | 48.9% | 48.1% | 50.4% | 49.6% |
| 1972 | 417,042 | 256,458 | Nixon, Richard M. | 160,584 | McGovern, George S. | | 95,874 R | 61.5% | 38.5% | 61.5% | 38.5% |
| 1968** | 392,936 | 169,254 | Nixon, Richard M. | 217,312 | Humphrey, Hubert H. | 6,370 | 48,058 D | 43.1% | 55.3% | 43.8% | 56.2% |
| 1964 | 380,965 | 118,701 | Goldwater, Barry M. | 262,264 | Johnson, Lyndon B. | | 143,563 D | 31.2% | 68.8% | 31.2% | 68.8% |
| 1960 | 421,767 | 240,608 | Nixon, Richard M. | 181,159 | Kennedy, John F. | | 59,449 R | 57.0% | 43.0% | 57.0% | 43.0% |
| 1956 | 351,706 | 249,238 | Eisenhower, Dwight D. | 102,468 | Stevenson, Adlai E. | | 146,770 R | 70.9% | 29.1% | 70.9% | 29.1% |
| 1952 | 351,786 | 232,353 | Eisenhower, Dwight D. | 118,806 | Stevenson, Adlai E. | 627 | 113,547 R | 66.0% | 33.8% | 66.2% | 33.8% |
| 1948 | 264,787 | 150,234 | Dewey, Thomas E. | 111,916 | Truman, Harry S. | 2,637 | 38,318 R | 56.7% | 42.3% | 57.3% | 42.7% |

In past elections, the other vote included: 2000 - 37,127 Green (Ralph Nader); 1996 - 85,970 Reform (Ross Perot); 1992 - 206,820 Independent (Perot), who placed second statewide; 1980 - 53,327 Independent (John Anderson); 1968 - 6,370 American Independent (George Wallace).

# MAINE

## POSTWAR VOTE FOR GOVERNOR

| Year | Total Vote | Republican Vote | Candidate | Democratic Vote | Candidate | Other Vote | Plurality | | Percentage Total Vote Rep. | Dem. | Major Vote Rep. | Dem. |
|---|---|---|---|---|---|---|---|---|---|---|---|---|
| 2002 | 505,190 | 209,496 | Cianchette, Peter E. | 238,179 | Baldacci, John | 57,515 | 28,683 | D | 41.5% | 47.1% | 46.8% | 53.2% |
| 1998** | 421,009 | 79,716 | Longley, James B., Jr. | 50,506 | Connolly, Thomas J. | 290,787 | 167,056 | I | 18.9% | 12.0% | 61.2% | 38.8% |
| 1994** | 511,308 | 117,990 | Collins, Susan | 172,951 | Brennan, Joseph E. | 220,367 | 7,878 | I | 23.1% | 33.8% | 40.6% | 59.4% |
| 1990 | 522,492 | 243,766 | McKernan, John R. | 230,038 | Brennan, Joseph E. | 48,688 | 13,728 | R | 46.7% | 44.0% | 51.4% | 48.6% |
| 1986** | 426,861 | 170,312 | McKernan, John R. | 128,744 | Tierney, James | 127,805 | 41,568 | R | 39.9% | 30.2% | 56.9% | 43.1% |
| 1982 | 460,295 | 172,949 | Cragin, Charles L. | 281,066 | Brennan, Joseph E. | 6,280 | 108,117 | D | 37.6% | 61.1% | 38.1% | 61.9% |
| 1978 | 370,258 | 126,862 | Palmer, Linwood E. | 176,493 | Brennan, Joseph E. | 66,903 | 49,631 | D | 34.3% | 47.7% | 41.8% | 58.2% |
| 1974** | 363,945 | 84,176 | Erwin, James S. | 132,219 | Mitchell, George J. | 147,550 | 10,245 | I | 23.1% | 36.3% | 38.9% | 61.1% |
| 1970 | 325,386 | 162,248 | Erwin, James S. | 163,138 | Curtis, Kenneth M. | | 890 | D | 49.9% | 50.1% | 49.9% | 50.1% |
| 1966 | 323,838 | 151,802 | Reed, John H. | 172,036 | Curtis, Kenneth M. | | 20,234 | D | 46.9% | 53.1% | 46.9% | 53.1% |
| 1962 | 292,725 | 146,604 | Reed, John H. | 146,121 | Dolloff, Maynard C. | | 483 | R | 50.1% | 49.9% | 50.1% | 49.9% |
| 1960S | 417,315 | 219,768 | Reed, John H. | 197,547 | Coffin, Frank M. | | 22,221 | R | 52.7% | 47.3% | 52.7% | 47.3% |
| 1958** | 280,295 | 134,572 | Hildreth, Horace A. | 145,723 | Clauson, Clinton A. | | 11,151 | D | 48.0% | 52.0% | 48.0% | 52.0% |
| 1956 | 304,649 | 124,395 | Trafton, Willis A. | 180,254 | Muskie, Edmund S. | | 55,859 | D | 40.8% | 59.2% | 40.8% | 59.2% |
| 1954 | 248,971 | 113,298 | Cross, Burton M. | 135,673 | Muskie, Edmund S. | | 22,375 | D | 45.5% | 54.5% | 45.5% | 54.5% |
| 1952 | 248,441 | 128,532 | Cross, Burton M. | 82,538 | Oliver, James C. | 37,371 | 45,994 | R | 51.7% | 33.2% | 60.9% | 39.1% |
| 1950 | 241,177 | 145,823 | Payne, Frederick G. | 94,304 | Grant, Earl S. | 1,050 | 51,519 | R | 60.5% | 39.1% | 60.7% | 39.3% |
| 1948 | 222,500 | 145,956 | Payne, Frederick G. | 76,544 | Lausier, Louis B. | | 69,412 | R | 65.6% | 34.4% | 65.6% | 34.4% |
| 1946 | 179,951 | 110,327 | Hildreth, Horace A. | 69,624 | Clark, F. Davis | | 40,703 | R | 61.3% | 38.7% | 61.3% | 38.7% |

In past elections, the other vote included: 1998 - 246,772 Independent (Angus King), who was reelected with 58.6 percent of the total vote; 1994 - 180,829 Independent (King), who was elected with 35.4 percent of the total vote; 1986 - 64,317 Independent (Sherry F. Huber), 63,474 Independent (John E. Menario); 1974 - 142,464 Independent (James B. Longley), who was elected with 39.1 percent of the total vote. The 1960 election was for a short term to fill a vacancy. The term of office of Maine's governor was increased from two to four years effective with the 1958 election.

## POSTWAR VOTE FOR SENATOR

| Year | Total Vote | Republican Vote | Candidate | Democratic Vote | Candidate | Other Vote | Rep.-Dem. Plurality | | Percentage Total Vote Rep. | Dem. | Major Vote Rep. | Dem. |
|---|---|---|---|---|---|---|---|---|---|---|---|---|
| 2002 | 504,899 | 295,041 | Collins, Susan | 209,858 | Pingree, Chellie | | 85,183 | R | 58.4% | 41.6% | 58.4% | 41.6% |
| 2000 | 634,872 | 437,689 | Snowe, Olympia J. | 197,183 | Lawrence, Mark | | 240,506 | R | 68.9% | 31.1% | 68.9% | 31.1% |
| 1996 | 606,777 | 298,422 | Collins, Susan | 266,226 | Brennan, Joseph E. | 42,129 | 32,196 | R | 49.2% | 43.9% | 52.9% | 47.1% |
| 1994 | 511,733 | 308,244 | Snowe, Olympia J. | 186,042 | Andrews, Thomas H. | 17,447 | 122,202 | R | 60.2% | 36.4% | 62.4% | 37.6% |
| 1990 | 520,320 | 319,167 | Cohen, William S. | 201,053 | Rolde, Neil | 100 | 118,114 | R | 61.3% | 38.6% | 61.4% | 38.6% |
| 1988 | 557,375 | 104,758 | Wyman, Jasper S. | 452,590 | Mitchell, George J. | 27 | 347,832 | D | 18.8% | 81.2% | 18.8% | 81.2% |
| 1984 | 551,406 | 404,414 | Cohen, William S. | 142,626 | Mitchell, Elizabeth H. | 4,366 | 261,788 | R | 73.3% | 25.9% | 73.9% | 26.1% |
| 1982 | 459,715 | 179,882 | Emery, David F. | 279,819 | Mitchell, George J. | 14 | 99,937 | D | 39.1% | 60.9% | 39.1% | 60.9% |
| 1978 | 375,172 | 212,294 | Cohen, William S. | 127,327 | Hathaway, William D. | 35,551 | 84,967 | R | 56.6% | 33.9% | 62.5% | 37.5% |
| 1976 | 486,254 | 193,489 | Monks, Robert A. G. | 292,704 | Muskie, Edmund S. | 61 | 99,215 | D | 39.8% | 60.2% | 39.8% | 60.2% |
| 1972 | 421,310 | 197,040 | Smith, Margaret Chase | 224,270 | Hathaway, William D. | | 27,230 | D | 46.8% | 53.2% | 46.8% | 53.2% |
| 1970 | 323,860 | 123,906 | Bishop, Neil S. | 199,954 | Muskie, Edmund S. | | 76,048 | D | 38.3% | 61.7% | 38.3% | 61.7% |
| 1966 | 319,535 | 188,291 | Smith, Margaret Chase | 131,136 | Violette, Elmer H. | 108 | 57,155 | R | 58.9% | 41.0% | 58.9% | 41.1% |
| 1964 | 380,551 | 127,040 | McIntire, Clifford | 253,511 | Muskie, Edmund S. | | 126,471 | D | 33.4% | 66.6% | 33.4% | 66.6% |
| 1960 | 416,699 | 256,890 | Smith, Margaret Chase | 159,809 | Cormier, Lucia M. | | 97,081 | R | 61.6% | 38.4% | 61.6% | 38.4% |
| 1958 | 284,226 | 111,522 | Payne, Frederick G. | 172,704 | Muskie, Edmund S. | | 61,182 | D | 39.2% | 60.8% | 39.2% | 60.8% |
| 1954 | 246,605 | 144,530 | Smith, Margaret Chase | 102,075 | Fullam, Paul A. | | 42,455 | R | 58.6% | 41.4% | 58.6% | 41.4% |
| 1952 | 237,164 | 139,205 | Payne, Frederick G. | 82,665 | Dube, Roger P. | 15,294 | 56,540 | R | 58.7% | 34.9% | 62.7% | 37.3% |
| 1948 | 223,256 | 159,182 | Smith, Margaret Chase | 64,074 | Scolten, Adrian H. | | 95,108 | R | 71.3% | 28.7% | 71.3% | 28.7% |
| 1946 | 175,014 | 111,215 | Brewster, Owen | 63,799 | MacDonald, Peter | | 47,416 | R | 63.5% | 36.5% | 63.5% | 36.5% |

# MAINE

Congressional districts first established for elections held in 2004
2 members

# MAINE

## PRESIDENT 2004

| 2000 Census Population | County | Total Vote | Republican | Democratic | Other | Rep.-Dem. Plurality | Percentage Total Vote Rep. | Dem. | Major Vote Rep. | Dem. |
|---|---|---|---|---|---|---|---|---|---|---|
| 103,793 | ANDROSCOGGIN | 56,067 | 24,519 | 30,503 | 1,045 | 5,984 D | 43.7% | 54.4% | 44.6% | 55.4% |
| 73,938 | AROOSTOOK | 37,733 | 17,564 | 19,569 | 600 | 2,005 D | 46.5% | 51.9% | 47.3% | 52.7% |
| 265,612 | CUMBERLAND | 162,962 | 65,384 | 94,846 | 2,732 | 29,462 D | 40.1% | 58.2% | 40.8% | 59.2% |
| 29,467 | FRANKLIN | 17,257 | 7,378 | 9,465 | 414 | 2,087 D | 42.8% | 54.8% | 43.8% | 56.2% |
| 51,791 | HANCOCK | 33,122 | 14,405 | 18,048 | 669 | 3,643 D | 43.5% | 54.5% | 44.4% | 55.6% |
| 117,114 | KENNEBEC | 66,772 | 29,761 | 35,616 | 1,395 | 5,855 D | 44.6% | 53.3% | 45.5% | 54.5% |
| 39,618 | KNOX | 23,247 | 10,103 | 12,690 | 454 | 2,587 D | 43.5% | 54.6% | 44.3% | 55.7% |
| 33,616 | LINCOLN | 22,142 | 10,370 | 11,351 | 421 | 981 D | 46.8% | 51.3% | 47.7% | 52.3% |
| 54,755 | OXFORD | 31,546 | 14,196 | 16,618 | 732 | 2,422 D | 45.0% | 52.7% | 46.1% | 53.9% |
| 144,919 | PENOBSCOT | 82,112 | 40,318 | 40,417 | 1,377 | 99 D | 49.1% | 49.2% | 49.9% | 50.1% |
| 17,235 | PISCATAQUIS | 9,940 | 5,299 | 4,409 | 232 | 890 R | 53.3% | 44.4% | 54.6% | 45.4% |
| 35,214 | SAGADAHOC | 21,079 | 9,497 | 11,107 | 475 | 1,610 D | 45.1% | 52.7% | 46.1% | 53.9% |
| 50,888 | SOMERSET | 27,108 | 12,953 | 13,555 | 600 | 602 D | 47.8% | 50.0% | 48.9% | 51.1% |
| 36,280 | WALDO | 22,322 | 10,309 | 11,555 | 458 | 1,246 D | 46.2% | 51.8% | 47.2% | 52.8% |
| 33,941 | WASHINGTON | 17,310 | 8,619 | 8,391 | 300 | 228 R | 49.8% | 48.5% | 50.7% | 49.3% |
| 186,742 | YORK | 110,033 | 49,526 | 58,702 | 1,805 | 9,176 D | 45.0% | 53.3% | 45.8% | 54.2% |
| 1,274,923 | TOTAL | 740,752 | 330,201 | 396,842 | 13,709 | 66,641 D | 44.6% | 53.6% | 45.4% | 54.6% |

| 2000 Census Population | City/Town | Total Vote | Republican | Democratic | Other | Rep.-Dem. Plurality | Rep. | Dem. | Rep. | Dem. |
|---|---|---|---|---|---|---|---|---|---|---|
| 23,203 | AUBURN | 12,317 | 5,219 | 6,869 | 229 | 1,650 D | 42.4% | 55.8% | 43.2% | 56.8% |
| 18,560 | AUGUSTA | 9,925 | 4,149 | 5,543 | 233 | 1,394 D | 41.8% | 55.8% | 42.8% | 57.2% |
| 31,473 | BANGOR | 16,565 | 7,135 | 9,162 | 268 | 2,027 D | 43.1% | 55.3% | 43.8% | 56.2% |
| 9,266 | BATH | 5,060 | 2,003 | 2,940 | 117 | 937 D | 39.6% | 58.1% | 40.5% | 59.5% |
| 6,381 | BELFAST | 3,879 | 1,533 | 2,270 | 76 | 737 D | 39.5% | 58.5% | 40.3% | 59.7% |
| 6,353 | BERWICK | 3,504 | 1,862 | 1,588 | 54 | 274 R | 53.1% | 45.3% | 54.0% | 46.0% |
| 20,942 | BIDDEFORD | 10,452 | 3,756 | 6,520 | 176 | 2,764 D | 35.9% | 62.4% | 36.6% | 63.4% |
| 8,987 | BREWER | 5,429 | 2,850 | 2,510 | 69 | 340 R | 52.5% | 46.2% | 53.2% | 46.8% |
| 21,172 | BRUNSWICK | 11,759 | 4,248 | 7,288 | 223 | 3,040 D | 36.1% | 62.0% | 36.8% | 63.2% |
| 7,452 | BUXTON | 4,482 | 2,252 | 2,172 | 58 | 80 R | 50.2% | 48.5% | 50.9% | 49.1% |
| 5,254 | CAMDEN | 3,483 | 1,153 | 2,277 | 53 | 1,124 D | 33.1% | 65.4% | 33.6% | 66.4% |
| 9,068 | CAPE ELIZABETH | 6,301 | 2,548 | 3,679 | 74 | 1,131 D | 40.4% | 58.4% | 40.9% | 59.1% |
| 8,312 | CARIBOU | 3,966 | 1,863 | 2,044 | 59 | 181 D | 47.0% | 51.5% | 47.7% | 52.3% |
| 7,159 | CUMBERLAND TOWN | 5,005 | 2,428 | 2,504 | 73 | 76 D | 48.5% | 50.0% | 49.2% | 50.8% |
| 5,954 | ELIOT | 3,938 | 1,721 | 2,164 | 53 | 443 D | 43.7% | 55.0% | 44.3% | 55.7% |
| 6,456 | ELLSWORTH | 4,066 | 2,096 | 1,896 | 74 | 200 R | 51.5% | 46.6% | 52.5% | 47.5% |
| 6,573 | FAIRFIELD | 3,487 | 1,492 | 1,917 | 78 | 425 D | 42.8% | 55.0% | 43.8% | 56.2% |
| 10,310 | FALMOUTH | 7,090 | 3,305 | 3,685 | 100 | 380 D | 46.6% | 52.0% | 47.3% | 52.7% |
| 7,410 | FARMINGTON | 4,125 | 1,540 | 2,484 | 101 | 944 D | 37.3% | 60.2% | 38.3% | 61.7% |
| 7,800 | FREEPORT | 5,016 | 1,906 | 3,007 | 103 | 1,101 D | 38.0% | 59.9% | 38.8% | 61.2% |
| 6,198 | GARDINER | 3,276 | 1,483 | 1,716 | 77 | 233 D | 45.3% | 52.4% | 46.4% | 53.6% |
| 14,141 | GORHAM | 8,655 | 4,133 | 4,393 | 129 | 260 D | 47.8% | 50.8% | 48.5% | 51.5% |
| 6,820 | GRAY | 4,403 | 2,208 | 2,102 | 93 | 106 R | 50.1% | 47.7% | 51.2% | 48.8% |
| 6,327 | HAMPDEN | 4,244 | 2,247 | 1,933 | 64 | 314 R | 52.9% | 45.5% | 53.8% | 46.2% |
| 5,239 | HARPSWELL | 3,654 | 1,583 | 2,004 | 67 | 421 D | 43.3% | 54.8% | 44.1% | 55.9% |
| 6,476 | HOULTON | 2,930 | 1,696 | 1,189 | 45 | 507 R | 57.9% | 40.6% | 58.8% | 41.2% |
| 4,985 | JAY | 2,817 | 974 | 1,790 | 53 | 816 D | 34.6% | 63.5% | 35.2% | 64.8% |
| 10,476 | KENNEBUNK | 7,154 | 3,328 | 3,709 | 117 | 381 D | 46.5% | 51.8% | 47.3% | 52.7% |
| 9,543 | KITTERY | 5,149 | 1,901 | 3,176 | 72 | 1,275 D | 36.9% | 61.7% | 37.4% | 62.6% |
| 35,690 | LEWISTON | 17,855 | 6,523 | 11,021 | 311 | 4,498 D | 36.5% | 61.7% | 37.2% | 62.8% |
| 2,361 | LIMESTONE | 1,034 | 441 | 574 | 19 | 133 D | 42.6% | 55.5% | 43.4% | 56.6% |
| 5,221 | LINCOLN TOWN | 2,596 | 1,461 | 1,082 | 53 | 379 R | 56.3% | 41.7% | 57.5% | 42.5% |
| 9,077 | LISBON | 4,851 | 2,374 | 2,372 | 105 | 2 R | 48.9% | 48.9% | 50.0% | 50.0% |
| 5,203 | MILLINOCKET | 2,894 | 1,188 | 1,647 | 59 | 459 D | 41.1% | 56.9% | 41.9% | 58.1% |
| 5,959 | OAKLAND | 3,281 | 1,501 | 1,716 | 64 | 215 D | 45.7% | 52.3% | 46.7% | 53.3% |

# MAINE

## PRESIDENT 2004

| 2000 Census Population | City/Town | Total Vote | Republican | Democratic | Other | Rep.-Dem. Plurality | | Percentage | | | |
|---|---|---|---|---|---|---|---|---|---|---|---|
| | | | | | | | | Total Vote | | Major Vote | |
| | | | | | | | | Rep. | Dem. | Rep. | Dem. |
| 8,856 | OLD ORCHARD BEACH | 5,428 | 2,095 | 3,240 | 93 | 1,145 | D | 38.6% | 59.7% | 39.3% | 60.7% |
| 8,130 | OLD TOWN | 4,483 | 1,674 | 2,729 | 80 | 1,055 | D | 37.3% | 60.9% | 38.0% | 62.0% |
| 9,112 | ORONO | 5,325 | 1,578 | 3,649 | 98 | 2,071 | D | 29.6% | 68.5% | 30.2% | 69.8% |
| 62,249 | PORTLAND | 36,916 | 9,455 | 26,800 | 661 | 17,345 | D | 25.6% | 72.6% | 26.1% | 73.9% |
| 9,511 | PRESQUE ISLE | 4,672 | 2,268 | 2,309 | 95 | 41 | D | 48.5% | 49.4% | 49.6% | 50.4% |
| 7,609 | ROCKLAND | 3,655 | 1,497 | 2,077 | 81 | 580 | D | 41.0% | 56.8% | 41.9% | 58.1% |
| 6,472 | RUMFORD | 3,297 | 1,151 | 2,060 | 86 | 909 | D | 34.9% | 62.5% | 35.8% | 64.2% |
| 16,822 | SACO | 9,969 | 3,948 | 5,892 | 129 | 1,944 | D | 39.6% | 59.1% | 40.1% | 59.9% |
| 20,806 | SANFORD | 10,406 | 4,634 | 5,582 | 190 | 948 | D | 44.5% | 53.6% | 45.4% | 54.6% |
| 16,970 | SCARBOROUGH | 11,355 | 5,569 | 5,651 | 135 | 82 | D | 49.0% | 49.8% | 49.6% | 50.4% |
| 8,824 | SKOWHEGAN | 4,392 | 1,798 | 2,511 | 83 | 713 | D | 40.9% | 57.2% | 41.7% | 58.3% |
| 6,671 | SOUTH BERWICK | 4,149 | 1,848 | 2,173 | 128 | 325 | D | 44.5% | 52.4% | 46.0% | 54.0% |
| 23,324 | SOUTH PORTLAND | 14,106 | 4,882 | 8,965 | 259 | 4,083 | D | 34.6% | 63.6% | 35.3% | 64.7% |
| 9,285 | STANDISH | 5,243 | 2,721 | 2,436 | 86 | 285 | R | 51.9% | 46.5% | 52.8% | 47.2% |
| 9,100 | TOPSHAM | 5,240 | 2,386 | 2,751 | 103 | 365 | D | 45.5% | 52.5% | 46.4% | 53.6% |
| 15,605 | WATERVILLE | 7,616 | 2,413 | 5,056 | 147 | 2,643 | D | 31.7% | 66.4% | 32.3% | 67.7% |
| 9,400 | WELLS | 5,779 | 2,814 | 2,879 | 86 | 65 | D | 48.7% | 49.8% | 49.4% | 50.6% |
| 16,142 | WESTBROOK | 8,929 | 3,744 | 5,047 | 138 | 1,303 | D | 41.9% | 56.5% | 42.6% | 57.4% |
| 14,904 | WINDHAM | 9,082 | 4,553 | 4,400 | 129 | 153 | R | 50.1% | 48.4% | 50.9% | 49.1% |
| 7,743 | WINSLOW | 4,369 | 1,799 | 2,492 | 78 | 693 | D | 41.2% | 57.0% | 41.9% | 58.1% |
| 6,232 | WINTHROP | 3,639 | 1,820 | 1,724 | 95 | 96 | R | 50.0% | 47.4% | 51.4% | 48.6% |
| 8,360 | YARMOUTH | 5,593 | 2,327 | 3,185 | 81 | 858 | D | 41.6% | 56.9% | 42.2% | 57.8% |
| 12,854 | YORK TOWN | 8,560 | 3,793 | 4,647 | 120 | 854 | D | 44.3% | 54.3% | 44.9% | 55.1% |

# MAINE

## HOUSE OF REPRESENTATIVES

| CD | Year | Total Vote | Republican | | Democratic | | Other Vote | Rep.-Dem. Plurality | | Percentage | | | |
|---|---|---|---|---|---|---|---|---|---|---|---|---|---|
| | | | Vote | Candidate | Vote | Candidate | | | | Total Vote | | Major Vote | |
| | | | | | | | | | | Rep. | Dem. | Rep. | Dem. |
| 1 | 2004 | 366,740 | 147,663 | Summers, Charles E. Jr. | 219,077 | Allen, Tom* | | 71,414 | D | 40.3% | 59.7% | 40.3% | 59.7% |
| 1 | 2002 | 270,577 | 97,931 | Joyce, Steven | 172,646 | Allen, Tom* | | 74,715 | D | 36.2% | 63.8% | 36.2% | 63.8% |
| 2 | 2004 | 343,436 | 135,547 | Hamel, Brian N. | 199,303 | Michaud, Michael H.* | 8,586 | 63,756 | D | 39.5% | 58.0% | 40.5% | 59.5% |
| 2 | 2002 | 224,717 | 107,849 | Raye, Kevin L. | 116,868 | Michaud, Michael H. | | 9,019 | D | 48.0% | 52.0% | 48.0% | 52.0% |
| Total | 2004 | 710,176 | 283,210 | | 418,380 | | 8,586 | 135,170 | D | 39.9% | 58.9% | 40.4% | 59.6% |
| Total | 2002 | 495,294 | 205,780 | | 289,514 | | | 83,734 | D | 41.5% | 58.5% | 41.5% | 58.5% |

An asterisk (*) denotes incumbent.

# MAINE

## GENERAL AND PRIMARY ELECTIONS

## 2004 GENERAL ELECTIONS

**President**  Other vote was 8,069 The Better Life (Ralph Nader); 2,936 Green Independent (David Cobb); 1,965 Libertarian (Michael Badnarik); 735 Constitution (Michael Peroutka); 4 write-in (Bill Van Auken).

**House**  Other vote was:

CD 1
CD 2  8,586 Socialist Equality (Carl Cooley).

## 2004 PRIMARY ELECTIONS

**Primary**  June 8, 2004

**Registration** (as of January 2004)

| | |
|---|---|
| Republican | 274,727 |
| Democratic | 297,831 |
| Green Independent | 19,006 |
| Unenrolled | 365,921 |
| TOTAL | 957,485 |

**Primary Type**  Semi-open—Registered voters in a political party could participate only in their party's primary. "Unenrolled" and new voters could vote in either party's primary by enrolling in that party on primary day.

Note:  An asterisk (*) denotes incumbent.

| | REPUBLICAN PRIMARIES | | | DEMOCRATIC PRIMARIES | | |
|---|---|---|---|---|---|---|
| Congressional District 1 | Charles E. Summers Jr. | 29,944 | 100.0% | Tom Allen* | 34,524 | 100.0% |
| Congressional District 2 | Brian N. Hamel | 23,832 | 100.0% | Michael H. Michaud* | 30,609 | 100.0% |

# MARYLAND

## GOVERNOR
Robert L. Ehrlich Jr. (R). Elected 2002 to a four-year term.

## SENATORS (2 Democrats)
Barbara A. Mikulski (D). Reelected 2004 to a six-year term. Previously elected 1998, 1992, 1986.

Paul S. Sarbanes (D). Reelected 2000 to a six-year term. Previously elected 1994, 1988, 1982, 1976.

## REPRESENTATIVES (6 Democrats, 2 Republicans)
1. Wayne T. Gilchrest (R)
2. C.A. Dutch Ruppersberger (D)
3. Benjamin L. Cardin (D)
4. Albert R. Wynn (D)
5. Steny H. Hoyer (D)
6. Roscoe G. Bartlett (R)
7. Elijah E. Cummings (D)
8. Chris Van Hollen (D)

## POSTWAR VOTE FOR PRESIDENT

| | | Republican | | Democratic | | Other | | Percentage Total Vote | | Major Vote | |
| Year | Total Vote | Vote | Candidate | Vote | Candidate | Vote | Plurality | Rep. | Dem. | Rep. | Dem. |
|---|---|---|---|---|---|---|---|---|---|---|---|
| 2004 | 2,386,678 | 1,024,703 | Bush, George W. | 1,334,493 | Kerry, John | 27,482 | 309,790 D | 42.9% | 55.9% | 43.4% | 56.6% |
| 2000** | 2,020,480 | 813,797 | Bush, George W. | 1,140,782 | Gore, Al | 65,901 | 326,985 D | 40.3% | 56.5% | 41.6% | 58.4% |
| 1996** | 1,780,870 | 681,530 | Dole, Bob | 966,207 | Clinton, Bill | 133,133 | 284,677 D | 38.3% | 54.3% | 41.4% | 58.6% |
| 1992** | 1,985,046 | 707,094 | Bush, George | 988,571 | Clinton, Bill | 289,381 | 281,477 D | 35.6% | 49.8% | 41.7% | 58.3% |
| 1988 | 1,714,358 | 876,167 | Bush, George | 826,304 | Dukakis, Michael S. | 11,887 | 49,863 R | 51.1% | 48.2% | 51.5% | 48.5% |
| 1984 | 1,675,873 | 879,918 | Reagan, Ronald | 787,935 | Mondale, Walter F. | 8,020 | 91,983 R | 52.5% | 47.0% | 52.8% | 47.2% |
| 1980** | 1,540,496 | 680,606 | Reagan, Ronald | 726,161 | Carter, Jimmy | 133,729 | 45,555 D | 44.2% | 47.1% | 48.4% | 51.6% |
| 1976 | 1,439,897 | 672,661 | Ford, Gerald R. | 759,612 | Carter, Jimmy | 7,624 | 86,951 D | 46.7% | 52.8% | 47.0% | 53.0% |
| 1972 | 1,353,812 | 829,305 | Nixon, Richard M. | 505,781 | McGovern, George S. | 18,726 | 323,524 R | 61.3% | 37.4% | 62.1% | 37.9% |
| 1968** | 1,235,039 | 517,995 | Nixon, Richard M. | 538,310 | Humphrey, Hubert H. | 178,734 | 20,315 D | 41.9% | 43.6% | 49.0% | 51.0% |
| 1964 | 1,116,457 | 385,495 | Goldwater, Barry M. | 730,912 | Johnson, Lyndon B. | 50 | 345,417 D | 34.5% | 65.5% | 34.5% | 65.5% |
| 1960 | 1,055,349 | 489,538 | Nixon, Richard M. | 565,808 | Kennedy, John F. | 3 | 76,270 D | 46.4% | 53.6% | 46.4% | 53.6% |
| 1956 | 932,827 | 559,738 | Eisenhower, Dwight D. | 372,613 | Stevenson, Adlai E. | 476 | 187,125 R | 60.0% | 39.9% | 60.0% | 40.0% |
| 1952 | 902,074 | 499,424 | Eisenhower, Dwight D. | 395,337 | Stevenson, Adlai E. | 7,313 | 104,087 R | 55.4% | 43.8% | 55.8% | 44.2% |
| 1948 | 596,748 | 294,814 | Dewey, Thomas E. | 286,521 | Truman, Harry S. | 15,413 | 8,293 R | 49.4% | 48.0% | 50.7% | 49.3% |

In past elections, the other vote included: 2000 - 53,768 Green (Ralph Nader); 1996 - 115,812 Reform (Ross Perot); 1992 - 281,414 Independent (Perot); 1980 - 119,537 Independent (John Anderson); 1968 - 178,734 American Independent (George Wallace).

# MARYLAND

## POSTWAR VOTE FOR GOVERNOR

| Year | Total Vote | Republican Vote | Republican Candidate | Democratic Vote | Democratic Candidate | Other Vote | Rep.-Dem. Plurality | Total Vote Rep. | Total Vote Dem. | Major Vote Rep. | Major Vote Dem. |
|------|-----------|------|-----------|------|-----------|------|------------|------|------|------|------|
| 2002 | 1,706,179 | 879,592 | Ehrlich, Robert L. Jr. | 813,422 | Townsend, Kathleen Kennedy | 13,165 | 66,170 R | 51.6% | 47.7% | 52.0% | 48.0% |
| 1998 | 1,535,978 | 688,357 | Sauerbrey, Ellen R. | 846,972 | Glendening, Parris N. | 649 | 158,615 D | 44.8% | 55.1% | 44.8% | 55.2% |
| 1994 | 1,410,300 | 702,101 | Sauerbrey, Ellen R. | 708,094 | Glendening, Parris N. | 105 | 5,993 D | 49.8% | 50.2% | 49.8% | 50.2% |
| 1990 | 1,111,088 | 446,980 | Shepard, William S. | 664,015 | Schaefer, William D. | 93 | 217,035 D | 40.2% | 59.8% | 40.2% | 59.8% |
| 1986 | 1,101,476 | 194,185 | Mooney, Thomas J. | 907,291 | Schaefer, William D. | | 713,106 D | 17.6% | 82.4% | 17.6% | 82.4% |
| 1982 | 1,139,149 | 432,826 | Pascal, Robert A. | 705,910 | Hughes, Harry | 413 | 273,084 D | 38.0% | 62.0% | 38.0% | 62.0% |
| 1978 | 1,011,963 | 293,635 | Beall, J. Glenn, Jr. | 718,328 | Hughes, Harry | | 424,693 D | 29.0% | 71.0% | 29.0% | 71.0% |
| 1974 | 949,097 | 346,449 | Gore, Louise | 602,648 | Mandel, Marvin | | 256,199 D | 36.5% | 63.5% | 36.5% | 63.5% |
| 1970 | 973,099 | 314,336 | Blain, C. Stanley | 639,579 | Mandel, Marvin | 19,184 | 325,243 D | 32.3% | 65.7% | 33.0% | 67.0% |
| 1966 | 918,761 | 455,318 | Agnew, Spiro T. | 373,543 | Mahoney, George P. | 89,900 | 81,775 R | 49.6% | 40.7% | 54.9% | 45.1% |
| 1962 | 775,101 | 343,051 | Small, Frank | 432,045 | Tawes, J. Millard | 5 | 88,994 D | 44.3% | 55.7% | 44.3% | 55.7% |
| 1958 | 763,234 | 278,173 | Devereux, James | 485,061 | Tawes, J. Millard | | 206,888 D | 36.4% | 63.6% | 36.4% | 63.6% |
| 1954 | 700,484 | 381,451 | McKeldin, Theodore | 319,033 | Byrd, Harry C. | | 62,418 R | 54.5% | 45.5% | 54.5% | 45.5% |
| 1950 | 645,631 | 369,807 | McKeldin, Theodore | 275,824 | Lane, William P. | | 93,983 R | 57.3% | 42.7% | 57.3% | 42.7% |
| 1946 | 489,836 | 221,752 | McKeldin, Theodore | 268,084 | Lane, William P. | | 46,332 D | 45.3% | 54.7% | 45.3% | 54.7% |

## POSTWAR VOTE FOR SENATOR

| Year | Total Vote | Republican Vote | Republican Candidate | Democratic Vote | Democratic Candidate | Other Vote | Rep.-Dem. Plurality | Total Vote Rep. | Total Vote Dem. | Major Vote Rep. | Major Vote Dem. |
|------|-----------|------|-----------|------|-----------|------|------------|------|------|------|------|
| 2004 | 2,323,183 | 783,055 | Pipkin, E.J. | 1,504,691 | Mikulski, Barbara A. | 35,437 | 721,636 D | 33.7% | 64.8% | 34.2% | 65.8% |
| 2000 | 1,946,898 | 715,178 | Rappaport, Paul | 1,230,013 | Sarbanes, Paul S. | 1,707 | 514,835 D | 36.7% | 63.2% | 36.8% | 63.2% |
| 1998 | 1,507,447 | 444,637 | Pierpont, Ross Z. | 1,062,810 | Mikulski, Barbara A. | | 618,173 D | 29.5% | 70.5% | 29.5% | 70.5% |
| 1994 | 1,369,104 | 559,908 | Brock, William E. | 809,125 | Sarbanes, Paul S. | 71 | 249,217 D | 40.9% | 59.1% | 40.9% | 59.1% |
| 1992 | 1,841,735 | 533,688 | Keyes, Alan L. | 1,307,610 | Mikulski, Barbara A. | 437 | 773,922 D | 29.0% | 71.0% | 29.0% | 71.0% |
| 1988 | 1,617,065 | 617,537 | Keyes, Alan L. | 999,166 | Sarbanes, Paul S. | 362 | 381,629 D | 38.2% | 61.8% | 38.2% | 61.8% |
| 1986 | 1,112,637 | 437,411 | Chavez, Linda | 675,225 | Mikulski, Barbara A. | 1 | 237,814 D | 39.3% | 60.7% | 39.3% | 60.7% |
| 1982 | 1,114,690 | 407,334 | Hogan, Lawrence J. | 707,356 | Sarbanes, Paul S. | | 300,022 D | 36.5% | 63.5% | 36.5% | 63.5% |
| 1980 | 1,286,088 | 850,970 | Mathias, Charles | 435,118 | Conroy, Edward T. | | 415,852 R | 66.2% | 33.8% | 66.2% | 33.8% |
| 1976 | 1,365,568 | 530,439 | Beall, J. Glenn, Jr. | 772,101 | Sarbanes, Paul S. | 63,028 | 241,662 D | 38.8% | 56.5% | 40.7% | 59.3% |
| 1974 | 877,786 | 503,223 | Mathias, Charles | 374,563 | Mikulski, Barbara A. | | 128,660 R | 57.3% | 42.7% | 57.3% | 42.7% |
| 1970 | 956,370 | 484,960 | Beall, J. Glenn, Jr. | 460,422 | Tydings, Joseph D. | 10,988 | 24,538 R | 50.7% | 48.1% | 51.3% | 48.7% |
| 1968 | 1,133,727 | 541,893 | Mathias, Charles | 443,367 | Brewster, Daniel B. | 148,467 | 98,526 R | 47.8% | 39.1% | 55.0% | 45.0% |
| 1964 | 1,081,049 | 402,393 | Beall, J. Glenn | 678,649 | Tydings, Joseph D. | 7 | 276,256 D | 37.2% | 62.8% | 37.2% | 62.8% |
| 1962 | 714,248 | 270,312 | Miller, Edward T. | 443,935 | Brewster, Daniel B. | 1 | 173,623 D | 37.8% | 62.2% | 37.8% | 62.2% |
| 1958 | 749,291 | 382,021 | Beall, J. Glenn | 367,270 | D'Alesandro, Thomas | | 14,751 R | 51.0% | 49.0% | 51.0% | 49.0% |
| 1956 | 892,167 | 473,059 | Butler, John Marshall | 419,108 | Mahoney, George P. | | 53,951 R | 53.0% | 47.0% | 53.0% | 47.0% |
| 1952 | 856,193 | 449,823 | Beall, J. Glenn | 406,370 | Mahoney, George P. | | 43,453 R | 52.5% | 47.5% | 52.5% | 47.5% |
| 1950 | 615,614 | 326,291 | Butler, John Marshall | 283,180 | Tydings, Millard E. | 6,143 | 43,111 R | 53.0% | 46.0% | 53.5% | 46.5% |
| 1946 | 472,232 | 235,000 | Markey, David John | 237,232 | O'Conor, Herbert R. | | 2,232 D | 49.8% | 50.2% | 49.8% | 50.2% |

# MARYLAND

Congressional districts first established for elections held in 2002
8 members

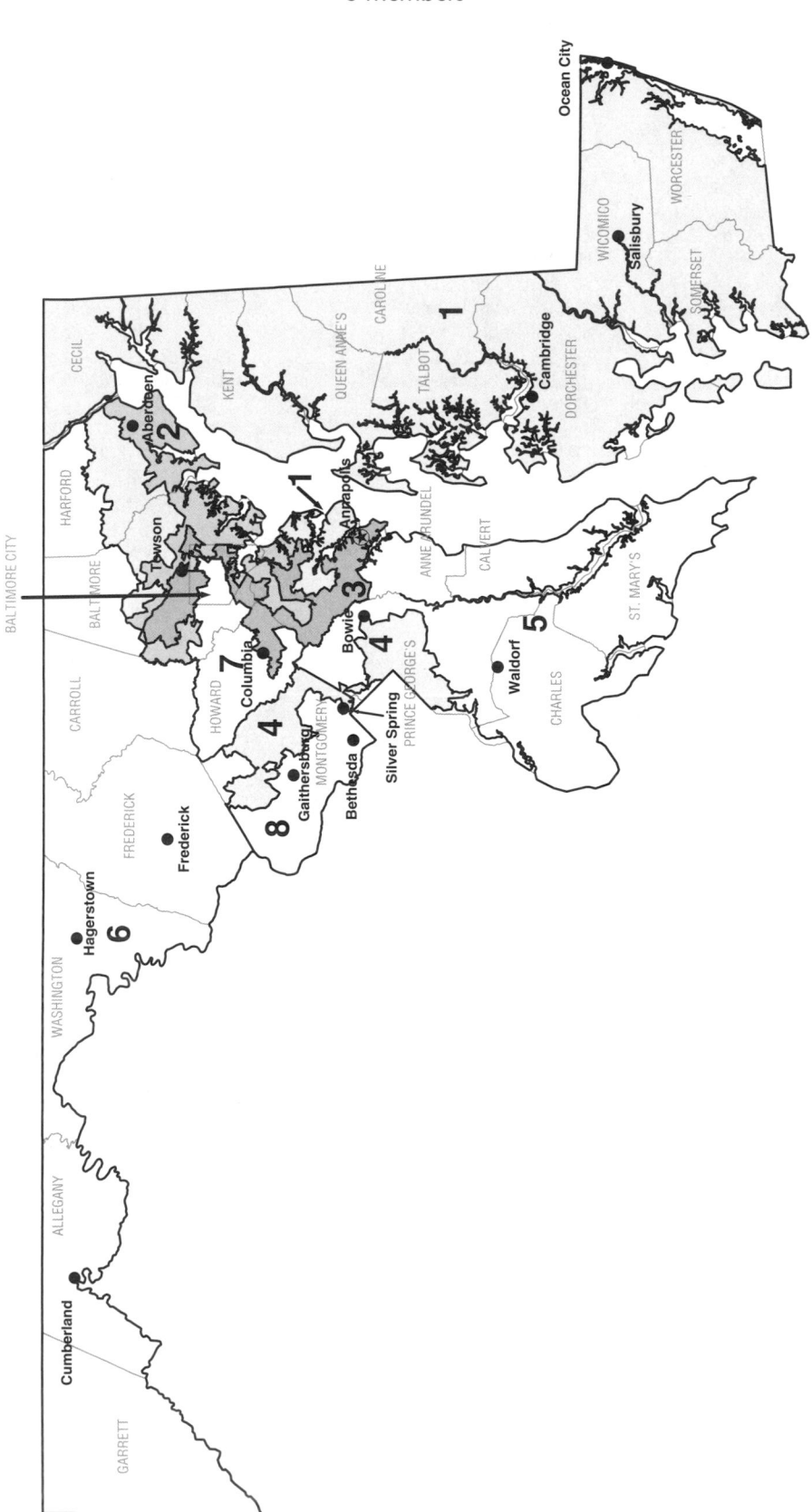

# MARYLAND

## Baltimore, Washington, D.C., Area

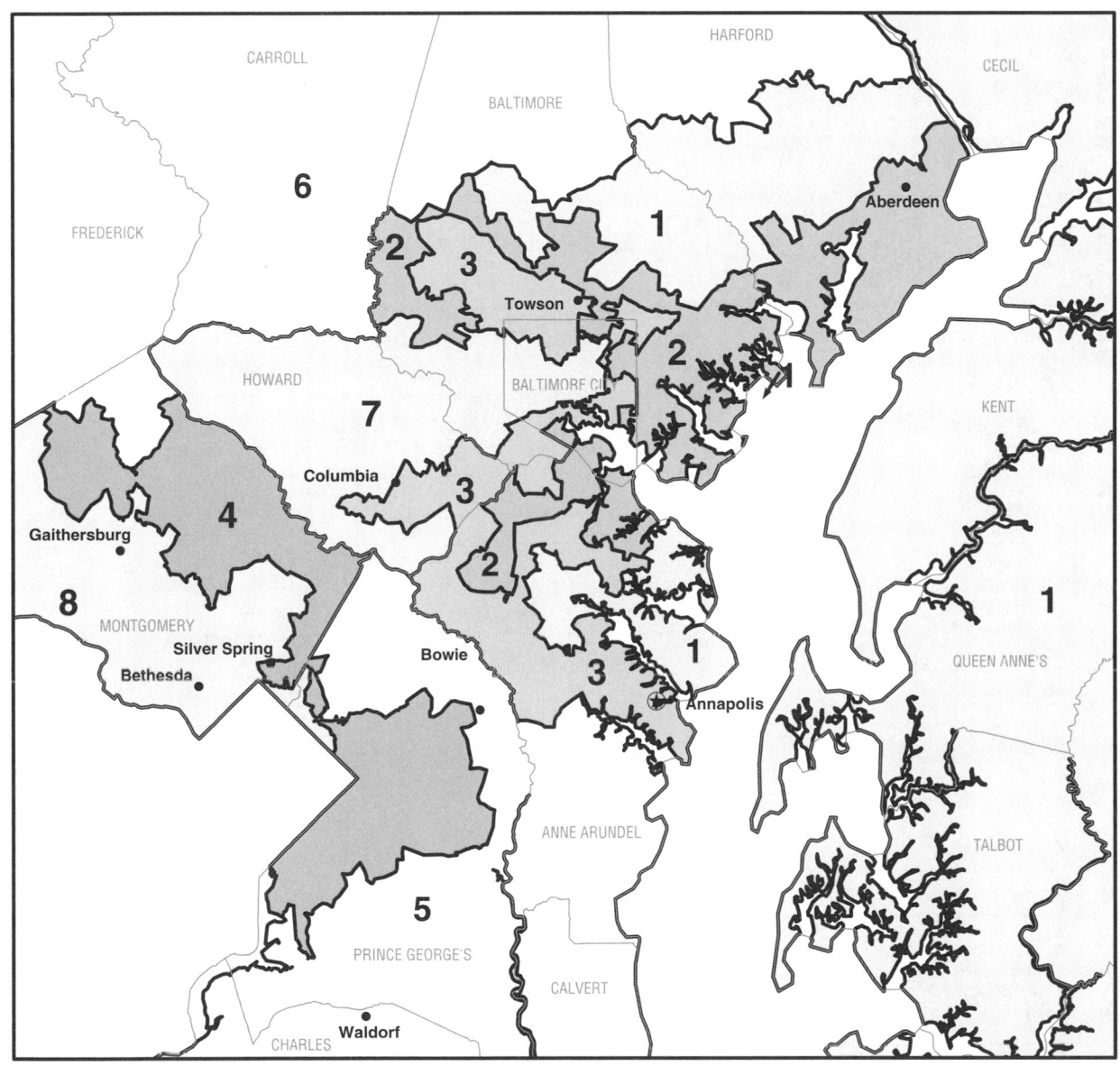

# MARYLAND

## PRESIDENT 2004

| 2000 Census Population | County | Total Vote | Republican | Democratic | Other | Rep.-Dem. Plurality | | Percentage | | | |
|---|---|---|---|---|---|---|---|---|---|---|---|
| | | | | | | | | Total Vote | | Major Vote | |
| | | | | | | | | Rep. | Dem. | Rep. | Dem. |
| 74,930 | ALLEGANY | 29,855 | 18,980 | 10,576 | 299 | 8,404 | R | 63.6% | 35.4% | 64.2% | 35.8% |
| 489,656 | ANNE ARUNDEL | 239,667 | 133,231 | 103,324 | 3,112 | 29,907 | R | 55.6% | 43.1% | 56.3% | 43.7% |
| 651,154 | BALTIMORE CITY | 213,563 | 36,230 | 175,022 | 2,311 | 138,792 | D | 17.0% | 82.0% | 17.2% | 82.8% |
| 754,292 | BALTIMORE COUNTY | 353,479 | 166,051 | 182,474 | 4,954 | 16,423 | D | 47.0% | 51.6% | 47.6% | 52.4% |
| 74,563 | CALVERT | 39,351 | 23,017 | 15,967 | 367 | 7,050 | R | 58.5% | 40.6% | 59.0% | 41.0% |
| 29,772 | CAROLINE | 11,356 | 7,396 | 3,810 | 150 | 3,586 | R | 65.1% | 33.6% | 66.0% | 34.0% |
| 150,897 | CARROLL | 79,349 | 55,275 | 22,974 | 1,100 | 32,301 | R | 69.7% | 29.0% | 70.6% | 29.4% |
| 85,951 | CECIL | 37,674 | 22,556 | 14,680 | 438 | 7,876 | R | 59.9% | 39.0% | 60.6% | 39.4% |
| 120,546 | CHARLES | 58,241 | 28,442 | 29,354 | 445 | 912 | D | 48.8% | 50.4% | 49.2% | 50.8% |
| 30,674 | DORCHESTER | 13,339 | 7,801 | 5,411 | 127 | 2,390 | R | 58.5% | 40.6% | 59.0% | 41.0% |
| 195,277 | FREDERICK | 100,594 | 59,934 | 39,503 | 1,157 | 20,431 | R | 59.6% | 39.3% | 60.3% | 39.7% |
| 29,846 | GARRETT | 12,484 | 9,085 | 3,291 | 108 | 5,794 | R | 72.8% | 26.4% | 73.4% | 26.6% |
| 218,590 | HARFORD | 112,728 | 71,565 | 39,685 | 1,478 | 31,880 | R | 63.5% | 35.2% | 64.3% | 35.7% |
| 247,842 | HOWARD | 133,810 | 59,724 | 72,257 | 1,829 | 12,533 | D | 44.6% | 54.0% | 45.3% | 54.7% |
| 19,197 | KENT | 9,285 | 4,900 | 4,278 | 107 | 622 | R | 52.8% | 46.1% | 53.4% | 46.6% |
| 873,341 | MONTGOMERY | 415,225 | 136,334 | 273,936 | 4,955 | 137,602 | D | 32.8% | 66.0% | 33.2% | 66.8% |
| 801,515 | PRINCE GEORGES | 318,474 | 55,532 | 260,532 | 2,410 | 205,000 | D | 17.4% | 81.8% | 17.6% | 82.4% |
| 40,563 | QUEEN ANNES | 21,794 | 14,489 | 7,070 | 235 | 7,419 | R | 66.5% | 32.4% | 67.2% | 32.8% |
| 86,211 | ST. MARYS | 37,916 | 23,725 | 13,776 | 415 | 9,949 | R | 62.6% | 36.3% | 63.3% | 36.7% |
| 24,747 | SOMERSET | 8,994 | 4,884 | 4,034 | 76 | 850 | R | 54.3% | 44.9% | 54.8% | 45.2% |
| 33,812 | TALBOT | 18,864 | 11,288 | 7,367 | 209 | 3,921 | R | 59.8% | 39.1% | 60.5% | 39.5% |
| 131,923 | WASHINGTON | 57,904 | 36,917 | 20,387 | 600 | 16,530 | R | 63.8% | 35.2% | 64.4% | 35.6% |
| 84,644 | WICOMICO | 37,503 | 21,998 | 15,137 | 368 | 6,861 | R | 58.7% | 40.4% | 59.2% | 40.8% |
| 46,543 | WORCESTER | 25,229 | 15,349 | 9,648 | 232 | 5,701 | R | 60.8% | 38.2% | 61.4% | 38.6% |
| 5,296,486 | TOTAL | 2,386,678 | 1,024,703 | 1,334,493 | 27,482 | 309,790 | D | 42.9% | 55.9% | 43.4% | 56.6% |

# MARYLAND

## SENATOR 2004

| 2000 Census Population | County | Total Vote | Republican | Democratic | Other | Rep.-Dem. Plurality | | Percentage | | | |
|---|---|---|---|---|---|---|---|---|---|---|---|
| | | | | | | | | Total Vote | | Major Vote | |
| | | | | | | | | Rep. | Dem. | Rep. | Dem. |
| 74,930 | ALLEGANY | 28,561 | 12,882 | 15,238 | 441 | 2,356 | D | 45.1% | 53.4% | 45.8% | 54.2% |
| 489,656 | ANNE ARUNDEL | 235,251 | 102,522 | 129,166 | 3,563 | 26,644 | D | 43.6% | 54.9% | 44.3% | 55.7% |
| 651,154 | BALTIMORE CITY | 199,972 | 23,759 | 172,427 | 3,786 | 148,668 | D | 11.9% | 86.2% | 12.1% | 87.9% |
| 754,292 | BALTIMORE COUNTY | 347,070 | 124,092 | 217,688 | 5,290 | 93,596 | D | 35.8% | 62.7% | 36.3% | 63.7% |
| 74,563 | CALVERT | 38,513 | 18,422 | 19,543 | 548 | 1,121 | D | 47.8% | 50.7% | 48.5% | 51.5% |
| 29,772 | CAROLINE | 11,134 | 5,439 | 5,543 | 152 | 104 | D | 48.9% | 49.8% | 49.5% | 50.5% |
| 150,897 | CARROLL | 78,156 | 44,704 | 32,391 | 1,061 | 12,313 | R | 57.2% | 41.4% | 58.0% | 42.0% |
| 85,951 | CECIL | 36,736 | 18,843 | 17,371 | 522 | 1,472 | R | 51.3% | 47.3% | 52.0% | 48.0% |
| 120,546 | CHARLES | 56,726 | 21,547 | 34,305 | 874 | 12,758 | D | 38.0% | 60.5% | 38.6% | 61.4% |
| 30,674 | DORCHESTER | 12,984 | 5,284 | 7,571 | 129 | 2,287 | D | 40.7% | 58.3% | 41.1% | 58.9% |
| 195,277 | FREDERICK | 97,965 | 47,081 | 49,336 | 1,548 | 2,255 | D | 48.1% | 50.4% | 48.8% | 51.2% |
| 29,846 | GARRETT | 12,014 | 7,330 | 4,540 | 144 | 2,790 | R | 61.0% | 37.8% | 61.8% | 38.2% |
| 218,590 | HARFORD | 111,196 | 56,465 | 53,444 | 1,287 | 3,021 | R | 50.8% | 48.1% | 51.4% | 48.6% |
| 247,842 | HOWARD | 131,230 | 46,610 | 82,479 | 2,141 | 35,869 | D | 35.5% | 62.9% | 36.1% | 63.9% |
| 19,197 | KENT | 9,088 | 3,860 | 5,117 | 111 | 1,257 | D | 42.5% | 56.3% | 43.0% | 57.0% |
| 873,341 | MONTGOMERY | 404,510 | 106,101 | 291,839 | 6,570 | 185,738 | D | 26.2% | 72.1% | 26.7% | 73.3% |
| 801,515 | PRINCE GEORGES | 308,649 | 39,863 | 264,088 | 4,698 | 224,225 | D | 12.9% | 85.6% | 13.1% | 86.9% |
| 40,563 | QUEEN ANNES | 21,542 | 11,964 | 9,332 | 246 | 2,632 | R | 55.5% | 43.3% | 56.2% | 43.8% |
| 86,211 | ST. MARYS | 36,867 | 17,802 | 18,440 | 625 | 638 | D | 48.3% | 50.0% | 49.1% | 50.9% |
| 24,747 | SOMERSET | 8,751 | 3,501 | 5,157 | 93 | 1,656 | D | 40.0% | 58.9% | 40.4% | 59.6% |
| 33,812 | TALBOT | 18,575 | 8,501 | 9,855 | 219 | 1,354 | D | 45.8% | 53.1% | 46.3% | 53.7% |
| 131,923 | WASHINGTON | 56,391 | 29,181 | 26,431 | 779 | 2,750 | R | 51.7% | 46.9% | 52.5% | 47.5% |
| 84,644 | WICOMICO | 36,608 | 16,348 | 19,866 | 394 | 3,518 | D | 44.7% | 54.3% | 45.1% | 54.9% |
| 46,543 | WORCESTER | 24,694 | 10,954 | 13,524 | 216 | 2,570 | D | 44.4% | 54.8% | 44.8% | 55.2% |
| 5,296,486 | TOTAL | 2,323,183 | 783,055 | 1,504,691 | 35,437 | 721,636 | D | 33.7% | 64.8% | 34.2% | 65.8% |

# MARYLAND

## HOUSE OF REPRESENTATIVES

| CD | Year | Total Vote | Republican | | Democratic | | Other Vote | Rep.-Dem. Plurality | Percentage | | | |
|---|---|---|---|---|---|---|---|---|---|---|---|---|
| | | | | | | | | | Total Vote | | Major Vote | |
| | | | Vote | Candidate | Vote | Candidate | | | Rep. | Dem. | Rep. | Dem. |
| 1 | 2004 | 323,526 | 245,149 | Gilchrest, Wayne T.* | 77,872 | Alexakis, Kostas | 505 | 167,277 R | 75.8% | 24.1% | 75.9% | 24.1% |
| 1 | 2002 | 250,413 | 192,004 | Gilchrest, Wayne T.* | 57,986 | Tamlyn, Ann D. | 423 | 134,018 R | 76.7% | 23.2% | 76.8% | 23.2% |
| 2 | 2004 | 247,295 | 75,812 | Brooks, Jane | 164,751 | Ruppersberger, C.A. Dutch* | 6,732 | 88,939 D | 30.7% | 66.6% | 31.5% | 68.5% |
| 2 | 2002 | 195,202 | 88,954 | Bentley, Helen Delich | 105,718 | Ruppersberger, C.A. Dutch | 530 | 16,764 D | 45.6% | 54.2% | 45.7% | 54.3% |
| 3 | 2004 | 287,219 | 97,008 | Duckworth, Robert P. | 182,066 | Cardin, Benjamin L.* | 8,145 | 85,058 D | 33.8% | 63.4% | 34.8% | 65.2% |
| 3 | 2002 | 221,543 | 75,721 | Conwell, Scott | 145,589 | Cardin, Benjamin L.* | 233 | 69,868 D | 34.2% | 65.7% | 34.2% | 65.8% |
| 4 | 2004 | 261,860 | 52,907 | McKinnis, John | 196,809 | Wynn, Albert R.* | 12,144 | 143,902 D | 20.2% | 75.2% | 21.2% | 78.8% |
| 4 | 2002 | 167,555 | 34,890 | Kimble, John B. | 131,644 | Wynn, Albert R.* | 1,021 | 96,754 D | 20.8% | 78.6% | 21.0% | 79.0% |
| 5 | 2004 | 298,335 | 87,189 | Jewitt, Brad | 204,867 | Hoyer, Steny H.* | 6,279 | 117,678 D | 29.2% | 68.7% | 29.9% | 70.1% |
| 5 | 2002 | 199,087 | 60,758 | Crawford, Joseph T. | 137,903 | Hoyer, Steny H.* | 426 | 77,145 D | 30.5% | 69.3% | 30.6% | 69.4% |
| 6 | 2004 | 305,857 | 206,076 | Bartlett, Roscoe G.* | 90,108 | Bosley, Kenneth T. | 9,673 | 115,968 R | 67.4% | 29.5% | 69.6% | 30.4% |
| 6 | 2002 | 223,611 | 147,825 | Bartlett, Roscoe G.* | 75,575 | DeArmon, Donald M. | 211 | 72,250 R | 66.1% | 33.8% | 66.2% | 33.8% |
| 7 | 2004 | 244,183 | 60,102 | Salazar, Tony | 179,189 | Cummings, Elijah E.* | 4,892 | 119,087 D | 24.6% | 73.4% | 25.1% | 74.9% |
| 7 | 2002 | 186,394 | 49,172 | Ward, Joseph E. | 137,047 | Cummings, Elijah E.* | 175 | 87,875 D | 26.4% | 73.5% | 26.4% | 73.6% |
| 8 | 2004 | 287,680 | 71,989 | Floyd, Chuck | 215,129 | Van Hollen, Chris* | 562 | 143,140 D | 25.0% | 74.8% | 25.1% | 74.9% |
| 8 | 2002 | 218,113 | 103,587 | Morella, Constance A.* | 112,788 | Van Hollen, Chris | 1,738 | 9,201 D | 47.5% | 51.7% | 47.9% | 52.1% |
| Total | 2004 | 2,255,955 | 896,232 | | 1,310,791 | | 48,932 | 414,559 D | 39.7% | 58.1% | 40.6% | 59.4% |
| Total | 2002 | 1,661,918 | 752,911 | | 904,250 | | 4,757 | 151,339 D | 45.3% | 54.4% | 45.4% | 54.6% |

An asterisk (*) denotes incumbent.

# MARYLAND

## GENERAL AND PRIMARY ELECTIONS

### 2004 GENERAL ELECTIONS

**President**  Other vote was 11,854 Populist (Ralph Nader); 6,094 Libertarian (Michael Badnarik); 3,632 Green (David Cobb); 3,421 Constitution (Michael Peroutka); 27 write-in (Joe Schriner); 7 write-in (John Joseph Kennedy); 4 write-in (Theodis "Ted" Brown Sr.); 2 write-in (Lawson Bone); 1 write-in (Robert A. Boyle II); 2,440 scattered write-in.

**Senator**  Other vote was 24,816 Green (Maria Allwine); 9,009 Constitution (Thomas Trump); 204 write-in (Robert Gemmill II); 109 write-in (Ray Bly); 47 write-in (Dennard A. Gayle-El Sr.); 1,252 scattered write-in.

**House**  Other vote was:

CD 1  505 scattered write-in.
CD 2  6,508 Green (Keith Salkowski); 224 scattered write-in.
CD 3  7,895 Green (Patsy Allen); 250 scattered write-in.
CD 4  11,885 Green (Theresa Mitchell Dudley); 6 write-in (John B. Kimble); 253 scattered write-in.
CD 5  4,224 Green (Bob S. Auerbach); 1,849 Constitution (Steve Krukar); 206 scattered write-in.
CD 6  9,324 Green (Gregory J. Hemingway); 349 scattered write-in.
CD 7  4,727 Green (Virginia T. Rodino); 165 scattered write-in.
CD 8  79 write-in (Lih Young); 483 scattered write-in.

# MARYLAND

## GENERAL AND PRIMARY ELECTIONS

## 2004 PRIMARY ELECTIONS

**Primary**  March 2, 2004

**Registration**
(as of Feb. 28, 2004)

| | |
|---|---|
| Republican | 842,287 |
| Democratic | 1,574,017 |
| Green | 6,206 |
| Others | 24,401 |
| Unaffiliated | 374,105 |
| TOTAL | 2,821,016 |

**Primary Type**  Closed—Only registered Democrats and Republicans could vote in their party's primary.

**Note:**  An asterisk (*) denotes incumbent.

| | REPUBLICAN PRIMARIES | | | DEMOCRATIC PRIMARIES | | |
|---|---|---|---|---|---|---|
| President | George W. Bush* | 151,943 | 100.0% | John Kerry | 286,955 | 59.6% |
| | | | | John Edwards | 123,006 | 25.5% |
| | | | | Al Sharpton | 21,810 | 4.5% |
| | | | | Howard Dean | 12,461 | 2.6% |
| | | | | Dennis J. Kucinich | 8,693 | 1.8% |
| | | | | Uncommitted | 8,527 | 1.8% |
| | | | | Joseph I. Lieberman | 5,245 | 1.1% |
| | | | | Wesley Clark | 4,230 | 0.9% |
| | | | | Mildred Glover | 4,039 | 0.8% |
| | | | | Carol Moseley Braun | 2,809 | 0.6% |
| | | | | Richard A. Gephardt | 2,146 | 0.4% |
| | | | | Lyndon H. LaRouche Jr. | 1,555 | 0.3% |
| | | | | TOTAL | 481,476 | |
| Senator | E.J. Pipkin | 70,229 | 50.6% | Barbara A. Mikulski* | 408,848 | 89.9% |
| | John Stafford | 14,661 | 10.6% | A. Robert Kaufman | 32,127 | 7.1% |
| | Eileen "Cookie Baker" Martin | 11,748 | 8.5% | Sid Altman | 13,901 | 3.1% |
| | Dorothy Corry Jennings | 10,401 | 7.5% | | | |
| | Earl S. Gordon | 8,233 | 5.9% | | | |
| | Gene Zarwell | 6,865 | 4.9% | | | |
| | Ray Bly | 6,244 | 4.5% | | | |
| | James A. Kodak | 5,328 | 3.8% | | | |
| | Corrogan R. Vaughn | 5,146 | 3.7% | | | |
| | TOTAL | 138,855 | | TOTAL | 454,876 | |
| Congressional District 1 | Wayne T. Gilchrest* | 23,590 | 61.9% | Ann D. Tamlyn | 14,492 | 36.5% |
| | Richard F. Colburn | 14,508 | 38.1% | Kostas Alexakis | 10,106 | 25.5% |
| | | | | Steven R. Eastaugh | 7,816 | 19.7% |
| | | | | Harry E. Simpson | 7,264 | 18.3% |
| | TOTAL | 38,098 | | TOTAL | 39,678 | |

Ann D. Tamlyn subsequently quit the race and was replaced on the general election ballot by Kostas Alexakis.

| | | | | | | |
|---|---|---|---|---|---|---|
| Congressional District 2 | Jane Brooks | 6,751 | 51.7% | C.A. Dutch Ruppersberger* | 41,509 | 100.0% |
| | Dave Harvilicz | 3,515 | 26.9% | | | |
| | Michael J. Littleton | 2,788 | 21.4% | | | |
| | TOTAL | 13,054 | | | | |
| Congressional District 3 | Robert P. Duckworth | 12,242 | 78.0% | Benjamin L. Cardin* | 54,398 | 89.8% |
| | Rick Hoover | 2,215 | 14.1% | John Rea | 6,163 | 10.2% |
| | Armand F. Girard | 1,245 | 7.9% | | | |
| | TOTAL | 15,702 | | TOTAL | 60,561 | |
| Congressional District 4 | John McKinnis | 2,258 | 32.0% | Albert R. Wynn* | 48,643 | 84.0% |
| | Roscoe M. Moore Jr. | 1,578 | 22.3% | George E. McDermott | 9,268 | 16.0% |
| | John B. Kimble | 1,131 | 16.0% | | | |
| | Patrick A. Schaeffer Jr. | 805 | 11.4% | | | |
| | William R. "Bill" Bernetich | 673 | 9.5% | | | |
| | Floyd W. Anderson Jr. | 618 | 8.7% | | | |
| | TOTAL | 7,063 | | TOTAL | 57,911 | |

# MARYLAND

## GENERAL AND PRIMARY ELECTIONS

| | REPUBLICAN PRIMARIES | | | DEMOCRATIC PRIMARIES | | |
|---|---|---|---|---|---|---|
| Congressional District 5 | Brad Jewitt | 5,545 | 37.5% | Steny H. Hoyer* | 49,218 | 100.0% |
| | Joseph T. Crawford | 4,992 | 33.8% | | | |
| | Patrick Edward Flaherty | 4,251 | 28.7% | | | |
| | TOTAL | 14,788 | | | | |
| Congressional District 6 | Roscoe G. Bartlett* | 31,867 | 70.3% | Kenneth T. Bosley | 7,704 | 22.9% |
| | Scott L. Rolle | 13,481 | 29.7% | Rodney D. Fox | 6,716 | 20.0% |
| | | | | Kevin M. Shaffer | 5,739 | 17.1% |
| | | | | James Daniel Benson | 5,524 | 16.4% |
| | | | | Richard Nacewicz | 4,911 | 14.6% |
| | | | | Ty Unglebower | 2,026 | 6.0% |
| | | | | Robert J. Rhudy | 981 | 2.9% |
| | TOTAL | 45,348 | | TOTAL | 33,601 | |
| Congressional District 7 | Tony Salazar | 4,815 | 52.2% | Elijah E. Cummings* | 53,015 | 91.4% |
| | Joseph E. Ward | 3,960 | 42.9% | Charles Curtis McPeek Sr. | 4,972 | 8.6% |
| | Almaajid Muhammad El | 452 | 4.9% | | | |
| | TOTAL | 9,227 | | TOTAL | 57,987 | |
| Congressional District 8 | Chuck Floyd | 8,778 | 57.2% | Chris Van Hollen* | 67,805 | 91.1% |
| | Robin Ficker | 4,255 | 27.7% | Deborah A. Vollmer | 4,847 | 6.5% |
| | Steve Rosen | 2,306 | 15.0% | Lih Young | 1,784 | 2.4% |
| | TOTAL | 15,339 | | TOTAL | 74,436 | |

# MASSACHUSETTS

## GOVERNOR
Mitt Romney (R). Elected 2002 to a four-year term.

## SENATORS (2 Democrats)
Edward M. Kennedy (D). Reelected 2000 to a six-year term. Previously elected 1994, 1988, 1982, 1976, 1970, 1964 and in 1962 to fill out the term vacated by the December 1960 resignation of Senator John F. Kennedy, who was elected president in November 1960.

John Kerry (D). Reelected 2002 to a six-year term. Previously elected 1996, 1990, 1984.

## REPRESENTATIVES (10 Democrats)
1. John W. Olver (D)
2. Richard E. Neal (D)
3. Jim McGovern (D)
4. Barney Frank (D)
5. Martin T. Meehan (D)
6. John F. Tierney (D)
7. Edward J. Markey (D)
8. Michael E. Capuano (D)
9. Stephen F. Lynch (D)
10. Bill Delahunt (D)

## POSTWAR VOTE FOR PRESIDENT

| Year | Total Vote | Republican | | Democratic | | Other Vote | Plurality | Percentage | | | |
|---|---|---|---|---|---|---|---|---|---|---|---|
| | | Vote | Candidate | Vote | Candidate | | | Total Vote | | Major Vote | |
| | | | | | | | | Rep. | Dem. | Rep. | Dem. |
| 2004 | 2,912,388 | 1,071,109 | Bush, George W. | 1,803,800 | Kerry, John | 37,479 | 732,691 D | 36.8% | 61.9% | 37.3% | 62.7% |
| 2000** | 2,702,984 | 878,502 | Bush, George W. | 1,616,487 | Gore, Al | 207,995 | 737,985 D | 32.5% | 59.8% | 35.2% | 64.8% |
| 1996** | 2,556,785 | 718,107 | Dole, Bob | 1,571,763 | Clinton, Bill | 266,915 | 853,656 D | 28.1% | 61.5% | 31.4% | 68.6% |
| 1992** | 2,773,700 | 805,049 | Bush, George | 1,318,662 | Clinton, Bill | 649,989 | 513,613 D | 29.0% | 47.5% | 37.9% | 62.1% |
| 1988 | 2,632,805 | 1,194,635 | Bush, George | 1,401,415 | Dukakis, Michael S. | 36,755 | 206,780 D | 45.4% | 53.2% | 46.0% | 54.0% |
| 1984 | 2,559,453 | 1,310,936 | Reagan, Ronald | 1,239,606 | Mondale, Walter F. | 8,911 | 71,330 R | 51.2% | 48.4% | 51.4% | 48.6% |
| 1980** | 2,524,298 | 1,057,631 | Reagan, Ronald | 1,053,802 | Carter, Jimmy | 412,865 | 3,829 R | 41.9% | 41.7% | 50.1% | 49.9% |
| 1976 | 2,547,558 | 1,030,276 | Ford, Gerald R. | 1,429,475 | Carter, Jimmy | 87,807 | 399,199 D | 40.4% | 56.1% | 41.9% | 58.1% |
| 1972 | 2,458,756 | 1,112,078 | Nixon, Richard M. | 1,332,540 | McGovern, George S. | 14,138 | 220,462 D | 45.2% | 54.2% | 45.5% | 54.5% |
| 1968** | 2,331,752 | 766,844 | Nixon, Richard M. | 1,469,218 | Humphrey, Hubert H. | 95,690 | 702,374 D | 32.9% | 63.0% | 34.3% | 65.7% |
| 1964 | 2,344,798 | 549,727 | Goldwater, Barry M. | 1,786,422 | Johnson, Lyndon B. | 8,649 | 1,236,695 D | 23.4% | 76.2% | 23.5% | 76.5% |
| 1960 | 2,469,480 | 976,750 | Nixon, Richard M. | 1,487,174 | Kennedy, John F. | 5,556 | 510,424 D | 39.6% | 60.2% | 39.6% | 60.4% |
| 1956 | 2,348,506 | 1,393,197 | Eisenhower, Dwight D. | 948,190 | Stevenson, Adlai E. | 7,119 | 445,007 R | 59.3% | 40.4% | 59.5% | 40.5% |
| 1952 | 2,383,398 | 1,292,325 | Eisenhower, Dwight D. | 1,083,525 | Stevenson, Adlai E. | 7,548 | 208,800 R | 54.2% | 45.5% | 54.4% | 45.6% |
| 1948 | 2,107,146 | 909,370 | Dewey, Thomas E. | 1,151,788 | Truman, Harry S. | 45,988 | 242,418 D | 43.2% | 54.7% | 44.1% | 55.9% |

In past elections, the other vote included: 2000 - 173,564 - Green (Ralph Nader); 1996 - 227,217 Reform (Ross Perot); 1992 - 630,731 Independent (Perot); 1980 - 382,539 Independent (John Anderson); 1968 - 87,088 American Independent (George Wallace).

# MASSACHUSETTS

## POSTWAR VOTE FOR GOVERNOR

| Year | Total Vote | Republican | | Democratic | | Other Vote | Rep.-Dem. Plurality | Percentage | | | |
|------|-----------|------|-----------|------|-----------|------|-----------|------|------|------|------|
| | | | | | | | | Total Vote | | Major Vote | |
| | | Vote | Candidate | Vote | Candidate | | | Rep. | Dem. | Rep. | Dem. |
| 2002 | 2,194,179 | 1,091,988 | Romney, Mitt | 985,981 | O'Brien, Shannon P. | 116,210 | 106,007 R | 49.8% | 44.9% | 52.6% | 47.4% |
| 1998 | 1,903,336 | 967,160 | Cellucci, Paul | 901,843 | Harshbarger, Scott | 34,333 | 65,317 R | 50.8% | 47.4% | 51.7% | 48.3% |
| 1994 | 2,164,318 | 1,533,430 | Weld, William F. | 611,650 | Roosevelt, Mark | 19,238 | 921,780 R | 70.9% | 28.3% | 71.5% | 28.5% |
| 1990 | 2,342,927 | 1,175,817 | Weld, William F. | 1,099,878 | Silber, John | 67,232 | 75,939 R | 50.2% | 46.9% | 51.7% | 48.3% |
| 1986 | 1,684,079 | 525,364 | Kariotis, George | 1,157,786 | Dukakis, Michael S. | 929 | 632,422 D | 31.2% | 68.7% | 31.2% | 68.8% |
| 1982 | 2,050,254 | 749,679 | Sears, John W. | 1,219,109 | Dukakis, Michael S. | 81,466 | 469,430 D | 36.6% | 59.5% | 38.1% | 61.9% |
| 1978 | 1,962,251 | 926,072 | Hatch, Francis W. | 1,030,294 | King, Edward J. | 5,885 | 104,222 D | 47.2% | 52.5% | 47.3% | 52.7% |
| 1974 | 1,854,798 | 784,353 | Sargent, Francis W. | 992,284 | Dukakis, Michael S. | 78,161 | 207,931 D | 42.3% | 53.5% | 44.1% | 55.9% |
| 1970 | 1,867,906 | 1,058,623 | Sargent, Francis W. | 799,269 | White, Kevin H. | 10,014 | 259,354 R | 56.7% | 42.8% | 57.0% | 43.0% |
| 1966** | 2,041,177 | 1,277,358 | Volpe, John A. | 752,720 | McCormack, Edward J. | 11,099 | 524,638 R | 62.6% | 36.9% | 62.9% | 37.1% |
| 1964 | 2,340,130 | 1,176,462 | Volpe, John A. | 1,153,416 | Bellotti, Francis X. | 10,252 | 23,046 R | 50.3% | 49.3% | 50.5% | 49.5% |
| 1962 | 2,109,089 | 1,047,891 | Volpe, John A. | 1,053,322 | Peabody, Endicott | 7,876 | 5,431 D | 49.7% | 49.9% | 49.9% | 50.1% |
| 1960 | 2,417,133 | 1,269,295 | Volpe, John A. | 1,130,810 | Ward, Joseph D. | 17,028 | 138,485 R | 52.5% | 46.8% | 52.9% | 47.1% |
| 1958 | 1,899,117 | 818,463 | Gibbons, Charles | 1,067,020 | Furcolo, Foster | 13,634 | 248,557 D | 43.1% | 56.2% | 43.4% | 56.6% |
| 1956 | 2,339,884 | 1,096,759 | Whittier, Sumner G. | 1,234,618 | Furcolo, Foster | 8,507 | 137,859 D | 46.9% | 52.8% | 47.0% | 53.0% |
| 1954 | 1,903,774 | 985,339 | Herter, Christian A. | 910,087 | Murphy, Robert F. | 8,348 | 75,252 R | 51.8% | 47.8% | 52.0% | 48.0% |
| 1952 | 2,356,298 | 1,175,955 | Herter, Christian A. | 1,161,499 | Dever, Paul A. | 18,844 | 14,456 R | 49.9% | 49.3% | 50.3% | 49.7% |
| 1950 | 1,910,180 | 824,069 | Coolidge, Arthur W. | 1,074,570 | Dever, Paul A. | 11,541 | 250,501 D | 43.1% | 56.3% | 43.4% | 56.6% |
| 1948 | 2,099,250 | 849,895 | Bradford, Robert F. | 1,239,247 | Dever, Paul A. | 10,108 | 389,352 D | 40.5% | 59.0% | 40.7% | 59.3% |
| 1946 | 1,683,452 | 911,152 | Bradford, Robert F. | 762,743 | Tobin, Maurice | 9,557 | 148,409 R | 54.1% | 45.3% | 54.4% | 45.6% |

The term of office of Massachusetts' governor was increased from two to four years effective with the 1966 election.

## POSTWAR VOTE FOR SENATOR

| Year | Total Vote | Republican | | Democratic | | Other Vote | Rep.-Dem. Plurality | Percentage | | | |
|------|-----------|------|-----------|------|-----------|------|-----------|------|------|------|------|
| | | | | | | | | Total Vote | | Major Vote | |
| | | Vote | Candidate | Vote | Candidate | | | Rep. | Dem. | Rep. | Dem. |
| 2002** | 2,006,758 | | — | 1,605,976 | Kerry, John | 400,782 | 1,605,976 D | | 80.0% | | 100.0% |
| 2000 | 2,599,420 | 334,341 | Robinson, Jack E. | 1,889,494 | Kennedy, Edward M. | 375,585 | 1,555,153 D | 12.9% | 72.7% | 15.0% | 85.0% |
| 1996 | 2,555,886 | 1,142,837 | Weld, William F. | 1,334,345 | Kerry, John | 78,704 | 191,508 D | 44.7% | 52.2% | 46.1% | 53.9% |
| 1994 | 2,179,964 | 894,005 | Romney, Mitt | 1,266,011 | Kennedy, Edward M. | 19,948 | 372,006 D | 41.0% | 58.1% | 41.4% | 58.6% |
| 1990 | 2,316,212 | 992,917 | Rappaport, Jim | 1,321,712 | Kerry, John | 1,583 | 328,795 D | 42.9% | 57.1% | 42.9% | 57.1% |
| 1988 | 2,606,225 | 884,267 | Malone, Joseph | 1,693,344 | Kennedy, Edward M. | 28,614 | 809,077 D | 33.9% | 65.0% | 34.3% | 65.7% |
| 1984 | 2,530,195 | 1,136,806 | Shamie, Raymond | 1,392,981 | Kerry, John | 408 | 256,175 D | 44.9% | 55.1% | 44.9% | 55.1% |
| 1982 | 2,050,769 | 784,602 | Shamie, Raymond | 1,247,084 | Kennedy, Edward M. | 19,083 | 462,482 D | 38.3% | 60.8% | 38.6% | 61.4% |
| 1978 | 1,985,700 | 890,584 | Brooke, Edward W. | 1,093,283 | Tsongas, Paul E. | 1,833 | 202,699 D | 44.8% | 55.1% | 44.9% | 55.1% |
| 1976 | 2,491,255 | 722,641 | Robertson, Michael | 1,726,657 | Kennedy, Edward M. | 41,957 | 1,004,016 D | 29.0% | 69.3% | 29.5% | 70.5% |
| 1972 | 2,370,676 | 1,505,932 | Brooke, Edward W. | 823,278 | Droney, John J. | 41,466 | 682,654 R | 63.5% | 34.7% | 64.7% | 35.3% |
| 1970 | 1,935,607 | 715,978 | Spaulding, Josiah A. | 1,202,856 | Kennedy, Edward M. | 16,773 | 486,878 D | 37.0% | 62.1% | 37.3% | 62.7% |
| 1966 | 1,999,949 | 1,213,473 | Brooke, Edward W. | 774,761 | Peabody, Endicott | 11,715 | 438,712 R | 60.7% | 38.7% | 61.0% | 39.0% |
| 1964 | 2,312,028 | 587,663 | Whitmore, Howard | 1,716,907 | Kennedy, Edward M. | 7,458 | 1,129,244 D | 25.4% | 74.3% | 25.5% | 74.5% |
| 1962S | 2,097,085 | 877,669 | Lodge, George C. | 1,162,611 | Kennedy, Edward M. | 56,805 | 284,942 D | 41.9% | 55.4% | 43.0% | 57.0% |
| 1960 | 2,417,813 | 1,358,556 | Saltonstall, Leverett | 1,050,725 | O'Connor, Thomas J. | 8,532 | 307,831 R | 56.2% | 43.5% | 56.4% | 43.6% |
| 1958 | 1,862,041 | 488,318 | Celeste, Vincent J. | 1,362,926 | Kennedy, John F. | 10,797 | 874,608 D | 26.2% | 73.2% | 26.4% | 73.6% |
| 1954 | 1,892,710 | 956,605 | Saltonstall, Leverett | 927,899 | Furcolo, Foster | 8,206 | 28,706 R | 50.5% | 49.0% | 50.8% | 49.2% |
| 1952 | 2,360,425 | 1,141,247 | Lodge, Henry Cabot | 1,211,984 | Kennedy, John F. | 7,194 | 70,737 D | 48.3% | 51.3% | 48.5% | 51.5% |
| 1948 | 2,055,798 | 1,088,475 | Saltonstall, Leverett | 954,398 | Fitzgerald, John I. | 12,925 | 134,077 R | 52.9% | 46.4% | 53.3% | 46.7% |
| 1946 | 1,662,063 | 989,736 | Lodge, Henry Cabot | 660,200 | Walsh, David I. | 12,127 | 329,536 R | 59.5% | 39.7% | 60.0% | 40.0% |

The Republican Party did not run a candidate in the 2002 Senate election. The 1962 election was for a short term to fill a vacancy.

# MASSACHUSETTS

Congressional districts first established for elections held in 2002
10 members

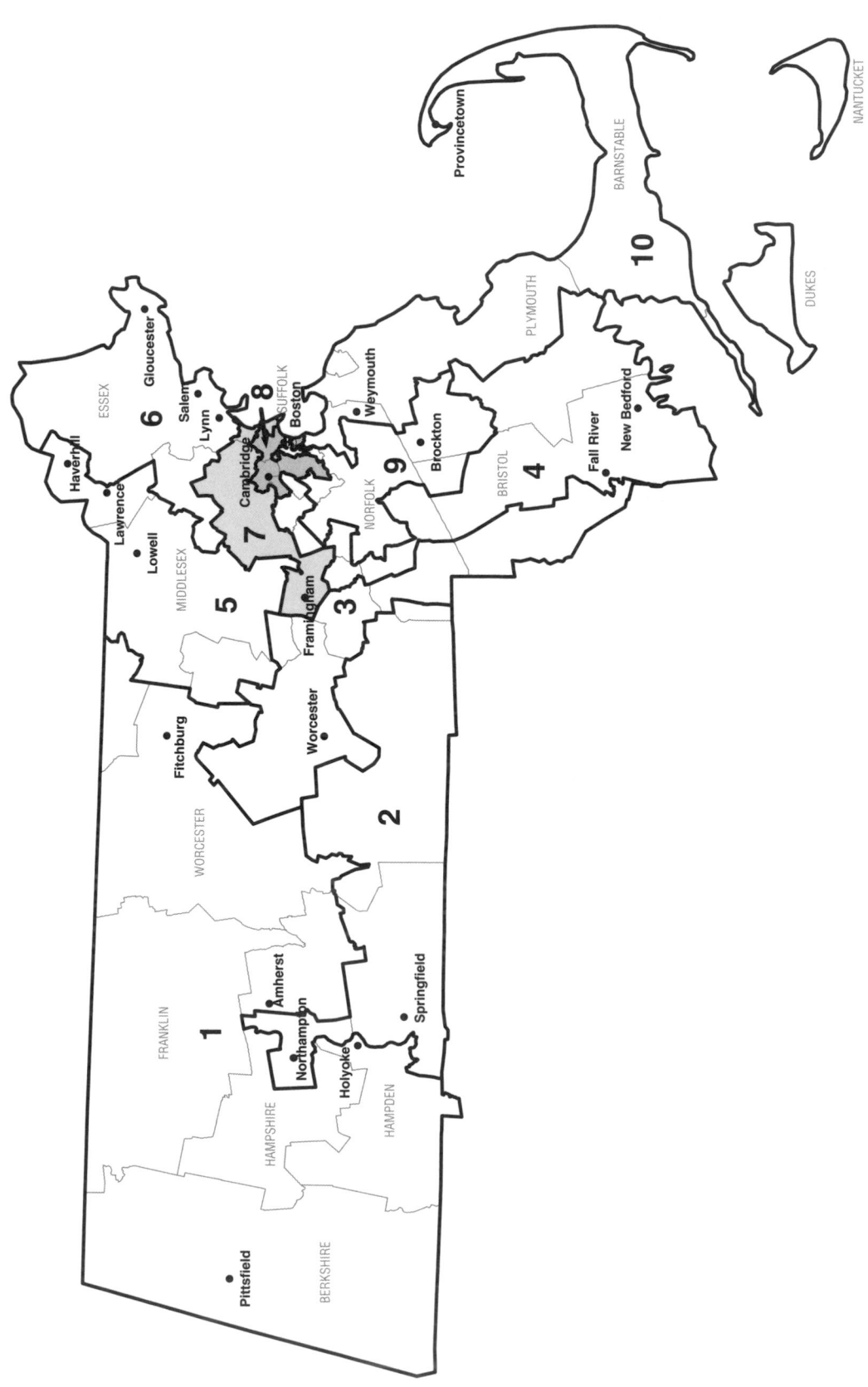

# MASSACHUSETTS

Boston Area

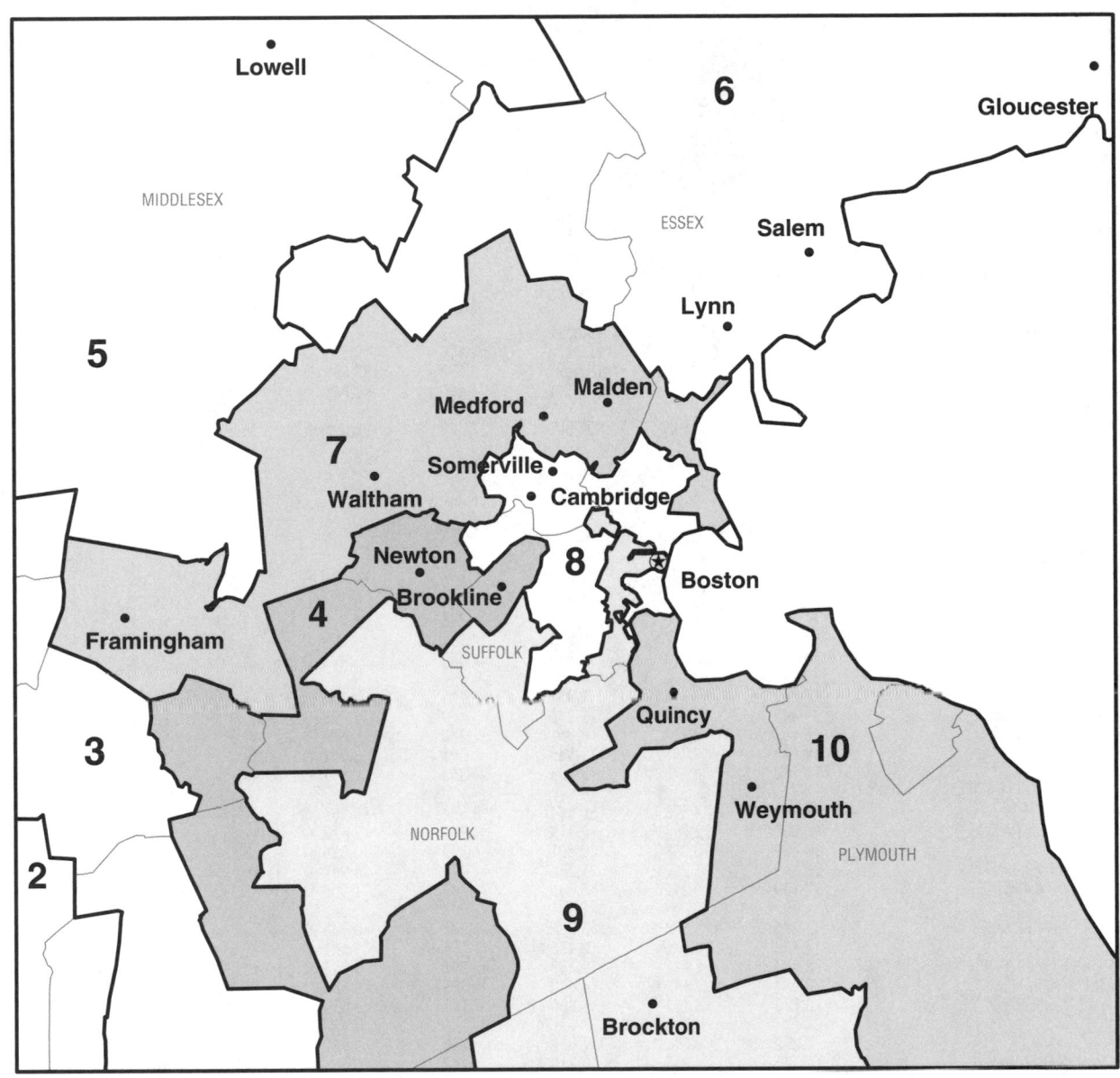

# MASSACHUSETTS

## PRESIDENT 2004

| 2000 Census Population | County | Total Vote | Republican | Democratic | Other | Rep.-Dem. Plurality | Percentage Total Vote Rep. | Dem. | Major Vote Rep. | Dem. |
|---|---|---|---|---|---|---|---|---|---|---|
| 222,230 | BARNSTABLE | 132,148 | 58,527 | 72,156 | 1,465 | 13,629 D | 44.3% | 54.6% | 44.8% | 55.2% |
| 134,953 | BERKSHIRE | 65,291 | 16,806 | 47,743 | 742 | 30,937 D | 25.7% | 73.1% | 26.0% | 74.0% |
| 534,678 | BRISTOL | 232,878 | 82,524 | 147,854 | 2,500 | 65,330 D | 35.4% | 63.5% | 35.8% | 64.2% |
| 14,987 | DUKES | 9,997 | 2,602 | 7,265 | 130 | 4,663 D | 26.0% | 72.7% | 26.4% | 73.6% |
| 723,419 | ESSEX | 333,233 | 135,114 | 194,068 | 4,051 | 58,954 D | 40.5% | 58.2% | 41.0% | 59.0% |
| 71,535 | FRANKLIN | 37,381 | 11,058 | 25,550 | 773 | 14,492 D | 29.6% | 68.4% | 30.2% | 69.8% |
| 456,228 | HAMPDEN | 186,639 | 70,925 | 113,710 | 2,004 | 42,785 D | 38.0% | 60.9% | 38.4% | 61.6% |
| 152,251 | HAMPSHIRE | 74,422 | 21,315 | 51,680 | 1,427 | 30,365 D | 28.6% | 69.4% | 29.2% | 70.8% |
| 1,465,396 | MIDDLESEX | 688,960 | 237,815 | 440,862 | 10,283 | 203,047 D | 34.5% | 64.0% | 35.0% | 65.0% |
| 9,520 | NANTUCKET | 5,724 | 2,040 | 3,608 | 76 | 1,568 D | 35.6% | 63.0% | 36.1% | 63.9% |
| 650,308 | NORFOLK | 331,137 | 127,763 | 199,392 | 3,982 | 71,629 D | 38.6% | 60.2% | 39.1% | 60.9% |
| 472,822 | PLYMOUTH | 233,297 | 105,603 | 125,178 | 2,516 | 19,575 D | 45.3% | 53.7% | 45.8% | 54.2% |
| 689,807 | SUFFOLK | 240,645 | 54,923 | 182,592 | 3,130 | 127,669 D | 22.8% | 75.9% | 23.1% | 76.9% |
| 750,963 | WORCESTER | 340,636 | 144,094 | 192,142 | 4,400 | 48,048 D | 42.3% | 56.4% | 42.9% | 57.1% |
| 6,349,097 | TOTAL | 2,912,388 | 1,071,109 | 1,803,800 | 37,479 | 732,691 D | 36.8% | 61.9% | 37.3% | 62.7% |

| 2000 Census Population | City/Town | Total Vote | Republican | Democratic | Other | Rep.-Dem. Plurality | Rep. | Dem. | Rep. | Dem. |
|---|---|---|---|---|---|---|---|---|---|---|
| 20,331 | ACTON | 10,738 | 3,485 | 7,063 | 190 | 3,578 D | 32.5% | 65.8% | 33.0% | 67.0% |
| 28,144 | AGAWAM | 13,776 | 5,957 | 7,691 | 128 | 1,734 D | 43.2% | 55.8% | 43.6% | 56.4% |
| 34,874 | AMHERST | 11,557 | 1,466 | 9,745 | 346 | 8,279 D | 12.7% | 84.3% | 13.1% | 86.9% |
| 31,247 | ANDOVER | 17,363 | 7,907 | 9,205 | 251 | 1,298 D | 45.5% | 53.0% | 46.2% | 53.8% |
| 42,389 | ARLINGTON | 24,733 | 6,428 | 17,856 | 449 | 11,428 D | 26.0% | 72.2% | 26.5% | 73.5% |
| 42,068 | ATTLEBORO | 17,842 | 7,714 | 9,857 | 271 | 2,143 D | 43.2% | 55.2% | 43.9% | 56.1% |
| 47,821 | BARNSTABLE | 25,443 | 11,938 | 13,236 | 269 | 1,298 D | 46.9% | 52.0% | 47.4% | 52.6% |
| 24,194 | BELMONT | 13,468 | 4,287 | 8,961 | 220 | 4,674 D | 31.8% | 66.5% | 32.4% | 67.6% |
| 39,862 | BEVERLY | 19,625 | 7,791 | 11,543 | 291 | 3,752 D | 39.7% | 58.8% | 40.3% | 59.7% |
| 38,981 | BILLERICA | 18,188 | 8,472 | 9,463 | 253 | 991 D | 46.6% | 52.0% | 47.2% | 52.8% |
| 589,141 | BOSTON | 208,236 | 44,518 | 160,884 | 2,834 | 116,366 D | 21.4% | 77.3% | 21.7% | 78.3% |
| 33,828 | BRAINTREE | 18,201 | 7,797 | 10,219 | 185 | 2,422 D | 42.8% | 56.1% | 43.3% | 56.7% |
| 94,304 | BROCKTON | 30,429 | 10,058 | 20,091 | 280 | 10,033 D | 33.1% | 66.0% | 33.4% | 66.6% |
| 57,107 | BROOKLINE | 26,949 | 5,269 | 21,256 | 424 | 15,987 D | 19.6% | 78.9% | 19.9% | 80.1% |
| 22,876 | BURLINGTON | 12,129 | 5,241 | 6,747 | 141 | 1,506 D | 43.2% | 55.6% | 43.7% | 56.3% |
| 101,355 | CAMBRIDGE | 42,295 | 5,338 | 35,886 | 1,071 | 30,548 D | 12.6% | 84.8% | 12.9% | 87.1% |
| 20,775 | CANTON | 11,458 | 4,875 | 6,476 | 107 | 1,601 D | 42.5% | 56.5% | 42.9% | 57.1% |
| 33,858 | CHELMSFORD | 18,464 | 8,485 | 9,688 | 291 | 1,203 D | 46.0% | 52.5% | 46.7% | 53.3% |
| 54,653 | CHICOPEE | 22,857 | 7,957 | 14,642 | 258 | 6,685 D | 34.8% | 64.1% | 35.2% | 64.8% |
| 16,993 | CONCORD | 10,173 | 3,182 | 6,800 | 191 | 3,618 D | 31.3% | 66.8% | 31.9% | 68.1% |
| 25,212 | DANVERS | 13,292 | 6,090 | 7,052 | 150 | 962 D | 45.8% | 53.1% | 46.3% | 53.7% |
| 30,666 | DARTMOUTH | 15,215 | 4,855 | 10,218 | 142 | 5,363 D | 31.9% | 67.2% | 32.2% | 67.8% |
| 23,464 | DEDHAM | 12,377 | 4,866 | 7,410 | 101 | 2,544 D | 39.3% | 59.9% | 39.6% | 60.4% |
| 28,562 | DRACUT | 13,746 | 6,671 | 6,974 | 101 | 303 D | 48.5% | 50.7% | 48.9% | 51.1% |
| 22,299 | EASTON | 11,460 | 5,436 | 5,878 | 146 | 442 D | 47.4% | 51.3% | 48.0% | 52.0% |
| 38,037 | EVERETT | 12,849 | 4,025 | 8,719 | 105 | 4,694 D | 31.3% | 67.9% | 31.6% | 68.4% |
| 91,938 | FALL RIVER | 31,560 | 7,369 | 23,859 | 332 | 16,490 D | 23.3% | 75.6% | 23.6% | 76.4% |
| 32,660 | FALMOUTH | 19,332 | 7,807 | 11,274 | 251 | 3,467 D | 40.4% | 58.3% | 40.9% | 59.1% |
| 39,102 | FITCHBURG | 13,621 | 5,023 | 8,433 | 165 | 3,410 D | 36.9% | 61.9% | 37.3% | 62.7% |
| 66,910 | FRAMINGHAM | 26,043 | 8,448 | 17,239 | 356 | 8,791 D | 32.4% | 66.2% | 32.9% | 67.1% |
| 29,560 | FRANKLIN | 15,424 | 6,974 | 8,268 | 182 | 1,294 D | 45.2% | 53.6% | 45.8% | 54.2% |
| 30,273 | GLOUCESTER | 14,948 | 5,185 | 9,536 | 227 | 4,351 D | 34.7% | 63.8% | 35.2% | 64.8% |
| 58,969 | HAVERHILL | 24,577 | 10,332 | 13,919 | 326 | 3,587 D | 42.0% | 56.6% | 42.6% | 57.4% |
| 19,882 | HINGHAM | 11,985 | 5,612 | 6,230 | 143 | 618 D | 46.8% | 52.0% | 47.4% | 52.6% |
| 39,838 | HOLYOKE | 14,724 | 4,514 | 10,033 | 177 | 5,519 D | 30.7% | 68.1% | 31.0% | 69.0% |
| 72,043 | LAWRENCE | 16,458 | 4,796 | 11,547 | 115 | 6,751 D | 29.1% | 70.2% | 29.3% | 70.7% |
| 41,303 | LEOMINSTER | 17,538 | 7,289 | 10,004 | 245 | 2,715 D | 41.6% | 57.0% | 42.2% | 57.8% |
| 30,355 | LEXINGTON | 17,427 | 4,834 | 12,334 | 259 | 7,500 D | 27.7% | 70.8% | 28.2% | 71.8% |
| 105,167 | LOWELL | 29,122 | 10,554 | 18,195 | 373 | 7,641 D | 36.2% | 62.5% | 36.7% | 63.3% |
| 89,050 | LYNN | 28,007 | 8,373 | 19,372 | 262 | 10,999 D | 29.9% | 69.2% | 30.2% | 69.8% |

# MASSACHUSETTS

## PRESIDENT 2004

| 2000 Census Population | City/Town | Total Vote | Republican | Democratic | Other | Rep.-Dem. Plurality | Percentage | | | |
|---|---|---|---|---|---|---|---|---|---|---|
| | | | | | | | Total Vote | | Major Vote | |
| | | | | | | | Rep. | Dem. | Rep. | Dem. |
| 56,340 | MALDEN | 19,969 | 5,730 | 14,011 | 228 | 8,281 D | 28.7% | 70.2% | 29.0% | 71.0% |
| 20,377 | MARBLEHEAD | 12,076 | 4,755 | 7,140 | 181 | 2,385 D | 39.4% | 59.1% | 40.0% | 60.0% |
| 36,255 | MARLBOROUGH | 15,459 | 6,407 | 8,825 | 227 | 2,418 D | 41.4% | 57.1% | 42.1% | 57.9% |
| 24,324 | MARSHFIELD | 13,502 | 6,387 | 6,951 | 164 | 564 D | 47.3% | 51.5% | 47.9% | 52.1% |
| 55,765 | MEDFORD | 26,018 | 7,932 | 17,737 | 349 | 9,805 D | 30.5% | 68.2% | 30.9% | 69.1% |
| 27,134 | MELROSE | 15,216 | 5,640 | 9,386 | 190 | 3,746 D | 37.1% | 61.7% | 37.5% | 62.5% |
| 43,789 | METHUEN | 19,287 | 9,075 | 10,037 | 175 | 962 D | 47.1% | 52.0% | 47.5% | 52.5% |
| 26,799 | MILFORD | 11,896 | 4,776 | 7,015 | 105 | 2,239 D | 40.1% | 59.0% | 40.5% | 59.5% |
| 26,062 | MILTON | 14,860 | 5,465 | 9,238 | 157 | 3,773 D | 36.8% | 62.2% | 37.2% | 62.8% |
| 32,170 | NATICK | 17,105 | 6,000 | 10,848 | 257 | 4,848 D | 35.1% | 63.4% | 35.6% | 64.4% |
| 28,911 | NEEDHAM | 16,821 | 5,846 | 10,775 | 200 | 4,929 D | 34.8% | 64.1% | 35.2% | 64.8% |
| 93,768 | NEW BEDFORD | 33,188 | 7,328 | 25,551 | 309 | 18,223 D | 22.1% | 77.0% | 22.3% | 77.7% |
| 83,829 | NEWTON | 42,622 | 10,025 | 32,061 | 536 | 22,036 D | 23.5% | 75.2% | 23.8% | 76.2% |
| 27,202 | NORTH ANDOVER | 13,812 | 6,891 | 6,760 | 161 | 131 R | 49.9% | 48.9% | 50.5% | 49.5% |
| 27,143 | NORTH ATTLEBOROUGH | 13,486 | 6,496 | 6,815 | 175 | 319 D | 48.2% | 50.5% | 48.8% | 51.2% |
| 28,978 | NORTHAMPTON | 15,397 | 2,793 | 12,233 | 371 | 9,440 D | 18.1% | 79.5% | 18.6% | 81.4% |
| 28,587 | NORWOOD | 13,914 | 5,568 | 8,162 | 184 | 2,594 D | 40.0% | 58.7% | 40.6% | 59.4% |
| 48,129 | PEABODY | 25,016 | 9,531 | 15,249 | 236 | 5,718 D | 38.1% | 61.0% | 38.5% | 61.5% |
| 45,793 | PITTSFIELD | 20,444 | 4,991 | 15,269 | 184 | 10,278 D | 24.4% | 74.7% | 24.6% | 75.4% |
| 51,701 | PLYMOUTH | 26,354 | 11,892 | 14,198 | 264 | 2,306 D | 45.1% | 53.9% | 45.6% | 54.4% |
| 88,025 | QUINCY | 37,999 | 13,373 | 24,173 | 453 | 10,800 D | 35.2% | 63.6% | 35.6% | 64.4% |
| 30,963 | RANDOLPH | 13,460 | 3,758 | 9,593 | 109 | 5,835 D | 27.9% | 71.3% | 28.1% | 71.9% |
| 23,708 | READING | 12,716 | 5,240 | 7,332 | 144 | 2,092 D | 41.2% | 57.7% | 41.7% | 58.3% |
| 47,283 | REVERE | 16,482 | 5,355 | 10,983 | 144 | 5,628 D | 32.5% | 66.6% | 32.8% | 67.2% |
| 40,407 | SALEM | 18,083 | 5,563 | 12,286 | 234 | 6,723 D | 30.8% | 67.9% | 31.2% | 68.8% |
| 26,078 | SAUGUS | 13,437 | 5,568 | 7,736 | 133 | 2,168 D | 41.4% | 57.6% | 41.9% | 58.1% |
| 17,863 | SCITUATE | 10,897 | 5,075 | 5,673 | 149 | 598 D | 46.6% | 52.1% | 47.2% | 52.8% |
| 31,640 | SHREWSBURY | 16,285 | 7,113 | 8,989 | 183 | 1,876 D | 43.7% | 55.2% | 44.2% | 55.8% |
| 77,478 | SOMERVILLE | 30,277 | 5,232 | 24,300 | 745 | 19,068 D | 17.3% | 80.3% | 17.7% | 82.3% |
| 152,082 | SPRINGFIELD | 47,073 | 13,028 | 33,583 | 462 | 20,555 D | 27.7% | 71.3% | 28.0% | 72.0% |
| 22,219 | STONEHAM | 11,795 | 4,741 | 6,952 | 102 | 2,211 D | 40.2% | 58.9% | 40.5% | 59.5% |
| 27,149 | STOUGHTON | 13,284 | 4,896 | 8,252 | 136 | 3,356 D | 36.9% | 62.1% | 37.2% | 62.8% |
| 55,976 | TAUNTON | 21,223 | 7,804 | 13,206 | 213 | 5,402 D | 36.8% | 62.2% | 37.1% | 62.9% |
| 28,851 | TEWKSBURY | 14,777 | 6,889 | 7,739 | 149 | 850 D | 46.6% | 52.4% | 47.1% | 52.9% |
| 24,804 | WAKEFIELD | 13,728 | 5,647 | 7,920 | 161 | 2,273 D | 41.1% | 57.7% | 41.6% | 58.4% |
| 22,824 | WALPOLE | 12,757 | 6,119 | 6,503 | 135 | 384 D | 48.0% | 51.0% | 48.5% | 51.5% |
| 59,226 | WALTHAM | 23,043 | 8,228 | 14,517 | 298 | 6,289 D | 35.7% | 63.0% | 36.2% | 63.8% |
| 32,986 | WATERTOWN | 15,416 | 4,191 | 10,970 | 255 | 6,779 D | 27.2% | 71.2% | 27.6% | 72.4% |
| 26,613 | WELLESLEY | 14,009 | 5,211 | 8,614 | 184 | 3,403 D | 37.2% | 61.5% | 37.7% | 62.3% |
| 27,899 | WEST SPRINGFIELD | 11,793 | 5,012 | 6,646 | 135 | 1,634 D | 42.5% | 56.4% | 43.0% | 57.0% |
| 40,072 | WESTFIELD | 16,841 | 7,568 | 9,064 | 209 | 1,496 D | 44.9% | 53.8% | 45.5% | 54.5% |
| 53,988 | WEYMOUTH | 26,561 | 10,912 | 15,367 | 282 | 4,455 D | 41.1% | 57.9% | 41.5% | 58.5% |
| 20,810 | WINCHESTER | 12,100 | 4,814 | 7,106 | 180 | 2,292 D | 39.8% | 58.7% | 40.4% | 59.6% |
| 37,258 | WOBURN | 18,233 | 7,743 | 10,322 | 168 | 2,579 D | 42.5% | 56.6% | 42.9% | 57.1% |
| 172,648 | WORCESTER | 56,656 | 17,648 | 38,264 | 744 | 20,616 D | 31.1% | 67.5% | 31.6% | 68.4% |
| 24,807 | YARMOUTH | 14,319 | 6,529 | 7,652 | 138 | 1,123 D | 45.6% | 53.4% | 46.0% | 54.0% |

# MASSACHUSETTS

## HOUSE OF REPRESENTATIVES

| | | | Republican | | Democratic | | Other | Rep.-Dem. | Percentage | | | |
|---|---|---|---|---|---|---|---|---|---|---|---|---|
| | | Total | | | | | | | Total Vote | | Major Vote | |
| CD | Year | Vote | Vote | Candidate | Vote | Candidate | Vote | Plurality | Rep. | Dem. | Rep. | Dem. |
| 1 | 2004 | 231,747 | | | 229,465 | Olver, John W.* | 2,282 | 229,465 D | | 99.0% | | 100.0% |
| 1 | 2002 | 204,019 | 66,061 | Kinnaman, Matthew W. | 137,841 | Olver, John W.* | 117 | 71,780 D | 32.4% | 67.6% | 32.4% | 67.6% |
| 2 | 2004 | 220,484 | | | 217,682 | Neal, Richard E.* | 2,802 | 217,682 D | | 98.7% | | 100.0% |
| 2 | 2002 | 154,728 | | | 153,387 | Neal, Richard E.* | 1,341 | 153,387 D | | 99.1% | | 100.0% |
| 3 | 2004 | 272,412 | 80,197 | Crews, Ronald A.. | 192,036 | McGovern, Jim* | 179 | 111,839 D | 29.4% | 70.5% | 29.5% | 70.5% |
| 3 | 2002 | 157,545 | | | 155,697 | McGovern, Jim* | 1,848 | 155,697 D | | 98.8% | | 100.0% |
| 4 | 2004 | 282,039 | | | 219,260 | Frank, Barney* | 62,779 | 219,260 D | | 77.7% | | 100.0% |
| 4 | 2002 | 167,816 | | | 166,125 | Frank, Barney* | 1,691 | 166,125 D | | 99.0% | | 100.0% |
| 5 | 2004 | 268,189 | 88,232 | Tierney, Thomas P. | 179,652 | Meehan, Martin T.* | 305 | 91,420 D | 32.9% | 67.0% | 32.9% | 67.1% |
| 5 | 2002 | 203,777 | 69,337 | McCarthy, Charles | 122,562 | Meehan, Martin T.* | 11,878 | 53,225 D | 34.0% | 60.1% | 36.1% | 63.9% |
| 6 | 2004 | 305,522 | 91,597 | O'Malley, Stephen P. Jr. | 213,458 | Tierney, John F.* | 467 | 121,861 D | 30.0% | 69.9% | 30.0% | 70.0% |
| 6 | 2002 | 238,615 | 75,462 | Smith, Mark C. | 162,900 | Tierney, John F.* | 253 | 87,438 D | 31.6% | 68.3% | 31.7% | 68.3% |
| 7 | 2004 | 275,099 | 60,334 | Chase, Kenneth G. | 202,399 | Markey, Edward J.* | 12,366 | 142,065 D | 21.9% | 73.6% | 23.0% | 77.0% |
| 7 | 2002 | 174,037 | | | 170,968 | Markey, Edward J.* | 3,069 | 170,968 D | | 98.2% | | 100.0% |
| 8 | 2004 | 168,081 | | | 165,852 | Capuano, Michael E.* | 2,229 | 165,852 D | | 98.7% | | 100.0% |
| 8 | 2002 | 112,356 | | | 111,861 | Capuano, Michael E.* | 495 | 111,861 D | | 99.6% | | 100.0% |
| 9 | 2004 | 220,312 | | | 218,167 | Lynch, Stephen F.* | 2,145 | 218,167 D | | 99.0% | | 100.0% |
| 9 | 2002 | 168,976 | | | 168,055 | Lynch, Stephen F.* | 921 | 168,055 D | | 99.5% | | 100.0% |
| 10 | 2004 | 337,070 | 114,879 | Jones, Michael J. | 222,013 | Delahunt, Bill* | 178 | 107,134 D | 34.1% | 65.9% | 34.1% | 65.9% |
| 10 | 2002 | 259,002 | 79,624 | Gonzaga, Luiz | 179,238 | Delahunt, Bill* | 140 | 99,614 D | 30.7% | 69.2% | 30.8% | 69.2% |
| Total | 2004 | 2,580,955 | 435,239 | | 2,059,984 | | 85,732 | 1,624,745 D | 16.9% | 79.8% | 17.4% | 82.6% |
| Total | 2002 | 1,840,871 | 290,484 | | 1,528,634 | | 21,753 | 1,238,150 D | 15.8% | 83.0% | 16.0% | 84.0% |

An asterisk (*) denotes incumbent.

# MASSACHUSETTS

## GENERAL AND PRIMARY ELECTIONS

### 2004 GENERAL ELECTIONS

**President**  Other vote was 15,022 Libertarian (Michael Badnarik); 10,623 Green-Rainbow (David Cobb); 4,806 write-in (Ralph Nader); 7,028 scattered write-in.

**House**  Other vote was:

CD 1  2,282 scattered write-in.
CD 2  2,802 scattered write-in.
CD 3  179 scattered write-in.
CD 4  62,293 Independent (Charles A. Morse); 486 scattered write-in.
CD 5  305 scattered write-in.
CD 6  467 scattered write-in.
CD 7  12,139 Independent (James O. Hall); 227 scattered write-in.
CD 8  2,229 scattered write-in.
CD 9  2,145 scattered write-in.
CD 10  178 scattered write-in.

# MASSACHUSETTS

## GENERAL AND PRIMARY ELECTIONS

## 2004 PRIMARY ELECTIONS

| | | | | |
|---|---|---|---|---|
| **Primary** | March 2, 2004 (President) | **Registration** | Republican | 515,860 |
| | September 14, 2004 (Congress) | (as of Aug. 25, 2004) | Democratic | 1,479,055 |
| | | | Libertarian | 22,794 |
| | | | Green-Rainbow | 9,176 |
| | | | Other Parties | 6,190 |
| | | | Unenrolled | 1,928,277 |
| | | | TOTAL | 3,961,352 |

**Primary Type**   Semi-open—Registered Democrats and Republicans could vote only in their party's primary. "Unenrolled" voters could participate in either party's primary.

Note:   An asterisk (*) denotes incumbent.

| | REPUBLICAN PRIMARIES | | | DEMOCRATIC PRIMARIES | | |
|---|---|---|---|---|---|---|
| **President** | George W. Bush* | 62,773 | 88.8% | John Kerry | 440,964 | 71.7% |
| | No Preference | 6,050 | 8.6% | John Edwards | 108,051 | 17.6% |
| | John Kerry (write-in) | 267 | 0.4% | Dennis J. Kucinich | 25,198 | 4.1% |
| | John McCain (write-in) | 75 | 0.1% | Howard Dean | 17,076 | 2.8% |
| | Ralph Nader (write-in) | 63 | 0.1% | Al Sharpton | 6,123 | 1.0% |
| | John Edwards (write-in) | 50 | 0.1% | Joseph I. Lieberman | 5,432 | 0.9% |
| | Scattered write-in | 1,376 | 1.9% | No Preference | 4,451 | 0.7% |
| | | | | Wesley Clark | 3,109 | 0.5% |
| | | | | Richard A. Gephardt | 1,455 | 0.2% |
| | | | | Carol Moseley Braun | 1,019 | 0.2% |
| | | | | Lyndon H. LaRouche Jr. | 970 | 0.2% |
| | | | | Ralph Nader (write-in) | 168 | |
| | | | | Jeremy Robinson-Leon (write-in) | 155 | |
| | | | | George W. Bush (write-in) | 91 | |
| | | | | Hillary Rodham Clinton (write-in) | 34 | |
| | | | | Scattered write-in | 892 | 0.1% |
| | TOTAL | 70,654 | | TOTAL | 615,188 | |
| **Congressional District 1** | *Steven E. Adam was listed on the primary ballot and received 660 votes. Another 675 votes were cast as scattered write-ins. However, Adam subsequently quit the race and no Republican candidate appeared on the general election ballot.* | | | John W. Olver* | 35,037 | 99.3% |
| | | | | Write-in | 259 | 0.7% |
| | | | | TOTAL | 35,296 | |
| **Congressional District 2** | *No Republican candidate filed for the primary. There were 623 scattered write-in votes.* | | | Richard E. Neal* | 29,707 | 99.1% |
| | | | | Write-in | 259 | 0.9% |
| | | | | TOTAL | 29,966 | |
| **Congressional District 3** | Ronald A. Crews | 8,443 | 98.8% | Jim McGovern* | 39,014 | 99.2% |
| | Write-in | 99 | 1.2% | Write-in | 322 | 0.8% |
| | TOTAL | 8,542 | | TOTAL | 39,336 | |
| **Congressional District 4** | *No Republican candidate filed for the primary. There were 535 scattered write-in votes.* | | | Barney Frank* | 22,019 | 99.3% |
| | | | | Write-in | 153 | 0.7% |
| | | | | TOTAL | 22,172 | |
| **Congressional District 5** | Thomas P. Tierney | 4,711 | 61.4% | Martin T. Meehan* | 19,418 | 98.6% |
| | Ilana Freedman | 2,918 | 38.1% | Write-in | 277 | 1.4% |
| | Write-in | 38 | 0.5% | | | |
| | TOTAL | 7,667 | | TOTAL | 19,695 | |
| **Congressional District 6** | Stephen P. O'Malley Jr. | 6,204 | 98.0% | John F. Tierney* | 27,660 | 99.4% |
| | Write-in | 124 | 2.0% | Write-in | 178 | 0.6% |
| | TOTAL | 6,328 | | TOTAL | 27,838 | |

# MASSACHUSETTS

## GENERAL AND PRIMARY ELECTIONS

| | REPUBLICAN PRIMARIES | | | DEMOCRATIC PRIMARIES | | |
|---|---|---|---|---|---|---|
| **Congressional District 7** | Kenneth G. Chase | 4,928 | 97.3% | Edward J. Markey* | 38,583 | 98.9% |
| | Write-in | 137 | 2.7% | Write-in | 410 | 1.1% |
| | TOTAL | 5,065 | | TOTAL | 38,993 | |
| **Congressional District 8** | *No Republican candidate filed for the primary. There were 403 scattered write-in votes.* | | | Michael E. Capuano* | 32,648 | 98.4% |
| | | | | Write-in | 523 | 1.6% |
| | | | | TOTAL | 33,171 | |
| **Congressional District 9** | *No Republican candidate filed for the primary. There were 651 scattered write-in votes.* | | | Stephen F. Lynch* | 37,035 | 98.8% |
| | | | | Write-in | 440 | 1.2% |
| | | | | TOTAL | 37,475 | |
| **Congressional District 10** | Michael J. Jones | 11,856 | 99.2% | Bill Delahunt* | 25,939 | 99.3% |
| | Write-in | 94 | 0.8% | Write-in | 190 | 0.7% |
| | TOTAL | 11,950 | | TOTAL | 26,129 | |

# MICHIGAN

## GOVERNOR
Jennifer M. Granholm (D). Elected 2002 to a four-year term.

## SENATORS (2 Democrats)
Carl Levin (D). Reelected 2002 to a six-year term. Previously elected 1996, 1990, 1984, 1978.

Debbie Stabenow (D). Elected 2000 to a six-year term.

## REPRESENTATIVES (9 Republicans, 6 Democrats)
1. Bart Stupak (D)
2. Peter Hoekstra (R)
3. Vernon J. Ehlers (R)
4. Dave Camp (R)
5. Dale E. Kildee (D)
6. Fred Upton (R)
7. Joe Schwarz (R)
8. Mike Rogers (R)
9. Joe Knollenberg (R)
10. Candice S. Miller (R)
11. Thaddeus McCotter (R)
12. Sander M. Levin (D)
13. Carolyn Cheeks Kilpatrick (D)
14. John Conyers Jr. (D)
15. John D. Dingell (D)

## POSTWAR VOTE FOR PRESIDENT

| Year | Total Vote | Republican Vote | Candidate | Democratic Vote | Candidate | Other Vote | Plurality | Total Vote Rep. | Total Vote Dem. | Major Vote Rep. | Major Vote Dem. |
|---|---|---|---|---|---|---|---|---|---|---|---|
| 2004 | 4,839,252 | 2,313,746 | Bush, George W. | 2,479,183 | Kerry, John | 46,323 | 165,437 D | 47.8% | 51.2% | 48.3% | 51.7% |
| 2000** | 4,232,711 | 1,953,139 | Bush, George W. | 2,170,418 | Gore, Al | 109,154 | 217,279 D | 46.1% | 51.3% | 47.4% | 52.6% |
| 1996** | 3,848,844 | 1,481,212 | Dole, Bob | 1,989,653 | Clinton, Bill | 377,979 | 508,441 D | 38.5% | 51.7% | 42.7% | 57.3% |
| 1992** | 4,274,673 | 1,554,940 | Bush, George | 1,871,182 | Clinton, Bill | 848,551 | 316,242 D | 36.4% | 43.8% | 45.4% | 54.6% |
| 1988 | 3,669,163 | 1,965,486 | Bush, George | 1,675,783 | Dukakis, Michael S. | 27,894 | 289,703 R | 53.6% | 45.7% | 54.0% | 46.0% |
| 1984 | 3,801,658 | 2,251,571 | Reagan, Ronald | 1,529,638 | Mondale, Walter F. | 20,449 | 721,933 R | 59.2% | 40.2% | 59.5% | 40.5% |
| 1980** | 3,909,725 | 1,915,225 | Reagan, Ronald | 1,661,532 | Carter, Jimmy | 332,968 | 253,693 R | 49.0% | 42.5% | 53.5% | 46.5% |
| 1976 | 3,653,749 | 1,893,742 | Ford, Gerald R. | 1,696,714 | Carter, Jimmy | 63,293 | 197,028 R | 51.8% | 46.4% | 52.7% | 47.3% |
| 1972 | 3,489,727 | 1,961,721 | Nixon, Richard M. | 1,459,435 | McGovern, George S. | 68,571 | 502,286 R | 56.2% | 41.8% | 57.3% | 42.7% |
| 1968** | 3,306,250 | 1,370,665 | Nixon, Richard M. | 1,593,082 | Humphrey, Hubert H. | 342,503 | 222,417 D | 41.5% | 48.2% | 46.2% | 53.8% |
| 1964 | 3,203,102 | 1,060,152 | Goldwater, Barry M. | 2,136,615 | Johnson, Lyndon B. | 6,335 | 1,076,463 D | 33.1% | 66.7% | 33.2% | 66.8% |
| 1960 | 3,318,097 | 1,620,428 | Nixon, Richard M. | 1,687,269 | Kennedy, John F. | 10,400 | 66,841 D | 48.8% | 50.9% | 49.0% | 51.0% |
| 1956 | 3,080,468 | 1,713,647 | Eisenhower, Dwight D. | 1,359,898 | Stevenson, Adlai E. | 6,923 | 353,749 R | 55.6% | 44.1% | 55.8% | 44.2% |
| 1952 | 2,798,592 | 1,551,529 | Eisenhower, Dwight D. | 1,230,657 | Stevenson, Adlai E. | 16,406 | 320,872 R | 55.4% | 44.0% | 55.8% | 44.2% |
| 1948 | 2,109,609 | 1,038,595 | Dewey, Thomas E. | 1,003,448 | Truman, Harry S. | 67,566 | 35,147 R | 49.2% | 47.6% | 50.9% | 49.1% |

In past elections, the other vote included: 2000 - 84,165 Green (Ralph Nader); 1996 - 336,670 Reform (Ross Perot); 1992 - 824,813 Independent (Perot); 1980 - 275,223 Independent (John Anderson); 1968 - 331,968 American Independent (George Wallace).

# MICHIGAN

## POSTWAR VOTE FOR GOVERNOR

| Year | Total Vote | Republican Vote | Republican Candidate | Democratic Vote | Democratic Candidate | Other Vote | Rep.-Dem. Plurality | Percentage Total Vote Rep. | Percentage Total Vote Dem. | Percentage Major Vote Rep. | Percentage Major Vote Dem. |
|------|-----------|-----------------|----------------------|-----------------|----------------------|------------|---------------------|------|------|------|------|
| 2002 | 3,177,565 | 1,506,104 | Posthumus, Dick | 1,633,796 | Granholm, Jennifer M. | 37,665 | 127,692 D | 47.4% | 51.4% | 48.0% | 52.0% |
| 1998 | 3,027,104 | 1,883,005 | Engler, John | 1,143,574 | Fieger, Geoffrey | 525 | 739,431 R | 62.2% | 37.8% | 62.2% | 37.8% |
| 1994 | 3,089,077 | 1,899,101 | Engler, John | 1,188,438 | Wolpe, Howard | 1,538 | 710,663 R | 61.5% | 38.5% | 61.5% | 38.5% |
| 1990 | 2,564,563 | 1,276,134 | Engler, John | 1,258,539 | Blanchard, James J. | 29,890 | 17,595 R | 49.8% | 49.1% | 50.3% | 49.7% |
| 1986 | 2,396,564 | 753,647 | Lucas, William | 1,632,138 | Blanchard, James J. | 10,779 | 878,491 D | 31.4% | 68.1% | 31.6% | 68.4% |
| 1982 | 3,040,008 | 1,369,582 | Headlee, Richard H. | 1,561,291 | Blanchard, James J. | 109,135 | 191,709 D | 45.1% | 51.4% | 46.7% | 53.3% |
| 1978 | 2,867,212 | 1,628,485 | Milliken, William G. | 1,237,256 | Fitzgerald, William | 1,471 | 391,229 R | 56.8% | 43.2% | 56.8% | 43.2% |
| 1974 | 2,657,017 | 1,356,865 | Milliken, William G. | 1,242,247 | Levin, Sander | 57,905 | 114,618 R | 51.1% | 46.8% | 52.2% | 47.8% |
| 1970 | 2,656,162 | 1,339,047 | Milliken, William G. | 1,294,638 | Levin, Sander | 22,477 | 44,409 R | 50.4% | 48.7% | 50.8% | 49.2% |
| 1966** | 2,461,909 | 1,490,430 | Romney, George W. | 963,383 | Ferency, Zolton A. | 8,096 | 527,047 R | 60.5% | 39.1% | 60.7% | 39.3% |
| 1964 | 3,158,102 | 1,764,355 | Romney, George W. | 1,381,442 | Staebler, Neil | 12,305 | 382,913 R | 55.9% | 43.7% | 56.1% | 43.9% |
| 1962 | 2,764,839 | 1,420,086 | Romney, George W. | 1,339,513 | Swainson, John B. | 5,240 | 80,573 R | 51.4% | 48.4% | 51.5% | 48.5% |
| 1960 | 3,255,991 | 1,602,022 | Bagwell, Paul D. | 1,643,634 | Swainson, John B. | 10,335 | 41,612 D | 49.2% | 50.5% | 49.4% | 50.6% |
| 1958 | 2,312,184 | 1,078,089 | Bagwell, Paul D. | 1,225,533 | Williams, G. Mennen | 8,562 | 147,444 D | 46.6% | 53.0% | 46.8% | 53.2% |
| 1956 | 3,049,651 | 1,376,376 | Cobo, Albert E. | 1,666,689 | Williams, G. Mennen | 6,586 | 290,313 D | 45.1% | 54.7% | 45.2% | 54.8% |
| 1954 | 2,187,027 | 963,300 | Leonard, Donald S. | 1,216,308 | Williams, G. Mennen | 7,419 | 253,008 D | 44.0% | 55.6% | 44.2% | 55.8% |
| 1952 | 2,865,980 | 1,423,275 | Alger, Fred M. | 1,431,893 | Williams, G. Mennen | 10,812 | 8,618 D | 49.7% | 50.0% | 49.8% | 50.2% |
| 1950 | 1,879,382 | 933,998 | Kelly, Harry F. | 935,152 | Williams, G. Mennen | 10,232 | 1,154 D | 49.7% | 49.8% | 50.0% | 50.0% |
| 1948 | 2,113,122 | 964,810 | Sigler, Kim | 1,128,664 | Williams, G. Mennen | 19,648 | 163,854 D | 45.7% | 53.4% | 46.1% | 53.9% |
| 1946 | 1,665,475 | 1,003,878 | Sigler, Kim | 644,540 | Van Wagoner, Murray | 17,057 | 359,338 R | 60.3% | 38.7% | 60.9% | 39.1% |

The term of office of Michigan's governor was increased from two to four years effective with the 1966 election.

## POSTWAR VOTE FOR SENATOR

| Year | Total Vote | Republican Vote | Republican Candidate | Democratic Vote | Democratic Candidate | Other Vote | Rep.-Dem. Plurality | Percentage Total Vote Rep. | Percentage Total Vote Dem. | Percentage Major Vote Rep. | Percentage Major Vote Dem. |
|------|-----------|-----------------|----------------------|-----------------|----------------------|------------|---------------------|------|------|------|------|
| 2002 | 3,129,287 | 1,185,545 | Raczkowski, Andrew | 1,896,614 | Levin, Carl | 47,128 | 711,069 D | 37.9% | 60.6% | 38.5% | 61.5% |
| 2000 | 4,167,685 | 1,994,693 | Abraham, Spencer | 2,061,952 | Stabenow, Debbie | 111,040 | 67,259 D | 47.9% | 49.5% | 49.2% | 50.8% |
| 1996 | 3,762,575 | 1,500,106 | Romney, Ronna | 2,195,738 | Levin, Carl | 66,731 | 695,632 D | 39.9% | 58.4% | 40.6% | 59.4% |
| 1994 | 3,043,385 | 1,578,770 | Abraham, Spencer | 1,300,960 | Carr, M. Robert | 163,655 | 277,810 R | 51.9% | 42.7% | 54.8% | 45.2% |
| 1990 | 2,560,494 | 1,055,695 | Schuette, Bill | 1,471,753 | Levin, Carl | 33,046 | 416,058 D | 41.2% | 57.5% | 41.8% | 58.2% |
| 1988 | 3,505,985 | 1,348,219 | Dunn, Jim | 2,116,865 | Riegle, Donald W. | 40,901 | 768,646 D | 38.5% | 60.4% | 38.9% | 61.1% |
| 1984 | 3,700,938 | 1,745,302 | Lousma, Jack | 1,915,831 | Levin, Carl | 39,805 | 170,529 D | 47.2% | 51.8% | 47.7% | 52.3% |
| 1982 | 2,994,334 | 1,223,288 | Ruppe, Philip E. | 1,728,793 | Riegle, Donald W. | 42,253 | 505,505 D | 40.9% | 57.7% | 41.4% | 58.6% |
| 1978 | 2,846,630 | 1,362,165 | Griffin, Robert P. | 1,484,193 | Levin, Carl | 272 | 122,028 D | 47.9% | 52.1% | 47.9% | 52.1% |
| 1976 | 3,490,664 | 1,635,087 | Esch, Marvin L. | 1,831,031 | Riegle, Donald W. | 24,546 | 195,944 D | 46.8% | 52.5% | 47.2% | 52.8% |
| 1972 | 3,406,906 | 1,781,065 | Griffin, Robert P. | 1,577,178 | Kelley, Frank J. | 48,663 | 203,887 R | 52.3% | 46.3% | 53.0% | 47.0% |
| 1970 | 2,610,839 | 858,470 | Romney, Lenore | 1,744,716 | Hart, Philip A. | 7,653 | 886,246 D | 32.9% | 66.8% | 33.0% | 67.0% |
| 1966 | 2,439,365 | 1,363,530 | Griffin, Robert P. | 1,069,484 | Williams, G. Mennen | 6,351 | 294,046 R | 55.9% | 43.8% | 56.0% | 44.0% |
| 1964 | 3,101,667 | 1,096,272 | Peterson, Elly M. | 1,996,912 | Hart, Philip A. | 8,483 | 900,640 D | 35.3% | 64.4% | 35.4% | 64.6% |
| 1960 | 3,226,647 | 1,548,873 | Bentley, Alvin M. | 1,669,179 | McNamara, Patrick V. | 8,595 | 120,306 D | 48.0% | 51.7% | 48.1% | 51.9% |
| 1958 | 2,271,644 | 1,046,963 | Potter, Charles E. | 1,216,966 | Hart, Philip A. | 7,715 | 170,003 D | 46.1% | 53.6% | 46.2% | 53.8% |
| 1954 | 2,144,840 | 1,049,420 | Ferguson, Homer | 1,088,550 | McNamara, Patrick V. | 6,870 | 39,130 D | 48.9% | 50.8% | 49.1% | 50.9% |
| 1952 | 2,821,133 | 1,428,352 | Potter, Charles E. | 1,383,416 | Moody, Blair | 9,365 | 44,936 R | 50.6% | 49.0% | 50.8% | 49.2% |
| 1948 | 2,062,097 | 1,045,156 | Ferguson, Homer | 1,000,329 | Hook, Frank E. | 16,612 | 44,827 R | 50.7% | 48.5% | 51.1% | 48.9% |
| 1946 | 1,618,720 | 1,085,570 | Vandenberg, Arthur | 517,923 | Lee, James H. | 15,227 | 567,647 R | 67.1% | 32.0% | 67.7% | 32.3% |

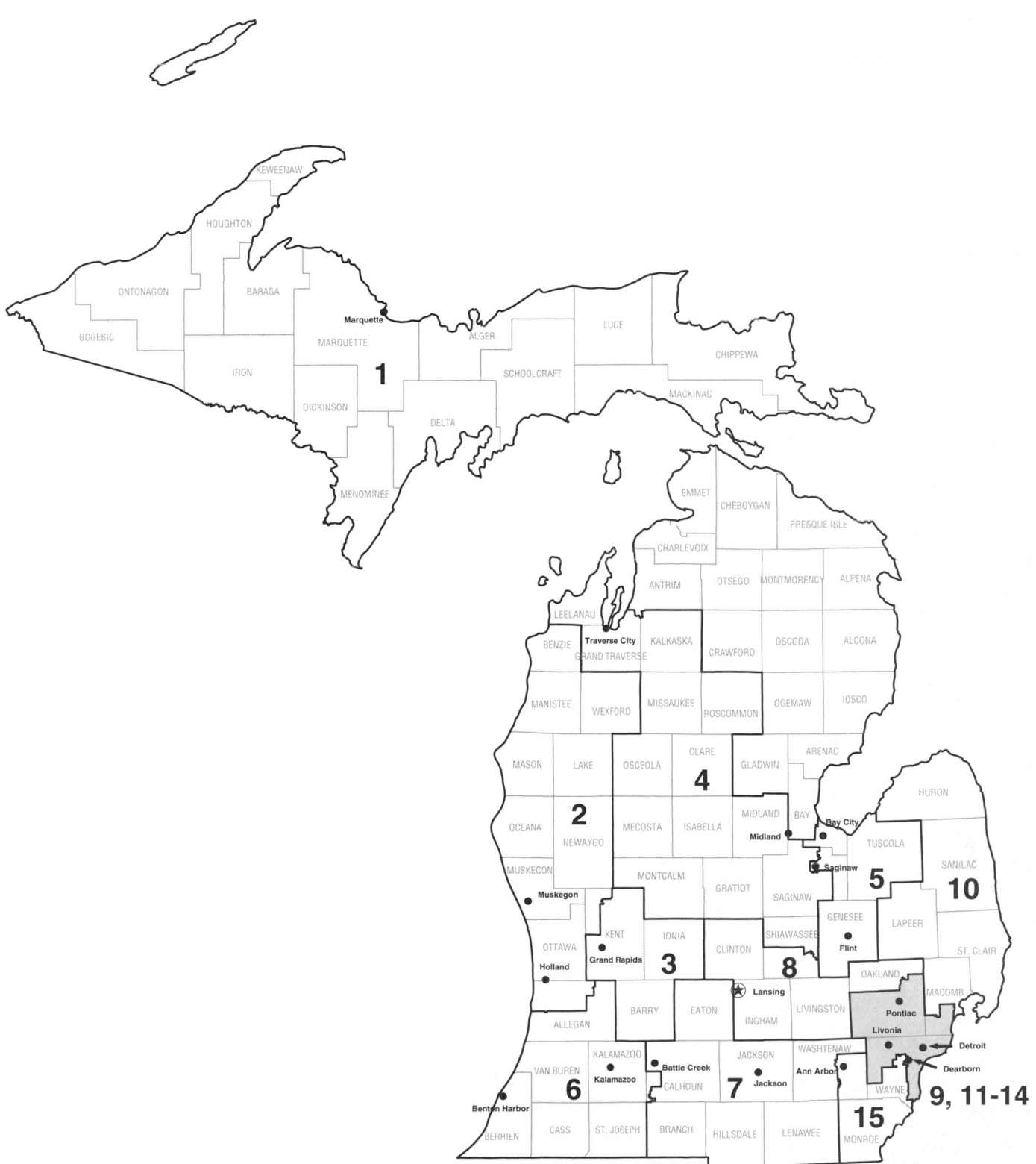

# MICHIGAN

Congressional districts first established for elections held in 2002
15 members

# MICHIGAN

Detroit Area

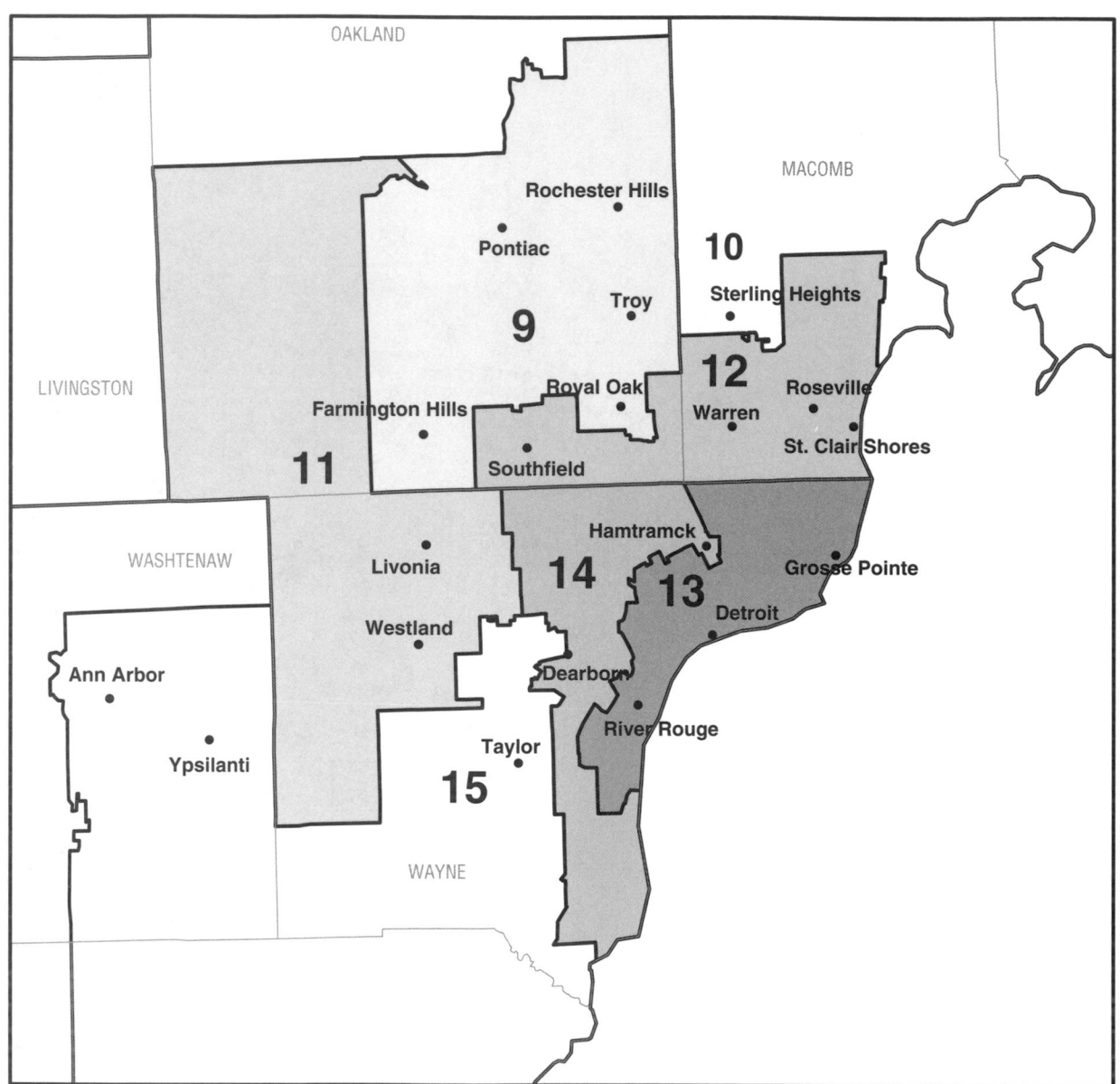

# MICHIGAN

## PRESIDENT 2004

| 2000 Census Population | County | Total Vote | Republican | Democratic | Other | Rep.-Dem. Plurality | Percentage | | | |
|---|---|---|---|---|---|---|---|---|---|---|
| | | | | | | | Total Vote | | Major Vote | |
| | | | | | | | Rep. | Dem. | Rep. | Dem. |
| 11,719 | ALCONA | 6,531 | 3,592 | 2,871 | 68 | 721 R | 55.0% | 44.0% | 55.6% | 44.4% |
| 9,862 | ALGER | 4,765 | 2,318 | 2,395 | 52 | 77 D | 48.6% | 50.3% | 49.2% | 50.8% |
| 105,665 | ALLEGAN | 53,907 | 34,022 | 19,355 | 530 | 14,667 R | 63.1% | 35.9% | 63.7% | 36.3% |
| 31,314 | ALPENA | 15,211 | 7,665 | 7,407 | 139 | 258 R | 50.4% | 48.7% | 50.9% | 49.1% |
| 23,110 | ANTRIM | 13,619 | 8,379 | 5,072 | 168 | 3,307 R | 61.5% | 37.2% | 62.3% | 37.7% |
| 17,269 | ARENAC | 8,216 | 4,071 | 4,076 | 69 | 5 D | 49.5% | 49.6% | 50.0% | 50.0% |
| 8,746 | BARAGA | 3,684 | 1,977 | 1,660 | 47 | 317 R | 53.7% | 45.1% | 54.4% | 45.6% |
| 56,755 | BARRY | 30,272 | 18,638 | 11,312 | 322 | 7,326 R | 61.6% | 37.4% | 62.2% | 37.8% |
| 110,157 | BAY | 57,059 | 25,448 | 31,049 | 562 | 5,601 D | 44.6% | 54.4% | 45.0% | 55.0% |
| 15,998 | BENZIE | 9,778 | 5,284 | 4,383 | 111 | 901 R | 54.0% | 44.8% | 54.7% | 45.3% |
| 162,453 | BERRIEN | 74,671 | 41,076 | 32,846 | 749 | 8,230 R | 55.0% | 44.0% | 55.6% | 44.4% |
| 45,787 | BRANCH | 17,967 | 10,784 | 7,004 | 179 | 3,780 R | 60.0% | 39.0% | 60.6% | 39.4% |
| 137,985 | CALHOUN | 62,667 | 32,093 | 29,891 | 683 | 2,202 R | 51.2% | 47.7% | 51.8% | 48.2% |
| 51,104 | CASS | 22,697 | 12,964 | 9,537 | 196 | 3,427 R | 57.1% | 42.0% | 57.6% | 42.4% |
| 26,090 | CHARLEVOIX | 14,139 | 8,214 | 5,729 | 196 | 2,485 R | 58.1% | 40.5% | 58.9% | 41.1% |
| 26,448 | CHEBOYGAN | 13,887 | 7,798 | 5,941 | 148 | 1,857 R | 56.2% | 42.8% | 56.8% | 43.2% |
| 38,543 | CHIPPEWA | 16,488 | 9,122 | 7,203 | 163 | 1,919 R | 55.3% | 43.7% | 55.9% | 44.1% |
| 31,252 | CLARE | 14,226 | 7,088 | 6,984 | 154 | 104 R | 49.8% | 49.1% | 50.4% | 49.6% |
| 64,753 | CLINTON | 37,807 | 21,989 | 15,483 | 335 | 6,506 R | 58.2% | 41.0% | 58.7% | 41.3% |
| 14,273 | CRAWFORD | 7,235 | 4,017 | 3,126 | 92 | 891 R | 55.5% | 43.2% | 56.2% | 43.8% |
| 38,520 | DELTA | 19,238 | 9,680 | 9,381 | 177 | 299 R | 50.3% | 48.8% | 50.8% | 49.2% |
| 27,472 | DICKINSON | 13,549 | 7,734 | 5,650 | 165 | 2,084 R | 57.1% | 41.7% | 57.8% | 42.2% |
| 103,655 | EATON | 55,755 | 29,781 | 25,411 | 563 | 4,370 R | 53.4% | 45.6% | 54.0% | 46.0% |
| 31,437 | EMMET | 17,372 | 10,332 | 6,846 | 194 | 3,486 R | 59.5% | 39.4% | 60.1% | 39.9% |
| 436,141 | GENESEE | 213,775 | 83,870 | 128,334 | 1,571 | 44,464 D | 39.2% | 60.0% | 39.5% | 60.5% |
| 26,023 | GLADWIN | 13,227 | 6,770 | 6,343 | 114 | 427 R | 51.2% | 48.0% | 51.6% | 48.4% |
| 17,370 | GOGEBIC | 8,452 | 3,935 | 4,421 | 96 | 486 D | 46.6% | 52.3% | 47.1% | 52.9% |
| 77,654 | GRAND TRAVERSE | 46,191 | 27,446 | 18,256 | 489 | 9,190 R | 59.4% | 39.5% | 60.1% | 39.9% |
| 42,285 | GRATIOT | 17,379 | 9,834 | 7,377 | 168 | 2,457 R | 56.6% | 42.4% | 57.1% | 42.9% |
| 46,527 | HILLSDALE | 20,216 | 12,804 | 7,123 | 289 | 5,681 R | 63.3% | 35.2% | 64.3% | 35.7% |
| 36,016 | HOUGHTON | 15,851 | 8,889 | 6,731 | 231 | 2,158 R | 56.1% | 42.5% | 56.9% | 43.1% |
| 36,079 | HURON | 17,466 | 9,671 | 7,629 | 166 | 2,042 R | 55.4% | 43.7% | 55.9% | 44.1% |
| 279,320 | INGHAM | 133,053 | 54,734 | 76,877 | 1,442 | 22,143 D | 41.1% | 57.8% | 41.6% | 58.4% |
| 61,518 | IONIA | 27,618 | 16,621 | 10,647 | 350 | 5,974 R | 60.2% | 38.6% | 61.0% | 39.0% |
| 27,339 | IOSCO | 14,006 | 7,301 | 6,557 | 148 | 744 R | 52.1% | 46.8% | 52.7% | 47.3% |
| 13,138 | IRON | 6,511 | 3,224 | 3,215 | 72 | 9 R | 49.5% | 49.4% | 50.1% | 49.9% |
| 63,351 | ISABELLA | 24,390 | 11,754 | 12,334 | 302 | 580 D | 48.2% | 50.6% | 48.8% | 51.2% |
| 158,422 | JACKSON | 71,795 | 40,029 | 31,025 | 741 | 9,004 R | 55.8% | 43.2% | 56.3% | 43.7% |
| 238,603 | KALAMAZOO | 119,783 | 57,147 | 61,462 | 1,174 | 4,315 D | 47.7% | 51.3% | 48.2% | 51.8% |
| 16,571 | KALKASKA | 8,380 | 5,084 | 3,189 | 107 | 1,895 R | 60.7% | 38.1% | 61.5% | 38.5% |
| 574,335 | KENT | 290,891 | 171,201 | 116,909 | 2,781 | 54,292 R | 58.9% | 40.2% | 59.4% | 40.6% |
| 2,301 | KEWEENAW | 1,439 | 781 | 630 | 28 | 151 R | 54.3% | 43.8% | 55.4% | 44.6% |
| 11,333 | LAKE | 5,246 | 2,503 | 2,675 | 68 | 172 D | 47.7% | 51.0% | 48.3% | 51.7% |
| 87,904 | LAPEER | 44,147 | 25,556 | 18,086 | 505 | 7,470 R | 57.9% | 41.0% | 58.6% | 41.4% |
| 21,119 | LEELANAU | 13,917 | 7,733 | 6,048 | 136 | 1,685 R | 55.6% | 43.5% | 56.1% | 43.9% |
| 98,890 | LENAWEE | 47,012 | 25,675 | 20,787 | 550 | 4,888 R | 54.6% | 44.2% | 55.3% | 44.7% |
| 156,951 | LIVINGSTON | 93,742 | 58,860 | 33,991 | 891 | 24,869 R | 62.8% | 36.3% | 63.4% | 36.6% |
| 7,024 | LUCE | 2,829 | 1,749 | 1,045 | 35 | 704 R | 61.8% | 36.9% | 62.6% | 37.4% |
| 11,943 | MACKINAC | 6,599 | 3,706 | 2,819 | 74 | 887 R | 56.2% | 42.7% | 56.8% | 43.2% |
| 788,149 | MACOMB | 402,410 | 202,166 | 196,160 | 4,084 | 6,006 R | 50.2% | 48.7% | 50.8% | 49.2% |
| 24,527 | MANISTEE | 12,740 | 6,295 | 6,272 | 173 | 23 R | 49.4% | 49.2% | 50.1% | 49.9% |
| 64,634 | MARQUETTE | 32,488 | 14,690 | 17,412 | 386 | 2,722 D | 45.2% | 53.6% | 45.8% | 54.2% |
| 28,274 | MASON | 14,611 | 8,124 | 6,333 | 154 | 1,791 R | 55.6% | 43.3% | 56.2% | 43.8% |
| 40,553 | MECOSTA | 17,581 | 9,710 | 7,730 | 141 | 1,980 R | 55.2% | 44.0% | 55.7% | 44.3% |
| 25,326 | MENOMINEE | 11,419 | 5,942 | 5,326 | 151 | 616 R | 52.0% | 46.6% | 52.7% | 47.3% |
| 82,874 | MIDLAND | 43,275 | 24,369 | 18,355 | 551 | 6,014 R | 56.3% | 42.4% | 57.0% | 43.0% |
| 14,478 | MISSAUKEE | 7,421 | 5,055 | 2,319 | 47 | 2,736 R | 68.1% | 31.2% | 68.6% | 31.4% |
| 145,945 | MONROE | 74,132 | 37,470 | 36,089 | 573 | 1,381 R | 50.5% | 48.7% | 50.9% | 49.1% |
| 61,266 | MONTCALM | 26,734 | 14,968 | 11,471 | 295 | 3,497 R | 56.0% | 42.9% | 56.6% | 43.4% |
| 10,315 | MONTMORENCY | 5,563 | 3,300 | 2,196 | 67 | 1,104 R | 59.3% | 39.5% | 60.0% | 40.0% |

# MICHIGAN

## PRESIDENT 2004

| 2000 Census Population | County | Total Vote | Republican | Democratic | Other | Rep.-Dem. Plurality | Percentage Total Vote Rep. | Total Vote Dem. | Major Vote Rep. | Major Vote Dem. |
|---|---|---|---|---|---|---|---|---|---|---|
| 170,200 | MUSKEGON | 80,313 | 35,302 | 44,282 | 729 | 8,980 D | 44.0% | 55.1% | 44.4% | 55.6% |
| 47,874 | NEWAYGO | 22,873 | 13,608 | 9,057 | 208 | 4,551 R | 59.5% | 39.6% | 60.0% | 40.0% |
| 1,194,156 | OAKLAND | 641,977 | 316,633 | 319,387 | 5,957 | 2,754 D | 49.3% | 49.8% | 49.8% | 50.2% |
| 26,873 | OCEANA | 12,297 | 6,677 | 5,441 | 179 | 1,236 R | 54.3% | 44.2% | 55.1% | 44.9% |
| 21,645 | OGEMAW | 10,796 | 5,454 | 5,215 | 127 | 239 R | 50.5% | 48.3% | 51.1% | 48.9% |
| 7,818 | ONTONAGON | 4,192 | 2,262 | 1,863 | 67 | 399 R | 54.0% | 44.4% | 54.8% | 45.2% |
| 23,197 | OSCEOLA | 11,188 | 6,599 | 4,467 | 122 | 2,132 R | 59.0% | 39.9% | 59.6% | 40.4% |
| 9,418 | OSCODA | 4,409 | 2,570 | 1,792 | 47 | 778 R | 58.3% | 40.6% | 58.9% | 41.1% |
| 23,301 | OTSEGO | 12,307 | 7,470 | 4,674 | 163 | 2,796 R | 60.7% | 38.0% | 61.5% | 38.5% |
| 238,314 | OTTAWA | 128,643 | 92,048 | 35,552 | 1,043 | 56,496 R | 71.6% | 27.6% | 72.1% | 27.9% |
| 14,411 | PRESQUE ISLE | 7,516 | 3,982 | 3,432 | 102 | 550 R | 53.0% | 45.7% | 53.7% | 46.3% |
| 25,469 | ROSCOMMON | 14,359 | 7,364 | 6,810 | 185 | 554 R | 51.3% | 47.4% | 52.0% | 48.0% |
| 210,039 | SAGINAW | 102,852 | 47,165 | 54,887 | 800 | 7,722 D | 45.9% | 53.4% | 46.2% | 53.8% |
| 164,235 | ST. CLAIR | 79,743 | 42,740 | 36,174 | 829 | 6,566 R | 53.6% | 45.4% | 54.2% | 45.8% |
| 62,422 | ST. JOSEPH | 25,239 | 15,340 | 9,648 | 251 | 5,692 R | 60.8% | 38.2% | 61.4% | 38.6% |
| 44,547 | SANILAC | 20,763 | 12,632 | 7,883 | 248 | 4,749 R | 60.8% | 38.0% | 61.6% | 38.4% |
| 8,903 | SCHOOLCRAFT | 4,441 | 2,267 | 2,137 | 37 | 130 R | 51.0% | 48.1% | 51.5% | 48.5% |
| 71,687 | SHIAWASSEE | 36,651 | 19,407 | 16,881 | 363 | 2,526 R | 53.0% | 46.1% | 53.5% | 46.5% |
| 58,266 | TUSCOLA | 28,338 | 15,389 | 12,631 | 318 | 2,758 R | 54.3% | 44.6% | 54.9% | 45.1% |
| 76,263 | VAN BUREN | 34,174 | 17,634 | 16,151 | 389 | 1,483 R | 51.6% | 47.3% | 52.2% | 47.8% |
| 322,895 | WASHTENAW | 173,264 | 61,455 | 109,953 | 1,856 | 48,498 D | 35.5% | 63.5% | 35.9% | 64.1% |
| 2,061,162 | WAYNE | 864,728 | 257,750 | 600,047 | 6,931 | 342,297 D | 29.8% | 69.4% | 30.0% | 70.0% |
| 30,484 | WEXFORD | 15,160 | 8,966 | 6,034 | 160 | 2,932 R | 59.1% | 39.8% | 59.8% | 40.2% |
| 9,938,444 | TOTAL | 4,839,252 | 2,313,746 | 2,479,183 | 46,323 | 165,437 D | 47.8% | 51.2% | 48.3% | 51.7% |

# MICHIGAN

## HOUSE OF REPRESENTATIVES

| CD | Year | Total Vote | Republican Vote | Republican Candidate | Democratic Vote | Democratic Candidate | Other Vote | Rep.-Dem. Plurality | Total Vote Rep. | Total Vote Dem. | Major Vote Rep. | Major Vote Dem. |
|---|---|---|---|---|---|---|---|---|---|---|---|---|
| 1 | 2004 | 322,674 | 105,706 | Hooper, Don | 211,571 | Stupak, Bart* | 5,397 | 105,865 D | 32.8% | 65.6% | 33.3% | 66.7% |
| 1 | 2002 | 222,687 | 69,254 | Hooper, Don | 150,701 | Stupak, Bart* | 2,732 | 81,447 D | 31.1% | 67.7% | 31.5% | 68.5% |
| 2 | 2004 | 325,005 | 225,343 | Hoekstra, Peter* | 94,040 | Kotos, Kimon | 5,622 | 131,303 R | 69.3% | 28.9% | 70.6% | 29.4% |
| 2 | 2002 | 222,907 | 156,937 | Hoekstra, Peter* | 61,749 | Wrisley, Jeff | 4,221 | 95,188 R | 70.4% | 27.7% | 71.8% | 28.2% |
| 3 | 2004 | 322,103 | 214,465 | Ehlers, Vernon J.* | 101,395 | Hickey, Peter | 6,243 | 113,070 R | 66.6% | 31.5% | 67.9% | 32.1% |
| 3 | 2002 | 218,855 | 153,131 | Ehlers, Vernon J.* | 61,987 | Lynnes, Kathryn | 3,737 | 91,144 R | 70.0% | 28.3% | 71.2% | 28.8% |
| 4 | 2004 | 318,924 | 205,274 | Camp, Dave* | 110,885 | Huckleberry, Mike | 2,765 | 94,389 R | 64.4% | 34.8% | 64.9% | 35.1% |
| 4 | 2002 | 218,573 | 149,090 | Camp, Dave* | 65,950 | Hollenbeck, Lawrence | 3,533 | 83,140 R | 68.2% | 30.2% | 69.3% | 30.7% |
| 5 | 2004 | 309,915 | 96,934 | Kirkwood, Myrah | 208,163 | Kildee, Dale E.* | 4,818 | 111,229 D | 31.3% | 67.2% | 31.8% | 68.2% |
| 5 | 2002 | 173,339 | | | 158,709 | Kildee, Dale E.* | 14,630 | 158,709 D | | 91.6% | | 100.0% |
| 6 | 2004 | 302,158 | 197,425 | Upton, Fred* | 97,978 | Elliott, Scott | 6,755 | 99,447 R | 65.3% | 32.4% | 66.8% | 33.2% |
| 6 | 2002 | 183,517 | 126,936 | Upton, Fred* | 53,793 | Giguere, Gary, Jr. | 2,788 | 73,143 R | 69.2% | 29.3% | 70.2% | 29.8% |
| 7 | 2004 | 301,642 | 176,053 | Schwarz, Joe | 109,527 | Renier, Sharon | 16,062 | 66,526 R | 58.4% | 36.3% | 61.6% | 38.4% |
| 7 | 2002 | 203,069 | 121,142 | Smith, Nick* | 78,412 | Simpson, Mike | 3,515 | 42,730 R | 59.7% | 38.6% | 60.7% | 39.3% |
| 8 | 2004 | 340,423 | 207,925 | Rogers, Mike* | 125,619 | Alexander, Robert | 6,879 | 82,306 R | 61.1% | 36.9% | 62.3% | 37.7% |
| 8 | 2002 | 230,597 | 156,525 | Rogers, Mike* | 70,920 | McAlpine, Frank | 3,152 | 85,605 R | 67.9% | 30.8% | 68.8% | 31.2% |

# MICHIGAN

## HOUSE OF REPRESENTATIVES

| CD | Year | Total Vote | Republican Vote | Republican Candidate | Democratic Vote | Democratic Candidate | Other Vote | Rep.-Dem. Plurality | Total Vote Rep. | Total Vote Dem. | Major Vote Rep. | Major Vote Dem. |
|----|------|-----------|-----------------|----------------------|-----------------|----------------------|-----------|---------------------|-----------------|-----------------|-----------------|-----------------|
| 9 | 2004 | 340,799 | 199,210 | Knollenberg, Joe* | 134,764 | Reifman, Steven | 6,825 | 64,446 R | 58.5% | 39.5% | 59.6% | 40.4% |
| 9 | 2002 | 242,880 | 141,102 | Knollenberg, Joe* | 96,856 | Fink, David | 4,922 | 44,246 R | 58.1% | 39.9% | 59.3% | 40.7% |
| 10 | 2004 | 331,868 | 227,720 | Miller, Candice S.* | 98,029 | Casey, Rob | 6,119 | 129,691 R | 68.6% | 29.5% | 69.9% | 30.1% |
| 10 | 2002 | 216,928 | 137,339 | Miller, Candice S. | 77,053 | Marlinga, Carl | 2,536 | 60,286 R | 63.3% | 35.5% | 64.1% | 35.9% |
| 11 | 2004 | 327,216 | 186,431 | McCotter, Thaddeus* | 134,301 | Truran, Phillip | 6,484 | 52,130 R | 57.0% | 41.0% | 58.1% | 41.9% |
| 11 | 2002 | 220,405 | 126,050 | McCotter, Thaddeus | 87,402 | Kelley, Kevin | 6,953 | 38,648 R | 57.2% | 39.7% | 59.1% | 40.9% |
| 12 | 2004 | 304,134 | 88,256 | Shafer, Randell | 210,827 | Levin, Sander M.* | 5,051 | 122,571 D | 29.0% | 69.3% | 29.5% | 70.5% |
| 12 | 2002 | 206,528 | 61,502 | Dean, Harvey | 140,970 | Levin, Sander M.* | 4,056 | 79,468 D | 29.8% | 68.3% | 30.4% | 69.6% |
| 13 | 2004 | 221,654 | 40,935 | Cassell, Cynthia | 173,246 | Kilpatrick, Carolyn Cheeks* | 7,473 | 132,311 D | 18.5% | 78.2% | 19.1% | 80.9% |
| 13 | 2002 | 131,941 | | | 120,869 | Kilpatrick, Carolyn Cheeks* | 11,072 | 120,869 D | | 91.6% | | 100.0% |
| 14 | 2004 | 254,580 | 35,089 | Pedraza, Veronica | 213,681 | Conyers, John, Jr.* | 5,810 | 178,592 D | 13.8% | 83.9% | 14.1% | 85.9% |
| 14 | 2002 | 174,608 | 26,544 | Stone, Dave | 145,285 | Conyers, John, Jr.* | 2,779 | 118,741 D | 15.2% | 83.2% | 15.4% | 84.6% |
| 15 | 2004 | 307,963 | 81,828 | Reamer, Dawn | 218,409 | Dingell, John D.* | 7,726 | 136,581 D | 26.6% | 70.9% | 27.3% | 72.7% |
| 15 | 2002 | 189,063 | 48,626 | Kaltenbach, Martin | 136,518 | Dingell, John D.* | 3,919 | 87,892 D | 25.7% | 72.2% | 26.3% | 73.7% |
| Total | 2004 | 4,631,058 | 2,288,594 | | 2,242,435 | | 100,029 | 46,159 R | 49.4% | 48.4% | 50.5% | 49.5% |
| Total | 2002 | 3,055,897 | 1,474,178 | | 1,507,174 | | 74,545 | 32,996 D | 48.2% | 49.3% | 49.4% | 50.6% |

An asterisk (*) denotes incumbent.

# MICHIGAN

## GENERAL AND PRIMARY ELECTIONS

## 2004 GENERAL ELECTIONS

**President**    Other vote was 24,035 No Party Affiliation (Ralph Nader); 10,552 Libertarian (Michael Badnarik); 5,325 Green (David Cobb); 4,980 U.S. Taxpayers (Michael Peroutka); 1,431 Natural Law (Walter F. Brown).

**House**    Other vote was:

CD 1    3,105 Green (David Newland); 2,292 Libertarian (John Loosemore).

CD 2    2,876 Libertarian (Steve VanTil); 2,746 U.S. Taxpayers (Ronald Graeser).

CD 3    3,695 Libertarian (Warren Adams); 2,548 U.S. Taxpayers (Marcel Sales).

CD 4    2,765 Libertarian (Albert Chia Jr.).

CD 5    2,468 Green (Harley Mikkelson); 2,350 Libertarian (Clint Foster).

CD 6    2,311 Green (Randall MacPhee); 2,275 Libertarian (Erwin Haas); 2,169 U.S. Taxpayers (W. Dennis FitzSimons).

CD 7    9,032 U.S. Taxpayers (David Horn); 3,996 Green (Jason Seagraves); 3,034 Libertarian (Kenneth Proctor).

CD 8    3,591 Libertarian (Will White); 3,288 U.S. Taxpayers (John Mangopoulos).

CD 9    6,825 Libertarian (Robert Schubring).

CD 10    3,966 Libertarian (Phoebe Basso); 2,153 Natural Law (Anthony America).

CD 11    6,484 Libertarian (Charles Basso Jr.).

CD 12    5,051 Libertarian (Dick Gach).

CD 13    4,261 Green (Thomas Lavigne); 3,211 Libertarian (Eric Gordon); 1 write-in (Osborne Hart).

CD 14    2,278 Libertarian (Michael Donahue); 2,224 Green (Lisa Weltman); 1,307 U.S. Taxpayers (Wilbert Sears); 1 write-in (Nathaniel Banks).

CD 15    3,400 Libertarian (Gregory Stempfle); 2,508 U.S. Taxpayers (Mike Eller); 1,818 No Party Affiliation (Jerome White).

# MICHIGAN

## GENERAL AND PRIMARY ELECTIONS

## 2004 PRIMARY ELECTIONS

| | | | |
|---|---|---|---|
| **Primary** | August 3, 2004 | **Registration** (as of July 6, 2004) | 6,916,340   No Party Registration |

**Primary Type**   Open—Any registered voter could participate in the primary of either party.

Note:   An asterisk (*) denotes incumbent.

| | REPUBLICAN PRIMARIES | | | DEMOCRATIC PRIMARIES | | |
|---|---|---|---|---|---|---|
| Congressional District 1 | Don Hooper | 39,964 | 100.0% | Bart Stupak* | 53,114 | 100.0% |
| Congressional District 2 | Peter Hoekstra* | 59,066 | 100.0% | Kimon Kotos | 18,603 | 100.0% |
| Congressional District 3 | Vernon J. Ehlers* | 91,241 | 100.0% | Peter Hickey | 26,006 | 100.0% |
| Congressional District 4 | Dave Camp* | 70,345 | 100.0% | Mike Huckleberry | 19,947 | 100.0% |
| Congressional District 5 | Myrah Kirkwood | 16,798 | 100.0% | Dale E. Kildee* | 62,626 | 100.0% |
| Congressional District 6 | Fred Upton* | 59,786 | 100.0% | Scott Elliott | 14,100 | 100.0% |
| Congressional District 7 | Joe Schwarz | 20,440 | 27.8% | Sharon Renier | 8,944 | 52.0% |
| | Brad Smith | 16,488 | 22.4% | Drew Walker | 4,204 | 24.4% |
| | Tim Walberg | 12,973 | 17.7% | Douglas Wilson | 4,057 | 23.6% |
| | Clark Bisbee | 10,301 | 14.0% | | | |
| | Gene DeRossett | 8,379 | 11.4% | | | |
| | Paul DeWeese | 4,886 | 6.7% | | | |
| | TOTAL | 73,467 | | TOTAL | 17,205 | |
| Congressional District 8 | Mike Rogers* | 53,418 | 100.0% | Robert Alexander | 13,114 | 59.4% |
| | | | | Matthew Ferguson | 8,978 | 40.6% |
| | | | | TOTAL | 22,092 | |
| Congressional District 9 | Joe Knollenberg* | 54,255 | 100.0% | Steven Reifman | 14,699 | 61.4% |
| | | | | Bart Baron | 9,257 | 38.6% |
| | | | | TOTAL | 23,956 | |
| Congressional District 10 | Candice S. Miller* | 60,012 | 100.0% | Rob Casey | 20,732 | 100.0% |
| Congressional District 11 | Thaddeus McCotter* | 32,619 | 100.0% | Phillip Truran | 15,762 | 68.9% |
| | | | | Mario Fundarski | 7,108 | 31.1% |
| | | | | TOTAL | 22,870 | |
| Congressional District 12 | Randell Shafer | 19,272 | 100.0% | Sander M. Levin* | 46,466 | 100.0% |
| Congressional District 13 | Cynthia Cassell | 6,218 | 100.0% | Carolyn Cheeks Kilpatrick* | 42,415 | 100.0% |
| Congressional District 14 | Veronica Pedraza | 5,402 | 100.0% | John Conyers Jr.* | 54,790 | 100.0% |
| Congressional District 15 | Dawn Reamer | 13,612 | 100.0% | John D. Dingell* | 45,348 | 100.0% |

# MINNESOTA

## GOVERNOR
Tim Pawlenty (R). Elected 2002 to a four-year term.

## SENATORS (1 Democrat, 1 Republican)
Norm Coleman (R). Elected 2002 to a six-year term.

Mark Dayton (D). Elected 2000 to a six-year term.

## REPRESENTATIVES (4 Democrats, 4 Republicans)
1. Gil Gutknecht (R)
2. John Kline (R)
3. Jim Ramstad (R)
4. Betty McCollum (D)
5. Martin Olav Sabo (D)
6. Mark Kennedy (R)
7. Collin C. Peterson (D)
8. James L. Oberstar (D)

## POSTWAR VOTE FOR PRESIDENT

| | | Republican | | Democratic | | | | Percentage | | | |
| | | | | | | | | Total Vote | | Major Vote | |
| Year | Total Vote | Vote | Candidate | Vote | Candidate | Other Vote | Plurality | Rep. | Dem. | Rep. | Dem. |
|---|---|---|---|---|---|---|---|---|---|---|---|
| 2004 | 2,828,387 | 1,346,695 | Bush, George W. | 1,445,014 | Kerry, John | 36,678 | 98,319 D | 47.6% | 51.1% | 48.2% | 51.8% |
| 2000** | 2,438,685 | 1,109,659 | Bush, George W. | 1,168,266 | Gore, Al | 160,760 | 58,607 D | 45.5% | 47.9% | 48.7% | 51.3% |
| 1996** | 2,192,640 | 766,476 | Dole, Bob | 1,120,438 | Clinton, Bill | 305,726 | 353,962 D | 35.0% | 51.1% | 40.6% | 59.4% |
| 1992** | 2,347,948 | 747,841 | Bush, George | 1,020,997 | Clinton, Bill | 579,110 | 273,156 D | 31.9% | 43.5% | 42.3% | 57.7% |
| 1988 | 2,096,790 | 962,337 | Bush, George | 1,109,471 | Dukakis, Michael S. | 24,982 | 147,134 D | 45.9% | 52.9% | 46.4% | 53.6% |
| 1984 | 2,084,449 | 1,032,603 | Reagan, Ronald | 1,036,364 | Mondale, Walter F. | 15,482 | 3,761 D | 49.5% | 49.7% | 49.9% | 50.1% |
| 1980** | 2,051,980 | 873,268 | Reagan, Ronald | 954,174 | Carter, Jimmy | 224,538 | 80,906 D | 42.6% | 46.5% | 47.8% | 52.2% |
| 1976 | 1,949,931 | 819,395 | Ford, Gerald R. | 1,070,440 | Carter, Jimmy | 60,096 | 251,045 D | 42.0% | 54.9% | 43.4% | 56.6% |
| 1972 | 1,741,652 | 898,269 | Nixon, Richard M. | 802,346 | McGovern, George S. | 41,037 | 95,923 R | 51.6% | 46.1% | 52.8% | 47.2% |
| 1968** | 1,588,506 | 658,643 | Nixon, Richard M. | 857,738 | Humphrey, Hubert H. | 72,125 | 199,095 D | 41.5% | 54.0% | 43.4% | 56.6% |
| 1964 | 1,554,462 | 559,624 | Goldwater, Barry M. | 991,117 | Johnson, Lyndon B. | 3,721 | 431,493 D | 36.0% | 63.8% | 36.1% | 63.9% |
| 1960 | 1,541,887 | 757,915 | Nixon, Richard M. | 779,933 | Kennedy, John F. | 4,039 | 22,018 D | 49.2% | 50.6% | 49.3% | 50.7% |
| 1956 | 1,340,005 | 719,302 | Eisenhower, Dwight D. | 617,525 | Stevenson, Adlai E. | 3,178 | 101,777 R | 53.7% | 46.1% | 53.8% | 46.2% |
| 1952 | 1,379,483 | 763,211 | Eisenhower, Dwight D. | 608,458 | Stevenson, Adlai E. | 7,814 | 154,753 R | 55.3% | 44.1% | 55.6% | 44.4% |
| 1948 | 1,212,226 | 483,617 | Dewey, Thomas E. | 692,966 | Truman, Harry S. | 35,643 | 209,349 D | 39.9% | 57.2% | 41.1% | 58.9% |

In past elections, the other vote included: 2000 - 126,696 Green (Nader); 1996 - 257,704 Reform (Ross Perot); 1992 - 562,506 Independent (Perot); 1980 - 174,990 Independent (John Anderson); 1968 - 68,931 American Independent (George Wallace).

# MINNESOTA

## POSTWAR VOTE FOR GOVERNOR

| Year | Total Vote | Republican | | Democratic | | Other Vote | Rep.-Dem. Plurality | Percentage | | | |
|------|------------|------------|-----------|------------|----------|------------|---------------------|------------|------|------------|------|
| | | | | | | | | Total Vote | | Major Vote | |
| | | Vote | Candidate | Vote | Candidate | | | Rep. | Dem. | Rep. | Dem. |
| 2002** | 2,252,473 | 999,473 | Pawlenty, Tim | 821,268 | Moe, Roger D. | 431,732 | 178,205 R | 44.4% | 36.5% | 54.9% | 45.1% |
| 1998** | 2,090,518 | 716,880 | Coleman, Norm | 587,060 | Humphrey, Hubert H., III | 786,578 | 56,523 V | 34.3% | 28.1% | 55.0% | 45.0% |
| 1994 | 1,765,590 | 1,094,165 | Carlson, Arne | 589,344 | Marty, John | 82,081 | 504,821 R | 62.0% | 33.4% | 65.0% | 35.0% |
| 1990 | 1,806,777 | 895,988 | Carlson, Arne | 836,218 | Perpich, Rudy | 74,571 | 59,770 R | 49.6% | 46.3% | 51.7% | 48.3% |
| 1986 | 1,415,989 | 606,755 | Ludeman, Cal R. | 790,138 | Perpich, Rudy | 19,096 | 183,383 D | 42.9% | 55.8% | 43.4% | 56.6% |
| 1982 | 1,789,539 | 715,796 | Whitney, Wheelock | 1,049,104 | Perpich, Rudy | 24,639 | 333,308 D | 40.0% | 58.6% | 40.6% | 59.4% |
| 1978 | 1,585,702 | 830,019 | Quie, Albert H. | 718,244 | Perpich, Rudy | 37,439 | 111,775 R | 52.3% | 45.3% | 53.6% | 46.4% |
| 1974 | 1,252,898 | 367,722 | Johnson, John W. | 786,787 | Anderson, Wendell R. | 98,389 | 419,065 D | 29.3% | 62.8% | 31.9% | 68.1% |
| 1970 | 1,365,443 | 621,780 | Head, Douglas M. | 737,921 | Anderson, Wendell R. | 5,742 | 116,141 D | 45.5% | 54.0% | 45.7% | 54.3% |
| 1966 | 1,295,058 | 680,593 | LeVander, Harold | 607,943 | Rolvaag, Karl F. | 6,522 | 72,650 R | 52.6% | 46.9% | 52.8% | 47.2% |
| 1962** | 1,246,904 | 619,751 | Andersen, Elmer L. | 619,842 | Rolvaag, Karl F. | 7,311 | 91 D | 49.7% | 49.7% | 50.0% | 50.0% |
| 1960 | 1,550,265 | 783,813 | Andersen, Elmer L. | 760,934 | Freeman, Orville L. | 5,518 | 22,879 R | 50.6% | 49.1% | 50.7% | 49.3% |
| 1958 | 1,159,915 | 490,731 | MacKinnon, George | 658,326 | Freeman, Orville L. | 10,858 | 167,595 D | 42.3% | 56.8% | 42.7% | 57.3% |
| 1956 | 1,422,161 | 685,196 | Nelsen, Ancher | 731,180 | Freeman, Orville L. | 5,785 | 45,984 D | 48.2% | 51.4% | 48.4% | 51.6% |
| 1954 | 1,151,417 | 538,865 | Anderson, C. Elmer | 607,099 | Freeman, Orville L. | 5,453 | 68,234 D | 46.8% | 52.7% | 47.0% | 53.0% |
| 1952 | 1,418,869 | 785,125 | Anderson, C. Elmer | 624,480 | Freeman, Orville L. | 9,264 | 160,645 R | 55.3% | 44.0% | 55.7% | 44.3% |
| 1950 | 1,046,632 | 635,800 | Youngdahl, Luther | 400,637 | Peterson, Harry H. | 10,195 | 235,163 R | 60.7% | 38.3% | 61.3% | 38.7% |
| 1948 | 1,210,894 | 643,572 | Youngdahl, Luther | 545,766 | Halsted, Charles L. | 21,556 | 97,806 R | 53.1% | 45.1% | 54.1% | 45.9% |
| 1946 | 880,348 | 519,067 | Youngdahl, Luther | 349,565 | Barker, Harold H. | 11,716 | 169,502 R | 59.0% | 39.7% | 59.8% | 40.2% |

In past elections, the other vote included: 2002 - 364,534 Independence (Timothy J. Penny); 1998 - 773,403 Reform (Jesse Ventura), who was elected with 37.0 percent of the total vote. The term of office of Minnesota's governor was increased from two to four years effective with the 1962 election.

## POSTWAR VOTE FOR SENATOR

| Year | Total Vote | Republican | | Democratic | | Other Vote | Rep.-Dem. Plurality | Percentage | | | |
|------|------------|------------|-----------|------------|----------|------------|---------------------|------------|------|------------|------|
| | | | | | | | | Total Vote | | Major Vote | |
| | | Vote | Candidate | Vote | Candidate | | | Rep. | Dem. | Rep. | Dem. |
| 2002** | 2,254,639 | 1,116,697 | Coleman, Norm | 1,067,246 | Mondale, Walter F. | 70,696 | 49,451 R | 49.5% | 47.3% | 51.1% | 48.9% |
| 2000 | 2,419,520 | 1,047,474 | Grams, Rod | 1,181,553 | Dayton, Mark | 190,493 | 134,079 D | 43.3% | 48.8% | 47.0% | 53.0% |
| 1996 | 2,183,062 | 901,282 | Boschwitz, Rudy | 1,098,493 | Wellstone, Paul | 183,287 | 197,211 D | 41.3% | 50.3% | 45.1% | 54.9% |
| 1994 | 1,772,929 | 869,653 | Grams, Rod | 781,860 | Wynia, Ann | 121,416 | 87,793 R | 49.1% | 44.1% | 52.7% | 47.3% |
| 1990 | 1,808,045 | 864,375 | Boschwitz, Rudy | 911,999 | Wellstone, Paul | 31,671 | 47,624 D | 47.8% | 50.4% | 48.7% | 51.3% |
| 1988 | 2,093,953 | 1,176,210 | Durenberger, David | 856,694 | Humphrey, Hubert H., III | 61,049 | 319,516 R | 56.2% | 40.9% | 57.9% | 42.1% |
| 1984 | 2,066,143 | 1,199,926 | Boschwitz, Rudy | 852,844 | Growe, Joan Anderson | 13,373 | 347,082 R | 58.1% | 41.3% | 58.5% | 41.5% |
| 1982 | 1,804,675 | 949,207 | Durenberger, David | 840,401 | Dayton, Mark | 15,067 | 108,806 R | 52.6% | 46.6% | 53.0% | 47.0% |
| 1978 | 1,580,778 | 894,092 | Boschwitz, Rudy | 638,375 | Anderson, Wendell R. | 48,311 | 255,717 R | 56.6% | 40.4% | 58.3% | 41.7% |
| 1978S | 1,560,724 | 957,908 | Durenberger, David | 538,675 | Short, Robert E. | 64,141 | 419,233 R | 61.4% | 34.5% | 64.0% | 36.0% |
| 1976 | 1,912,068 | 478,611 | Brekke, Gerald W. | 1,290,736 | Humphrey, Hubert H. | 142,721 | 812,125 D | 25.0% | 67.5% | 27.1% | 72.9% |
| 1972 | 1,731,653 | 742,121 | Hansen, Philip | 981,340 | Mondale, Walter F. | 8,192 | 239,219 D | 42.9% | 56.7% | 43.1% | 56.9% |
| 1970 | 1,364,887 | 568,025 | MacGregor, Clark | 788,256 | Humphrey, Hubert H. | 8,606 | 220,231 D | 41.6% | 57.8% | 41.9% | 58.1% |
| 1966 | 1,271,426 | 574,868 | Forsythe, Robert A. | 685,840 | Mondale, Walter F. | 10,718 | 110,972 D | 45.2% | 53.9% | 45.6% | 54.4% |
| 1964 | 1,543,590 | 605,933 | Whitney, Wheelock | 931,353 | McCarthy, Eugene J. | 6,304 | 325,420 D | 39.3% | 60.3% | 39.4% | 60.6% |
| 1960 | 1,536,839 | 648,586 | Peterson, P. K. | 884,168 | Humphrey, Hubert H. | 4,085 | 235,582 D | 42.2% | 57.5% | 42.3% | 57.7% |
| 1958 | 1,150,883 | 536,629 | Thye, Edward J. | 608,847 | McCarthy, Eugene J. | 5,407 | 72,218 D | 46.6% | 52.9% | 46.8% | 53.2% |
| 1954 | 1,138,952 | 479,619 | Bjornson, Val | 642,193 | Humphrey, Hubert H. | 17,140 | 162,574 D | 42.1% | 56.4% | 42.8% | 57.2% |
| 1952 | 1,387,419 | 785,649 | Thye, Edward J. | 590,011 | Carlson, William E. | 11,759 | 195,638 R | 56.6% | 42.5% | 57.1% | 42.9% |
| 1948 | 1,220,250 | 485,801 | Ball, Joseph H. | 729,494 | Humphrey, Hubert H. | 4,955 | 243,693 D | 39.8% | 59.8% | 40.0% | 60.0% |
| 1946 | 878,731 | 517,775 | Thye, Edward J. | 349,520 | Jorgenson, Theodore | 11,436 | 168,255 R | 58.9% | 39.8% | 59.7% | 40.3% |

In October 2002 the Democratic incumbent, Paul Wellstone, was killed in an airplane crash. Walter F. Mondale was named to replace him on the general election ballot. One of the 1978 elections was for a short term to fill a vacancy.

# MINNESOTA

Congressional districts first established for elections held in 2002
8 members

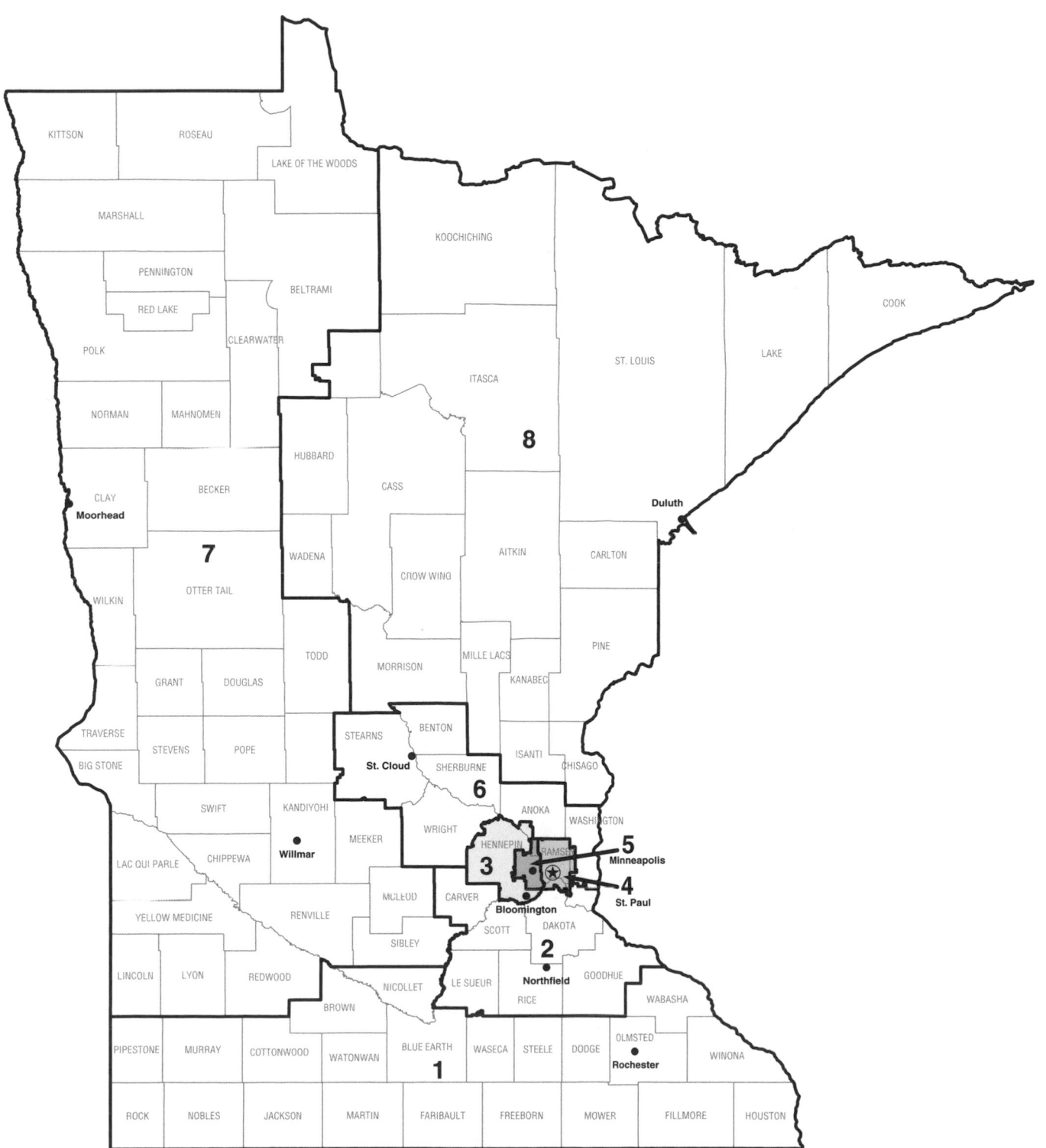

# MINNESOTA

Minneapolis-St. Paul Area

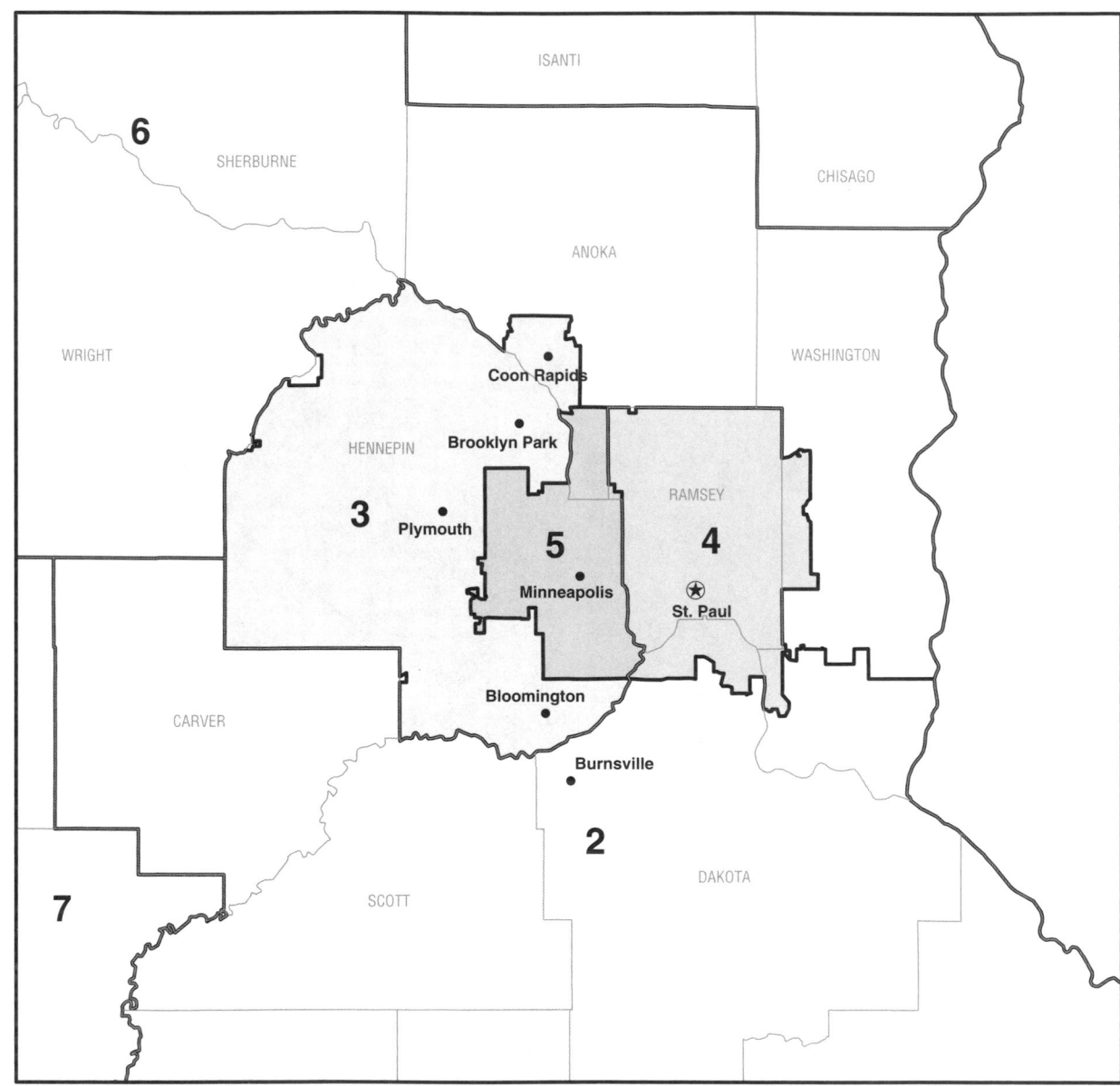

# MINNESOTA

## PRESIDENT 2004

| 2000 Census Population | County | Total Vote | Republican | Democratic | Other | Rep.-Dem. Plurality | Percentage | | | |
|---|---|---|---|---|---|---|---|---|---|---|
| | | | | | | | Total Vote | | Major Vote | |
| | | | | | | | Rep. | Dem. | Rep. | Dem. |
| 15,301 | AITKIN | 9,452 | 4,768 | 4,539 | 145 | 229 R | 50.4% | 48.0% | 51.2% | 48.8% |
| 298,084 | ANOKA | 174,066 | 91,853 | 80,226 | 1,987 | 11,627 R | 52.8% | 46.1% | 53.4% | 46.6% |
| 30,000 | BECKER | 16,801 | 9,795 | 6,756 | 250 | 3,039 R | 58.3% | 40.2% | 59.2% | 40.8% |
| 39,650 | BELTRAMI | 21,131 | 10,237 | 10,592 | 302 | 355 D | 48.4% | 50.1% | 49.1% | 50.9% |
| 34,226 | BENTON | 18,384 | 10,043 | 8,059 | 282 | 1,984 R | 54.6% | 43.8% | 55.5% | 44.5% |
| 5,820 | BIG STONE | 3,067 | 1,483 | 1,536 | 48 | 53 D | 48.4% | 50.1% | 49.1% | 50.9% |
| 55,941 | BLUE EARTH | 33,119 | 15,737 | 16,865 | 517 | 1,128 D | 47.5% | 50.9% | 48.3% | 51.7% |
| 26,911 | BROWN | 13,778 | 8,395 | 5,158 | 225 | 3,237 R | 60.9% | 37.4% | 61.9% | 38.1% |
| 31,671 | CARLTON | 18,334 | 6,642 | 11,462 | 230 | 4,820 D | 36.2% | 62.5% | 36.7% | 63.3% |
| 70,205 | CARVER | 45,411 | 28,510 | 16,456 | 445 | 12,054 R | 62.8% | 36.2% | 63.4% | 36.6% |
| 27,150 | CASS | 15,910 | 8,875 | 6,835 | 200 | 2,040 R | 55.8% | 43.0% | 56.5% | 43.5% |
| 13,088 | CHIPPEWA | 6,606 | 3,089 | 3,424 | 93 | 335 D | 46.8% | 51.8% | 47.4% | 52.6% |
| 41,101 | CHISAGO | 28,260 | 15,705 | 12,219 | 336 | 3,486 R | 55.6% | 43.2% | 56.2% | 43.8% |
| 51,229 | CLAY | 27,737 | 14,365 | 12,989 | 383 | 1,376 R | 51.8% | 46.8% | 52.5% | 47.5% |
| 8,423 | CLEARWATER | 4,361 | 2,438 | 1,871 | 52 | 567 R | 55.9% | 42.9% | 56.6% | 43.4% |
| 5,168 | COOK | 3,303 | 1,489 | 1,733 | 81 | 244 D | 45.1% | 52.5% | 46.2% | 53.8% |
| 12,167 | COTTONWOOD | 6,369 | 3,557 | 2,726 | 86 | 831 R | 55.8% | 42.8% | 56.6% | 43.4% |
| 55,099 | CROW WING | 33,545 | 19,106 | 14,005 | 434 | 5,101 R | 57.0% | 41.7% | 57.7% | 42.3% |
| 355,904 | DAKOTA | 215,846 | 108,959 | 104,635 | 2,252 | 4,324 R | 50.5% | 48.5% | 51.0% | 49.0% |
| 17,731 | DODGE | 9,868 | 5,593 | 4,117 | 158 | 1,476 R | 56.7% | 41.7% | 57.6% | 42.4% |
| 32,821 | DOUGLAS | 20,309 | 11,793 | 8,219 | 297 | 3,574 R | 58.1% | 40.5% | 58.9% | 41.1% |
| 16,181 | FARIBAULT | 8,681 | 4,794 | 3,767 | 120 | 1,027 R | 55.2% | 43.4% | 56.0% | 44.0% |
| 21,122 | FILLMORE | 11,698 | 5,694 | 5,825 | 179 | 131 D | 48.7% | 49.8% | 49.4% | 50.6% |
| 32,584 | FREEBORN | 17,666 | 7,681 | 9,733 | 252 | 2,052 D | 43.5% | 55.1% | 44.1% | 55.9% |
| 44,127 | GOODHUE | 25,608 | 13,134 | 12,103 | 371 | 1,031 R | 51.3% | 47.3% | 52.0% | 48.0% |
| 6,289 | GRANT | 3,819 | 1,893 | 1,856 | 70 | 37 R | 49.6% | 48.6% | 50.5% | 49.5% |
| 1,116,200 | HENNEPIN | 646,981 | 255,133 | 383,841 | 8,007 | 128,708 D | 39.4% | 59.3% | 39.9% | 60.1% |
| 19,718 | HOUSTON | 11,082 | 5,631 | 5,276 | 175 | 355 R | 50.8% | 47.6% | 51.6% | 48.4% |
| 18,376 | HUBBARD | 11,340 | 6,444 | 4,741 | 155 | 1,703 R | 56.8% | 41.8% | 57.6% | 42.4% |
| 31,287 | ISANTI | 19,313 | 11,190 | 7,883 | 240 | 3,307 R | 57.9% | 40.8% | 58.7% | 41.3% |
| 43,992 | ITASCA | 24,367 | 10,705 | 13,290 | 372 | 2,585 D | 43.9% | 54.5% | 44.6% | 55.4% |
| 11,268 | JACKSON | 5,779 | 3,024 | 2,652 | 103 | 372 R | 52.3% | 45.9% | 53.3% | 46.7% |
| 14,996 | KANABEC | 8,248 | 4,527 | 3,592 | 129 | 935 R | 54.9% | 43.5% | 55.8% | 44.2% |
| 41,203 | KANDIYOHI | 21,349 | 11,704 | 9,337 | 308 | 2,367 R | 54.8% | 43.7% | 55.6% | 44.4% |
| 5,285 | KITTSON | 2,682 | 1,307 | 1,333 | 42 | 26 D | 48.7% | 49.7% | 49.5% | 50.5% |
| 14,355 | KOOCHICHING | 7,309 | 3,539 | 3,662 | 108 | 123 D | 48.4% | 50.1% | 49.1% | 50.9% |
| 8,067 | LAC QUI PARLE | 4,541 | 2,093 | 2,390 | 58 | 297 D | 46.1% | 52.6% | 46.7% | 53.3% |
| 11,058 | LAKE | 7,071 | 2,769 | 4,212 | 90 | 1,443 D | 39.2% | 59.6% | 39.7% | 60.3% |
| 4,522 | LAKE OF THE WOODS | 2,400 | 1,428 | 921 | 51 | 507 R | 59.5% | 38.4% | 60.8% | 39.2% |
| 25,426 | LE SUEUR | 14,424 | 7,746 | 6,466 | 212 | 1,280 R | 53.7% | 44.8% | 54.5% | 45.5% |
| 6,429 | LINCOLN | 3,342 | 1,736 | 1,558 | 48 | 178 R | 51.9% | 46.6% | 52.7% | 47.3% |
| 25,425 | LYON | 12,673 | 7,203 | 5,292 | 178 | 1,911 R | 56.8% | 41.8% | 57.6% | 42.4% |
| 34,898 | MCLEOD | 18,412 | 11,407 | 6,712 | 293 | 4,695 R | 62.0% | 36.5% | 63.0% | 37.0% |
| 5,190 | MAHNOMEN | 2,508 | 1,132 | 1,339 | 37 | 207 D | 45.1% | 53.4% | 45.8% | 54.2% |
| 10,155 | MARSHALL | 5,562 | 3,187 | 2,308 | 67 | 879 R | 57.3% | 41.5% | 58.0% | 42.0% |
| 21,802 | MARTIN | 11,047 | 6,311 | 4,590 | 146 | 1,721 R | 57.1% | 41.5% | 57.9% | 42.1% |
| 22,644 | MEEKER | 12,334 | 6,854 | 5,292 | 188 | 1,562 R | 55.6% | 42.9% | 56.4% | 43.6% |
| 22,330 | MILLE LACS | 13,065 | 7,194 | 5,677 | 194 | 1,517 R | 55.1% | 43.5% | 55.9% | 44.1% |
| 31,712 | MORRISON | 16,758 | 9,698 | 6,794 | 266 | 2,904 R | 57.9% | 40.5% | 58.8% | 41.2% |
| 38,603 | MOWER | 20,222 | 7,591 | 12,334 | 297 | 4,743 D | 37.5% | 61.0% | 38.1% | 61.9% |
| 9,165 | MURRAY | 4,998 | 2,719 | 2,218 | 61 | 501 R | 54.4% | 44.4% | 55.1% | 44.9% |
| 29,771 | NICOLLET | 17,741 | 8,689 | 8,797 | 255 | 108 D | 49.0% | 49.6% | 49.7% | 50.3% |
| 20,832 | NOBLES | 9,204 | 5,159 | 3,898 | 147 | 1,261 R | 56.1% | 42.4% | 57.0% | 43.0% |
| 7,442 | NORMAN | 3,810 | 1,794 | 1,954 | 62 | 160 D | 47.1% | 51.3% | 47.9% | 52.1% |
| 124,277 | OLMSTED | 71,575 | 37,371 | 33,285 | 919 | 4,086 R | 52.2% | 46.5% | 52.9% | 47.1% |
| 57,159 | OTTER TAIL | 32,178 | 19,734 | 12,038 | 406 | 7,696 R | 61.3% | 37.4% | 62.1% | 37.9% |
| 13,584 | PENNINGTON | 7,017 | 3,767 | 3,117 | 133 | 650 R | 53.7% | 44.4% | 54.7% | 45.3% |
| 26,530 | PINE | 14,518 | 7,033 | 7,228 | 257 | 195 D | 48.4% | 49.8% | 49.3% | 50.7% |
| 9,895 | PIPESTONE | 5,032 | 3,066 | 1,900 | 66 | 1,166 R | 60.9% | 37.8% | 61.7% | 38.3% |
| 31,369 | POLK | 15,668 | 8,724 | 6,729 | 215 | 1,995 R | 55.7% | 42.9% | 56.5% | 43.5% |

# MINNESOTA

## PRESIDENT 2004

| 2000 Census Population | County | Total Vote | Republican | Democratic | Other | Rep.-Dem. Plurality | Percentage | | | |
|---|---|---|---|---|---|---|---|---|---|---|
| | | | | | | | Total Vote | | Major Vote | |
| | | | | | | | Rep. | Dem. | Rep. | Dem. |
| 11,236 | POPE | 6,700 | 3,303 | 3,301 | 96 | 2 R | 49.3% | 49.3% | 50.0% | 50.0% |
| 511,035 | RAMSEY | 272,577 | 97,096 | 171,846 | 3,635 | 74,750 D | 35.6% | 63.0% | 36.1% | 63.9% |
| 4,299 | RED LAKE | 2,177 | 1,164 | 963 | 50 | 201 R | 53.5% | 44.2% | 54.7% | 45.3% |
| 16,815 | REDWOOD | 8,139 | 4,898 | 3,104 | 137 | 1,794 R | 60.2% | 38.1% | 61.2% | 38.8% |
| 17,154 | RENVILLE | 8,349 | 4,430 | 3,787 | 132 | 643 R | 53.1% | 45.4% | 53.9% | 46.1% |
| 56,665 | RICE | 30,745 | 13,881 | 16,425 | 439 | 2,544 D | 45.1% | 53.4% | 45.8% | 54.2% |
| 9,721 | ROCK | 5,191 | 3,111 | 2,000 | 80 | 1,111 R | 59.9% | 38.5% | 60.9% | 39.1% |
| 16,338 | ROSEAU | 7,911 | 5,355 | 2,442 | 114 | 2,913 R | 67.7% | 30.9% | 68.7% | 31.3% |
| 200,528 | ST. LOUIS | 119,565 | 40,112 | 77,958 | 1,495 | 37,846 D | 33.5% | 65.2% | 34.0% | 66.0% |
| 89,498 | SCOTT | 60,639 | 36,055 | 23,958 | 626 | 12,097 R | 59.5% | 39.5% | 60.1% | 39.9% |
| 64,417 | SHERBURNE | 41,454 | 25,182 | 15,816 | 456 | 9,366 R | 60.7% | 38.2% | 61.4% | 38.6% |
| 15,356 | SIBLEY | 7,949 | 4,669 | 3,109 | 171 | 1,560 R | 58.7% | 39.1% | 60.0% | 40.0% |
| 133,166 | STEARNS | 75,577 | 41,726 | 32,659 | 1,192 | 9,067 R | 55.2% | 43.2% | 56.1% | 43.9% |
| 33,680 | STEELE | 18,695 | 10,389 | 7,994 | 312 | 2,395 R | 55.6% | 42.8% | 56.5% | 43.5% |
| 10,053 | STEVENS | 5,949 | 3,030 | 2,821 | 98 | 209 R | 50.9% | 47.4% | 51.8% | 48.2% |
| 11,956 | SWIFT | 5,735 | 2,481 | 3,165 | 89 | 684 D | 43.3% | 55.2% | 43.9% | 56.1% |
| 24,426 | TODD | 12,214 | 6,945 | 5,034 | 235 | 1,911 R | 56.9% | 41.2% | 58.0% | 42.0% |
| 4,134 | TRAVERSE | 2,141 | 1,076 | 1,026 | 39 | 50 R | 50.3% | 47.9% | 51.2% | 48.8% |
| 21,610 | WABASHA | 11,835 | 6,120 | 5,548 | 167 | 572 R | 51.7% | 46.9% | 52.5% | 47.5% |
| 13,713 | WADENA | 7,093 | 4,214 | 2,791 | 88 | 1,423 R | 59.4% | 39.3% | 60.2% | 39.8% |
| 19,526 | WASECA | 9,800 | 5,457 | 4,179 | 164 | 1,278 R | 55.7% | 42.6% | 56.6% | 43.4% |
| 201,130 | WASHINGTON | 128,449 | 65,751 | 61,395 | 1,303 | 4,356 R | 51.2% | 47.8% | 51.7% | 48.3% |
| 11,876 | WATONWAN | 5,583 | 2,970 | 2,514 | 99 | 456 R | 53.2% | 45.0% | 54.2% | 45.8% |
| 7,138 | WILKIN | 3,527 | 2,303 | 1,169 | 55 | 1,134 R | 65.3% | 33.1% | 66.3% | 33.7% |
| 49,985 | WINONA | 27,422 | 12,686 | 14,231 | 505 | 1,545 D | 46.3% | 51.9% | 47.1% | 52.9% |
| 89,986 | WRIGHT | 59,534 | 36,176 | 22,618 | 740 | 13,558 R | 60.8% | 38.0% | 61.5% | 38.5% |
| 11,080 | YELLOW MEDICINE | 5,758 | 2,878 | 2,799 | 81 | 79 R | 50.0% | 48.6% | 50.7% | 49.3% |
| 4,919,479 | TOTAL | 2,828,387 | 1,346,695 | 1,445,014 | 36,678 | 98,319 D | 47.6% | 51.1% | 48.2% | 51.8% |

# MINNESOTA

## HOUSE OF REPRESENTATIVES

| CD | Year | Total Vote | Republican Vote | Candidate | Democratic Vote | Candidate | Other Vote | Rep.-Dem. Plurality | | Total Vote Rep. | Total Vote Dem. | Major Vote Rep. | Major Vote Dem. |
|----|------|-----------|-----------------|-----------|-----------------|-----------|-----------|---------------------|---|------|------|------|------|
| 1 | 2004 | 324,055 | 193,132 | Gutknecht, Gil* | 115,088 | Pomeroy, Leigh | 15,835 | 78,044 | R | 59.6% | 35.5% | 62.7% | 37.3% |
| 1 | 2002 | 265,982 | 163,570 | Gutknecht, Gil* | 92,165 | Andreasen, Steve | 10,247 | 71,405 | R | 61.5% | 34.7% | 64.0% | 36.0% |
| 2 | 2004 | 365,945 | 206,313 | Kline, John* | 147,527 | Daly, Teresa | 12,105 | 58,786 | R | 56.4% | 40.3% | 58.3% | 41.7% |
| 2 | 2002 | 286,860 | 152,970 | Kline, John | 121,121 | Luther, Bill* | 12,769 | 31,849 | R | 53.3% | 42.2% | 55.8% | 44.2% |
| 3 | 2004 | 358,892 | 231,871 | Ramstad, Jim* | 126,665 | Watts, Deborah | 356 | 105,206 | R | 64.6% | 35.3% | 64.7% | 35.3% |
| 3 | 2002 | 296,218 | 213,334 | Ramstad, Jim* | 82,575 | Stanton, Darryl | 309 | 130,759 | R | 72.0% | 27.9% | 72.1% | 27.9% |
| 4 | 2004 | 317,299 | 105,467 | Bataglia, Patrice | 182,387 | McCollum, Betty* | 29,445 | 76,920 | D | 33.2% | 57.5% | 36.6% | 63.4% |
| 4 | 2002 | 264,540 | 89,705 | Billington, Clyde | 164,597 | McCollum, Betty* | 10,238 | 74,892 | D | 33.9% | 62.2% | 35.3% | 64.7% |
| 5 | 2004 | 313,526 | 76,600 | Mathias, Daniel | 218,434 | Sabo, Martin Olav* | 18,492 | 141,834 | D | 24.4% | 69.7% | 26.0% | 74.0% |
| 5 | 2002 | 255,982 | 66,271 | Mathias, Daniel | 171,572 | Sabo, Martin Olav* | 18,139 | 105,301 | D | 25.9% | 67.0% | 27.9% | 72.1% |
| 6 | 2004 | 377,224 | 203,669 | Kennedy, Mark* | 173,309 | Wetterling, Patty | 246 | 30,360 | R | 54.0% | 45.9% | 54.0% | 46.0% |
| 6 | 2002 | 287,312 | 164,747 | Kennedy, Mark* | 100,738 | Robert, Janet | 21,827 | 64,009 | R | 57.3% | 35.1% | 62.1% | 37.9% |
| 7 | 2004 | 314,257 | 106,349 | Sturrock, David E. | 207,628 | Peterson, Collin C.* | 280 | 101,279 | D | 33.8% | 66.1% | 33.9% | 66.1% |
| 7 | 2002 | 260,813 | 90,342 | Stevens, Dan | 170,234 | Peterson, Collin C.* | 237 | 79,892 | D | 34.6% | 65.3% | 34.7% | 65.3% |
| 8 | 2004 | 350,483 | 112,693 | Groettum, Mark | 228,586 | Oberstar, James L.* | 9,204 | 115,893 | D | 32.2% | 65.2% | 33.0% | 67.0% |
| 8 | 2002 | 283,931 | 88,673 | Lemen, Bob | 194,909 | Oberstar, James L.* | 349 | 106,236 | D | 31.2% | 68.6% | 31.3% | 68.7% |
| Total | 2004 | 2,721,681 | 1,236,094 | | 1,399,624 | | 85,963 | 163,530 | D | 45.4% | 51.4% | 46.9% | 53.1% |
| Total | 2002 | 2,201,638 | 1,029,612 | | 1,097,911 | | 74,115 | 68,299 | D | 46.8% | 49.9% | 48.4% | 51.6% |

An asterisk (*) denotes incumbent.

# MINNESOTA

## GENERAL AND PRIMARY ELECTIONS

## 2004 GENERAL ELECTIONS

**President**  Other vote was 18,683 Better Life (Ralph Nader); 4,639 Libertarian (Michael Badnarik); 4,408 Green (David Cobb); 3,074 Constitution (Michael Peroutka); 2,387 Christian Freedom (Thomas J. Harens); 539 Socialist Equality (Bill Van Auken); 416 Socialist Workers (Roger Calero); 4 write-in (John Joseph Kennedy); 2 write-in (Walter F. Brown); 2 write-in (Debra Joyce Renderos); 2 write-in (Martin Wishnatsky); 1 write-in (Joy Elaina Graham-Pendergast); 2,521 scattered write-in.

**House**  Other vote was:

CD 1  15,569 Independence (Gregory Mikkelson); 2 write-in (Pedro "Jesus" Romero); 264 scattered write-in.
CD 2  11,822 Independence (Doug Williams); 283 scattered write-in.
CD 3  356 scattered write-in.
CD 4  29,099 Independence (Peter F. Vento); 346 scattered write-in.
CD 5  17,984 Green (Jay Pond); 508 scattered write-in.
CD 6  246 scattered write-in.
CD 7  280 scattered write-in.
CD 8  8,933 Green (Van Presley); 271 scattered write-in.

# MINNESOTA

## GENERAL AND PRIMARY ELECTIONS

## 2004 PRIMARY ELECTIONS

| | |
|---|---|
| **Primary** | September 14, 2004 |

| | | |
|---|---|---|
| **Registration** (as of poll opening time on Sept. 14, 2004) | 2,872,540 | No Party Registration |

**Primary Type**   Open—Any registered voter could participate in the primary of the party of their choice.

Note:   An asterisk (*) denotes incumbent.

| | REPUBLICAN PRIMARIES | | | DEMOCRATIC PRIMARIES | | |
|---|---|---|---|---|---|---|
| Congressional District 1 | Gil Gutknecht* | 17,651 | 100.0% | Leigh Pomeroy | 12,682 | 100.0% |
| Congressional District 2 | John Kline* | 12,710 | 100.0% | Teresa Daly | 10,206 | 100.0% |
| Congressional District 3 | Jim Ramstad* <br> Burton Hanson <br> TOTAL | 19,232 <br> 2,159 <br> 21,391 | 89.9% <br> 10.1% | Deborah Watts | 7,438 | 100.0% |
| Congressional District 4 | Patrice Bataglia <br> Jack Shepard <br> TOTAL | 7,969 <br> 2,417 <br> 10,386 | 76.7% <br> 23.3% | Betty McCollum* | 16,529 | 100.0% |
| Congressional District 5 | Daniel Mathias | 5,840 | 100.0% | Martin Olav Sabo* <br> Dick Franson <br> TOTAL | 23,047 <br> 2,264 <br> 25,311 | 91.1% <br> 8.9% |
| Congressional District 6 | Mark Kennedy* | 11,817 | 100.0% | Patty Wetterling | 10,385 | 100.0% |
| Congressional District 7 | David E. Sturrock | 10,882 | 100.0% | Collin C. Peterson* | 16,036 | 100.0% |
| Congressional District 8 | Mark Groettum | 13,429 | 100.0% | James L. Oberstar* <br> Michael H. Johnson <br> TOTAL | 37,353 <br> 6,314 <br> 43,667 | 85.5% <br> 14.5% |

# MISSISSIPPI

## GOVERNOR
Haley Barbour (R). Elected 2003 to a four-year term.

## SENATORS (2 Republicans)
Thad Cochran (R). Reelected 2002 to a six-year term. Previously elected 1996, 1990, 1984, 1978.

Trent Lott (R). Reelected 2000 to a six-year term. Previously elected 1994, 1988.

## REPRESENTATIVES (2 Democrats, 2 Republicans)
1. Roger Wicker (R)
2. Bennie Thompson (D)
3. Charles W. "Chip" Pickering Jr. (R)
4. Gene Taylor (D)

## POSTWAR VOTE FOR PRESIDENT

| | | Republican | | Democratic | | Other | | Total Vote | | Major Vote | |
|---|---|---|---|---|---|---|---|---|---|---|---|
| Year | Total Vote | Vote | Candidate | Vote | Candidate | Vote | Plurality | Rep. | Dem. | Rep. | Dem. |
| 2004 | 1,152,145 | 684,981 | Bush, George W. | 458,094 | Kerry, John | 9,070 | 226,887 R | 59.5% | 39.8% | 59.9% | 40.1% |
| 2000** | 994,184 | 572,844 | Bush, George W. | 404,614 | Gore, Al | 16,726 | 168,230 R | 57.6% | 40.7% | 58.6% | 41.4% |
| 1996** | 893,857 | 439,838 | Dole, Bob | 394,022 | Clinton, Bill | 59,997 | 45,816 R | 49.2% | 44.1% | 52.7% | 47.3% |
| 1992** | 981,793 | 487,793 | Bush, George | 400,258 | Clinton, Bill | 93,742 | 87,535 R | 49.7% | 40.8% | 54.9% | 45.1% |
| 1988 | 931,527 | 557,890 | Bush, George | 363,921 | Dukakis, Michael S. | 9,716 | 193,969 R | 59.9% | 39.1% | 60.5% | 39.5% |
| 1984 | 941,104 | 582,377 | Reagan, Ronald | 352,192 | Mondale, Walter F. | 6,535 | 230,185 R | 61.9% | 37.4% | 62.3% | 37.7% |
| 1980** | 892,620 | 441,089 | Reagan, Ronald | 429,281 | Carter, Jimmy | 22,250 | 11,808 R | 49.4% | 48.1% | 50.7% | 49.3% |
| 1976 | 769,361 | 366,846 | Ford, Gerald R. | 381,309 | Carter, Jimmy | 21,206 | 14,463 D | 47.7% | 49.6% | 49.0% | 51.0% |
| 1972 | 645,963 | 505,125 | Nixon, Richard M. | 126,782 | McGovern, George S. | 14,056 | 378,343 R | 78.2% | 19.6% | 79.9% | 20.1% |
| 1968** | 654,509 | 88,516 | Nixon, Richard M. | 150,644 | Humphrey, Hubert H. | 415,349 | 264,705 A | 13.5% | 23.0% | 37.0% | 63.0% |
| 1964 | 409,146 | 356,528 | Goldwater, Barry M. | 52,618 | Johnson, Lyndon B. | | 303,910 R | 87.1% | 12.9% | 87.1% | 12.9% |
| 1960** | 298,171 | 73,561 | Nixon, Richard M. | 108,362 | Kennedy, John F. | 116,248 | 7,886 U | 24.7% | 36.3% | 40.4% | 59.6% |
| 1956 | 248,104 | 60,685 | Eisenhower, Dwight D. | 144,453 | Stevenson, Adlai E. | 42,966 | 83,768 D | 24.5% | 58.2% | 29.6% | 70.4% |
| 1952 | 285,532 | 112,966 | Eisenhower, Dwight D. | 172,566 | Stevenson, Adlai E. | | 59,600 D | 39.6% | 60.4% | 39.6% | 60.4% |
| 1948** | 192,190 | 5,043 | Dewey, Thomas E. | 19,384 | Truman, Harry S. | 167,763 | 148,154 SR | 2.6% | 10.1% | 20.6% | 79.4% |

In past elections, the other vote included: 2000 - 8,122 Green (Ralph Nader); 1996 - 52,222 Reform (Ross Perot); 1992 - 85,626 Independent (Perot); 1980 - 12,036 Independent (John Anderson); 1968 - 415,349 American Independent (George Wallace); 1960 - 116,248 Unpledged Independent Democratic electors; 1948 - 167,538 States' Rights (Strom Thurmond).

# MISSISSIPPI

## POSTWAR VOTE FOR GOVERNOR

| Year | Total Vote | Republican Vote | Republican Candidate | Democratic Vote | Democratic Candidate | Other Vote | Rep.-Dem. Plurality | Total Vote Rep. | Total Vote Dem. | Major Vote Rep. | Major Vote Dem. |
|---|---|---|---|---|---|---|---|---|---|---|---|
| 2003 | 894,487 | 470,404 | Barbour, Haley | 409,787 | Musgrove, Ronnie | 14,296 | 60,617 R | 52.6% | 45.8% | 53.4% | 46.6% |
| 1999** | 763,938 | 370,691 | Parker, Mike | 379,034 | Musgrove, Ronnie | 14,213 | 8,343 D | 48.5% | 49.6% | 49.4% | 50.6% |
| 1995 | 819,471 | 455,261 | Fordice, Kirk | 364,210 | Molpus, Dick | | 91,051 R | 55.6% | 44.4% | 55.6% | 44.4% |
| 1991 | 711,188 | 361,500 | Fordice, Kirk | 338,435 | Mabus, Ray | 11,253 | 23,065 R | 50.8% | 47.6% | 51.6% | 48.4% |
| 1987 | 721,695 | 336,006 | Reed, Jack | 385,689 | Mabus, Ray | | 49,683 D | 46.6% | 53.4% | 46.6% | 53.4% |
| 1983 | 742,737 | 288,764 | Bramlett, Leon | 409,209 | Allain, William A. | 44,764 | 120,445 D | 38.9% | 55.1% | 41.4% | 58.6% |
| 1979 | 677,322 | 263,702 | Carmichael, Gil | 413,620 | Winter, William F. | | 149,918 D | 38.9% | 61.1% | 38.9% | 61.1% |
| 1975 | 708,033 | 319,632 | Carmichael, Gil | 369,568 | Finch, Cliff | 18,833 | 49,936 D | 45.1% | 52.2% | 46.4% | 53.6% |
| 1971 | 780,537 | | — | 601,122 | Waller, William L. | 179,415 | 601,122 D | | 77.0% | | 100.0% |
| 1967 | 448,697 | 133,379 | Phillips, Rubel L. | 315,318 | Williams, John Bell | | 181,939 D | 29.7% | 70.3% | 29.7% | 70.3% |
| 1963 | 363,971 | 138,515 | Phillips, Rubel L. | 225,456 | Johnson, Paul B. | | 86,941 D | 38.1% | 61.9% | 38.1% | 61.9% |
| 1959 | 57,671 | | — | 57,671 | Barnett, Ross R. | | 57,671 D | | 100.0% | | 100.0% |
| 1955 | 40,707 | | — | 40,707 | Coleman, James P. | | 40,707 D | | 100.0% | | 100.0% |
| 1951 | 43,422 | | — | 43,422 | White, Hugh | | 43,422 D | | 100.0% | | 100.0% |
| 1947 | 166,095 | | — | 161,993 | Wright, Fielding L. | 4,102 | 161,993 D | | 97.5% | | 100.0% |

In 1999 no candidate received a majority of the vote. Democrat Ronnie Musgrove was elected in January 2000 by the Mississippi House of Representatives.

## POSTWAR VOTE FOR SENATOR

| Year | Total Vote | Republican Vote | Republican Candidate | Democratic Vote | Democratic Candidate | Other Vote | Rep.-Dem. Plurality | Total Vote Rep. | Total Vote Dem. | Major Vote Rep. | Major Vote Dem. |
|---|---|---|---|---|---|---|---|---|---|---|---|
| 2002 | 630,495 | 533,269 | Cochran, Thad | | — | 97,226 | 533,269 R | 84.6% | | 100.0% | |
| 2000 | 994,144 | 654,941 | Lott, Trent | 314,090 | Brown, Troy | 25,113 | 340,851 R | 65.9% | 31.6% | 67.6% | 32.4% |
| 1996 | 878,662 | 624,154 | Cochran, Thad | 240,647 | Hunt, James W. | 13,861 | 383,507 R | 71.0% | 27.4% | 72.2% | 27.8% |
| 1994 | 608,085 | 418,333 | Lott, Trent | 189,752 | Harper, Ken | | 228,581 R | 68.8% | 31.2% | 68.8% | 31.2% |
| 1990 | 274,244 | 274,244 | Cochran, Thad | | — | | 274,244 R | 100.0% | | 100.0% | |
| 1988 | 946,719 | 510,380 | Lott, Trent | 436,339 | Dowdy, Wayne | | 74,041 R | 53.9% | 46.1% | 53.9% | 46.1% |
| 1984 | 952,240 | 580,314 | Cochran, Thad | 371,926 | Winter, William F. | | 208,388 R | 60.9% | 39.1% | 60.9% | 39.1% |
| 1982 | 645,026 | 230,927 | Barbour, Haley | 414,099 | Stennis, John | | 183,172 D | 35.8% | 64.2% | 35.8% | 64.2% |
| 1978** | 583,936 | 263,089 | Cochran, Thad | 185,454 | Dantin, Maurice | 135,393 | 77,635 R | 45.1% | 31.8% | 58.7% | 41.3% |
| 1976 | 554,433 | | — | 554,433 | Stennis, John | | 554,433 D | | 100.0% | | 100.0% |
| 1972 | 645,746 | 249,779 | Carmichael, Gil | 375,102 | Eastland, James O. | 20,865 | 125,323 D | 38.7% | 58.1% | 40.0% | 60.0% |
| 1970 | 324,215 | | — | 286,622 | Stennis, John | 37,593 | 286,622 D | | 88.4% | | 100.0% |
| 1966 | 393,900 | 105,150 | Walker, Prentiss | 258,248 | Eastland, James O. | 30,502 | 153,098 D | 26.7% | 65.6% | 28.9% | 71.1% |
| 1964 | 343,364 | | — | 343,364 | Stennis, John | | 343,364 D | | 100.0% | | 100.0% |
| 1960 | 266,148 | 21,807 | Moore, Joe A. | 244,341 | Eastland, James O. | | 222,534 D | 8.2% | 91.8% | 8.2% | 91.8% |
| 1958 | 61,039 | | — | 61,039 | Stennis, John | | 61,039 D | | 100.0% | | 100.0% |
| 1954 | 105,526 | 4,678 | White, James A. | 100,848 | Eastland, James O. | | 96,170 D | 4.4% | 95.6% | 4.4% | 95.6% |
| 1952 | 233,919 | | — | 233,919 | Stennis, John | | 233,919 D | | 100.0% | | 100.0% |
| 1948 | 151,478 | | — | 151,478 | Eastland, James O. | | 151,478 D | | 100.0% | | 100.0% |
| 1947S | 193,709 | | [See note below] | | | | D | | | | |
| 1946 | 46,747 | | — | 46,747 | Bilbo, Theodore | | 46,747 D | | 100.0% | | 100.0% |

In past elections, the other vote included: 1978 - 133,646 Independent (Charles Evers). The 1947 election was for a short term to fill a vacancy and was held without party designation or nomination; John Stennis polled 52,068 votes (26.9 percent of the total vote) and won the election with a 6,343-vote plurality. Other votes included: 45,725 W. M. Colmer; 43,642 Forrest B. Jackson; 27,159 Paul B. Johnson; 24,492 John E. Rankin.

# MISSISSIPPI

Congressional districts first established for elections held in 2002
4 members

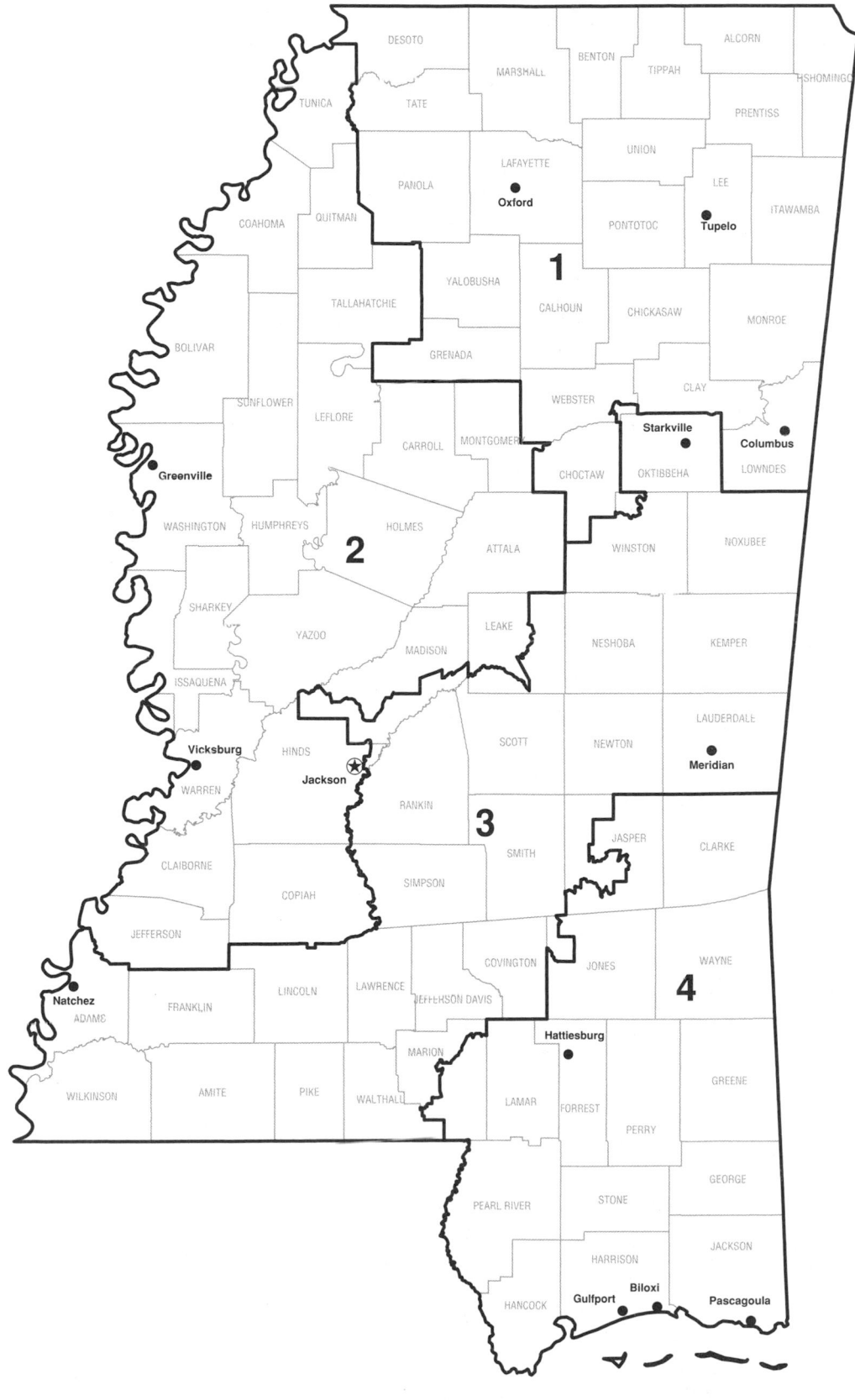

# MISSISSIPPI

## PRESIDENT 2004

| 2000 Census Population | County | Total Vote | Republican | Democratic | Other | Rep.-Dem. Plurality | Percentage Total Vote Rep. | Dem. | Major Vote Rep. | Dem. |
|---|---|---|---|---|---|---|---|---|---|---|
| 34,340 | ADAMS | 15,470 | 6,996 | 8,423 | 51 | 1,427 D | 45.2% | 54.4% | 45.4% | 54.6% |
| 34,558 | ALCORN | 14,239 | 8,634 | 5,454 | 151 | 3,180 R | 60.6% | 38.3% | 61.3% | 38.7% |
| 13,599 | AMITE | 7,197 | 4,147 | 3,012 | 38 | 1,135 R | 57.6% | 41.9% | 57.9% | 42.1% |
| 19,661 | ATTALA | 8,207 | 5,014 | 3,145 | 48 | 1,869 R | 61.1% | 38.3% | 61.5% | 38.5% |
| 8,026 | BENTON | 4,247 | 1,969 | 2,245 | 33 | 276 D | 46.4% | 52.9% | 46.7% | 53.3% |
| 40,633 | BOLIVAR | 15,307 | 5,535 | 9,631 | 141 | 4,096 D | 36.2% | 62.9% | 36.5% | 63.5% |
| 15,069 | CALHOUN | 6,389 | 4,131 | 2,234 | 24 | 1,897 R | 64.7% | 35.0% | 64.9% | 35.1% |
| 10,769 | CARROLL | 5,592 | 3,664 | 1,900 | 28 | 1,764 R | 65.5% | 34.0% | 65.9% | 34.1% |
| 19,440 | CHICKASAW | 8,343 | 4,193 | 4,078 | 72 | 115 R | 50.3% | 48.9% | 50.7% | 49.3% |
| 9,758 | CHOCTAW | 4,082 | 2,694 | 1,366 | 22 | 1,328 R | 66.0% | 33.5% | 66.4% | 33.6% |
| 11,831 | CLAIBORNE | 5,355 | 950 | 4,362 | 43 | 3,412 D | 17.7% | 81.5% | 17.9% | 82.1% |
| 17,955 | CLARKE | 7,505 | 5,068 | 2,402 | 35 | 2,666 R | 67.5% | 32.0% | 67.8% | 32.2% |
| 21,979 | CLAY | 9,139 | 4,342 | 4,753 | 44 | 411 D | 47.5% | 52.0% | 47.7% | 52.3% |
| 30,622 | COAHOMA | 10,608 | 3,676 | 6,805 | 127 | 3,129 D | 34.7% | 64.1% | 35.1% | 64.9% |
| 28,757 | COPIAH | 11,388 | 6,374 | 4,961 | 53 | 1,413 R | 56.0% | 43.6% | 56.2% | 43.8% |
| 19,407 | COVINGTON | 8,252 | 5,044 | 3,158 | 50 | 1,886 R | 61.1% | 38.3% | 61.5% | 38.5% |
| 107,199 | DE SOTO | 50,200 | 36,306 | 13,583 | 311 | 22,723 R | 72.3% | 27.1% | 72.8% | 27.2% |
| 72,604 | FORREST | 26,733 | 16,318 | 10,220 | 195 | 6,098 R | 61.0% | 38.2% | 61.5% | 38.5% |
| 8,448 | FRANKLIN | 4,491 | 2,893 | 1,574 | 24 | 1,319 R | 64.4% | 35.0% | 64.8% | 35.2% |
| 19,144 | GEORGE | 8,001 | 6,223 | 1,724 | 54 | 4,499 R | 77.8% | 21.5% | 78.3% | 21.7% |
| 13,299 | GREENE | 5,299 | 3,850 | 1,421 | 28 | 2,429 R | 72.7% | 26.8% | 73.0% | 27.0% |
| 23,263 | GRENADA | 10,105 | 5,872 | 4,180 | 53 | 1,692 R | 58.1% | 41.4% | 58.4% | 41.6% |
| 42,967 | HANCOCK | 17,869 | 12,581 | 5,107 | 181 | 7,474 R | 70.4% | 28.6% | 71.1% | 28.9% |
| 189,601 | HARRISON | 63,267 | 39,703 | 23,076 | 488 | 16,627 R | 62.8% | 36.5% | 63.2% | 36.8% |
| 250,800 | HINDS | 92,500 | 36,975 | 54,845 | 680 | 17,870 D | 40.0% | 59.3% | 40.3% | 59.7% |
| 21,609 | HOLMES | 8,383 | 1,961 | 6,366 | 56 | 4,405 D | 23.4% | 75.9% | 23.5% | 76.5% |
| 11,206 | HUMPHREYS | 4,899 | 1,679 | 3,168 | 52 | 1,489 D | 34.3% | 64.7% | 34.6% | 65.4% |
| 2,274 | ISSAQUENA | 970 | 439 | 516 | 15 | 77 D | 45.3% | 53.2% | 46.0% | 54.0% |
| 22,770 | ITAWAMBA | 9,710 | 6,833 | 2,802 | 75 | 4,031 R | 70.4% | 28.9% | 70.9% | 29.1% |
| 131,420 | JACKSON | 51,049 | 35,134 | 15,572 | 343 | 19,562 R | 68.8% | 30.5% | 69.3% | 30.7% |
| 18,149 | JASPER | 8,009 | 3,855 | 4,117 | 37 | 262 D | 48.1% | 51.4% | 48.4% | 51.6% |
| 9,740 | JEFFERSON | 3,466 | 630 | 2,821 | 15 | 2,191 D | 18.2% | 81.4% | 18.3% | 81.7% |
| 13,962 | JEFFERSON DAVIS | 5,765 | 2,668 | 2,959 | 138 | 291 D | 46.3% | 51.3% | 47.4% | 52.6% |
| 64,958 | JONES | 26,666 | 19,125 | 7,398 | 143 | 11,727 R | 71.7% | 27.7% | 72.1% | 27.9% |
| 10,453 | KEMPER | 4,603 | 2,109 | 2,465 | 29 | 356 D | 45.8% | 53.6% | 46.1% | 53.9% |
| 38,744 | LAFAYETTE | 15,388 | 9,004 | 6,218 | 166 | 2,786 R | 58.5% | 40.4% | 59.2% | 40.8% |
| 39,070 | LAMAR | 20,465 | 16,410 | 3,923 | 132 | 12,487 R | 80.2% | 19.2% | 80.7% | 19.3% |
| 78,161 | LAUDERDALE | 30,166 | 19,736 | 10,292 | 138 | 9,444 R | 65.4% | 34.1% | 65.7% | 34.3% |
| 13,258 | LAWRENCE | 6,306 | 3,956 | 2,308 | 42 | 1,648 R | 62.7% | 36.6% | 63.2% | 36.8% |
| 20,940 | LEAKE | 8,212 | 4,962 | 3,212 | 38 | 1,750 R | 60.4% | 39.1% | 60.7% | 39.3% |
| 75,755 | LEE | 30,621 | 20,254 | 10,127 | 240 | 10,127 R | 66.1% | 33.1% | 66.7% | 33.3% |
| 37,947 | LEFLORE | 12,463 | 4,635 | 7,566 | 262 | 2,931 D | 37.2% | 60.7% | 38.0% | 62.0% |
| 33,166 | LINCOLN | 14,491 | 10,008 | 4,418 | 65 | 5,590 R | 69.1% | 30.5% | 69.4% | 30.6% |
| 61,586 | LOWNDES | 24,268 | 13,690 | 10,408 | 170 | 3,282 R | 56.4% | 42.9% | 56.8% | 43.2% |
| 74,674 | MADISON | 37,724 | 24,257 | 13,268 | 199 | 10,989 R | 64.3% | 35.2% | 64.6% | 35.4% |
| 25,595 | MARION | 11,947 | 7,999 | 3,888 | 60 | 4,111 R | 67.0% | 32.5% | 67.3% | 32.7% |
| 34,993 | MARSHALL | 14,649 | 5,975 | 8,591 | 83 | 2,616 D | 40.8% | 58.6% | 41.0% | 59.0% |
| 38,014 | MONROE | 15,632 | 9,308 | 6,237 | 87 | 3,071 R | 59.5% | 39.9% | 59.9% | 40.1% |
| 12,189 | MONTGOMERY | 5,496 | 3,002 | 2,473 | 21 | 529 R | 54.6% | 45.0% | 54.8% | 45.2% |
| 28,684 | NESHOBA | 10,418 | 7,780 | 2,600 | 38 | 5,180 R | 74.7% | 25.0% | 75.0% | 25.0% |
| 21,838 | NEWTON | 8,487 | 6,165 | 2,280 | 42 | 3,885 R | 72.6% | 26.9% | 73.0% | 27.0% |
| 12,548 | NOXUBEE | 6,097 | 1,723 | 4,346 | 28 | 2,623 D | 28.3% | 71.3% | 28.4% | 71.6% |
| 42,902 | OKTIBBEHA | 16,279 | 9,068 | 7,015 | 196 | 2,053 R | 55.7% | 43.1% | 56.4% | 43.6% |
| 34,274 | PANOLA | 13,440 | 6,769 | 6,615 | 56 | 154 R | 50.4% | 49.2% | 50.6% | 49.4% |
| 48,621 | PEARL RIVER | 19,487 | 14,896 | 4,472 | 119 | 10,424 R | 76.4% | 22.9% | 76.9% | 23.1% |
| 12,138 | PERRY | 5,030 | 3,747 | 1,261 | 22 | 2,486 R | 74.5% | 25.1% | 74.8% | 25.2% |
| 38,940 | PIKE | 16,632 | 8,660 | 7,881 | 91 | 779 R | 52.1% | 47.4% | 52.4% | 47.6% |
| 26,726 | PONTOTOC | 11,240 | 8,480 | 2,660 | 100 | 5,820 R | 75.4% | 23.7% | 76.1% | 23.9% |
| 25,556 | PRENTISS | 9,932 | 6,538 | 3,327 | 67 | 3,211 R | 65.8% | 33.5% | 66.3% | 33.7% |
| 10,117 | QUITMAN | 3,416 | 1,360 | 2,032 | 24 | 672 D | 39.8% | 59.5% | 40.1% | 59.9% |

# MISSISSIPPI

## PRESIDENT 2004

| 2000 Census Population | County | Total Vote | Republican | Democratic | Other | Rep.-Dem. Plurality | Percentage | | | |
|---|---|---|---|---|---|---|---|---|---|---|
| | | | | | | | Total Vote | | Major Vote | |
| | | | | | | | Rep. | Dem. | Rep. | Dem. |
| 115,327 | RANKIN | 54,717 | 43,054 | 11,005 | 658 | 32,049 R | 78.7% | 20.1% | 79.6% | 20.4% |
| 28,423 | SCOTT | 10,228 | 6,395 | 3,802 | 31 | 2,593 R | 62.5% | 37.2% | 62.7% | 37.3% |
| 6,580 | SHARKEY | 3,093 | 1,120 | 1,560 | 413 | 440 D | 36.2% | 50.4% | 41.8% | 58.2% |
| 27,639 | SIMPSON | 10,474 | 7,138 | 3,272 | 64 | 3,866 R | 68.1% | 31.2% | 68.6% | 31.4% |
| 16,182 | SMITH | 7,120 | 5,577 | 1,496 | 47 | 4,081 R | 78.3% | 21.0% | 78.8% | 21.2% |
| 13,622 | STONE | 5,735 | 4,146 | 1,528 | 61 | 2,618 R | 72.3% | 26.6% | 73.1% | 26.9% |
| 34,369 | SUNFLOWER | 10,015 | 3,534 | 6,359 | 122 | 2,825 D | 35.3% | 63.5% | 35.7% | 64.3% |
| 14,903 | TALLAHATCHIE | 6,217 | 2,737 | 3,420 | 60 | 683 D | 44.0% | 55.0% | 44.5% | 55.5% |
| 25,370 | TATE | 11,167 | 6,760 | 4,347 | 60 | 2,413 R | 60.5% | 38.9% | 60.9% | 39.1% |
| 20,826 | TIPPAH | 9,275 | 6,174 | 3,016 | 85 | 3,158 R | 66.6% | 32.5% | 67.2% | 32.8% |
| 19,163 | TISHOMINGO | 8,326 | 5,379 | 2,846 | 101 | 2,533 R | 64.6% | 34.2% | 65.4% | 34.6% |
| 9,227 | TUNICA | 3,129 | 950 | 2,140 | 39 | 1,190 D | 30.4% | 68.4% | 30.7% | 69.3% |
| 25,362 | UNION | 10,819 | 7,906 | 2,839 | 74 | 5,067 R | 73.1% | 26.2% | 73.6% | 26.4% |
| 15,156 | WALTHALL | 6,352 | 3,888 | 2,435 | 29 | 1,453 R | 61.2% | 38.3% | 61.5% | 38.5% |
| 49,644 | WARREN | 19,679 | 11,356 | 8,224 | 99 | 3,132 R | 57.7% | 41.8% | 58.0% | 42.0% |
| 62,977 | WASHINGTON | 19,597 | 7,731 | 11,569 | 297 | 3,838 D | 39.4% | 59.0% | 40.1% | 59.9% |
| 21,216 | WAYNE | 8,794 | 5,562 | 3,193 | 39 | 2,369 R | 63.2% | 36.3% | 63.5% | 36.5% |
| 10,294 | WEBSTER | 5,065 | 3,708 | 1,341 | 16 | 2,367 R | 73.2% | 26.5% | 73.4% | 26.6% |
| 10,312 | WILKINSON | 4,385 | 1,563 | 2,794 | 28 | 1,231 D | 35.6% | 63.7% | 35.9% | 64.1% |
| 20,160 | WINSTON | 9,409 | 5,386 | 3,978 | 45 | 1,408 R | 57.2% | 42.3% | 57.5% | 42.5% |
| 13,051 | YALOBUSHA | 5,971 | 3,278 | 2,656 | 37 | 622 R | 54.9% | 44.5% | 55.2% | 44.8% |
| 28,149 | YAZOO | 10,987 | 5,672 | 5,013 | 302 | 659 R | 51.6% | 45.6% | 53.1% | 46.9% |
| 2,844,658 | TOTAL | 1,152,145 | 684,981 | 458,094 | 9,070 | 226,887 R | 59.5% | 39.8% | 59.9% | 40.1% |

# MISSISSIPPI

## GOVERNOR 2003

| 2000 Census Population | County | Total Vote | Republican | Democratic | Other | Rep.-Dem. Plurality | Percentage | | | |
|---|---|---|---|---|---|---|---|---|---|---|
| | | | | | | | Total Vote | | Major Vote | |
| | | | | | | | Rep. | Dem. | Rep. | Dem. |
| 34,340 | ADAMS | 12,677 | 5,123 | 7,464 | 90 | 2,341 D | 40.4% | 58.9% | 40.7% | 59.3% |
| 34,558 | ALCORN | 10,339 | 5,613 | 4,401 | 325 | 1,212 R | 54.3% | 42.6% | 56.1% | 43.9% |
| 13,599 | AMITE | 5,907 | 2,974 | 2,811 | 122 | 163 R | 50.3% | 47.6% | 51.4% | 48.6% |
| 19,661 | ATTALA | 6,841 | 3,636 | 3,109 | 96 | 527 R | 53.2% | 45.4% | 53.9% | 46.1% |
| 8,026 | BENTON | 3,055 | 1,091 | 1,902 | 62 | 811 D | 35.7% | 62.3% | 36.5% | 63.5% |
| 40,633 | BOLIVAR | 11,387 | 3,995 | 7,176 | 216 | 3,181 D | 35.1% | 63.0% | 35.8% | 64.2% |
| 15,069 | CALHOUN | 5,867 | 3,303 | 2,440 | 124 | 863 R | 56.3% | 41.6% | 57.5% | 42.5% |
| 10,769 | CARROLL | 4,684 | 2,919 | 1,712 | 53 | 1,207 R | 62.3% | 36.5% | 63.0% | 37.0% |
| 19,440 | CHICKASAW | 6,829 | 2,873 | 3,850 | 106 | 977 D | 42.1% | 56.4% | 42.7% | 57.3% |
| 9,758 | CHOCTAW | 3,441 | 2,117 | 1,290 | 34 | 827 R | 61.5% | 37.5% | 62.1% | 37.9% |
| 11,831 | CLAIBORNE | 4,538 | 804 | 3,683 | 51 | 2,879 D | 17.7% | 81.2% | 17.9% | 82.1% |
| 17,955 | CLARKE | 7,216 | 4,142 | 2,938 | 136 | 1,204 R | 57.4% | 40.7% | 58.5% | 41.5% |
| 21,979 | CLAY | 8,316 | 3,375 | 4,827 | 114 | 1,452 D | 40.6% | 58.0% | 41.1% | 58.9% |
| 30,622 | COAHOMA | 6,608 | 2,414 | 4,090 | 104 | 1,676 D | 36.5% | 61.9% | 37.1% | 62.9% |
| 28,757 | COPIAH | 10,436 | 4,951 | 5,357 | 128 | 406 D | 47.4% | 51.3% | 48.0% | 52.0% |
| 19,407 | COVINGTON | 7,288 | 3,931 | 3,164 | 193 | 767 R | 53.9% | 43.4% | 55.4% | 44.6% |
| 107,199 | DE SOTO | 27,935 | 18,689 | 8,876 | 370 | 9,813 R | 66.9% | 31.8% | 67.8% | 32.2% |
| 72,604 | FORREST | 18,970 | 11,134 | 7,562 | 274 | 3,572 R | 58.7% | 39.9% | 59.6% | 40.4% |
| 8,448 | FRANKLIN | 3,664 | 2,024 | 1,537 | 103 | 487 R | 55.2% | 41.9% | 56.8% | 43.2% |
| 19,144 | GEORGE | 6,101 | 3,485 | 2,492 | 124 | 993 R | 57.1% | 40.8% | 58.3% | 41.7% |
| 13,299 | GREENE | 4,053 | 2,176 | 1,815 | 62 | 361 R | 53.7% | 44.8% | 54.5% | 45.5% |
| 23,263 | GRENADA | 7,246 | 3,979 | 3,215 | 52 | 764 R | 54.9% | 44.4% | 55.3% | 44.7% |
| 42,967 | HANCOCK | 12,737 | 7,085 | 5,328 | 324 | 1,757 R | 55.6% | 41.8% | 57.1% | 42.9% |
| 189,601 | HARRISON | 43,759 | 23,641 | 19,310 | 808 | 4,331 R | 54.0% | 44.1% | 55.0% | 45.0% |
| 250,800 | HINDS | 72,515 | 29,057 | 42,700 | 758 | 13,643 D | 40.1% | 58.9% | 40.5% | 59.5% |

# MISSISSIPPI

## GOVERNOR 2003

| 2000 Census Population | County | Total Vote | Republican | Democratic | Other | Rep.-Dem. Plurality | Percentage Total Vote Rep. | Dem. | Major Vote Rep. | Dem. |
|---:|---|---:|---:|---:|---:|---:|---:|---:|---:|---:|
| 21,609 | HOLMES | 6,787 | 1,663 | 5,052 | 72 | 3,389 D | 24.5% | 74.4% | 24.8% | 75.2% |
| 11,206 | HUMPHREYS | 4,681 | 1,701 | 2,901 | 79 | 1,200 D | 36.3% | 62.0% | 37.0% | 63.0% |
| 2,274 | ISSAQUENA | 952 | 330 | 603 | 19 | 273 D | 34.7% | 63.3% | 35.4% | 64.6% |
| 22,770 | ITAWAMBA | 7,534 | 4,047 | 3,301 | 186 | 746 R | 53.7% | 43.8% | 55.1% | 44.9% |
| 131,420 | JACKSON | 36,390 | 21,818 | 13,908 | 664 | 7,910 R | 60.0% | 38.2% | 61.1% | 38.9% |
| 18,149 | JASPER | 6,534 | 2,770 | 3,697 | 67 | 927 D | 42.4% | 56.6% | 42.8% | 57.2% |
| 9,740 | JEFFERSON | 3,453 | 503 | 2,914 | 36 | 2,411 D | 14.6% | 84.4% | 14.7% | 85.3% |
| 13,962 | JEFFERSON DAVIS | 5,666 | 2,226 | 3,378 | 62 | 1,152 D | 39.3% | 59.6% | 39.7% | 60.3% |
| 64,958 | JONES | 22,043 | 13,341 | 8,298 | 404 | 5,043 R | 60.5% | 37.6% | 61.7% | 38.3% |
| 10,453 | KEMPER | 4,685 | 1,872 | 2,759 | 54 | 887 D | 40.0% | 58.9% | 40.4% | 59.6% |
| 38,744 | LAFAYETTE | 11,037 | 6,172 | 4,716 | 149 | 1,456 R | 55.9% | 42.7% | 56.7% | 43.3% |
| 39,070 | LAMAR | 14,875 | 10,838 | 3,640 | 397 | 7,198 R | 72.9% | 24.5% | 74.9% | 25.1% |
| 78,161 | LAUDERDALE | 22,745 | 14,786 | 7,707 | 252 | 7,079 R | 65.0% | 33.9% | 65.7% | 34.3% |
| 13,258 | LAWRENCE | 5,464 | 2,726 | 2,644 | 94 | 82 R | 49.9% | 48.4% | 50.8% | 49.2% |
| 20,940 | LEAKE | 6,634 | 3,500 | 3,061 | 73 | 439 R | 52.8% | 46.1% | 53.3% | 46.7% |
| 75,755 | LEE | 23,346 | 13,249 | 9,690 | 407 | 3,559 R | 56.8% | 41.5% | 57.8% | 42.2% |
| 37,947 | LEFLORE | 9,485 | 3,808 | 5,468 | 209 | 1,660 D | 40.1% | 57.6% | 41.1% | 58.9% |
| 33,166 | LINCOLN | 12,669 | 7,274 | 5,175 | 220 | 2,099 R | 57.4% | 40.8% | 58.4% | 41.6% |
| 61,586 | LOWNDES | 18,837 | 9,938 | 8,732 | 167 | 1,206 R | 52.8% | 46.4% | 53.2% | 46.8% |
| 74,674 | MADISON | 30,037 | 18,020 | 11,713 | 304 | 6,307 R | 60.0% | 39.0% | 60.6% | 39.4% |
| 25,595 | MARION | 10,000 | 6,066 | 3,804 | 130 | 2,262 R | 60.7% | 38.0% | 61.5% | 38.5% |
| 34,993 | MARSHALL | 8,243 | 3,094 | 5,043 | 106 | 1,949 D | 37.5% | 61.2% | 38.0% | 62.0% |
| 38,014 | MONROE | 13,063 | 6,181 | 6,680 | 202 | 499 D | 47.3% | 51.1% | 48.1% | 51.9% |
| 12,189 | MONTGOMERY | 4,722 | 2,430 | 2,242 | 50 | 188 R | 51.5% | 47.5% | 52.0% | 48.0% |
| 28,684 | NESHOBA | 8,957 | 5,559 | 3,276 | 122 | 2,283 R | 62.1% | 36.6% | 62.9% | 37.1% |
| 21,838 | NEWTON | 7,602 | 4,819 | 2,687 | 96 | 2,132 R | 63.4% | 35.3% | 64.2% | 35.8% |
| 12,548 | NOXUBEE | 5,236 | 1,368 | 3,819 | 49 | 2,451 D | 26.1% | 72.9% | 26.4% | 73.6% |
| 42,902 | OKTIBBEHA | 13,116 | 6,828 | 6,107 | 181 | 721 R | 52.1% | 46.6% | 52.8% | 47.2% |
| 34,274 | PANOLA | 10,845 | 4,140 | 6,624 | 81 | 2,484 D | 38.2% | 61.1% | 38.5% | 61.5% |
| 48,621 | PEARL RIVER | 14,281 | 8,782 | 5,138 | 361 | 3,644 R | 61.5% | 36.0% | 63.1% | 36.9% |
| 12,138 | PERRY | 4,040 | 2,503 | 1,485 | 52 | 1,018 R | 62.0% | 36.8% | 62.8% | 37.2% |
| 38,940 | PIKE | 13,700 | 6,048 | 7,452 | 200 | 1,404 D | 44.1% | 54.4% | 44.8% | 55.2% |
| 26,726 | PONTOTOC | 8,968 | 5,533 | 3,217 | 218 | 2,316 R | 61.7% | 35.9% | 63.2% | 36.8% |
| 25,556 | PRENTISS | 8,740 | 4,226 | 4,347 | 167 | 121 D | 48.4% | 49.7% | 49.3% | 50.7% |
| 10,117 | QUITMAN | 3,712 | 1,175 | 2,475 | 62 | 1,300 D | 31.7% | 66.7% | 32.2% | 67.8% |
| 115,327 | RANKIN | 38,610 | 28,633 | 9,151 | 826 | 19,482 R | 74.2% | 23.7% | 75.8% | 24.2% |
| 28,423 | SCOTT | 8,253 | 4,582 | 3,612 | 59 | 970 R | 55.5% | 43.8% | 55.9% | 44.1% |
| 6,580 | SHARKEY | 2,611 | 1,011 | 1,561 | 39 | 550 D | 38.7% | 59.8% | 39.3% | 60.7% |
| 27,639 | SIMPSON | 10,145 | 5,655 | 4,240 | 250 | 1,415 R | 55.7% | 41.8% | 57.2% | 42.8% |
| 16,182 | SMITH | 7,126 | 4,499 | 2,482 | 145 | 2,017 R | 63.1% | 34.8% | 64.4% | 35.6% |
| 13,622 | STONE | 5,433 | 3,056 | 2,124 | 253 | 932 R | 56.2% | 39.1% | 59.0% | 41.0% |
| 34,369 | SUNFLOWER | 7,154 | 2,772 | 4,307 | 75 | 1,535 D | 38.7% | 60.2% | 39.2% | 60.8% |
| 14,903 | TALLAHATCHIE | 5,153 | 2,150 | 2,928 | 75 | 778 D | 41.7% | 56.8% | 42.3% | 57.7% |
| 25,370 | TATE | 7,232 | 3,898 | 3,247 | 87 | 651 R | 53.9% | 44.9% | 54.6% | 45.4% |
| 20,826 | TIPPAH | 7,310 | 3,891 | 3,271 | 148 | 620 R | 53.2% | 44.7% | 54.3% | 45.7% |
| 19,163 | TISHOMINGO | 6,971 | 3,777 | 2,948 | 246 | 829 R | 54.2% | 42.3% | 56.2% | 43.8% |
| 9,227 | TUNICA | 2,773 | 823 | 1,882 | 68 | 1,059 D | 29.7% | 67.9% | 30.4% | 69.6% |
| 25,362 | UNION | 8,704 | 4,906 | 3,599 | 199 | 1,307 R | 56.4% | 41.3% | 57.7% | 42.3% |
| 15,156 | WALTHALL | 5,088 | 2,552 | 2,478 | 58 | 74 R | 50.2% | 48.7% | 50.7% | 49.3% |
| 49,644 | WARREN | 15,906 | 8,525 | 7,171 | 210 | 1,354 R | 53.6% | 45.1% | 54.3% | 45.7% |
| 62,977 | WASHINGTON | 14,215 | 5,383 | 8,720 | 112 | 3,337 D | 37.9% | 61.3% | 38.2% | 61.8% |
| 21,216 | WAYNE | 7,621 | 3,867 | 3,646 | 108 | 221 R | 50.7% | 47.8% | 51.5% | 48.5% |
| 10,294 | WEBSTER | 4,773 | 3,136 | 1,558 | 79 | 1,578 R | 65.7% | 32.6% | 66.8% | 33.2% |
| 10,312 | WILKINSON | 4,226 | 1,321 | 2,775 | 130 | 1,454 D | 31.3% | 65.7% | 32.3% | 67.7% |
| 20,160 | WINSTON | 8,866 | 4,437 | 4,325 | 104 | 112 R | 50.0% | 48.8% | 50.6% | 49.4% |
| 13,051 | YALOBUSHA | 4,612 | 2,154 | 2,406 | 52 | 252 D | 46.7% | 52.2% | 47.2% | 52.8% |
| 28,149 | YAZOO | 10,217 | 5,511 | 4,554 | 152 | 957 R | 53.9% | 44.6% | 54.8% | 45.2% |
| 2,844,658 | TOTAL | 894,487 | 470,404 | 409,787 | 14,296 | 60,617 R | 52.6% | 45.8% | 53.4% | 46.6% |

# MISSISSIPPI

## HOUSE OF REPRESENTATIVES

| CD | Year | Total Vote | Republican Vote | Republican Candidate | Democratic Vote | Democratic Candidate | Other Vote | Rep.-Dem. Plurality | Total Vote Rep. | Total Vote Dem. | Major Vote Rep. | Major Vote Dem. |
|----|------|-----------|-----------------|----------------------|-----------------|----------------------|-----------|---------------------|-----------------|-----------------|-----------------|-----------------|
| 1 | 2004 | 277,584 | 219,328 | Wicker, Roger* | | | 58,256 | 219,328 R | 79.0% | | 100.0% | |
| 1 | 2002 | 133,567 | 95,404 | Wicker, Roger* | 32,318 | Weathers, Rex N. | 5,845 | 63,086 R | 71.4% | 24.2% | 74.7% | 25.3% |
| 2 | 2004 | 264,869 | 107,647 | LeSueur, Clinton B. | 154,626 | Thompson, Bennie* | 2,596 | 46,979 D | 40.6% | 58.4% | 41.0% | 59.0% |
| 2 | 2002 | 163,050 | 69,711 | LeSueur, Clinton B. | 89,913 | Thompson, Bennie* | 3,426 | 20,202 D | 42.8% | 55.1% | 43.7% | 56.3% |
| 3 | 2004 | 293,368 | 234,874 | Pickering, Charles W. "Chip" Jr.* | | | 58,494 | 234,874 R | 80.1% | | 100.0% | |
| 3 | 2002 | 219,151 | 139,329 | Pickering, Charles W. "Chip" Jr.* | 76,184 | Shows, Ronnie* | 3,638 | 63,145 R | 63.6% | 34.8% | 64.6% | 35.4% |
| 4 | 2004 | 280,382 | 96,740 | Lott, Michael | 181,614 | Taylor, Gene* | 2,028 | 84,874 D | 34.5% | 64.8% | 34.8% | 65.2% |
| 4 | 2002 | 161,868 | 34,373 | Mertz, Karl Cleveland | 121,742 | Taylor, Gene* | 5,753 | 87,369 D | 21.2% | 75.2% | 22.0% | 78.0% |
| Total | 2004 | 1,116,203 | 658,589 | | 336,240 | | 121,374 | 322,349 R | 59.0% | 30.1% | 66.2% | 33.8% |
| Total | 2002 | 677,636 | 338,817 | | 320,157 | | 18,662 | 18,660 R | 50.0% | 47.2% | 51.4% | 48.6% |

An asterisk (*) denotes incumbent.

# MISSISSIPPI

## GENERAL AND PRIMARY ELECTIONS

### 2003–2004 GENERAL ELECTIONS

**President**
Other vote was 3,177 Reform (Ralph Nader); 1,793 Libertarian (Michael Badnarik); 1,759 Constitution (Michael Peroutka), 1,268 Independent (James Harris); 1,073 Green (David Cobb).

**Governor (2003)**
Other vote was 6,317 Constitution (John Thomas Cripps); 4,070 Reform (Shawn O'Hara); 3,909 Green (Sherman Lee Dillon).

**House**
Other vote was:

CD 1   58,256 Reform (Barbara Dale Washer).
CD 2   2,596 Reform (Shawn O'Hara).
CD 3   40,426 Independent (Jim Giles); 18,068 Reform (Lamonica L. Magee).
CD 4   2,028 Reform (Tracella Lou O'Hara Hill).

### 2003–2004 PRIMARY ELECTIONS

**Primary**
August 5, 2003 (Governor)
March 9, 2004

**Registration**
(as of April 2004)
1,791,666   No Party Registration

**Primary Type**
Open—Any registered voter could participate in the primary of either party.

262

# MISSISSIPPI

## GENERAL AND PRIMARY ELECTIONS

Note: An asterisk (*) denotes incumbent. The names of unopposed candidates do not have to appear on the primary ballot; therefore, in some cases, no votes were cast for these candidates.

| | REPUBLICAN PRIMARIES | | | DEMOCRATIC PRIMARIES | | |
|---|---|---|---|---|---|---|
| President | No Republican Primary | | | John Kerry | 59,815 | 78.4% |
| | | | | John Edwards | 5,582 | 7.3% |
| | | | | Al Sharpton | 3,933 | 5.2% |
| | | | | Howard Dean | 1,997 | 2.6% |
| | | | | Wesley Clark | 1,878 | 2.5% |
| | | | | Uncommitted | 1,370 | 1.8% |
| | | | | Dennis J. Kucinich | 768 | 1.0% |
| | | | | Joseph I. Lieberman | 716 | 0.9% |
| | | | | Lyndon H. LaRouche Jr. | 239 | 0.3% |
| | | | | TOTAL | 76,298 | |
| Governor (2003) | Haley Barbour | 158,284 | 83.3% | Ronnie Musgrove* | 392,264 | 75.8% |
| | Mitch Tyner | 31,768 | 16.7% | Gilbert Fountain | 39,685 | 7.7% |
| | | | | Elder McClendon | 30,421 | 5.9% |
| | | | | Katie Perrone | 28,154 | 5.4% |
| | | | | Catherine Starr | 26,821 | 5.2% |
| | TOTAL | 190,052 | | TOTAL | 517,345 | |
| Congressional District 1 | Roger Wicker* | Unopposed | | No Democratic candidate | | |
| Congressional District 2 | Clinton B. LeSueur | 14,468 | 84.8% | Bennie Thompson* | 24,316 | 100.0% |
| | Stephanie Summers-O'Neal | 1,319 | 7.7% | | | |
| | James Broadwater | 1,266 | 7.4% | | | |
| | Write-in | 3 | | | | |
| | TOTAL | 17,056 | | | | |
| Congressional District 3 | Charles W. "Chip" Pickering Jr.* | Unopposed | | No Democratic candidate | | |
| Congressional District 4 | Michael Lott | 5,991 | 84.8% | Gene Taylor* | 938 | 100.0% |
| | Karl Cleveland Mertz | 530 | 7.5% | | | |
| | Steven A. McCaleb | 512 | 7.2% | | | |
| | Write-in | 31 | 0.4% | | | |
| | TOTAL | 7,064 | | | | |

# MISSOURI

## GOVERNOR
Matt Blunt (R). Elected 2004 to a four-year term.

## SENATORS (2 Republicans)
Christopher S. Bond (R). Reelected 2004 to a six-year term. Previously elected 1998, 1992, 1986.

Jim Talent (R). Elected 2002 to fill the remaining four years of the term won by the late Mel Carnahan in 2000. Carnahan died in a plane crash in October 2000, but his name remained on the ballot. His widow, Jean Carnahan, was appointed to fill the seat until a special election could be held in 2002.

## REPRESENTATIVES (5 Republicans, 4 Democrats)
1. William Lacy Clay (D)
2. Todd Akin (R)
3. Russ Carnahan (D)
4. Ike Skelton (D)
5. Emanuel Cleaver II (D)
6. Sam Graves (R)
7. Roy Blunt (R)
8. Jo Ann Emerson (R)
9. Kenny Hulshof (R)

## POSTWAR VOTE FOR PRESIDENT

| Year | Total Vote | Republican Vote | Republican Candidate | Democratic Vote | Democratic Candidate | Other Vote | Plurality | Total Vote Rep. | Total Vote Dem. | Major Vote Rep. | Major Vote Dem. |
|------|-----------|-----------------|---------------------|-----------------|---------------------|-----------|-----------|-------|-------|-------|-------|
| 2004 | 2,731,364 | 1,455,713 | Bush, George W. | 1,259,171 | Kerry, John | 16,480 | 196,542 R | 53.3% | 46.1% | 53.6% | 46.4% |
| 2000** | 2,359,892 | 1,189,924 | Bush, George W. | 1,111,138 | Gore, Al | 58,830 | 78,786 R | 50.4% | 47.1% | 51.7% | 48.3% |
| 1996** | 2,158,065 | 890,016 | Dole, Bob | 1,025,935 | Clinton, Bill | 242,114 | 135,919 D | 41.2% | 47.5% | 46.5% | 53.5% |
| 1992** | 2,391,565 | 811,159 | Bush, George | 1,053,873 | Clinton, Bill | 526,533 | 242,714 D | 33.9% | 44.1% | 43.5% | 56.5% |
| 1988 | 2,093,713 | 1,084,953 | Bush, George | 1,001,619 | Dukakis, Michael S. | 7,141 | 83,334 R | 51.8% | 47.8% | 52.0% | 48.0% |
| 1984 | 2,122,783 | 1,274,188 | Reagan, Ronald | 848,583 | Mondale, Walter F. | 12 | 425,605 R | 60.0% | 40.0% | 60.0% | 40.0% |
| 1980** | 2,099,824 | 1,074,181 | Reagan, Ronald | 931,182 | Carter, Jimmy | 94,461 | 142,999 R | 51.2% | 44.3% | 53.6% | 46.4% |
| 1976 | 1,953,600 | 927,443 | Ford, Gerald R. | 998,387 | Carter, Jimmy | 27,770 | 70,944 D | 47.5% | 51.1% | 48.2% | 51.8% |
| 1972 | 1,855,803 | 1,153,852 | Nixon, Richard M. | 697,147 | McGovern, George S. | 4,804 | 456,705 R | 62.2% | 37.6% | 62.3% | 37.7% |
| 1968** | 1,809,502 | 811,932 | Nixon, Richard M. | 791,444 | Humphrey, Hubert H. | 206,126 | 20,488 R | 44.9% | 43.7% | 50.6% | 49.4% |
| 1964 | 1,817,879 | 653,535 | Goldwater, Barry M. | 1,164,344 | Johnson, Lyndon B. | | 510,809 D | 36.0% | 64.0% | 36.0% | 64.0% |
| 1960 | 1,934,422 | 962,221 | Nixon, Richard M. | 972,201 | Kennedy, John F. | | 9,980 D | 49.7% | 50.3% | 49.7% | 50.3% |
| 1956 | 1,832,562 | 914,289 | Eisenhower, Dwight D. | 918,273 | Stevenson, Adlai E. | | 3,984 D | 49.9% | 50.1% | 49.9% | 50.1% |
| 1952 | 1,892,062 | 959,429 | Eisenhower, Dwight D. | 929,830 | Stevenson, Adlai E. | 2,803 | 29,599 R | 50.7% | 49.1% | 50.8% | 49.2% |
| 1948 | 1,578,628 | 655,039 | Dewey, Thomas E. | 917,315 | Truman, Harry S. | 6,274 | 262,276 D | 41.5% | 58.1% | 41.7% | 58.3% |

In past elections, the other vote included: 2000 - 38,515 Green (Ralph Nader); 1996 - 217,188 Reform (Ross Perot); 1992 - 518,741 Independent (Perot); 1980 - 77,920 Independent (John Anderson); 1968 - 206,126 American Independent (George Wallace).

# MISSOURI

## POSTWAR VOTE FOR GOVERNOR

| Year | Total Vote | Republican | | Democratic | | Other Vote | Rep.-Dem. Plurality | Percentage | | | |
|---|---|---|---|---|---|---|---|---|---|---|---|
| | | | | | | | | Total Vote | | Major Vote | |
| | | Vote | Candidate | Vote | Candidate | | | Rep. | Dem. | Rep. | Dem. |
| 2004 | 2,719,599 | 1,382,419 | Blunt, Matt | 1,301,442 | McCaskill, Claire | 35,738 | 80,977 R | 50.8% | 47.9% | 51.5% | 48.5% |
| 2000 | 2,346,830 | 1,131,307 | Talent, Jim | 1,152,752 | Holden, Bob | 62,771 | 21,445 D | 48.2% | 49.1% | 49.5% | 50.5% |
| 1996 | 2,142,518 | 866,268 | Kelly, Margaret | 1,224,801 | Carnahan, Mel | 51,449 | 358,533 D | 40.4% | 57.2% | 41.4% | 58.6% |
| 1992 | 2,344,121 | 968,574 | Webster, William L. | 1,375,425 | Carnahan, Mel | 122 | 406,851 D | 41.3% | 58.7% | 41.3% | 58.7% |
| 1988 | 2,085,928 | 1,339,531 | Ashcroft, John | 724,919 | Hearnes, Betty C. | 21,478 | 614,612 R | 64.2% | 34.8% | 64.9% | 35.1% |
| 1984 | 2,108,210 | 1,194,506 | Ashcroft, John | 913,700 | Rothman, Kenneth J. | 4 | 280,806 R | 56.7% | 43.3% | 56.7% | 43.3% |
| 1980 | 2,088,028 | 1,098,950 | Bond, Christopher S. | 981,884 | Teasdale, Joseph P. | 7,194 | 117,066 R | 52.6% | 47.0% | 52.8% | 47.2% |
| 1976 | 1,933,575 | 958,110 | Bond, Christopher S. | 971,184 | Teasdale, Joseph P. | 4,281 | 13,074 D | 49.6% | 50.2% | 49.7% | 50.3% |
| 1972 | 1,865,683 | 1,029,451 | Bond, Christopher S. | 832,751 | Dowd, Edward L. | 3,481 | 196,700 R | 55.2% | 44.6% | 55.3% | 44.7% |
| 1968 | 1,764,602 | 691,797 | Roos, Lawrence K. | 1,072,805 | Hearnes, Warren E. | | 381,008 D | 39.2% | 60.8% | 39.2% | 60.8% |
| 1964 | 1,789,600 | 678,949 | Shepley, Ethan | 1,110,651 | Hearnes, Warren E. | | 431,702 D | 37.9% | 62.1% | 37.9% | 62.1% |
| 1960 | 1,887,331 | 792,131 | Farmer, Edward G. | 1,095,200 | Dalton, John M. | | 303,069 D | 42.0% | 58.0% | 42.0% | 58.0% |
| 1956 | 1,808,338 | 866,810 | Hocker, Lon | 941,528 | Blair, James T. | | 74,718 D | 47.9% | 52.1% | 47.9% | 52.1% |
| 1952 | 1,871,095 | 886,370 | Elliott, Howard | 983,166 | Donnelly, Phil M. | 1,559 | 96,796 D | 47.4% | 52.5% | 47.4% | 52.6% |
| 1948 | 1,567,338 | 670,064 | Thompson, Murray | 893,092 | Smith, Forrest | 4,182 | 223,028 D | 42.8% | 57.0% | 42.9% | 57.1% |

## POSTWAR VOTE FOR SENATOR

| Year | Total Vote | Republican | | Democratic | | Other Vote | Rep.-Dem. Plurality | Percentage | | | |
|---|---|---|---|---|---|---|---|---|---|---|---|
| | | | | | | | | Total Vote | | Major Vote | |
| | | Vote | Candidate | Vote | Candidate | | | Rep. | Dem. | Rep. | Dem. |
| 2004 | 2,706,402 | 1,518,089 | Bond, Christopher S. | 1,158,261 | Farmer, Nancy | 30,052 | 359,828 R | 56.1% | 42.8% | 56.7% | 43.3% |
| 2002S | 1,877,620 | 935,032 | Talent, Jim | 913,778 | Carnahan, Jean | 28,810 | 21,254 R | 49.8% | 48.7% | 50.6% | 49.4% |
| 2000** | 2,361,586 | 1,142,852 | Ashcroft, John | 1,191,812 | Carnahan, Mel | 26,922 | 48,960 D | 48.4% | 50.5% | 49.0% | 51.0% |
| 1998 | 1,576,857 | 830,625 | Bond, Christopher S. | 690,208 | Nixon, Jeremiah W. | 56,024 | 140,417 R | 52.7% | 43.8% | 54.6% | 45.4% |
| 1994 | 1,775,116 | 1,060,149 | Ashcroft, John | 633,697 | Wheat, Alan | 81,270 | 426,452 R | 59.7% | 35.7% | 62.6% | 37.4% |
| 1992 | 2,354,925 | 1,221,901 | Bond, Christopher S. | 1,057,967 | Rothman-Serot, Geri | 75,057 | 163,934 R | 51.9% | 44.9% | 53.6% | 46.4% |
| 1988 | 2,078,875 | 1,407,416 | Danforth, John C. | 660,045 | Nixon, Jeremiah W. | 11,414 | 747,371 R | 67.7% | 31.8% | 68.1% | 31.9% |
| 1986 | 1,477,327 | 777,612 | Bond, Christopher S. | 699,624 | Woods, Harriett | 91 | 77,988 R | 52.6% | 47.4% | 52.6% | 47.4% |
| 1982 | 1,543,521 | 784,876 | Danforth, John C. | 758,629 | Woods, Harriett | 16 | 26,247 R | 50.8% | 49.1% | 50.9% | 49.1% |
| 1980 | 2,066,965 | 985,399 | McNary, Gene | 1,074,859 | Eagleton, Thomas F. | 6,707 | 89,460 D | 47.7% | 52.0% | 47.8% | 52.2% |
| 1976 | 1,914,777 | 1,090,067 | Danforth, John C. | 813,571 | Hearnes, Warren E. | 11,139 | 276,496 R | 56.9% | 42.5% | 57.3% | 42.7% |
| 1974 | 1,224,303 | 480,900 | Curtis, Thomas B. | 735,433 | Eagleton, Thomas F. | 7,970 | 254,533 D | 39.3% | 60.1% | 39.5% | 60.5% |
| 1970 | 1,283,912 | 617,903 | Danforth, John C. | 655,431 | Symington, Stuart | 10,578 | 37,528 D | 48.1% | 51.0% | 48.5% | 51.5% |
| 1968 | 1,737,958 | 850,544 | Curtis, Thomas B. | 887,414 | Eagleton, Thomas F. | | 36,870 D | 48.9% | 51.1% | 48.9% | 51.1% |
| 1964 | 1,783,043 | 596,377 | Bradshaw, Jean P. | 1,186,666 | Symington, Stuart | | 590,289 D | 33.4% | 66.6% | 33.4% | 66.6% |
| 1962 | 1,222,259 | 555,330 | Kemper, Crosby | 666,929 | Long, Edward V. | | 111,599 D | 45.4% | 54.6% | 45.4% | 54.6% |
| 1960S | 1,880,232 | 880,576 | Hocker, Lon | 999,656 | Long, Edward V. | | 119,080 D | 46.8% | 53.2% | 46.8% | 53.2% |
| 1958 | 1,173,903 | 393,847 | Palmer, Hazel | 780,056 | Symington, Stuart | | 386,209 D | 33.6% | 66.4% | 33.6% | 66.4% |
| 1956 | 1,800,984 | 785,048 | Douglas, Herbert | 1,015,936 | Hennings, Thomas C. | | 230,888 D | 43.6% | 56.4% | 43.6% | 56.4% |
| 1952 | 1,868,083 | 858,170 | Kem, James P. | 1,008,523 | Symington, Stuart | 1,390 | 150,353 D | 45.9% | 54.0% | 46.0% | 54.0% |
| 1950 | 1,279,414 | 592,922 | Donnell, Forrest C. | 685,732 | Hennings, Thomas C. | 760 | 92,810 D | 46.3% | 53.6% | 46.4% | 53.6% |
| 1946 | 1,084,100 | 572,556 | Kem, James P. | 511,544 | Briggs, Frank P. | | 61,012 R | 52.8% | 47.2% | 52.8% | 47.2% |

In October 2000 the Democratic candidate, Mel Carnahan, was killed in an airplane crash but his name remained on the ballot and he won the election in November. Subsequently, his widow, Jean Carnahan, was appointed to fill the seat until an election could be held in 2002 for the remaining four years of the term. The 1960 election was for a short term to fill a vacancy.

# MISSOURI

Congressional districts first established for elections held in 2002
9 members

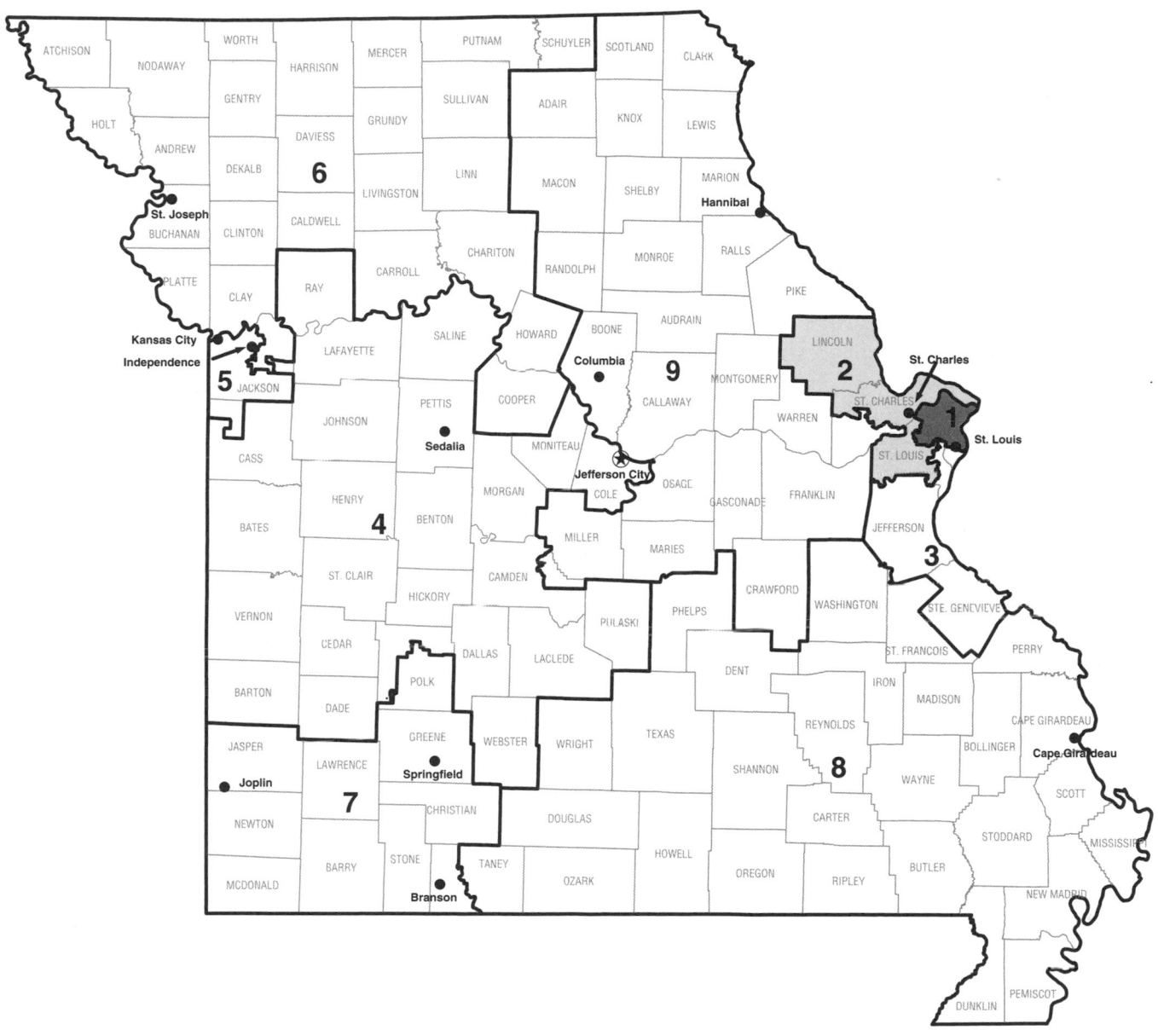

# MISSOURI

## PRESIDENT 2004

| 2000 Census Population | County | Total Vote | Republican | Democratic | Other | Rep.-Dem. Plurality | Percentage Total Vote Rep. | Dem. | Major Vote Rep. | Dem. |
|---|---|---|---|---|---|---|---|---|---|---|
| 24,977 | ADAIR | 11,404 | 6,367 | 4,938 | 99 | 1,429 R | 55.8% | 43.3% | 56.3% | 43.7% |
| 16,492 | ANDREW | 8,266 | 5,135 | 3,069 | 62 | 2,066 R | 62.1% | 37.1% | 62.6% | 37.4% |
| 6,430 | ATCHISON | 3,156 | 2,137 | 1,005 | 14 | 1,132 R | 67.7% | 31.8% | 68.0% | 32.0% |
| 25,853 | AUDRAIN | 10,683 | 6,294 | 4,318 | 71 | 1,976 R | 58.9% | 40.4% | 59.3% | 40.7% |
| 34,010 | BARRY | 13,927 | 9,599 | 4,223 | 105 | 5,376 R | 68.9% | 30.3% | 69.4% | 30.6% |
| 12,541 | BARTON | 5,991 | 4,572 | 1,373 | 46 | 3,199 R | 76.3% | 22.9% | 76.9% | 23.1% |
| 16,653 | BATES | 8,466 | 5,004 | 3,398 | 64 | 1,606 R | 59.1% | 40.1% | 59.6% | 40.4% |
| 17,180 | BENTON | 9,009 | 5,575 | 3,381 | 53 | 2,194 R | 61.9% | 37.5% | 62.2% | 37.8% |
| 12,029 | BOLLINGER | 5,895 | 4,102 | 1,754 | 39 | 2,348 R | 69.6% | 29.8% | 70.0% | 30.0% |
| 135,454 | BOONE | 76,046 | 37,801 | 37,643 | 602 | 158 R | 49.7% | 49.5% | 50.1% | 49.9% |
| 85,998 | BUCHANAN | 37,950 | 19,812 | 17,799 | 339 | 2,013 R | 52.2% | 46.9% | 52.7% | 47.3% |
| 40,867 | BUTLER | 16,441 | 11,696 | 4,666 | 79 | 7,030 R | 71.1% | 28.4% | 71.5% | 28.5% |
| 8,969 | CALDWELL | 4,268 | 2,593 | 1,645 | 30 | 948 R | 60.8% | 38.5% | 61.2% | 38.8% |
| 40,766 | CALLAWAY | 17,773 | 11,108 | 6,559 | 106 | 4,549 R | 62.5% | 36.9% | 62.9% | 37.1% |
| 37,051 | CAMDEN | 19,519 | 13,122 | 6,296 | 101 | 6,826 R | 67.2% | 32.3% | 67.6% | 32.4% |
| 68,693 | CAPE GIRARDEAU | 34,565 | 23,814 | 10,568 | 183 | 13,246 R | 68.9% | 30.6% | 69.3% | 30.7% |
| 10,285 | CARROLL | 4,741 | 3,155 | 1,568 | 18 | 1,587 R | 66.5% | 33.1% | 66.8% | 33.2% |
| 5,941 | CARTER | 2,779 | 1,797 | 964 | 18 | 833 R | 64.7% | 34.7% | 65.1% | 34.9% |
| 82,092 | CASS | 44,217 | 27,253 | 16,681 | 283 | 10,572 R | 61.6% | 37.7% | 62.0% | 38.0% |
| 13,733 | CEDAR | 6,203 | 4,238 | 1,910 | 55 | 2,328 R | 68.3% | 30.8% | 68.9% | 31.1% |
| 8,438 | CHARITON | 4,340 | 2,421 | 1,892 | 27 | 529 R | 55.8% | 43.6% | 56.1% | 43.9% |
| 54,285 | CHRISTIAN | 31,348 | 22,102 | 9,059 | 187 | 13,043 R | 70.5% | 28.9% | 70.9% | 29.1% |
| 7,416 | CLARK | 3,736 | 1,899 | 1,794 | 43 | 105 R | 50.8% | 48.0% | 51.4% | 48.6% |
| 184,006 | CLAY | 96,460 | 51,193 | 44,670 | 597 | 6,523 R | 53.1% | 46.3% | 53.4% | 46.6% |
| 18,979 | CLINTON | 9,540 | 5,287 | 4,165 | 88 | 1,122 R | 55.4% | 43.7% | 55.9% | 44.1% |
| 71,397 | COLE | 36,701 | 24,752 | 11,753 | 196 | 12,999 R | 67.4% | 32.0% | 67.8% | 32.2% |
| 16,670 | COOPER | 7,508 | 5,058 | 2,400 | 50 | 2,658 R | 67.4% | 32.0% | 67.8% | 32.2% |
| 22,804 | CRAWFORD | 9,381 | 5,686 | 3,632 | 63 | 2,054 R | 60.6% | 38.7% | 61.0% | 39.0% |
| 7,923 | DADE | 4,089 | 2,963 | 1,104 | 22 | 1,859 R | 72.5% | 27.0% | 72.9% | 27.1% |
| 15,661 | DALLAS | 7,259 | 4,788 | 2,407 | 64 | 2,381 R | 66.0% | 33.2% | 66.5% | 33.5% |
| 8,016 | DAVIESS | 3,794 | 2,351 | 1,402 | 41 | 949 R | 62.0% | 37.0% | 62.6% | 37.4% |
| 11,597 | DE KALB | 4,686 | 2,941 | 1,707 | 38 | 1,234 R | 62.8% | 36.4% | 63.3% | 36.7% |
| 14,927 | DENT | 6,304 | 4,369 | 1,865 | 70 | 2,504 R | 69.3% | 29.6% | 70.1% | 29.9% |
| 13,084 | DOUGLAS | 6,327 | 4,498 | 1,741 | 88 | 2,757 R | 71.1% | 27.5% | 72.1% | 27.9% |
| 33,155 | DUNKLIN | 11,677 | 6,720 | 4,901 | 56 | 1,819 R | 57.5% | 42.0% | 57.8% | 42.2% |
| 93,807 | FRANKLIN | 45,318 | 26,429 | 18,556 | 333 | 7,873 R | 58.3% | 40.9% | 58.8% | 41.2% |
| 15,342 | GASCONADE | 7,171 | 4,753 | 2,355 | 63 | 2,398 R | 66.3% | 32.8% | 66.9% | 33.1% |
| 6,861 | GENTRY | 3,312 | 2,085 | 1,201 | 26 | 884 R | 63.0% | 36.3% | 63.5% | 36.5% |
| 240,391 | GREENE | 125,266 | 77,885 | 46,657 | 724 | 31,228 R | 62.2% | 37.2% | 62.5% | 37.5% |
| 10,432 | GRUNDY | 4,808 | 3,172 | 1,561 | 75 | 1,611 R | 66.0% | 32.5% | 67.0% | 33.0% |
| 8,850 | HARRISON | 4,048 | 2,729 | 1,279 | 40 | 1,450 R | 67.4% | 31.6% | 68.1% | 31.9% |
| 21,997 | HENRY | 10,877 | 6,361 | 4,461 | 55 | 1,900 R | 58.5% | 41.0% | 58.8% | 41.2% |
| 8,940 | HICKORY | 4,866 | 2,791 | 2,043 | 32 | 748 R | 57.4% | 42.0% | 57.7% | 42.3% |
| 5,351 | HOLT | 2,691 | 1,864 | 811 | 16 | 1,053 R | 69.3% | 30.1% | 69.7% | 30.3% |
| 10,212 | HOWARD | 4,921 | 2,915 | 1,972 | 34 | 943 R | 59.2% | 40.1% | 59.6% | 40.4% |
| 37,238 | HOWELL | 16,379 | 11,097 | 5,118 | 164 | 5,979 R | 67.8% | 31.2% | 68.4% | 31.6% |
| 10,697 | IRON | 4,679 | 2,477 | 2,157 | 45 | 320 R | 52.9% | 46.1% | 53.5% | 46.5% |
| 654,880 | JACKSON | 174,570 | 94,439 | 79,029 | 1,102 | 15,410 R | 54.1% | 45.3% | 54.4% | 45.6% |
| 104,686 | JASPER | 45,085 | 31,846 | 13,002 | 237 | 18,844 R | 70.6% | 28.8% | 71.0% | 29.0% |
| 198,099 | JEFFERSON | 93,264 | 46,624 | 46,057 | 583 | 567 R | 50.0% | 49.4% | 50.3% | 49.7% |
| 48,258 | JOHNSON | 20,236 | 12,257 | 7,790 | 189 | 4,467 R | 60.6% | 38.5% | 61.1% | 38.9% |
| *See Note | KANSAS CITY | 141,423 | 36,061 | 104,625 | 737 | 68,564 D | 25.5% | 74.0% | 25.6% | 74.4% |
| 4,361 | KNOX | 1,978 | 1,207 | 761 | 10 | 446 R | 61.0% | 38.5% | 61.3% | 38.7% |
| 32,513 | LACLEDE | 14,869 | 10,578 | 4,213 | 78 | 6,365 R | 71.1% | 28.3% | 71.5% | 28.5% |
| 32,960 | LAFAYETTE | 16,182 | 9,656 | 6,412 | 114 | 3,244 R | 59.7% | 39.6% | 60.1% | 39.9% |
| 35,204 | LAWRENCE | 15,806 | 11,194 | 4,506 | 106 | 6,688 R | 70.8% | 28.5% | 71.3% | 28.7% |
| 10,494 | LEWIS | 4,644 | 2,862 | 1,754 | 28 | 1,108 R | 61.6% | 37.8% | 62.0% | 38.0% |
| 38,944 | LINCOLN | 19,839 | 11,316 | 8,368 | 155 | 2,948 R | 57.0% | 42.2% | 57.5% | 42.5% |
| 13,754 | LINN | 5,898 | 3,422 | 2,440 | 36 | 982 R | 58.0% | 41.4% | 58.4% | 41.6% |
| 14,558 | LIVINGSTON | 6,346 | 4,029 | 2,278 | 39 | 1,751 R | 63.5% | 35.9% | 63.9% | 36.1% |

# MISSOURI
## PRESIDENT 2004

| 2000 Census Population | County | Total Vote | Republican | Democratic | Other | Rep.-Dem. Plurality | Percentage Total Vote Rep. | Dem. | Major Vote Rep. | Dem. |
|---|---|---|---|---|---|---|---|---|---|---|
| 21,681 | MCDONALD | 7,725 | 5,443 | 2,215 | 67 | 3,228 R | 70.5% | 28.7% | 71.1% | 28.9% |
| 15,762 | MACON | 7,570 | 4,673 | 2,856 | 41 | 1,817 R | 61.7% | 37.7% | 62.1% | 37.9% |
| 11,800 | MADISON | 4,918 | 2,905 | 1,972 | 41 | 933 R | 59.1% | 40.1% | 59.6% | 40.4% |
| 8,903 | MARIES | 4,424 | 2,825 | 1,563 | 36 | 1,262 R | 63.9% | 35.3% | 64.4% | 35.6% |
| 28,289 | MARION | 12,453 | 7,815 | 4,568 | 70 | 3,247 R | 62.8% | 36.7% | 63.1% | 36.9% |
| 3,757 | MERCER | 1,817 | 1,207 | 582 | 28 | 625 R | 66.4% | 32.0% | 67.5% | 32.5% |
| 23,564 | MILLER | 10,831 | 7,797 | 2,959 | 75 | 4,838 R | 72.0% | 27.3% | 72.5% | 27.5% |
| 13,427 | MISSISSIPPI | 5,298 | 2,903 | 2,374 | 21 | 529 R | 54.8% | 44.8% | 55.0% | 45.0% |
| 14,827 | MONITEAU | 6,691 | 4,743 | 1,913 | 35 | 2,830 R | 70.9% | 28.6% | 71.3% | 28.7% |
| 9,311 | MONROE | 4,307 | 2,632 | 1,647 | 28 | 985 R | 61.1% | 38.2% | 61.5% | 38.5% |
| 12,136 | MONTGOMERY | 5,760 | 3,563 | 2,147 | 50 | 1,416 R | 61.9% | 37.3% | 62.4% | 37.6% |
| 19,309 | MORGAN | 8,771 | 5,657 | 3,053 | 61 | 2,604 R | 64.5% | 34.8% | 64.9% | 35.1% |
| 19,760 | NEW MADRID | 7,907 | 4,154 | 3,716 | 37 | 438 R | 52.5% | 47.0% | 52.8% | 47.2% |
| 52,636 | NEWTON | 23,889 | 17,187 | 6,564 | 138 | 10,623 R | 71.9% | 27.5% | 72.4% | 27.6% |
| 21,912 | NODAWAY | 10,119 | 6,226 | 3,830 | 63 | 2,396 R | 61.5% | 37.8% | 61.9% | 38.1% |
| 10,344 | OREGON | 4,673 | 2,769 | 1,823 | 81 | 946 R | 59.3% | 39.0% | 60.3% | 39.7% |
| 13,062 | OSAGE | 6,671 | 4,975 | 1,673 | 23 | 3,302 R | 74.6% | 25.1% | 74.8% | 25.2% |
| 9,542 | OZARK | 4,707 | 3,083 | 1,561 | 63 | 1,522 R | 65.5% | 33.2% | 66.4% | 33.6% |
| 20,047 | PEMISCOT | 6,806 | 3,398 | 3,381 | 27 | 17 R | 49.9% | 49.7% | 50.1% | 49.9% |
| 18,132 | PERRY | 8,247 | 5,583 | 2,621 | 43 | 2,962 R | 67.7% | 31.8% | 68.1% | 31.9% |
| 39,403 | PETTIS | 17,496 | 11,603 | 5,801 | 92 | 5,802 R | 66.3% | 33.2% | 66.7% | 33.3% |
| 39,825 | PHELPS | 18,700 | 11,874 | 6,666 | 160 | 5,208 R | 63.5% | 35.6% | 64.0% | 36.0% |
| 18,351 | PIKE | 8,040 | 4,314 | 3,670 | 56 | 644 R | 53.7% | 45.6% | 54.0% | 46.0% |
| 73,781 | PLATTE | 41,970 | 23,302 | 18,412 | 256 | 4,890 R | 55.5% | 43.9% | 55.9% | 44.1% |
| 26,992 | POLK | 12,453 | 8,586 | 3,775 | 92 | 4,811 R | 68.9% | 30.3% | 69.5% | 30.5% |
| 41,165 | PULASKI | 12,221 | 8,618 | 3,551 | 52 | 5,067 R | 70.5% | 29.1% | 70.8% | 29.2% |
| 5,223 | PUTNAM | 2,445 | 1,660 | 772 | 13 | 888 R | 67.9% | 31.6% | 68.3% | 31.7% |
| 9,626 | RALLS | 5,034 | 2,986 | 2,031 | 17 | 955 R | 59.3% | 40.3% | 59.5% | 40.5% |
| 24,663 | RANDOLPH | 10,198 | 6,551 | 3,586 | 61 | 2,965 R | 64.2% | 35.2% | 64.6% | 35.4% |
| 23,354 | RAY | 10,788 | 5,673 | 5,034 | 81 | 639 R | 52.6% | 46.7% | 53.0% | 47.0% |
| 6,689 | REYNOLDS | 3,364 | 1,896 | 1,449 | 19 | 447 R | 56.4% | 43.1% | 56.7% | 43.3% |
| 13,509 | RIPLEY | 5,653 | 3,693 | 1,907 | 53 | 1,786 R | 65.3% | 33.7% | 65.9% | 34.1% |
| 283,883 | ST. CHARLES | 163,488 | 95,826 | 66,855 | 807 | 28,971 R | 58.6% | 40.9% | 58.9% | 41.1% |
| 9,652 | ST. CLAIR | 4,965 | 3,098 | 1,841 | 26 | 1,257 R | 62.4% | 37.1% | 62.7% | 37.3% |
| 55,641 | ST. FRANCOIS | 22,933 | 12,087 | 10,748 | 98 | 1,339 R | 52.7% | 46.9% | 52.9% | 47.1% |
| 1,016,315 | ST. LOUIS COUNTY | 542,983 | 244,969 | 295,284 | 2,730 | 50,315 D | 45.1% | 54.4% | 45.3% | 54.7% |
| 348,189 | ST. LOUIS CITY | 144,638 | 27,793 | 116,133 | 712 | 88,340 D | 19.2% | 80.3% | 19.3% | 80.7% |
| 17,842 | STE. GENEVIEVE | 8,146 | 3,791 | 4,281 | 74 | 490 D | 46.5% | 52.6% | 47.0% | 53.0% |
| 23,756 | SALINE | 9,939 | 5,389 | 4,479 | 71 | 910 R | 54.2% | 45.1% | 54.6% | 45.4% |
| 4,170 | SCHUYLER | 2,031 | 1,124 | 894 | 13 | 230 R | 55.3% | 44.0% | 55.7% | 44.3% |
| 4,983 | SCOTLAND | 2,197 | 1,352 | 828 | 17 | 524 R | 61.5% | 37.7% | 62.0% | 38.0% |
| 40,422 | SCOTT | 17,448 | 11,330 | 6,057 | 61 | 5,273 R | 64.9% | 34.7% | 65.2% | 34.8% |
| 8,324 | SHANNON | 4,167 | 2,511 | 1,618 | 38 | 893 R | 60.3% | 38.8% | 60.8% | 39.2% |
| 6,799 | SHELBY | 3,502 | 2,280 | 1,201 | 21 | 1,079 R | 65.1% | 34.3% | 65.5% | 34.5% |
| 29,705 | STODDARD | 13,252 | 9,242 | 3,946 | 64 | 5,296 R | 69.7% | 29.8% | 70.1% | 29.9% |
| 28,658 | STONE | 15,189 | 10,534 | 4,578 | 77 | 5,956 R | 69.4% | 30.1% | 69.7% | 30.3% |
| 7,219 | SULLIVAN | 3,089 | 1,880 | 1,178 | 31 | 702 R | 60.9% | 38.1% | 61.5% | 38.5% |
| 39,703 | TANEY | 19,280 | 13,578 | 5,601 | 101 | 7,977 R | 70.4% | 29.1% | 70.8% | 29.2% |
| 23,003 | TEXAS | 11,018 | 7,234 | 3,664 | 120 | 3,570 R | 65.7% | 33.3% | 66.4% | 33.6% |
| 20,454 | VERNON | 8,992 | 5,732 | 3,206 | 54 | 2,526 R | 63.7% | 35.7% | 64.1% | 35.9% |
| 24,525 | WARREN | 13,432 | 7,883 | 5,461 | 88 | 2,422 R | 58.7% | 40.7% | 59.1% | 40.9% |
| 23,344 | WASHINGTON | 9,178 | 4,641 | 4,459 | 78 | 182 R | 50.6% | 48.6% | 51.0% | 49.0% |
| 13,259 | WAYNE | 6,204 | 3,919 | 2,250 | 35 | 1,669 R | 63.2% | 36.3% | 63.5% | 36.5% |
| 31,045 | WEBSTER | 14,944 | 10,194 | 4,657 | 93 | 5,537 R | 68.2% | 31.2% | 68.6% | 31.4% |
| 2,382 | WORTH | 1,132 | 691 | 436 | 5 | 255 R | 61.0% | 38.5% | 61.3% | 38.7% |
| 17,955 | WRIGHT | 8,346 | 6,090 | 2,188 | 68 | 3,902 R | 73.0% | 26.2% | 73.6% | 26.4% |
| 5,595,211 | TOTAL | 2,731,364 | 1,455,713 | 1,259,171 | 16,480 | 196,542 R | 53.3% | 46.1% | 53.6% | 46.4% |

Note: Kansas City has established its own election board and reports its results separately from Jackson County.

# MISSOURI

## GOVERNOR 2004

| 2000 Census Population | County | Total Vote | Republican | Democratic | Other | Rep.-Dem. Plurality | Percentage Total Vote Rep. | Dem. | Major Vote Rep. | Dem. |
|---|---|---|---|---|---|---|---|---|---|---|
| 24,977 | ADAIR | 11,255 | 7,019 | 4,094 | 142 | 2,925 R | 62.4% | 36.4% | 63.2% | 36.8% |
| 16,492 | ANDREW | 8,239 | 5,001 | 3,143 | 95 | 1,858 R | 60.7% | 38.1% | 61.4% | 38.6% |
| 6,430 | ATCHISON | 3,100 | 1,973 | 1,082 | 45 | 891 R | 63.6% | 34.9% | 64.6% | 35.4% |
| 25,853 | AUDRAIN | 10,662 | 6,047 | 4,500 | 115 | 1,547 R | 56.7% | 42.2% | 57.3% | 42.7% |
| 34,010 | BARRY | 13,911 | 9,594 | 4,147 | 170 | 5,447 R | 69.0% | 29.8% | 69.8% | 30.2% |
| 12,541 | BARTON | 5,971 | 4,743 | 1,164 | 64 | 3,579 R | 79.4% | 19.5% | 80.3% | 19.7% |
| 16,653 | BATES | 8,416 | 4,479 | 3,795 | 142 | 684 R | 53.2% | 45.1% | 54.1% | 45.9% |
| 17,180 | BENTON | 8,979 | 5,088 | 3,767 | 124 | 1,321 R | 56.7% | 42.0% | 57.5% | 42.5% |
| 12,029 | BOLLINGER | 5,802 | 3,902 | 1,843 | 57 | 2,059 R | 67.3% | 31.8% | 67.9% | 32.1% |
| 135,454 | BOONE | 75,356 | 35,666 | 38,489 | 1,201 | 2,823 D | 47.3% | 51.1% | 48.1% | 51.9% |
| 85,998 | BUCHANAN | 37,913 | 18,967 | 18,317 | 629 | 650 R | 50.0% | 48.3% | 50.9% | 49.1% |
| 40,867 | BUTLER | 16,328 | 10,796 | 5,364 | 168 | 5,432 R | 66.1% | 32.9% | 66.8% | 33.2% |
| 8,969 | CALDWELL | 4,289 | 2,419 | 1,796 | 74 | 623 R | 56.4% | 41.9% | 57.4% | 42.6% |
| 40,766 | CALLAWAY | 17,727 | 10,153 | 7,373 | 201 | 2,780 R | 57.3% | 41.6% | 57.9% | 42.1% |
| 37,051 | CAMDEN | 19,541 | 11,956 | 7,401 | 184 | 4,555 R | 61.2% | 37.9% | 61.8% | 38.2% |
| 68,693 | CAPE GIRARDEAU | 34,373 | 22,433 | 11,511 | 429 | 10,922 R | 65.3% | 33.5% | 66.1% | 33.9% |
| 10,285 | CARROLL | 4,703 | 2,828 | 1,830 | 45 | 998 R | 60.1% | 38.9% | 60.7% | 39.3% |
| 5,941 | CARTER | 2,613 | 1,563 | 1,022 | 28 | 541 R | 59.8% | 39.1% | 60.5% | 39.5% |
| 82,092 | CASS | 43,969 | 23,538 | 19,772 | 659 | 3,766 R | 53.5% | 45.0% | 54.3% | 45.7% |
| 13,733 | CEDAR | 6,177 | 4,096 | 1,979 | 102 | 2,117 R | 66.3% | 32.0% | 67.4% | 32.6% |
| 8,438 | CHARITON | 4,326 | 2,350 | 1,941 | 35 | 409 R | 54.3% | 44.9% | 54.8% | 45.2% |
| 54,285 | CHRISTIAN | 31,191 | 21,400 | 9,443 | 348 | 11,957 R | 68.6% | 30.3% | 69.4% | 30.6% |
| 7,416 | CLARK | 3,686 | 2,469 | 1,129 | 88 | 1,340 R | 67.0% | 30.6% | 68.6% | 31.4% |
| 184,006 | CLAY | 95,856 | 44,763 | 49,573 | 1,520 | 4,810 D | 46.7% | 51.7% | 47.5% | 52.5% |
| 18,979 | CLINTON | 9,504 | 4,663 | 4,705 | 136 | 42 D | 49.1% | 49.5% | 49.8% | 50.2% |
| 71,397 | COLE | 36,668 | 23,147 | 13,229 | 292 | 9,918 R | 63.1% | 36.1% | 63.6% | 36.4% |
| 16,670 | COOPER | 7,500 | 4,593 | 2,826 | 81 | 1,767 R | 61.2% | 37.7% | 61.9% | 38.1% |
| 22,804 | CRAWFORD | 9,397 | 5,422 | 3,845 | 130 | 1,577 R | 57.7% | 40.9% | 58.5% | 41.5% |
| 7,923 | DADE | 4,079 | 2,938 | 1,102 | 39 | 1,836 R | 72.0% | 27.0% | 72.7% | 27.3% |
| 15,661 | DALLAS | 7,242 | 4,708 | 2,421 | 113 | 2,287 R | 65.0% | 33.4% | 66.0% | 34.0% |
| 8,016 | DAVIESS | 3,766 | 2,091 | 1,618 | 57 | 473 R | 55.5% | 43.0% | 56.4% | 43.6% |
| 11,597 | DE KALB | 4,678 | 2,710 | 1,890 | 78 | 820 R | 57.9% | 40.4% | 58.9% | 41.1% |
| 14,927 | DENT | 6,324 | 4,122 | 2,092 | 110 | 2,030 R | 65.2% | 33.1% | 66.3% | 33.7% |
| 13,084 | DOUGLAS | 6,296 | 4,412 | 1,788 | 96 | 2,624 R | 70.1% | 28.4% | 71.2% | 28.8% |
| 33,155 | DUNKLIN | 11,465 | 6,015 | 5,302 | 148 | 713 R | 52.5% | 46.2% | 53.2% | 46.8% |
| 93,807 | FRANKLIN | 45,369 | 25,557 | 19,195 | 617 | 6,362 R | 56.3% | 42.3% | 57.1% | 42.9% |
| 15,342 | GASCONADE | 7,185 | 4,696 | 2,412 | 77 | 2,284 R | 65.4% | 33.6% | 66.1% | 33.9% |
| 6,861 | GENTRY | 3,300 | 1,901 | 1,354 | 45 | 547 R | 57.6% | 41.0% | 58.4% | 41.6% |
| 240,391 | GREENE | 124,736 | 76,645 | 46,470 | 1,621 | 30,175 R | 61.4% | 37.3% | 62.3% | 37.7% |
| 10,432 | GRUNDY | 4,817 | 2,836 | 1,890 | 91 | 946 R | 58.9% | 39.2% | 60.0% | 40.0% |
| 8,850 | HARRISON | 4,023 | 2,556 | 1,417 | 50 | 1,139 R | 63.5% | 35.2% | 64.3% | 35.7% |
| 21,997 | HENRY | 10,840 | 5,471 | 5,235 | 134 | 236 R | 50.5% | 48.3% | 51.1% | 48.9% |
| 8,940 | HICKORY | 4,864 | 2,750 | 2,051 | 63 | 699 R | 56.5% | 42.2% | 57.3% | 42.7% |
| 5,351 | HOLT | 2,677 | 1,776 | 873 | 28 | 903 R | 66.3% | 32.6% | 67.0% | 33.0% |
| 10,212 | HOWARD | 4,914 | 2,578 | 2,277 | 59 | 301 R | 52.5% | 46.3% | 53.1% | 46.9% |
| 37,238 | HOWELL | 16,328 | 10,595 | 5,466 | 267 | 5,129 R | 64.9% | 33.5% | 66.0% | 34.0% |
| 10,697 | IRON | 4,660 | 2,359 | 2,215 | 86 | 144 R | 50.6% | 47.5% | 51.6% | 48.4% |
| 654,880 | JACKSON | 173,788 | 82,771 | 88,570 | 2,447 | 5,799 D | 47.6% | 51.0% | 48.3% | 51.7% |
| 104,686 | JASPER | 44,665 | 33,293 | 10,853 | 519 | 22,440 R | 74.5% | 24.3% | 75.4% | 24.6% |
| 198,099 | JEFFERSON | 93,224 | 45,891 | 45,909 | 1,424 | 18 D | 49.2% | 49.2% | 50.0% | 50.0% |
| 48,258 | JOHNSON | 20,109 | 10,767 | 8,958 | 384 | 1,809 R | 53.5% | 44.5% | 54.6% | 45.4% |
| *See Note | KANSAS CITY | 140,548 | 32,285 | 106,234 | 2,029 | 73,949 D | 23.0% | 75.6% | 23.3% | 76.7% |
| 4,361 | KNOX | 1,970 | 1,328 | 623 | 19 | 705 R | 67.4% | 31.6% | 68.1% | 31.9% |
| 32,513 | LACLEDE | 14,865 | 9,993 | 4,724 | 148 | 5,269 R | 67.2% | 31.8% | 67.9% | 32.1% |
| 32,960 | LAFAYETTE | 16,123 | 8,541 | 7,351 | 231 | 1,190 R | 53.0% | 45.6% | 53.7% | 46.3% |
| 35,204 | LAWRENCE | 15,763 | 11,069 | 4,500 | 194 | 6,569 R | 70.2% | 28.5% | 71.1% | 28.9% |
| 10,494 | LEWIS | 4,601 | 3,084 | 1,441 | 76 | 1,643 R | 67.0% | 31.3% | 68.2% | 31.8% |
| 38,944 | LINCOLN | 19,768 | 10,626 | 8,824 | 318 | 1,802 R | 53.8% | 44.6% | 54.6% | 45.4% |
| 13,754 | LINN | 5,901 | 3,252 | 2,588 | 61 | 664 R | 55.1% | 43.9% | 55.7% | 44.3% |
| 14,558 | LIVINGSTON | 6,318 | 3,680 | 2,580 | 58 | 1,100 R | 58.2% | 40.8% | 58.8% | 41.2% |

# MISSOURI

## GOVERNOR 2004

| 2000 Census Population | County | Total Vote | Republican | Democratic | Other | Rep.-Dem. Plurality | Percentage Total Vote Rep. | Dem. | Major Vote Rep. | Dem. |
|---|---|---|---|---|---|---|---|---|---|---|
| 21,681 | MCDONALD | 7,664 | 5,622 | 1,894 | 148 | 3,728 R | 73.4% | 24.7% | 74.8% | 25.2% |
| 15,762 | MACON | 7,479 | 4,598 | 2,781 | 100 | 1,817 R | 61.5% | 37.2% | 62.3% | 37.7% |
| 11,800 | MADISON | 4,872 | 2,819 | 1,972 | 81 | 847 R | 57.9% | 40.5% | 58.8% | 41.2% |
| 8,903 | MARIES | 4,407 | 2,688 | 1,665 | 54 | 1,023 R | 61.0% | 37.8% | 61.8% | 38.2% |
| 28,289 | MARION | 12,370 | 8,292 | 3,930 | 148 | 4,362 R | 67.0% | 31.8% | 67.8% | 32.2% |
| 3,757 | MERCER | 1,775 | 1,237 | 519 | 19 | 718 R | 69.7% | 29.2% | 70.4% | 29.6% |
| 23,564 | MILLER | 10,819 | 7,331 | 3,370 | 118 | 3,961 R | 67.8% | 31.1% | 68.5% | 31.5% |
| 13,427 | MISSISSIPPI | 5,258 | 2,558 | 2,645 | 55 | 87 D | 48.6% | 50.3% | 49.2% | 50.8% |
| 14,827 | MONITEAU | 6,706 | 4,480 | 2,178 | 48 | 2,302 R | 66.8% | 32.5% | 67.3% | 32.7% |
| 9,311 | MONROE | 4,293 | 2,576 | 1,670 | 47 | 906 R | 60.0% | 38.9% | 60.7% | 39.3% |
| 12,136 | MONTGOMERY | 5,743 | 3,480 | 2,186 | 77 | 1,294 R | 60.6% | 38.1% | 61.4% | 38.6% |
| 19,309 | MORGAN | 8,762 | 5,273 | 3,377 | 112 | 1,896 R | 60.2% | 38.5% | 61.0% | 39.0% |
| 19,760 | NEW MADRID | 7,855 | 3,737 | 4,036 | 82 | 299 D | 47.6% | 51.4% | 48.1% | 51.9% |
| 52,636 | NEWTON | 23,839 | 17,935 | 5,662 | 242 | 12,273 R | 75.2% | 23.8% | 76.0% | 24.0% |
| 21,912 | NODAWAY | 10,030 | 5,424 | 4,456 | 150 | 968 R | 54.1% | 44.4% | 54.9% | 45.1% |
| 10,344 | OREGON | 4,625 | 2,579 | 1,950 | 96 | 629 R | 55.8% | 42.2% | 56.9% | 43.1% |
| 13,062 | OSAGE | 6,678 | 4,586 | 2,044 | 48 | 2,542 R | 68.7% | 30.6% | 69.2% | 30.8% |
| 9,542 | OZARK | 4,678 | 2,949 | 1,628 | 101 | 1,321 R | 63.0% | 34.8% | 64.4% | 35.6% |
| 20,047 | PEMISCOT | 6,599 | 2,965 | 3,528 | 106 | 563 D | 44.9% | 53.5% | 45.7% | 54.3% |
| 18,132 | PERRY | 8,197 | 5,293 | 2,822 | 82 | 2,471 R | 64.6% | 34.4% | 65.2% | 34.8% |
| 39,403 | PETTIS | 17,517 | 10,038 | 7,293 | 186 | 2,745 R | 57.3% | 41.6% | 57.9% | 42.1% |
| 39,825 | PHELPS | 18,565 | 10,970 | 7,341 | 254 | 3,629 R | 59.1% | 39.5% | 59.9% | 40.1% |
| 18,351 | PIKE | 7,982 | 4,416 | 3,434 | 132 | 982 R | 55.3% | 43.0% | 56.3% | 43.7% |
| 73,781 | PLATTE | 41,684 | 20,137 | 20,970 | 577 | 833 D | 48.3% | 50.3% | 49.0% | 51.0% |
| 26,992 | POLK | 12,409 | 8,418 | 3,835 | 156 | 4,583 R | 67.8% | 30.9% | 68.7% | 31.3% |
| 41,165 | PULASKI | 11,486 | 7,466 | 3,882 | 138 | 3,584 R | 65.0% | 33.8% | 65.8% | 34.2% |
| 5,223 | PUTNAM | 2,415 | 1,757 | 624 | 34 | 1,133 R | 72.8% | 25.8% | 73.8% | 26.2% |
| 9,626 | RALLS | 5,010 | 3,090 | 1,866 | 54 | 1,224 R | 61.7% | 37.2% | 62.3% | 37.7% |
| 24,663 | RANDOLPH | 10,140 | 5,841 | 4,167 | 132 | 1,674 R | 57.6% | 41.1% | 58.4% | 41.6% |
| 23,354 | RAY | 10,776 | 5,073 | 5,531 | 172 | 458 D | 47.1% | 51.3% | 47.8% | 52.2% |
| 6,689 | REYNOLDS | 3,257 | 1,746 | 1,470 | 41 | 276 R | 53.6% | 45.1% | 54.3% | 45.7% |
| 13,509 | RIPLEY | 5,567 | 3,332 | 2,136 | 99 | 1,196 R | 59.9% | 38.4% | 60.9% | 39.1% |
| 283,883 | ST. CHARLES | 163,372 | 91,323 | 70,184 | 1,865 | 21,139 R | 55.9% | 43.0% | 56.5% | 43.5% |
| 9,652 | ST. CLAIR | 4,961 | 2,888 | 2,004 | 69 | 884 R | 58.2% | 40.4% | 59.0% | 41.0% |
| 55,641 | ST. FRANCOIS | 22,831 | 11,903 | 10,601 | 327 | 1,302 R | 52.1% | 46.4% | 52.9% | 47.1% |
| 1,016,315 | ST. LOUIS COUNTY | 541,550 | 238,783 | 296,624 | 6,143 | 57,841 D | 44.1% | 54.8% | 44.6% | 55.4% |
| 348,189 | ST. LOUIS CITY | 143,828 | 29,667 | 111,940 | 2,221 | 82,273 D | 20.6% | 77.8% | 21.0% | 79.0% |
| 17,842 | STE. GENEVIEVE | 8,199 | 3,845 | 4,208 | 146 | 363 D | 46.9% | 51.3% | 47.7% | 52.3% |
| 23,756 | SALINE | 9,885 | 4,691 | 5,071 | 123 | 380 D | 47.5% | 51.3% | 48.1% | 51.9% |
| 4,170 | SCHUYLER | 2,003 | 1,278 | 697 | 28 | 581 R | 63.8% | 34.8% | 64.7% | 35.3% |
| 4,983 | SCOTLAND | 2,148 | 1,507 | 615 | 26 | 892 R | 70.2% | 28.6% | 71.0% | 29.0% |
| 40,422 | SCOTT | 17,376 | 10,198 | 7,004 | 174 | 3,194 R | 58.7% | 40.3% | 59.3% | 40.7% |
| 8,324 | SHANNON | 4,123 | 2,391 | 1,652 | 80 | 739 R | 58.0% | 40.1% | 59.1% | 40.9% |
| 6,799 | SHELBY | 3,471 | 2,316 | 1,116 | 39 | 1,200 R | 66.7% | 32.2% | 67.5% | 32.5% |
| 29,705 | STODDARD | 13,228 | 8,152 | 4,940 | 136 | 3,212 R | 61.6% | 37.3% | 62.3% | 37.7% |
| 28,658 | STONE | 15,135 | 10,176 | 4,791 | 168 | 5,385 R | 67.2% | 31.7% | 68.0% | 32.0% |
| 7,219 | SULLIVAN | 3,089 | 1,929 | 1,105 | 55 | 824 R | 62.4% | 35.8% | 63.6% | 36.4% |
| 39,703 | TANEY | 19,174 | 13,207 | 5,734 | 233 | 7,473 R | 68.9% | 29.9% | 69.7% | 30.3% |
| 23,003 | TEXAS | 11,014 | 6,644 | 4,177 | 193 | 2,467 R | 60.3% | 37.9% | 61.4% | 38.6% |
| 20,454 | VERNON | 8,971 | 5,989 | 2,868 | 114 | 3,121 R | 66.8% | 32.0% | 67.6% | 32.4% |
| 24,525 | WARREN | 13,352 | 7,488 | 5,689 | 175 | 1,799 R | 56.1% | 42.6% | 56.8% | 43.2% |
| 23,344 | WASHINGTON | 9,177 | 4,622 | 4,393 | 162 | 229 R | 50.4% | 47.9% | 51.3% | 48.7% |
| 13,259 | WAYNE | 6,202 | 3,649 | 2,472 | 81 | 1,177 R | 58.8% | 39.9% | 59.6% | 40.4% |
| 31,045 | WEBSTER | 14,918 | 10,086 | 4,651 | 181 | 5,435 R | 67.6% | 31.2% | 68.4% | 31.6% |
| 2,382 | WORTH | 1,133 | 662 | 461 | 10 | 201 R | 58.4% | 40.7% | 58.9% | 41.1% |
| 17,955 | WRIGHT | 8,344 | 5,955 | 2,280 | 109 | 3,675 R | 71.4% | 27.3% | 72.3% | 27.7% |
| 5,595,211 | TOTAL | 2,719,599 | 1,382,419 | 1,301,442 | 35,738 | 80,977 R | 50.8% | 47.9% | 51.5% | 48.5% |

Note: Kansas City has established its own election board and reports its results separately from Jackson County.

# MISSOURI
## SENATOR 2004

| 2000 Census Population | County | Total Vote | Republican | Democratic | Other | Rep.-Dem. Plurality | Percentage | | | |
|---|---|---|---|---|---|---|---|---|---|---|
| | | | | | | | Total Vote | | Major Vote | |
| | | | | | | | Rep. | Dem. | Rep. | Dem. |
| 24,977 | ADAIR | 11,190 | 7,497 | 3,561 | 132 | 3,936 R | 67.0% | 31.8% | 67.8% | 32.2% |
| 16,492 | ANDREW | 8,221 | 5,544 | 2,599 | 78 | 2,945 R | 67.4% | 31.6% | 68.1% | 31.9% |
| 6,430 | ATCHISON | 3,107 | 2,236 | 847 | 24 | 1,389 R | 72.0% | 27.3% | 72.5% | 27.5% |
| 25,853 | AUDRAIN | 10,659 | 7,121 | 3,456 | 82 | 3,665 R | 66.8% | 32.4% | 67.3% | 32.7% |
| 34,010 | BARRY | 13,867 | 9,775 | 3,933 | 159 | 5,842 R | 70.5% | 28.4% | 71.3% | 28.7% |
| 12,541 | BARTON | 5,962 | 4,826 | 1,068 | 68 | 3,758 R | 80.9% | 17.9% | 81.9% | 18.1% |
| 16,653 | BATES | 8,416 | 5,108 | 3,214 | 94 | 1,894 R | 60.7% | 38.2% | 61.4% | 38.6% |
| 17,180 | BENTON | 8,963 | 5,644 | 3,216 | 103 | 2,428 R | 63.0% | 35.9% | 63.7% | 36.3% |
| 12,029 | BOLLINGER | 5,798 | 4,161 | 1,594 | 43 | 2,567 R | 71.8% | 27.5% | 72.3% | 27.7% |
| 135,454 | BOONE | 74,984 | 42,345 | 31,467 | 1,172 | 10,878 R | 56.5% | 42.0% | 57.4% | 42.6% |
| 85,998 | BUCHANAN | 37,788 | 21,790 | 15,389 | 609 | 6,401 R | 57.7% | 40.7% | 58.6% | 41.4% |
| 40,867 | BUTLER | 16,281 | 11,903 | 4,225 | 153 | 7,678 R | 73.1% | 26.0% | 73.8% | 26.2% |
| 8,969 | CALDWELL | 4,239 | 2,697 | 1,473 | 69 | 1,224 R | 63.6% | 34.7% | 64.7% | 35.3% |
| 40,766 | CALLAWAY | 17,644 | 11,362 | 6,054 | 228 | 5,308 R | 64.4% | 34.3% | 65.2% | 34.8% |
| 37,051 | CAMDEN | 19,467 | 13,427 | 5,826 | 214 | 7,601 R | 69.0% | 29.9% | 69.7% | 30.3% |
| 68,693 | CAPE GIRARDEAU | 34,340 | 24,190 | 9,780 | 370 | 14,410 R | 70.4% | 28.5% | 71.2% | 28.8% |
| 10,285 | CARROLL | 4,700 | 3,337 | 1,331 | 32 | 2,006 R | 71.0% | 28.3% | 71.5% | 28.5% |
| 5,941 | CARTER | 2,716 | 1,861 | 829 | 26 | 1,032 R | 68.5% | 30.5% | 69.2% | 30.8% |
| 82,092 | CASS | 43,840 | 27,931 | 15,390 | 519 | 12,541 R | 63.7% | 35.1% | 64.5% | 35.5% |
| 13,733 | CEDAR | 6,143 | 4,285 | 1,761 | 97 | 2,524 R | 69.8% | 28.7% | 70.9% | 29.1% |
| 8,438 | CHARITON | 4,318 | 2,699 | 1,587 | 32 | 1,112 R | 62.5% | 36.8% | 63.0% | 37.0% |
| 54,285 | CHRISTIAN | 31,144 | 22,370 | 8,482 | 292 | 13,888 R | 71.8% | 27.2% | 72.5% | 27.5% |
| 7,416 | CLARK | 3,703 | 2,449 | 1,180 | 74 | 1,269 R | 66.1% | 31.9% | 67.5% | 32.5% |
| 184,006 | CLAY | 95,470 | 53,892 | 40,357 | 1,221 | 13,535 R | 56.4% | 42.3% | 57.2% | 42.8% |
| 18,979 | CLINTON | 9,466 | 5,352 | 3,974 | 140 | 1,378 R | 56.5% | 42.0% | 57.4% | 42.6% |
| 71,397 | COLE | 36,563 | 25,857 | 10,370 | 336 | 15,487 R | 70.7% | 28.4% | 71.4% | 28.6% |
| 16,670 | COOPER | 7,496 | 5,263 | 2,160 | 73 | 3,103 R | 70.2% | 28.8% | 70.9% | 29.1% |
| 22,804 | CRAWFORD | 9,340 | 5,557 | 3,667 | 116 | 1,890 R | 59.5% | 39.3% | 60.2% | 39.8% |
| 7,923 | DADE | 4,038 | 3,039 | 966 | 33 | 2,073 R | 75.3% | 23.9% | 75.9% | 24.1% |
| 15,661 | DALLAS | 7,220 | 4,882 | 2,240 | 98 | 2,642 R | 67.6% | 31.0% | 68.5% | 31.5% |
| 8,016 | DAVIESS | 3,761 | 2,409 | 1,298 | 54 | 1,111 R | 64.1% | 34.5% | 65.0% | 35.0% |
| 11,597 | DE KALB | 4,669 | 3,054 | 1,553 | 62 | 1,501 R | 65.4% | 33.3% | 66.3% | 33.7% |
| 14,927 | DENT | 6,299 | 4,356 | 1,847 | 96 | 2,509 R | 69.2% | 29.3% | 70.2% | 29.8% |
| 13,084 | DOUGLAS | 6,286 | 4,535 | 1,642 | 109 | 2,893 R | 72.1% | 26.1% | 73.4% | 26.6% |
| 33,155 | DUNKLIN | 11,416 | 6,840 | 4,450 | 126 | 2,390 R | 59.9% | 39.0% | 60.6% | 39.4% |
| 93,807 | FRANKLIN | 45,243 | 26,317 | 18,376 | 550 | 7,941 R | 58.2% | 40.6% | 58.9% | 41.1% |
| 15,342 | GASCONADE | 7,167 | 4,964 | 2,135 | 68 | 2,829 R | 69.3% | 29.8% | 69.9% | 30.1% |
| 6,861 | GENTRY | 3,294 | 2,180 | 1,080 | 34 | 1,100 R | 66.2% | 32.8% | 66.9% | 33.1% |
| 240,391 | GREENE | 124,068 | 81,119 | 41,372 | 1,577 | 39,747 R | 65.4% | 33.3% | 66.2% | 33.8% |
| 10,432 | GRUNDY | 4,819 | 3,371 | 1,352 | 96 | 2,019 R | 70.0% | 28.1% | 71.4% | 28.6% |
| 8,850 | HARRISON | 3,949 | 2,852 | 1,066 | 31 | 1,786 R | 72.2% | 27.0% | 72.8% | 27.2% |
| 21,997 | HENRY | 10,790 | 6,410 | 4,258 | 122 | 2,152 R | 59.4% | 39.5% | 60.1% | 39.9% |
| 8,940 | HICKORY | 4,842 | 2,935 | 1,847 | 60 | 1,088 R | 60.6% | 38.1% | 61.4% | 38.6% |
| 5,351 | HOLT | 2,673 | 2,002 | 652 | 19 | 1,350 R | 74.9% | 24.4% | 75.4% | 24.6% |
| 10,212 | HOWARD | 4,904 | 3,121 | 1,721 | 62 | 1,400 R | 63.6% | 35.1% | 64.5% | 35.5% |
| 37,238 | HOWELL | 16,280 | 11,477 | 4,569 | 234 | 6,908 R | 70.5% | 28.1% | 71.5% | 28.5% |
| 10,697 | IRON | 4,659 | 2,499 | 2,087 | 73 | 412 R | 53.6% | 44.8% | 54.5% | 45.5% |
| 654,880 | JACKSON | 172,872 | 98,548 | 72,306 | 2,018 | 26,242 R | 57.0% | 41.8% | 57.7% | 42.3% |
| 104,686 | JASPER | 44,460 | 33,399 | 10,547 | 514 | 22,852 R | 75.1% | 23.7% | 76.0% | 24.0% |
| 198,099 | JEFFERSON | 92,875 | 47,203 | 44,469 | 1,203 | 2,734 R | 50.8% | 47.9% | 51.5% | 48.5% |
| 48,258 | JOHNSON | 20,105 | 12,574 | 7,194 | 337 | 5,380 R | 62.5% | 35.8% | 63.6% | 36.4% |
| *See Note | KANSAS CITY | 139,960 | 43,118 | 95,244 | 1,598 | 52,126 D | 30.8% | 68.1% | 31.2% | 68.8% |
| 4,361 | KNOX | 1,978 | 1,406 | 558 | 14 | 848 R | 71.1% | 28.2% | 71.6% | 28.4% |
| 32,513 | LACLEDE | 14,812 | 10,894 | 3,775 | 143 | 7,119 R | 73.5% | 25.5% | 74.3% | 25.7% |
| 32,960 | LAFAYETTE | 16,089 | 9,980 | 5,966 | 143 | 4,014 R | 62.0% | 37.1% | 62.6% | 37.4% |
| 35,204 | LAWRENCE | 15,745 | 11,265 | 4,284 | 196 | 6,981 R | 71.5% | 27.2% | 72.4% | 27.6% |
| 10,494 | LEWIS | 4,605 | 3,129 | 1,423 | 53 | 1,706 R | 67.9% | 30.9% | 68.7% | 31.3% |
| 38,944 | LINCOLN | 19,733 | 11,033 | 8,429 | 271 | 2,604 R | 55.9% | 42.7% | 56.7% | 43.3% |
| 13,754 | LINN | 5,882 | 3,652 | 2,186 | 44 | 1,466 R | 62.1% | 37.2% | 62.6% | 37.4% |
| 14,558 | LIVINGSTON | 6,307 | 4,258 | 1,995 | 54 | 2,263 R | 67.5% | 31.6% | 68.1% | 31.9% |

# MISSOURI

## SENATOR 2004

| 2000 Census Population | County | Total Vote | Republican | Democratic | Other | Rep.-Dem. Plurality | Percentage Total Vote Rep. | Dem. | Major Vote Rep. | Dem. |
|---|---|---|---|---|---|---|---|---|---|---|
| 21,681 | MCDONALD | 7,649 | 5,617 | 1,895 | 137 | 3,722 R | 73.4% | 24.8% | 74.8% | 25.2% |
| 15,762 | MACON | 7,501 | 5,143 | 2,301 | 57 | 2,842 R | 68.6% | 30.7% | 69.1% | 30.9% |
| 11,800 | MADISON | 4,885 | 3,002 | 1,823 | 60 | 1,179 R | 61.5% | 37.3% | 62.2% | 37.8% |
| 8,903 | MARIES | 4,413 | 3,018 | 1,344 | 51 | 1,674 R | 68.4% | 30.5% | 69.2% | 30.8% |
| 28,289 | MARION | 12,356 | 8,424 | 3,813 | 119 | 4,611 R | 68.2% | 30.9% | 68.8% | 31.2% |
| 3,757 | MERCER | 1,751 | 1,297 | 425 | 29 | 872 R | 74.1% | 24.3% | 75.3% | 24.7% |
| 23,564 | MILLER | 10,792 | 8,049 | 2,626 | 117 | 5,423 R | 74.6% | 24.3% | 75.4% | 24.6% |
| 13,427 | MISSISSIPPI | 5,257 | 2,937 | 2,287 | 33 | 650 R | 55.9% | 43.5% | 56.2% | 43.8% |
| 14,827 | MONITEAU | 6,687 | 4,925 | 1,703 | 59 | 3,222 R | 73.7% | 25.5% | 74.3% | 25.7% |
| 9,311 | MONROE | 4,290 | 2,857 | 1,390 | 43 | 1,467 R | 66.6% | 32.4% | 67.3% | 32.7% |
| 12,136 | MONTGOMERY | 5,739 | 3,823 | 1,840 | 76 | 1,983 R | 66.6% | 32.1% | 67.5% | 32.5% |
| 19,309 | MORGAN | 8,741 | 5,896 | 2,756 | 89 | 3,140 R | 67.5% | 31.5% | 68.1% | 31.9% |
| 19,760 | NEW MADRID | 7,852 | 4,173 | 3,611 | 68 | 562 R | 53.1% | 46.0% | 53.6% | 46.4% |
| 52,636 | NEWTON | 23,785 | 18,198 | 5,356 | 231 | 12,842 R | 76.5% | 22.5% | 77.3% | 22.7% |
| 21,912 | NODAWAY | 10,004 | 6,774 | 3,144 | 86 | 3,630 R | 67.7% | 31.4% | 68.3% | 31.7% |
| 10,344 | OREGON | 4,615 | 2,800 | 1,725 | 90 | 1,075 R | 60.7% | 37.4% | 61.9% | 38.1% |
| 13,062 | OSAGE | 6,681 | 5,048 | 1,584 | 49 | 3,464 R | 75.6% | 23.7% | 76.1% | 23.9% |
| 9,542 | OZARK | 4,659 | 3,128 | 1,445 | 86 | 1,683 R | 67.1% | 31.0% | 68.4% | 31.6% |
| 20,047 | PEMISCOT | 6,495 | 3,341 | 3,037 | 117 | 304 R | 51.4% | 46.8% | 52.4% | 47.6% |
| 18,132 | PERRY | 8,189 | 5,917 | 2,212 | 60 | 3,705 R | 72.3% | 27.0% | 72.8% | 27.2% |
| 39,403 | PETTIS | 17,447 | 11,700 | 5,546 | 201 | 6,154 R | 67.1% | 31.8% | 67.8% | 32.2% |
| 39,825 | PHELPS | 18,478 | 12,151 | 6,079 | 248 | 6,072 R | 65.8% | 32.9% | 66.7% | 33.3% |
| 18,351 | PIKE | 7,978 | 4,646 | 3,252 | 80 | 1,394 R | 58.2% | 40.8% | 58.8% | 41.2% |
| 73,781 | PLATTE | 41,488 | 24,370 | 16,640 | 478 | 7,730 R | 58.7% | 40.1% | 59.4% | 40.6% |
| 26,992 | POLK | 12,325 | 8,698 | 3,470 | 157 | 5,228 R | 70.6% | 28.2% | 71.5% | 28.5% |
| 41,165 | PULASKI | 12,085 | 8,669 | 3,265 | 151 | 5,404 R | 71.7% | 27.0% | 72.6% | 27.4% |
| 5,223 | PUTNAM | 2,415 | 1,848 | 547 | 20 | 1,301 R | 76.5% | 22.7% | 77.2% | 22.8% |
| 9,626 | RALLS | 5,005 | 3,155 | 1,813 | 37 | 1,342 R | 63.0% | 36.2% | 63.5% | 36.5% |
| 24,663 | RANDOLPH | 10,148 | 6,728 | 3,294 | 126 | 3,434 R | 66.3% | 32.5% | 67.1% | 32.9% |
| 23,354 | RAY | 10,746 | 5,780 | 4,815 | 151 | 965 R | 53.8% | 44.8% | 54.6% | 45.4% |
| 6,689 | REYNOLDS | 3,208 | 1,887 | 1,293 | 28 | 594 R | 58.8% | 40.3% | 59.3% | 40.7% |
| 13,509 | RIPLEY | 5,579 | 3,763 | 1,719 | 97 | 2,044 R | 67.4% | 30.8% | 68.6% | 31.4% |
| 283,883 | ST. CHARLES | 162,757 | 97,631 | 63,545 | 1,581 | 34,086 R | 60.0% | 39.0% | 60.6% | 39.4% |
| 9,652 | ST. CLAIR | 4,947 | 3,140 | 1,762 | 45 | 1,378 R | 63.5% | 35.6% | 64.1% | 35.9% |
| 55,641 | ST. FRANCOIS | 22,774 | 12,401 | 10,122 | 251 | 2,279 R | 54.5% | 44.4% | 55.1% | 44.9% |
| 1,016,315 | ST. LOUIS COUNTY | 536,430 | 254,285 | 277,503 | 4,642 | 23,218 D | 47.4% | 51.7% | 47.8% | 52.2% |
| 348,189 | ST. LOUIS CITY | 142,268 | 31,468 | 109,228 | 1,572 | 77,760 D | 22.1% | 76.8% | 22.4% | 77.6% |
| 17,842 | STE. GENEVIEVE | 8,176 | 4,111 | 3,935 | 130 | 176 R | 50.3% | 48.1% | 51.1% | 48.9% |
| 23,756 | SALINE | 9,873 | 5,886 | 3,894 | 93 | 1,992 R | 59.6% | 39.4% | 60.2% | 39.8% |
| 4,170 | SCHUYLER | 2,000 | 1,308 | 668 | 24 | 640 R | 65.4% | 33.4% | 66.2% | 33.8% |
| 4,983 | SCOTLAND | 2,166 | 1,635 | 510 | 21 | 1,125 R | 75.5% | 23.5% | 76.2% | 23.8% |
| 40,422 | SCOTT | 17,355 | 11,345 | 5,878 | 132 | 5,467 R | 65.4% | 33.9% | 65.9% | 34.1% |
| 8,324 | SHANNON | 4,053 | 2,550 | 1,452 | 51 | 1,098 R | 62.9% | 35.8% | 63.7% | 36.3% |
| 6,799 | SHELBY | 3,468 | 2,450 | 994 | 24 | 1,456 R | 70.6% | 28.7% | 71.1% | 28.9% |
| 29,705 | STODDARD | 13,171 | 9,123 | 3,946 | 102 | 5,177 R | 69.3% | 30.0% | 69.8% | 30.2% |
| 28,658 | STONE | 15,101 | 10,753 | 4,205 | 143 | 6,548 R | 71.2% | 27.8% | 71.9% | 28.1% |
| 7,219 | SULLIVAN | 3,089 | 2,175 | 879 | 35 | 1,296 R | 70.4% | 28.5% | 71.2% | 28.8% |
| 39,703 | TANEY | 19,062 | 13,630 | 5,183 | 249 | 8,447 R | 71.5% | 27.2% | 72.4% | 27.6% |
| 23,003 | TEXAS | 10,970 | 7,178 | 3,627 | 165 | 3,551 R | 65.4% | 33.1% | 66.4% | 33.6% |
| 20,454 | VERNON | 8,948 | 6,145 | 2,699 | 104 | 3,446 R | 68.7% | 30.2% | 69.5% | 30.5% |
| 24,525 | WARREN | 13,289 | 7,921 | 5,208 | 160 | 2,713 R | 59.6% | 39.2% | 60.3% | 39.7% |
| 23,344 | WASHINGTON | 9,140 | 4,768 | 4,240 | 132 | 528 R | 52.2% | 46.4% | 52.9% | 47.1% |
| 13,259 | WAYNE | 6,192 | 3,974 | 2,153 | 65 | 1,821 R | 64.2% | 34.8% | 64.9% | 35.1% |
| 31,045 | WEBSTER | 14,863 | 10,281 | 4,431 | 151 | 5,850 R | 69.2% | 29.8% | 69.9% | 30.1% |
| 2,382 | WORTH | 1,125 | 755 | 365 | 5 | 390 R | 67.1% | 32.4% | 67.4% | 32.6% |
| 17,955 | WRIGHT | 8,317 | 6,114 | 2,107 | 96 | 4,007 R | 73.5% | 25.3% | 74.4% | 25.6% |
| 5,595,211 | TOTAL | 2,706,402 | 1,518,089 | 1,158,261 | 30,052 | 359,828 R | 56.1% | 42.8% | 56.7% | 43.3% |

Note: Kansas City has established its own election board and reports its results separately from Jackson County.

# MISSOURI

## HOUSE OF REPRESENTATIVES

| CD | Year | Total Vote | Republican Vote | Republican Candidate | Democratic Vote | Democratic Candidate | Other Vote | Rep.-Dem. Plurality | Percentage Total Vote Rep. | Dem. | Major Vote Rep. | Dem. |
|----|------|-----------|-----------------|----------------------|-----------------|----------------------|-----------|---------------------|------------|------|------|------|
| 1 | 2004 | 283,771 | 64,791 | Farr, Leslie L. II | 213,658 | Clay, William Lacy* | 5,322 | 148,867 D | 22.8% | 75.3% | 23.3% | 76.7% |
| 1 | 2002 | 191,055 | 51,755 | Schwadron, Richard | 133,946 | Clay, William Lacy* | 5,354 | 82,191 D | 27.1% | 70.1% | 27.9% | 72.1% |
| 2 | 2004 | 349,867 | 228,725 | Akin, Todd* | 115,366 | Weber, George D. | 5,776 | 113,359 R | 65.4% | 33.0% | 66.5% | 33.5% |
| 2 | 2002 | 248,828 | 167,057 | Akin, Todd* | 77,223 | Hogan, John | 4,548 | 89,834 R | 67.1% | 31.0% | 68.4% | 31.6% |
| 3 | 2004 | 277,916 | 125,422 | Federer, Bill | 146,894 | Carnahan, Russ | 5,600 | 21,472 D | 45.1% | 52.9% | 46.1% | 53.9% |
| 3 | 2002 | 206,878 | 80,551 | Enz, Catherine S. | 122,181 | Gephardt, Richard A.* | 4,146 | 41,630 D | 38.9% | 59.1% | 39.7% | 60.3% |
| 4 | 2004 | 288,226 | 93,334 | Noland, James A. "Jim" | 190,800 | Skelton, Ike* | 4,092 | 97,466 D | 32.4% | 66.2% | 32.8% | 67.2% |
| 4 | 2002 | 210,238 | 64,451 | Noland, James A. "Jim" | 142,204 | Skelton, Ike* | 3,583 | 77,753 D | 30.7% | 67.6% | 31.2% | 68.8% |
| 5 | 2004 | 293,025 | 123,431 | Patterson, Jeanne | 161,727 | Cleaver, Emanuel II | 7,867 | 38,296 D | 42.1% | 55.2% | 43.3% | 56.7% |
| 5 | 2002 | 186,167 | 60,245 | Gordon, Steve | 122,645 | McCarthy, Karen* | 3,277 | 62,400 D | 32.4% | 65.9% | 32.9% | 67.1% |
| 6 | 2004 | 307,855 | 196,516 | Graves, Sam* | 106,987 | Broomfield, Charles S. | 4,352 | 89,529 R | 63.8% | 34.8% | 64.7% | 35.3% |
| 6 | 2002 | 208,088 | 131,151 | Graves, Sam* | 73,202 | Rinehart, Cathy | 3,735 | 57,949 R | 63.0% | 35.2% | 64.2% | 35.8% |
| 7 | 2004 | 298,205 | 210,080 | Blunt, Roy* | 84,356 | Newberry, Jim | 3,769 | 125,724 R | 70.4% | 28.3% | 71.3% | 28.7% |
| 7 | 2002 | 199,863 | 149,519 | Blunt, Roy* | 45,964 | Lapham, Ron | 4,380 | 103,555 R | 74.8% | 23.0% | 76.5% | 23.5% |
| 8 | 2004 | 268,711 | 194,039 | Emerson, Jo Ann* | 71,543 | Henderson, Dean | 3,129 | 122,496 R | 72.2% | 26.6% | 73.1% | 26.9% |
| 8 | 2002 | 188,321 | 135,144 | Emerson, Jo Ann* | 50,686 | Curtis, Gene | 2,491 | 84,458 R | 71.8% | 26.9% | 72.7% | 27.3% |
| 9 | 2004 | 299,447 | 193,429 | Hulshof, Kenny* | 101,343 | Jacobsen, Linda | 4,675 | 92,086 R | 64.6% | 33.8% | 65.6% | 34.4% |
| 9 | 2002 | 214,125 | 146,032 | Hulshof, Kenny* | 61,126 | Deichman, Donald M. "Don" | 6,967 | 84,906 R | 68.2% | 28.5% | 70.5% | 29.5% |
| Total | 2004 | 2,667,023 | 1,429,767 | | 1,192,674 | | 44,582 | 237,093 R | 53.6% | 44.7% | 54.5% | 45.5% |
| Total | 2002 | 1,853,563 | 985,905 | | 829,177 | | 38,481 | 156,728 R | 53.2% | 44.7% | 54.3% | 45.7% |

An asterisk (*) denotes incumbent.

# MISSOURI

## GENERAL AND PRIMARY ELECTIONS

## 2004 GENERAL ELECTIONS

**President**  Other vote was 9,831 Libertarian (Michael Badnarik); 5,355 Constitution (Michael Peroutka); 1,294 write-in (Ralph Nader).

**Governor**  Other vote was 24,378 Libertarian (John M. Swenson); 11,299 Constitution (Robert Wells); 61 write-in (Kenneth J. Johnson).

**Senator**  Other vote was 19,648 Libertarian (Kevin Tull); 10,404 Constitution (Don Griffin).

**House**  Other vote was:

CD 1  3,937 Libertarian (Terry Chadwick); 1,385 Constitution (Robert Rehbein).
CD 2  4,822 Libertarian (Darla Maloney); 954 Constitution (David Leefe).
CD 3  4,367 Libertarian (Kevin C. Babcock); 1,222 Constitution (William J. Renaud); 11 write-in (Joseph L. Badaracco).
CD 4  2,827 Libertarian (Bill Lower); 1,265 Constitution (Raymond Lister).
CD 5  5,827 Libertarian (Rick Bailie); 2,040 Constitution (Darin Rodenberg).
CD 6  4,352 Libertarian (Erik Buck).
CD 7  2,767 Libertarian (Kevin Craig); 1,002 Constitution (Steve Alger).
CD 8  1,810 Libertarian (Stan Cuff); 1,319 Constitution (Leonard J. Davidson).
CD 9  3,228 Libertarian (Tamara A. Millay); 1,447 Constitution (Chris Earl).

# MISSOURI

## GENERAL AND PRIMARY ELECTIONS

### 2004 PRIMARY ELECTIONS

| | | |
|---|---|---|
| **Primary** | February 3, 2004 (President) | **Registration** 3,681,844 No Party |
| | August 3, 2004 (Congress) | (as of November 2002) Registration |

**Primary Type**  Open—Any registered voter could participate in the primary of the party of their choice.

Note:   An asterisk (*) denotes incumbent.

| | REPUBLICAN PRIMARIES | | | DEMOCRATIC PRIMARIES | | |
|---|---|---|---|---|---|---|
| President | George W. Bush* | 117,007 | 95.1% | John Kerry | 211,745 | 50.6% |
| | Uncommitted | 3,830 | 3.1% | John Edwards | 103,088 | 24.6% |
| | Bill Wyatt | 1,268 | 1.0% | Howard Dean | 36,288 | 8.7% |
| | Blake Ashby | 981 | 0.8% | Wesley Clark | 18,340 | 4.4% |
| | | | | Joseph I. Lieberman | 14,727 | 3.5% |
| | | | | Al Sharpton | 14,308 | 3.4% |
| | | | | Richard A. Gephardt | 8,281 | 2.0% |
| | | | | Dennis J. Kucinich | 4,875 | 1.2% |
| | | | | Uncommitted | 4,311 | 1.0% |
| | | | | Carol Moseley Braun | 1,088 | 0.3% |
| | | | | Lyndon H. LaRouche Jr. | 953 | 0.2% |
| | | | | Fern Penna | 335 | 0.1% |
| | TOTAL | 123,086 | | TOTAL | 418,339 | |
| Governor | Matt Blunt | 534,393 | 88.4% | Claire McCaskill | 437,780 | 51.6% |
| | Karen Lee Dee Skelton-Memhardt | 26,089 | 4.3% | Bob Holden* | 383,734 | 45.3% |
| | Jennie Lee "Jen" Sievers | 18,733 | 3.1% | Jim LePage | 16,761 | 2.0% |
| | Jeff Killian | 10,423 | 1.7% | Jeffery A. Emrick | 9,473 | 1.1% |
| | Roy W. Lang | 8,750 | 1.4% | | | |
| | Martin Lindstedt | 6,369 | 1.1% | | | |
| | TOTAL | 604,757 | | TOTAL | 847,748 | |
| Senator | Christopher S. Bond* | 541,998 | 88.1% | Nancy Farmer | 544,830 | 73.7% |
| | Mike Steger | 73,354 | 11.9% | Charles Berry | 143,229 | 19.4% |
| | | | | Ronald Bonar | 51,375 | 6.9% |
| | TOTAL | 615,352 | | TOTAL | 739,434 | |
| Congressional District 1 | Leslie L. Farr II | 20,136 | 100.0% | William Lacy Clay* | 92,094 | 100.0% |
| Congressional District 2 | Todd Akin* | 80,673 | 100.0% | George D. Weber | 36,470 | 54.8% |
| | | | | John Hogan | 30,117 | 45.2% |
| | | | | TOTAL | 66,587 | |
| Congressional District 3 | Bill Federer | 28,427 | 75.2% | Russ Carnahan | 24,507 | 22.9% |
| | Joan McGivney | 9,371 | 24.8% | Jeff Smith | 22,783 | 21.3% |
| | | | | Steve Stoll | 19,372 | 18.1% |
| | | | | Joan Barry | 18,922 | 17.7% |
| | | | | Mariano V. Favazza | 9,647 | 9.0% |
| | | | | Mark Smith | 7,400 | 6.9% |
| | | | | Jo Ann Karll | 2,667 | 2.5% |
| | | | | Mike Evans | 644 | 0.6% |
| | | | | Corey Mohn | 590 | 0.6% |
| | | | | Michael R. Bram | 469 | 0.4% |
| | TOTAL | 37,798 | | TOTAL | 107,001 | |
| Congressional District 4 | James A. "Jim" Noland | 40,428 | 52.4% | Ike Skelton* | 77,219 | 100.0% |
| | Steve Morrow | 19,131 | 24.8% | | | |
| | Jeff Parnell | 17,643 | 22.9% | | | |
| | TOTAL | 77,202 | | | | |
| Congressional District 5 | Jeanne Patterson | 23,354 | 55.0% | Emanuel Cleaver II | 72,810 | 60.0% |
| | Steve Dennis | 8,937 | 21.0% | Jamie Metzl | 48,607 | 40.0% |
| | Clay Chastain | 6,518 | 15.4% | | | |
| | Annalisa Zapien-Pina | 2,024 | 4.8% | | | |
| | Joyce P. Lea | 1,629 | 3.8% | | | |
| | TOTAL | 42,462 | | TOTAL | 121,417 | |

# MISSOURI

## GENERAL AND PRIMARY ELECTIONS

| | REPUBLICAN PRIMARIES | | | DEMOCRATIC PRIMARIES | | |
|---|---|---|---|---|---|---|
| **Congressional District 6** | Sam Graves* | 69,412 | 100.0% | Charles S. Broomfield | 53,548 | 62.0% |
| | | | | Jeff Bailey | 32,839 | 38.0% |
| | | | | TOTAL | 86,387 | |
| **Congressional District 7** | Roy Blunt* | 111,293 | 100.0% | Jim Newberry | 23,983 | 47.7% |
| | | | | Jack Truman | 12,915 | 25.7% |
| | | | | Doug Burlison | 9,656 | 19.2% |
| | | | | Ron Lapham | 3,743 | 7.4% |
| | | | | TOTAL | 50,297 | |
| **Congressional District 8** | Jo Ann Emerson* | 65,052 | 88.6% | Dean Henderson | 37,213 | 57.0% |
| | Richard Allen Kline | 8,401 | 11.4% | Jerry Cass | 28,040 | 43.0% |
| | TOTAL | 73,453 | | TOTAL | 65,253 | |
| **Congressional District 9** | Kenny Hulshof* | 62,956 | 100.0% | Linda Jacobsen | 78,059 | 100.0% |

# MONTANA

## GOVERNOR
Brian Schweitzer (D). Elected 2004 to a four-year term.

## SENATORS (1 Democrat, 1 Republican)
Max Baucus (D). Reelected 2002 to a six-year term. Previously elected 1996, 1990, 1984, 1978.

Conrad Burns (R). Reelected 2000 to a six-year term. Previously elected 1994, 1988.

## REPRESENTATIVE (1 Republican)
At Large. Denny Rehberg (R)

## POSTWAR VOTE FOR PRESIDENT

| | | Republican | | Democratic | | Other | | Percentage Total Vote | | Major Vote | |
|---|---|---|---|---|---|---|---|---|---|---|---|
| Year | Total Vote | Vote | Candidate | Vote | Candidate | Vote | Plurality | Rep. | Dem. | Rep. | Dem. |
| 2004 | 450,445 | 266,063 | Bush, George W. | 173,710 | Kerry, John | 10,672 | 92,353 R | 59.1% | 38.6% | 60.5% | 39.5% |
| 2000** | 410,997 | 240,178 | Bush, George W. | 137,126 | Gore, Al | 33,693 | 103,052 R | 58.4% | 33.4% | 63.7% | 36.3% |
| 1996** | 407,261 | 179,652 | Dole, Bob | 167,922 | Clinton, Bill | 59,687 | 11,730 R | 44.1% | 41.2% | 51.7% | 48.3% |
| 1992** | 410,611 | 144,207 | Bush, George | 154,507 | Clinton, Bill | 111,897 | 10,300 D | 35.1% | 37.6% | 48.3% | 51.7% |
| 1988 | 365,674 | 190,412 | Bush, George | 168,936 | Dukakis, Michael S. | 6,326 | 21,476 R | 52.1% | 46.2% | 53.0% | 47.0% |
| 1984 | 384,377 | 232,450 | Reagan, Ronald | 146,742 | Mondale, Walter F. | 5,185 | 85,708 R | 60.5% | 38.2% | 61.3% | 38.7% |
| 1980** | 363,952 | 206,814 | Reagan, Ronald | 118,032 | Carter, Jimmy | 39,106 | 88,782 R | 56.8% | 32.4% | 63.7% | 36.3% |
| 1976 | 328,734 | 173,703 | Ford, Gerald R. | 149,259 | Carter, Jimmy | 5,772 | 24,444 R | 52.8% | 45.4% | 53.8% | 46.2% |
| 1972 | 317,603 | 183,976 | Nixon, Richard M. | 120,197 | McGovern, George S. | 13,430 | 63,779 R | 57.9% | 37.8% | 60.5% | 39.5% |
| 1968** | 274,404 | 138,835 | Nixon, Richard M. | 114,117 | Humphrey, Hubert H. | 21,452 | 24,718 R | 50.6% | 41.6% | 54.9% | 45.1% |
| 1964 | 278,628 | 113,032 | Goldwater, Barry M. | 164,246 | Johnson, Lyndon B. | 1,350 | 51,214 D | 40.6% | 58.9% | 40.8% | 59.2% |
| 1960 | 277,579 | 141,841 | Nixon, Richard M. | 134,891 | Kennedy, John F. | 847 | 6,950 R | 51.1% | 48.6% | 51.3% | 48.7% |
| 1956 | 271,171 | 154,933 | Eisenhower, Dwight D. | 116,238 | Stevenson, Adlai E. | | 38,695 R | 57.1% | 42.9% | 57.1% | 42.9% |
| 1952 | 265,037 | 157,394 | Eisenhower, Dwight D. | 106,213 | Stevenson, Adlai E. | 1,430 | 51,181 R | 59.4% | 40.1% | 59.7% | 40.3% |
| 1948 | 224,278 | 96,770 | Dewey, Thomas E. | 119,071 | Truman, Harry S. | 8,437 | 22,301 D | 43.1% | 53.1% | 44.8% | 55.2% |

In past elections, the other vote included: 2000 - 24,437 Green (Ralph Nader); 1996 - 55,229 Reform (Ross Perot); 1992 - 107,225 Independent (Perot); 1980 - 29,281 Independent (John Anderson); 1968 - 20,015 American Independent (George Wallace).

# MONTANA

## POSTWAR VOTE FOR GOVERNOR

| | | Republican | | Democratic | | | | Percentage | | | |
| | | | | | | Other | Rep.-Dem. | Total Vote | | Major Vote | |
| Year | Total Vote | Vote | Candidate | Vote | Candidate | Vote | Plurality | Rep. | Dem. | Rep. | Dem. |
|---|---|---|---|---|---|---|---|---|---|---|---|
| 2004 | 446,146 | 205,313 | Brown, Bob | 225,016 | Schweitzer, Brian | 15,817 | 19,703 D | 46.0% | 50.4% | 47.7% | 52.3% |
| 2000 | 410,192 | 209,135 | Martz, Judy | 193,131 | O'Keefe, Mark | 7,926 | 16,004 R | 51.0% | 47.1% | 52.0% | 48.0% |
| 1996** | 405,175 | 320,768 | Racicot, Marc | 84,407 | Jacobson, Judy | | 236,361 R | 79.2% | 20.8% | 79.2% | 20.8% |
| 1992 | 407,842 | 209,401 | Racicot, Marc | 198,421 | Bradley, Dorothy | 20 | 10,980 R | 51.3% | 48.7% | 51.3% | 48.7% |
| 1988 | 367,021 | 190,604 | Stephens, Stan | 169,313 | Judge, Thomas L. | 7,104 | 21,291 R | 51.9% | 46.1% | 53.0% | 47.0% |
| 1984 | 378,970 | 100,070 | Goodover, Pat M. | 266,578 | Schwinden, Ted | 12,322 | 166,508 D | 26.4% | 70.3% | 27.3% | 72.7% |
| 1980 | 360,466 | 160,892 | Ramirez, Jack | 199,574 | Schwinden, Ted | | 38,682 D | 44.6% | 55.4% | 44.6% | 55.4% |
| 1976 | 316,720 | 115,848 | Woodahl, Robert | 195,420 | Judge, Thomas L. | 5,452 | 79,572 D | 36.6% | 61.7% | 37.2% | 62.8% |
| 1972 | 318,754 | 146,231 | Smith, Ed | 172,523 | Judge, Thomas L. | | 26,292 D | 45.9% | 54.1% | 45.9% | 54.1% |
| 1968 | 278,112 | 116,432 | Babcock, Tim M. | 150,481 | Anderson, Forrest H. | 11,199 | 34,049 D | 41.9% | 54.1% | 43.6% | 56.4% |
| 1964 | 280,975 | 144,113 | Babcock, Tim M. | 136,862 | Renne, Roland | | 7,251 R | 51.3% | 48.7% | 51.3% | 48.7% |
| 1960 | 279,881 | 154,230 | Nutter, Donald G. | 125,651 | Cannon, Paul | | 28,579 R | 55.1% | 44.9% | 55.1% | 44.9% |
| 1956 | 270,366 | 138,878 | Aronson, J. Hugo | 131,488 | Olsen, Arnold H. | | 7,390 R | 51.4% | 48.6% | 51.4% | 48.6% |
| 1952 | 263,792 | 134,423 | Aronson, J. Hugo | 129,369 | Bonner, John W. | | 5,054 R | 51.0% | 49.0% | 51.0% | 49.0% |
| 1948 | 222,964 | 97,792 | Ford, Sam C. | 124,267 | Bonner, John W. | 905 | 26,475 D | 43.9% | 55.7% | 44.0% | 56.0% |

In 1996 the Democratic vote total included 7,936 absentee ballots cast for the party's initial gubernatorial candidate, Chet Blaylock, who died in October.

## POSTWAR VOTE FOR SENATOR

| | | Republican | | Democratic | | | | Percentage | | | |
| | | | | | | Other | Rep.-Dem. | Total Vote | | Major Vote | |
| Year | Total Vote | Vote | Candidate | Vote | Candidate | Vote | Plurality | Rep. | Dem. | Rep. | Dem. |
|---|---|---|---|---|---|---|---|---|---|---|---|
| 2002 | 326,537 | 103,611 | Taylor, Mike | 204,853 | Baucus, Max | 18,073 | 101,242 D | 31.7% | 62.7% | 33.6% | 66.4% |
| 2000 | 411,601 | 208,082 | Burns, Conrad | 194,430 | Schweitzer, Brian | 9,089 | 13,652 R | 50.6% | 47.2% | 51.7% | 48.3% |
| 1996 | 407,490 | 182,111 | Rehberg, Denny | 201,935 | Baucus, Max | 23,444 | 19,824 D | 44.7% | 49.6% | 47.4% | 52.6% |
| 1994 | 350,409 | 218,542 | Burns, Conrad | 131,845 | Mudd, Jack | 22 | 86,697 R | 62.4% | 37.6% | 62.4% | 37.6% |
| 1990 | 319,336 | 93,836 | Kolstad, Allen C. | 217,563 | Baucus, Max | 7,937 | 123,727 D | 29.4% | 68.1% | 30.1% | 69.9% |
| 1988 | 365,254 | 189,445 | Burns, Conrad | 175,809 | Melcher, John | | 13,636 R | 51.9% | 48.1% | 51.9% | 48.1% |
| 1984 | 379,155 | 154,308 | Cozzens, Chuck | 215,704 | Baucus, Max | 9,143 | 61,396 D | 40.7% | 56.9% | 41.7% | 58.3% |
| 1982 | 321,062 | 133,789 | Williams, Larry | 174,861 | Melcher, John | 12,412 | 41,072 D | 41.7% | 54.5% | 43.3% | 56.7% |
| 1978 | 287,942 | 127,589 | Williams, Larry | 160,353 | Baucus, Max | | 32,764 D | 44.3% | 55.7% | 44.3% | 55.7% |
| 1976 | 321,445 | 115,213 | Burger, Stanley C. | 206,232 | Melcher, John | | 91,019 D | 35.8% | 64.2% | 35.8% | 64.2% |
| 1972 | 314,925 | 151,316 | Hibbard, Henry S. | 163,609 | Metcalf, Lee | | 12,293 D | 48.0% | 52.0% | 48.0% | 52.0% |
| 1970 | 247,869 | 97,809 | Wallace, Harold E. | 150,060 | Mansfield, Mike | | 52,251 D | 39.5% | 60.5% | 39.5% | 60.5% |
| 1966 | 259,863 | 121,697 | Babcock, Tim M. | 138,166 | Metcalf, Lee | | 16,469 D | 46.8% | 53.2% | 46.8% | 53.2% |
| 1964 | 280,010 | 99,367 | Blewett, Alex | 180,643 | Mansfield, Mike | | 81,276 D | 35.5% | 64.5% | 35.5% | 64.5% |
| 1960 | 276,612 | 136,281 | Fjare, Orvin B. | 140,331 | Metcalf, Lee | | 4,050 D | 49.3% | 50.7% | 49.3% | 50.7% |
| 1958 | 229,483 | 54,573 | Welch, Lou W. | 174,910 | Mansfield, Mike | | 120,337 D | 23.8% | 76.2% | 23.8% | 76.2% |
| 1954 | 227,454 | 112,863 | D'Ewart, Wesley A. | 114,591 | Murray, James E. | | 1,728 D | 49.6% | 50.4% | 49.6% | 50.4% |
| 1952 | 262,297 | 127,360 | Ecton, Zales N. | 133,109 | Mansfield, Mike | 1,828 | 5,749 D | 48.6% | 50.7% | 48.9% | 51.1% |
| 1948 | 221,003 | 94,458 | David, Tom J. | 125,193 | Murray, James E. | 1,352 | 30,735 D | 42.7% | 56.6% | 43.0% | 57.0% |
| 1946 | 190,566 | 101,901 | Ecton, Zales N. | 86,476 | Erickson, Leif | 2,189 | 15,425 R | 53.5% | 45.4% | 54.1% | 45.9% |

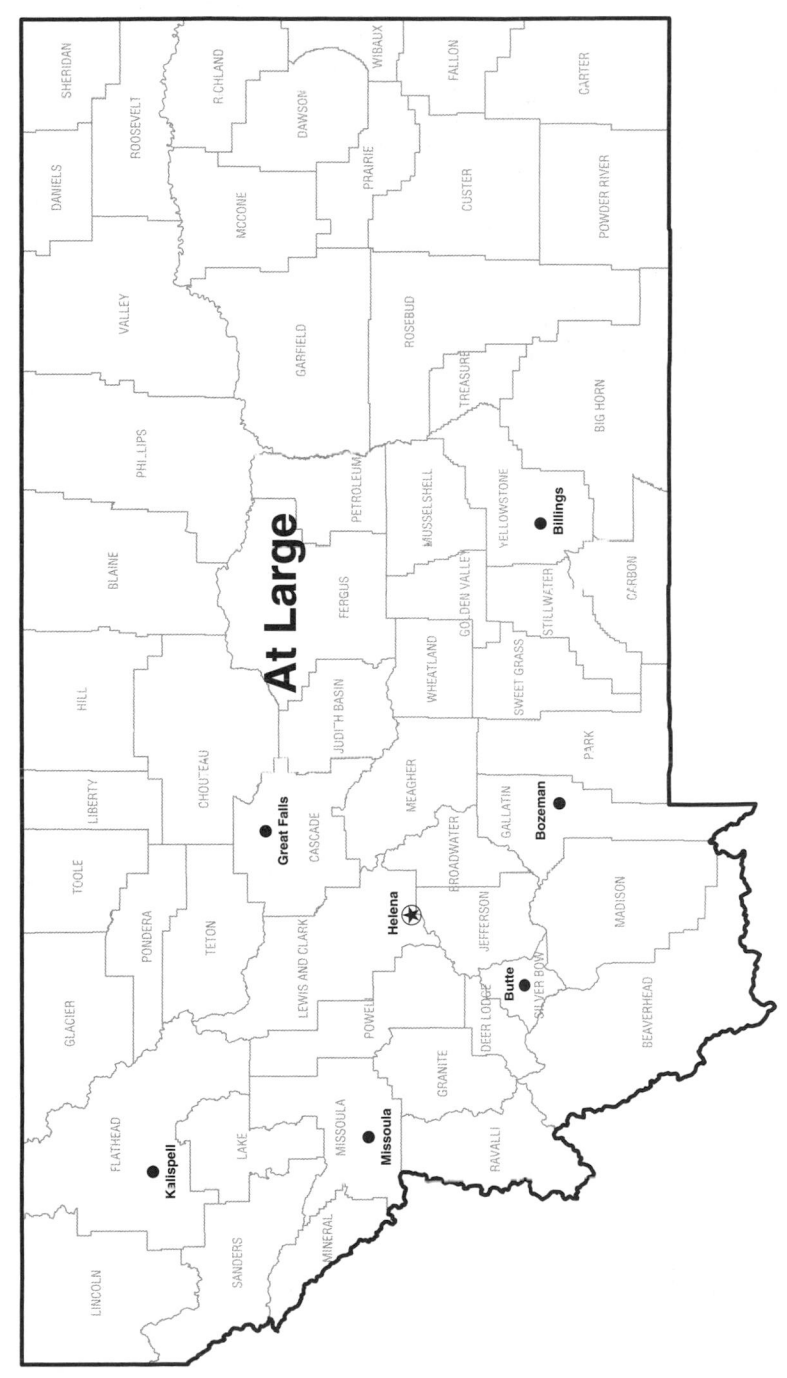

# MONTANA

One member At Large

# MONTANA

## PRESIDENT 2004

| 2000 Census Population | County | Total Vote | Republican | Democratic | Other | Rep.-Dem. Plurality | Percentage Total Vote Rep. | Dem. | Major Vote Rep. | Dem. |
|---|---|---|---|---|---|---|---|---|---|---|
| 9,202 | BEAVERHEAD | 4,242 | 3,067 | 1,103 | 72 | 1,964 R | 72.3% | 26.0% | 73.5% | 26.5% |
| 12,671 | BIG HORN | 4,311 | 2,028 | 2,215 | 68 | 187 D | 47.0% | 51.4% | 47.8% | 52.2% |
| 7,009 | BLAINE | 2,768 | 1,424 | 1,300 | 44 | 124 R | 51.4% | 47.0% | 52.3% | 47.7% |
| 4,385 | BROADWATER | 2,356 | 1,778 | 533 | 45 | 1,245 R | 75.5% | 22.6% | 76.9% | 23.1% |
| 9,552 | CARBON | 5,321 | 3,342 | 1,847 | 132 | 1,495 R | 62.8% | 34.7% | 64.4% | 35.6% |
| 1,360 | CARTER | 709 | 623 | 76 | 10 | 547 R | 87.9% | 10.7% | 89.1% | 10.9% |
| 80,357 | CASCADE | 33,459 | 19,028 | 13,701 | 730 | 5,327 R | 56.9% | 40.9% | 58.1% | 41.9% |
| 5,970 | CHOUTEAU | 2,921 | 1,913 | 946 | 62 | 967 R | 65.5% | 32.4% | 66.9% | 33.1% |
| 11,696 | CUSTER | 5,048 | 3,297 | 1,630 | 121 | 1,667 R | 65.3% | 32.3% | 66.9% | 33.1% |
| 2,017 | DANIELS | 1,119 | 764 | 326 | 29 | 438 R | 68.3% | 29.1% | 70.1% | 29.9% |
| 9,059 | DAWSON | 4,484 | 2,884 | 1,494 | 106 | 1,390 R | 64.3% | 33.3% | 65.9% | 34.1% |
| 9,417 | DEER LODGE | 4,543 | 1,725 | 2,700 | 118 | 975 D | 38.0% | 59.4% | 39.0% | 61.0% |
| 2,837 | FALLON | 1,491 | 1,178 | 289 | 24 | 889 R | 79.0% | 19.4% | 80.3% | 19.7% |
| 11,893 | FERGUS | 6,127 | 4,425 | 1,582 | 120 | 2,843 R | 72.2% | 25.8% | 73.7% | 26.3% |
| 74,471 | FLATHEAD | 38,678 | 26,019 | 11,587 | 1,072 | 14,432 R | 67.3% | 30.0% | 69.2% | 30.8% |
| 67,831 | GALLATIN | 39,842 | 22,392 | 16,405 | 1,045 | 5,987 R | 56.2% | 41.2% | 57.7% | 42.3% |
| 1,279 | GARFIELD | 655 | 590 | 52 | 13 | 538 R | 90.1% | 7.9% | 91.9% | 8.1% |
| 13,247 | GLACIER | 4,562 | 1,828 | 2,641 | 93 | 813 D | 40.1% | 57.9% | 40.9% | 59.1% |
| 1,042 | GOLDEN VALLEY | 522 | 396 | 119 | 7 | 277 R | 75.9% | 22.8% | 76.9% | 23.1% |
| 2,830 | GRANITE | 1,605 | 1,144 | 404 | 57 | 740 R | 71.3% | 25.2% | 73.9% | 26.1% |
| 16,673 | HILL | 6,657 | 3,505 | 2,997 | 155 | 508 R | 52.7% | 45.0% | 53.9% | 46.1% |
| 10,049 | JEFFERSON | 5,868 | 3,844 | 1,881 | 143 | 1,963 R | 65.5% | 32.1% | 67.1% | 32.9% |
| 2,329 | JUDITH BASIN | 1,286 | 944 | 322 | 20 | 622 R | 73.4% | 25.0% | 74.6% | 25.4% |
| 26,507 | LAKE | 12,576 | 7,245 | 4,960 | 371 | 2,285 R | 57.6% | 39.4% | 59.4% | 40.6% |
| 55,716 | LEWIS AND CLARK | 29,843 | 16,494 | 12,717 | 632 | 3,777 R | 55.3% | 42.6% | 56.5% | 43.5% |
| 2,158 | LIBERTY | 1,033 | 734 | 281 | 18 | 453 R | 71.1% | 27.2% | 72.3% | 27.7% |
| 18,837 | LINCOLN | 8,449 | 5,889 | 2,320 | 240 | 3,569 R | 69.7% | 27.5% | 71.7% | 28.3% |
| 1,977 | MCCONE | 1,137 | 791 | 320 | 26 | 471 R | 69.6% | 28.1% | 71.2% | 28.8% |
| 6,851 | MADISON | 3,933 | 2,868 | 983 | 82 | 1,885 R | 72.9% | 25.0% | 74.5% | 25.5% |
| 1,932 | MEAGHER | 973 | 698 | 247 | 28 | 451 R | 71.7% | 25.4% | 73.9% | 26.1% |
| 3,884 | MINERAL | 1,837 | 1,242 | 542 | 53 | 700 R | 67.6% | 29.5% | 69.6% | 30.4% |
| 95,802 | MISSOULA | 52,454 | 23,989 | 26,983 | 1,482 | 2,994 D | 45.7% | 51.4% | 47.1% | 52.9% |
| 4,497 | MUSSELSHELL | 2,247 | 1,663 | 538 | 46 | 1,125 R | 74.0% | 23.9% | 75.6% | 24.4% |
| 15,694 | PARK | 8,218 | 4,771 | 3,199 | 248 | 1,572 R | 58.1% | 38.9% | 59.9% | 40.1% |
| 493 | PETROLEUM | 292 | 228 | 55 | 9 | 173 R | 78.1% | 18.8% | 80.6% | 19.4% |
| 4,601 | PHILLIPS | 2,170 | 1,677 | 456 | 37 | 1,221 R | 77.3% | 21.0% | 78.6% | 21.4% |
| 6,424 | PONDERA | 2,860 | 1,853 | 956 | 51 | 897 R | 64.8% | 33.4% | 66.0% | 34.0% |
| 1,858 | POWDER RIVER | 1,029 | 856 | 154 | 19 | 702 R | 83.2% | 15.0% | 84.8% | 15.2% |
| 7,180 | POWELL | 2,830 | 1,993 | 761 | 76 | 1,232 R | 70.4% | 26.9% | 72.4% | 27.6% |
| 1,199 | PRAIRIE | 736 | 546 | 181 | 9 | 365 R | 74.2% | 24.6% | 75.1% | 24.9% |
| 36,070 | RAVALLI | 19,867 | 13,279 | 6,144 | 444 | 7,135 R | 66.8% | 30.9% | 68.4% | 31.6% |
| 9,667 | RICHLAND | 4,308 | 3,110 | 1,120 | 78 | 1,990 R | 72.2% | 26.0% | 73.5% | 26.5% |
| 10,620 | ROOSEVELT | 4,028 | 1,762 | 2,195 | 71 | 433 D | 43.7% | 54.5% | 44.5% | 55.5% |
| 9,383 | ROSEBUD | 3,585 | 1,982 | 1,520 | 83 | 462 R | 55.3% | 42.4% | 56.6% | 43.4% |
| 10,227 | SANDERS | 5,153 | 3,461 | 1,502 | 190 | 1,959 R | 67.2% | 29.1% | 69.7% | 30.3% |
| 4,105 | SHERIDAN | 2,038 | 1,159 | 846 | 33 | 313 R | 56.9% | 41.5% | 57.8% | 42.2% |
| 34,606 | SILVER BOW | 16,084 | 6,381 | 9,307 | 396 | 2,926 D | 39.7% | 57.9% | 40.7% | 59.3% |
| 8,195 | STILLWATER | 4,213 | 3,090 | 1,025 | 98 | 2,065 R | 73.3% | 24.3% | 75.1% | 24.9% |
| 3,609 | SWEET GRASS | 1,983 | 1,509 | 445 | 29 | 1,064 R | 76.1% | 22.4% | 77.2% | 22.8% |
| 6,445 | TETON | 3,359 | 2,232 | 1,047 | 80 | 1,185 R | 66.4% | 31.2% | 68.1% | 31.9% |
| 5,267 | TOOLE | 2,311 | 1,583 | 690 | 38 | 893 R | 68.5% | 29.9% | 69.6% | 30.4% |
| 861 | TREASURE | 482 | 348 | 121 | 13 | 227 R | 72.2% | 25.1% | 74.2% | 25.8% |
| 7,675 | VALLEY | 4,018 | 2,476 | 1,431 | 111 | 1,045 R | 61.6% | 35.6% | 63.4% | 36.6% |
| 2,259 | WHEATLAND | 979 | 706 | 250 | 23 | 456 R | 72.1% | 25.5% | 73.8% | 26.2% |
| 1,068 | WIBAUX | 560 | 407 | 144 | 9 | 263 R | 72.7% | 25.7% | 73.9% | 26.1% |
| 129,352 | YELLOWSTONE | 66,286 | 40,903 | 24,120 | 1,263 | 16,783 R | 61.7% | 36.4% | 62.9% | 37.1% |
| 902,195 | TOTAL | 450,445 | 266,063 | 173,710 | 10,672 | 92,353 R | 59.1% | 38.6% | 60.5% | 39.5% |

# MONTANA

## GOVERNOR 2004

| 2000 Census Population | County | Total Vote | Republican | Democratic | Other | Rep.-Dem. Plurality | Total Vote Rep. | Dem. | Major Vote Rep. | Dem. |
|---|---|---|---|---|---|---|---|---|---|---|
| 9,202 | BEAVERHEAD | 4,184 | 2,419 | 1,638 | 127 | 781 R | 57.8% | 39.1% | 59.6% | 40.4% |
| 12,671 | BIG HORN | 4,270 | 1,445 | 2,543 | 282 | 1,098 D | 33.8% | 59.6% | 36.2% | 63.8% |
| 7,009 | BLAINE | 2,727 | 996 | 1,588 | 143 | 592 D | 36.5% | 58.2% | 38.5% | 61.5% |
| 4,385 | BROADWATER | 2,339 | 1,380 | 895 | 64 | 485 R | 59.0% | 38.3% | 60.7% | 39.3% |
| 9,552 | CARBON | 5,274 | 2,471 | 2,627 | 176 | 156 D | 46.9% | 49.8% | 48.5% | 51.5% |
| 1,360 | CARTER | 697 | 529 | 150 | 18 | 379 R | 75.9% | 21.5% | 77.9% | 22.1% |
| 80,357 | CASCADE | 33,524 | 13,848 | 18,659 | 1,017 | 4,811 D | 41.3% | 55.7% | 42.6% | 57.4% |
| 5,970 | CHOUTEAU | 2,885 | 1,556 | 1,238 | 91 | 318 R | 53.9% | 42.9% | 55.7% | 44.3% |
| 11,696 | CUSTER | 5,069 | 2,558 | 2,368 | 143 | 190 R | 50.5% | 46.7% | 51.9% | 48.1% |
| 2,017 | DANIELS | 1,076 | 583 | 470 | 23 | 113 R | 54.2% | 43.7% | 55.4% | 44.6% |
| 9,059 | DAWSON | 4,435 | 2,193 | 2,143 | 99 | 50 R | 49.4% | 48.3% | 50.6% | 49.4% |
| 9,417 | DEER LODGE | 4,514 | 1,096 | 3,231 | 187 | 2,135 D | 24.3% | 71.6% | 25.3% | 74.7% |
| 2,837 | FALLON | 1,445 | 883 | 522 | 40 | 361 R | 61.1% | 36.1% | 62.8% | 37.2% |
| 11,893 | FERGUS | 6,083 | 3,509 | 2,426 | 148 | 1,083 R | 57.7% | 39.9% | 59.1% | 40.9% |
| 74,471 | FLATHEAD | 38,225 | 21,970 | 14,967 | 1,288 | 7,003 R | 57.5% | 39.2% | 59.5% | 40.5% |
| 67,831 | GALLATIN | 39,274 | 19,036 | 18,575 | 1,663 | 461 R | 48.5% | 47.3% | 50.6% | 49.4% |
| 1,279 | GARFIELD | 642 | 482 | 150 | 10 | 332 R | 75.1% | 23.4% | 76.3% | 23.7% |
| 13,247 | GLACIER | 4,543 | 1,275 | 2,994 | 274 | 1,719 D | 28.1% | 65.9% | 29.9% | 70.1% |
| 1,042 | GOLDEN VALLEY | 512 | 309 | 190 | 13 | 119 R | 60.4% | 37.1% | 61.9% | 38.1% |
| 2,830 | GRANITE | 1,570 | 889 | 605 | 76 | 284 R | 56.6% | 38.5% | 59.5% | 40.5% |
| 16,673 | HILL | 6,579 | 2,407 | 3,886 | 286 | 1,479 D | 36.6% | 59.1% | 38.2% | 61.8% |
| 10,049 | JEFFERSON | 5,811 | 2,953 | 2,649 | 209 | 304 R | 50.8% | 45.6% | 52.7% | 47.3% |
| 2,329 | JUDITH BASIN | 1,268 | 799 | 442 | 27 | 357 R | 63.0% | 34.9% | 64.4% | 35.6% |
| 26,507 | LAKE | 12,473 | 5,882 | 5,998 | 593 | 116 D | 47.2% | 48.1% | 49.5% | 50.5% |
| 55,716 | LEWIS AND CLARK | 29,959 | 13,343 | 15,891 | 725 | 2,548 D | 44.5% | 53.0% | 45.6% | 54.4% |
| 2,158 | LIBERTY | 1,027 | 565 | 448 | 14 | 117 R | 55.0% | 43.6% | 55.8% | 44.2% |
| 18,837 | LINCOLN | 8,281 | 4,647 | 3,286 | 348 | 1,361 R | 56.1% | 39.7% | 58.6% | 41.4% |
| 1,977 | MCCONE | 1,128 | 618 | 482 | 28 | 136 R | 54.8% | 42.7% | 56.2% | 43.8% |
| 6,851 | MADISON | 3,908 | 2,340 | 1,416 | 152 | 924 R | 59.9% | 36.2% | 62.3% | 37.7% |
| 1,932 | MEAGHER | 958 | 557 | 371 | 30 | 186 R | 58.1% | 38.7% | 60.0% | 40.0% |
| 3,884 | MINERAL | 1,798 | 875 | 838 | 85 | 37 R | 48.7% | 46.6% | 51.1% | 48.9% |
| 95,802 | MISSOULA | 51,775 | 18,269 | 31,532 | 1,974 | 13,263 D | 35.3% | 60.9% | 36.7% | 63.3% |
| 4,497 | MUSSELSHELL | 2,221 | 1,316 | 819 | 86 | 497 R | 59.3% | 36.9% | 61.6% | 38.4% |
| 15,694 | PARK | 8,120 | 3,855 | 3,915 | 350 | 60 D | 47.5% | 48.2% | 49.6% | 50.4% |
| 493 | PETROLEUM | 289 | 185 | 95 | 9 | 90 R | 64.0% | 32.9% | 66.1% | 33.9% |
| 4,601 | PHILLIPS | 2,131 | 1,243 | 830 | 58 | 413 R | 58.3% | 38.9% | 60.0% | 40.0% |
| 6,424 | PONDERA | 2,843 | 1,376 | 1,373 | 94 | 3 R | 48.4% | 48.3% | 50.1% | 49.9% |
| 1,858 | POWDER RIVER | 994 | 673 | 291 | 30 | 382 R | 67.7% | 29.3% | 69.8% | 30.2% |
| 7,180 | POWELL | 2,808 | 1,446 | 1,248 | 114 | 198 R | 51.5% | 44.4% | 53.7% | 46.3% |
| 1,199 | PRAIRIE | 735 | 457 | 260 | 18 | 197 R | 62.2% | 35.4% | 63.7% | 36.3% |
| 36,070 | RAVALLI | 19,593 | 10,182 | 8,775 | 636 | 1,407 R | 52.0% | 44.8% | 53.7% | 46.3% |
| 9,667 | RICHLAND | 4,235 | 2,454 | 1,679 | 102 | 775 R | 57.9% | 39.6% | 59.4% | 40.6% |
| 10,620 | ROOSEVELT | 3,948 | 1,323 | 2,377 | 248 | 1,054 D | 33.5% | 60.2% | 35.8% | 64.2% |
| 9,383 | ROSEBUD | 3,564 | 1,378 | 1,990 | 196 | 612 D | 38.7% | 55.8% | 40.9% | 59.1% |
| 10,227 | SANDERS | 5,048 | 2,741 | 2,124 | 183 | 617 R | 54.3% | 42.1% | 56.3% | 43.7% |
| 4,105 | SHERIDAN | 1,994 | 949 | 1,005 | 40 | 56 D | 47.6% | 50.4% | 48.6% | 51.4% |
| 34,606 | SILVER BOW | 15,970 | 4,190 | 11,161 | 619 | 6,971 D | 26.2% | 69.9% | 27.3% | 72.7% |
| 8,195 | STILLWATER | 4,151 | 2,246 | 1,774 | 131 | 472 R | 54.1% | 42.7% | 55.9% | 44.1% |
| 3,609 | SWEET GRASS | 1,950 | 1,266 | 640 | 44 | 626 R | 64.9% | 32.8% | 66.4% | 33.6% |
| 6,445 | TETON | 3,331 | 1,748 | 1,492 | 91 | 256 R | 52.5% | 44.8% | 54.0% | 46.0% |
| 5,267 | TOOLE | 2,272 | 1,133 | 1,055 | 84 | 78 R | 49.9% | 46.4% | 51.8% | 48.2% |
| 861 | TREASURE | 469 | 259 | 188 | 22 | 71 R | 55.2% | 40.1% | 57.9% | 42.1% |
| 7,675 | VALLEY | 3,986 | 1,621 | 2,215 | 150 | 594 D | 40.7% | 55.6% | 42.3% | 57.7% |
| 2,259 | WHEATLAND | 972 | 583 | 368 | 21 | 215 R | 60.0% | 37.9% | 61.3% | 38.7% |
| 1,068 | WIBAUX | 538 | 308 | 218 | 12 | 90 R | 57.2% | 40.5% | 58.6% | 41.4% |
| 129,352 | YELLOWSTONE | 65,731 | 29,699 | 33,906 | 2,126 | 4,207 D | 45.2% | 51.6% | 46.7% | 53.3% |
| 902,195 | TOTAL | 446,146 | 205,313 | 225,016 | 15,817 | 19,703 D | 46.0% | 50.4% | 47.7% | 52.3% |

# MONTANA

## HOUSE OF REPRESENTATIVES

| CD | Year | Total Vote | Republican Vote | Republican Candidate | Democratic Vote | Democratic Candidate | Other Vote | Rep.-Dem. Plurality | Total Vote Rep. | Total Vote Dem. | Major Vote Rep. | Major Vote Dem. |
|----|------|-----------|-----------------|----------------------|-----------------|----------------------|------------|---------------------|-----------------|-----------------|-----------------|-----------------|
| AL | 2004 | 444,230 | 286,076 | Rehberg, Denny* | 145,606 | Velazquez, Tracy | 12,548 | 140,470 R | 64.4% | 32.8% | 66.3% | 33.7% |
| AL | 2002 | 331,321 | 214,100 | Rehberg, Denny* | 108,233 | Kelly, Steve | 8,988 | 105,867 R | 64.6% | 32.7% | 66.4% | 33.6% |
| AL | 2000 | 410,523 | 211,418 | Rehberg, Denny | 189,971 | Keenan, Nancy | 9,134 | 21,447 R | 51.5% | 46.3% | 52.7% | 47.3% |
| AL | 1998 | 331,551 | 175,748 | Hill, Rick* | 147,073 | Deschamps, Dusty | 8,730 | 28,675 R | 53.0% | 44.4% | 54.4% | 45.6% |
| AL | 1996 | 404,426 | 211,975 | Hill, Rick | 174,516 | Yellowtail, Bill | 17,935 | 37,459 R | 52.4% | 43.2% | 54.8% | 45.2% |
| AL | 1994 | 352,133 | 148,715 | Jamison, Cy | 171,372 | Williams, Pat* | 32,046 | 22,657 D | 42.2% | 48.7% | 46.5% | 53.5% |
| AL | 1992 | 403,735 | 189,570 | Marlenee, Ron* | 203,711 | Williams, Pat* | 10,454 | 14,141 D | 47.0% | 50.5% | 48.2% | 51.8% |

An asterisk (*) denotes incumbent.

# MONTANA

## GENERAL AND PRIMARY ELECTIONS

### 2004 GENERAL ELECTIONS

**President**  Other vote was 6,168 Independent (Ralph Nader); 1,764 Constitution (Michael Peroutka); 1,733 Libertarian (Michael Badnarik); 996 Green (David Cobb); 6 write-in (John Joseph Kennedy); 3 write-in (Robert Leslie Beattie); 2 write-in (Walter F. Brown).

**Governor**  Other vote was 8,393 Green (Bob Kelleher); 7,424 Libertarian (Stanley R. Jones).

**House**  Other vote was:

**At Large**  12,548 Libertarian (Mike Fellows).

### 2004 PRIMARY ELECTIONS

**Primary**  June 8, 2004          **Registration**  595,668  No Party Registration
                                    (as of June 8, 2004)

**Primary Type**  Open—Any registered voter could participate in the primary of either party.

Note:  An asterisk (*) denotes incumbent.

| REPUBLICAN PRIMARIES | | | DEMOCRATIC PRIMARIES | | |
|----------------------|--|--|----------------------|--|--|
| **President** | George W. Bush* | 106,407 | 94.4% | John Kerry | 63,611 | 68.0% |
| | No Preference | 6,340 | 5.6% | Dennis J. Kucinich | 9,686 | 10.4% |
| | Nancy Warrick (write-in) | 1 | | John Edwards | 8,516 | 9.1% |
| | | | | No Preference | 6,899 | 7.4% |
| | | | | Wesley Clark | 4,081 | 4.4% |
| | | | | Lyndon H. LaRouche Jr. | 750 | 0.8% |
| | TOTAL | 112,748 | | TOTAL | 93,543 | |
| **Governor** | Bob Brown | 43,145 | 39.2% | Brian Schweitzer | 68,738 | 72.5% |
| | Pat Davison | 25,319 | 23.0% | John Vincent | 26,057 | 27.5% |
| | Ken Miller | 24,313 | 22.1% | | | |
| | Tom Keating | 17,421 | 15.8% | | | |
| | TOTAL | 110,198 | | TOTAL | 94,795 | |
| **House At Large** | Denny Rehberg* | 107,309 | 100.0% | Tracy Velazquez | 72,001 | 100.0% |

# NEBRASKA

## GOVERNOR
Dave Heineman (R). Became governor January 21, 2005, upon the resignation of Mike Johanns (R) to become U.S. secretary of agriculture.

## SENATORS (1 Democrat, 1 Republican)
Chuck Hagel (R). Reelected 2002 to a six-year term. Previously elected 1996.

Ben Nelson (D). Elected 2000 to a six-year term.

## REPRESENTATIVES (3 Republicans)
1. Jeff Fortenberry (R)          3. Tom Osborne (R)
2. Lee Terry (R)

## POSTWAR VOTE FOR PRESIDENT

| Year | Total Vote | Republican Vote | Republican Candidate | Democratic Vote | Democratic Candidate | Other Vote | Plurality | Total Vote Rep. | Total Vote Dem. | Major Vote Rep. | Major Vote Dem. |
|------|-----------|------|-----------|------|-----------|------|-----------|------|------|------|------|
| 2004 | 778,186 | 512,814 | Bush, George W. | 254,328 | Kerry, John | 11,044 | 258,486 R | 65.9% | 32.7% | 66.8% | 33.2% |
| 2000** | 697,019 | 433,862 | Bush, George W. | 231,780 | Gore, Al | 31,377 | 202,082 R | 62.2% | 33.3% | 65.2% | 34.8% |
| 1996** | 677,415 | 363,467 | Dole, Bob | 236,761 | Clinton, Bill | 77,187 | 126,706 R | 53.7% | 35.0% | 60.6% | 39.4% |
| 1992** | 737,546 | 343,678 | Bush, George | 216,864 | Clinton, Bill | 177,004 | 126,814 R | 46.6% | 29.4% | 61.3% | 38.7% |
| 1988 | 661,465 | 397,956 | Bush, George | 259,235 | Dukakis, Michael S. | 4,274 | 138,721 R | 60.2% | 39.2% | 60.6% | 39.4% |
| 1984 | 652,090 | 460,054 | Reagan, Ronald | 187,866 | Mondale, Walter F. | 4,170 | 272,188 R | 70.6% | 28.8% | 71.0% | 29.0% |
| 1980** | 640,854 | 419,937 | Reagan, Ronald | 166,851 | Carter, Jimmy | 54,066 | 253,086 R | 65.5% | 26.0% | 71.6% | 28.4% |
| 1976 | 607,668 | 359,705 | Ford, Gerald R. | 233,692 | Carter, Jimmy | 14,271 | 126,013 R | 59.2% | 38.5% | 60.6% | 39.4% |
| 1972 | 576,289 | 406,298 | Nixon, Richard M. | 169,991 | McGovern, George S. | | 236,307 R | 70.5% | 29.5% | 70.5% | 29.5% |
| 1968** | 536,851 | 321,163 | Nixon, Richard M. | 170,784 | Humphrey, Hubert H. | 44,904 | 150,379 R | 59.8% | 31.8% | 65.3% | 34.7% |
| 1964 | 584,154 | 276,847 | Goldwater, Barry M. | 307,307 | Johnson, Lyndon B. | | 30,460 D | 47.4% | 52.6% | 47.4% | 52.6% |
| 1960 | 613,095 | 380,553 | Nixon, Richard M. | 232,542 | Kennedy, John F. | | 148,011 R | 62.1% | 37.9% | 62.1% | 37.9% |
| 1956 | 577,137 | 378,108 | Eisenhower, Dwight D. | 199,029 | Stevenson, Adlai E. | | 179,079 R | 65.5% | 34.5% | 65.5% | 34.5% |
| 1952 | 609,660 | 421,603 | Eisenhower, Dwight D. | 188,057 | Stevenson, Adlai E. | | 233,546 R | 69.2% | 30.8% | 69.2% | 30.8% |
| 1948 | 488,940 | 264,774 | Dewey, Thomas E. | 224,165 | Truman, Harry S. | 1 | 40,609 R | 54.2% | 45.8% | 54.2% | 45.8% |

In past elections, the other vote included: 2000 - 24,540 Green (Ralph Nader); 1996 - 71,278 Reform (Ross Perot); 1992 - 174,104 Independent (Perot); 1980 - 44,993 Independent (John Anderson); 1968 - 44,904 American Independent (George Wallace).

# NEBRASKA

## POSTWAR VOTE FOR GOVERNOR

| Year | Total Vote | Republican Vote | Republican Candidate | Democratic Vote | Democratic Candidate | Other Vote | Rep.-Dem. Plurality | Total Vote Rep. | Total Vote Dem. | Major Vote Rep. | Major Vote Dem. |
|---|---|---|---|---|---|---|---|---|---|---|---|
| 2002 | 480,991 | 330,349 | Johanns, Mike | 132,348 | Dean, Stormy | 18,294 | 198,001 R | 68.7% | 27.5% | 71.4% | 28.6% |
| 1998 | 545,238 | 293,910 | Johanns, Mike | 250,678 | Hoppner, Bill | 650 | 43,232 R | 53.9% | 46.0% | 54.0% | 46.0% |
| 1994 | 579,561 | 148,230 | Spence, Gene | 423,270 | Nelson, Ben | 8,061 | 275,040 D | 25.6% | 73.0% | 25.9% | 74.1% |
| 1990 | 586,542 | 288,741 | Orr, Kay | 292,771 | Nelson, Ben | 5,030 | 4,030 D | 49.2% | 49.9% | 49.7% | 50.3% |
| 1986 | 564,422 | 298,325 | Orr, Kay | 265,156 | Boosalis, Helen | 941 | 33,169 R | 52.9% | 47.0% | 52.9% | 47.1% |
| 1982 | 547,902 | 270,203 | Thone, Charles | 277,436 | Kerrey, Bob | 263 | 7,233 D | 49.3% | 50.6% | 49.3% | 50.7% |
| 1978 | 492,423 | 275,473 | Thone, Charles | 216,754 | Whelan, Gerald T. | 196 | 58,719 R | 55.9% | 44.0% | 56.0% | 44.0% |
| 1974 | 451,306 | 159,780 | Marvel, Richard D. | 267,012 | Exon, J. J. | 24,514 | 107,232 D | 35.4% | 59.2% | 37.4% | 62.6% |
| 1970 | 461,619 | 201,994 | Tiemann, Norbert T. | 248,552 | Exon, J. J. | 11,073 | 46,558 D | 43.8% | 53.8% | 44.8% | 55.2% |
| 1966** | 486,396 | 299,245 | Tiemann, Norbert T. | 186,985 | Sorensen, Philip C. | 166 | 112,260 R | 61.5% | 38.4% | 61.5% | 38.5% |
| 1964 | 578,090 | 231,029 | Burney, Dwight W. | 347,026 | Morrison, Frank B. | 35 | 115,997 D | 40.0% | 60.0% | 40.0% | 60.0% |
| 1962 | 464,585 | 221,885 | Seaton, Fred A. | 242,669 | Morrison, Frank B. | 31 | 20,784 D | 47.8% | 52.2% | 47.8% | 52.2% |
| 1960 | 598,971 | 287,302 | Cooper, John R. | 311,344 | Morrison, Frank B. | 325 | 24,042 D | 48.0% | 52.0% | 48.0% | 52.0% |
| 1958 | 421,067 | 209,705 | Anderson, Victor E. | 211,345 | Brooks, Ralph G. | 17 | 1,640 D | 49.8% | 50.2% | 49.8% | 50.2% |
| 1956 | 567,933 | 308,293 | Anderson, Victor E. | 228,048 | Sorrell, Frank | 31,592 | 80,245 R | 54.3% | 40.2% | 57.5% | 42.5% |
| 1954 | 414,841 | 250,080 | Anderson, Victor E. | 164,753 | Ritchie, William | 8 | 85,327 R | 60.3% | 39.7% | 60.3% | 39.7% |
| 1952 | 595,714 | 366,009 | Crosby, Robert B. | 229,700 | Raecke, Walter R. | 5 | 136,309 R | 61.4% | 38.6% | 61.4% | 38.6% |
| 1950 | 449,720 | 247,081 | Peterson, Val | 202,638 | Raecke, Walter R. | 1 | 44,443 R | 54.9% | 45.1% | 54.9% | 45.1% |
| 1948 | 476,352 | 286,119 | Peterson, Val | 190,214 | Sorrell, Frank | 19 | 95,905 R | 60.1% | 39.9% | 60.1% | 39.9% |
| 1946 | 380,835 | 249,468 | Peterson, Val | 131,367 | Sorrell, Frank | | 118,101 R | 65.5% | 34.5% | 65.5% | 34.5% |

The term of office of Nebraska's governor was increased from two to four years effective with the 1966 election.

## POSTWAR VOTE FOR SENATOR

| Year | Total Vote | Republican Vote | Republican Candidate | Democratic Vote | Democratic Candidate | Other Vote | Rep.-Dem. Plurality | Total Vote Rep. | Total Vote Dem. | Major Vote Rep. | Major Vote Dem. |
|---|---|---|---|---|---|---|---|---|---|---|---|
| 2002 | 480,217 | 397,438 | Hagel, Chuck | 70,290 | Matulka, Charlie A. | 12,489 | 327,148 R | 82.8% | 14.6% | 85.0% | 15.0% |
| 2000 | 692,344 | 337,967 | Stenberg, Don | 353,097 | Nelson, Ben | 1,280 | 15,130 D | 48.8% | 51.0% | 48.9% | 51.1% |
| 1996 | 676,789 | 379,933 | Hagel, Chuck | 281,904 | Nelson, Ben | 14,952 | 98,029 R | 56.1% | 41.7% | 57.4% | 42.6% |
| 1994 | 579,205 | 260,668 | Stoney, Jan | 317,297 | Kerrey, Bob | 1,240 | 56,629 D | 45.0% | 54.8% | 45.1% | 54.9% |
| 1990 | 593,828 | 243,013 | Daub, Harold J. | 349,779 | Exon, J. J. | 1,036 | 106,766 D | 40.9% | 58.9% | 41.0% | 59.0% |
| 1988 | 667,860 | 278,250 | Karnes, David | 378,717 | Kerrey, Bob | 10,893 | 100,467 D | 41.7% | 56.7% | 42.4% | 57.6% |
| 1984 | 639,668 | 307,147 | Hoch, Nancy | 332,217 | Exon, J. J. | 304 | 25,070 D | 48.0% | 51.9% | 48.0% | 52.0% |
| 1982 | 545,647 | 155,760 | Keck, Jim | 363,350 | Zorinsky, Edward | 26,537 | 207,590 D | 28.5% | 66.6% | 30.0% | 70.0% |
| 1978 | 494,368 | 159,806 | Shasteen, Donald | 334,276 | Exon, J. J. | 286 | 174,470 D | 32.3% | 67.6% | 32.3% | 67.7% |
| 1976 | 598,314 | 284,284 | McCollister, John Y. | 313,809 | Zorinsky, Edward | 221 | 29,525 D | 47.5% | 52.4% | 47.5% | 52.5% |
| 1972 | 568,580 | 301,841 | Curtis, Carl T. | 265,922 | Carpenter, Terry | 817 | 35,919 R | 53.1% | 46.8% | 53.2% | 46.8% |
| 1970 | 458,966 | 240,894 | Hruska, Roman L. | 217,681 | Morrison, Frank B. | 391 | 23,213 R | 52.5% | 47.4% | 52.5% | 47.5% |
| 1966 | 485,101 | 296,116 | Curtis, Carl T. | 187,950 | Morrison, Frank B. | 1,035 | 108,166 R | 61.0% | 38.7% | 61.2% | 38.8% |
| 1964 | 563,401 | 345,772 | Hruska, Roman L. | 217,605 | Arndt, Raymond W. | 24 | 128,167 R | 61.4% | 38.6% | 61.4% | 38.6% |
| 1960 | 598,743 | 352,748 | Curtis, Carl T. | 245,837 | Conrad, Robert | 158 | 106,911 R | 58.9% | 41.1% | 58.9% | 41.1% |
| 1958 | 417,385 | 232,227 | Hruska, Roman L. | 185,152 | Morrison, Frank B. | 6 | 47,075 R | 55.6% | 44.4% | 55.6% | 44.4% |
| 1954 | 418,691 | 255,695 | Curtis, Carl T. | 162,990 | Neville, Keith | 6 | 92,705 R | 61.1% | 38.9% | 61.1% | 38.9% |
| 1954S | 411,225 | 250,341 | Hruska, Roman L. | 160,881 | Green, James F. | 3 | 89,460 R | 60.9% | 39.1% | 60.9% | 39.1% |
| 1952 | 591,749 | 408,971 | Butler, Hugh | 164,660 | Long, Stanley D. | 18,118 | 244,311 R | 69.1% | 27.8% | 71.3% | 28.7% |
| 1952S | 581,750 | 369,841 | Griswold, Dwight | 211,898 | Ritchie, William | 11 | 157,943 R | 63.6% | 36.4% | 63.6% | 36.4% |
| 1948 | 471,895 | 267,575 | Wherry, Kenneth S. | 204,320 | Carpenter, Terry | | 63,255 R | 56.7% | 43.3% | 56.7% | 43.3% |
| 1946 | 382,958 | 271,208 | Butler, Hugh | 111,750 | Mekota, John E. | | 159,458 R | 70.8% | 29.2% | 70.8% | 29.2% |

One each of the 1954 and 1952 elections was for a short term to fill a vacancy.

# NEBRASKA

Congressional districts first established for elections held in 2002
3 members

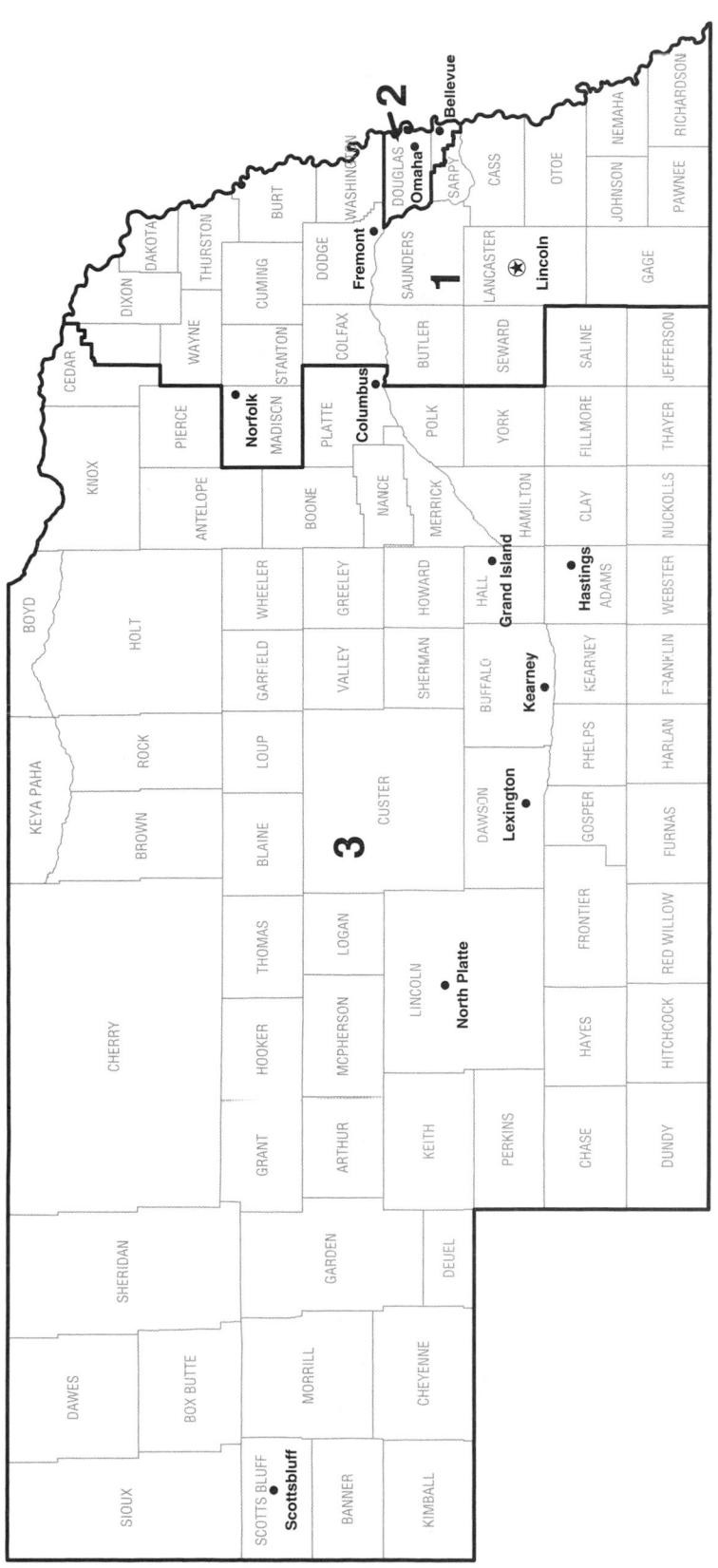

# NEBRASKA

## PRESIDENT 2004

| 2000 Census Population | County | Total Vote | Republican | Democratic | Other | Rep.-Dem. Plurality | Percentage Total Vote Rep. | Dem. | Major Vote Rep. | Dem. |
|---|---|---|---|---|---|---|---|---|---|---|
| 31,151 | ADAMS | 13,286 | 9,233 | 3,791 | 262 | 5,442 R | 69.5% | 28.5% | 70.9% | 29.1% |
| 7,452 | ANTELOPE | 3,424 | 2,761 | 613 | 50 | 2,148 R | 80.6% | 17.9% | 81.8% | 18.2% |
| 444 | ARTHUR | 266 | 240 | 24 | 2 | 216 R | 90.2% | 9.0% | 90.9% | 9.1% |
| 819 | BANNER | 437 | 379 | 56 | 2 | 323 R | 86.7% | 12.8% | 87.1% | 12.9% |
| 583 | BLAINE | 339 | 301 | 38 | | 263 R | 88.8% | 11.2% | 88.8% | 11.2% |
| 6,259 | BOONE | 2,895 | 2,309 | 546 | 40 | 1,763 R | 79.8% | 18.9% | 80.9% | 19.1% |
| 12,158 | BOX BUTTE | 5,152 | 3,396 | 1,657 | 99 | 1,739 R | 65.9% | 32.2% | 67.2% | 32.8% |
| 2,438 | BOYD | 1,148 | 911 | 228 | 9 | 683 R | 79.4% | 19.9% | 80.0% | 20.0% |
| 3,525 | BROWN | 1,733 | 1,426 | 268 | 39 | 1,158 R | 82.3% | 15.5% | 84.2% | 15.8% |
| 42,259 | BUFFALO | 18,608 | 14,222 | 4,100 | 286 | 10,122 R | 76.4% | 22.0% | 77.6% | 22.4% |
| 7,791 | BURT | 3,668 | 2,349 | 1,272 | 47 | 1,077 R | 64.0% | 34.7% | 64.9% | 35.1% |
| 8,767 | BUTLER | 4,168 | 3,016 | 1,068 | 84 | 1,948 R | 72.4% | 25.6% | 73.8% | 26.2% |
| 24,334 | CASS | 11,529 | 7,763 | 3,619 | 147 | 4,144 R | 67.3% | 31.4% | 68.2% | 31.8% |
| 9,615 | CEDAR | 4,536 | 3,387 | 1,083 | 66 | 2,304 R | 74.7% | 23.9% | 75.8% | 24.2% |
| 4,068 | CHASE | 1,973 | 1,652 | 302 | 19 | 1,350 R | 83.7% | 15.3% | 84.5% | 15.5% |
| 6,148 | CHERRY | 3,042 | 2,509 | 483 | 50 | 2,026 R | 82.5% | 15.9% | 83.9% | 16.1% |
| 9,830 | CHEYENNE | 4,746 | 3,791 | 893 | 62 | 2,898 R | 79.9% | 18.8% | 80.9% | 19.1% |
| 7,039 | CLAY | 3,337 | 2,543 | 743 | 51 | 1,800 R | 76.2% | 22.3% | 77.4% | 22.6% |
| 10,441 | COLFAX | 3,633 | 2,589 | 990 | 54 | 1,599 R | 71.3% | 27.3% | 72.3% | 27.7% |
| 10,203 | CUMING | 4,349 | 3,330 | 966 | 53 | 2,364 R | 76.6% | 22.2% | 77.5% | 22.5% |
| 11,793 | CUSTER | 5,612 | 4,518 | 1,040 | 54 | 3,478 R | 80.5% | 18.5% | 81.3% | 18.7% |
| 20,253 | DAKOTA | 6,615 | 3,526 | 3,027 | 62 | 499 R | 53.3% | 45.8% | 53.8% | 46.2% |
| 9,060 | DAWES | 3,994 | 2,809 | 1,119 | 66 | 1,690 R | 70.3% | 28.0% | 71.5% | 28.5% |
| 24,365 | DAWSON | 7,956 | 6,149 | 1,728 | 79 | 4,421 R | 77.3% | 21.7% | 78.1% | 21.9% |
| 2,098 | DEUEL | 1,053 | 820 | 222 | 11 | 598 R | 77.9% | 21.1% | 78.7% | 21.3% |
| 6,339 | DIXON | 3,009 | 2,028 | 938 | 43 | 1,090 R | 67.4% | 31.2% | 68.4% | 31.6% |
| 36,160 | DODGE | 16,172 | 10,716 | 5,250 | 206 | 5,466 R | 66.3% | 32.5% | 67.1% | 32.9% |
| 463,585 | DOUGLAS | 207,071 | 120,813 | 83,330 | 2,928 | 37,483 R | 58.3% | 40.2% | 59.2% | 40.8% |
| 2,292 | DUNDY | 1,053 | 858 | 186 | 9 | 672 R | 81.5% | 17.7% | 82.2% | 17.8% |
| 6,634 | FILLMORE | 3,193 | 2,314 | 828 | 51 | 1,486 R | 72.5% | 25.9% | 73.6% | 26.4% |
| 3,574 | FRANKLIN | 1,714 | 1,277 | 412 | 25 | 865 R | 74.5% | 24.0% | 75.6% | 24.4% |
| 3,099 | FRONTIER | 1,467 | 1,160 | 275 | 32 | 885 R | 79.1% | 18.7% | 80.8% | 19.2% |
| 5,324 | FURNAS | 2,467 | 1,950 | 492 | 25 | 1,458 R | 79.0% | 19.9% | 79.9% | 20.1% |
| 22,993 | GAGE | 10,384 | 6,575 | 3,655 | 154 | 2,920 R | 63.3% | 35.2% | 64.3% | 35.7% |
| 2,292 | GARDEN | 1,183 | 970 | 201 | 12 | 769 R | 82.0% | 17.0% | 82.8% | 17.2% |
| 1,902 | GARFIELD | 1,017 | 806 | 196 | 15 | 610 R | 79.3% | 19.3% | 80.4% | 19.6% |
| 2,143 | GOSPER | 1,119 | 890 | 222 | 7 | 668 R | 79.5% | 19.8% | 80.0% | 20.0% |
| 747 | GRANT | 396 | 352 | 41 | 3 | 311 R | 88.9% | 10.4% | 89.6% | 10.4% |
| 2,714 | GREELEY | 1,248 | 865 | 361 | 22 | 504 R | 69.3% | 28.9% | 70.6% | 29.4% |
| 53,534 | HALL | 21,154 | 14,592 | 6,228 | 334 | 8,364 R | 69.0% | 29.4% | 70.1% | 29.9% |
| 9,403 | HAMILTON | 4,866 | 3,785 | 1,012 | 69 | 2,773 R | 77.8% | 20.8% | 78.9% | 21.1% |
| 3,786 | HARLAN | 1,897 | 1,467 | 398 | 32 | 1,069 R | 77.3% | 21.0% | 78.7% | 21.3% |
| 1,068 | HAYES | 598 | 524 | 66 | 8 | 458 R | 87.6% | 11.0% | 88.8% | 11.2% |
| 3,111 | HITCHCOCK | 1,486 | 1,171 | 296 | 19 | 875 R | 78.8% | 19.9% | 79.8% | 20.2% |
| 11,551 | HOLT | 5,174 | 4,217 | 894 | 63 | 3,323 R | 81.5% | 17.3% | 82.5% | 17.5% |
| 783 | HOOKER | 461 | 392 | 64 | 5 | 328 R | 85.0% | 13.9% | 86.0% | 14.0% |
| 6,567 | HOWARD | 2,979 | 2,020 | 900 | 59 | 1,120 R | 67.8% | 30.2% | 69.2% | 30.8% |
| 8,333 | JEFFERSON | 4,011 | 2,600 | 1,352 | 59 | 1,248 R | 64.8% | 33.7% | 65.8% | 34.2% |
| 4,488 | JOHNSON | 2,394 | 1,470 | 885 | 39 | 585 R | 61.4% | 37.0% | 62.4% | 37.6% |
| 6,882 | KEARNEY | 3,379 | 2,621 | 707 | 51 | 1,914 R | 77.6% | 20.9% | 78.8% | 21.2% |
| 8,875 | KEITH | 4,137 | 3,356 | 743 | 38 | 2,613 R | 81.1% | 18.0% | 81.9% | 18.1% |
| 983 | KEYA PAHA | 549 | 442 | 98 | 9 | 344 R | 80.5% | 17.9% | 81.9% | 18.1% |
| 4,089 | KIMBALL | 1,877 | 1,491 | 366 | 20 | 1,125 R | 79.4% | 19.5% | 80.3% | 19.7% |
| 9,374 | KNOX | 4,213 | 3,062 | 1,086 | 65 | 1,976 R | 72.7% | 25.8% | 73.8% | 26.2% |
| 250,291 | LANCASTER | 124,509 | 69,764 | 52,747 | 1,998 | 17,017 R | 56.0% | 42.4% | 56.9% | 43.1% |
| 34,632 | LINCOLN | 16,199 | 11,056 | 4,905 | 238 | 6,151 R | 68.3% | 30.3% | 69.3% | 30.7% |
| 774 | LOGAN | 429 | 357 | 67 | 5 | 290 R | 83.2% | 15.6% | 84.2% | 15.8% |
| 712 | LOUP | 386 | 314 | 68 | 4 | 246 R | 81.3% | 17.6% | 82.2% | 17.8% |
| 533 | MCPHERSON | 312 | 259 | 49 | 4 | 210 R | 83.0% | 15.7% | 84.1% | 15.9% |
| 35,226 | MADISON | 14,089 | 10,981 | 2,934 | 174 | 8,047 R | 77.9% | 20.8% | 78.9% | 21.1% |

# NEBRASKA

## PRESIDENT 2004

| 2000 Census Population | County | Total Vote | Republican | Democratic | Other | Rep.-Dem. Plurality | Percentage Total Vote Rep. | Dem. | Major Vote Rep. | Dem. |
|---|---|---|---|---|---|---|---|---|---|---|
| 8,204 | MERRICK | 3,657 | 2,771 | 833 | 53 | 1,938 R | 75.8% | 22.8% | 76.9% | 23.1% |
| 5,440 | MORRILL | 2,293 | 1,755 | 495 | 43 | 1,260 R | 76.5% | 21.6% | 78.0% | 22.0% |
| 4,038 | NANCE | 1,731 | 1,237 | 459 | 35 | 778 R | 71.5% | 26.5% | 72.9% | 27.1% |
| 7,576 | NEMAHA | 3,715 | 2,595 | 1,066 | 54 | 1,529 R | 69.9% | 28.7% | 70.9% | 29.1% |
| 5,057 | NUCKOLLS | 2,471 | 1,884 | 541 | 46 | 1,343 R | 76.2% | 21.9% | 77.7% | 22.3% |
| 15,396 | OTOE | 7,386 | 5,018 | 2,275 | 93 | 2,743 R | 67.9% | 30.8% | 68.8% | 31.2% |
| 3,087 | PAWNEE | 1,483 | 986 | 481 | 16 | 505 R | 66.5% | 32.4% | 67.2% | 32.8% |
| 3,200 | PERKINS | 1,558 | 1,285 | 262 | 11 | 1,023 R | 82.5% | 16.8% | 83.1% | 16.9% |
| 9,747 | PHELPS | 4,743 | 3,872 | 830 | 41 | 3,042 R | 81.6% | 17.5% | 82.3% | 17.7% |
| 7,857 | PIERCE | 3,398 | 2,824 | 546 | 28 | 2,278 R | 83.1% | 16.1% | 83.8% | 16.2% |
| 31,662 | PLATTE | 13,987 | 11,130 | 2,657 | 200 | 8,473 R | 79.6% | 19.0% | 80.7% | 19.3% |
| 5,639 | POLK | 2,727 | 2,146 | 549 | 32 | 1,597 R | 78.7% | 20.1% | 79.6% | 20.4% |
| 11,448 | RED WILLOW | 5,258 | 4,129 | 1,055 | 74 | 3,074 R | 78.5% | 20.1% | 79.6% | 20.4% |
| 9,531 | RICHARDSON | 4,278 | 2,924 | 1,297 | 57 | 1,627 R | 68.3% | 30.3% | 69.3% | 30.7% |
| 1,756 | ROCK | 883 | 740 | 130 | 13 | 610 R | 83.8% | 14.7% | 85.1% | 14.9% |
| 13,843 | SALINE | 5,566 | 3,071 | 2,420 | 75 | 651 R | 55.2% | 43.5% | 55.9% | 44.1% |
| 122,595 | SARPY | 58,334 | 40,163 | 17,455 | 716 | 22,708 R | 68.9% | 29.9% | 69.7% | 30.3% |
| 19,830 | SAUNDERS | 9,489 | 6,441 | 2,884 | 164 | 3,557 R | 67.9% | 30.4% | 69.1% | 30.9% |
| 36,951 | SCOTTS BLUFF | 14,390 | 10,378 | 3,843 | 169 | 6,535 R | 72.1% | 26.7% | 73.0% | 27.0% |
| 16,496 | SEWARD | 7,565 | 5,353 | 2,114 | 98 | 3,239 R | 70.8% | 27.9% | 71.7% | 28.3% |
| 6,198 | SHERIDAN | 2,599 | 2,136 | 430 | 33 | 1,706 R | 82.2% | 16.5% | 83.2% | 16.8% |
| 3,318 | SHERMAN | 1,643 | 1,072 | 541 | 30 | 531 R | 65.2% | 32.9% | 66.5% | 33.5% |
| 1,475 | SIOUX | 809 | 677 | 123 | 9 | 554 R | 83.7% | 15.2% | 84.6% | 15.4% |
| 6,455 | STANTON | 2,745 | 2,159 | 559 | 27 | 1,600 R | 78.7% | 20.4% | 79.4% | 20.6% |
| 6,055 | THAYER | 2,878 | 2,075 | 764 | 39 | 1,311 R | 72.1% | 26.5% | 73.1% | 26.9% |
| 729 | THOMAS | 444 | 378 | 60 | 6 | 318 R | 85.1% | 13.5% | 86.3% | 13.7% |
| 7,171 | THURSTON | 2,387 | 1,154 | 1,212 | 21 | 58 D | 48.3% | 50.8% | 48.8% | 51.2% |
| 4,647 | VALLEY | 2,391 | 1,801 | 564 | 26 | 1,237 R | 75.3% | 23.6% | 76.2% | 23.8% |
| 18,780 | WASHINGTON | 9,950 | 7,083 | 2,754 | 113 | 4,329 R | 71.2% | 27.7% | 72.0% | 28.0% |
| 9,851 | WAYNE | 4,085 | 2,971 | 1,059 | 55 | 1,912 R | 72.7% | 25.9% | 73.7% | 26.3% |
| 4,061 | WEBSTER | 2,002 | 1,403 | 557 | 42 | 846 R | 70.1% | 27.8% | 71.6% | 28.4% |
| 886 | WHEELER | 453 | 366 | 81 | 6 | 285 R | 80.8% | 17.9% | 81.9% | 18.1% |
| 14,598 | YORK | 6,797 | 5,393 | 1,304 | 100 | 4,089 R | 79.3% | 19.2% | 80.5% | 19.5% |
| 1,711,263 | TOTAL | 778,186 | 512,814 | 254,328 | 11,044 | 258,486 R | 65.9% | 32.7% | 66.8% | 33.2% |

# NEBRASKA

## HOUSE OF REPRESENTATIVES

| CD | Year | Total Vote | Republican Vote | Republican Candidate | Democratic Vote | Democratic Candidate | Other Vote | Rep.-Dem. Plurality | Percentage Total Vote Rep. | Dem. | Major Vote Rep. | Dem. |
|---|---|---|---|---|---|---|---|---|---|---|---|---|
| 1 | 2004 | 265,072 | 143,756 | Fortenberry, Jeff | 113,971 | Connealy, Matt | 7,345 | 29,785 R | 54.2% | 43.0% | 55.8% | 44.2% |
| 1 | 2002 | 155,844 | 133,013 | Bereuter, Doug* | | | 22,831 | 133,013 R | 85.4% | | 100.0% | |
| 2 | 2004 | 249,764 | 152,608 | Terry, Lee* | 90,292 | Thompson, Nancy | 6,864 | 62,316 R | 61.1% | 36.2% | 62.8% | 37.2% |
| 2 | 2002 | 142,014 | 89,917 | Terry, Lee* | 46,843 | Simon, Jim | 5,254 | 43,074 R | 63.3% | 33.0% | 65.7% | 34.3% |
| 3 | 2004 | 250,136 | 218,751 | Osborne, Tom* | 26,434 | Anderson, Donna J. | 4,951 | 192,317 R | 87.5% | 10.6% | 89.2% | 10.8% |
| 3 | 2002 | 175,956 | 163,939 | Osborne, Tom* | | | 12,017 | 163,939 R | 93.2% | | 100.0% | |
| Total | 2004 | 764,972 | 515,115 | | 230,697 | | 19,160 | 284,418 R | 67.3% | 30.2% | 69.1% | 30.9% |
| Total | 2002 | 473,814 | 386,869 | | 46,843 | | 40,102 | 340,026 R | 81.6% | 9.9% | 89.2% | 10.8% |

An asterisk (*) denotes incumbent.

# NEBRASKA

## GENERAL AND PRIMARY ELECTIONS

## 2004 GENERAL ELECTIONS

| | |
|---|---|
| **President** | Other vote was 5,698 By Petition (Ralph Nader); 2,041 Libertarian (Michael Badnarik); 1,314 Nebraska (Michael Peroutka); 978 Green (David Cobb); 82 By Petition (Roger Calero); 931 scattered write-in. |
| **House** | Other vote was: |

| | |
|---|---|
| CD 1 | 7,345 Green (Steven R. Larrick). |
| CD 2 | 4,656 Libertarian (Jack Graziano); 2,208 Green (Dante Silvatierra). |
| CD 3 | 3,396 Nebraska (Joseph A. Rosberg); 1,555 Green (Roy Guisinger). |

## 2004 PRIMARY ELECTIONS

| | | | | |
|---|---|---|---|---|
| **Primary** | May 11, 2004 | **Registration** (as of May 11, 2004) | Republican | 544,979 |
| | | | Democratic | 378,157 |
| | | | Libertarian | 4,206 |
| | | | Nebraska | 3,321 |
| | | | Green | 158 |
| | | | Nonpartisan | 157,021 |
| | | | TOTAL | 1,087,842 |

**Primary Type** Semi-open—Registered Democrats and Republicans could vote only in their party's primary. Voters registered as nonpartisan could participate in either party's primary for the Senate and House (but not president).

Note:   An asterisk (*) denotes incumbent. Ballots cast by nonpartisan voters in primaries for the House and Senate were tallied separately but were included in the overall totals, which are listed below.

| | REPUBLICAN PRIMARIES | | | DEMOCRATIC PRIMARIES | | |
|---|---|---|---|---|---|---|
| **President** | George W. Bush* | 121,355 | 100.0% | John Kerry | 52,479 | 73.3% |
| | | | | John Edwards | 10,031 | 14.0% |
| | | | | Howard Dean | 5,400 | 7.5% |
| | | | | Dennis J. Kucinich | 1,490 | 2.1% |
| | | | | Al Sharpton | 1,367 | 1.9% |
| | | | | Lyndon H. LaRouche Jr. | 805 | 1.1% |
| | | | | TOTAL | 71,572 | |
| **Congressional District 1** | Jeff Fortenberry | 18,735 | 39.2% | Matt Connealy | 14,807 | 50.2% |
| | Curt Bromm | 15,708 | 32.9% | Janet Stewart | 9,857 | 33.4% |
| | Greg Ruehle | 10,077 | 21.1% | Charlie Matulka | 2,750 | 9.3% |
| | Bob Van Valkenburg | 1,044 | 2.2% | Phil Chase | 2,080 | 7.1% |
| | Daniel Manning | 1,027 | 2.2% | | | |
| | Greg Walburn | 696 | 1.5% | | | |
| | Andrew J. Ringsmuth | 469 | 1.0% | | | |
| | TOTAL | 47,756 | | TOTAL | 29,494 | |
| **Congressional District 2** | Lee Terry* | 23,463 | 100.0% | Nancy Thompson | 18,573 | 100.0% |
| **Congressional District 3** | Tom Osborne* | 58,558 | 100.0% | Donna J. Anderson | 19,747 | 100.0% |

# NEVADA

## GOVERNOR
Kenny Guinn (R). Reelected 2002 to a four-year term. Previously elected 1998.

## SENATORS (1 Democrat, 1 Republican)
John Ensign (R). Elected 2000 to a six-year term.

Harry Reid (D). Reelected 2004 to a six-year term. Previously elected 1998, 1992, 1986.

## REPRESENTATIVES (2 Republicans, 1 Democrat)
1. Shelley Berkley (D)          3. Jon Porter (R)
2. Jim Gibbons (R)

## POSTWAR VOTE FOR PRESIDENT

| | | Republican | | Democratic | | Other | | Percentage | | | |
| | Total | | | | | | | Total Vote | | Major Vote | |
| Year | Vote | Vote | Candidate | Vote | Candidate | Vote | Plurality | Rep. | Dem. | Rep. | Dem. |
|---|---|---|---|---|---|---|---|---|---|---|---|
| 2004 | 829,587 | 418,690 | Bush, George W. | 397,190 | Kerry, John | 13,707 | 21,500 R | 50.5% | 47.9% | 51.3% | 48.7% |
| 2000** | 608,970 | 301,575 | Bush, George W. | 279,978 | Gore, Al | 27,417 | 21,597 R | 49.5% | 46.0% | 51.9% | 48.1% |
| 1996** | 464,279 | 199,244 | Dole, Bob | 203,974 | Clinton, Bill | 61,061 | 4,730 D | 42.9% | 43.9% | 49.4% | 50.6% |
| 1992** | 506,318 | 175,828 | Bush, George | 189,148 | Clinton, Bill | 141,342 | 13,320 D | 34.7% | 37.4% | 48.2% | 51.8% |
| 1988 | 350,067 | 206,040 | Bush, George | 132,738 | Dukakis, Michael S. | 11,289 | 73,302 R | 58.9% | 37.9% | 60.8% | 39.2% |
| 1984 | 286,667 | 188,770 | Reagan, Ronald | 91,655 | Mondale, Walter F. | 6,242 | 97,115 R | 65.8% | 32.0% | 67.3% | 32.7% |
| 1980** | 247,885 | 155,017 | Reagan, Ronald | 66,666 | Carter, Jimmy | 26,202 | 88,351 R | 62.5% | 26.9% | 69.9% | 30.1% |
| 1976 | 201,876 | 101,273 | Ford, Gerald R. | 92,479 | Carter, Jimmy | 8,124 | 8,794 R | 50.2% | 45.8% | 52.3% | 47.7% |
| 1972 | 181,766 | 115,750 | Nixon, Richard M. | 66,016 | McGovern, George S. | | 49,734 R | 63.7% | 36.3% | 63.7% | 36.3% |
| 1968** | 154,218 | 73,188 | Nixon, Richard M. | 60,598 | Humphrey, Hubert H. | 20,432 | 12,590 R | 47.5% | 39.3% | 54.7% | 45.3% |
| 1964 | 135,433 | 56,094 | Goldwater, Barry M. | 79,339 | Johnson, Lyndon B. | | 23,245 D | 41.4% | 58.6% | 41.4% | 58.6% |
| 1960 | 107,267 | 52,387 | Nixon, Richard M. | 54,880 | Kennedy, John F. | | 2,493 D | 48.8% | 51.2% | 48.8% | 51.2% |
| 1956 | 96,689 | 56,049 | Eisenhower, Dwight D. | 40,640 | Stevenson, Adlai E. | | 15,409 R | 58.0% | 42.0% | 58.0% | 42.0% |
| 1952 | 82,190 | 50,502 | Eisenhower, Dwight D. | 31,688 | Stevenson, Adlai E. | | 18,814 R | 61.4% | 38.6% | 61.4% | 38.6% |
| 1948 | 62,117 | 29,357 | Dewey, Thomas E. | 31,291 | Truman, Harry S. | 1,469 | 1,934 D | 47.3% | 50.4% | 48.4% | 51.6% |

In past elections, the other vote included: 2000 - 15,008 Green (Ralph Nader); 1996 - 43,986 Reform (Ross Perot); 1992 - 132,580 Independent (Perot); 1980 - 17,651 Independent (John Anderson); 1968 - 20,432 American Independent (George Wallace).

# NEVADA

## POSTWAR VOTE FOR GOVERNOR

| Year | Total Vote | Republican | | Democratic | | Other Vote | Rep.-Dem. Plurality | Percentage | | | |
|---|---|---|---|---|---|---|---|---|---|---|---|
| | | | | | | | | Total Vote | | Major Vote | |
| | | Vote | Candidate | Vote | Candidate | | | Rep. | Dem. | Rep. | Dem. |
| 2002 | 504,079 | 344,001 | Guinn, Kenny | 110,935 | Neal, Joe | 49,143 | 233,066 R | 68.2% | 22.0% | 75.6% | 24.4% |
| 1998 | 433,630 | 223,892 | Guinn, Kenny | 182,281 | Jones, Jan Laverty | 27,457 | 41,611 R | 51.6% | 42.0% | 55.1% | 44.9% |
| 1994 | 379,676 | 156,875 | Gibbons, Jim | 200,026 | Miller, Robert J. | 22,775 | 43,151 D | 41.3% | 52.7% | 44.0% | 56.0% |
| 1990 | 320,743 | 95,789 | Gallaway, Jim | 207,878 | Miller, Robert J. | 17,076 | 112,089 D | 29.9% | 64.8% | 31.5% | 68.5% |
| 1986 | 260,375 | 65,081 | Cafferata, Patty | 187,268 | Bryan, Richard H. | 8,026 | 122,187 D | 25.0% | 71.9% | 25.8% | 74.2% |
| 1982 | 239,751 | 100,104 | List, Robert F. | 128,132 | Bryan, Richard H. | 11,515 | 28,028 D | 41.8% | 53.4% | 43.9% | 56.1% |
| 1978 | 192,445 | 108,097 | List, Robert F. | 76,361 | Rose, Robert E. | 7,987 | 31,736 R | 56.2% | 39.7% | 58.6% | 41.4% |
| 1974 | 169,358 | 28,959 | Crumpler, Shirley | 114,114 | O'Callaghan, Mike | 26,285 | 85,155 D | 17.1% | 67.4% | 20.2% | 79.8% |
| 1970 | 146,991 | 64,400 | Fike, Ed | 70,697 | O'Callaghan, Mike | 11,894 | 6,297 D | 43.8% | 48.1% | 47.7% | 52.3% |
| 1966 | 137,677 | 71,807 | Laxalt, Paul | 65,870 | Sawyer, Grant | | 5,937 R | 52.2% | 47.8% | 52.2% | 47.8% |
| 1962 | 96,929 | 32,145 | Gragson, Oran K. | 64,784 | Sawyer, Grant | | 32,639 D | 33.2% | 66.8% | 33.2% | 66.8% |
| 1958 | 84,889 | 34,025 | Russell, Charles H. | 50,864 | Sawyer, Grant | | 16,839 D | 40.1% | 59.9% | 40.1% | 59.9% |
| 1954 | 78,462 | 41,665 | Russell, Charles H. | 36,797 | Pittman, Vail | | 4,868 R | 53.1% | 46.9% | 53.1% | 46.9% |
| 1950 | 61,773 | 35,609 | Russell, Charles H. | 26,164 | Pittman, Vail | | 9,445 R | 57.6% | 42.4% | 57.6% | 42.4% |
| 1946 | 49,902 | 21,247 | Jepson, Melvin E. | 28,655 | Pittman, Vail | | 7,408 D | 42.6% | 57.4% | 42.6% | 57.4% |

## POSTWAR VOTE FOR SENATOR

| Year | Total Vote | Republican | | Democratic | | Other Vote | Rep.-Dem. Plurality | Percentage | | | |
|---|---|---|---|---|---|---|---|---|---|---|---|
| | | | | | | | | Total Vote | | Major Vote | |
| | | Vote | Candidate | Vote | Candidate | | | Rep. | Dem. | Rep. | Dem. |
| 2004 | 810,068 | 284,640 | Ziser, Richard | 494,805 | Reid, Harry | 30,623 | 210,165 D | 35.1% | 61.1% | 36.5% | 63.5% |
| 2000 | 600,250 | 330,687 | Ensign, John | 238,260 | Bernstein, Ed | 31,303 | 92,427 R | 55.1% | 39.7% | 58.1% | 41.9% |
| 1998 | 435,790 | 208,222 | Ensign, John | 208,650 | Reid, Harry | 18,918 | 428 D | 47.8% | 47.9% | 49.9% | 50.1% |
| 1994 | 380,530 | 156,020 | Furman, Hal | 193,804 | Bryan, Richard H. | 30,706 | 37,784 D | 41.0% | 50.9% | 44.6% | 55.4% |
| 1992 | 495,887 | 199,413 | Dahl, Demar | 253,150 | Reid, Harry | 43,324 | 53,737 D | 40.2% | 51.0% | 44.1% | 55.9% |
| 1988 | 349,649 | 161,336 | Hecht, Chic | 175,548 | Bryan, Richard H. | 12,765 | 14,212 D | 46.1% | 50.2% | 47.9% | 52.1% |
| 1986 | 261,932 | 116,606 | Santini, James | 130,955 | Reid, Harry | 14,371 | 14,349 D | 44.5% | 50.0% | 47.1% | 52.9% |
| 1982 | 240,394 | 120,377 | Hecht, Chic | 114,720 | Cannon, Howard W. | 5,297 | 5,657 R | 50.1% | 47.7% | 51.2% | 48.8% |
| 1980 | 246,436 | 144,224 | Laxalt, Paul | 92,129 | Gojack, Mary | 10,083 | 52,095 R | 58.5% | 37.4% | 61.0% | 39.0% |
| 1976 | 201,980 | 63,471 | Towell, David | 127,295 | Cannon, Howard W. | 11,214 | 63,824 D | 31.4% | 63.0% | 33.3% | 66.7% |
| 1974 | 169,473 | 79,605 | Laxalt, Paul | 78,981 | Reid, Harry | 10,887 | 624 R | 47.0% | 46.6% | 50.2% | 49.8% |
| 1970 | 147,768 | 60,838 | Raggio, William J. | 85,187 | Cannon, Howard W. | 1,743 | 24,349 D | 41.2% | 57.6% | 41.7% | 58.3% |
| 1968 | 152,690 | 69,068 | Fike, Ed | 83,622 | Bible, Alan | | 14,554 D | 45.2% | 54.8% | 45.2% | 54.8% |
| 1964 | 134,624 | 67,288 | Laxalt, Paul | 67,336 | Cannon, Howard W. | | 48 D | 50.0% | 50.0% | 50.0% | 50.0% |
| 1962 | 97,192 | 33,749 | Wright, William B. | 63,443 | Bible, Alan | | 29,694 D | 34.7% | 65.3% | 34.7% | 65.3% |
| 1958 | 84,492 | 35,760 | Malone, George W. | 48,732 | Cannon, Howard W. | | 12,972 D | 42.3% | 57.7% | 42.3% | 57.7% |
| 1956 | 96,389 | 45,712 | Young, Clifton | 50,677 | Bible, Alan | | 4,965 D | 47.4% | 52.6% | 47.4% | 52.6% |
| 1954S | 77,513 | 32,470 | Brown, Ernest S. | 45,043 | Bible, Alan | | 12,573 D | 41.9% | 58.1% | 41.9% | 58.1% |
| 1952 | 81,090 | 41,906 | Malone, George W. | 39,184 | Mechling, Thomas B. | | 2,722 R | 51.7% | 48.3% | 51.7% | 48.3% |
| 1950 | 61,762 | 25,933 | Marshall, George E. | 35,829 | McCarran, Pat | | 9,896 D | 42.0% | 58.0% | 42.0% | 58.0% |
| 1946 | 50,354 | 27,801 | Malone, George W. | 22,553 | Bunker, Berkeley | | 5,248 R | 55.2% | 44.8% | 55.2% | 44.8% |

The 1954 election was for a short term to fill a vacancy.

# NEVADA

Congressional districts first established for elections held in 2002
3 members

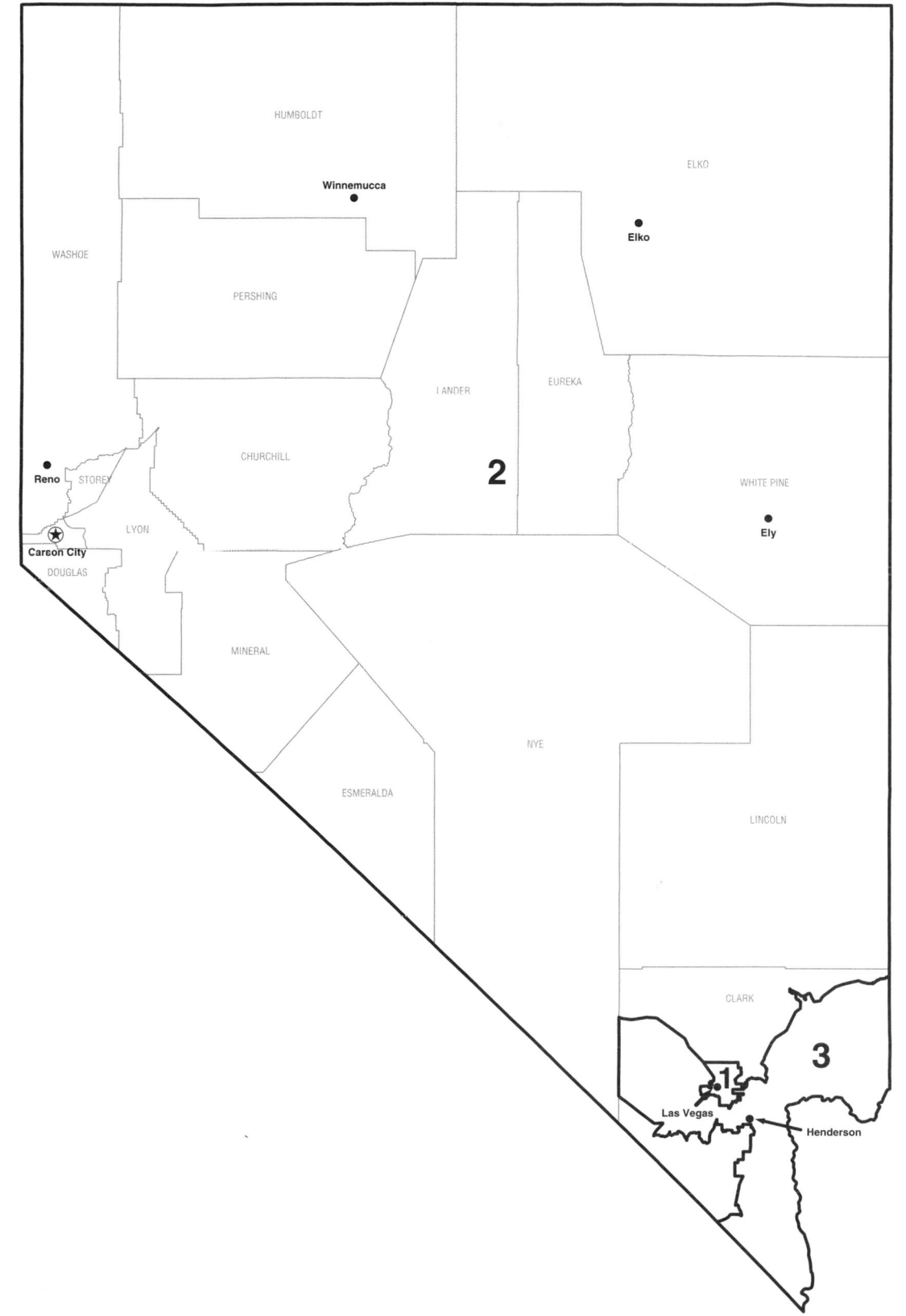

# NEVADA

## PRESIDENT 2004

| 2000 Census Population | County | Total Vote | Republican | Democratic | Other | Rep.-Dem. Plurality | Percentage | | | |
|---|---|---|---|---|---|---|---|---|---|---|
| | | | | | | | Total Vote | | Major Vote | |
| | | | | | | | Rep. | Dem. | Rep. | Dem. |
| 52,457 | CARSON CITY | 23,106 | 13,171 | 9,441 | 494 | 3,730 R | 57.0% | 40.9% | 58.2% | 41.8% |
| 23,982 | CHURCHILL | 10,237 | 7,335 | 2,705 | 197 | 4,630 R | 71.7% | 26.4% | 73.1% | 26.9% |
| 1,375,765 | CLARK | 545,397 | 255,337 | 281,767 | 8,293 | 26,430 D | 46.8% | 51.7% | 47.5% | 52.5% |
| 41,259 | DOUGLAS | 23,898 | 15,192 | 8,275 | 431 | 6,917 R | 63.6% | 34.6% | 64.7% | 35.3% |
| 45,291 | ELKO | 15,309 | 11,938 | 3,050 | 321 | 8,888 R | 78.0% | 19.9% | 79.7% | 20.3% |
| 971 | ESMERALDA | 481 | 367 | 99 | 15 | 268 R | 76.3% | 20.6% | 78.8% | 21.2% |
| 1,651 | EUREKA | 738 | 571 | 144 | 23 | 427 R | 77.4% | 19.5% | 79.9% | 20.1% |
| 16,106 | HUMBOLDT | 5,367 | 3,896 | 1,361 | 110 | 2,535 R | 72.6% | 25.4% | 74.1% | 25.9% |
| 5,794 | LANDER | 2,053 | 1,602 | 414 | 37 | 1,188 R | 78.0% | 20.2% | 79.5% | 20.5% |
| 4,165 | LINCOLN | 2,047 | 1,579 | 418 | 50 | 1,161 R | 77.1% | 20.4% | 79.1% | 20.9% |
| 34,501 | LYON | 17,151 | 11,136 | 5,637 | 378 | 5,499 R | 64.9% | 32.9% | 66.4% | 33.6% |
| 5,071 | MINERAL | 2,327 | 1,336 | 931 | 60 | 405 R | 57.4% | 40.0% | 58.9% | 41.1% |
| 32,485 | NYE | 14,510 | 8,487 | 5,616 | 407 | 2,871 R | 58.5% | 38.7% | 60.2% | 39.8% |
| 6,693 | PERSHING | 1,917 | 1,341 | 538 | 38 | 803 R | 70.0% | 28.1% | 71.4% | 28.6% |
| 3,399 | STOREY | 2,168 | 1,253 | 871 | 44 | 382 R | 57.8% | 40.2% | 59.0% | 41.0% |
| 339,486 | WASHOE | 159,079 | 81,545 | 74,841 | 2,693 | 6,704 R | 51.3% | 47.0% | 52.1% | 47.9% |
| 9,181 | WHITE PINE | 3,802 | 2,604 | 1,082 | 116 | 1,522 R | 68.5% | 28.5% | 70.6% | 29.4% |
| 1,998,257 | TOTAL | 829,587 | 418,690 | 397,190 | 13,707 | 21,500 R | 50.5% | 47.9% | 51.3% | 48.7% |

# NEVADA

## SENATOR 2004

| 2000 Census Population | County | Total Vote | Republican | Democratic | Other | Rep.-Dem. Plurality | Percentage | | | |
|---|---|---|---|---|---|---|---|---|---|---|
| | | | | | | | Total Vote | | Major Vote | |
| | | | | | | | Rep. | Dem. | Rep. | Dem. |
| 52,457 | CARSON CITY | 22,819 | 9,559 | 12,478 | 782 | 2,919 D | 41.9% | 54.7% | 43.4% | 56.6% |
| 23,982 | CHURCHILL | 10,122 | 5,647 | 3,995 | 480 | 1,652 R | 55.8% | 39.5% | 58.6% | 41.4% |
| 1,375,765 | CLARK | 531,702 | 167,104 | 345,694 | 18,904 | 178,590 D | 31.4% | 65.0% | 32.6% | 67.4% |
| 41,259 | DOUGLAS | 23,309 | 12,120 | 10,409 | 780 | 1,711 R | 52.0% | 44.7% | 53.8% | 46.2% |
| 45,291 | ELKO | 14,997 | 7,912 | 6,084 | 1,001 | 1,828 R | 52.8% | 40.6% | 56.5% | 43.5% |
| 971 | ESMERALDA | 477 | 257 | 162 | 58 | 95 R | 53.9% | 34.0% | 61.3% | 38.7% |
| 1,651 | EUREKA | 734 | 404 | 267 | 63 | 137 R | 55.0% | 36.4% | 60.2% | 39.8% |
| 16,106 | HUMBOLDT | 5,260 | 2,431 | 2,524 | 305 | 93 D | 46.2% | 48.0% | 49.1% | 50.9% |
| 5,794 | LANDER | 2,024 | 989 | 908 | 127 | 81 R | 48.9% | 44.9% | 52.1% | 47.9% |
| 4,165 | LINCOLN | 2,024 | 1,128 | 745 | 151 | 383 R | 55.7% | 36.8% | 60.2% | 39.8% |
| 34,501 | LYON | 16,846 | 8,633 | 7,526 | 687 | 1,107 R | 51.2% | 44.7% | 53.4% | 46.6% |
| 5,071 | MINERAL | 2,277 | 591 | 1,565 | 121 | 974 D | 26.0% | 68.7% | 27.4% | 72.6% |
| 32,485 | NYE | 14,053 | 5,798 | 7,521 | 734 | 1,723 D | 41.3% | 53.5% | 43.5% | 56.5% |
| 6,693 | PERSHING | 1,892 | 817 | 960 | 115 | 143 D | 43.2% | 50.7% | 46.0% | 54.0% |
| 3,399 | STOREY | 2,131 | 914 | 1,133 | 84 | 219 D | 42.9% | 53.2% | 44.7% | 55.3% |
| 339,486 | WASHOE | 155,652 | 58,994 | 90,706 | 5,952 | 31,712 D | 37.9% | 58.3% | 39.4% | 60.6% |
| 9,181 | WHITE PINE | 3,749 | 1,342 | 2,128 | 279 | 786 D | 35.8% | 56.8% | 38.7% | 61.3% |
| 1,998,257 | TOTAL | 810,068 | 284,640 | 494,805 | 30,623 | 210,165 D | 35.1% | 61.1% | 36.5% | 63.5% |

# NEVADA

## HOUSE OF REPRESENTATIVES

| CD | Year | Total Vote | Republican Vote | Republican Candidate | Democratic Vote | Democratic Candidate | Other Vote | Rep.-Dem. Plurality | Total Vote Rep. | Total Vote Dem. | Major Vote Rep. | Major Vote Dem. |
|----|------|-----------|-----------------|----------------------|-----------------|----------------------|------------|---------------------|-----------------|-----------------|-----------------|-----------------|
| 1 | 2004 | 202,436 | 63,005 | Mickelson, Russ | 133,569 | Berkley, Shelley* | 5,862 | 70,564 D | 31.1% | 66.0% | 32.1% | 67.9% |
| 1 | 2002 | 119,714 | 51,148 | Boggs-McDonald, Lynette Maria | 64,312 | Berkley, Shelley* | 4,254 | 13,164 D | 42.7% | 53.7% | 44.3% | 55.7% |
| 2 | 2004 | 291,079 | 195,466 | Gibbons, Jim* | 79,978 | Cochran, Angie G. | 15,635 | 115,488 R | 67.2% | 27.5% | 71.0% | 29.0% |
| 2 | 2002 | 201,200 | 149,574 | Gibbons, Jim* | 40,189 | Souza, Travis O. | 11,437 | 109,385 R | 74.3% | 20.0% | 78.8% | 21.2% |
| 3 | 2004 | 297,918 | 162,240 | Porter, Jon* | 120,365 | Gallagher, Tom | 15,313 | 41,875 R | 54.5% | 40.4% | 57.4% | 42.6% |
| 3 | 2002 | 178,994 | 100,378 | Porter, Jon | 66,659 | Herrera, Dario | 11,957 | 33,719 R | 56.1% | 37.2% | 60.1% | 39.9% |
| Total | 2004 | 791,433 | 420,711 | | 333,912 | | 36,810 | 86,799 R | 53.2% | 42.2% | 55.8% | 44.2% |
| Total | 2002 | 499,908 | 301,100 | | 171,160 | | 27,648 | 129,940 R | 60.2% | 34.2% | 63.8% | 36.2% |

An asterisk (*) denotes incumbent.

# NEVADA

## GENERAL AND PRIMARY ELECTIONS

## 2004 GENERAL ELECTIONS

**President** Other vote was 4,838 Independent (Ralph Nader); 3,688 "None of these Candidates"; 3,176 Libertarian (Michael Badnarik); 1,152 Independent American (Michael Peroutka); 853 Green (David Cobb).

**Senator** Other vote was 12,968 "None of these Candidates"; 9,559 Libertarian (Thomas L. Hurst); 6,001 Independent American (David Schumann); 2,095 Natural Law (Gary Marinch).

**House** Other vote was:

CD 1 5,862 Libertarian (Jim Duensing).
CD 2 10,638 Independent American (Janine Hansen); 4,997 Libertarian (Brendan J. Trainor).
CD 3 9,260 Libertarian (Joseph P. Silvestri); 6,053 Independent American (Richard Wayne O'Dell).

## 2004 PRIMARY ELECTIONS

**Primary** September 7, 2004

**Registration** (as of Sept. 7, 2004)

| | |
|---|---|
| Republican | 382,630 |
| Democratic | 383,651 |
| Independent American | 24,726 |
| Libertarian | 5,490 |
| Green | 2,942 |
| Natural Law | 985 |
| Reform | 215 |
| Other | 2,239 |
| Nonpartisan | 143,103 |
| TOTAL | 945,981 |

**Primary Type** Closed—Only registered Democrats and Republicans could vote in their party's primary.

# NEVADA

## GENERAL AND PRIMARY ELECTIONS

Note: An asterisk (*) denotes incumbent. The names of unopposed candidates did not appear on the primary ballot; therefore, no votes were cast for these candidates.

| | REPUBLICAN PRIMARIES | | | DEMOCRATIC PRIMARIES | | |
|---|---|---|---|---|---|---|
| **Senator** | Richard Ziser | 40,533 | 33.5% | Harry Reid* | Unopposed | |
| | Kenneth Wegner | 21,406 | 17.7% | | | |
| | Robert Brown | 19,553 | 16.2% | | | |
| | None of these Candidates | 16,827 | 13.9% | | | |
| | Royle William Melton | 10,552 | 8.7% | | | |
| | Cherie M. Tilley | 10,357 | 8.6% | | | |
| | Carlo Poliak | 1,769 | 1.5% | | | |
| | TOTAL | 120,997 | | | | |
| **Congressional District 1** | Russ Mickelson | 11,868 | 63.5% | Shelley Berkley* | 27,765 | 83.2% |
| | Lewis A. Byer | 4,806 | 25.7% | Ann Reynolds | 3,208 | 9.6% |
| | Francisco E. Tamez | 2,026 | 10.8% | Brian Kral | 2,412 | 7.2% |
| | TOTAL | 18,700 | | TOTAL | 33,385 | |
| **Congressional District 2** | Jim Gibbons* | Unopposed | | Angie G. Cochran | 18,319 | 50.6% |
| | | | | David Jerome Bennett | 17,859 | 49.4% |
| | | | | TOTAL | 36,178 | |
| **Congressional District 3** | Jon Porter* | Unopposed | | Tom Gallagher | 23,349 | 69.5% |
| | | | | Shanna Phillips | 2,573 | 7.7% |
| | | | | Anna Nevenic | 2,239 | 6.7% |
| | | | | Rick Devoe | 2,217 | 6.6% |
| | | | | Mark Budetich | 1,833 | 5.5% |
| | | | | Ron Von Felden | 1,383 | 4.1% |
| | | | | TOTAL | 33,594 | |

# NEW HAMPSHIRE

## GOVERNOR
John Lynch (D). Elected 2004 to a two-year term.

## SENATORS (2 Republicans)
Judd Gregg (R). Reelected 2004 to a six-year term. Previously elected 1998, 1992.

John E. Sununu (R). Elected 2002 to a six-year term.

## REPRESENTATIVES (2 Republicans)
1. Jeb Bradley (R)    2. Charles Bass (R)

## POSTWAR VOTE FOR PRESIDENT

| | | Republican | | Democratic | | Other | | Percentage | | | |
| | Total | | | | | | | Total Vote | | Major Vote | |
| Year | Vote | Vote | Candidate | Vote | Candidate | Vote | Plurality | Rep. | Dem. | Rep. | Dem. |
|---|---|---|---|---|---|---|---|---|---|---|---|
| 2004 | 677,738 | 331,237 | Bush, George W. | 340,511 | Kerry, John | 5,990 | 9,274 D | 48.9% | 50.2% | 49.3% | 50.7% |
| 2000** | 569,081 | 273,559 | Bush, George W. | 266,348 | Gore, Al | 29,174 | 7,211 R | 48.1% | 46.8% | 50.7% | 49.3% |
| 1996** | 499,175 | 196,532 | Dole, Bob | 246,214 | Clinton, Bill | 56,429 | 49,682 D | 39.4% | 49.3% | 44.4% | 55.6% |
| 1992** | 537,943 | 202,484 | Bush, George | 209,040 | Clinton, Bill | 126,419 | 6,556 D | 37.6% | 38.9% | 49.2% | 50.8% |
| 1988 | 451,074 | 281,537 | Bush, George | 163,696 | Dukakis, Michael S. | 5,841 | 117,841 R | 62.4% | 36.3% | 63.2% | 36.8% |
| 1984 | 389,066 | 267,051 | Reagan, Ronald | 120,395 | Mondale, Walter F. | 1,620 | 146,656 R | 68.6% | 30.9% | 68.9% | 31.1% |
| 1980** | 383,990 | 221,705 | Reagan, Ronald | 108,864 | Carter, Jimmy | 53,421 | 112,841 R | 57.7% | 28.4% | 67.1% | 32.9% |
| 1976 | 339,618 | 185,935 | Ford, Gerald R. | 147,635 | Carter, Jimmy | 6,048 | 38,300 R | 54.7% | 43.5% | 55.7% | 44.3% |
| 1972 | 334,055 | 213,724 | Nixon, Richard M. | 116,435 | McGovern, George S. | 3,896 | 97,289 R | 64.0% | 34.9% | 64.7% | 35.3% |
| 1968** | 297,298 | 154,903 | Nixon, Richard M. | 130,589 | Humphrey, Hubert H. | 11,806 | 24,314 R | 52.1% | 43.9% | 54.3% | 45.7% |
| 1964 | 288,093 | 104,029 | Goldwater, Barry M. | 184,064 | Johnson, Lyndon B. | | 80,035 D | 36.1% | 63.9% | 36.1% | 63.9% |
| 1960 | 295,761 | 157,989 | Nixon, Richard M. | 137,772 | Kennedy, John F. | | 20,217 R | 53.4% | 46.6% | 53.4% | 46.6% |
| 1956 | 266,994 | 176,519 | Eisenhower, Dwight D. | 90,364 | Stevenson, Adlai E. | 111 | 86,155 R | 66.1% | 33.8% | 66.1% | 33.9% |
| 1952 | 272,950 | 166,287 | Eisenhower, Dwight D. | 106,663 | Stevenson, Adlai E. | | 59,624 R | 60.9% | 39.1% | 60.9% | 39.1% |
| 1948 | 231,440 | 121,299 | Dewey, Thomas E. | 107,995 | Truman, Harry S. | 2,146 | 13,304 R | 52.4% | 46.7% | 52.9% | 47.1% |

In past elections, the other vote included: 2000 - 22,198 Green (Ralph Nader); 1996 - 48,390 Reform (Ross Perot); 1992 - 121,337 Independent (Perot); 1980 - 49,693 Independent (John Anderson); 1968 - 11,173 American Independent (George Wallace).

## POSTWAR VOTE FOR GOVERNOR

| | | Republican | | Democratic | | Other | Rep.-Dem. | Percentage | | | |
| | Total | | | | | | | Total Vote | | Major Vote | |
| Year | Vote | Vote | Candidate | Vote | Candidate | Vote | Plurality | Rep. | Dem. | Rep. | Dem. |
|---|---|---|---|---|---|---|---|---|---|---|---|
| 2004 | 667,020 | 325,981 | Benson, Craig | 340,299 | Lynch, John | 740 | 14,318 D | 48.9% | 51.0% | 48.9% | 51.1% |
| 2002 | 442,976 | 259,663 | Benson, Craig | 169,277 | Fernald, Mark | 14,036 | 90,386 R | 58.6% | 38.2% | 60.5% | 39.5% |
| 2000 | 564,953 | 246,952 | Humphrey, Gordon J. | 275,038 | Shaheen, Jeanne | 42,963 | 28,086 D | 43.7% | 48.7% | 47.3% | 52.7% |
| 1998 | 318,940 | 98,473 | Lucas, Jay | 210,769 | Shaheen, Jeanne | 9,698 | 112,296 D | 30.9% | 66.1% | 31.8% | 68.2% |
| 1996 | 497,040 | 196,321 | Lamontagne, Ovide | 284,175 | Shaheen, Jeanne | 16,544 | 87,854 D | 39.5% | 57.2% | 40.9% | 59.1% |
| 1994 | 311,882 | 218,134 | Merrill, Steve | 79,686 | King, Wayne D. | 14,062 | 138,448 R | 69.9% | 25.6% | 73.2% | 26.8% |
| 1992 | 516,170 | 289,170 | Merrill, Steve | 206,232 | Arnesen, Deborah A. | 20,768 | 82,938 R | 56.0% | 40.0% | 58.4% | 41.6% |
| 1990 | 295,018 | 177,773 | Gregg, Judd | 101,923 | Grandmaison, J. Joseph | 15,322 | 75,850 R | 60.3% | 34.5% | 63.6% | 36.4% |
| 1988 | 441,923 | 267,064 | Gregg, Judd | 172,543 | McEachern, Paul | 2,316 | 94,521 R | 60.4% | 39.0% | 60.8% | 39.2% |
| 1986 | 251,107 | 134,824 | Sununu, John H. | 116,142 | McEachern, Paul | 141 | 18,682 R | 53.7% | 46.3% | 53.7% | 46.3% |
| 1984 | 383,910 | 256,574 | Sununu, John H. | 127,156 | Spirou, Chris | 180 | 129,418 R | 66.8% | 33.1% | 66.9% | 33.1% |
| 1982 | 282,588 | 145,389 | Sununu, John H. | 132,317 | Gallen, Hugh J. | 4,882 | 13,072 R | 51.4% | 46.8% | 52.4% | 47.6% |
| 1980 | 384,031 | 156,178 | Thomson, Meldrim | 226,436 | Gallen, Hugh J. | 1,417 | 70,258 D | 40.7% | 59.0% | 40.8% | 59.2% |
| 1978 | 269,587 | 122,464 | Thomson, Meldrim | 133,133 | Gallen, Hugh J. | 13,990 | 10,669 D | 45.4% | 49.4% | 47.9% | 52.1% |
| 1976 | 342,669 | 197,589 | Thomson, Meldrim | 145,015 | Spanos, Harry V. | 65 | 52,574 R | 57.7% | 42.3% | 57.7% | 42.3% |

# NEW HAMPSHIRE

## POSTWAR VOTE FOR GOVERNOR

| Year | Total Vote | Republican | | Democratic | | Other Vote | Rep.-Dem. Plurality | Percentage | | | |
|---|---|---|---|---|---|---|---|---|---|---|---|
| | | Vote | Candidate | Vote | Candidate | | | Total Vote | | Major Vote | |
| | | | | | | | | Rep. | Dem. | Rep. | Dem. |
| 1974 | 226,665 | 115,933 | Thomson, Meldrim | 110,591 | Leonard, Richard W. | 141 | 5,342 R | 51.1% | 48.8% | 51.2% | 48.8% |
| 1972** | 323,102 | 133,702 | Thomson, Meldrim | 126,107 | Crowley, Roger J. | 63,293 | 7,595 R | 41.4% | 39.0% | 51.5% | 48.5% |
| 1970 | 222,441 | 102,298 | Peterson, Walter R. | 98,098 | Crowley, Roger J. | 22,045 | 4,200 R | 46.0% | 44.1% | 51.0% | 49.0% |
| 1968 | 285,342 | 149,902 | Peterson, Walter R. | 135,378 | Bussiere, Emile R. | 62 | 14,524 R | 52.5% | 47.4% | 52.5% | 47.5% |
| 1966 | 233,642 | 107,259 | Gregg, Hugh | 125,882 | King, John W. | 501 | 18,623 D | 45.9% | 53.9% | 46.0% | 54.0% |
| 1964 | 285,863 | 94,824 | Pillsbury, John | 190,863 | King, John W. | 176 | 96,039 D | 33.2% | 66.8% | 33.2% | 66.8% |
| 1962 | 230,048 | 94,567 | Pillsbury, John | 135,481 | King, John W. | | 40,914 D | 41.1% | 58.9% | 41.1% | 58.9% |
| 1960 | 290,527 | 161,123 | Powell, Wesley | 129,404 | Boutin, Bernard L. | | 31,719 R | 55.5% | 44.5% | 55.5% | 44.5% |
| 1958 | 206,745 | 106,790 | Powell, Wesley | 99,955 | Boutin, Bernard L. | | 6,835 R | 51.7% | 48.3% | 51.7% | 48.3% |
| 1956 | 258,695 | 141,578 | Dwinell, Lane | 117,117 | Shaw, John | | 24,461 R | 54.7% | 45.3% | 54.7% | 45.3% |
| 1954 | 194,631 | 107,287 | Dwinell, Lane | 87,344 | Shaw, John | | 19,943 R | 55.1% | 44.9% | 55.1% | 44.9% |
| 1952 | 265,715 | 167,791 | Gregg, Hugh | 97,924 | Craig, William H. | | 69,867 R | 63.1% | 36.9% | 63.1% | 36.9% |
| 1950 | 191,239 | 108,907 | Adams, Sherman | 82,258 | Bingham, Robert P. | 74 | 26,649 R | 56.9% | 43.0% | 57.0% | 43.0% |
| 1948 | 222,571 | 116,212 | Adams, Sherman | 105,207 | Hill, Herbert W. | 1,152 | 11,005 R | 52.2% | 47.3% | 52.5% | 47.5% |
| 1946 | 163,451 | 103,204 | Dale, Charles M. | 60,247 | Keefe, F. Clyde | | 42,957 R | 63.1% | 36.9% | 63.1% | 36.9% |

In past elections, the other vote included: 1972 - 63,199 Independent (Malcolm McLane).

## POSTWAR VOTE FOR SENATOR

| Year | Total Vote | Republican | | Democratic | | Other Vote | Rep.-Dem. Plurality | Percentage | | | |
|---|---|---|---|---|---|---|---|---|---|---|---|
| | | Vote | Candidate | Vote | Candidate | | | Total Vote | | Major Vote | |
| | | | | | | | | Rep. | Dem. | Rep. | Dem. |
| 2004 | 657,086 | 434,847 | Gregg, Judd | 221,549 | Haddock, Doris Granny D. | 690 | 213,298 R | 66.2% | 33.7% | 66.2% | 33.8% |
| 2002 | 447,135 | 227,229 | Sununu, John E. | 207,478 | Shaheen, Jeanne | 12,428 | 19,751 R | 50.8% | 46.4% | 52.3% | 47.7% |
| 1998 | 314,956 | 213,477 | Gregg, Judd | 88,883 | Condodemetraky, George | 12,596 | 124,594 R | 67.8% | 28.2% | 70.6% | 29.4% |
| 1996 | 492,598 | 242,304 | Smith, Robert C. | 227,397 | Swett, Dick | 22,897 | 14,907 R | 49.2% | 46.2% | 51.6% | 48.4% |
| 1992 | 518,416 | 249,591 | Gregg, Judd | 234,982 | Rauh, John | 33,843 | 14,609 R | 48.1% | 45.3% | 51.5% | 48.5% |
| 1990 | 291,393 | 189,792 | Smith, Robert C. | 91,299 | Durkin, John A. | 10,302 | 98,493 R | 65.1% | 31.3% | 67.5% | 32.5% |
| 1986 | 244,797 | 154,090 | Rudman, Warren | 79,225 | Peabody, Endicott | 11,482 | 74,865 R | 62.9% | 32.4% | 66.0% | 34.0% |
| 1984 | 384,406 | 225,828 | Humphrey, Gordon J. | 157,447 | D'Amours, Norman E. | 1,131 | 68,381 R | 58.7% | 41.0% | 58.9% | 41.1% |
| 1980 | 375,064 | 195,563 | Rudman, Warren | 179,455 | Durkin, John A. | 46 | 16,108 R | 52.1% | 47.8% | 52.1% | 47.9% |
| 1978 | 263,779 | 133,745 | Humphrey, Gordon J. | 127,945 | McIntyre, Thomas J. | 2,089 | 5,800 R | 50.7% | 48.5% | 51.1% | 48.9% |
| 1975S | 262,682 | 113,007 | Wyman, Louis C. | 140,778 | Durkin, John A. | 8,897 | 27,771 D | 43.0% | 53.6% | 44.5% | 55.5% |
| 1974** | 223,363 | 110,926 | Wyman, Louis C. | 110,924 | Durkin, John A. | 1,513 | 2 R | 49.7% | 49.7% | 50.0% | 50.0% |
| 1972 | 324,354 | 139,852 | Powell, Wesley | 184,495 | McIntyre, Thomas J. | 7 | 44,643 D | 43.1% | 56.9% | 43.1% | 56.9% |
| 1968 | 286,989 | 170,163 | Cotton, Norris | 116,816 | King, John W. | 10 | 53,347 R | 59.3% | 40.7% | 59.3% | 40.7% |
| 1966 | 229,305 | 105,241 | Thyng, Harrison R. | 123,888 | McIntyre, Thomas J. | 176 | 18,647 D | 45.9% | 54.0% | 45.9% | 54.1% |
| 1962 | 224,479 | 134,035 | Cotton, Norris | 90,444 | Catalfo, Alfred | | 43,591 R | 59.7% | 40.3% | 59.7% | 40.3% |
| 1962S | 224,811 | 107,199 | Bass, Perkins | 117,612 | McIntyre, Thomas J. | | 10,413 D | 47.7% | 52.3% | 47.7% | 52.3% |
| 1960 | 287,545 | 173,521 | Bridges, Styles | 114,024 | Hill, Herbert W. | | 59,497 R | 60.3% | 39.7% | 60.3% | 39.7% |
| 1956 | 251,943 | 161,424 | Cotton, Norris | 90,519 | Pickett, Laurence M. | | 70,905 R | 64.1% | 35.9% | 64.1% | 35.9% |
| 1954 | 194,536 | 117,150 | Bridges, Styles | 77,386 | Morin, Gerard L. | | 39,764 R | 60.2% | 39.8% | 60.2% | 39.8% |
| 1954S | 189,558 | 114,068 | Cotton, Norris | 75,490 | Bentley, Stanley J. | | 38,578 R | 60.2% | 39.8% | 60.2% | 39.8% |
| 1950 | 190,573 | 106,142 | Tobey, Charles W. | 72,473 | Kelley, Emmet J. | 11,958 | 33,669 R | 55.7% | 38.0% | 59.4% | 40.6% |
| 1948 | 222,898 | 129,600 | Bridges, Styles | 91,760 | Fortin, Alfred E. | 1,538 | 37,840 R | 58.1% | 41.2% | 58.5% | 41.5% |

Following the closely contested 1974 election, neither candidate was seated and the 1975 special election was held for the remaining years of that term. One each of the 1962 and 1954 elections were for short terms to fill vacancies.

# NEW HAMPSHIRE

Congressional districts first established for elections held in 2002
2 members

# NEW HAMPSHIRE

## PRESIDENT 2004

| 2000 Census Population | County | Total Vote | Republican | Democratic | Other | Rep.-Dem. Plurality | Percentage Total Vote Rep. | Dem. | Major Vote Rep. | Dem. |
|---|---|---|---|---|---|---|---|---|---|---|
| 56,325 | BELKNAP | 32,298 | 17,920 | 14,080 | 298 | 3,840 R | 55.5% | 43.6% | 56.0% | 44.0% |
| 43,666 | CARROLL | 28,222 | 14,614 | 13,319 | 289 | 1,295 R | 51.8% | 47.2% | 52.3% | 47.7% |
| 73,825 | CHESHIRE | 41,347 | 16,463 | 24,438 | 446 | 7,975 D | 39.8% | 59.1% | 40.3% | 59.7% |
| 33,111 | COOS | 16,925 | 8,143 | 8,585 | 197 | 442 D | 48.1% | 50.7% | 48.7% | 51.3% |
| 81,743 | GRAFTON | 46,971 | 20,277 | 26,180 | 514 | 5,903 D | 43.2% | 55.7% | 43.6% | 56.4% |
| 380,841 | HILLSBOROUGH | 195,427 | 99,724 | 94,121 | 1,582 | 5,603 R | 51.0% | 48.2% | 51.4% | 48.6% |
| 136,225 | MERRIMACK | 76,647 | 36,060 | 39,975 | 612 | 3,915 D | 47.0% | 52.2% | 47.4% | 52.6% |
| 277,359 | ROCKINGHAM | 158,816 | 82,069 | 75,437 | 1,310 | 6,632 R | 51.7% | 47.5% | 52.1% | 47.9% |
| 112,233 | STRAFFORD | 59,281 | 25,825 | 32,942 | 514 | 7,117 D | 43.6% | 55.6% | 43.9% | 56.1% |
| 40,458 | SULLIVAN | 21,804 | 10,142 | 11,434 | 228 | 1,292 D | 46.5% | 52.4% | 47.0% | 53.0% |
| 1,235,786 | TOTAL | 677,738 | 331,237 | 340,511 | 5,990 | 9,274 D | 48.9% | 50.2% | 49.3% | 50.7% |
|  | City/Town |  |  |  |  |  |  |  |  |  |
| 10,769 | AMHERST | 7,146 | 3,637 | 3,469 | 40 | 168 R | 50.9% | 48.5% | 51.2% | 48.8% |
| 6,178 | ATKINSON | 4,326 | 2,457 | 1,836 | 33 | 621 R | 56.8% | 42.4% | 57.2% | 42.8% |
| 7,475 | BARRINGTON | 4,346 | 2,086 | 2,216 | 44 | 130 D | 48.0% | 51.0% | 48.5% | 51.5% |
| 18,274 | BEDFORD | 10,920 | 6,836 | 4,047 | 37 | 2,789 R | 62.6% | 37.1% | 62.8% | 37.2% |
| 6,716 | BELMONT | 3,349 | 1,882 | 1,431 | 36 | 451 R | 56.2% | 42.7% | 56.8% | 43.2% |
| 10,331 | BERLIN | 4,881 | 1,741 | 3,097 | 43 | 1,356 D | 35.7% | 63.5% | 36.0% | 64.0% |
| 7,138 | BOW | 4,713 | 2,403 | 2,276 | 34 | 127 R | 51.0% | 48.3% | 51.4% | 48.6% |
| 13,151 | CLAREMONT | 5,891 | 2,575 | 3,253 | 63 | 678 D | 43.7% | 55.2% | 44.2% | 55.8% |
| 40,687 | CONCORD | 21,069 | 8,210 | 12,675 | 184 | 4,465 D | 39.0% | 60.2% | 39.3% | 60.7% |
| 8,604 | CONWAY | 5,110 | 2,300 | 2,752 | 58 | 452 D | 45.0% | 53.9% | 45.5% | 54.5% |
| 34,021 | DERRY | 14,912 | 8,038 | 6,760 | 114 | 1,278 R | 53.9% | 45.3% | 54.3% | 45.7% |
| 26,884 | DOVER | 15,533 | 6,206 | 9,225 | 102 | 3,019 D | 40.0% | 59.4% | 40.2% | 59.8% |
| 12,664 | DURHAM | 6,101 | 1,772 | 4,272 | 57 | 2,500 D | 29.0% | 70.0% | 29.3% | 70.7% |
| 5,476 | EPPING | 3,133 | 1,555 | 1,551 | 27 | 4 R | 49.6% | 49.5% | 50.1% | 49.9% |
| 14,058 | EXETER | 8,259 | 3,544 | 4,659 | 56 | 1,115 D | 42.9% | 56.4% | 43.2% | 56.8% |
| 5,774 | FARMINGTON | 2,852 | 1,452 | 1,379 | 21 | 73 R | 50.9% | 48.4% | 51.3% | 48.7% |
| 8,405 | FRANKLIN | 3,760 | 1,813 | 1,920 | 27 | 107 D | 48.2% | 51.1% | 48.6% | 51.4% |
| 6,803 | GILFORD | 4,582 | 2,626 | 1,924 | 32 | 702 R | 57.3% | 42.0% | 57.7% | 42.3% |
| 16,929 | GOFFSTOWN | 8,808 | 5,008 | 3,734 | 66 | 1,274 R | 56.9% | 42.4% | 57.3% | 42.7% |
| 8,297 | HAMPSTEAD | 4,943 | 2,856 | 2,046 | 41 | 810 R | 57.8% | 41.4% | 58.3% | 41.7% |
| 14,937 | HAMPTON | 9,451 | 4,645 | 4,729 | 77 | 84 D | 49.1% | 50.0% | 49.6% | 50.4% |
| 10,850 | HANOVER | 6,655 | 1,444 | 5,152 | 59 | 3,708 D | 21.7% | 77.4% | 21.9% | 78.1% |
| 7,015 | HOLLIS | 4,858 | 2,425 | 2,398 | 35 | 27 R | 49.9% | 49.4% | 50.3% | 49.7% |
| 11,721 | HOOKSETT | 6,467 | 3,784 | 2,656 | 27 | 1,128 R | 58.5% | 41.1% | 58.8% | 41.2% |
| 22,928 | HUDSON | 11,674 | 6,172 | 5,390 | 112 | 782 R | 52.9% | 46.2% | 53.4% | 46.6% |
| 5,476 | JAFFREY | 2,985 | 1,459 | 1,495 | 31 | 36 D | 48.9% | 50.1% | 49.4% | 50.6% |
| 22,563 | KEENE | 12,483 | 4,004 | 8,378 | 101 | 4,374 D | 32.1% | 67.1% | 32.3% | 67.7% |
| 5,862 | KINGSTON | 3,272 | 1,806 | 1,430 | 36 | 376 R | 55.2% | 43.7% | 55.8% | 44.2% |
| 16,411 | LACONIA | 7,866 | 4,286 | 3,511 | 69 | 775 R | 54.5% | 44.6% | 55.0% | 45.0% |
| 12,568 | LEBANON | 6,402 | 2,302 | 4,048 | 52 | 1,746 D | 36.0% | 63.2% | 36.3% | 63.7% |
| 7,360 | LITCHFIELD | 4,155 | 2,386 | 1,747 | 22 | 639 R | 57.4% | 42.0% | 57.7% | 42.3% |
| 5,845 | LITTLETON | 3,033 | 1,659 | 1,337 | 37 | 322 R | 54.7% | 44.1% | 55.4% | 44.6% |
| 23,236 | LONDONDERRY | 12,214 | 6,888 | 5,222 | 104 | 1,666 R | 56.4% | 42.8% | 56.9% | 43.1% |
| 107,006 | MANCHESTER | 46,736 | 23,286 | 23,116 | 334 | 170 R | 49.8% | 49.5% | 50.2% | 49.8% |
| 25,119 | MERRIMACK TOWN | 14,739 | 7,927 | 6,682 | 130 | 1,245 R | 53.8% | 45.3% | 54.3% | 45.7% |
| 13,535 | MILFORD | 7,351 | 3,757 | 3,516 | 78 | 241 R | 51.1% | 47.8% | 51.7% | 48.3% |
| 86,605 | NASHUA | 39,958 | 18,016 | 21,587 | 355 | 3,571 D | 45.1% | 54.0% | 45.5% | 54.5% |
| 8,027 | NEWMARKET | 4,820 | 1,830 | 2,939 | 51 | 1,109 D | 38.0% | 61.0% | 38.4% | 61.6% |
| 6,269 | NEWPORT | 2,919 | 1,458 | 1,425 | 36 | 33 R | 49.9% | 48.8% | 50.6% | 49.4% |
| 10,914 | PELHAM | 6,523 | 3,725 | 2,755 | 43 | 970 R | 57.1% | 42.2% | 57.5% | 42.5% |
| 6,897 | PEMBROKE | 3,606 | 1,824 | 1,752 | 30 | 72 R | 50.6% | 48.6% | 51.0% | 49.0% |
| 5,883 | PETERBOROUGH | 3,774 | 1,439 | 2,310 | 25 | 871 D | 38.1% | 61.2% | 38.4% | 61.6% |
| 7,747 | PLAISTOW | 4,151 | 2,331 | 1,804 | 16 | 527 R | 56.2% | 43.5% | 56.4% | 43.6% |
| 5,892 | PLYMOUTH | 3,540 | 1,209 | 2,300 | 31 | 1,091 D | 34.2% | 65.0% | 34.5% | 65.5% |
| 20,784 | PORTSMOUTH | 12,736 | 4,185 | 8,436 | 115 | 4,251 D | 32.9% | 66.2% | 33.2% | 66.8% |

# NEW HAMPSHIRE

## PRESIDENT 2004

| 2000 Census Population | City/Town | Total Vote | Republican | Democratic | Other | Rep.-Dem. Plurality | Percentage Total Vote Rep. | Dem. | Major Vote Rep. | Dem. |
|---|---|---|---|---|---|---|---|---|---|---|
| 9,674 | RAYMOND | 4,800 | 2,630 | 2,127 | 43 | 503 R | 54.8% | 44.3% | 55.3% | 44.7% |
| 28,461 | ROCHESTER | 13,456 | 6,658 | 6,672 | 126 | 14 D | 49.5% | 49.6% | 49.9% | 50.1% |
| 28,112 | SALEM | 14,364 | 7,797 | 6,472 | 95 | 1,325 R | 54.3% | 45.1% | 54.6% | 45.4% |
| 7,934 | SEABROOK | 4,283 | 2,223 | 2,023 | 37 | 200 R | 51.9% | 47.2% | 52.4% | 47.6% |
| 11,477 | SOMERSWORTH | 5,511 | 2,355 | 3,101 | 55 | 746 D | 42.7% | 56.3% | 43.2% | 56.8% |
| 6,800 | SWANZEY | 3,502 | 1,520 | 1,950 | 32 | 430 D | 43.4% | 55.7% | 43.8% | 56.2% |
| 7,776 | WEARE | 4,390 | 2,549 | 1,795 | 46 | 754 R | 58.1% | 40.9% | 58.7% | 41.3% |
| 10,709 | WINDHAM | 7,074 | 4,204 | 2,829 | 41 | 1,375 R | 59.4% | 40.0% | 59.8% | 40.2% |

# NEW HAMPSHIRE

## GOVERNOR 2004

| 2000 Census Population | County | Total Vote | Republican | Democratic | Other | Rep.-Dem. Plurality | Percentage Total Vote Rep. | Dem. | Major Vote Rep. | Dem. |
|---|---|---|---|---|---|---|---|---|---|---|
| 56,325 | BELKNAP | 31,947 | 17,598 | 14,304 | 45 | 3,294 R | 55.1% | 44.8% | 55.2% | 44.8% |
| 43,666 | CARROLL | 27,820 | 15,797 | 12,003 | 20 | 3,794 R | 56.8% | 43.1% | 56.8% | 43.2% |
| 73,825 | CHESHIRE | 40,411 | 16,225 | 24,085 | 101 | 7,860 D | 40.1% | 59.6% | 40.3% | 59.7% |
| 33,111 | COOS | 16,688 | 7,790 | 8,884 | 14 | 1,094 D | 46.7% | 53.2% | 46.7% | 53.3% |
| 81,743 | GRAFTON | 45,930 | 20,842 | 25,043 | 45 | 4,201 D | 45.4% | 54.5% | 45.4% | 54.6% |
| 380,841 | HILLSBOROUGH | 192,416 | 100,867 | 91,344 | 205 | 9,523 R | 52.4% | 47.5% | 52.5% | 47.5% |
| 136,225 | MERRIMACK | 75,935 | 30,443 | 45,403 | 89 | 14,960 D | 40.1% | 59.8% | 40.1% | 59.9% |
| 277,359 | ROCKINGHAM | 156,200 | 80,174 | 75,885 | 141 | 4,289 R | 51.3% | 48.6% | 51.4% | 48.6% |
| 112,233 | STRAFFORD | 58,229 | 26,261 | 31,912 | 56 | 5,651 D | 45.1% | 54.8% | 45.1% | 54.9% |
| 40,458 | SULLIVAN | 21,444 | 9,984 | 11,436 | 24 | 1,452 D | 46.6% | 53.3% | 46.6% | 53.4% |
| 1,235,786 | TOTAL | 667,020 | 325,981 | 340,299 | 740 | 14,318 D | 48.9% | 51.0% | 48.9% | 51.1% |

| 2000 Census Population | City/Town | Total Vote | Republican | Democratic | Other | Rep.-Dem. Plurality | Percentage Total Vote Rep. | Dem. | Major Vote Rep. | Dem. |
|---|---|---|---|---|---|---|---|---|---|---|
| 10,769 | AMHERST | 7,080 | 3,736 | 3,336 | 8 | 400 R | 52.8% | 47.1% | 52.8% | 47.2% |
| 6,178 | ATKINSON | 4,251 | 2,535 | 1,713 | 3 | 822 R | 59.6% | 40.3% | 59.7% | 40.3% |
| 7,475 | BARRINGTON | 4,287 | 2,018 | 2,262 | 7 | 244 D | 47.1% | 52.8% | 47.1% | 52.9% |
| 18,274 | BEDFORD | 10,802 | 6,763 | 4,039 | | 2,724 R | 62.6% | 37.4% | 62.6% | 37.4% |
| 6,716 | BELMONT | 3,302 | 1,797 | 1,499 | 6 | 298 R | 54.4% | 45.4% | 54.5% | 45.5% |
| 10,331 | BERLIN | 4,837 | 1,698 | 3,134 | 5 | 1,436 D | 35.1% | 64.8% | 35.1% | 64.9% |
| 7,138 | BOW | 4,672 | 1,917 | 2,748 | 7 | 831 D | 41.0% | 58.8% | 41.1% | 58.9% |
| 13,151 | CLAREMONT | 5,801 | 2,476 | 3,320 | 5 | 844 D | 42.7% | 57.2% | 42.7% | 57.3% |
| 40,687 | CONCORD | 20,852 | 6,052 | 14,759 | 41 | 8,707 D | 29.0% | 70.8% | 29.1% | 70.9% |
| 8,604 | CONWAY | 4,988 | 2,551 | 2,432 | 5 | 119 R | 51.1% | 48.8% | 51.2% | 48.8% |
| 34,021 | DERRY | 14,677 | 7,903 | 6,774 | | 1,129 R | 53.8% | 46.2% | 53.8% | 46.2% |
| 26,884 | DOVER | 15,260 | 6,332 | 8,926 | 2 | 2,594 D | 41.5% | 58.5% | 41.5% | 58.5% |
| 12,664 | DURHAM | 5,754 | 1,735 | 3,999 | 20 | 2,264 D | 30.2% | 69.5% | 30.3% | 69.7% |
| 5,476 | EPPING | 3,092 | 1,576 | 1,516 | | 60 R | 51.0% | 49.0% | 51.0% | 49.0% |
| 14,058 | EXETER | 8,115 | 3,396 | 4,714 | 5 | 1,318 D | 41.8% | 58.1% | 41.9% | 58.1% |
| 5,774 | FARMINGTON | 2,831 | 1,562 | 1,269 | | 293 R | 55.2% | 44.8% | 55.2% | 44.8% |
| 8,405 | FRANKLIN | 3,739 | 1,649 | 2,086 | 4 | 437 D | 44.1% | 55.8% | 44.1% | 55.9% |
| 6,803 | GILFORD | 4,539 | 2,637 | 1,900 | 2 | 737 R | 58.1% | 41.9% | 58.1% | 41.9% |
| 16,929 | GOFFSTOWN | 8,697 | 4,912 | 3,779 | 6 | 1,133 R | 56.5% | 43.5% | 56.5% | 43.5% |
| 8,297 | HAMPSTEAD | 4,849 | 2,844 | 2,003 | 2 | 841 R | 58.7% | 41.3% | 58.7% | 41.3% |

# NEW HAMPSHIRE

## GOVERNOR 2004

| 2000 Census Population | City/Town | Total Vote | Republican | Democratic | Other | Rep.-Dem. Plurality | Percentage Total Vote Rep. | Dem. | Major Vote Rep. | Dem. |
|---|---|---|---|---|---|---|---|---|---|---|
| 14,937 | HAMPTON | 9,308 | 4,279 | 5,021 | 8 | 742 D | 46.0% | 53.9% | 46.0% | 54.0% |
| 10,850 | HANOVER | 6,210 | 1,557 | 4,641 | 12 | 3,084 D | 25.1% | 74.7% | 25.1% | 74.9% |
| 7,015 | HOLLIS | 4,777 | 2,532 | 2,240 | 5 | 292 R | 53.0% | 46.9% | 53.1% | 46.9% |
| 11,721 | HOOKSETT | 6,402 | 3,626 | 2,774 | 2 | 852 R | 56.6% | 43.3% | 56.7% | 43.3% |
| 22,928 | HUDSON | 11,476 | 6,412 | 5,054 | 10 | 1,358 R | 55.9% | 44.0% | 55.9% | 44.1% |
| 5,476 | JAFFREY | 2,918 | 1,386 | 1,525 | 7 | 139 D | 47.5% | 52.3% | 47.6% | 52.4% |
| 22,563 | KEENE | 12,157 | 3,898 | 8,217 | 42 | 4,319 D | 32.1% | 67.6% | 32.2% | 67.8% |
| 5,862 | KINGSTON | 3,213 | 1,774 | 1,439 | | 335 R | 55.2% | 44.8% | 55.2% | 44.8% |
| 16,411 | LACONIA | 7,790 | 4,174 | 3,594 | 22 | 580 R | 53.6% | 46.1% | 53.7% | 46.3% |
| 12,568 | LEBANON | 6,286 | 2,447 | 3,830 | 9 | 1,383 D | 38.9% | 60.9% | 39.0% | 61.0% |
| 7,360 | LITCHFIELD | 4,103 | 2,428 | 1,671 | 4 | 757 R | 59.2% | 40.7% | 59.2% | 40.8% |
| 5,845 | LITTLETON | 2,992 | 1,602 | 1,390 | | 212 R | 53.5% | 46.5% | 53.5% | 46.5% |
| 23,236 | LONDONDERRY | 12,054 | 6,911 | 5,119 | 24 | 1,792 R | 57.3% | 42.5% | 57.4% | 42.6% |
| 107,006 | MANCHESTER | 46,105 | 23,523 | 22,521 | 61 | 1,002 R | 51.0% | 48.8% | 51.1% | 48.9% |
| 25,119 | MERRIMACK TOWN | 14,515 | 7,873 | 6,610 | 32 | 1,263 R | 54.2% | 45.5% | 54.4% | 45.6% |
| 13,535 | MILFORD | 7,249 | 3,877 | 3,361 | 11 | 516 R | 53.5% | 46.4% | 53.6% | 46.4% |
| 86,605 | NASHUA | 39,135 | 18,801 | 20,303 | 31 | 1,502 D | 48.0% | 51.9% | 48.1% | 51.9% |
| 8,027 | NEWMARKET | 4,724 | 1,830 | 2,890 | 4 | 1,060 D | 38.7% | 61.2% | 38.8% | 61.2% |
| 6,269 | NEWPORT | 2,884 | 1,443 | 1,438 | 3 | 5 R | 50.0% | 49.9% | 50.1% | 49.9% |
| 10,914 | PELHAM | 6,334 | 3,652 | 2,679 | 3 | 973 R | 57.7% | 42.3% | 57.7% | 42.3% |
| 6,897 | PEMBROKE | 3,562 | 1,509 | 2,047 | 6 | 538 D | 42.4% | 57.5% | 42.4% | 57.6% |
| 5,883 | PETERBOROUGH | 3,708 | 1,315 | 2,382 | 11 | 1,067 D | 35.5% | 64.2% | 35.6% | 64.4% |
| 7,747 | PLAISTOW | 4,057 | 2,326 | 1,729 | 2 | 597 R | 57.3% | 42.6% | 57.4% | 42.6% |
| 5,892 | PLYMOUTH | 3,478 | 1,339 | 2,129 | 10 | 790 D | 38.5% | 61.2% | 38.6% | 61.4% |
| 20,784 | PORTSMOUTH | 12,497 | 3,921 | 8,554 | 22 | 4,633 D | 31.4% | 68.4% | 31.4% | 68.6% |
| 9,674 | RAYMOND | 4,728 | 2,635 | 2,087 | 6 | 548 R | 55.7% | 44.1% | 55.8% | 44.2% |
| 28,461 | ROCHESTER | 13,327 | 6,844 | 6,469 | 14 | 375 R | 51.4% | 48.5% | 51.4% | 48.6% |
| 28,112 | SALEM | 14,086 | 7,905 | 6,177 | 4 | 1,728 R | 56.1% | 43.9% | 56.1% | 43.9% |
| 7,934 | SEABROOK | 4,200 | 2,137 | 2,059 | 4 | 78 R | 50.9% | 49.0% | 50.9% | 49.1% |
| 11,477 | SOMERSWORTH | 5,438 | 2,396 | 3,037 | 5 | 641 D | 44.1% | 55.8% | 44.1% | 55.9% |
| 6,800 | SWANZEY | 3,437 | 1,501 | 1,936 | | 435 D | 43.7% | 56.3% | 43.7% | 56.3% |
| 7,776 | WEARE | 4,340 | 2,491 | 1,847 | 2 | 644 R | 57.4% | 42.6% | 57.4% | 42.6% |
| 10,709 | WINDHAM | 6,927 | 4,223 | 2,701 | 3 | 1,522 R | 61.0% | 39.0% | 61.0% | 39.0% |

# NEW HAMPSHIRE

## SENATOR 2004

| 2000 Census Population | County | Total Vote | Republican | Democratic | Other | Rep.-Dem. Plurality | Percentage Total Vote Rep. | Dem. | Major Vote Rep. | Dem. |
|---|---|---|---|---|---|---|---|---|---|---|
| 56,325 | BELKNAP | 31,613 | 22,949 | 8,643 | 21 | 14,306 R | 72.6% | 27.3% | 72.6% | 27.4% |
| 43,666 | CARROLL | 27,544 | 18,663 | 8,868 | 13 | 9,795 R | 67.8% | 32.2% | 67.8% | 32.2% |
| 73,825 | CHESHIRE | 40,090 | 21,901 | 18,116 | 73 | 3,785 R | 54.6% | 45.2% | 54.7% | 45.3% |
| 33,111 | COOS | 16,514 | 11,819 | 4,684 | 11 | 7,135 R | 71.6% | 28.4% | 71.6% | 28.4% |
| 81,743 | GRAFTON | 45,372 | 27,323 | 17,990 | 59 | 9,333 R | 60.2% | 39.7% | 60.3% | 39.7% |
| 380,841 | HILLSBOROUGH | 189,335 | 128,739 | 60,409 | 187 | 68,330 R | 68.0% | 31.9% | 68.1% | 31.9% |
| 136,225 | MERRIMACK | 75,000 | 49,804 | 25,117 | 79 | 24,687 R | 66.4% | 33.5% | 66.5% | 33.5% |
| 277,359 | ROCKINGHAM | 152,968 | 104,087 | 48,739 | 142 | 55,348 R | 68.0% | 31.9% | 68.1% | 31.9% |
| 112,233 | STRAFFORD | 57,444 | 36,321 | 21,037 | 86 | 15,284 R | 63.2% | 36.6% | 63.3% | 36.7% |
| 40,458 | SULLIVAN | 21,206 | 13,241 | 7,946 | 19 | 5,295 R | 62.4% | 37.5% | 62.5% | 37.5% |
| 1,235,786 | TOTAL | 657,086 | 434,847 | 221,549 | 690 | 213,298 R | 66.2% | 33.7% | 66.2% | 33.8% |

# NEW HAMPSHIRE

## SENATOR 2004

| 2000 Census Population | City/Town | Total Vote | Republican | Democratic | Other | Rep.-Dem. Plurality | | Percentage | | | |
|---|---|---|---|---|---|---|---|---|---|---|---|
| | | | | | | | | Total Vote | | Major Vote | |
| | | | | | | | | Rep. | Dem. | Rep. | Dem. |
| 10,769 | AMHERST | 6,945 | 4,773 | 2,158 | 14 | 2,615 | R | 68.7% | 31.1% | 68.9% | 31.1% |
| 6,178 | ATKINSON | 4,157 | 3,012 | 1,144 | 1 | 1,868 | R | 72.5% | 27.5% | 72.5% | 27.5% |
| 7,475 | BARRINGTON | 4,213 | 2,800 | 1,405 | 8 | 1,395 | R | 66.5% | 33.3% | 66.6% | 33.4% |
| 18,274 | BEDFORD | 10,661 | 8,311 | 2,350 | | 5,961 | R | 78.0% | 22.0% | 78.0% | 22.0% |
| 6,716 | BELMONT | 3,270 | 2,403 | 862 | 5 | 1,541 | R | 73.5% | 26.4% | 73.6% | 26.4% |
| 10,331 | BERLIN | 4,795 | 3,349 | 1,443 | 3 | 1,906 | R | 69.8% | 30.1% | 69.9% | 30.1% |
| 7,138 | BOW | 4,624 | 3,285 | 1,327 | 12 | 1,958 | R | 71.0% | 28.7% | 71.2% | 28.8% |
| 13,151 | CLAREMONT | 5,717 | 3,610 | 2,102 | 5 | 1,508 | R | 63.1% | 36.8% | 63.2% | 36.8% |
| 40,687 | CONCORD | 20,532 | 12,470 | 8,021 | 41 | 4,449 | R | 60.7% | 39.1% | 60.9% | 39.1% |
| 8,604 | CONWAY | 4,966 | 2,999 | 1,962 | 5 | 1,037 | R | 60.4% | 39.5% | 60.5% | 39.5% |
| 34,021 | DERRY | 14,340 | 9,675 | 4,661 | 4 | 5,014 | R | 67.5% | 32.5% | 67.5% | 32.5% |
| 26,884 | DOVER | 15,161 | 9,001 | 6,133 | 27 | 2,868 | R | 59.4% | 40.5% | 59.5% | 40.5% |
| 12,664 | DURHAM | 5,674 | 2,783 | 2,876 | 15 | 93 | D | 49.0% | 50.7% | 49.2% | 50.8% |
| 5,476 | EPPING | 3,048 | 2,101 | 946 | 1 | 1,155 | R | 68.9% | 31.0% | 69.0% | 31.0% |
| 14,058 | EXETER | 7,950 | 4,870 | 3,075 | 5 | 1,795 | R | 61.3% | 38.7% | 61.3% | 38.7% |
| 5,774 | FARMINGTON | 2,786 | 1,936 | 850 | | 1,086 | R | 69.5% | 30.5% | 69.5% | 30.5% |
| 8,405 | FRANKLIN | 3,681 | 2,425 | 1,254 | 2 | 1,171 | R | 65.9% | 34.1% | 65.9% | 34.1% |
| 6,803 | GILFORD | 4,475 | 3,397 | 1,078 | | 2,319 | R | 75.9% | 24.1% | 75.9% | 24.1% |
| 16,929 | GOFFSTOWN | 8,569 | 6,406 | 2,163 | | 4,243 | R | 74.8% | 25.2% | 74.8% | 25.2% |
| 8,297 | HAMPSTEAD | 4,748 | 3,477 | 1,271 | | 2,206 | R | 73.2% | 26.8% | 73.2% | 26.8% |
| 14,937 | HAMPTON | 9,122 | 6,086 | 3,031 | 5 | 3,055 | R | 66.7% | 33.2% | 66.8% | 33.2% |
| 10,850 | HANOVER | 6,217 | 2,284 | 3,920 | 13 | 1,636 | D | 36.7% | 63.1% | 36.8% | 63.2% |
| 7,015 | HOLLIS | 4,679 | 3,301 | 1,374 | 4 | 1,927 | R | 70.5% | 29.4% | 70.6% | 29.4% |
| 11,721 | HOOKSETT | 6,323 | 4,789 | 1,533 | 1 | 3,256 | R | 75.7% | 24.2% | 75.8% | 24.2% |
| 22,928 | HUDSON | 11,250 | 7,740 | 3,498 | 12 | 4,242 | R | 68.8% | 31.1% | 68.9% | 31.1% |
| 5,476 | JAFFREY | 2,917 | 1,804 | 1,106 | 7 | 698 | R | 61.8% | 37.9% | 62.0% | 38.0% |
| 22,563 | KEENE | 12,028 | 5,913 | 6,100 | 15 | 187 | D | 49.2% | 50.7% | 49.2% | 50.8% |
| 5,862 | KINGSTON | 3,130 | 2,182 | 946 | 2 | 1,236 | R | 69.7% | 30.2% | 69.8% | 30.2% |
| 16,411 | LACONIA | 7,767 | 5,604 | 2,160 | 3 | 3,444 | R | 72.2% | 27.8% | 72.2% | 27.8% |
| 12,568 | LEBANON | 6,215 | 3,290 | 2,914 | 11 | 376 | R | 52.9% | 46.9% | 53.0% | 47.0% |
| 7,360 | LITCHFIELD | 4,010 | 2,969 | 1,041 | | 1,928 | R | 74.0% | 26.0% | 74.0% | 26.0% |
| 5,845 | LITTLETON | 2,985 | 2,204 | 776 | 5 | 1,428 | R | 73.8% | 26.0% | 74.0% | 26.0% |
| 23,236 | LONDONDERRY | 11,799 | 8,450 | 3,324 | 25 | 5,126 | R | 71.6% | 28.2% | 71.8% | 28.2% |
| 107,006 | MANCHESTER | 45,461 | 31,468 | 13,942 | 51 | 17,526 | R | 69.2% | 30.7% | 69.3% | 30.7% |
| 25,119 | MERRIMACK TOWN | 14,245 | 10,057 | 4,186 | 2 | 5,871 | R | 70.6% | 29.4% | 70.6% | 29.4% |
| 13,535 | MILFORD | 7,148 | 4,889 | 2,247 | 12 | 2,642 | R | 68.4% | 31.4% | 68.5% | 31.5% |
| 86,605 | NASHUA | 38,348 | 24,305 | 13,994 | 49 | 10,311 | R | 63.4% | 36.5% | 63.5% | 36.5% |
| 8,027 | NEWMARKET | 4,613 | 2,697 | 1,913 | 3 | 784 | R | 58.5% | 41.5% | 58.5% | 41.5% |
| 6,269 | NEWPORT | 2,847 | 1,905 | 939 | 3 | 966 | R | 66.9% | 33.0% | 67.0% | 33.0% |
| 10,914 | PELHAM | 6,130 | 4,213 | 1,915 | 2 | 2,298 | R | 68.7% | 31.2% | 68.8% | 31.3% |
| 6,897 | PEMBROKE | 3,516 | 2,475 | 1,038 | 3 | 1,437 | R | 70.4% | 29.5% | 70.5% | 29.5% |
| 5,883 | PETERBOROUGH | 3,718 | 1,868 | 1,846 | 4 | 22 | R | 50.2% | 49.7% | 50.3% | 49.7% |
| 7,747 | PLAISTOW | 3,978 | 2,763 | 1,213 | 2 | 1,550 | R | 69.5% | 30.5% | 69.5% | 30.5% |
| 5,892 | PLYMOUTH | 3,351 | 1,814 | 1,531 | 6 | 283 | R | 54.1% | 45.7% | 54.2% | 45.8% |
| 20,784 | PORTSMOUTH | 12,201 | 6,655 | 5,517 | 29 | 1,138 | R | 54.5% | 45.2% | 54.7% | 45.3% |
| 9,674 | RAYMOND | 4,657 | 3,272 | 1,372 | 13 | 1,900 | R | 70.3% | 29.5% | 70.5% | 29.5% |
| 28,461 | ROCHESTER | 13,086 | 9,079 | 3,991 | 16 | 5,088 | R | 69.4% | 30.5% | 69.5% | 30.5% |
| 28,112 | SALEM | 13,734 | 9,393 | 4,337 | 4 | 5,056 | R | 68.4% | 31.6% | 68.4% | 31.6% |
| 7,934 | SEABROOK | 4,092 | 2,670 | 1,419 | 3 | 1,251 | R | 65.2% | 34.7% | 65.3% | 34.7% |
| 11,477 | SOMERSWORTH | 5,345 | 3,393 | 1,943 | 9 | 1,450 | R | 63.5% | 36.4% | 63.6% | 36.4% |
| 6,800 | SWANZEY | 3,419 | 2,068 | 1,350 | 1 | 718 | R | 60.5% | 39.5% | 60.5% | 39.5% |
| 7,776 | WEARE | 4,304 | 3,102 | 1,195 | 7 | 1,907 | R | 72.1% | 27.8% | 72.2% | 27.8% |
| 10,709 | WINDHAM | 6,761 | 4,999 | 1,758 | 4 | 3,241 | R | 73.9% | 26.0% | 74.0% | 26.0% |

# NEW HAMPSHIRE

## HOUSE OF REPRESENTATIVES

| CD | Year | Total Vote | Republican Vote | Republican Candidate | Democratic Vote | Democratic Candidate | Other Vote | Rep.-Dem. Plurality | Percentage Total Vote Rep. | Dem. | Major Vote Rep. | Dem. |
|----|------|-----------|-----------------|----------------------|-----------------|----------------------|-----------|---------------------|-------------------|------|------|------|
| 1 | 2004 | 323,372 | 204,836 | Bradley, Jeb* | 118,226 | Nadeau, Justin | 310 | 86,610 R | 63.3% | 36.6% | 63.4% | 36.6% |
| 1 | 2002 | 221,987 | 128,993 | Bradley, Jeb | 85,426 | Clark, Martha Fuller | 7,568 | 43,567 R | 58.1% | 38.5% | 60.2% | 39.8% |
| 2 | 2004 | 328,194 | 191,188 | Bass, Charles* | 125,280 | Hodes, Paul W. | 11,726 | 65,908 R | 58.3% | 38.2% | 60.4% | 39.6% |
| 2 | 2002 | 221,456 | 125,804 | Bass, Charles* | 90,479 | Swett, Katrina | 5,173 | 35,325 R | 56.8% | 40.9% | 58.2% | 41.8% |
| Total | 2004 | 651,566 | 396,024 | | 243,506 | | 12,036 | 152,518 R | 60.8% | 37.4% | 61.9% | 38.1% |
| Total | 2002 | 443,443 | 254,797 | | 175,905 | | 12,741 | 78,892 R | 57.5% | 39.7% | 59.2% | 40.8% |

An asterisk (*) denotes incumbent.

# NEW HAMPSHIRE

## GENERAL AND PRIMARY ELECTIONS

## 2004 GENERAL ELECTIONS

**President**    Other vote was 4,479 Independent (Ralph Nader); 372 write-in (Michael Badnarik); 357 write-in (John McCain); 161 write-in (Michael Peroutka); 42 write-in (Howard Dean); 14 write-in (Wesley Clark); 14 write-in (Wesley Powell); 8 write-in (Dennis Kucinich); 5 write-in (John Edwards); 538 scattered write-in.

**Governor**    Other vote was 740 scattered write-in.

**Senator**    Other vote was 102 write-in (Kenneth Blevens); 588 scattered write-in.

**House**    Other vote was:

  CD 1    310 scattered write-in.
  CD 2    11,311 Libertarian (Richard B. Kahn); 415 scattered write-in.

## 2004 PRIMARY ELECTIONS

**Primary**    September 14, 2004

| **Registration** (as of Sept. 14, 2004) | | |
|---|---|---|
| | Republican | 246,266 |
| | Democratic | 207,284 |
| | Undeclared | 281,504 |
| | TOTAL | 735,054 |

**Primary Type**    Semi-open—Registered Democrats and Republicans could vote only in their party's primary. "Undeclared" voters could participate in either party's primary.

# NEW HAMPSHIRE

## GENERAL AND PRIMARY ELECTIONS

Note: An asterisk (*) denotes incumbent.

| | REPUBLICAN PRIMARIES | | | DEMOCRATIC PRIMARIES | | |
|---|---|---|---|---|---|---|
| **President** | George W. Bush* | 53,962 | 79.8% | John Kerry | 84,377 | 38.4% |
| | Richard P. Bosa | 841 | 1.2% | Howard Dean | 57,761 | 26.3% |
| | John Buchanan | 836 | 1.2% | Wesley Clark | 27,314 | 12.4% |
| | John Donald Rigazio | 803 | 1.2% | John Edwards | 26,487 | 12.1% |
| | Robert Edward Haines | 579 | 0.9% | Joseph I. Lieberman | 18,911 | 8.6% |
| | Michael Callis | 388 | 0.6% | Dennis J. Kucinich | 3,114 | 1.4% |
| | Blake Ashby | 264 | 0.4% | Richard A. Gephardt | 419 | 0.2% |
| | Millie Howard | 239 | 0.4% | Al Sharpton | 347 | 0.2% |
| | "Tom" Laughlin | 154 | 0.2% | Lyndon H. LaRouche Jr. | 90 | |
| | "Bill" Wyatt | 153 | 0.2% | Willie Felix Carter | 86 | |
| | "Jim" Taylor | 124 | 0.2% | Carol Moseley Braun | 81 | |
| | Mark "Dick" Harnes | 87 | 0.1% | Edward Thomas O'Donnell Jr. | 79 | |
| | Cornelius E. O'Connor | 77 | 0.1% | Katherine Bateman | 68 | |
| | George Gostigian | 52 | 0.1% | "Randy" Crow | 60 | |
| | Write-in | 9,065 | 13.4% | Vincent S. Hamm | 58 | |
| | | | | Robert H. Linnell | 49 | |
| | | | | Gerry Dokka | 42 | |
| | | | | Caroline Pettinato Killeen | 31 | |
| | | | | R. Randy Lee | 15 | |
| | | | | Harry W. Braun III | 13 | |
| | | | | Mildred Glover | 11 | |
| | | | | Fern Penna | 8 | |
| | | | | Leonard Dennis Talbow | 8 | |
| | | | | Write-in | 358 | 0.2% |
| | TOTAL | 67,624 | | TOTAL | 219,787 | |

*Among the Republican write-ins were 2,819 votes for John Kerry, 1,789 for Howard Dean, 1,407 for Wesley Clark, 1,088 for John Edwards, and 914 for Joseph I. Lieberman.*

*Among the Democratic write-ins were 257 votes for George W. Bush.*

| | REPUBLICAN PRIMARIES | | | DEMOCRATIC PRIMARIES | | |
|---|---|---|---|---|---|---|
| **Governor** | Craig Benson* | 49,097 | 74.0% | John Lynch | 43,798 | 74.3% |
| | Charles A. Tarbell | 13,621 | 20.5% | Paul McEachern | 14,403 | 24.4% |
| | Write-in | 3,632 | 5.5% | Write-in | 761 | 1.3% |
| | TOTAL | 66,350 | | TOTAL | 58,962 | |
| **Senator** | Judd Gregg* | 60,597 | 91.6% | Doris Granny D. Haddock | 46,745 | 98.0% |
| | Tom Alciere | 2,682 | 4.1% | Write-in | 934 | 2.0% |
| | Michael D. Tipa | 2,563 | 3.9% | | | |
| | Write-in | 322 | 0.5% | | | |
| | TOTAL | 66,164 | | TOTAL | 47,679 | |
| **Congressional District 1** | Jeb Bradley* | 27,285 | 89.5% | Justin Nadeau | 12,150 | 52.8% |
| | R. "Bob" Tillman Bevill | 3,076 | 10.1% | Peter J. Duffy | 5,813 | 25.3% |
| | Write-in | 120 | 0.4% | "Bob" Bruce | 4,049 | 17.6% |
| | | | | Travis Joseph Liles | 831 | 3.6% |
| | | | | Write-in | 177 | 0.8% |
| | TOTAL | 30,481 | | TOTAL | 23,020 | |
| **Congressional District 2** | Charles Bass* | 25,414 | 71.2% | Paul W. Hodes | 15,161 | 60.0% |
| | Mark Brady | 10,167 | 28.5% | "Chris" Owen | 9,792 | 38.8% |
| | Write-in | 96 | 0.3% | Write-in | 311 | 1.2% |
| | TOTAL | 35,677 | | TOTAL | 25,264 | |

# NEW JERSEY

## GOVERNOR
Richard J. Codey (D). Became acting governor November 16, 2004, following the resignation of James E. McGreevey (D).

## SENATORS (2 Democrats)
Jon Corzine (D). Elected 2000 to a six-year term.

Frank R. Lautenberg (D). Elected 2002 to a six-year term. Previously elected 1994, 1988, 1982.

## REPRESENTATIVES (7 Democrats, 6 Republicans)
1. Robert E. Andrews (D)
2. Frank A. LoBiondo (R)
3. H. James Saxton (R)
4. Christopher H. Smith (R)
5. Scott Garrett (R)
6. Frank Pallone Jr. (D)
7. Mike Ferguson (R)
8. Bill Pascrell Jr. (D)
9. Steven R. Rothman (D)
10. Donald M. Payne (D)
11. Rodney Frelinghuysen (R)
12. Rush D. Holt (D)
13. Robert Menendez (D)

## POSTWAR VOTE FOR PRESIDENT

| | | Republican | | Democratic | | Other | | Total Vote | | Major Vote | |
|---|---|---|---|---|---|---|---|---|---|---|---|
| Year | Total Vote | Vote | Candidate | Vote | Candidate | Vote | Plurality | Rep. | Dem. | Rep. | Dem. |
| 2004 | 3,611,691 | 1,670,003 | Bush, George W. | 1,911,430 | Kerry, John | 30,258 | 241,427 D | 46.2% | 52.9% | 46.6% | 53.4% |
| 2000** | 3,187,226 | 1,284,173 | Bush, George W. | 1,788,850 | Gore, Al | 114,203 | 504,677 D | 40.3% | 56.1% | 41.8% | 58.2% |
| 1996** | 3,075,807 | 1,103,078 | Dole, Bob | 1,652,329 | Clinton, Bill | 320,400 | 549,251 D | 35.9% | 53.7% | 40.0% | 60.0% |
| 1992** | 3,343,594 | 1,356,865 | Bush, George | 1,436,206 | Clinton, Bill | 550,523 | 79,341 D | 40.6% | 43.0% | 48.6% | 51.4% |
| 1988 | 3,099,553 | 1,743,192 | Bush, George | 1,320,352 | Dukakis, Michael S. | 36,009 | 422,840 R | 56.2% | 42.6% | 56.9% | 43.1% |
| 1984 | 3,217,862 | 1,933,630 | Reagan, Ronald | 1,261,323 | Mondale, Walter F. | 22,909 | 672,307 R | 60.1% | 39.2% | 60.5% | 39.5% |
| 1980** | 2,975,684 | 1,546,557 | Reagan, Ronald | 1,147,364 | Carter, Jimmy | 281,763 | 399,193 R | 52.0% | 38.6% | 57.4% | 42.6% |
| 1976 | 3,014,472 | 1,509,688 | Ford, Gerald R. | 1,444,653 | Carter, Jimmy | 60,131 | 65,035 R | 50.1% | 47.9% | 51.1% | 48.9% |
| 1972 | 2,997,229 | 1,845,502 | Nixon, Richard M. | 1,102,211 | McGovern, George S. | 49,516 | 743,291 R | 61.6% | 36.8% | 62.6% | 37.4% |
| 1968** | 2,875,395 | 1,325,467 | Nixon, Richard M. | 1,264,206 | Humphrey, Hubert H. | 285,722 | 61,261 R | 46.1% | 44.0% | 51.2% | 48.8% |
| 1964 | 2,847,663 | 964,174 | Goldwater, Barry M. | 1,868,231 | Johnson, Lyndon B. | 15,258 | 904,057 D | 33.9% | 65.6% | 34.0% | 66.0% |
| 1960 | 2,773,111 | 1,363,324 | Nixon, Richard M. | 1,385,415 | Kennedy, John F. | 24,372 | 22,091 D | 49.2% | 50.0% | 49.6% | 50.4% |
| 1956 | 2,484,312 | 1,606,942 | Eisenhower, Dwight D. | 850,337 | Stevenson, Adlai E. | 27,033 | 756,605 R | 64.7% | 34.2% | 65.4% | 34.6% |
| 1952 | 2,418,554 | 1,373,613 | Eisenhower, Dwight D. | 1,015,902 | Stevenson, Adlai E. | 29,039 | 357,711 R | 56.8% | 42.0% | 57.5% | 42.5% |
| 1948 | 1,949,555 | 981,124 | Dewey, Thomas E. | 895,455 | Truman, Harry S. | 72,976 | 85,669 R | 50.3% | 45.9% | 52.3% | 47.7% |

In past elections, the other vote included: 2000 - 94,554 Green (Ralph Nader); 1996 - 262,134 Reform (Ross Perot); 1992 - 521,829 Independent (Perot); 1980 - 234,632 Independent (John Anderson); 1968 - 262,187 American Independent (George Wallace).

# NEW JERSEY

## POSTWAR VOTE FOR GOVERNOR

| Year | Total Vote | Republican | | Democratic | | Other Vote | Rep.-Dem. Plurality | Percentage | | | |
|------|-----------|------------|-----------|------------|-----------|------------|---------------------|------------|------|-----------|------|
| | | Vote | Candidate | Vote | Candidate | | | Total Vote | | Major Vote | |
| | | | | | | | | Rep. | Dem. | Rep. | Dem. |
| 2001 | 2,227,165 | 928,174 | Schundler, Bret | 1,256,853 | McGreevey, James E. | 42,138 | 328,679 D | 41.7% | 56.4% | 42.5% | 57.5% |
| 1997 | 2,418,344 | 1,133,394 | Whitman, Christine T. | 1,107,968 | McGreevey, James E. | 176,982 | 25,426 R | 46.9% | 45.8% | 50.6% | 49.4% |
| 1993 | 2,505,964 | 1,236,124 | Whitman, Christine T. | 1,210,031 | Florio, James J. | 59,809 | 26,093 R | 49.3% | 48.3% | 50.5% | 49.5% |
| 1989 | 2,253,764 | 838,553 | Courter, James A. | 1,379,937 | Florio, James J. | 35,274 | 541,384 D | 37.2% | 61.2% | 37.8% | 62.2% |
| 1985 | 1,972,624 | 1,372,631 | Kean, Thomas H. | 578,402 | Shapiro, Peter | 21,591 | 794,229 R | 69.6% | 29.3% | 70.4% | 29.6% |
| 1981 | 2,317,239 | 1,145,999 | Kean, Thomas H. | 1,144,202 | Florio, James J. | 27,038 | 1,797 R | 49.5% | 49.4% | 50.0% | 50.0% |
| 1977 | 2,126,264 | 888,880 | Bateman, Raymond H. | 1,184,564 | Byrne, Brendan T. | 52,820 | 295,684 D | 41.8% | 55.7% | 42.9% | 57.1% |
| 1973 | 2,122,009 | 676,235 | Sandman, Charles W. | 1,414,613 | Byrne, Brendan T. | 31,161 | 738,378 D | 31.9% | 66.7% | 32.3% | 67.7% |
| 1969 | 2,366,606 | 1,411,905 | Cahill, William T. | 911,003 | Meyner, Robert B. | 43,698 | 500,902 R | 59.7% | 38.5% | 60.8% | 39.2% |
| 1965 | 2,229,583 | 915,996 | Dumont, Wayne | 1,279,568 | Hughes, Richard J. | 34,019 | 363,572 D | 41.1% | 57.4% | 41.7% | 58.3% |
| 1961 | 2,152,662 | 1,049,274 | Mitchell, James P. | 1,084,194 | Hughes, Richard J. | 19,194 | 34,920 D | 48.7% | 50.4% | 49.2% | 50.8% |
| 1957 | 2,018,488 | 897,321 | Forbes, Malcolm S. | 1,101,130 | Meyner, Robert B. | 20,037 | 203,809 D | 44.5% | 54.6% | 44.9% | 55.1% |
| 1953 | 1,810,812 | 809,068 | Troast, Paul L. | 962,710 | Meyner, Robert B. | 39,034 | 153,642 D | 44.7% | 53.2% | 45.7% | 54.3% |
| 1949** | 1,718,788 | 885,882 | Driscoll, Alfred | 810,022 | Wene, Elmer H. | 22,884 | 75,860 R | 51.5% | 47.1% | 52.2% | 47.8% |
| 1946 | 1,414,527 | 807,378 | Driscoll, Alfred | 585,960 | Hansen, Lewis G. | 21,189 | 221,418 R | 57.1% | 41.4% | 57.9% | 42.1% |

The term of office of New Jersey's governor was increased from three to four years effective with the 1949 election.

## POSTWAR VOTE FOR SENATOR

| Year | Total Vote | Republican | | Democratic | | Other Vote | Rep.-Dem. Plurality | Percentage | | | |
|------|-----------|------------|-----------|------------|-----------|------------|---------------------|------------|------|-----------|------|
| | | Vote | Candidate | Vote | Candidate | | | Total Vote | | Major Vote | |
| | | | | | | | | Rep. | Dem. | Rep. | Dem. |
| 2002 | 2,112,604 | 928,439 | Forrester, Douglas R. | 1,138,193 | Lautenberg, Frank R. | 45,972 | 209,754 D | 43.9% | 53.9% | 44.9% | 55.1% |
| 2000 | 3,015,662 | 1,420,267 | Franks, Bob | 1,511,237 | Corzine, Jon | 84,158 | 90,970 D | 47.1% | 50.1% | 48.4% | 51.6% |
| 1996 | 2,884,106 | 1,227,817 | Zimmer, Dick | 1,519,328 | Torricelli, Robert G. | 136,961 | 291,511 D | 42.6% | 52.7% | 44.7% | 55.3% |
| 1994 | 2,054,887 | 966,244 | Haytaian, Garabed | 1,033,487 | Lautenberg, Frank R. | 55,156 | 67,243 D | 47.0% | 50.3% | 48.3% | 51.7% |
| 1990 | 1,938,454 | 918,874 | Whitman, Christine T. | 977,810 | Bradley, Bill | 41,770 | 58,936 D | 47.4% | 50.4% | 48.4% | 51.6% |
| 1988 | 2,987,634 | 1,349,937 | Dawkins, Peter M. | 1,599,905 | Lautenberg, Frank R. | 37,792 | 249,968 D | 45.2% | 53.6% | 45.8% | 54.2% |
| 1984 | 3,096,456 | 1,080,100 | Mochary, Mary V. | 1,986,644 | Bradley, Bill | 29,712 | 906,544 D | 34.9% | 64.2% | 35.2% | 64.8% |
| 1982 | 2,193,945 | 1,047,626 | Fenwick, Millicent | 1,117,549 | Lautenberg, Frank R. | 28,770 | 69,923 D | 47.8% | 50.9% | 48.4% | 51.6% |
| 1978 | 1,957,515 | 844,200 | Bell, Jeffrey | 1,082,960 | Bradley, Bill | 30,355 | 238,760 D | 43.1% | 55.3% | 43.8% | 56.2% |
| 1976 | 2,771,390 | 1,054,508 | Norcross, David F. | 1,681,140 | Williams, Harrison | 35,742 | 626,632 D | 38.0% | 60.7% | 38.5% | 61.5% |
| 1972 | 2,791,907 | 1,743,854 | Case, Clifford P. | 963,573 | Krebs, Paul J. | 84,480 | 780,281 R | 62.5% | 34.5% | 64.4% | 35.6% |
| 1970 | 2,142,105 | 903,026 | Gross, Nelson G. | 1,157,074 | Williams, Harrison | 82,005 | 254,048 D | 42.2% | 54.0% | 43.8% | 56.2% |
| 1966 | 2,131,188 | 1,279,343 | Case, Clifford P. | 788,021 | Wilentz, Warren W. | 63,824 | 491,322 R | 60.0% | 37.0% | 61.9% | 38.1% |
| 1964 | 2,710,441 | 1,011,610 | Shanley, Bernard M. | 1,678,051 | Williams, Harrison | 20,780 | 666,441 D | 37.3% | 61.9% | 37.6% | 62.4% |
| 1960 | 2,664,556 | 1,483,832 | Case, Clifford P. | 1,151,385 | Lord, Thorn | 29,339 | 332,447 R | 55.7% | 43.2% | 56.3% | 43.7% |
| 1958 | 1,881,329 | 882,287 | Kean, Robert W. | 966,832 | Williams, Harrison | 32,210 | 84,545 D | 46.9% | 51.4% | 47.7% | 52.3% |
| 1954 | 1,770,557 | 861,528 | Case, Clifford P. | 858,158 | Howell, Charles R. | 50,871 | 3,370 R | 48.7% | 48.5% | 50.1% | 49.9% |
| 1952 | 2,318,232 | 1,286,782 | Smith, H. Alexander | 1,011,187 | Alexander, Archibald | 20,263 | 275,595 R | 55.5% | 43.6% | 56.0% | 44.0% |
| 1948 | 1,869,882 | 934,720 | Hendrickson, Robert | 884,414 | Alexander, Archibald | 50,748 | 50,306 R | 50.0% | 47.3% | 51.4% | 48.6% |
| 1946 | 1,367,155 | 799,808 | Smith, H. Alexander | 548,458 | Brunner, George E. | 18,889 | 251,350 R | 58.5% | 40.1% | 59.3% | 40.7% |

# NEW JERSEY

Congressional districts first established for elections held in 2002
13 members

# NEW JERSEY

### Northern New Jersey Gateway Area

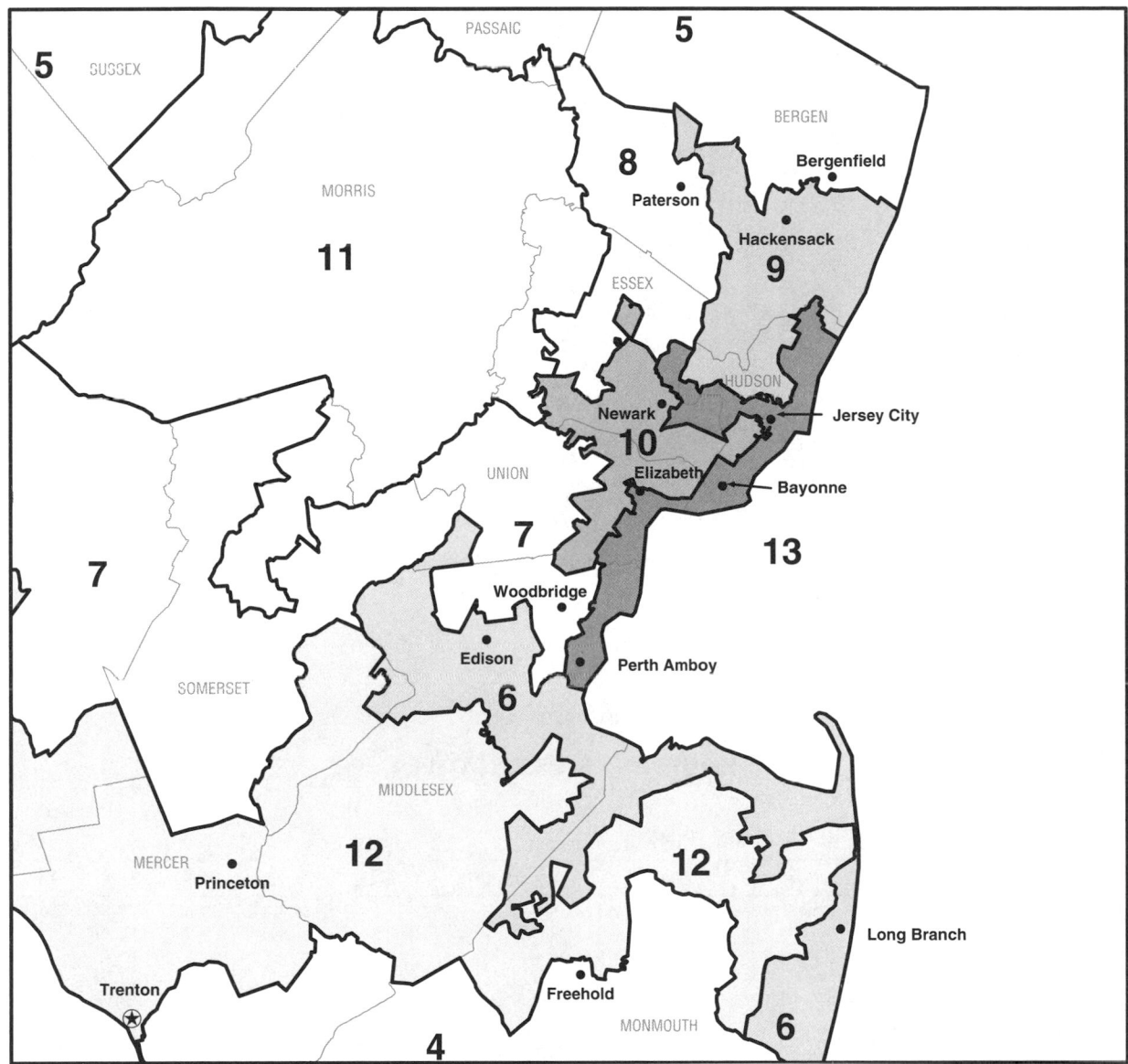

# NEW JERSEY

## PRESIDENT 2004

| 2000 Census Population | County | Total Vote | Republican | Democratic | Other | Rep.-Dem. Plurality | Total Vote Rep. | Total Vote Dem. | Major Vote Rep. | Major Vote Dem. |
|---|---|---|---|---|---|---|---|---|---|---|
| 252,552 | ATLANTIC | 106,097 | 49,487 | 55,746 | 864 | 6,259 D | 46.6% | 52.5% | 47.0% | 53.0% |
| 884,118 | BERGEN | 400,244 | 189,833 | 207,666 | 2,745 | 17,833 D | 47.4% | 51.9% | 47.8% | 52.2% |
| 423,394 | BURLINGTON | 207,956 | 95,936 | 110,411 | 1,609 | 14,475 D | 46.1% | 53.1% | 46.5% | 53.5% |
| 508,932 | CAMDEN | 220,933 | 81,427 | 137,765 | 1,741 | 56,338 D | 36.9% | 62.4% | 37.1% | 62.9% |
| 102,326 | CAPE MAY | 50,762 | 28,832 | 21,475 | 455 | 7,357 R | 56.8% | 42.3% | 57.3% | 42.7% |
| 146,438 | CUMBERLAND | 53,185 | 24,362 | 27,875 | 948 | 3,513 D | 45.8% | 52.4% | 46.6% | 53.4% |
| 793,633 | ESSEX | 289,348 | 83,374 | 203,681 | 2,293 | 120,307 D | 28.8% | 70.4% | 29.0% | 71.0% |
| 254,673 | GLOUCESTER | 127,964 | 60,033 | 66,835 | 1,096 | 6,802 D | 46.9% | 52.2% | 47.3% | 52.7% |
| 608,975 | HUDSON | 189,446 | 60,646 | 127,447 | 1,353 | 66,801 D | 32.0% | 67.3% | 32.2% | 67.8% |
| 121,989 | HUNTERDON | 66,680 | 39,888 | 26,050 | 742 | 13,838 R | 59.8% | 39.1% | 60.5% | 39.5% |
| 350,761 | MERCER | 149,510 | 56,604 | 91,580 | 1,326 | 34,976 D | 37.9% | 61.3% | 38.2% | 61.8% |
| 750,162 | MIDDLESEX | 295,805 | 126,492 | 166,628 | 2,685 | 40,136 D | 42.8% | 56.3% | 43.2% | 56.8% |
| 615,301 | MONMOUTH | 299,939 | 163,650 | 133,773 | 2,516 | 29,877 R | 54.6% | 44.6% | 55.0% | 45.0% |
| 470,212 | MORRIS | 235,154 | 135,241 | 98,066 | 1,847 | 37,175 R | 57.5% | 41.7% | 58.0% | 42.0% |
| 510,916 | OCEAN | 256,306 | 154,204 | 99,839 | 2,263 | 54,365 R | 60.2% | 39.0% | 60.7% | 39.3% |
| 489,049 | PASSAIC | 171,311 | 75,200 | 94,962 | 1,149 | 19,762 D | 43.9% | 55.4% | 44.2% | 55.8% |
| 64,285 | SALEM | 29,781 | 15,721 | 13,749 | 311 | 1,972 R | 52.8% | 46.2% | 53.3% | 46.7% |
| 297,490 | SOMERSET | 140,279 | 72,508 | 66,476 | 1,295 | 6,032 R | 51.7% | 47.4% | 52.2% | 47.8% |
| 144,166 | SUSSEX | 69,396 | 44,506 | 23,990 | 900 | 20,516 R | 64.1% | 34.6% | 65.0% | 35.0% |
| 522,541 | UNION | 203,387 | 82,517 | 119,372 | 1,498 | 36,855 D | 40.6% | 58.7% | 40.9% | 59.1% |
| 102,437 | WARREN | 48,208 | 29,542 | 18,044 | 622 | 11,498 R | 61.3% | 37.4% | 62.1% | 37.9% |
| 8,414,350 | TOTAL | 3,611,691 | 1,670,003 | 1,911,430 | 30,258 | 241,427 D | 46.2% | 52.9% | 46.6% | 53.4% |

# NEW JERSEY

## HOUSE OF REPRESENTATIVES

| CD | Year | Total Vote | Republican Vote | Republican Candidate | Democratic Vote | Democratic Candidate | Other Vote | Rep.-Dem. Plurality | Total Vote Rep. | Total Vote Dem. | Major Vote Rep. | Major Vote Dem. |
|---|---|---|---|---|---|---|---|---|---|---|---|---|
| 1 | 2004 | 268,203 | 66,109 | Hutchison, S. Daniel | 201,163 | Andrews, Robert E.* | 931 | 135,054 D | 24.6% | 75.0% | 24.7% | 75.3% |
| 1 | 2002 | 131,389 | | | 121,846 | Andrews, Robert E.* | 9,543 | 121,846 D | | 92.7% | | 100.0% |
| 2 | 2004 | 265,442 | 172,779 | LoBiondo, Frank A.* | 86,792 | Robb, Timothy J. | 5,871 | 85,987 R | 65.1% | 32.7% | 66.6% | 33.4% |
| 2 | 2002 | 168,799 | 116,834 | LoBiondo, Frank A.* | 47,735 | Farkas, Steven A. | 4,230 | 69,099 R | 69.2% | 28.3% | 71.0% | 29.0% |
| 3 | 2004 | 308,862 | 195,938 | Saxton, H. James* | 107,034 | Conaway, Herb | 5,890 | 88,904 R | 63.4% | 34.7% | 64.7% | 35.3% |
| 3 | 2002 | 189,739 | 123,375 | Saxton, H. James* | 64,364 | Strada, Richard | 2,000 | 59,011 R | 65.0% | 33.9% | 65.7% | 34.3% |
| 4 | 2004 | 287,553 | 192,671 | Smith, Christopher H.* | 92,826 | Vasquez, Amy | 2,056 | 99,845 R | 67.0% | 32.3% | 67.5% | 32.5% |
| 4 | 2002 | 174,301 | 115,293 | Smith, Christopher H.* | 55,967 | Brennan, Mary | 3,041 | 59,326 R | 66.1% | 32.1% | 67.3% | 32.7% |
| 5 | 2004 | 297,425 | 171,220 | Garrett, Scott* | 122,259 | Wolfe, Dorothea Anne | 3,946 | 48,961 R | 57.6% | 41.1% | 58.3% | 41.7% |
| 5 | 2002 | 199,851 | 118,881 | Garrett, Scott | 76,504 | Sumers, Anne | 4,466 | 42,377 R | 59.5% | 38.3% | 60.8% | 39.2% |
| 6 | 2004 | 230,151 | 70,942 | Fernandez, Sylvester | 153,981 | Pallone, Frank Jr.* | 5,228 | 83,039 D | 30.8% | 66.9% | 31.5% | 68.5% |
| 6 | 2002 | 137,495 | 42,479 | Medrow, Ric | 91,379 | Pallone, Frank Jr.* | 3,637 | 48,900 D | 30.9% | 66.5% | 31.7% | 68.3% |
| 7 | 2004 | 285,847 | 162,597 | Ferguson, Mike* | 119,081 | Brozak, Steve | 4,169 | 43,516 R | 56.9% | 41.7% | 57.7% | 42.3% |
| 7 | 2002 | 183,002 | 106,055 | Ferguson, Mike* | 74,879 | Carden, Tim | 2,068 | 31,176 R | 58.0% | 40.9% | 58.6% | 41.4% |
| 8 | 2004 | 218,820 | 62,747 | Ajjan, George | 152,001 | Pascrell, Bill Jr.* | 4,072 | 89,254 D | 28.7% | 69.5% | 29.2% | 70.8% |
| 8 | 2002 | 131,819 | 40,318 | Silverman, Jared | 88,101 | Pascrell, Bill Jr.* | 3,400 | 47,783 D | 30.6% | 66.8% | 31.4% | 68.6% |
| 9 | 2004 | 216,251 | 68,564 | Trawinski, Edward | 146,038 | Rothman, Steven R.* | 1,649 | 77,474 D | 31.7% | 67.5% | 31.9% | 68.1% |
| 9 | 2002 | 139,196 | 42,088 | Glass, Joseph | 97,108 | Rothman, Steven R.* | | 55,020 D | 30.2% | 69.8% | 30.2% | 69.8% |

# NEW JERSEY

## HOUSE OF REPRESENTATIVES

| | | Total | Republican | | Democratic | | Other | Rep.-Dem. | Percentage | | | |
| | | | | | | | | | Total Vote | | Major Vote | |
| CD | Year | Vote | Vote | Candidate | Vote | Candidate | Vote | Plurality | Rep. | Dem. | Rep. | Dem. |
|---|---|---|---|---|---|---|---|---|---|---|---|---|
| 10 | 2004 | 160,713 | | | 155,697 | Payne, Donald M.* | 5,016 | 155,697 D | | 96.9% | | 100.0% |
| 10 | 2002 | 102,346 | 15,913 | Wirtz, Andrew | 86,433 | Payne, Donald M.* | | 70,520 D | 15.5% | 84.5% | 15.5% | 84.5% |
| | | | | | | | | | | | | |
| 11 | 2004 | 296,002 | 200,915 | Frelinghuysen, Rodney* | 91,811 | Buell, James W. | 3,276 | 109,104 R | 67.9% | 31.0% | 68.6% | 31.4% |
| 11 | 2002 | 183,678 | 132,938 | Frelinghuysen, Rodney* | 48,477 | Pawar, Vij | 2,263 | 84,461 R | 72.4% | 26.4% | 73.3% | 26.7% |
| | | | | | | | | | | | | |
| 12 | 2004 | 289,785 | 115,014 | Spadea, Bill | 171,691 | Holt, Rush D.* | 3,080 | 56,677 D | 39.7% | 59.2% | 40.1% | 59.9% |
| 12 | 2002 | 171,713 | 62,938 | Soaries, DeForest "Buster" | 104,806 | Holt, Rush D.* | 3,969 | 41,868 D | 36.7% | 61.0% | 37.5% | 62.5% |
| | | | | | | | | | | | | |
| 13 | 2004 | 159,541 | 35,288 | Piatkowski, Richard W. | 121,018 | Menendez, Robert* | 3,235 | 85,730 D | 22.1% | 75.9% | 22.6% | 77.4% |
| 13 | 2002 | 92,731 | 16,852 | Geron, James | 72,605 | Menendez, Robert* | 3,274 | 55,753 D | 18.2% | 78.3% | 18.8% | 81.2% |
| | | | | | | | | | | | | |
| Total | 2004 | 3,284,595 | 1,514,784 | | 1,721,392 | | 48,419 | 206,608 D | 46.1% | 52.4% | 46.8% | 53.2% |
| Total | 2002 | 2,006,059 | 933,964 | | 1,030,204 | | 41,891 | 96,240 D | 46.6% | 51.4% | 47.6% | 52.4% |

An asterisk (*) denotes incumbent.

# NEW JERSEY

## GENERAL AND PRIMARY ELECTIONS

## 2004 GENERAL ELECTIONS

**President**    Other vote was 19,418 Independent (Ralph Nader); 4,514 Libertarian (Michael Badnarik); 2,750 Constitution (Michael Peroutka); 1,807 Green (David Cobb); 664 Socialist (Walter F. Brown); 575 Socialist Equality (Bill Van Auken); 530 Socialist Workers (Roger Calero).

**House**    Other vote was:

CD 1    931 E Pluribus Unum (Arturo Fulvio Croce).

CD 2    1,993 Jobs Equality Business (Willie Norwood); 1,767 Libertarian (Michael J. Matthews Jr.); 1,516 Green (Jose David Alcantara); 595 Socialist (Costantino Rozzo).

CD 3    4,914 U.S. Marijuana (R. Edward Forchion); 976 Libertarian (Frank Orland).

CD 4    2,056 Libertarian (Richard Edgar).

CD 5    1,857 Libertarian (Victor Kaplan); 1,515 NJ Conservative (Thomas A. Phelan); 574 Socialist (Gregory Pason).

CD 6    2,829 Libertarian (Virginia A. Flynn); 2,399 Help Middlesex/Monmouth/Somerset/Union Residents (Mac Dara F.X. Lyden).

CD 7    2,153 Libertarian (Thomas D. Abrams); 2,016 Independent (Matthew Angus Williams).

CD 8    4,072 Green (Joseph A. Fortunato).

CD 9    1,649 Libertarian (David Daly).

CD 10    2,927 Green (Toy-Ling Washington); 2,089 Socialist Workers (Sara J. Lobman).

CD 11    1,746 Immigration Moratorium Now (John Mele); 1,530 Libertarian (Austin S. Lett).

CD 12    1,562 Libertarian (Ken Chazotte); 1,518 Green (Daryl M. Brooks).

CD 13    1,282 Pro Life Conservative (Dick Hester); 1,066 Politicos son Corruptus (Herbert H. Shaw); 887 Socialist Workers (Angela L. Lariscy).

# NEW JERSEY

## GENERAL AND PRIMARY ELECTIONS

## 2004 PRIMARY ELECTIONS

| | | | | |
|---|---|---|---|---|
| Primary | June 8, 2004 | Registration (as of June 8, 2004) | Republican | 865,237 |
| | | | Democratic | 1,130,812 |
| | | | Independent | 15,357 |
| | | | Green | 493 |
| | | | Libertarian | 355 |
| | | | Other | 164 |
| | | | Unaffiliated | 2,611,586 |
| | | | TOTAL | 4,624,004 |

**Primary Type**   Semi-open—Registered Democrats and Republicans could vote only in their party's primary. "Unaffiliated" voters could participate in either party's primary if they were willing to become a member of that party.

Note:   An asterisk (*) denotes incumbent.

| | REPUBLICAN PRIMARIES | | | DEMOCRATIC PRIMARIES | | |
|---|---|---|---|---|---|---|
| President | George W. Bush* | 141,752 | 100.0% | John Kerry | 198,213 | 92.3% |
| | | | | Dennis J. Kucinich | 9,251 | 4.3% |
| | | | | Lyndon H. LaRouche Jr. | 4,514 | 2.1% |
| | | | | George H. Ballard III | 2,826 | 1.3% |
| | | | | TOTAL | 214,804 | |
| Congressional District 1 | S. Daniel Hutchison | 4,188 | 50.1% | Robert E. Andrews* | 20,961 | 100.0% |
| | John Cusack | 4,176 | 49.9% | | | |
| | TOTAL | 8,364 | | | | |
| Congressional District 2 | Frank A. LoBiondo* | 13,844 | 100.0% | Timothy J. Robb | 11,121 | 100.0% |
| Congressional District 3 | H. James Saxton* | 16,354 | 100.0% | Herb Conaway | 12,083 | 100.0% |
| Congressional District 4 | Christopher H. Smith* | 14,376 | 100.0% | Amy Vasquez | 9,588 | 100.0% |
| Congressional District 5 | Scott Garrett* | 21,523 | 100.0% | Dorothea Anne Wolfe | 7,588 | 82.7% |
| | | | | Frank Fracasso | 1,587 | 17.3% |
| | | | | TOTAL | 9,175 | |
| Congressional District 6 | Sylvester Fernandez | 5,623 | 100.0% | Frank Pallone Jr.* | 14,451 | 100.0% |
| Congressional District 7 | Mike Ferguson* | 13,456 | 100.0% | Steve Brozak | 9,094 | 100.0% |
| Congressional District 8 | George Ajjan | 4,506 | 100.0% | Bill Pascrell Jr.* | 12,143 | 100.0% |
| Congressional District 9 | No Republican candidate filed for the primary. Edward Trawinski received 211 write-in votes. | | | Steven R. Rothman* | 18,366 | 100.0% |
| Congressional District 10 | No Republican candidate | | | Donald M. Payne* | 26,063 | 100.0% |
| Congressional District 11 | Rodney Frelinghuysen* | 24,997 | 100.0% | James W. Buell | 8,548 | 100.0% |
| Congressional District 12 | Bill Spadea | 8,271 | 100.0% | Rush D. Holt* | 14,832 | 100.0% |
| Congressional District 13 | Richard W. Piatkowski | 3,199 | 100.0% | Robert Menendez* | 34,807 | 87.2% |
| | | | | Steven Fulop | 5,099 | 12.8% |
| | | | | TOTAL | 39,906 | |

# NEW MEXICO

## GOVERNOR
Bill Richardson (D). Elected 2002 to a four-year term.

## SENATORS (1 Democrat, 1 Republican)
Jeff Bingaman (D). Reelected 2000 to a six-year term. Previously elected 1994, 1988, 1982.

Pete V. Domenici (R). Reelected 2002 to a six-year term. Previously elected 1996, 1990, 1984, 1978, 1972.

## REPRESENTATIVES (2 Republicans, 1 Democrat)
1. Heather A. Wilson (R)
2. Steve Pearce (R)
3. Tom Udall (D)

## POSTWAR VOTE FOR PRESIDENT

| Year | Total Vote | Republican Vote | Republican Candidate | Democratic Vote | Democratic Candidate | Other Vote | Plurality | Total Vote Rep. | Total Vote Dem. | Major Vote Rep. | Major Vote Dem. |
|------|-----------|-----------------|----------------------|-----------------|----------------------|-----------|-----------|-----------------|-----------------|------------------|------------------|
| 2004 | 756,304 | 376,930 | Bush, George W. | 370,942 | Kerry, John | 8,432 | 5,988 R | 49.8% | 49.0% | 50.4% | 49.6% |
| 2000** | 598,605 | 286,417 | Bush, George W. | 286,783 | Gore, Al | 25,405 | 366 D | 47.8% | 47.9% | 50.0% | 50.0% |
| 1996** | 556,074 | 232,751 | Dole, Bob | 273,495 | Clinton, Bill | 49,828 | 40,744 D | 41.9% | 49.2% | 46.0% | 54.0% |
| 1992** | 569,986 | 212,824 | Bush, George | 261,617 | Clinton, Bill | 95,545 | 48,793 D | 37.3% | 45.9% | 44.9% | 55.1% |
| 1988 | 521,287 | 270,341 | Bush, George | 244,497 | Dukakis, Michael S. | 6,449 | 25,844 R | 51.9% | 46.9% | 52.5% | 47.5% |
| 1984 | 514,370 | 307,101 | Reagan, Ronald | 201,769 | Mondale, Walter F. | 5,500 | 105,332 R | 59.7% | 39.2% | 60.3% | 39.7% |
| 1980** | 456,971 | 250,779 | Reagan, Ronald | 167,826 | Carter, Jimmy | 38,366 | 82,953 R | 54.9% | 36.7% | 59.9% | 40.1% |
| 1976 | 418,409 | 211,419 | Ford, Gerald R. | 201,148 | Carter, Jimmy | 5,842 | 10,271 R | 50.5% | 48.1% | 51.2% | 48.8% |
| 1972 | 386,241 | 235,606 | Nixon, Richard M. | 141,084 | McGovern, George S. | 9,551 | 94,522 R | 61.0% | 36.5% | 62.5% | 37.5% |
| 1968** | 327,350 | 169,692 | Nixon, Richard M. | 130,081 | Humphrey, Hubert H. | 27,577 | 39,611 R | 51.8% | 39.7% | 56.6% | 43.4% |
| 1964 | 328,645 | 132,838 | Goldwater, Barry M. | 194,015 | Johnson, Lyndon B. | 1,792 | 61,177 D | 40.4% | 59.0% | 40.6% | 59.4% |
| 1960 | 311,107 | 153,733 | Nixon, Richard M. | 156,027 | Kennedy, John F. | 1,347 | 2,294 D | 49.4% | 50.2% | 49.6% | 50.4% |
| 1956 | 253,926 | 146,788 | Eisenhower, Dwight D. | 106,098 | Stevenson, Adlai E. | 1,040 | 40,690 R | 57.8% | 41.8% | 58.0% | 42.0% |
| 1952 | 238,608 | 132,170 | Eisenhower, Dwight D. | 105,661 | Stevenson, Adlai E. | 777 | 26,509 R | 55.4% | 44.3% | 55.6% | 44.4% |
| 1948 | 187,063 | 80,303 | Dewey, Thomas E. | 105,464 | Truman, Harry S. | 1,296 | 25,161 D | 42.9% | 56.4% | 43.2% | 56.8% |

In past elections, the other vote included: 2000 - 21,251 Green (Ralph Nader); 1996 - 32,257 Reform (Ross Perot); 1992 - 91,895 Independent (Perot); 1980 - 29,459 Independent (John Anderson); 1968 - 25,737 American Independent (George Wallace).

# NEW MEXICO

## POSTWAR VOTE FOR GOVERNOR

| Year | Total Vote | Republican Vote | Republican Candidate | Democratic Vote | Democratic Candidate | Other Vote | Rep.-Dem. Plurality | Total Vote Rep. | Total Vote Dem. | Major Vote Rep. | Major Vote Dem. |
|---|---|---|---|---|---|---|---|---|---|---|---|
| 2002 | 484,233 | 189,074 | Sanchez, John A. | 268,693 | Richardson, Bill | 26,466 | 79,619 D | 39.0% | 55.5% | 41.3% | 58.7% |
| 1998 | 498,703 | 271,948 | Johnson, Gary E. | 226,755 | Chavez, Martin J. | | 45,193 R | 54.5% | 45.5% | 54.5% | 45.5% |
| 1994 | 467,621 | 232,945 | Johnson, Gary E. | 186,686 | King, Bruce | 47,990 | 46,259 R | 49.8% | 39.9% | 55.5% | 44.5% |
| 1990 | 411,236 | 185,692 | Bond, Frank M. | 224,564 | King, Bruce | 980 | 38,872 D | 45.2% | 54.6% | 45.3% | 54.7% |
| 1986 | 394,833 | 209,455 | Carruthers, Garrey E. | 185,378 | Powell. Ray B. | | 24,077 R | 53.0% | 47.0% | 53.0% | 47.0% |
| 1982 | 407,466 | 191,626 | Irick, John B. | 215,840 | Anaya, Toney | | 24,214 D | 47.0% | 53.0% | 47.0% | 53.0% |
| 1978 | 345,577 | 170,848 | Skeen, Joseph R. | 174,631 | King, Bruce | 98 | 3,783 D | 49.4% | 50.5% | 49.5% | 50.5% |
| 1974 | 328,742 | 160,430 | Skeen, Joseph R. | 164,172 | Apodaca, Jerry | 4,140 | 3,742 D | 48.8% | 49.9% | 49.4% | 50.6% |
| 1970** | 290,375 | 134,640 | Domenici, Pete V. | 148,835 | King, Bruce | 6,900 | 14,195 D | 46.4% | 51.3% | 47.5% | 52.5% |
| 1968 | 318,975 | 160,140 | Cargo, David F. | 157,230 | Chavez, Fabian | 1,605 | 2,910 R | 50.2% | 49.3% | 50.5% | 49.5% |
| 1966 | 260,232 | 134,625 | Cargo, David F. | 125,587 | Lusk, Thomas E. | 20 | 9,038 R | 51.7% | 48.3% | 51.7% | 48.3% |
| 1964 | 318,042 | 126,540 | Tucker, Merle H. | 191,497 | Campbell, Jack M. | 5 | 64,957 D | 39.8% | 60.2% | 39.8% | 60.2% |
| 1962 | 247,135 | 116,184 | Mechem, Edwin L. | 130,933 | Campbell, Jack M. | 18 | 14,749 D | 47.0% | 53.0% | 47.0% | 53.0% |
| 1960 | 305,542 | 153,765 | Mechem, Edwin L. | 151,777 | Burroughs, John | | 1,988 R | 50.3% | 49.7% | 50.3% | 49.7% |
| 1958 | 205,048 | 101,567 | Mechem, Edwin L. | 103,481 | Burroughs, John | | 1,914 D | 49.5% | 50.5% | 49.5% | 50.5% |
| 1956 | 251,751 | 131,488 | Mechem, Edwin L. | 120,263 | Simms, John F. | | 11,225 R | 52.2% | 47.8% | 52.2% | 47.8% |
| 1954 | 193,956 | 83,373 | Stockton, Alvin | 110,583 | Simms, John F. | | 27,210 D | 43.0% | 57.0% | 43.0% | 57.0% |
| 1952 | 240,150 | 129,116 | Mechem, Edwin L. | 111,034 | Grantham, Everett | | 18,082 R | 53.8% | 46.2% | 53.8% | 46.2% |
| 1950 | 180,205 | 96,846 | Mechem, Edwin L. | 83,359 | Miles, John E. | | 13,487 R | 53.7% | 46.3% | 53.7% | 46.3% |
| 1948 | 189,992 | 86,023 | Lujan, Manuel | 103,969 | Mabry, Thomas J. | | 17,946 D | 45.3% | 54.7% | 45.3% | 54.7% |
| 1946 | 132,930 | 62,875 | Safford, Edward L. | 70,055 | Mabry, Thomas J. | | 7,180 D | 47.3% | 52.7% | 47.3% | 52.7% |

The term of New Mexico's governor was increased from two to four years effective with the 1970 election.

## POSTWAR VOTE FOR SENATOR

| Year | Total Vote | Republican Vote | Republican Candidate | Democratic Vote | Democratic Candidate | Other Vote | Rep.-Dem. Plurality | Total Vote Rep. | Total Vote Dem. | Major Vote Rep. | Major Vote Dem. |
|---|---|---|---|---|---|---|---|---|---|---|---|
| 2002 | 483,340 | 314,301 | Domenici, Pete V. | 169,039 | Tristani, Gloria | | 145,262 R | 65.0% | 35.0% | 65.0% | 35.0% |
| 2000 | 589,526 | 225,517 | Redmond, Bill | 363,744 | Bingaman, Jeff | 265 | 138,227 D | 38.3% | 61.7% | 38.3% | 61.7% |
| 1996 | 551,821 | 357,171 | Domenici, Pete V. | 164,356 | Trujillo, Art | 30,294 | 192,815 R | 64.7% | 29.8% | 68.5% | 31.5% |
| 1994 | 463,196 | 213,025 | McMillan, Colin R. | 249,989 | Bingaman, Jeff | 182 | 36,964 D | 46.0% | 54.0% | 46.0% | 54.0% |
| 1990 | 406,938 | 296,712 | Domenici, Pete V. | 110,033 | Benavides, Tom R. | 193 | 186,679 R | 72.9% | 27.0% | 72.9% | 27.1% |
| 1988 | 508,598 | 186,579 | Valentine, William | 321,983 | Bingaman, Jeff | 36 | 135,404 D | 36.7% | 63.3% | 36.7% | 63.3% |
| 1984 | 502,634 | 361,371 | Domenici, Pete V. | 141,253 | Pratt, Judith A. | 10 | 220,118 R | 71.9% | 28.1% | 71.9% | 28.1% |
| 1982 | 404,810 | 187,128 | Schmitt, Harrison | 217,682 | Bingaman, Jeff | | 30,554 D | 46.2% | 53.8% | 46.2% | 53.8% |
| 1978 | 343,554 | 183,442 | Domenici, Pete V. | 160,045 | Anaya, Toney | 67 | 23,397 R | 53.4% | 46.6% | 53.4% | 46.6% |
| 1976 | 413,141 | 234,681 | Schmitt, Harrison | 176,382 | Montoya, Joseph M. | 2,078 | 58,299 R | 56.8% | 42.7% | 57.1% | 42.9% |
| 1972 | 378,330 | 204,253 | Domenici, Pete V. | 173,815 | Daniels, Jack | 262 | 30,438 R | 54.0% | 45.9% | 54.0% | 46.0% |
| 1970 | 289,906 | 135,004 | Carter, Anderson | 151,486 | Montoya, Joseph M. | 3,416 | 16,482 D | 46.6% | 52.3% | 47.1% | 52.9% |
| 1966 | 258,203 | 120,988 | Carter, Anderson | 137,205 | Anderson, Clinton P. | 10 | 16,217 D | 46.9% | 53.1% | 46.9% | 53.1% |
| 1964 | 325,774 | 147,562 | Mechem, Edwin L. | 178,209 | Montoya, Joseph M. | 3 | 30,647 D | 45.3% | 54.7% | 45.3% | 54.7% |
| 1960 | 300,551 | 109,897 | Colwes, William F. | 190,654 | Anderson, Clinton P. | | 80,757 D | 36.6% | 63.4% | 36.6% | 63.4% |
| 1958 | 203,323 | 75,827 | Atchley, Forrest S. | 127,496 | Chavez, Dennis | | 51,669 D | 37.3% | 62.7% | 37.3% | 62.7% |
| 1954 | 194,422 | 83,071 | Mechem, Edwin L. | 111,351 | Anderson, Clinton P. | | 28,280 D | 42.7% | 57.3% | 42.7% | 57.3% |
| 1952 | 239,711 | 117,168 | Hurley, Patrick J. | 122,543 | Chavez, Dennis | | 5,375 D | 48.9% | 51.1% | 48.9% | 51.1% |
| 1948 | 188,495 | 80,226 | Hurley, Patrick J. | 108,269 | Anderson, Clinton P. | | 28,043 D | 42.6% | 57.4% | 42.6% | 57.4% |
| 1946 | 133,282 | 64,632 | Hurley, Patrick J. | 68,650 | Chavez, Dennis | | 4,018 D | 48.5% | 51.5% | 48.5% | 51.5% |

# NEW MEXICO

Congressional districts first established for elections held in 2002
3 members

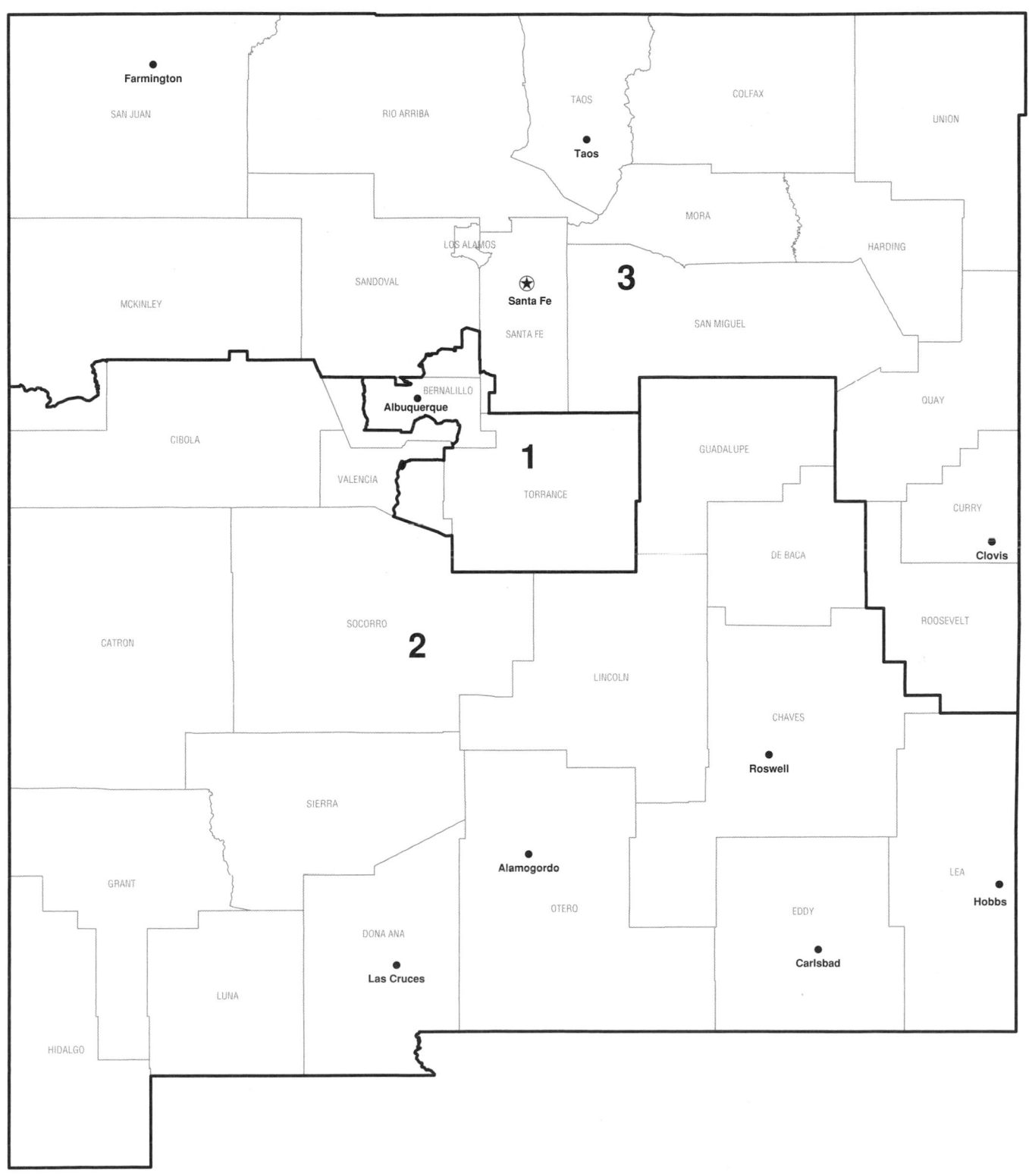

# NEW MEXICO

## PRESIDENT 2004

| 2000 Census Population | County | Total Vote | Republican | Democratic | Other | Rep.-Dem. Plurality | Percentage Total Vote Rep. | Dem. | Major Vote Rep. | Dem. |
|---|---|---|---|---|---|---|---|---|---|---|
| 556,678 | BERNALILLO | 256,811 | 121,454 | 132,252 | 3,105 | 10,798 D | 47.3% | 51.5% | 47.9% | 52.1% |
| 3,543 | CATRON | 1,993 | 1,427 | 551 | 15 | 876 R | 71.6% | 27.6% | 72.1% | 27.9% |
| 61,382 | CHAVES | 21,705 | 14,773 | 6,726 | 206 | 8,047 R | 68.1% | 31.0% | 68.7% | 31.3% |
| 25,595 | CIBOLA | 7,487 | 3,477 | 3,913 | 97 | 436 D | 46.4% | 52.3% | 47.1% | 52.9% |
| 14,189 | COLFAX | 5,968 | 3,082 | 2,824 | 62 | 258 R | 51.6% | 47.3% | 52.2% | 47.8% |
| 45,044 | CURRY | 14,286 | 10,649 | 3,541 | 96 | 7,108 R | 74.5% | 24.8% | 75.0% | 25.0% |
| 2,240 | DE BACA | 993 | 706 | 281 | 6 | 425 R | 71.1% | 28.3% | 71.5% | 28.5% |
| 174,682 | DONA ANA | 61,960 | 29,548 | 31,762 | 650 | 2,214 D | 47.7% | 51.3% | 48.2% | 51.8% |
| 51,658 | EDDY | 20,270 | 13,268 | 6,880 | 122 | 6,388 R | 65.5% | 33.9% | 65.9% | 34.1% |
| 31,002 | GRANT | 13,392 | 6,135 | 7,095 | 162 | 960 D | 45.8% | 53.0% | 46.4% | 53.6% |
| 4,680 | GUADALUPE | 2,267 | 914 | 1,340 | 13 | 426 D | 40.3% | 59.1% | 40.6% | 59.4% |
| 810 | HARDING | 644 | 380 | 259 | 5 | 121 R | 59.0% | 40.2% | 59.5% | 40.5% |
| 5,932 | HIDALGO | 1,964 | 1,081 | 861 | 22 | 220 R | 55.0% | 43.8% | 55.7% | 44.3% |
| 55,511 | LEA | 18,181 | 14,430 | 3,646 | 105 | 10,784 R | 79.4% | 20.1% | 79.8% | 20.2% |
| 19,411 | LINCOLN | 9,014 | 6,070 | 2,822 | 122 | 3,248 R | 67.3% | 31.3% | 68.3% | 31.7% |
| 18,343 | LOS ALAMOS | 11,197 | 5,810 | 5,206 | 181 | 604 R | 51.9% | 46.5% | 52.7% | 47.3% |
| 25,016 | LUNA | 7,593 | 4,164 | 3,340 | 89 | 824 R | 54.8% | 44.0% | 55.5% | 44.5% |
| 74,798 | MCKINLEY | 20,623 | 7,351 | 13,051 | 221 | 5,700 D | 35.6% | 63.3% | 36.0% | 64.0% |
| 5,180 | MORA | 2,826 | 928 | 1,876 | 22 | 948 D | 32.8% | 66.4% | 33.1% | 66.9% |
| 62,298 | OTERO | 20,764 | 14,066 | 6,433 | 265 | 7,633 R | 67.7% | 31.0% | 68.6% | 31.4% |
| 10,155 | QUAY | 4,117 | 2,661 | 1,422 | 34 | 1,239 R | 64.6% | 34.5% | 65.2% | 34.8% |
| 41,190 | RIO ARRIBA | 14,999 | 5,149 | 9,753 | 97 | 4,604 D | 34.3% | 65.0% | 34.6% | 65.4% |
| 18,018 | ROOSEVELT | 7,144 | 4,997 | 2,082 | 65 | 2,915 R | 69.9% | 29.1% | 70.6% | 29.4% |
| 89,908 | SANDOVAL | 44,541 | 22,628 | 21,421 | 492 | 1,207 R | 50.8% | 48.1% | 51.4% | 48.6% |
| 113,801 | SAN JUAN | 45,006 | 29,525 | 14,843 | 638 | 14,682 R | 65.6% | 33.0% | 66.5% | 33.5% |
| 30,126 | SAN MIGUEL | 12,116 | 3,313 | 8,683 | 120 | 5,370 D | 27.3% | 71.7% | 27.6% | 72.4% |
| 129,292 | SANTA FE | 66,200 | 18,466 | 47,074 | 660 | 28,608 D | 27.9% | 71.1% | 28.2% | 71.8% |
| 13,270 | SIERRA | 5,157 | 3,162 | 1,926 | 69 | 1,236 R | 61.3% | 37.3% | 62.1% | 37.9% |
| 18,078 | SOCORRO | 7,851 | 3,696 | 4,025 | 130 | 329 D | 47.1% | 51.3% | 47.9% | 52.1% |
| 29,979 | TAOS | 14,835 | 3,666 | 10,987 | 182 | 7,321 D | 24.7% | 74.1% | 25.0% | 75.0% |
| 16,911 | TORRANCE | 6,507 | 4,026 | 2,386 | 95 | 1,640 R | 61.9% | 36.7% | 62.8% | 37.2% |
| 4,174 | UNION | 1,881 | 1,454 | 411 | 16 | 1,043 R | 77.3% | 21.9% | 78.0% | 22.0% |
| 66,152 | VALENCIA | 26,012 | 14,474 | 11,270 | 268 | 3,204 R | 55.6% | 43.3% | 56.2% | 43.8% |
| 1,819,046 | TOTAL | 756,304 | 376,930 | 370,942 | 8,432 | 5,988 R | 49.8% | 49.0% | 50.4% | 49.6% |

# NEW MEXICO

## HOUSE OF REPRESENTATIVES

| CD | Year | Total Vote | Republican Vote | Republican Candidate | Democratic Vote | Democratic Candidate | Other Vote | Rep.-Dem. Plurality | Percentage Total Vote Rep. | Dem. | Major Vote Rep. | Dem. |
|---|---|---|---|---|---|---|---|---|---|---|---|---|
| 1 | 2004 | 270,905 | 147,372 | Wilson, Heather A.* | 123,339 | Romero, Richard M. | 194 | 24,033 R | 54.4% | 45.5% | 54.4% | 45.6% |
| 1 | 2002 | 172,945 | 95,711 | Wilson, Heather A.* | 77,234 | Romero, Richard M. | | 18,477 R | 55.3% | 44.7% | 55.3% | 44.7% |
| 2 | 2004 | 216,790 | 130,498 | Pearce, Steve* | 86,292 | King, Gary K. | | 44,206 R | 60.2% | 39.8% | 60.2% | 39.8% |
| 2 | 2002 | 141,629 | 79,631 | Pearce, Steve | 61,916 | Smith, John Arthur | 82 | 17,715 R | 56.2% | 43.7% | 56.3% | 43.7% |
| 3 | 2004 | 255,204 | 79,935 | Tucker, Gregory M. | 175,269 | Udall, Tom* | | 95,334 D | 31.3% | 68.7% | 31.3% | 68.7% |
| 3 | 2002 | 122,950 | | | 122,950 | Udall, Tom* | | 122,950 D | | 100.0% | | 100.0% |
| Total | 2004 | 742,899 | 357,805 | | 384,900 | | 194 | 27,095 D | 48.2% | 51.8% | 48.2% | 51.8% |
| Total | 2002 | 437,524 | 175,342 | | 262,100 | | 82 | 86,758 D | 40.1% | 59.9% | 40.1% | 59.9% |

An asterisk (*) denotes incumbent.

# NEW MEXICO

## GENERAL AND PRIMARY ELECTIONS

## 2004 GENERAL ELECTIONS

**President**    Other vote was 4,053 Independent (Ralph Nader); 2,382 Libertarian (Michael Badnarik); 1,226 Green (David Cobb); 771 Constitution (Michael Peroutka).

**House**    Other vote was:

CD 1    194 write-in (Orlin G. Cole).
CD 2
CD 3

## 2004 PRIMARY ELECTIONS

| **Primary** | June 1, 2004 | **Registration** (as of May 5, 2004) | Republican | 310,061 |
|---|---|---|---|---|
| | | | Democratic | 498,991 |
| | | | Green | 10,107 |
| | | | Other Parties | 17,602 |
| | | | No Party | 121,618 |
| | | | TOTAL | 958,379 |

**Primary Type**    Closed—Only registered Democrats and Republicans could vote in their party's primary.

Note:    An asterisk (*) denotes incumbent.

| | REPUBLICAN PRIMARIES | | | DEMOCRATIC PRIMARIES | | |
|---|---|---|---|---|---|---|
| President | George W. Bush* | 49,165 | 100.0% | No Democratic primary | | |
| Congressional District 1 | Heather A. Wilson* | 15,690 | 100.0% | Richard M. Romero | 20,632 | 58.3% |
| | | | | Miles Jay Nelson | 14,768 | 41.7% |
| | | | | TOTAL | 35,400 | |
| Congressional District 2 | Steve Pearce* | 18,644 | 100.0% | Gary K. King | 22,779 | 64.9% |
| | | | | Jeff Steinborn | 12,335 | 35.1% |
| | | | | TOTAL | 35,114 | |
| Congressional District 3 | Gregory M. Tucker | 14,038 | 100.0% | Tom Udall* | 50,871 | 100.0% |

# NEW YORK

## GOVERNOR
George E. Pataki (R). Reelected 2002 to a four-year term. Previously elected 1998, 1994.

## SENATORS (2 Democrats)
Hillary Rodham Clinton (D). Elected 2000 to a six-year term.

Charles E. Schumer (D). Reelected 2004 to a six-year term. Previously elected 1998.

## REPRESENTATIVES (20 Democrats, 9 Republicans)

1. Timothy H. Bishop (D)
2. Steve Israel (D)
3. Peter T. King (R)
4. Carolyn McCarthy (D)
5. Gary L. Ackerman (D)
6. Gregory W. Meeks (D)
7. Joseph Crowley (D)
8. Jerrold Nadler (D)
9. Anthony Weiner (D)
10. Edolphus Towns (D)
11. Major R. Owens (D)
12. Nydia M. Velázquez (D)
13. Vito J. Fossella (R)
14. Carolyn B. Maloney (D)
15. Charles B. Rangel (D)
16. Jose E. Serrano (D)
17. Eliot L. Engel (D)
18. Nita M. Lowey (D)
19. Sue W. Kelly (R)
20. John E. Sweeney (R)
21. Michael R. McNulty (D)
22. Maurice D. Hinchey (D)
23. John M. McHugh (R)
24. Sherwood Boehlert (R)
25. James T. Walsh (R)
26. Thomas M. Reynolds (R)
27. Brian Higgins (D)
28. Louise M. Slaughter (D)
29. John R. "Randy" Kuhl Jr. (R)

## POSTWAR VOTE FOR PRESIDENT

| | | Republican | | Democratic | | Other | | Percentage | | | |
| | | | | | | | | Total Vote | | Major Vote | |
| Year | Total Vote | Vote | Candidate | Vote | Candidate | Vote | Plurality | Rep. | Dem. | Rep. | Dem. |
|---|---|---|---|---|---|---|---|---|---|---|---|
| 2004 | 7,391,036 | 2,962,567 | Bush, George W. | 4,314,280 | Kerry, John | 114,189 | 1,351,713 D | 40.1% | 58.4% | 40.7% | 59.3% |
| 2000** | 6,821,999 | 2,403,374 | Bush, George W. | 4,107,697 | Gore, Al | 310,928 | 1,704,323 D | 35.2% | 60.2% | 36.9% | 63.1% |
| 1996** | 6,316,129 | 1,933,492 | Dole, Bob | 3,756,177 | Clinton, Bill | 626,460 | 1,822,685 D | 30.6% | 59.5% | 34.0% | 66.0% |
| 1992** | 6,926,925 | 2,346,649 | Bush, George | 3,444,450 | Clinton, Bill | 1,135,826 | 1,097,801 D | 33.9% | 49.7% | 40.5% | 59.5% |
| 1988 | 6,485,683 | 3,081,871 | Bush, George | 3,347,882 | Dukakis, Michael S. | 55,930 | 266,011 D | 47.5% | 51.6% | 47.9% | 52.1% |
| 1984 | 6,806,810 | 3,664,763 | Reagan, Ronald | 3,119,609 | Mondale, Walter F. | 22,438 | 545,154 R | 53.8% | 45.8% | 54.0% | 46.0% |
| 1980** | 6,201,959 | 2,893,831 | Reagan, Ronald | 2,728,372 | Carter, Jimmy | 579,756 | 165,459 R | 46.7% | 44.0% | 51.5% | 48.5% |
| 1976 | 6,534,170 | 3,100,791 | Ford, Gerald R. | 3,389,558 | Carter, Jimmy | 43,821 | 288,767 D | 47.5% | 51.9% | 47.8% | 52.2% |
| 1972 | 7,165,919 | 4,192,778 | Nixon, Richard M. | 2,951,084 | McGovern, George S. | 22,057 | 1,241,694 R | 58.5% | 41.2% | 58.7% | 41.3% |
| 1968** | 6,791,688 | 3,007,932 | Nixon, Richard M. | 3,378,470 | Humphrey, Hubert H. | 405,286 | 370,538 D | 44.3% | 49.7% | 47.1% | 52.9% |
| 1964 | 7,166,275 | 2,243,559 | Goldwater, Barry M. | 4,913,102 | Johnson, Lyndon B. | 9,614 | 2,669,543 D | 31.3% | 68.6% | 31.3% | 68.7% |
| 1960 | 7,291,079 | 3,446,419 | Nixon, Richard M. | 3,830,085 | Kennedy, John F. | 14,575 | 383,666 D | 47.3% | 52.5% | 47.4% | 52.6% |
| 1956 | 7,095,971 | 4,345,506 | Eisenhower, Dwight D. | 2,747,944 | Stevenson, Adlai E. | 2,521 | 1,597,562 R | 61.2% | 38.7% | 61.3% | 38.7% |
| 1952 | 7,128,239 | 3,952,813 | Eisenhower, Dwight D. | 3,104,601 | Stevenson, Adlai E. | 70,825 | 848,212 R | 55.5% | 43.6% | 56.0% | 44.0% |
| 1948** | 6,177,337 | 2,841,163 | Dewey, Thomas E. | 2,780,204 | Truman, Harry S. | 555,970 | 60,959 R | 46.0% | 45.0% | 50.5% | 49.5% |

In past elections, the other vote included: 2000 - 244,030 Green (Ralph Nader); 1996 - 503,458 Reform (Ross Perot); 1992 - 1,090,721 Independent (Perot); 1980 - 467,801 Independent (John Anderson); 1968 - 358,864 American Independent (George Wallace); 1948 - 509,559 Progressive (Henry Wallace).

# NEW YORK

## POSTWAR VOTE FOR GOVERNOR

| Year | Total Vote | Republican | | Democratic | | Other Vote | Rep.-Dem. Plurality | Percentage | | | |
|---|---|---|---|---|---|---|---|---|---|---|---|
| | | | | | | | | Total Vote | | Major Vote | |
| | | Vote | Candidate | Vote | Candidate | | | Rep. | Dem. | Rep. | Dem. |
| 2002** | 4,579,078 | 2,262,255 | Pataki, George E. | 1,534,064 | McCall, H. Carl | 782,759 | 728,191 R | 49.4% | 33.5% | 59.6% | 40.4% |
| 1998 | 4,735,236 | 2,571,991 | Pataki, George E. | 1,570,317 | Vallone, Peter F. | 592,928 | 1,001,674 R | 54.3% | 33.2% | 62.1% | 37.9% |
| 1994 | 5,208,762 | 2,538,702 | Pataki, George E. | 2,364,904 | Cuomo, Mario M. | 305,156 | 173,798 R | 48.7% | 45.4% | 51.8% | 48.2% |
| 1990** | 4,056,896 | 865,948 | Rinfret, Pierre A. | 2,157,087 | Cuomo, Mario M. | 1,033,861 | 1,291,139 D | 21.3% | 53.2% | 28.6% | 71.4% |
| 1986 | 4,294,124 | 1,363,810 | O'Rourke, Andrew P. | 2,775,229 | Cuomo, Mario M. | 155,085 | 1,411,419 D | 31.8% | 64.6% | 32.9% | 67.1% |
| 1982 | 5,254,891 | 2,494,827 | Lehrman, Lew | 2,675,213 | Cuomo, Mario M. | 84,851 | 180,386 D | 47.5% | 50.9% | 48.3% | 51.7% |
| 1978 | 4,768,820 | 2,156,404 | Duryea, Perry B. | 2,429,272 | Carey, Hugh L. | 183,144 | 272,868 D | 45.2% | 50.9% | 47.0% | 53.0% |
| 1974 | 5,293,176 | 2,219,667 | Wilson, Malcolm | 3,028,503 | Carey, Hugh L. | 45,006 | 808,836 D | 41.9% | 57.2% | 42.3% | 57.7% |
| 1970 | 6,013,064 | 3,151,432 | Rockefeller, Nelson A. | 2,421,426 | Goldberg, Arthur | 440,206 | 730,006 R | 52.4% | 40.3% | 56.5% | 43.5% |
| 1966** | 6,031,585 | 2,690,626 | Rockefeller, Nelson A. | 2,298,363 | O'Connor, Frank D. | 1,042,596 | 392,263 R | 44.6% | 38.1% | 53.9% | 46.1% |
| 1962 | 5,805,631 | 3,081,587 | Rockefeller, Nelson A. | 2,552,418 | Morgenthau, Robert M. | 171,626 | 529,169 R | 53.1% | 44.0% | 54.7% | 45.3% |
| 1958 | 5,712,665 | 3,126,929 | Rockefeller, Nelson A. | 2,553,895 | Harriman, Averell | 31,841 | 573,034 R | 54.7% | 44.7% | 55.0% | 45.0% |
| 1954 | 5,161,942 | 2,549,613 | Ives, Irving M. | 2,560,738 | Harriman, Averell | 51,591 | 11,125 D | 49.4% | 49.6% | 49.9% | 50.1% |
| 1950 | 5,308,889 | 2,819,523 | Dewey, Thomas E. | 2,246,855 | Lynch, Walter A. | 242,511 | 572,668 R | 53.1% | 42.3% | 55.7% | 44.3% |
| 1946 | 4,964,552 | 2,825,633 | Dewey, Thomas E. | 2,138,482 | Mead, James M. | 437 | 687,151 R | 56.9% | 43.1% | 56.9% | 43.1% |

In past elections, the other vote included: 2002 - 654,016 Independence (B. Thomas Golisano); 1990 - 827,614 Conservative (Herbert I. London); 1966 - 510,023 Conservative (Paul L. Adams); 507,234 Liberal (Franklin Roosevelt Jr.).

## POSTWAR VOTE FOR SENATOR

| Year | Total Vote | Republican | | Democratic | | Other Vote | Rep.-Dem. Plurality | Percentage | | | |
|---|---|---|---|---|---|---|---|---|---|---|---|
| | | | | | | | | Total Vote | | Major Vote | |
| | | Vote | Candidate | Vote | Candidate | | | Rep. | Dem. | Rep. | Dem. |
| 2004 | 6,702,875 | 1,625,069 | Mills, Howard | 4,769,824 | Schumer, Charles E. | 307,982 | 3,144,755 D | 24.2% | 71.2% | 25.4% | 74.6% |
| 2000 | 6,779,839 | 2,915,730 | Lazio, Rick A. | 3,747,310 | Clinton, Hillary Rodham | 116,799 | 831,580 D | 43.0% | 55.3% | 43.8% | 56.2% |
| 1998 | 4,670,805 | 2,058,988 | D'Amato, Alfonse M. | 2,551,065 | Schumer, Charles E. | 60,752 | 492,077 D | 44.1% | 54.6% | 44.7% | 55.3% |
| 1994 | 4,794,601 | 1,988,308 | Castro, Bernadette | 2,646,541 | Moynihan, Daniel P. | 159,752 | 658,233 D | 41.5% | 55.2% | 42.9% | 57.1% |
| 1992 | 6,458,826 | 3,166,994 | D'Amato, Alfonse M. | 3,086,200 | Abrams, Robert | 205,632 | 80,794 R | 49.0% | 47.8% | 50.6% | 49.4% |
| 1988 | 6,040,980 | 1,875,784 | McMillan, Robert | 4,048,649 | Moynihan, Daniel P. | 116,547 | 2,172,865 D | 31.1% | 67.0% | 31.7% | 68.3% |
| 1986 | 4,179,447 | 2,378,197 | D'Amato, Alfonse M. | 1,723,216 | Green, Mark | 78,034 | 654,981 R | 56.9% | 41.2% | 58.0% | 42.0% |
| 1982 | 4,967,729 | 1,696,766 | Sullivan, Florence M. | 3,232,146 | Moynihan, Daniel P. | 38,817 | 1,535,380 D | 34.2% | 65.1% | 34.4% | 65.6% |
| 1980 | 6,014,914 | 2,699,652 | D'Amato, Alfonse M. | 2,618,661 | Holtzman, Elizabeth | 696,601 | 80,991 R | 44.9% | 43.5% | 50.8% | 49.2% |
| 1976 | 6,319,755 | 2,836,633 | Buckley, James L. | 3,422,594 | Moynihan, Daniel P. | 60,528 | 585,961 D | 44.9% | 54.2% | 45.3% | 54.7% |
| 1974 | 5,163,600 | 2,340,188 | Javits, Jacob K. | 1,973,781 | Clark, Ramsey | 849,631 | 366,407 R | 45.3% | 38.2% | 54.2% | 45.8% |
| 1970** | 5,904,782 | 1,434,472 | Goodell, Charles | 2,171,232 | Ottinger, Richard L. | 2,299,078 | 116,958 C | 24.3% | 36.8% | 39.8% | 60.2% |
| 1968** | 6,581,587 | 3,269,772 | Javits, Jacob K. | 2,150,695 | O'Dwyer, Paul | 1,161,120 | 1,119,077 R | 49.7% | 32.7% | 60.3% | 39.7% |
| 1964 | 7,151,686 | 3,104,056 | Keating, Kenneth B. | 3,823,749 | Kennedy, Robert F. | 223,881 | 719,693 D | 43.4% | 53.5% | 44.8% | 55.2% |
| 1962 | 5,700,186 | 3,269,417 | Javits, Jacob K. | 2,289,341 | Donovan, James B. | 141,428 | 980,076 R | 57.4% | 40.2% | 58.8% | 41.2% |
| 1958 | 5,602,088 | 2,842,942 | Keating, Kenneth B. | 2,709,950 | Hogan, Frank S. | 49,196 | 132,992 R | 50.7% | 48.4% | 51.2% | 48.8% |
| 1956 | 6,991,136 | 3,723,933 | Javits, Jacob K. | 3,265,159 | Wagner, Robert F. | 2,044 | 458,774 R | 53.3% | 46.7% | 53.3% | 46.7% |
| 1952 | 6,980,259 | 3,853,934 | Ives, Irving M. | 2,521,736 | Cashmore, John | 604,589 | 1,332,198 R | 55.2% | 36.1% | 60.4% | 39.6% |
| 1950 | 5,228,403 | 2,367,353 | Hanley, Joe R. | 2,632,313 | Lehman, Herbert H. | 228,737 | 264,960 D | 45.3% | 50.3% | 47.4% | 52.6% |
| 1949S | 4,966,878 | 2,384,381 | Dulles, John Foster | 2,582,438 | Lehman, Herbert H. | 59 | 198,057 D | 48.0% | 52.0% | 48.0% | 52.0% |
| 1946 | 4,867,564 | 2,559,365 | Ives, Irving M. | 2,308,112 | Lehman, Herbert H. | 87 | 251,253 R | 52.6% | 47.4% | 52.6% | 47.4% |

In past elections, the other vote included: 1970 - 2,288,190 Conservative (James L. Buckley), who won the election with 38.8 percent of the total vote; 1968 - 1,139,402 Conservative (Buckley). In 1970 Buckley was also the nominee of the Independent Alliance Party. The 1949 election was for a short term to fill a vacancy.

# NEW YORK

Congressional districts first established for elections held in 2002
29 members

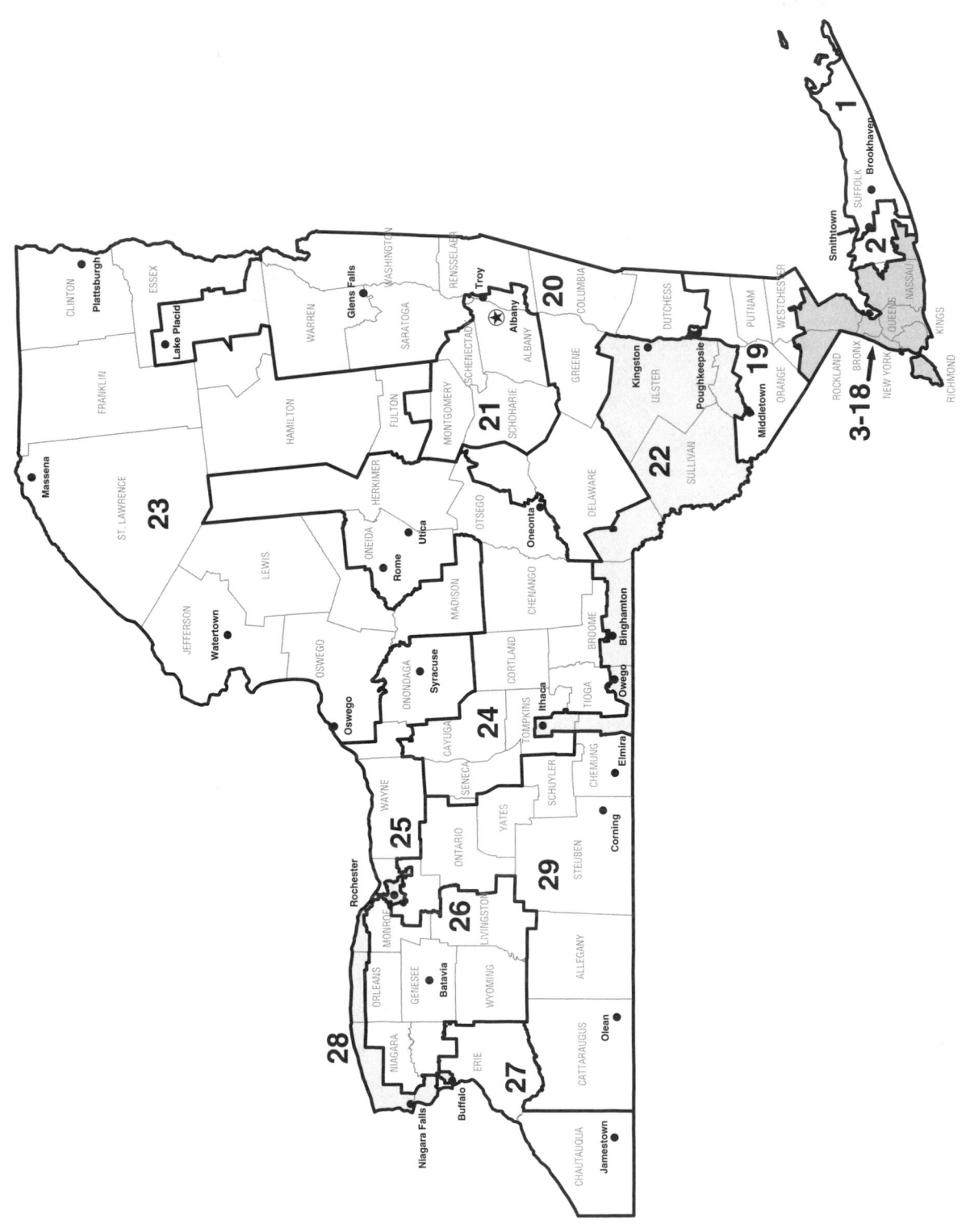

# NEW YORK

New York City Area

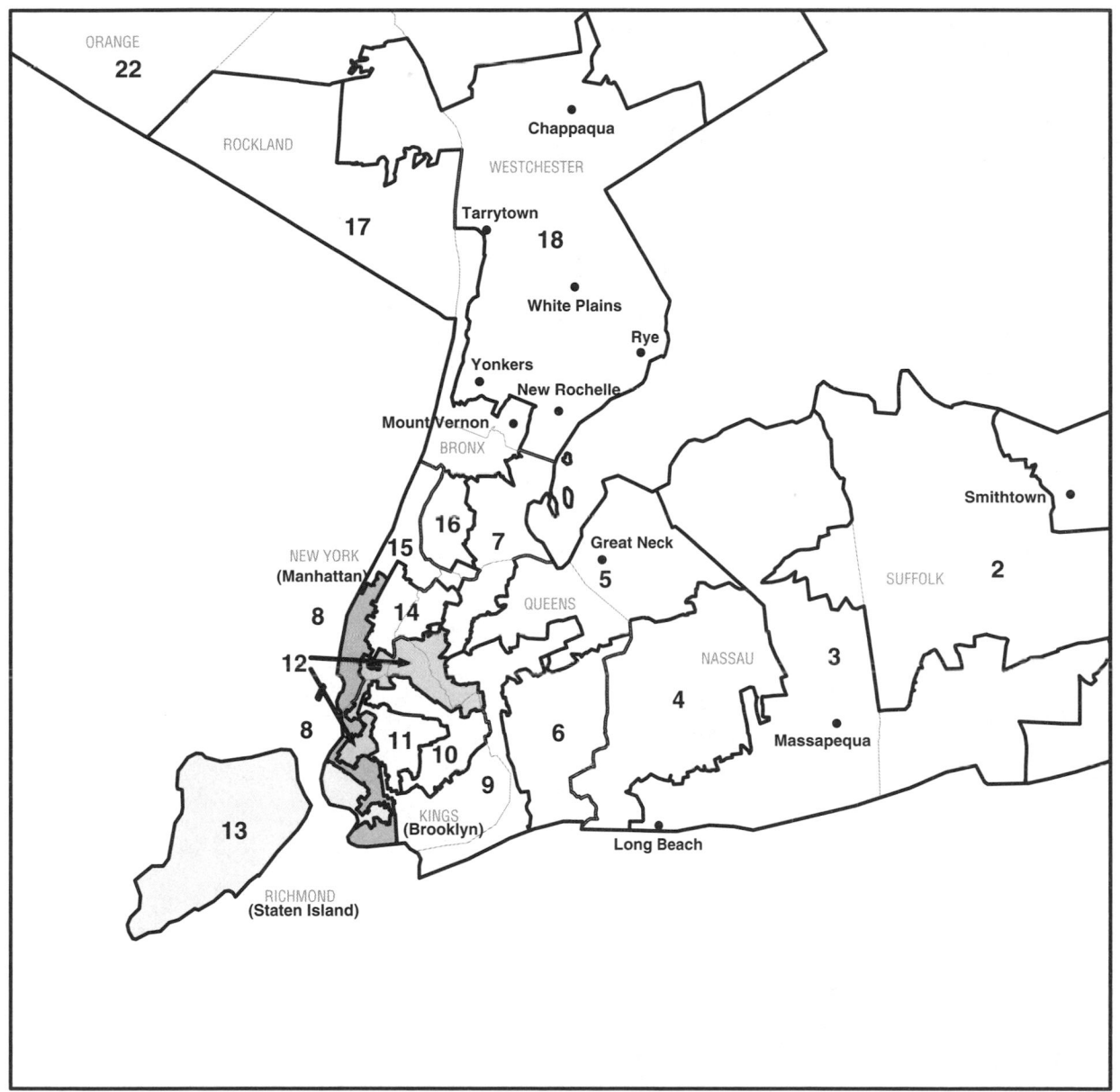

ORANGE
**22**

ROCKLAND

WESTCHESTER

Chappaqua

Tarrytown

**18**

**17**

White Plains

Rye

Yonkers

New Rochelle

Mount Vernon

BRONX

**16**

**7**

Great Neck

NEW YORK
(Manhattan)

**15**

**5**

QUEENS

Smithtown

SUFFOLK

**2**

**8**

**14**

NASSAU

**3**

**12**

**6**

**4**

**8**

**11**

**10**

Massapequa

**9**

KINGS
(Brooklyn)

**13**

RICHMOND
(Staten Island)

Long Beach

# NEW YORK

## PRESIDENT 2004

| 2000 Census Population | County | Total Vote | Republican | Democratic | Other | Rep.-Dem. Plurality | Percentage | | | |
|---|---|---|---|---|---|---|---|---|---|---|
| | | | | | | | Total Vote | | Major Vote | |
| | | | | | | | Rep. | Dem. | Rep. | Dem. |
| 294,565 | ALBANY | 147,199 | 54,872 | 89,323 | 3,004 | 34,451 D | 37.3% | 60.7% | 38.1% | 61.9% |
| 49,927 | ALLEGANY | 19,270 | 12,310 | 6,566 | 394 | 5,744 R | 63.9% | 34.1% | 65.2% | 34.8% |
| 1,332,650 | BRONX | 342,929 | 56,701 | 283,994 | 2,234 | 227,293 D | 16.5% | 82.8% | 16.6% | 83.4% |
| 200,536 | BROOME | 91,890 | 43,568 | 46,281 | 2,041 | 2,713 D | 47.4% | 50.4% | 48.5% | 51.5% |
| 83,955 | CATTARAUGUS | 34,262 | 20,051 | 13,514 | 697 | 6,537 R | 58.5% | 39.4% | 59.7% | 40.3% |
| 81,963 | CAYUGA | 36,052 | 17,743 | 17,534 | 775 | 209 R | 49.2% | 48.6% | 50.3% | 49.7% |
| 139,750 | CHAUTAUQUA | 60,942 | 32,434 | 27,257 | 1,251 | 5,177 R | 53.2% | 44.7% | 54.3% | 45.7% |
| 91,070 | CHEMUNG | 39,075 | 21,321 | 17,080 | 674 | 4,241 R | 54.6% | 43.7% | 55.5% | 44.5% |
| 51,401 | CHENANGO | 21,341 | 11,582 | 9,277 | 482 | 2,305 R | 54.3% | 43.5% | 55.5% | 44.5% |
| 79,894 | CLINTON | 33,736 | 15,330 | 17,624 | 782 | 2,294 D | 45.4% | 52.2% | 46.5% | 53.5% |
| 63,094 | COLUMBIA | 31,103 | 14,457 | 15,929 | 717 | 1,472 D | 46.5% | 51.2% | 47.6% | 52.4% |
| 48,599 | CORTLAND | 22,760 | 11,613 | 10,670 | 477 | 943 R | 51.0% | 46.9% | 52.1% | 47.9% |
| 48,055 | DELAWARE | 21,166 | 11,958 | 8,724 | 484 | 3,234 R | 56.5% | 41.2% | 57.8% | 42.2% |
| 280,150 | DUTCHESS | 123,881 | 63,372 | 58,232 | 2,277 | 5,140 R | 51.2% | 47.0% | 52.1% | 47.9% |
| 950,265 | ERIE | 445,138 | 184,423 | 251,090 | 9,625 | 66,667 D | 41.4% | 56.4% | 42.3% | 57.7% |
| 38,851 | ESSEX | 19,082 | 9,869 | 8,768 | 445 | 1,101 R | 51.7% | 45.9% | 53.0% | 47.0% |
| 51,134 | FRANKLIN | 18,316 | 8,383 | 9,543 | 390 | 1,160 D | 45.8% | 52.1% | 46.8% | 53.2% |
| 55,073 | FULTON | 22,215 | 12,570 | 9,202 | 443 | 3,368 R | 56.6% | 41.4% | 57.7% | 42.3% |
| 60,370 | GENESEE | 27,580 | 16,725 | 10,331 | 524 | 6,394 R | 60.6% | 37.5% | 61.8% | 38.2% |
| 48,195 | GREENE | 22,398 | 12,996 | 8,933 | 469 | 4,063 R | 58.0% | 39.9% | 59.3% | 40.7% |
| 5,379 | HAMILTON | 3,692 | 2,475 | 1,145 | 72 | 1,330 R | 67.0% | 31.0% | 68.4% | 31.6% |
| 64,427 | HERKIMER | 28,310 | 16,024 | 11,675 | 611 | 4,349 R | 56.6% | 41.2% | 57.9% | 42.1% |
| 111,738 | JEFFERSON | 38,800 | 21,231 | 16,860 | 709 | 4,371 R | 54.7% | 43.5% | 55.7% | 44.3% |
| 2,465,326 | KINGS | 687,780 | 167,149 | 514,973 | 5,658 | 347,824 D | 24.3% | 74.9% | 24.5% | 75.5% |
| 26,944 | LEWIS | 11,397 | 6,624 | 4,546 | 227 | 2,078 R | 58.1% | 39.9% | 59.3% | 40.7% |
| 64,328 | LIVINGSTON | 29,948 | 17,729 | 11,504 | 715 | 6,225 R | 59.2% | 38.4% | 60.6% | 39.4% |
| 69,441 | MADISON | 30,287 | 16,537 | 13,121 | 629 | 3,416 R | 54.6% | 43.3% | 55.8% | 44.2% |
| 735,343 | MONROE | 342,981 | 163,545 | 173,497 | 5,939 | 9,952 D | 47.7% | 50.6% | 48.5% | 51.5% |
| 49,708 | MONTGOMERY | 21,221 | 11,338 | 9,449 | 434 | 1,889 R | 53.4% | 44.5% | 54.5% | 45.5% |
| 1,334,544 | NASSAU | 618,343 | 288,355 | 323,070 | 6,918 | 34,715 D | 46.6% | 52.2% | 47.2% | 52.8% |
| 1,537,195 | NEW YORK | 641,747 | 107,405 | 526,765 | 7,577 | 419,360 D | 16.7% | 82.1% | 16.9% | 83.1% |
| 219,846 | NIAGARA | 96,580 | 47,111 | 47,602 | 1,867 | 491 D | 48.8% | 49.3% | 49.7% | 50.3% |
| 235,469 | ONEIDA | 95,369 | 52,392 | 40,792 | 2,185 | 11,600 R | 54.9% | 42.8% | 56.2% | 43.8% |
| 458,336 | ONONDAGA | 214,589 | 94,006 | 116,381 | 4,202 | 22,375 D | 43.8% | 54.2% | 44.7% | 55.3% |
| 100,224 | ONTARIO | 50,102 | 27,999 | 21,166 | 937 | 6,833 R | 55.9% | 42.2% | 56.9% | 43.1% |
| 341,367 | ORANGE | 144,673 | 79,089 | 63,394 | 2,190 | 15,695 R | 54.7% | 43.8% | 55.5% | 44.5% |
| 44,171 | ORLEANS | 16,573 | 10,317 | 5,959 | 297 | 4,358 R | 62.3% | 36.0% | 63.4% | 36.6% |
| 122,377 | OSWEGO | 51,607 | 26,325 | 24,133 | 1,149 | 2,192 R | 51.0% | 46.8% | 52.2% | 47.8% |
| 61,676 | OTSEGO | 26,652 | 13,342 | 12,723 | 587 | 619 R | 50.1% | 47.7% | 51.2% | 48.8% |
| 95,745 | PUTNAM | 46,563 | 26,356 | 19,575 | 632 | 6,781 R | 56.6% | 42.0% | 57.4% | 42.6% |
| 2,229,379 | QUEENS | 605,062 | 165,954 | 433,835 | 5,273 | 267,881 D | 27.4% | 71.7% | 27.7% | 72.3% |
| 152,538 | RENSSELAER | 72,514 | 34,734 | 36,075 | 1,705 | 1,341 D | 47.9% | 49.7% | 49.1% | 50.9% |
| 443,728 | RICHMOND | 160,126 | 90,325 | 68,448 | 1,353 | 21,877 R | 56.4% | 42.7% | 56.9% | 43.1% |
| 286,753 | ROCKLAND | 131,231 | 65,130 | 64,191 | 1,910 | 939 R | 49.6% | 48.9% | 50.4% | 49.6% |
| 111,931 | ST. LAWRENCE | 41,755 | 18,029 | 22,857 | 869 | 4,828 D | 43.2% | 54.7% | 44.1% | 55.9% |
| 200,635 | SARATOGA | 106,873 | 56,158 | 48,730 | 1,985 | 7,428 R | 52.5% | 45.6% | 53.5% | 46.5% |
| 146,555 | SCHENECTADY | 69,469 | 32,066 | 35,971 | 1,432 | 3,905 D | 46.2% | 51.8% | 47.1% | 52.9% |
| 31,582 | SCHOHARIE | 14,557 | 8,591 | 5,630 | 336 | 2,961 R | 59.0% | 38.7% | 60.4% | 39.6% |
| 19,224 | SCHUYLER | 8,590 | 4,960 | 3,445 | 185 | 1,515 R | 57.7% | 40.1% | 59.0% | 41.0% |
| 33,342 | SENECA | 15,325 | 7,981 | 6,979 | 365 | 1,002 R | 52.1% | 45.5% | 53.3% | 46.7% |
| 98,726 | STEUBEN | 42,284 | 26,980 | 14,523 | 781 | 12,457 R | 63.8% | 34.3% | 65.0% | 35.0% |
| 1,419,369 | SUFFOLK | 638,712 | 309,949 | 315,909 | 12,854 | 5,960 R | 48.5% | 49.5% | 49.5% | 50.5% |
| 73,966 | SULLIVAN | 30,966 | 15,319 | 15,034 | 613 | 285 R | 49.5% | 48.6% | 50.5% | 49.5% |
| 51,784 | TIOGA | 23,902 | 13,762 | 9,694 | 446 | 4,068 R | 57.6% | 40.6% | 58.7% | 41.3% |
| 96,501 | TOMPKINS | 42,402 | 13,994 | 27,229 | 1,179 | 13,235 D | 33.0% | 64.2% | 33.9% | 66.1% |
| 177,749 | ULSTER | 87,712 | 37,821 | 47,602 | 2,289 | 9,781 D | 43.1% | 54.3% | 44.3% | 55.7% |
| 63,303 | WARREN | 31,059 | 16,969 | 13,405 | 685 | 3,564 R | 54.6% | 43.2% | 55.9% | 44.1% |
| 61,042 | WASHINGTON | 25,103 | 13,827 | 10,624 | 652 | 3,203 R | 55.1% | 42.3% | 56.5% | 43.5% |
| 93,765 | WAYNE | 41,200 | 24,709 | 15,709 | 782 | 9,000 R | 60.0% | 38.1% | 61.1% | 38.9% |
| 923,459 | WESTCHESTER | 395,770 | 159,628 | 229,849 | 6,293 | 70,221 D | 40.3% | 58.1% | 41.0% | 59.0% |
| 43,424 | WYOMING | 18,164 | 11,745 | 6,134 | 285 | 5,611 R | 64.7% | 33.8% | 65.7% | 34.3% |
| 24,621 | YATES | 10,711 | 6,309 | 4,205 | 197 | 2,104 R | 58.9% | 39.3% | 60.0% | 40.0% |
| 18,976,457 | TOTAL | 7,391,036 | 2,962,567 | 4,314,280 | 114,189 | 1,351,713 D | 40.1% | 58.4% | 40.7% | 59.3% |

# NEW YORK CITY

## PRESIDENT 2004

| 2000 Census Population | County | Total Vote | Republican | Democratic | Other | Rep.-Dem. Plurality | | Percentage | | | |
|---|---|---|---|---|---|---|---|---|---|---|---|
| | | | | | | | | Total Vote | | Major Vote | |
| | | | | | | | | Rep. | Dem. | Rep. | Dem. |
| 1,332,650 | BRONX | 342,929 | 56,701 | 283,994 | 2,234 | 227,293 | D | 16.5% | 82.8% | 16.6% | 83.4% |
| 2,465,326 | KINGS | 687,780 | 167,149 | 514,973 | 5,658 | 347,824 | D | 24.3% | 74.9% | 24.5% | 75.5% |
| 1,537,195 | NEW YORK | 641,747 | 107,405 | 526,765 | 7,577 | 419,360 | D | 16.7% | 82.1% | 16.9% | 83.1% |
| 2,229,379 | QUEENS | 605,062 | 165,954 | 433,835 | 5,273 | 267,881 | D | 27.4% | 71.7% | 27.7% | 72.3% |
| 443,728 | RICHMOND | 160,126 | 90,325 | 68,448 | 1,353 | 21,877 | R | 56.4% | 42.7% | 56.9% | 43.1% |
| 8,008,278 | TOTAL | 2,437,644 | 587,534 | 1,828,015 | 22,095 | 1,240,481 | D | 24.1% | 75.0% | 24.3% | 75.7% |

# NEW YORK

## SENATOR 2004

| 2000 Census Population | County | Total Vote | Republican | Democratic | Other | Rep.-Dem. Plurality | | Percentage | | | |
|---|---|---|---|---|---|---|---|---|---|---|---|
| | | | | | | | | Total Vote | | Major Vote | |
| | | | | | | | | Rep. | Dem. | Rep. | Dem. |
| 294,565 | ALBANY | 136,411 | 34,800 | 95,247 | 6,364 | 60,447 | D | 25.5% | 69.8% | 26.8% | 73.2% |
| 49,927 | ALLEGANY | 17,254 | 7,856 | 8,399 | 999 | 543 | D | 45.5% | 48.7% | 48.3% | 51.7% |
| 1,332,650 | BRONX | 297,763 | 21,935 | 269,768 | 6,060 | 247,833 | D | 7.4% | 90.6% | 7.5% | 92.5% |
| 200,536 | BROOME | 83,179 | 27,768 | 51,339 | 4,072 | 23,571 | D | 33.4% | 61.7% | 35.1% | 64.9% |
| 83,955 | CATTARAUGUS | 30,888 | 12,194 | 17,104 | 1,590 | 4,910 | D | 39.5% | 55.4% | 41.6% | 58.4% |
| 81,963 | CAYUGA | 31,980 | 11,107 | 18,719 | 2,154 | 7,612 | D | 34.7% | 58.5% | 37.2% | 62.8% |
| 139,750 | CHAUTAUQUA | 55,132 | 18,545 | 34,116 | 2,471 | 15,571 | D | 33.6% | 61.9% | 35.2% | 64.8% |
| 91,070 | CHEMUNG | 34,969 | 13,165 | 20,242 | 1,562 | 7,077 | D | 37.6% | 57.9% | 39.4% | 60.6% |
| 51,401 | CHENANGO | 19,235 | 8,171 | 9,880 | 1,184 | 1,709 | D | 42.5% | 51.4% | 45.3% | 54.7% |
| 79,894 | CLINTON | 29,800 | 9,873 | 18,509 | 1,418 | 8,636 | D | 33.1% | 62.1% | 34.8% | 65.2% |
| 63,094 | COLUMBIA | 28,354 | 9,868 | 16,926 | 1,560 | 7,058 | D | 34.8% | 59.7% | 36.8% | 63.2% |
| 48,599 | CORTLAND | 20,020 | 7,366 | 11,486 | 1,168 | 4,120 | D | 36.8% | 57.4% | 39.1% | 60.9% |
| 48,055 | DELAWARE | 19,144 | 8,423 | 9,600 | 1,121 | 1,177 | D | 44.0% | 50.1% | 46.7% | 53.3% |
| 280,150 | DUTCHESS | 111,267 | 38,170 | 66,100 | 6,997 | 27,930 | D | 34.3% | 59.4% | 36.6% | 63.4% |
| 950,265 | ERIE | 403,107 | 91,985 | 290,210 | 20,912 | 198,225 | D | 22.8% | 72.0% | 24.1% | 75.9% |
| 38,851 | ESSEX | 16,525 | 6,693 | 8,726 | 1,106 | 2,033 | D | 40.5% | 52.8% | 43.4% | 56.6% |
| 51,134 | FRANKLIN | 16,026 | 5,443 | 9,913 | 670 | 4,470 | D | 34.0% | 61.9% | 35.4% | 64.6% |
| 55,073 | FULTON | 19,379 | 7,913 | 10,207 | 1,259 | 2,294 | D | 40.8% | 52.7% | 43.7% | 56.3% |
| 60,370 | GENESEE | 24,495 | 9,584 | 13,454 | 1,457 | 3,870 | D | 39.1% | 54.9% | 41.6% | 58.4% |
| 48,195 | GREENE | 20,753 | 9,150 | 10,352 | 1,251 | 1,202 | D | 44.1% | 49.9% | 46.9% | 53.1% |
| 5,379 | HAMILTON | 3,309 | 1,697 | 1,434 | 178 | 263 | R | 51.3% | 43.3% | 54.2% | 45.8% |
| 64,427 | HERKIMER | 24,407 | 8,754 | 13,919 | 1,734 | 5,165 | D | 35.9% | 57.0% | 38.6% | 61.4% |
| 111,738 | JEFFERSON | 34,970 | 10,846 | 22,463 | 1,661 | 11,617 | D | 31.0% | 64.2% | 32.6% | 67.4% |
| 2,465,326 | KINGS | 615,990 | 56,823 | 542,759 | 16,408 | 485,936 | D | 9.2% | 88.1% | 9.5% | 90.5% |
| 26,944 | LEWIS | 10,136 | 3,700 | 5,929 | 507 | 2,229 | D | 36.5% | 58.5% | 38.4% | 61.6% |
| 64,328 | LIVINGSTON | 26,447 | 10,814 | 14,236 | 1,397 | 3,422 | D | 40.9% | 53.8% | 43.2% | 56.8% |
| 69,441 | MADISON | 27,223 | 9,984 | 15,359 | 1,880 | 5,375 | D | 36.7% | 56.4% | 39.4% | 60.6% |
| 735,343 | MONROE | 309,145 | 87,655 | 204,268 | 17,222 | 116,613 | D | 28.4% | 66.1% | 30.0% | 70.0% |
| 49,708 | MONTGOMERY | 18,346 | 6,235 | 10,895 | 1,216 | 4,660 | D | 34.0% | 59.4% | 36.4% | 63.6% |
| 1,334,544 | NASSAU | 582,486 | 161,395 | 387,085 | 34,006 | 225,690 | D | 27.7% | 66.5% | 29.4% | 70.6% |
| 1,537,195 | NEW YORK | 586,309 | 59,560 | 512,902 | 13,847 | 453,342 | D | 10.2% | 87.5% | 10.4% | 89.6% |
| 219,846 | NIAGARA | 86,249 | 25,137 | 56,314 | 4,798 | 31,177 | D | 29.1% | 65.3% | 30.9% | 69.1% |
| 235,469 | ONEIDA | 87,905 | 29,195 | 52,655 | 6,055 | 23,460 | D | 33.2% | 59.9% | 35.7% | 64.3% |
| 458,336 | ONONDAGA | 199,265 | 61,500 | 125,318 | 12,447 | 63,818 | D | 30.9% | 62.9% | 32.9% | 67.1% |
| 100,224 | ONTARIO | 45,078 | 15,951 | 26,849 | 2,278 | 10,898 | D | 35.4% | 59.6% | 37.3% | 62.7% |
| 341,367 | ORANGE | 132,653 | 53,011 | 73,135 | 6,507 | 20,124 | D | 40.0% | 55.1% | 42.0% | 58.0% |
| 44,171 | ORLEANS | 14,619 | 6,161 | 7,668 | 790 | 1,507 | D | 42.1% | 52.5% | 44.6% | 55.4% |
| 122,377 | OSWEGO | 45,969 | 17,167 | 25,890 | 2,912 | 8,723 | D | 37.3% | 56.3% | 39.9% | 60.1% |
| 61,676 | OTSEGO | 23,890 | 8,638 | 13,632 | 1,620 | 4,994 | D | 36.2% | 57.1% | 38.8% | 61.2% |
| 95,745 | PUTNAM | 41,396 | 14,557 | 24,001 | 2,838 | 9,444 | D | 35.2% | 58.0% | 37.8% | 62.2% |

# NEW YORK

## SENATOR 2004

| 2000 Census Population | County | Total Vote | Republican | Democratic | Other | Rep.-Dem. Plurality | Percentage | | | |
|---|---|---|---|---|---|---|---|---|---|---|
| | | | | | | | Total Vote | | Major Vote | |
| | | | | | | | Rep. | Dem. | Rep. | Dem. |
| 2,229,379 | QUEENS | 538,027 | 71,453 | 450,332 | 16,242 | 378,879 D | 13.3% | 83.7% | 13.7% | 86.3% |
| 152,538 | RENSSELAER | 66,494 | 21,431 | 40,911 | 4,152 | 19,480 D | 32.2% | 61.5% | 34.4% | 65.6% |
| 443,728 | RICHMOND | 143,065 | 37,727 | 98,123 | 7,215 | 60,396 D | 26.4% | 68.6% | 27.8% | 72.2% |
| 286,753 | ROCKLAND | 119,714 | 32,993 | 81,155 | 5,566 | 48,162 D | 27.6% | 67.8% | 28.9% | 71.1% |
| 111,931 | ST. LAWRENCE | 36,863 | 9,237 | 25,724 | 1,902 | 16,487 D | 25.1% | 69.8% | 26.4% | 73.6% |
| 200,635 | SARATOGA | 97,532 | 38,846 | 53,309 | 5,377 | 14,463 D | 39.8% | 54.7% | 42.2% | 57.8% |
| 146,555 | SCHENECTADY | 63,884 | 20,316 | 39,521 | 4,047 | 19,205 D | 31.8% | 61.9% | 34.0% | 66.0% |
| 31,582 | SCHOHARIE | 13,450 | 5,991 | 6,750 | 709 | 759 D | 44.5% | 50.2% | 47.0% | 53.0% |
| 19,224 | SCHUYLER | 7,748 | 3,227 | 4,088 | 433 | 861 D | 41.6% | 52.8% | 44.1% | 55.9% |
| 33,342 | SENECA | 13,545 | 4,595 | 8,228 | 722 | 3,633 D | 33.9% | 60.7% | 35.8% | 64.2% |
| 98,726 | STEUBEN | 36,316 | 16,379 | 18,167 | 1,770 | 1,788 D | 45.1% | 50.0% | 47.4% | 52.6% |
| 1,419,369 | SUFFOLK | 586,913 | 163,470 | 391,950 | 31,493 | 228,480 D | 27.9% | 66.8% | 29.4% | 70.6% |
| 73,966 | SULLIVAN | 28,313 | 9,080 | 17,582 | 1,651 | 8,502 D | 32.1% | 62.1% | 34.1% | 65.9% |
| 51,784 | TIOGA | 21,702 | 9,602 | 10,872 | 1,228 | 1,270 D | 44.2% | 50.1% | 46.9% | 53.1% |
| 96,501 | TOMPKINS | 38,071 | 9,504 | 25,930 | 2,637 | 16,426 D | 25.0% | 68.1% | 26.8% | 73.2% |
| 177,749 | ULSTER | 81,020 | 24,029 | 51,689 | 5,302 | 27,660 D | 29.7% | 63.8% | 31.7% | 68.3% |
| 63,303 | WARREN | 27,887 | 10,889 | 15,611 | 1,387 | 4,722 D | 39.0% | 56.0% | 41.1% | 58.9% |
| 61,042 | WASHINGTON | 22,158 | 9,000 | 11,947 | 1,211 | 2,947 D | 40.6% | 53.9% | 43.0% | 57.0% |
| 93,765 | WAYNE | 36,482 | 14,986 | 19,083 | 2,413 | 4,097 D | 41.1% | 52.3% | 44.0% | 56.0% |
| 923,459 | WESTCHESTER | 366,272 | 92,685 | 258,134 | 15,453 | 165,449 D | 25.3% | 70.5% | 26.4% | 73.6% |
| 43,424 | WYOMING | 16,395 | 6,929 | 8,494 | 972 | 1,565 D | 42.3% | 51.8% | 44.9% | 55.1% |
| 24,621 | YATES | 9,551 | 3,911 | 5,216 | 424 | 1,305 D | 40.9% | 54.6% | 42.9% | 57.1% |
| 18,976,457 | TOTAL | 6,702,875 | 1,625,069 | 4,769,824 | 307,982 | 3,144,755 D | 24.2% | 71.2% | 25.4% | 74.6% |

# NEW YORK CITY

## SENATOR 2004

| 2000 Census Population | County | Total Vote | Republican | Democratic | Other | Rep.-Dem. Plurality | Percentage | | | |
|---|---|---|---|---|---|---|---|---|---|---|
| | | | | | | | Total Vote | | Major Vote | |
| | | | | | | | Rep. | Dem. | Rep. | Dem. |
| 1,332,650 | BRONX | 297,763 | 21,935 | 269,768 | 6,060 | 247,833 D | 7.4% | 90.6% | 7.5% | 92.5% |
| 2,465,326 | KINGS | 615,990 | 56,823 | 542,759 | 16,408 | 485,936 D | 9.2% | 88.1% | 9.5% | 90.5% |
| 1,537,195 | NEW YORK | 586,309 | 59,560 | 512,902 | 13,847 | 453,342 D | 10.2% | 87.5% | 10.4% | 89.6% |
| 2,229,379 | QUEENS | 538,027 | 71,453 | 450,332 | 16,242 | 378,879 D | 13.3% | 83.7% | 13.7% | 86.3% |
| 443,728 | RICHMOND | 143,065 | 37,727 | 98,123 | 7,215 | 60,396 D | 26.4% | 68.6% | 27.8% | 72.2% |
| 8,008,278 | TOTAL | 2,181,154 | 247,498 | 1,873,884 | 59,772 | 1,626,386 D | 11.3% | 85.9% | 11.7% | 88.3% |

# NEW YORK

## HOUSE OF REPRESENTATIVES

| CD | Year | Total Vote | Republican Vote | Republican Candidate | Democratic Vote | Democratic Candidate | Other Vote | Rep.-Dem. Plurality | Total Vote Rep. | Total Vote Dem. | Major Vote Rep. | Major Vote Dem. |
|---|---|---|---|---|---|---|---|---|---|---|---|---|
| 1 | 2004 | 278,209 | 121,855 | # Manger, William M. Jr. | 156,354 | # Bishop, Timothy H.* | | 34,499 D | 43.8% | 56.2% | 43.8% | 56.2% |
| 1 | 2002 | 167,791 | 81,524 | # Grucci, Felix J., Jr.* | 84,276 | # Bishop, Timothy H. | 1,991 | 2,752 D | 48.6% | 50.2% | 49.2% | 50.8% |
| 2 | 2004 | 242,543 | 80,950 | # Hoffmann, Richard | 161,593 | # Israel, Steve* | | 80,643 D | 33.4% | 66.6% | 33.4% | 66.6% |
| 2 | 2002 | 146,126 | 59,117 | # Finley, Joseph P. | 85,451 | # Israel, Steve* | 1,558 | 26,334 D | 40.5% | 58.5% | 40.9% | 59.1% |
| 3 | 2004 | 271,996 | 171,259 | # King, Peter T.* | 100,737 | Mathies, Blair H. Jr. | | 70,522 R | 63.0% | 37.0% | 63.0% | 37.0% |
| 3 | 2002 | 169,072 | 121,537 | # King, Peter T.* | 46,022 | Finz, Stuart L. | 1,513 | 75,515 R | 71.9% | 27.2% | 72.5% | 27.5% |
| 4 | 2004 | 254,110 | 94,141 | # Garner, James A. | 159,969 | # McCarthy, Carolyn* | | 65,828 D | 37.0% | 63.0% | 37.0% | 63.0% |
| 4 | 2002 | 168,540 | 72,882 | # O'Grady, Marilyn F. | 94,806 | # McCarthy, Carolyn* | 852 | 21,924 D | 43.2% | 56.3% | 43.5% | 56.5% |
| 5 | 2004 | 167,841 | 46,867 | # Graves, Stephen | 119,726 | # Ackerman, Gary L.* | 1,248 | 72,859 D | 27.9% | 71.3% | 28.1% | 71.9% |
| 5 | 2002 | 74,491 | | | 68,773 | # Ackerman, Gary L.* | 5,718 | 68,773 D | | 92.3% | | 100.0% |
| 6 | 2004 | 129,688 | | | 129,688 | # Meeks, Gregory W.* | | 129,688 D | | 100.0% | | 100.0% |
| 6 | 2002 | 75,431 | | | 72,799 | # Meeks, Gregory W.* | 2,632 | 72,799 D | | 96.5% | | 100.0% |
| 7 | 2004 | 128,823 | 24,548 | # Cinquemain, Joseph | 104,275 | # Crowley, Joseph* | | 79,727 D | 19.1% | 80.9% | 19.1% | 80.9% |
| 7 | 2002 | 69,539 | 18,572 | # Brawley, Kevin | 50,967 | # Crowley, Joseph* | | 32,395 D | 26.7% | 73.3% | 26.7% | 73.3% |
| 8 | 2004 | 201,322 | 39,240 | # Hort, Peter | 162,082 | # Nadler, Jerrold* | | 122,842 D | 19.5% | 80.5% | 19.5% | 80.5% |
| 8 | 2002 | 106,481 | 19,674 | # Farrin, Jim | 81,002 | # Nadler, Jerrold* | 5,805 | 61,328 D | 18.5% | 76.1% | 19.5% | 80.5% |
| 9 | 2004 | 158,476 | 45,451 | # Cronin, Gerard J. | 113,025 | # Weiner, Anthony* | | 67,574 D | 28.7% | 71.3% | 28.7% | 71.3% |
| 9 | 2002 | 92,435 | 31,698 | # Donohue, Alfred F. | 60,737 | # Weiner, Anthony* | | 29,039 D | 34.3% | 65.7% | 34.3% | 65.7% |
| 10 | 2004 | 148,766 | 11,099 | Clarke, Harvey R. | 136,113 | # Towns, Edolphus* | 1,554 | 125,014 D | 7.5% | 91.5% | 7.5% | 92.5% |
| 10 | 2002 | 75,498 | | | 73,859 | # Towns, Edolphus* | 1,639 | 73,859 D | | 97.8% | | 100.0% |
| 11 | 2004 | 154,198 | | | 144,999 | # Owens, Major R.* | 9,199 | 144,999 D | | 94.0% | | 100.0% |
| 11 | 2002 | 88,864 | 11,149 | # Cleary, Susan | 76,917 | # Owens, Major R.* | 798 | 65,768 D | 12.5% | 86.6% | 12.7% | 87.3% |
| 12 | 2004 | 124,962 | 17,166 | # Rodriguez, Paul A. | 107,796 | # Velázquez, Nydia M.* | | 90,630 D | 13.7% | 86.3% | 13.7% | 86.3% |
| 12 | 2002 | 50,527 | | | 48,408 | # Velázquez, Nydia M.* | 2,119 | 48,408 D | | 95.8% | | 100.0% |
| 13 | 2004 | 191,434 | 112,934 | # Fossella, Vito J.* | 78,500 | # Barbaro, Frank J. | | 34,434 R | 59.0% | 41.0% | 59.0% | 41.0% |
| 13 | 2002 | 103,693 | 72,204 | # Fossella, Vito J.* | 29,366 | # Mattsson, Arne M. | 2,123 | 42,838 R | 69.6% | 28.3% | 71.1% | 28.9% |
| 14 | 2004 | 230,311 | 43,623 | # Srdanovic, Anton | 186,688 | # Maloney, Carolyn B.* | | 143,065 D | 18.9% | 81.1% | 18.9% | 81.1% |
| 14 | 2002 | 127,479 | 31,548 | # Srdanovic, Anton | 95,931 | # Maloney, Carolyn B.* | | 64,383 D | 24.7% | 75.3% | 24.7% | 75.3% |
| 15 | 2004 | 177,051 | 12,355 | Jefferson, Kenneth P. Jr. | 161,351 | # Rangel, Charles B.* | 3,345 | 148,996 D | 7.0% | 91.1% | 7.1% | 92.9% |
| 15 | 2002 | 95,375 | 11,008 | # Fields, Jessie A. | 84,367 | # Rangel, Charles B.* | | 73,359 D | 11.5% | 88.5% | 11.5% | 88.5% |
| 16 | 2004 | 117,248 | 5,610 | # Mohamed, Ali | 111,638 | # Serrano, Jose E.* | | 106,028 D | 4.8% | 95.2% | 4.8% | 95.2% |
| 16 | 2002 | 55,082 | 4,366 | # Dellavalle, Frank | 50,716 | # Serrano, Jose E.* | | 46,350 D | 7.9% | 92.1% | 7.9% | 92.1% |
| 17 | 2004 | 184,536 | 40,524 | Brennan, Matt I. | 140,530 | # Engel, Eliot L.* | 3,482 | 100,006 D | 22.0% | 76.2% | 22.4% | 77.6% |
| 17 | 2002 | 123,843 | 42,634 | # Vanderhoef, C. Scott | 77,535 | # Engel, Eliot L.* | 3,674 | 34,901 D | 34.4% | 62.6% | 35.5% | 64.5% |
| 18 | 2004 | 244,690 | 73,975 | Hoffman, Richard A. | 170,715 | # Lowey, Nita M.* | | 96,740 D | 30.2% | 69.8% | 30.2% | 69.8% |
| 18 | 2002 | 107,515 | | | 98,957 | # Lowey, Nita M.* | 8,558 | 98,957 D | | 92.0% | | 100.0% |
| 19 | 2004 | 262,830 | 175,401 | # Kelly, Sue W.* | 87,429 | Jaliman, Michael | | 87,972 R | 66.7% | 33.3% | 66.7% | 33.3% |
| 19 | 2002 | 173,112 | 121,129 | # Kelly, Sue W.* | 44,967 | Selendy, Janine M.H. | 7,016 | 76,162 R | 70.0% | 26.0% | 72.9% | 27.1% |
| 20 | 2004 | 286,736 | 188,753 | # Sweeney, John E.* | 96,630 | Kelly, Doris F. | 1,353 | 92,123 R | 65.8% | 33.7% | 66.1% | 33.9% |
| 20 | 2002 | 191,278 | 140,238 | # Sweeney, John E.* | 45,878 | Stoppenbach, Frank | 5,162 | 94,360 R | 73.3% | 24.0% | 75.3% | 24.7% |
| 21 | 2004 | 274,154 | 80,121 | Redlich, Warren | 194,033 | # McNulty, Michael R.* | | 113,912 D | 29.2% | 70.8% | 29.2% | 70.8% |
| 21 | 2002 | 214,854 | 53,525 | Rosenstein, Charles B. | 161,329 | # McNulty, Michael R.* | | 107,804 D | 24.9% | 75.1% | 24.9% | 75.1% |

# NEW YORK

## HOUSE OF REPRESENTATIVES

| | | Total | Republican | | Democratic | | Other | Rep.-Dem. | Percentage | | | |
|---|---|---|---|---|---|---|---|---|---|---|---|---|
| | | | | | | | | | Total Vote | | Major Vote | |
| CD | Year | Vote | Vote | Candidate | Vote | Candidate | Vote | Plurality | Rep. | Dem. | Rep. | Dem. |
| 22 | 2004 | 249,370 | 81,881 | Brenner, William A. | 167,489 | # Hinchey, Maurice D.* | | 85,608 D | 32.8% | 67.2% | 32.8% | 67.2% |
| 22 | 2002 | 176,484 | 58,008 | # Hall, Eric | 113,280 | # Hinchey, Maurice D.* | 5,196 | 55,272 D | 32.9% | 64.2% | 33.9% | 66.1% |
| 23 | 2004 | 226,527 | 160,079 | # McHugh, John M.* | 66,448 | Johnson, Robert J. | | 93,631 R | 70.7% | 29.3% | 70.7% | 29.3% |
| 23 | 2002 | 124,682 | 124,682 | # McHugh, John M.* | | | | 124,682 R | 100.0% | | 100.0% | |
| 24 | 2004 | 251,368 | 143,000 | # Boehlert, Sherwood* | 85,140 | Miller, Jeffrey A. | 23,228 | 57,860 R | 56.9% | 33.9% | 62.7% | 37.3% |
| 24 | 2002 | 152,777 | 108,017 | Boehlert, Sherwood* | | | 44,760 | 108,017 R | 70.7% | | 100.0% | |
| 25 | 2004 | 209,169 | 189,063 | # Walsh, James T.* | | | 20,106 | 189,063 R | 90.4% | | 100.0% | |
| 25 | 2002 | 200,031 | 144,610 | # Walsh, James T.* | 53,290 | Aldersley, Stephanie | 2,131 | 91,320 R | 72.3% | 26.6% | 73.1% | 26.9% |
| 26 | 2004 | 283,079 | 157,466 | # Reynolds, Thomas M.* | 125,613 | # Davis, Jack | | 31,853 R | 55.6% | 44.4% | 55.6% | 44.4% |
| 26 | 2002 | 183,459 | 135,089 | # Reynolds, Thomas M.* | 41,140 | Nariman, Ayesha F. | 7,230 | 93,949 R | 73.6% | 22.4% | 76.7% | 23.3% |
| 27 | 2004 | 282,890 | 139,558 | # Naples, Nancy A. | 143,332 | # Higgins, Brian | | 3,774 D | 49.3% | 50.7% | 49.3% | 50.7% |
| 27 | 2002 | 173,919 | 120,117 | # Quinn, Jack* | 47,811 | # Crotty, Peter | 5,991 | 72,306 R | 69.1% | 27.5% | 71.5% | 28.5% |
| 28 | 2004 | 219,876 | 54,543 | # Laba, Michael D. | 159,655 | # Slaughter, Louise M.* | 5,678 | 105,112 D | 24.8% | 72.6% | 25.5% | 74.5% |
| 28 | 2002 | 158,604 | 59,547 | # Wojtaszek, Henry F. | 99,057 | # Slaughter, Louise M.* | | 39,510 D | 37.5% | 62.5% | 37.5% | 62.5% |
| 29 | 2004 | 270,215 | 136,883 | Kuhl, John R. "Randy" Jr. | 110,241 | # Barend, Samara | 23,091 | 26,642 R | 50.7% | 40.8% | 55.4% | 44.6% |
| 29 | 2002 | 174,631 | 127,657 | # Houghton, Amo* | 37,128 | Peters, Kisun J. | 9,846 | 90,529 R | 73.1% | 21.3% | 77.5% | 22.5% |
| Total | 2004 | 6,222,418 | 2,448,345 | | 3,681,789 | | 92,284 | 1,233,444 D | 39.3% | 59.2% | 39.9% | 60.1% |
| Total | 2002 | 3,821,613 | 1,770,532 | | 1,924,769 | | 126,312 | 154,237 D | 46.3% | 50.4% | 47.9% | 52.1% |

A pound sign (#) indicates that the candidate received votes on the ballot line of one or more other parties. Each candidate's total vote is listed above.

An asterisk (*) denotes incumbent.

# NEW YORK

## GENERAL AND PRIMARY ELECTIONS

### 2004 GENERAL ELECTIONS

**President** — Other vote was 99,873 Ralph Nader (84,247 on the Independence Party line; 15,626 on the Peace and Justice line); 11,607 Libertarian (Michael Badnarik); 2,405 Socialist Workers (Roger Calero); 207 write-in (Michael Peroutka); 87 write-in (David Cobb); 4 write-in (Michael Halpin); 4 write-in (John Joseph Kennedy); 2 write-in (Bill Van Auken).

**Senator** — Other vote was 220,960 Conservative (Marilyn O'Grady); 36,942 Green (David E. McReynolds); 19,073 Libertarian (Donald Silberger); 16,196 Builders (Abraham Hirschfeld); 14,811 Socialist Workers (Martin Koppel).

**House** — Other vote was:

CD 1
CD 2
CD 3
CD 4
CD 5    1,248 For All Americans (Gonzalo Policarpio).
CD 6
CD 7
CD 8

# NEW YORK
## GENERAL AND PRIMARY ELECTIONS

## 2004 GENERAL ELECTIONS

CD 9
CD 10    1,554 Conservative (Mariana Blume).
CD 11    4,721 Independence (Lorraine Stevens); 4,478 Conservative (Sol Lieberman).
CD 12
CD 13
CD 14
CD 15    3,345 Independence (Jessie Fields).
CD 16
CD 17    3,482 Conservative (Kevin Brawley).
CD 18
CD 19
CD 20    1,353 Centrist (Morris N. Guller).
CD 21
CD 22
CD 23
CD 24    23,228 Conservative (David L. Walrath).
CD 25    20,106 Peace and Justice (Howie Hawkins).
CD 26
CD 27
CD 28    5,678 Independence (Francina J. Cartonia).
CD 29    17,272 Conservative (Mark W. Assini); 5,819 Independence (John Ciampoli).

Note: Candidates in New York can appear on the ballot line of more than one party. In the presidential election, for instance, George W. Bush received 2,806,993 on the Republican line and another 155,574 votes on the Conservative line, for a total of 2,962,567 votes. John Kerry received 4,180,755 votes on the Democratic line and 133,525 votes on the Working Families line, for a total of 4,314,280 votes. In the New York tables, votes received by each Democratic and Republican candidate on the ballot lines of other parties are combined into one overall vote, which is credited to the major party of which they are a member.

## 2004 PRIMARY ELECTIONS

**Primary**  March 2, 2004 (President)
September 14, 2004 (Congress)

**Registration** (as of March 1, 2004)

| | |
|---|---|
| Republican | 3,083,584 |
| Democratic | 5,175,514 |
| Independence | 280,532 |
| Conservative | 156,959 |
| Liberal | 79,088 |
| Right to Life | 45,861 |
| Green | 38,492 |
| Working Families | 21,334 |
| Other | 2,194,096 |
| TOTAL | 11,075,460 |

**Primary Type**  Closed—Only registered Democrats and Republicans could vote in their party's primary.

# NEW YORK

## GENERAL AND PRIMARY ELECTIONS

Note: An asterisk (*) denotes incumbent. Names of unopposed candidates did not appear on the primary ballot; therefore, no votes were cast for these candidates.

| | REPUBLICAN PRIMARIES | | | DEMOCRATIC PRIMARIES | | |
|---|---|---|---|---|---|---|
| President | No Republican primary | | | John Kerry | 437,754 | 61.2% |
| | | | | John Edwards | 143,960 | 20.1% |
| | | | | Al Sharpton | 57,456 | 8.0% |
| | | | | Dennis J. Kucinich | 36,680 | 5.1% |
| | | | | Howard Dean | 20,471 | 2.9% |
| | | | | Joseph I. Lieberman | 9,314 | 1.3% |
| | | | | Richard A. Gephardt | 3,954 | 0.6% |
| | | | | Wesley Clark | 3,517 | 0.5% |
| | | | | Lyndon H. LaRouche Jr. | 2,527 | 0.4% |
| | | | | TOTAL | 715,633 | |
| Senator | Howard Mills | Unopposed | | Charles E. Schumer* | Unopposed | |
| Congressional District 1 | William M. Manger Jr. | Unopposed | | Timothy H. Bishop* | Unopposed | |
| Congressional District 2 | Richard Hoffmann | Unopposed | | Steve Israel* | Unopposed | |
| Congressional District 3 | Peter T. King* | 8,110 | 83.6% | Blair H. Mathies Jr. | Unopposed | |
| | Robert Previdi | 1,564 | 16.1% | | | |
| | Write-in | 22 | 0.2% | | | |
| | TOTAL | 9,696 | | | | |
| Congressional District 4 | James A. Garner | Unopposed | | Carolyn McCarthy* | Unopposed | |
| Congressional District 5 | Stephen Graves | 1,461 | 74.9% | Gary L. Ackerman* | Unopposed | |
| | Gonzalo Policarpio | 481 | 24.7% | | | |
| | Write-in | 8 | 0.4% | | | |
| | TOTAL | 1,950 | | | | |
| Congressional District 6 | No Republican candidate | | | Gregory W. Meeks* | Unopposed | |
| Congressional District 7 | Joseph Cinquemain | Unopposed | | Joseph Crowley* | 15,738 | 63.4% |
| | | | | Dennis Coleman | 4,716 | 19.0% |
| | | | | Aniello V. Grimaldi | 2,280 | 9.2% |
| | | | | Curtis Brooks | 2,102 | 8.5% |
| | | | | Write-in | 6 | |
| | | | | TOTAL | 24,842 | |
| Congressional District 8 | Peter Hort | Unopposed | | Jerrold Nadler* | Unopposed | |
| Congressional District 9 | Gerard J. Cronin | Unopposed | | Anthony Weiner* | Unopposed | |
| Congressional District 10 | Harvey R. Clarke | Unopposed | | Edolphus Towns* | Unopposed | |
| Congressional District 11 | No Republican candidate | | | Major R. Owens* | 14,718 | 45.4% |
| | | | | Yvette D. Clarke | 9,371 | 28.9% |
| | | | | Tracy L. Boyland | 7,119 | 22.0% |
| | | | | Gabriel A. Pearse | 1,179 | 3.6% |
| | | | | Write-in | 3 | |
| | | | | TOTAL | 32,390 | |
| Congressional District 12 | Paul A. Rodriguez | Unopposed | | Nydia M. Velázquez* | Unopposed | |
| Congressional District 13 | Vito J. Fossella* | Unopposed | | Frank J. Barbaro | Unopposed | |
| Congressional District 14 | Anton Srdanovic | Unopposed | | Carolyn B. Maloney* | Unopposed | |

# NEW YORK

## GENERAL AND PRIMARY ELECTIONS

| | REPUBLICAN PRIMARIES | | | DEMOCRATIC PRIMARIES | | |
|---|---|---|---|---|---|---|
| Congressional District 15 | Kenneth P. Jefferson Jr. | Unopposed | | Charles B. Rangel* | 19,087 | 76.0% |
| | | | | Ruben Dario Vargas | 3,254 | 12.9% |
| | | | | Geoffrey G. Johnson | 2,779 | 11.1% |
| | | | | Write-in | 8 | |
| | | | | TOTAL | 25,128 | |
| Congressional District 16 | Ali Mohamed | Unopposed | | Jose E. Serrano* | Unopposed | |
| Congressional District 17 | Matt I. Brennan | Unopposed | | Eliot L. Engel* | 18,854 | 58.8% |
| | | | | Kevin M. McAdams | 6,416 | 20.0% |
| | | | | Jessica Flagg | 3,225 | 10.1% |
| | | | | Write-in | 3,543 | 11.1% |
| | | | | TOTAL | 32,038 | |
| Congressional District 18 | Richard A. Hoffman | 2,439 | 44.5% | Nita M. Lowey* | Unopposed | |
| | Jim Russell | 2,260 | 41.2% | | | |
| | Write-in | 784 | 14.3% | | | |
| | TOTAL | 5,483 | | | | |
| Congressional District 19 | Sue W. Kelly* | Unopposed | | Michael Jaliman | 5,440 | 58.0% |
| | | | | Janine Selendy | 3,722 | 39.7% |
| | | | | Write-in | 211 | 2.3% |
| | | | | TOTAL | 9,373 | |
| Congressional District 20 | John E. Sweeney* | Unopposed | | Doris F. Kelly | 4,350 | 63.7% |
| | | | | John J. Coleman | 2,427 | 35.5% |
| | | | | Write-in | 56 | 0.8% |
| | | | | TOTAL | 6,833 | |
| Congressional District 21 | Warren Redlich | Unopposed | | Michael R. McNulty* | Unopposed | |
| Congressional District 22 | William A. Brenner | 6,793 | 50.9% | Maurice D. Hinchey* | Unopposed | |
| | Paul Slobodian | 4,663 | 35.0% | | | |
| | Write-in | 1,883 | 14.1% | | | |
| | TOTAL | 13,339 | | | | |
| Congressional District 23 | John M. McHugh* | Unopposed | | Robert J. Johnson | Unopposed | |
| Congressional District 24 | Sherwood Boehlert* | 22,908 | 58.9% | Jeffrey A. Miller | Unopposed | |
| | David L. Walrath | 15,394 | 39.6% | | | |
| | Write-in | 588 | 1.5% | | | |
| | TOTAL | 38,890 | | | | |
| Congressional District 25 | James T. Walsh* | Unopposed | | No Democratic candidate | | |
| Congressional District 26 | Thomas M. Reynolds* | Unopposed | | Jack Davis | Unopposed | |
| Congressional District 27 | Nancy A. Naples | Unopposed | | Brian Higgins | 18,790 | 44.4% |
| | | | | Paul T. Clark | 11,150 | 26.4% |
| | | | | Michael J. Collesano | 5,042 | 11.9% |
| | | | | Mark W. Thomas | 3,961 | 9.4% |
| | | | | Peter Crotty | 1,401 | 3.3% |
| | | | | Write-in | 1,962 | 4.6% |
| | | | | TOTAL | 42,306 | |
| Congressional District 28 | Michael D. Laba | Unopposed | | Louise M. Slaughter* | 19,966 | 78.9% |
| | | | | Francina Cartonia | 3,202 | 12.6% |
| | | | | Write-in | 2,149 | 8.5% |
| | | | | TOTAL | 25,317 | |
| Congressional District 29 | John R. "Randy" Kuhl Jr. | 25,552 | 64.0% | Samara Barend | 9,082 | 79.7% |
| | Mark W. Assini | 13,303 | 33.3% | Jeremy Weir Alderson | 2,204 | 19.3% |
| | Write-in | 1,074 | 2.7% | Write-in | 112 | 1.0% |
| | TOTAL | 39,929 | | TOTAL | 11,398 | |

# NORTH CAROLINA

## GOVERNOR
Michael F. Easley (D). Reelected 2004 to a four-year term. Previously elected 2000.

## SENATORS (2 Republicans)
Richard M. Burr (R). Elected 2004 to a six-year term.

Elizabeth Dole (R). Elected 2002 to a six-year term.

## REPRESENTATIVES (7 Republicans, 6 Democrats)
1. G.K. Butterfield (D)
2. Bob Etheridge (D)
3. Walter B. Jones (R)
4. David E. Price (D)
5. Virginia Foxx (R)
6. Howard Coble (R)
7. Mike McIntyre (D)
8. Robin Hayes (R)
9. Sue Myrick (R)
10. Patrick T. McHenry (R)
11. Charles H. Taylor (R)
12. Melvin Watt (D)
13. Brad Miller (D)

## POSTWAR VOTE FOR PRESIDENT

| Year | Total Vote | Republican Vote | Candidate | Democratic Vote | Candidate | Other Vote | Plurality | Percentage Total Vote Rep. | Dem. | Major Vote Rep. | Dem. |
|------|-----------|-----------------|-----------|-----------------|-----------|------------|-----------|------|------|------|------|
| 2004 | 3,501,007 | 1,961,166 | Bush, George W. | 1,525,849 | Kerry, John | 13,992 | 435,317 R | 56.0% | 43.6% | 56.2% | 43.8% |
| 2000 | 2,911,262 | 1,631,163 | Bush, George W. | 1,257,692 | Gore, Al | 22,407 | 373,471 R | 56.0% | 43.2% | 56.5% | 43.5% |
| 1996** | 2,515,807 | 1,225,938 | Dole, Bob | 1,107,849 | Clinton, Bill | 182,020 | 118,089 R | 48.7% | 44.0% | 52.5% | 47.5% |
| 1992** | 2,611,850 | 1,134,661 | Bush, George | 1,114,042 | Clinton, Bill | 363,147 | 20,619 R | 43.4% | 42.7% | 50.5% | 49.5% |
| 1988 | 2,134,370 | 1,237,258 | Bush, George | 890,167 | Dukakis, Michael S. | 6,945 | 347,091 R | 58.0% | 41.7% | 58.2% | 41.8% |
| 1984 | 2,175,361 | 1,346,481 | Reagan, Ronald | 824,287 | Mondale, Walter F. | 4,593 | 522,194 R | 61.9% | 37.9% | 62.0% | 38.0% |
| 1980** | 1,855,833 | 915,018 | Reagan, Ronald | 875,635 | Carter, Jimmy | 65,180 | 39,383 R | 49.3% | 47.2% | 51.1% | 48.9% |
| 1976 | 1,678,914 | 741,960 | Ford, Gerald R. | 927,365 | Carter, Jimmy | 9,589 | 185,405 D | 44.2% | 55.2% | 44.4% | 55.6% |
| 1972 | 1,518,612 | 1,054,889 | Nixon, Richard M. | 438,705 | McGovern, George S. | 25,018 | 616,184 R | 69.5% | 28.9% | 70.6% | 29.4% |
| 1968** | 1,587,493 | 627,192 | Nixon, Richard M. | 464,113 | Humphrey, Hubert H. | 496,188 | 131,004 R | 39.5% | 29.2% | 57.5% | 42.5% |
| 1964 | 1,424,983 | 624,844 | Goldwater, Barry M. | 800,139 | Johnson, Lyndon B. | | 175,295 D | 43.8% | 56.2% | 43.8% | 56.2% |
| 1960 | 1,368,556 | 655,420 | Nixon, Richard M. | 713,136 | Kennedy, John F. | | 57,716 D | 47.9% | 52.1% | 47.9% | 52.1% |
| 1956 | 1,165,592 | 575,062 | Eisenhower, Dwight D. | 590,530 | Stevenson, Adlai E. | | 15,468 D | 49.3% | 50.7% | 49.3% | 50.7% |
| 1952 | 1,210,910 | 558,107 | Eisenhower, Dwight D. | 652,803 | Stevenson, Adlai E. | | 94,696 D | 46.1% | 53.9% | 46.1% | 53.9% |
| 1948** | 791,209 | 258,572 | Dewey, Thomas E. | 459,070 | Truman, Harry S. | 73,567 | 200,498 D | 32.7% | 58.0% | 36.0% | 64.0% |

In past elections, the other vote included: 1996 - 168,059 Reform (Ross Perot); 1992 - 357,864 Independent (Perot); 1980 - 52,800 Independent (John Anderson); 1968 - 496,188 American Independent (George Wallace), who came in second statewide; 1948 - 69,652 States' Rights (Strom Thurmond).

# NORTH CAROLINA

## POSTWAR VOTE FOR GOVERNOR

| Year | Total Vote | Republican Vote | Republican Candidate | Democratic Vote | Democratic Candidate | Other Vote | Rep.-Dem. Plurality | Total Vote Rep. | Total Vote Dem. | Major Vote Rep. | Major Vote Dem. |
|---|---|---|---|---|---|---|---|---|---|---|---|
| 2004 | 3,486,688 | 1,495,021 | Ballantine, Patrick J. | 1,939,154 | Easley, Michael F. | 52,513 | 444,133 D | 42.9% | 55.6% | 43.5% | 56.5% |
| 2000 | 2,942,062 | 1,360,960 | Vinroot, Richard | 1,530,324 | Easley, Michael F. | 50,778 | 169,364 D | 46.3% | 52.0% | 47.1% | 52.9% |
| 1996 | 2,566,185 | 1,097,053 | Hayes, Robin | 1,436,638 | Hunt, James B. | 32,494 | 339,585 D | 42.8% | 56.0% | 43.3% | 56.7% |
| 1992 | 2,595,184 | 1,121,955 | Gardner, James C. | 1,368,246 | Hunt, James B. | 104,983 | 246,291 D | 43.2% | 52.7% | 45.1% | 54.9% |
| 1988 | 2,180,025 | 1,222,338 | Martin, James G. | 957,687 | Jordan, Robert B. | | 264,651 R | 56.1% | 43.9% | 56.1% | 43.9% |
| 1984 | 2,226,727 | 1,208,167 | Martin, James G. | 1,011,209 | Edmisten, Rufus | 7,351 | 196,958 R | 54.3% | 45.4% | 54.4% | 45.6% |
| 1980 | 1,847,432 | 691,449 | Lake, Beverly | 1,143,145 | Hunt, James B. | 12,838 | 451,696 D | 37.4% | 61.9% | 37.7% | 62.3% |
| 1976 | 1,663,824 | 564,102 | Flaherty, David T. | 1,081,293 | Hunt, James B. | 18,429 | 517,191 D | 33.9% | 65.0% | 34.3% | 65.7% |
| 1972 | 1,504,785 | 767,470 | Holshouser, James E. | 729,104 | Bowles, Hargrove | 8,211 | 38,366 R | 51.0% | 48.5% | 51.3% | 48.7% |
| 1968 | 1,558,308 | 737,075 | Gardner, James C. | 821,233 | Scott, Robert W. | | 84,158 D | 47.3% | 52.7% | 47.3% | 52.7% |
| 1964 | 1,396,508 | 606,165 | Gavin, Robert L. | 790,343 | Moore, Dan K. | | 184,178 D | 43.4% | 56.6% | 43.4% | 56.6% |
| 1960 | 1,350,360 | 613,975 | Gavin, Robert L. | 735,248 | Sanford, Terry | 1,137 | 121,273 D | 45.5% | 54.4% | 45.5% | 54.5% |
| 1956 | 1,135,859 | 375,379 | Hayes, Kyle | 760,480 | Hodges, Luther H. | | 385,101 D | 33.0% | 67.0% | 33.0% | 67.0% |
| 1952 | 1,179,635 | 383,329 | Seawell, H. F. | 796,306 | Umstead, William B. | | 412,977 D | 32.5% | 67.5% | 32.5% | 67.5% |
| 1948 | 780,525 | 206,166 | Pritchard, George | 570,995 | Scott, William Kerr | 3,364 | 364,829 D | 26.4% | 73.2% | 26.5% | 73.5% |

## POSTWAR VOTE FOR SENATOR

| Year | Total Vote | Republican Vote | Republican Candidate | Democratic Vote | Democratic Candidate | Other Vote | Rep.-Dem. Plurality | Total Vote Rep. | Total Vote Dem. | Major Vote Rep. | Major Vote Dem. |
|---|---|---|---|---|---|---|---|---|---|---|---|
| 2004 | 3,472,082 | 1,791,450 | Burr, Richard M. | 1,632,527 | Bowles, Erskine | 48,105 | 158,923 R | 51.6% | 47.0% | 52.3% | 47.7% |
| 2002 | 2,331,181 | 1,248,664 | Dole, Elizabeth | 1,047,983 | Bowles, Erskine | 34,534 | 200,681 R | 53.6% | 45.0% | 54.4% | 45.6% |
| 1998 | 2,012,143 | 945,943 | Faircloth, Lauch | 1,029,237 | Edwards, John | 36,963 | 83,294 D | 47.0% | 51.2% | 47.9% | 52.1% |
| 1996 | 2,556,456 | 1,345,833 | Helms, Jesse | 1,173,875 | Gantt, Harvey B. | 36,748 | 171,958 R | 52.6% | 45.9% | 53.4% | 46.6% |
| 1992 | 2,577,891 | 1,297,892 | Faircloth, Lauch | 1,194,015 | Sanford, Terry | 85,984 | 103,877 R | 50.3% | 46.3% | 52.1% | 47.9% |
| 1990 | 2,069,585 | 1,087,331 | Helms, Jesse | 981,573 | Gantt, Harvy B. | 681 | 105,758 R | 52.5% | 47.4% | 52.6% | 47.4% |
| 1986 | 1,591,330 | 767,668 | Broyhill, James T. | 823,662 | Sanford, Terry | | 55,994 D | 48.2% | 51.8% | 48.2% | 51.8% |
| 1984 | 2,239,051 | 1,156,768 | Helms, Jesse | 1,070,488 | Hunt, James B. | 11,795 | 86,280 R | 51.7% | 47.8% | 51.9% | 48.1% |
| 1980 | 1,797,665 | 898,064 | East, John P. | 887,653 | Morgan, Robert | 11,948 | 10,411 R | 50.0% | 49.4% | 50.3% | 49.7% |
| 1978 | 1,135,814 | 619,151 | Helms, Jesse | 516,663 | Ingram, John | | 102,488 R | 54.5% | 45.5% | 54.5% | 45.5% |
| 1974 | 1,020,367 | 377,618 | Stevens, William E. | 633,775 | Morgan, Robert | 8,974 | 256,157 D | 37.0% | 62.1% | 37.3% | 62.7% |
| 1972 | 1,472,541 | 795,248 | Helms, Jesse | 677,293 | Galifianakis, Nick | | 117,955 R | 54.0% | 46.0% | 54.0% | 46.0% |
| 1968 | 1,437,340 | 566,934 | Somers, Robert V. | 870,406 | Ervin, Sam J. | | 303,472 D | 39.4% | 60.6% | 39.4% | 60.6% |
| 1966 | 901,978 | 400,502 | Shallcross, John S. | 501,440 | Jordan, B. Everett | 36 | 100,938 D | 44.4% | 55.6% | 44.4% | 55.6% |
| 1962 | 813,155 | 321,635 | Greene, Claude L. | 491,520 | Ervin, Sam J. | | 169,885 D | 39.6% | 60.4% | 39.6% | 60.4% |
| 1960 | 1,291,485 | 497,964 | Hayes, Kyle | 793,521 | Jordan, B. Everett | | 295,557 D | 38.6% | 61.4% | 38.6% | 61.4% |
| 1958S | 616,469 | 184,977 | Clarke, Richard C. | 431,492 | Jordan, B. Everett | | 246,515 D | 30.0% | 70.0% | 30.0% | 70.0% |
| 1956 | 1,098,828 | 367,475 | Johnson, Joel A. | 731,353 | Ervin, Sam J. | | 363,878 D | 33.4% | 66.6% | 33.4% | 66.6% |
| 1954 | 619,634 | 211,322 | West, Paul C. | 408,312 | Scott, William Kerr | | 196,990 D | 34.1% | 65.9% | 34.1% | 65.9% |
| 1954S | 410,574 | | — | 410,574 | Ervin, Sam J. | | 410,574 D | | 100.0% | | 100.0% |
| 1950 | 548,276 | 171,804 | Leavitt, Halsey B. | 376,472 | Hoey, Clyde R. | | 204,668 D | 31.3% | 68.7% | 31.3% | 68.7% |
| 1950S | 544,924 | 177,753 | Gavin, E. L. | 364,912 | Smith, Willis | 2,259 | 187,159 D | 32.6% | 67.0% | 32.8% | 67.2% |
| 1948 | 764,559 | 220,307 | Wilkinson, John A. | 540,762 | Broughton, J. M. | 3,490 | 320,455 D | 28.8% | 70.7% | 28.9% | 71.1% |

The 1958 election and one each of the 1954 and 1950 elections were for short terms to fill vacancies.

# NORTH CAROLINA

Congressional districts first established for elections held in 2002
13 members

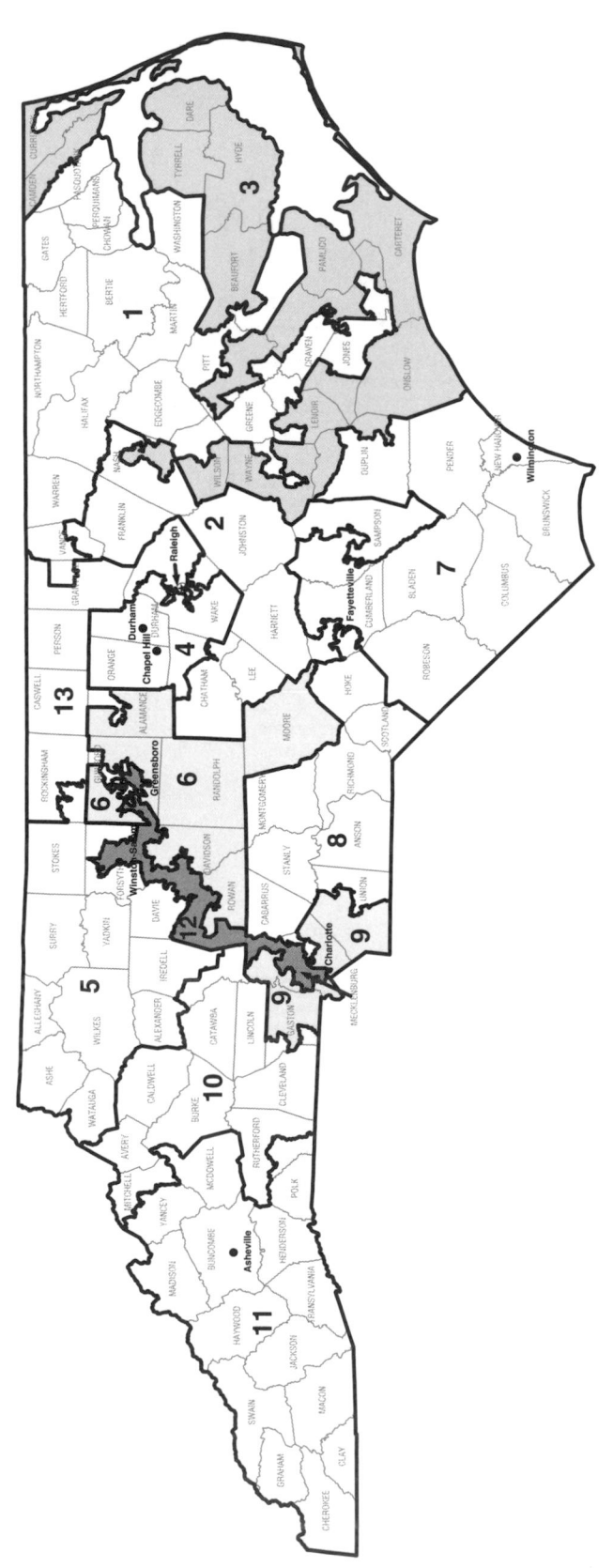

329

# NORTH CAROLINA

Central North Carolina Area

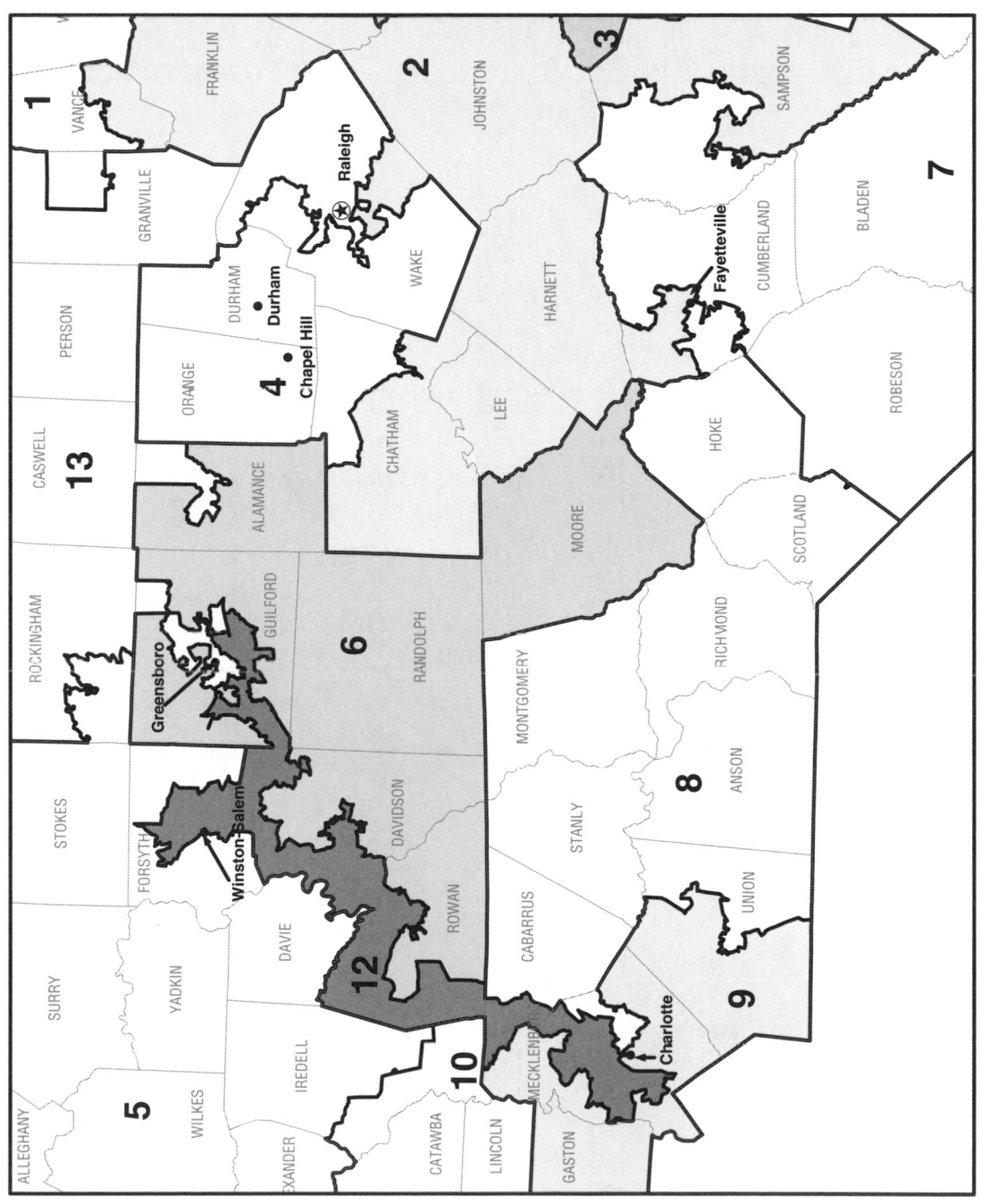

# NORTH CAROLINA

## PRESIDENT 2004

| 2000 Census Population | County | Total Vote | Republican | Democratic | Other | Rep.-Dem. Plurality | Percentage Total Vote Rep. | Dem. | Major Vote Rep. | Dem. |
|---:|---|---:|---:|---:|---:|---:|---:|---:|---:|---:|
| 130,800 | ALAMANCE | 54,175 | 33,302 | 20,686 | 187 | 12,616 R | 61.5% | 38.2% | 61.7% | 38.3% |
| 33,603 | ALEXANDER | 15,600 | 10,928 | 4,618 | 54 | 6,310 R | 70.1% | 29.6% | 70.3% | 29.7% |
| 10,677 | ALLEGHANY | 4,827 | 2,883 | 1,922 | 22 | 961 R | 59.7% | 39.8% | 60.0% | 40.0% |
| 25,275 | ANSON | 9,225 | 3,796 | 5,413 | 16 | 1,617 D | 41.1% | 58.7% | 41.2% | 58.8% |
| 24,384 | ASHE | 11,823 | 7,292 | 4,477 | 54 | 2,815 R | 61.7% | 37.9% | 62.0% | 38.0% |
| 17,167 | AVERY | 7,524 | 5,678 | 1,805 | 41 | 3,873 R | 75.5% | 24.0% | 75.9% | 24.1% |
| 44,958 | BEAUFORT | 19,522 | 12,432 | 7,025 | 65 | 5,407 R | 63.7% | 36.0% | 63.9% | 36.1% |
| 19,773 | BERTIE | 8,032 | 3,057 | 4,938 | 37 | 1,881 D | 38.1% | 61.5% | 38.2% | 61.8% |
| 32,278 | BLADEN | 12,313 | 6,174 | 6,109 | 30 | 65 R | 50.1% | 49.6% | 50.3% | 49.7% |
| 73,143 | BRUNSWICK | 37,977 | 22,925 | 14,903 | 149 | 8,022 R | 60.4% | 39.2% | 60.6% | 39.4% |
| 206,330 | BUNCOMBE | 105,013 | 52,491 | 51,868 | 654 | 623 R | 50.0% | 49.4% | 50.3% | 49.7% |
| 89,148 | BURKE | 30,762 | 18,922 | 11,728 | 112 | 7,194 R | 61.5% | 38.1% | 61.7% | 38.3% |
| 131,063 | CABARRUS | 60,824 | 40,780 | 19,803 | 241 | 20,977 R | 67.0% | 32.6% | 67.3% | 32.7% |
| 77,415 | CALDWELL | 31,348 | 21,186 | 9,999 | 163 | 11,187 R | 67.6% | 31.9% | 67.9% | 32.1% |
| 6,885 | CAMDEN | 3,830 | 2,480 | 1,339 | 11 | 1,141 R | 64.8% | 35.0% | 64.9% | 35.1% |
| 59,383 | CARTERET | 25,575 | 17,716 | 7,732 | 127 | 9,984 R | 69.3% | 30.2% | 69.6% | 30.4% |
| 23,501 | CASWELL | 9,437 | 4,868 | 4,539 | 30 | 329 R | 51.6% | 48.1% | 51.7% | 48.3% |
| 141,685 | CATAWBA | 58,688 | 39,602 | 18,858 | 228 | 20,744 R | 67.5% | 32.1% | 67.7% | 32.3% |
| 49,329 | CHATHAM | 25,922 | 12,892 | 12,897 | 133 | 5 D | 49.7% | 49.8% | 50.0% | 50.0% |
| 24,298 | CHEROKEE | 11,199 | 7,517 | 3,635 | 47 | 3,882 R | 67.1% | 32.5% | 67.4% | 32.6% |
| 14,526 | CHOWAN | 5,386 | 2,967 | 2,406 | 13 | 561 R | 55.1% | 44.7% | 55.2% | 44.8% |
| 8,775 | CLAY | 4,866 | 3,209 | 1,628 | 29 | 1,581 R | 65.9% | 33.5% | 66.3% | 33.7% |
| 96,287 | CLEVELAND | 37,079 | 22,750 | 14,215 | 114 | 8,535 R | 61.4% | 38.3% | 61.5% | 38.5% |
| 54,749 | COLUMBUS | 21,191 | 10,773 | 10,343 | 75 | 430 R | 50.8% | 48.8% | 51.0% | 49.0% |
| 91,436 | CRAVEN | 37,756 | 23,575 | 14,019 | 162 | 9,556 R | 62.4% | 37.1% | 62.7% | 37.3% |
| 302,963 | CUMBERLAND | 95,226 | 49,139 | 45,788 | 299 | 3,351 R | 51.6% | 48.1% | 51.8% | 48.2% |
| 18,190 | CURRITUCK | 8,976 | 6,013 | 2,909 | 54 | 3,104 R | 67.0% | 32.4% | 67.4% | 32.6% |
| 29,967 | DARE | 15,548 | 9,345 | 6,136 | 67 | 3,209 R | 60.1% | 39.5% | 60.4% | 39.6% |
| 147,246 | DAVIDSON | 59,496 | 42,075 | 17,191 | 230 | 24,884 R | 70.7% | 28.9% | 71.0% | 29.0% |
| 34,835 | DAVIE | 16,680 | 12,372 | 4,233 | 75 | 8,139 R | 74.2% | 25.4% | 74.5% | 25.5% |
| 49,063 | DUPLIN | 16,583 | 9,611 | 6,923 | 49 | 2,688 R | 58.0% | 41.7% | 58.1% | 41.9% |
| 223,314 | DURHAM | 109,651 | 34,614 | 74,524 | 513 | 39,910 D | 31.6% | 68.0% | 31.7% | 68.3% |
| 55,606 | EDGECOMBE | 21,079 | 8,163 | 12,877 | 39 | 4,714 D | 38.7% | 61.1% | 38.8% | 61.2% |
| 306,067 | FORSYTH | 139,125 | 75,294 | 63,340 | 491 | 11,954 R | 54.1% | 45.5% | 54.3% | 45.7% |
| 47,260 | FRANKLIN | 20,918 | 11,540 | 9,286 | 92 | 2,254 R | 55.2% | 44.4% | 55.4% | 44.6% |
| 190,365 | GASTON | 63,755 | 43,252 | 20,254 | 249 | 22,998 R | 67.8% | 31.8% | 68.1% | 31.9% |
| 10,516 | GATES | 4,053 | 1,924 | 2,121 | 8 | 197 D | 47.5% | 52.3% | 47.6% | 52.4% |
| 7,993 | GRAHAM | 3,987 | 2,693 | 1,272 | 22 | 1,421 R | 67.5% | 31.9% | 67.9% | 32.1% |
| 48,498 | GRANVILLE | 18,601 | 9,491 | 9,057 | 53 | 434 R | 51.0% | 48.7% | 51.2% | 48.8% |
| 18,974 | GREENE | 6,472 | 3,800 | 2,665 | 7 | 1,135 R | 58.7% | 41.2% | 58.8% | 41.2% |
| 421,048 | GUILFORD | 199,314 | 98,254 | 100,042 | 1,018 | 1,788 D | 49.3% | 50.2% | 49.5% | 50.5% |
| 57,370 | HALIFAX | 19,647 | 8,088 | 11,528 | 31 | 3,440 D | 41.2% | 58.7% | 41.2% | 58.8% |
| 91,025 | HARNETT | 32,571 | 20,922 | 11,563 | 86 | 9,359 R | 64.2% | 35.5% | 64.4% | 35.6% |
| 54,033 | HAYWOOD | 25,932 | 14,545 | 11,237 | 150 | 3,308 R | 56.1% | 43.3% | 56.4% | 43.6% |
| 89,173 | HENDERSON | 43,234 | 28,025 | 15,003 | 206 | 13,022 R | 64.8% | 34.7% | 65.1% | 34.9% |
| 22,601 | HERTFORD | 8,132 | 2,942 | 5,141 | 49 | 2,199 D | 36.2% | 63.2% | 36.4% | 63.6% |
| 33,646 | HOKE | 11,088 | 5,257 | 5,794 | 37 | 537 D | 47.4% | 52.3% | 47.6% | 52.4% |
| 5,826 | HYDE | 2,293 | 1,235 | 1,048 | 10 | 187 R | 53.9% | 45.7% | 54.1% | 45.9% |
| 122,660 | IREDELL | 56,973 | 38,675 | 18,065 | 233 | 20,610 R | 67.9% | 31.7% | 68.2% | 31.8% |
| 33,121 | JACKSON | 14,174 | 7,351 | 6,737 | 86 | 614 R | 51.9% | 47.5% | 52.2% | 47.8% |
| 121,965 | JOHNSTON | 54,357 | 36,903 | 17,266 | 188 | 19,637 R | 67.9% | 31.8% | 68.1% | 31.9% |
| 10,381 | JONES | 4,513 | 2,607 | 1,893 | 13 | 714 R | 57.8% | 41.9% | 57.9% | 42.1% |
| 49,040 | LEE | 19,543 | 11,834 | 7,657 | 52 | 4,177 R | 60.6% | 39.2% | 60.7% | 39.3% |
| 59,648 | LENOIR | 23,179 | 12,939 | 10,207 | 33 | 2,732 R | 55.8% | 44.0% | 55.9% | 44.1% |
| 63,780 | LINCOLN | 29,579 | 20,052 | 9,434 | 93 | 10,618 R | 67.8% | 31.9% | 68.0% | 32.0% |
| 42,151 | MCDOWELL | 16,002 | 10,590 | 5,330 | 82 | 5,260 R | 66.2% | 33.3% | 66.5% | 33.5% |
| 29,811 | MACON | 15,024 | 9,448 | 5,489 | 87 | 3,959 R | 62.9% | 36.5% | 63.3% | 36.7% |
| 19,635 | MADISON | 9,463 | 5,175 | 4,234 | 54 | 941 R | 54.7% | 44.7% | 55.0% | 45.0% |
| 25,593 | MARTIN | 10,452 | 5,334 | 5,102 | 16 | 232 R | 51.0% | 48.8% | 51.1% | 48.9% |
| 695,454 | MECKLENBURG | 323,102 | 155,084 | 166,828 | 1,190 | 11,744 D | 48.0% | 51.6% | 48.2% | 51.8% |

# NORTH CAROLINA

## PRESIDENT 2004

| 2000 Census Population | County | Total Vote | Republican | Democratic | Other | Rep.-Dem. Plurality | Percentage | | | |
|---|---|---|---|---|---|---|---|---|---|---|
| | | | | | | | Total Vote | | Major Vote | |
| | | | | | | | Rep. | Dem. | Rep. | Dem. |
| 15,687 | MITCHELL | 7,798 | 5,686 | 2,080 | 32 | 3,606 R | 72.9% | 26.7% | 73.2% | 26.8% |
| 26,822 | MONTGOMERY | 10,080 | 5,745 | 4,313 | 22 | 1,432 R | 57.0% | 42.8% | 57.1% | 42.9% |
| 74,769 | MOORE | 38,382 | 24,714 | 13,555 | 113 | 11,159 R | 64.4% | 35.3% | 64.6% | 35.4% |
| 87,420 | NASH | 37,673 | 21,902 | 15,693 | 78 | 6,209 R | 58.1% | 41.7% | 58.3% | 41.7% |
| 160,307 | NEW HANOVER | 81,247 | 45,351 | 35,572 | 324 | 9,779 R | 55.8% | 43.8% | 56.0% | 44.0% |
| 22,086 | NORTHAMPTON | 8,770 | 3,176 | 5,584 | 10 | 2,408 D | 36.2% | 63.7% | 36.3% | 63.7% |
| 150,355 | ONSLOW | 37,277 | 25,890 | 11,250 | 137 | 14,640 R | 69.5% | 30.2% | 69.7% | 30.3% |
| 118,227 | ORANGE | 64,153 | 20,771 | 42,910 | 472 | 22,139 D | 32.4% | 66.9% | 32.6% | 67.4% |
| 12,934 | PAMLICO | 6,038 | 3,679 | 2,335 | 24 | 1,344 R | 60.9% | 38.7% | 61.2% | 38.8% |
| 34,897 | PASQUOTANK | 13,648 | 6,609 | 6,984 | 55 | 375 D | 48.4% | 51.2% | 48.6% | 51.4% |
| 41,082 | PENDER | 17,085 | 10,037 | 6,999 | 49 | 3,038 R | 58.7% | 41.0% | 58.9% | 41.1% |
| 11,368 | PERQUIMANS | 4,958 | 2,965 | 1,971 | 22 | 994 R | 59.8% | 39.8% | 60.1% | 39.9% |
| 35,623 | PERSON | 15,214 | 8,973 | 6,198 | 43 | 2,775 R | 59.0% | 40.7% | 59.1% | 40.9% |
| 133,798 | PITT | 53,643 | 28,590 | 24,924 | 129 | 3,666 R | 53.3% | 46.5% | 53.4% | 46.6% |
| 18,324 | POLK | 9,021 | 5,140 | 3,787 | 94 | 1,353 R | 57.0% | 42.0% | 57.6% | 42.4% |
| 130,454 | RANDOLPH | 50,910 | 37,771 | 12,966 | 173 | 24,805 R | 74.2% | 25.5% | 74.4% | 25.6% |
| 46,564 | RICHMOND | 16,145 | 7,709 | 8,383 | 53 | 674 D | 47.7% | 51.9% | 47.9% | 52.1% |
| 123,339 | ROBESON | 33,871 | 15,909 | 17,868 | 94 | 1,959 D | 47.0% | 52.8% | 47.1% | 52.9% |
| 91,928 | ROCKINGHAM | 37,388 | 22,840 | 14,430 | 118 | 8,410 R | 61.1% | 38.6% | 61.3% | 38.7% |
| 130,340 | ROWAN | 51,867 | 34,915 | 16,735 | 217 | 18,180 R | 67.3% | 32.3% | 67.6% | 32.4% |
| 62,899 | RUTHERFORD | 24,658 | 16,343 | 8,184 | 131 | 8,159 R | 66.3% | 33.2% | 66.6% | 33.4% |
| 60,161 | SAMPSON | 22,288 | 12,600 | 9,649 | 39 | 2,951 R | 56.5% | 43.3% | 56.6% | 43.4% |
| 35,998 | SCOTLAND | 11,547 | 5,141 | 6,386 | 20 | 1,245 D | 44.5% | 55.3% | 44.6% | 55.4% |
| 58,100 | STANLY | 25,553 | 17,814 | 7,650 | 89 | 10,164 R | 69.7% | 29.9% | 70.0% | 30.0% |
| 44,711 | STOKES | 19,414 | 13,583 | 5,767 | 64 | 7,816 R | 70.0% | 29.7% | 70.2% | 29.8% |
| 71,219 | SURRY | 25,992 | 17,587 | 8,304 | 101 | 9,283 R | 67.7% | 31.9% | 67.9% | 32.1% |
| 12,968 | SWAIN | 5,044 | 2,593 | 2,419 | 32 | 174 R | 51.4% | 48.0% | 51.7% | 48.3% |
| 29,334 | TRANSYLVANIA | 15,588 | 9,386 | 6,097 | 105 | 3,289 R | 60.2% | 39.1% | 60.6% | 39.4% |
| 4,149 | TYRRELL | 1,590 | 855 | 731 | 4 | 124 R | 53.8% | 46.0% | 53.9% | 46.1% |
| 123,677 | UNION | 61,001 | 42,820 | 17,974 | 207 | 24,846 R | 70.2% | 29.5% | 70.4% | 29.6% |
| 42,954 | VANCE | 15,677 | 6,884 | 8,762 | 31 | 1,878 D | 43.9% | 55.9% | 44.0% | 56.0% |
| 627,846 | WAKE | 348,844 | 177,324 | 169,909 | 1,611 | 7,415 R | 50.8% | 48.7% | 51.1% | 48.9% |
| 19,972 | WARREN | 8,027 | 2,840 | 5,171 | 16 | 2,331 D | 35.4% | 64.4% | 35.5% | 64.5% |
| 13,723 | WASHINGTON | 5,471 | 2,484 | 2,969 | 18 | 485 D | 45.4% | 54.3% | 45.6% | 54.4% |
| 42,695 | WATAUGA | 24,050 | 12,659 | 11,232 | 159 | 1,427 R | 52.6% | 46.7% | 53.0% | 47.0% |
| 113,329 | WAYNE | 40,046 | 24,883 | 15,076 | 87 | 9,807 R | 62.1% | 37.6% | 62.3% | 37.7% |
| 65,632 | WILKES | 27,154 | 19,197 | 7,862 | 95 | 11,335 R | 70.7% | 29.0% | 70.9% | 29.1% |
| 73,814 | WILSON | 30,535 | 16,264 | 14,206 | 65 | 2,058 R | 53.3% | 46.5% | 53.4% | 46.6% |
| 36,348 | YADKIN | 15,313 | 11,816 | 3,451 | 46 | 8,365 R | 77.2% | 22.5% | 77.4% | 22.6% |
| 17,774 | YANCEY | 9,431 | 4,940 | 4,434 | 57 | 506 R | 52.4% | 47.0% | 52.7% | 47.3% |
| 8,049,313 | TOTAL | 3,501,007 | 1,961,166 | 1,525,849 | 13,992 | 435,317 R | 56.0% | 43.6% | 56.2% | 43.8% |

# NORTH CAROLINA

## GOVERNOR 2004

| 2000 Census Population | County | Total Vote | Republican | Democratic | Other | Rep.-Dem. Plurality | | Percentage | | | |
|---|---|---|---|---|---|---|---|---|---|---|---|
| | | | | | | | | Total Vote | | Major Vote | |
| | | | | | | | | Rep. | Dem. | Rep. | Dem. |
| 130,800 | ALAMANCE | 53,978 | 25,774 | 27,435 | 769 | 1,661 | D | 47.7% | 50.8% | 48.4% | 51.6% |
| 33,603 | ALEXANDER | 15,754 | 8,460 | 7,061 | 233 | 1,399 | R | 53.7% | 44.8% | 54.5% | 45.5% |
| 10,677 | ALLEGHANY | 4,655 | 1,886 | 2,699 | 70 | 813 | D | 40.5% | 58.0% | 41.1% | 58.9% |
| 25,275 | ANSON | 9,213 | 2,523 | 6,591 | 99 | 4,068 | D | 27.4% | 71.5% | 27.7% | 72.3% |
| 24,384 | ASHE | 11,836 | 5,512 | 6,132 | 192 | 620 | D | 46.6% | 51.8% | 47.3% | 52.7% |
| 17,167 | AVERY | 7,553 | 4,877 | 2,516 | 160 | 2,361 | R | 64.6% | 33.3% | 66.0% | 34.0% |
| 44,958 | BEAUFORT | 19,722 | 8,140 | 11,285 | 297 | 3,145 | D | 41.3% | 57.2% | 41.9% | 58.1% |
| 19,773 | BERTIE | 7,860 | 2,056 | 5,737 | 67 | 3,681 | D | 26.2% | 73.0% | 26.4% | 73.6% |
| 32,278 | BLADEN | 12,099 | 3,897 | 8,086 | 116 | 4,189 | D | 32.2% | 66.8% | 32.5% | 67.5% |
| 73,143 | BRUNSWICK | 37,654 | 16,020 | 21,156 | 478 | 5,136 | D | 42.5% | 56.2% | 43.1% | 56.9% |
| 206,330 | BUNCOMBE | 101,968 | 40,551 | 58,863 | 2,554 | 18,312 | D | 39.8% | 57.7% | 40.8% | 59.2% |
| 89,148 | BURKE | 32,104 | 16,470 | 15,112 | 522 | 1,358 | R | 51.3% | 47.1% | 52.1% | 47.9% |
| 131,063 | CABARRUS | 60,756 | 30,518 | 29,276 | 962 | 1,242 | R | 50.2% | 48.2% | 51.0% | 49.0% |
| 77,415 | CALDWELL | 31,314 | 16,724 | 14,061 | 529 | 2,663 | R | 53.4% | 44.9% | 54.3% | 45.7% |
| 6,885 | CAMDEN | 3,743 | 1,748 | 1,929 | 66 | 181 | D | 46.7% | 51.5% | 47.5% | 52.5% |
| 59,383 | CARTERET | 24,953 | 12,927 | 11,606 | 420 | 1,321 | R | 51.8% | 46.5% | 52.7% | 47.3% |
| 23,501 | CASWELL | 9,382 | 3,521 | 5,747 | 114 | 2,226 | D | 37.5% | 61.3% | 38.0% | 62.0% |
| 141,685 | CATAWBA | 57,161 | 30,643 | 25,656 | 862 | 4,987 | R | 53.6% | 44.9% | 54.4% | 45.6% |
| 49,329 | CHATHAM | 25,123 | 9,813 | 14,917 | 393 | 5,104 | D | 39.1% | 59.4% | 39.7% | 60.3% |
| 24,298 | CHEROKEE | 10,930 | 5,952 | 4,807 | 171 | 1,145 | R | 54.5% | 44.0% | 55.3% | 44.7% |
| 14,526 | CHOWAN | 5,124 | 2,070 | 2,961 | 93 | 891 | D | 40.4% | 57.8% | 41.1% | 58.9% |
| 8,775 | CLAY | 4,773 | 2,653 | 2,015 | 105 | 638 | R | 55.6% | 42.2% | 56.8% | 43.2% |
| 96,287 | CLEVELAND | 37,275 | 16,614 | 20,204 | 457 | 3,590 | D | 44.6% | 54.2% | 45.1% | 54.9% |
| 54,749 | COLUMBUS | 21,046 | 7,348 | 13,454 | 244 | 6,106 | D | 34.9% | 63.9% | 35.3% | 64.7% |
| 91,436 | CRAVEN | 37,309 | 17,877 | 18,938 | 494 | 1,061 | D | 47.9% | 50.8% | 48.6% | 51.4% |
| 302,963 | CUMBERLAND | 95,864 | 35,229 | 59,168 | 1,467 | 23,939 | D | 36.7% | 61.7% | 37.3% | 62.7% |
| 18,190 | CURRITUCK | 8,821 | 4,367 | 4,167 | 287 | 200 | R | 49.5% | 47.2% | 51.2% | 48.8% |
| 29,967 | DARE | 15,600 | 6,441 | 8,746 | 413 | 2,305 | D | 41.3% | 56.1% | 42.4% | 57.6% |
| 147,246 | DAVIDSON | 59,334 | 31,301 | 27,050 | 983 | 4,251 | R | 52.8% | 45.6% | 53.6% | 46.4% |
| 34,835 | DAVIE | 16,558 | 9,680 | 6,541 | 337 | 3,139 | R | 58.5% | 39.5% | 59.7% | 40.3% |
| 49,063 | DUPLIN | 16,576 | 6,913 | 9,502 | 161 | 2,589 | D | 41.7% | 57.3% | 42.1% | 57.9% |
| 223,314 | DURHAM | 109,456 | 27,773 | 79,929 | 1,754 | 52,156 | D | 25.4% | 73.0% | 25.8% | 74.2% |
| 55,606 | EDGECOMBE | 20,976 | 4,853 | 15,960 | 163 | 11,107 | D | 23.1% | 76.1% | 23.3% | 76.7% |
| 306,067 | FORSYTH | 138,815 | 58,965 | 77,829 | 2,021 | 18,864 | D | 42.5% | 56.1% | 43.1% | 56.9% |
| 47,260 | FRANKLIN | 20,954 | 8,070 | 12,577 | 307 | 4,507 | D | 38.5% | 60.0% | 39.1% | 60.9% |
| 190,365 | GASTON | 63,818 | 33,882 | 28,960 | 976 | 4,922 | R | 53.1% | 45.4% | 53.9% | 46.1% |
| 10,516 | GATES | 4,090 | 1,368 | 2,668 | 54 | 1,300 | D | 33.4% | 65.2% | 33.9% | 66.1% |
| 7,993 | GRAHAM | 3,883 | 2,002 | 1,813 | 68 | 189 | R | 51.6% | 46.7% | 52.5% | 47.5% |
| 48,498 | GRANVILLE | 18,658 | 6,723 | 11,699 | 236 | 4,976 | D | 36.0% | 62.7% | 36.5% | 63.5% |
| 18,974 | GREENE | 6,463 | 2,728 | 3,684 | 51 | 956 | D | 42.2% | 57.0% | 42.5% | 57.5% |
| 421,048 | GUILFORD | 198,261 | 75,203 | 119,965 | 3,093 | 44,762 | D | 37.9% | 60.5% | 38.5% | 61.5% |
| 57,370 | HALIFAX | 19,723 | 4,968 | 14,604 | 151 | 9,636 | D | 25.2% | 74.0% | 25.4% | 74.6% |
| 91,025 | HARNETT | 32,441 | 15,475 | 16,510 | 456 | 1,035 | D | 47.7% | 50.9% | 48.4% | 51.6% |
| 54,033 | HAYWOOD | 26,255 | 10,362 | 15,434 | 459 | 5,072 | D | 39.5% | 58.8% | 40.2% | 59.8% |
| 89,173 | HENDERSON | 42,844 | 22,923 | 19,361 | 560 | 3,562 | R | 53.5% | 45.2% | 54.2% | 45.8% |
| 22,601 | HERTFORD | 8,094 | 2,015 | 5,982 | 97 | 3,967 | D | 24.9% | 73.9% | 25.2% | 74.8% |
| 33,646 | HOKE | 11,041 | 3,525 | 7,347 | 169 | 3,822 | D | 31.9% | 66.5% | 32.4% | 67.6% |
| 5,826 | HYDE | 2,252 | 841 | 1,391 | 20 | 550 | D | 37.3% | 61.8% | 37.7% | 62.3% |
| 122,660 | IREDELL | 56,795 | 29,406 | 26,449 | 940 | 2,957 | R | 51.8% | 46.6% | 52.6% | 47.4% |
| 33,121 | JACKSON | 14,247 | 5,873 | 8,057 | 317 | 2,184 | D | 41.2% | 56.6% | 42.2% | 57.8% |
| 121,965 | JOHNSTON | 54,525 | 27,668 | 26,275 | 582 | 1,393 | R | 50.7% | 48.2% | 51.3% | 48.7% |
| 10,381 | JONES | 4,555 | 1,847 | 2,670 | 38 | 823 | D | 40.5% | 58.6% | 40.9% | 59.1% |
| 49,040 | LEE | 19,425 | 8,146 | 11,044 | 235 | 2,898 | D | 41.9% | 56.9% | 42.4% | 57.6% |
| 59,648 | LENOIR | 22,986 | 9,964 | 12,898 | 124 | 2,934 | D | 43.3% | 56.1% | 43.6% | 56.4% |
| 63,780 | LINCOLN | 29,685 | 15,584 | 13,654 | 447 | 1,930 | R | 52.5% | 46.0% | 53.3% | 46.7% |
| 42,151 | MCDOWELL | 15,956 | 7,969 | 7,740 | 247 | 229 | R | 49.9% | 48.5% | 50.7% | 49.3% |
| 29,811 | MACON | 14,775 | 7,457 | 7,156 | 162 | 301 | R | 50.5% | 48.4% | 51.0% | 49.0% |
| 19,635 | MADISON | 9,342 | 4,047 | 5,135 | 160 | 1,088 | D | 43.3% | 55.0% | 44.1% | 55.9% |
| 25,593 | MARTIN | 10,527 | 3,246 | 7,174 | 107 | 3,928 | D | 30.8% | 68.1% | 31.2% | 68.8% |
| 695,454 | MECKLENBURG | 319,166 | 127,521 | 186,801 | 4,844 | 59,280 | D | 40.0% | 58.5% | 40.6% | 59.4% |

# NORTH CAROLINA

## GOVERNOR 2004

| 2000 Census Population | County | Total Vote | Republican | Democratic | Other | Rep.-Dem. Plurality | Percentage | | | |
|---:|---|---:|---:|---:|---:|---:|---|---|---|---|
| | | | | | | | Total Vote | | Major Vote | |
| | | | | | | | Rep. | Dem. | Rep. | Dem. |
| 15,687 | MITCHELL | 7,764 | 4,946 | 2,691 | 127 | 2,255 R | 63.7% | 34.7% | 64.8% | 35.2% |
| 26,822 | MONTGOMERY | 10,111 | 4,335 | 5,640 | 136 | 1,305 D | 42.9% | 55.8% | 43.5% | 56.5% |
| 74,769 | MOORE | 37,837 | 19,311 | 18,210 | 316 | 1,101 R | 51.0% | 48.1% | 51.5% | 48.5% |
| 87,420 | NASH | 38,158 | 14,452 | 23,385 | 321 | 8,933 D | 37.9% | 61.3% | 38.2% | 61.8% |
| 160,307 | NEW HANOVER | 81,198 | 36,502 | 43,421 | 1,275 | 6,919 D | 45.0% | 53.5% | 45.7% | 54.3% |
| 22,086 | NORTHAMPTON | 8,767 | 2,087 | 6,604 | 76 | 4,517 D | 23.8% | 75.3% | 24.0% | 76.0% |
| 150,355 | ONSLOW | 37,324 | 18,957 | 17,499 | 868 | 1,458 R | 50.8% | 46.9% | 52.0% | 48.0% |
| 118,227 | ORANGE | 63,706 | 16,782 | 45,681 | 1,243 | 28,899 D | 26.3% | 71.7% | 26.9% | 73.1% |
| 12,934 | PAMLICO | 5,987 | 2,552 | 3,361 | 74 | 809 D | 42.6% | 56.1% | 43.2% | 56.8% |
| 34,897 | PASQUOTANK | 13,271 | 4,894 | 8,146 | 231 | 3,252 D | 36.9% | 61.4% | 37.5% | 62.5% |
| 41,082 | PENDER | 17,043 | 7,797 | 9,040 | 206 | 1,243 D | 45.7% | 53.0% | 46.3% | 53.7% |
| 11,368 | PERQUIMANS | 4,887 | 2,221 | 2,594 | 72 | 373 D | 45.4% | 53.1% | 46.1% | 53.9% |
| 35,623 | PERSON | 15,192 | 5,795 | 9,204 | 193 | 3,409 D | 38.1% | 60.6% | 38.6% | 61.4% |
| 133,798 | PITT | 53,072 | 21,809 | 30,722 | 541 | 8,913 D | 41.1% | 57.9% | 41.5% | 58.5% |
| 18,324 | POLK | 9,172 | 4,264 | 4,746 | 162 | 482 D | 46.5% | 51.7% | 47.3% | 52.7% |
| 130,454 | RANDOLPH | 51,688 | 30,240 | 20,634 | 814 | 9,606 R | 58.5% | 39.9% | 59.4% | 40.6% |
| 46,564 | RICHMOND | 16,193 | 5,188 | 10,697 | 308 | 5,509 D | 32.0% | 66.1% | 32.7% | 67.3% |
| 123,339 | ROBESON | 34,800 | 10,000 | 24,462 | 338 | 14,462 D | 28.7% | 70.3% | 29.0% | 71.0% |
| 91,928 | ROCKINGHAM | 37,284 | 15,411 | 21,199 | 674 | 5,788 D | 41.3% | 56.9% | 42.1% | 57.9% |
| 130,340 | ROWAN | 51,698 | 26,195 | 24,508 | 995 | 1,687 R | 50.7% | 47.4% | 51.7% | 48.3% |
| 62,899 | RUTHERFORD | 24,118 | 11,725 | 12,062 | 331 | 337 D | 48.6% | 50.0% | 49.3% | 50.7% |
| 60,161 | SAMPSON | 22,508 | 9,483 | 12,830 | 195 | 3,347 D | 42.1% | 57.0% | 42.5% | 57.5% |
| 35,998 | SCOTLAND | 10,637 | 3,897 | 6,595 | 145 | 2,698 D | 36.6% | 62.0% | 37.1% | 62.9% |
| 58,100 | STANLY | 25,132 | 13,306 | 11,454 | 372 | 1,852 R | 52.9% | 45.6% | 53.7% | 46.3% |
| 44,711 | STOKES | 19,772 | 10,125 | 9,323 | 324 | 802 R | 51.2% | 47.2% | 52.1% | 47.9% |
| 71,219 | SURRY | 25,321 | 12,302 | 12,655 | 364 | 353 D | 48.6% | 50.0% | 49.3% | 50.7% |
| 12,968 | SWAIN | 5,044 | 2,026 | 2,939 | 79 | 913 D | 40.2% | 58.3% | 40.8% | 59.2% |
| 29,334 | TRANSYLVANIA | 15,345 | 7,506 | 7,538 | 301 | 32 D | 48.9% | 49.1% | 49.9% | 50.1% |
| 4,149 | TYRRELL | 1,574 | 550 | 1,006 | 18 | 456 D | 34.9% | 63.9% | 35.3% | 64.7% |
| 123,677 | UNION | 59,541 | 34,444 | 24,355 | 742 | 10,089 R | 57.8% | 40.9% | 58.6% | 41.4% |
| 42,954 | VANCE | 15,933 | 4,614 | 11,177 | 142 | 6,563 D | 29.0% | 70.2% | 29.2% | 70.8% |
| 627,846 | WAKE | 349,542 | 138,650 | 205,535 | 5,357 | 66,885 D | 39.7% | 58.8% | 40.3% | 59.7% |
| 19,972 | WARREN | 8,041 | 1,994 | 5,992 | 55 | 3,998 D | 24.8% | 74.5% | 25.0% | 75.0% |
| 13,723 | WASHINGTON | 5,478 | 1,702 | 3,668 | 108 | 1,966 D | 31.1% | 67.0% | 31.7% | 68.3% |
| 42,695 | WATAUGA | 23,685 | 10,645 | 12,392 | 648 | 1,747 D | 44.9% | 52.3% | 46.2% | 53.8% |
| 113,329 | WAYNE | 40,519 | 19,440 | 20,652 | 427 | 1,212 D | 48.0% | 51.0% | 48.5% | 51.5% |
| 65,632 | WILKES | 27,771 | 15,008 | 12,377 | 386 | 2,631 R | 54.0% | 44.6% | 54.8% | 45.2% |
| 73,814 | WILSON | 30,350 | 11,874 | 18,267 | 209 | 6,393 D | 39.1% | 60.2% | 39.4% | 60.6% |
| 36,348 | YADKIN | 15,709 | 9,023 | 6,434 | 252 | 2,589 R | 57.4% | 41.0% | 58.4% | 41.6% |
| 17,774 | YANCEY | 9,470 | 4,060 | 5,275 | 135 | 1,215 D | 42.9% | 55.7% | 43.5% | 56.5% |
| 8,049,313 | TOTAL | 3,486,688 | 1,495,021 | 1,939,154 | 52,513 | 444,133 D | 42.9% | 55.6% | 43.5% | 56.5% |

# NORTH CAROLINA

## SENATOR 2004

| 2000 Census Population | County | Total Vote | Republican | Democratic | Other | Rep.-Dem. Plurality | Percentage | | | |
|---|---|---|---|---|---|---|---|---|---|---|
| | | | | | | | Total Vote | | Major Vote | |
| | | | | | | | Rep. | Dem. | Rep. | Dem. |
| 130,800 | ALAMANCE | 53,912 | 30,614 | 22,580 | 718 | 8,034 R | 56.8% | 41.9% | 57.6% | 42.4% |
| 33,603 | ALEXANDER | 15,725 | 10,073 | 5,430 | 222 | 4,643 R | 64.1% | 34.5% | 65.0% | 35.0% |
| 10,677 | ALLEGHANY | 4,727 | 2,754 | 1,908 | 65 | 846 R | 58.3% | 40.4% | 59.1% | 40.9% |
| 25,275 | ANSON | 9,193 | 3,367 | 5,734 | 92 | 2,367 D | 36.6% | 62.4% | 37.0% | 63.0% |
| 24,384 | ASHE | 11,846 | 7,021 | 4,651 | 174 | 2,370 R | 59.3% | 39.3% | 60.2% | 39.8% |
| 17,167 | AVERY | 7,236 | 5,157 | 1,917 | 162 | 3,240 R | 71.3% | 26.5% | 72.9% | 27.1% |
| 44,958 | BEAUFORT | 19,646 | 11,109 | 8,231 | 306 | 2,878 R | 56.5% | 41.9% | 57.4% | 42.6% |
| 19,773 | BERTIE | 7,921 | 2,640 | 5,227 | 54 | 2,587 D | 33.3% | 66.0% | 33.6% | 66.4% |
| 32,278 | BLADEN | 11,877 | 5,073 | 6,661 | 143 | 1,588 D | 42.7% | 56.1% | 43.2% | 56.8% |
| 73,143 | BRUNSWICK | 37,305 | 20,554 | 16,128 | 623 | 4,426 R | 55.1% | 43.2% | 56.0% | 44.0% |
| 206,330 | BUNCOMBE | 100,631 | 46,763 | 51,745 | 2,123 | 4,982 D | 46.5% | 51.4% | 47.5% | 52.5% |
| 89,148 | BURKE | 32,085 | 18,371 | 13,137 | 577 | 5,234 R | 57.3% | 40.9% | 58.3% | 41.7% |
| 131,063 | CABARRUS | 60,768 | 37,494 | 22,206 | 1,068 | 15,288 R | 61.7% | 36.5% | 62.8% | 37.2% |
| 77,415 | CALDWELL | 31,268 | 19,612 | 11,079 | 577 | 8,533 R | 62.7% | 35.4% | 63.9% | 36.1% |
| 6,885 | CAMDEN | 3,721 | 2,083 | 1,576 | 62 | 507 R | 56.0% | 42.4% | 56.9% | 43.1% |
| 59,383 | CARTERET | 25,408 | 16,082 | 8,875 | 451 | 7,207 R | 63.3% | 34.9% | 64.4% | 35.6% |
| 23,501 | CASWELL | 9,400 | 4,559 | 4,737 | 104 | 178 D | 48.5% | 50.4% | 49.0% | 51.0% |
| 141,685 | CATAWBA | 56,940 | 35,946 | 20,153 | 841 | 15,793 R | 63.1% | 35.4% | 64.1% | 35.9% |
| 49,329 | CHATHAM | 25,751 | 11,816 | 13,601 | 334 | 1,785 D | 45.9% | 52.8% | 46.5% | 53.5% |
| 24,298 | CHEROKEE | 10,548 | 6,426 | 3,966 | 156 | 2,460 R | 60.9% | 37.6% | 61.8% | 38.2% |
| 14,526 | CHOWAN | 5,185 | 2,457 | 2,638 | 90 | 181 D | 47.4% | 50.9% | 48.2% | 51.8% |
| 8,775 | CLAY | 4,743 | 2,896 | 1,749 | 98 | 1,147 R | 61.1% | 36.9% | 62.3% | 37.7% |
| 96,287 | CLEVELAND | 37,200 | 20,324 | 16,342 | 534 | 3,982 R | 54.6% | 43.9% | 55.4% | 44.6% |
| 54,749 | COLUMBUS | 20,863 | 8,721 | 11,860 | 282 | 3,139 D | 41.8% | 56.8% | 42.4% | 57.6% |
| 91,436 | CRAVEN | 37,290 | 21,402 | 15,299 | 589 | 6,103 R | 57.4% | 41.0% | 58.3% | 41.7% |
| 302,963 | CUMBERLAND | 95,573 | 44,145 | 50,097 | 1,331 | 5,952 D | 46.2% | 52.4% | 46.8% | 53.2% |
| 18,190 | CURRITUCK | 8,391 | 5,007 | 3,172 | 212 | 1,835 R | 59.7% | 37.8% | 61.2% | 38.8% |
| 29,967 | DARE | 15,601 | 8,215 | 6,995 | 391 | 1,220 R | 52.7% | 44.8% | 54.0% | 46.0% |
| 147,246 | DAVIDSON | 59,395 | 38,913 | 19,530 | 952 | 19,383 R | 65.5% | 32.9% | 66.6% | 33.4% |
| 34,835 | DAVIE | 16,604 | 11,861 | 4,505 | 238 | 7,356 R | 71.4% | 27.1% | 72.5% | 27.5% |
| 49,063 | DUPLIN | 16,573 | 8,613 | 7,768 | 192 | 845 R | 52.0% | 46.9% | 52.6% | 47.4% |
| 223,314 | DURHAM | 109,718 | 32,217 | 76,294 | 1,207 | 44,077 D | 29.4% | 69.5% | 29.7% | 70.3% |
| 55,606 | EDGECOMBE | 21,089 | 7,072 | 13,822 | 195 | 6,750 D | 33.5% | 65.5% | 33.8% | 66.2% |
| 306,067 | FORSYTH | 139,467 | 74,108 | 63,899 | 1,460 | 10,209 R | 53.1% | 45.8% | 53.7% | 46.3% |
| 47,260 | FRANKLIN | 20,914 | 10,421 | 10,197 | 296 | 224 R | 49.8% | 48.8% | 50.5% | 49.5% |
| 190,365 | GASTON | 63,700 | 39,857 | 22,750 | 1,093 | 17,107 R | 62.6% | 35.7% | 63.7% | 36.3% |
| 10,516 | GATES | 4,059 | 1,654 | 2,352 | 53 | 698 D | 40.7% | 57.9% | 41.3% | 58.7% |
| 7,993 | GRAHAM | 3,774 | 2,267 | 1,445 | 62 | 822 R | 60.1% | 38.3% | 61.1% | 38.9% |
| 48,498 | GRANVILLE | 18,468 | 8,447 | 9,806 | 215 | 1,359 D | 45.7% | 53.1% | 46.3% | 53.7% |
| 18,974 | GREENE | 6,492 | 3,400 | 3,043 | 49 | 357 R | 52.4% | 46.9% | 52.8% | 47.2% |
| 421,048 | GUILFORD | 198,614 | 89,926 | 106,315 | 2,373 | 16,389 D | 45.3% | 53.5% | 45.8% | 54.2% |
| 57,370 | HALIFAX | 19,731 | 7,110 | 12,457 | 164 | 5,347 D | 36.0% | 63.1% | 36.3% | 63.7% |
| 91,025 | HARNETT | 32,365 | 18,501 | 13,417 | 447 | 5,084 R | 57.2% | 41.5% | 58.0% | 42.0% |
| 54,033 | HAYWOOD | 26,141 | 12,949 | 12,710 | 482 | 239 R | 49.5% | 48.6% | 50.5% | 49.5% |
| 89,173 | HENDERSON | 41,634 | 25,430 | 15,652 | 552 | 9,778 R | 61.1% | 37.6% | 61.9% | 38.1% |
| 22,601 | HERTFORD | 7,986 | 2,478 | 5,428 | 80 | 2,950 D | 31.0% | 68.0% | 31.3% | 68.7% |
| 33,646 | HOKE | 10,901 | 4,431 | 6,271 | 199 | 1,840 D | 40.6% | 57.5% | 41.4% | 58.6% |
| 5,826 | HYDE | 2,206 | 1,060 | 1,118 | 28 | 58 D | 48.1% | 50.7% | 48.7% | 51.3% |
| 122,660 | IREDELL | 56,935 | 35,600 | 20,402 | 933 | 15,198 R | 62.5% | 35.8% | 63.6% | 36.4% |
| 33,121 | JACKSON | 14,104 | 6,656 | 7,220 | 228 | 564 D | 47.2% | 51.2% | 48.0% | 52.0% |
| 121,965 | JOHNSTON | 53,876 | 33,334 | 19,966 | 576 | 13,368 R | 61.9% | 37.1% | 62.5% | 37.5% |
| 10,381 | JONES | 4,536 | 2,392 | 2,092 | 52 | 300 R | 52.7% | 46.1% | 53.3% | 46.7% |
| 49,040 | LEE | 19,371 | 10,218 | 8,900 | 253 | 1,318 R | 52.7% | 45.9% | 53.4% | 46.6% |
| 59,648 | LENOIR | 22,864 | 11,707 | 11,012 | 145 | 695 R | 51.2% | 48.2% | 51.5% | 48.5% |
| 63,780 | LINCOLN | 29,635 | 18,422 | 10,657 | 556 | 7,765 R | 62.2% | 36.0% | 63.4% | 36.6% |
| 42,151 | MCDOWELL | 15,815 | 9,366 | 6,179 | 270 | 3,187 R | 59.2% | 39.1% | 60.3% | 39.7% |
| 29,811 | MACON | 14,454 | 8,399 | 5,896 | 159 | 2,503 R | 58.1% | 40.8% | 58.8% | 41.2% |
| 19,635 | MADISON | 9,118 | 4,490 | 4,479 | 149 | 11 R | 49.2% | 49.1% | 50.1% | 49.9% |
| 25,593 | MARTIN | 10,492 | 4,615 | 5,779 | 98 | 1,164 D | 44.0% | 55.1% | 44.4% | 55.6% |
| 695,454 | MECKLENBURG | 319,722 | 141,653 | 173,964 | 4,105 | 32,311 D | 44.3% | 54.4% | 44.9% | 55.1% |

# NORTH CAROLINA

## SENATOR 2004

| 2000 Census Population | County | Total Vote | Republican | Democratic | Other | Rep.-Dem. Plurality | | Percentage | | | |
|---|---|---|---|---|---|---|---|---|---|---|---|
| | | | | | | | | Total Vote | | Major Vote | |
| | | | | | | | | Rep. | Dem. | Rep. | Dem. |
| 15,687 | MITCHELL | 7,689 | 5,340 | 2,208 | 141 | 3,132 | R | 69.4% | 28.7% | 70.7% | 29.3% |
| 26,822 | MONTGOMERY | 10,072 | 5,234 | 4,693 | 145 | 541 | R | 52.0% | 46.6% | 52.7% | 47.3% |
| 74,769 | MOORE | 37,590 | 22,522 | 14,708 | 360 | 7,814 | R | 59.9% | 39.1% | 60.5% | 39.5% |
| 87,420 | NASH | 37,928 | 19,985 | 17,611 | 332 | 2,374 | R | 52.7% | 46.4% | 53.2% | 46.8% |
| 160,307 | NEW HANOVER | 79,088 | 41,231 | 36,218 | 1,639 | 5,013 | R | 52.1% | 45.8% | 53.2% | 46.8% |
| 22,086 | NORTHAMPTON | 8,756 | 2,822 | 5,861 | 73 | 3,039 | D | 32.2% | 66.9% | 32.5% | 67.5% |
| 150,355 | ONSLOW | 36,088 | 22,790 | 12,542 | 756 | 10,248 | R | 63.2% | 34.8% | 64.5% | 35.5% |
| 118,227 | ORANGE | 64,119 | 19,797 | 43,476 | 846 | 23,679 | D | 30.9% | 67.8% | 31.3% | 68.7% |
| 12,934 | PAMLICO | 6,014 | 3,326 | 2,605 | 83 | 721 | R | 55.3% | 43.3% | 56.1% | 43.9% |
| 34,897 | PASQUOTANK | 13,279 | 5,669 | 7,426 | 184 | 1,757 | D | 42.7% | 55.9% | 43.3% | 56.7% |
| 41,082 | PENDER | 16,824 | 9,182 | 7,390 | 252 | 1,792 | R | 54.6% | 43.9% | 55.4% | 44.6% |
| 11,368 | PERQUIMANS | 4,872 | 2,566 | 2,242 | 64 | 324 | R | 52.7% | 46.0% | 53.4% | 46.6% |
| 35,623 | PERSON | 15,098 | 8,212 | 6,701 | 185 | 1,511 | R | 54.4% | 44.4% | 55.1% | 44.9% |
| 133,798 | PITT | 52,908 | 26,489 | 26,019 | 400 | 470 | R | 50.1% | 49.2% | 50.4% | 49.6% |
| 18,324 | POLK | 9,153 | 4,825 | 4,169 | 159 | 656 | R | 52.7% | 45.5% | 53.6% | 46.4% |
| 130,454 | RANDOLPH | 51,486 | 35,495 | 15,199 | 792 | 20,296 | R | 68.9% | 29.5% | 70.0% | 30.0% |
| 46,564 | RICHMOND | 16,129 | 6,574 | 9,221 | 334 | 2,647 | D | 40.8% | 57.2% | 41.6% | 58.4% |
| 123,339 | ROBESON | 34,410 | 13,025 | 20,896 | 489 | 7,871 | D | 37.9% | 60.7% | 38.4% | 61.6% |
| 91,928 | ROCKINGHAM | 37,182 | 21,224 | 15,435 | 523 | 5,789 | R | 57.1% | 41.5% | 57.9% | 42.1% |
| 130,340 | ROWAN | 51,552 | 31,998 | 18,543 | 1,011 | 13,455 | R | 62.1% | 36.0% | 63.3% | 36.7% |
| 62,899 | RUTHERFORD | 24,088 | 14,061 | 9,669 | 358 | 4,392 | R | 58.4% | 40.1% | 59.3% | 40.7% |
| 60,161 | SAMPSON | 22,369 | 11,574 | 10,626 | 169 | 948 | R | 51.7% | 47.5% | 52.1% | 47.9% |
| 35,998 | SCOTLAND | 10,731 | 4,336 | 6,282 | 113 | 1,946 | D | 40.4% | 58.5% | 40.8% | 59.2% |
| 58,100 | STANLY | 25,015 | 16,036 | 8,603 | 376 | 7,433 | R | 64.1% | 34.4% | 65.1% | 34.9% |
| 44,711 | STOKES | 19,858 | 13,456 | 6,138 | 264 | 7,318 | R | 67.8% | 30.9% | 68.7% | 31.3% |
| 71,219 | SURRY | 25,754 | 16,740 | 8,735 | 279 | 8,005 | R | 65.0% | 33.9% | 65.7% | 34.3% |
| 12,968 | SWAIN | 5,011 | 2,344 | 2,587 | 80 | 243 | D | 46.8% | 51.6% | 47.5% | 52.5% |
| 29,334 | TRANSYLVANIA | 15,284 | 8,586 | 6,421 | 277 | 2,165 | R | 56.2% | 42.0% | 57.2% | 42.8% |
| 4,149 | TYRRELL | 1,539 | 658 | 857 | 24 | 199 | D | 42.8% | 55.7% | 43.4% | 56.6% |
| 123,677 | UNION | 59,537 | 39,383 | 19,451 | 703 | 19,932 | R | 66.1% | 32.7% | 66.9% | 33.1% |
| 42,954 | VANCE | 15,885 | 6,137 | 9,633 | 115 | 3,496 | D | 38.6% | 60.6% | 38.9% | 61.1% |
| 627,846 | WAKE | 344,674 | 163,069 | 177,324 | 4,281 | 14,255 | D | 47.3% | 51.4% | 47.9% | 52.1% |
| 19,972 | WARREN | 8,025 | 2,510 | 5,424 | 91 | 2,914 | D | 31.3% | 67.6% | 31.6% | 68.4% |
| 13,723 | WASHINGTON | 5,469 | 2,126 | 3,285 | 58 | 1,159 | D | 38.9% | 60.1% | 39.3% | 60.7% |
| 42,695 | WATAUGA | 23,774 | 12,207 | 10,987 | 580 | 1,220 | R | 51.3% | 46.2% | 52.6% | 47.4% |
| 113,329 | WAYNE | 40,461 | 23,026 | 17,116 | 319 | 5,910 | R | 56.9% | 42.3% | 57.4% | 42.6% |
| 65,632 | WILKES | 27,576 | 18,173 | 8,967 | 436 | 9,206 | R | 65.9% | 32.5% | 67.0% | 33.0% |
| 73,814 | WILSON | 30,205 | 14,416 | 15,566 | 223 | 1,150 | D | 47.7% | 51.5% | 48.1% | 51.9% |
| 36,348 | YADKIN | 15,635 | 11,464 | 3,956 | 215 | 7,508 | R | 73.3% | 25.3% | 74.3% | 25.7% |
| 17,774 | YANCEY | 9,448 | 4,594 | 4,718 | 136 | 124 | D | 48.6% | 49.9% | 49.3% | 50.7% |
| 8,049,313 | TOTAL | 3,472,082 | 1,791,450 | 1,632,527 | 48,105 | 158,923 | R | 51.6% | 47.0% | 52.3% | 47.7% |

# NORTH CAROLINA

## HOUSE OF REPRESENTATIVES

| CD | Year | Total Vote | Republican Vote | Candidate | Democratic Vote | Candidate | Other Vote | Rep.-Dem. Plurality | Total Vote Rep. | Total Vote Dem. | Major Vote Rep. | Major Vote Dem. |
|---|---|---|---|---|---|---|---|---|---|---|---|---|
| 1 | 2004 | 215,175 | 77,508 | Dority, Greg | 137,667 | Butterfield, G.K.* | | 60,159 D | 36.0% | 64.0% | 36.0% | 64.0% |
| 1 | 2002 | 146,157 | 50,907 | Dority, Greg | 93,157 | Ballance, Frank W. Jr. | 2,093 | 42,250 D | 34.8% | 63.7% | 35.3% | 64.7% |
| 2 | 2004 | 232,890 | 87,811 | Creech, Billy J. | 145,079 | Etheridge, Bob* | | 57,268 D | 37.7% | 62.3% | 37.7% | 62.3% |
| 2 | 2002 | 153,184 | 50,965 | Ellen, Joseph L. | 100,121 | Etheridge, Bob* | 2,098 | 49,156 D | 33.3% | 65.4% | 33.7% | 66.3% |
| 3 | 2004 | 243,090 | 171,863 | Jones, Walter B.* | 71,227 | Eaton, Roger A. | | 100,636 R | 70.7% | 29.3% | 70.7% | 29.3% |
| 3 | 2002 | 144,934 | 131,448 | Jones, Walter B.* | | | 13,486 | 131,448 R | 90.7% | | 100.0% | |
| 4 | 2004 | 339,234 | 121,717 | Batchelor, Todd A. | 217,441 | Price, David E.* | 76 | 95,724 D | 35.9% | 64.1% | 35.9% | 64.1% |
| 4 | 2002 | 216,046 | 78,095 | Nguyen, Tuan A. | 132,185 | Price, David E.* | 5,766 | 54,090 D | 36.1% | 61.2% | 37.1% | 62.9% |
| 5 | 2004 | 284,817 | 167,546 | Foxx, Virginia | 117,271 | Harrell, Jim A. Jr. | | 50,275 R | 58.8% | 41.2% | 58.8% | 41.2% |
| 5 | 2002 | 196,437 | 137,879 | Burr, Richard M.* | 58,558 | Crawford, David | | 79,321 R | 70.2% | 29.8% | 70.2% | 29.8% |
| 6 | 2004 | 283,623 | 207,470 | Coble, Howard* | 76,153 | Jordan, William W. | | 131,317 R | 73.1% | 26.9% | 73.1% | 26.9% |
| 6 | 2002 | 167,497 | 151,430 | Coble, Howard* | | | 16,067 | 151,430 R | 90.4% | | 100.0% | |
| 7 | 2004 | 246,466 | 66,084 | Plonk, Ken | 180,382 | McIntyre, Mike* | | 114,298 D | 26.8% | 73.2% | 26.8% | 73.2% |
| 7 | 2002 | 166,654 | 45,537 | Adams, James R. | 118,543 | McIntyre, Mike* | 2,574 | 73,006 D | 27.3% | 71.1% | 27.8% | 72.2% |
| 8 | 2004 | 225,171 | 125,070 | Hayes, Robin* | 100,101 | Troutman, Beth | | 24,969 R | 55.5% | 44.5% | 55.5% | 44.5% |
| 8 | 2002 | 149,736 | 80,298 | Hayes, Robin* | 66,819 | Kouri, Chris | 2,619 | 13,479 R | 53.6% | 44.6% | 54.6% | 45.4% |
| 9 | 2004 | 300,101 | 210,783 | Myrick, Sue* | 89,318 | Flynn, Jack | | 121,465 R | 70.2% | 29.8% | 70.2% | 29.8% |
| 9 | 2002 | 193,443 | 140,095 | Myrick, Sue* | 49,974 | McGuire, Ed | 3,374 | 90,121 R | 72.4% | 25.8% | 73.7% | 26.3% |
| 10 | 2004 | 246,117 | 157,884 | McHenry, Patrick T. | 88,233 | Fischer, Anne N. | | 69,651 R | 64.1% | 35.9% | 64.1% | 35.9% |
| 10 | 2002 | 173,292 | 102,768 | Ballenger, Cass* | 65,587 | Daugherty, Ron | 4,937 | 37,181 R | 59.3% | 37.8% | 61.0% | 39.0% |
| 11 | 2004 | 290,897 | 159,709 | Taylor, Charles H.* | 131,188 | Keever, Patsy | | 28,521 R | 54.9% | 45.1% | 54.9% | 45.1% |
| 11 | 2002 | 202,260 | 112,335 | Taylor, Charles H.* | 86,664 | Neill, Sam | 3,261 | 25,671 R | 55.5% | 42.8% | 56.5% | 43.5% |
| 12 | 2004 | 231,806 | 76,898 | Fisher, Ada M. | 154,908 | Watt, Melvin* | | 78,010 D | 33.2% | 66.8% | 33.2% | 66.8% |
| 12 | 2002 | 151,239 | 49,588 | Kish, Jeff | 98,821 | Watt, Melvin* | 2,830 | 49,233 D | 32.8% | 65.3% | 33.4% | 66.6% |
| 13 | 2004 | 273,684 | 112,788 | Johnson, Virginia | 160,896 | Miller, Brad* | | 48,108 D | 41.2% | 58.8% | 41.2% | 58.8% |
| 13 | 2002 | 183,270 | 77,688 | Grant, Carolyn W. | 100,287 | Miller, Brad | 5,295 | 22,599 D | 42.4% | 54.7% | 43.7% | 56.3% |
| Total | 2004 | 3,413,071 | 1,743,131 | | 1,669,864 | | 76 | 73,267 R | 51.1% | 48.9% | 51.1% | 48.9% |
| Total | 2002 | 2,244,149 | 1,209,033 | | 970,716 | | 64,400 | 238,317 R | 53.9% | 43.3% | 55.5% | 44.5% |

An asterisk (*) denotes incumbent.

# NORTH CAROLINA

## GENERAL AND PRIMARY ELECTIONS

### 2004 GENERAL ELECTIONS

**President**  Other vote was 11,731 Libertarian (Michael Badnarik); 1,805 write-in (Ralph Nader); 348 write-in (Walter F. Brown); 108 write-in (David Cobb).

**Governor**  Other vote was 52,513 Libertarian (Barbara Howe).

**Senator**  Other vote was 47,743 Libertarian (Tom Bailey); 362 write-in (Walker F. Rucker).

# NORTH CAROLINA

## GENERAL AND PRIMARY ELECTIONS

## 2004 GENERAL ELECTIONS

| House | Other vote was: |
|---|---|
| CD 1 | |
| CD 2 | |
| CD 3 | |
| CD 4 | 76 write-in (Maximilian Longley). |
| CD 5 | |
| CD 6 | |
| CD 7 | |
| CD 8 | |
| CD 9 | |
| CD 10 | |
| CD 11 | |
| CD 12 | |
| CD 13 | |

## 2004 PRIMARY ELECTIONS

| | | | |
|---|---|---|---|
| **Primary** | July 20, 2004 | **Registration** (as of June 19, 2004) | Republican 1,762,644 |
| | | | Democratic 2,419,206 |
| **Primary Runoff** | August 17, 2004 | | Libertarian 10,608 |
| | | | Unaffiliated 923,390 |
| | | | TOTAL 5,115,848 |

**Primary Type**  Semi-open—Registered Democrats and Republicans could vote only in their party's primary. Unaffiliated voters could participate in the primary of either party. The total number of registered voters was listed as 5,115,849 by state election officials on the eve of the 2004 primary, but adds to 5,115,848.

Note: An asterisk (*) denotes incumbent. The names of unopposed candidates did not appear on the primary ballot; therefore, no votes were cast for these candidates.

| | REPUBLICAN PRIMARIES | | | DEMOCRATIC PRIMARIES | | |
|---|---|---|---|---|---|---|
| Governor | Patrick J. Ballantine | 110,726 | 30.4% | Michael F. Easley* | 379,498 | 85.4% |
| | Richard Vinroot | 109,217 | 30.0% | Rickey Kipfer | 65,061 | 14.6% |
| | Bill Cobey | 97,461 | 26.7% | | | |
| | Dan Barrett | 19,097 | 5.2% | | | |
| | Fern H. Shubert | 14,445 | 4.0% | | | |
| | George W. Little | 13,474 | 3.7% | | | |
| | TOTAL | 364,420 | | TOTAL | 444,559 | |
| Senator | Richard M. Burr | 302,319 | 87.9% | Erskine Bowles | Unopposed | |
| | John Ross Hendrix | 25,971 | 7.6% | | | |
| | Albert Lee Wiley Jr. | 15,585 | 4.5% | | | |
| | TOTAL | 343,875 | | | | |
| Congressional District 1 | Greg Dority | 7,526 | 80.7% | G.K. Butterfield | 43,257 | 71.4% |
| | Jerry N. Williford | 1,795 | 19.3% | Samuel "Sam" S. Davis III | 7,577 | 12.5% |
| | | | | Christine L. Fitch | 4,301 | 7.1% |
| | | | | Donald "Don" Davis | 3,296 | 5.4% |
| | | | | Darryl Smith | 2,111 | 3.5% |
| | TOTAL | 9,321 | | TOTAL | 60,542 | |
| Congressional District 2 | Billy J. Creech | 12,890 | 79.7% | Bob Etheridge* | Unopposed | |
| | Robert Rogan | 3,277 | 20.3% | | | |
| | TOTAL | 16,167 | | | | |

# NORTH CAROLINA

## GENERAL AND PRIMARY ELECTIONS

| | REPUBLICAN PRIMARIES | | | DEMOCRATIC PRIMARIES | | |
|---|---|---|---|---|---|---|
| **Congressional District 3** | Walter B. Jones* | Unopposed | | Roger A. Eaton | Unopposed | |
| **Congressional District 4** | Todd A. Batchelor | 11,531 | 45.4% | David E. Price* | Unopposed | |
| | Robert E. "Whit" Whitfield | 7,954 | 31.3% | | | |
| | James C. Powers | 3,116 | 12.3% | | | |
| | Howard Mason | 2,787 | 11.0% | | | |
| | TOTAL | 25,388 | | | | |
| **Congressional District 5** | Vernon L. Robinson | 13,824 | 23.6% | Jim A. Harrell Jr. | 17,481 | 73.3% |
| | Virginia Foxx | 13,119 | 22.4% | Roger N. Kirkman | 3,784 | 15.9% |
| | Ed Broyhill | 12,608 | 21.5% | Andrew Winfrey | 2,574 | 10.8% |
| | Jay Helvey | 8,517 | 14.5% | | | |
| | Nathan Tabor | 7,660 | 13.1% | | | |
| | Joseph H. "Joe" Byrd | 1,457 | 2.5% | | | |
| | Edward L. "Ed" Powell | 969 | 1.7% | | | |
| | David Stephen Vanhoy | 473 | 0.8% | | | |
| | TOTAL | 58,627 | | TOTAL | 23,839 | |
| | PRIMARY RUNOFF | | | | | |
| | Virginia Foxx | 23,092 | 54.6% | | | |
| | Vernon L. Robinson | 19,201 | 45.4% | | | |
| | TOTAL | 42,293 | | | | |
| **Congressional District 6** | Howard Coble* | Unopposed | | William W. Jordan | 11,871 | 66.5% |
| | | | | Rick Miller | 5,993 | 33.5% |
| | | | | TOTAL | 17,864 | |
| **Congressional District 7** | Ken Plonk | Unopposed | | Mike McIntyre* | Unopposed | |
| **Congressional District 8** | Robin Hayes* | Unopposed | | Beth Troutman | 19,838 | 72.5% |
| | | | | Mark Ortiz | 7,515 | 27.5% |
| | | | | TOTAL | 27,353 | |
| **Congressional District 9** | Sue Myrick* | Unopposed | | Jack Flynn | Unopposed | |
| **Congressional District 10** | David Huffman | 14,280 | 35.0% | Anne N. Fischer | 8,538 | 50.6% |
| | Patrick T. McHenry | 10,760 | 26.3% | John F. Cole | 8,340 | 49.4% |
| | Sandy Lyons | 8,000 | 19.6% | | | |
| | George A. Moretz | 7,812 | 19.1% | | | |
| | TOTAL | 40,852 | | TOTAL | 16,878 | |
| | PRIMARY RUNOFF | | | | | |
| | Patrick T. McHenry | 15,015 | 50.1% | | | |
| | David Huffman | 14,930 | 49.9% | | | |
| | TOTAL | 29,945 | | | | |
| **Congressional District 11** | Charles H. Taylor* | Unopposed | | Patsy Keever | 26,385 | 81.5% |
| | | | | Clyde Michael Morgan | 5,972 | 18.5% |
| | | | | TOTAL | 32,357 | |
| **Congressional District 12** | Ada M. Fisher | Unopposed | | Melvin Watt* | 24,374 | 85.2% |
| | | | | Kimberly "Kim" Holley | 4,241 | 14.8% |
| | | | | TOTAL | 28,615 | |
| **Congressional District 13** | Virginia Johnson | 13,644 | 55.5% | Brad Miller* | Unopposed | |
| | Graham Boyd | 10,958 | 44.5% | | | |
| | TOTAL | 24,602 | | | | |

# NORTH DAKOTA

## GOVERNOR

John Hoeven (R). Reelected 2004 to a four-year term. Previously elected 2000.

## SENATORS (2 Democrats)

Kent Conrad (D). Reelected 2000 to a six-year term. Previously elected 1994 and in a special election December 1992 to fill the remaining two years of the term vacated by the death of Senator Quentin N. Burdick (D), who died in September 1992; elected 1986 to a six-year term.

Byron L. Dorgan (D). Reelected 2004 to a six-year term. Previously elected 1998, 1992.

## REPRESENTATIVES (1 Democrat)

At Large. Earl Pomeroy (D)

## POSTWAR VOTE FOR PRESIDENT

| Year | Total Vote | Republican | | Democratic | | Other Vote | Plurality | Percentage | | | |
| | | Vote | Candidate | Vote | Candidate | | | Total Vote | | Major Vote | |
| | | | | | | | | Rep. | Dem. | Rep. | Dem. |
|---|---|---|---|---|---|---|---|---|---|---|---|
| 2004 | 312,833 | 196,651 | Bush, George W. | 111,052 | Kerry, John | 5,130 | 85,599 R | 62.9% | 35.5% | 63.9% | 36.1% |
| 2000** | 288,256 | 174,852 | Bush, George W. | 95,284 | Gore, Al | 18,120 | 79,568 R | 60.7% | 33.1% | 64.7% | 35.3% |
| 1996** | 266,411 | 125,050 | Dole, Bob | 106,905 | Clinton, Bill | 34,456 | 18,145 R | 46.9% | 40.1% | 53.9% | 46.1% |
| 1992** | 308,133 | 136,244 | Bush, George | 99,168 | Clinton, Bill | 72,721 | 37,076 R | 44.2% | 32.2% | 57.9% | 42.1% |
| 1988 | 297,261 | 166,559 | Bush, George | 127,739 | Dukakis, Michael S. | 2,963 | 38,820 R | 56.0% | 43.0% | 56.6% | 43.4% |
| 1984 | 308,971 | 200,336 | Reagan, Ronald | 104,429 | Mondale, Walter F. | 4,206 | 95,907 R | 64.8% | 33.8% | 65.7% | 34.3% |
| 1980** | 301,545 | 193,695 | Reagan, Ronald | 79,189 | Carter, Jimmy | 28,661 | 114,506 R | 64.2% | 26.3% | 71.0% | 29.0% |
| 1976 | 297,188 | 153,470 | Ford, Gerald R. | 136,078 | Carter, Jimmy | 7,640 | 17,392 R | 51.6% | 45.8% | 53.0% | 47.0% |
| 1972 | 280,514 | 174,109 | Nixon, Richard M. | 100,384 | McGovern, George S. | 6,021 | 73,725 R | 62.1% | 35.8% | 63.4% | 36.6% |
| 1968** | 247,882 | 138,669 | Nixon, Richard M. | 94,769 | Humphrey, Hubert H. | 14,444 | 43,900 R | 55.9% | 38.2% | 59.4% | 40.6% |
| 1964 | 258,389 | 108,207 | Goldwater, Barry M. | 149,784 | Johnson, Lyndon B. | 398 | 41,577 D | 41.9% | 58.0% | 41.9% | 58.1% |
| 1960 | 278,431 | 154,310 | Nixon, Richard M. | 123,963 | Kennedy, John F. | 158 | 30,347 R | 55.4% | 44.5% | 55.5% | 44.5% |
| 1956 | 253,991 | 156,766 | Eisenhower, Dwight D. | 96,742 | Stevenson, Adlai E. | 483 | 60,024 R | 61.7% | 38.1% | 61.8% | 38.2% |
| 1952 | 270,127 | 191,712 | Eisenhower, Dwight D. | 76,694 | Stevenson, Adlai E. | 1,721 | 115,018 R | 71.0% | 28.4% | 71.4% | 28.6% |
| 1948 | 220,716 | 115,139 | Dewey, Thomas E. | 95,812 | Truman, Harry S. | 9,765 | 19,327 R | 52.2% | 43.4% | 54.6% | 45.4% |

In past elections, the other vote included: 2000 - 9,486 Green (Ralph Nader); 1996 - 32,515 Reform (Ross Perot); 1992 - 71,084 Independent (Perot); 1980 - 23,640 Independent (John Anderson); 1968 - 14,244 American Independent (George Wallace).

# NORTH DAKOTA

## POSTWAR VOTE FOR GOVERNOR

| Year | Total Vote | Republican Vote | Republican Candidate | Democratic Vote | Democratic Candidate | Other Vote | Rep.-Dem. Plurality | Total Vote Rep. | Total Vote Dem. | Major Vote Rep. | Major Vote Dem. |
|------|-----------|-----------------|----------------------|-----------------|----------------------|------------|---------------------|-----------------|-----------------|-----------------|-----------------|
| 2004 | 309,873 | 220,803 | Hoeven, John | 84,877 | Satrom, Joseph A. | 4,193 | 135,926 R | 71.3% | 27.4% | 72.2% | 27.8% |
| 2000 | 289,412 | 159,255 | Hoeven, John | 130,144 | Heitkamp, Heidi | 13 | 29,111 R | 55.0% | 45.0% | 55.0% | 45.0% |
| 1996 | 264,298 | 174,937 | Schafer, Edward T. | 89,349 | Kaldor, Lee | 12 | 85,588 R | 66.2% | 33.8% | 66.2% | 33.8% |
| 1992 | 304,861 | 176,398 | Schafer, Edward T. | 123,845 | Spaeth, Nicholas | 4,618 | 52,553 R | 57.9% | 40.6% | 58.8% | 41.2% |
| 1988 | 299,080 | 119,986 | Mallberg, Leon L. | 179,094 | Sinner, George | | 59,108 D | 40.1% | 59.9% | 40.1% | 59.9% |
| 1984 | 314,382 | 140,460 | Olson, Allen I. | 173,922 | Sinner, George | | 33,462 D | 44.7% | 55.3% | 44.7% | 55.3% |
| 1980 | 302,621 | 162,230 | Olson, Allen I. | 140,391 | Link, Arthur A. | | 21,839 R | 53.6% | 46.4% | 53.6% | 46.4% |
| 1976 | 297,249 | 138,321 | Elkin, Richard | 153,309 | Link, Arthur A. | 5,619 | 14,988 D | 46.5% | 51.6% | 47.4% | 52.6% |
| 1972 | 281,931 | 138,032 | Larsen, Richard | 143,899 | Link, Arthur A. | | 5,867 D | 49.0% | 51.0% | 49.0% | 51.0% |
| 1968 | 248,000 | 108,382 | McCarney, Robert P. | 135,955 | Guy, William L. | 3,663 | 27,573 D | 43.7% | 54.8% | 44.4% | 55.6% |
| 1964** | 262,661 | 116,247 | Halcrow, Donald M. | 146,414 | Guy, William L. | | 30,167 D | 44.3% | 55.7% | 44.3% | 55.7% |
| 1962 | 228,509 | 113,251 | Andrews, Mark | 115,258 | Guy, William L. | | 2,007 D | 49.6% | 50.4% | 49.6% | 50.4% |
| 1960 | 275,375 | 122,486 | Dahl, C. P. | 136,148 | Guy, William L. | 16,741 | 13,662 D | 44.5% | 49.4% | 47.4% | 52.6% |
| 1958 | 210,599 | 111,836 | Davis, John E. | 98,763 | Lord, John F. | | 13,073 R | 53.1% | 46.9% | 53.1% | 46.9% |
| 1956 | 252,435 | 147,566 | Davis, John E. | 104,869 | Warner, Wallace E. | | 42,697 R | 58.5% | 41.5% | 58.5% | 41.5% |
| 1954 | 193,501 | 124,253 | Brunsdale, C. Norman | 69,248 | Bymers, Cornelius | | 55,005 R | 64.2% | 35.8% | 64.2% | 35.8% |
| 1952 | 253,934 | 199,944 | Brunsdale, C. Norman | 53,990 | Johnson, Ole C. | | 145,954 R | 78.7% | 21.3% | 78.7% | 21.3% |
| 1950 | 183,772 | 121,822 | Brunsdale, C. Norman | 61,950 | Byerly, Clyde G. | | 59,872 R | 66.3% | 33.7% | 66.3% | 33.7% |
| 1948 | 214,858 | 131,764 | Aandahl, Fred G. | 80,555 | Henry, Howard | 2,539 | 51,209 R | 61.3% | 37.5% | 62.1% | 37.9% |
| 1946 | 169,391 | 116,672 | Aandahl, Fred G. | 52,719 | Burdick, Quentin N. | | 63,953 R | 68.9% | 31.1% | 68.9% | 31.1% |

The term of office of North Dakota's governor was increased from two to four years effective with the 1964 election.

## POSTWAR VOTE FOR SENATOR

| Year | Total Vote | Republican Vote | Republican Candidate | Democratic Vote | Democratic Candidate | Other Vote | Rep.-Dem. Plurality | Total Vote Rep. | Total Vote Dem. | Major Vote Rep. | Major Vote Dem. |
|------|-----------|-----------------|----------------------|-----------------|----------------------|------------|---------------------|-----------------|-----------------|-----------------|-----------------|
| 2004 | 310,696 | 98,553 | Liffrig, Mike | 212,143 | Dorgan, Byron L. | | 113,590 D | 31.7% | 68.3% | 31.7% | 68.3% |
| 2000 | 287,539 | 111,069 | Sand, Duane | 176,470 | Conrad, Kent | | 65,401 D | 38.6% | 61.4% | 38.6% | 61.4% |
| 1998 | 213,358 | 75,013 | Nalewaja, Donna | 134,747 | Dorgan, Byron L. | 3,598 | 59,734 D | 35.2% | 63.2% | 35.8% | 64.2% |
| 1994 | 236,547 | 99,390 | Clayburg, Ben | 137,157 | Conrad, Kent | | 37,767 D | 42.0% | 58.0% | 42.0% | 58.0% |
| 1992 | 303,957 | 118,162 | Sydness, Steve | 179,347 | Dorgan, Byron L. | 6,448 | 61,185 D | 38.9% | 59.0% | 39.7% | 60.3% |
| 1992S | 163,311 | 55,194 | Dalrymple, Jack | 103,246 | Conrad, Kent | 4,871 | 48,052 D | 33.8% | 63.2% | 34.8% | 65.2% |
| 1988 | 289,170 | 112,937 | Striden, Earl | 171,899 | Burdick, Quentin N. | 4,334 | 58,962 D | 39.1% | 59.4% | 39.6% | 60.4% |
| 1986 | 288,998 | 141,797 | Andrews, Mark | 143,932 | Conrad, Kent | 3,269 | 2,135 D | 49.1% | 49.8% | 49.6% | 50.4% |
| 1982 | 262,465 | 89,304 | Knorr, Gene | 164,873 | Burdick, Quentin N. | 8,288 | 75,569 D | 34.0% | 62.8% | 35.1% | 64.9% |
| 1980 | 299,272 | 210,347 | Andrews, Mark | 86,658 | Johanneson, Kent | 2,267 | 123,689 R | 70.3% | 29.0% | 70.8% | 29.2% |
| 1976 | 283,062 | 103,466 | Stroup, Richard | 175,772 | Burdick, Quentin N. | 3,824 | 72,306 D | 36.6% | 62.1% | 37.1% | 62.9% |
| 1974 | 235,661 | 114,117 | Young, Milton R. | 113,931 | Guy, William L. | 7,613 | 186 R | 48.4% | 48.3% | 50.0% | 50.0% |
| 1970 | 219,560 | 82,996 | Kleppe, Tom | 134,519 | Burdick, Quentin N. | 2,045 | 51,523 D | 37.8% | 61.3% | 38.2% | 61.8% |
| 1968 | 239,776 | 154,968 | Young, Milton R. | 80,815 | Lashkowitz, Herschel | 3,993 | 74,153 R | 64.6% | 33.7% | 65.7% | 34.3% |
| 1964 | 258,945 | 109,681 | Kleppe, Tom | 149,264 | Burdick, Quentin N. | | 39,583 D | 42.4% | 57.6% | 42.4% | 57.6% |
| 1962 | 223,737 | 135,705 | Young, Milton R. | 88,032 | Lanier, William | | 47,673 R | 60.7% | 39.3% | 60.7% | 39.3% |
| 1960S | 210,349 | 103,475 | Davis, John E. | 104,593 | Burdick, Quentin N. | 2,281 | 1,118 D | 49.2% | 49.7% | 49.7% | 50.3% |
| 1958 | 204,635 | 117,070 | Langer, William | 84,892 | Vendsel, Raymond | 2,673 | 32,178 R | 57.2% | 41.5% | 58.0% | 42.0% |
| 1956 | 244,161 | 155,305 | Young, Milton R. | 87,919 | Burdick, Quentin N. | 937 | 67,386 R | 63.6% | 36.0% | 63.9% | 36.1% |
| 1952 | 237,995 | 157,907 | Langer, William | 55,347 | Morrison, Harold A. | 24,741 | 102,560 R | 66.3% | 23.3% | 74.0% | 26.0% |
| 1950 | 186,716 | 126,209 | Young, Milton R. | 60,507 | O'Brien, Harry | | 65,702 R | 67.6% | 32.4% | 67.6% | 32.4% |
| 1946** | 165,382 | 88,210 | Langer, William | 38,368 | Larson, Abner B. | 38,804 | 49,842 R | 53.3% | 23.2% | 69.7% | 30.3% |
| 1946S | 136,852 | 75,998 | Young, Milton R. | 37,507 | Lanier, William | 23,347 | 38,491 R | 55.5% | 27.4% | 67.0% | 33.0% |

One of the 1992 elections was for a short term to fill a vacancy and the special election was held in December. The 1960 and 1946 special elections were held in June for short terms to fill vacancies. In 1946 other vote was for Arthur Thompson (Independent) who received 23.5 percent of the total vote and finished second.

# NORTH DAKOTA

One member At Large

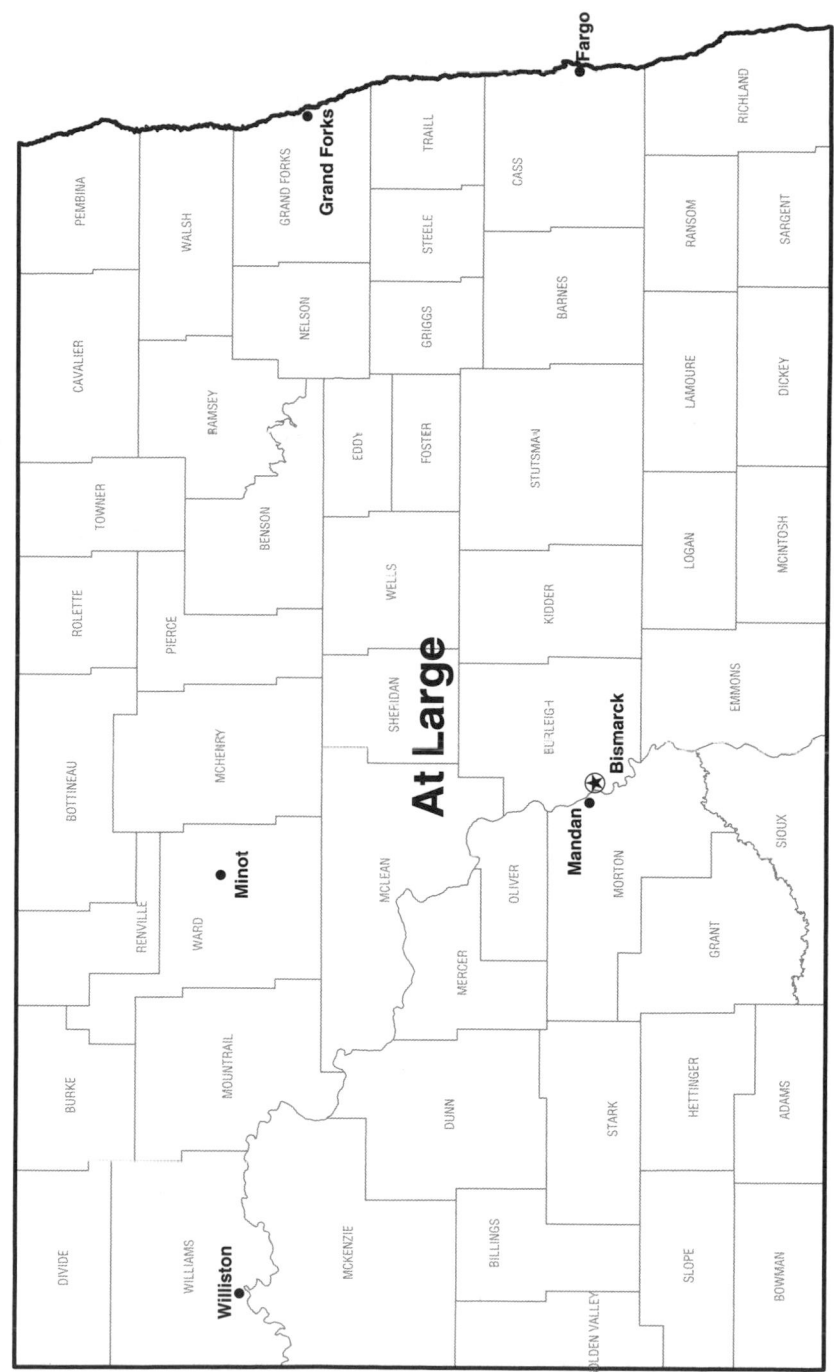

# NORTH DAKOTA

## PRESIDENT 2004

| 2000 Census Population | County | Total Vote | Republican | Democratic | Other | Rep.-Dem. Plurality | Percentage Total Vote Rep. | Dem. | Major Vote Rep. | Dem. |
|---|---|---|---|---|---|---|---|---|---|---|
| 2,593 | ADAMS | 1,291 | 915 | 353 | 23 | 562 R | 70.9% | 27.3% | 72.2% | 27.8% |
| 11,775 | BARNES | 5,813 | 3,541 | 2,186 | 86 | 1,355 R | 60.9% | 37.6% | 61.8% | 38.2% |
| 6,964 | BENSON | 2,246 | 1,002 | 1,196 | 48 | 194 D | 44.6% | 53.3% | 45.6% | 54.4% |
| 888 | BILLINGS | 564 | 449 | 99 | 16 | 350 R | 79.6% | 17.6% | 81.9% | 18.1% |
| 7,149 | BOTTINEAU | 3,674 | 2,468 | 1,168 | 38 | 1,300 R | 67.2% | 31.8% | 67.9% | 32.1% |
| 3,242 | BOWMAN | 1,716 | 1,280 | 397 | 39 | 883 R | 74.6% | 23.1% | 76.3% | 23.7% |
| 2,242 | BURKE | 1,165 | 808 | 336 | 21 | 472 R | 69.4% | 28.8% | 70.6% | 29.4% |
| 69,416 | BURLEIGH | 38,814 | 26,577 | 11,621 | 616 | 14,956 R | 68.5% | 29.9% | 69.6% | 30.4% |
| 123,138 | CASS | 66,711 | 39,619 | 26,010 | 1,082 | 13,609 R | 59.4% | 39.0% | 60.4% | 39.6% |
| 4,831 | CAVALIER | 2,444 | 1,522 | 887 | 35 | 635 R | 62.3% | 36.3% | 63.2% | 36.8% |
| 5,757 | DICKEY | 2,821 | 1,890 | 883 | 48 | 1,007 R | 67.0% | 31.3% | 68.2% | 31.8% |
| 2,283 | DIVIDE | 1,268 | 751 | 487 | 30 | 264 R | 59.2% | 38.4% | 60.7% | 39.3% |
| 3,600 | DUNN | 1,774 | 1,178 | 571 | 25 | 607 R | 66.4% | 32.2% | 67.4% | 32.6% |
| 2,757 | EDDY | 1,213 | 655 | 534 | 24 | 121 R | 54.0% | 44.0% | 55.1% | 44.9% |
| 4,331 | EMMONS | 2,113 | 1,449 | 611 | 53 | 838 R | 68.6% | 28.9% | 70.3% | 29.7% |
| 3,759 | FOSTER | 1,766 | 1,219 | 518 | 29 | 701 R | 69.0% | 29.3% | 70.2% | 29.8% |
| 1,924 | GOLDEN VALLEY | 927 | 719 | 195 | 13 | 524 R | 77.6% | 21.0% | 78.7% | 21.3% |
| 66,109 | GRAND FORKS | 30,470 | 17,298 | 12,646 | 526 | 4,652 R | 56.8% | 41.5% | 57.8% | 42.2% |
| 2,841 | GRANT | 1,242 | 952 | 264 | 26 | 688 R | 76.7% | 21.3% | 78.3% | 21.7% |
| 2,754 | GRIGGS | 1,439 | 907 | 505 | 27 | 402 R | 63.0% | 35.1% | 64.2% | 35.8% |
| 2,715 | HETTINGER | 1,494 | 1,044 | 405 | 45 | 639 R | 69.9% | 27.1% | 72.0% | 28.0% |
| 2,753 | KIDDER | 1,369 | 902 | 433 | 34 | 469 R | 65.9% | 31.6% | 67.6% | 32.4% |
| 4,701 | LA MOURE | 2,335 | 1,592 | 712 | 31 | 880 R | 68.2% | 30.5% | 69.1% | 30.9% |
| 2,308 | LOGAN | 1,130 | 844 | 265 | 21 | 579 R | 74.7% | 23.5% | 76.1% | 23.9% |
| 5,987 | MCHENRY | 2,820 | 1,744 | 1,030 | 46 | 714 R | 61.8% | 36.5% | 62.9% | 37.1% |
| 3,390 | MCINTOSH | 1,722 | 1,254 | 436 | 32 | 818 R | 72.8% | 25.3% | 74.2% | 25.8% |
| 5,737 | MCKENZIE | 2,762 | 1,897 | 847 | 18 | 1,050 R | 68.7% | 30.7% | 69.1% | 30.9% |
| 9,311 | MCLEAN | 4,750 | 3,014 | 1,664 | 72 | 1,350 R | 63.5% | 35.0% | 64.4% | 35.6% |
| 8,644 | MERCER | 4,617 | 3,285 | 1,245 | 87 | 2,040 R | 71.2% | 27.0% | 72.5% | 27.5% |
| 25,303 | MORTON | 12,633 | 8,325 | 4,073 | 235 | 4,252 R | 65.9% | 32.2% | 67.1% | 32.9% |
| 6,631 | MOUNTRAIL | 3,030 | 1,527 | 1,465 | 38 | 62 R | 50.4% | 48.3% | 51.0% | 49.0% |
| 3,715 | NELSON | 1,922 | 1,107 | 778 | 37 | 329 R | 57.6% | 40.5% | 58.7% | 41.3% |
| 2,065 | OLIVER | 1,119 | 790 | 310 | 19 | 480 R | 70.6% | 27.7% | 71.8% | 28.2% |
| 8,585 | PEMBINA | 3,856 | 2,466 | 1,321 | 69 | 1,145 R | 64.0% | 34.3% | 65.1% | 34.9% |
| 4,675 | PIERCE | 2,195 | 1,475 | 686 | 34 | 789 R | 67.2% | 31.3% | 68.3% | 31.7% |
| 12,066 | RAMSEY | 4,900 | 2,943 | 1,885 | 72 | 1,058 R | 60.1% | 38.5% | 61.0% | 39.0% |
| 5,890 | RANSOM | 2,602 | 1,352 | 1,199 | 51 | 153 R | 52.0% | 46.1% | 53.0% | 47.0% |
| 2,610 | RENVILLE | 1,469 | 953 | 497 | 19 | 456 R | 64.9% | 33.8% | 65.7% | 34.3% |
| 17,998 | RICHLAND | 8,215 | 5,264 | 2,821 | 130 | 2,443 R | 64.1% | 34.3% | 65.1% | 34.9% |
| 13,674 | ROLETTE | 4,044 | 1,392 | 2,564 | 88 | 1,172 D | 34.4% | 63.4% | 35.2% | 64.8% |
| 4,366 | SARGENT | 2,200 | 1,147 | 1,021 | 32 | 126 R | 52.1% | 46.4% | 52.9% | 47.1% |
| 1,710 | SHERIDAN | 944 | 727 | 200 | 17 | 527 R | 77.0% | 21.2% | 78.4% | 21.6% |
| 4,044 | SIOUX | 1,140 | 319 | 804 | 17 | 485 D | 28.0% | 70.5% | 28.4% | 71.6% |
| 767 | SLOPE | 432 | 335 | 89 | 8 | 246 R | 77.5% | 20.6% | 79.0% | 21.0% |
| 22,636 | STARK | 10,400 | 7,220 | 3,013 | 167 | 4,207 R | 69.4% | 29.0% | 70.6% | 29.4% |
| 2,258 | STEELE | 1,213 | 586 | 616 | 11 | 30 D | 48.3% | 50.8% | 48.8% | 51.2% |
| 21,908 | STUTSMAN | 10,122 | 6,517 | 3,438 | 167 | 3,079 R | 64.4% | 34.0% | 65.5% | 34.5% |
| 2,876 | TOWNER | 1,391 | 754 | 606 | 31 | 148 R | 54.2% | 43.6% | 55.4% | 44.6% |
| 8,477 | TRAILL | 4,248 | 2,543 | 1,651 | 54 | 892 R | 59.9% | 38.9% | 60.6% | 39.4% |
| 12,389 | WALSH | 5,186 | 3,194 | 1,905 | 87 | 1,289 R | 61.6% | 36.7% | 62.6% | 37.4% |
| 58,795 | WARD | 25,612 | 17,008 | 8,236 | 368 | 8,772 R | 66.4% | 32.2% | 67.4% | 32.6% |
| 5,102 | WELLS | 2,561 | 1,654 | 858 | 49 | 796 R | 64.6% | 33.5% | 65.8% | 34.2% |
| 19,761 | WILLIAMS | 8,929 | 6,278 | 2,512 | 139 | 3,766 R | 70.3% | 28.1% | 71.4% | 28.6% |
| 642,200 | TOTAL | 312,833 | 196,651 | 111,052 | 5,130 | 85,599 R | 62.9% | 35.5% | 63.9% | 36.1% |

# NORTH DAKOTA

## GOVERNOR 2004

| 2000 Census Population | County | Total Vote | Republican | Democratic | Other | Rep.-Dem. Plurality | Percentage | | | |
|---|---|---|---|---|---|---|---|---|---|---|
| | | | | | | | Total Vote | | Major Vote | |
| | | | | | | | Rep. | Dem. | Rep. | Dem. |
| 2,593 | ADAMS | 1,282 | 984 | 278 | 20 | 706 R | 76.8% | 21.7% | 78.0% | 22.0% |
| 11,775 | BARNES | 5,784 | 4,121 | 1,597 | 66 | 2,524 R | 71.2% | 27.6% | 72.1% | 27.9% |
| 6,964 | BENSON | 2,241 | 1,257 | 947 | 37 | 310 R | 56.1% | 42.3% | 57.0% | 43.0% |
| 888 | BILLINGS | 560 | 438 | 115 | 7 | 323 R | 78.2% | 20.5% | 79.2% | 20.8% |
| 7,149 | BOTTINEAU | 3,663 | 2,819 | 787 | 57 | 2,032 R | 77.0% | 21.5% | 78.2% | 21.8% |
| 3,242 | BOWMAN | 1,709 | 1,358 | 317 | 34 | 1,041 R | 79.5% | 18.5% | 81.1% | 18.9% |
| 2,242 | BURKE | 1,153 | 894 | 243 | 16 | 651 R | 77.5% | 21.1% | 78.6% | 21.4% |
| 69,416 | BURLEIGH | 38,579 | 27,675 | 10,369 | 535 | 17,306 R | 71.7% | 26.9% | 72.7% | 27.3% |
| 123,138 | CASS | 65,875 | 45,814 | 19,315 | 746 | 26,499 R | 69.5% | 29.3% | 70.3% | 29.7% |
| 4,831 | CAVALIER | 2,452 | 1,863 | 528 | 61 | 1,335 R | 76.0% | 21.5% | 77.9% | 22.1% |
| 5,757 | DICKEY | 2,795 | 2,044 | 710 | 41 | 1,334 R | 73.1% | 25.4% | 74.2% | 25.8% |
| 2,283 | DIVIDE | 1,262 | 907 | 339 | 16 | 568 R | 71.9% | 26.9% | 72.8% | 27.2% |
| 3,600 | DUNN | 1,766 | 1,268 | 469 | 29 | 799 R | 71.8% | 26.6% | 73.0% | 27.0% |
| 2,757 | EDDY | 1,210 | 817 | 373 | 20 | 444 R | 67.5% | 30.8% | 68.7% | 31.3% |
| 4,331 | EMMONS | 2,081 | 1,483 | 558 | 40 | 925 R | 71.3% | 26.8% | 72.7% | 27.3% |
| 3,759 | FOSTER | 1,764 | 1,330 | 414 | 20 | 916 R | 75.4% | 23.5% | 76.3% | 23.7% |
| 1,924 | GOLDEN VALLEY | 921 | 754 | 158 | 9 | 596 R | 81.9% | 17.2% | 82.7% | 17.3% |
| 66,109 | GRAND FORKS | 29,787 | 21,450 | 7,870 | 467 | 13,580 R | 72.0% | 26.4% | 73.2% | 26.8% |
| 2,841 | GRANT | 1,243 | 965 | 257 | 21 | 708 R | 77.6% | 20.7% | 79.0% | 21.0% |
| 2,754 | GRIGGS | 1,418 | 1,022 | 384 | 12 | 638 R | 72.1% | 27.1% | 72.7% | 27.3% |
| 2,715 | HETTINGER | 1,498 | 1,058 | 418 | 22 | 640 R | 70.6% | 27.9% | 71.7% | 28.3% |
| 2,753 | KIDDER | 1,350 | 863 | 440 | 47 | 423 R | 63.9% | 32.6% | 66.2% | 33.8% |
| 4,701 | LA MOURE | 2,328 | 1,707 | 607 | 14 | 1,100 R | 73.3% | 26.1% | 73.8% | 26.2% |
| 2,308 | LOGAN | 1,134 | 856 | 258 | 20 | 598 R | 75.5% | 22.8% | 76.8% | 23.2% |
| 5,987 | MCHENRY | 2,821 | 1,959 | 810 | 52 | 1,149 R | 69.4% | 28.7% | 70.7% | 29.3% |
| 3,390 | MCINTOSH | 1,712 | 1,344 | 351 | 17 | 993 R | 78.5% | 20.5% | 79.3% | 20.7% |
| 5,737 | MCKENZIE | 2,736 | 2,082 | 614 | 40 | 1,468 R | 76.1% | 22.4% | 77.2% | 22.8% |
| 9,311 | MCLEAN | 4,732 | 3,245 | 1,430 | 57 | 1,815 R | 68.6% | 30.2% | 69.4% | 30.6% |
| 8,644 | MERCER | 4,612 | 3,358 | 1,208 | 46 | 2,150 R | 72.8% | 26.2% | 73.5% | 26.5% |
| 25,303 | MORTON | 12,586 | 8,735 | 3,663 | 188 | 5,072 R | 69.4% | 29.1% | 70.5% | 29.5% |
| 6,631 | MOUNTRAIL | 3,027 | 1,898 | 1,085 | 44 | 813 R | 62.7% | 35.8% | 63.6% | 36.4% |
| 3,715 | NELSON | 1,908 | 1,308 | 582 | 18 | 726 R | 68.6% | 30.5% | 69.2% | 30.8% |
| 2,065 | OLIVER | 1,122 | 824 | 280 | 18 | 544 R | 73.4% | 25.0% | 74.6% | 25.4% |
| 8,585 | PEMBINA | 3,849 | 2,960 | 832 | 57 | 2,128 R | 76.9% | 21.6% | 78.1% | 21.9% |
| 4,675 | PIERCE | 2,183 | 1,626 | 529 | 28 | 1,097 R | 74.5% | 24.2% | 75.5% | 24.5% |
| 12,066 | RAMSEY | 4,890 | 3,599 | 1,223 | 68 | 2,376 R | 73.6% | 25.0% | 74.6% | 25.4% |
| 5,890 | RANSOM | 2,587 | 1,656 | 904 | 27 | 752 R | 64.0% | 34.9% | 64.7% | 35.3% |
| 2,610 | RENVILLE | 1,454 | 1,078 | 362 | 14 | 716 R | 74.1% | 24.9% | 74.9% | 25.1% |
| 17,998 | RICHLAND | 8,110 | 5,720 | 2,302 | 88 | 3,418 R | 70.5% | 28.4% | 71.3% | 28.7% |
| 13,674 | ROLETTE | 4,004 | 1,812 | 2,106 | 86 | 294 D | 45.3% | 52.6% | 46.2% | 53.8% |
| 4,366 | SARGENT | 2,191 | 1,321 | 845 | 25 | 476 R | 60.3% | 38.6% | 61.0% | 39.0% |
| 1,710 | SHERIDAN | 936 | 724 | 199 | 13 | 525 R | 77.4% | 21.3% | 78.4% | 21.6% |
| 4,044 | SIOUX | 1,121 | 525 | 572 | 24 | 47 D | 46.8% | 51.0% | 47.9% | 52.1% |
| 767 | SLOPE | 430 | 333 | 86 | 11 | 247 R | 77.4% | 20.0% | 79.5% | 20.5% |
| 22,636 | STARK | 10,323 | 7,877 | 2,306 | 140 | 5,571 R | 76.3% | 22.3% | 77.4% | 22.6% |
| 2,258 | STEELE | 1,216 | 656 | 551 | 9 | 105 R | 53.9% | 45.3% | 54.3% | 45.7% |
| 21,908 | STUTSMAN | 10,032 | 7,110 | 2,761 | 161 | 4,349 R | 70.9% | 27.5% | 72.0% | 28.0% |
| 2,876 | TOWNER | 1,390 | 968 | 404 | 18 | 564 R | 69.6% | 29.1% | 70.6% | 29.4% |
| 8,477 | TRAILL | 4,224 | 2,710 | 1,469 | 45 | 1,241 R | 64.2% | 34.8% | 64.8% | 35.2% |
| 12,389 | WALSH | 5,188 | 3,940 | 1,189 | 59 | 2,751 R | 75.9% | 22.9% | 76.8% | 23.2% |
| 58,795 | WARD | 25,204 | 18,934 | 5,945 | 325 | 12,989 R | 75.1% | 23.6% | 76.1% | 23.9% |
| 5,102 | WELLS | 2,571 | 1,819 | 722 | 30 | 1,097 R | 70.8% | 28.1% | 71.6% | 28.4% |
| 19,761 | WILLIAMS | 8,859 | 6,935 | 1,796 | 128 | 5,139 R | 78.3% | 20.3% | 79.4% | 20.6% |
| 642,200 | TOTAL | 309,873 | 220,803 | 84,877 | 4,193 | 135,926 R | 71.3% | 27.4% | 72.2% | 27.8% |

# NORTH DAKOTA

## SENATOR 2004

| 2000 Census Population | County | Total Vote | Republican | Democratic | Other | Rep.-Dem. Plurality | Percentage | | | |
|---|---|---|---|---|---|---|---|---|---|---|
| | | | | | | | Total Vote | | Major Vote | |
| | | | | | | | Rep. | Dem. | Rep. | Dem. |
| 2,593 | ADAMS | 1,281 | 477 | 804 | | 327 D | 37.2% | 62.8% | 37.2% | 62.8% |
| 11,775 | BARNES | 5,802 | 1,716 | 4,086 | | 2,370 D | 29.6% | 70.4% | 29.6% | 70.4% |
| 6,964 | BENSON | 2,255 | 531 | 1,724 | | 1,193 D | 23.5% | 76.5% | 23.5% | 76.5% |
| 888 | BILLINGS | 558 | 267 | 291 | | 24 D | 47.8% | 52.2% | 47.8% | 52.2% |
| 7,149 | BOTTINEAU | 3,627 | 1,100 | 2,527 | | 1,427 D | 30.3% | 69.7% | 30.3% | 69.7% |
| 3,242 | BOWMAN | 1,708 | 710 | 998 | | 288 D | 41.6% | 58.4% | 41.6% | 58.4% |
| 2,242 | BURKE | 1,173 | 335 | 838 | | 503 D | 28.6% | 71.4% | 28.6% | 71.4% |
| 69,416 | BURLEIGH | 38,415 | 14,885 | 23,530 | | 8,645 D | 38.7% | 61.3% | 38.7% | 61.3% |
| 123,138 | CASS | 66,074 | 19,343 | 46,731 | | 27,388 D | 29.3% | 70.7% | 29.3% | 70.7% |
| 4,831 | CAVALIER | 2,466 | 708 | 1,758 | | 1,050 D | 28.7% | 71.3% | 28.7% | 71.3% |
| 5,757 | DICKEY | 2,807 | 1,203 | 1,604 | | 401 D | 42.9% | 57.1% | 42.9% | 57.1% |
| 2,283 | DIVIDE | 1,257 | 277 | 980 | | 703 D | 22.0% | 78.0% | 22.0% | 78.0% |
| 3,600 | DUNN | 1,766 | 591 | 1,175 | | 584 D | 33.5% | 66.5% | 33.5% | 66.5% |
| 2,757 | EDDY | 1,226 | 300 | 926 | | 626 D | 24.5% | 75.5% | 24.5% | 75.5% |
| 4,331 | EMMONS | 2,113 | 873 | 1,240 | | 367 D | 41.3% | 58.7% | 41.3% | 58.7% |
| 3,759 | FOSTER | 1,766 | 500 | 1,266 | | 766 D | 28.3% | 71.7% | 28.3% | 71.7% |
| 1,924 | GOLDEN VALLEY | 931 | 402 | 529 | | 127 D | 43.2% | 56.8% | 43.2% | 56.8% |
| 66,109 | GRAND FORKS | 29,988 | 8,393 | 21,595 | | 13,202 D | 28.0% | 72.0% | 28.0% | 72.0% |
| 2,841 | GRANT | 1,247 | 510 | 737 | | 227 D | 40.9% | 59.1% | 40.9% | 59.1% |
| 2,754 | GRIGGS | 1,432 | 438 | 994 | | 556 D | 30.6% | 69.4% | 30.6% | 69.4% |
| 2,715 | HETTINGER | 1,490 | 550 | 940 | | 390 D | 36.9% | 63.1% | 36.9% | 63.1% |
| 2,753 | KIDDER | 1,364 | 503 | 861 | | 358 D | 36.9% | 63.1% | 36.9% | 63.1% |
| 4,701 | LA MOURE | 2,323 | 816 | 1,507 | | 691 D | 35.1% | 64.9% | 35.1% | 64.9% |
| 2,308 | LOGAN | 1,132 | 417 | 715 | | 298 D | 36.8% | 63.2% | 36.8% | 63.2% |
| 5,987 | MCHENRY | 2,815 | 775 | 2,040 | | 1,265 D | 27.5% | 72.5% | 27.5% | 72.5% |
| 3,390 | MCINTOSH | 1,732 | 665 | 1,067 | | 402 D | 38.4% | 61.6% | 38.4% | 61.6% |
| 5,737 | MCKENZIE | 2,736 | 963 | 1,773 | | 810 D | 35.2% | 64.8% | 35.2% | 64.8% |
| 9,311 | MCLEAN | 4,738 | 1,567 | 3,171 | | 1,604 D | 33.1% | 66.9% | 33.1% | 66.9% |
| 8,644 | MERCER | 4,612 | 1,854 | 2,758 | | 904 D | 40.2% | 59.8% | 40.2% | 59.8% |
| 25,303 | MORTON | 12,571 | 4,676 | 7,895 | | 3,219 D | 37.2% | 62.8% | 37.2% | 62.8% |
| 6,631 | MOUNTRAIL | 3,032 | 643 | 2,389 | | 1,746 D | 21.2% | 78.8% | 21.2% | 78.8% |
| 3,715 | NELSON | 1,931 | 488 | 1,443 | | 955 D | 25.3% | 74.7% | 25.3% | 74.7% |
| 2,065 | OLIVER | 1,122 | 449 | 673 | | 224 D | 40.0% | 60.0% | 40.0% | 60.0% |
| 8,585 | PEMBINA | 3,865 | 1,240 | 2,625 | | 1,385 D | 32.1% | 67.9% | 32.1% | 67.9% |
| 4,675 | PIERCE | 2,198 | 719 | 1,479 | | 760 D | 32.7% | 67.3% | 32.7% | 67.3% |
| 12,066 | RAMSEY | 4,929 | 1,362 | 3,567 | | 2,205 D | 27.6% | 72.4% | 27.6% | 72.4% |
| 5,890 | RANSOM | 2,606 | 546 | 2,060 | | 1,514 D | 21.0% | 79.0% | 21.0% | 79.0% |
| 2,610 | RENVILLE | 1,468 | 390 | 1,078 | | 688 D | 26.6% | 73.4% | 26.6% | 73.4% |
| 17,998 | RICHLAND | 8,148 | 2,369 | 5,779 | | 3,410 D | 29.1% | 70.9% | 29.1% | 70.9% |
| 13,674 | ROLETTE | 4,053 | 668 | 3,385 | | 2,717 D | 16.5% | 83.5% | 16.5% | 83.5% |
| 4,366 | SARGENT | 2,197 | 514 | 1,683 | | 1,169 D | 23.4% | 76.6% | 23.4% | 76.6% |
| 1,710 | SHERIDAN | 941 | 429 | 512 | | 83 D | 45.6% | 54.4% | 45.6% | 54.4% |
| 4,044 | SIOUX | 1,142 | 146 | 996 | | 850 D | 12.8% | 87.2% | 12.8% | 87.2% |
| 767 | SLOPE | 435 | 184 | 251 | | 67 D | 42.3% | 57.7% | 42.3% | 57.7% |
| 22,636 | STARK | 10,347 | 3,618 | 6,729 | | 3,111 D | 35.0% | 65.0% | 35.0% | 65.0% |
| 2,258 | STEELE | 1,219 | 209 | 1,010 | | 801 D | 17.1% | 82.9% | 17.1% | 82.9% |
| 21,908 | STUTSMAN | 10,106 | 3,170 | 6,936 | | 3,766 D | 31.4% | 68.6% | 31.4% | 68.6% |
| 2,876 | TOWNER | 1,402 | 334 | 1,068 | | 734 D | 23.8% | 76.2% | 23.8% | 76.2% |
| 8,477 | TRAILL | 4,239 | 1,085 | 3,154 | | 2,069 D | 25.6% | 74.4% | 25.6% | 74.4% |
| 12,389 | WALSH | 5,208 | 1,541 | 3,667 | | 2,126 D | 29.6% | 70.4% | 29.6% | 70.4% |
| 58,795 | WARD | 25,255 | 8,073 | 17,182 | | 9,109 D | 32.0% | 68.0% | 32.0% | 68.0% |
| 5,102 | WELLS | 2,571 | 887 | 1,684 | | 797 D | 34.5% | 65.5% | 34.5% | 65.5% |
| 19,761 | WILLIAMS | 8,877 | 3,144 | 5,733 | | 2,589 D | 35.4% | 64.6% | 35.4% | 64.6% |
| 642,200 | TOTAL | 310,696 | 98,553 | 212,143 | | 113,590 D | 31.7% | 68.3% | 31.7% | 68.3% |

# NORTH DAKOTA

## HOUSE OF REPRESENTATIVES

| | | | Republican | | Democratic | | Other | Rep.-Dem. | Percentage | | | |
|---|---|---|---|---|---|---|---|---|---|---|---|---|
| | | | | | | | | | Total Vote | | Major Vote | |
| CD | Year | Total Vote | Vote | Candidate | Vote | Candidate | Vote | Plurality | Rep. | Dem. | Rep. | Dem. |
| AL | 2004 | 310,814 | 125,684 | Sand, Duane | 185,130 | Pomeroy, Earl* | | 59,446 D | 40.4% | 59.6% | 40.4% | 59.6% |
| AL | 2002 | 231,030 | 109,957 | Clayburgh, Rick | 121,073 | Pomeroy, Earl* | | 11,116 D | 47.6% | 52.4% | 47.6% | 52.4% |
| AL | 2000 | 285,658 | 127,251 | Dorso, John | 151,173 | Pomeroy, Earl* | 7,234 | 23,922 D | 44.5% | 52.9% | 45.7% | 54.3% |
| AL | 1998 | 215,469 | 75,013 | Cramer, Kevin | 134,747 | Pomeroy, Earl* | 5,709 | 59,734 D | 34.8% | 62.5% | 35.8% | 64.2% |
| AL | 1996 | 263,010 | 113,684 | Cramer, Kevin | 144,833 | Pomeroy, Earl* | 4,493 | 31,149 D | 43.2% | 55.1% | 44.0% | 56.0% |
| AL | 1994 | 235,389 | 105,988 | Porter, Gary | 123,134 | Pomeroy, Earl* | 6,267 | 17,146 D | 45.0% | 52.3% | 46.3% | 53.7% |
| AL | 1992 | 297,898 | 117,442 | Korsmo, John T. | 169,273 | Pomeroy, Earl | 11,183 | 51,831 D | 39.4% | 56.8% | 41.0% | 59.0% |
| AL | 1990 | 233,979 | 81,443 | Schafer, Edward | 152,530 | Dorgan, Byron L.* | 6 | 71,087 D | 34.8% | 65.2% | 34.8% | 65.2% |
| AL | 1988 | 299,982 | 84,475 | Sydness, Steve | 212,583 | Dorgan, Byron L.* | 2,924 | 128,108 D | 28.2% | 70.9% | 28.4% | 71.6% |
| AL | 1986 | 286,361 | 66,989 | Vinje, Syver | 216,258 | Dorgan, Byron L.* | 3,114 | 149,269 D | 23.4% | 75.5% | 23.7% | 76.3% |
| AL | 1984 | 308,729 | 65,761 | Altenburg, Lois I. | 242,968 | Dorgan, Byron L.* | | 177,207 D | 21.3% | 78.7% | 21.3% | 78.7% |
| AL | 1982 | 260,499 | 72,241 | Jones, Kent | 186,534 | Dorgan, Byron L.* | 1,724 | 114,293 D | 27.7% | 71.6% | 27.9% | 72.1% |
| AL | 1980 | 293,076 | 124,707 | Smykowski, Jim | 166,437 | Dorgan, Byron L. | 1,932 | 41,730 D | 42.6% | 56.8% | 42.8% | 57.2% |
| AL | 1978 | 220,348 | 147,746 | Andrews, Mark* | 68,016 | Hagen, Bruce | 4,586 | 79,730 R | 67.1% | 30.9% | 68.5% | 31.5% |
| AL | 1976 | 289,881 | 181,018 | Andrews, Mark* | 104,263 | Omdahl, Lloyd B. | 4,600 | 76,755 R | 62.4% | 36.0% | 63.5% | 36.5% |
| AL | 1974 | 233,688 | 130,184 | Andrews, Mark* | 103,504 | Dorgan, Byron L. | | 26,680 R | 55.7% | 44.3% | 55.7% | 44.3% |
| AL | 1972 | 268,721 | 195,360 | Andrews, Mark* | 72,850 | Ista, Richard | 511 | 122,510 R | 72.7% | 27.1% | 72.8% | 27.2% |

An asterisk (*) denotes incumbent.

# NORTH DAKOTA

## GENERAL AND PRIMARY ELECTIONS

## 2004 GENERAL ELECTIONS

**President**    Other vote was 3,756 Independent (Ralph Nader); 851 Libertarian (Michael Badnarik); 514 Constitution (Michael Peroutka); 9 write-in (Martin Wishnatsky).

**Governor**    Other vote was 4,193 Independent (Roland Riemers).

**Senator**

**House**
  At Large

## 2004 PRIMARY ELECTIONS

**Primary**    June 8, 2004                **Registration**                No Formal Registration

**Primary Type**    Open—Any person of voting age could participate in the primary of either party.

Note:   An asterisk (*) denotes incumbent.

| | REPUBLICAN PRIMARIES | | | DEMOCRATIC PRIMARIES | | |
|---|---|---|---|---|---|---|
| Governor | John Hoeven* | 42,135 | 100.0% | Joseph A. Satrom | 35,597 | 100.0% |
| Senator | Mike Liffrig | 39,329 | 100.0% | Byron L. Dorgan* | 39,636 | 100.0% |
| House At Large | Duane Sand | 39,815 | 100.0% | Earl Pomeroy* | 38,925 | 100.0% |

# OHIO

## GOVERNOR
Bob Taft (R). Reelected 2002 to a four-year term. Previously elected 1998.

## SENATORS (2 Republicans)
Mike DeWine (R). Reelected 2000 to a six-year term. Previously elected 1994.

George V. Voinovich (R). Reelected 2004 to a six-year term. Previously elected 1998.

## REPRESENTATIVES (12 Republicans, 6 Democrats)
1. Steve Chabot (R)
2. Jean Schmidt (R)
3. Michael R. Turner (R)
4. Michael G. Oxley (R)
5. Paul E. Gillmor (R)
6. Ted Strickland (D)
7. David L. Hobson (R)
8. John A. Boehner (R)
9. Marcy Kaptur (D)
10. Dennis J. Kucinich (D)
11. Stephanie Tubbs Jones (D)
12. Pat Tiberi (R)
13. Sherrod Brown (D)
14. Steven C. LaTourette (R)
15. Deborah Pryce (R)
16. Ralph Regula (R)
17. Tim Ryan (D)
18. Bob Ney (R)

## POSTWAR VOTE FOR PRESIDENT

| Year | Total Vote | Republican Vote | Republican Candidate | Democratic Vote | Democratic Candidate | Other Vote | Plurality | Total Vote Rep. | Total Vote Dem. | Major Vote Rep. | Major Vote Dem. |
|------|-----------|------|------|------|------|------|------|------|------|------|------|
| 2004 | 5,627,908 | 2,859,768 | Bush, George W. | 2,741,167 | Kerry, John | 26,973 | 118,601 R | 50.8% | 48.7% | 51.1% | 48.9% |
| 2000** | 4,701,998 | 2,350,363 | Bush, George W. | 2,183,628 | Gore, Al | 168,007 | 166,735 R | 50.0% | 46.4% | 51.8% | 48.2% |
| 1996** | 4,534,434 | 1,859,883 | Dole, Bob | 2,148,222 | Clinton, Bill | 526,329 | 288,339 D | 41.0% | 47.4% | 46.4% | 53.6% |
| 1992** | 4,939,967 | 1,894,310 | Bush, George | 1,984,942 | Clinton, Bill | 1,060,715 | 90,632 D | 38.3% | 40.2% | 48.8% | 51.2% |
| 1988 | 4,393,699 | 2,416,549 | Bush, George | 1,939,629 | Dukakis, Michael S. | 37,521 | 476,920 R | 55.0% | 44.1% | 55.5% | 44.5% |
| 1984 | 4,547,619 | 2,678,560 | Reagan, Ronald | 1,825,440 | Mondale, Walter F. | 43,619 | 853,120 R | 58.9% | 40.1% | 59.5% | 40.5% |
| 1980** | 4,283,603 | 2,206,545 | Reagan, Ronald | 1,752,414 | Carter, Jimmy | 324,644 | 454,131 R | 51.5% | 40.9% | 55.7% | 44.3% |
| 1976 | 4,111,873 | 2,000,505 | Ford, Gerald R. | 2,011,621 | Carter, Jimmy | 99,747 | 11,116 D | 48.7% | 48.9% | 49.9% | 50.1% |
| 1972 | 4,094,787 | 2,441,827 | Nixon, Richard M. | 1,558,889 | McGovern, George S. | 94,071 | 882,938 R | 59.6% | 38.1% | 61.0% | 39.0% |
| 1968** | 3,959,698 | 1,791,014 | Nixon, Richard M. | 1,700,586 | Humphrey, Hubert H. | 468,098 | 90,428 R | 45.2% | 42.9% | 51.3% | 48.7% |
| 1964 | 3,969,196 | 1,470,865 | Goldwater, Barry M. | 2,498,331 | Johnson, Lyndon B. | | 1,027,466 D | 37.1% | 62.9% | 37.1% | 62.9% |
| 1960 | 4,161,859 | 2,217,611 | Nixon, Richard M. | 1,944,248 | Kennedy, John F. | | 273,363 R | 53.3% | 46.7% | 53.3% | 46.7% |
| 1956 | 3,702,265 | 2,262,610 | Eisenhower, Dwight D. | 1,439,655 | Stevenson, Adlai E. | | 822,955 R | 61.1% | 38.9% | 61.1% | 38.9% |
| 1952 | 3,700,758 | 2,100,391 | Eisenhower, Dwight D. | 1,600,367 | Stevenson, Adlai E. | | 500,024 R | 56.8% | 43.2% | 56.8% | 43.2% |
| 1948 | 2,936,071 | 1,445,684 | Dewey, Thomas E. | 1,452,791 | Truman, Harry S. | 37,596 | 7,107 D | 49.2% | 49.5% | 49.9% | 50.1% |

In past elections, the other vote included: 2000 - 117,799 Green (Ralph Nader); 1996 - 483,207 Reform (Ross Perot); 1992 - 1,036,426 Independent (Perot); 1980 - 254,472 Independent (John Anderson); 1968 - 467,495 American Independent (George Wallace).

# OHIO

## POSTWAR VOTE FOR GOVERNOR

| Year | Total Vote | Republican Vote | Republican Candidate | Democratic Vote | Democratic Candidate | Other Vote | Rep.-Dem. Plurality | Percentage Total Vote Rep. | Total Vote Dem. | Major Vote Rep. | Major Vote Dem. |
|---|---|---|---|---|---|---|---|---|---|---|---|
| 2002 | 3,228,992 | 1,865,007 | Taft, Bob | 1,236,924 | Hagan, Timothy | 127,061 | 628,083 R | 57.8% | 38.3% | 60.1% | 39.9% |
| 1998 | 3,354,213 | 1,678,721 | Taft, Bob | 1,498,956 | Fisher, Lee | 176,536 | 179,765 R | 50.0% | 44.7% | 52.8% | 47.2% |
| 1994 | 3,346,238 | 2,401,572 | Voinovich, George V. | 835,849 | Burch, Robert L. | 108,817 | 1,565,723 R | 71.8% | 25.0% | 74.2% | 25.8% |
| 1990 | 3,477,650 | 1,938,103 | Voinovich, George V. | 1,539,416 | Celebrezze, Anthony J. | 131 | 398,687 R | 55.7% | 44.3% | 55.7% | 44.3% |
| 1986 | 3,066,611 | 1,207,264 | Rhodes, James A. | 1,858,372 | Celeste, Richard F. | 975 | 651,108 D | 39.4% | 60.6% | 39.4% | 60.6% |
| 1982 | 3,356,721 | 1,303,962 | Brown, Clarence, Jr. | 1,981,882 | Celeste, Richard F. | 70,877 | 677,920 D | 38.8% | 59.0% | 39.7% | 60.3% |
| 1978 | 2,843,351 | 1,402,167 | Rhodes, James A. | 1,354,631 | Celeste, Richard F. | 86,553 | 47,536 R | 49.3% | 47.6% | 50.9% | 49.1% |
| 1974 | 3,072,010 | 1,493,679 | Rhodes, James A. | 1,482,191 | Gilligan, John J. | 96,140 | 11,488 R | 48.6% | 48.2% | 50.2% | 49.8% |
| 1970 | 3,184,133 | 1,382,659 | Cloud, Roger | 1,725,560 | Gilligan, John J. | 75,914 | 342,901 D | 43.4% | 54.2% | 44.5% | 55.5% |
| 1966 | 2,887,331 | 1,795,277 | Rhodes, James A. | 1,092,054 | Reams, Frazier, Jr. | | 703,223 R | 62.2% | 37.8% | 62.2% | 37.8% |
| 1962 | 3,116,711 | 1,836,190 | Rhodes, James A. | 1,280,521 | DiSalle, Michael V. | | 555,669 R | 58.9% | 41.1% | 58.9% | 41.1% |
| 1958** | 3,284,134 | 1,414,874 | O'Neill, C. William | 1,869,260 | DiSalle, Michael V. | | 454,386 D | 43.1% | 56.9% | 43.1% | 56.9% |
| 1956 | 3,542,091 | 1,984,988 | O'Neill, C. William | 1,557,103 | DiSalle, Michael V. | | 427,885 R | 56.0% | 44.0% | 56.0% | 44.0% |
| 1954 | 2,597,790 | 1,192,528 | Rhodes, James A. | 1,405,262 | Lausche, Frank J. | | 212,734 D | 45.9% | 54.1% | 45.9% | 54.1% |
| 1952 | 3,605,168 | 1,590,058 | Taft, Charles P. | 2,015,110 | Lausche, Frank J. | | 425,052 D | 44.1% | 55.9% | 44.1% | 55.9% |
| 1950 | 2,892,819 | 1,370,570 | Ebright, Don H. | 1,522,249 | Lausche, Frank J. | | 151,679 D | 47.4% | 52.6% | 47.4% | 52.6% |
| 1948 | 3,018,289 | 1,398,514 | Herbert, Thomas J. | 1,619,775 | Lausche, Frank J. | | 221,261 D | 46.3% | 53.7% | 46.3% | 53.7% |
| 1946 | 2,303,750 | 1,166,550 | Herbert, Thomas J. | 1,125,997 | Lausche, Frank J. | 11,203 | 40,553 R | 50.6% | 48.9% | 50.9% | 49.1% |

The term of office of Ohio's governor was increased from two to four years effective with the 1958 election.

## POSTWAR VOTE FOR SENATOR

| Year | Total Vote | Republican Vote | Republican Candidate | Democratic Vote | Democratic Candidate | Other Vote | Rep.-Dem. Plurality | Percentage Total Vote Rep. | Total Vote Dem. | Major Vote Rep. | Major Vote Dem. |
|---|---|---|---|---|---|---|---|---|---|---|---|
| 2004 | 5,426,196 | 3,464,651 | Voinovich, George V. | 1,961,249 | Fingerhut, Eric D. | 296 | 1,503,402 R | 63.9% | 36.1% | 63.9% | 36.1% |
| 2000 | 4,448,801 | 2,665,512 | DeWine, Mike | 1,595,066 | Celeste, Ted | 188,223 | 1,070,446 R | 59.9% | 35.9% | 62.6% | 37.4% |
| 1998 | 3,404,351 | 1,922,087 | Voinovich, George V. | 1,482,054 | Boyle, Mary O. | 210 | 440,033 R | 56.5% | 43.5% | 56.5% | 43.5% |
| 1994 | 3,436,884 | 1,836,556 | DeWine, Mike | 1,348,213 | Hyatt, Joel | 252,115 | 488,343 R | 53.4% | 39.2% | 57.7% | 42.3% |
| 1992 | 4,793,953 | 2,028,300 | DeWine, Mike | 2,444,419 | Glenn, John H. | 321,234 | 416,119 D | 42.3% | 51.0% | 45.3% | 54.7% |
| 1988 | 4,352,905 | 1,872,716 | Voinovich, George V. | 2,480,038 | Metzenbaum, Howard | 151 | 607,322 D | 43.0% | 57.0% | 43.0% | 57.0% |
| 1986 | 3,121,189 | 1,171,893 | Kindness, Thomas N. | 1,949,208 | Glenn, John H. | 88 | 777,315 D | 37.5% | 62.5% | 37.5% | 62.5% |
| 1982 | 3,395,463 | 1,396,790 | Pfeifer, Paul E. | 1,923,767 | Metzenbaum, Howard | 74,906 | 526,977 D | 41.1% | 56.7% | 42.1% | 57.9% |
| 1980 | 4,027,303 | 1,137,695 | Betts, James E. | 2,770,786 | Glenn, John H. | 118,822 | 1,633,091 D | 28.2% | 68.8% | 29.1% | 70.9% |
| 1976 | 3,920,613 | 1,823,774 | Taft, Robert A., Jr. | 1,941,113 | Metzenbaum, Howard | 155,726 | 117,339 D | 46.5% | 49.5% | 48.4% | 51.6% |
| 1974 | 2,987,951 | 918,133 | Perk, Ralph J. | 1,930,670 | Glenn, John H. | 139,148 | 1,012,537 D | 30.7% | 64.6% | 32.2% | 67.8% |
| 1970 | 3,151,274 | 1,565,682 | Taft, Robert A., Jr. | 1,495,262 | Metzenbaum, Howard | 90,330 | 70,420 R | 49.7% | 47.4% | 51.2% | 48.8% |
| 1968 | 3,743,121 | 1,928,964 | Saxbe, William B. | 1,814,152 | Gilligan, John J. | 5 | 114,812 R | 51.5% | 48.5% | 51.5% | 48.5% |
| 1964 | 3,830,389 | 1,906,781 | Taft, Robert A., Jr. | 1,923,608 | Young, Stephen M. | | 16,827 D | 49.8% | 50.2% | 49.8% | 50.2% |
| 1962 | 2,994,986 | 1,151,173 | Briley, John M. | 1,843,813 | Lausche, Frank J. | | 692,640 D | 38.4% | 61.6% | 38.4% | 61.6% |
| 1958 | 3,149,410 | 1,497,199 | Bricker, John W. | 1,652,211 | Young, Stephen M. | | 155,012 D | 47.5% | 52.5% | 47.5% | 52.5% |
| 1956 | 3,525,499 | 1,660,910 | Bender, George H. | 1,864,589 | Lausche, Frank J. | | 203,679 D | 47.1% | 52.9% | 47.1% | 52.9% |
| 1954S | 2,512,778 | 1,257,874 | Bender, George H. | 1,254,904 | Burke, Thomas A. | | 2,970 R | 50.1% | 49.9% | 50.1% | 49.9% |
| 1952 | 3,442,291 | 1,878,961 | Bricker, John W. | 1,563,330 | DiSalle, Michael V. | | 315,631 R | 54.6% | 45.4% | 54.6% | 45.4% |
| 1950 | 2,860,102 | 1,645,643 | Taft, Robert A. | 1,214,459 | Ferguson, Joseph T. | | 431,184 R | 57.5% | 42.5% | 57.5% | 42.5% |
| 1946 | 2,237,269 | 1,275,774 | Bricker, John W. | 947,610 | Huffman, James W. | 13,885 | 328,164 R | 57.0% | 42.4% | 57.4% | 42.6% |

The 1954 election was for a short term to fill a vacancy.

348

# OHIO

Congressional districts first established for elections held in 2002
18 members

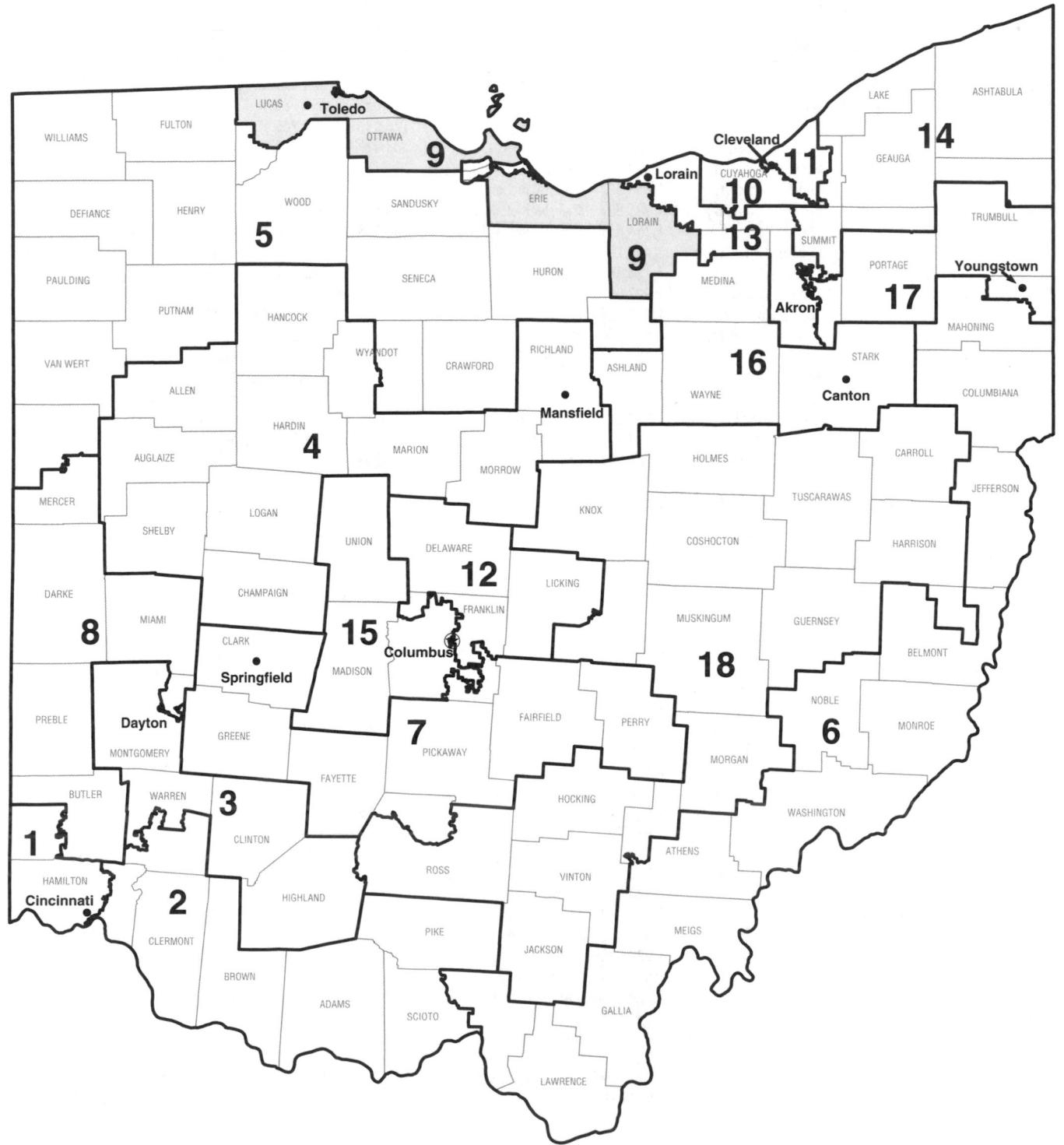

# OHIO

## Cleveland Area

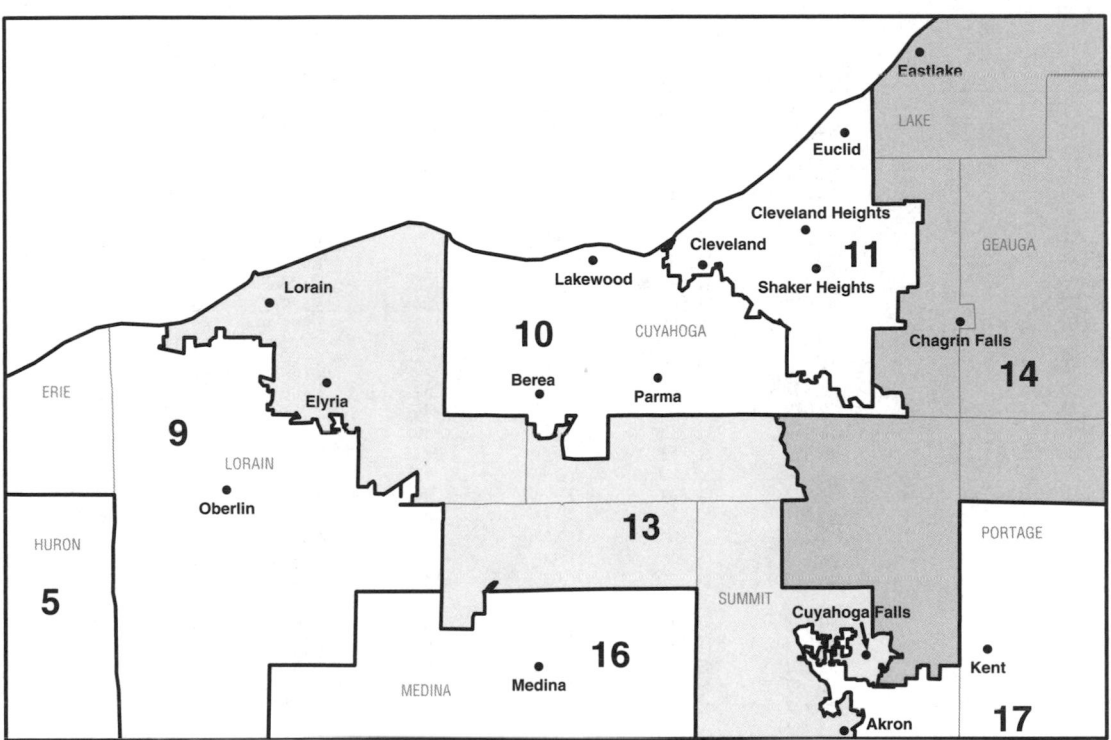

## Columbus Area

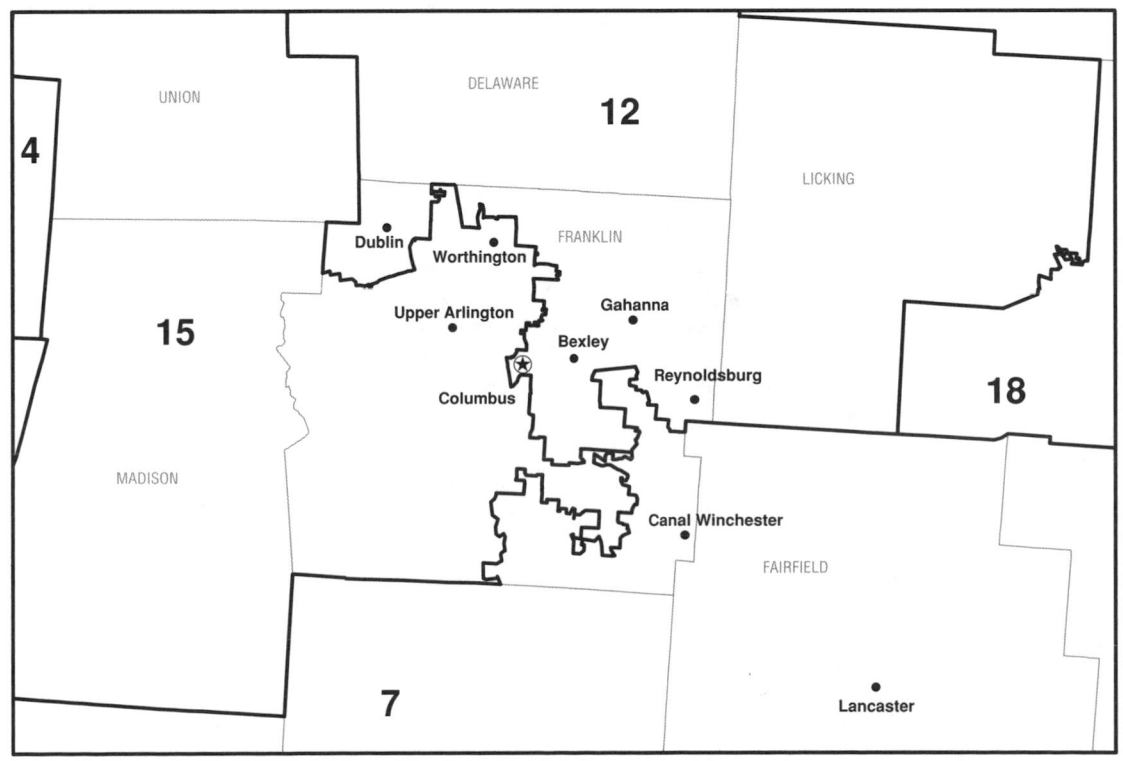

# OHIO

## PRESIDENT 2004

| 2000 Census Population | County | Total Vote | Republican | Democratic | Other | Rep.-Dem. Plurality | Percentage | | | |
|---|---|---|---|---|---|---|---|---|---|---|
| | | | | | | | Total Vote | | Major Vote | |
| | | | | | | | Rep. | Dem. | Rep. | Dem. |
| 27,330 | ADAMS | 12,000 | 7,653 | 4,281 | 66 | 3,372 R | 63.8% | 35.7% | 64.1% | 35.9% |
| 108,473 | ALLEN | 49,256 | 32,580 | 16,470 | 206 | 16,110 R | 66.1% | 33.4% | 66.4% | 33.6% |
| 52,523 | ASHLAND | 24,979 | 16,209 | 8,576 | 194 | 7,633 R | 64.9% | 34.3% | 65.4% | 34.6% |
| 102,728 | ASHTABULA | 45,407 | 21,038 | 24,060 | 309 | 3,022 D | 46.3% | 53.0% | 46.6% | 53.4% |
| 62,223 | ATHENS | 30,045 | 10,847 | 18,998 | 200 | 8,151 D | 36.1% | 63.2% | 36.3% | 63.7% |
| 46,611 | AUGLAIZE | 23,034 | 17,016 | 5,903 | 115 | 11,113 R | 73.9% | 25.6% | 74.2% | 25.8% |
| 70,226 | BELMONT | 33,322 | 15,589 | 17,576 | 157 | 1,987 D | 46.8% | 52.7% | 47.0% | 53.0% |
| 42,285 | BROWN | 19,892 | 12,647 | 7,140 | 105 | 5,507 R | 63.6% | 35.9% | 63.9% | 36.1% |
| 332,807 | BUTLER | 166,819 | 109,872 | 56,243 | 704 | 53,629 R | 65.9% | 33.7% | 66.1% | 33.9% |
| 28,836 | CARROLL | 14,112 | 7,695 | 6,300 | 117 | 1,395 R | 54.5% | 44.6% | 55.0% | 45.0% |
| 38,890 | CHAMPAIGN | 18,776 | 11,718 | 6,968 | 90 | 4,750 R | 62.4% | 37.1% | 62.7% | 37.3% |
| 144,742 | CLARK | 68,807 | 34,941 | 33,535 | 331 | 1,406 R | 50.8% | 48.7% | 51.0% | 49.0% |
| 177,977 | CLERMONT | 89,079 | 62,949 | 25,887 | 243 | 37,062 R | 70.7% | 29.1% | 70.9% | 29.1% |
| 40,543 | CLINTON | 18,414 | 12,938 | 5,417 | 59 | 7,521 R | 70.3% | 29.4% | 70.5% | 29.5% |
| 112,075 | COLUMBIANA | 49,465 | 25,753 | 23,429 | 283 | 2,324 R | 52.1% | 47.4% | 52.4% | 47.6% |
| 36,655 | COSHOCTON | 17,303 | 9,839 | 7,378 | 86 | 2,461 R | 56.9% | 42.6% | 57.1% | 42.9% |
| 46,966 | CRAWFORD | 21,801 | 13,885 | 7,773 | 143 | 6,112 R | 63.7% | 35.7% | 64.1% | 35.9% |
| 1,393,978 | CUYAHOGA | 673,777 | 221,600 | 448,503 | 3,674 | 226,903 D | 32.9% | 66.6% | 33.1% | 66.9% |
| 53,309 | DARKE | 26,313 | 18,306 | 7,846 | 161 | 10,460 R | 69.6% | 29.8% | 70.0% | 30.0% |
| 39,500 | DEFIANCE | 18,516 | 11,397 | 6,975 | 144 | 4,422 R | 61.6% | 37.7% | 62.0% | 38.0% |
| 109,989 | DELAWARE | 80,456 | 53,143 | 27,048 | 265 | 26,095 R | 66.1% | 33.6% | 66.3% | 33.7% |
| 79,551 | ERIE | 40,085 | 18,597 | 21,421 | 67 | 2,824 D | 46.4% | 53.4% | 46.5% | 53.5% |
| 122,759 | FAIRFIELD | 67,882 | 42,715 | 24,783 | 384 | 17,932 R | 62.9% | 36.5% | 63.3% | 36.7% |
| 28,433 | FAYETTE | 11,757 | 7,376 | 4,334 | 47 | 3,042 R | 62.7% | 36.9% | 63.0% | 37.0% |
| 1,068,978 | FRANKLIN | 525,827 | 237,253 | 285,801 | 2,773 | 48,548 D | 45.1% | 54.4% | 45.4% | 54.6% |
| 42,084 | FULTON | 21,954 | 13,640 | 8,224 | 90 | 5,416 R | 62.1% | 37.5% | 62.4% | 37.6% |
| 31,069 | GALLIA | 13,993 | 8,576 | 5,366 | 51 | 3,210 R | 61.3% | 38.3% | 61.5% | 38.5% |
| 90,895 | GEAUGA | 50,442 | 30,370 | 19,850 | 222 | 10,520 R | 60.2% | 39.4% | 60.5% | 39.5% |
| 147,886 | GREENE | 79,282 | 48,388 | 30,531 | 363 | 17,857 R | 61.0% | 38.5% | 61.3% | 38.7% |
| 40,792 | GUERNSEY | 17,840 | 9,962 | 7,768 | 110 | 2,194 R | 55.8% | 43.5% | 56.2% | 43.8% |
| 845,303 | HAMILTON | 424,025 | 222,616 | 199,679 | 1,730 | 22,937 R | 52.5% | 47.1% | 52.7% | 47.3% |
| 71,295 | HANCOCK | 35,619 | 25,105 | 10,352 | 162 | 14,753 R | 70.5% | 29.1% | 70.8% | 29.2% |
| 31,945 | HARDIN | 13,392 | 8,441 | 4,891 | 60 | 3,550 R | 63.0% | 36.5% | 63.3% | 36.7% |
| 15,856 | HARRISON | 8,109 | 4,274 | 3,780 | 55 | 494 R | 52.7% | 46.6% | 53.1% | 46.9% |
| 29,210 | HENRY | 15,105 | 9,902 | 5,111 | 92 | 4,791 R | 65.6% | 33.8% | 66.0% | 34.0% |
| 40,875 | HIGHLAND | 18,481 | 12,211 | 6,194 | 76 | 6,017 R | 66.1% | 33.5% | 66.3% | 33.7% |
| 28,241 | HOCKING | 13,199 | 6,936 | 6,175 | 88 | 761 R | 52.5% | 46.8% | 52.9% | 47.1% |
| 38,943 | HOLMES | 11,220 | 8,468 | 2,697 | 55 | 5,771 R | 75.5% | 24.0% | 75.8% | 24.2% |
| 59,487 | HURON | 25,558 | 14,817 | 10,568 | 173 | 4,249 R | 58.0% | 41.3% | 58.4% | 41.6% |
| 32,641 | JACKSON | 14,334 | 8,585 | 5,700 | 49 | 2,885 R | 59.9% | 39.8% | 60.1% | 39.9% |
| 73,894 | JEFFERSON | 36,372 | 17,185 | 19,024 | 163 | 1,839 D | 47.2% | 52.3% | 47.5% | 52.5% |
| 54,500 | KNOX | 27,045 | 17,068 | 9,820 | 157 | 7,248 R | 63.1% | 36.3% | 63.5% | 36.5% |
| 227,511 | LAKE | 121,823 | 62,193 | 59,049 | 581 | 3,144 R | 51.1% | 48.5% | 51.3% | 48.7% |
| 62,319 | LAWRENCE | 27,710 | 15,455 | 12,120 | 135 | 3,335 R | 55.8% | 43.7% | 56.0% | 44.0% |
| 145,491 | LICKING | 79,420 | 49,016 | 30,053 | 351 | 18,963 R | 61.7% | 37.8% | 62.0% | 38.0% |
| 46,005 | LOGAN | 21,398 | 14,471 | 6,825 | 102 | 7,646 R | 67.6% | 31.9% | 68.0% | 32.0% |
| 284,664 | LORAIN | 140,742 | 61,203 | 78,970 | 569 | 17,767 D | 43.5% | 56.1% | 43.7% | 56.3% |
| 455,054 | LUCAS | 220,430 | 87,160 | 132,715 | 555 | 45,555 D | 39.5% | 60.2% | 39.6% | 60.4% |
| 40,213 | MADISON | 17,398 | 11,117 | 6,203 | 78 | 4,914 R | 63.9% | 35.7% | 64.2% | 35.8% |
| 257,555 | MAHONING | 132,904 | 48,761 | 83,194 | 949 | 34,433 D | 36.7% | 62.6% | 37.0% | 63.0% |
| 66,217 | MARION | 29,258 | 17,171 | 11,930 | 157 | 5,241 R | 58.7% | 40.8% | 59.0% | 41.0% |
| 151,095 | MEDINA | 84,878 | 48,196 | 36,272 | 410 | 11,924 R | 56.8% | 42.7% | 57.1% | 42.9% |
| 23,072 | MEIGS | 10,771 | 6,272 | 4,438 | 61 | 1,834 R | 58.2% | 41.2% | 58.6% | 41.4% |
| 40,924 | MERCER | 20,890 | 15,650 | 5,118 | 122 | 10,532 R | 74.9% | 24.5% | 75.4% | 24.6% |
| 98,868 | MIAMI | 51,760 | 33,992 | 17,606 | 162 | 16,386 R | 65.7% | 34.0% | 65.9% | 34.1% |
| 15,180 | MONROE | 7,729 | 3,424 | 4,243 | 62 | 819 D | 44.3% | 54.9% | 44.7% | 55.3% |
| 559,062 | MONTGOMERY | 282,584 | 138,371 | 142,997 | 1,216 | 4,626 D | 49.0% | 50.6% | 49.2% | 50.8% |
| 14,897 | MORGAN | 6,703 | 3,758 | 2,875 | 70 | 883 R | 56.1% | 42.9% | 56.7% | 43.3% |
| 31,628 | MORROW | 16,328 | 10,474 | 5,775 | 79 | 4,699 R | 64.1% | 35.4% | 64.5% | 35.5% |
| 84,585 | MUSKINGUM | 38,866 | 22,254 | 16,421 | 191 | 5,833 R | 57.3% | 42.3% | 57.5% | 42.5% |

# OHIO

## PRESIDENT 2004

| 2000 Census Population | County | Total Vote | Republican | Democratic | Other | Rep.-Dem. Plurality | Percentage | | | |
|---|---|---|---|---|---|---|---|---|---|---|
| | | | | | | | Total Vote | | Major Vote | |
| | | | | | | | Rep. | Dem. | Rep. | Dem. |
| 14,058 | NOBLE | 6,540 | 3,841 | 2,654 | 45 | 1,187 R | 58.7% | 40.6% | 59.1% | 40.9% |
| 40,985 | OTTAWA | 23,259 | 12,073 | 11,118 | 68 | 955 R | 51.9% | 47.8% | 52.1% | 47.9% |
| 20,293 | PAULDING | 9,879 | 6,206 | 3,610 | 63 | 2,596 R | 62.8% | 36.5% | 63.2% | 36.8% |
| 34,078 | PERRY | 15,189 | 7,856 | 7,257 | 76 | 599 R | 51.7% | 47.8% | 52.0% | 48.0% |
| 52,727 | PICKAWAY | 22,852 | 14,161 | 8,579 | 112 | 5,582 R | 62.0% | 37.5% | 62.3% | 37.7% |
| 27,695 | PIKE | 12,576 | 6,520 | 5,989 | 67 | 531 R | 51.8% | 47.6% | 52.1% | 47.9% |
| 152,061 | PORTAGE | 76,647 | 35,583 | 40,675 | 389 | 5,092 D | 46.4% | 53.1% | 46.7% | 53.3% |
| 42,337 | PREBLE | 21,127 | 13,734 | 7,274 | 119 | 6,460 R | 65.0% | 34.4% | 65.4% | 34.6% |
| 34,726 | PUTNAM | 18,849 | 14,370 | 4,392 | 87 | 9,978 R | 76.2% | 23.3% | 76.6% | 23.4% |
| 128,852 | RICHLAND | 61,840 | 36,872 | 24,638 | 330 | 12,234 R | 59.6% | 39.8% | 59.9% | 40.1% |
| 73,345 | ROSS | 31,671 | 17,231 | 13,978 | 462 | 3,253 R | 54.4% | 44.1% | 55.2% | 44.8% |
| 61,792 | SANDUSKY | 29,014 | 16,224 | 12,686 | 104 | 3,538 R | 55.9% | 43.7% | 56.1% | 43.9% |
| 79,195 | SCIOTO | 35,203 | 18,259 | 16,827 | 117 | 1,432 R | 51.9% | 47.8% | 52.0% | 48.0% |
| 58,683 | SENECA | 26,991 | 15,886 | 10,957 | 148 | 4,929 R | 58.9% | 40.6% | 59.2% | 40.8% |
| 47,910 | SHELBY | 22,855 | 16,204 | 6,535 | 116 | 9,669 R | 70.9% | 28.6% | 71.3% | 28.7% |
| 378,098 | STARK | 188,459 | 92,215 | 95,337 | 907 | 3,122 D | 48.9% | 50.6% | 49.2% | 50.8% |
| 542,899 | SUMMIT | 276,320 | 118,558 | 156,587 | 1,175 | 38,029 D | 42.9% | 56.7% | 43.1% | 56.9% |
| 225,116 | TRUMBULL | 108,145 | 40,977 | 66,673 | 495 | 25,696 D | 37.9% | 61.7% | 38.1% | 61.9% |
| 90,914 | TUSCARAWAS | 42,906 | 23,829 | 18,853 | 224 | 4,976 R | 55.5% | 43.9% | 55.8% | 44.2% |
| 40,909 | UNION | 22,631 | 15,870 | 6,665 | 96 | 9,205 R | 70.1% | 29.5% | 70.4% | 29.6% |
| 29,659 | VAN WERT | 14,827 | 10,678 | 4,095 | 54 | 6,583 R | 72.0% | 27.6% | 72.3% | 27.7% |
| 12,806 | VINTON | 5,928 | 3,249 | 2,651 | 28 | 598 R | 54.8% | 44.7% | 55.1% | 44.9% |
| 158,383 | WARREN | 94,422 | 68,037 | 26,044 | 341 | 41,993 R | 72.1% | 27.6% | 72.3% | 27.7% |
| 63,251 | WASHINGTON | 30,216 | 17,532 | 12,538 | 146 | 4,994 R | 58.0% | 41.5% | 58.3% | 41.7% |
| 111,564 | WAYNE | 51,848 | 31,879 | 19,786 | 183 | 12,093 R | 61.5% | 38.2% | 61.7% | 38.3% |
| 39,188 | WILLIAMS | 18,639 | 12,040 | 6,481 | 118 | 5,559 R | 64.6% | 34.8% | 65.0% | 35.0% |
| 121,065 | WOOD | 63,346 | 33,592 | 29,401 | 353 | 4,191 R | 53.0% | 46.4% | 53.3% | 46.7% |
| 22,908 | WYANDOT | 11,043 | 7,254 | 3,708 | 81 | 3,546 R | 65.7% | 33.6% | 66.2% | 33.8% |
| 11,353,140 | TOTAL | 5,627,908 | 2,859,768 | 2,741,167 | 26,973 | 118,601 R | 50.8% | 48.7% | 51.1% | 48.9% |

# OHIO

## SENATOR 2004

| 2000 Census Population | County | Total Vote | Republican | Democratic | Other | Rep.-Dem. Plurality | Percentage | | | |
|---|---|---|---|---|---|---|---|---|---|---|
| | | | | | | | Total Vote | | Major Vote | |
| | | | | | | | Rep. | Dem. | Rep. | Dem. |
| 27,330 | ADAMS | 11,514 | 8,303 | 3,211 | | 5,092 R | 72.1% | 27.9% | 72.1% | 27.9% |
| 108,473 | ALLEN | 46,569 | 33,463 | 13,106 | | 20,357 R | 71.9% | 28.1% | 71.9% | 28.1% |
| 52,523 | ASHLAND | 24,529 | 18,207 | 6,322 | | 11,885 R | 74.2% | 25.8% | 74.2% | 25.8% |
| 102,728 | ASHTABULA | 44,376 | 25,998 | 18,378 | | 7,620 R | 58.6% | 41.4% | 58.6% | 41.4% |
| 62,223 | ATHENS | 28,771 | 14,992 | 13,778 | 1 | 1,214 R | 52.1% | 47.9% | 52.1% | 47.9% |
| 46,611 | AUGLAIZE | 22,556 | 17,771 | 4,785 | | 12,986 R | 78.8% | 21.2% | 78.8% | 21.2% |
| 70,226 | BELMONT | 32,337 | 18,868 | 13,469 | | 5,399 R | 58.3% | 41.7% | 58.3% | 41.7% |
| 42,285 | BROWN | 19,205 | 13,730 | 5,474 | 1 | 8,256 R | 71.5% | 28.5% | 71.5% | 28.5% |
| 332,807 | BUTLER | 160,660 | 117,117 | 43,537 | 6 | 73,580 R | 72.9% | 27.1% | 72.9% | 27.1% |
| 28,836 | CARROLL | 13,757 | 9,309 | 4,448 | | 4,861 R | 67.7% | 32.3% | 67.7% | 32.3% |
| 38,890 | CHAMPAIGN | 18,217 | 13,480 | 4,737 | | 8,743 R | 74.0% | 26.0% | 74.0% | 26.0% |
| 144,742 | CLARK | 67,414 | 43,383 | 24,031 | | 19,352 R | 64.4% | 35.6% | 64.4% | 35.6% |
| 177,977 | CLERMONT | 86,649 | 66,499 | 20,143 | 7 | 46,356 R | 76.7% | 23.2% | 76.8% | 23.2% |
| 40,543 | CLINTON | 17,788 | 14,056 | 3,732 | | 10,324 R | 79.0% | 21.0% | 79.0% | 21.0% |
| 112,075 | COLUMBIANA | 48,175 | 30,306 | 17,869 | | 12,437 R | 62.9% | 37.1% | 62.9% | 37.1% |
| 36,655 | COSHOCTON | 16,837 | 11,696 | 5,141 | | 6,555 R | 69.5% | 30.5% | 69.5% | 30.5% |
| 46,966 | CRAWFORD | 21,403 | 15,423 | 5,980 | | 9,443 R | 72.1% | 27.9% | 72.1% | 27.9% |
| 1,393,978 | CUYAHOGA | 637,303 | 334,204 | 303,085 | 14 | 31,119 R | 52.4% | 47.6% | 52.4% | 47.6% |
| 53,309 | DARKE | 25,807 | 19,906 | 5,901 | | 14,005 R | 77.1% | 22.9% | 77.1% | 22.9% |
| 39,500 | DEFIANCE | 18,057 | 12,778 | 5,279 | | 7,499 R | 70.8% | 29.2% | 70.8% | 29.2% |

# OHIO

## SENATOR 2004

| 2000 Census Population | County | Total Vote | Republican | Democratic | Other | Rep.-Dem. Plurality | Percentage | | | |
|---|---|---|---|---|---|---|---|---|---|---|
| | | | | | | | Total Vote | | Major Vote | |
| | | | | | | | Rep. | Dem. | Rep. | Dem. |
| 109,989 | DELAWARE | 77,823 | 59,921 | 17,902 | | 42,019 R | 77.0% | 23.0% | 77.0% | 23.0% |
| 79,551 | ERIE | 39,356 | 23,833 | 15,521 | 2 | 8,312 R | 60.6% | 39.4% | 60.6% | 39.4% |
| 122,759 | FAIRFIELD | 66,009 | 48,980 | 17,027 | 2 | 31,953 R | 74.2% | 25.8% | 74.2% | 25.8% |
| 28,433 | FAYETTE | 11,392 | 8,724 | 2,668 | | 6,056 R | 76.6% | 23.4% | 76.6% | 23.4% |
| 1,068,978 | FRANKLIN | 495,389 | 295,601 | 199,677 | 111 | 95,924 R | 59.7% | 40.3% | 59.7% | 40.3% |
| 42,084 | FULTON | 21,381 | 16,342 | 5,039 | | 11,303 R | 76.4% | 23.6% | 76.4% | 23.6% |
| 31,069 | GALLIA | 13,078 | 9,439 | 3,639 | | 5,800 R | 72.2% | 27.8% | 72.2% | 27.8% |
| 90,895 | GEAUGA | 49,540 | 36,165 | 13,371 | 4 | 22,794 R | 73.0% | 27.0% | 73.0% | 27.0% |
| 147,886 | GREENE | 77,224 | 55,043 | 22,180 | 1 | 32,863 R | 71.3% | 28.7% | 71.3% | 28.7% |
| 40,792 | GUERNSEY | 17,408 | 11,330 | 6,076 | 2 | 5,254 R | 65.1% | 34.9% | 65.1% | 34.9% |
| 845,303 | HAMILTON | 407,431 | 255,406 | 151,912 | 113 | 103,494 R | 62.7% | 37.3% | 62.7% | 37.3% |
| 71,295 | HANCOCK | 34,725 | 27,626 | 7,096 | 3 | 20,530 R | 79.6% | 20.4% | 79.6% | 20.4% |
| 31,945 | HARDIN | 13,067 | 9,336 | 3,731 | | 5,605 R | 71.4% | 28.6% | 71.4% | 28.6% |
| 15,856 | HARRISON | 7,896 | 5,082 | 2,814 | | 2,268 R | 64.4% | 35.6% | 64.4% | 35.6% |
| 29,210 | HENRY | 14,927 | 11,628 | 3,299 | | 8,329 R | 77.9% | 22.1% | 77.9% | 22.1% |
| 40,875 | HIGHLAND | 17,927 | 13,395 | 4,532 | | 8,863 R | 74.7% | 25.3% | 74.7% | 25.3% |
| 28,241 | HOCKING | 12,823 | 8,481 | 4,342 | | 4,139 R | 66.1% | 33.9% | 66.1% | 33.9% |
| 38,943 | HOLMES | 10,927 | 8,986 | 1,941 | | 7,045 R | 82.2% | 17.8% | 82.2% | 17.8% |
| 59,487 | HURON | 25,015 | 18,019 | 6,996 | | 11,023 R | 72.0% | 28.0% | 72.0% | 28.0% |
| 32,641 | JACKSON | 13,715 | 9,871 | 3,844 | | 6,027 R | 72.0% | 28.0% | 72.0% | 28.0% |
| 73,894 | JEFFERSON | 35,136 | 20,970 | 14,166 | | 6,804 R | 59.7% | 40.3% | 59.7% | 40.3% |
| 54,500 | KNOX | 26,088 | 18,507 | 7,581 | | 10,926 R | 70.9% | 29.1% | 70.9% | 29.1% |
| 227,511 | LAKE | 116,243 | 76,682 | 39,561 | | 37,121 R | 66.0% | 34.0% | 66.0% | 34.0% |
| 62,319 | LAWRENCE | 26,564 | 17,222 | 9,342 | | 7,880 R | 64.8% | 35.2% | 64.8% | 35.2% |
| 145,491 | LICKING | 76,966 | 55,952 | 21,014 | | 34,938 R | 72.7% | 27.3% | 72.7% | 27.3% |
| 46,005 | LOGAN | 20,804 | 16,191 | 4,613 | | 11,578 R | 77.8% | 22.2% | 77.8% | 22.2% |
| 284,664 | LORAIN | 136,921 | 79,485 | 57,436 | | 22,049 R | 58.1% | 41.9% | 58.1% | 41.9% |
| 455,054 | LUCAS | 211,795 | 121,535 | 90,250 | 10 | 31,285 R | 57.4% | 42.6% | 57.4% | 42.6% |
| 40,213 | MADISON | 16,811 | 12,828 | 3,983 | | 8,845 R | 76.3% | 23.7% | 76.3% | 23.7% |
| 257,555 | MAHONING | 127,958 | 66,554 | 61,403 | 1 | 5,151 R | 52.0% | 48.0% | 52.0% | 48.0% |
| 66,217 | MARION | 28,658 | 19,817 | 8,841 | | 10,976 R | 69.1% | 30.9% | 69.1% | 30.9% |
| 151,095 | MEDINA | 82,899 | 58,239 | 24,660 | | 33,579 R | 70.3% | 29.7% | 70.3% | 29.7% |
| 23,072 | MEIGS | 10,236 | 7,110 | 3,126 | | 3,984 R | 69.5% | 30.5% | 69.5% | 30.5% |
| 40,924 | MERCER | 20,713 | 16,334 | 4,379 | | 11,955 R | 78.9% | 21.1% | 78.9% | 21.1% |
| 98,868 | MIAMI | 50,171 | 37,659 | 12,510 | 2 | 25,149 R | 75.1% | 24.9% | 75.1% | 24.9% |
| 15,180 | MONROE | 7,505 | 4,121 | 3,384 | | 737 R | 54.9% | 45.1% | 54.9% | 45.1% |
| 559,062 | MONTGOMERY | 273,676 | 170,942 | 102,734 | | 68,208 R | 62.5% | 37.5% | 62.5% | 37.5% |
| 14,897 | MORGAN | 6,467 | 4,472 | 1,995 | | 2,477 R | 69.2% | 30.8% | 69.2% | 30.8% |
| 31,628 | MORROW | 15,899 | 11,795 | 4,104 | | 7,691 R | 74.2% | 25.8% | 74.2% | 25.8% |
| 84,585 | MUSKINGUM | 37,547 | 26,367 | 11,180 | | 15,187 R | 70.2% | 29.8% | 70.2% | 29.8% |
| 14,058 | NOBLE | 6,345 | 4,289 | 2,056 | | 2,233 R | 67.6% | 32.4% | 67.6% | 32.4% |
| 40,985 | OTTAWA | 22,651 | 15,425 | 7,224 | 2 | 8,201 R | 68.1% | 31.9% | 68.1% | 31.9% |
| 20,293 | PAULDING | 9,520 | 6,385 | 3,134 | 1 | 3,251 R | 67.1% | 32.9% | 67.1% | 32.9% |
| 34,078 | PERRY | 14,691 | 9,657 | 5,034 | | 4,623 R | 65.7% | 34.3% | 65.7% | 34.3% |
| 52,727 | PICKAWAY | 21,968 | 15,650 | 6,315 | 3 | 9,335 R | 71.2% | 28.7% | 71.2% | 28.8% |
| 27,695 | PIKE | 12,256 | 7,516 | 4,740 | | 2,776 R | 61.3% | 38.7% | 61.3% | 38.7% |
| 152,061 | PORTAGE | 74,147 | 44,185 | 29,962 | | 14,223 R | 59.6% | 40.4% | 59.6% | 40.4% |
| 42,337 | PREBLE | 20,552 | 15,169 | 5,383 | | 9,786 R | 73.8% | 26.2% | 73.8% | 26.2% |
| 34,726 | PUTNAM | 18,465 | 14,671 | 3,794 | | 10,877 R | 79.5% | 20.5% | 79.5% | 20.5% |
| 128,852 | RICHLAND | 60,133 | 40,663 | 19,469 | 1 | 21,194 R | 67.6% | 32.4% | 67.6% | 32.4% |
| 73,345 | ROSS | 30,640 | 20,634 | 10,006 | | 10,628 R | 67.3% | 32.7% | 67.3% | 32.7% |
| 61,792 | SANDUSKY | 28,735 | 20,407 | 8,327 | 1 | 12,080 R | 71.0% | 29.0% | 71.0% | 29.0% |
| 79,195 | SCIOTO | 34,181 | 20,998 | 13,183 | | 7,815 R | 61.4% | 38.6% | 61.4% | 38.6% |
| 58,683 | SENECA | 26,352 | 18,913 | 7,439 | | 11,474 R | 71.8% | 28.2% | 71.8% | 28.2% |
| 47,910 | SHELBY | 22,171 | 17,060 | 5,111 | | 11,949 R | 76.9% | 23.1% | 76.9% | 23.1% |
| 378,098 | STARK | 185,507 | 118,558 | 66,949 | | 51,609 R | 63.9% | 36.1% | 63.9% | 36.1% |
| 542,899 | SUMMIT | 270,428 | 153,906 | 116,522 | | 37,384 R | 56.9% | 43.1% | 56.9% | 43.1% |
| 225,116 | TRUMBULL | 104,495 | 54,638 | 49,856 | 1 | 4,782 R | 52.3% | 47.7% | 52.3% | 47.7% |
| 90,914 | TUSCARAWAS | 41,504 | 27,307 | 14,197 | | 13,110 R | 65.8% | 34.2% | 65.8% | 34.2% |
| 40,909 | UNION | 22,040 | 17,505 | 4,534 | 1 | 12,971 R | 79.4% | 20.6% | 79.4% | 20.6% |

# OHIO

## SENATOR 2004

| 2000 Census Population | County | Total Vote | Republican | Democratic | Other | Rep.-Dem. Plurality | Percentage | | | |
|---|---|---|---|---|---|---|---|---|---|---|
| | | | | | | | Total Vote | | Major Vote | |
| | | | | | | | Rep. | Dem. | Rep. | Dem. |
| 29,659 | VAN WERT | 14,418 | 10,697 | 3,721 | | 6,976 R | 74.2% | 25.8% | 74.2% | 25.8% |
| 12,806 | VINTON | 5,676 | 3,740 | 1,936 | | 1,804 R | 65.9% | 34.1% | 65.9% | 34.1% |
| 158,383 | WARREN | 91,335 | 72,083 | 19,251 | 1 | 52,832 R | 78.9% | 21.1% | 78.9% | 21.1% |
| 63,251 | WASHINGTON | 29,030 | 18,876 | 10,149 | 5 | 8,727 R | 65.0% | 35.0% | 65.0% | 35.0% |
| 111,564 | WAYNE | 50,580 | 36,559 | 14,021 | | 22,538 R | 72.3% | 27.7% | 72.3% | 27.7% |
| 39,188 | WILLIAMS | 18,066 | 13,563 | 4,503 | | 9,060 R | 75.1% | 24.9% | 75.1% | 24.9% |
| 121,065 | WOOD | 61,462 | 41,821 | 19,641 | | 22,180 R | 68.0% | 32.0% | 68.0% | 32.0% |
| 22,908 | WYANDOT | 10,814 | 8,297 | 2,517 | | 5,780 R | 76.7% | 23.3% | 76.7% | 23.3% |
| 11,353,140 | TOTAL | 5,426,196 | 3,464,651 | 1,961,249 | 296 | 1,503,402 R | 63.9% | 36.1% | 63.9% | 36.1% |

# OHIO

## HOUSE OF REPRESENTATIVES

| CD | Year | Total Vote | Republican | | Democratic | | Other Vote | Rep.-Dem. Plurality | Percentage | | | |
|---|---|---|---|---|---|---|---|---|---|---|---|---|
| | | | Vote | Candidate | Vote | Candidate | | | Total Vote | | Major Vote | |
| | | | | | | | | | Rep. | Dem. | Rep. | Dem. |
| 1 | 2004 | 289,863 | 173,430 | Chabot, Steve* | 116,235 | Harris, Greg | 198 | 57,195 R | 59.8% | 40.1% | 59.9% | 40.1% |
| 1 | 2002 | 170,928 | 110,760 | Chabot, Steve* | 60,168 | Harris, Greg | | 50,592 R | 64.8% | 35.2% | 64.8% | 35.2% |
| 2 | 2004 | 316,760 | 227,102 | Portman, Rob* | 89,598 | Sanders, Charles | 60 | 137,504 R | 71.7% | 28.3% | 71.7% | 28.3% |
| 2 | 2002 | 188,016 | 139,218 | Portman, Rob* | 48,785 | Sanders, Charles | 13 | 90,433 R | 74.0% | 25.9% | 74.1% | 25.9% |
| 3 | 2004 | 316,738 | 197,290 | Turner, Michael R.* | 119,448 | Mitakides, Jane | | 77,842 R | 62.3% | 37.7% | 62.3% | 37.7% |
| 3 | 2002 | 189,951 | 111,630 | Turner, Michael R. | 78,307 | Carne, Rick | 14 | 33,323 R | 58.8% | 41.2% | 58.8% | 41.2% |
| 4 | 2004 | 286,345 | 167,807 | Oxley, Michael G.* | 118,538 | Konop, Ben | | 49,269 R | 58.6% | 41.4% | 58.6% | 41.4% |
| 4 | 2002 | 177,727 | 120,001 | Oxley, Michael G.* | 57,726 | Clark, Jim | | 62,275 R | 67.5% | 32.5% | 67.5% | 32.5% |
| 5 | 2004 | 293,305 | 196,649 | Gillmor, Paul E.* | 96,656 | Weirauch, Robin | | 99,993 R | 67.0% | 33.0% | 67.0% | 33.0% |
| 5 | 2002 | 188,254 | 126,286 | Gillmor, Paul E.* | 51,872 | Anderson, Roger | 10,096 | 74,414 R | 67.1% | 27.6% | 70.9% | 29.1% |
| 6 | 2004 | 223,989 | | | 223,844 | Strickland, Ted* | 145 | 223,844 D | | 99.9% | | 100.0% |
| 6 | 2002 | 191,615 | 77,643 | Halleck, Mike | 113,972 | Strickland, Ted* | | 36,329 D | 40.5% | 59.5% | 40.5% | 59.5% |
| 7 | 2004 | 287,151 | 186,534 | Hobson, David L.* | 100,617 | Anastasio, Kara | | 85,917 R | 65.0% | 35.0% | 65.0% | 35.0% |
| 7 | 2002 | 167,632 | 113,252 | Hobson, David L.* | 45,568 | Anastasio, Kara | 8,812 | 67,684 R | 67.6% | 27.2% | 71.3% | 28.7% |
| 8 | 2004 | 292,249 | 201,675 | Boehner, John A.* | 90,574 | Hardenbrook, Jeff | | 111,101 R | 69.0% | 31.0% | 69.0% | 31.0% |
| 8 | 2002 | 169,391 | 119,947 | Boehner, John A.* | 49,444 | Hardenbrook, Jeff | | 70,503 R | 70.8% | 29.2% | 70.8% | 29.2% |
| 9 | 2004 | 301,132 | 95,983 | Kaczala, Larry A. | 205,149 | Kaptur, Marcy* | | 109,166 D | 31.9% | 68.1% | 31.9% | 68.1% |
| 9 | 2002 | 178,717 | 46,481 | Emery, Ed | 132,236 | Kaptur, Marcy* | | 85,755 D | 26.0% | 74.0% | 26.0% | 74.0% |
| 10 | 2004 | 287,212 | 96,463 | Herman, Edward Fitzpatrick | 172,406 | Kucinich, Dennis J.* | 18,343 | 75,943 D | 33.6% | 60.0% | 35.9% | 64.1% |
| 10 | 2002 | 175,536 | 41,778 | Heben, Jon | 129,997 | Kucinich, Dennis J.* | 3,761 | 88,219 D | 23.8% | 74.1% | 24.3% | 75.7% |
| 11 | 2004 | 222,371 | | | 222,371 | Jones, Stephanie Tubbs* | | 222,371 D | | 100.0% | | 100.0% |
| 11 | 2002 | 152,736 | 36,146 | Pappano, Patrick | 116,590 | Jones, Stephanie Tubbs* | | 80,444 D | 23.7% | 76.3% | 23.7% | 76.3% |
| 12 | 2004 | 321,046 | 198,912 | Tiberi, Pat* | 122,109 | Brown, Edward | 25 | 76,803 R | 62.0% | 38.0% | 62.0% | 38.0% |
| 12 | 2002 | 181,689 | 116,982 | Tiberi, Pat* | 64,707 | Brown, Edward | | 52,275 R | 64.4% | 35.6% | 64.4% | 35.6% |
| 13 | 2004 | 298,094 | 97,090 | Lucas, Robert | 201,004 | Brown, Sherrod* | | 103,914 D | 32.6% | 67.4% | 32.6% | 67.4% |
| 13 | 2002 | 178,382 | 55,357 | Oliveros, Ed | 123,025 | Brown, Sherrod* | | 67,668 D | 31.0% | 69.0% | 31.0% | 69.0% |

# OHIO
## HOUSE OF REPRESENTATIVES

| CD | Year | Total Vote | Republican Vote | Republican Candidate | Democratic Vote | Democratic Candidate | Other Vote | Rep.-Dem. Plurality | Total Vote Rep. | Total Vote Dem. | Major Vote Rep. | Major Vote Dem. |
|---|---|---|---|---|---|---|---|---|---|---|---|---|
| 14 | 2004 | 321,366 | 201,652 | LaTourette, Steven C.* | 119,714 | Cafaro, Capri S. | | 81,938 R | 62.7% | 37.3% | 62.7% | 37.3% |
| 14 | 2002 | 186,372 | 134,413 | LaTourette, Steven C.* | 51,846 | Blanchard, Dale | 113 | 82,567 R | 72.1% | 27.8% | 72.2% | 27.8% |
| 15 | 2004 | 277,435 | 166,520 | Pryce, Deborah* | 110,915 | Brown, Mark | | 55,605 R | 60.0% | 40.0% | 60.0% | 40.0% |
| 15 | 2002 | 162,479 | 108,193 | Pryce, Deborah* | 54,286 | Brown, Mark | | 53,907 R | 66.6% | 33.4% | 66.6% | 33.4% |
| 16 | 2004 | 304,361 | 202,544 | Regula, Ralph* | 101,817 | Seemann, Jeff | | 100,727 R | 66.5% | 33.5% | 66.5% | 33.5% |
| 16 | 2002 | 188,378 | 129,734 | Regula, Ralph* | 58,644 | Rice, Jim | | 71,090 R | 68.9% | 31.1% | 68.9% | 31.1% |
| 17 | 2004 | 275,671 | 62,871 | Cusimano, Frank V. | 212,800 | Ryan, Tim* | | 149,929 D | 22.8% | 77.2% | 22.8% | 77.2% |
| 17 | 2002 | 184,674 | 62,188 | Benjamin, Ann Womer | 94,441 | Ryan, Tim | 28,045 | 32,253 D | 33.7% | 51.1% | 39.7% | 60.3% |
| 18 | 2004 | 268,420 | 177,600 | Ney, Bob* | 90,820 | Thomas, Brian R. | | 86,780 R | 66.2% | 33.8% | 66.2% | 33.8% |
| 18 | 2002 | 125,546 | 125,546 | Ney, Bob* | | | | 125,546 R | 100.0% | | 100.0% | |
| Total | 2004 | 5,183,508 | 2,650,122 | | 2,514,615 | | 18,771 | 135,507 R | 51.1% | 48.5% | 51.3% | 48.7% |
| Total | 2002 | 3,158,023 | 1,775,555 | | 1,331,614 | | 50,854 | 443,941 R | 56.2% | 42.2% | 57.1% | 42.9% |

An asterisk (*) denotes incumbent.

# OHIO
## GENERAL AND PRIMARY ELECTION

## 2004 GENERAL ELECTIONS

**President**     Other vote was 14,676 Other Party Candidate (Michael Badnarik); 11,939 Other Party Candidate (Michael Peroutka); 192 write-in (David Cobb); 114 write-in (Joe Schriner); 22 write-in (James Harris); 17 write-in (Richard A. Duncan); 11 write-in (Thomas F. Zych); 2 write-in (John Parker).

**Senator**     Other vote was 296 write-in (Helen Meyers).

**House**     Other vote was:

CD 1     198 write-in (Rich Stevenson).
CD 2     60 write-in (James Condit Jr.).
CD 3
CD 4
CD 5
CD 6     145 write-in (John Stephen Luchansky).
CD 7
CD 8
CD 9
CD 10     18,343 Non-Partisan (Barbara Anne Ferris).
CD 11
CD 12     25 write-in (Chuck Spingola).
CD 13
CD 14
CD 15
CD 16
CD 17
CD 18

Note:     In Ohio, only the Democratic Party and Republican Party are recognized. Other candidates are listed on the ballot either as "Other Party Candidate" or "Non-Partisan."

# OHIO

## GENERAL AND PRIMARY ELECTIONS

## 2004 PRIMARY ELECTIONS

| | | | | |
|---|---|---|---|---|
| **Primary** | March 2, 2004 | **Registration** (as of March 2, 2004) | 7,204,856 | No Formal System of Party Registration |

**Primary Type** Open—Any registered voter can participate in the primary of either party. However, records are kept of voter participation in recent primaries, and in some counties voters who have cast a ballot in recent years in one party's primary can be challenged if they attempt to participate in the other party's primary. They may be asked to sign an affidavit affirming the fact that they are voting in the opposing party's primary and will be considered a member of the other party because of their primary ballot cast.

Note: An asterisk (*) denotes incumbent. The Democratic presidential primary vote was compiled by the Ohio secretary of state by congressional district. *America Votes* aggregated the results into statewide totals for each candidate.

| | REPUBLICAN PRIMARIES | | | DEMOCRATIC PRIMARIES | | |
|---|---|---|---|---|---|---|
| President | George W. Bush* | 793,833 | 100.0% | John Kerry | 632,599 | 51.8% |
| | | | | John Edwards | 416,106 | 34.1% |
| | | | | Dennis J. Kucinich | 110,067 | 9.0% |
| | | | | Howard Dean | 30,983 | 2.5% |
| | | | | Joseph I. Lieberman | 14,676 | 1.2% |
| | | | | Wesley Clark | 12,577 | 1.0% |
| | | | | Lyndon H. LaRouche Jr. | 4,018 | 0.3% |
| | | | | TOTAL | 1,221,026 | |
| Senator | George V. Voinovich* | 640,082 | 76.6% | Eric D. Fingerhut | 672,989 | 70.8% |
| | John Mitchel | 195,476 | 23.4% | Norbert G. Dennerll | 277,721 | 29.2% |
| | TOTAL | 835,558 | | TOTAL | 950,710 | |
| Congressional District 1 | Steve Chabot* | 38,730 | 100.0% | Greg Harris | 18,659 | 60.9% |
| | | | | Richard Lerner | 11,972 | 39.1% |
| | | | | TOTAL | 30,631 | |
| Congressional District 2 | Rob Portman* | 63,796 | 100.0% | Charles Sanders | 20,979 | 65.3% |
| | | | | Mark A. Crummie | 11,124 | 34.7% |
| | | | | TOTAL | 32,103 | |
| Congressional District 3 | Michael R. Turner* | 48,482 | 100.0% | Jane Mitakides | 38,851 | 100.0% |
| Congressional District 4 | Michael G. Oxley* | 65,979 | 100.0% | Ben Konop | 37,742 | 100.0% |
| Congressional District 5 | Paul E. Gillmor* | 59,083 | 100.0% | Robin Weirauch | 39,089 | 100.0% |
| Congressional District 6 | No Republican candidate | | | Ted Strickland* | 73,405 | 83.0% |
| | | | | Diane DiCarlo Murphy | 15,054 | 17.0% |
| | | | | TOTAL | 88,459 | |
| Congressional District 7 | David L. Hobson* | 57,445 | 100.0% | Kara Anastasio | 41,476 | 100.0% |
| Congressional District 8 | John A. Boehner* | 55,149 | 100.0% | Jeff Hardenbrook | 31,435 | 100.0% |
| Congressional District 9 | Larry A. Kaczala | 11,908 | 67.2% | Marcy Kaptur* | 58,053 | 100.0% |
| | Ed Emery | 4,522 | 25.5% | | | |
| | Luis T.J. Leal | 1,278 | 7.2% | | | |
| | TOTAL | 17,708 | | | | |
| Congressional District 10 | Edward Fitzpatrick Herman | 8,548 | 41.8% | Dennis J. Kucinich* | 74,692 | 85.5% |
| | Bruce Cobbeldick | 4,336 | 21.2% | George Pulling | 12,639 | 14.5% |
| | Bill Smith | 3,959 | 19.3% | | | |
| | Matt Webb | 3,620 | 17.7% | | | |
| | TOTAL | 20,463 | | TOTAL | 87,331 | |
| Congressional District 11 | No Republican candidate | | | Stephanie Tubbs Jones* | 87,275 | 100.0% |

# OHIO

## GENERAL AND PRIMARY ELECTIONS

| REPUBLICAN PRIMARIES | | | | DEMOCRATIC PRIMARIES | | |
|---|---|---|---|---|---|---|
| Congressional District 12 | Pat Tiberi* | 47,446 | 100.0% | Edward Brown | 40,029 | 100.0% |
| Congressional District 13 | Robert Lucas | 16,058 | 58.7% | Sherrod Brown* | 69,455 | 100.0% |
| | Joe Ortega | 11,295 | 41.3% | | | |
| | TOTAL | 27,353 | | | | |
| Congressional District 14 | Steven C. LaTourette* | 48,192 | 100.0% | Capri S. Cafaro | 34,774 | 53.9% |
| | | | | Ed Jerse | 12,045 | 18.7% |
| | | | | Herb Hammer | 9,393 | 14.5% |
| | | | | Charles L. Wolfe | 4,493 | 7.0% |
| | | | | Dale Virgil Blanchard | 3,857 | 6.0% |
| | | | | TOTAL | 64,562 | |
| Congressional District 15 | Deborah Pryce* | 36,860 | 83.6% | Mark Brown | 18,944 | 50.2% |
| | Charlie Morrison II | 7,254 | 16.4% | Ignacio M. Garcia | 9,966 | 26.4% |
| | | | | W. Raymond Mills | 8,843 | 23.4% |
| | TOTAL | 44,114 | | TOTAL | 37,753 | |
| Congressional District 16 | Ralph Regula* | 53,481 | 100.0% | Jeff Seemann | 51,622 | 100.0% |
| Congressional District 17 | Frank V. Cusimano | 17,445 | 100.0% | Tim Ryan* | 97,564 | 100.0% |
| Congressional District 18 | Bob Ney* | 45,259 | 100.0% | Brian R. Thomas | 24,263 | 52.3% |
| | | | | Paul E. Richards | 22,110 | 47.7% |
| | | | | TOTAL | 46,373 | |

# OKLAHOMA

## GOVERNOR
Brad Henry (D). Elected 2002 to a four-year term.

## SENATORS (2 Republicans)
Tom Coburn (R). Elected 2004 to a six-year term.

James M. Inhofe (R). Reelected 2002 to a six-year term. Previously elected 1996 and 1994 to fill out the remaining two years of the term vacated when David L. Boren (D) resigned to become president of the University of Oklahoma.

## REPRESENTATIVES (4 Republicans, 1 Democrat)
1. John Sullivan (R)
2. Dan Boren (D)
3. Frank D. Lucas (R)
4. Tom Cole (R)
5. Ernest Istook (R)

## POSTWAR VOTE FOR PRESIDENT

| Year | Total Vote | Republican Vote | Candidate | Democratic Vote | Candidate | Other Vote | Plurality | | Total Vote Rep. | Dem. | Major Vote Rep. | Dem. |
|---|---|---|---|---|---|---|---|---|---|---|---|---|
| 2004 | 1,463,758 | 959,792 | Bush, George W. | 503,966 | Kerry, John | | 455,826 | R | 65.6% | 34.4% | 65.6% | 34.4% |
| 2000 | 1,234,229 | 744,337 | Bush, George W. | 474,276 | Gore, Al | 15,616 | 270,061 | R | 60.3% | 38.4% | 61.1% | 38.9% |
| 1996** | 1,206,713 | 582,315 | Dole, Bob | 488,105 | Clinton, Bill | 136,293 | 94,210 | R | 48.3% | 40.4% | 54.4% | 45.6% |
| 1992** | 1,390,359 | 592,929 | Bush, George | 473,066 | Clinton, Bill | 324,364 | 119,863 | R | 42.6% | 34.0% | 55.6% | 44.4% |
| 1988 | 1,171,036 | 678,367 | Bush, George | 483,423 | Dukakis, Michael S. | 9,246 | 194,944 | R | 57.9% | 41.3% | 58.4% | 41.6% |
| 1984 | 1,255,676 | 861,530 | Reagan, Ronald | 385,080 | Mondale, Walter F. | 9,066 | 476,450 | R | 68.6% | 30.7% | 69.1% | 30.9% |
| 1980** | 1,149,708 | 695,570 | Reagan, Ronald | 402,026 | Carter, Jimmy | 52,112 | 293,544 | R | 60.5% | 35.0% | 63.4% | 36.6% |
| 1976 | 1,092,251 | 545,708 | Ford, Gerald R. | 532,442 | Carter, Jimmy | 14,101 | 13,266 | R | 50.0% | 48.7% | 50.6% | 49.4% |
| 1972 | 1,029,900 | 759,025 | Nixon, Richard M. | 247,147 | McGovern, George S. | 23,728 | 511,878 | R | 73.7% | 24.0% | 75.4% | 24.6% |
| 1968** | 943,086 | 449,697 | Nixon, Richard M. | 301,658 | Humphrey, Hubert H. | 191,731 | 148,039 | R | 47.7% | 32.0% | 59.9% | 40.1% |
| 1964 | 932,499 | 412,665 | Goldwater, Barry M. | 519,834 | Johnson, Lyndon B. | | 107,169 | D | 44.3% | 55.7% | 44.3% | 55.7% |
| 1960 | 903,150 | 533,039 | Nixon, Richard M. | 370,111 | Kennedy, John F. | | 162,928 | R | 59.0% | 41.0% | 59.0% | 41.0% |
| 1956 | 859,350 | 473,769 | Eisenhower, Dwight D. | 385,581 | Stevenson, Adlai E. | | 88,188 | R | 55.1% | 44.9% | 55.1% | 44.9% |
| 1952 | 948,984 | 518,045 | Eisenhower, Dwight D. | 430,939 | Stevenson, Adlai E. | | 87,106 | R | 54.6% | 45.4% | 54.6% | 45.4% |
| 1948 | 721,599 | 268,817 | Dewey, Thomas E. | 452,782 | Truman, Harry S. | | 183,965 | D | 37.3% | 62.7% | 37.3% | 62.7% |

In past elections, the other vote included: 1996 - 130,788 Reform (Ross Perot); 1992 - 319,878 Independent (Perot); 1980 - 38,284 Independent (John Anderson); 1968 - 191,731 American Independent (George Wallace).

# OKLAHOMA

## POSTWAR VOTE FOR GOVERNOR

| Year | Total Vote | Republican | | Democratic | | Other Vote | Rep.-Dem. Plurality | Percentage | | | |
|------|------------|------------|-----------|------------|-----------|------------|---------------------|------------|------|------|------|
| | | Vote | Candidate | Vote | Candidate | | | Total Vote | | Major Vote | |
| | | | | | | | | Rep. | Dem. | Rep. | Dem. |
| 2002** | 1,035,620 | 441,277 | Largent, Steve | 448,143 | Henry, Brad | 146,200 | 6,866 D | 42.6% | 43.3% | 49.6% | 50.4% |
| 1998 | 873,585 | 505,498 | Keating, Frank | 357,552 | Boyd, Laura | 10,535 | 147,946 R | 57.9% | 40.9% | 58.6% | 41.4% |
| 1994** | 995,012 | 466,740 | Keating, Frank | 294,936 | Mildren, Jack | 233,336 | 171,804 R | 46.9% | 29.6% | 61.3% | 38.7% |
| 1990 | 911,314 | 297,584 | Price, Bill | 523,196 | Walters, David | 90,534 | 225,612 D | 32.7% | 57.4% | 36.3% | 63.7% |
| 1986 | 909,925 | 431,762 | Bellmon, Henry | 405,295 | Walters, David | 72,868 | 26,467 R | 47.5% | 44.5% | 51.6% | 48.4% |
| 1982 | 883,130 | 332,207 | Daxon, Tom | 548,159 | Nigh, George | 2,764 | 215,952 D | 37.6% | 62.1% | 37.7% | 62.3% |
| 1978 | 777,414 | 367,055 | Shotts, Ron | 402,240 | Nigh, George | 8,119 | 35,185 D | 47.2% | 51.7% | 47.7% | 52.3% |
| 1974 | 804,848 | 290,459 | Inhofe, James M. | 514,389 | Boren, David L. | | 223,930 D | 36.1% | 63.9% | 36.1% | 63.9% |
| 1970 | 698,790 | 336,157 | Bartlett, Dewey F. | 338,338 | Hall, David | 24,295 | 2,181 D | 48.1% | 48.4% | 49.8% | 50.2% |
| 1966 | 677,258 | 377,078 | Bartlett, Dewey F. | 296,328 | Moore, Preston J. | 3,852 | 80,750 R | 55.7% | 43.8% | 56.0% | 44.0% |
| 1962 | 709,763 | 392,316 | Bellmon, Henry | 315,357 | Atkinson, W. P. | 2,090 | 76,959 R | 55.3% | 44.4% | 55.4% | 44.6% |
| 1958 | 538,839 | 107,495 | Ferguson, Phil | 399,504 | Edmondson, J. Howard | 31,840 | 292,009 D | 19.9% | 74.1% | 21.2% | 78.8% |
| 1954 | 609,194 | 251,808 | Sparks, Reuben K. | 357,386 | Gary, Raymond | | 105,578 D | 41.3% | 58.7% | 41.3% | 58.7% |
| 1950 | 644,276 | 313,205 | Ferguson, Jo O. | 329,308 | Murray, Johnston | 1,763 | 16,103 D | 48.6% | 51.1% | 48.7% | 51.3% |
| 1946 | 494,599 | 227,426 | Flynn, Olney F. | 259,491 | Turner, Roy J. | 7,682 | 32,065 D | 46.0% | 52.5% | 46.7% | 53.3% |

In past elections, the other vote included: 2002 - 146,200 Independent (Gary L. Richardson); 1994 - 233,336 Independent (Wes Watkins).

## POSTWAR VOTE FOR SENATOR

| Year | Total Vote | Republican | | Democratic | | Other Vote | Rep.-Dem. Plurality | Percentage | | | |
|------|------------|------------|-----------|------------|-----------|------------|---------------------|------------|------|------|------|
| | | Vote | Candidate | Vote | Candidate | | | Total Vote | | Major Vote | |
| | | | | | | | | Rep. | Dem. | Rep. | Dem. |
| 2004 | 1,446,846 | 763,433 | Coburn, Tom | 596,750 | Carson, Brad | 86,663 | 166,683 R | 52.8% | 41.2% | 56.1% | 43.9% |
| 2002 | 1,018,424 | 583,579 | Inhofe, James M. | 369,789 | Walters, David | 65,056 | 213,790 R | 57.3% | 36.3% | 61.2% | 38.8% |
| 1998 | 859,713 | 570,682 | Nickles, Don | 268,898 | Carroll, Don E. | 20,133 | 301,784 R | 66.4% | 31.3% | 68.0% | 32.0% |
| 1996 | 1,183,150 | 670,610 | Inhofe, James M. | 474,162 | Boren, Jim | 38,378 | 196,448 R | 56.7% | 40.1% | 58.6% | 41.4% |
| 1994S | 982,430 | 542,390 | Inhofe, James M. | 392,488 | McCurdy, Dave | 47,552 | 149,902 R | 55.2% | 40.0% | 58.0% | 42.0% |
| 1992 | 1,294,423 | 757,876 | Nickles, Don | 494,350 | Lewis, Steve | 42,197 | 263,526 R | 58.5% | 38.2% | 60.5% | 39.5% |
| 1990 | 884,498 | 148,814 | Jones, Stephen | 735,684 | Boren, David L. | | 586,870 D | 16.8% | 83.2% | 16.8% | 83.2% |
| 1986 | 893,666 | 493,436 | Nickles, Don | 400,230 | Jones, James R. | | 93,206 R | 55.2% | 44.8% | 55.2% | 44.8% |
| 1984 | 1,197,937 | 280,638 | Crozier, Will E. | 906,131 | Boren, David L. | 11,168 | 625,493 D | 23.4% | 75.6% | 23.6% | 76.4% |
| 1980 | 1,098,294 | 587,252 | Nickles, Don | 478,283 | Coats, Andrew | 32,759 | 108,969 R | 53.5% | 43.5% | 55.1% | 44.9% |
| 1978 | 754,264 | 247,857 | Kamm, Robert B. | 493,953 | Boren, David L. | 12,454 | 246,096 D | 32.9% | 65.5% | 33.4% | 66.6% |
| 1974 | 791,809 | 390,997 | Bellmon, Henry | 387,162 | Edmondson, Ed | 13,650 | 3,835 R | 49.4% | 48.9% | 50.2% | 49.8% |
| 1972 | 1,005,148 | 516,934 | Bartlett, Dewey F. | 478,212 | Edmondson, Ed | 10,002 | 38,722 R | 51.4% | 47.6% | 51.9% | 48.1% |
| 1968 | 909,119 | 470,120 | Bellmon, Henry | 419,658 | Monroney, A. S. Mike | 19,341 | 50,462 R | 51.7% | 46.2% | 52.8% | 47.2% |
| 1966 | 638,742 | 295,585 | Patterson, Pat J. | 343,157 | Harris, Fred R. | | 47,572 D | 46.3% | 53.7% | 46.3% | 53.7% |
| 1964S | 912,174 | 445,392 | Wilkinson, Bud | 466,782 | Harris, Fred R. | | 21,390 D | 48.8% | 51.2% | 48.8% | 51.2% |
| 1962 | 664,712 | 307,966 | Crawford, B. Hayden | 353,890 | Monroney, A. S. Mike | 2,856 | 45,924 D | 46.3% | 53.2% | 46.5% | 53.5% |
| 1960 | 864,475 | 385,646 | Crawford, B. Hayden | 474,116 | Kerr, Robert S. | 4,713 | 88,470 D | 44.6% | 54.8% | 44.9% | 55.1% |
| 1956 | 831,142 | 371,146 | McKeever, Douglas | 459,996 | Monroney, A. S. Mike | | 88,850 D | 44.7% | 55.3% | 44.7% | 55.3% |
| 1954 | 600,120 | 262,013 | Mock, Fred M. | 335,127 | Kerr, Robert S. | 2,980 | 73,114 D | 43.7% | 55.8% | 43.9% | 56.1% |
| 1950 | 631,177 | 285,224 | Alexander, W. H. | 345,953 | Monroney, A. S. Mike | | 60,729 D | 45.2% | 54.8% | 45.2% | 54.8% |
| 1948 | 708,931 | 265,169 | Rizley, Ross | 441,654 | Kerr, Robert S. | 2,108 | 176,485 D | 37.4% | 62.3% | 37.5% | 62.5% |

The 1994 and 1964 elections were for short terms to fill a vacancy.

359

# OKLAHOMA

Congressional districts first established for elections held in 2002
5 members

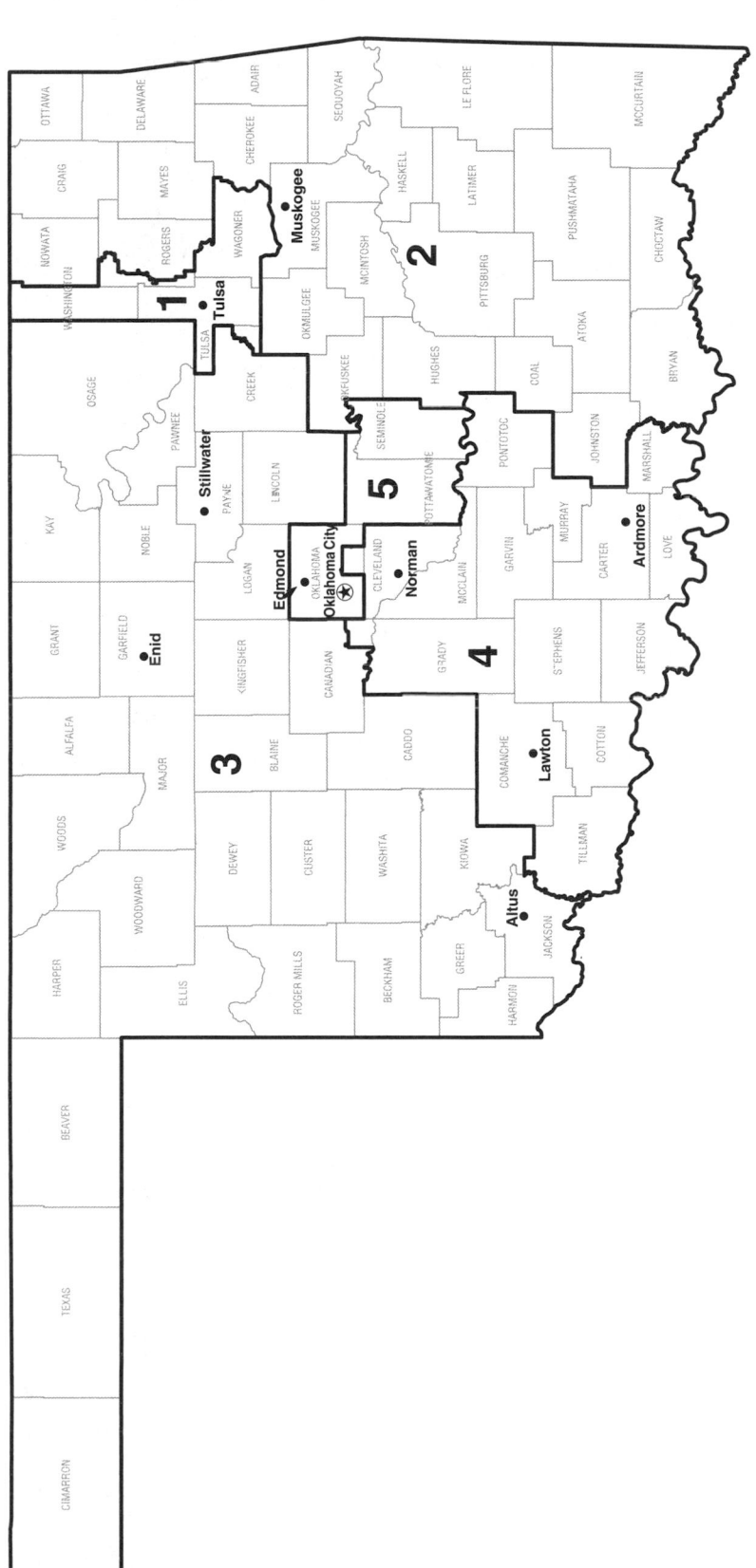

# OKLAHOMA

## PRESIDENT 2004

| 2000 Census Population | County | Total Vote | Republican | Democratic | Other | Rep.-Dem. Plurality | Percentage Total Vote | | Major Vote | |
|---|---|---|---|---|---|---|---|---|---|---|
| | | | | | | | Rep. | Dem. | Rep. | Dem. |
| 21,038 | ADAIR | 7,533 | 4,971 | 2,562 | | 2,409 R | 66.0% | 34.0% | 66.0% | 34.0% |
| 6,105 | ALFALFA | 2,671 | 2,201 | 470 | | 1,731 R | 82.4% | 17.6% | 82.4% | 17.6% |
| 13,879 | ATOKA | 5,088 | 3,142 | 1,946 | | 1,196 R | 61.8% | 38.2% | 61.8% | 38.2% |
| 5,857 | BEAVER | 2,569 | 2,272 | 297 | | 1,975 R | 88.4% | 11.6% | 88.4% | 11.6% |
| 19,799 | BECKHAM | 7,385 | 5,454 | 1,931 | | 3,523 R | 73.9% | 26.1% | 73.9% | 26.1% |
| 11,976 | BLAINE | 4,421 | 3,199 | 1,222 | | 1,977 R | 72.4% | 27.6% | 72.4% | 27.6% |
| 36,534 | BRYAN | 14,360 | 8,615 | 5,745 | | 2,870 R | 60.0% | 40.0% | 60.0% | 40.0% |
| 30,150 | CADDO | 10,407 | 6,491 | 3,916 | | 2,575 R | 62.4% | 37.6% | 62.4% | 37.6% |
| 87,697 | CANADIAN | 43,009 | 33,297 | 9,712 | | 23,585 R | 77.4% | 22.6% | 77.4% | 22.6% |
| 45,621 | CARTER | 18,644 | 12,178 | 6,466 | | 5,712 R | 65.3% | 34.7% | 65.3% | 34.7% |
| 42,521 | CHEROKEE | 18,192 | 9,569 | 8,623 | | 946 R | 52.6% | 47.4% | 52.6% | 47.4% |
| 15,342 | CHOCTAW | 5,807 | 3,168 | 2,639 | | 529 R | 54.6% | 45.4% | 54.6% | 45.4% |
| 3,148 | CIMARRON | 1,426 | 1,242 | 184 | | 1,058 R | 87.1% | 12.9% | 87.1% | 12.9% |
| 208,016 | CLEVELAND | 99,727 | 65,720 | 34,007 | | 31,713 R | 65.9% | 34.1% | 65.9% | 34.1% |
| 6,031 | COAL | 2,599 | 1,396 | 1,203 | | 193 R | 53.7% | 46.3% | 53.7% | 46.3% |
| 114,996 | COMANCHE | 33,192 | 21,170 | 12,022 | | 9,148 R | 63.8% | 36.2% | 63.8% | 36.2% |
| 6,614 | COTTON | 2,640 | 1,742 | 898 | | 844 R | 66.0% | 34.0% | 66.0% | 34.0% |
| 14,950 | CRAIG | 6,398 | 3,894 | 2,504 | | 1,390 R | 60.9% | 39.1% | 60.9% | 39.1% |
| 67,367 | CREEK | 28,777 | 18,848 | 9,929 | | 8,919 R | 65.5% | 34.5% | 65.5% | 34.5% |
| 26,142 | CUSTER | 10,640 | 7,839 | 2,801 | | 5,038 R | 73.7% | 26.3% | 73.7% | 26.3% |
| 37,077 | DELAWARE | 15,608 | 10,017 | 5,591 | | 4,426 R | 64.2% | 35.8% | 64.2% | 35.8% |
| 4,743 | DEWEY | 2,251 | 1,843 | 408 | | 1,435 R | 81.9% | 18.1% | 81.9% | 18.1% |
| 4,075 | ELLIS | 2,080 | 1,685 | 395 | | 1,290 R | 81.0% | 19.0% | 81.0% | 19.0% |
| 57,813 | GARFIELD | 23,271 | 17,685 | 5,586 | | 12,099 R | 76.0% | 24.0% | 76.0% | 24.0% |
| 27,210 | GARVIN | 11,317 | 7,610 | 3,707 | | 3,903 R | 67.2% | 32.8% | 67.2% | 32.8% |
| 45,516 | GRADY | 20,106 | 14,136 | 5,970 | | 8,166 R | 70.3% | 29.7% | 70.3% | 29.7% |
| 5,144 | GRANT | 2,521 | 1,950 | 571 | | 1,379 R | 77.4% | 22.6% | 77.4% | 22.6% |
| 6,061 | GREER | 2,248 | 1,529 | 719 | | 810 R | 68.0% | 32.0% | 68.0% | 32.0% |
| 3,283 | HARMON | 1,192 | 838 | 354 | | 484 R | 70.3% | 29.7% | 70.3% | 29.7% |
| 3,562 | HARPER | 1,665 | 1,397 | 268 | | 1,129 R | 83.9% | 16.1% | 83.9% | 16.1% |
| 11,792 | HASKELL | 5,324 | 2,946 | 2,378 | | 568 R | 55.3% | 44.7% | 55.3% | 44.7% |
| 14,154 | HUGHES | 5,349 | 3,066 | 2,283 | | 783 R | 57.3% | 42.7% | 57.3% | 42.7% |
| 28,439 | JACKSON | 9,256 | 7,024 | 2,232 | | 4,792 R | 75.9% | 24.1% | 75.9% | 24.1% |
| 6,818 | JEFFERSON | 2,603 | 1,546 | 1,057 | | 489 R | 59.4% | 40.6% | 59.4% | 40.6% |
| 10,513 | JOHNSTON | 4,348 | 2,635 | 1,713 | | 922 R | 60.6% | 39.4% | 60.6% | 39.4% |
| 48,080 | KAY | 20,078 | 14,121 | 5,957 | | 8,164 R | 70.3% | 29.7% | 70.3% | 29.7% |
| 13,926 | KINGFISHER | 6,652 | 5,630 | 1,022 | | 4,608 R | 84.6% | 15.4% | 84.6% | 15.4% |
| 10,227 | KIOWA | 4,023 | 2,610 | 1,413 | | 1,197 R | 64.9% | 35.1% | 64.9% | 35.1% |
| 10,692 | LATIMER | 4,480 | 2,535 | 1,945 | | 590 R | 56.6% | 43.4% | 56.6% | 43.4% |
| 48,109 | LE FLORE | 17,424 | 10,683 | 6,741 | | 3,942 R | 61.3% | 38.7% | 61.3% | 38.7% |
| 32,080 | LINCOLN | 14,190 | 10,149 | 4,041 | | 6,108 R | 71.5% | 28.5% | 71.5% | 28.5% |
| 33,924 | LOGAN | 16,343 | 11,474 | 4,869 | | 6,605 R | 70.2% | 29.8% | 70.2% | 29.8% |
| 8,831 | LOVE | 3,833 | 2,295 | 1,538 | | 757 R | 59.9% | 40.1% | 59.9% | 40.1% |
| 27,740 | MCCLAIN | 13,783 | 10,041 | 3,742 | | 6,299 R | 72.9% | 27.1% | 72.9% | 27.1% |
| 34,402 | MCCURTAIN | 11,156 | 7,472 | 3,684 | | 3,788 R | 67.0% | 33.0% | 67.0% | 33.0% |
| 19,456 | MCINTOSH | 9,180 | 4,692 | 4,488 | | 204 R | 51.1% | 48.9% | 51.1% | 48.9% |
| 7,545 | MAJOR | 3,659 | 3,122 | 537 | | 2,585 R | 85.3% | 14.7% | 85.3% | 14.7% |
| 13,184 | MARSHALL | 5,451 | 3,363 | 2,088 | | 1,275 R | 61.7% | 38.3% | 61.7% | 38.3% |
| 38,369 | MAYES | 16,879 | 9,946 | 6,933 | | 3,013 R | 58.9% | 41.1% | 58.9% | 41.1% |
| 12,623 | MURRAY | 5,795 | 3,665 | 2,130 | | 1,535 R | 63.2% | 36.8% | 63.2% | 36.8% |
| 69,451 | MUSKOGEE | 27,709 | 15,124 | 12,585 | | 2,539 R | 54.6% | 45.4% | 54.6% | 45.4% |
| 11,411 | NOBLE | 5,328 | 3,993 | 1,335 | | 2,658 R | 74.9% | 25.1% | 74.9% | 25.1% |
| 10,569 | NOWATA | 4,465 | 2,805 | 1,660 | | 1,145 R | 62.8% | 37.2% | 62.8% | 37.2% |
| 11,814 | OKFUSKEE | 4,285 | 2,542 | 1,743 | | 799 R | 59.3% | 40.7% | 59.3% | 40.7% |
| 660,448 | OKLAHOMA | 272,039 | 174,741 | 97,298 | | 77,443 R | 64.2% | 35.8% | 64.2% | 35.8% |
| 39,685 | OKMULGEE | 15,730 | 8,363 | 7,367 | | 996 R | 53.2% | 46.8% | 53.2% | 46.8% |
| 44,437 | OSAGE | 19,535 | 11,467 | 8,068 | | 3,399 R | 58.7% | 41.3% | 58.7% | 41.3% |
| 33,194 | OTTAWA | 12,529 | 7,443 | 5,086 | | 2,357 R | 59.4% | 40.6% | 59.4% | 40.6% |
| 16,612 | PAWNEE | 6,976 | 4,412 | 2,564 | | 1,848 R | 63.2% | 36.8% | 63.2% | 36.8% |
| 68,190 | PAYNE | 29,661 | 19,560 | 10,101 | | 9,459 R | 65.9% | 34.1% | 65.9% | 34.1% |

# OKLAHOMA

## PRESIDENT 2004

| 2000 Census Population | County | Total Vote | Republican | Democratic | Other | Rep.-Dem. Plurality | Percentage | | | |
|---|---|---|---|---|---|---|---|---|---|---|
| | | | | | | | Total Vote | | Major Vote | |
| | | | | | | | Rep. | Dem. | Rep. | Dem. |
| 43,953 | PITTSBURG | 18,586 | 11,134 | 7,452 | | 3,682 R | 59.9% | 40.1% | 59.9% | 40.1% |
| 35,143 | PONTOTOC | 14,812 | 9,647 | 5,165 | | 4,482 R | 65.1% | 34.9% | 65.1% | 34.9% |
| 65,521 | POTTAWATOMIE | 25,853 | 17,215 | 8,638 | | 8,577 R | 66.6% | 33.4% | 66.6% | 33.4% |
| 11,667 | PUSHMATAHA | 4,797 | 2,863 | 1,934 | | 929 R | 59.7% | 40.3% | 59.7% | 40.3% |
| 3,436 | ROGER MILLS | 1,770 | 1,388 | 382 | | 1,006 R | 78.4% | 21.6% | 78.4% | 21.6% |
| 70,641 | ROGERS | 36,894 | 24,976 | 11,918 | | 13,058 R | 67.7% | 32.3% | 67.7% | 32.3% |
| 24,894 | SEMINOLE | 9,272 | 5,624 | 3,648 | | 1,976 R | 60.7% | 39.3% | 60.7% | 39.3% |
| 38,972 | SEQUOYAH | 14,775 | 8,865 | 5,910 | | 2,955 R | 60.0% | 40.0% | 60.0% | 40.0% |
| 43,182 | STEPHENS | 19,161 | 13,646 | 5,515 | | 8,131 R | 71.2% | 28.8% | 71.2% | 28.8% |
| 20,107 | TEXAS | 6,466 | 5,450 | 1,016 | | 4,434 R | 84.3% | 15.7% | 84.3% | 15.7% |
| 9,287 | TILLMAN | 3,448 | 2,273 | 1,175 | | 1,098 R | 65.9% | 34.1% | 65.9% | 34.1% |
| 563,299 | TULSA | 253,672 | 163,452 | 90,220 | | 73,232 R | 64.4% | 35.6% | 64.4% | 35.6% |
| 57,491 | WAGONER | 28,238 | 19,081 | 9,157 | | 9,924 R | 67.6% | 32.4% | 67.6% | 32.4% |
| 48,996 | WASHINGTON | 23,413 | 16,551 | 6,862 | | 9,689 R | 70.7% | 29.3% | 70.7% | 29.3% |
| 11,508 | WASHITA | 5,045 | 3,705 | 1,340 | | 2,365 R | 73.4% | 26.6% | 73.4% | 26.6% |
| 9,089 | WOODS | 4,098 | 3,166 | 932 | | 2,234 R | 77.3% | 22.7% | 77.3% | 22.7% |
| 18,486 | WOODWARD | 7,651 | 6,193 | 1,458 | | 4,735 R | 80.9% | 19.1% | 80.9% | 19.1% |
| 3,450,654 | TOTAL | 1,463,758 | 959,792 | 503,966 | | 455,826 R | 65.6% | 34.4% | 65.6% | 34.4% |

# OKLAHOMA

## SENATOR 2004

| 2000 Census Population | County | Total Vote | Republican | Democratic | Other | Rep.-Dem. Plurality | Percentage | | | |
|---|---|---|---|---|---|---|---|---|---|---|
| | | | | | | | Total Vote | | Major Vote | |
| | | | | | | | Rep. | Dem. | Rep. | Dem. |
| 21,038 | ADAIR | 7,493 | 3,160 | 4,049 | 284 | 889 D | 42.2% | 54.0% | 43.8% | 56.2% |
| 6,105 | ALFALFA | 2,623 | 1,522 | 852 | 249 | 670 R | 58.0% | 32.5% | 64.1% | 35.9% |
| 13,879 | ATOKA | 5,036 | 2,273 | 2,491 | 272 | 218 D | 45.1% | 49.5% | 47.7% | 52.3% |
| 5,857 | BEAVER | 2,531 | 1,841 | 579 | 111 | 1,262 R | 72.7% | 22.9% | 76.1% | 23.9% |
| 19,799 | BECKHAM | 7,330 | 3,645 | 3,129 | 556 | 516 R | 49.7% | 42.7% | 53.8% | 46.2% |
| 11,976 | BLAINE | 4,357 | 2,223 | 1,688 | 446 | 535 R | 51.0% | 38.7% | 56.8% | 43.2% |
| 36,534 | BRYAN | 14,093 | 6,026 | 7,250 | 817 | 1,224 D | 42.8% | 51.4% | 45.4% | 54.6% |
| 30,150 | CADDO | 10,264 | 4,205 | 5,156 | 903 | 951 D | 41.0% | 50.2% | 44.9% | 55.1% |
| 87,697 | CANADIAN | 42,422 | 27,482 | 11,738 | 3,202 | 15,744 R | 64.8% | 27.7% | 70.1% | 29.9% |
| 45,621 | CARTER | 18,347 | 8,682 | 7,943 | 1,722 | 739 R | 47.3% | 43.3% | 52.2% | 47.8% |
| 42,521 | CHEROKEE | 18,167 | 7,140 | 10,414 | 613 | 3,274 D | 39.3% | 57.3% | 40.7% | 59.3% |
| 15,342 | CHOCTAW | 5,731 | 2,044 | 3,438 | 249 | 1,394 D | 35.7% | 60.0% | 37.3% | 62.7% |
| 3,148 | CIMARRON | 1,395 | 959 | 375 | 61 | 584 R | 68.7% | 26.9% | 71.9% | 28.1% |
| 208,016 | CLEVELAND | 98,393 | 54,431 | 36,248 | 7,714 | 18,183 R | 55.3% | 36.8% | 60.0% | 40.0% |
| 6,031 | COAL | 2,575 | 945 | 1,488 | 142 | 543 D | 36.7% | 57.8% | 38.8% | 61.2% |
| 114,996 | COMANCHE | 32,617 | 15,393 | 14,762 | 2,462 | 631 R | 47.2% | 45.3% | 51.0% | 49.0% |
| 6,614 | COTTON | 2,591 | 1,085 | 1,307 | 199 | 222 D | 41.9% | 50.4% | 45.4% | 54.6% |
| 14,950 | CRAIG | 6,386 | 2,791 | 3,351 | 244 | 560 D | 43.7% | 52.5% | 45.4% | 54.6% |
| 67,367 | CREEK | 28,576 | 15,205 | 12,046 | 1,325 | 3,159 R | 53.2% | 42.2% | 55.8% | 44.2% |
| 26,142 | CUSTER | 10,507 | 5,860 | 3,793 | 854 | 2,067 R | 55.8% | 36.1% | 60.7% | 39.3% |
| 37,077 | DELAWARE | 15,471 | 7,324 | 7,584 | 563 | 260 D | 47.3% | 49.0% | 49.1% | 50.9% |
| 4,743 | DEWEY | 2,218 | 1,209 | 805 | 204 | 404 R | 54.5% | 36.3% | 60.0% | 40.0% |
| 4,075 | ELLIS | 2,062 | 1,178 | 678 | 206 | 500 R | 57.1% | 32.9% | 63.5% | 36.5% |
| 57,813 | GARFIELD | 23,023 | 13,469 | 7,122 | 2,432 | 6,347 R | 58.5% | 30.9% | 65.4% | 34.6% |
| 27,210 | GARVIN | 11,157 | 5,408 | 4,674 | 1,075 | 734 R | 48.5% | 41.9% | 53.6% | 46.4% |
| 45,516 | GRADY | 19,863 | 10,820 | 7,115 | 1,928 | 3,705 R | 54.5% | 35.8% | 60.3% | 39.7% |
| 5,144 | GRANT | 2,501 | 1,290 | 922 | 289 | 368 R | 51.6% | 36.9% | 58.3% | 41.7% |
| 6,061 | GREER | 2,200 | 1,011 | 1,058 | 131 | 47 D | 46.0% | 48.1% | 48.9% | 51.1% |
| 3,283 | HARMON | 1,165 | 495 | 587 | 83 | 92 D | 42.5% | 50.4% | 45.7% | 54.3% |
| 3,562 | HARPER | 1,627 | 955 | 526 | 146 | 429 R | 58.7% | 32.3% | 64.5% | 35.5% |

# OKLAHOMA

## SENATOR 2004

| 2000 Census Population | County | Total Vote | Republican | Democratic | Other | Rep.-Dem. Plurality | | Percentage | | | |
|---|---|---|---|---|---|---|---|---|---|---|---|
| | | | | | | | | Total Vote | | Major Vote | |
| | | | | | | | | Rep. | Dem. | Rep. | Dem. |
| 11,792 | HASKELL | 5,293 | 2,118 | 3,045 | 130 | 927 | D | 40.0% | 57.5% | 41.0% | 59.0% |
| 14,154 | HUGHES | 5,293 | 2,132 | 2,811 | 350 | 679 | D | 40.3% | 53.1% | 43.1% | 56.9% |
| 28,439 | JACKSON | 9,115 | 5,005 | 3,471 | 639 | 1,534 | R | 54.9% | 38.1% | 59.0% | 41.0% |
| 6,818 | JEFFERSON | 2,551 | 997 | 1,360 | 194 | 363 | D | 39.1% | 53.3% | 42.3% | 57.7% |
| 10,513 | JOHNSTON | 4,279 | 1,616 | 2,384 | 279 | 768 | D | 37.8% | 55.7% | 40.4% | 59.6% |
| 48,080 | KAY | 19,891 | 11,141 | 7,136 | 1,614 | 4,005 | R | 56.0% | 35.9% | 61.0% | 39.0% |
| 13,926 | KINGFISHER | 6,570 | 4,410 | 1,568 | 592 | 2,842 | R | 67.1% | 23.9% | 73.8% | 26.2% |
| 10,227 | KIOWA | 3,968 | 1,593 | 2,066 | 309 | 473 | D | 40.1% | 52.1% | 43.5% | 56.5% |
| 10,692 | LATIMER | 4,429 | 1,731 | 2,493 | 205 | 762 | D | 39.1% | 56.3% | 41.0% | 59.0% |
| 48,109 | LE FLORE | 17,139 | 7,759 | 8,813 | 567 | 1,054 | D | 45.3% | 51.4% | 46.8% | 53.2% |
| 32,080 | LINCOLN | 14,048 | 7,690 | 5,025 | 1,333 | 2,665 | R | 54.7% | 35.8% | 60.5% | 39.5% |
| 33,924 | LOGAN | 16,152 | 9,432 | 5,496 | 1,224 | 3,936 | R | 58.4% | 34.0% | 63.2% | 36.8% |
| 8,831 | LOVE | 3,759 | 1,519 | 1,898 | 342 | 379 | D | 40.4% | 50.5% | 44.5% | 55.5% |
| 27,740 | MCCLAIN | 13,594 | 7,845 | 4,552 | 1,197 | 3,293 | R | 57.7% | 33.5% | 63.3% | 36.7% |
| 34,402 | MCCURTAIN | 10,958 | 5,390 | 5,211 | 357 | 179 | R | 49.2% | 47.6% | 50.8% | 49.2% |
| 19,456 | MCINTOSH | 9,148 | 3,685 | 5,259 | 204 | 1,574 | D | 40.3% | 57.5% | 41.2% | 58.8% |
| 7,545 | MAJOR | 3,610 | 2,333 | 961 | 316 | 1,372 | R | 64.6% | 26.6% | 70.8% | 29.2% |
| 13,184 | MARSHALL | 5,354 | 2,364 | 2,554 | 436 | 190 | D | 44.2% | 47.7% | 48.1% | 51.9% |
| 38,369 | MAYES | 16,795 | 7,343 | 8,893 | 559 | 1,550 | D | 43.7% | 53.0% | 45.2% | 54.8% |
| 12,623 | MURRAY | 5,705 | 2,385 | 2,793 | 527 | 408 | D | 41.8% | 49.0% | 46.1% | 53.9% |
| 69,451 | MUSKOGEE | 27,654 | 13,093 | 13,906 | 655 | 813 | D | 47.3% | 50.3% | 48.5% | 51.5% |
| 11,411 | NOBLE | 5,258 | 2,955 | 1,700 | 603 | 1,255 | R | 56.2% | 32.3% | 63.5% | 36.5% |
| 10,569 | NOWATA | 4,430 | 2,080 | 2,164 | 186 | 84 | D | 47.0% | 48.8% | 49.0% | 51.0% |
| 11,814 | OKFUSKEE | 4,241 | 1,859 | 2,193 | 189 | 334 | D | 43.8% | 51.7% | 45.9% | 54.1% |
| 660,448 | OKLAHOMA | 268,205 | 147,793 | 102,171 | 18,241 | 45,622 | R | 55.1% | 38.1% | 59.1% | 40.9% |
| 39,685 | OKMULGEE | 15,628 | 6,360 | 8,775 | 493 | 2,415 | D | 40.7% | 56.1% | 42.0% | 58.0% |
| 44,437 | OSAGE | 19,362 | 8,746 | 9,703 | 913 | 957 | D | 45.2% | 50.1% | 47.4% | 52.6% |
| 33,194 | OTTAWA | 12,383 | 5,234 | 6,742 | 407 | 1,508 | D | 42.3% | 54.4% | 43.7% | 56.3% |
| 16,612 | PAWNEE | 6,919 | 3,416 | 3,116 | 387 | 300 | R | 49.4% | 45.0% | 52.3% | 47.7% |
| 68,190 | PAYNE | 29,374 | 16,047 | 11,229 | 2,098 | 4,818 | R | 54.6% | 38.2% | 58.8% | 41.2% |
| 43,953 | PITTSBURG | 18,468 | 7,684 | 9,818 | 966 | 2,134 | D | 41.6% | 53.2% | 43.9% | 56.1% |
| 35,143 | PONTOTOC | 14,625 | 7,042 | 6,525 | 1,058 | 517 | R | 48.2% | 44.6% | 51.9% | 48.1% |
| 65,521 | POTTAWATOMIE | 25,531 | 13,300 | 9,948 | 2,283 | 3,352 | R | 52.1% | 39.0% | 57.2% | 42.8% |
| 11,667 | PUSHMATAHA | 4,731 | 1,778 | 2,699 | 254 | 921 | D | 37.6% | 57.0% | 39.7% | 60.3% |
| 3,436 | ROGER MILLS | 1,750 | 1,029 | 594 | 127 | 435 | R | 58.8% | 33.9% | 63.4% | 36.6% |
| 70,641 | ROGERS | 36,655 | 19,645 | 15,740 | 1,270 | 3,905 | R | 53.6% | 42.9% | 55.5% | 44.5% |
| 24,894 | SEMINOLE | 9,161 | 4,128 | 4,304 | 729 | 176 | D | 45.1% | 47.0% | 49.0% | 51.0% |
| 38,972 | SEQUOYAH | 14,581 | 6,468 | 7,700 | 413 | 1,232 | D | 44.4% | 52.8% | 45.7% | 54.3% |
| 43,182 | STEPHENS | 18,897 | 10,138 | 7,116 | 1,643 | 3,022 | R | 53.6% | 37.7% | 58.8% | 41.2% |
| 20,107 | TEXAS | 6,360 | 4,576 | 1,554 | 230 | 3,022 | R | 71.9% | 24.4% | 74.6% | 25.4% |
| 9,287 | TILLMAN | 3,368 | 1,288 | 1,874 | 206 | 586 | D | 38.2% | 55.6% | 40.7% | 59.3% |
| 563,299 | TULSA | 251,012 | 141,020 | 101,128 | 8,864 | 39,892 | R | 56.2% | 40.3% | 58.2% | 41.8% |
| 57,491 | WAGONER | 28,060 | 15,963 | 11,162 | 935 | 4,801 | R | 56.9% | 39.8% | 58.8% | 41.2% |
| 48,996 | WASHINGTON | 23,214 | 13,951 | 8,259 | 1,004 | 5,692 | R | 60.1% | 35.6% | 62.8% | 37.2% |
| 11,508 | WASHITA | 5,001 | 2,484 | 2,076 | 441 | 408 | R | 49.7% | 41.5% | 54.5% | 45.5% |
| 9,089 | WOODS | 4,031 | 2,208 | 1,369 | 454 | 839 | R | 54.8% | 34.0% | 61.7% | 38.3% |
| 18,486 | WOODWARD | 7,575 | 4,589 | 2,228 | 758 | 2,361 | R | 60.6% | 29.4% | 67.3% | 32.7% |
| 3,450,654 | TOTAL | 1,446,846 | 763,433 | 596,750 | 86,663 | 166,683 | R | 52.8% | 41.2% | 56.1% | 43.9% |

# OKLAHOMA

## HOUSE OF REPRESENTATIVES

| CD | Year | Total Vote | Republican Vote | Republican Candidate | Democratic Vote | Democratic Candidate | Other Vote | Rep.-Dem. Plurality | Percentage Total Vote Rep. | Dem. | Major Vote Rep. | Dem. |
|---|---|---|---|---|---|---|---|---|---|---|---|---|
| 1 | 2004 | 310,934 | 187,145 | Sullivan, John* | 116,731 | Dodd, Doug | 7,058 | 70,414 R | 60.2% | 37.5% | 61.6% | 38.4% |
| 1 | 2002 | 214,955 | 119,566 | Sullivan, John* | 90,649 | Dodd, Doug | 4,740 | 28,917 R | 55.6% | 42.2% | 56.9% | 43.1% |
| 2 | 2004 | 272,542 | 92,963 | Smalley, Wayland | 179,579 | Boren, Dan | | 86,616 D | 34.1% | 65.9% | 34.1% | 65.9% |
| 2 | 2002 | 197,982 | 51,234 | Pharaoh, Kent | 146,748 | Carson, Brad* | | 95,514 D | 25.9% | 74.1% | 25.9% | 74.1% |
| 3 | 2004 | 262,131 | 215,510 | Lucas, Frank D.* | | | 46,621 | 215,510 R | 82.2% | | 100.0% | |
| 3 | 2002 | 196,090 | 148,206 | Lucas, Frank D.* | | | 47,884 | 148,206 R | 75.6% | | 100.0% | |
| 4 | 2004 | 255,854 | 198,985 | Cole, Tom* | | | 56,869 | 198,985 R | 77.8% | | 100.0% | |
| 4 | 2002 | 197,774 | 106,452 | Cole, Tom | 91,322 | Roberts, Darryl | | 15,130 R | 53.8% | 46.2% | 53.8% | 46.2% |
| 5 | 2004 | 273,149 | 180,430 | Istook, Ernest* | 92,719 | Smith, Bert | | 87,711 R | 66.1% | 33.9% | 66.1% | 33.9% |
| 5 | 2002 | 195,051 | 121,374 | Istook, Ernest* | 63,208 | Barlow, Lou | 10,469 | 58,166 R | 62.2% | 32.4% | 65.8% | 34.2% |
| Total | 2004 | 1,374,610 | 875,033 | | 389,029 | | 110,548 | 486,004 R | 63.7% | 28.3% | 69.2% | 30.8% |
| Total | 2002 | 1,001,852 | 546,832 | | 391,927 | | 63,093 | 154,905 R | 54.6% | 39.1% | 58.3% | 41.7% |

An asterisk (*) denotes incumbent.

# OKLAHOMA

## GENERAL AND PRIMARY ELECTIONS

## 2004 GENERAL ELECTIONS

**President**

**Senator**    Other vote was 86,663 Independent (Sheila Bilyeu).

**House**    Other vote was:

CD 1    7,058 Independent (John Krymski).
CD 2
CD 3    46,621 Independent (Gregory M. Wilson).
CD 4    56,869 Independent (Charlene K. Bradshaw).
CD 5

## 2004 PRIMARY ELECTIONS

| **Primary** | February 3, 2004 (President) | **Registration** | Republican | 742,758 |
|---|---|---|---|---|
| | July 27, 2004 (Congress) | (as of June 30, 2004) | Democratic | 1,048,538 |
| | | | Libertarian | 545 |
| | | | Reform | 27 |
| | | | Independent | 204,696 |
| | | | TOTAL | 1,996,564 |

**Primary Type**    Closed—Only registered Democrats and Republicans could vote in their party's primary.

# OKLAHOMA

## GENERAL AND PRIMARY ELECTIONS

Note: An asterisk (*) denotes incumbent. The names of unopposed candidates did not appear on the primary ballot; therefore, no votes were cast for these candidates.

| | REPUBLICAN PRIMARIES | | | DEMOCRATIC PRIMARIES | | |
|---|---|---|---|---|---|---|
| **President** | George W. Bush* | 59,577 | 90.0% | Wesley Clark | 90,526 | 29.9% |
| | Bill Wyatt | 6,621 | 10.0% | John Edwards | 89,310 | 29.5% |
| | | | | John Kerry | 81,073 | 26.8% |
| | | | | Joseph I. Lieberman | 19,680 | 6.5% |
| | | | | Howard Dean | 12,734 | 4.2% |
| | | | | Al Sharpton | 3,939 | 1.3% |
| | | | | Dennis J. Kucinich | 2,544 | 0.8% |
| | | | | Richard A. Gephardt | 1,890 | 0.6% |
| | | | | Lyndon H. LaRouche Jr. | 689 | 0.2% |
| | TOTAL | 66,198 | | TOTAL | 302,385 | |
| **Senator** | Tom Coburn | 145,974 | 61.2% | Brad Carson | 280,026 | 79.4% |
| | Kirk Humphreys | 59,877 | 25.1% | Carroll Fisher | 28,385 | 8.0% |
| | Bob Anthony | 29,596 | 12.4% | Jim Rogers | 20,179 | 5.7% |
| | Jay Richard Hunt | 2,944 | 1.2% | Monte E. Johnson | 17,274 | 4.9% |
| | | | | W.B.G. Woodson | 6,932 | 2.0% |
| | TOTAL | 238,391 | | TOTAL | 352,796 | |
| **Congressional District 1** | John Sullivan* | 44,082 | 70.4% | Doug Dodd | Unopposed | |
| | Bill Wortman | 15,778 | 25.2% | | | |
| | Evelyn L. Rogers | 2,779 | 4.4% | | | |
| | TOTAL | 62,639 | | | | |
| **Congressional District 2** | Wayland Smalley | 11,851 | 51.9% | Dan Boren | 73,421 | 57.7% |
| | Damon Harris | 6,664 | 29.2% | Kalyn Free | 46,061 | 36.2% |
| | Raymond Wickson | 4,321 | 18.9% | Bryan J. Bigby | 5,328 | 4.2% |
| | | | | Vern L. Cassity | 2,497 | 2.0% |
| | TOTAL | 22,836 | | TOTAL | 127,307 | |
| **Congressional District 3** | Frank D. Lucas* | Unopposed | | No Democratic candidate | | |
| **Congressional District 4** | Tom Cole* | Unopposed | | No Democratic candidate | | 48.3% |
| **Congressional District 5** | Ernest Istook* | Unopposed | | Bert Smith | 26,903 | 61.4% |
| | | | | Harley Venters | 16,920 | 38.6% |
| | | | | TOTAL | 43,823 | |

# OREGON

## GOVERNOR
Theodore R. Kulongoski (D). Elected 2002 to a four-year term.

## SENATORS (1 Democrat, 1 Republican)
Gordon H. Smith (R). Reelected 2002 to a six-year term. Previously elected 1996.

Ron Wyden (D). Reelected 2004 to a six-year term. Previously elected 1998 and in a special election January 30, 1996, to serve the remaining three years of the term vacated when Senator Robert W. Packwood (R) resigned.

## REPRESENTATIVES (4 Democrats, 1 Republican)
1. David Wu (D)
2. Greg Walden (R)
3. Earl Blumenauer (D)
4. Peter A. DeFazio (D)
5. Darlene Hooley (D)

## POSTWAR VOTE FOR PRESIDENT

| Year | Total Vote | Republican Vote | Republican Candidate | Democratic Vote | Democratic Candidate | Other Vote | Plurality | Percentage Total Vote Rep. | Percentage Total Vote Dem. | Percentage Major Vote Rep. | Percentage Major Vote Dem. |
|------|-----------|----------------|---------------------|-----------------|---------------------|-----------|-----------|------|------|------|------|
| 2004 | 1,836,782 | 866,831 | Bush, George W. | 943,163 | Kerry, John | 26,788 | 76,332 D | 47.2% | 51.3% | 47.9% | 52.1% |
| 2000** | 1,533,968 | 713,577 | Bush, George W. | 720,342 | Gore, Al | 100,049 | 6,765 D | 46.5% | 47.0% | 49.8% | 50.2% |
| 1996** | 1,377,760 | 538,152 | Dole, Bob | 649,641 | Clinton, Bill | 189,967 | 111,489 D | 39.1% | 47.2% | 45.3% | 54.7% |
| 1992** | 1,462,643 | 475,757 | Bush, George | 621,314 | Clinton, Bill | 365,572 | 145,557 D | 32.5% | 42.5% | 43.4% | 56.6% |
| 1988 | 1,201,694 | 560,126 | Bush, George | 616,206 | Dukakis, Michael S. | 25,362 | 56,080 D | 46.6% | 51.3% | 47.6% | 52.4% |
| 1984 | 1,226,527 | 685,700 | Reagan, Ronald | 536,479 | Mondale, Walter F. | 4,348 | 149,221 R | 55.9% | 43.7% | 56.1% | 43.9% |
| 1980** | 1,181,516 | 571,044 | Reagan, Ronald | 456,890 | Carter, Jimmy | 153,582 | 114,154 R | 48.3% | 38.7% | 55.6% | 44.4% |
| 1976 | 1,029,876 | 492,120 | Ford, Gerald R. | 490,407 | Carter, Jimmy | 47,349 | 1,713 R | 47.8% | 47.6% | 50.1% | 49.9% |
| 1972 | 927,946 | 486,686 | Nixon, Richard M. | 392,760 | McGovern, George S. | 48,500 | 93,926 R | 52.4% | 42.3% | 55.3% | 44.7% |
| 1968** | 819,622 | 408,433 | Nixon, Richard M. | 358,866 | Humphrey, Hubert H. | 52,323 | 49,567 R | 49.8% | 43.8% | 53.2% | 46.8% |
| 1964 | 786,305 | 282,779 | Goldwater, Barry M. | 501,017 | Johnson, Lyndon B. | 2,509 | 218,238 D | 36.0% | 63.7% | 36.1% | 63.9% |
| 1960 | 776,421 | 408,060 | Nixon, Richard M. | 367,402 | Kennedy, John F. | 959 | 40,658 R | 52.6% | 47.3% | 52.6% | 47.4% |
| 1956 | 736,132 | 406,393 | Eisenhower, Dwight D. | 329,204 | Stevenson, Adlai E. | 535 | 77,189 R | 55.2% | 44.7% | 55.2% | 44.8% |
| 1952 | 695,059 | 420,815 | Eisenhower, Dwight D. | 270,579 | Stevenson, Adlai E. | 3,665 | 150,236 R | 60.5% | 38.9% | 60.9% | 39.1% |
| 1948 | 524,080 | 260,904 | Dewey, Thomas E. | 243,147 | Truman, Harry S. | 20,029 | 17,757 R | 49.8% | 46.4% | 51.8% | 48.2% |

In past elections, the other vote included: 2000 - 77,357 Green (Ralph Nader); 1996 - 121,221 Reform (Ross Perot); 1992 - 354,091 Independent (Perot); 1980 - 112,389 Independent (John Anderson); 1968 - 49,683 American Independent (George Wallace).

# OREGON

## POSTWAR VOTE FOR GOVERNOR

| Year | Total Vote | Republican | | Democratic | | Other Vote | Rep.-Dem. Plurality | Percentage | | | |
|------|-----------|------|-----------|------|-----------|------|-----------|-----------|-----------|-----------|-----------|
| | | | | | | | | Total Vote | | Major Vote | |
| | | Vote | Candidate | Vote | Candidate | | | Rep. | Dem. | Rep. | Dem. |
| 2002 | 1,260,497 | 581,785 | Mannix, Kevin L. | 618,004 | Kulongoski, Theodore R. | 60,708 | 36,219 D | 46.2% | 49.0% | 48.5% | 51.5% |
| 1998 | 1,113,098 | 334,001 | Sizemore, Bill | 717,061 | Kitzhaber, John | 62,036 | 383,060 D | 30.0% | 64.4% | 31.8% | 68.2% |
| 1994 | 1,221,010 | 517,874 | Smith, Denny | 622,083 | Kitzhaber, John | 81,053 | 104,209 D | 42.4% | 50.9% | 45.4% | 54.6% |
| 1990 | 1,112,847 | 444,646 | Frohnmayer, Dave | 508,749 | Roberts, Barbara | 159,452 | 64,103 D | 40.0% | 45.7% | 46.6% | 53.4% |
| 1986 | 1,059,630 | 506,986 | Paulus, Norma | 549,456 | Goldschmidt, Neil | 3,188 | 42,470 D | 47.8% | 51.9% | 48.0% | 52.0% |
| 1982 | 1,042,009 | 639,841 | Atiyeh, Victor | 374,316 | Kulongoski, Theodore R. | 27,852 | 265,525 R | 61.4% | 35.9% | 63.1% | 36.9% |
| 1978 | 911,143 | 498,452 | Atiyeh, Victor | 409,411 | Straub, Robert W. | 3,280 | 89,041 R | 54.7% | 44.9% | 54.9% | 45.1% |
| 1974 | 770,574 | 324,751 | Atiyeh, Victor | 444,812 | Straub, Robert W. | 1,011 | 120,061 D | 42.1% | 57.7% | 42.2% | 57.8% |
| 1970 | 666,394 | 369,964 | McCall, Tom | 293,892 | Straub, Robert W. | 2,538 | 76,072 R | 55.5% | 44.1% | 55.7% | 44.3% |
| 1966 | 682,862 | 377,346 | McCall, Tom | 305,008 | Straub, Robert W. | 508 | 72,338 R | 55.3% | 44.7% | 55.3% | 44.7% |
| 1962 | 637,407 | 345,497 | Hatfield, Mark | 265,359 | Thornton, Robert Y. | 26,551 | 80,138 R | 54.2% | 41.6% | 56.6% | 43.4% |
| 1958 | 599,994 | 331,900 | Hatfield, Mark | 267,934 | Holmes, Robert D. | 160 | 63,966 R | 55.3% | 44.7% | 55.3% | 44.7% |
| 1956S | 731,279 | 361,840 | Smith, Elmo E. | 369,439 | Holmes, Robert D. | | 7,599 D | 49.5% | 50.5% | 49.5% | 50.5% |
| 1954 | 566,701 | 322,522 | Patterson, Paul | 244,179 | Carson, Joseph K. | | 78,343 R | 56.9% | 43.1% | 56.9% | 43.1% |
| 1950 | 505,910 | 334,160 | McKay, Douglas | 171,750 | Flegel, Austin F. | | 162,410 R | 66.1% | 33.9% | 66.1% | 33.9% |
| 1948S | 509,633 | 271,295 | McKay, Douglas | 226,958 | Wallace, Lew | 11,380 | 44,337 R | 53.2% | 44.5% | 54.4% | 45.6% |
| 1946 | 344,155 | 237,681 | Snell, Earl | 106,474 | Donaugh, Carl C. | | 131,207 R | 69.1% | 30.9% | 69.1% | 30.9% |

The 1956 and 1948 elections were for short terms to fill vacancies.

## POSTWAR VOTE FOR SENATOR

| Year | Total Vote | Republican | | Democratic | | Other Vote | Rep.-Dem. Plurality | Percentage | | | |
|------|-----------|------|-----------|------|-----------|------|-----------|-----------|-----------|-----------|-----------|
| | | | | | | | | Total Vote | | Major Vote | |
| | | Vote | Candidate | Vote | Candidate | | | Rep. | Dem. | Rep. | Dem. |
| 2004 | 1,780,550 | 565,254 | King, Al | 1,128,728 | Wyden, Ron | 86,568 | 563,474 D | 31.7% | 63.4% | 33.4% | 66.6% |
| 2002 | 1,267,221 | 712,287 | Smith, Gordon H. | 501,898 | Bradbury, Bill | 53,036 | 210,389 R | 56.2% | 39.6% | 58.7% | 41.3% |
| 1998 | 1,117,747 | 377,739 | Lim, John | 682,425 | Wyden, Ron | 57,583 | 304,686 D | 33.8% | 61.1% | 35.6% | 64.4% |
| 1996 | 1,360,230 | 677,336 | Smith, Gordon H. | 624,370 | Bruggere, Tom | 58,524 | 52,966 R | 49.8% | 45.9% | 52.0% | 48.0% |
| 1996S | 1,196,608 | 553,519 | Smith, Gordon H. | 571,739 | Wyden, Ron | 71,350 | 18,220 D | 46.3% | 47.8% | 49.2% | 50.8% |
| 1992 | 1,376,033 | 717,455 | Packwood, Robert W. | 639,851 | AuCoin, Les | 18,727 | 77,604 R | 52.1% | 46.5% | 52.9% | 47.1% |
| 1990 | 1,099,255 | 590,095 | Hatfield, Mark | 507,743 | Lonsdale, Harry | 1,417 | 82,352 R | 53.7% | 46.2% | 53.8% | 46.2% |
| 1986 | 1,042,555 | 656,317 | Packwood, Robert W. | 375,735 | Bauman, Rick | 10,503 | 280,582 R | 63.0% | 36.0% | 63.6% | 36.4% |
| 1984 | 1,214,735 | 808,152 | Hatfield, Mark | 406,122 | Hendriksen, Margie | 461 | 402,030 R | 66.5% | 33.4% | 66.6% | 33.4% |
| 1980 | 1,140,494 | 594,290 | Packwood, Robert W. | 501,963 | Kulongoski, Theodore R. | 44,241 | 92,327 R | 52.1% | 44.0% | 54.2% | 45.8% |
| 1978 | 892,518 | 550,165 | Hatfield, Mark | 341,616 | Cook, Vernon | 737 | 208,549 R | 61.6% | 38.3% | 61.7% | 38.3% |
| 1974 | 766,414 | 420,984 | Packwood, Robert W. | 338,591 | Roberts, Betty | 6,839 | 82,393 R | 54.9% | 44.2% | 55.4% | 44.6% |
| 1972 | 920,833 | 494,671 | Hatfield, Mark | 425,036 | Morse, Wayne L. | 1,126 | 69,635 R | 53.7% | 46.2% | 53.8% | 46.2% |
| 1968 | 814,176 | 408,646 | Packwood, Robert W. | 405,353 | Morse, Wayne L. | 177 | 3,293 R | 50.2% | 49.8% | 50.2% | 49.8% |
| 1966 | 685,067 | 354,391 | Hatfield, Mark | 330,374 | Duncan, Robert B. | 302 | 24,017 R | 51.7% | 48.2% | 51.8% | 48.2% |
| 1962 | 636,558 | 291,587 | Unander, Sig | 344,716 | Morse, Wayne L. | 255 | 53,129 D | 45.8% | 54.2% | 45.8% | 54.2% |
| 1960 | 755,875 | 343,009 | Smith, Elmo E. | 412,757 | Neuberger, Maurine | 109 | 69,748 D | 45.4% | 54.6% | 45.4% | 54.6% |
| 1956 | 732,254 | 335,405 | McKay, Douglas | 396,849 | Morse, Wayne L. | | 61,444 D | 45.8% | 54.2% | 45.8% | 54.2% |
| 1954 | 569,088 | 283,313 | Cordon, Guy | 285,775 | Neuberger, Richard L. | | 2,462 D | 49.8% | 50.2% | 49.8% | 50.2% |
| 1950 | 503,455 | 376,510 | Morse, Wayne L. | 116,780 | Latourette, Howard | 10,165 | 259,730 R | 74.8% | 23.2% | 76.3% | 23.7% |
| 1948 | 498,570 | 299,295 | Cordon, Guy | 199,275 | Wilson, Manley J. | | 100,020 R | 60.0% | 40.0% | 60.0% | 40.0% |

One of the 1996 elections was for a short term to fill a vacancy, and was held in January.

# OREGON

Congressional districts first established for elections held in 2002
5 members

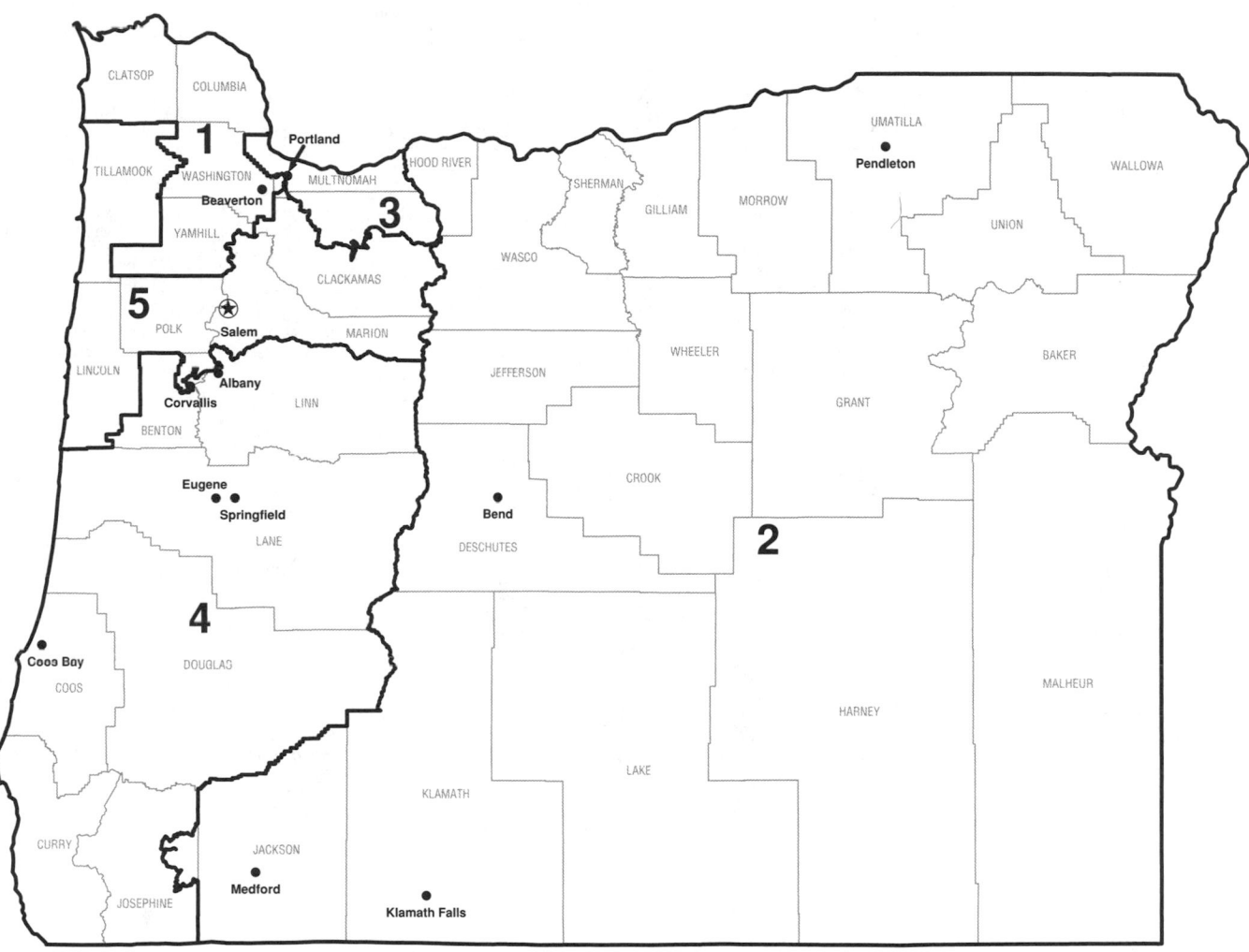

# OREGON

## PRESIDENT 2004

| 2000 Census Population | County | Total Vote | Republican | Democratic | Other | Rep.-Dem. Plurality | Percentage Total Vote Rep. | Dem. | Major Vote Rep. | Dem. |
|---|---|---|---|---|---|---|---|---|---|---|
| 16,741 | BAKER | 9,034 | 6,253 | 2,616 | 165 | 3,637 R | 69.2% | 29.0% | 70.5% | 29.5% |
| 78,153 | BENTON | 45,735 | 18,460 | 26,515 | 760 | 8,055 D | 40.4% | 58.0% | 41.0% | 59.0% |
| 338,391 | CLACKAMAS | 195,000 | 97,691 | 95,129 | 2,180 | 2,562 R | 50.1% | 48.8% | 50.7% | 49.3% |
| 35,630 | CLATSOP | 19,309 | 8,503 | 10,461 | 345 | 1,958 D | 44.0% | 54.2% | 44.8% | 55.2% |
| 43,560 | COLUMBIA | 24,917 | 11,868 | 12,563 | 486 | 695 D | 47.6% | 50.4% | 48.6% | 51.4% |
| 62,779 | COOS | 33,362 | 18,291 | 14,393 | 678 | 3,898 R | 54.8% | 43.1% | 56.0% | 44.0% |
| 19,182 | CROOK | 10,051 | 6,830 | 3,024 | 197 | 3,806 R | 68.0% | 30.1% | 69.3% | 30.7% |
| 21,137 | CURRY | 12,799 | 7,332 | 5,220 | 247 | 2,112 R | 57.3% | 40.8% | 58.4% | 41.6% |
| 115,367 | DESCHUTES | 74,048 | 41,757 | 31,179 | 1,112 | 10,578 R | 56.4% | 42.1% | 57.3% | 42.7% |
| 100,399 | DOUGLAS | 54,984 | 35,956 | 18,089 | 939 | 17,867 R | 65.4% | 32.9% | 66.5% | 33.5% |
| 1,915 | GILLIAM | 1,138 | 755 | 370 | 13 | 385 R | 66.3% | 32.5% | 67.1% | 32.9% |
| 7,935 | GRANT | 4,061 | 3,204 | 780 | 77 | 2,424 R | 78.9% | 19.2% | 80.4% | 19.6% |
| 7,609 | HARNEY | 3,702 | 2,815 | 839 | 48 | 1,976 R | 76.0% | 22.7% | 77.0% | 23.0% |
| 20,411 | HOOD RIVER | 9,859 | 4,124 | 5,587 | 148 | 1,463 D | 41.8% | 56.7% | 42.5% | 57.5% |
| 181,269 | JACKSON | 102,189 | 56,519 | 44,366 | 1,304 | 12,153 R | 55.3% | 43.4% | 56.0% | 44.0% |
| 19,009 | JEFFERSON | 8,115 | 4,762 | 3,243 | 110 | 1,519 R | 58.7% | 40.0% | 59.5% | 40.5% |
| 75,726 | JOSEPHINE | 42,275 | 26,241 | 15,214 | 820 | 11,027 R | 62.1% | 36.0% | 63.3% | 36.7% |
| 63,775 | KLAMATH | 31,515 | 22,733 | 8,264 | 518 | 14,469 R | 72.1% | 26.2% | 73.3% | 26.7% |
| 7,422 | LAKE | 3,905 | 3,039 | 802 | 64 | 2,237 R | 77.8% | 20.5% | 79.1% | 20.9% |
| 322,959 | LANE | 185,872 | 75,007 | 107,769 | 3,096 | 32,762 D | 40.4% | 58.0% | 41.0% | 59.0% |
| 44,479 | LINCOLN | 24,325 | 10,160 | 13,753 | 412 | 3,593 D | 41.8% | 56.5% | 42.5% | 57.5% |
| 103,069 | LINN | 52,041 | 31,260 | 19,940 | 841 | 11,320 R | 60.1% | 38.3% | 61.1% | 38.9% |
| 31,615 | MALHEUR | 10,846 | 8,123 | 2,577 | 146 | 5,546 R | 74.9% | 23.8% | 75.9% | 24.1% |
| 284,834 | MARION | 129,619 | 69,900 | 57,671 | 2,048 | 12,229 R | 53.9% | 44.5% | 54.8% | 45.2% |
| 10,995 | MORROW | 4,149 | 2,732 | 1,361 | 56 | 1,371 R | 65.8% | 32.8% | 66.7% | 33.3% |
| 660,486 | MULTNOMAH | 362,694 | 98,439 | 259,585 | 4,670 | 161,146 D | 27.1% | 71.6% | 27.5% | 72.5% |
| 62,380 | POLK | 35,489 | 19,508 | 15,484 | 497 | 4,024 R | 55.0% | 43.6% | 55.7% | 44.3% |
| 1,934 | SHERMAN | 1,104 | 694 | 390 | 20 | 304 R | 62.9% | 35.3% | 64.0% | 36.0% |
| 24,262 | TILLAMOOK | 13,951 | 7,003 | 6,750 | 198 | 253 R | 50.2% | 48.4% | 50.9% | 49.1% |
| 70,548 | UMATILLA | 26,322 | 17,068 | 8,884 | 370 | 8,184 R | 64.8% | 33.8% | 65.8% | 34.2% |
| 24,530 | UNION | 13,519 | 8,879 | 4,428 | 212 | 4,451 R | 65.7% | 32.8% | 66.7% | 33.3% |
| 7,226 | WALLOWA | 4,521 | 3,132 | 1,269 | 120 | 1,863 R | 69.3% | 28.1% | 71.2% | 28.8% |
| 23,791 | WASCO | 12,002 | 6,119 | 5,691 | 192 | 428 R | 51.0% | 47.4% | 51.8% | 48.2% |
| 445,342 | WASHINGTON | 231,308 | 107,223 | 121,140 | 2,945 | 13,917 D | 46.4% | 52.4% | 47.0% | 53.0% |
| 1,547 | WHEELER | 880 | 612 | 245 | 23 | 367 R | 69.5% | 27.8% | 71.4% | 28.6% |
| 84,992 | YAMHILL | 42,142 | 23,839 | 17,572 | 731 | 6,267 R | 56.6% | 41.7% | 57.6% | 42.4% |
| 3,421,399 | TOTAL | 1,836,782 | 866,831 | 943,163 | 26,788 | 76,332 D | 47.2% | 51.3% | 47.9% | 52.1% |

# OREGON

## SENATOR 2004

| 2000 Census Population | County | Total Vote | Republican | Democratic | Other | Rep.-Dem. Plurality | | Percentage | | | |
|---|---|---|---|---|---|---|---|---|---|---|---|
| | | | | | | | | Total Vote | | Major Vote | |
| | | | | | | | | Rep. | Dem. | Rep. | Dem. |
| 16,741 | BAKER | 8,813 | 4,077 | 4,391 | 345 | 314 | D | 46.3% | 49.8% | 48.1% | 51.9% |
| 78,153 | BENTON | 44,301 | 13,635 | 28,090 | 2,576 | 14,455 | D | 30.8% | 63.4% | 32.7% | 67.3% |
| 338,391 | CLACKAMAS | 188,024 | 63,929 | 117,113 | 6,982 | 53,184 | D | 34.0% | 62.3% | 35.3% | 64.7% |
| 35,630 | CLATSOP | 18,328 | 5,167 | 12,076 | 1,085 | 6,909 | D | 28.2% | 65.9% | 30.0% | 70.0% |
| 43,560 | COLUMBIA | 24,285 | 7,422 | 15,504 | 1,359 | 8,082 | D | 30.6% | 63.8% | 32.4% | 67.6% |
| 62,779 | COOS | 32,636 | 12,930 | 18,148 | 1,558 | 5,218 | D | 39.6% | 55.6% | 41.6% | 58.4% |
| 19,182 | CROOK | 9,787 | 3,816 | 5,623 | 348 | 1,807 | D | 39.0% | 57.5% | 40.4% | 59.6% |
| 21,137 | CURRY | 12,490 | 5,000 | 6,868 | 622 | 1,868 | D | 40.0% | 55.0% | 42.1% | 57.9% |
| 115,367 | DESCHUTES | 71,836 | 24,842 | 43,301 | 3,693 | 18,459 | D | 34.6% | 60.3% | 36.5% | 63.5% |
| 100,399 | DOUGLAS | 53,237 | 24,352 | 26,396 | 2,489 | 2,044 | D | 45.7% | 49.6% | 48.0% | 52.0% |
| 1,915 | GILLIAM | 1,118 | 358 | 726 | 34 | 368 | D | 32.0% | 64.9% | 33.0% | 67.0% |
| 7,935 | GRANT | 3,901 | 1,912 | 1,828 | 161 | 84 | R | 49.0% | 46.9% | 51.1% | 48.9% |
| 7,609 | HARNEY | 3,616 | 1,860 | 1,647 | 109 | 213 | R | 51.4% | 45.5% | 53.0% | 47.0% |
| 20,411 | HOOD RIVER | 9,559 | 2,718 | 6,361 | 480 | 3,643 | D | 28.4% | 66.5% | 29.9% | 70.1% |
| 181,269 | JACKSON | 99,428 | 35,130 | 60,094 | 4,204 | 24,964 | D | 35.3% | 60.4% | 36.9% | 63.1% |
| 19,009 | JEFFERSON | 7,961 | 2,548 | 5,118 | 295 | 2,570 | D | 32.0% | 64.3% | 33.2% | 66.8% |
| 75,726 | JOSEPHINE | 41,213 | 17,360 | 21,772 | 2,081 | 4,412 | D | 42.1% | 52.8% | 44.4% | 55.6% |
| 63,775 | KLAMATH | 30,915 | 13,925 | 15,950 | 1,040 | 2,025 | D | 45.0% | 51.6% | 46.6% | 53.4% |
| 7,422 | LAKE | 3,829 | 1,786 | 1,922 | 121 | 136 | D | 46.6% | 50.2% | 48.2% | 51.8% |
| 322,959 | LANE | 180,299 | 53,551 | 116,500 | 10,248 | 62,949 | D | 29.7% | 64.6% | 31.5% | 68.5% |
| 44,479 | LINCOLN | 23,791 | 6,793 | 15,686 | 1,312 | 8,893 | D | 28.6% | 65.9% | 30.2% | 69.8% |
| 103,069 | LINN | 50,468 | 21,355 | 26,906 | 2,207 | 5,551 | D | 42.3% | 53.3% | 44.2% | 55.8% |
| 31,615 | MALHEUR | 10,556 | 5,720 | 4,422 | 414 | 1,298 | R | 54.2% | 41.9% | 56.4% | 43.6% |
| 284,834 | MARION | 125,827 | 47,363 | 73,228 | 5,236 | 25,865 | D | 37.6% | 58.2% | 39.3% | 60.7% |
| 10,995 | MORROW | 4,056 | 1,577 | 2,328 | 151 | 751 | D | 38.9% | 57.4% | 40.4% | 59.6% |
| 660,486 | MULTNOMAH | 352,447 | 60,907 | 269,834 | 21,706 | 208,927 | D | 17.3% | 76.6% | 18.4% | 81.6% |
| 62,380 | POLK | 34,377 | 13,503 | 19,474 | 1,400 | 5,971 | D | 39.3% | 56.6% | 40.9% | 59.1% |
| 1,934 | SHERMAN | 1,079 | 366 | 685 | 28 | 319 | D | 33.9% | 63.5% | 34.8% | 65.2% |
| 24,262 | TILLAMOOK | 13,530 | 4,398 | 8,526 | 606 | 4,128 | D | 32.5% | 63.0% | 34.0% | 66.0% |
| 70,548 | UMATILLA | 25,379 | 9,735 | 14,716 | 928 | 4,981 | D | 38.4% | 58.0% | 39.8% | 60.2% |
| 24,530 | UNION | 13,115 | 5,077 | 7,548 | 490 | 2,471 | D | 38.7% | 57.6% | 40.2% | 59.8% |
| 7,226 | WALLOWA | 4,375 | 1,762 | 2,439 | 174 | 677 | D | 40.3% | 55.7% | 41.9% | 58.1% |
| 23,791 | WASCO | 11,716 | 3,539 | 7,683 | 494 | 4,144 | D | 30.2% | 65.6% | 31.5% | 68.5% |
| 445,342 | WASHINGTON | 222,785 | 70,582 | 142,569 | 9,634 | 71,987 | D | 31.7% | 64.0% | 33.1% | 66.9% |
| 1,547 | WHEELER | 858 | 316 | 494 | 48 | 178 | D | 36.8% | 57.6% | 39.0% | 61.0% |
| 84,992 | YAMHILL | 40,615 | 15,943 | 22,762 | 1,910 | 6,819 | D | 39.3% | 56.0% | 41.2% | 58.8% |
| 3,421,399 | TOTAL | 1,780,550 | 565,254 | 1,128,728 | 86,568 | 563,474 | D | 31.7% | 63.4% | 33.4% | 66.6% |

# OREGON

## HOUSE OF REPRESENTATIVES

| | | | Republican | | Democratic | | | | Percentage | | | |
|---|---|---|---|---|---|---|---|---|---|---|---|---|
| | | | | | | | | | Total Vote | | Major Vote | |
| CD | Year | Total Vote | Vote | Candidate | Vote | Candidate | Other Vote | Rep.-Dem. Plurality | Rep. | Dem. | Rep. | Dem. |
| 1 | 2004 | 354,338 | 135,164 | Ameri, Goli | 203,771 | Wu, David* | 15,403 | 68,607 D | 38.1% | 57.5% | 39.9% | 60.1% |
| 1 | 2002 | 238,036 | 80,917 | Greenfield, Jim | 149,215 | Wu, David* | 7,904 | 68,298 D | 34.0% | 62.7% | 35.2% | 64.8% |
| 2 | 2004 | 346,865 | 248,461 | Walden, Greg* | 88,914 | McColgan, John C. | 9,490 | 159,547 R | 71.6% | 25.6% | 73.6% | 26.4% |
| 2 | 2002 | 252,284 | 181,295 | Walden, Greg* | 64,991 | Buckley, Peter | 5,998 | 116,304 R | 71.9% | 25.8% | 73.6% | 26.4% |
| 3 | 2004 | 346,560 | 82,045 | Mars, Tami | 245,559 | Blumenauer, Earl* | 18,956 | 163,514 D | 23.7% | 70.9% | 25.0% | 75.0% |
| 3 | 2002 | 234,977 | 62,821 | Seale, Sarah | 156,851 | Blumenauer, Earl* | 15,305 | 94,030 D | 26.7% | 66.8% | 28.6% | 71.4% |
| 4 | 2004 | 374,909 | 140,882 | Feldkamp, Jim | 228,611 | DeFazio, Peter A.* | 5,416 | 87,729 D | 37.6% | 61.0% | 38.1% | 61.9% |
| 4 | 2002 | 263,481 | 90,523 | VanLeeuwen, Liz | 168,150 | DeFazio, Peter A.* | 4,808 | 77,627 D | 34.4% | 63.8% | 35.0% | 65.0% |
| 5 | 2004 | 349,634 | 154,993 | Zupancic, Jim | 184,833 | Hooley, Darlene* | 9,808 | 29,840 D | 44.3% | 52.9% | 45.6% | 54.4% |
| 5 | 2002 | 251,537 | 113,441 | Boquist, Brian J. | 137,713 | Hooley, Darlene* | 383 | 24,272 D | 45.1% | 54.7% | 45.2% | 54.8% |
| Total | 2004 | 1,772,306 | 761,545 | | 951,688 | | 59,073 | 190,143 D | 43.0% | 53.7% | 44.5% | 55.5% |
| Total | 2002 | 1,240,315 | 528,997 | | 676,920 | | 34,398 | 147,923 D | 42.7% | 54.6% | 43.9% | 56.1% |

An asterisk (*) denotes incumbent.

# OREGON

## GENERAL AND PRIMARY ELECTIONS

### 2004 GENERAL ELECTIONS

**President**     Other vote was 7,260 Libertarian (Michael Badnarik); 5,315 Pacific Green (David Cobb); 5,257 Constitution (Michael Peroutka); 8,956 write-in.

**Senator**     Other vote was 43,053 Pacific Green (Teresa Keane); 29,582 Libertarian (Dan Fitzgerald); 12,397 Constitution (David Brownlow); 1,536 write-in.

**House**     Other vote was:

CD 1     13,882 Constitution (Dean Wolf); 1,521 write-in.
CD 2     4,792 Libertarian (Jim Lindsay); 4,060 Constitution (Jack Alan Brown Jr.); 638 write-in.
CD 3     10,678 Socialist (Walter F. "Walt" Brown); 7,119 Constitution (Dale Winegarden); 1,159 write-in.
CD 4     3,190 Libertarian (Jacob Boone); 1,799 Constitution (Michael Paul Marsh); 427 write-in.
CD 5     6,463 Libertarian (Jerry Defoe); 2,971 Constitution (Joseph H. Bitz); 374 write-in.

### 2004 PRIMARY ELECTIONS

**Primary**     May 18, 2004

| **Registration** (as of April 30, 2004) | | |
|---|---|---|
| | Republican | 681,519 |
| | Democratic | 734,199 |
| | Libertarian | 15,204 |
| | Pacific Green | 13,683 |
| | Constitution | 2,229 |
| | Socialist | 298 |
| | Other | 33,363 |
| | Non-Affiliated | 399,813 |
| | TOTAL | 1,880,308 |

**Primary Type**     Closed—Only registered Democrats and Republicans could vote in their party's primary.

# OREGON

## GENERAL AND PRIMARY ELECTIONS

Note: An asterisk (*) denotes incumbent. The primary and general election were conducted entirely by mail.

| | REPUBLICAN PRIMARIES | | | DEMOCRATIC PRIMARIES | | |
|---|---|---|---|---|---|---|
| **President** | George W. Bush* | 293,806 | 94.9% | John Kerry | 289,804 | 78.6% |
| | Write-in | 15,700 | 5.1% | Dennis J. Kucinich | 60,019 | 16.3% |
| | | | | Lyndon H. LaRouche Jr. | 8,571 | 2.3% |
| | | | | Write-in | 10,150 | 2.8% |
| | TOTAL | 309,506 | | TOTAL | 368,544 | |
| **Senator** | Al King | 85,035 | 35.2% | Ron Wyden* | 345,219 | 99.0% |
| | Bruce Broussard | 53,084 | 22.0% | Write-in | 3,387 | 1.0% |
| | Thomas Lee Abshier | 51,879 | 21.5% | | | |
| | E. Bowerman | 18,779 | 7.8% | | | |
| | Philip Petrie | 15,838 | 6.5% | | | |
| | Pavel Goberman | 12,230 | 5.1% | | | |
| | Write-in | 4,990 | 2.1% | | | |
| | TOTAL | 241,835 | | TOTAL | 348,606 | |
| **Congressional District 1** | Goli Ameri | 26,451 | 48.2% | David Wu* | 62,001 | 99.0% |
| | Jason DC Meshell | 14,495 | 26.4% | Write-in | 631 | 1.0% |
| | Tim Phillips | 13,316 | 24.3% | | | |
| | Write-in | 591 | 1.1% | | | |
| | TOTAL | 54,853 | | TOTAL | 62,632 | |
| **Congressional District 2** | Greg Walden* | 79,686 | 99.3% | John C. McColgan | 45,521 | 97.9% |
| | Write-in | 549 | 0.7% | Write-in | 997 | 2.1% |
| | TOTAL | 80,235 | | TOTAL | 46,518 | |
| **Congressional District 3** | Tami Mars | 21,572 | 94.0% | Earl Blumenauer* | 76,811 | 89.0% |
| | Write-in | 1,374 | 6.0% | John Sweeney | 9,207 | 10.7% |
| | | | | Write-in | 280 | 0.3% |
| | TOTAL | 22,946 | | TOTAL | 86,298 | |
| **Congressional District 4** | Jim Feldkamp | 51,500 | 97.8% | Peter A. DeFazio* | 78,414 | 99.2% |
| | Write-in | 1,183 | 2.2% | Write-in | 610 | 0.8% |
| | TOTAL | 52,683 | | TOTAL | 79,024 | |
| **Congressional District 5** | Jim Zupancic | 37,856 | 55.8% | Darlene Hooley* | 59,407 | 85.1% |
| | Jackie Winters | 29,529 | 43.5% | Andrew Kaza | 10,027 | 14.4% |
| | Write-in | 426 | 0.6% | Write-in | 366 | 0.5% |
| | TOTAL | 67,811 | | TOTAL | 69,800 | |

# PENNSYLVANIA

## GOVERNOR
Edward G. Rendell (D). Elected 2002 to a four-year term.

## SENATORS (2 Republicans)
Rick Santorum (R). Reelected 2000 to a six-year term. Previously elected 1994.

Arlen Specter (R). Reelected 2004 to a six-year term. Previously elected 1998, 1992, 1986, 1980.

## REPRESENTATIVES (12 Republicans, 7 Democrats)
1. Robert A. Brady (D)
2. Chaka Fattah (D)
3. Phil English (R)
4. Melissa A. Hart (R)
5. John E. Peterson (R)
6. Jim Gerlach (R)
7. Curt Weldon (R)
8. Michael G. Fitzpatrick (R)
9. Bill Shuster (R)
10. Don Sherwood (R)
11. Paul E. Kanjorski (D)
12. John P. Murtha (D)
13. Allyson Y. Schwartz (D)
14. Mike Doyle (D)
15. Charlie Dent (R)
16. Joe Pitts (R)
17. Tim Holden (D)
18. Tim Murphy (R)
19. Todd R. Platts (R)

## POSTWAR VOTE FOR PRESIDENT

| | Total | Republican | | Democratic | | Other | | Percentage | | | |
| | | | | | | | | Total Vote | | Major Vote | |
| Year | Vote | Vote | Candidate | Vote | Candidate | Vote | Plurality | Rep. | Dem. | Rep. | Dem. |
|---|---|---|---|---|---|---|---|---|---|---|---|
| 2004 | 5,769,590 | 2,793,847 | Bush, George W. | 2,938,095 | Kerry, John | 37,648 | 144,248 D | 48.4% | 50.9% | 48.7% | 51.3% |
| 2000** | 4,913,119 | 2,281,127 | Bush, George W. | 2,485,967 | Gore, Al | 146,025 | 204,840 D | 46.4% | 50.6% | 47.9% | 52.1% |
| 1996** | 4,506,118 | 1,801,169 | Dole, Bob | 2,215,819 | Clinton, Bill | 489,130 | 414,650 D | 40.0% | 49.2% | 44.8% | 55.2% |
| 1992** | 4,959,810 | 1,791,841 | Bush, George | 2,239,164 | Clinton, Bill | 928,805 | 447,323 D | 36.1% | 45.1% | 44.5% | 55.5% |
| 1988 | 4,536,251 | 2,300,087 | Bush, George | 2,194,944 | Dukakis, Michael S. | 41,220 | 105,143 R | 50.7% | 48.4% | 51.2% | 48.8% |
| 1984 | 4,844,903 | 2,584,323 | Reagan, Ronald | 2,228,131 | Mondale, Walter F. | 32,449 | 356,192 R | 53.3% | 46.0% | 53.7% | 46.3% |
| 1980** | 4,561,501 | 2,261,872 | Reagan, Ronald | 1,937,540 | Carter, Jimmy | 362,089 | 324,332 R | 49.6% | 42.5% | 53.9% | 46.1% |
| 1976 | 4,620,787 | 2,205,604 | Ford, Gerald R. | 2,328,677 | Carter, Jimmy | 86,506 | 123,073 D | 47.7% | 50.4% | 48.6% | 51.4% |
| 1972 | 4,592,106 | 2,714,521 | Nixon, Richard M. | 1,796,951 | McGovern, George S. | 80,634 | 917,570 R | 59.1% | 39.1% | 60.2% | 39.8% |
| 1968** | 4,747,928 | 2,090,017 | Nixon, Richard M. | 2,259,405 | Humphrey, Hubert H. | 398,506 | 169,388 D | 44.0% | 47.6% | 48.1% | 51.9% |
| 1964 | 4,822,690 | 1,673,657 | Goldwater, Barry M. | 3,130,954 | Johnson, Lyndon B. | 18,079 | 1,457,297 D | 34.7% | 64.9% | 34.8% | 65.2% |
| 1960 | 5,006,541 | 2,439,956 | Nixon, Richard M. | 2,556,282 | Kennedy, John F. | 10,303 | 116,326 D | 48.7% | 51.1% | 48.8% | 51.2% |
| 1956 | 4,576,503 | 2,585,252 | Eisenhower, Dwight D. | 1,981,769 | Stevenson, Adlai E. | 9,482 | 603,483 R | 56.5% | 43.3% | 56.6% | 43.4% |
| 1952 | 4,580,969 | 2,415,789 | Eisenhower, Dwight D. | 2,146,269 | Stevenson, Adlai E. | 18,911 | 269,520 R | 52.7% | 46.9% | 53.0% | 47.0% |
| 1948 | 3,735,348 | 1,902,197 | Dewey, Thomas E. | 1,752,426 | Truman, Harry S. | 80,725 | 149,771 R | 50.9% | 46.9% | 52.0% | 48.0% |

In past elections, the other vote included: 2000 - 103,392 Green (Ralph Nader); 1996 - 430,984 Reform (Ross Perot); 1992 - 902,667 Independent (Perot); 1980 - 292,921 Independent (John Anderson); 1968 - 378,582 American Independent (George Wallace).

# PENNSYLVANIA

## POSTWAR VOTE FOR GOVERNOR

| Year | Total Vote | Republican Vote | Republican Candidate | Democratic Vote | Democratic Candidate | Other Vote | Rep.-Dem. Plurality | Total Vote Rep. | Total Vote Dem. | Major Vote Rep. | Major Vote Dem. |
|---|---|---|---|---|---|---|---|---|---|---|---|
| 2002 | 3,583,179 | 1,589,408 | Fisher, Mike | 1,913,235 | Rendell, Edward G. | 80,536 | 323,827 D | 44.4% | 53.4% | 45.4% | 54.6% |
| 1998** | 3,025,152 | 1,736,844 | Ridge, Thomas J. | 938,745 | Itkin, Ivan | 349,563 | 798,099 R | 57.4% | 31.0% | 64.9% | 35.1% |
| 1994** | 3,585,526 | 1,627,976 | Ridge, Thomas J. | 1,430,099 | Singel, Mark S. | 527,451 | 197,877 R | 45.4% | 39.9% | 53.2% | 46.8% |
| 1990 | 3,052,760 | 987,516 | Hafer, Barbara | 2,065,244 | Casey, Robert | | 1,077,728 D | 32.3% | 67.7% | 32.3% | 67.7% |
| 1986 | 3,388,275 | 1,638,268 | Scranton, William W., III | 1,717,484 | Casey, Robert | 32,523 | 79,216 D | 48.4% | 50.7% | 48.8% | 51.2% |
| 1982 | 3,683,985 | 1,872,784 | Thornburgh, Richard L. | 1,772,353 | Ertel, Allen E. | 38,848 | 100,431 R | 50.8% | 48.1% | 51.4% | 48.6% |
| 1978 | 3,741,969 | 1,966,042 | Thornburgh, Richard L. | 1,737,888 | Flaherty, Peter | 38,039 | 228,154 R | 52.5% | 46.4% | 53.1% | 46.9% |
| 1974 | 3,491,234 | 1,578,917 | Lewis, Andrew L. | 1,878,252 | Shapp, Milton | 34,065 | 299,335 D | 45.2% | 53.8% | 45.7% | 54.3% |
| 1970 | 3,700,060 | 1,542,854 | Broderick, Raymond | 2,043,029 | Shapp, Milton | 114,177 | 500,175 D | 41.7% | 55.2% | 43.0% | 57.0% |
| 1966 | 4,050,668 | 2,110,349 | Shafer, Raymond P. | 1,868,719 | Shapp, Milton | 71,600 | 241,630 R | 52.1% | 46.1% | 53.0% | 47.0% |
| 1962 | 4,378,042 | 2,424,918 | Scranton, William W. | 1,938,627 | Dilworth, Richardson | 14,497 | 486,291 R | 55.4% | 44.3% | 55.6% | 44.4% |
| 1958 | 3,986,918 | 1,948,769 | McGonigle, A. T. | 2,024,852 | Lawrence, David | 13,297 | 76,083 D | 48.9% | 50.8% | 49.0% | 51.0% |
| 1954 | 3,720,457 | 1,717,070 | Wood, Lloyd H. | 1,996,266 | Leader, George M. | 7,121 | 279,196 D | 46.2% | 53.7% | 46.2% | 53.8% |
| 1950 | 3,540,059 | 1,796,119 | Fine, John S. | 1,710,355 | Dilworth, Richardson | 33,585 | 85,764 R | 50.7% | 48.3% | 51.2% | 48.8% |
| 1946 | 3,123,994 | 1,828,462 | Duff, James H. | 1,270,947 | Rice, John S. | 24,585 | 557,515 R | 58.5% | 40.7% | 59.0% | 41.0% |

In past elections, the other vote included: 1998 - 315,761 Constitutional (Peg Luksik); 1994 - 460,269 Constitutional (Luksik).

## POSTWAR VOTE FOR SENATOR

| Year | Total Vote | Republican Vote | Republican Candidate | Democratic Vote | Democratic Candidate | Other Vote | Rep.-Dem. Plurality | Total Vote Rep. | Total Vote Dem. | Major Vote Rep. | Major Vote Dem. |
|---|---|---|---|---|---|---|---|---|---|---|---|
| 2004 | 5,559,105 | 2,925,080 | Specter, Arlen | 2,334,126 | Hoeffel, Joseph M. | 299,899 | 590,954 R | 52.6% | 42.0% | 55.6% | 44.4% |
| 2000 | 4,735,504 | 2,481,962 | Santorum, Rick | 2,154,908 | Klink, Ron | 98,634 | 327,054 R | 52.4% | 45.5% | 53.5% | 46.5% |
| 1998 | 2,957,772 | 1,814,180 | Specter, Arlen | 1,028,839 | Lloyd, Bill | 114,753 | 785,341 R | 61.3% | 34.8% | 63.8% | 36.2% |
| 1994 | 3,513,361 | 1,735,691 | Santorum, Rick | 1,648,481 | Wofford, Harris | 129,189 | 87,210 R | 49.4% | 46.9% | 51.3% | 48.7% |
| 1992 | 4,802,410 | 2,358,125 | Specter, Arlen | 2,224,966 | Yeakel, Lynn | 219,319 | 133,159 R | 49.1% | 46.3% | 51.5% | 48.5% |
| 1991S | 3,382,746 | 1,521,986 | Thornburgh, Richard | 1,860,760 | Wofford, Harris | | 338,774 D | 45.0% | 55.0% | 45.0% | 55.0% |
| 1988 | 4,366,598 | 2,901,715 | Heinz, H. John | 1,416,764 | Vignola, Joseph C. | 48,119 | 1,484,951 R | 66.5% | 32.4% | 67.2% | 32.8% |
| 1986 | 3,378,226 | 1,906,537 | Specter, Arlen | 1,448,219 | Edgar, Robert W. | 23,470 | 458,318 R | 56.4% | 42.9% | 56.8% | 43.2% |
| 1982 | 3,604,108 | 2,136,418 | Heinz, H. John | 1,412,965 | Wecht, Cyril H. | 54,725 | 723,453 R | 59.3% | 39.2% | 60.2% | 39.8% |
| 1980 | 4,418,042 | 2,230,404 | Specter, Arlen | 2,122,391 | Flaherty, Peter | 65,247 | 108,013 R | 50.5% | 48.0% | 51.2% | 48.8% |
| 1976 | 4,546,353 | 2,381,891 | Heinz, H. John | 2,126,977 | Green, William J., III | 37,485 | 254,914 R | 52.4% | 46.8% | 52.8% | 47.2% |
| 1974 | 3,477,812 | 1,843,317 | Schweiker, Richard S. | 1,596,121 | Flaherty, Peter | 38,374 | 247,196 R | 53.0% | 45.9% | 53.6% | 46.4% |
| 1970 | 3,644,305 | 1,874,106 | Scott, Hugh | 1,653,774 | Sesler, William G. | 116,425 | 220,332 R | 51.4% | 45.4% | 53.1% | 46.9% |
| 1968 | 4,624,218 | 2,399,762 | Schweiker, Richard S. | 2,117,662 | Clark, Joseph S. | 106,794 | 282,100 R | 51.9% | 45.8% | 53.1% | 46.9% |
| 1964 | 4,803,835 | 2,429,858 | Scott, Hugh | 2,359,223 | Blatt, Genevieve | 14,754 | 70,635 R | 50.6% | 49.1% | 50.7% | 49.3% |
| 1962 | 4,383,475 | 2,134,649 | Van Zandt, James E. | 2,238,383 | Clark, Joseph S. | 10,443 | 103,734 D | 48.7% | 51.1% | 48.8% | 51.2% |
| 1958 | 3,988,622 | 2,042,586 | Scott, Hugh | 1,929,821 | Leader, George M. | 16,215 | 112,765 R | 51.2% | 48.4% | 51.4% | 48.6% |
| 1956 | 4,529,874 | 2,250,671 | Duff, James H. | 2,268,641 | Clark, Joseph S. | 10,562 | 17,970 D | 49.7% | 50.1% | 49.8% | 50.2% |
| 1952 | 4,519,761 | 2,331,034 | Martin, Edward | 2,168,546 | Bard, Guy Kurtz | 20,181 | 162,488 R | 51.6% | 48.0% | 51.8% | 48.2% |
| 1950 | 3,548,703 | 1,820,400 | Duff, James H. | 1,694,076 | Myers, Francis J. | 34,227 | 126,324 R | 51.3% | 47.7% | 51.8% | 48.2% |
| 1946 | 3,127,860 | 1,853,458 | Martin, Edward | 1,245,338 | Guffey, Joseph F. | 29,064 | 608,120 R | 59.3% | 39.8% | 59.8% | 40.2% |

The 1991 election was for a short term to fill a vacancy.

374

# PENNSYLVANIA

Congressional districts first established for elections held in 2004
19 members

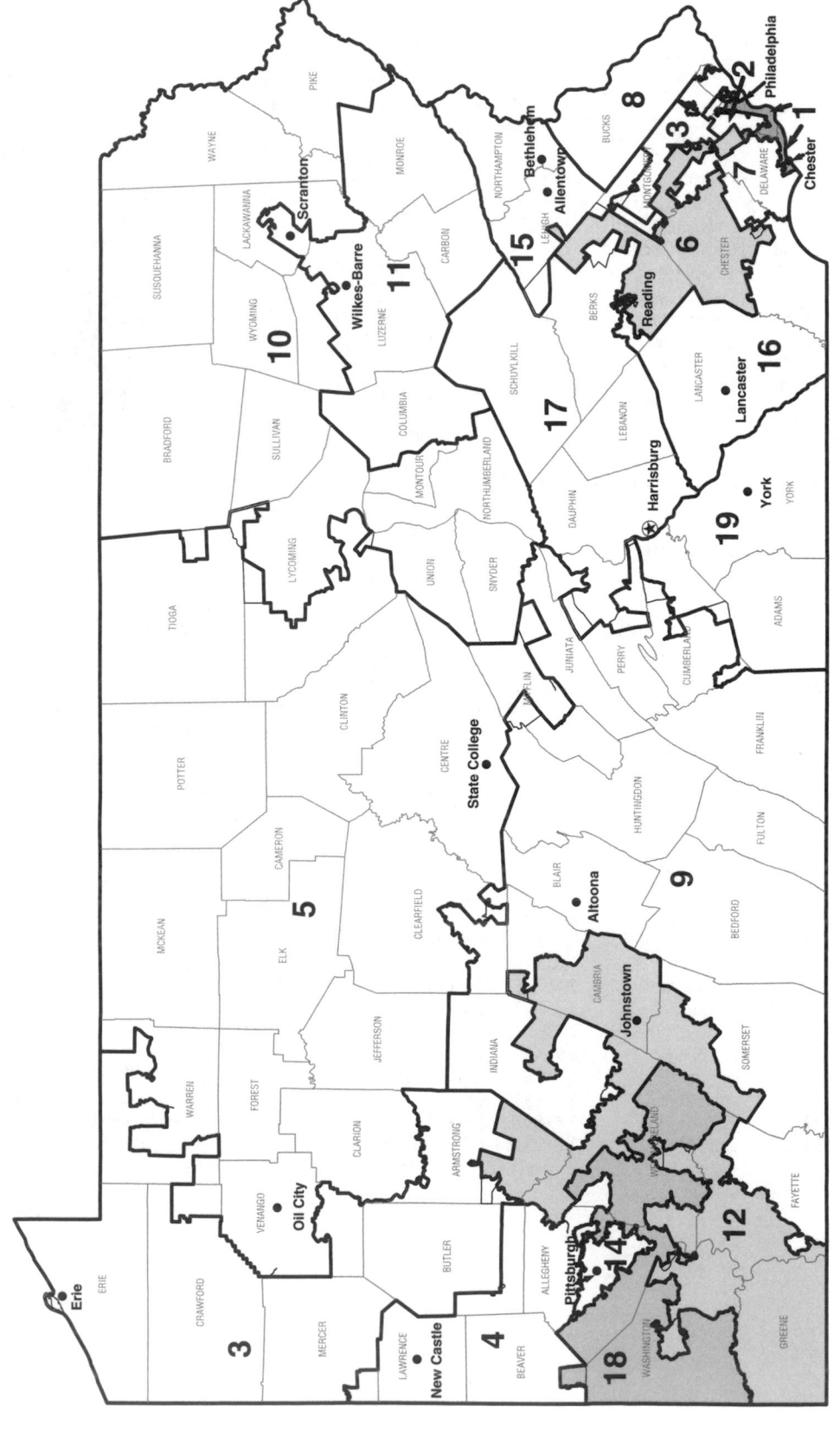

# PENNSYLVANIA

## Philadelphia Area

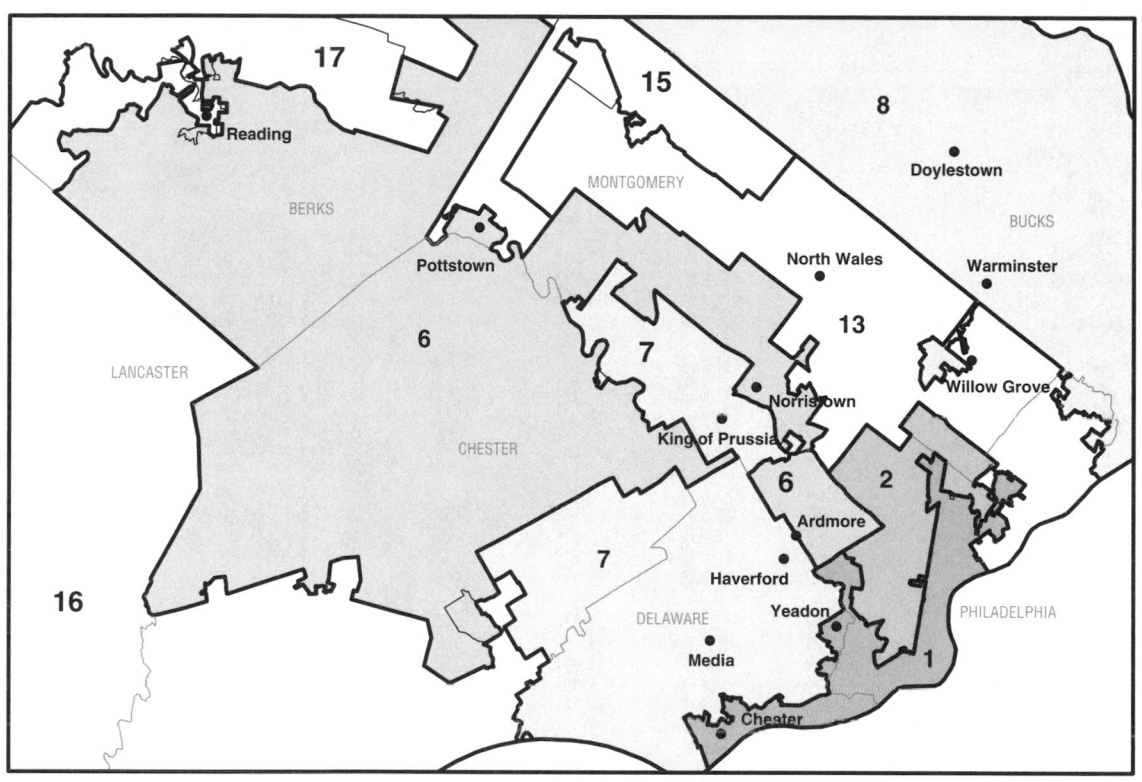

## Pittsburgh Area

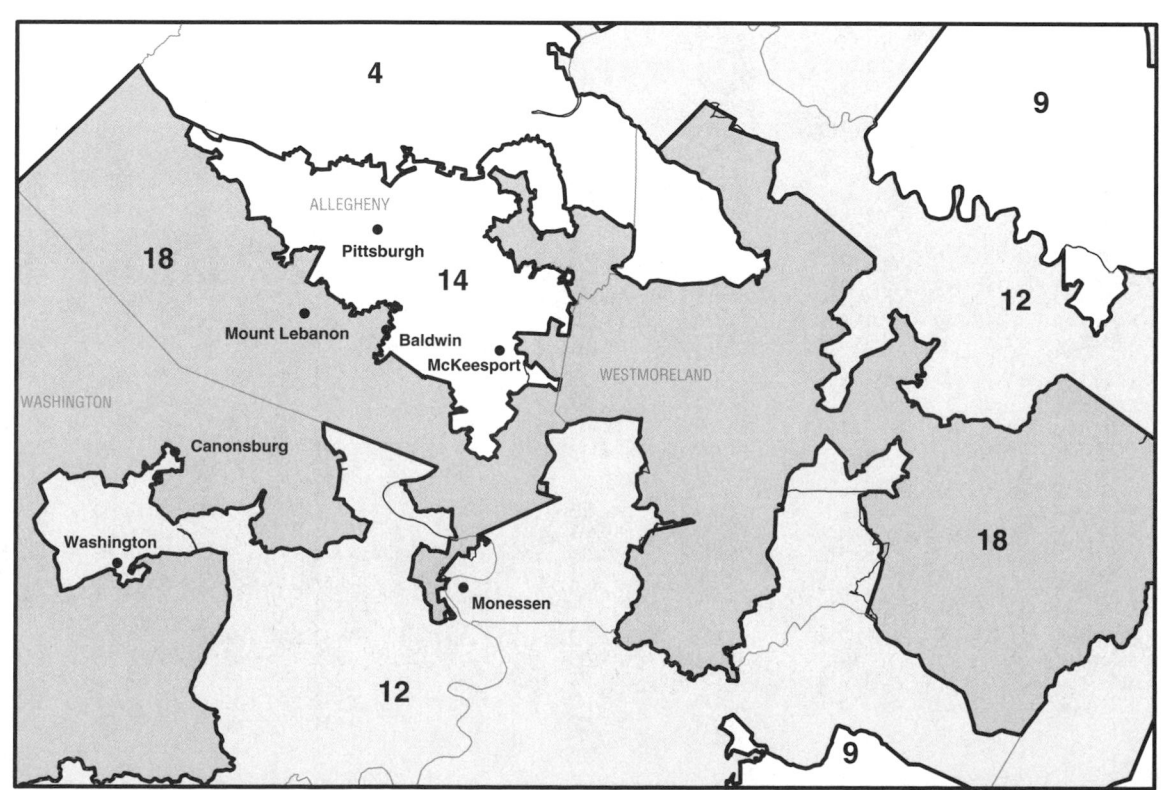

# PENNSYLVANIA

## PRESIDENT 2004

| 2000 Census Population | County | Total Vote | Republican | Democratic | Other | Rep.-Dem. Plurality | Percentage | | | |
|---|---|---|---|---|---|---|---|---|---|---|
| | | | | | | | Total Vote | | Major Vote | |
| | | | | | | | Rep. | Dem. | Rep. | Dem. |
| 91,292 | ADAMS | 42,228 | 28,247 | 13,764 | 217 | 14,483 R | 66.9% | 32.6% | 67.2% | 32.8% |
| 1,281,666 | ALLEGHENY | 645,469 | 271,925 | 368,912 | 4,632 | 96,987 D | 42.1% | 57.2% | 42.4% | 57.6% |
| 72,392 | ARMSTRONG | 31,097 | 18,925 | 12,025 | 147 | 6,900 R | 60.9% | 38.7% | 61.1% | 38.9% |
| 181,412 | BEAVER | 82,543 | 39,916 | 42,146 | 481 | 2,230 D | 48.4% | 51.1% | 48.6% | 51.4% |
| 49,984 | BEDFORD | 22,679 | 16,606 | 6,016 | 57 | 10,590 R | 73.2% | 26.5% | 73.4% | 26.6% |
| 373,638 | BERKS | 164,487 | 87,122 | 76,309 | 1,056 | 10,813 R | 53.0% | 46.4% | 53.3% | 46.7% |
| 129,144 | BLAIR | 54,178 | 35,751 | 18,105 | 322 | 17,646 R | 66.0% | 33.4% | 66.4% | 33.6% |
| 62,761 | BRADFORD | 25,652 | 16,942 | 8,590 | 120 | 8,352 R | 66.0% | 33.5% | 66.4% | 33.6% |
| 597,635 | BUCKS | 319,816 | 154,469 | 163,438 | 1,909 | 8,969 D | 48.3% | 51.1% | 48.6% | 51.4% |
| 174,083 | BUTLER | 85,425 | 54,959 | 30,090 | 376 | 24,869 R | 64.3% | 35.2% | 64.6% | 35.4% |
| 152,598 | CAMBRIA | 66,983 | 34,048 | 32,591 | 344 | 1,457 R | 50.8% | 48.7% | 51.1% | 48.9% |
| 5,974 | CAMERON | 2,406 | 1,599 | 794 | 13 | 805 R | 66.5% | 33.0% | 66.8% | 33.2% |
| 58,802 | CARBON | 25,043 | 12,519 | 12,223 | 301 | 296 R | 50.0% | 48.8% | 50.6% | 49.4% |
| 135,758 | CENTRE | 64,253 | 33,133 | 30,733 | 387 | 2,400 R | 51.6% | 47.8% | 51.9% | 48.1% |
| 433,501 | CHESTER | 230,823 | 120,036 | 109,708 | 1,079 | 10,328 R | 52.0% | 47.5% | 52.2% | 47.8% |
| 41,765 | CLARION | 17,184 | 11,063 | 6,049 | 72 | 5,014 R | 64.4% | 35.2% | 64.7% | 35.3% |
| 83,382 | CLEARFIELD | 34,233 | 20,533 | 13,518 | 182 | 7,015 R | 60.0% | 39.5% | 60.3% | 39.7% |
| 37,914 | CLINTON | 13,967 | 8,035 | 5,823 | 109 | 2,212 R | 57.5% | 41.7% | 58.0% | 42.0% |
| 64,151 | COLUMBIA | 26,869 | 16,052 | 10,679 | 138 | 5,373 R | 59.7% | 39.7% | 60.1% | 39.9% |
| 90,366 | CRAWFORD | 38,322 | 21,965 | 16,013 | 344 | 5,952 R | 57.3% | 41.8% | 57.8% | 42.2% |
| 213,674 | CUMBERLAND | 106,082 | 67,648 | 37,928 | 506 | 29,720 R | 63.8% | 35.8% | 64.1% | 35.9% |
| 251,798 | DAUPHIN | 121,208 | 65,296 | 55,299 | 613 | 9,997 R | 53.9% | 45.6% | 54.1% | 45.9% |
| 550,864 | DELAWARE | 284,538 | 120,425 | 162,601 | 1,512 | 42,176 D | 42.3% | 57.1% | 42.5% | 57.5% |
| 35,112 | ELK | 14,550 | 7,872 | 6,602 | 76 | 1,270 R | 54.1% | 45.4% | 54.4% | 45.6% |
| 280,843 | ERIE | 125,898 | 57,372 | 67,921 | 605 | 10,549 D | 45.6% | 53.9% | 45.8% | 54.2% |
| 148,644 | FAYETTE | 54,707 | 25,045 | 29,120 | 542 | 4,075 D | 45.8% | 53.2% | 46.2% | 53.8% |
| 4,946 | FOREST | 2,573 | 1,571 | 989 | 13 | 582 R | 61.1% | 38.4% | 61.4% | 38.6% |
| 129,313 | FRANKLIN | 58,569 | 41,817 | 16,562 | 190 | 25,255 R | 71.4% | 28.3% | 71.6% | 28.4% |
| 14,261 | FULTON | 6,271 | 4,772 | 1,475 | 24 | 3,297 R | 76.1% | 23.5% | 76.4% | 23.6% |
| 40,672 | GREENE | 15,565 | 7,786 | 7,674 | 105 | 112 R | 50.0% | 49.3% | 50.4% | 49.6% |
| 45,586 | HUNTINGDON | 18,058 | 12,126 | 5,879 | 53 | 6,247 R | 67.2% | 32.6% | 67.3% | 32.7% |
| 89,605 | INDIANA | 36,248 | 20,254 | 15,831 | 163 | 4,423 R | 55.9% | 43.7% | 56.1% | 43.9% |
| 45,932 | JEFFERSON | 19,560 | 13,371 | 6,073 | 116 | 7,298 R | 68.4% | 31.0% | 68.8% | 31.2% |
| 22,821 | JUNIATA | 10,006 | 7,144 | 2,797 | 65 | 4,347 R | 71.4% | 28.0% | 71.9% | 28.1% |
| 213,295 | LACKAWANNA | 105,819 | 44,766 | 59,573 | 1,480 | 14,807 D | 42.3% | 56.3% | 42.9% | 57.1% |
| 470,658 | LANCASTER | 221,278 | 145,591 | 74,328 | 1,359 | 71,263 R | 65.8% | 33.6% | 66.2% | 33.8% |
| 94,643 | LAWRENCE | 43,442 | 21,938 | 21,387 | 117 | 551 R | 50.5% | 49.2% | 50.6% | 49.4% |
| 120,327 | LEBANON | 55,665 | 37,089 | 18,109 | 467 | 18,980 R | 66.6% | 32.5% | 67.2% | 32.8% |
| 312,090 | LEHIGH | 145,091 | 70,160 | 73,940 | 991 | 3,780 D | 48.4% | 51.0% | 48.7% | 51.3% |
| 319,250 | LUZERNE | 136,028 | 64,953 | 69,573 | 1,502 | 4,620 D | 47.7% | 51.1% | 48.3% | 51.7% |
| 120,044 | LYCOMING | 50,049 | 33,961 | 15,681 | 407 | 18,280 R | 67.9% | 31.3% | 68.4% | 31.6% |
| 45,936 | MCKEAN | 17,426 | 10,941 | 6,294 | 191 | 4,647 R | 62.8% | 36.1% | 63.5% | 36.5% |
| 120,293 | MERCER | 51,564 | 26,311 | 24,831 | 422 | 1,480 R | 51.0% | 48.2% | 51.4% | 48.6% |
| 46,486 | MIFFLIN | 16,802 | 11,726 | 4,889 | 187 | 6,837 R | 69.8% | 29.1% | 70.6% | 29.4% |
| 138,687 | MONROE | 56,342 | 27,971 | 27,967 | 404 | 4 R | 49.6% | 49.6% | 50.0% | 50.0% |
| 750,097 | MONTGOMERY | 399,591 | 175,741 | 222,048 | 1,802 | 46,307 D | 44.0% | 55.6% | 44.2% | 55.8% |
| 18,236 | MONTOUR | 7,624 | 4,903 | 2,666 | 55 | 2,237 R | 64.3% | 35.0% | 64.8% | 35.2% |
| 267,066 | NORTHAMPTON | 126,740 | 62,102 | 63,446 | 1,192 | 1,344 D | 49.0% | 50.1% | 49.5% | 50.5% |
| 94,556 | NORTHUMBERLAND | 37,134 | 22,262 | 14,602 | 270 | 7,660 R | 60.0% | 39.3% | 60.4% | 39.6% |
| 43,602 | PERRY | 19,427 | 13,919 | 5,423 | 85 | 8,496 R | 71.6% | 27.9% | 72.0% | 28.0% |
| 1,517,550 | PHILADELPHIA | 674,069 | 130,099 | 542,205 | 1,765 | 412,106 D | 19.3% | 80.4% | 19.4% | 80.6% |
| 46,302 | PIKE | 21,299 | 12,444 | 8,656 | 199 | 3,788 R | 58.4% | 40.6% | 59.0% | 41.0% |
| 18,080 | POTTER | 7,962 | 5,640 | 2,268 | 54 | 3,372 R | 70.8% | 28.5% | 71.3% | 28.7% |
| 150,336 | SCHUYLKILL | 65,269 | 35,640 | 29,231 | 398 | 6,409 R | 54.6% | 44.8% | 54.9% | 45.1% |
| 37,546 | SNYDER | 14,983 | 10,566 | 4,348 | 69 | 6,218 R | 70.5% | 29.0% | 70.8% | 29.2% |
| 80,023 | SOMERSET | 36,778 | 23,802 | 12,842 | 134 | 10,960 R | 64.7% | 34.9% | 65.0% | 35.0% |
| 6,556 | SULLIVAN | 3,285 | 2,056 | 1,213 | 16 | 843 R | 62.6% | 36.9% | 62.9% | 37.1% |
| 42,238 | SUSQUEHANNA | 19,040 | 11,573 | 7,351 | 116 | 4,222 R | 60.8% | 38.6% | 61.2% | 38.8% |
| 41,373 | TIOGA | 17,571 | 12,019 | 5,437 | 115 | 6,582 R | 68.4% | 30.9% | 68.9% | 31.1% |
| 41,624 | UNION | 16,123 | 10,334 | 5,700 | 89 | 4,634 R | 64.1% | 35.4% | 64.5% | 35.5% |

# PENNSYLVANIA

## PRESIDENT 2004

| 2000 Census Population | County | Total Vote | Republican | Democratic | Other | Rep.-Dem. Plurality | | Percentage | | | |
|---|---|---|---|---|---|---|---|---|---|---|---|
| | | | | | | | | Total Vote | | Major Vote | |
| | | | | | | | | Rep. | Dem. | Rep. | Dem. |
| 57,565 | VENANGO | 23,659 | 14,472 | 9,024 | 163 | 5,448 | R | 61.2% | 38.1% | 61.6% | 38.4% |
| 43,863 | WARREN | 19,273 | 10,999 | 8,044 | 230 | 2,955 | R | 57.1% | 41.7% | 57.8% | 42.2% |
| 202,897 | WASHINGTON | 96,177 | 47,673 | 48,225 | 279 | 552 | D | 49.6% | 50.1% | 49.7% | 50.3% |
| 47,722 | WAYNE | 21,967 | 13,713 | 8,060 | 194 | 5,653 | R | 62.4% | 36.7% | 63.0% | 37.0% |
| 369,993 | WESTMORELAND | 178,696 | 100,087 | 77,774 | 835 | 22,313 | R | 56.0% | 43.5% | 56.3% | 43.7% |
| 28,080 | WYOMING | 12,832 | 7,782 | 4,982 | 68 | 2,800 | R | 60.6% | 38.8% | 61.0% | 39.0% |
| 381,751 | YORK | 179,269 | 114,270 | 63,701 | 1,298 | 50,569 | R | 63.7% | 35.5% | 64.2% | 35.8% |
| 12,281,054 | TOTAL | 5,769,590 | 2,793,847 | 2,938,095 | 37,648 | 144,248 | D | 48.4% | 50.9% | 48.7% | 51.3% |

Note: The statewide totals for "Total Vote" and "Other" include 2,656 write-in votes for Ralph Nader and 1,170 scattered write-ins that were not included in the county-by-county returns.

# PENNSYLVANIA

## SENATOR 2004

| 2000 Census Population | County | Total Vote | Republican | Democratic | Other | Rep.-Dem. Plurality | | Percentage | | | |
|---|---|---|---|---|---|---|---|---|---|---|---|
| | | | | | | | | Total Vote | | Major Vote | |
| | | | | | | | | Rep. | Dem. | Rep. | Dem. |
| 91,292 | ADAMS | 40,747 | 26,840 | 10,654 | 3,253 | 16,186 | R | 65.9% | 26.1% | 71.6% | 28.4% |
| 1,281,666 | ALLEGHENY | 619,037 | 279,698 | 298,010 | 41,329 | 18,312 | D | 45.2% | 48.1% | 48.4% | 51.6% |
| 72,392 | ARMSTRONG | 30,793 | 17,504 | 9,831 | 3,458 | 7,673 | R | 56.8% | 31.9% | 64.0% | 36.0% |
| 181,412 | BEAVER | 83,030 | 37,599 | 38,352 | 7,079 | 753 | D | 45.3% | 46.2% | 49.5% | 50.5% |
| 49,984 | BEDFORD | 21,958 | 14,786 | 5,347 | 1,825 | 9,439 | R | 67.3% | 24.4% | 73.4% | 26.6% |
| 373,638 | BERKS | 159,082 | 90,319 | 60,355 | 8,408 | 29,964 | R | 56.8% | 37.9% | 59.9% | 40.1% |
| 129,144 | BLAIR | 53,483 | 34,362 | 14,613 | 4,508 | 19,749 | R | 64.2% | 27.3% | 70.2% | 29.8% |
| 62,761 | BRADFORD | 24,895 | 17,516 | 6,173 | 1,206 | 11,343 | R | 70.4% | 24.8% | 73.9% | 26.1% |
| 597,635 | BUCKS | 310,875 | 175,923 | 126,676 | 8,276 | 49,247 | R | 56.6% | 40.7% | 58.1% | 41.9% |
| 174,083 | BUTLER | 83,888 | 48,413 | 25,507 | 9,968 | 22,906 | R | 57.7% | 30.4% | 65.5% | 34.5% |
| 152,598 | CAMBRIA | 66,184 | 33,745 | 28,030 | 4,409 | 5,715 | R | 51.0% | 42.4% | 54.6% | 45.4% |
| 5,974 | CAMERON | 2,374 | 1,412 | 692 | 270 | 720 | R | 59.5% | 29.1% | 67.1% | 32.9% |
| 58,802 | CARBON | 24,107 | 13,545 | 9,593 | 969 | 3,952 | R | 56.2% | 39.8% | 58.5% | 41.5% |
| 135,758 | CENTRE | 62,973 | 33,902 | 24,458 | 4,613 | 9,444 | R | 53.8% | 38.8% | 58.1% | 41.9% |
| 433,501 | CHESTER | 224,896 | 133,329 | 82,551 | 9,016 | 50,778 | R | 59.3% | 36.7% | 61.8% | 38.2% |
| 41,765 | CLARION | 17,378 | 10,336 | 4,854 | 2,188 | 5,482 | R | 59.5% | 27.9% | 68.0% | 32.0% |
| 83,382 | CLEARFIELD | 33,786 | 19,107 | 11,556 | 3,123 | 7,551 | R | 56.6% | 34.2% | 62.3% | 37.7% |
| 37,914 | CLINTON | 13,449 | 7,967 | 4,612 | 870 | 3,355 | R | 59.2% | 34.3% | 63.3% | 36.7% |
| 64,151 | COLUMBIA | 26,361 | 16,666 | 8,260 | 1,435 | 8,406 | R | 63.2% | 31.3% | 66.9% | 33.1% |
| 90,366 | CRAWFORD | 36,348 | 23,213 | 11,309 | 1,826 | 11,904 | R | 63.9% | 31.1% | 67.2% | 32.8% |
| 213,674 | CUMBERLAND | 103,984 | 67,880 | 27,268 | 8,836 | 40,612 | R | 65.3% | 26.2% | 71.3% | 28.7% |
| 251,798 | DAUPHIN | 117,693 | 68,693 | 40,562 | 8,438 | 28,131 | R | 58.4% | 34.5% | 62.9% | 37.1% |
| 550,864 | DELAWARE | 275,203 | 144,316 | 125,407 | 5,480 | 18,909 | R | 52.4% | 45.6% | 53.5% | 46.5% |
| 35,112 | ELK | 14,339 | 8,170 | 5,200 | 969 | 2,970 | R | 57.0% | 36.3% | 61.1% | 38.9% |
| 280,843 | ERIE | 116,715 | 69,937 | 42,627 | 4,151 | 27,310 | R | 59.9% | 36.5% | 62.1% | 37.9% |
| 148,644 | FAYETTE | 50,217 | 22,228 | 24,284 | 3,705 | 2,056 | D | 44.3% | 48.4% | 47.8% | 52.2% |
| 4,946 | FOREST | 2,559 | 1,596 | 782 | 181 | 814 | R | 62.4% | 30.6% | 67.1% | 32.9% |
| 129,313 | FRANKLIN | 57,636 | 40,291 | 13,422 | 3,923 | 26,869 | R | 69.9% | 23.3% | 75.0% | 25.0% |
| 14,261 | FULTON | 6,000 | 4,367 | 1,271 | 362 | 3,096 | R | 72.8% | 21.2% | 77.5% | 22.5% |
| 40,672 | GREENE | 15,703 | 7,795 | 6,799 | 1,109 | 996 | R | 49.6% | 43.3% | 53.4% | 46.6% |
| 45,586 | HUNTINGDON | 17,806 | 11,632 | 4,849 | 1,325 | 6,783 | R | 65.3% | 27.2% | 70.6% | 29.4% |
| 89,605 | INDIANA | 36,072 | 19,616 | 12,590 | 3,866 | 7,026 | R | 54.4% | 34.9% | 60.9% | 39.1% |
| 45,932 | JEFFERSON | 19,163 | 11,782 | 5,294 | 2,087 | 6,488 | R | 61.5% | 27.6% | 69.0% | 31.0% |
| 22,821 | JUNIATA | 9,938 | 6,923 | 2,260 | 755 | 4,663 | R | 69.7% | 22.7% | 75.4% | 24.6% |
| 213,295 | LACKAWANNA | 99,736 | 54,797 | 41,604 | 3,335 | 13,193 | R | 54.9% | 41.7% | 56.8% | 43.2% |

# PENNSYLVANIA

## SENATOR 2004

| 2000 Census Population | County | Total Vote | Republican | Democratic | Other | Rep.-Dem. Plurality | Percentage Total Vote Rep. | Dem. | Major Vote Rep. | Dem. |
|---|---|---|---|---|---|---|---|---|---|---|
| 470,658 | LANCASTER | 213,566 | 131,771 | 57,078 | 24,717 | 74,693 R | 61.7% | 26.7% | 69.8% | 30.2% |
| 94,643 | LAWRENCE | 41,961 | 21,021 | 18,116 | 2,824 | 2,905 R | 50.1% | 43.2% | 53.7% | 46.3% |
| 120,327 | LEBANON | 52,921 | 35,336 | 13,182 | 4,403 | 22,154 R | 66.8% | 24.9% | 72.8% | 27.2% |
| 312,090 | LEHIGH | 137,822 | 73,610 | 58,386 | 5,826 | 15,224 R | 53.4% | 42.4% | 55.8% | 44.2% |
| 319,250 | LUZERNE | 127,839 | 71,615 | 51,154 | 5,070 | 20,461 R | 56.0% | 40.0% | 58.3% | 41.7% |
| 120,044 | LYCOMING | 47,614 | 31,153 | 12,879 | 3,582 | 18,274 R | 65.4% | 27.0% | 70.8% | 29.2% |
| 45,936 | MCKEAN | 16,315 | 11,078 | 4,340 | 897 | 6,738 R | 67.9% | 26.6% | 71.9% | 28.1% |
| 120,293 | MERCER | 51,073 | 26,401 | 21,511 | 3,161 | 4,890 R | 51.7% | 42.1% | 55.1% | 44.9% |
| 46,486 | MIFFLIN | 16,365 | 11,380 | 3,983 | 1,002 | 7,397 R | 69.5% | 24.3% | 74.1% | 25.9% |
| 138,687 | MONROE | 53,852 | 29,944 | 22,354 | 1,554 | 7,590 R | 55.6% | 41.5% | 57.3% | 42.7% |
| 750,097 | MONTGOMERY | 390,148 | 203,895 | 175,709 | 10,544 | 28,186 R | 52.3% | 45.0% | 53.7% | 46.3% |
| 18,236 | MONTOUR | 7,505 | 4,907 | 2,122 | 476 | 2,785 R | 65.4% | 28.3% | 69.8% | 30.2% |
| 267,066 | NORTHAMPTON | 119,974 | 64,502 | 50,777 | 4,695 | 13,725 R | 53.8% | 42.3% | 56.0% | 44.0% |
| 94,556 | NORTHUMBERLAND | 35,291 | 22,162 | 11,041 | 2,088 | 11,121 R | 62.8% | 31.3% | 66.7% | 33.3% |
| 43,602 | PERRY | 19,133 | 13,099 | 4,065 | 1,969 | 9,034 R | 68.5% | 21.2% | 76.3% | 23.7% |
| 1,517,550 | PHILADELPHIA | 641,014 | 181,922 | 451,901 | 7,191 | 269,979 D | 28.4% | 70.5% | 28.7% | 71.3% |
| 46,302 | PIKE | 20,307 | 12,774 | 6,977 | 556 | 5,797 R | 62.9% | 34.4% | 64.7% | 35.3% |
| 18,080 | POTTER | 7,830 | 5,600 | 1,692 | 538 | 3,908 R | 71.5% | 21.6% | 76.8% | 23.2% |
| 150,336 | SCHUYLKILL | 63,415 | 39,118 | 21,207 | 3,090 | 17,911 R | 61.7% | 33.4% | 64.8% | 35.2% |
| 37,546 | SNYDER | 14,617 | 10,035 | 3,365 | 1,217 | 6,670 R | 68.7% | 23.0% | 74.9% | 25.1% |
| 80,023 | SOMERSET | 36,220 | 21,941 | 11,618 | 2,661 | 10,323 R | 60.6% | 32.1% | 65.4% | 34.6% |
| 6,556 | SULLIVAN | 3,124 | 2,056 | 912 | 156 | 1,144 R | 65.8% | 29.2% | 69.3% | 30.7% |
| 42,238 | SUSQUEHANNA | 18,655 | 12,385 | 5,288 | 982 | 7,097 R | 66.4% | 28.3% | 70.1% | 29.9% |
| 41,373 | TIOGA | 17,214 | 11,989 | 3,864 | 1,361 | 8,125 R | 69.6% | 22.4% | 75.6% | 24.4% |
| 41,624 | UNION | 15,787 | 9,996 | 4,744 | 1,047 | 5,252 R | 63.3% | 30.1% | 67.8% | 32.2% |
| 57,565 | VENANGO | 23,357 | 14,244 | 6,746 | 2,367 | 7,498 R | 61.0% | 28.9% | 67.9% | 32.1% |
| 43,863 | WARREN | 18,151 | 11,432 | 5,280 | 1,439 | 6,152 R | 63.0% | 29.1% | 68.4% | 31.6% |
| 202,897 | WASHINGTON | 94,766 | 46,493 | 40,534 | 7,739 | 5,959 R | 49.1% | 42.8% | 53.4% | 46.6% |
| 47,722 | WAYNE | 21,020 | 14,129 | 6,102 | 789 | 8,027 R | 67.2% | 29.0% | 69.8% | 30.2% |
| 369,993 | WESTMORELAND | 169,274 | 86,126 | 66,728 | 16,420 | 19,398 R | 50.9% | 39.4% | 56.3% | 43.7% |
| 28,080 | WYOMING | 12,680 | 8,460 | 3,297 | 923 | 5,163 R | 66.7% | 26.0% | 72.0% | 28.0% |
| 381,751 | YORK | 171,307 | 108,301 | 51,522 | 11,484 | 56,779 R | 63.2% | 30.1% | 67.8% | 32.2% |
| 12,281,054 | TOTAL | 5,559,105 | 2,925,080 | 2,334,126 | 299,899 | 590,954 R | 52.6% | 42.0% | 55.6% | 44.4% |

Note: The statewide totals for "Total Vote" and "Other" include 580 scattered write-in votes that were not included in the county-by-county returns.

# PENNSYLVANIA

## HOUSE OF REPRESENTATIVES

| CD | Year | Total Vote | Republican Vote | Republican Candidate | Democratic Vote | Democratic Candidate | Other Vote | Rep.-Dem. Plurality | Total Vote Rep. | Total Vote Dem. | Major Vote Rep. | Major Vote Dem. |
|----|------|-----------|-----------------|----------------------|-----------------|----------------------|-----------|---------------------|-----------------|-----------------|-----------------|-----------------|
| 1 | 2004 | 248,587 | 33,266 | Williams, Deborah L. | 214,462 | Brady, Robert A.* | 859 | 181,196 D | 13.4% | 86.3% | 13.4% | 86.6% |
| 1 | 2002 | 140,090 | 17,444 | Delaney, Marie G. | 121,076 | Brady, Robert A.* | 1,570 | 103,632 D | 12.5% | 86.4% | 12.6% | 87.4% |
| 2 | 2004 | 287,637 | 34,411 | Bolno, Stewart | 253,226 | Fattah, Chaka* | | 218,815 D | 12.0% | 88.0% | 12.0% | 88.0% |
| 2 | 2002 | 171,611 | 20,988 | Dougherty, Thomas G. | 150,623 | Fattah, Chaka* | | 129,635 D | 12.2% | 87.8% | 12.2% | 87.8% |
| 3 | 2004 | 277,323 | 166,580 | English, Phil* | 110,684 | Porter, Steven | 59 | 55,896 R | 60.1% | 39.9% | 60.1% | 39.9% |
| 3 | 2002 | 150,329 | 116,763 | English, Phil* | | | 33,566 | 116,763 R | 77.7% | | 100.0% | |
| 4 | 2004 | 323,945 | 204,329 | Hart, Melissa A.* | 116,303 | Drobac, Stevan Jr. | 3,313 | 88,026 R | 63.1% | 35.9% | 63.7% | 36.3% |
| 4 | 2002 | 202,218 | 130,534 | Hart, Melissa A.* | 71,674 | Drobac, Stevan Jr. | 10 | 58,860 R | 64.6% | 35.4% | 64.6% | 35.4% |
| 5 | 2004 | 219,198 | 192,852 | Peterson, John E.* | | | 26,346 | 192,852 R | 88.0% | | 100.0% | |
| 5 | 2002 | 143,211 | 124,942 | Peterson, John E.* | | | 18,269 | 124,942 R | 87.2% | | 100.0% | |
| 6 | 2004 | 314,386 | 160,348 | Gerlach, Jim* | 153,977 | Murphy, Lois | 61 | 6,371 R | 51.0% | 49.0% | 51.0% | 49.0% |
| 6 | 2002 | 201,791 | 103,648 | Gerlach, Jim | 98,128 | Wofford, Dan | 15 | 5,520 R | 51.4% | 48.6% | 51.4% | 48.6% |
| 7 | 2004 | 334,547 | 196,556 | Weldon, Curt* | 134,932 | Scoles, Paul | 3,059 | 61,624 R | 58.8% | 40.3% | 59.3% | 40.7% |
| 7 | 2002 | 221,351 | 146,296 | Weldon, Curt* | 75,055 | Lennon, Peter A. | | 71,241 R | 66.1% | 33.9% | 66.1% | 33.9% |
| 8 | 2004 | 331,276 | 183,229 | Fitzpatrick, Michael G. | 143,427 | Schrader, Virginia Waters | 4,620 | 39,802 R | 55.3% | 43.3% | 56.1% | 43.9% |
| 8 | 2002 | 203,687 | 127,475 | Greenwood, James C.* | 76,178 | Reece, Timothy T. | 34 | 51,297 R | 62.6% | 37.4% | 62.6% | 37.4% |
| 9 | 2004 | 265,272 | 184,320 | Shuster, Bill* | 80,787 | Politis, Paul I. | 165 | 103,533 R | 69.5% | 30.5% | 69.5% | 30.5% |
| 9 | 2002 | 174,849 | 124,184 | Shuster, Bill* | 50,558 | Henry, John R. | 107 | 73,626 R | 71.0% | 28.9% | 71.1% | 28.9% |
| 10 | 2004 | 206,839 | 191,967 | Sherwood, Don* | | | 14,872 | 191,967 R | 92.8% | | 100.0% | |
| 10 | 2002 | 164,159 | 152,017 | # Sherwood, Don* | | | 12,142 | 152,017 R | 92.6% | | 100.0% | |
| 11 | 2004 | 181,285 | | | 171,147 | Kanjorksi, Paul E.* | 10,138 | 171,147 D | | 94.4% | | 100.0% |
| 11 | 2002 | 168,615 | 71,543 | Barletta, Louis J. | 93,758 | Kanjorksi, Paul E.* | 3,314 | 22,215 D | 42.4% | 55.6% | 43.3% | 56.7% |
| 12 | 2004 | 204,710 | | | 204,504 | Murtha, John P.* | 206 | 204,504 D | | 99.9% | | 100.0% |
| 12 | 2002 | 169,028 | 44,818 | Choby, Bill | 124,201 | Murtha, John P.* | 9 | 79,383 D | 26.5% | 73.5% | 26.5% | 73.5% |
| 13 | 2004 | 308,124 | 127,205 | Brown, Melissa | 171,763 | Schwartz, Allyson Y. | 9,156 | 44,558 D | 41.3% | 55.7% | 42.5% | 57.5% |
| 13 | 2002 | 211,867 | 100,295 | Brown, Melissa | 107,945 | Hoeffel, Joseph M.* | 3,627 | 7,650 D | 47.3% | 50.9% | 48.2% | 51.8% |
| 14 | 2004 | 220,299 | | | 220,139 | Doyle, Mike* | 160 | 220,139 D | | 99.9% | | 100.0% |
| 14 | 2002 | 123,412 | | | 123,323 | Doyle, Mike* | 89 | 123,323 D | | 99.9% | | 100.0% |
| 15 | 2004 | 291,147 | 170,634 | Dent, Charlie | 114,646 | Driscoll, Joe | 5,867 | 55,988 R | 58.6% | 39.4% | 59.8% | 40.2% |
| 15 | 2002 | 171,713 | 98,493 | Toomey, Patrick J.* | 73,212 | O'Brien, Edward J. | 8 | 25,281 R | 57.4% | 42.6% | 57.4% | 42.6% |
| 16 | 2004 | 285,313 | 183,620 | Pitts, Joe* | 98,410 | Herr, Lois K. | 3,283 | 85,210 R | 64.4% | 34.5% | 65.1% | 34.9% |
| 16 | 2002 | 134,597 | 119,046 | Pitts, Joe* | | | 15,551 | 119,046 R | 88.4% | | 100.0% | |
| 17 | 2004 | 291,793 | 113,592 | Paterno, Scott | 172,412 | Holden, Tim* | 5,789 | 58,820 D | 38.9% | 59.1% | 39.7% | 60.3% |
| 17 | 2002 | 201,291 | 97,802 | Gekas, George W.* | 103,483 | Holden, Tim* | 6 | 5,681 D | 48.6% | 51.4% | 48.6% | 51.4% |
| 18 | 2004 | 315,342 | 197,894 | Murphy, Tim* | 117,420 | Boles, Mark G. | 28 | 80,474 R | 62.8% | 37.2% | 62.8% | 37.2% |
| 18 | 2002 | 199,349 | 119,885 | Murphy, Tim | 79,451 | Machek, Jack | 13 | 40,434 R | 60.1% | 39.9% | 60.1% | 39.9% |
| 19 | 2004 | 245,251 | 224,274 | Platts, Todd R.* | | | 20,977 | 224,274 R | 91.4% | | 100.0% | |
| 19 | 2002 | 157,145 | 143,097 | Platts, Todd R.* | | | 14,048 | 143,097 R | 91.1% | | 100.0% | |
| Total | 2004 | 5,152,274 | 2,565,077 | | 2,478,239 | | 108,958 | 86,838 R | 49.8% | 48.1% | 50.9% | 49.1% |
| Total | 2002 | 3,310,313 | 1,859,270 | | 1,348,665 | | 102,378 | 510,605 R | 56.2% | 40.7% | 58.0% | 42.0% |

A pound sign (#) indicates that the candidate had the endorsement of more than one party.

An asterisk (*) denotes incumbent.

# PENNSYLVANIA

## GENERAL AND PRIMARY ELECTIONS

## 2004 GENERAL ELECTIONS

| | |
|---|---|
| **President** | Other vote was 21,185 Libertarian (Michael Badnarik); 6,319 Green (David Cobb); 6,318 Constitution (Michael Peroutka); 2,656 write-in (Ralph Nader); 1,170 scattered write-in. |
| **Senator** | Other vote was 220,056 Constitution (James N. Clymer); 79,263 Libertarian (Betsy Summers); 580 scattered write-in. |
| **House** | Other vote was: |

| | |
|---|---|
| CD 1 | 857 Randolph for Congress (Christopher Randolph); 2 write-in. |
| CD 2 | |
| CD 3 | 59 write-in. |
| CD 4 | 3,285 Healthcare (Steven B. Larchuk); 28 write-in. |
| CD 5 | 26,239 Libertarian (Thomas A. Martin); 107 write-in. |
| CD 6 | 61 write-in. |
| CD 7 | 3,039 Libertarian (David Jahn); 20 write-in. |
| CD 8 | 3,710 Libertarian (Arthur L. Farnsworth); 898 Constitution (Erich G. Lukas); 12 write-in. |
| CD 9 | 165 write-in. |
| CD 10 | 14,805 Constitution (Veronica A. Hannevig); 67 write-in. |
| CD 11 | 10,105 Constitution (Kenneth C. Brenneman); 33 write-in. |
| CD 12 | 206 write-in. |
| CD 13 | 5,291 Constitution (John P. McDermott); 3,865 Libertarian (Chuck Moulton). |
| CD 14 | 160 write-in. |
| CD 15 | 3,660 Libertarian (Richard J. Piotrowski); 2,194 Green (Greta Browne); 13 write-in. |
| CD 16 | 3,269 Green (William R. Hagen); 14 write-in. |
| CD 17 | 5,782 Libertarian (Russ Diamond); 7 write-in. |
| CD 18 | 28 write-in. |
| CD 19 | 8,890 Green (Charles J. Steel); 8,456 Libertarian (Michael Mickey Paoletta); 3,474 Constitution (Lester B. Searer); 157 write-in. |

## 2004 PRIMARY ELECTIONS

| | | | | |
|---|---|---|---|---|
| **Primary** | April 27, 2004 | **Registration** (as of April 2004) | Republican | 3,230,496 |
| | | | Democratic | 3,706,122 |
| | | | Libertarian | 30,853 |
| | | | Green | 12,415 |
| | | | Other | 800,696 |
| | | | TOTAL | 7,780,582 |

**Primary Type** Closed—Only registered Democrats and Republicans could vote in their party's primary.

Note:  An asterisk (*) denotes incumbent.

| | REPUBLICAN PRIMARIES | | | DEMOCRATIC PRIMARIES | | |
|---|---|---|---|---|---|---|
| President | George W. Bush* | 861,555 | 100.0% | John Kerry | 585,683 | 74.1% |
| | | | | Howard Dean | 79,799 | 10.1% |
| | | | | John Edwards | 76,762 | 9.7% |
| | | | | Dennis J. Kucinich | 30,110 | 3.8% |
| | | | | Lyndon H. LaRouche Jr. | 17,528 | 2.2% |
| | | | | TOTAL | 789,882 | |
| Senator | Arlen Specter* | 530,839 | 50.8% | Joseph M. Hoeffel | 595,816 | 100.0% |
| | Patrick J. Toomey | 513,693 | 49.2% | | | |
| | TOTAL | 1,044,532 | | | | |

# PENNSYLVANIA

## GENERAL AND PRIMARY ELECTIONS

| | REPUBLICAN PRIMARIES | | | DEMOCRATIC PRIMARIES | | |
|---|---|---|---|---|---|---|
| Congressional District 1 | Deborah L. Williams | 6,486 | 100.0% | Robert A. Brady* | 45,426 | 100.0% |
| Congressional District 2 | Stewart Bolno | 7,058 | 100.0% | Chaka Fattah* | 61,456 | 100.0% |
| Congressional District 3 | Phil English* | 50,634 | 100.0% | Steven Porter | 32,544 | 100.0% |
| Congressional District 4 | Melissa A. Hart* | 53,721 | 100.0% | Stevan Drobac Jr.<br>Eric A. Wafer<br>TOTAL | 29,024<br>18,529<br>47,553 | 61.0%<br>39.0% |
| Congressional District 5 | John E. Peterson*<br>Bob Perry<br>TOTAL | 47,216<br>13,501<br>60,717 | 77.8%<br>22.2% | No Democratic candidate | | |
| Congressional District 6 | Jim Gerlach* | 50,809 | 100.0% | Lois Murphy | 23,310 | 100.0% |
| Congressional District 7 | Curt Weldon* | 66,816 | 100.0% | Greg Phillips<br><br>*After the primary, Greg Phillips withdrew from the race. He was replaced on the general election ballot by Paul Scoles.* | 15,552 | 100.0% |
| Congressional District 8 | James C. Greenwood*<br>Joseph V. Montone<br>TOTAL<br><br>*After the primary, James C. Greenwood decided not to seek reelection. He was replaced on the general election ballot by Michael G. Fitzpatrick.* | 38,279<br>17,098<br>55,377 | 69.1%<br>30.9% | Virginia Waters Schrader<br>Tom Lingenfelter<br>TOTAL | 17,313<br>10,941<br>28,254 | 61.3%<br>38.7% |
| Congressional District 9 | Bill Shuster*<br>Michael DelGrosso<br>TOTAL | 43,097<br>40,845<br>83,942 | 51.3%<br>48.7% | Paul I. Politis | 28,092 | 100.0% |
| Congressional District 10 | Don Sherwood* | 54,115 | 100.0% | No Democratic candidate | | |
| Congressional District 11 | No Republican candidate | | | Paul E. Kanjorski* | 35,055 | 100.0% |
| Congressional District 12 | No Republican candidate | | | John P. Murtha* | 61,190 | 100.0% |
| Congressional District 13 | Melissa Brown<br>Ellen M. Bard<br>Al Taubenberger<br>TOTAL | 22,656<br>20,341<br>15,492<br>58,489 | 38.7%<br>34.8%<br>26.5% | Allyson Y. Schwartz<br>Joe Torsella<br><br>TOTAL | 24,309<br>22,232<br><br>46,541 | 52.2%<br>47.8% |
| Congressional District 14 | No Republican candidate | | | Mike Doyle* | 63,033 | 100.0% |
| Congressional District 15 | Charlie Dent<br>Joe Pascuzzo<br>Brian O'Neill<br>TOTAL | 25,376<br>16,152<br>7,749<br>49,277 | 51.5%<br>32.8%<br>15.7% | Joe Driscoll<br>Richard J. Orloski<br><br>TOTAL | 18,768<br>14,535<br><br>33,303 | 56.4%<br>43.6% |
| Congressional District 16 | Joe Pitts* | 54,345 | 100.0% | Lois K. Herr | 12,522 | 100.0% |
| Congressional District 17 | Scott Paterno<br>Ron Hostetler<br>William B. Lynch<br>Susan C. Sue Helm<br>Frank Ryan<br>Mark Stewart<br>TOTAL | 19,258<br>15,370<br>12,172<br>9,128<br>9,061<br>6,935<br>71,924 | 26.8%<br>21.4%<br>16.9%<br>12.7%<br>12.6%<br>9.6% | Tim Holden* | 31,127 | 100.0% |
| Congressional District 18 | Tim Murphy* | 47,737 | 100.0% | Mark G. Boles | 42,743 | 47.0% |
| Congressional District 19 | Todd R. Platts* | 65,207 | 100.0% | No Democratic candidate | | |

# RHODE ISLAND

## GOVERNOR
Donald L. Carcieri (R). Elected 2002 to a four-year term.

## SENATORS (1 Democrat, 1 Republican)
Lincoln Chafee (R). Elected 2000 to a six-year term. Previously appointed to complete the term of his late father, John H. Chafee, beginning Nov. 4, 1999.

Jack Reed (D). Reelected 2002 to a six-year term. Previously elected 1996.

## REPRESENTATIVES (2 Democrats)
1. Patrick J. Kennedy (D)          2. Jim Langevin (D)

## POSTWAR VOTE FOR PRESIDENT

| Year | Total Vote | Republican Vote | Republican Candidate | Democratic Vote | Democratic Candidate | Other Vote | Plurality | Total Vote Rep. | Total Vote Dem. | Major Vote Rep. | Major Vote Dem. |
|------|-----------|-----------------|----------------------|-----------------|----------------------|-----------|-----------|--------|--------|--------|--------|
| 2004 | 437,134 | 169,046 | Bush, George W. | 259,760 | Kerry, John | 8,328 | 90,714 D | 38.7% | 59.4% | 39.4% | 60.6% |
| 2000** | 409,047 | 130,555 | Bush, George W. | 249,508 | Gore, Al | 28,984 | 118,953 D | 31.9% | 61.0% | 34.4% | 65.6% |
| 1996** | 390,284 | 104,683 | Dole, Bob | 233,050 | Clinton, Bill | 52,551 | 128,367 D | 26.8% | 59.7% | 31.0% | 69.0% |
| 1992** | 453,477 | 131,601 | Bush, George | 213,299 | Clinton, Bill | 108,577 | 81,698 D | 29.0% | 47.0% | 38.2% | 61.8% |
| 1988 | 404,620 | 177,761 | Bush, George | 225,123 | Dukakis, Michael S. | 1,736 | 47,362 D | 43.9% | 55.6% | 44.1% | 55.9% |
| 1984 | 410,492 | 212,080 | Reagan, Ronald | 197,106 | Mondale, Walter F. | 1,306 | 14,974 R | 51.7% | 48.0% | 51.8% | 48.2% |
| 1980** | 416,072 | 154,793 | Reagan, Ronald | 198,342 | Carter, Jimmy | 62,937 | 43,549 D | 37.2% | 47.7% | 43.8% | 56.2% |
| 1976 | 411,170 | 181,249 | Ford, Gerald R. | 227,636 | Carter, Jimmy | 2,285 | 46,387 D | 44.1% | 55.4% | 44.3% | 55.7% |
| 1972 | 415,808 | 220,383 | Nixon, Richard M. | 194,645 | McGovern, George S. | 780 | 25,738 R | 53.0% | 46.8% | 53.1% | 46.9% |
| 1968** | 385,000 | 122,359 | Nixon, Richard M. | 246,518 | Humphrey, Hubert H. | 16,123 | 124,159 D | 31.8% | 64.0% | 33.2% | 66.8% |
| 1964 | 390,091 | 74,615 | Goldwater, Barry M. | 315,463 | Johnson, Lyndon B. | 13 | 240,848 D | 19.1% | 80.9% | 19.1% | 80.9% |
| 1960 | 405,535 | 147,502 | Nixon, Richard M. | 258,032 | Kennedy, John F. | 1 | 110,530 D | 36.4% | 63.6% | 36.4% | 63.6% |
| 1956 | 387,609 | 225,819 | Eisenhower, Dwight D. | 161,790 | Stevenson, Adlai E. | | 64,029 R | 58.3% | 41.7% | 58.3% | 41.7% |
| 1952 | 414,498 | 210,935 | Eisenhower, Dwight D. | 203,293 | Stevenson, Adlai E. | 270 | 7,642 R | 50.9% | 49.0% | 50.9% | 49.1% |
| 1948 | 327,702 | 135,787 | Dewey, Thomas E. | 188,736 | Truman, Harry S. | 3,179 | 52,949 D | 41.4% | 57.6% | 41.8% | 58.2% |

In past elections, the other vote included: 2000 - 25,052 Green (Ralph Nader); 1996 - 43,723 Reform (Ross Perot); 1992 - 105,045 Independent (Perot); 1980 - 59,819 Independent (John Anderson); 1968 - 15,678 American Independent (George Wallace).

# RHODE ISLAND

## POSTWAR VOTE FOR GOVERNOR

| Year | Total Vote | Republican | | Democratic | | Other Vote | Rep.-Dem. Plurality | Percentage | | | |
|------|------------|------------|------------|------------|------------|------------|---------------------|------------|------------|------------|------------|
| | | Vote | Candidate | Vote | Candidate | | | Total Vote | | Major Vote | |
| | | | | | | | | Rep. | Dem. | Rep. | Dem. |
| 2002 | 332,655 | 181,827 | Carcieri, Donald L. | 150,229 | York, Myrth | 599 | 31,598 R | 54.7% | 45.2% | 54.8% | 45.2% |
| 1998 | 306,445 | 156,180 | Almond, Lincoln C. | 129,105 | York, Myrth | 21,160 | 27,075 R | 51.0% | 42.1% | 54.7% | 45.3% |
| 1994** | 361,377 | 171,194 | Almond, Lincoln C. | 157,361 | York, Myrth | 32,822 | 13,833 R | 47.4% | 43.5% | 52.1% | 47.9% |
| 1992 | 425,026 | 145,590 | Leonard, Elizabeth Ann | 261,484 | Sundlun, Bruce G. | 17,952 | 115,894 D | 34.3% | 61.5% | 35.8% | 64.2% |
| 1990 | 356,672 | 92,177 | DiPrete, Edward | 264,411 | Sundlun, Bruce G. | 84 | 172,234 D | 25.8% | 74.1% | 25.8% | 74.2% |
| 1988 | 400,516 | 203,550 | DiPrete, Edward | 196,936 | Sundlun, Bruce G. | 30 | 6,614 R | 50.8% | 49.2% | 50.8% | 49.2% |
| 1986 | 322,724 | 208,822 | DiPrete, Edward | 104,508 | Sundlun, Bruce G. | 9,394 | 104,314 R | 64.7% | 32.4% | 66.6% | 33.4% |
| 1984 | 408,375 | 245,059 | DiPrete, Edward | 163,311 | Solomon, Anthony J. | 5 | 81,748 R | 60.0% | 40.0% | 60.0% | 40.0% |
| 1982 | 337,259 | 79,602 | Marzullo, Vincent | 247,208 | Garrahy, J. Joseph | 10,449 | 167,606 D | 23.6% | 73.3% | 24.4% | 75.6% |
| 1980 | 405,916 | 106,729 | Cianci, Vincent A. | 299,174 | Garrahy, J. Joseph | 13 | 192,445 D | 26.3% | 73.7% | 26.3% | 73.7% |
| 1978 | 314,363 | 96,596 | Almond, Lincoln C. | 197,386 | Garrahy, J. Joseph | 20,381 | 100,790 D | 30.7% | 62.8% | 32.9% | 67.1% |
| 1976 | 398,683 | 178,254 | Taft, James L. | 218,561 | Garrahy, J. Joseph | 1,868 | 40,307 D | 44.7% | 54.8% | 44.9% | 55.1% |
| 1974 | 321,660 | 69,224 | Nugent, James W. | 252,436 | Noel, Philip W. | | 183,212 D | 21.5% | 78.5% | 21.5% | 78.5% |
| 1972 | 412,866 | 194,315 | DeSimone, Herbert F. | 216,953 | Noel, Philip W. | 1,598 | 22,638 D | 47.1% | 52.5% | 47.2% | 52.8% |
| 1970 | 346,342 | 171,549 | DeSimone, Herbert F. | 173,420 | Licht, Frank | 1,373 | 1,871 D | 49.5% | 50.1% | 49.7% | 50.3% |
| 1968 | 383,725 | 187,958 | Chafee, John H. | 195,766 | Licht, Frank | 1 | 7,808 D | 49.0% | 51.0% | 49.0% | 51.0% |
| 1966 | 332,064 | 210,202 | Chafee, John H. | 121,862 | Hobbs, Horace E. | | 88,340 R | 63.3% | 36.7% | 63.3% | 36.7% |
| 1964 | 391,668 | 239,501 | Chafee, John H. | 152,165 | Gallogly, Edward P. | 2 | 87,336 R | 61.1% | 38.9% | 61.1% | 38.9% |
| 1962 | 327,506 | 163,952 | Chafee, John H. | 163,554 | Notte, John A. | | 398 D | 50.1% | 49.9% | 50.1% | 49.9% |
| 1960 | 401,362 | 174,044 | Del Sesto, Christopher | 227,318 | Notte, John A. | | 53,274 D | 43.4% | 56.6% | 43.4% | 56.6% |
| 1958 | 346,780 | 176,505 | Del Sesto, Christopher | 170,275 | Roberts, Dennis J. | | 6,230 R | 50.9% | 49.1% | 50.9% | 49.1% |
| 1956 | 383,919 | 191,604 | Del Sesto, Christopher | 192,315 | Roberts, Dennis J. | | 711 D | 49.9% | 50.1% | 49.9% | 50.1% |
| 1954 | 328,670 | 137,131 | Lewis, Dean J. | 189,595 | Roberts, Dennis J. | 1,944 | 52,464 D | 41.7% | 57.7% | 42.0% | 58.0% |
| 1952 | 409,689 | 194,102 | Archambault, Raoul | 215,587 | Roberts, Dennis J. | | 21,485 D | 47.4% | 52.6% | 47.4% | 52.6% |
| 1950 | 296,809 | 120,684 | Lachapelle, E. T. | 176,125 | Roberts, Dennis J. | | 55,441 D | 40.7% | 59.3% | 40.7% | 59.3% |
| 1948 | 323,863 | 124,441 | Ruerat, Albert P. | 198,056 | Pastore, John O. | 1,366 | 73,615 D | 38.4% | 61.2% | 38.6% | 61.4% |
| 1946 | 275,341 | 126,456 | Murphy, John G. | 148,885 | Pastore, John O. | | 22,429 D | 45.9% | 54.1% | 45.9% | 54.1% |

The term of office of Rhode Island's governor was increased to four from two years effective with the 1994 election.

## POSTWAR VOTE FOR SENATOR

| Year | Total Vote | Republican | | Democratic | | Other Vote | Rep.-Dem. Plurality | Percentage | | | |
|------|------------|------------|------------|------------|------------|------------|---------------------|------------|------------|------------|------------|
| | | Vote | Candidate | Vote | Candidate | | | Total Vote | | Major Vote | |
| | | | | | | | | Rep. | Dem. | Rep. | Dem. |
| 2002 | 323,912 | 69,881 | Tingle, Robert G. | 253,922 | Reed, Jack | 109 | 184,041 D | 21.6% | 78.4% | 21.6% | 78.4% |
| 2000 | 391,537 | 222,588 | Chafee, Lincoln | 161,023 | Weygand, Bob | 7,926 | 61,565 R | 56.8% | 41.1% | 58.0% | 42.0% |
| 1996 | 363,378 | 127,368 | Mayer, Nancy | 230,676 | Reed, Jack | 5,334 | 103,308 D | 35.1% | 63.5% | 35.6% | 64.4% |
| 1994 | 345,388 | 222,856 | Chafee, John H. | 122,532 | Kushner, Linda J. | | 100,324 R | 64.5% | 35.5% | 64.5% | 35.5% |
| 1990 | 364,062 | 138,947 | Schneider, Claudine | 225,105 | Pell, Claiborne | 10 | 86,158 D | 38.2% | 61.8% | 38.2% | 61.8% |
| 1988 | 397,996 | 217,273 | Chafee, John H. | 180,717 | Licht, Richard A. | 6 | 36,556 R | 54.6% | 45.4% | 54.6% | 45.4% |
| 1984 | 395,285 | 108,492 | Leonard, Barbara | 286,780 | Pell, Claiborne | 13 | 178,288 D | 27.4% | 72.6% | 27.4% | 72.6% |
| 1982 | 342,779 | 175,495 | Chafee, John H. | 167,283 | Michaelson, Julius C. | 1 | 8,212 R | 51.2% | 48.8% | 51.2% | 48.8% |
| 1978 | 305,618 | 76,061 | Reynolds, James G. | 229,557 | Pell, Claiborne | | 153,496 D | 24.9% | 75.1% | 24.9% | 75.1% |
| 1976 | 398,906 | 230,329 | Chafee, John H. | 167,665 | Lorber, Richard P. | 912 | 62,664 R | 57.7% | 42.0% | 57.9% | 42.1% |
| 1972 | 413,432 | 188,990 | Chafee, John H. | 221,942 | Pell, Claiborne | 2,500 | 32,952 D | 45.7% | 53.7% | 46.0% | 54.0% |
| 1970 | 341,222 | 107,351 | McLaughlin, John | 230,469 | Pastore, John O. | 3,402 | 123,118 D | 31.5% | 67.5% | 31.8% | 68.2% |
| 1966 | 324,173 | 104,838 | Briggs, Ruth M. | 219,331 | Pell, Claiborne | 4 | 114,493 D | 32.3% | 67.7% | 32.3% | 67.7% |
| 1964 | 386,322 | 66,715 | Lagueux, Ronald R. | 319,607 | Pastore, John O. | | 252,892 D | 17.3% | 82.7% | 17.3% | 82.7% |
| 1960 | 399,983 | 124,408 | Archambault, Raoul | 275,575 | Pell, Claiborne | | 151,167 D | 31.1% | 68.9% | 31.1% | 68.9% |
| 1958 | 344,519 | 122,353 | Ewing, Bayard | 222,166 | Pastore, John O. | | 99,813 D | 35.5% | 64.5% | 35.5% | 64.5% |
| 1954 | 326,624 | 132,970 | Sundlun, Walter I. | 193,654 | Green, Theodore F. | | 60,684 D | 40.7% | 59.3% | 40.7% | 59.3% |
| 1952 | 410,978 | 185,850 | Ewing, Bayard | 225,128 | Pastore, John O. | | 39,278 D | 45.2% | 54.8% | 45.2% | 54.8% |
| 1950S | 297,909 | 114,184 | Levy, Austin T. | 183,725 | Pastore, John O. | | 69,541 D | 38.3% | 61.7% | 38.3% | 61.7% |
| 1948 | 320,420 | 130,262 | Hazard, Thomas P. | 190,158 | Green, Theodore F. | | 59,896 D | 40.7% | 59.3% | 40.7% | 59.3% |
| 1946 | 273,528 | 122,780 | Dyer, W. Gurnee | 150,748 | McGrath, J. Howard | | 27,968 D | 44.9% | 55.1% | 44.9% | 55.1% |

The 1950 election was for a short term to fill a vacancy.

# RHODE ISLAND

Congressional districts first established for elections held in 2002
2 members

PROVIDENCE

**1**

**Pawtucket**

**Providence**

**Cranston**

BRISTOL

**Warwick**

**Bristol**

KENT

**2**

NEWPORT

WASHINGTON

**1**

**Newport**

**Kingston**

**Westerly**

**New Shoreham**

**2**

# RHODE ISLAND

## PRESIDENT 2004

| 2000 Census Population | County | Total Vote | Republican | Democratic | Other | Rep.-Dem. Plurality | Percentage | | | |
|---|---|---|---|---|---|---|---|---|---|---|
| | | | | | | | Total Vote | | Major Vote | |
| | | | | | | | Rep. | Dem. | Rep. | Dem. |
| 50,648 | BRISTOL | 24,677 | 9,855 | 14,448 | 374 | 4,593 D | 39.9% | 58.5% | 40.6% | 59.4% |
| 167,090 | KENT | 77,842 | 33,699 | 42,830 | 1,313 | 9,131 D | 43.3% | 55.0% | 44.0% | 56.0% |
| 85,433 | NEWPORT | 40,337 | 16,622 | 22,992 | 723 | 6,370 D | 41.2% | 57.0% | 42.0% | 58.0% |
| 621,602 | PROVIDENCE | 230,947 | 82,337 | 144,811 | 3,799 | 62,474 D | 35.7% | 62.7% | 36.2% | 63.8% |
| 123,546 | WASHINGTON | 62,486 | 26,533 | 34,679 | 1,274 | 8,146 D | 42.5% | 55.5% | 43.3% | 56.7% |
| 1,048,319 | TOTAL | 437,134 | 169,046 | 259,760 | 8,328 | 90,714 D | 38.7% | 59.4% | 39.4% | 60.6% |

Note: The statewide totals for "Total Vote" and "Other" include 845 scattered write-in votes that were not included in the county-by-county returns.

| | City/Town | | | | | | | | | |
|---|---|---|---|---|---|---|---|---|---|---|
| 16,819 | BARRINGTON | 9,450 | 4,020 | 5,291 | 139 | 1,271 D | 42.5% | 56.0% | 43.2% | 56.8% |
| 22,469 | BRISTOL TOWN | 10,427 | 4,000 | 6,276 | 151 | 2,276 D | 38.4% | 60.2% | 38.9% | 61.1% |
| 15,796 | BURRILLVILLE | 6,339 | 3,024 | 3,204 | 111 | 180 D | 47.7% | 50.5% | 48.6% | 51.4% |
| 18,928 | CENTRAL FALLS | 3,498 | 807 | 2,647 | 44 | 1,840 D | 23.1% | 75.7% | 23.4% | 76.6% |
| 7,859 | CHARLESTOWN | 4,202 | 1,838 | 2,279 | 85 | 441 D | 43.7% | 54.2% | 44.6% | 55.4% |
| 33,668 | COVENTRY | 15,939 | 7,249 | 8,417 | 273 | 1,168 D | 45.5% | 52.8% | 46.3% | 53.7% |
| 79,269 | CRANSTON | 35,281 | 14,471 | 20,331 | 479 | 5,860 D | 41.0% | 57.6% | 41.6% | 58.4% |
| 31,840 | CUMBERLAND | 15,871 | 6,874 | 8,753 | 244 | 1,879 D | 43.3% | 55.2% | 44.0% | 56.0% |
| 12,948 | EAST GREENWICH | 7,108 | 3,690 | 3,289 | 129 | 401 R | 51.9% | 46.3% | 52.9% | 47.1% |
| 48,688 | EAST PROVIDENCE | 20,332 | 6,359 | 13,655 | 318 | 7,296 D | 31.3% | 67.2% | 31.8% | 68.2% |
| 6,045 | EXETER | 3,011 | 1,439 | 1,506 | 66 | 67 D | 47.8% | 50.0% | 48.9% | 51.1% |
| 4,274 | FOSTER | 2,404 | 1,121 | 1,224 | 59 | 103 D | 46.6% | 50.9% | 47.8% | 52.2% |
| 9,948 | GLOCESTER | 4,873 | 2,357 | 2,425 | 93 | 68 D | 48.3% | 49.7% | 49.3% | 50.7% |
| 7,836 | HOPKINTON | 3,532 | 1,589 | 1,838 | 105 | 249 D | 45.0% | 52.0% | 46.4% | 53.6% |
| 5,622 | JAMESTOWN | 3,591 | 1,372 | 2,133 | 86 | 761 D | 38.2% | 59.4% | 39.1% | 60.9% |
| 28,195 | JOHNSTON | 13,904 | 5,848 | 7,870 | 186 | 2,022 D | 42.1% | 56.6% | 42.6% | 57.4% |
| 20,898 | LINCOLN | 10,910 | 4,966 | 5,783 | 161 | 817 D | 45.5% | 53.0% | 46.2% | 53.8% |
| 3,593 | LITTLE COMPTON | 2,307 | 1,056 | 1,195 | 56 | 139 D | 45.8% | 51.8% | 46.9% | 53.1% |
| 17,334 | MIDDLETOWN | 7,299 | 3,146 | 4,024 | 129 | 878 D | 43.1% | 55.1% | 43.9% | 56.1% |
| 16,361 | NARRAGANSETT | 8,518 | 3,444 | 4,921 | 153 | 1,477 D | 40.4% | 57.8% | 41.2% | 58.8% |
| 26,475 | NEWPORT CITY | 10,360 | 3,699 | 6,475 | 186 | 2,776 D | 35.7% | 62.5% | 36.4% | 63.6% |
| 1,010 | NEW SHOREHAM | 1,069 | 338 | 696 | 35 | 358 D | 31.6% | 65.1% | 32.7% | 67.3% |
| 26,326 | NORTH KINGSTOWN | 14,230 | 6,536 | 7,430 | 264 | 894 D | 45.9% | 52.2% | 46.8% | 53.2% |
| 32,411 | NORTH PROVIDENCE | 15,542 | 5,662 | 9,671 | 209 | 4,009 D | 36.4% | 62.2% | 36.9% | 63.1% |
| 10,618 | NORTH SMITHFIELD | 5,754 | 2,716 | 2,961 | 77 | 245 D | 47.2% | 51.5% | 47.8% | 52.2% |
| 72,958 | PAWTUCKET | 22,359 | 6,394 | 15,567 | 398 | 9,173 D | 28.6% | 69.6% | 29.1% | 70.9% |
| 17,149 | PORTSMOUTH | 9,348 | 4,337 | 4,868 | 143 | 531 D | 46.4% | 52.1% | 47.1% | 52.9% |
| 173,618 | PROVIDENCE CITY | 46,634 | 9,787 | 35,917 | 930 | 26,130 D | 21.0% | 77.0% | 21.4% | 78.6% |
| 7,222 | RICHMOND | 3,528 | 1,591 | 1,853 | 84 | 262 D | 45.1% | 52.5% | 46.2% | 53.8% |
| 10,324 | SCITUATE | 5,634 | 3,001 | 2,510 | 123 | 491 R | 53.3% | 44.6% | 54.5% | 45.5% |
| 20,613 | SMITHFIELD | 9,434 | 4,425 | 4,861 | 148 | 436 D | 46.9% | 51.5% | 47.7% | 52.3% |
| 27,921 | SOUTH KINGSTOWN | 13,314 | 4,949 | 8,091 | 274 | 3,142 D | 37.2% | 60.8% | 38.0% | 62.0% |
| 15,260 | TIVERTON | 7,432 | 3,012 | 4,297 | 123 | 1,285 D | 40.5% | 57.8% | 41.2% | 58.8% |
| 11,360 | WARREN | 4,800 | 1,835 | 2,881 | 84 | 1,046 D | 38.2% | 60.0% | 38.9% | 61.1% |
| 85,808 | WARWICK | 40,467 | 16,640 | 23,164 | 663 | 6,524 D | 41.1% | 57.2% | 41.8% | 58.2% |
| 22,966 | WESTERLY | 11,082 | 4,809 | 6,065 | 208 | 1,256 D | 43.4% | 54.7% | 44.2% | 55.8% |
| 5,085 | WEST GREENWICH | 2,834 | 1,466 | 1,300 | 68 | 166 R | 51.7% | 45.9% | 53.0% | 47.0% |
| 29,581 | WEST WARWICK | 11,494 | 4,654 | 6,660 | 180 | 2,006 D | 40.5% | 57.9% | 41.1% | 58.9% |
| 43,224 | WOONSOCKET | 12,176 | 4,525 | 7,432 | 219 | 2,907 D | 37.2% | 61.0% | 37.8% | 62.2% |
| 1,048,319 | TOTAL | 437,134 | 169,046 | 259,760 | 8,328 | 90,714 D | 38.7% | 59.4% | 39.4% | 60.6% |

Note: The statewide totals for "Total Vote" and "Other" include 845 scattered write-in votes that were not included in the city/town returns.

# RHODE ISLAND

## HOUSE OF REPRESENTATIVES

| CD | Year | Total Vote | Republican Vote | Republican Candidate | Democratic Vote | Democratic Candidate | Other Vote | Rep.-Dem. Plurality | Total Vote Rep. | Total Vote Dem. | Major Vote Rep. | Major Vote Dem. |
|---|---|---|---|---|---|---|---|---|---|---|---|---|
| 1 | 2004 | 195,010 | 69,819 | Rogers, David W. | 124,923 | Kennedy, Patrick J.* | 268 | 55,104 D | 35.8% | 64.1% | 35.9% | 64.1% |
| 1 | 2002 | 159,066 | 59,370 | Rogers, David W. | 95,286 | Kennedy, Patrick J.* | 4,410 | 35,916 D | 37.3% | 59.9% | 38.4% | 61.6% |
| 2 | 2004 | 207,165 | 43,139 | Barton, Arthur Chuck III | 154,392 | Langevin, Jim* | 9,634 | 111,253 D | 20.8% | 74.5% | 21.8% | 78.2% |
| 2 | 2002 | 169,580 | 37,767 | Matson, John O. | 129,390 | Langevin, Jim* | 2,423 | 91,623 D | 22.3% | 76.3% | 22.6% | 77.4% |
| Total | 2004 | 402,175 | 112,958 | | 279,315 | | 9,902 | 166,357 D | 28.1% | 69.5% | 28.8% | 71.2% |
| Total | 2002 | 328,646 | 97,137 | | 224,676 | | 6,833 | 127,539 D | 29.6% | 68.4% | 30.2% | 69.8% |

An asterisk (*) denotes incumbent.

# RHODE ISLAND

## GENERAL AND PRIMARY ELECTIONS

### 2004 GENERAL ELECTIONS

**President** — Other vote was 4,651 Reform (Ralph Nader); 1,333 Green (David Cobb); 907 Libertarian (Michael Badnarik); 339 Constitution (Michael Peroutka); 253 Workers World (John Parker); 845 write-in.

**House** — Other vote was:

CD 1 — 6 write-in (Mark Binder); 262 scattered write-in.
CD 2 — 6,196 Independent (Edward M. Morabito); 3,303 Socialist (Dorman J. Hayes Jr.); 5 write-in (Patrick Kennedy); 130 scattered write-in.

### 2004 PRIMARY ELECTIONS

**Primary** — March 2, 2004 (President); September 14, 2004 (Congress)

**Registration** (as of Sept. 14, 2004)

| | |
|---|---|
| Republican | 65,377 |
| Democratic | 235,940 |
| Green | 89 |
| Unaffiliated | 314,629 |
| TOTAL | 616,035 |

**Primary Type** — Semi-open—Registered Democrats and Republicans could vote only in their party's primary. Unaffiliated voters could participate in either party's primary if they were willing to become a member of that party.

# RHODE ISLAND

## GENERAL AND PRIMARY ELECTIONS

Note:   An asterisk (*) denotes incumbent.

| | REPUBLICAN PRIMARIES | | | DEMOCRATIC PRIMARIES | | |
|---|---|---|---|---|---|---|
| President | George W. Bush* | 2,152 | 84.9% | John Kerry | 25,466 | 71.2% |
| | Uncommitted | 314 | 12.4% | John Edwards | 6,635 | 18.6% |
| | Write-in | 69 | 2.7% | Howard Dean | 1,425 | 4.0% |
| | | | | Dennis J. Kucinich | 1,054 | 2.9% |
| | | | | Uncommitted | 415 | 1.2% |
| | | | | Joseph I. Lieberman | 303 | 0.8% |
| | | | | Wesley Clark | 237 | 0.7% |
| | | | | Lyndon H. LaRouche Jr. | 63 | 0.2% |
| | | | | Al Sharpton (write-in) | 38 | 0.1% |
| | | | | Scattered write-in | 123 | 0.3% |
| | TOTAL | 2,535 | | TOTAL | 35,759 | |
| Congressional District 1 | David W. Rogers | 385 | 100.0% | Patrick J. Kennedy* | 22,684 | 75.5% |
| | | | | Mark Binder | 7,359 | 24.5% |
| | | | | TOTAL | 30,043 | |
| Congressional District 2 | Arthur Chuck Barton III | 7,216 | 100.0% | Jim Langevin* | 19,244 | 85.6% |
| | | | | John D. Hamilton | 3,230 | 14.4% |
| | | | | TOTAL | 22,474 | |

# SOUTH CAROLINA

## GOVERNOR
Mark Sanford (R). Elected 2002 to a four-year term.

## SENATORS (2 Republicans)
Jim DeMint (R). Elected 2004 to a six-year term.

Lindsey Graham (R). Elected 2002 to a six-year term.

## REPRESENTATIVES (4 Republicans, 2 Democrats)
1. Henry E. Brown Jr. (R)
2. Joe Wilson (R)
3. J. Gresham Barrett (R)
4. Bob Inglis (R)
5. John M. Spratt Jr. (D)
6. James E. Clyburn (D)

## POSTWAR VOTE FOR PRESIDENT

| | | Republican | | Democratic | | Other | | Percentage | | | |
| | | | | | | | | Total Vote | | Major Vote | |
| Year | Total Vote | Vote | Candidate | Vote | Candidate | Vote | Plurality | Rep. | Dem. | Rep. | Dem. |
|---|---|---|---|---|---|---|---|---|---|---|---|
| 2004 | 1,617,730 | 937,974 | Bush, George W. | 661,699 | Kerry, John | 18,057 | 276,275 R | 58.0% | 40.9% | 58.6% | 41.4% |
| 2000** | 1,382,717 | 785,937 | Bush, George W. | 565,561 | Gore, Al | 31,219 | 220,376 R | 56.8% | 40.9% | 58.2% | 41.8% |
| 1996** | 1,151,689 | 573,458 | Dole, Bob | 506,283 | Clinton, Bill | 71,948 | 67,175 R | 49.8% | 44.0% | 53.1% | 46.9% |
| 1992** | 1,202,527 | 577,507 | Bush, George | 479,514 | Clinton, Bill | 145,506 | 97,993 R | 48.0% | 39.9% | 54.6% | 45.4% |
| 1988 | 986,009 | 606,443 | Bush, George | 370,554 | Dukakis, Michael S. | 9,012 | 235,889 R | 61.5% | 37.6% | 62.1% | 37.9% |
| 1984 | 968,529 | 615,539 | Reagan, Ronald | 344,459 | Mondale, Walter F. | 8,531 | 271,080 R | 63.6% | 35.6% | 64.1% | 35.9% |
| 1980** | 894,071 | 441,841 | Reagan, Ronald | 430,385 | Carter, Jimmy | 21,845 | 11,456 R | 49.4% | 48.1% | 50.7% | 49.3% |
| 1976 | 802,583 | 346,149 | Ford, Gerald R. | 450,807 | Carter, Jimmy | 5,627 | 104,658 D | 43.1% | 56.2% | 43.4% | 56.6% |
| 1972 | 673,960 | 477,044 | Nixon, Richard M. | 186,824 | McGovern, George S. | 10,092 | 290,220 R | 70.8% | 27.7% | 71.9% | 28.1% |
| 1968** | 666,978 | 254,062 | Nixon, Richard M. | 197,486 | Humphrey, Hubert H. | 215,430 | 38,632 R | 38.1% | 29.6% | 56.3% | 43.7% |
| 1964 | 524,779 | 309,048 | Goldwater, Barry M. | 215,723 | Johnson, Lyndon B. | 8 | 93,325 R | 58.9% | 41.1% | 58.9% | 41.1% |
| 1960 | 386,688 | 188,558 | Nixon, Richard M. | 198,129 | Kennedy, John F. | 1 | 9,571 D | 48.8% | 51.2% | 48.8% | 51.2% |
| 1956** | 300,583 | 75,700 | Eisenhower, Dwight D. | 136,372 | Stevenson, Adlai E. | 88,511 | 47,863 D | 25.2% | 45.4% | 35.7% | 64.3% |
| 1952 | 341,087 | 168,082 | Eisenhower, Dwight D. | 173,004 | Stevenson, Adlai E. | 1 | 4,922 D | 49.3% | 50.7% | 49.3% | 50.7% |
| 1948** | 142,571 | 5,386 | Dewey, Thomas E. | 34,423 | Truman, Harry S. | 102,762 | 68,184 SR | 3.8% | 24.1% | 13.5% | 86.5% |

In past elections, the other vote included: 2000 - 20,200 Green (Ralph Nader); 1996 - 64,386 Reform (Ross Perot); 1992 - 138,872 Independent (Perot); 1980 - 14,153 Independent (John Anderson); 1968 - 215,430 American Independent (George Wallace), which finished second in South Carolina; 1956 - 88,509 Independent states' rights electors, which placed second; 1948 - 102,607 States' Rights (Strom Thurmond), which won South Carolina with 72.0 percent of the vote.

# SOUTH CAROLINA

## POSTWAR VOTE FOR GOVERNOR

| Year | Total Vote | Republican Vote | Republican Candidate | Democratic Vote | Democratic Candidate | Other Vote | Rep.-Dem. Plurality | Total Vote Rep. | Total Vote Dem. | Major Vote Rep. | Major Vote Dem. |
|------|-----------|-----------------|---------------------|-----------------|---------------------|------------|---------------------|-----------------|-----------------|-----------------|-----------------|
| 2002 | 1,107,725 | 585,422 | Sanford, Mark | 521,140 | Hodges, Jim | 1,163 | 64,282 R | 52.8% | 47.0% | 52.9% | 47.1% |
| 1998 | 1,070,869 | 484,088 | Beasley, David | 570,070 | Hodges, Jim | 16,711 | 85,982 D | 45.2% | 53.2% | 45.9% | 54.1% |
| 1994 | 933,850 | 470,756 | Beasley, David | 447,002 | Theodore, Nick A. | 16,092 | 23,754 R | 50.4% | 47.9% | 51.3% | 48.7% |
| 1990 | 760,965 | 528,831 | Campbell, Carroll | 212,034 | Mitchell, Theo | 20,100 | 316,797 R | 69.5% | 27.9% | 71.4% | 28.6% |
| 1986 | 753,751 | 384,565 | Campbell, Carroll | 361,325 | Daniel, Mike | 7,861 | 23,240 R | 51.0% | 47.9% | 51.6% | 48.4% |
| 1982 | 671,625 | 202,806 | Workman, W. D. | 468,819 | Riley, Richard W. | | 266,013 D | 30.2% | 69.8% | 30.2% | 69.8% |
| 1978 | 627,182 | 236,946 | Young, Edward L. | 384,898 | Riley, Richard W. | 5,338 | 147,952 D | 37.8% | 61.4% | 38.1% | 61.9% |
| 1974 | 523,199 | 266,109 | Edwards, James B. | 248,938 | Dorn, W. J. Bryan | 8,152 | 17,171 R | 50.9% | 47.6% | 51.7% | 48.3% |
| 1970 | 484,857 | 221,233 | Watson, Albert W. | 250,551 | West, John C. | 13,073 | 29,318 D | 45.6% | 51.7% | 46.9% | 53.1% |
| 1966 | 439,942 | 184,088 | Rogers, Joseph O. | 255,854 | McNair, Robert E. | | 71,766 D | 41.8% | 58.2% | 41.8% | 58.2% |
| 1962 | 253,721 | | — | 253,704 | Russell, Donald S. | 17 | 253,704 D | | 100.0% | | 100.0% |
| 1958 | 77,740 | | — | 77,714 | Hollings, Ernest F. | 26 | 77,714 D | | 100.0% | | 100.0% |
| 1954 | 214,212 | | — | 214,204 | Timmerman, George B. | 8 | 214,204 D | | 100.0% | | 100.0% |
| 1950 | 50,642 | | — | 50,633 | Byrnes, James F. | 9 | 50,633 D | | 100.0% | | 100.0% |
| 1946 | 26,520 | | — | 26,520 | Thurmond, Strom | | 26,520 D | | 100.0% | | 100.0% |

## POSTWAR VOTE FOR SENATOR

| Year | Total Vote | Republican Vote | Republican Candidate | Democratic Vote | Democratic Candidate | Other Vote | Rep.-Dem. Plurality | Total Vote Rep. | Total Vote Dem. | Major Vote Rep. | Major Vote Dem. |
|------|-----------|-----------------|---------------------|-----------------|---------------------|------------|---------------------|-----------------|-----------------|-----------------|-----------------|
| 2004 | 1,597,221 | 857,167 | DeMint, Jim | 704,384 | Tenenbaum, Inez | 35,670 | 152,783 R | 53.7% | 44.1% | 54.9% | 45.1% |
| 2002 | 1,102,948 | 600,010 | Graham, Lindsey | 487,359 | Sanders, Alex | 15,579 | 112,651 R | 54.4% | 44.2% | 55.2% | 44.8% |
| 1998 | 1,068,367 | 488,132 | Inglis, Bob | 562,791 | Hollings, Ernest F. | 17,444 | 74,659 D | 45.7% | 52.7% | 46.4% | 53.6% |
| 1996 | 1,161,372 | 619,859 | Thurmond, Strom | 510,951 | Close, Elliott Springs | 30,562 | 108,908 R | 53.4% | 44.0% | 54.8% | 45.2% |
| 1992 | 1,180,438 | 554,175 | Hartnett, Thomas F. | 591,030 | Hollings, Ernest F. | 35,233 | 36,855 D | 46.9% | 50.1% | 48.4% | 51.6% |
| 1990 | 750,716 | 482,032 | Thurmond, Strom | 244,112 | Cunningham, Bob | 24,572 | 237,920 R | 64.2% | 32.5% | 66.4% | 33.6% |
| 1986 | 737,962 | 262,886 | McMaster, Henry D. | 465,500 | Hollings, Ernest F. | 9,576 | 202,614 D | 35.6% | 63.1% | 36.1% | 63.9% |
| 1984 | 965,130 | 644,815 | Thurmond, Strom | 306,982 | Purvis, Melvin | 13,333 | 337,833 R | 66.8% | 31.8% | 67.7% | 32.3% |
| 1980 | 870,594 | 257,946 | Mays, Marshall T. | 612,554 | Hollings, Ernest F. | 94 | 354,608 D | 29.6% | 70.4% | 29.6% | 70.4% |
| 1978 | 632,852 | 351,733 | Thurmond, Strom | 281,119 | Ravenel, Charles D. | | 70,614 R | 55.6% | 44.4% | 55.6% | 44.4% |
| 1974 | 512,397 | 146,645 | Bush, Gwenyfred | 356,126 | Hollings, Ernest F. | 9,626 | 209,481 D | 28.6% | 69.5% | 29.2% | 70.8% |
| 1972 | 672,246 | 426,601 | Thurmond, Strom | 245,457 | Zeigler, Eugene N. | 188 | 181,144 R | 63.5% | 36.5% | 63.5% | 36.5% |
| 1968 | 652,855 | 248,780 | Parker, Marshall | 404,060 | Hollings, Ernest F. | 15 | 155,280 D | 38.1% | 61.9% | 38.1% | 61.9% |
| 1966 | 436,252 | 271,297 | Thurmond, Strom | 164,955 | Morrah, Bradley | | 106,342 R | 62.2% | 37.8% | 62.2% | 37.8% |
| 1966S | 435,822 | 212,032 | Parker, Marshall | 223,790 | Hollings, Ernest F. | | 11,758 D | 48.7% | 51.3% | 48.7% | 51.3% |
| 1962 | 312,647 | 133,930 | Workman, W.D. | 178,712 | Johnston, Olin D. | 5 | 44,782 D | 42.8% | 57.2% | 42.8% | 57.2% |
| 1960 | 330,266 | | — | 330,164 | Thurmond, Strom | 102 | 330,164 D | | 100.0% | | 100.0% |
| 1956 | 279,845 | 49,695 | Crawford, Leon P. | 230,150 | Johnston, Olin D. | | 180,455 D | 17.8% | 82.2% | 17.8% | 82.2% |
| 1956S | 251,907 | | — | 251,907 | Thurmond, Strom | | 251,907 D | | 100.0% | | 100.0% |
| 1954** | 227,232 | | — | 83,525 | Brown, Edgar A. | 143,707 | 59,919 ID | | 36.8% | | 100.0% |
| 1950 | 50,277 | | — | 50,240 | Johnston, Olin D. | 37 | 50,240 D | | 99.9% | | 100.0% |
| 1948 | 141,006 | 5,008 | Gerald, J. Bates | 135,998 | Maybank, Burnet R. | | 130,990 D | 3.6% | 96.4% | 3.6% | 96.4% |

One each of the 1966 and 1956 elections was for a short term to fill a vacancy. In 1954 Strom Thurmond polled 143,444 votes as an Independent Democratic write-in candidate (63.1 percent of the total vote) and won the election with a 59,919-vote plurality over the Democratic candidate.

# SOUTH CAROLINA

Congressional districts first established for elections held in 2002
6 members

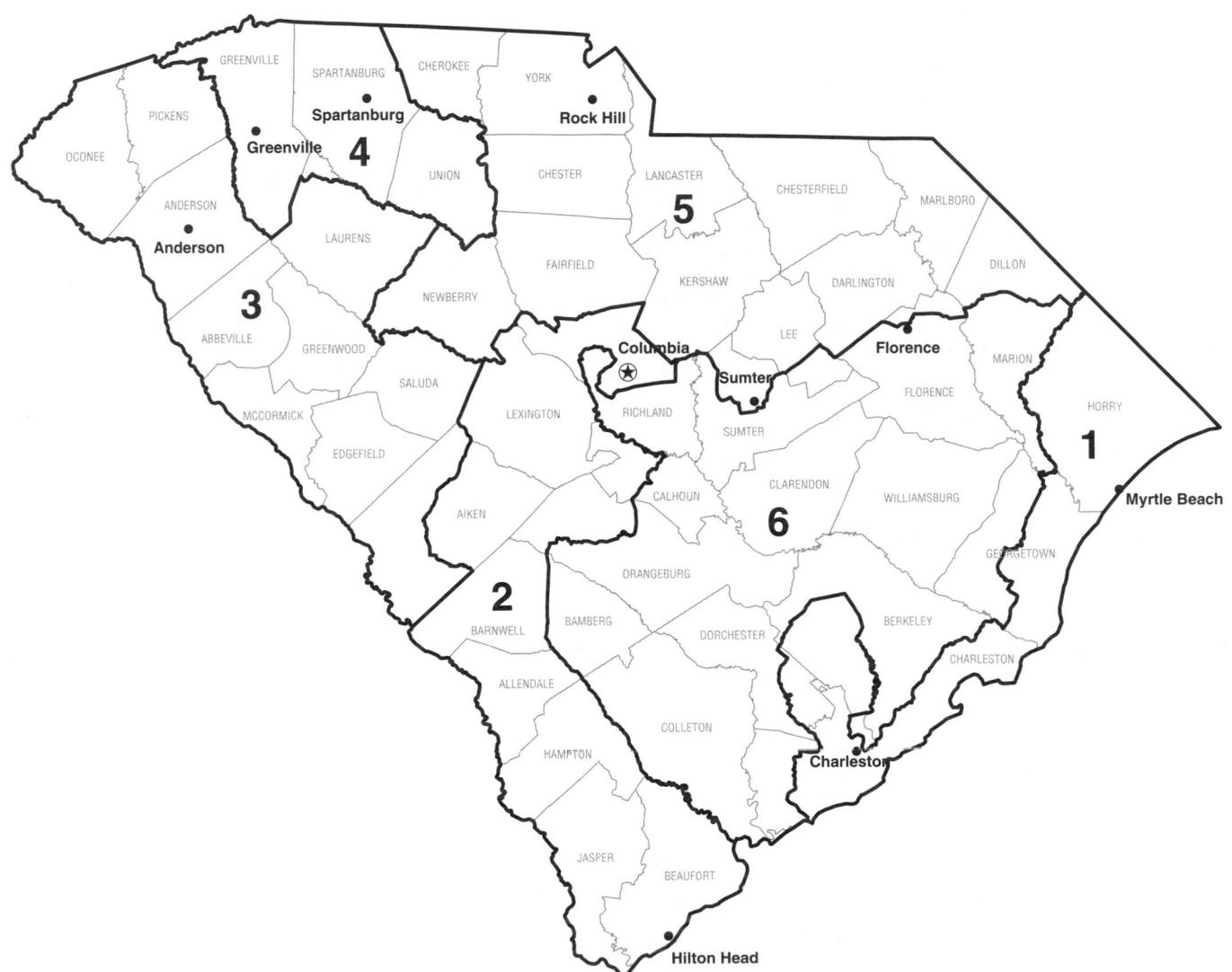

# SOUTH CAROLINA

## PRESIDENT 2004

| 2000 Census Population | County | Total Vote | Republican | Democratic | Other | Rep.-Dem. Plurality | Percentage Total Vote Rep. | Dem. | Major Vote Rep. | Dem. |
|---|---|---|---|---|---|---|---|---|---|---|
| 26,167 | ABBEVILLE | 9,925 | 5,436 | 4,389 | 100 | 1,047 R | 54.8% | 44.2% | 55.3% | 44.7% |
| 142,552 | AIKEN | 59,492 | 39,077 | 19,799 | 616 | 19,278 R | 65.7% | 33.3% | 66.4% | 33.6% |
| 11,211 | ALLENDALE | 3,591 | 985 | 2,565 | 41 | 1,580 D | 27.4% | 71.4% | 27.7% | 72.3% |
| 165,740 | ANDERSON | 64,722 | 43,355 | 20,697 | 670 | 22,658 R | 67.0% | 32.0% | 67.7% | 32.3% |
| 16,658 | BAMBERG | 6,036 | 2,138 | 3,841 | 57 | 1,703 D | 35.4% | 63.6% | 35.8% | 64.2% |
| 23,478 | BARNWELL | 8,685 | 4,606 | 3,982 | 97 | 624 R | 53.0% | 45.8% | 53.6% | 46.4% |
| 120,937 | BEAUFORT | 55,235 | 33,331 | 21,505 | 399 | 11,826 R | 60.3% | 38.9% | 60.8% | 39.2% |
| 142,651 | BERKELEY | 52,937 | 32,104 | 20,142 | 691 | 11,962 R | 60.6% | 38.0% | 61.4% | 38.6% |
| 15,185 | CALHOUN | 6,919 | 3,448 | 3,393 | 78 | 55 R | 49.8% | 49.0% | 50.4% | 49.6% |
| 309,969 | CHARLESTON | 136,316 | 70,297 | 63,758 | 2,261 | 6,539 R | 51.6% | 46.8% | 52.4% | 47.6% |
| 52,537 | CHEROKEE | 18,714 | 12,090 | 6,466 | 158 | 5,624 R | 64.6% | 34.6% | 65.2% | 34.8% |
| 34,068 | CHESTER | 11,729 | 5,798 | 5,790 | 141 | 8 R | 49.4% | 49.4% | 50.0% | 50.0% |
| 42,768 | CHESTERFIELD | 14,049 | 7,252 | 6,729 | 68 | 523 R | 51.6% | 47.9% | 51.9% | 48.1% |
| 32,502 | CLARENDON | 13,200 | 6,061 | 7,087 | 52 | 1,026 D | 45.9% | 53.7% | 46.1% | 53.9% |
| 38,264 | COLLETON | 14,106 | 7,264 | 6,699 | 143 | 565 R | 51.5% | 47.5% | 52.0% | 48.0% |
| 67,394 | DARLINGTON | 25,454 | 13,416 | 11,829 | 209 | 1,587 R | 52.7% | 46.5% | 53.1% | 46.9% |
| 30,722 | DILLON | 9,235 | 4,301 | 4,832 | 102 | 531 D | 46.6% | 52.3% | 47.1% | 52.9% |
| 96,413 | DORCHESTER | 41,317 | 26,006 | 14,733 | 578 | 11,273 R | 62.9% | 35.7% | 63.8% | 36.2% |
| 74,595 | EDGEFIELD | 9,746 | 5,611 | 4,051 | 84 | 1,560 R | 57.6% | 41.6% | 58.1% | 41.9% |
| 23,454 | FAIRFIELD | 9,435 | 3,531 | 5,764 | 140 | 2,233 D | 37.4% | 61.1% | 38.0% | 62.0% |
| 125,761 | FLORENCE | 49,545 | 27,689 | 21,442 | 414 | 6,247 R | 55.9% | 43.3% | 56.4% | 43.6% |
| 55,797 | GEORGETOWN | 23,593 | 12,606 | 10,602 | 385 | 2,004 R | 53.4% | 44.9% | 54.3% | 45.7% |
| 379,616 | GREENVILLE | 168,833 | 111,481 | 55,347 | 2,005 | 56,134 R | 66.0% | 32.8% | 66.8% | 33.2% |
| 66,271 | GREENWOOD | 23,442 | 14,264 | 8,954 | 224 | 5,310 R | 60.8% | 38.2% | 61.4% | 38.6% |
| 21,386 | HAMPTON | 8,016 | 3,097 | 4,832 | 87 | 1,735 D | 38.6% | 60.3% | 39.1% | 60.9% |
| 196,629 | HORRY | 81,347 | 50,447 | 29,547 | 1,353 | 20,900 R | 62.0% | 36.3% | 63.1% | 36.9% |
| 20,678 | JASPER | 6,846 | 2,933 | 3,840 | 73 | 907 D | 42.8% | 56.1% | 43.3% | 56.7% |
| 52,647 | KERSHAW | 22,915 | 14,160 | 8,515 | 240 | 5,645 R | 61.8% | 37.2% | 62.4% | 37.6% |
| 61,351 | LANCASTER | 20,814 | 12,916 | 7,631 | 267 | 5,285 R | 62.1% | 36.7% | 62.9% | 37.1% |
| 69,567 | LAURENS | 23,829 | 14,466 | 9,205 | 158 | 5,261 R | 60.7% | 38.6% | 61.1% | 38.9% |
| 20,119 | LEE | 7,898 | 2,901 | 4,960 | 37 | 2,059 D | 36.7% | 62.8% | 36.9% | 63.1% |
| 216,014 | LEXINGTON | 93,432 | 67,132 | 25,393 | 907 | 41,739 R | 71.9% | 27.2% | 72.6% | 27.4% |
| 9,958 | MCCORMICK | 5,122 | 2,396 | 2,648 | 78 | 252 D | 46.8% | 51.7% | 47.5% | 52.5% |
| 35,466 | MARION | 13,507 | 5,589 | 7,767 | 151 | 2,178 D | 41.4% | 57.5% | 41.8% | 58.2% |
| 28,818 | MARLBORO | 8,560 | 3,423 | 4,984 | 153 | 1,561 D | 40.0% | 58.2% | 40.7% | 59.3% |
| 36,108 | NEWBERRY | 12,409 | 7,654 | 4,483 | 272 | 3,171 R | 61.7% | 36.1% | 63.1% | 36.9% |
| 66,215 | OCONEE | 27,532 | 18,811 | 8,395 | 326 | 10,416 R | 68.3% | 30.5% | 69.1% | 30.9% |
| 91,582 | ORANGEBURG | 37,564 | 12,695 | 24,698 | 171 | 12,003 D | 33.8% | 65.7% | 34.0% | 66.0% |
| 110,757 | PICKENS | 40,510 | 29,759 | 10,287 | 464 | 19,472 R | 73.5% | 25.4% | 74.3% | 25.7% |
| 320,677 | RICHLAND | 133,801 | 56,212 | 76,283 | 1,306 | 20,071 D | 42.0% | 57.0% | 42.4% | 57.6% |
| 19,181 | SALUDA | 7,578 | 4,537 | 3,001 | 40 | 1,536 R | 59.9% | 39.6% | 60.2% | 39.8% |
| 253,791 | SPARTANBURG | 96,758 | 62,004 | 33,633 | 1,121 | 28,371 R | 64.1% | 34.8% | 64.8% | 35.2% |
| 104,646 | SUMTER | 37,003 | 18,074 | 18,695 | 234 | 621 D | 48.8% | 50.5% | 49.2% | 50.8% |
| 29,881 | UNION | 11,934 | 6,592 | 5,236 | 106 | 1,356 R | 55.2% | 43.9% | 55.7% | 44.3% |
| 37,217 | WILLIAMSBURG | 13,918 | 4,795 | 9,044 | 79 | 4,249 D | 34.5% | 65.0% | 34.6% | 65.4% |
| 164,614 | YORK | 70,181 | 45,234 | 24,226 | 721 | 21,008 R | 64.5% | 34.5% | 65.1% | 34.9% |
| 4,012,012 | TOTAL | 1,617,730 | 937,974 | 661,699 | 18,057 | 276,275 R | 58.0% | 40.9% | 58.6% | 41.4% |

# SOUTH CAROLINA

## SENATOR 2004

| 2000 Census Population | County | Total Vote | Republican | Democratic | Other | Rep.-Dem. Plurality | Percentage | | | |
|---|---|---|---|---|---|---|---|---|---|---|
| | | | | | | | Total Vote | | Major Vote | |
| | | | | | | | Rep. | Dem. | Rep. | Dem. |
| 26,167 | ABBEVILLE | 9,743 | 4,954 | 4,592 | 197 | 362 R | 50.8% | 47.1% | 51.9% | 48.1% |
| 142,552 | AIKEN | 58,107 | 36,446 | 20,674 | 987 | 15,772 R | 62.7% | 35.6% | 63.8% | 36.2% |
| 11,211 | ALLENDALE | 3,382 | 921 | 2,388 | 73 | 1,467 D | 27.2% | 70.6% | 27.8% | 72.2% |
| 165,740 | ANDERSON | 63,933 | 39,554 | 22,890 | 1,489 | 16,664 R | 61.9% | 35.8% | 63.3% | 36.7% |
| 16,658 | BAMBERG | 5,944 | 1,883 | 3,973 | 88 | 2,090 D | 31.7% | 66.8% | 32.2% | 67.8% |
| 23,478 | BARNWELL | 8,522 | 4,233 | 4,131 | 158 | 102 R | 49.7% | 48.5% | 50.6% | 49.4% |
| 120,937 | BEAUFORT | 54,048 | 31,724 | 20,884 | 1,440 | 10,840 R | 58.7% | 38.6% | 60.3% | 39.7% |
| 142,651 | BERKELEY | 52,227 | 29,759 | 21,248 | 1,220 | 8,511 R | 57.0% | 40.7% | 58.3% | 41.7% |
| 15,185 | CALHOUN | 6,806 | 3,118 | 3,562 | 126 | 444 D | 45.8% | 52.3% | 46.7% | 53.3% |
| 309,969 | CHARLESTON | 133,526 | 65,088 | 65,197 | 3,241 | 109 D | 48.7% | 48.8% | 50.0% | 50.0% |
| 52,537 | CHEROKEE | 18,335 | 10,658 | 7,167 | 510 | 3,491 R | 58.1% | 39.1% | 59.8% | 40.2% |
| 34,068 | CHESTER | 11,162 | 4,944 | 5,977 | 241 | 1,033 D | 44.3% | 53.5% | 45.3% | 54.7% |
| 42,768 | CHESTERFIELD | 14,171 | 6,195 | 7,674 | 302 | 1,479 D | 43.7% | 54.2% | 44.7% | 55.3% |
| 32,502 | CLARENDON | 13,514 | 5,575 | 7,768 | 171 | 2,193 D | 41.3% | 57.5% | 41.8% | 58.2% |
| 38,264 | COLLETON | 13,663 | 6,531 | 6,905 | 227 | 374 D | 47.8% | 50.5% | 48.6% | 51.4% |
| 67,394 | DARLINGTON | 25,179 | 12,191 | 12,531 | 457 | 340 D | 48.4% | 49.8% | 49.3% | 50.7% |
| 30,722 | DILLON | 9,476 | 4,174 | 5,075 | 227 | 901 D | 44.0% | 53.6% | 45.1% | 54.9% |
| 96,413 | DORCHESTER | 40,341 | 23,818 | 15,517 | 1,006 | 8,301 R | 59.0% | 38.5% | 60.6% | 39.4% |
| 24,595 | EDGEFIELD | 9,652 | 5,145 | 4,355 | 152 | 790 R | 53.3% | 45.1% | 54.2% | 45.8% |
| 23,454 | FAIRFIELD | 9,260 | 3,072 | 5,998 | 190 | 2,926 D | 33.2% | 64.8% | 33.9% | 66.1% |
| 125,761 | FLORENCE | 48,820 | 25,917 | 22,236 | 667 | 3,681 R | 53.1% | 45.5% | 53.8% | 46.2% |
| 55,797 | GEORGETOWN | 23,637 | 11,718 | 11,500 | 419 | 218 R | 49.6% | 48.7% | 50.5% | 49.5% |
| 379,616 | GREENVILLE | 167,262 | 105,471 | 57,886 | 3,905 | 47,585 R | 63.1% | 34.6% | 64.6% | 35.4% |
| 66,271 | GREENWOOD | 22,959 | 12,859 | 9,632 | 468 | 3,227 R | 56.0% | 42.0% | 57.2% | 42.8% |
| 21,386 | HAMPTON | 7,714 | 2,659 | 4,855 | 200 | 2,196 D | 34.5% | 62.9% | 35.4% | 64.6% |
| 196,629 | HORRY | 79,260 | 45,819 | 31,478 | 1,963 | 14,341 R | 57.8% | 39.7% | 59.3% | 40.7% |
| 20,678 | JASPER | 6,591 | 2,738 | 3,763 | 90 | 1,025 D | 41.5% | 57.1% | 42.1% | 57.9% |
| 52,647 | KERSHAW | 22,428 | 12,634 | 9,354 | 440 | 3,280 R | 56.3% | 41.7% | 57.5% | 42.5% |
| 61,351 | LANCASTER | 20,677 | 11,106 | 8,986 | 585 | 2,120 R | 53.7% | 43.5% | 55.3% | 44.7% |
| 69,567 | LAURENS | 23,589 | 12,951 | 10,124 | 514 | 2,827 R | 54.9% | 42.9% | 56.1% | 43.9% |
| 20,119 | LEE | 8,058 | 2,619 | 5,345 | 94 | 2,726 D | 32.5% | 66.3% | 32.9% | 67.1% |
| 216,014 | LEXINGTON | 92,554 | 59,467 | 30,885 | 2,202 | 28,582 R | 64.3% | 33.4% | 65.8% | 34.2% |
| 9,958 | MCCORMICK | 5,183 | 2,338 | 2,782 | 63 | 444 D | 45.1% | 53.7% | 45.7% | 54.3% |
| 35,466 | MARION | 12,939 | 4,935 | 7,734 | 270 | 2,799 D | 38.1% | 59.8% | 39.0% | 61.0% |
| 28,818 | MARLBORO | 8,323 | 2,900 | 5,055 | 368 | 2,155 D | 34.8% | 60.7% | 36.5% | 63.5% |
| 36,108 | NEWBERRY | 12,448 | 6,894 | 5,224 | 330 | 1,670 R | 55.4% | 42.0% | 56.9% | 43.1% |
| 66,215 | OCONEE | 27,064 | 17,185 | 9,330 | 549 | 7,855 R | 63.5% | 34.5% | 64.8% | 35.2% |
| 91,582 | ORANGEBURG | 38,087 | 11,812 | 25,663 | 612 | 13,851 D | 31.0% | 67.4% | 31.5% | 68.5% |
| 110,757 | PICKENS | 39,975 | 27,465 | 11,545 | 965 | 15,920 R | 68.7% | 28.9% | 70.4% | 29.6% |
| 320,677 | RICHLAND | 133,493 | 49,729 | 80,688 | 3,076 | 30,959 D | 37.3% | 60.4% | 38.1% | 61.9% |
| 19,181 | SALUDA | 7,601 | 4,177 | 3,288 | 136 | 889 R | 55.0% | 43.3% | 56.0% | 44.0% |
| 253,791 | SPARTANBURG | 95,393 | 56,006 | 36,550 | 2,837 | 19,456 R | 58.7% | 38.3% | 60.5% | 39.5% |
| 104,646 | SUMTER | 37,963 | 16,744 | 20,643 | 576 | 3,899 D | 44.1% | 54.4% | 44.8% | 55.2% |
| 29,881 | UNION | 11,473 | 5,704 | 5,481 | 288 | 223 R | 49.7% | 47.8% | 51.0% | 49.0% |
| 37,217 | WILLIAMSBURG | 14,172 | 4,560 | 9,400 | 212 | 4,840 D | 32.2% | 66.3% | 32.7% | 67.3% |
| 164,614 | YORK | 68,567 | 40,777 | 26,451 | 1,339 | 14,326 R | 59.5% | 38.6% | 60.7% | 39.3% |
| 4,012,012 | TOTAL | 1,597,221 | 857,167 | 704,384 | 35,670 | 152,783 R | 53.7% | 44.1% | 54.9% | 45.1% |

# SOUTH CAROLINA
## HOUSE OF REPRESENTATIVES

| | | | Republican | | Democratic | | Other | Rep.-Dem. | Total Vote | | Major Vote | |
|---|---|---|---|---|---|---|---|---|---|---|---|---|
| CD | Year | Total Vote | Vote | Candidate | Vote | Candidate | Vote | Plurality | Rep. | Dem. | Rep. | Dem. |
| 1 | 2004 | 212,308 | 186,448 | Brown, Henry E. Jr.* | | | 25,860 | 186,448 R | 87.8% | | 100.0% | |
| 1 | 2002 | 142,425 | 127,562 | Brown, Henry E. Jr.* | | | 14,863 | 127,562 R | 89.6% | | 100.0% | |
| 2 | 2004 | 279,870 | 181,862 | Wilson, Joe* | 93,249 | Ellisor, Michael R. | 4,759 | 88,613 R | 65.0% | 33.3% | 66.1% | 33.9% |
| 2 | 2002 | 171,359 | 144,149 | Wilson, Joe* | | | 27,210 | 144,149 R | 84.1% | | 100.0% | |
| 3 | 2004 | 191,999 | 191,052 | Barrett, J. Gresham* | | | 947 | 191,052 R | 99.5% | | 100.0% | |
| 3 | 2002 | 178,195 | 119,644 | Barrett, J. Gresham | 55,743 | Brightharp, George L. | 2,808 | 63,901 R | 67.1% | 31.3% | 68.2% | 31.8% |
| 4 | 2004 | 270,594 | 188,795 | Inglis, Bob | 78,376 | Brown, Brandon P. | 3,423 | 110,419 R | 69.8% | 29.0% | 70.7% | 29.3% |
| 4 | 2002 | 177,417 | 122,422 | DeMint, Jim* | 52,635 # | Ashy, Peter J. | 2,360 | 69,787 R | 69.0% | 29.7% | 69.9% | 30.1% |
| 5 | 2004 | 242,518 | 89,568 | Spencer, Albert F. | 152,867 | Spratt, John M. Jr.* | 83 | 63,299 D | 36.9% | 63.0% | 36.9% | 63.1% |
| 5 | 2002 | 141,972 | | | 121,912 | Spratt, John M. Jr.* | 20,060 | 121,912 D | | 85.9% | | 100.0% |
| 6 | 2004 | 241,829 | 79,600 # | McLeod, Gary | 161,987 | Clyburn, James E.* | 242 | 82,387 D | 32.9% | 67.0% | 32.9% | 67.1% |
| 6 | 2002 | 174,066 | 55,760 | McLeod, Gary | 116,586 | Clyburn, James E.* | 1,720 | 60,826 D | 32.0% | 67.0% | 32.4% | 67.6% |
| Total | 2004 | 1,439,118 | 917,325 | | 486,479 | | 35,314 | 430,846 R | 63.7% | 33.8% | 65.3% | 34.7% |
| Total | 2002 | 985,434 | 569,537 | | 346,876 | | 69,021 | 222,661 R | 57.8% | 35.2% | 62.1% | 37.9% |

A pound sign (#) indicates that candidate received votes on the ballot line of another party.

An asterisk (*) denotes incumbent.

# SOUTH CAROLINA
## GENERAL AND PRIMARY ELECTIONS

## 2004 GENERAL ELECTIONS

**President** Other vote was 5,520 Independence (Ralph Nader); 5,317 Constitution (Michael Peroutka); 3,608 Libertarian (Michael Badnarik); 2,124 United Citizens (Walter F. Brown); 1,488 Green (David Cobb).

**Senator** Other vote was 13,464 Constitution (Patrick Tyndall); 10,678 Libertarian (Rebekah E. Sutherland); 5,859 United Citizens (Tee Ferguson); 4,383 Green-Independence (Efia Nwangaza); 1,286 write-in. (Efia Nwangaza received 4,245 votes on the Green Party ballot line and 138 votes on the Independence Party ballot line.)

**House** Other vote was:

CD 1    25,674 Green (James E. Dunn); 186 write-in.
CD 2    4,447 Constitution (Steve Lefemine); 312 write-in.
CD 3    947 write-in.
CD 4    3,273 Green (C. Faye Walters); 150 write-in.
CD 5    83 write-in.
CD 6    242 write-in. (Republican Gary McLeod received 4,157 votes on the Constitution Party ballot line.)

# SOUTH CAROLINA

## GENERAL AND PRIMARY ELECTIONS

## 2004 PRIMARY ELECTIONS

| | | | | |
|---|---|---|---|---|
| **Primary** | February 3, 2004 (President)<br>June 8, 2004 (Congress) | **Registration**<br>(as of June 8, 2004) | 2,157,442 | No Party Registration |

**Primary Runoff** June 22, 2004

**Primary Type** Open—Any registered voter could participate in either the Democratic or Republican primary, although any voter who participated in one party's primary could not vote in a primary runoff of the other party.

Note: An asterisk (*) denotes incumbent. The names of unopposed candidates did not appear on the primary ballot; therefore, no votes were cast for these candidates.

| | REPUBLICAN PRIMARIES | | | DEMOCRATIC PRIMARIES | | |
|---|---|---|---|---|---|---|
| President | No Republican primary | | | John Edwards | 132,660 | 45.1% |
| | | | | John Kerry | 87,620 | 29.8% |
| | | | | Al Sharpton | 28,495 | 9.7% |
| | | | | Wesley Clark | 21,218 | 7.2% |
| | | | | Howard Dean | 13,984 | 4.8% |
| | | | | Joseph I. Lieberman | 7,101 | 2.4% |
| | | | | Dennis J. Kucinich | 1,344 | 0.5% |
| | | | | Richard A. Gephardt | 828 | 0.3% |
| | | | | Carol Moseley Braun | 593 | 0.2% |
| | | | | TOTAL | 293,843 | |
| Senator | David Beasley | 107,847 | 36.6% | Inez Tenenbaum | 126,720 | 75.5% |
| | Jim DeMint | 77,567 | 26.3% | Ben Frasier | 41,070 | 24.5% |
| | Thomas Ravenal | 73,167 | 24.8% | | | |
| | Charlie Condon | 27,694 | 9.4% | | | |
| | Mark McBride | 6,479 | 2.2% | | | |
| | Orly Benny Davis | 1,915 | 0.6% | | | |
| | TOTAL | 294,669 | | TOTAL | 167,790 | |
| | PRIMARY RUNOFF | | | | | |
| | Jim DeMint | 154,644 | 59.2% | | | |
| | David Beasley | 106,480 | 40.8% | | | |
| | TOTAL | 261,124 | | | | |
| Congressional District 1 | Henry E. Brown Jr.* | 47,066 | 83.5% | No Democratic candidate | | |
| | Bob Batchelder | 9,326 | 16.5% | | | |
| | TOTAL | 56,392 | | | | |
| Congressional District 2 | Joe Wilson* | Unopposed | | Michael R. Ellisor | Unopposed | |
| Congressional District 3 | J. Gresham Barrett* | Unopposed | | No Democratic candidate | | |
| Congressional District 4 | Bob Inglis | 52,125 | 84.2% | Brandon P. Brown | 8,895 | 58.8% |
| | Carole Wells | 7,140 | 11.5% | Andrew Wittman | 6,245 | 41.2% |
| | Jack Adams | 2,628 | 4.2% | | | |
| | TOTAL | 61,893 | | TOTAL | 15,140 | |
| Congressional District 5 | Albert F. Spencer | Unopposed | | John M. Spratt Jr.* | Unopposed | |
| Congressional District 6 | Gary McLeod | 16,855 | 78.8% | James E. Clyburn* | Unopposed | |
| | Michael Reino | 4,544 | 21.2% | | | |
| | TOTAL | 21,399 | | | | |

# SOUTH DAKOTA

## GOVERNOR
Mike Rounds (R). Elected 2002 to a four-year term.

## SENATORS (1 Democrat, 1 Republican)
Tim Johnson (D). Reelected 2002 to a six-year term. Previously elected 1996.

John Thune (R). Elected 2004 to a six-year term.

## REPRESENTATIVE (1 Democrat)
At Large. Stephanie Herseth (D)

## POSTWAR VOTE FOR PRESIDENT

| Year | Total Vote | Republican | | Democratic | | Other Vote | Plurality | Percentage | | | |
|------|-----------|-------|-----------|-------|-----------|------|-----------|------|------|------|------|
| | | | | | | | | Total Vote | | Major Vote | |
| | | Vote | Candidate | Vote | Candidate | | | Rep. | Dem. | Rep. | Dem. |
| 2004 | 388,215 | 232,584 | Bush, George W. | 149,244 | Kerry, John | 6,387 | 83,340 R | 59.9% | 38.4% | 60.9% | 39.1% |
| 2000 | 316,269 | 190,700 | Bush, George W. | 118,804 | Gore, Al | 6,765 | 71,896 R | 60.3% | 37.6% | 61.6% | 38.4% |
| 1996** | 323,826 | 150,543 | Dole, Bob | 139,333 | Clinton, Bill | 33,950 | 11,210 R | 46.5% | 43.0% | 51.9% | 48.1% |
| 1992** | 336,254 | 136,718 | Bush, George | 124,888 | Clinton, Bill | 74,648 | 11,830 R | 40.7% | 37.1% | 52.3% | 47.7% |
| 1988 | 312,991 | 165,415 | Bush, George | 145,560 | Dukakis, Michael S. | 2,016 | 19,855 R | 52.8% | 46.5% | 53.2% | 46.8% |
| 1984 | 317,867 | 200,267 | Reagan, Ronald | 116,113 | Mondale, Walter F. | 1,487 | 84,154 R | 63.0% | 36.5% | 63.3% | 36.7% |
| 1980** | 327,703 | 198,343 | Reagan, Ronald | 103,855 | Carter, Jimmy | 25,505 | 94,488 R | 60.5% | 31.7% | 65.6% | 34.4% |
| 1976 | 300,678 | 151,505 | Ford, Gerald R. | 147,068 | Carter, Jimmy | 2,105 | 4,437 R | 50.4% | 48.9% | 50.7% | 49.3% |
| 1972 | 307,415 | 166,476 | Nixon, Richard M. | 139,945 | McGovern, George S. | 994 | 26,531 R | 54.2% | 45.5% | 54.3% | 45.7% |
| 1968** | 281,264 | 149,841 | Nixon, Richard M. | 118,023 | Humphrey, Hubert H. | 13,400 | 31,818 R | 53.3% | 42.0% | 55.9% | 44.1% |
| 1964 | 293,118 | 130,108 | Goldwater, Barry M. | 163,010 | Johnson, Lyndon B. | | 32,902 D | 44.4% | 55.6% | 44.4% | 55.6% |
| 1960 | 306,487 | 178,417 | Nixon, Richard M. | 128,070 | Kennedy, John F. | | 50,347 R | 58.2% | 41.8% | 58.2% | 41.8% |
| 1956 | 293,857 | 171,569 | Eisenhower, Dwight D. | 122,288 | Stevenson, Adlai E. | | 49,281 R | 58.4% | 41.6% | 58.4% | 41.6% |
| 1952 | 294,283 | 203,857 | Eisenhower, Dwight D. | 90,426 | Stevenson, Adlai E. | | 113,431 R | 69.3% | 30.7% | 69.3% | 30.7% |
| 1948 | 250,105 | 129,651 | Dewey, Thomas E. | 117,653 | Truman, Harry S. | 2,801 | 11,998 R | 51.8% | 47.0% | 52.4% | 47.6% |

In past elections, the other vote included: 1996 - 31,250 Reform (Ross Perot); 1992 - 73,295 Independent (Perot); 1980 - 21,431 Independent (John Anderson); 1968 - 13,400 American Independent (George Wallace).

# SOUTH DAKOTA

## POSTWAR VOTE FOR GOVERNOR

| Year | Total Vote | Republican | | Democratic | | Other Vote | Rep.-Dem. Plurality | Percentage | | | |
|------|-----------|-----------|-----------|-----------|-----------|-----------|-----------|-----------|-----------|-----------|-----------|
| | | | | | | | | Total Vote | | Major Vote | |
| | | Vote | Candidate | Vote | Candidate | | | Rep. | Dem. | Rep. | Dem. |
| 2002 | 334,559 | 189,920 | Rounds, Mike | 140,263 | Abbott, Jim | 4,376 | 49,657 R | 56.8% | 41.9% | 57.5% | 42.5% |
| 1998 | 260,187 | 166,621 | Janklow, Bill | 85,473 | Hunhoff, Bernie | 8,093 | 81,148 R | 64.0% | 32.9% | 66.1% | 33.9% |
| 1994 | 311,613 | 172,515 | Janklow, Bill | 126,273 | Beddow, Jim | 12,825 | 46,242 R | 55.4% | 40.5% | 57.7% | 42.3% |
| 1990 | 256,723 | 151,198 | Mickelson, George S. | 105,525 | Samuelson, Bob L. | | 45,673 R | 58.9% | 41.1% | 58.9% | 41.1% |
| 1986 | 294,441 | 152,543 | Mickelson, George S. | 141,898 | Herseth, R. Lars | | 10,645 R | 51.8% | 48.2% | 51.8% | 48.2% |
| 1982 | 278,562 | 197,426 | Janklow, Bill | 81,136 | O'Connor, Michael J. | | 116,290 R | 70.9% | 29.1% | 70.9% | 29.1% |
| 1978 | 259,795 | 147,116 | Janklow, Bill | 112,679 | McKellips, Roger | | 34,437 R | 56.6% | 43.4% | 56.6% | 43.4% |
| 1974** | 278,228 | 129,077 | Olson, John E. | 149,151 | Kneip, Richard F. | | 20,074 D | 46.4% | 53.6% | 46.4% | 53.6% |
| 1972 | 308,177 | 123,165 | Thompson, Carveth | 185,012 | Kneip, Richard F. | | 61,847 D | 40.0% | 60.0% | 40.0% | 60.0% |
| 1970 | 239,963 | 108,347 | Farrar, Frank | 131,616 | Kneip, Richard F. | | 23,269 D | 45.2% | 54.8% | 45.2% | 54.8% |
| 1968 | 276,906 | 159,646 | Farrar, Frank | 117,260 | Chamberlin, Robert | | 42,386 R | 57.7% | 42.3% | 57.7% | 42.3% |
| 1966 | 228,214 | 131,710 | Boe, Nils A. | 96,504 | Chamberlin, Robert | | 35,206 R | 57.7% | 42.3% | 57.7% | 42.3% |
| 1964 | 290,570 | 150,151 | Boe, Nils A. | 140,419 | Lindley, John F. | | 9,732 R | 51.7% | 48.3% | 51.7% | 48.3% |
| 1962 | 256,120 | 143,682 | Gubbrud, Archie M. | 112,438 | Herseth, Ralph | | 31,244 R | 56.1% | 43.9% | 56.1% | 43.9% |
| 1960 | 304,625 | 154,530 | Gubbrud, Archie M. | 150,095 | Herseth, Ralph | | 4,435 R | 50.7% | 49.3% | 50.7% | 49.3% |
| 1958 | 258,281 | 125,520 | Saunders, Phil | 132,761 | Herseth, Ralph | | 7,241 D | 48.6% | 51.4% | 48.6% | 51.4% |
| 1956 | 292,017 | 158,819 | Foss, Joe J. | 133,198 | Herseth, Ralph | | 25,621 R | 54.4% | 45.6% | 54.4% | 45.6% |
| 1954 | 236,255 | 133,878 | Foss, Joe J. | 102,377 | Martin, Ed C. | | 31,501 R | 56.7% | 43.3% | 56.7% | 43.3% |
| 1952 | 289,515 | 203,102 | Anderson, Sigurd | 86,413 | Iverson, Sherman A. | | 116,689 R | 70.2% | 29.8% | 70.2% | 29.8% |
| 1950 | 253,316 | 154,254 | Anderson, Sigurd | 99,062 | Robbie, Joseph | | 55,192 R | 60.9% | 39.1% | 60.9% | 39.1% |
| 1948 | 245,372 | 149,883 | Mickelson, George | 95,489 | Volz, Harold J. | | 54,394 R | 61.1% | 38.9% | 61.1% | 38.9% |
| 1946 | 162,292 | 108,998 | Mickelson, George | 53,294 | Haeder, Richard | | 55,704 R | 67.2% | 32.8% | 67.2% | 32.8% |

The term of office of South Dakota's governor was increased from two to four years effective with the 1974 election.

## POSTWAR VOTE FOR SENATOR

| Year | Total Vote | Republican | | Democratic | | Other Vote | Rep.-Dem. Plurality | Percentage | | | |
|------|-----------|-----------|-----------|-----------|-----------|-----------|-----------|-----------|-----------|-----------|-----------|
| | | | | | | | | Total Vote | | Major Vote | |
| | | Vote | Candidate | Vote | Candidate | | | Rep. | Dem. | Rep. | Dem. |
| 2004 | 391,188 | 197,848 | Thune, John | 193,340 | Daschle, Tom | | 4,508 R | 50.6% | 49.4% | 50.6% | 49.4% |
| 2002 | 337,508 | 166,957 | Thune, John | 167,481 | Johnson, Tim | 3,070 | 524 D | 49.5% | 49.6% | 49.9% | 50.1% |
| 1998 | 262,111 | 95,431 | Schmidt, Ron | 162,884 | Daschle, Tom | 3,796 | 67,453 D | 36.4% | 62.1% | 36.9% | 63.1% |
| 1996 | 324,487 | 157,954 | Pressler, Larry | 166,533 | Johnson, Tim | | 8,579 D | 48.7% | 51.3% | 48.7% | 51.3% |
| 1992 | 334,495 | 108,733 | Haar, Charlene | 217,095 | Daschle, Tom | 8,667 | 108,362 D | 32.5% | 64.9% | 33.4% | 66.6% |
| 1990 | 258,976 | 135,682 | Pressler, Larry | 116,727 | Muenster, Ted | 6,567 | 18,955 R | 52.4% | 45.1% | 53.8% | 46.2% |
| 1986 | 295,830 | 143,173 | Abdnor, James | 152,657 | Daschle, Tom | | 9,484 D | 48.4% | 51.6% | 48.4% | 51.6% |
| 1984 | 315,713 | 235,176 | Pressler, Larry | 80,537 | Cunningham, George V. | | 154,639 R | 74.5% | 25.5% | 74.5% | 25.5% |
| 1980 | 327,478 | 190,594 | Abdnor, James | 129,018 | McGovern, George S. | 7,866 | 61,576 R | 58.2% | 39.4% | 59.6% | 40.4% |
| 1978 | 255,599 | 170,832 | Pressler, Larry | 84,767 | Barnett, Don | | 86,065 R | 66.8% | 33.2% | 66.8% | 33.2% |
| 1974 | 278,884 | 130,955 | Thorsness, Leo K. | 147,929 | McGovern, George S. | | 16,974 D | 47.0% | 53.0% | 47.0% | 53.0% |
| 1972 | 306,386 | 131,613 | Hirsch, Robert W. | 174,773 | Abourezk, James | | 43,160 D | 43.0% | 57.0% | 43.0% | 57.0% |
| 1968 | 279,912 | 120,951 | Gubbrud, Archie M. | 158,961 | McGovern, George S. | | 38,010 D | 43.2% | 56.8% | 43.2% | 56.8% |
| 1966 | 227,080 | 150,517 | Mundt, Karl E. | 76,563 | Wright, Donn H. | | 73,954 R | 66.3% | 33.7% | 66.3% | 33.7% |
| 1962 | 254,319 | 126,861 | Bottum, Joe H. | 127,458 | McGovern, George S. | | 597 D | 49.9% | 50.1% | 49.9% | 50.1% |
| 1960 | 305,442 | 160,181 | Mundt, Karl E. | 145,261 | McGovern, George S. | | 14,920 R | 52.4% | 47.6% | 52.4% | 47.6% |
| 1956 | 290,622 | 147,621 | Case, Francis | 143,001 | Holum, Kenneth | | 4,620 R | 50.8% | 49.2% | 50.8% | 49.2% |
| 1954 | 235,745 | 135,071 | Mundt, Karl E. | 100,674 | Holum, Kenneth | | 34,397 R | 57.3% | 42.7% | 57.3% | 42.7% |
| 1950 | 251,362 | 160,670 | Case, Francis | 90,692 | Engel, John A. | | 69,978 R | 63.9% | 36.1% | 63.9% | 36.1% |
| 1948 | 242,833 | 144,084 | Mundt, Karl E. | 98,749 | Engel, John A. | | 45,335 R | 59.3% | 40.7% | 59.3% | 40.7% |

# SOUTH DAKOTA

One member At Large

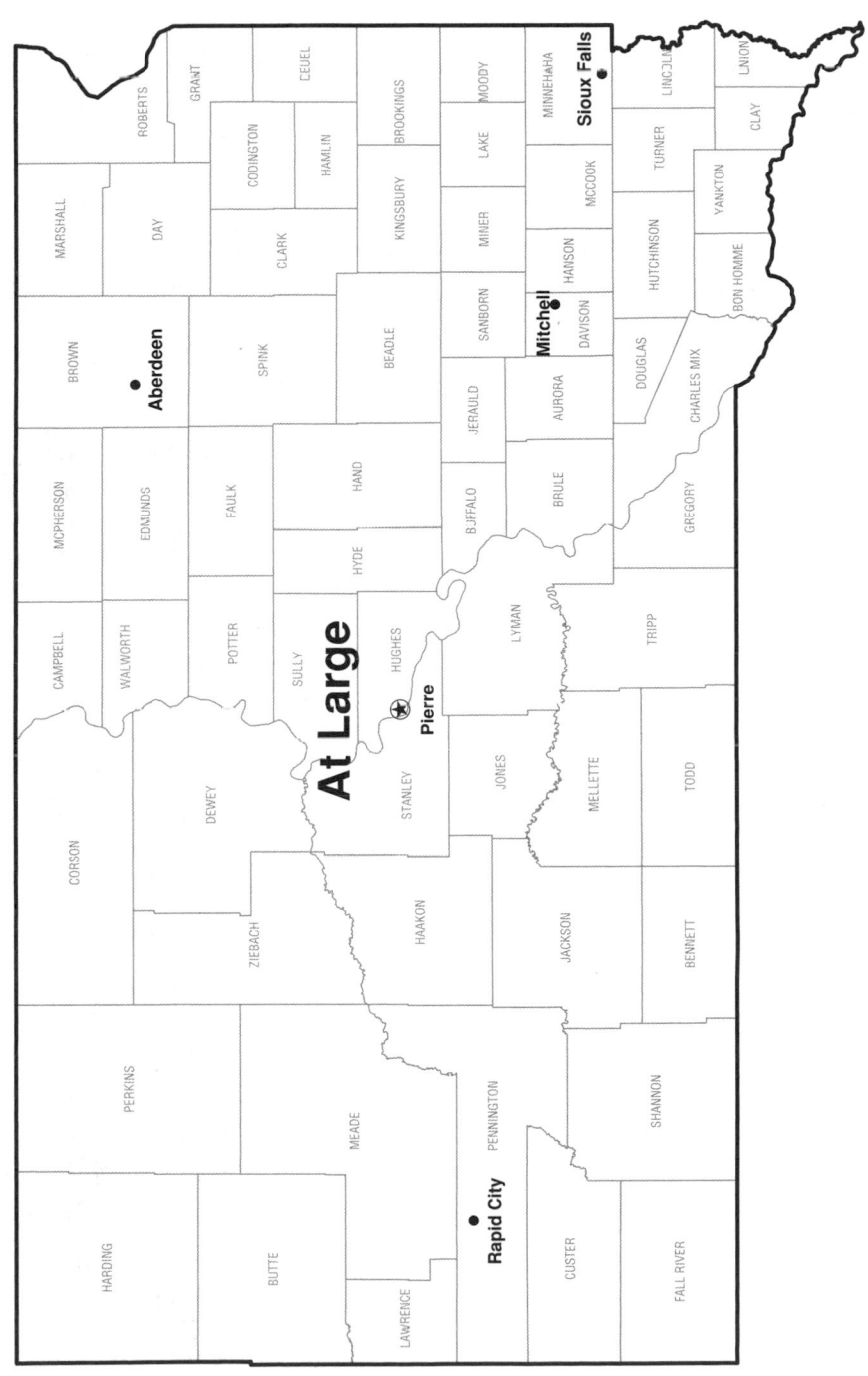

# SOUTH DAKOTA

## PRESIDENT 2004

| 2000 Census Population | County | Total Vote | Republican | Democratic | Other | Rep.-Dem. Plurality | Percentage | | | |
|---|---|---|---|---|---|---|---|---|---|---|
| | | | | | | | Total Vote | | Major Vote | |
| | | | | | | | Rep. | Dem. | Rep. | Dem. |
| 3,058 | AURORA | 1,649 | 1,009 | 620 | 20 | 389 R | 61.2% | 37.6% | 61.9% | 38.1% |
| 17,023 | BEADLE | 8,480 | 4,917 | 3,443 | 120 | 1,474 R | 58.0% | 40.6% | 58.8% | 41.2% |
| 3,574 | BENNETT | 1,630 | 833 | 759 | 38 | 74 R | 51.1% | 46.6% | 52.3% | 47.7% |
| 7,260 | BON HOMME | 3,408 | 2,063 | 1,293 | 52 | 770 R | 60.5% | 37.9% | 61.5% | 38.5% |
| 28,220 | BROOKINGS | 13,375 | 7,662 | 5,443 | 270 | 2,219 R | 57.3% | 40.7% | 58.5% | 41.5% |
| 35,460 | BROWN | 18,599 | 10,386 | 7,943 | 270 | 2,443 R | 55.8% | 42.7% | 56.7% | 43.3% |
| 5,364 | BRULE | 2,629 | 1,544 | 1,040 | 45 | 504 R | 58.7% | 39.6% | 59.8% | 40.2% |
| 2,032 | BUFFALO | 841 | 223 | 603 | 15 | 380 D | 26.5% | 71.7% | 27.0% | 73.0% |
| 9,094 | BUTTE | 4,271 | 3,166 | 1,009 | 96 | 2,157 R | 74.1% | 23.6% | 75.8% | 24.2% |
| 1,782 | CAMPBELL | 959 | 708 | 239 | 12 | 469 R | 73.8% | 24.9% | 74.8% | 25.2% |
| 9,350 | CHARLES MIX | 4,798 | 2,556 | 2,155 | 87 | 401 R | 53.3% | 44.9% | 54.3% | 45.7% |
| 4,143 | CLARK | 2,327 | 1,435 | 875 | 17 | 560 R | 61.7% | 37.6% | 62.1% | 37.9% |
| 13,537 | CLAY | 6,136 | 2,692 | 3,315 | 129 | 623 D | 43.9% | 54.0% | 44.8% | 55.2% |
| 25,897 | CODINGTON | 12,751 | 7,778 | 4,803 | 170 | 2,975 R | 61.0% | 37.7% | 61.8% | 38.2% |
| 4,181 | CORSON | 1,724 | 720 | 972 | 32 | 252 D | 41.8% | 56.4% | 42.6% | 57.4% |
| 7,275 | CUSTER | 4,304 | 2,922 | 1,272 | 110 | 1,650 R | 67.9% | 29.6% | 69.7% | 30.3% |
| 18,741 | DAVISON | 8,952 | 5,561 | 3,263 | 128 | 2,298 R | 62.1% | 36.4% | 63.0% | 37.0% |
| 6,267 | DAY | 3,540 | 1,671 | 1,817 | 52 | 146 D | 47.2% | 51.3% | 47.9% | 52.1% |
| 4,498 | DEUEL | 2,412 | 1,406 | 961 | 45 | 445 R | 58.3% | 39.8% | 59.4% | 40.6% |
| 5,972 | DEWEY | 2,564 | 921 | 1,606 | 37 | 685 D | 35.9% | 62.6% | 36.4% | 63.6% |
| 3,458 | DOUGLAS | 2,012 | 1,596 | 393 | 23 | 1,203 R | 79.3% | 19.5% | 80.2% | 19.8% |
| 4,367 | EDMUNDS | 2,234 | 1,434 | 765 | 35 | 669 R | 64.2% | 34.2% | 65.2% | 34.8% |
| 7,453 | FALL RIVER | 3,845 | 2,413 | 1,326 | 106 | 1,087 R | 62.8% | 34.5% | 64.5% | 35.5% |
| 2,640 | FAULK | 1,369 | 945 | 418 | 6 | 527 R | 69.0% | 30.5% | 69.3% | 30.7% |
| 7,847 | GRANT | 4,090 | 2,392 | 1,633 | 65 | 759 R | 58.5% | 39.9% | 59.4% | 40.6% |
| 4,792 | GREGORY | 2,546 | 1,685 | 813 | 48 | 872 R | 66.2% | 31.9% | 67.5% | 32.5% |
| 2,196 | HAAKON | 1,240 | 1,007 | 219 | 14 | 788 R | 81.2% | 17.7% | 82.1% | 17.9% |
| 5,540 | HAMLIN | 3,011 | 1,946 | 1,015 | 50 | 931 R | 64.6% | 33.7% | 65.7% | 34.3% |
| 3,741 | HAND | 2,187 | 1,482 | 668 | 37 | 814 R | 67.8% | 30.5% | 68.9% | 31.1% |
| 3,139 | HANSON | 2,150 | 1,379 | 745 | 26 | 634 R | 64.1% | 34.7% | 64.9% | 35.1% |
| 1,353 | HARDING | 815 | 704 | 94 | 17 | 610 R | 86.4% | 11.5% | 88.2% | 11.8% |
| 16,481 | HUGHES | 8,835 | 6,017 | 2,697 | 121 | 3,320 R | 68.1% | 30.5% | 69.0% | 31.0% |
| 8,075 | HUTCHINSON | 4,147 | 2,899 | 1,177 | 71 | 1,722 R | 69.9% | 28.4% | 71.1% | 28.9% |
| 1,671 | HYDE | 900 | 631 | 259 | 10 | 372 R | 70.1% | 28.8% | 70.9% | 29.1% |
| 2,930 | JACKSON | 1,271 | 726 | 508 | 37 | 218 R | 57.1% | 40.0% | 58.8% | 41.2% |
| 2,295 | JERAULD | 1,236 | 736 | 482 | 18 | 254 R | 59.5% | 39.0% | 60.4% | 39.6% |
| 1,193 | JONES | 717 | 565 | 134 | 18 | 431 R | 78.8% | 18.7% | 80.8% | 19.2% |
| 5,815 | KINGSBURY | 3,014 | 1,804 | 1,163 | 47 | 641 R | 59.9% | 38.6% | 60.8% | 39.2% |
| 11,276 | LAKE | 6,007 | 3,359 | 2,509 | 139 | 850 R | 55.9% | 41.8% | 57.2% | 42.8% |
| 21,802 | LAWRENCE | 11,619 | 7,489 | 3,857 | 273 | 3,632 R | 64.5% | 33.2% | 66.0% | 34.0% |
| 24,131 | LINCOLN | 17,066 | 11,161 | 5,703 | 202 | 5,458 R | 65.4% | 33.4% | 66.2% | 33.8% |
| 3,895 | LYMAN | 1,940 | 1,029 | 872 | 39 | 157 R | 53.0% | 44.9% | 54.1% | 45.9% |
| 5,832 | MCCOOK | 3,271 | 2,017 | 1,201 | 53 | 816 R | 61.7% | 36.7% | 62.7% | 37.3% |
| 2,904 | MCPHERSON | 1,579 | 1,180 | 369 | 30 | 811 R | 74.7% | 23.4% | 76.2% | 23.8% |
| 4,576 | MARSHALL | 2,364 | 1,242 | 1,099 | 23 | 143 R | 52.5% | 46.5% | 53.1% | 46.9% |
| 24,253 | MEADE | 11,504 | 8,347 | 2,941 | 216 | 5,406 R | 72.6% | 25.6% | 73.9% | 26.1% |
| 2,083 | MELLETTE | 931 | 553 | 361 | 17 | 192 R | 59.4% | 38.8% | 60.5% | 39.5% |
| 2,884 | MINER | 1,470 | 810 | 641 | 19 | 169 R | 55.1% | 43.6% | 55.8% | 44.2% |
| 148,281 | MINNEHAHA | 77,632 | 44,189 | 32,314 | 1,129 | 11,875 R | 56.9% | 41.6% | 57.8% | 42.2% |
| 6,595 | MOODY | 3,451 | 1,790 | 1,609 | 52 | 181 R | 51.9% | 46.6% | 52.7% | 47.3% |
| 88,565 | PENNINGTON | 44,968 | 29,976 | 14,213 | 779 | 15,763 R | 66.7% | 31.6% | 67.8% | 32.2% |
| 3,363 | PERKINS | 1,813 | 1,329 | 418 | 66 | 911 R | 73.3% | 23.1% | 76.1% | 23.9% |
| 2,693 | POTTER | 1,618 | 1,143 | 463 | 12 | 680 R | 70.6% | 28.6% | 71.2% | 28.8% |
| 10,016 | ROBERTS | 4,982 | 2,396 | 2,527 | 59 | 131 D | 48.1% | 50.7% | 48.7% | 51.3% |
| 2,675 | SANBORN | 1,426 | 817 | 581 | 28 | 236 R | 57.3% | 40.7% | 58.4% | 41.6% |
| 12,466 | SHANNON | 4,214 | 526 | 3,566 | 122 | 3,040 D | 12.5% | 84.6% | 12.9% | 87.1% |
| 7,454 | SPINK | 3,774 | 2,259 | 1,478 | 37 | 781 R | 59.9% | 39.2% | 60.4% | 39.6% |
| 2,772 | STANLEY | 1,623 | 1,129 | 464 | 30 | 665 R | 69.6% | 28.6% | 70.9% | 29.1% |
| 1,556 | SULLY | 917 | 702 | 201 | 14 | 501 R | 76.6% | 21.9% | 77.7% | 22.3% |
| 9,050 | TODD | 3,524 | 889 | 2,543 | 92 | 1,654 D | 25.2% | 72.2% | 25.9% | 74.1% |

# SOUTH DAKOTA

## PRESIDENT 2004

| 2000 Census Population | County | Total Vote | Republican | Democratic | Other | Rep.-Dem. Plurality | | Total Vote Rep. | Dem. | Major Vote Rep. | Dem. |
|---|---|---|---|---|---|---|---|---|---|---|---|
| 6,430 | TRIPP | 3,245 | 2,230 | 972 | 43 | 1,258 R | | 68.7% | 30.0% | 69.6% | 30.4% |
| 8,849 | TURNER | 4,834 | 3,084 | 1,646 | 104 | 1,438 R | | 63.8% | 34.1% | 65.2% | 34.8% |
| 12,584 | UNION | 7,048 | 3,987 | 3,000 | 61 | 987 R | | 56.6% | 42.6% | 57.1% | 42.9% |
| 5,974 | WALWORTH | 2,880 | 1,967 | 878 | 35 | 1,089 R | | 68.3% | 30.5% | 69.1% | 30.9% |
| 21,652 | YANKTON | 10,431 | 6,003 | 4,237 | 191 | 1,766 R | | 57.5% | 40.6% | 58.6% | 41.4% |
| 2,519 | ZIEBACH | 1,116 | 447 | 641 | 28 | 194 D | | 40.1% | 57.4% | 41.1% | 58.9% |
| 754,844 | TOTAL | 388,215 | 232,584 | 149,244 | 6,387 | 83,340 R | | 59.9% | 38.4% | 60.9% | 39.1% |

# SOUTH DAKOTA

## SENATOR 2004

| 2000 Census Population | County | Total Vote | Republican | Democratic | Other | Rep.-Dem. Plurality | | Total Vote Rep. | Dem. | Major Vote Rep. | Dem. |
|---|---|---|---|---|---|---|---|---|---|---|---|
| 3,058 | AURORA | 1,650 | 752 | 898 | | 146 D | | 45.6% | 54.4% | 45.6% | 54.4% |
| 17,023 | BEADLE | 8,518 | 3,784 | 4,734 | | 950 D | | 44.4% | 55.6% | 44.4% | 55.6% |
| 3,574 | BENNETT | 1,675 | 729 | 946 | | 217 D | | 43.5% | 56.5% | 43.5% | 56.5% |
| 7,260 | BON HOMME | 3,524 | 1,678 | 1,846 | | 168 D | | 47.6% | 52.4% | 47.6% | 52.4% |
| 28,220 | BROOKINGS | 13,451 | 6,255 | 7,196 | | 941 D | | 46.5% | 53.5% | 46.5% | 53.5% |
| 35,460 | BROWN | 18,731 | 7,981 | 10,750 | | 2,769 D | | 42.6% | 57.4% | 42.6% | 57.4% |
| 5,364 | BRULE | 2,661 | 1,279 | 1,382 | | 103 D | | 48.1% | 51.9% | 48.1% | 51.9% |
| 2,032 | BUFFALO | 881 | 168 | 713 | | 545 D | | 19.1% | 80.9% | 19.1% | 80.9% |
| 9,094 | BUTTE | 4,281 | 2,763 | 1,518 | | 1,245 R | | 64.5% | 35.5% | 64.5% | 35.5% |
| 1,782 | CAMPBELL | 964 | 577 | 387 | | 190 R | | 59.9% | 40.1% | 59.9% | 40.1% |
| 9,350 | CHARLES MIX | 4,858 | 2,179 | 2,679 | | 500 D | | 44.9% | 55.1% | 44.9% | 55.1% |
| 4,143 | CLARK | 2,354 | 1,109 | 1,245 | | 136 D | | 47.1% | 52.9% | 47.1% | 52.9% |
| 13,537 | CLAY | 6,161 | 2,252 | 3,909 | | 1,657 D | | 36.6% | 63.4% | 36.6% | 63.4% |
| 25,897 | CODINGTON | 12,850 | 6,714 | 6,136 | | 578 R | | 52.2% | 47.8% | 52.2% | 47.8% |
| 4,181 | CORSON | 1,772 | 647 | 1,125 | | 478 D | | 36.5% | 63.5% | 36.5% | 63.5% |
| 7,275 | CUSTER | 4,383 | 2,751 | 1,632 | | 1,119 R | | 62.8% | 37.2% | 62.8% | 37.2% |
| 18,741 | DAVISON | 9,023 | 4,583 | 4,440 | | 143 R | | 50.8% | 49.2% | 50.8% | 49.2% |
| 6,267 | DAY | 3,607 | 1,270 | 2,337 | | 1,067 D | | 35.2% | 64.8% | 35.2% | 64.8% |
| 4,498 | DEUEL | 2,448 | 1,083 | 1,365 | | 282 D | | 44.2% | 55.8% | 44.2% | 55.8% |
| 5,972 | DEWEY | 2,625 | 705 | 1,920 | | 1,215 D | | 26.9% | 73.1% | 26.9% | 73.1% |
| 3,458 | DOUGLAS | 2,026 | 1,391 | 635 | | 756 R | | 68.7% | 31.3% | 68.7% | 31.3% |
| 4,367 | EDMUNDS | 2,302 | 1,201 | 1,101 | | 100 R | | 52.2% | 47.8% | 52.2% | 47.8% |
| 7,453 | FALL RIVER | 3,931 | 2,207 | 1,724 | | 483 R | | 56.1% | 43.9% | 56.1% | 43.9% |
| 2,640 | FAULK | 1,379 | 744 | 635 | | 109 R | | 54.0% | 46.0% | 54.0% | 46.0% |
| 7,847 | GRANT | 4,110 | 1,986 | 2,124 | | 138 D | | 48.3% | 51.7% | 48.3% | 51.7% |
| 4,792 | GREGORY | 2,568 | 1,426 | 1,142 | | 284 R | | 55.5% | 44.5% | 55.5% | 44.5% |
| 2,196 | HAAKON | 1,243 | 873 | 370 | | 503 R | | 70.2% | 29.8% | 70.2% | 29.8% |
| 5,540 | HAMLIN | 3,040 | 1,649 | 1,391 | | 258 R | | 54.2% | 45.8% | 54.2% | 45.8% |
| 3,741 | HAND | 2,243 | 1,103 | 1,140 | | 37 D | | 49.2% | 50.8% | 49.2% | 50.8% |
| 3,139 | HANSON | 2,145 | 1,207 | 938 | | 269 R | | 56.3% | 43.7% | 56.3% | 43.7% |
| 1,353 | HARDING | 817 | 642 | 175 | | 467 R | | 78.6% | 21.4% | 78.6% | 21.4% |
| 16,481 | HUGHES | 8,884 | 5,035 | 3,849 | | 1,186 R | | 56.7% | 43.3% | 56.7% | 43.3% |
| 8,075 | HUTCHINSON | 4,258 | 2,605 | 1,653 | | 952 R | | 61.2% | 38.8% | 61.2% | 38.8% |
| 1,671 | HYDE | 911 | 532 | 379 | | 153 R | | 58.4% | 41.6% | 58.4% | 41.6% |
| 2,930 | JACKSON | 1,309 | 652 | 657 | | 5 D | | 49.8% | 50.2% | 49.8% | 50.2% |
| 2,295 | JERAULD | 1,280 | 540 | 740 | | 200 D | | 42.2% | 57.8% | 42.2% | 57.8% |
| 1,193 | JONES | 728 | 518 | 210 | | 308 R | | 71.2% | 28.8% | 71.2% | 28.8% |
| 5,815 | KINGSBURY | 3,062 | 1,374 | 1,688 | | 314 D | | 44.9% | 55.1% | 44.9% | 55.1% |
| 11,276 | LAKE | 6,074 | 2,683 | 3,391 | | 708 D | | 44.2% | 55.8% | 44.2% | 55.8% |
| 21,802 | LAWRENCE | 11,670 | 6,755 | 4,915 | | 1,840 R | | 57.9% | 42.1% | 57.9% | 42.1% |

# SOUTH DAKOTA

## SENATOR 2004

| 2000 Census Population | County | Total Vote | Republican | Democratic | Other | Rep.-Dem. Plurality | Percentage | | | |
|---|---|---|---|---|---|---|---|---|---|---|
| | | | | | | | Total Vote | | Major Vote | |
| | | | | | | | Rep. | Dem. | Rep. | Dem. |
| 24,131 | LINCOLN | 17,139 | 9,671 | 7,468 | | 2,203 R | 56.4% | 43.6% | 56.4% | 43.6% |
| 3,895 | LYMAN | 1,953 | 841 | 1,112 | | 271 D | 43.1% | 56.9% | 43.1% | 56.9% |
| 5,832 | MCCOOK | 3,305 | 1,686 | 1,619 | | 67 R | 51.0% | 49.0% | 51.0% | 49.0% |
| 2,904 | MCPHERSON | 1,601 | 1,005 | 596 | | 409 R | 62.8% | 37.2% | 62.8% | 37.2% |
| 4,576 | MARSHALL | 2,392 | 970 | 1,422 | | 452 D | 40.6% | 59.4% | 40.6% | 59.4% |
| 24,253 | MEADE | 11,519 | 7,380 | 4,139 | | 3,241 R | 64.1% | 35.9% | 64.1% | 35.9% |
| 2,083 | MELLETTE | 974 | 479 | 495 | | 16 D | 49.2% | 50.8% | 49.2% | 50.8% |
| 2,884 | MINER | 1,477 | 589 | 888 | | 299 D | 39.9% | 60.1% | 39.9% | 60.1% |
| 148,281 | MINNEHAHA | 77,779 | 38,105 | 39,674 | | 1,569 D | 49.0% | 51.0% | 49.0% | 51.0% |
| 6,595 | MOODY | 3,493 | 1,451 | 2,042 | | 591 D | 41.5% | 58.5% | 41.5% | 58.5% |
| 88,565 | PENNINGTON | 45,037 | 26,681 | 18,356 | | 8,325 R | 59.2% | 40.8% | 59.2% | 40.8% |
| 3,363 | PERKINS | 1,825 | 1,128 | 697 | | 431 R | 61.8% | 38.2% | 61.8% | 38.2% |
| 2,693 | POTTER | 1,632 | 944 | 688 | | 256 R | 57.8% | 42.2% | 57.8% | 42.2% |
| 10,016 | ROBERTS | 5,020 | 2,115 | 2,905 | | 790 D | 42.1% | 57.9% | 42.1% | 57.9% |
| 2,675 | SANBORN | 1,446 | 607 | 839 | | 232 D | 42.0% | 58.0% | 42.0% | 58.0% |
| 12,466 | SHANNON | 4,451 | 564 | 3,887 | | 3,323 D | 12.7% | 87.3% | 12.7% | 87.3% |
| 7,454 | SPINK | 3,813 | 1,689 | 2,124 | | 435 D | 44.3% | 55.7% | 44.3% | 55.7% |
| 2,772 | STANLEY | 1,630 | 905 | 725 | | 180 R | 55.5% | 44.5% | 55.5% | 44.5% |
| 1,556 | SULLY | 932 | 598 | 334 | | 264 R | 64.2% | 35.8% | 64.2% | 35.8% |
| 9,050 | TODD | 3,661 | 776 | 2,885 | | 2,109 D | 21.2% | 78.8% | 21.2% | 78.8% |
| 6,430 | TRIPP | 3,269 | 1,829 | 1,440 | | 389 R | 55.9% | 44.1% | 55.9% | 44.1% |
| 8,849 | TURNER | 4,861 | 2,620 | 2,241 | | 379 R | 53.9% | 46.1% | 53.9% | 46.1% |
| 12,584 | UNION | 7,057 | 3,706 | 3,351 | | 355 R | 52.5% | 47.5% | 52.5% | 47.5% |
| 5,974 | WALWORTH | 2,928 | 1,630 | 1,298 | | 332 R | 55.7% | 44.3% | 55.7% | 44.3% |
| 21,652 | YANKTON | 10,462 | 5,128 | 5,334 | | 206 D | 49.0% | 51.0% | 49.0% | 51.0% |
| 2,519 | ZIEBACH | 1,135 | 369 | 766 | | 397 D | 32.5% | 67.5% | 32.5% | 67.5% |
| 754,844 | TOTAL | 391,188 | 197,848 | 193,340 | | 4,508 R | 50.6% | 49.4% | 50.6% | 49.4% |

# SOUTH DAKOTA

## HOUSE OF REPRESENTATIVES

| CD | Year | Total Vote | Republican | | Democratic | | Other Vote | Rep.-Dem. Plurality | Percentage | | | |
|---|---|---|---|---|---|---|---|---|---|---|---|---|
| | | | Vote | Candidate | Vote | Candidate | | | Total Vote | | Major Vote | |
| | | | | | | | | | Rep. | Dem. | Rep. | Dem. |
| AL | 2004 | 389,468 | 178,823 | Diedrich, Larry | 207,837 | Herseth, Stephanie* | 2,808 | 29,014 D | 45.9% | 53.4% | 46.2% | 53.8% |
| AL | 2002 | 336,807 | 180,023 | Janklow, Bill | 153,656 | Herseth, Stephanie | 3,128 | 26,367 R | 53.4% | 45.6% | 54.0% | 46.0% |
| AL | 2000 | 314,761 | 231,083 | Thune, John* | 78,321 | Hohn, Curt | 5,357 | 152,762 R | 73.4% | 24.9% | 74.7% | 25.3% |
| AL | 1998 | 258,590 | 194,157 | Thune, John* | 64,433 | Moser, Jeff | | 129,724 R | 75.1% | 24.9% | 75.1% | 24.9% |
| AL | 1996 | 323,203 | 186,393 | Thune, John | 119,547 | Weiland, Rick | 17,263 | 66,846 R | 57.7% | 37.0% | 60.9% | 39.1% |
| AL | 1994 | 305,922 | 112,054 | Berkhout, Jan | 183,036 | Johnson, Tim* | 10,832 | 70,982 D | 36.6% | 59.8% | 38.0% | 62.0% |
| AL | 1992 | 332,902 | 89,375 | Timmer, John | 230,070 | Johnson, Tim* | 13,457 | 140,695 D | 26.8% | 69.1% | 28.0% | 72.0% |
| AL | 1990 | 257,298 | 83,484 | Frankenfeld, Don | 173,814 | Johnson, Tim* | | 90,330 D | 32.4% | 67.6% | 32.4% | 67.6% |
| AL | 1988 | 311,916 | 88,157 | Volk, David | 223,759 | Johnson, Tim* | | 135,602 D | 28.3% | 71.7% | 28.3% | 71.7% |
| AL | 1986 | 289,723 | 118,261 | Bell, Dale | 171,462 | Johnson, Tim | | 53,201 D | 40.8% | 59.2% | 40.8% | 59.2% |
| AL | 1984 | 316,222 | 134,821 | Bell, Dale | 181,401 | Daschle, Tom* | | 46,580 D | 42.6% | 57.4% | 42.6% | 57.4% |
| AL | 1982 | 275,652 | 133,530 | Roberts, Clint | 142,122 | Daschle, Tom* | | 8,592 D | 48.4% | 51.6% | 48.4% | 51.6% |

An asterisk (*) denotes incumbent.

# SOUTH DAKOTA

## GENERAL AND PRIMARY ELECTIONS

## 2004 GENERAL ELECTIONS

**President**   Other vote was 4,320 Independent (Ralph Nader); 1,103 Constitution (Michael Peroutka); 964 Libertarian (Michael Badnarik).

**Senator**

**House**   Other vote was:

At Large   2,808 Libertarian (Terry Begay).

## 2004 PRIMARY ELECTIONS

**Primary**   June 1, 2004

| **Registration** (active registrants as of May 17, 2004) | | |
|---|---|---|
| Republican | 223,861 |
| Democratic | 179,869 |
| Libertarian | 1,049 |
| Constitution | 66 |
| Other | 60,128 |
| TOTAL | 464,973 |

**Primary Type**   Closed—Only registered Democrats and Republicans could vote in their party's primary. In addition to the active registered voters, there were 52,865 inactive voters at the time of the 2004 primary.

Note:   An asterisk (*) denotes incumbent. The names of unopposed candidates did not appear on the primary ballot; therefore, no votes were cast for these candidates.

| | REPUBLICAN PRIMARIES | | DEMOCRATIC PRIMARIES | | |
|---|---|---|---|---|---|
| **President** | No Republican primary | | John Kerry | 69,473 | 82.3% |
| | | | Uncommitted | 5,105 | 6.0% |
| | | | Howard Dean | 4,838 | 5.7% |
| | | | Lyndon H. LaRouche Jr. | 2,943 | 3.5% |
| | | | Dennis J. Kucinich | 2,046 | 2.4% |
| | | | TOTAL | 84,405 | |
| **Senator** | John Thune | Unopposed | Tom Daschle* | Unopposed | |
| **House At Large** | Larry Diedrich | Unopposed | Stephanie Herseth* | Unopposed | |

# TENNESSEE

## GOVERNOR
Phil Bredesen (D). Elected 2002 to a four-year term.

## SENATORS (2 Republicans)
Lamar Alexander (R). Elected 2002 to a six-year term.

Bill Frist (R). Reelected 2000 to a six-year term. Previously elected 1994.

## REPRESENTATIVES (5 Democrats, 4 Republicans)
1. Bill Jenkins (R)
2. John J. "Jimmy" Duncan Jr. (R)
3. Zach Wamp (R)
4. Lincoln Davis (D)
5. Jim Cooper (D)
6. Bart Gordon (D)
7. Marsha Blackburn (R)
8. John Tanner (D)
9. Harold E. Ford Jr. (D)

## POSTWAR VOTE FOR PRESIDENT

| | | Republican | | Democratic | | Other | | Percentage | | | |
| | | | | | | | | Total Vote | | Major Vote | |
| Year | Total Vote | Vote | Candidate | Vote | Candidate | Vote | Plurality | Rep. | Dem. | Rep. | Dem. |
|---|---|---|---|---|---|---|---|---|---|---|---|
| 2004 | 2,437,319 | 1,384,375 | Bush, George W. | 1,036,477 | Kerry, John | 16,467 | 347,898 R | 56.8% | 42.5% | 57.2% | 42.8% |
| 2000** | 2,076,181 | 1,061,949 | Bush, George W. | 981,720 | Gore, Al | 32,512 | 80,229 R | 51.1% | 47.3% | 52.0% | 48.0% |
| 1996** | 1,894,105 | 863,530 | Dole, Bob | 909,146 | Clinton, Bill | 121,429 | 45,616 D | 45.6% | 48.0% | 48.7% | 51.3% |
| 1992** | 1,982,638 | 841,300 | Bush, George | 933,521 | Clinton, Bill | 207,817 | 92,221 D | 42.4% | 47.1% | 47.4% | 52.6% |
| 1988 | 1,636,250 | 947,233 | Bush, George | 679,794 | Dukakis, Michael S. | 9,223 | 267,439 R | 57.9% | 41.5% | 58.2% | 41.8% |
| 1984 | 1,711,994 | 990,212 | Reagan, Ronald | 711,714 | Mondale, Walter F. | 10,068 | 278,498 R | 57.8% | 41.6% | 58.2% | 41.8% |
| 1980** | 1,617,616 | 787,761 | Reagan, Ronald | 783,051 | Carter, Jimmy | 46,804 | 4,710 R | 48.7% | 48.4% | 50.1% | 49.9% |
| 1976 | 1,476,345 | 633,969 | Ford, Gerald R. | 825,879 | Carter, Jimmy | 16,497 | 191,910 D | 42.9% | 55.9% | 43.4% | 56.6% |
| 1972 | 1,201,182 | 813,147 | Nixon, Richard M. | 357,293 | McGovern, George S. | 30,742 | 455,854 R | 67.7% | 29.7% | 69.5% | 30.5% |
| 1968** | 1,248,617 | 472,592 | Nixon, Richard M. | 351,233 | Humphrey, Hubert H. | 424,792 | 47,800 R | 37.8% | 28.1% | 57.4% | 42.6% |
| 1964 | 1,143,946 | 508,965 | Goldwater, Barry M. | 634,947 | Johnson, Lyndon B. | 34 | 125,982 D | 44.5% | 55.5% | 44.5% | 55.5% |
| 1960 | 1,051,792 | 556,577 | Nixon, Richard M. | 481,453 | Kennedy, John F. | 13,762 | 75,124 R | 52.9% | 45.8% | 53.6% | 46.4% |
| 1956 | 939,404 | 462,288 | Eisenhower, Dwight D. | 456,507 | Stevenson, Adlai E. | 20,609 | 5,781 R | 49.2% | 48.6% | 50.3% | 49.7% |
| 1952 | 892,553 | 446,147 | Eisenhower, Dwight D. | 443,710 | Stevenson, Adlai E. | 2,696 | 2,437 R | 50.0% | 49.7% | 50.1% | 49.9% |
| 1948** | 550,283 | 202,914 | Dewey, Thomas E. | 270,402 | Truman, Harry S. | 76,967 | 67,488 D | 36.9% | 49.1% | 42.9% | 57.1% |

In past elections, the other vote included: 2000 - 19,781 Green (Ralph Nader); 1996 - 105,918 Reform (Ross Perot); 1992 - 199,968 Independent (Perot); 1980 - 35,991 Independent (John Anderson); 1968 - 424,792 American Independent (George Wallace), which finished second in Tennessee; 1948 - 73,815 States' Rights (Strom Thurmond).

# TENNESSEE

## POSTWAR VOTE FOR GOVERNOR

| Year | Total Vote | Republican Vote | Republican Candidate | Democratic Vote | Democratic Candidate | Other Vote | Plurality | Total Vote Rep. | Total Vote Dem. | Major Vote Rep. | Major Vote Dem. |
|---|---|---|---|---|---|---|---|---|---|---|---|
| 2002 | 1,653,167 | 786,803 | Hilleary, Van | 837,284 | Bredesen, Phil | 29,080 | 50,481 D | 47.6% | 50.6% | 48.4% | 51.6% |
| 1998 | 976,236 | 669,973 | Sundquist, Don | 287,750 | Hooker, John J. | 18,513 | 382,223 R | 68.6% | 29.5% | 70.0% | 30.0% |
| 1994 | 1,487,130 | 807,104 | Sundquist, Don | 664,252 | Bredesen, Phil | 15,774 | 142,852 R | 54.3% | 44.7% | 54.9% | 45.1% |
| 1990 | 790,441 | 289,348 | Henry, Dwight | 480,885 | McWherter, Ned | 20,208 | 191,537 D | 36.6% | 60.8% | 37.6% | 62.4% |
| 1986 | 1,210,339 | 553,449 | Dunn, Winfield | 656,602 | McWherter, Ned | 288 | 103,153 D | 45.7% | 54.2% | 45.7% | 54.3% |
| 1982 | 1,238,927 | 737,963 | Alexander, Lamar | 500,937 | Tyree, Randy | 27 | 237,026 R | 59.6% | 40.4% | 59.6% | 40.4% |
| 1978 | 1,189,695 | 661,959 | Alexander, Lamar | 523,495 | Butcher, Jake | 4,241 | 138,464 R | 55.6% | 44.0% | 55.8% | 44.2% |
| 1974 | 1,040,714 | 455,467 | Alexander, Lamar | 576,833 | Blanton, Ray | 8,414 | 121,366 D | 43.8% | 55.4% | 44.1% | 55.9% |
| 1970 | 1,108,247 | 575,777 | Dunn, Winfield | 509,521 | Hooker, John J. | 22,949 | 66,256 R | 52.0% | 46.0% | 53.1% | 46.9% |
| 1966** | 656,566 | | — | 532,998 | Ellington, Buford | 123,568 | 532,998 D | | 81.2% | | 100.0% |
| 1962** | 621,064 | 100,190 | Patty, Hubert D. | 315,648 | Clement, Frank G. | 205,226 | 111,883 D | 16.1% | 50.8% | 24.1% | 75.9% |
| 1958** | 432,545 | 35,938 | Wall, Thomas P. | 248,874 | Ellington, Buford | 147,733 | 112,475 D | 8.3% | 57.5% | 12.6% | 87.4% |
| 1954** | 322,586 | | — | 281,291 | Clement, Frank G. | 41,295 | 281,291 D | | 87.2% | | 100.0% |
| 1952 | 806,771 | 166,377 | Witt, R. Beecher | 640,290 | Clement, Frank G. | 104 | 473,913 D | 20.6% | 79.4% | 20.6% | 79.4% |
| 1950 | 236,194 | | — | 184,437 | Browning, Gordon | 51,757 | 184,437 D | | 78.1% | | 100.0% |
| 1948 | 543,881 | 179,957 | Acuff, Roy | 363,903 | Browning, Gordon | 21 | 183,946 D | 33.1% | 66.9% | 33.1% | 66.9% |
| 1946 | 229,456 | 73,222 | Lowe, W. O. | 149,937 | McCord, Jim Nance | 6,297 | 76,715 D | 31.9% | 65.3% | 32.8% | 67.2% |

In past elections, the other vote included: 1966 - 64,602 Independent (H. L. Crawford), who finished second; 50,221 Independent (Charles Moffett); 1962 - 203,765 Independent (William R. Anderson), who finished second; 1958 - 136,399 Independent (Jim Nance McCord), who finished second. In the 1958 and 1962 elections, the plurality of the winning Democratic candidate is listed over the Independent runner-up. In other elections, the plurality is the difference between the Republican and Democratic vote. The term of office of Tennessee's governor was increased from two to four years effective with the 1954 election.

## POSTWAR VOTE FOR SENATOR

| Year | Total Vote | Republican Vote | Republican Candidate | Democratic Vote | Democratic Candidate | Other Vote | Rep.-Dem. Plurality | Total Vote Rep. | Total Vote Dem. | Major Vote Rep. | Major Vote Dem. |
|---|---|---|---|---|---|---|---|---|---|---|---|
| 2002 | 1,642,421 | 891,420 | Alexander, Lamar | 728,295 | Clement, Bob | 22,706 | 163,125 R | 54.3% | 44.3% | 55.0% | 45.0% |
| 2000 | 1,928,613 | 1,255,444 | Frist, Bill | 621,152 | Clark, Jeff | 52,017 | 634,292 R | 65.1% | 32.2% | 66.9% | 33.1% |
| 1996 | 1,778,664 | 1,091,554 | Thompson, Fred | 654,937 | Gordon, Houston | 32,173 | 436,617 R | 61.4% | 36.8% | 62.5% | 37.5% |
| 1994 | 1,480,391 | 834,226 | Frist, Bill | 623,164 | Sasser, James R. | 23,001 | 211,062 R | 56.4% | 42.1% | 57.2% | 42.8% |
| 1994S | 1,465,862 | 885,998 | Thompson, Fred | 565,930 | Cooper, Jim | 13,934 | 320,068 R | 60.4% | 38.6% | 61.0% | 39.0% |
| 1990 | 783,922 | 233,703 | Hawkins, William R. | 530,898 | Gore, Al | 19,321 | 297,195 D | 29.8% | 67.7% | 30.6% | 69.4% |
| 1988 | 1,567,181 | 541,033 | Anderson, Bill | 1,020,061 | Sasser, James R. | 6,087 | 479,028 D | 34.5% | 65.1% | 34.7% | 65.3% |
| 1984 | 1,648,064 | 557,016 | Ashe, Victor | 1,000,607 | Gore, Al | 90,441 | 443,591 D | 33.8% | 60.7% | 35.8% | 64.2% |
| 1982 | 1,259,785 | 479,642 | Beard, Robin L. | 780,113 | Sasser, James R. | 30 | 300,471 D | 38.1% | 61.9% | 38.1% | 61.9% |
| 1978 | 1,157,094 | 642,644 | Baker, Howard H., Jr. | 466,228 | Eskind, Jane | 48,222 | 176,416 R | 55.5% | 40.3% | 58.0% | 42.0% |
| 1976 | 1,432,046 | 673,231 | Brock, William E. | 751,180 | Sasser, James R. | 7,635 | 77,949 D | 47.0% | 52.5% | 47.3% | 52.7% |
| 1972 | 1,164,195 | 716,539 | Baker, Howard H., Jr. | 440,599 | Blanton, Ray | 7,057 | 275,940 R | 61.5% | 37.8% | 61.9% | 38.1% |
| 1970 | 1,097,041 | 562,645 | Brock, William E. | 519,858 | Gore, Albert | 14,538 | 42,787 R | 51.3% | 47.4% | 52.0% | 48.0% |
| 1966 | 866,961 | 483,063 | Baker, Howard H., Jr. | 383,843 | Clement, Frank G. | 55 | 99,220 R | 55.7% | 44.3% | 55.7% | 44.3% |
| 1964 | 1,064,018 | 493,475 | Kuykendall, Daniel H. | 570,542 | Gore, Albert | 1 | 77,067 D | 46.4% | 53.6% | 46.4% | 53.6% |
| 1964S | 1,091,093 | 517,330 | Baker, Howard H., Jr. | 568,905 | Bass, Ross | 4,858 | 51,575 D | 47.4% | 52.1% | 47.6% | 52.4% |
| 1960 | 828,519 | 234,053 | Frazier, A. Bradley | 594,460 | Kefauver, Estes | 6 | 360,407 D | 28.2% | 71.7% | 28.2% | 71.8% |
| 1958 | 401,666 | 76,371 | Atkins, Hobart F. | 317,324 | Gore, Albert | 7,971 | 240,953 D | 19.0% | 79.0% | 19.4% | 80.6% |
| 1954 | 356,094 | 106,971 | Wall, Thomas P. | 249,121 | Kefauver, Estes | 2 | 142,150 D | 30.0% | 70.0% | 30.0% | 70.0% |
| 1952 | 735,219 | 153,479 | Atkins, Hobart F. | 545,432 | Gore, Albert | 36,308 | 391,953 D | 20.9% | 74.2% | 22.0% | 78.0% |
| 1948 | 499,218 | 166,947 | Reece, B. Carroll | 326,142 | Kefauver, Estes | 6,129 | 159,195 D | 33.4% | 65.3% | 33.9% | 66.1% |
| 1946 | 218,714 | 57,238 | Ladd, William B. | 145,654 | McKellar, Kenneth | 15,822 | 88,416 D | 26.2% | 66.6% | 28.2% | 71.8% |

One each of the 1994 and 1964 elections was for a short term to fill a vacancy.

# TENNESSEE

Congressional districts first established for elections held in 2002
9 members

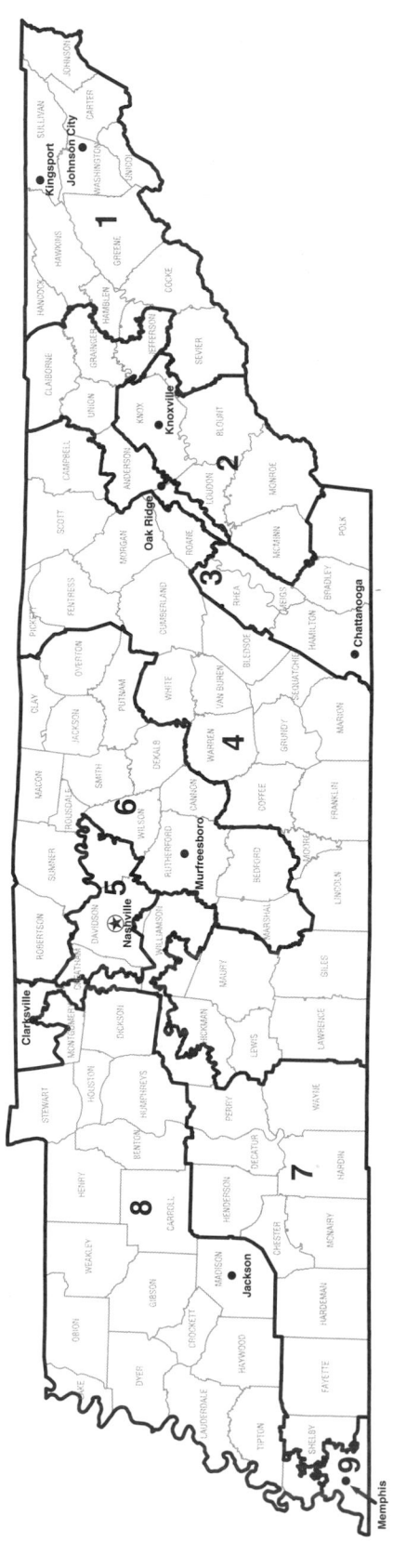

# TENNESSEE

## PRESIDENT 2004

| 2000 Census Population | County | Total Vote | Republican | Democratic | Other | Rep.-Dem. Plurality | Percentage Total Vote Rep. | Dem. | Major Vote Rep. | Dem. |
|---|---|---|---|---|---|---|---|---|---|---|
| 71,330 | ANDERSON | 31,682 | 18,510 | 12,896 | 276 | 5,614 R | 58.4% | 40.7% | 58.9% | 41.1% |
| 37,586 | BEDFORD | 13,706 | 8,351 | 5,268 | 87 | 3,083 R | 60.9% | 38.4% | 61.3% | 38.7% |
| 16,537 | BENTON | 7,090 | 3,161 | 3,869 | 60 | 708 D | 44.6% | 54.6% | 45.0% | 55.0% |
| 12,367 | BLEDSOE | 4,809 | 2,849 | 1,927 | 33 | 922 R | 59.2% | 40.1% | 59.7% | 40.3% |
| 105,823 | BLOUNT | 48,712 | 33,241 | 15,047 | 424 | 18,194 R | 68.2% | 30.9% | 68.8% | 31.2% |
| 87,965 | BRADLEY | 35,637 | 25,951 | 9,431 | 255 | 16,520 R | 72.8% | 26.5% | 73.3% | 26.7% |
| 39,854 | CAMPBELL | 14,118 | 7,859 | 6,163 | 96 | 1,696 R | 55.7% | 43.7% | 56.0% | 44.0% |
| 12,826 | CANNON | 5,481 | 2,931 | 2,515 | 35 | 416 R | 53.5% | 45.9% | 53.8% | 46.2% |
| 29,475 | CARROLL | 11,757 | 6,605 | 5,070 | 82 | 1,535 R | 56.2% | 43.1% | 56.6% | 43.4% |
| 56,742 | CARTER | 22,313 | 15,768 | 6,395 | 150 | 9,373 R | 70.7% | 28.7% | 71.1% | 28.9% |
| 35,912 | CHEATHAM | 15,697 | 9,676 | 5,918 | 103 | 3,758 R | 61.6% | 37.7% | 62.0% | 38.0% |
| 15,540 | CHESTER | 6,357 | 4,086 | 2,242 | 29 | 1,844 R | 64.3% | 35.3% | 64.6% | 35.4% |
| 29,862 | CLAIBORNE | 10,540 | 6,448 | 4,034 | 58 | 2,414 R | 61.2% | 38.3% | 61.5% | 38.5% |
| 7,976 | CLAY | 3,357 | 1,650 | 1,675 | 32 | 25 D | 49.2% | 49.9% | 49.6% | 50.4% |
| 33,565 | COCKE | 12,311 | 8,297 | 3,935 | 79 | 4,362 R | 67.4% | 32.0% | 67.8% | 32.2% |
| 48,014 | COFFEE | 20,167 | 11,793 | 8,243 | 131 | 3,550 R | 58.5% | 40.9% | 58.9% | 41.1% |
| 14,532 | CROCKETT | 5,722 | 3,242 | 2,459 | 21 | 783 R | 56.7% | 43.0% | 56.9% | 43.1% |
| 46,802 | CUMBERLAND | 23,637 | 15,144 | 8,327 | 166 | 6,817 R | 64.1% | 35.2% | 64.5% | 35.5% |
| 569,891 | DAVIDSON | 242,302 | 107,839 | 132,737 | 1,726 | 24,898 D | 44.5% | 54.8% | 44.8% | 55.2% |
| 11,731 | DECATUR | 4,879 | 2,566 | 2,268 | 45 | 298 R | 52.6% | 46.5% | 53.1% | 46.9% |
| 17,423 | DE KALB | 7,173 | 3,685 | 3,445 | 43 | 240 R | 51.4% | 48.0% | 51.7% | 48.3% |
| 43,156 | DICKSON | 19,298 | 10,567 | 8,597 | 134 | 1,970 R | 54.8% | 44.5% | 55.1% | 44.9% |
| 37,279 | DYER | 13,809 | 8,447 | 5,287 | 75 | 3,160 R | 61.2% | 38.3% | 61.5% | 38.5% |
| 28,806 | FAYETTE | 14,737 | 8,962 | 5,696 | 79 | 3,266 R | 60.8% | 38.7% | 61.1% | 38.9% |
| 16,625 | FENTRESS | 6,700 | 4,293 | 2,371 | 36 | 1,922 R | 64.1% | 35.4% | 64.4% | 35.6% |
| 39,270 | FRANKLIN | 17,077 | 9,129 | 7,800 | 148 | 1,329 R | 53.5% | 45.7% | 53.9% | 46.1% |
| 48,152 | GIBSON | 19,221 | 10,596 | 8,511 | 114 | 2,085 R | 55.1% | 44.3% | 55.5% | 44.5% |
| 29,447 | GILES | 11,537 | 6,163 | 5,273 | 101 | 890 R | 53.4% | 45.7% | 53.9% | 46.1% |
| 20,659 | GRAINGER | 7,527 | 4,907 | 2,569 | 51 | 2,338 R | 65.2% | 34.1% | 65.6% | 34.4% |
| 62,909 | GREENE | 24,194 | 16,382 | 7,635 | 177 | 8,747 R | 67.7% | 31.6% | 68.2% | 31.8% |
| 14,332 | GRUNDY | 4,929 | 2,107 | 2,789 | 33 | 682 D | 42.7% | 56.6% | 43.0% | 57.0% |
| 58,128 | HAMBLEN | 22,318 | 14,742 | 7,433 | 143 | 7,309 R | 66.1% | 33.3% | 66.5% | 33.5% |
| 307,896 | HAMILTON | 136,936 | 78,547 | 57,302 | 1,087 | 21,245 R | 57.4% | 41.8% | 57.8% | 42.2% |
| 6,786 | HANCOCK | 2,551 | 1,756 | 777 | 18 | 979 R | 68.8% | 30.5% | 69.3% | 30.7% |
| 28,105 | HARDEMAN | 10,466 | 4,704 | 5,685 | 77 | 981 D | 44.9% | 54.3% | 45.3% | 54.7% |
| 25,578 | HARDIN | 9,954 | 6,087 | 3,834 | 33 | 2,253 R | 61.2% | 38.5% | 61.4% | 38.6% |
| 53,563 | HAWKINS | 20,233 | 13,447 | 6,684 | 102 | 6,763 R | 66.5% | 33.0% | 66.8% | 33.2% |
| 19,797 | HAYWOOD | 7,548 | 3,140 | 4,359 | 49 | 1,219 D | 41.6% | 57.8% | 41.9% | 58.1% |
| 25,522 | HENDERSON | 10,096 | 6,585 | 3,448 | 63 | 3,137 R | 65.2% | 34.2% | 65.6% | 34.4% |
| 31,115 | HENRY | 13,177 | 7,340 | 5,732 | 105 | 1,608 R | 55.7% | 43.5% | 56.2% | 43.8% |
| 22,295 | HICKMAN | 8,673 | 4,359 | 4,263 | 51 | 96 R | 50.3% | 49.2% | 50.6% | 49.4% |
| 8,088 | HOUSTON | 3,598 | 1,440 | 2,126 | 32 | 686 D | 40.0% | 59.1% | 40.4% | 59.6% |
| 17,929 | HUMPHREYS | 7,793 | 3,261 | 4,485 | 47 | 1,224 D | 41.8% | 57.6% | 42.1% | 57.9% |
| 10,984 | JACKSON | 5,056 | 2,026 | 2,998 | 32 | 972 D | 40.1% | 59.3% | 40.3% | 59.7% |
| 44,294 | JEFFERSON | 17,215 | 11,625 | 5,469 | 121 | 6,156 R | 67.5% | 31.8% | 68.0% | 32.0% |
| 17,499 | JOHNSON | 6,480 | 4,634 | 1,812 | 34 | 2,822 R | 71.5% | 28.0% | 71.9% | 28.1% |
| 382,032 | KNOX | 178,419 | 110,803 | 66,013 | 1,603 | 44,790 R | 62.1% | 37.0% | 62.7% | 37.3% |
| 7,954 | LAKE | 4,740 | 2,078 | 2,634 | 28 | 556 D | 43.8% | 55.6% | 44.1% | 55.9% |
| 27,101 | LAUDERDALE | 8,682 | 4,164 | 4,474 | 44 | 310 D | 48.0% | 51.5% | 48.2% | 51.8% |
| 39,926 | LAWRENCE | 16,658 | 9,959 | 6,592 | 107 | 3,367 R | 59.8% | 39.6% | 60.2% | 39.8% |
| 11,367 | LEWIS | 5,054 | 2,819 | 2,192 | 43 | 627 R | 55.8% | 43.4% | 56.3% | 43.7% |
| 31,340 | LINCOLN | 12,457 | 7,829 | 4,546 | 82 | 3,283 R | 62.8% | 36.5% | 63.3% | 36.7% |
| 39,086 | LOUDON | 19,864 | 14,041 | 5,708 | 115 | 8,333 R | 70.7% | 28.7% | 71.1% | 28.9% |
| 49,015 | MCMINN | 18,003 | 11,980 | 5,891 | 132 | 6,089 R | 66.5% | 32.7% | 67.0% | 33.0% |
| 24,653 | MCNAIRY | 9,924 | 5,787 | 4,101 | 36 | 1,686 R | 58.3% | 41.3% | 58.5% | 41.5% |
| 20,386 | MACON | 7,433 | 4,670 | 2,738 | 25 | 1,932 R | 62.8% | 36.8% | 63.0% | 37.0% |
| 91,837 | MADISON | 38,675 | 21,679 | 16,840 | 156 | 4,839 R | 56.1% | 43.5% | 56.3% | 43.7% |
| 27,776 | MARION | 11,492 | 5,862 | 5,548 | 82 | 314 R | 51.0% | 48.3% | 51.4% | 48.6% |
| 26,767 | MARSHALL | 10,615 | 5,825 | 4,722 | 68 | 1,103 R | 54.9% | 44.5% | 55.2% | 44.8% |
| 69,498 | MAURY | 30,043 | 17,505 | 12,379 | 159 | 5,126 R | 58.3% | 41.2% | 58.6% | 41.4% |

# TENNESSEE

## PRESIDENT 2004

| 2000 Census Population | County | Total Vote | Republican | Democratic | Other | Rep.-Dem. Plurality | Percentage Total Vote Rep. | Dem. | Major Vote Rep. | Dem. |
|---|---|---|---|---|---|---|---|---|---|---|
| 11,086 | MEIGS | 4,132 | 2,500 | 1,595 | 37 | 905 R | 60.5% | 38.6% | 61.1% | 38.9% |
| 38,961 | MONROE | 15,568 | 10,123 | 5,354 | 91 | 4,769 R | 65.0% | 34.4% | 65.4% | 34.6% |
| 134,768 | MONTGOMERY | 48,998 | 28,627 | 20,070 | 301 | 8,557 R | 58.4% | 41.0% | 58.8% | 41.2% |
| 5,740 | MOORE | 2,774 | 1,668 | 1,084 | 22 | 584 R | 60.1% | 39.1% | 60.6% | 39.4% |
| 19,757 | MORGAN | 7,360 | 4,401 | 2,924 | 35 | 1,477 R | 59.8% | 39.7% | 60.1% | 39.9% |
| 32,450 | OBION | 13,535 | 7,859 | 5,549 | 127 | 2,310 R | 58.1% | 41.0% | 58.6% | 41.4% |
| 20,118 | OVERTON | 8,510 | 3,941 | 4,518 | 51 | 577 D | 46.3% | 53.1% | 46.6% | 53.4% |
| 7,631 | PERRY | 3,150 | 1,522 | 1,579 | 49 | 57 D | 48.3% | 50.1% | 49.1% | 50.9% |
| 4,945 | PICKETT | 2,645 | 1,600 | 1,033 | 12 | 567 R | 60.5% | 39.1% | 60.8% | 39.2% |
| 16,050 | POLK | 6,700 | 3,924 | 2,724 | 52 | 1,200 R | 58.6% | 40.7% | 59.0% | 41.0% |
| 62,315 | PUTNAM | 26,442 | 15,637 | 10,566 | 239 | 5,071 R | 59.1% | 40.0% | 59.7% | 40.3% |
| 28,400 | RHEA | 11,054 | 7,301 | 3,665 | 88 | 3,636 R | 66.0% | 33.2% | 66.6% | 33.4% |
| 51,910 | ROANE | 23,338 | 14,467 | 8,706 | 165 | 5,761 R | 62.0% | 37.3% | 62.4% | 37.6% |
| 54,433 | ROBERTSON | 25,323 | 15,331 | 9,865 | 127 | 5,466 R | 60.5% | 39.0% | 60.8% | 39.2% |
| 182,023 | RUTHERFORD | 84,409 | 52,200 | 31,647 | 562 | 20,553 R | 61.8% | 37.5% | 62.3% | 37.7% |
| 21,127 | SCOTT | 7,628 | 4,509 | 3,086 | 33 | 1,423 R | 59.1% | 40.5% | 59.4% | 40.6% |
| 11,370 | SEQUATCHIE | 4,983 | 2,951 | 1,986 | 46 | 965 R | 59.2% | 39.9% | 59.8% | 40.2% |
| 71,170 | SEVIER | 30,970 | 22,143 | 8,621 | 206 | 13,522 R | 71.5% | 27.8% | 72.0% | 28.0% |
| 897,472 | SHELBY | 377,282 | 158,137 | 216,945 | 2,200 | 58,808 D | 41.9% | 57.5% | 42.2% | 57.8% |
| 17,712 | SMITH | 7,828 | 3,739 | 4,044 | 45 | 305 D | 47.8% | 51.7% | 48.0% | 52.0% |
| 12,370 | STEWART | 5,583 | 2,675 | 2,860 | 48 | 185 D | 47.9% | 51.2% | 48.3% | 51.7% |
| 153,048 | SULLIVAN | 62,639 | 42,555 | 19,637 | 447 | 22,918 R | 67.9% | 31.3% | 68.4% | 31.6% |
| 130,449 | SUMNER | 61,968 | 40,181 | 21,458 | 329 | 18,723 R | 64.8% | 34.6% | 65.2% | 34.8% |
| 51,271 | TIPTON | 21,677 | 14,178 | 7,379 | 120 | 6,799 R | 65.4% | 34.0% | 65.8% | 34.2% |
| 7,259 | TROUSDALE | 3,191 | 1,314 | 1,851 | 26 | 537 D | 41.2% | 58.0% | 41.5% | 58.5% |
| 17,667 | UNICOI | 7,463 | 5,030 | 2,374 | 59 | 2,656 R | 67.4% | 31.8% | 67.9% | 32.1% |
| 17,808 | UNION | 6,710 | 4,145 | 2,524 | 41 | 1,621 R | 61.8% | 37.6% | 62.2% | 37.8% |
| 5,508 | VAN BUREN | 2,347 | 1,120 | 1,209 | 18 | 89 D | 47.7% | 51.5% | 48.1% | 51.9% |
| 38,276 | WARREN | 14,400 | 7,503 | 6,808 | 89 | 695 R | 52.1% | 47.3% | 52.4% | 47.6% |
| 107,198 | WASHINGTON | 45,006 | 29,735 | 14,944 | 327 | 14,791 R | 66.1% | 33.2% | 66.6% | 33.4% |
| 16,842 | WAYNE | 5,984 | 3,999 | 1,951 | 34 | 2,048 R | 66.8% | 32.6% | 67.2% | 32.8% |
| 34,895 | WEAKLEY | 13,496 | 7,817 | 5,588 | 91 | 2,229 R | 57.9% | 41.4% | 58.3% | 41.7% |
| 23,102 | WHITE | 9,495 | 5,269 | 4,147 | 79 | 1,122 R | 55.5% | 43.7% | 56.0% | 44.0% |
| 126,638 | WILLIAMSON | 79,650 | 57,451 | 21,732 | 467 | 35,719 R | 72.1% | 27.3% | 72.6% | 27.4% |
| 88,809 | WILSON | 44,452 | 28,924 | 15,277 | 251 | 13,647 R | 65.1% | 34.4% | 65.4% | 34.6% |
| 5,689,283 | TOTAL | 2,437,319 | 1,384,375 | 1,036,477 | 16,467 | 347,898 R | 56.8% | 42.5% | 57.2% | 42.8% |

# TENNESSEE

## HOUSE OF REPRESENTATIVES

| CD | Year | Total Vote | Republican Vote | Candidate | Democratic Vote | Candidate | Other Vote | Rep.-Dem. Plurality | Percentage Total Vote Rep. | Dem. | Major Vote Rep. | Dem. |
|---|---|---|---|---|---|---|---|---|---|---|---|---|
| 1 | 2004 | 233,560 | 172,543 | Jenkins, Bill* | 56,361 | Leonard, Graham | 4,656 | 116,182 R | 73.9% | 24.1% | 75.4% | 24.6% |
| 1 | 2002 | 128,886 | 127,300 | Jenkins, Bill* | | | 1,586 | 127,300 R | 98.8% | | 100.0% | |
| 2 | 2004 | 272,928 | 215,795 | Duncan, John J. "Jimmy" Jr.* | 52,155 | Greene, John | 4,978 | 163,640 R | 79.1% | 19.1% | 80.5% | 19.5% |
| 2 | 2002 | 185,981 | 146,887 | Duncan, John J. "Jimmy" Jr.* | 37,035 | Greene, John | 2,059 | 109,852 R | 79.0% | 19.9% | 79.9% | 20.1% |
| 3 | 2004 | 256,636 | 166,154 | Wamp, Zach* | 84,295 | Wolfe, John | 6,187 | 81,859 R | 64.7% | 32.8% | 66.3% | 33.7% |
| 3 | 2002 | 173,921 | 112,254 | Wamp, Zach* | 58,824 | Wolfe, John | 2,843 | 53,430 R | 64.5% | 33.8% | 65.6% | 34.4% |
| 4 | 2004 | 252,646 | 109,993 | Bowling, Janice | 138,459 | Davis, Lincoln* | 4,194 | 28,466 D | 43.5% | 54.8% | 44.3% | 55.7% |
| 4 | 2002 | 184,300 | 85,680 | Bowling, Janice | 95,989 | Davis, Lincoln | 2,631 | 10,309 D | 46.5% | 52.1% | 47.2% | 52.8% |
| 5 | 2004 | 243,963 | 74,978 | Knapp, Scott | 168,970 | Cooper, Jim* | 15 | 93,992 D | 30.7% | 69.3% | 30.7% | 69.3% |
| 5 | 2002 | 170,886 | 56,825 | Duvall, Robert | 108,903 | Cooper, Jim | 5,158 | 52,078 D | 33.3% | 63.7% | 34.3% | 65.7% |

# TENNESSEE

## HOUSE OF REPRESENTATIVES

| CD | Year | Total Vote | Republican Vote | Republican Candidate | Democratic Vote | Democratic Candidate | Other Vote | Rep.-Dem. Plurality | | Total Vote Rep. | Total Vote Dem. | Major Vote Rep. | Major Vote Dem. |
|----|------|-----------|-----------------|----------------------|-----------------|----------------------|------------|---------------------|--|-----|------|------|------|
| 6 | 2004 | 260,642 | 87,523 | Demas, Nick | 167,448 | Gordon, Bart* | 5,671 | 79,925 | D | 33.6% | 64.2% | 34.3% | 65.7% |
| 6 | 2002 | 177,547 | 57,401 | Garrison, Robert L. | 117,034 | Gordon, Bart* | 3,112 | 59,633 | D | 32.3% | 65.9% | 32.9% | 67.1% |
| 7 | 2004 | 232,404 | 232,404 | Blackburn, Marsha* | | | | 232,404 | R | 100.0% | | 100.0% | |
| 7 | 2002 | 195,558 | 138,314 | Blackburn, Marsha | 51,790 | Barron, Tim | 5,454 | 86,524 | R | 70.7% | 26.5% | 72.8% | 27.2% |
| 8 | 2004 | 233,567 | 59,853 | Hart, James L. | 173,623 | Tanner, John* | 91 | 113,770 | D | 25.6% | 74.3% | 25.6% | 74.4% |
| 8 | 2002 | 167,970 | 45,853 | McClain, Mat | 117,811 | Tanner, John* | 4,306 | 71,958 | D | 27.3% | 70.1% | 28.0% | 72.0% |
| 9 | 2004 | 232,392 | 41,578 | Fort, Ruben M. | 190,648 | Ford, Harold E. Jr.* | 166 | 149,070 | D | 17.9% | 82.0% | 17.9% | 82.1% |
| 9 | 2002 | 144,260 | | | 120,904 | Ford, Harold E. Jr.* | 23,356 | 120,904 | D | | 83.8% | | 100.0% |
| Total | 2004 | 2,218,738 | 1,160,821 | | 1,031,959 | | 25,958 | 128,862 | R | 52.3% | 46.5% | 52.9% | 47.1% |
| Total | 2002 | 1,529,309 | 770,514 | | 708,290 | | 50,505 | 62,224 | R | 50.4% | 46.3% | 52.1% | 47.9% |

An asterisk (*) denotes incumbent.

# TENNESSEE

## GENERAL AND PRIMARY ELECTIONS

### 2004 GENERAL ELECTIONS

**President** — Other vote was 8,992 Independent (Ralph Nader); 4,866 Independent (Michael Badnarik); 2,570 Independent (Michael Peroutka); 33 write-in (David Cobb); 6 write-in (Walter F. Brown).

**House** — Other vote was:

CD 1 — 3,061 Independent (Ralph J. Ball); 1,595 Independent (Michael Peavler).
CD 2 — 4,978 Independent (Charles E. Howard).
CD 3 — 3,018 Independent (June Griffin); 1,696 Independent (Doug Vandagriff); 1,473 Independent (Jean Howard-Hill).
CD 4 — 4,194 Independent (Ken Martin).
CD 5 — 15 write-in (Thomas F. Kovach).
CD 6 — 3,869 Independent (J. Patrick Lyons); 1,802 Independent (Norman R. Saliba).
CD 7 —
CD 8 — 91 write-in (Dennis Bertrand).
CD 9 — 166 write-in (Jim Maynard).

Note: In Tennessee all third-party candidates were listed as Independents regardless of party affiliation.

### 2004 PRIMARY ELECTIONS

**Primary** — February 10, 2004 (President); August 5, 2004 (Congress)

**Registration** (as of June 1, 2004—includes 425,359 inactive registrants) — 3,532,364 No Party Registration

**Primary Type** — Open—Any registered voter could participate in either the Democratic or Republican primary.

# TENNESSEE

## GENERAL AND PRIMARY ELECTIONS

Note: An asterisk (*) denotes incumbent.

| | REPUBLICAN PRIMARIES | | | DEMOCRATIC PRIMARIES | | |
|---|---|---|---|---|---|---|
| President | George W. Bush* | 94,557 | 95.5% | John Kerry | 151,527 | 41.0% |
| | Uncommitted | 4,504 | 4.5% | John Edwards | 97,914 | 26.5% |
| | | | | Wesley Clark | 85,315 | 23.1% |
| | | | | Howard Dean | 16,128 | 4.4% |
| | | | | Al Sharpton | 6,107 | 1.7% |
| | | | | Joseph I. Lieberman | 3,213 | 0.9% |
| | | | | Uncommitted | 2,727 | 0.7% |
| | | | | Carol Moseley Braun | 2,490 | 0.7% |
| | | | | Dennis J. Kucinich | 2,279 | 0.6% |
| | | | | Richard A. Gephardt | 1,402 | 0.4% |
| | | | | Lyndon H. LaRouche Jr. | 283 | 0.1% |
| | TOTAL | 99,061 | | TOTAL | 369,385 | |
| Congressional District 1 | Bill Jenkins* | 32,726 | 89.7% | Graham Leonard | 4,834 | 47.0% |
| | David R. Smith II | 3,747 | 10.3% | William Malcolm Earp Jr. | 2,770 | 26.9% |
| | | | | Lewis Hopkins Jr. | 2,686 | 26.1% |
| | TOTAL | 36,473 | | TOTAL | 10,290 | |
| Congressional District 2 | John J. "Jimmy" Duncan Jr.* | 41,362 | 91.5% | John Greene | 6,169 | 51.6% |
| | Debbie Jones Howard | 3,861 | 8.5% | Robert R. "Bob" Scott | 5,782 | 48.4% |
| | TOTAL | 45,223 | | TOTAL | 11,951 | |
| Congressional District 3 | Zach Wamp* | 30,183 | 90.1% | John Wolfe | 14,766 | 59.5% |
| | Timothy A. Sevier | 3,334 | 9.9% | Betty F. Williamson | 10,037 | 40.5% |
| | TOTAL | 33,517 | | TOTAL | 24,803 | |
| Congressional District 4 | Janice Bowling | 19,246 | 86.9% | Lincoln Davis* | 36,462 | 91.4% |
| | Dale Harvey | 2,431 | 11.0% | Harvey Howard | 3,435 | 8.6% |
| | Don Cuva | 465 | 2.1% | | | |
| | TOTAL | 22,142 | | TOTAL | 39,897 | |
| Congressional District 5 | Scott Knapp | 8,110 | 100.0% | Jim Cooper* | 22,396 | 100.0% |
| Congressional District 6 | Nick Demas | 7,657 | 51.5% | Bart Gordon* | 28,524 | 93.2% |
| | Elizabeth Hall | 7,205 | 48.5% | Robert C. Hall | 2,066 | 6.8% |
| | TOTAL | 14,862 | | TOTAL | 30,590 | |
| Congressional District 7 | Marsha Blackburn* | 24,233 | 100.0% | No Democratic candidate | | |
| Congressional District 8 | James L. Hart | 8,227 | 78.5% | John Tanner* | 28,427 | 100.0% |
| | Dennis Bertrand (write-in) | 2,253 | 21.5% | | | |
| | TOTAL | 10,480 | | | | |
| Congressional District 9 | Ruben M. Fort | 12,532 | 100.0% | Harold E. Ford Jr.* | 33,708 | 100.0% |

# TEXAS

## GOVERNOR

Rick Perry (R). Elected 2002 to a four-year term. Assumed office Dec. 21, 2000, following the resignation of president-elect George W. Bush.

## SENATORS (2 Republicans)

John Cornyn (R). Elected 2002 to a six-year term.

Kay Bailey Hutchison (R). Reelected 2000 to a six-year term. Previously elected 1994 and in a special election June 5, 1993, to fill out the remaining year and a half of the term vacated when Senator Lloyd Bentsen (D) resigned to become Secretary of the Treasury.

## REPRESENTATIVES (21 Republicans, 11 Democrats)

1. Louie Gohmert (R)
2. Ted Poe (R)
3. Sam Johnson (R)
4. Ralph M. Hall (R)
5. Jeb Hensarling (R)
6. Joe L. Barton (R)
7. John Culberson (R)
8. Kevin Brady (R)
9. Al Green (D)
10. Michael McCaul (R)
11. K. Michael Conaway (R)
12. Kay Granger (R)
13. William M. "Mac" Thornberry (R)
14. Ron Paul (R)
15. Ruben Hinojosa (D)
16. Silvestre Reyes (D)
17. Chet Edwards (D)
18. Sheila Jackson-Lee (D)
19. Randy Neugebauer (R)
20. Charlie Gonzalez (D)
21. Lamar Smith (R)
22. Tom DeLay (R)
23. Henry Bonilla (R)
24. Kenny Marchant (R)
25. Lloyd Doggett (D)
26. Michael C. Burgess (R)
27. Solomon P. Ortiz (D)
28. Henry Cuellar (D)
29. Gene Green (D)
30. Eddie Bernice Johnson (D)
31. John Carter (R)
32. Pete Sessions (R)

## POSTWAR VOTE FOR PRESIDENT

| Year | Total Vote | Republican Vote | Republican Candidate | Democratic Vote | Democratic Candidate | Other Vote | Plurality | Total Vote Rep. | Total Vote Dem. | Major Vote Rep. | Major Vote Dem. |
|------|-----------|------|-----------|------|-----------|------|-----------|------|------|------|------|
| 2004 | 7,410,765 | 4,526,917 | Bush, George W. | 2,832,704 | Kerry, John | 51,144 | 1,694,213 R | 61.1% | 38.2% | 61.5% | 38.5% |
| 2000** | 6,407,637 | 3,799,639 | Bush, George W. | 2,433,746 | Gore, Al | 174,252 | 1,365,893 R | 59.3% | 38.0% | 61.0% | 39.0% |
| 1996** | 5,611,644 | 2,736,167 | Dole, Bob | 2,459,683 | Clinton, Bill | 415,794 | 276,484 R | 48.8% | 43.8% | 52.7% | 47.3% |
| 1992** | 6,154,018 | 2,496,071 | Bush, George | 2,281,815 | Clinton, Bill | 1,376,132 | 214,256 R | 40.6% | 37.1% | 52.2% | 47.8% |
| 1988 | 5,427,410 | 3,036,829 | Bush, George | 2,352,748 | Dukakis, Michael S. | 37,833 | 684,081 R | 56.0% | 43.3% | 56.3% | 43.7% |
| 1984 | 5,397,571 | 3,433,428 | Reagan, Ronald | 1,949,276 | Mondale, Walter F. | 14,867 | 1,484,152 R | 63.6% | 36.1% | 63.8% | 36.2% |
| 1980** | 4,541,636 | 2,510,705 | Reagan, Ronald | 1,881,147 | Carter, Jimmy | 149,784 | 629,558 R | 55.3% | 41.4% | 57.2% | 42.8% |
| 1976 | 4,071,884 | 1,953,300 | Ford, Gerald R. | 2,082,319 | Carter, Jimmy | 36,265 | 129,019 D | 48.0% | 51.1% | 48.4% | 51.6% |
| 1972 | 3,471,281 | 2,298,896 | Nixon, Richard M. | 1,154,289 | McGovern, George S. | 18,096 | 1,144,607 R | 66.2% | 33.3% | 66.6% | 33.4% |
| 1968** | 3,079,216 | 1,227,844 | Nixon, Richard M. | 1,266,804 | Humphrey, Hubert H. | 584,568 | 38,960 D | 39.9% | 41.1% | 49.2% | 50.8% |
| 1964 | 2,626,811 | 958,566 | Goldwater, Barry M. | 1,663,185 | Johnson, Lyndon B. | 5,060 | 704,619 D | 36.5% | 63.3% | 36.6% | 63.4% |
| 1960 | 2,311,084 | 1,121,310 | Nixon, Richard M. | 1,167,567 | Kennedy, John F. | 22,207 | 46,257 D | 48.5% | 50.5% | 49.0% | 51.0% |
| 1956 | 1,955,168 | 1,080,619 | Eisenhower, Dwight D. | 859,958 | Stevenson, Adlai E. | 14,591 | 220,661 R | 55.3% | 44.0% | 55.7% | 44.3% |
| 1952 | 2,075,946 | 1,102,878 | Eisenhower, Dwight D. | 969,228 | Stevenson, Adlai E. | 3,840 | 133,650 R | 53.1% | 46.7% | 53.2% | 46.8% |
| 1948** | 1,249,577 | 303,467 | Dewey, Thomas E. | 824,235 | Truman, Harry S. | 121,875 | 520,768 D | 24.3% | 66.0% | 26.9% | 73.1% |

In past elections, the other vote included: 2000 - 137,994 Green (Ralph Nader); 1996 - 378,537 Reform (Ross Perot); 1992 - 1,354,781 Independent (Perot); 1980 - 111,613 Independent (John Anderson); 1968 - 584,269 American Independent (Wallace); 1948 - 113,920 States' Rights (Strom Thurmond).

# TEXAS

## POSTWAR VOTE FOR GOVERNOR

| Year | Total Vote | Republican Vote | Candidate | Democratic Vote | Candidate | Other Vote | Rep.-Dem. Plurality | Total Vote Rep. | Dem. | Major Vote Rep. | Dem. |
|---|---|---|---|---|---|---|---|---|---|---|---|
| 2002 | 4,553,987 | 2,632,591 | Perry, Rick | 1,819,798 | Sanchez, Tony | 101,598 | 812,793 R | 57.8% | 40.0% | 59.1% | 40.9% |
| 1998 | 3,738,483 | 2,551,454 | Bush, George W. | 1,165,444 | Mauro, Garry | 21,585 | 1,386,010 R | 68.2% | 31.2% | 68.6% | 31.4% |
| 1994 | 4,396,242 | 2,350,994 | Bush, George W. | 2,016,928 | Richards, Ann | 28,320 | 334,066 R | 53.5% | 45.9% | 53.8% | 46.2% |
| 1990 | 3,892,746 | 1,826,431 | Williams, Clayton | 1,925,670 | Richards, Ann | 140,645 | 99,239 D | 46.9% | 49.5% | 48.7% | 51.3% |
| 1986 | 3,441,460 | 1,813,779 | Clements, William P. | 1,584,515 | White, Mark | 43,166 | 229,264 R | 52.7% | 46.0% | 53.4% | 46.6% |
| 1982 | 3,191,091 | 1,465,937 | Clements, William P. | 1,697,870 | White, Mark | 27,284 | 231,933 D | 45.9% | 53.2% | 46.3% | 53.7% |
| 1978 | 2,369,764 | 1,183,839 | Clements, William P. | 1,166,979 | Hill, John | 18,946 | 16,860 R | 50.0% | 49.2% | 50.4% | 49.6% |
| 1974** | 1,654,984 | 514,725 | Granberry, Jim | 1,016,334 | Briscoe, Dolph | 123,925 | 501,609 D | 31.1% | 61.4% | 33.6% | 66.4% |
| 1972 | 3,410,128 | 1,534,060 | Grover, Henry C. | 1,633,970 | Briscoe, Dolph | 242,098 | 99,910 D | 45.0% | 47.9% | 48.4% | 51.6% |
| 1970 | 2,235,847 | 1,037,723 | Eggers, Paul W. | 1,197,726 | Smith, Preston | 398 | 160,003 D | 46.4% | 53.6% | 46.4% | 53.6% |
| 1968 | 2,916,509 | 1,254,333 | Eggers, Paul W. | 1,662,019 | Smith, Preston | 157 | 407,686 D | 43.0% | 57.0% | 43.0% | 57.0% |
| 1966 | 1,425,861 | 368,025 | Kennerly, T. E. | 1,037,517 | Connally, John B. | 20,319 | 669,492 D | 25.8% | 72.8% | 26.2% | 73.8% |
| 1964 | 2,544,753 | 661,675 | Crichton, Jack | 1,877,793 | Connally, John B. | 5,285 | 1,216,118 D | 26.0% | 73.8% | 26.1% | 73.9% |
| 1962 | 1,569,181 | 715,025 | Cox, Jack | 847,036 | Connally, John B. | 7,120 | 132,011 D | 45.6% | 54.0% | 45.8% | 54.2% |
| 1960 | 2,250,718 | 612,963 | Steger, William M. | 1,637,755 | Daniel, Price | | 1,024,792 D | 27.2% | 72.8% | 27.2% | 72.8% |
| 1958 | 789,133 | 94,098 | Mayer, Edwin S. | 695,035 | Daniel, Price | | 600,937 D | 11.9% | 88.1% | 11.9% | 88.1% |
| 1956 | 1,828,161 | 271,088 | Bryant, William R. | 1,433,051 | Daniel, Price | 124,022 | 1,161,963 D | 14.8% | 78.4% | 15.9% | 84.1% |
| 1954 | 636,892 | 66,154 | Adams, Tod R. | 569,533 | Shivers, Allan | 1,205 | 503,379 D | 10.4% | 89.4% | 10.4% | 89.6% |
| 1952 | 1,881,202 | | — | 1,844,530 | Shivers, Allan | 36,672 | 1,844,530 D | | 98.1% | | 100.0% |
| 1950 | 394,747 | 39,737 | Currie, Ralph W. | 355,010 | Shivers, Allan | | 315,273 D | 10.1% | 89.9% | 10.1% | 89.9% |
| 1948 | 1,208,860 | 177,399 | Lane, Alvin H. | 1,024,160 | Jester, Beauford | 7,301 | 846,761 D | 14.7% | 84.7% | 14.8% | 85.2% |
| 1946 | 378,744 | 33,231 | Nolte, Eugene | 345,513 | Jester, Beauford | | 312,282 D | 8.8% | 91.2% | 8.8% | 91.2% |

The term of office of Texas' governor was increased from two to four years effective with the 1974 election.

## POSTWAR VOTE FOR SENATOR

| Year | Total Vote | Republican Vote | Candidate | Democratic Vote | Candidate | Other Vote | Rep.-Dem. Plurality | Total Vote Rep. | Dem. | Major Vote Rep. | Dem. |
|---|---|---|---|---|---|---|---|---|---|---|---|
| 2002 | 4,514,012 | 2,496,243 | Cornyn, John | 1,955,758 | Kirk, Ron | 62,011 | 540,485 R | 55.3% | 43.3% | 56.1% | 43.9% |
| 2000 | 6,276,652 | 4,082,091 | Hutchison, Kay Bailey | 2,030,315 | Kelly, Gene | 164,246 | 2,051,776 R | 65.0% | 32.3% | 66.8% | 33.2% |
| 1996 | 5,527,441 | 3,027,680 | Gramm, Phil | 2,428,776 | Morales, Victor M. | 70,985 | 598,904 R | 54.8% | 43.9% | 55.5% | 44.5% |
| 1994 | 4,279,940 | 2,604,218 | Hutchison, Kay Bailey | 1,639,615 | Fisher, Richard | 36,107 | 964,603 R | 60.8% | 38.3% | 61.4% | 38.6% |
| 1993S | 1,765,254 | 1,188,716 | Hutchison, Kay Bailey | 576,538 | Krueger, Robert | | 612,178 R | 67.3% | 32.7% | 67.3% | 32.7% |
| 1990 | 3,822,157 | 2,302,357 | Gramm, Phil | 1,429,986 | Parmer, Hugh | 89,814 | 872,371 R | 60.2% | 37.4% | 61.7% | 38.3% |
| 1988 | 5,323,606 | 2,129,228 | Boulter, Beau | 3,149,806 | Bentsen, Lloyd | 44,572 | 1,020,578 D | 40.0% | 59.2% | 40.3% | 59.7% |
| 1984 | 5,319,178 | 3,116,348 | Gramm, Phil | 2,202,557 | Doggett, Lloyd | 273 | 913,791 R | 58.6% | 41.4% | 58.6% | 41.4% |
| 1982 | 3,103,167 | 1,256,759 | Collins, James M. | 1,818,223 | Bentsen, Lloyd | 28,185 | 561,464 D | 40.5% | 58.6% | 40.9% | 59.1% |
| 1978 | 2,312,540 | 1,151,376 | Tower, John G. | 1,139,149 | Krueger, Robert | 22,015 | 12,227 R | 49.8% | 49.3% | 50.3% | 49.7% |
| 1976 | 3,874,516 | 1,636,370 | Steelman, Alan | 2,199,956 | Bentsen, Lloyd | 38,190 | 563,586 D | 42.2% | 56.8% | 42.7% | 57.3% |
| 1972 | 3,413,903 | 1,822,877 | Tower, John G. | 1,511,985 | Sanders, Barefoot | 79,041 | 310,892 R | 53.4% | 44.3% | 54.7% | 45.3% |
| 1970 | 2,231,671 | 1,035,794 | Bush, George | 1,194,069 | Bentsen, Lloyd | 1,808 | 158,275 D | 46.4% | 53.5% | 46.5% | 53.5% |
| 1966 | 1,493,182 | 842,501 | Tower, John G. | 643,855 | Carr, Waggoner | 6,826 | 198,646 R | 56.4% | 43.1% | 56.7% | 43.3% |
| 1964 | 2,603,856 | 1,134,337 | Bush, George | 1,463,958 | Yarborough, Ralph | 5,561 | 329,621 D | 43.6% | 56.2% | 43.7% | 56.3% |
| 1961S | 886,091 | 448,217 | Tower, John G. | 437,874 | Blakley, William A. | | 10,343 R | 50.6% | 49.4% | 50.6% | 49.4% |
| 1960 | 2,253,784 | 926,653 | Tower, John G. | 1,306,625 | Johnson, Lyndon B. | 20,506 | 379,972 D | 41.1% | 58.0% | 41.5% | 58.5% |
| 1958 | 787,128 | 185,926 | Whittenburg, Roy | 587,030 | Yarborough, Ralph | 14,172 | 401,104 D | 23.6% | 74.6% | 24.1% | 75.9% |
| 1957S | 957,298 | | [See note below] | | | | D | | | | |
| 1954 | 636,475 | 94,131 | Watson, Carlos G. | 539,319 | Johnson, Lyndon B. | 3,025 | 445,188 D | 14.8% | 84.7% | 14.9% | 85.1% |
| 1952 | 1,895,192 | | — | 1,895,192 | Daniel, Price | | 1,895,192 D | | 100.0% | | 100.0% |
| 1948 | 1,061,563 | 349,665 | Porter, Jack | 702,985 | Johnson, Lyndon B. | 8,913 | 353,320 D | 32.9% | 66.2% | 33.2% | 66.8% |
| 1946 | 380,681 | 43,750 | Sells, Murray C. | 336,931 | Connally, Tom | | 293,181 D | 11.5% | 88.5% | 11.5% | 88.5% |

The June 1993 election was for a short term to fill a vacancy; the vote above was for the special election runoff. The 1961 and 1957 elections were also for short terms to fill vacancies. Although neither vote was held with official party designations, the 1961 vote above was a runoff contest between unofficial party candidates. In 1957 there was a single ballot without a runoff and Democrat Ralph Yarborough polled 364,605 votes (38.1 percent of the total vote) and won the election with a 73,802-vote plurality.

# TEXAS

Congressional districts first established for elections held in 2004
32 members

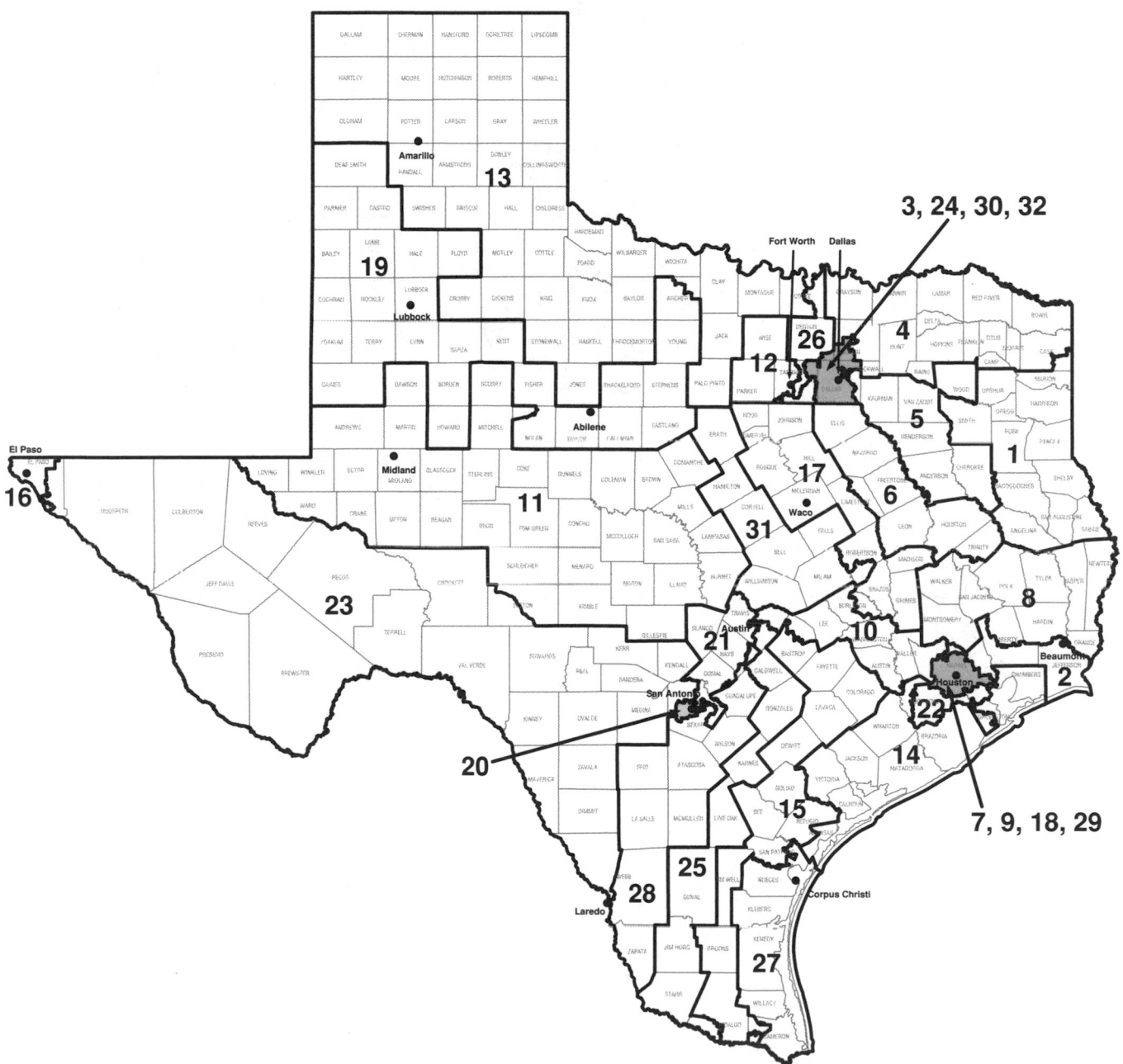

# TEXAS

## Houston Area

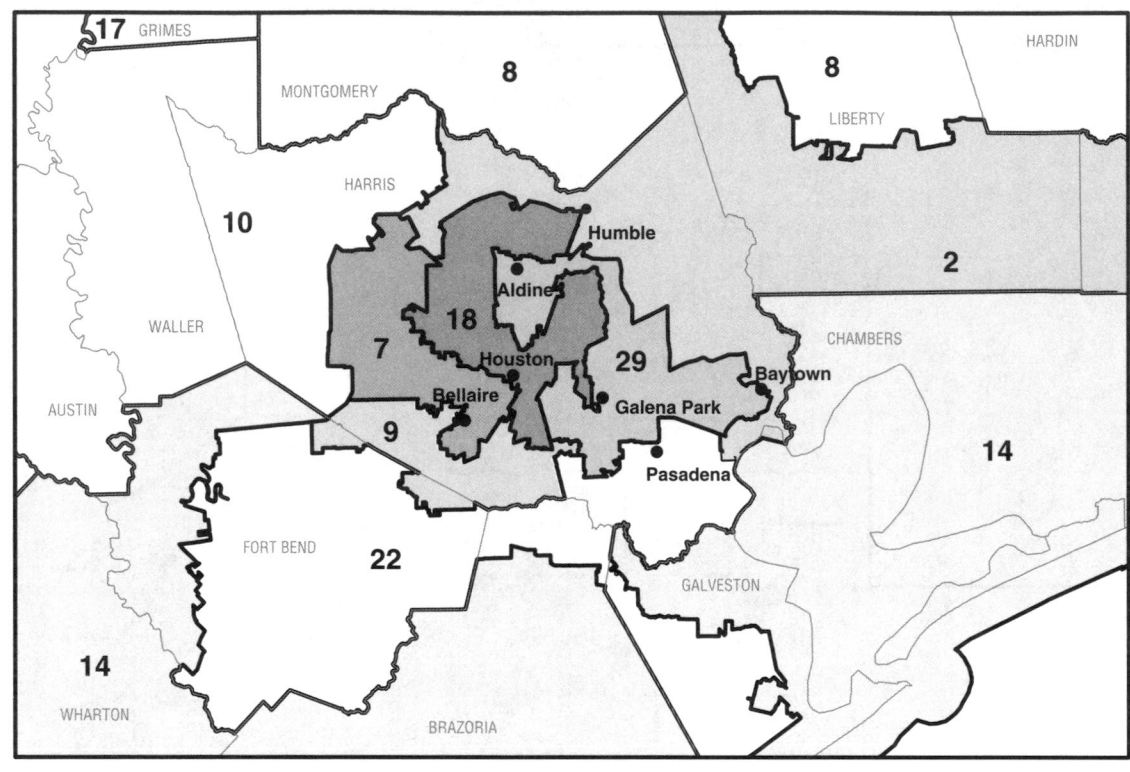

# TEXAS

Dallas-Fort Worth Area

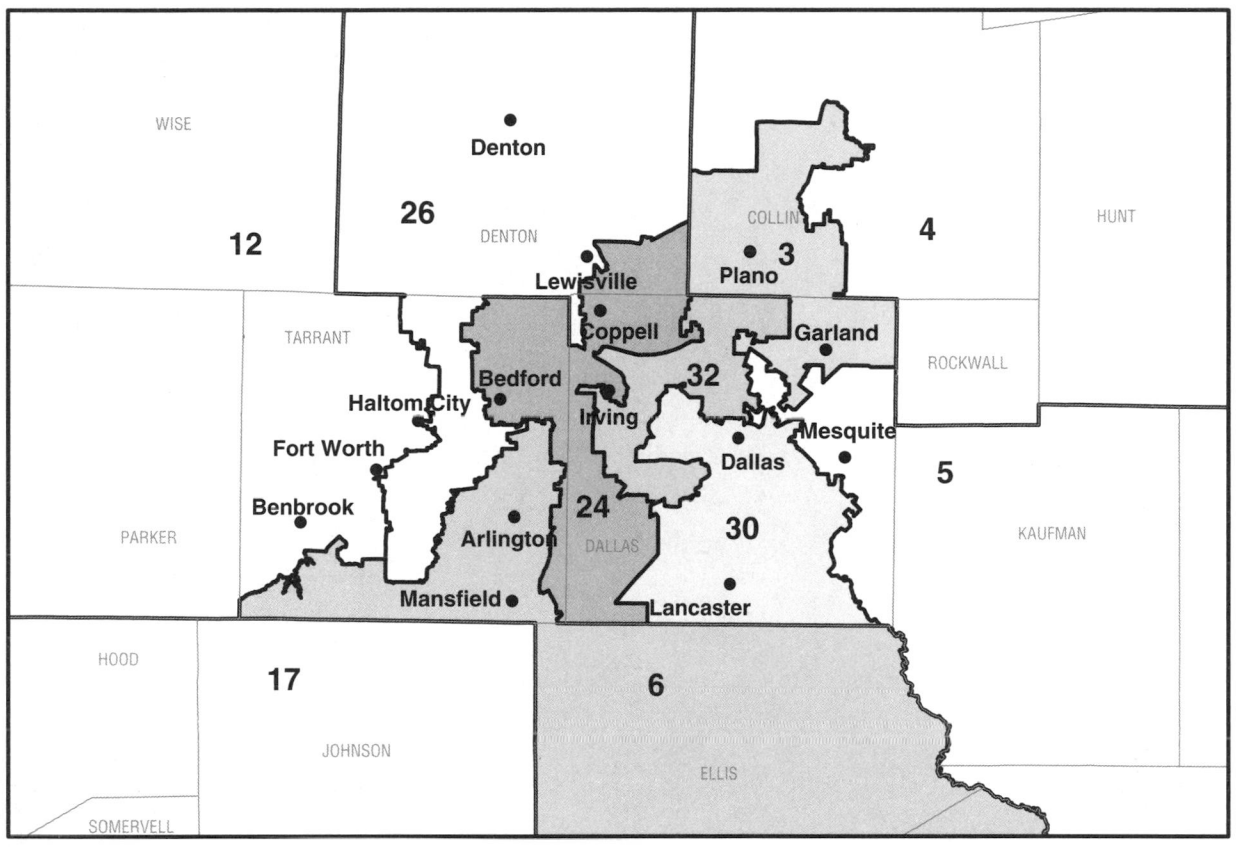

# TEXAS

## PRESIDENT 2004

| 2000 Census Population | County | Total Vote | Republican | Democratic | Other | Rep.-Dem. Plurality | Total Vote Rep. | Dem. | Major Vote Rep. | Dem. |
|---|---|---|---|---|---|---|---|---|---|---|
| 55,109 | ANDERSON | 16,301 | 11,525 | 4,678 | 98 | 6,847 R | 70.7% | 28.7% | 71.1% | 28.9% |
| 13,004 | ANDREWS | 4,536 | 3,837 | 677 | 22 | 3,160 R | 84.6% | 14.9% | 85.0% | 15.0% |
| 80,130 | ANGELINA | 28,364 | 18,932 | 9,302 | 130 | 9,630 R | 66.7% | 32.8% | 67.1% | 32.9% |
| 22,497 | ARANSAS | 9,268 | 6,569 | 2,640 | 59 | 3,929 R | 70.9% | 28.5% | 71.3% | 28.7% |
| 8,854 | ARCHER | 4,451 | 3,556 | 878 | 17 | 2,678 R | 79.9% | 19.7% | 80.2% | 19.8% |
| 2,148 | ARMSTRONG | 1,004 | 830 | 170 | 4 | 660 R | 82.7% | 16.9% | 83.0% | 17.0% |
| 38,628 | ATASCOSA | 12,116 | 7,635 | 4,421 | 60 | 3,214 R | 63.0% | 36.5% | 63.3% | 36.7% |
| 23,590 | AUSTIN | 10,702 | 8,072 | 2,582 | 48 | 5,490 R | 75.4% | 24.1% | 75.8% | 24.2% |
| 6,594 | BAILEY | 2,412 | 1,882 | 525 | 5 | 1,357 R | 78.0% | 21.8% | 78.2% | 21.8% |
| 17,645 | BANDERA | 8,741 | 6,933 | 1,738 | 70 | 5,195 R | 79.3% | 19.9% | 80.0% | 20.0% |
| 57,733 | BASTROP | 23,441 | 13,290 | 9,794 | 357 | 3,496 R | 56.7% | 41.8% | 57.6% | 42.4% |
| 4,093 | BAYLOR | 1,640 | 1,169 | 467 | 4 | 702 R | 71.3% | 28.5% | 71.5% | 28.5% |
| 32,359 | BEE | 9,518 | 5,428 | 4,045 | 45 | 1,383 R | 57.0% | 42.5% | 57.3% | 42.7% |
| 237,974 | BELL | 79,724 | 52,135 | 27,165 | 424 | 24,970 R | 65.4% | 34.1% | 65.7% | 34.3% |
| 1,392,931 | BEXAR | 475,314 | 260,698 | 210,976 | 3,640 | 49,722 R | 54.8% | 44.4% | 55.3% | 44.7% |
| 8,418 | BLANCO | 4,584 | 3,277 | 1,267 | 40 | 2,010 R | 71.5% | 27.6% | 72.1% | 27.9% |
| 729 | BORDEN | 359 | 303 | 55 | 1 | 248 R | 84.4% | 15.3% | 84.6% | 15.4% |
| 17,204 | BOSQUE | 7,586 | 5,737 | 1,815 | 34 | 3,922 R | 75.6% | 23.9% | 76.0% | 24.0% |
| 89,306 | BOWIE | 33,760 | 21,791 | 11,880 | 89 | 9,911 R | 64.5% | 35.2% | 64.7% | 35.3% |
| 241,767 | BRAZORIA | 93,248 | 63,662 | 28,904 | 682 | 34,758 R | 68.3% | 31.0% | 68.8% | 31.2% |
| 152,415 | BRAZOS | 54,309 | 37,594 | 16,128 | 587 | 21,466 R | 69.2% | 29.7% | 70.0% | 30.0% |
| 8,866 | BREWSTER | 3,760 | 1,980 | 1,729 | 51 | 251 R | 52.7% | 46.0% | 53.4% | 46.6% |
| 1,790 | BRISCOE | 811 | 620 | 191 | | 429 R | 76.4% | 23.6% | 76.4% | 23.6% |
| 7,976 | BROOKS | 2,674 | 845 | 1,823 | 6 | 978 D | 31.6% | 68.2% | 31.7% | 68.3% |
| 37,674 | BROWN | 14,253 | 11,640 | 2,523 | 90 | 9,117 R | 81.7% | 17.7% | 82.2% | 17.8% |
| 16,470 | BURLESON | 6,721 | 4,405 | 2,276 | 40 | 2,129 R | 65.5% | 33.9% | 65.9% | 34.1% |
| 34,147 | BURNET | 15,742 | 11,456 | 4,147 | 139 | 7,309 R | 72.8% | 26.3% | 73.4% | 26.6% |
| 32,194 | CALDWELL | 11,587 | 6,436 | 5,052 | 99 | 1,384 R | 55.5% | 43.6% | 56.0% | 44.0% |
| 20,647 | CALHOUN | 6,929 | 4,348 | 2,561 | 20 | 1,787 R | 62.8% | 37.0% | 62.9% | 37.1% |
| 12,905 | CALLAHAN | 5,654 | 4,542 | 1,073 | 39 | 3,469 R | 80.3% | 19.0% | 80.9% | 19.1% |
| 335,227 | CAMERON | 69,156 | 34,801 | 33,998 | 357 | 803 R | 50.3% | 49.2% | 50.6% | 49.4% |
| 11,549 | CAMP | 4,439 | 2,638 | 1,778 | 23 | 860 R | 59.4% | 40.1% | 59.7% | 40.3% |
| 6,516 | CARSON | 2,944 | 2,450 | 485 | 9 | 1,965 R | 83.2% | 16.5% | 83.5% | 16.5% |
| 30,438 | CASS | 12,049 | 7,383 | 4,630 | 36 | 2,753 R | 61.3% | 38.4% | 61.5% | 38.5% |
| 8,285 | CASTRO | 2,430 | 1,794 | 631 | 5 | 1,163 R | 73.8% | 26.0% | 74.0% | 26.0% |
| 26,031 | CHAMBERS | 11,649 | 8,618 | 2,953 | 78 | 5,665 R | 74.0% | 25.3% | 74.5% | 25.5% |
| 46,659 | CHEROKEE | 15,839 | 11,329 | 4,439 | 71 | 6,890 R | 71.5% | 28.0% | 71.8% | 28.2% |
| 7,688 | CHILDRESS | 2,144 | 1,629 | 511 | 4 | 1,118 R | 76.0% | 23.8% | 76.1% | 23.9% |
| 11,006 | CLAY | 5,288 | 3,971 | 1,299 | 18 | 2,672 R | 75.1% | 24.6% | 75.4% | 24.6% |
| 3,730 | COCHRAN | 1,110 | 856 | 249 | 5 | 607 R | 77.1% | 22.4% | 77.5% | 22.5% |
| 3,864 | COKE | 1,610 | 1,338 | 266 | 6 | 1,072 R | 83.1% | 16.5% | 83.4% | 16.6% |
| 9,235 | COLEMAN | 3,826 | 3,035 | 778 | 13 | 2,257 R | 79.3% | 20.3% | 79.6% | 20.4% |
| 491,675 | COLLIN | 245,154 | 174,435 | 68,935 | 1,784 | 105,500 R | 71.2% | 28.1% | 71.7% | 28.3% |
| 3,206 | COLLINGSWORTH | 1,398 | 1,051 | 346 | 1 | 705 R | 75.2% | 24.7% | 75.2% | 24.8% |
| 20,390 | COLORADO | 7,690 | 5,488 | 2,161 | 41 | 3,327 R | 71.4% | 28.1% | 71.7% | 28.3% |
| 78,021 | COMAL | 41,043 | 31,574 | 9,153 | 316 | 22,421 R | 76.9% | 22.3% | 77.5% | 22.5% |
| 14,026 | COMANCHE | 5,268 | 3,813 | 1,431 | 24 | 2,382 R | 72.4% | 27.2% | 72.7% | 27.3% |
| 3,966 | CONCHO | 1,193 | 911 | 270 | 12 | 641 R | 76.4% | 22.6% | 77.1% | 22.9% |
| 36,363 | COOKE | 15,107 | 11,908 | 3,142 | 57 | 8,766 R | 78.8% | 20.8% | 79.1% | 20.9% |
| 74,978 | CORYELL | 17,625 | 12,421 | 5,122 | 82 | 7,299 R | 70.5% | 29.1% | 70.8% | 29.2% |
| 1,904 | COTTLE | 768 | 549 | 214 | 5 | 335 R | 71.5% | 27.9% | 72.0% | 28.0% |
| 3,996 | CRANE | 1,574 | 1,314 | 254 | 6 | 1,060 R | 83.5% | 16.1% | 83.8% | 16.2% |
| 4,099 | CROCKETT | 1,728 | 1,248 | 473 | 7 | 775 R | 72.2% | 27.4% | 72.5% | 27.5% |
| 7,072 | CROSBY | 2,275 | 1,647 | 622 | 6 | 1,025 R | 72.4% | 27.3% | 72.6% | 27.4% |
| 2,975 | CULBERSON | 788 | 407 | 375 | 6 | 32 R | 51.6% | 47.6% | 52.0% | 48.0% |
| 6,222 | DALLAM | 1,782 | 1,473 | 305 | 4 | 1,168 R | 82.7% | 17.1% | 82.8% | 17.2% |
| 2,218,899 | DALLAS | 687,709 | 346,246 | 336,641 | 4,822 | 9,605 R | 50.3% | 49.0% | 50.7% | 49.3% |
| 14,985 | DAWSON | 4,545 | 3,419 | 1,114 | 12 | 2,305 R | 75.2% | 24.5% | 75.4% | 24.6% |
| 18,561 | DEAF SMITH | 5,291 | 4,139 | 1,133 | 19 | 3,006 R | 78.2% | 21.4% | 78.5% | 21.5% |
| 5,327 | DELTA | 2,082 | 1,447 | 627 | 8 | 820 R | 69.5% | 30.1% | 69.8% | 30.2% |

# TEXAS

## PRESIDENT 2004

| 2000 Census Population | County | Total Vote | Republican | Democratic | Other | Rep.-Dem. Plurality | Percentage Total Vote Rep. | Dem. | Major Vote Rep. | Dem. |
|---|---|---|---|---|---|---|---|---|---|---|
| 432,976 | DENTON | 201,410 | 140,891 | 59,346 | 1,173 | 81,545 R | 70.0% | 29.5% | 70.4% | 29.6% |
| 20,013 | DE WITT | 6,732 | 5,100 | 1,610 | 22 | 3,490 R | 75.8% | 23.9% | 76.0% | 24.0% |
| 2,762 | DICKENS | 1,063 | 815 | 245 | 3 | 570 R | 76.7% | 23.0% | 76.9% | 23.1% |
| 10,248 | DIMMIT | 3,566 | 1,188 | 2,365 | 13 | 1,177 D | 33.3% | 66.3% | 33.4% | 66.6% |
| 3,828 | DONLEY | 1,784 | 1,429 | 349 | 6 | 1,080 R | 80.1% | 19.6% | 80.4% | 19.6% |
| 13,120 | DUVAL | 4,091 | 1,160 | 2,916 | 15 | 1,756 D | 28.4% | 71.3% | 28.5% | 71.5% |
| 18,297 | EASTLAND | 6,857 | 5,249 | 1,582 | 26 | 3,667 R | 76.5% | 23.1% | 76.8% | 23.2% |
| 121,123 | ECTOR | 36,310 | 27,502 | 8,579 | 229 | 18,923 R | 75.7% | 23.6% | 76.2% | 23.8% |
| 2,162 | EDWARDS | 963 | 745 | 217 | 1 | 528 R | 77.4% | 22.5% | 77.4% | 22.6% |
| 111,360 | ELLIS | 46,444 | 34,602 | 11,640 | 202 | 22,962 R | 74.5% | 25.1% | 74.8% | 25.2% |
| 679,622 | EL PASO | 169,573 | 73,261 | 95,142 | 1,170 | 21,881 D | 43.2% | 56.1% | 43.5% | 56.5% |
| 33,001 | ERATH | 12,281 | 9,506 | 2,710 | 65 | 6,796 R | 77.4% | 22.1% | 77.8% | 22.2% |
| 18,576 | FALLS | 5,902 | 3,454 | 2,427 | 21 | 1,027 R | 58.5% | 41.1% | 58.7% | 41.3% |
| 31,242 | FANNIN | 11,960 | 7,893 | 4,001 | 66 | 3,892 R | 66.0% | 33.5% | 66.4% | 33.6% |
| 21,804 | FAYETTE | 10,397 | 7,527 | 2,803 | 67 | 4,724 R | 72.4% | 27.0% | 72.9% | 27.1% |
| 4,344 | FISHER | 1,923 | 1,161 | 758 | 4 | 403 R | 60.4% | 39.4% | 60.5% | 39.5% |
| 7,771 | FLOYD | 2,584 | 2,032 | 545 | 7 | 1,487 R | 78.6% | 21.1% | 78.9% | 21.1% |
| 1,622 | FOARD | 587 | 347 | 235 | 5 | 112 R | 59.1% | 40.0% | 59.6% | 40.4% |
| 354,452 | FORT BEND | 163,169 | 93,625 | 68,722 | 822 | 24,903 R | 57.4% | 42.1% | 57.7% | 42.3% |
| 9,458 | FRANKLIN | 4,217 | 3,185 | 1,011 | 21 | 2,174 R | 75.5% | 24.0% | 75.9% | 24.1% |
| 17,867 | FREESTONE | 7,161 | 5,057 | 2,070 | 34 | 2,987 R | 70.6% | 28.9% | 71.0% | 29.0% |
| 16,252 | FRIO | 3,930 | 1,991 | 1,931 | 8 | 60 R | 50.7% | 49.1% | 50.8% | 49.2% |
| 14,467 | GAINES | 4,164 | 3,540 | 608 | 16 | 2,932 R | 85.0% | 14.6% | 85.3% | 14.7% |
| 250,158 | GALVESTON | 105,981 | 61,290 | 43,919 | 772 | 17,371 R | 57.8% | 41.4% | 58.3% | 41.7% |
| 4,872 | GARZA | 1,812 | 1,480 | 326 | 6 | 1,154 R | 81.7% | 18.0% | 81.9% | 18.1% |
| 20,814 | GILLESPIE | 11,553 | 9,297 | 2,104 | 152 | 7,193 R | 80.5% | 18.2% | 81.5% | 18.5% |
| 1,406 | GLASSCOCK | 533 | 488 | 44 | 1 | 444 R | 91.6% | 8.3% | 91.7% | 8.3% |
| 6,928 | GOLIAD | 3,501 | 2,267 | 1,219 | 15 | 1,048 R | 64.8% | 34.8% | 65.0% | 35.0% |
| 18,628 | GONZALES | 6,022 | 4,291 | 1,709 | 22 | 2,582 R | 71.3% | 28.4% | 71.5% | 28.5% |
| 22,744 | GRAY | 8,572 | 7,260 | 1,289 | 23 | 5,971 R | 84.7% | 15.0% | 84.9% | 15.1% |
| 110,595 | GRAYSON | 44,423 | 30,777 | 13,452 | 194 | 17,325 R | 69.3% | 30.3% | 69.6% | 30.4% |
| 111,379 | GREGG | 42,398 | 29,939 | 12,306 | 153 | 17,633 R | 70.6% | 29.0% | 70.9% | 29.1% |
| 23,552 | GRIMES | 8,030 | 5,263 | 2,713 | 54 | 2,550 R | 65.5% | 33.8% | 66.0% | 34.0% |
| 89,023 | GUADALUPE | 38,752 | 28,208 | 10,290 | 254 | 17,918 R | 72.8% | 26.6% | 73.3% | 26.7% |
| 36,602 | HALE | 10,154 | 8,025 | 2,078 | 51 | 5,947 R | 79.0% | 20.5% | 79.4% | 20.6% |
| 3,782 | HALL | 1,277 | 860 | 413 | 4 | 447 R | 67.3% | 32.3% | 67.6% | 32.4% |
| 8,229 | HAMILTON | 3,730 | 2,856 | 845 | 29 | 2,011 R | 76.6% | 22.7% | 77.2% | 22.8% |
| 5,369 | HANSFORD | 2,147 | 1,903 | 240 | 4 | 1,663 R | 88.6% | 11.2% | 88.8% | 11.2% |
| 4,724 | HARDEMAN | 1,702 | 1,214 | 480 | 8 | 734 R | 71.3% | 28.2% | 71.7% | 28.3% |
| 48,073 | HARDIN | 20,710 | 15,030 | 5,608 | 72 | 9,422 R | 72.6% | 27.1% | 72.8% | 27.2% |
| 3,400,578 | HARRIS | 1,067,968 | 584,723 | 475,865 | 7,380 | 108,858 R | 54.8% | 44.6% | 55.1% | 44.9% |
| 62,110 | HARRISON | 26,223 | 16,473 | 9,642 | 108 | 6,831 R | 62.8% | 36.8% | 63.1% | 36.9% |
| 5,537 | HARTLEY | 2,059 | 1,736 | 315 | 8 | 1,421 R | 84.3% | 15.3% | 84.6% | 15.4% |
| 6,093 | HASKELL | 2,416 | 1,539 | 867 | 10 | 672 R | 63.7% | 35.9% | 64.0% | 36.0% |
| 97,589 | HAYS | 47,823 | 27,021 | 20,110 | 692 | 6,911 R | 56.5% | 42.1% | 57.3% | 42.7% |
| 3,351 | HEMPHILL | 1,643 | 1,380 | 257 | 6 | 1,123 R | 84.0% | 15.6% | 84.3% | 15.7% |
| 73,277 | HENDERSON | 28,849 | 20,210 | 8,505 | 134 | 11,705 R | 70.1% | 29.5% | 70.4% | 29.6% |
| 569,463 | HIDALGO | 113,683 | 50,931 | 62,369 | 383 | 11,438 D | 44.8% | 54.9% | 45.0% | 55.0% |
| 32,321 | HILL | 13,053 | 9,225 | 3,751 | 77 | 5,474 R | 70.7% | 28.7% | 71.1% | 28.9% |
| 22,716 | HOCKLEY | 7,577 | 6,160 | 1,385 | 32 | 4,775 R | 81.3% | 18.3% | 81.6% | 18.4% |
| 41,100 | HOOD | 21,293 | 16,280 | 4,865 | 148 | 11,415 R | 76.5% | 22.8% | 77.0% | 23.0% |
| 31,960 | HOPKINS | 12,062 | 8,582 | 3,443 | 37 | 5,139 R | 71.1% | 28.5% | 71.4% | 28.6% |
| 23,185 | HOUSTON | 8,806 | 5,848 | 2,921 | 37 | 2,927 R | 66.4% | 33.2% | 66.7% | 33.3% |
| 33,627 | HOWARD | 10,201 | 7,480 | 2,663 | 58 | 4,817 R | 73.3% | 26.1% | 73.7% | 26.3% |
| 3,344 | HUDSPETH | 886 | 577 | 302 | 7 | 275 R | 65.1% | 34.1% | 65.6% | 34.4% |
| 76,596 | HUNT | 28,194 | 20,065 | 7,971 | 158 | 12,094 R | 71.2% | 28.3% | 71.6% | 28.4% |
| 23,857 | HUTCHINSON | 9,369 | 7,839 | 1,503 | 27 | 6,336 R | 83.7% | 16.0% | 83.9% | 16.1% |
| 1,771 | IRION | 828 | 684 | 141 | 3 | 543 R | 82.6% | 17.0% | 82.9% | 17.1% |
| 8,763 | JACK | 3,126 | 2,470 | 643 | 13 | 1,827 R | 79.0% | 20.6% | 79.3% | 20.7% |
| 14,391 | JACKSON | 5,077 | 3,766 | 1,296 | 15 | 2,470 R | 74.2% | 25.5% | 74.4% | 25.6% |

# TEXAS

## PRESIDENT 2004

| 2000 Census Population | County | Total Vote | Republican | Democratic | Other | Rep.-Dem. Plurality | Percentage Total Vote Rep. | Dem. | Major Vote Rep. | Dem. |
|---|---|---|---|---|---|---|---|---|---|---|
| 35,604 | JASPER | 12,873 | 8,347 | 4,471 | 55 | 3,876 R | 64.8% | 34.7% | 65.1% | 34.9% |
| 2,207 | JEFF DAVIS | 1,167 | 764 | 378 | 25 | 386 R | 65.5% | 32.4% | 66.9% | 33.1% |
| 252,051 | JEFFERSON | 91,866 | 44,423 | 47,066 | 377 | 2,643 D | 48.4% | 51.2% | 48.6% | 51.4% |
| 5,281 | JIM HOGG | 2,065 | 712 | 1,344 | 9 | 632 D | 34.5% | 65.1% | 34.6% | 65.4% |
| 39,326 | JIM WELLS | 12,691 | 5,817 | 6,824 | 50 | 1,007 D | 45.8% | 53.8% | 46.0% | 54.0% |
| 126,811 | JOHNSON | 47,422 | 34,818 | 12,325 | 279 | 22,493 R | 73.4% | 26.0% | 73.9% | 26.1% |
| 20,785 | JONES | 5,931 | 4,254 | 1,658 | 19 | 2,596 R | 71.7% | 28.0% | 72.0% | 28.0% |
| 15,446 | KARNES | 4,673 | 3,114 | 1,543 | 16 | 1,571 R | 66.6% | 33.0% | 66.9% | 33.1% |
| 71,313 | KAUFMAN | 30,366 | 21,304 | 8,947 | 115 | 12,357 R | 70.2% | 29.5% | 70.4% | 29.6% |
| 23,743 | KENDALL | 14,072 | 11,434 | 2,532 | 106 | 8,902 R | 81.3% | 18.0% | 81.9% | 18.1% |
| 414 | KENEDY | 169 | 82 | 85 | 2 | 3 D | 48.5% | 50.3% | 49.1% | 50.9% |
| 859 | KENT | 522 | 382 | 138 | 2 | 244 R | 73.2% | 26.4% | 73.5% | 26.5% |
| 43,653 | KERR | 21,246 | 16,538 | 4,557 | 151 | 11,981 R | 77.8% | 21.4% | 78.4% | 21.6% |
| 4,468 | KIMBLE | 1,816 | 1,482 | 324 | 10 | 1,158 R | 81.6% | 17.8% | 82.1% | 17.9% |
| 356 | KING | 156 | 137 | 18 | 1 | 119 R | 87.8% | 11.5% | 88.4% | 11.6% |
| 3,379 | KINNEY | 1,600 | 1,051 | 542 | 7 | 509 R | 65.7% | 33.9% | 66.0% | 34.0% |
| 31,549 | KLEBERG | 9,973 | 5,366 | 4,550 | 57 | 816 R | 53.8% | 45.6% | 54.1% | 45.9% |
| 4,253 | KNOX | 1,552 | 1,081 | 464 | 7 | 617 R | 69.7% | 29.9% | 70.0% | 30.0% |
| 48,499 | LAMAR | 17,470 | 12,054 | 5,338 | 78 | 6,716 R | 69.0% | 30.6% | 69.3% | 30.7% |
| 14,709 | LAMB | 4,271 | 3,410 | 857 | 4 | 2,553 R | 79.8% | 20.1% | 79.9% | 20.1% |
| 17,762 | LAMPASAS | 7,025 | 5,422 | 1,593 | 10 | 3,829 R | 77.2% | 22.7% | 77.3% | 22.7% |
| 5,866 | LA SALLE | 2,230 | 989 | 1,229 | 12 | 240 D | 44.3% | 55.1% | 44.6% | 55.4% |
| 19,210 | LAVACA | 8,177 | 5,974 | 2,152 | 51 | 3,822 R | 73.1% | 26.3% | 73.5% | 26.5% |
| 15,657 | LEE | 6,088 | 4,160 | 1,899 | 29 | 2,261 R | 68.3% | 31.2% | 68.7% | 31.3% |
| 15,335 | LEON | 6,799 | 5,023 | 1,754 | 22 | 3,269 R | 73.9% | 25.8% | 74.1% | 25.9% |
| 70,154 | LIBERTY | 21,691 | 14,821 | 6,780 | 90 | 8,041 R | 68.3% | 31.3% | 68.6% | 31.4% |
| 22,051 | LIMESTONE | 7,818 | 5,028 | 2,752 | 38 | 2,276 R | 64.3% | 35.2% | 64.6% | 35.4% |
| 3,057 | LIPSCOMB | 1,337 | 1,147 | 184 | 6 | 963 R | 85.8% | 13.8% | 86.2% | 13.8% |
| 12,309 | LIVE OAK | 4,201 | 3,147 | 1,036 | 18 | 2,111 R | 74.9% | 24.7% | 75.2% | 24.8% |
| 17,044 | LLANO | 9,563 | 7,241 | 2,257 | 65 | 4,984 R | 75.7% | 23.6% | 76.2% | 23.8% |
| 67 | LOVING | 80 | 65 | 12 | 3 | 53 R | 81.3% | 15.0% | 84.4% | 15.6% |
| 242,628 | LUBBOCK | 93,151 | 70,135 | 22,472 | 544 | 47,663 R | 75.3% | 24.1% | 75.7% | 24.3% |
| 6,550 | LYNN | 2,271 | 1,776 | 490 | 5 | 1,286 R | 78.2% | 21.6% | 78.4% | 21.6% |
| 8,205 | MCCULLOCH | 3,220 | 2,465 | 745 | 10 | 1,720 R | 76.6% | 23.1% | 76.8% | 23.2% |
| 213,517 | MCLENNAN | 79,254 | 52,090 | 26,760 | 404 | 25,330 R | 65.7% | 33.8% | 66.1% | 33.9% |
| 851 | MCMULLEN | 564 | 467 | 95 | 2 | 372 R | 82.8% | 16.8% | 83.1% | 16.9% |
| 12,940 | MADISON | 4,101 | 2,837 | 1,235 | 29 | 1,602 R | 69.2% | 30.1% | 69.7% | 30.3% |
| 10,941 | MARION | 4,348 | 2,441 | 1,884 | 23 | 557 R | 56.1% | 43.3% | 56.4% | 43.6% |
| 4,746 | MARTIN | 1,807 | 1,514 | 288 | 5 | 1,226 R | 83.8% | 15.9% | 84.0% | 16.0% |
| 3,738 | MASON | 2,077 | 1,600 | 459 | 18 | 1,141 R | 77.0% | 22.1% | 77.7% | 22.3% |
| 37,957 | MATAGORDA | 12,521 | 8,119 | 4,355 | 47 | 3,764 R | 64.8% | 34.8% | 65.1% | 34.9% |
| 47,297 | MAVERICK | 10,034 | 4,025 | 5,948 | 61 | 1,923 D | 40.1% | 59.3% | 40.4% | 59.6% |
| 39,304 | MEDINA | 14,826 | 10,389 | 4,322 | 115 | 6,067 R | 70.1% | 29.2% | 70.6% | 29.4% |
| 2,360 | MENARD | 1,103 | 761 | 331 | 11 | 430 R | 69.0% | 30.0% | 69.7% | 30.3% |
| 116,009 | MIDLAND | 44,834 | 36,585 | 8,005 | 244 | 28,580 R | 81.6% | 17.9% | 82.0% | 18.0% |
| 24,238 | MILAM | 8,783 | 5,291 | 3,445 | 47 | 1,846 R | 60.2% | 39.2% | 60.6% | 39.4% |
| 5,151 | MILLS | 2,231 | 1,794 | 416 | 21 | 1,378 R | 80.4% | 18.6% | 81.2% | 18.8% |
| 9,698 | MITCHELL | 2,558 | 1,912 | 639 | 7 | 1,273 R | 74.7% | 25.0% | 75.0% | 25.0% |
| 19,117 | MONTAGUE | 7,897 | 5,910 | 1,946 | 41 | 3,964 R | 74.8% | 24.6% | 75.2% | 24.8% |
| 293,768 | MONTGOMERY | 133,988 | 104,654 | 28,628 | 706 | 76,026 R | 78.1% | 21.4% | 78.5% | 21.5% |
| 20,121 | MOORE | 5,628 | 4,601 | 1,009 | 18 | 3,592 R | 81.8% | 17.9% | 82.0% | 18.0% |
| 13,048 | MORRIS | 5,278 | 2,818 | 2,437 | 23 | 381 R | 53.4% | 46.2% | 53.6% | 46.4% |
| 1,426 | MOTLEY | 684 | 564 | 113 | 7 | 451 R | 82.5% | 16.5% | 83.3% | 16.7% |
| 59,203 | NACOGDOCHES | 21,466 | 14,160 | 7,152 | 154 | 7,008 R | 66.0% | 33.3% | 66.4% | 33.6% |
| 45,124 | NAVARRO | 16,034 | 10,715 | 5,259 | 60 | 5,456 R | 66.8% | 32.8% | 67.1% | 32.9% |
| 15,072 | NEWTON | 5,700 | 3,159 | 2,513 | 28 | 646 R | 55.4% | 44.1% | 55.7% | 44.3% |
| 15,802 | NOLAN | 5,289 | 3,722 | 1,541 | 26 | 2,181 R | 70.4% | 29.1% | 70.7% | 29.3% |
| 313,645 | NUECES | 104,560 | 59,359 | 44,439 | 762 | 14,920 R | 56.8% | 42.5% | 57.2% | 42.8% |
| 9,006 | OCHILTREE | 3,177 | 2,922 | 251 | 4 | 2,671 R | 92.0% | 7.9% | 92.1% | 7.9% |
| 2,185 | OLDHAM | 843 | 733 | 108 | 2 | 625 R | 87.0% | 12.8% | 87.2% | 12.8% |

# TEXAS

## PRESIDENT 2004

| 2000 Census Population | County | Total Vote | Republican | Democratic | Other | Rep.-Dem. Plurality | Percentage | | | |
|---|---|---|---|---|---|---|---|---|---|---|
| | | | | | | | Total Vote | | Major Vote | |
| | | | | | | | Rep. | Dem. | Rep. | Dem. |
| 84,966 | ORANGE | 31,908 | 20,292 | 11,476 | 140 | 8,816 R | 63.6% | 36.0% | 63.9% | 36.1% |
| 27,026 | PALO PINTO | 10,014 | 7,137 | 2,816 | 61 | 4,321 R | 71.3% | 28.1% | 71.7% | 28.3% |
| 22,756 | PANOLA | 10,007 | 7,021 | 2,958 | 28 | 4,063 R | 70.2% | 29.6% | 70.4% | 29.6% |
| 88,495 | PARKER | 40,957 | 31,795 | 8,966 | 196 | 22,829 R | 77.6% | 21.9% | 78.0% | 22.0% |
| 10,016 | PARMER | 2,773 | 2,375 | 389 | 9 | 1,986 R | 85.6% | 14.0% | 85.9% | 14.1% |
| 16,809 | PECOS | 4,428 | 3,167 | 1,242 | 19 | 1,925 R | 71.5% | 28.0% | 71.8% | 28.2% |
| 41,133 | POLK | 20,846 | 13,778 | 6,964 | 104 | 6,814 R | 66.1% | 33.4% | 66.4% | 33.6% |
| 113,546 | POTTER | 29,056 | 21,401 | 7,489 | 166 | 13,912 R | 73.7% | 25.8% | 74.1% | 25.9% |
| 7,304 | PRESIDIO | 1,890 | 715 | 1,159 | 16 | 444 D | 37.8% | 61.3% | 38.2% | 61.8% |
| 9,139 | RAINS | 4,229 | 2,998 | 1,213 | 18 | 1,785 R | 70.9% | 28.7% | 71.2% | 28.8% |
| 104,312 | RANDALL | 48,587 | 40,520 | 7,849 | 218 | 32,671 R | 83.4% | 16.2% | 83.8% | 16.2% |
| 3,326 | REAGAN | 1,143 | 956 | 184 | 3 | 772 R | 83.6% | 16.1% | 83.9% | 16.1% |
| 3,047 | REAL | 1,645 | 1,314 | 325 | 6 | 989 R | 79.9% | 19.8% | 80.2% | 19.8% |
| 14,314 | RED RIVER | 5,490 | 3,379 | 2,097 | 14 | 1,282 R | 61.5% | 38.2% | 61.7% | 38.3% |
| 13,137 | REEVES | 3,395 | 1,777 | 1,600 | 18 | 177 R | 52.3% | 47.1% | 52.6% | 47.4% |
| 7,828 | REFUGIO | 3,455 | 2,212 | 1,232 | 11 | 980 R | 64.0% | 35.7% | 64.2% | 35.8% |
| 887 | ROBERTS | 507 | 461 | 46 | | 415 R | 90.9% | 9.1% | 90.9% | 9.1% |
| 16,000 | ROBERTSON | 6,795 | 3,792 | 2,979 | 24 | 813 R | 55.8% | 43.8% | 56.0% | 44.0% |
| 43,080 | ROCKWALL | 25,581 | 20,120 | 5,320 | 141 | 14,800 R | 78.7% | 20.8% | 79.1% | 20.9% |
| 11,495 | RUNNELS | 4,049 | 3,239 | 792 | 18 | 2,447 R | 80.0% | 19.6% | 80.4% | 19.6% |
| 47,372 | RUSK | 18,344 | 13,390 | 4,899 | 55 | 8,491 R | 73.0% | 26.7% | 73.2% | 26.8% |
| 10,469 | SABINE | 4,639 | 3,138 | 1,476 | 25 | 1,662 R | 67.6% | 31.8% | 68.0% | 32.0% |
| 8,946 | SAN AUGUSTINE | 3,757 | 2,235 | 1,506 | 16 | 729 R | 59.5% | 40.1% | 59.7% | 40.3% |
| 22,246 | SAN JACINTO | 8,125 | 5,394 | 2,688 | 43 | 2,706 R | 66.4% | 33.1% | 66.7% | 33.3% |
| 67,138 | SAN PATRICIO | 21,320 | 13,474 | 7,764 | 82 | 5,710 R | 63.2% | 36.4% | 63.4% | 36.6% |
| 6,186 | SAN SABA | 2,431 | 1,894 | 529 | 8 | 1,365 R | 77.9% | 21.8% | 78.2% | 21.8% |
| 2,935 | SCHLEICHER | 1,329 | 1,012 | 312 | 5 | 700 R | 76.1% | 23.5% | 76.4% | 23.6% |
| 16,361 | SCURRY | 5,572 | 4,576 | 981 | 15 | 3,595 R | 82.1% | 17.6% | 82.3% | 17.7% |
| 3,302 | SHACKELFORD | 1,527 | 1,292 | 229 | 6 | 1,063 R | 84.6% | 15.0% | 84.9% | 15.1% |
| 25,224 | SHELBY | 9,279 | 6,295 | 2,951 | 33 | 3,344 R | 67.8% | 31.8% | 68.1% | 31.9% |
| 3,186 | SHERMAN | 1,066 | 942 | 124 | | 818 R | 88.4% | 11.6% | 88.4% | 11.6% |
| 174,706 | SMITH | 73,664 | 53,392 | 19,970 | 302 | 33,422 R | 72.5% | 27.1% | 72.8% | 27.2% |
| 6,809 | SOMERVELL | 3,551 | 2,701 | 831 | 19 | 1,870 R | 76.1% | 23.4% | 76.5% | 23.5% |
| 53,597 | STARR | 9,781 | 2,552 | 7,199 | 30 | 4,647 D | 26.1% | 73.6% | 26.2% | 73.8% |
| 9,674 | STEPHENS | 3,519 | 2,803 | 703 | 13 | 2,100 R | 79.7% | 20.0% | 79.9% | 20.1% |
| 1,393 | STERLING | 615 | 544 | 71 | | 473 R | 88.5% | 11.5% | 88.5% | 11.5% |
| 1,693 | STONEWALL | 752 | 499 | 250 | 3 | 249 R | 66.4% | 33.2% | 66.6% | 33.4% |
| 4,077 | SUTTON | 1,453 | 1,173 | 280 | | 893 R | 80.7% | 19.3% | 80.7% | 19.3% |
| 8,378 | SWISHER | 2,120 | 1,487 | 626 | 7 | 861 R | 70.1% | 29.5% | 70.4% | 29.6% |
| 1,446,219 | TARRANT | 560,141 | 349,462 | 207,286 | 3,393 | 142,176 R | 62.4% | 37.0% | 62.8% | 37.2% |
| 126,555 | TAYLOR | 48,099 | 37,197 | 10,648 | 254 | 26,549 R | 77.3% | 22.1% | 77.7% | 22.3% |
| 1,081 | TERRELL | 469 | 306 | 159 | 4 | 147 R | 65.2% | 33.9% | 65.8% | 34.2% |
| 12,761 | TERRY | 3,970 | 3,166 | 794 | 10 | 2,372 R | 79.7% | 20.0% | 79.9% | 20.1% |
| 1,850 | THROCKMORTON | 863 | 656 | 202 | 5 | 454 R | 76.0% | 23.4% | 76.5% | 23.5% |
| 28,118 | TITUS | 8,907 | 5,709 | 3,173 | 25 | 2,536 R | 64.1% | 35.6% | 64.3% | 35.7% |
| 104,010 | TOM GREEN | 37,417 | 28,185 | 9,007 | 225 | 19,178 R | 75.3% | 24.1% | 75.8% | 24.2% |
| 812,280 | TRAVIS | 352,113 | 147,885 | 197,235 | 6,993 | 49,350 D | 42.0% | 56.0% | 42.9% | 57.1% |
| 13,779 | TRINITY | 6,213 | 3,985 | 2,204 | 24 | 1,781 R | 64.1% | 35.5% | 64.4% | 35.6% |
| 20,871 | TYLER | 7,745 | 5,043 | 2,659 | 43 | 2,384 R | 65.1% | 34.3% | 65.5% | 34.5% |
| 35,291 | UPSHUR | 14,526 | 10,232 | 4,225 | 69 | 6,007 R | 70.4% | 29.1% | 70.8% | 29.2% |
| 3,404 | UPTON | 1,197 | 1,009 | 185 | 3 | 824 R | 84.3% | 15.5% | 84.5% | 15.5% |
| 25,926 | UVALDE | 8,483 | 5,148 | 3,298 | 37 | 1,850 R | 60.7% | 38.9% | 61.0% | 39.0% |
| 44,856 | VAL VERDE | 11,795 | 6,968 | 4,757 | 70 | 2,211 R | 59.1% | 40.3% | 59.4% | 40.6% |
| 48,140 | VAN ZANDT | 19,856 | 14,976 | 4,822 | 58 | 10,154 R | 75.4% | 24.3% | 75.6% | 24.4% |
| 84,088 | VICTORIA | 29,602 | 20,875 | 8,553 | 174 | 12,322 R | 70.5% | 28.9% | 70.9% | 29.1% |
| 61,758 | WALKER | 17,822 | 11,710 | 5,977 | 135 | 5,733 R | 65.7% | 33.5% | 66.2% | 33.8% |
| 32,663 | WALLER | 13,881 | 7,679 | 6,145 | 57 | 1,534 R | 55.3% | 44.3% | 55.5% | 44.5% |
| 10,909 | WARD | 3,768 | 2,856 | 901 | 11 | 1,955 R | 75.8% | 23.9% | 76.0% | 24.0% |
| 30,373 | WASHINGTON | 13,063 | 9,597 | 3,389 | 77 | 6,208 R | 73.5% | 25.9% | 73.9% | 26.1% |
| 193,117 | WEBB | 41,556 | 17,753 | 23,654 | 149 | 5,901 D | 42.7% | 56.9% | 42.9% | 57.1% |

# TEXAS

## PRESIDENT 2004

| 2000 Census Population | County | Total Vote | Republican | Democratic | Other | Rep.-Dem. Plurality | Percentage | | | |
|---|---|---|---|---|---|---|---|---|---|---|
| | | | | | | | Total Vote | | Major Vote | |
| | | | | | | | Rep. | Dem. | Rep. | Dem. |
| 41,188 | WHARTON | 14,039 | 9,288 | 4,702 | 49 | 4,586 R | 66.2% | 33.5% | 66.4% | 33.6% |
| 5,284 | WHEELER | 2,394 | 1,960 | 420 | 14 | 1,540 R | 81.9% | 17.5% | 82.4% | 17.6% |
| 131,664 | WICHITA | 45,545 | 32,472 | 12,819 | 254 | 19,653 R | 71.3% | 28.1% | 71.7% | 28.3% |
| 14,676 | WILBARGER | 4,990 | 3,685 | 1,284 | 21 | 2,401 R | 73.8% | 25.7% | 74.2% | 25.8% |
| 20,082 | WILLACY | 4,962 | 2,209 | 2,734 | 19 | 525 D | 44.5% | 55.1% | 44.7% | 55.3% |
| 249,967 | WILLIAMSON | 128,198 | 83,284 | 43,117 | 1,797 | 40,167 R | 65.0% | 33.6% | 65.9% | 34.1% |
| 32,408 | WILSON | 14,885 | 10,400 | 4,409 | 76 | 5,991 R | 69.9% | 29.6% | 70.2% | 29.8% |
| 7,173 | WINKLER | 2,002 | 1,604 | 391 | 7 | 1,213 R | 80.1% | 19.5% | 80.4% | 19.6% |
| 48,793 | WISE | 20,047 | 15,177 | 4,783 | 87 | 10,394 R | 75.7% | 23.9% | 76.0% | 24.0% |
| 36,752 | WOOD | 16,929 | 12,831 | 4,034 | 64 | 8,797 R | 75.8% | 23.8% | 76.1% | 23.9% |
| 7,322 | YOAKUM | 2,613 | 2,228 | 376 | 9 | 1,852 R | 85.3% | 14.4% | 85.6% | 14.4% |
| 17,943 | YOUNG | 7,409 | 5,874 | 1,511 | 24 | 4,363 R | 79.3% | 20.4% | 79.5% | 20.5% |
| 12,182 | ZAPATA | 2,898 | 1,228 | 1,662 | 8 | 434 D | 42.4% | 57.3% | 42.5% | 57.5% |
| 11,600 | ZAVALA | 3,118 | 777 | 2,332 | 9 | 1,555 D | 24.9% | 74.8% | 25.0% | 75.0% |
| 20,851,820 | TOTAL | 7,410,765 | 4,526,917 | 2,832,704 | 51,144 | 1,694,213 R | 61.1% | 38.2% | 61.5% | 38.5% |

# TEXAS

## HOUSE OF REPRESENTATIVES

| CD | Year | Total Vote | Republican | | Democratic | | Other Vote | Rep.-Dem. Plurality | Percentage | | | |
|---|---|---|---|---|---|---|---|---|---|---|---|---|
| | | | Vote | Candidate | Vote | Candidate | | | Total Vote | | Major Vote | |
| | | | | | | | | | Rep. | Dem. | Rep. | Dem. |
| 1 | 2004 | 255,507 | 157,068 | Gohmert, Louie | 96,281 | Sandlin, Max* | 2,158 | 60,787 R | 61.5% | 37.7% | 62.0% | 38.0% |
| 2 | 2004 | 252,038 | 139,951 | Poe, Ted | 108,156 | Lampson, Nick* | 3,931 | 31,795 R | 55.5% | 42.9% | 56.4% | 43.6% |
| 3 | 2004 | 210,352 | 180,099 | Johnson, Sam* | | | 30,253 | 180,099 R | 85.6% | | 100.0% | |
| 4 | 2004 | 267,942 | 182,866 | Hall, Ralph M.* | 81,585 | Nickerson, Jim | 3,491 | 101,281 R | 68.2% | 30.4% | 69.1% | 30.9% |
| 5 | 2004 | 230,845 | 148,816 | Hensarling, Jeb* | 75,911 | Bernstein, Bill | 6,118 | 72,905 R | 64.5% | 32.9% | 66.2% | 33.8% |
| 6 | 2004 | 255,627 | 168,767 | Barton, Joe L.* | 83,609 | Meyer, Morris | 3,251 | 85,158 R | 66.0% | 32.7% | 66.9% | 33.1% |
| 7 | 2004 | 273,651 | 175,440 | Culberson, John* | 91,126 | Martinez, John | 7,085 | 84,314 R | 64.1% | 33.3% | 65.8% | 34.2% |
| 8 | 2004 | 260,628 | 179,599 | Brady, Kevin* | 77,324 | Wright, James "Jim" | 3,705 | 102,275 R | 68.9% | 29.7% | 69.9% | 30.1% |
| 9 | 2004 | 158,566 | 42,132 | Molina, Arlette | 114,462 | Green, Al | 1,972 | 72,330 D | 26.6% | 72.2% | 26.9% | 73.1% |
| 10 | 2004 | 231,643 | 182,113 | McCaul, Michael | | | 49,530 | 182,113 R | 78.6% | | 100.0% | |
| 11 | 2004 | 230,977 | 177,291 | Conaway, K. Michael | 50,339 | Raasch, Wayne | 3,347 | 126,952 R | 76.8% | 21.8% | 77.9% | 22.1% |
| 12 | 2004 | 239,538 | 173,222 | Granger, Kay* | 66,316 | Alvarado, Felix | | 106,906 R | 72.3% | 27.7% | 72.3% | 27.7% |
| 13 | 2004 | 205,241 | 189,448 | Thornberry, William M. "Mac"* | | | 15,793 | 189,448 R | 92.3% | | 100.0% | |
| 14 | 2004 | 173,668 | 173,668 | Paul, Ron* | | | | 173,668 R | 100.0% | | 100.0% | |
| 15 | 2004 | 166,358 | 67,917 | Thamm, Michael D. | 96,089 | Hinojosa, Rubén* | 2,352 | 28,172 D | 40.8% | 57.8% | 41.4% | 58.6% |
| 16 | 2004 | 160,773 | 49,972 | Brigham, David | 108,577 | Reyes, Silvestre* | 2,224 | 58,605 D | 31.1% | 67.5% | 31.5% | 68.5% |
| 17 | 2004 | 244,748 | 116,049 | Wohlgemuth, Arlene | 125,309 | Edwards, Chet* | 3,390 | 9,260 D | 47.4% | 51.2% | 48.1% | 51.9% |

# TEXAS

## HOUSE OF REPRESENTATIVES

| CD | Year | Total Vote | Republican | | Democratic | | Other Vote | Rep.-Dem. Plurality | Percentage | | | |
|----|------|-----------|------|-----------|------|-----------|-----------|------------------|-----------|------|-----------|------|
| | | | | | | | | | Total Vote | | Major Vote | |
| | | | Vote | Candidate | Vote | Candidate | | | Rep. | Dem. | Rep. | Dem. |
| 18 | 2004 | 152,988 | | | 136,018 | Jackson-Lee, Sheila* | 16,970 | 136,018 D | | 88.9% | | 100.0% |
| 19 | 2004 | 233,514 | 136,459 | Neugebauer, Randy* | 93,531 | Stenholm, Charles W.* | 3,524 | 42,928 R | 58.4% | 40.1% | 59.3% | 40.7% |
| 20 | 2004 | 171,804 | 54,976 | Scott, Roger | 112,480 | Gonzalez, Charlie* | 4,348 | 57,504 D | 32.0% | 65.5% | 32.8% | 67.2% |
| 21 | 2004 | 341,119 | 209,774 | Smith, Lamar* | 121,129 | Smith, Rhett R. | 10,216 | 88,645 R | 61.5% | 35.5% | 63.4% | 36.6% |
| 22 | 2004 | 272,620 | 150,386 | DeLay, Tom* | 112,034 | Morrison, Richard R. | 10,200 | 38,352 R | 55.2% | 41.1% | 57.3% | 42.7% |
| 23 | 2004 | 246,503 | 170,716 | Bonilla, Henry* | 72,480 | Sullivan, Joe | 3,307 | 98,236 R | 69.3% | 29.4% | 70.2% | 29.8% |
| 24 | 2004 | 241,374 | 154,435 | Marchant, Kenny | 82,599 | Page, Gary R. | 4,340 | 71,836 R | 64.0% | 34.2% | 65.2% | 34.8% |
| 25 | 2004 | 160,217 | 49,252 | Klein, Rebecca Armendariz | 108,309 | Doggett, Lloyd* | 2,656 | 59,057 D | 30.7% | 67.6% | 31.3% | 68.7% |
| 26 | 2004 | 274,539 | 180,519 | Burgess, Michael C.* | 89,809 | Reyes, Lico | 4,211 | 90,710 R | 65.8% | 32.7% | 66.8% | 33.2% |
| 27 | 2004 | 177,536 | 61,955 | Vaden, William "Willie" | 112,081 | Ortiz, Solomon P.* | 3,500 | 50,126 D | 34.9% | 63.1% | 35.6% | 64.4% |
| 28 | 2004 | 180,166 | 69,538 | Hopson, James "Jim" F. | 106,323 | Cuellar, Henry | 4,305 | 36,785 D | 38.6% | 59.0% | 39.5% | 60.5% |
| 29 | 2004 | 83,124 | | | 78,256 | Green, Gene* | 4,868 | 78,256 D | | 94.1% | | 100.0% |
| 30 | 2004 | 155,334 | | | 144,513 | Johnson, Eddie Bernice* | 10,821 | 144,513 D | | 93.0% | | 100.0% |
| 31 | 2004 | 247,427 | 160,247 | Carter, John* | 80,292 | Porter, Jon | 6,888 | 79,955 R | 64.8% | 32.5% | 66.6% | 33.4% |
| 32 | 2004 | 202,236 | 109,859 | Sessions, Pete* | 89,030 | Frost, Martin* | 3,347 | 20,829 R | 54.3% | 44.0% | 55.2% | 44.8% |
| Total | 2004 | 6,958,603 | 4,012,534 | | 2,713,968 | | 232,101 | 1,298,566 R | 57.7% | 39.0% | 59.7% | 40.3% |
| Total | 2002 | 4,295,210 | 2,290,723 | | 1,885,178 | | 119,309 | 405,545 R | 53.3% | 43.9% | 54.9% | 45.1% |

An asterisk (*) denotes incumbent.

Note: Congressional district lines in Texas were redrawn between the elections of 2002 and 2004. The results from 2002, and a map of the Texas congressional district lines that year, can be found in *America Votes 25*.

# TEXAS

## GENERAL AND PRIMARY ELECTIONS

## 2004 GENERAL ELECTIONS

**President**    Other vote was 38,787 Libertarian (Michael Badnarik); 9,159 write-in (Ralph Nader); 1,636 write-in (Michael Peroutka); 1,014 write-in (David Cobb); 219 write-in (Andrew J. Falk); 126 write-in (John Joseph Kennedy); 111 write-in (Walter F. Brown); 92 write-in (Deborah Elaine Allen).

**House**    Other vote was:

| | |
|---|---|
| CD 1 | 2,158 Libertarian (Dean L. Tucker). |
| CD 2 | 3,931 Libertarian (Sandra Leigh Saulsbury). |
| CD 3 | 16,966 Independent (Paul Jenkins); 13,287 Libertarian (James Vessels). |
| CD 4 | 3,491 Libertarian (Kevin D. Anderson). |
| CD 5 | 6,118 Libertarian (John Gonzalez). |
| CD 6 | 3,251 Libertarian (Stephen Schrader). |
| CD 7 | 3,713 Independent (Paul Staton); 3,372 Libertarian (Drew Parks). |
| CD 8 | 3,705 Libertarian (Paul Hansen). |
| CD 9 | 1,972 Libertarian (Stacey Lynn Bourland). |
| CD 10 | 35,569 Libertarian (Robert Fritsche); 13,961 write-in (Lorenzo Sadun). |
| CD 11 | 3,347 Libertarian (Jeffrey Blunt). |
| CD 12 | |
| CD 13 | 15,793 Libertarian (M.J. "Smitty" Smith). |
| CD 14 | |
| CD 15 | 2,352 Libertarian (William R. Cady). |
| CD 16 | 2,224 Libertarian (Brad Clardy). |
| CD 17 | 3,390 Libertarian (Clyde L. Garland). |
| CD 18 | 9,787 Independent (Tom Bazán); 7,183 Libertarian (Brent Sullivan). |
| CD 19 | 3,524 Libertarian (Richard Peterson). |
| CD 20 | 2,377 Libertarian (Jessie Bouley); 1,971 Independent (Michael Idrogo). |
| CD 21 | 10,216 Libertarian (Jason Pratt). |
| CD 22 | 5,314 Independent (Michael Fjetland); 4,886 Libertarian (Tom Morrison). |
| CD 23 | 3,307 Libertarian (Nazirite "Comrade" Perez). |
| CD 24 | 4,340 Libertarian (James H. Lawrence). |
| CD 25 | 2,656 Libertarian (James Werner). |
| CD 26 | 4,211 Libertarian (James Gholston). |
| CD 27 | 3,500 Libertarian (Christopher J. Claytor). |
| CD 28 | 4,305 Libertarian (Ken Ashby). |
| CD 29 | 4,868 Libertarian (Clifford L. Messina). |
| CD 30 | 10,821 Libertarian (John Davis). |
| CD 31 | 6,888 Libertarian (Celeste Adams). |
| CD 32 | 3,347 Libertarian (Michael David Needleman). |

## 2004 PRIMARY ELECTIONS

**Primary**    March 9, 2004                 **Registration**    12,264,663  No Party Registration
                                             (as of March 9, 2004)

**Primary Runoff**    April 13, 2004

**Primary Type**    Open—Registered voters could participate in the Democratic or Republican primary, although if they voted in the primary of one party they could not vote in the runoff of the other party.

# TEXAS

## GENERAL AND PRIMARY ELECTIONS

Note:   An asterisk (*) denotes incumbent.

| | REPUBLICAN PRIMARIES | | | DEMOCRATIC PRIMARIES | | |
|---|---|---|---|---|---|---|
| President | George W. Bush* | 635,948 | 92.5% | John Kerry | 563,237 | 67.1% |
| | Uncommitted | 51,667 | 7.5% | John Edwards | 120,413 | 14.3% |
| | | | | Howard Dean | 40,035 | 4.8% |
| | | | | Al Sharpton | 31,020 | 3.7% |
| | | | | Joseph I. Lieberman | 25,245 | 3.0% |
| | | | | Wesley Clark | 18,437 | 2.2% |
| | | | | Dennis J. Kucinich | 15,475 | 1.8% |
| | | | | Richard A. Gephardt | 12,160 | 1.4% |
| | | | | Lyndon H. LaRouche Jr. | 6,871 | 0.8% |
| | | | | Randy Crow | 6,338 | 0.8% |
| | TOTAL | 687,615 | | TOTAL | 839,231 | |
| Congressional District 1 | Louie Gohmert | 19,421 | 41.7% | Max Sandlin* | 26,400 | 100.0% |
| | John Graves | 13,933 | 29.9% | | | |
| | Wayne Christian | 6,854 | 14.7% | | | |
| | Lyle Thorstenson | 4,604 | 9.9% | | | |
| | Emily Mathews | 1,266 | 2.7% | | | |
| | Larry Thornton | 457 | 1.0% | | | |
| | TOTAL | 46,535 | | | | |
| | PRIMARY RUNOFF | | | | | |
| | Louie Gohmert | 16,841 | 57.2% | | | |
| | John Graves | 12,618 | 42.8% | | | |
| | TOTAL | 29,459 | | | | |
| Congressional District 2 | Ted Poe | 14,932 | 61.1% | Nick Lampson* | 27,284 | 100.0% |
| | George Fastuca | 3,668 | 15.0% | | | |
| | Clint Moore | 2,868 | 11.7% | | | |
| | Mark Henry | 2,423 | 9.9% | | | |
| | John Nickell | 285 | 1.2% | | | |
| | Andrew J. Bolton | 246 | 1.0% | | | |
| | TOTAL | 24,422 | | | | |
| Congressional District 3 | Sam Johnson* | 12,429 | 84.1% | No Democratic candidate | | |
| | Brian Rubarts | 2,357 | 15.9% | | | |
| | TOTAL | 14,786 | | | | |
| Congressional District 4 | Ralph M. Hall* | 22,484 | 77.2% | Jim Nickerson | 24,141 | 65.9% |
| | Mike Murphy | 3,524 | 12.1% | Jerry D. Ashford Jr. | 12,513 | 34.1% |
| | Mike Mosher | 3,122 | 10.7% | | | |
| | TOTAL | 29,130 | | TOTAL | 36,654 | |
| Congressional District 5 | Jeb Hensarling* | 18,756 | 100.0% | Bill Bernstein | 14,012 | 100.0% |
| Congressional District 6 | Joe L. Barton* | 13,486 | 100.0% | Morris Meyer | 13,564 | 100.0% |
| Congressional District 7 | John Culberson* | 26,561 | 92.2% | John Martinez | 10,372 | 100.0% |
| | Sam Texas | 2,245 | 7.8% | | | |
| | TOTAL | 28,806 | | | | |
| Congressional District 8 | Kevin Brady* | 26,445 | 100.0% | James "Jim" Wright | 32,535 | 100.0% |
| Congressional District 9 | Arlette Molina | 4,836 | 81.0% | Al Green | 18,034 | 66.5% |
| | A.R. Hassan | 1,132 | 19.0% | Chris Bell* | 8,492 | 31.3% |
| | | | | Beverly A. Spencer | 607 | 2.2% |
| | TOTAL | 5,968 | | TOTAL | 27,133 | |

# TEXAS

## GENERAL AND PRIMARY ELECTIONS

| | REPUBLICAN PRIMARIES | | | DEMOCRATIC PRIMARIES | | |
|---|---|---|---|---|---|---|
| **Congressional District 10** | Ben Streusand | 9,364 | 28.2% | No Democratic candidate | | |
| | Michael McCaul | 7,953 | 23.9% | | | |
| | John Devine | 7,096 | 21.3% | | | |
| | Dave Phillips | 4,460 | 13.4% | | | |
| | Teresa Doggett Taylor | 1,494 | 4.5% | | | |
| | Pat Elliott | 1,245 | 3.7% | | | |
| | John Kelley | 952 | 2.9% | | | |
| | Brad Tashenberg | 695 | 2.1% | | | |
| | TOTAL | 33,259 | | | | |
| | PRIMARY RUNOFF | | | | | |
| | Michael McCaul | 15,084 | 63.1% | | | |
| | Ben Streusand | 8,803 | 36.9% | | | |
| | TOTAL | 23,887 | | | | |
| **Congressional District 11** | K. Michael Conaway | 38,792 | 74.5% | Wayne Raasch | 13,948 | 100.0% |
| | Bill Lester | 13,255 | 25.5% | | | |
| | TOTAL | 52,047 | | | | |
| **Congressional District 12** | Kay Granger* | 17,964 | 100.0% | Felix Alvarado | 10,452 | 100.0% |
| **Congressional District 13** | William M. "Mac" Thornberry* | 40,801 | 100.0% | No Democratic candidate | | |
| **Congressional District 14** | Ron Paul* | 21,095 | 100.0% | No Democratic candidate | | |
| **Congressional District 15** | Alexander Hamilton | 3,795 | 41.5% | Rubén Hinojosa* | 44,427 | 100.0% |
| | Michael D. Thamm | 3,398 | 37.1% | | | |
| | Paul B. Haring | 1,954 | 21.4% | | | |
| | TOTAL | 9,147 | | | | |
| | PRIMARY RUNOFF | | | | | |
| | Michael D. Thamm | 2,830 | 60.8% | | | |
| | Alexander Hamilton | 1,823 | 39.2% | | | |
| | TOTAL | 4,653 | | | | |
| **Congressional District 16** | David Brigham | 4,127 | 53.2% | Silvestre Reyes* | 27,469 | 100.0% |
| | Bobby Ortiz | 3,626 | 46.8% | | | |
| | TOTAL | 7,753 | | | | |
| **Congressional District 17** | Arlene Wohlgemuth | 15,627 | 41.3% | Chet Edwards* | 17,754 | 100.0% |
| | Dot Snyder | 11,568 | 30.5% | | | |
| | Dave McIntyre | 10,681 | 28.2% | | | |
| | TOTAL | 37,876 | | | | |
| | PRIMARY RUNOFF | | | | | |
| | Arlene Wohlgemuth | 16,694 | 54.9% | | | |
| | Dot Snyder | 13,713 | 45.1% | | | |
| | TOTAL | 30,407 | | | | |
| **Congressional District 18** | No Republican candidate | | | Sheila Jackson-Lee* | 19,565 | 100.0% |
| **Congressional District 19** | Randy Neugebauer* | 24,712 | 100.0% | Charles W. Stenholm* | 16,576 | 100.0% |
| **Congressional District 20** | Roger Scott | 4,832 | 100.0% | Charlie Gonzalez* | 16,804 | 100.0% |
| **Congressional District 21** | Lamar Smith* | 28,144 | 100.0% | Rhett R. Smith | 26,297 | 100.0% |
| **Congressional District 22** | Tom DeLay* | 15,490 | 100.0% | Richard R. Morrison | 7,303 | 71.4% |
| | | | | Erik Saenz | 2,920 | 28.6% |
| | | | | TOTAL | 10,223 | |
| **Congressional District 23** | Henry Bonilla* | 21,299 | 100.0% | Joe Sullivan | 29,061 | 63.8% |
| | | | | Virgil W. Yanta | 16,523 | 36.2% |
| | | | | TOTAL | 45,584 | |

# TEXAS

## GENERAL AND PRIMARY ELECTIONS

| | REPUBLICAN PRIMARIES | | | DEMOCRATIC PRIMARIES | | |
|---|---|---|---|---|---|---|
| **Congressional District 24** | Kenny Marchant | 9,073 | 73.5% | Gary R. Page | 6,572 | 100.0% |
| | Cynthia Newman | 1,103 | 8.9% | | | |
| | Bill Dunn | 1,096 | 8.9% | | | |
| | Terry Waldrum | 1,074 | 8.7% | | | |
| | TOTAL | 12,346 | | | | |
| **Congressional District 25** | Rebecca Armendariz Klein | 3,679 | 67.3% | Lloyd Doggett* | 40,306 | 64.4% |
| | Regner A. Capener | 1,788 | 32.7% | Leticia Hinojosa | 22,305 | 35.6% |
| | TOTAL | 5,467 | | TOTAL | 62,611 | |
| **Congressional District 26** | Michael C. Burgess* | 17,184 | 100.0% | Lico Reyes | 10,880 | 100.0% |
| **Congressional District 27** | William "Willie" Vaden | 5,582 | 69.9% | Solomon P. Ortiz* | 44,849 | 100.0% |
| | Jesus A. Caquias | 2,401 | 30.1% | | | |
| | TOTAL | 7,983 | | | | |
| **Congressional District 28** | James "Jim" F. Hopson | 4,856 | 49.1% | Henry Cuellar | 24,651 | 50.2% |
| | Francisco "Quico" Canseco | 2,115 | 21.4% | Ciro D. Rodriguez* | 24,448 | 49.8% |
| | Chris Bellamy | 1,478 | 14.9% | | | |
| | Gabriel "Gabe" Perales Jr. | 1,445 | 14.6% | | | |
| | TOTAL | 9,894 | | TOTAL | 49,099 | |
| | PRIMARY RUNOFF | | | | | |
| | James "Jim" F. Hopson | 1,886 | 64.4% | | | |
| | Francisco "Quico" Canseco | 1,044 | 35.6% | | | |
| | TOTAL | 2,930 | | | | |
| **Congressional District 29** | No Republican candidate | | | Gene Green* | 9,337 | 100.0% |
| **Congressional District 30** | No Republican candidate | | | Eddie Bernice Johnson* | 25,719 | 100.0% |
| **Congressional District 31** | John Carter* | 25,293 | 69.5% | Jon Porter | 14,909 | 100.0% |
| | Wes Riddle | 8,215 | 22.6% | | | |
| | Dick Armbrust | 2,868 | 7.9% | | | |
| | TOTAL | 36,376 | | | | |
| **Congressional District 32** | Pete Sessions* | 11,819 | 100.0% | Martin Frost* | 9,943 | 100.0% |

# UTAH

## GOVERNOR
Jon Huntsman Jr. (R). Elected 2004 to a four-year term.

## SENATORS (2 Republicans)
Robert F. Bennett (R). Reelected 2004 to a six-year term. Previously elected 1998, 1992.

Orrin G. Hatch (R). Reelected 2000 to a six-year term. Previously elected 1994, 1988, 1982, 1976.

## REPRESENTATIVES (2 Republicans, 1 Democrat)
1. Rob Bishop (R)　　　2. Jim Matheson (D)　　　3. Chris Cannon (R)

## POSTWAR VOTE FOR PRESIDENT

| Year | Total Vote | Republican Vote | Candidate | Democratic Vote | Candidate | Other Vote | Plurality | | Total Vote Rep. | Total Vote Dem. | Major Vote Rep. | Major Vote Dem. |
|---|---|---|---|---|---|---|---|---|---|---|---|---|
| 2004 | 927,844 | 663,742 | Bush, George W. | 241,199 | Kerry, John | 22,903 | 422,543 | R | 71.5% | 26.0% | 73.3% | 26.7% |
| 2000** | 770,754 | 515,096 | Bush, George W. | 203,053 | Gore, Al | 52,605 | 312,043 | R | 66.8% | 26.3% | 71.7% | 28.3% |
| 1996** | 665,629 | 361,911 | Dole, Bob | 221,633 | Clinton, Bill | 82,085 | 140,278 | R | 54.4% | 33.3% | 62.0% | 38.0% |
| 1992** | 743,999 | 322,632 | Bush, George | 183,429 | Clinton, Bill | 237,938 | 119,232 | R | 43.4% | 24.7% | 63.8% | 36.2% |
| 1988 | 647,008 | 428,442 | Bush, George | 207,343 | Dukakis, Michael S. | 11,223 | 221,099 | R | 66.2% | 32.0% | 67.4% | 32.6% |
| 1984 | 629,656 | 469,105 | Reagan, Ronald | 155,369 | Mondale, Walter F. | 5,182 | 313,736 | R | 74.5% | 24.7% | 75.1% | 24.9% |
| 1980** | 604,222 | 439,687 | Reagan, Ronald | 124,266 | Carter, Jimmy | 40,269 | 315,421 | R | 72.8% | 20.6% | 78.0% | 22.0% |
| 1976 | 541,198 | 337,908 | Ford, Gerald R. | 182,110 | Carter, Jimmy | 21,180 | 155,798 | R | 62.4% | 33.6% | 65.0% | 35.0% |
| 1972 | 478,476 | 323,643 | Nixon, Richard M. | 126,284 | McGovern, George S. | 28,549 | 197,359 | R | 67.6% | 26.4% | 71.9% | 28.1% |
| 1968** | 422,568 | 238,728 | Nixon, Richard M. | 156,665 | Humphrey, Hubert H. | 27,175 | 82,063 | R | 56.5% | 37.1% | 60.4% | 39.6% |
| 1964 | 401,413 | 181,785 | Goldwater, Barry M. | 219,628 | Johnson, Lyndon B. | | 37,843 | D | 45.3% | 54.7% | 45.3% | 54.7% |
| 1960 | 374,709 | 205,361 | Nixon, Richard M. | 169,248 | Kennedy, John F. | 100 | 36,113 | R | 54.8% | 45.2% | 54.8% | 45.2% |
| 1956 | 333,995 | 215,631 | Eisenhower, Dwight D. | 118,364 | Stevenson, Adlai E. | | 97,267 | R | 64.6% | 35.4% | 64.6% | 35.4% |
| 1952 | 329,554 | 194,190 | Eisenhower, Dwight D. | 135,364 | Stevenson, Adlai E. | | 58,826 | R | 58.9% | 41.1% | 58.9% | 41.1% |
| 1948 | 276,306 | 124,402 | Dewey, Thomas E. | 149,151 | Truman, Harry S. | 2,753 | 24,749 | D | 45.0% | 54.0% | 45.5% | 54.5% |

In past elections, the other vote included: 2000 - 35,850 Green (Ralph Nader); 1996 - 66,461 Reform (Ross Perot); 1992 - 203,400 Independent (Perot), who finished second in Utah; 1980 - 30,284 Independent (John Anderson); 1968 - 26,906 American Independent (George Wallace).

# UTAH

## POSTWAR VOTE FOR GOVERNOR

| Year | Total Vote | Republican Vote | Republican Candidate | Democratic Vote | Democratic Candidate | Other Vote | Rep.-Dem. Plurality | Total Vote Rep. | Total Vote Dem. | Major Vote Rep. | Major Vote Dem. |
|---|---|---|---|---|---|---|---|---|---|---|---|
| 2004 | 919,960 | 531,190 | Huntsman, Jon Jr. | 380,359 | Matheson, Scott M. Jr. | 8,411 | 150,831 R | 57.7% | 41.3% | 58.3% | 41.7% |
| 2000 | 761,806 | 424,837 | Leavitt, Michael O. | 321,979 | Orton, Bill | 14,990 | 102,858 R | 55.8% | 42.3% | 56.9% | 43.1% |
| 1996 | 671,879 | 503,693 | Leavitt, Michael O. | 156,616 | Bradley, Jim | 11,570 | 347,077 R | 75.0% | 23.3% | 76.3% | 23.7% |
| 1992** | 762,549 | 321,713 | Leavitt, Michael O. | 177,181 | Hanson, Stewart | 263,655 | 65,960 R | 42.2% | 23.2% | 64.5% | 35.5% |
| 1988** | 649,114 | 260,462 | Bangerter, Norman H. | 249,321 | Wilson, Ted | 139,331 | 11,141 R | 40.1% | 38.4% | 51.1% | 48.9% |
| 1984 | 629,619 | 351,792 | Bangerter, Norman H. | 275,669 | Owens, Wayne | 2,158 | 76,123 R | 55.9% | 43.8% | 56.1% | 43.9% |
| 1980 | 600,019 | 266,578 | Wright, Bob | 330,974 | Matheson, Scott M. | 2,467 | 64,396 D | 44.4% | 55.2% | 44.6% | 55.4% |
| 1976 | 539,649 | 248,027 | Romney, Vernon B. | 280,706 | Matheson, Scott M. | 10,916 | 32,679 D | 46.0% | 52.0% | 46.9% | 53.1% |
| 1972 | 476,447 | 144,449 | Strike, Nicholas L. | 331,998 | Rampton, Calvin L. | | 187,549 D | 30.3% | 69.7% | 30.3% | 69.7% |
| 1968 | 421,012 | 131,729 | Buehner, Carl W. | 289,283 | Rampton, Calvin L. | | 157,554 D | 31.3% | 68.7% | 31.3% | 68.7% |
| 1964 | 398,256 | 171,300 | Melich, Mitchell | 226,956 | Rampton, Calvin L. | | 55,656 D | 43.0% | 57.0% | 43.0% | 57.0% |
| 1960 | 371,489 | 195,634 | Clyde, George D. | 175,855 | Barlocker, W. A. | | 19,779 R | 52.7% | 47.3% | 52.7% | 47.3% |
| 1956** | 332,889 | 127,164 | Clyde, George D. | 111,297 | Romney, L. C. | 94,428 | 15,867 R | 38.2% | 33.4% | 53.3% | 46.7% |
| 1952 | 327,704 | 180,516 | Lee, J. Bracken | 147,188 | Glade, Earl J. | | 33,328 R | 55.1% | 44.9% | 55.1% | 44.9% |
| 1948 | 275,067 | 151,253 | Lee, J. Bracken | 123,814 | Maw, Herbert B. | | 27,439 R | 55.0% | 45.0% | 55.0% | 45.0% |

In past elections, the other vote included: 1992 - 255,753 Independent (Merrill Cook), who finished second; 1988 - 136,651 Independent (Cook); 1956 - 94,428 Independent (J. Bracken Lee).

## POSTWAR VOTE FOR SENATOR

| Year | Total Vote | Republican Vote | Republican Candidate | Democratic Vote | Democratic Candidate | Other Vote | Rep.-Dem. Plurality | Total Vote Rep. | Total Vote Dem. | Major Vote Rep. | Major Vote Dem. |
|---|---|---|---|---|---|---|---|---|---|---|---|
| 2004 | 911,726 | 626,640 | Bennett, Robert F. | 258,955 | Van Dam, R. Paul | 26,131 | 367,685 R | 68.7% | 28.4% | 70.8% | 29.2% |
| 2000 | 769,704 | 504,803 | Hatch, Orrin G. | 242,569 | Howell, Scott N. | 22,332 | 262,234 R | 65.6% | 31.5% | 67.5% | 32.5% |
| 1998 | 494,909 | 316,652 | Bennett, Robert F. | 163,172 | Leckman, Scott | 15,085 | 153,480 R | 64.0% | 33.0% | 66.0% | 34.0% |
| 1994 | 519,323 | 357,297 | Hatch, Orrin G. | 146,938 | Shea, Patrick A. | 15,088 | 210,359 R | 68.8% | 28.3% | 70.9% | 29.1% |
| 1992 | 758,479 | 420,069 | Bennett, Robert F. | 301,228 | Owens, Wayne | 37,182 | 118,841 R | 55.4% | 39.7% | 58.2% | 41.8% |
| 1988 | 640,702 | 430,089 | Hatch, Orrin G. | 203,364 | Moss, Brian H. | 7,249 | 226,725 R | 67.1% | 31.7% | 67.9% | 32.1% |
| 1986 | 435,111 | 314,608 | Garn, E. J. | 115,523 | Oliver, Craig | 4,980 | 199,085 R | 72.3% | 26.6% | 73.1% | 26.9% |
| 1982 | 530,802 | 309,332 | Hatch, Orrin G. | 219,482 | Wilson, Ted | 1,988 | 89,850 R | 58.3% | 41.3% | 58.5% | 41.5% |
| 1980 | 594,298 | 437,675 | Garn, E. J. | 151,454 | Berman, Dan | 5,169 | 286,221 R | 73.6% | 25.5% | 74.3% | 25.7% |
| 1976 | 540,108 | 290,221 | Hatch, Orrin G. | 241,948 | Moss, Frank E. | 7,939 | 48,273 R | 53.7% | 44.8% | 54.5% | 45.5% |
| 1974 | 420,642 | 210,299 | Garn, E. J. | 185,377 | Owens, Wayne | 24,966 | 24,922 R | 50.0% | 44.1% | 53.1% | 46.9% |
| 1970 | 374,303 | 159,004 | Burton, Laurence J. | 210,207 | Moss, Frank E. | 5,092 | 51,203 D | 42.5% | 56.2% | 43.1% | 56.9% |
| 1968 | 419,262 | 225,075 | Bennett, Wallace F. | 192,168 | Weilenmann, Milton | 2,019 | 32,907 R | 53.7% | 45.8% | 53.9% | 46.1% |
| 1964 | 397,384 | 169,562 | Wilkinson, Ernest L. | 227,822 | Moss, Frank E. | | 58,260 D | 42.7% | 57.3% | 42.7% | 57.3% |
| 1962 | 318,411 | 166,755 | Bennett, Wallace F. | 151,656 | King, David S. | | 15,099 R | 52.4% | 47.6% | 52.4% | 47.6% |
| 1958** | 291,311 | 101,471 | Watkins, Arthur V. | 112,827 | Moss, Frank E. | 77,013 | 11,356 D | 34.8% | 38.7% | 47.4% | 52.6% |
| 1956 | 330,381 | 178,261 | Bennett, Wallace F. | 152,120 | Hopkin, Alonzo F. | | 26,141 R | 54.0% | 46.0% | 54.0% | 46.0% |
| 1952 | 327,033 | 177,435 | Watkins, Arthur V. | 149,598 | Granger, Walter K. | | 27,837 R | 54.3% | 45.7% | 54.3% | 45.7% |
| 1950 | 264,440 | 142,427 | Bennett, Wallace F. | 121,198 | Thomas, Elbert D. | 815 | 21,229 R | 53.9% | 45.8% | 54.0% | 46.0% |
| 1946 | 197,399 | 101,142 | Watkins, Arthur V. | 96,257 | Murdock, Abe | | 4,885 R | 51.2% | 48.8% | 51.2% | 48.8% |

In past elections, the other vote included: 1958 - 77,013 Independent (J. Bracken Lee).

# UTAH

Congressional districts first established for elections held in 2002
3 members

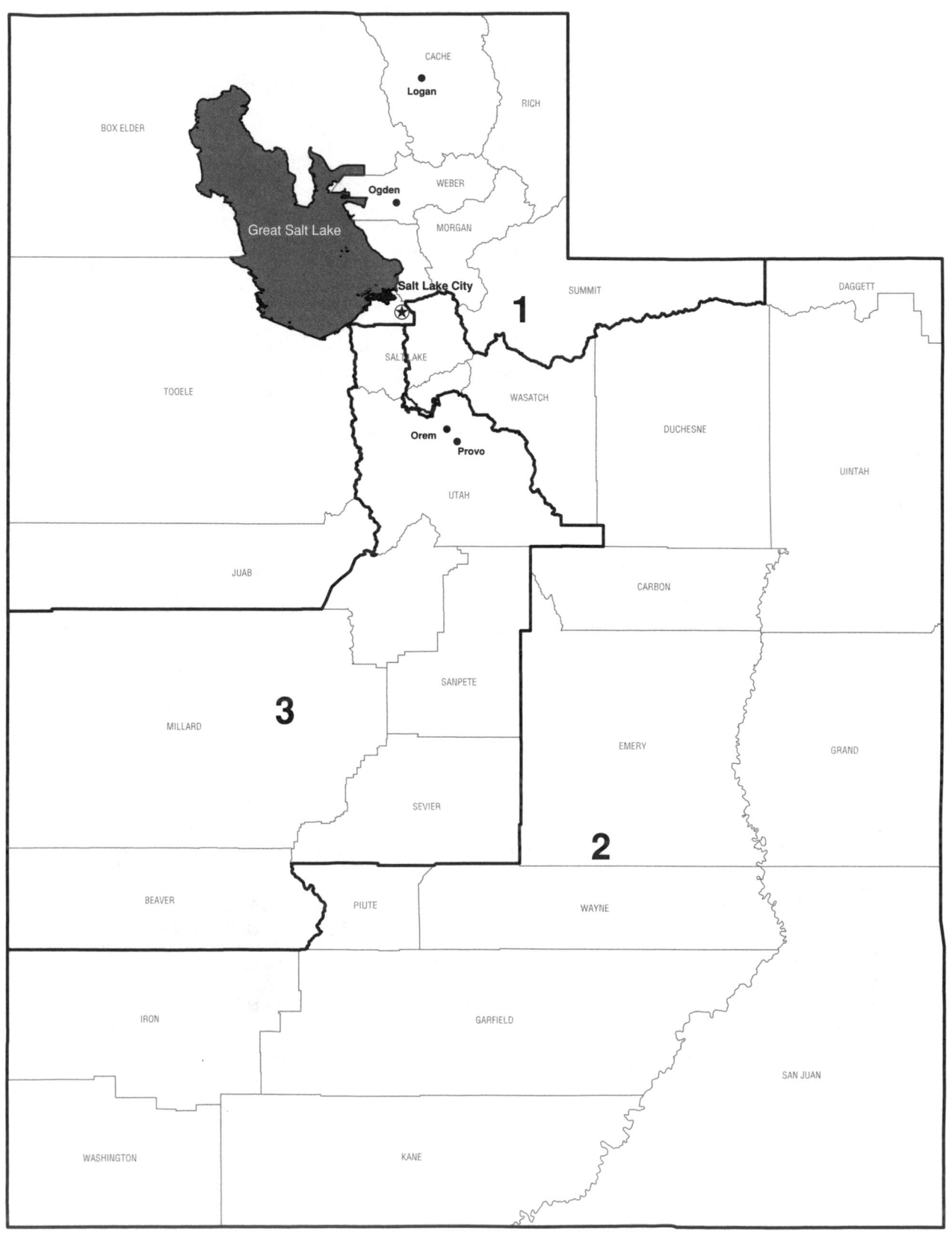

427

# UTAH

## PRESIDENT 2004

| 2000 Census Population | County | Total Vote | Republican | Democratic | Other | Rep.-Dem. Plurality | | Total Vote Rep. | Total Vote Dem. | Major Vote Rep. | Major Vote Dem. |
|---|---|---|---|---|---|---|---|---|---|---|---|
| 6,005 | BEAVER | 2,544 | 2,023 | 493 | 28 | 1,530 | R | 79.5% | 19.4% | 80.4% | 19.6% |
| 42,745 | BOX ELDER | 18,368 | 15,751 | 2,244 | 373 | 13,507 | R | 85.8% | 12.2% | 87.5% | 12.5% |
| 91,391 | CACHE | 39,731 | 32,486 | 6,375 | 870 | 26,111 | R | 81.8% | 16.0% | 83.6% | 16.4% |
| 20,422 | CARBON | 8,508 | 4,950 | 3,415 | 143 | 1,535 | R | 58.2% | 40.1% | 59.2% | 40.8% |
| 921 | DAGGETT | 499 | 380 | 108 | 11 | 272 | R | 76.2% | 21.6% | 77.9% | 22.1% |
| 238,994 | DAVIS | 109,268 | 86,187 | 20,893 | 2,188 | 65,294 | R | 78.9% | 19.1% | 80.5% | 19.5% |
| 14,371 | DUCHESNE | 5,556 | 4,742 | 738 | 76 | 4,004 | R | 85.3% | 13.3% | 86.5% | 13.5% |
| 10,860 | EMERY | 4,678 | 3,781 | 831 | 66 | 2,950 | R | 80.8% | 17.8% | 82.0% | 18.0% |
| 4,735 | GARFIELD | 2,162 | 1,848 | 264 | 50 | 1,584 | R | 85.5% | 12.2% | 87.5% | 12.5% |
| 8,485 | GRAND | 4,165 | 2,130 | 1,858 | 177 | 272 | R | 51.1% | 44.6% | 53.4% | 46.6% |
| 33,779 | IRON | 15,446 | 12,815 | 2,267 | 364 | 10,548 | R | 83.0% | 14.7% | 85.0% | 15.0% |
| 8,238 | JUAB | 3,417 | 2,681 | 605 | 131 | 2,076 | R | 78.5% | 17.7% | 81.6% | 18.4% |
| 6,046 | KANE | 3,051 | 2,414 | 576 | 61 | 1,838 | R | 79.1% | 18.9% | 80.7% | 19.3% |
| 12,405 | MILLARD | 4,877 | 4,084 | 626 | 167 | 3,458 | R | 83.7% | 12.8% | 86.7% | 13.3% |
| 7,129 | MORGAN | 3,841 | 3,301 | 472 | 68 | 2,829 | R | 85.9% | 12.3% | 87.5% | 12.5% |
| 1,435 | PIUTE | 773 | 646 | 123 | 4 | 523 | R | 83.6% | 15.9% | 84.0% | 16.0% |
| 1,961 | RICH | 1,037 | 922 | 109 | 6 | 813 | R | 88.9% | 10.5% | 89.4% | 10.6% |
| 898,387 | SALT LAKE | 362,138 | 215,728 | 135,949 | 10,461 | 79,779 | R | 59.6% | 37.5% | 61.3% | 38.7% |
| 14,413 | SAN JUAN | 4,950 | 2,971 | 1,906 | 73 | 1,065 | R | 60.0% | 38.5% | 60.9% | 39.1% |
| 22,763 | SANPETE | 8,507 | 7,004 | 1,189 | 314 | 5,815 | R | 82.3% | 14.0% | 85.5% | 14.5% |
| 18,842 | SEVIER | 7,641 | 6,597 | 920 | 124 | 5,677 | R | 86.3% | 12.0% | 87.8% | 12.2% |
| 29,736 | SUMMIT | 15,312 | 7,936 | 6,977 | 399 | 959 | R | 51.8% | 45.6% | 53.2% | 46.8% |
| 40,735 | TOOELE | 16,664 | 12,181 | 4,130 | 353 | 8,051 | R | 73.1% | 24.8% | 74.7% | 25.3% |
| 25,224 | UINTAH | 9,957 | 8,518 | 1,266 | 173 | 7,252 | R | 85.5% | 12.7% | 87.1% | 12.9% |
| 368,536 | UTAH | 149,173 | 128,269 | 17,357 | 3,547 | 110,912 | R | 86.0% | 11.6% | 88.1% | 11.9% |
| 15,215 | WASATCH | 7,512 | 5,503 | 1,854 | 155 | 3,649 | R | 73.3% | 24.7% | 74.8% | 25.2% |
| 90,354 | WASHINGTON | 44,018 | 35,633 | 7,513 | 872 | 28,120 | R | 81.0% | 17.1% | 82.6% | 17.4% |
| 2,509 | WAYNE | 1,360 | 1,062 | 279 | 19 | 783 | R | 78.1% | 20.5% | 79.2% | 20.8% |
| 196,533 | WEBER | 72,691 | 51,199 | 19,862 | 1,630 | 31,337 | R | 70.4% | 27.3% | 72.0% | 28.0% |
| 2,233,169 | TOTAL | 927,844 | 663,742 | 241,199 | 22,903 | 422,543 | R | 71.5% | 26.0% | 73.3% | 26.7% |

# UTAH

## GOVERNOR 2004

| 2000 Census Population | County | Total Vote | Republican | Democratic | Other | Rep.-Dem. Plurality | | Total Vote Rep. | Total Vote Dem. | Major Vote Rep. | Major Vote Dem. |
|---|---|---|---|---|---|---|---|---|---|---|---|
| 6,005 | BEAVER | 2,549 | 1,541 | 991 | 17 | 550 | R | 60.5% | 38.9% | 60.9% | 39.1% |
| 42,745 | BOX ELDER | 18,294 | 12,631 | 5,497 | 166 | 7,134 | R | 69.0% | 30.0% | 69.7% | 30.3% |
| 91,391 | CACHE | 39,245 | 25,307 | 13,660 | 278 | 11,647 | R | 64.5% | 34.8% | 64.9% | 35.1% |
| 20,422 | CARBON | 8,411 | 3,232 | 5,111 | 68 | 1,879 | D | 38.4% | 60.8% | 38.7% | 61.3% |
| 921 | DAGGETT | 481 | 287 | 194 | | 93 | R | 59.7% | 40.3% | 59.7% | 40.3% |
| 238,994 | DAVIS | 108,053 | 68,545 | 38,726 | 782 | 29,819 | R | 63.4% | 35.8% | 63.9% | 36.1% |
| 14,371 | DUCHESNE | 5,525 | 3,939 | 1,550 | 36 | 2,389 | R | 71.3% | 28.1% | 71.8% | 28.2% |
| 10,860 | EMERY | 4,658 | 2,754 | 1,848 | 56 | 906 | R | 59.1% | 39.7% | 59.8% | 40.2% |
| 4,735 | GARFIELD | 2,140 | 1,562 | 558 | 20 | 1,004 | R | 73.0% | 26.1% | 73.7% | 26.3% |
| 8,485 | GRAND | 4,123 | 1,811 | 2,239 | 73 | 428 | D | 43.9% | 54.3% | 44.7% | 55.3% |
| 33,779 | IRON | 15,336 | 10,673 | 4,526 | 137 | 6,147 | R | 69.6% | 29.5% | 70.2% | 29.8% |
| 8,238 | JUAB | 3,393 | 1,995 | 1,363 | 35 | 632 | R | 58.8% | 40.2% | 59.4% | 40.6% |
| 6,046 | KANE | 3,022 | 2,168 | 823 | 31 | 1,345 | R | 71.7% | 27.2% | 72.5% | 27.5% |
| 12,405 | MILLARD | 4,854 | 3,150 | 1,654 | 50 | 1,496 | R | 64.9% | 34.1% | 65.6% | 34.4% |
| 7,129 | MORGAN | 3,832 | 2,535 | 1,272 | 25 | 1,263 | R | 66.2% | 33.2% | 66.6% | 33.4% |

# UTAH

## GOVERNOR 2004

| 2000 Census Population | County | Total Vote | Republican | Democratic | Other | Rep.-Dem. Plurality | Percentage | | | |
|---|---|---|---|---|---|---|---|---|---|---|
| | | | | | | | Total Vote | | Major Vote | |
| | | | | | | | Rep. | Dem. | Rep. | Dem. |
| 1,435 | PIUTE | 756 | 517 | 237 | 2 | 280 R | 68.4% | 31.3% | 68.6% | 31.4% |
| 1,961 | RICH | 1,025 | 706 | 317 | 2 | 389 R | 68.9% | 30.9% | 69.0% | 31.0% |
| 898,387 | SALT LAKE | 360,681 | 168,818 | 188,002 | 3,861 | 19,184 D | 46.8% | 52.1% | 47.3% | 52.7% |
| 14,413 | SAN JUAN | 4,871 | 2,555 | 2,244 | 72 | 311 R | 52.5% | 46.1% | 53.2% | 46.8% |
| 22,763 | SANPETE | 8,330 | 5,441 | 2,799 | 90 | 2,642 R | 65.3% | 33.6% | 66.0% | 34.0% |
| 18,842 | SEVIER | 7,591 | 5,059 | 2,470 | 62 | 2,589 R | 66.6% | 32.5% | 67.2% | 32.8% |
| 29,736 | SUMMIT | 15,096 | 6,151 | 8,822 | 123 | 2,671 D | 40.7% | 58.4% | 41.1% | 58.9% |
| 40,735 | TOOELE | 16,479 | 9,181 | 7,106 | 192 | 2,075 R | 55.7% | 43.1% | 56.4% | 43.6% |
| 25,224 | UINTAH | 9,842 | 7,345 | 2,399 | 98 | 4,946 R | 74.6% | 24.4% | 75.4% | 24.6% |
| 368,536 | UTAH | 147,355 | 107,429 | 38,921 | 1,005 | 68,508 R | 72.9% | 26.4% | 73.4% | 26.6% |
| 15,215 | WASATCH | 7,438 | 4,353 | 3,032 | 53 | 1,321 R | 58.5% | 40.8% | 58.9% | 41.1% |
| 90,354 | WASHINGTON | 43,313 | 31,295 | 11,683 | 335 | 19,612 R | 72.3% | 27.0% | 72.8% | 27.2% |
| 2,509 | WAYNE | 1,338 | 880 | 458 | | 422 R | 65.8% | 34.2% | 65.8% | 34.2% |
| 196,533 | WEBER | 71,929 | 39,330 | 31,857 | 742 | 7,473 R | 54.7% | 44.3% | 55.2% | 44.8% |
| 2,233,169 | TOTAL | 919,960 | 531,190 | 380,359 | 8,411 | 150,831 R | 57.7% | 41.3% | 58.3% | 41.7% |

# UTAH

## SENATOR 2004

| 2000 Census Population | County | Total Vote | Republican | Democratic | Other | Rep.-Dem. Plurality | Percentage | | | |
|---|---|---|---|---|---|---|---|---|---|---|
| | | | | | | | Total Vote | | Major Vote | |
| | | | | | | | Rep. | Dem. | Rep. | Dem. |
| 6,005 | BEAVER | 2,484 | 1,799 | 623 | 62 | 1,176 R | 72.4% | 25.1% | 74.3% | 25.7% |
| 42,745 | BOX ELDER | 18,149 | 14,924 | 2,726 | 499 | 12,198 R | 82.2% | 15.0% | 84.6% | 15.4% |
| 91,391 | CACHE | 38,955 | 31,153 | 6,834 | 968 | 24,319 R | 80.0% | 17.5% | 82.0% | 18.0% |
| 20,422 | CARBON | 8,241 | 4,197 | 3,806 | 238 | 391 R | 50.9% | 46.2% | 52.4% | 47.6% |
| 921 | DAGGETT | 451 | 328 | 120 | 3 | 208 R | 72.7% | 26.6% | 73.2% | 26.8% |
| 238,994 | DAVIS | 107,526 | 81,724 | 23,044 | 2,758 | 58,680 R | 76.0% | 21.4% | 78.0% | 22.0% |
| 14,371 | DUCHESNE | 5,442 | 4,417 | 890 | 135 | 3,527 R | 81.2% | 16.4% | 83.2% | 16.8% |
| 10,860 | EMERY | 4,630 | 3,450 | 1,063 | 117 | 2,387 R | 74.5% | 23.0% | 76.4% | 23.6% |
| 4,735 | GARFIELD | 2,101 | 1,713 | 341 | 47 | 1,372 R | 81.5% | 16.2% | 83.4% | 16.6% |
| 8,485 | GRAND | 4,042 | 2,101 | 1,787 | 154 | 314 R | 52.0% | 44.2% | 54.0% | 46.0% |
| 33,779 | IRON | 15,099 | 12,176 | 2,442 | 481 | 9,734 R | 80.6% | 16.2% | 83.3% | 16.7% |
| 8,238 | JUAB | 3,373 | 2,410 | 788 | 175 | 1,622 R | 71.4% | 23.4% | 75.4% | 24.6% |
| 6,046 | KANE | 2,988 | 2,296 | 612 | 80 | 1,684 R | 76.8% | 20.5% | 79.0% | 21.0% |
| 12,405 | MILLARD | 4,826 | 3,716 | 848 | 262 | 2,868 R | 77.0% | 17.6% | 81.4% | 18.6% |
| 7,129 | MORGAN | 3,788 | 3,056 | 641 | 91 | 2,415 R | 80.7% | 16.9% | 82.7% | 17.3% |
| 1,435 | PIUTE | 686 | 573 | 109 | 4 | 464 R | 83.5% | 15.9% | 84.0% | 16.0% |
| 1,961 | RICH | 965 | 823 | 134 | 8 | 689 R | 85.3% | 13.9% | 86.0% | 14.0% |
| 898,387 | SALT LAKE | 357,472 | 204,974 | 142,277 | 10,221 | 62,697 R | 57.3% | 39.8% | 59.0% | 41.0% |
| 14,413 | SAN JUAN | 4,867 | 2,860 | 1,846 | 161 | 1,014 R | 58.8% | 37.9% | 60.8% | 39.2% |
| 22,763 | SANPETE | 8,338 | 6,334 | 1,515 | 489 | 4,819 R | 76.0% | 18.2% | 80.7% | 19.3% |
| 18,842 | SEVIER | 7,571 | 6,198 | 1,151 | 222 | 5,047 R | 81.9% | 15.2% | 84.3% | 15.7% |
| 29,736 | SUMMIT | 14,882 | 7,488 | 7,073 | 321 | 415 R | 50.3% | 47.5% | 51.4% | 48.6% |
| 40,735 | TOOELE | 16,283 | 10,873 | 4,800 | 610 | 6,073 R | 66.8% | 29.5% | 69.4% | 30.6% |
| 25,224 | UINTAH | 9,731 | 7,947 | 1,472 | 312 | 6,475 R | 81.7% | 15.1% | 84.4% | 15.6% |
| 368,536 | UTAH | 145,972 | 121,241 | 20,521 | 4,210 | 100,720 R | 83.1% | 14.1% | 85.5% | 14.5% |
| 15,215 | WASATCH | 7,356 | 5,146 | 2,008 | 202 | 3,138 R | 70.0% | 27.3% | 71.9% | 28.1% |
| 90,354 | WASHINGTON | 42,890 | 33,846 | 7,842 | 1,202 | 26,004 R | 78.9% | 18.3% | 81.2% | 18.8% |
| 2,509 | WAYNE | 1,227 | 951 | 264 | 12 | 687 R | 77.5% | 21.5% | 78.3% | 21.7% |
| 196,533 | WEBER | 71,391 | 47,926 | 21,378 | 2,087 | 26,548 R | 67.1% | 29.9% | 69.2% | 30.8% |
| 2,233,169 | TOTAL | 911,726 | 626,640 | 258,955 | 26,131 | 367,685 R | 68.7% | 28.4% | 70.8% | 29.2% |

# UTAH

## HOUSE OF REPRESENTATIVES

| CD | Year | Total Vote | Republican Vote | Republican Candidate | Democratic Vote | Democratic Candidate | Other Vote | Rep.-Dem. Plurality | Total Vote Rep. | Total Vote Dem. | Major Vote Rep. | Major Vote Dem. |
|----|------|-----------|-----------------|----------------------|-----------------|----------------------|------------|---------------------|-----------------|-----------------|-----------------|-----------------|
| 1 | 2004 | 293,961 | 199,615 | Bishop, Rob* | 85,630 | Thompson, Steven | 8,716 | 113,985 R | 67.9% | 29.1% | 70.0% | 30.0% |
| 1 | 2002 | 179,412 | 109,265 | Bishop, Rob | 66,104 | Thomas, Dave | 4,043 | 43,161 R | 60.9% | 36.8% | 62.3% | 37.7% |
| 2 | 2004 | 341,968 | 147,778 | Swallow, John | 187,250 | Matheson, Jim* | 6,940 | 39,472 D | 43.2% | 54.8% | 44.1% | 55.9% |
| 2 | 2002 | 224,098 | 109,123 | Swallow, John | 110,764 | Matheson, Jim* | 4,211 | 1,641 D | 48.7% | 49.4% | 49.6% | 50.4% |
| 3 | 2004 | 272,928 | 173,010 | Cannon, Chris* | 88,748 | Babka, Beau | 11,170 | 84,262 R | 63.4% | 32.5% | 66.1% | 33.9% |
| 3 | 2002 | 153,643 | 103,598 | Cannon, Chris* | 44,533 | Woodside, Nancy Jane | 5,512 | 59,065 R | 67.4% | 29.0% | 69.9% | 30.1% |
| Total | 2004 | 908,857 | 520,403 | | 361,628 | | 26,826 | 158,775 R | 57.3% | 39.8% | 59.0% | 41.0% |
| Total | 2002 | 557,153 | 321,986 | | 221,401 | | 13,766 | 100,585 R | 57.8% | 39.7% | 59.3% | 40.7% |

An asterisk (*) denotes incumbent.

# UTAH

## GENERAL AND PRIMARY ELECTIONS

## 2004 GENERAL ELECTIONS

**President** Other vote was 11,305 Unaffiliated (Ralph Nader); 6,841 Constitution (Michael Peroutka); 3,375 Libertarian (Michael Badnarik); 946 Personal Choice (Charles Jay); 393 Socialist Workers (James Harris); 39 write-in (David Cobb); 2 write-in (Lawrence Topham); 1 write-in (Joe Schriner); 1 write-in (John Joseph Kennedy).

**Governor** Other vote was 8,399 Personal Choice (Ken Larsen); 12 write-in (Stoney Fonua).

**Senator** Other vote was 17,289 Constitution (Gary R. Van Horn); 8,824 Personal Choice (Joe Labonte); 16 write-in (Cody Judy); 2 write-in (Nola Tuaone).

**House** Other vote was:

CD 1     4,510 Constitution (Charles Johnston); 4,206 Personal Choice (Richard W. Soderberg).

CD 2     3,541 Constitution (Jeremy Paul Petersen); 2,189 Green (Patrick S. Diehl); 1,210 Personal Choice (Ronald R. Amos).

CD 3     5,089 Constitution (Ronald Winfield); 3,691 Libertarian (Jim Dexter); 2,390 Personal Choice (Curtis Darrell James).

## 2004 PRIMARY ELECTIONS

**Primary** February 24, 2004 (President)     **Registration**     1,189,779     In process of
June 22, 2004 (Congress)     (as of June 22, 2004)     instituting registration by party

**Primary Type** Any registered voter could participate in the Democratic primary. Only registered Republicans could vote in the Republican primary. (As of June 2005, there were 417,147 registered Republicans in Utah, 95,738 registered Democrats.)

430

# UTAH

## GENERAL AND PRIMARY ELECTIONS

Note: An asterisk (*) denotes incumbent. Candidates in Utah are usually nominated by convention. It is up to each party to determine the percentage of the convention vote that is needed to force a primary.

| | REPUBLICAN PRIMARIES | | | DEMOCRATIC PRIMARIES | | |
|---|---|---|---|---|---|---|
| President | No Republican primary | | | John Kerry | 19,232 | 55.2% |
| | | | | John Edwards | 10,384 | 29.8% |
| | | | | Dennis J. Kucinich | 2,590 | 7.4% |
| | | | | Howard Dean | 1,335 | 3.8% |
| | | | | Wesley Clark | 489 | 1.4% |
| | | | | Joseph I. Lieberman | 402 | 1.2% |
| | | | | Uncommitted | 298 | 0.9% |
| | | | | Richard A. Gephardt | 124 | 0.4% |
| | | | | TOTAL | 34,854 | |
| Governor | Jon Huntsman Jr. | 102,955 | 66.4% | Scott M. Matheson Jr. | Nominated by convention | |
| | Nolan Karras | 52,048 | 33.6% | | | |
| | TOTAL | 155,003 | | | | |
| Senator | Robert F. Bennett* | Nominated by convention | | R. Paul Van Dam | Nominated by convention | |
| Congressional District 1 | Rob Bishop* | Nominated by convention | | Steven Thompson | Nominated by convention | |
| Congressional District 2 | John Swallow | 28,137 | 53.0% | Jim Matheson* | Nominated by convention | |
| | Tim Bridgewater | 24,960 | 47.0% | | | |
| | TOTAL | 53,097 | | | | |
| Congressional District 3 | Chris Cannon* | 27,663 | 58.4% | Beau Babka | Nominated by convention | |
| | Matt Throckmorton | 19,672 | 41.6% | | | |
| | TOTAL | 47,335 | | | | |

# VERMONT

## GOVERNOR

Jim Douglas (R). Reelected 2004 to a two-year term. Previously elected January 2003 by the state legislature. Douglas had finished first in the 2002 general election but failed to win a majority of the vote as required by Vermont law.

## SENATORS (1 Democrat, 1 Independent)

James M. Jeffords (I). Reelected 2000 to a six-year term. Previously elected 1994, 1988. Announced switch in party affiliation from Republican to Independent May 24, 2001, effective at the close of business June 5, 2001.

Patrick J. Leahy (D). Reelected 2004 to a six-year term. Previously elected 1998, 1992, 1986, 1980, 1974.

## REPRESENTATIVES (1 Independent)

At Large. Bernard Sanders (I)

## POSTWAR VOTE FOR PRESIDENT

| | | Republican | | Democratic | | | | Percentage | | | |
| | | | | | | | | Total Vote | | Major Vote | |
| Year | Total Vote | Vote | Candidate | Vote | Candidate | Other Vote | Plurality | Rep. | Dem. | Rep. | Dem. |
|---|---|---|---|---|---|---|---|---|---|---|---|
| 2004 | 312,309 | 121,180 | Bush, George W. | 184,067 | Kerry, John | 7,062 | 62,887 D | 38.8% | 58.9% | 39.7% | 60.3% |
| 2000** | 294,308 | 119,775 | Bush, George W. | 149,022 | Gore, Al | 25,511 | 29,247 D | 40.7% | 50.6% | 44.6% | 55.4% |
| 1996** | 258,449 | 80,352 | Dole, Bob | 137,894 | Clinton, Bill | 40,203 | 57,542 D | 31.1% | 53.4% | 36.8% | 63.2% |
| 1992** | 289,701 | 88,122 | Bush, George | 133,592 | Clinton, Bill | 67,987 | 45,470 D | 30.4% | 46.1% | 39.7% | 60.3% |
| 1988 | 243,328 | 124,331 | Bush, George | 115,775 | Dukakis, Michael S. | 3,222 | 8,556 R | 51.1% | 47.6% | 51.8% | 48.2% |
| 1984 | 234,561 | 135,865 | Reagan, Ronald | 95,730 | Mondale, Walter F. | 2,966 | 40,135 R | 57.9% | 40.8% | 58.7% | 41.3% |
| 1980** | 213,299 | 94,628 | Reagan, Ronald | 81,952 | Carter, Jimmy | 36,719 | 12,676 R | 44.4% | 38.4% | 53.6% | 46.4% |
| 1976 | 187,765 | 102,085 | Ford, Gerald R. | 80,954 | Carter, Jimmy | 4,726 | 21,131 R | 54.4% | 43.1% | 55.8% | 44.2% |
| 1972 | 186,947 | 117,149 | Nixon, Richard M. | 68,174 | McGovern, George S. | 1,624 | 48,975 R | 62.7% | 36.5% | 63.2% | 36.8% |
| 1968** | 161,404 | 85,142 | Nixon, Richard M. | 70,255 | Humphrey, Hubert H. | 6,007 | 14,887 R | 52.8% | 43.5% | 54.8% | 45.2% |
| 1964 | 163,089 | 54,942 | Goldwater, Barry M. | 108,127 | Johnson, Lyndon B. | 20 | 53,185 D | 33.7% | 66.3% | 33.7% | 66.3% |
| 1960 | 167,324 | 98,131 | Nixon, Richard M. | 69,186 | Kennedy, John F. | 7 | 28,945 R | 58.6% | 41.3% | 58.6% | 41.4% |
| 1956 | 152,978 | 110,390 | Eisenhower, Dwight D. | 42,549 | Stevenson, Adlai E. | 39 | 67,841 R | 72.2% | 27.8% | 72.2% | 27.8% |
| 1952 | 153,557 | 109,717 | Eisenhower, Dwight D. | 43,355 | Stevenson, Adlai E. | 485 | 66,362 R | 71.5% | 28.2% | 71.7% | 28.3% |
| 1948 | 123,382 | 75,926 | Dewey, Thomas E. | 45,557 | Truman, Harry S. | 1,899 | 30,369 R | 61.5% | 36.9% | 62.5% | 37.5% |

In past elections, the other vote included: 2000 - 20,374 Green (Ralph Nader); 1996 - 31,024 Reform (Ross Perot); 1992 - 65,991 Independent (Perot); 1980 - 31,761 Independent (John Anderson); 1968 - 5,104 American Independent (George Wallace).

# VERMONT

## POSTWAR VOTE FOR GOVERNOR

| Year | Total Vote | Republican Vote | Republican Candidate | Democratic Vote | Democratic Candidate | Other Vote | Rep.-Dem. Plurality | Percentage Total Vote Rep. | Dem. | Major Vote Rep. | Dem. |
|---|---|---|---|---|---|---|---|---|---|---|---|
| 2004 | 309,285 | 181,540 | Douglas, Jim | 117,327 | Clavelle, Peter | 10,418 | 64,213 R | 58.7% | 37.9% | 60.7% | 39.3% |
| 2002** | 230,161 | 103,436 | Douglas, Jim | 97,565 | Racine, Doug | 29,160 | 5,871 R | 44.9% | 42.4% | 51.5% | 48.5% |
| 2000 | 293,473 | 111,359 | Dwyer, Ruth | 148,059 | Dean, Howard B. | 34,055 | 36,700 D | 37.9% | 50.5% | 42.9% | 57.1% |
| 1998 | 218,120 | 89,726 | Dwyer, Ruth | 121,425 | Dean, Howard B. | 6,969 | 31,699 D | 41.1% | 55.7% | 42.5% | 57.5% |
| 1996 | 254,648 | 57,161 | Gropper, John L. | 179,544 | Dean, Howard B. | 17,943 | 122,383 D | 22.4% | 70.5% | 24.1% | 75.9% |
| 1994 | 212,046 | 40,292 | Kelley, David F. | 145,661 | Dean, Howard B. | 26,093 | 105,369 D | 19.0% | 68.7% | 21.7% | 78.3% |
| 1992 | 285,728 | 65,837 | McClaughry, John | 213,523 | Dean, Howard B. | 6,368 | 147,686 D | 23.0% | 74.7% | 23.6% | 76.4% |
| 1990 | 211,422 | 109,540 | Snelling, Richard A. | 97,321 | Welch, Peter | 4,561 | 12,219 R | 51.8% | 46.0% | 53.0% | 47.0% |
| 1988 | 243,130 | 105,319 | Bernhardt, Michael | 134,594 | Kunin, Madeleine M. | 3,253 | 29,275 D | 43.3% | 55.4% | 43.9% | 56.1% |
| 1986** | 196,716 | 75,162 | Smith, Peter | 92,379 | Kunin, Madeleine M. | 29,175 | 17,217 D | 38.2% | 47.0% | 44.9% | 55.1% |
| 1984 | 233,753 | 113,264 | Easton, John J. | 116,938 | Kunin, Madeleine M. | 3,551 | 3,674 D | 48.5% | 50.0% | 49.2% | 50.8% |
| 1982 | 169,251 | 93,111 | Snelling, Richard A. | 74,394 | Kunin, Madeleine M. | 1,746 | 18,717 R | 55.0% | 44.0% | 55.6% | 44.4% |
| 1980 | 210,381 | 123,229 | Snelling, Richard A. | 77,363 | Diamond, J. Jerome | 9,789 | 45,866 R | 58.6% | 36.8% | 61.4% | 38.6% |
| 1978 | 124,482 | 78,181 | Snelling, Richard A. | 42,482 | Granai, Edwin C. | 3,819 | 35,699 R | 62.8% | 34.1% | 64.8% | 35.2% |
| 1976 | 185,929 | 99,268 | Snelling, Richard A. | 75,262 | Hackel, Stella B. | 11,399 | 24,006 R | 53.4% | 40.5% | 56.9% | 43.1% |
| 1974 | 141,156 | 53,672 | Kennedy, Walter L. | 79,842 | Salmon, Thomas P. | 7,642 | 26,170 D | 38.0% | 56.6% | 40.2% | 59.8% |
| 1972 | 189,237 | 82,491 | Hackett, Luther F. | 104,533 | Salmon, Thomas P. | 2,213 | 22,042 D | 43.6% | 55.2% | 44.1% | 55.9% |
| 1970 | 153,528 | 87,458 | Davis, Deane C. | 66,028 | O'Brien, Leo | 42 | 21,430 R | 57.0% | 43.0% | 57.0% | 43.0% |
| 1968 | 161,089 | 89,387 | Davis, Deane C. | 71,656 | Daley, John J. | 46 | 17,731 R | 55.5% | 44.5% | 55.5% | 44.5% |
| 1966 | 136,262 | 57,577 | Snelling, Richard A. | 78,669 | Hoff, Philip H. | 16 | 21,092 D | 42.3% | 57.7% | 42.3% | 57.7% |
| 1964 | 164,199 | 57,576 | Foote, Ralph A. | 106,611 | Hoff, Philip H. | 12 | 49,035 D | 35.1% | 64.9% | 35.1% | 64.9% |
| 1962 | 121,422 | 60,035 | Keyser, F. Ray | 61,383 | Hoff, Philip H. | 4 | 1,348 D | 49.4% | 50.6% | 49.4% | 50.6% |
| 1960 | 164,632 | 92,861 | Keyser, F. Ray | 71,755 | Niquette, Russell F. | 16 | 21,106 R | 56.4% | 43.6% | 56.4% | 43.6% |
| 1958 | 123,728 | 62,222 | Stafford, Robert T. | 61,503 | Leddy, Bernard J. | 3 | 719 R | 50.3% | 49.7% | 50.3% | 49.7% |
| 1956 | 153,809 | 88,379 | Johnson, Joseph B. | 65,420 | Branon, E. Frank | 10 | 22,959 R | 57.5% | 42.5% | 57.5% | 42.5% |
| 1954 | 114,360 | 59,778 | Johnson, Joseph B. | 54,554 | Branon, E. Frank | 28 | 5,224 R | 52.3% | 47.7% | 52.3% | 47.7% |
| 1952 | 150,862 | 78,338 | Emerson, Lee E. | 60,051 | Larrow, Robert W. | 12,473 | 18,287 R | 51.9% | 39.8% | 56.6% | 43.4% |
| 1950 | 87,155 | 64,915 | Emerson, Lee E. | 22,227 | Moran, J. Edward | 13 | 42,688 R | 74.5% | 25.5% | 74.5% | 25.5% |
| 1948 | 120,183 | 86,394 | Gibson, Ernest W., Jr. | 33,588 | Ryan, Charles F. | 201 | 52,806 R | 71.9% | 27.9% | 72.0% | 28.0% |
| 1946 | 72,044 | 57,849 | Gibson, Ernest W., Jr. | 14,096 | Coburn, Berthold | 99 | 43,753 R | 80.3% | 19.6% | 80.4% | 19.6% |

In 2002 and 1986, in the absence of a majority for any candidate, the state legislature elected the governor—Republican Jim Douglas in January 2003, Democrat Madeleine M. Kunin in January 1987.

## POSTWAR VOTE FOR SENATOR

| Year | Total Vote | Republican Vote | Republican Candidate | Democratic Vote | Democratic Candidate | Other Vote | Rep.-Dem. Plurality | Percentage Total Vote Rep. | Dem. | Major Vote Rep. | Dem. |
|---|---|---|---|---|---|---|---|---|---|---|---|
| 2004 | 307,208 | 75,398 | McMullen, Jack | 216,972 | Leahy, Patrick J. | 14,838 | 141,574 D | 24.5% | 70.6% | 25.8% | 74.2% |
| 2000 | 288,500 | 189,133 | Jeffords, James M. | 73,352 | Flanagan, Ed | 26,015 | 115,781 R | 65.6% | 25.4% | 72.1% | 27.9% |
| 1998 | 214,036 | 48,051 | Tuttle, Fred H. | 154,567 | Leahy, Patrick J. | 11,418 | 106,516 D | 22.4% | 72.2% | 23.7% | 76.3% |
| 1994 | 211,672 | 106,505 | Jeffords, James M. | 85,868 | Backus, Jan | 19,299 | 20,637 R | 50.3% | 40.6% | 55.4% | 44.6% |
| 1992 | 285,739 | 123,854 | Douglas, Jim | 154,762 | Leahy, Patrick J. | 7,123 | 30,908 D | 43.3% | 54.2% | 44.5% | 55.5% |
| 1988 | 240,111 | 163,203 | Jeffords, James M. | 71,469 | Gray, William | 5,439 | 91,736 R | 68.0% | 29.8% | 69.5% | 30.5% |
| 1986 | 196,532 | 67,798 | Snelling, Richard A. | 124,123 | Leahy, Patrick J. | 4,611 | 56,325 D | 34.5% | 63.2% | 35.3% | 64.7% |
| 1982 | 168,003 | 84,450 | Stafford, Robert T. | 79,340 | Guest, James A. | 4,213 | 5,110 R | 50.3% | 47.2% | 51.6% | 48.4% |
| 1980 | 209,124 | 101,421 | Ledbetter, Stewart M. | 104,176 | Leahy, Patrick J. | 3,527 | 2,755 D | 48.5% | 49.8% | 49.3% | 50.7% |
| 1976 | 189,060 | 94,481 | Stafford, Robert T. | 85,682 | Salmon, Thomas P. | 8,897 | 8,799 R | 50.0% | 45.3% | 52.4% | 47.6% |
| 1974 | 142,772 | 66,223 | Mallary, Richard W. | 70,629 | Leahy, Patrick J. | 5,920 | 4,406 D | 46.4% | 49.5% | 48.4% | 51.6% |
| 1972S | 71,348 | 45,888 | Stafford, Robert T. | 23,842 | Major, Randolph T. | 1,618 | 22,046 R | 64.3% | 33.4% | 65.8% | 34.2% |
| 1970 | 154,899 | 91,198 | Prouty, Winston L. | 62,271 | Hoff, Philip H. | 1,430 | 28,927 R | 58.9% | 40.2% | 59.4% | 40.6% |
| 1968** | 157,375 | 157,154 | Aiken, George D. | — | | 221 | 157,154 R | 99.9% | | 100.0% | |
| 1964 | 164,350 | 87,879 | Prouty, Winston L. | 76,457 | Fayette, Frederick J. | 14 | 11,422 R | 53.5% | 46.5% | 53.5% | 46.5% |
| 1962 | 121,571 | 81,241 | Aiken, George D. | 40,134 | Johnson, W. Robert | 196 | 41,107 R | 66.8% | 33.0% | 66.9% | 33.1% |
| 1958 | 124,442 | 64,900 | Prouty, Winston L. | 59,536 | Fayette, Frederick J. | 6 | 5,364 R | 52.2% | 47.8% | 52.2% | 47.8% |
| 1956 | 155,289 | 103,101 | Aiken, George D. | 52,184 | O'Shea, Bernard G. | 4 | 50,917 R | 66.4% | 33.6% | 66.4% | 33.6% |
| 1952 | 154,052 | 111,406 | Flanders, Ralph E. | 42,630 | Johnston, Allan R. | 16 | 68,776 R | 72.3% | 27.7% | 72.3% | 27.7% |
| 1950 | 89,171 | 69,543 | Aiken, George D. | 19,608 | Bigelow, James E. | 20 | 49,935 R | 78.0% | 22.0% | 78.0% | 22.0% |
| 1946 | 73,340 | 54,729 | Flanders, Ralph E. | 18,594 | McDevitt, Charles P. | 17 | 36,135 R | 74.6% | 25.4% | 74.6% | 25.4% |

The 1972 election was for a short term to fill a vacancy. In 1968 the Republican candidate won both major party nominations.

# VERMONT

One member At Large

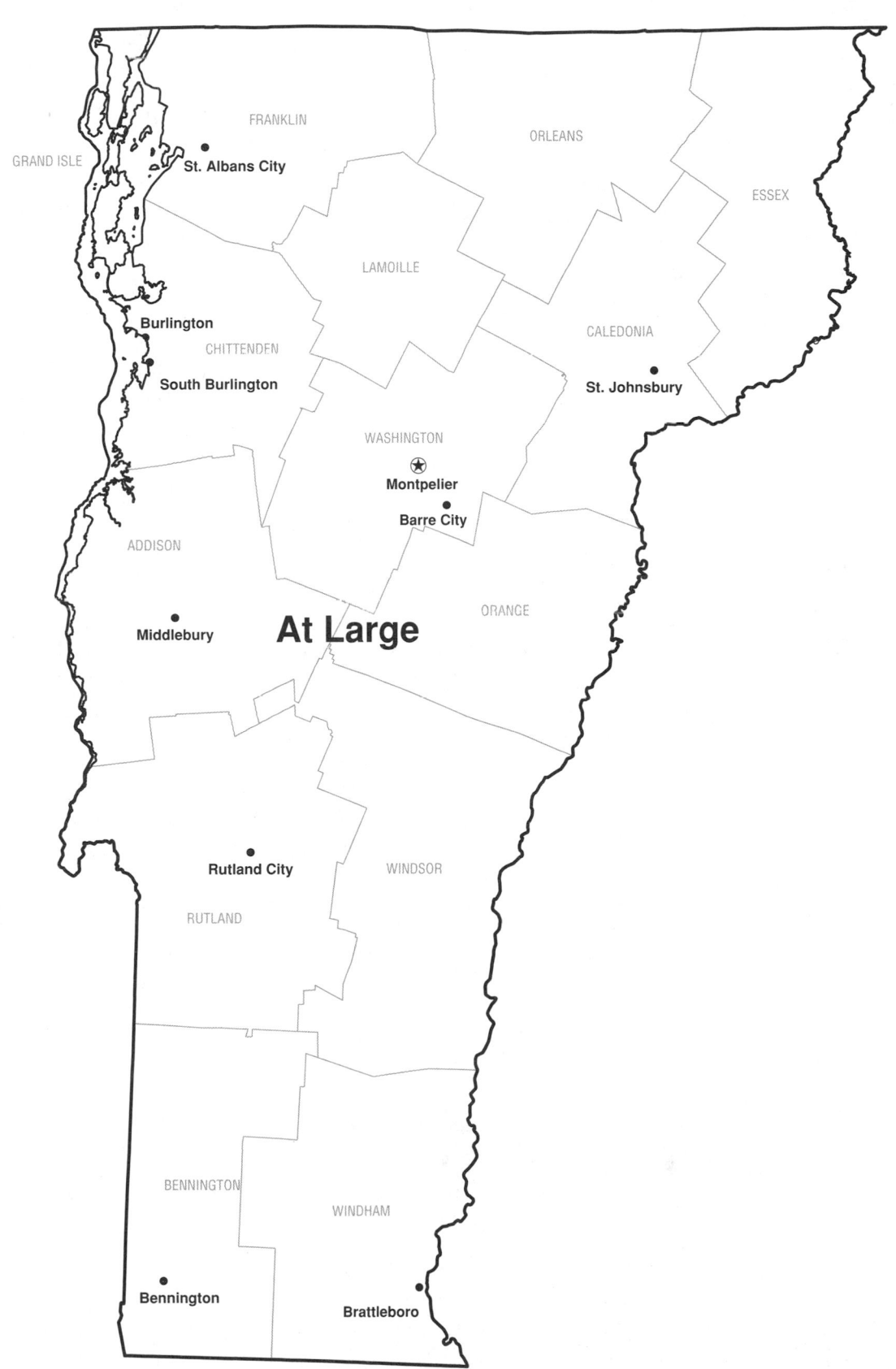

# VERMONT

## PRESIDENT 2004

| 2000 Census Population | County | Total Vote | Republican | Democratic | Other | Rep.-Dem. Plurality | | Percentage | | | |
|---|---|---|---|---|---|---|---|---|---|---|---|
| | | | | | | | | Total Vote | | Major Vote | |
| | | | | | | | | Rep. | Dem. | Rep. | Dem. |
| 35,974 | ADDISON | 18,579 | 7,077 | 11,147 | 355 | 4,070 | D | 38.1% | 60.0% | 38.8% | 61.2% |
| 36,994 | BENNINGTON | 19,065 | 7,616 | 11,069 | 380 | 3,453 | D | 39.9% | 58.1% | 40.8% | 59.2% |
| 29,702 | CALEDONIA | 14,211 | 6,765 | 7,106 | 340 | 341 | D | 47.6% | 50.0% | 48.8% | 51.2% |
| 146,571 | CHITTENDEN | 77,696 | 26,422 | 49,369 | 1,905 | 22,947 | D | 34.0% | 63.5% | 34.9% | 65.1% |
| 6,459 | ESSEX | 2,937 | 1,591 | 1,276 | 70 | 315 | R | 54.2% | 43.4% | 55.5% | 44.5% |
| 45,417 | FRANKLIN | 19,920 | 8,936 | 10,598 | 386 | 1,662 | D | 44.9% | 53.2% | 45.7% | 54.3% |
| 6,901 | GRAND ISLE | 4,077 | 1,754 | 2,246 | 77 | 492 | D | 43.0% | 55.1% | 43.9% | 56.2% |
| 23,233 | LAMOILLE | 12,181 | 4,260 | 7,636 | 285 | 3,376 | D | 35.0% | 62.7% | 35.8% | 64.2% |
| 28,226 | ORANGE | 14,895 | 6,421 | 8,159 | 315 | 1,738 | D | 43.1% | 54.8% | 44.0% | 56.0% |
| 26,277 | ORLEANS | 12,242 | 5,666 | 6,330 | 246 | 664 | D | 46.3% | 51.7% | 47.2% | 52.8% |
| 63,400 | RUTLAND | 30,975 | 14,440 | 15,904 | 631 | 1,464 | D | 46.6% | 51.3% | 47.6% | 52.4% |
| 58,039 | WASHINGTON | 31,448 | 11,461 | 19,177 | 810 | 7,716 | D | 36.4% | 61.0% | 37.4% | 62.6% |
| 44,216 | WINDHAM | 23,316 | 7,280 | 15,489 | 547 | 8,209 | D | 31.2% | 66.4% | 32.0% | 68.0% |
| 57,418 | WINDSOR | 30,767 | 11,491 | 18,561 | 715 | 7,070 | D | 37.3% | 60.3% | 38.2% | 61.8% |
| 608,827 | TOTAL | 312,309 | 121,180 | 184,067 | 7,062 | 62,887 | D | 38.8% | 58.9% | 39.7% | 60.3% |
| | **City/Town** | | | | | | | | | | |
| 9,291 | BARRE CITY | 3,819 | 1,703 | 2,037 | 79 | 334 | D | 44.6% | 53.3% | 45.5% | 54.5% |
| 7,602 | BARRE TOWN | 4,200 | 2,228 | 1,908 | 64 | 320 | R | 53.0% | 45.4% | 53.9% | 46.1% |
| 15,737 | BENNINGTON | 6,855 | 2,471 | 4,252 | 132 | 1,781 | D | 36.0% | 62.0% | 36.8% | 63.2% |
| 12,005 | BRATTLEBORO | 6,063 | 1,408 | 4,500 | 155 | 3,092 | D | 23.2% | 74.2% | 23.8% | 76.2% |
| 38,889 | BURLINGTON | 19,273 | 4,035 | 14,468 | 770 | 10,433 | D | 20.9% | 75.1% | 21.8% | 78.2% |
| 16,986 | COLCHESTER | 7,657 | 3,126 | 4,406 | 125 | 1,280 | D | 40.8% | 57.5% | 41.5% | 58.5% |
| 4,604 | DERBY | 2,152 | 1,012 | 1,104 | 36 | 92 | D | 47.0% | 51.3% | 47.8% | 52.2% |
| 18,626 | ESSEX | 10,295 | 4,349 | 5,760 | 186 | 1,411 | D | 42.2% | 55.9% | 43.0% | 57.0% |
| 10,367 | HARTFORD | 4,870 | 1,896 | 2,914 | 60 | 1,018 | D | 38.9% | 59.8% | 39.4% | 60.6% |
| 5,015 | JERICHO | 2,994 | 1,129 | 1,804 | 61 | 675 | D | 37.7% | 60.3% | 38.5% | 61.5% |
| 5,448 | LYNDON | 2,218 | 1,144 | 1,029 | 45 | 115 | R | 51.6% | 46.4% | 52.6% | 47.4% |
| 4,180 | MANCHESTER | 2,392 | 1,037 | 1,309 | 46 | 272 | D | 43.4% | 54.7% | 44.2% | 55.8% |
| 8,183 | MIDDLEBURY | 3,384 | 933 | 2,390 | 61 | 1,457 | D | 27.6% | 70.6% | 28.1% | 71.9% |
| 9,479 | MILTON | 4,464 | 2,253 | 2,130 | 81 | 123 | R | 50.5% | 47.7% | 51.4% | 48.6% |
| 8,035 | MONTPELIER | 4,719 | 1,048 | 3,536 | 135 | 2,488 | D | 22.2% | 74.9% | 22.9% | 77.1% |
| 5,139 | MORRISTOWN | 2,481 | 881 | 1,551 | 49 | 670 | D | 35.5% | 62.5% | 36.2% | 63.8% |
| 5,791 | NORTHFIELD | 2,349 | 1,050 | 1,228 | 71 | 178 | D | 44.7% | 52.3% | 46.1% | 53.9% |
| 4,853 | RANDOLPH | 2,329 | 914 | 1,348 | 67 | 434 | D | 39.2% | 57.9% | 40.4% | 59.6% |
| 4,090 | RICHMOND | 2,427 | 848 | 1,532 | 47 | 684 | D | 34.9% | 63.1% | 35.6% | 64.4% |
| 5,309 | ROCKINGHAM | 2,453 | 743 | 1,656 | 54 | 913 | D | 30.3% | 67.5% | 31.0% | 69.0% |
| 17,292 | RUTLAND CITY | 7,570 | 3,293 | 4,142 | 135 | 849 | D | 43.5% | 54.7% | 44.3% | 55.7% |
| 4,038 | RUTLAND TOWN | 2,455 | 1,309 | 1,104 | 42 | 205 | R | 53.3% | 45.0% | 54.2% | 45.8% |
| 6,944 | SHELBURNE | 4,370 | 1,493 | 2,800 | 77 | 1,307 | D | 34.2% | 64.1% | 34.8% | 65.2% |
| 15,814 | SOUTH BURLINGTON | 8,994 | 3,229 | 5,609 | 156 | 2,380 | D | 35.9% | 62.4% | 36.5% | 63.5% |
| 9,078 | SPRINGFIELD | 4,497 | 1,823 | 2,562 | 112 | 739 | D | 40.5% | 57.0% | 41.6% | 58.4% |
| 7,650 | ST. ALBANS CITY | 2,709 | 1,045 | 1,602 | 62 | 557 | D | 38.6% | 59.1% | 39.5% | 60.5% |
| 5,086 | ST. ALBANS TOWN | 2,575 | 1,209 | 1,328 | 38 | 119 | D | 47.0% | 51.6% | 47.7% | 52.3% |
| 7,571 | ST. JOHNSBURY | 3,123 | 1,488 | 1,577 | 58 | 89 | D | 47.6% | 50.5% | 48.5% | 51.5% |
| 2,548 | SWANTON | 2,513 | 1,184 | 1,302 | 27 | 118 | D | 47.1% | 51.8% | 47.6% | 52.4% |
| 4,915 | WATERBURY | 2,913 | 983 | 1,848 | 82 | 865 | D | 33.7% | 63.4% | 34.7% | 65.3% |
| 7,650 | WILLISTON | 4,975 | 1,931 | 2,938 | 106 | 1,007 | D | 38.8% | 59.1% | 39.7% | 60.3% |
| 6,561 | WINOOSKI | 2,529 | 781 | 1,685 | 63 | 904 | D | 30.9% | 66.6% | 31.7% | 68.3% |
| 3,232 | WOODSTOCK | 2,006 | 708 | 1,260 | 38 | 552 | D | 35.3% | 62.8% | 36.0% | 64.0% |

# VERMONT

## GOVERNOR 2004

| 2000 Census Population | County | Total Vote | Republican | Democratic | Other | Rep.-Dem. Plurality | Percentage | | | |
|---|---|---|---|---|---|---|---|---|---|---|
| | | | | | | | Total Vote | | Major Vote | |
| | | | | | | | Rep. | Dem. | Rep. | Dem. |
| 35,974 | ADDISON | 18,501 | 11,342 | 6,691 | 468 | 4,651 R | 61.3% | 36.2% | 62.9% | 37.1% |
| 36,994 | BENNINGTON | 18,720 | 11,162 | 6,650 | 908 | 4,512 R | 59.6% | 35.5% | 62.7% | 37.3% |
| 29,702 | CALEDONIA | 14,102 | 9,080 | 4,542 | 480 | 4,538 R | 64.4% | 32.2% | 66.7% | 33.3% |
| 146,571 | CHITTENDEN | 76,832 | 44,515 | 30,034 | 2,283 | 14,481 R | 57.9% | 39.1% | 59.7% | 40.3% |
| 6,459 | ESSEX | 2,893 | 1,974 | 793 | 126 | 1,181 R | 68.2% | 27.4% | 71.3% | 28.7% |
| 45,417 | FRANKLIN | 19,871 | 13,541 | 5,859 | 471 | 7,682 R | 68.1% | 29.5% | 69.8% | 30.2% |
| 6,901 | GRAND ISLE | 4,056 | 2,558 | 1,363 | 135 | 1,195 R | 63.1% | 33.6% | 65.2% | 34.8% |
| 23,233 | LAMOILLE | 12,103 | 7,124 | 4,532 | 447 | 2,592 R | 58.9% | 37.4% | 61.1% | 38.9% |
| 28,226 | ORANGE | 14,782 | 8,648 | 5,657 | 477 | 2,991 R | 58.5% | 38.3% | 60.5% | 39.5% |
| 26,277 | ORLEANS | 12,188 | 7,709 | 4,075 | 404 | 3,634 R | 63.3% | 33.4% | 65.4% | 34.6% |
| 63,400 | RUTLAND | 30,730 | 19,821 | 9,951 | 958 | 9,870 R | 64.5% | 32.4% | 66.6% | 33.4% |
| 58,039 | WASHINGTON | 31,250 | 17,398 | 13,010 | 842 | 4,388 R | 55.7% | 41.6% | 57.2% | 42.8% |
| 44,216 | WINDHAM | 22,878 | 9,747 | 11,886 | 1,245 | 2,139 D | 42.6% | 52.0% | 45.1% | 54.9% |
| 57,418 | WINDSOR | 30,379 | 16,921 | 12,284 | 1,174 | 4,637 R | 55.7% | 40.4% | 57.9% | 42.1% |
| 608,827 | TOTAL | 309,285 | 181,540 | 117,327 | 10,418 | 64,213 R | 58.7% | 37.9% | 60.7% | 39.3% |
| | City/Town | | | | | | | | | |
| 9,291 | BARRE CITY | 3,810 | 2,396 | 1,309 | 105 | 1,087 R | 62.9% | 34.4% | 64.7% | 35.3% |
| 7,602 | BARRE TOWN | 4,188 | 3,036 | 1,092 | 60 | 1,944 R | 72.5% | 26.1% | 73.5% | 26.5% |
| 15,737 | BENNINGTON | 6,721 | 3,746 | 2,588 | 387 | 1,158 R | 55.7% | 38.5% | 59.1% | 40.9% |
| 12,005 | BRATTLEBORO | 5,952 | 2,085 | 3,554 | 313 | 1,469 D | 35.0% | 59.7% | 37.0% | 63.0% |
| 38,889 | BURLINGTON | 18,849 | 7,759 | 10,139 | 951 | 2,380 D | 41.2% | 53.8% | 43.4% | 56.6% |
| 16,986 | COLCHESTER | 7,620 | 5,071 | 2,356 | 193 | 2,715 R | 66.5% | 30.9% | 68.3% | 31.7% |
| 4,604 | DERBY | 2,138 | 1,422 | 663 | 53 | 759 R | 66.5% | 31.0% | 68.2% | 31.8% |
| 18,626 | ESSEX | 10,218 | 7,054 | 2,961 | 203 | 4,093 R | 69.0% | 29.0% | 70.4% | 29.6% |
| 10,367 | HARTFORD | 4,787 | 2,774 | 1,873 | 140 | 901 R | 57.9% | 39.1% | 59.7% | 40.3% |
| 5,015 | JERICHO | 2,968 | 1,847 | 1,044 | 77 | 803 R | 62.2% | 35.2% | 63.9% | 36.1% |
| 5,448 | LYNDON | 2,201 | 1,500 | 625 | 76 | 875 R | 68.2% | 28.4% | 70.6% | 29.4% |
| 4,180 | MANCHESTER | 2,366 | 1,567 | 726 | 73 | 841 R | 66.2% | 30.7% | 68.3% | 31.7% |
| 8,183 | MIDDLEBURY | 3,347 | 1,925 | 1,363 | 59 | 562 R | 57.5% | 40.7% | 58.5% | 41.5% |
| 9,479 | MILTON | 4,442 | 3,225 | 1,136 | 81 | 2,089 R | 72.6% | 25.6% | 74.0% | 26.0% |
| 8,035 | MONTPELIER | 4,683 | 1,933 | 2,613 | 137 | 680 D | 41.3% | 55.8% | 42.5% | 57.5% |
| 5,139 | MORRISTOWN | 2,464 | 1,479 | 916 | 69 | 563 R | 60.0% | 37.2% | 61.8% | 38.2% |
| 5,791 | NORTHFIELD | 2,332 | 1,551 | 721 | 60 | 830 R | 66.5% | 30.9% | 68.3% | 31.7% |
| 4,853 | RANDOLPH | 2,319 | 1,378 | 868 | 73 | 510 R | 59.4% | 37.4% | 61.4% | 38.6% |
| 4,090 | RICHMOND | 2,411 | 1,413 | 929 | 69 | 484 R | 58.6% | 38.5% | 60.3% | 39.7% |
| 5,309 | ROCKINGHAM | 2,411 | 1,019 | 1,234 | 158 | 215 D | 42.3% | 51.2% | 45.2% | 54.8% |
| 17,292 | RUTLAND CITY | 7,523 | 4,729 | 2,582 | 212 | 2,147 R | 62.9% | 34.3% | 64.7% | 35.3% |
| 4,038 | RUTLAND TOWN | 2,442 | 1,814 | 589 | 39 | 1,225 R | 74.3% | 24.1% | 75.5% | 24.5% |
| 6,944 | SHELBURNE | 4,322 | 2,596 | 1,646 | 80 | 950 R | 60.1% | 38.1% | 61.2% | 38.8% |
| 15,814 | SOUTH BURLINGTON | 8,900 | 5,560 | 3,161 | 179 | 2,399 R | 62.5% | 35.5% | 63.8% | 36.2% |
| 9,078 | SPRINGFIELD | 4,435 | 2,578 | 1,652 | 205 | 926 R | 58.1% | 37.2% | 60.9% | 39.1% |
| 7,650 | ST. ALBANS CITY | 2,694 | 1,720 | 895 | 79 | 825 R | 63.8% | 33.2% | 65.8% | 34.2% |
| 5,086 | ST. ALBANS TOWN | 2,571 | 1,900 | 621 | 50 | 1,279 R | 73.9% | 24.2% | 75.4% | 24.6% |
| 7,571 | ST. JOHNSBURY | 3,098 | 2,072 | 942 | 84 | 1,130 R | 66.9% | 30.4% | 68.7% | 31.3% |
| 2,548 | SWANTON | 2,522 | 1,742 | 741 | 39 | 1,001 R | 69.1% | 29.4% | 70.2% | 29.8% |
| 4,915 | WATERBURY | 2,891 | 1,726 | 1,092 | 73 | 634 R | 59.7% | 37.8% | 61.2% | 38.8% |
| 7,650 | WILLISTON | 4,928 | 3,386 | 1,454 | 88 | 1,932 R | 68.7% | 29.5% | 70.0% | 30.0% |
| 6,561 | WINOOSKI | 2,522 | 1,301 | 1,140 | 81 | 161 R | 51.6% | 45.2% | 53.3% | 46.7% |
| 3,232 | WOODSTOCK | 1,979 | 1,127 | 795 | 57 | 332 R | 56.9% | 40.2% | 58.6% | 41.4% |

# VERMONT

## SENATOR 2004

| 2000 Census Population | County | Total Vote | Republican | Democratic | Other | Rep.-Dem. Plurality | Percentage Total Vote Rep. | Dem. | Major Vote Rep. | Dem. |
|---|---|---|---|---|---|---|---|---|---|---|
| 35,974 | ADDISON | 18,305 | 4,372 | 13,243 | 690 | 8,871 D | 23.9% | 72.3% | 24.8% | 75.2% |
| 36,994 | BENNINGTON | 18,571 | 5,136 | 12,179 | 1,256 | 7,043 D | 27.7% | 65.6% | 29.7% | 70.3% |
| 29,702 | CALEDONIA | 13,966 | 4,268 | 9,030 | 668 | 4,762 D | 30.6% | 64.7% | 32.1% | 67.9% |
| 146,571 | CHITTENDEN | 76,693 | 16,290 | 57,688 | 2,715 | 41,398 D | 21.2% | 75.2% | 22.0% | 78.0% |
| 6,459 | ESSEX | 2,831 | 923 | 1,697 | 211 | 774 D | 32.6% | 59.9% | 35.2% | 64.8% |
| 45,417 | FRANKLIN | 19,706 | 4,693 | 14,304 | 709 | 9,611 D | 23.8% | 72.6% | 24.7% | 75.3% |
| 6,901 | GRAND ISLE | 4,015 | 1,008 | 2,868 | 139 | 1,860 D | 25.1% | 71.4% | 26.0% | 74.0% |
| 23,233 | LAMOILLE | 12,001 | 2,786 | 8,620 | 595 | 5,834 D | 23.2% | 71.8% | 24.4% | 75.6% |
| 28,226 | ORANGE | 14,614 | 4,001 | 9,883 | 730 | 5,882 D | 27.4% | 67.6% | 28.8% | 71.2% |
| 26,277 | ORLEANS | 12,069 | 3,135 | 8,430 | 504 | 5,295 D | 26.0% | 69.8% | 27.1% | 72.9% |
| 63,400 | RUTLAND | 30,458 | 9,812 | 19,175 | 1,471 | 9,363 D | 32.2% | 63.0% | 33.8% | 66.2% |
| 58,039 | WASHINGTON | 31,076 | 6,814 | 23,025 | 1,237 | 16,211 D | 21.9% | 74.1% | 22.8% | 77.2% |
| 44,216 | WINDHAM | 22,704 | 4,954 | 16,085 | 1,665 | 11,131 D | 21.8% | 70.8% | 23.5% | 76.5% |
| 57,418 | WINDSOR | 30,199 | 7,206 | 20,745 | 2,248 | 13,539 D | 23.9% | 68.7% | 25.8% | 74.2% |
| 608,827 | TOTAL | 307,208 | 75,398 | 216,972 | 14,838 | 141,574 D | 24.5% | 70.6% | 25.8% | 74.2% |

| 2000 Census Population | City/Town | Total Vote | Republican | Democratic | Other | Rep.-Dem. Plurality | Total Vote Rep. | Dem. | Major Vote Rep. | Dem. |
|---|---|---|---|---|---|---|---|---|---|---|
| 9,291 | BARRE CITY | 3,774 | 1,002 | 2,638 | 134 | 1,636 D | 26.6% | 69.9% | 27.5% | 72.5% |
| 7,602 | BARRE TOWN | 4,172 | 1,373 | 2,679 | 120 | 1,306 D | 32.9% | 64.2% | 33.9% | 66.1% |
| 15,737 | BENNINGTON | 6,678 | 1,480 | 4,712 | 486 | 3,232 D | 22.2% | 70.6% | 23.9% | 76.1% |
| 12,005 | BRATTLEBORO | 5,942 | 956 | 4,602 | 384 | 3,646 D | 16.1% | 77.4% | 17.2% | 82.8% |
| 38,889 | BURLINGTON | 18,860 | 2,569 | 15,078 | 1,213 | 12,509 D | 13.6% | 79.9% | 14.6% | 85.4% |
| 16,986 | COLCHESTER | 7,602 | 1,825 | 5,574 | 203 | 3,749 D | 24.0% | 73.3% | 24.7% | 75.3% |
| 4,604 | DERBY | 2,137 | 575 | 1,498 | 64 | 923 D | 26.9% | 70.1% | 27.7% | 72.3% |
| 18,626 | ESSEX | 10,189 | 2,707 | 7,257 | 225 | 4,550 D | 26.6% | 71.2% | 27.2% | 72.8% |
| 10,367 | HARTFORD | 4,798 | 1,173 | 3,380 | 245 | 2,207 D | 24.4% | 70.4% | 25.8% | 74.2% |
| 5,015 | JERICHO | 2,974 | 759 | 2,141 | 74 | 1,382 D | 25.5% | 72.0% | 26.2% | 73.8% |
| 5,448 | LYNDON | 2,187 | 712 | 1,380 | 95 | 668 D | 32.6% | 63.1% | 34.0% | 66.0% |
| 4,180 | MANCHESTER | 2,331 | 831 | 1,372 | 128 | 541 D | 35.6% | 58.9% | 37.7% | 62.3% |
| 8,183 | MIDDLEBURY | 3,340 | 628 | 2,612 | 100 | 1,984 D | 18.8% | 78.2% | 19.4% | 80.6% |
| 9,479 | MILTON | 4,408 | 1,308 | 2,985 | 115 | 1,677 D | 29.7% | 67.7% | 30.5% | 69.5% |
| 8,035 | MONTPELIER | 4,672 | 652 | 3,814 | 206 | 3,162 D | 14.0% | 81.6% | 14.6% | 85.4% |
| 5,139 | MORRISTOWN | 2,452 | 546 | 1,803 | 103 | 1,257 D | 22.3% | 73.5% | 23.2% | 76.8% |
| 5,791 | NORTHFIELD | 2,309 | 536 | 1,686 | 87 | 1,150 D | 23.2% | 73.0% | 24.1% | 75.9% |
| 4,853 | RANDOLPH | 2,308 | 579 | 1,652 | 77 | 1,073 D | 25.1% | 71.6% | 26.0% | 74.0% |
| 4,090 | RICHMOND | 2,409 | 523 | 1,827 | 59 | 1,304 D | 21.7% | 75.8% | 22.3% | 77.7% |
| 5,309 | ROCKINGHAM | 2,405 | 420 | 1,770 | 215 | 1,350 D | 17.5% | 73.6% | 19.2% | 80.8% |
| 17,292 | RUTLAND CITY | 7,483 | 2,179 | 4,973 | 331 | 2,794 D | 29.1% | 66.5% | 30.5% | 69.5% |
| 4,038 | RUTLAND TOWN | 2,425 | 984 | 1,378 | 63 | 394 D | 40.6% | 56.8% | 41.7% | 58.3% |
| 6,944 | SHELBURNE | 4,322 | 939 | 3,279 | 104 | 2,340 D | 21.7% | 75.9% | 22.3% | 77.7% |
| 15,814 | SOUTH BURLINGTON | 8,881 | 1,961 | 6,727 | 193 | 4,766 D | 22.1% | 75.7% | 22.6% | 77.4% |
| 9,078 | SPRINGFIELD | 4,439 | 975 | 2,839 | 625 | 1,864 D | 22.0% | 64.0% | 25.6% | 74.4% |
| 7,650 | ST. ALBANS CITY | 2,684 | 519 | 2,078 | 87 | 1,559 D | 19.3% | 77.4% | 20.0% | 80.0% |
| 5,086 | ST. ALBANS TOWN | 2,549 | 632 | 1,843 | 74 | 1,211 D | 24.8% | 72.3% | 25.5% | 74.5% |
| 7,571 | ST. JOHNSBURY | 3,076 | 977 | 1,968 | 131 | 991 D | 31.8% | 64.0% | 33.2% | 66.8% |
| 2,548 | SWANTON | 2,502 | 613 | 1,839 | 50 | 1,226 D | 24.5% | 73.5% | 25.0% | 75.0% |
| 4,915 | WATERBURY | 2,885 | 539 | 2,242 | 104 | 1,703 D | 18.7% | 77.7% | 19.4% | 80.6% |
| 7,650 | WILLISTON | 4,914 | 1,266 | 3,547 | 101 | 2,281 D | 25.8% | 72.2% | 26.3% | 73.7% |
| 6,561 | WINOOSKI | 2,492 | 444 | 1,929 | 119 | 1,485 D | 17.8% | 77.4% | 18.7% | 81.3% |
| 3,232 | WOODSTOCK | 1,976 | 535 | 1,364 | 77 | 829 D | 27.1% | 69.0% | 28.2% | 71.8% |

# VERMONT

## HOUSE OF REPRESENTATIVES

| | | Total | Republican | | Democratic | | Other | | Percentage | | | |
| | | | | | | | | | Total Vote | | Major Vote | |
| CD | Year | Vote | Vote | Candidate | Vote | Candidate | Vote | Plurallty | Rep. | Dem. | Rep. | Dem. |
|---|---|---|---|---|---|---|---|---|---|---|---|---|
| AL | 2004 | 305,008 | 74,271 | Parke, Greg | 21,684 | Drown, Larry | 209,053 | 131,503 I | 24.4% | 67.5% (I) | | |
| AL | 2002 | 225,476 | 72,813 | Meub, William "Bill" | | | 152,663 | 72,067 I | 32.3% | 64.3% (I) | | |
| AL | 2000 | 283,366 | 51,977 | Kerin, Karen Ann | 14,918 | #Diamondstone, Pete | 216,471 | 144,141 I | 18.3% | 69.2% (I) | | |
| AL | 1998 | 215,133 | 70,740 | Candon, Mark | | | 144,393 | 65,663 I | 32.9% | 63.4% (I) | | |
| AL | 1996 | 254,706 | 83,021 | Sweetser, Susan W. | 23,830 | Long, Jack | 147,855 | 57,657 I | 32.6% | 55.2% (I) | | |
| AL | 1994 | 211,449 | 98,523 | Carroll, John | | | 112,926 | 6,979 I | 46.6% | 49.9% (I) | | |
| AL | 1992 | 281,626 | 86,901 | Philbin, Timothy | 22,279 | Young, Lewis E. | 172,446 | 75,823 I | 30.9% | 57.8% (I) | | |
| AL | 1990 | 209,856 | 82,938 | Smith, Peter* | 6,315 | Sandoval, Dolores | 120,603 | 34,584 I | 39.5% | 56.0% (I) | | |
| AL | 1988 | 240,131 | 98,937 | Smith, Peter | 45,330 | Poirier, Paul N. | 95,864 | 53,607 R | 41.2% | 18.9% | 68.6% | 31.4% |
| AL | 1986 | 188,954 | 168,403 | #Jeffords, James M.* | | | 20,551 | 168,403 R | 89.1% | | 100.0% | |
| AL | 1984 | 226,297 | 148,025 | Jeffords, James M.* | 60,360 | Pollina, Anthony | 17,912 | 87,665 R | 65.4% | 26.7% | 71.0% | 29.0% |
| AL | 1982 | 164,951 | 114,191 | Jeffords, James M.* | 38,296 | Kaplan, Mark A. | 12,464 | 75,895 R | 69.2% | 23.2% | 74.9% | 25.1% |
| AL | 1980 | 194,697 | 154,274 | Jeffords, James M.* | | | 40,423 | 154,274 R | 79.2% | | 100.0% | |
| AL | 1978 | 120,502 | 90,688 | Jeffords, James M.* | 23,228 | Dietz, S. Marie | 6,586 | 67,460 R | 75.3% | 19.3% | 79.6% | 20.4% |
| AL | 1976 | 184,783 | 124,458 | Jeffords, James M.* | 60,202 | #Burgess, John A. | 123 | 64,256 R | 67.4% | 32.6% | 67.4% | 32.6% |
| AL | 1974 | 140,899 | 74,561 | Jeffords, James M. | 56,342 | #Cain, Francis J. | 9,996 | 18,219 R | 52.9% | 40.0% | 57.0% | 43.0% |
| AL | 1972 | 186,028 | 120,924 | Mallary, Richard W. | 65,062 | Meyer, William H. | 42 | 55,862 R | 65.0% | 35.0% | 65.0% | 35.0% |
| AL | 1970 | 152,557 | 103,806 | Stafford, Robert T.* | 44,415 | O'Shea, Bernard G. | 4,336 | 59,391 R | 68.0% | 29.1% | 70.0% | 30.0% |
| AL | 1968 | 157,133 | 156,956 | #Stafford, Robert T.* | | | 177 | 156,956 R | 99.9% | | 100.0% | |
| AL | 1966 | 135,748 | 89,097 | Stafford, Robert T.* | 46,643 | Ryan, William J. | 8 | 42,454 R | 65.6% | 34.4% | 65.6% | 34.4% |
| AL | 1964 | 163,452 | 92,252 | Stafford, Robert T.* | 71,193 | O'Shea, Bernard G. | 7 | 21,059 R | 56.4% | 43.6% | 56.4% | 43.6% |
| AL | 1962 | 121,381 | 68,822 | Stafford, Robert T.* | 52,535 | Raynolds, Harold | 24 | 16,287 R | 56.7% | 43.3% | 56.7% | 43.3% |
| AL | 1960 | 166,035 | 94,905 | Stafford, Robert T. | 71,111 | Meyer, William H. | 19 | 23,794 R | 57.2% | 42.8% | 57.2% | 42.8% |
| AL | 1958 | 122,702 | 59,536 | Arthur, Harold J. | 63,131 | Meyer, William H. | 35 | 3,595 D | 48.5% | 51.5% | 48.5% | 51.5% |
| AL | 1956 | 154,536 | 103,736 | Prouty, Winston L.* | 50,797 | St. Amour, Camille | 3 | 52,939 R | 67.1% | 32.9% | 67.1% | 32.9% |
| AL | 1954 | 114,289 | 70,143 | Prouty, Winston L.* | 44,141 | Baylan, John J. | 5 | 26,002 R | 61.4% | 38.6% | 61.4% | 38.6% |
| AL | 1952 | 153,060 | 109,871 | Prouty, Winston L.* | 43,187 | Comings, Herbert B. | 2 | 66,684 R | 71.8% | 28.2% | 71.8% | 28.2% |
| AL | 1950 | 88,851 | 65,248 | Prouty, Winston L. | 22,709 | Comings, Herbert B. | 894 | 42,539 R | 73.4% | 25.6% | 74.2% | 25.8% |
| AL | 1948 | 121,968 | 74,076 | Plumley, Charles A.* | 47,767 | Ready, Robert W. | 125 | 26,309 R | 60.7% | 39.2% | 60.8% | 39.2% |
| AL | 1946 | 73,066 | 46,985 | Plumley, Charles A.* | 26,056 | Caldbeck, Matthew J. | 25 | 20,929 R | 64.3% | 35.7% | 64.3% | 35.7% |

An asterisk (*) denotes incumbent. Seat was won in 1990, 1992,1994, 1996, 1998, 2000, 2002, and 2004 by Bernard Sanders, an Independent. Other vote for those years includes the total for Sanders and other independent and minor party candidates. However, plurality and percent of total vote figures since 1990 compare the Republican candidate and Sanders only. For earlier years the comparison is between the Republican and Democratic candidates. A pound sign (#) indicates that a candidate received votes from another party.

Democratic candidates since 1990 have received the following shares of the total vote: 2004 - Larry Drown, 7.1 percent; 2000 - Pete Diamondstone, 5.3 percent; 1996 - Jack Long, 9.4 percent; 1992 - Lewis E. Young, 7.9 percent; 1990 - Dolores Sandoval, 3.0 percent.

# VERMONT

## GENERAL AND PRIMARY ELECTIONS

## 2002 GENERAL ELECTIONS

**President**    Other vote was 4,494 Independent (Ralph Nader); 1,102 Libertarian (Michael Badnarik); 265 Liberty Union (John Parker); 244 Socialist Workers (Roger Calero); 957 write-in.

**Governor**    Other vote was 4,221 Marijuana (Cris Ericson); 2,431 Independent (Patricia Hejny); 2,263 Libertarian (Hardy Machia); 1,298 Liberty Union (Peter Diamondstone); 205 write-in.

**Senator**    Other vote was 6,486 Marijuana (Cris Ericson); 3,999 Vermont Green (Craig Hill); 3,300 Independent (Keith Stern); 879 Liberty Union (Ben Mitchell); 174 write-in.

**House**    Other vote was:

  At Large    205,774 Independent (Bernard Sanders); 3,018 Liberty Union (Jane Newton); 261 write-in. (Sanders was elected with 67.5 percent of the total vote.)

# VERMONT

## GENERAL AND PRIMARY ELECTIONS

## 2004 PRIMARY ELECTIONS

**Primary**　March 2, 2004 (President)　　**Registration**　420,554　No Party Registration
September 14, 2004 (Congress)　(as of Sept. 14, 2004)

**Primary Type**　Open—Any registered voter could participate in the primary of any recognized party.

Note:　An asterisk (*) denotes incumbent.

| | REPUBLICAN PRIMARIES | | | DEMOCRATIC PRIMARIES | | |
|---|---|---|---|---|---|---|
| President | George W. Bush* | 25,415 | 96.7% | Howard Dean | 44,393 | 53.6% |
| | Write-in | 874 | 3.3% | John Kerry | 26,171 | 31.6% |
| | | | | John Edwards (write-in) | 5,113 | 6.2% |
| | | | | Dennis J. Kucinich | 3,396 | 4.1% |
| | | | | Wesley Clark | 2,749 | 3.3% |
| | | | | Lyndon H. LaRouche Jr. | 386 | 0.5% |
| | | | | Write-in | 673 | 0.8% |
| | TOTAL | 26,289 | | TOTAL | 82,881 | |
| Governor | Jim Douglas* | 15,806 | 98.7% | Peter Clavelle | 23,218 | 94.6% |
| | Write-in | 202 | 1.3% | Write-in | 1,313 | 5.4% |
| | TOTAL | 16,008 | | TOTAL | 24,531 | |
| Senator | Jack McMullen | 9,591 | 67.7% | Patrick J. Leahy* | 27,459 | 94.3% |
| | Peter D. Moss | 2,058 | 14.5% | Craig Hill | 1,573 | 5.4% |
| | Ben Mitchell | 1,715 | 12.1% | Write-in | 81 | 0.3% |
| | Write-in | 806 | 5.7% | | | |
| | TOTAL | 14,170 | | TOTAL | 29,113 | |
| House At Large | Greg Parke | 12,660 | 98.0% | Larry Drown | 14,870 | 86.1% |
| | Write-in | 255 | 2.0% | Bernard Sanders* (write-in) | 1,878 | 10.9% |
| | | | | Write-in | 515 | 3.0% |
| | TOTAL | 12,915 | | TOTAL | 17,263 | |

# VIRGINIA

## GOVERNOR
Mark Warner (D). Elected 2001 to a four-year term.

## SENATORS (2 Republicans)
George Allen (R). Elected 2000 to a six-year term.

John W. Warner (R). Reelected 2002 to a six-year term. Previously elected 1996, 1990, 1984, 1978.

## REPRESENTATIVES (8 Republicans, 3 Democrats)
1. Jo Ann Davis (R)
2. Thelma Drake (R)
3. Robert C. Scott (D)
4. J. Randy Forbes (R)
5. Virgil H. Goode Jr. (R)
6. Robert W. Goodlatte (R)
7. Eric Cantor (R)
8. James P. Moran (D)
9. Rick Boucher (D)
10. Frank R. Wolf (R)
11. Thomas M. Davis III (R)

## POSTWAR VOTE FOR PRESIDENT

| Year | Total Vote | Republican Vote | Candidate | Democratic Vote | Candidate | Other Vote | Plurality | Total Vote Rep. | Total Vote Dem. | Major Vote Rep. | Major Vote Dem. |
|------|-----------|------|-----------|------|-----------|------|-----------|------|------|------|------|
| 2004 | 3,198,367 | 1,716,959 | Bush, George W. | 1,454,742 | Kerry, John | 26,666 | 262,217 R | 53.7% | 45.5% | 54.1% | 45.9% |
| 2000** | 2,739,447 | 1,437,490 | Bush, George W. | 1,217,290 | Gore, Al | 84,667 | 220,200 R | 52.5% | 44.4% | 54.1% | 45.9% |
| 1996** | 2,416,642 | 1,138,350 | Dole, Bob | 1,091,060 | Clinton, Bill | 187,232 | 47,290 R | 47.1% | 45.1% | 51.1% | 48.9% |
| 1992** | 2,558,665 | 1,150,517 | Bush, George | 1,038,650 | Clinton, Bill | 369,498 | 111,867 R | 45.0% | 40.6% | 52.6% | 47.4% |
| 1988 | 2,191,609 | 1,309,162 | Bush, George | 859,799 | Dukakis, Michael S. | 22,648 | 449,363 R | 59.7% | 39.2% | 60.4% | 39.6% |
| 1984 | 2,146,635 | 1,337,078 | Reagan, Ronald | 796,250 | Mondale, Walter F. | 13,307 | 540,828 R | 62.3% | 37.1% | 62.7% | 37.3% |
| 1980** | 1,866,032 | 989,609 | Reagan, Ronald | 752,174 | Carter, Jimmy | 124,249 | 237,435 R | 53.0% | 40.3% | 56.8% | 43.2% |
| 1976 | 1,697,094 | 836,554 | Ford, Gerald R. | 813,896 | Carter, Jimmy | 46,644 | 22,658 R | 49.3% | 48.0% | 50.7% | 49.3% |
| 1972 | 1,457,019 | 988,493 | Nixon, Richard M. | 438,887 | McGovern, George S. | 29,639 | 549,606 R | 67.8% | 30.1% | 69.3% | 30.7% |
| 1968** | 1,361,491 | 590,319 | Nixon, Richard M. | 442,387 | Humphrey, Hubert H. | 328,785 | 147,932 R | 43.4% | 32.5% | 57.2% | 42.8% |
| 1964 | 1,042,267 | 481,334 | Goldwater, Barry M. | 558,038 | Johnson, Lyndon B. | 2,895 | 76,704 D | 46.2% | 53.5% | 46.3% | 53.7% |
| 1960 | 771,449 | 404,521 | Nixon, Richard M. | 362,327 | Kennedy, John F. | 4,601 | 42,194 R | 52.4% | 47.0% | 52.8% | 47.2% |
| 1956 | 697,978 | 386,459 | Eisenhower, Dwight D. | 267,760 | Stevenson, Adlai E. | 43,759 | 118,699 R | 55.4% | 38.4% | 59.1% | 40.9% |
| 1952 | 619,689 | 349,037 | Eisenhower, Dwight D. | 268,677 | Stevenson, Adlai E. | 1,975 | 80,360 R | 56.3% | 43.4% | 56.5% | 43.5% |
| 1948** | 419,256 | 172,070 | Dewey, Thomas E. | 200,786 | Truman, Harry S. | 46,400 | 28,716 D | 41.0% | 47.9% | 46.1% | 53.9% |

In past elections, the other vote included: 2000 - 59,398 Green (Ralph Nader); 1996 - 159,861 Reform (Ross Perot); 1992 - 348,639 Independent (Perot); 1980 - 95,418 Independent (John Anderson); 1968 - 321,833 American Independent (George Wallace); 1948 - 43,393 States' Rights (Strom Thurmond).

# VIRGINIA

## POSTWAR VOTE FOR GOVERNOR

| Year | Total Vote | Republican Vote | Republican Candidate | Democratic Vote | Democratic Candidate | Other Vote | Plurality | Percentage Total Vote Rep. | Percentage Total Vote Dem. | Percentage Major Vote Rep. | Percentage Major Vote Dem. |
|---|---|---|---|---|---|---|---|---|---|---|---|
| 2001 | 1,886,721 | 887,234 | Earley, Mark L. | 984,177 | Warner, Mark | 15,310 | 96,943 D | 47.0% | 52.2% | 47.4% | 52.6% |
| 1997 | 1,736,314 | 969,062 | Gilmore, James S., III | 738,971 | Beyer, Donald S., Jr. | 28,281 | 230,091 R | 55.8% | 42.6% | 56.7% | 43.3% |
| 1993 | 1,793,916 | 1,045,319 | Allen, George | 733,527 | Terry, Mary Sue | 15,070 | 311,792 R | 58.3% | 40.9% | 58.8% | 41.2% |
| 1989 | 1,789,078 | 890,195 | Coleman, J. Marshall | 896,936 | Wilder, L. Douglas | 1,947 | 6,741 D | 49.8% | 50.1% | 49.8% | 50.2% |
| 1985 | 1,343,243 | 601,652 | Durrette, Wyatt B. | 741,438 | Baliles, Gerald L. | 153 | 139,786 D | 44.8% | 55.2% | 44.8% | 55.2% |
| 1981 | 1,420,611 | 659,398 | Coleman, J. Marshall | 760,357 | Robb, Charles S. | 856 | 100,959 D | 46.4% | 53.5% | 46.4% | 53.6% |
| 1977 | 1,250,940 | 699,302 | Dalton, John | 541,319 | Howell, Henry | 10,319 | 157,983 R | 55.9% | 43.3% | 56.4% | 43.6% |
| 1973** | 1,035,495 | 525,075 | Godwin, Mills E. | — | | 510,420 | 14,972 R | 50.7% | | 100.0% | |
| 1969 | 915,764 | 480,869 | Holton, Linwood | 415,695 | Battle, William C. | 19,200 | 65,174 R | 52.5% | 45.4% | 53.6% | 46.4% |
| 1965 | 562,789 | 212,207 | Holton, Linwood | 269,526 | Godwin, Mills E. | 81,056 | 57,319 D | 37.7% | 47.9% | 44.1% | 55.9% |
| 1961 | 394,490 | 142,567 | Pearson, H. Clyde | 251,861 | Harrison, Albertis | 62 | 109,294 D | 36.1% | 63.8% | 36.1% | 63.9% |
| 1957 | 517,655 | 188,628 | Dalton, Ted | 326,921 | Almond, J. Lindsay | 2,106 | 138,293 D | 36.4% | 63.2% | 36.6% | 63.4% |
| 1953 | 414,025 | 183,328 | Dalton, Ted | 226,998 | Stanley, Thomas B. | 3,699 | 43,670 D | 44.3% | 54.8% | 44.7% | 55.3% |
| 1949 | 262,350 | 71,991 | Johnson, Walter | 184,772 | Battle, John S. | 5,587 | 112,781 D | 27.4% | 70.4% | 28.0% | 72.0% |
| 1945 | 168,783 | 52,386 | Landreth, S. Floyd | 112,355 | Tuck, William M. | 4,042 | 59,969 D | 31.0% | 66.6% | 31.8% | 68.2% |

In past elections, the other vote included: 1973 - 510,103 Independent (Henry Howell). In that election the plurality reflects the difference between the Republican and Independent vote. In other elections, the plurality is the difference between the Republican and Democratic vote.

## POSTWAR VOTE FOR SENATOR

| Year | Total Vote | Republican Vote | Republican Candidate | Democratic Vote | Democratic Candidate | Other Vote | Plurality | Percentage Total Vote Rep. | Percentage Total Vote Dem. | Percentage Major Vote Rep. | Percentage Major Vote Dem. |
|---|---|---|---|---|---|---|---|---|---|---|---|
| 2002 | 1,489,422 | 1,229,894 | Warner, John W. | — | | 259,528 | 1,229,894 R | 82.6% | | 100.0% | |
| 2000 | 2,718,301 | 1,420,460 | Allen, George | 1,296,093 | Robb, Charles S. | 1,748 | 124,367 R | 52.3% | 47.7% | 52.3% | 47.7% |
| 1996 | 2,354,715 | 1,235,744 | Warner, John W. | 1,115,982 | Warner, Mark R. | 2,989 | 119,762 R | 52.5% | 47.4% | 52.5% | 47.5% |
| 1994** | 2,057,463 | 882,213 | North, Oliver L. | 938,376 | Robb, Charles S. | 236,874 | 56,163 D | 42.9% | 45.6% | 48.5% | 51.5% |
| 1990 | 1,083,690 | 876,782 | Warner, John W. | — | | 206,908 | 876,782 R | 80.9% | | 100.0% | |
| 1988 | 2,068,897 | 593,652 | Dawkins, Maurice A. | 1,474,086 | Robb, Charles S. | 1,159 | 880,434 D | 28.7% | 71.2% | 28.7% | 71.3% |
| 1984 | 2,007,487 | 1,406,194 | Warner, John W. | 601,142 | Harrison, Edythe C. | 151 | 805,052 R | 70.0% | 29.9% | 70.1% | 29.9% |
| 1982 | 1,415,622 | 724,571 | Trible, Paul | 690,839 | Davis, Richard | 212 | 33,732 R | 51.2% | 48.8% | 51.2% | 48.8% |
| 1978 | 1,222,256 | 613,232 | Warner, John W. | 608,511 | Miller, Andrew P. | 513 | 4,721 R | 50.2% | 49.8% | 50.2% | 49.8% |
| 1976** | 1,557,500 | | — | 596,009 | Zumwalt, Elmo R. | 961,491 | 294,769 I | | 38.3% | | 100.0% |
| 1972 | 1,396,268 | 718,337 | Scott, William L. | 643,963 | Spong, William B. | 33,968 | 74,374 R | 51.4% | 46.1% | 52.7% | 47.3% |
| 1970** | 946,751 | 145,031 | Garland, Ray | 295,057 | Rawlings, George C. | 506,663 | 211,576 I | 15.3% | 31.2% | 33.0% | 67.0% |
| 1966 | 733,879 | 245,681 | Ould, James P. | 429,855 | Spong, William B. | 58,343 | 184,174 D | 33.5% | 58.6% | 36.4% | 63.6% |
| 1966S | 729,839 | 272,804 | Traylor, Lawrence M. | 389,028 | Byrd, Harry Flood, Jr. | 68,007 | 116,224 D | 37.4% | 53.3% | 41.2% | 58.8% |
| 1964 | 928,363 | 176,624 | May, Richard A. | 592,260 | Byrd, Harry Flood | 159,479 | 415,636 D | 19.0% | 63.8% | 23.0% | 77.0% |
| 1960 | 622,820 | | — | 506,169 | Robertson, A. Willis | 116,651 | 506,169 D | | 81.3% | | 100.0% |
| 1958 | 457,640 | | — | 317,221 | Byrd, Harry Flood | 140,419 | 317,221 D | | 69.3% | | 100.0% |
| 1954 | 306,510 | | — | 244,844 | Robertson, A. Willis | 61,666 | 244,844 D | | 79.9% | | 100.0% |
| 1952 | 543,516 | | — | 398,677 | Byrd, Harry Flood | 144,839 | 398,677 D | | 73.4% | | 100.0% |
| 1948 | 386,178 | 118,546 | Woods, Robert | 253,865 | Robertson, A. Willis | 13,767 | 135,319 D | 30.7% | 65.7% | 31.8% | 68.2% |
| 1946 | 252,863 | 77,005 | Parsons, Lester S. | 163,960 | Byrd, Harry Flood | 11,898 | 86,955 D | 30.5% | 64.8% | 32.0% | 68.0% |
| 1946S | 248,962 | 72,253 | Woods, Robert | 169,680 | Robertson, A. Willis | 7,029 | 97,427 D | 29.0% | 68.2% | 29.9% | 70.1% |

In past elections, the other vote included: 1994 - 235,324 Independent (J. Marshall Coleman); 1976 - 890,778 Independent (Harry Flood Byrd Jr.), who won the election with 57.2 percent of the total vote; 1970 - 506,633 Independent (Harry Flood Byrd Jr.), who won the election with 53.5 percent of the total vote. In the 1970 and 1976 elections Byrd's plurality is listed over the Democratic candidate, who in each case finished second. In other elections the plurality is the difference between the Republican and Democratic vote. One each of the 1966 and 1946 elections was for a short term to fill a vacancy.

# VIRGINIA

Congressional districts first established for elections held in 2002
11 members

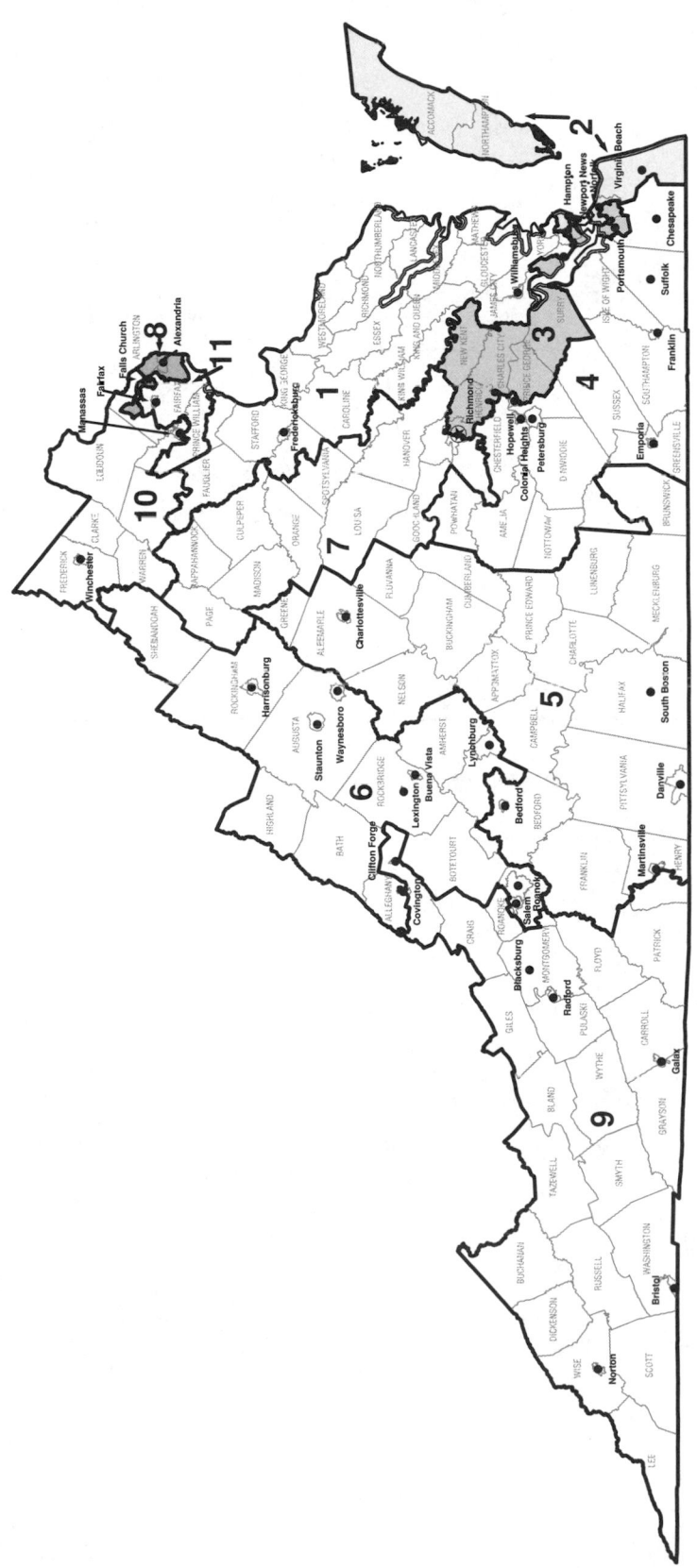

# VIRGINIA

## Northern Virginia Area

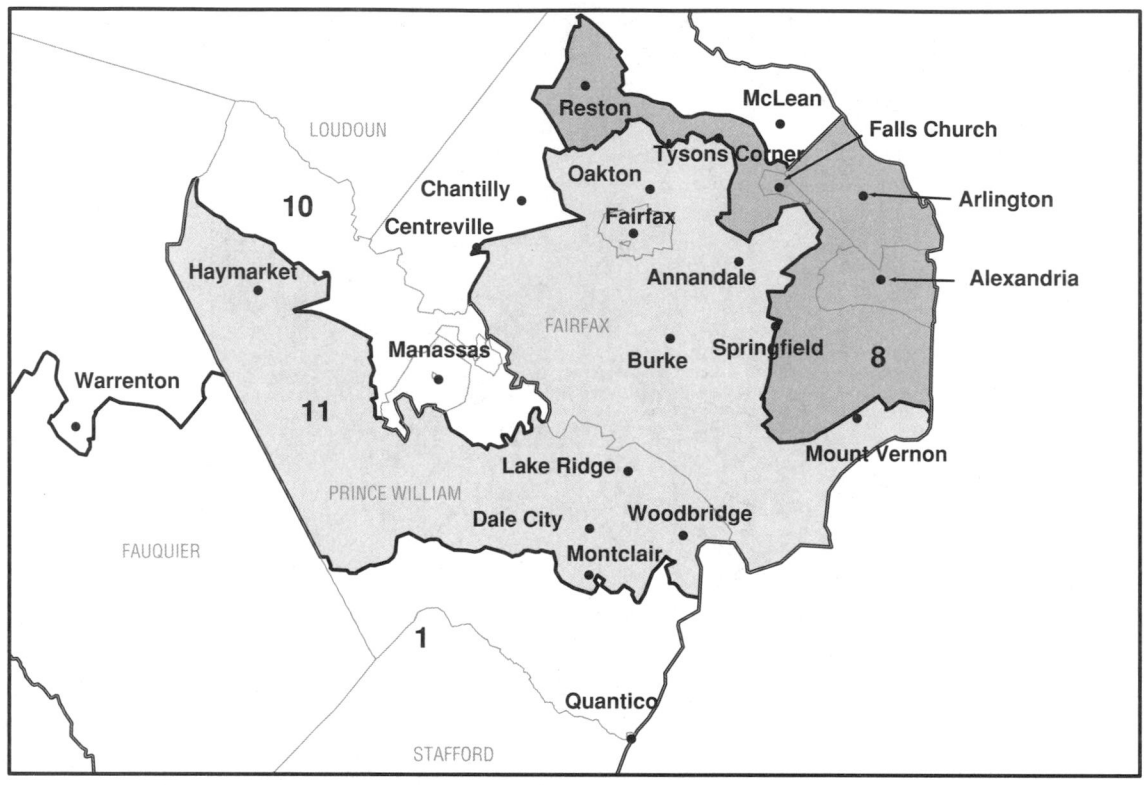

## Hampton Roads, Virginia Beach Area

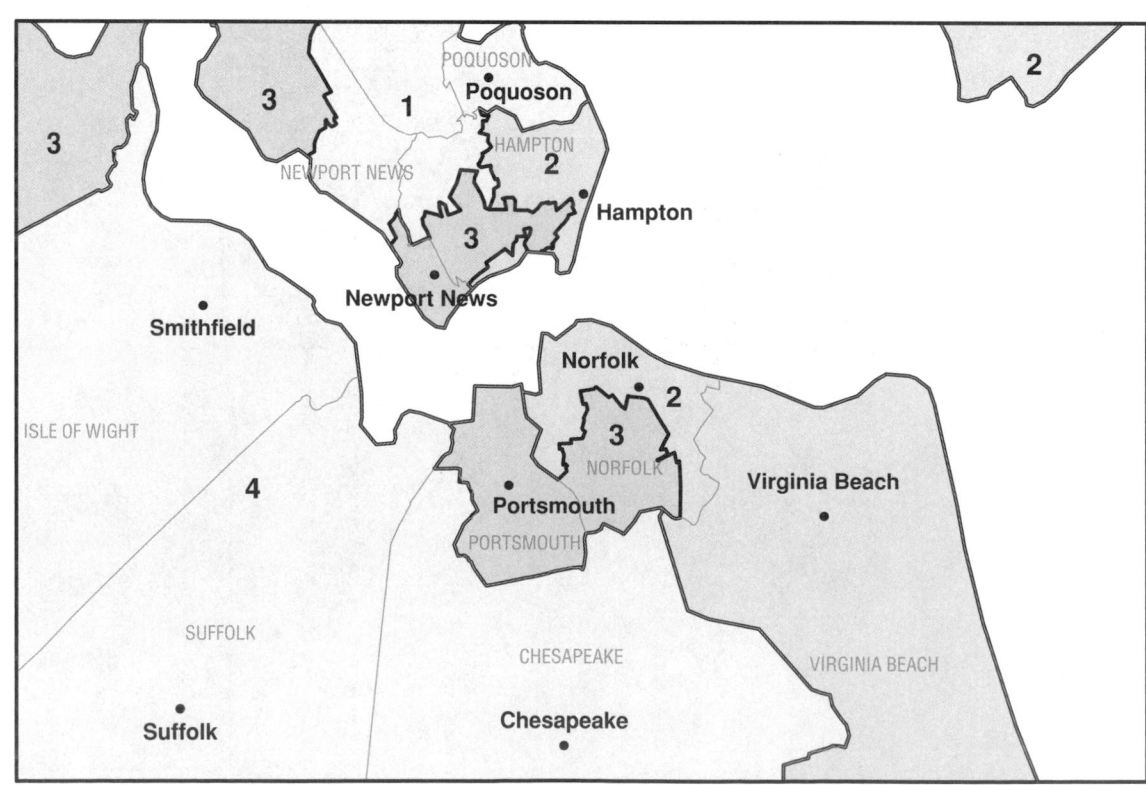

# VIRGINIA

## PRESIDENT 2004

| 2000 Census Population | County | Total Vote | Republican | Democratic | Other | Rep.-Dem. Plurality | Total Vote Rep. | Dem. | Major Vote Rep. | Dem. |
|---|---|---|---|---|---|---|---|---|---|---|
| 38,305 | ACCOMACK | 13,356 | 7,726 | 5,518 | 112 | 2,208 R | 57.8% | 41.3% | 58.3% | 41.7% |
| 79,236 | ALBEMARLE | 43,726 | 21,189 | 22,088 | 449 | 899 D | 48.5% | 50.5% | 49.0% | 51.0% |
| 17,215 | ALLEGHANY | 7,195 | 3,962 | 3,203 | 30 | 759 R | 55.1% | 44.5% | 55.3% | 44.7% |
| 11,400 | AMELIA | 5,397 | 3,499 | 1,862 | 36 | 1,637 R | 64.8% | 34.5% | 65.3% | 34.7% |
| 31,894 | AMHERST | 12,695 | 7,758 | 4,866 | 71 | 2,892 R | 61.1% | 38.3% | 61.5% | 38.5% |
| 13,705 | APPOMATTOX | 6,655 | 4,366 | 2,191 | 98 | 2,175 R | 65.6% | 32.9% | 66.6% | 33.4% |
| 189,453 | ARLINGTON | 94,650 | 29,635 | 63,987 | 1,028 | 34,352 D | 31.3% | 67.6% | 31.7% | 68.3% |
| 65,615 | AUGUSTA | 29,704 | 22,100 | 7,019 | 585 | 15,081 R | 74.4% | 23.6% | 75.9% | 24.1% |
| 5,048 | BATH | 2,282 | 1,432 | 828 | 22 | 604 R | 62.8% | 36.3% | 63.4% | 36.6% |
| 60,371 | BEDFORD COUNTY | 31,404 | 21,925 | 9,102 | 377 | 12,823 R | 69.8% | 29.0% | 70.7% | 29.3% |
| 6,871 | BLAND | 2,865 | 1,962 | 846 | 57 | 1,116 R | 68.5% | 29.5% | 69.9% | 30.1% |
| 30,496 | BOTETOURT | 15,797 | 10,865 | 4,801 | 131 | 6,064 R | 68.8% | 30.4% | 69.4% | 30.6% |
| 18,419 | BRUNSWICK | 6,926 | 2,852 | 4,062 | 12 | 1,210 D | 41.2% | 58.6% | 41.2% | 58.8% |
| 26,978 | BUCHANAN | 9,829 | 4,507 | 5,275 | 47 | 768 D | 45.9% | 53.7% | 46.1% | 53.9% |
| 15,623 | BUCKINGHAM | 6,027 | 3,185 | 2,789 | 53 | 396 R | 52.8% | 46.3% | 53.3% | 46.7% |
| 51,078 | CAMPBELL | 22,997 | 15,891 | 6,862 | 244 | 9,029 R | 69.1% | 29.8% | 69.8% | 30.2% |
| 22,121 | CAROLINE | 9,954 | 4,999 | 4,878 | 77 | 121 R | 50.2% | 49.0% | 50.6% | 49.4% |
| 29,245 | CARROLL | 12,128 | 8,173 | 3,888 | 67 | 4,285 R | 67.4% | 32.1% | 67.8% | 32.2% |
| 6,926 | CHARLES CITY | 3,439 | 1,254 | 2,155 | 30 | 901 D | 36.5% | 62.7% | 36.8% | 63.2% |
| 12,472 | CHARLOTTE | 5,438 | 3,166 | 2,223 | 49 | 943 R | 58.2% | 40.9% | 58.7% | 41.3% |
| 259,903 | CHESTERFIELD | 133,814 | 83,745 | 49,346 | 723 | 34,399 R | 62.6% | 36.9% | 62.9% | 37.1% |
| 12,652 | CLARKE | 6,505 | 3,741 | 2,699 | 65 | 1,042 R | 57.5% | 41.5% | 58.1% | 41.9% |
| 5,091 | CRAIG | 2,621 | 1,706 | 901 | 14 | 805 R | 65.1% | 34.4% | 65.4% | 34.6% |
| 34,262 | CULPEPER | 15,605 | 10,026 | 5,476 | 103 | 4,550 R | 64.2% | 35.1% | 64.7% | 35.3% |
| 9,017 | CUMBERLAND | 4,126 | 2,377 | 1,721 | 28 | 656 R | 57.6% | 41.7% | 58.0% | 42.0% |
| 16,395 | DICKENSON | 7,406 | 3,591 | 3,761 | 54 | 170 D | 48.5% | 50.8% | 48.8% | 51.2% |
| 24,533 | DINWIDDIE | 10,839 | 6,193 | 4,569 | 77 | 1,624 R | 57.1% | 42.2% | 57.5% | 42.5% |
| 9,989 | ESSEX | 4,344 | 2,304 | 2,007 | 33 | 297 R | 53.0% | 46.2% | 53.4% | 46.6% |
| 969,749 | FAIRFAX COUNTY | 461,379 | 211,980 | 245,671 | 3,728 | 33,691 D | 45.9% | 53.2% | 46.3% | 53.7% |
| 55,139 | FAUQUIER | 29,915 | 19,011 | 10,712 | 192 | 8,299 R | 63.6% | 35.8% | 64.0% | 36.0% |
| 13,874 | FLOYD | 6,734 | 4,162 | 2,488 | 84 | 1,674 R | 61.8% | 36.9% | 62.6% | 37.4% |
| 20,047 | FLUVANNA | 10,957 | 6,458 | 4,415 | 84 | 2,043 R | 58.9% | 40.3% | 59.4% | 40.6% |
| 47,286 | FRANKLIN COUNTY | 22,223 | 14,048 | 8,002 | 173 | 6,046 R | 63.2% | 36.0% | 63.7% | 36.3% |
| 59,209 | FREDERICK | 28,540 | 19,386 | 8,853 | 301 | 10,533 R | 67.9% | 31.0% | 68.6% | 31.4% |
| 16,657 | GILES | 7,498 | 4,320 | 3,047 | 131 | 1,273 R | 57.6% | 40.6% | 58.6% | 41.4% |
| 34,780 | GLOUCESTER | 16,333 | 11,084 | 5,105 | 144 | 5,979 R | 67.9% | 31.3% | 68.5% | 31.5% |
| 16,863 | GOOCHLAND | 10,338 | 6,668 | 3,583 | 87 | 3,085 R | 64.5% | 34.7% | 65.0% | 35.0% |
| 17,917 | GRAYSON | 7,137 | 4,655 | 2,430 | 52 | 2,225 R | 65.2% | 34.0% | 65.7% | 34.3% |
| 15,244 | GREENE | 6,939 | 4,570 | 2,240 | 129 | 2,330 R | 65.9% | 32.3% | 67.1% | 32.9% |
| 11,560 | GREENSVILLE | 4,258 | 1,732 | 2,514 | 12 | 782 D | 40.7% | 59.0% | 40.8% | 59.2% |
| 37,355 | HALIFAX | 14,656 | 8,363 | 6,220 | 73 | 2,143 R | 57.1% | 42.4% | 57.3% | 42.7% |
| 86,320 | HANOVER | 49,611 | 35,404 | 13,941 | 266 | 21,463 R | 71.4% | 28.1% | 71.7% | 28.3% |
| 262,300 | HENRICO | 133,418 | 71,809 | 60,864 | 745 | 10,945 R | 53.8% | 45.6% | 54.1% | 45.9% |
| 57,930 | HENRY | 23,458 | 13,358 | 9,851 | 249 | 3,507 R | 56.9% | 42.0% | 57.6% | 42.4% |
| 2,536 | HIGHLAND | 1,520 | 982 | 522 | 16 | 460 R | 64.6% | 34.3% | 65.3% | 34.7% |
| 29,728 | ISLE OF WIGHT | 15,871 | 9,929 | 5,871 | 71 | 4,058 R | 62.6% | 37.0% | 62.8% | 37.2% |
| 48,102 | JAMES CITY | 31,090 | 18,949 | 11,934 | 207 | 7,015 R | 60.9% | 38.4% | 61.4% | 38.6% |
| 6,630 | KING AND QUEEN | 3,286 | 1,737 | 1,506 | 43 | 231 R | 52.9% | 45.8% | 53.6% | 46.4% |
| 16,803 | KING GEORGE | 7,921 | 5,124 | 2,739 | 58 | 2,385 R | 64.7% | 34.6% | 65.2% | 34.8% |
| 13,146 | KING WILLIAM | 6,872 | 4,397 | 2,436 | 39 | 1,961 R | 64.0% | 35.4% | 64.3% | 35.7% |
| 11,567 | LANCASTER | 6,230 | 3,724 | 2,477 | 29 | 1,247 R | 59.8% | 39.8% | 60.1% | 39.9% |
| 23,589 | LEE | 9,770 | 5,664 | 4,005 | 101 | 1,659 R | 58.0% | 41.0% | 58.6% | 41.4% |
| 169,599 | LOUDOUN | 108,430 | 60,382 | 47,271 | 777 | 13,111 R | 55.7% | 43.6% | 56.1% | 43.9% |
| 25,627 | LOUISA | 12,035 | 7,083 | 4,844 | 108 | 2,239 R | 58.9% | 40.2% | 59.4% | 40.6% |
| 13,146 | LUNENBURG | 5,245 | 2,858 | 2,362 | 25 | 496 R | 54.5% | 45.0% | 54.8% | 45.2% |
| 12,520 | MADISON | 5,772 | 3,556 | 2,176 | 40 | 1,380 R | 61.6% | 37.7% | 62.0% | 38.0% |
| 9,207 | MATHEWS | 5,129 | 3,497 | 1,589 | 43 | 1,908 R | 68.2% | 31.0% | 68.8% | 31.2% |
| 32,380 | MECKLENBURG | 12,780 | 7,319 | 5,293 | 168 | 2,026 R | 57.3% | 41.4% | 58.0% | 42.0% |
| 9,932 | MIDDLESEX | 5,377 | 3,336 | 1,914 | 127 | 1,422 R | 62.0% | 35.6% | 63.5% | 36.5% |
| 83,629 | MONTGOMERY | 31,515 | 17,070 | 14,128 | 317 | 2,942 R | 54.2% | 44.8% | 54.7% | 45.3% |

# VIRGINIA

## PRESIDENT 2004

| 2000 Census Population | County | Total Vote | Republican | Democratic | Other | Rep.-Dem. Plurality | Percentage Total Vote Rep. | Dem. | Major Vote Rep. | Dem. |
|---|---|---|---|---|---|---|---|---|---|---|
| 14,445 | NELSON | 7,139 | 3,539 | 3,543 | 57 | 4 D | 49.6% | 49.6% | 50.0% | 50.0% |
| 13,462 | NEW KENT | 7,946 | 5,414 | 2,443 | 89 | 2,971 R | 68.1% | 30.7% | 68.9% | 31.1% |
| 13,093 | NORTHAMPTON | 5,499 | 2,669 | 2,775 | 55 | 106 D | 48.5% | 50.5% | 49.0% | 51.0% |
| 12,259 | NORTHUMBERLAND | 6,409 | 3,832 | 2,548 | 29 | 1,284 R | 59.8% | 39.8% | 60.1% | 39.9% |
| 15,725 | NOTTOWAY | 6,030 | 3,303 | 2,635 | 92 | 668 R | 54.8% | 43.7% | 55.6% | 44.4% |
| 25,881 | ORANGE | 12,928 | 7,749 | 5,015 | 164 | 2,734 R | 59.9% | 38.8% | 60.7% | 39.3% |
| 23,177 | PAGE | 9,603 | 6,221 | 3,324 | 58 | 2,897 R | 64.8% | 34.6% | 65.2% | 34.8% |
| 19,407 | PATRICK | 8,215 | 5,507 | 2,572 | 136 | 2,935 R | 67.0% | 31.3% | 68.2% | 31.8% |
| 61,745 | PITTSYLVANIA | 27,417 | 17,673 | 9,274 | 470 | 8,399 R | 64.5% | 33.8% | 65.6% | 34.4% |
| 22,377 | POWHATAN | 12,163 | 8,955 | 3,112 | 96 | 5,843 R | 73.6% | 25.6% | 74.2% | 25.8% |
| 19,720 | PRINCE EDWARD | 7,316 | 3,571 | 3,632 | 113 | 61 D | 48.8% | 49.6% | 49.6% | 50.4% |
| 33,047 | PRINCE GEORGE | 13,254 | 8,131 | 5,066 | 57 | 3,065 R | 61.3% | 38.2% | 61.6% | 38.4% |
| 280,813 | PRINCE WILLIAM | 132,063 | 69,776 | 61,271 | 1,016 | 8,505 R | 52.8% | 46.4% | 53.2% | 46.8% |
| 35,127 | PULASKI | 14,251 | 8,769 | 5,310 | 172 | 3,459 R | 61.5% | 37.3% | 62.3% | 37.7% |
| 6,983 | RAPPAHANNOCK | 4,050 | 2,172 | 1,837 | 41 | 335 R | 53.6% | 45.4% | 54.2% | 45.8% |
| 8,809 | RICHMOND COUNTY | 3,361 | 2,082 | 1,243 | 36 | 839 R | 61.9% | 37.0% | 62.6% | 37.4% |
| 85,778 | ROANOKE COUNTY | 46,973 | 30,596 | 16,082 | 295 | 14,514 R | 65.1% | 34.2% | 65.5% | 34.5% |
| 20,808 | ROCKBRIDGE | 9,181 | 5,412 | 3,627 | 142 | 1,785 R | 58.9% | 39.5% | 59.9% | 40.1% |
| 67,725 | ROCKINGHAM | 29,216 | 21,737 | 7,273 | 206 | 14,464 R | 74.4% | 24.9% | 74.9% | 25.1% |
| 30,308 | RUSSELL | 11,423 | 6,077 | 5,167 | 179 | 910 R | 53.2% | 45.2% | 54.0% | 46.0% |
| 23,403 | SCOTT | 9,967 | 6,479 | 3,324 | 164 | 3,155 R | 65.0% | 33.4% | 66.1% | 33.9% |
| 35,075 | SHENANDOAH | 17,146 | 11,820 | 5,186 | 140 | 6,634 R | 68.9% | 30.2% | 69.5% | 30.5% |
| 33,081 | SMYTH | 12,319 | 7,906 | 4,143 | 270 | 3,763 R | 64.2% | 33.6% | 65.6% | 34.4% |
| 17,482 | SOUTHAMPTON | 7,492 | 4,018 | 3,431 | 43 | 587 R | 53.6% | 45.8% | 53.9% | 46.1% |
| 90,395 | SPOTSYLVANIA | 45,445 | 28,527 | 16,623 | 295 | 11,904 R | 62.8% | 36.6% | 63.2% | 36.8% |
| 92,446 | STAFFORD | 45,986 | 28,500 | 17,208 | 278 | 11,292 R | 62.0% | 37.4% | 62.4% | 37.6% |
| 6,829 | SURRY | 3,522 | 1,543 | 1,954 | 25 | 411 D | 43.8% | 55.5% | 44.1% | 55.9% |
| 12,504 | SUSSEX | 4,345 | 1,890 | 2,420 | 35 | 530 D | 43.5% | 55.7% | 43.9% | 56.1% |
| 44,598 | TAZEWELL | 17,480 | 10,039 | 7,184 | 257 | 2,855 R | 57.4% | 41.1% | 58.3% | 41.7% |
| 31,584 | WARREN | 14,068 | 8,600 | 5,241 | 227 | 3,359 R | 61.1% | 37.3% | 62.1% | 37.9% |
| 51,103 | WASHINGTON | 22,514 | 14,749 | 7,339 | 426 | 7,410 R | 65.5% | 32.6% | 66.8% | 33.2% |
| 16,718 | WESTMORELAND | 6,848 | 3,433 | 3,370 | 45 | 63 R | 50.1% | 49.2% | 50.5% | 49.5% |
| 40,123 | WISE | 14,312 | 8,330 | 5,802 | 180 | 2,528 R | 58.2% | 40.5% | 58.9% | 41.1% |
| 27,599 | WYTHE | 11,554 | 7,911 | 3,581 | 62 | 4,330 R | 68.5% | 31.0% | 68.8% | 31.2% |
| 56,297 | YORK | 29,880 | 19,396 | 10,276 | 208 | 9,120 R | 64.9% | 34.4% | 65.4% | 34.6% |
| | **City/Town** | | | | | | | | | |
| 128,283 | ALEXANDRIA | 61,515 | 19,844 | 41,116 | 555 | 21,272 D | 32.3% | 66.8% | 32.6% | 67.4% |
| 6,299 | BEDFORD CITY | 2,542 | 1,472 | 1,042 | 28 | 430 R | 57.9% | 41.0% | 58.6% | 41.4% |
| 17,367 | BRISTOL | 6,724 | 4,275 | 2,400 | 49 | 1,875 R | 63.6% | 35.7% | 64.0% | 36.0% |
| 6,349 | BUENA VISTA | 2,389 | 1,417 | 936 | 36 | 481 R | 59.3% | 39.2% | 60.2% | 39.8% |
| 45,049 | CHARLOTTESVILLE | 15,450 | 4,172 | 11,088 | 190 | 6,916 D | 27.0% | 71.8% | 27.3% | 72.7% |
| 199,184 | CHESAPEAKE | 91,541 | 52,283 | 38,744 | 514 | 13,539 R | 57.1% | 42.3% | 57.4% | 42.6% |
| 16,897 | COLONIAL HEIGHTS | 8,231 | 6,129 | 2,061 | 41 | 4,068 R | 74.5% | 25.0% | 74.8% | 25.2% |
| 6,303 | COVINGTON | 2,301 | 1,104 | 1,179 | 18 | 75 D | 48.0% | 51.2% | 48.4% | 51.6% |
| 48,411 | DANVILLE | 19,112 | 9,399 | 9,436 | 277 | 37 D | 49.2% | 49.4% | 49.9% | 50.1% |
| 5,665 | EMPORIA | 2,221 | 970 | 1,247 | 4 | 277 D | 43.7% | 56.1% | 43.8% | 56.2% |
| 21,498 | FAIRFAX CITY | 10,546 | 5,045 | 5,395 | 106 | 350 D | 47.8% | 51.2% | 48.3% | 51.7% |
| 10,377 | FALLS CHURCH | 6,098 | 2,074 | 3,944 | 80 | 1,870 D | 34.0% | 64.7% | 34.5% | 65.5% |
| 8,346 | FRANKLIN CITY | 3,536 | 1,613 | 1,910 | 13 | 297 D | 45.6% | 54.0% | 45.8% | 54.2% |
| 19,279 | FREDERICKSBURG | 7,542 | 3,390 | 4,085 | 67 | 695 D | 44.9% | 54.2% | 45.4% | 54.6% |
| 6,837 | GALAX | 2,335 | 1,336 | 987 | 12 | 349 R | 57.2% | 42.3% | 57.5% | 42.5% |
| 146,437 | HAMPTON | 55,741 | 23,399 | 32,016 | 326 | 8,617 D | 42.0% | 57.4% | 42.2% | 57.8% |
| 40,468 | HARRISONBURG | 11,030 | 6,165 | 4,726 | 139 | 1,439 R | 55.9% | 42.8% | 56.6% | 43.4% |
| 22,354 | HOPEWELL | 7,936 | 4,251 | 3,573 | 112 | 678 R | 53.6% | 45.0% | 54.3% | 45.7% |
| 6,867 | LEXINGTON | 2,349 | 982 | 1,340 | 27 | 358 D | 41.8% | 57.0% | 42.3% | 57.7% |
| 65,269 | LYNCHBURG | 26,340 | 14,400 | 11,727 | 213 | 2,673 R | 54.7% | 44.5% | 55.1% | 44.9% |

# VIRGINIA

## PRESIDENT 2004

| 2000 Census Population | City/Town | Total Vote | Republican | Democratic | Other | Rep.-Dem. Plurality | Percentage Total Vote Rep. | Dem. | Percentage Major Vote Rep. | Dem. |
|---|---|---|---|---|---|---|---|---|---|---|
| 35,135 | MANASSAS | 12,903 | 7,257 | 5,562 | 84 | 1,695 R | 56.2% | 43.1% | 56.6% | 43.4% |
| 10,290 | MANASSAS PARK | 3,332 | 1,807 | 1,498 | 27 | 309 R | 54.2% | 45.0% | 54.7% | 45.3% |
| 15,416 | MARTINSVILLE | 5,603 | 2,538 | 3,036 | 29 | 498 D | 45.3% | 54.2% | 45.5% | 54.5% |
| 180,150 | NEWPORT NEWS | 67,952 | 32,208 | 35,319 | 425 | 3,111 D | 47.4% | 52.0% | 47.7% | 52.3% |
| 234,403 | NORFOLK | 70,570 | 26,401 | 43,518 | 651 | 17,117 D | 37.4% | 61.7% | 37.8% | 62.2% |
| 3,904 | NORTON | 1,504 | 768 | 725 | 11 | 43 R | 51.1% | 48.2% | 51.4% | 48.6% |
| 33,740 | PETERSBURG | 11,949 | 2,238 | 9,682 | 29 | 7,444 D | 18.7% | 81.0% | 18.8% | 81.2% |
| 11,566 | POQUOSON | 6,480 | 5,004 | 1,424 | 52 | 3,580 R | 77.2% | 22.0% | 77.8% | 22.2% |
| 100,565 | PORTSMOUTH | 39,534 | 15,212 | 24,112 | 210 | 8,900 D | 38.5% | 61.0% | 38.7% | 61.3% |
| 15,859 | RADFORD | 4,845 | 2,564 | 2,244 | 37 | 320 R | 52.9% | 46.3% | 53.3% | 46.7% |
| 197,790 | RICHMOND CITY | 74,325 | 21,637 | 52,167 | 521 | 30,530 D | 29.1% | 70.2% | 29.3% | 70.7% |
| 94,911 | ROANOKE CITY | 36,000 | 16,661 | 18,862 | 477 | 2,201 D | 46.3% | 52.4% | 46.9% | 53.1% |
| 24,747 | SALEM | 11,484 | 7,115 | 4,254 | 115 | 2,861 R | 62.0% | 37.0% | 62.6% | 37.4% |
| 23,853 | STAUNTON | 9,629 | 5,805 | 3,756 | 68 | 2,049 R | 60.3% | 39.0% | 60.7% | 39.3% |
| 63,677 | SUFFOLK | 32,189 | 16,763 | 15,233 | 193 | 1,530 R | 52.1% | 47.3% | 52.4% | 47.6% |
| 425,257 | VIRGINIA BEACH | 175,687 | 103,752 | 70,666 | 1,269 | 33,086 R | 59.1% | 40.2% | 59.5% | 40.5% |
| 19,520 | WAYNESBORO | 7,963 | 5,092 | 2,792 | 79 | 2,300 R | 63.9% | 35.1% | 64.6% | 35.4% |
| 11,998 | WILLIAMSBURG | 4,320 | 2,064 | 2,216 | 40 | 152 D | 47.8% | 51.3% | 48.2% | 51.8% |
| 23,585 | WINCHESTER | 9,343 | 5,283 | 3,967 | 93 | 1,316 R | 56.5% | 42.5% | 57.1% | 42.9% |
| 7,078,515 | TOTAL | 3,198,367 | 1,716,959 | 1,454,742 | 26,666 | 262,217 R | 53.7% | 45.5% | 54.1% | 45.9% |

# VIRGINIA

## HOUSE OF REPRESENTATIVES

| CD | Year | Total Vote | Republican Vote | Republican Candidate | Democratic Vote | Democratic Candidate | Other Vote | Rep.-Dem. Plurality | Percentage Total Vote Rep. | Dem. | Percentage Major Vote Rep. | Dem. |
|---|---|---|---|---|---|---|---|---|---|---|---|---|
| 1 | 2004 | 286,534 | 225,071 | Davis, Jo Ann* | | | 61,463 | 225,071 R | 78.5% | | 100.0% | |
| 1 | 2002 | 117,997 | 113,168 | Davis, Jo Ann* | | | 4,829 | 113,168 R | 95.9% | | 100.0% | |
| 2 | 2004 | 241,380 | 132,946 | Drake, Thelma | 108,180 | Ashe, David B. | 254 | 24,766 R | 55.1% | 44.8% | 55.1% | 44.9% |
| 2 | 2002 | 124,846 | 103,807 | Schrock, Ed* | | | 21,039 | 103,807 R | 83.1% | | 100.0% | |
| 3 | 2004 | 229,892 | 70,194 | Sears, Winsome E. | 159,373 | Scott, Robert C.* | 325 | 89,179 D | 30.5% | 69.3% | 30.6% | 69.4% |
| 3 | 2002 | 91,073 | | | 87,521 | Scott, Robert C.* | 3,552 | 87,521 D | | 96.1% | | 100.0% |
| 4 | 2004 | 283,027 | 182,444 | Forbes, J. Randy* | 100,413 | Menefee, Jonathan R. | 170 | 82,031 R | 64.5% | 35.5% | 64.5% | 35.5% |
| 4 | 2002 | 111,041 | 108,733 | Forbes, J. Randy* | | | 2,308 | 108,733 R | 97.9% | | 100.0% | |
| 5 | 2004 | 270,758 | 172,431 | Goode, Virgil H. Jr.* | 98,237 | Weed, Al C. II | 90 | 74,194 R | 63.7% | 36.3% | 63.7% | 36.3% |
| 5 | 2002 | 150,233 | 95,360 | Goode, Virgil H. Jr.* | 54,805 | Richards, Meredith M. | 68 | 40,555 R | 63.5% | 36.5% | 63.5% | 36.5% |
| 6 | 2004 | 213,648 | 206,560 | Goodlatte, Robert W.* | | | 7,088 | 206,560 R | 96.7% | | 100.0% | |
| 6 | 2002 | 108,732 | 105,530 | Goodlatte, Robert W.* | | | 3,202 | 105,530 R | 97.1% | | 100.0% | |
| 7 | 2004 | 305,658 | 230,765 | Cantor, Eric* | | | 74,893 | 230,765 R | 75.5% | | 100.0% | |
| 7 | 2002 | 163,665 | 113,658 | Cantor, Eric* | 49,854 | Jones, Ben L. "Cooter" | 153 | 63,804 R | 69.4% | 30.5% | 69.5% | 30.5% |
| 8 | 2004 | 287,919 | 106,231 | Cheney, Lisa Marie | 171,986 | Moran, James P.* | 9,702 | 65,755 D | 36.9% | 59.7% | 38.2% | 61.8% |
| 8 | 2002 | 171,799 | 64,121 | Tate, Scott C. | 102,759 | Moran, James P.* | 4,919 | 38,638 D | 37.3% | 59.8% | 38.4% | 61.6% |
| 9 | 2004 | 252,947 | 98,499 | Triplett, Kevin R. | 150,039 | Boucher, Rick* | 4,409 | 51,540 D | 38.9% | 59.3% | 39.6% | 60.4% |
| 9 | 2002 | 152,183 | 52,076 | Katzen, Jay K. | 100,075 | Boucher, Rick* | 32 | 47,999 D | 34.2% | 65.8% | 34.2% | 65.8% |
| 10 | 2004 | 323,011 | 205,982 | Wolf, Frank R.* | 116,654 | Socas, James R. | 375 | 89,328 R | 63.8% | 36.1% | 63.8% | 36.2% |
| 10 | 2002 | 161,615 | 115,917 | Wolf, Frank R.* | 45,464 | Stevens, John B. Jr. | 234 | 70,453 R | 71.7% | 28.1% | 71.8% | 28.2% |

# VIRGINIA

## HOUSE OF REPRESENTATIVES

| CD | Year | Total Vote | Republican Vote | Republican Candidate | Democratic Vote | Democratic Candidate | Other Vote | Rep.-Dem. Plurality | Total Vote Rep. | Total Vote Dem. | Major Vote Rep. | Major Vote Dem. |
|----|------|-----------|----------|----------------------|-------|---------------------|-----------|--------------------|----------|----------|----------|----------|
| 11 | 2004 | 309,233 | 186,299 | Davis, Thomas M. III* | 118,305 | Longmyer, Ken | 4,629 | 67,994 R | 60.2% | 38.3% | 61.2% | 38.8% |
| 11 | 2002 | 163,298 | 135,379 | Davis, Thomas M. III* | | | 27,919 | 135,379 R | 82.9% | | 100.0% | |
| Total | 2004 | 3,004,007 | 1,817,422 | | 1,023,187 | | 163,398 | 794,235 R | 60.5% | 34.1% | 64.0% | 36.0% |
| Total | 2002 | 1,516,482 | 1,007,749 | | 440,478 | | 68,255 | 567,271 R | 66.5% | 29.0% | 69.6% | 30.4% |

An asterisk (*) denotes incumbent.

# VIRGINIA

## GENERAL AND PRIMARY ELECTIONS

### 2004 GENERAL ELECTIONS

**President**   Other vote was 11,032 Libertarian (Michael Badnarik); 10,161 Constitution (Michael Peroutka); 2,393 write-in (Ralph Nader); 104 write-in (David Cobb); 23 write-in (Walter F. Brown); 1 write-in (Joseph Spence); 2,952 scattered write-in.

**House**   Other vote was:

CD 1   57,434 Independent (William A. Lee); 4,029 write-in.
CD 2   254 write-in.
CD 3   325 write-in.
CD 4   170 write-in.
CD 5   90 write-in.
CD 6   7,088 write-in.
CD 7   74,325 Independent (W. Brad Blanton); 568 write-in.
CD 8   9,004 Independent (James T. Hurysz); 698 write-in.
CD 9   4,341 Independent (Seth A. Davis); 68 write-in.
CD 10   375 write-in.
CD 11   4,338 Independent (Joseph P. Oddo); 291 write-in.

### 2004 PRIMARY ELECTIONS

**Primary**   February 10, 2004 (President)
June 8, 2004 (Congress)

**Registration** (as of May 10, 2004—includes 285,820 inactive registrants and 1,352 overseas voters)   4,318,058   No Party Registration

**Primary Type**   Open—Any registered voter could participate in the primary of either party.

# VIRGINIA

## GENERAL AND PRIMARY ELECTIONS

Note: An asterisk (*) denotes incumbent. The state parties and local party committees have the option of holding a primary or nominating candidates by convention or committee. If a primary was called and only one candidate filed to run in it, then no primary was held.

| | REPUBLICAN PRIMARIES | | DEMOCRATIC PRIMARIES | | |
|---|---|---|---|---|---|
| President | No Republican primary | | John Kerry | 204,142 | 51.5% |
| | | | John Edwards | 105,504 | 26.6% |
| | | | Wesley Clark | 36,572 | 9.2% |
| | | | Howard Dean | 27,637 | 7.0% |
| | | | Al Sharpton | 12,864 | 3.2% |
| | | | Dennis J. Kucinich | 5,016 | 1.3% |
| | | | Joseph I. Lieberman | 2,866 | 0.7% |
| | | | Lyndon H. LaRouche Jr. | 1,042 | 0.3% |
| | | | Richard A. Gephardt | 580 | 0.1% |
| | | | TOTAL | 396,223 | |
| Congressional District 1 | Jo Ann Davis* | Unopposed | No Democratic candidate | | |
| Congressional District 2 | *Ed Schrock ran unopposed for the Republican nomination but subsequently withdrew from the race. He was replaced on the general election ballot by Thelma Drake.* | | David B. Ashe | Unopposed | |
| Congressional District 3 | Winsome E. Sears | Nominated by convention | Robert C. Scott* | Unopposed | |
| Congressional District 4 | J. Randy Forbes* | Unopposed | Jonathan R. Menefee | Nominated by convention | |
| Congressional District 5 | Virgil H. Goode Jr.* | Unopposed | Al C. Weed II | Nominated by convention | |
| Congressional District 6 | Robert W. Goodlatte* | Unopposed | No Democratic candidate | | |
| Congressional District 7 | Eric Cantor* | Unopposed | No Democratic candidate | | |
| Congressional District 8 | Lisa Marie Cheney | Nominated by convention | James P. Moran* | 24,121 | 58.6% |
| | | | Andrew M. Rosenberg | 17,067 | 41.4% |
| | | | TOTAL | 41,188 | |
| Congressional District 9 | Kevin R. Triplett | Nominated by convention | Rick Boucher* | Nominated by convention | |
| Congressional District 10 | Frank R. Wolf* | Unopposed | James R. Socas | Nominated by convention | |
| Congressional District 11 | Thomas M. Davis III* | Unopposed | Ken Longmyer | *No candidate filed. Ken Longmyer was subsequently named as the Democratic candidate.* | |

# WASHINGTON

## GOVERNOR
Christine Gregoire (D). Elected 2004 to a four-year term.

## SENATORS (2 Democrats)
Maria Cantwell (D). Elected 2000 to a six-year term.

Patty Murray (D). Reelected 2004 to a six-year term. Previously elected 1998, 1992.

## REPRESENTATIVES (6 Democrats, 3 Republicans)
1. Jay Inslee (D)
2. Rick Larsen (D)
3. Brian Baird (D)
4. Doc Hastings (R)
5. Cathy McMorris (R)
6. Norm Dicks (D)
7. Jim McDermott (D)
8. Dave Reichert (R)
9. Adam Smith (D)

## POSTWAR VOTE FOR PRESIDENT

| Year | Total Vote | Republican Vote | Republican Candidate | Democratic Vote | Democratic Candidate | Other Vote | Plurality | Total Vote Rep. | Total Vote Dem. | Major Vote Rep. | Major Vote Dem. |
|------|-----------|-----------------|---------------------|-----------------|---------------------|-----------|-----------|-------|-------|-------|-------|
| 2004 | 2,859,084 | 1,304,894 | Bush, George W. | 1,510,201 | Kerry, John | 43,989 | 205,307 D | 45.6% | 52.8% | 46.4% | 53.6% |
| 2000** | 2,487,433 | 1,108,864 | Bush, George W. | 1,247,652 | Gore, Al | 130,917 | 138,788 D | 44.6% | 50.2% | 47.1% | 52.9% |
| 1996** | 2,253,837 | 840,712 | Dole, Bob | 1,123,323 | Clinton, Bill | 289,802 | 282,611 D | 37.3% | 49.8% | 42.8% | 57.2% |
| 1992** | 2,288,230 | 731,234 | Bush, George | 993,037 | Clinton, Bill | 563,959 | 261,803 D | 32.0% | 43.4% | 42.4% | 57.6% |
| 1988 | 1,865,253 | 903,835 | Bush, George | 933,516 | Dukakis, Michael S. | 27,902 | 29,681 D | 48.5% | 50.0% | 49.2% | 50.8% |
| 1984 | 1,883,910 | 1,051,670 | Reagan, Ronald | 807,352 | Mondale, Walter F. | 24,888 | 244,318 R | 55.8% | 42.9% | 56.6% | 43.4% |
| 1980** | 1,742,394 | 865,244 | Reagan, Ronald | 650,193 | Carter, Jimmy | 226,957 | 215,051 R | 49.7% | 37.3% | 57.1% | 42.9% |
| 1976 | 1,555,534 | 777,732 | Ford, Gerald R. | 717,323 | Carter, Jimmy | 60,479 | 60,409 R | 50.0% | 46.1% | 52.0% | 48.0% |
| 1972 | 1,470,847 | 837,135 | Nixon, Richard M. | 568,334 | McGovern, George S. | 65,378 | 268,801 R | 56.9% | 38.6% | 59.6% | 40.4% |
| 1968** | 1,304,281 | 588,510 | Nixon, Richard M. | 616,037 | Humphrey, Hubert H. | 99,734 | 27,527 D | 45.1% | 47.2% | 48.9% | 51.1% |
| 1964 | 1,258,556 | 470,366 | Goldwater, Barry M. | 779,881 | Johnson, Lyndon B. | 8,309 | 309,515 D | 37.4% | 62.0% | 37.6% | 62.4% |
| 1960 | 1,241,572 | 629,273 | Nixon, Richard M. | 599,298 | Kennedy, John F. | 13,001 | 29,975 R | 50.7% | 48.3% | 51.2% | 48.8% |
| 1956 | 1,150,889 | 620,430 | Eisenhower, Dwight D. | 523,002 | Stevenson, Adlai E. | 7,457 | 97,428 R | 53.9% | 45.4% | 54.3% | 45.7% |
| 1952 | 1,102,708 | 599,107 | Eisenhower, Dwight D. | 492,845 | Stevenson, Adlai E. | 10,756 | 106,262 R | 54.3% | 44.7% | 54.9% | 45.1% |
| 1948 | 905,058 | 386,314 | Dewey, Thomas E. | 476,165 | Truman, Harry S. | 42,579 | 89,851 D | 42.7% | 52.6% | 44.8% | 55.2% |

In past elections, the other vote included: 2000 - 103,002 Green (Ralph Nader); 1996 - 201,003 Reform (Ross Perot); 1992 - 541,780 Independent (Perot); 1980 - 185,073 Independent (John Anderson); 1968 - 96,990 American Independent (George Wallace).

# WASHINGTON

## POSTWAR VOTE FOR GOVERNOR

| Year | Total Vote | Republican Vote | Republican Candidate | Democratic Vote | Democratic Candidate | Other Vote | Rep.-Dem. Plurality | Percentage Total Vote Rep. | Percentage Total Vote Dem. | Percentage Major Vote Rep. | Percentage Major Vote Dem. |
|---|---|---|---|---|---|---|---|---|---|---|---|
| 2004** | 2,810,058 | 1,373,232 | Rossi, Dino | 1,373,361 | Gregoire, Christine | 63,465 | 129 D | 48.9% | 48.9% | 50.0% | 50.0% |
| 2000 | 2,469,852 | 980,060 | Carlson, John | 1,441,973 | Locke, Gary | 47,819 | 461,913 D | 39.7% | 58.4% | 40.5% | 59.5% |
| 1996 | 2,237,030 | 940,538 | Craswell, Ellen | 1,296,492 | Locke, Gary | | 355,954 D | 42.0% | 58.0% | 42.0% | 58.0% |
| 1992 | 2,270,826 | 1,086,216 | Eikenberry, Ken | 1,184,315 | Lowry, Mike | 295 | 98,099 D | 47.8% | 52.2% | 47.8% | 52.2% |
| 1988 | 1,874,929 | 708,481 | Williams, Bob | 1,166,448 | Gardner, Booth | | 457,967 D | 37.8% | 62.2% | 37.8% | 62.2% |
| 1984 | 1,888,987 | 881,994 | Spellman, John D. | 1,006,993 | Gardner, Booth | | 124,999 D | 46.7% | 53.3% | 46.7% | 53.3% |
| 1980 | 1,730,896 | 981,083 | Spellman, John D. | 749,813 | McDermott, James A. | | 231,270 R | 56.7% | 43.3% | 56.7% | 43.3% |
| 1976 | 1,546,382 | 687,039 | Spellman, John D. | 821,797 | Ray, Dixy Lee | 37,546 | 134,758 D | 44.4% | 53.1% | 45.5% | 54.5% |
| 1972 | 1,472,542 | 747,825 | Evans, Daniel J. | 630,613 | Rosellini, Albert D. | 94,104 | 117,212 R | 50.8% | 42.8% | 54.3% | 45.7% |
| 1968 | 1,265,355 | 692,378 | Evans, Daniel J. | 560,262 | O'Connell, John J. | 12,715 | 132,116 R | 54.7% | 44.3% | 55.3% | 44.7% |
| 1964 | 1,250,274 | 697,256 | Evans, Daniel J. | 548,692 | Rosellini, Albert D. | 4,326 | 148,564 R | 55.8% | 43.9% | 56.0% | 44.0% |
| 1960 | 1,215,748 | 594,122 | Andrews, Lloyd J. | 611,987 | Rosellini, Albert D. | 9,639 | 17,865 D | 48.9% | 50.3% | 49.3% | 50.7% |
| 1956 | 1,128,977 | 508,041 | Anderson, Emmett T. | 616,773 | Rosellini, Albert D. | 4,163 | 108,732 D | 45.0% | 54.6% | 45.2% | 54.8% |
| 1952 | 1,078,497 | 567,822 | Langlie, Arthur B. | 510,675 | Mitchell, Hugh B. | | 57,147 R | 52.6% | 47.4% | 52.6% | 47.4% |
| 1948 | 883,141 | 445,958 | Langlie, Arthur B. | 417,035 | Wallgren, Mon C. | 20,148 | 28,923 R | 50.5% | 47.2% | 51.7% | 48.3% |

In 2004, the initial official vote count put Republican Dino Rossi ahead by 261 votes. A machine recount reduced Rossi's margin to 42 votes. A subsequent manual recount gave Democrat Christine Gregoire the election by a margin of 129 votes (see above), and she was inaugurated governor.

## POSTWAR VOTE FOR SENATOR

| Year | Total Vote | Republican Vote | Republican Candidate | Democratic Vote | Democratic Candidate | Other Vote | Rep.-Dem. Plurality | Percentage Total Vote Rep. | Percentage Total Vote Dem. | Percentage Major Vote Rep. | Percentage Major Vote Dem. |
|---|---|---|---|---|---|---|---|---|---|---|---|
| 2004 | 2,818,651 | 1,204,584 | Nethercutt, George | 1,549,708 | Murray, Patty | 64,359 | 345,124 D | 42.7% | 55.0% | 43.7% | 56.3% |
| 2000 | 2,461,379 | 1,197,208 | Gorton, Slade | 1,199,437 | Cantwell, Maria | 64,734 | 2,229 D | 48.6% | 48.7% | 50.0% | 50.0% |
| 1998 | 1,888,561 | 785,377 | Smith, Linda | 1,103,184 | Murray, Patty | | 317,807 D | 41.6% | 58.4% | 41.6% | 58.4% |
| 1994 | 1,700,173 | 947,821 | Gorton, Slade | 752,352 | Sims, Ron | | 195,469 R | 55.7% | 44.3% | 55.7% | 44.3% |
| 1992 | 2,219,162 | 1,020,829 | Chandler, Rod | 1,197,973 | Murray, Patty | 360 | 177,144 D | 46.0% | 54.0% | 46.0% | 54.0% |
| 1988 | 1,848,542 | 944,359 | Gorton, Slade | 904,183 | Lowry, Mike | | 40,176 R | 51.1% | 48.9% | 51.1% | 48.9% |
| 1986 | 1,337,367 | 650,931 | Gorton, Slade | 677,471 | Adams, Brock | 8,965 | 26,540 D | 48.7% | 50.7% | 49.0% | 51.0% |
| 1983S | 1,213,307 | 672,326 | Evans, Daniel J. | 540,981 | Lowry, Mike | | 131,345 R | 55.4% | 44.6% | 55.4% | 44.6% |
| 1982 | 1,368,476 | 332,273 | Jewett, Doug | 943,655 | Jackson, Henry M. | 92,548 | 611,382 D | 24.3% | 69.0% | 26.0% | 74.0% |
| 1980 | 1,728,369 | 936,317 | Gorton, Slade | 792,052 | Magnuson, Warren G. | | 144,265 R | 54.2% | 45.8% | 54.2% | 45.8% |
| 1976 | 1,491,111 | 361,546 | Brown, George M. | 1,071,219 | Jackson, Henry M. | 58,346 | 709,673 D | 24.2% | 71.8% | 25.2% | 74.8% |
| 1974 | 1,007,847 | 363,626 | Metcalf, Jack | 611,811 | Magnuson, Warren G. | 32,410 | 248,185 D | 36.1% | 60.7% | 37.3% | 62.7% |
| 1970 | 1,066,807 | 170,790 | Elicker, Charles W. | 879,385 | Jackson, Henry M. | 16,632 | 708,595 D | 16.0% | 82.4% | 16.3% | 83.7% |
| 1968 | 1,236,063 | 435,894 | Metcalf, Jack | 796,183 | Magnuson, Warren G. | 3,986 | 360,289 D | 35.3% | 64.4% | 35.4% | 64.6% |
| 1964 | 1,213,088 | 337,138 | Andrews, Lloyd J. | 875,950 | Jackson, Henry M. | | 538,812 D | 27.8% | 72.2% | 27.8% | 72.2% |
| 1962 | 943,229 | 446,204 | Christensen, Richard G. | 491,365 | Magnuson, Warren G. | 5,660 | 45,161 D | 47.3% | 52.1% | 47.6% | 52.4% |
| 1958 | 886,822 | 278,271 | Bantz, William B. | 597,040 | Jackson, Henry M. | 11,511 | 318,769 D | 31.4% | 67.3% | 31.8% | 68.2% |
| 1956 | 1,122,217 | 436,652 | Langlie, Arthur B. | 685,565 | Magnuson, Warren G. | | 248,913 D | 38.9% | 61.1% | 38.9% | 61.1% |
| 1952 | 1,058,735 | 460,884 | Cain, Harry P. | 595,288 | Jackson, Henry M. | 2,563 | 134,404 D | 43.5% | 56.2% | 43.6% | 56.4% |
| 1950 | 744,783 | 342,464 | Williams, Walter | 397,719 | Magnuson, Warren G. | 4,600 | 55,255 D | 46.0% | 53.4% | 46.3% | 53.7% |
| 1946 | 660,342 | 358,847 | Cain, Harry P. | 298,683 | Mitchell, Hugh B. | 2,812 | 60,164 R | 54.3% | 45.2% | 54.6% | 45.4% |

The 1983 election was for a short term to fill a vacancy.

450

# WASHINGTON

Congressional districts first established for elections held in 2002
9 members

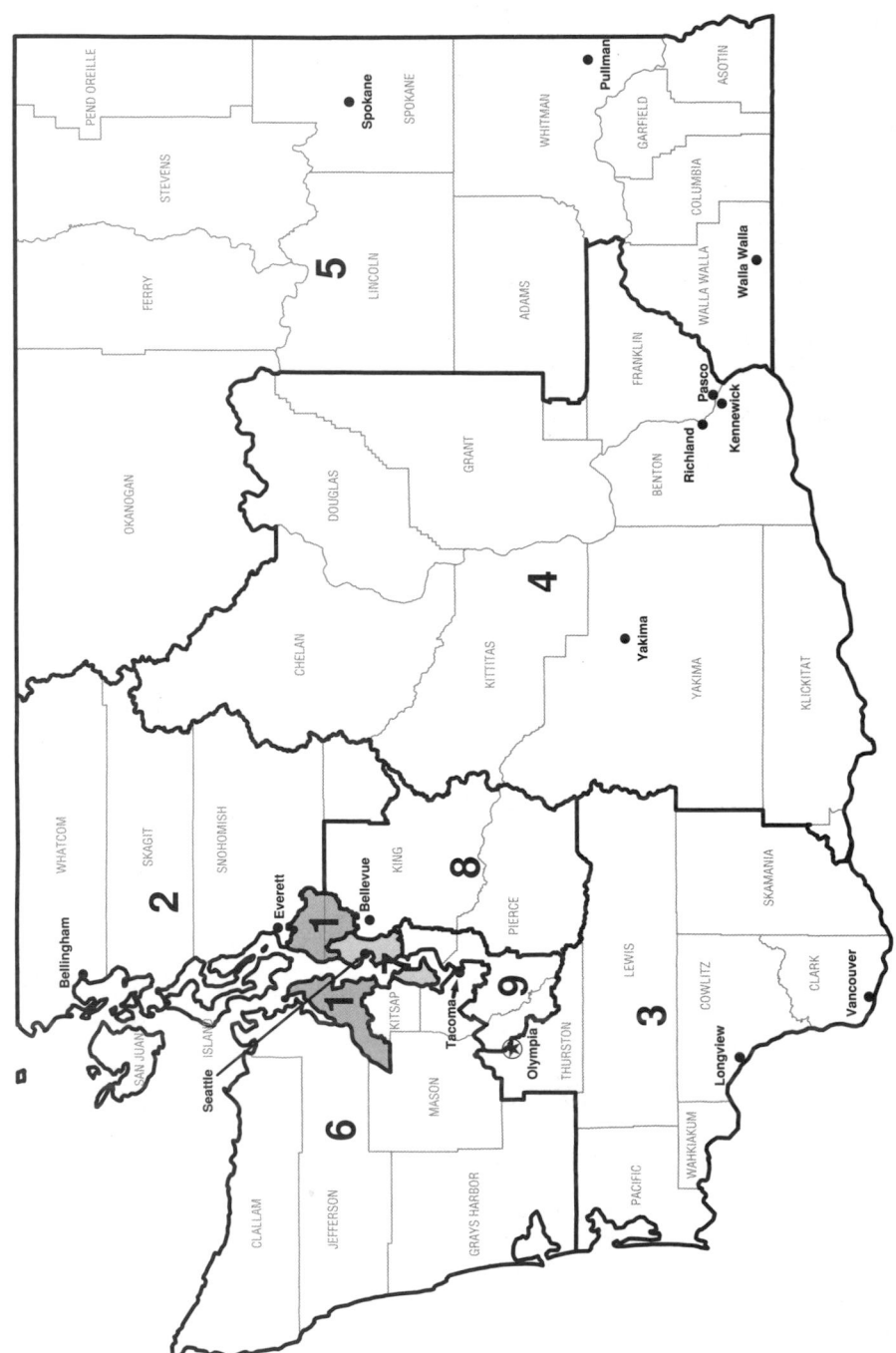

# WASHINGTON

## Seattle, Puget Sound Area

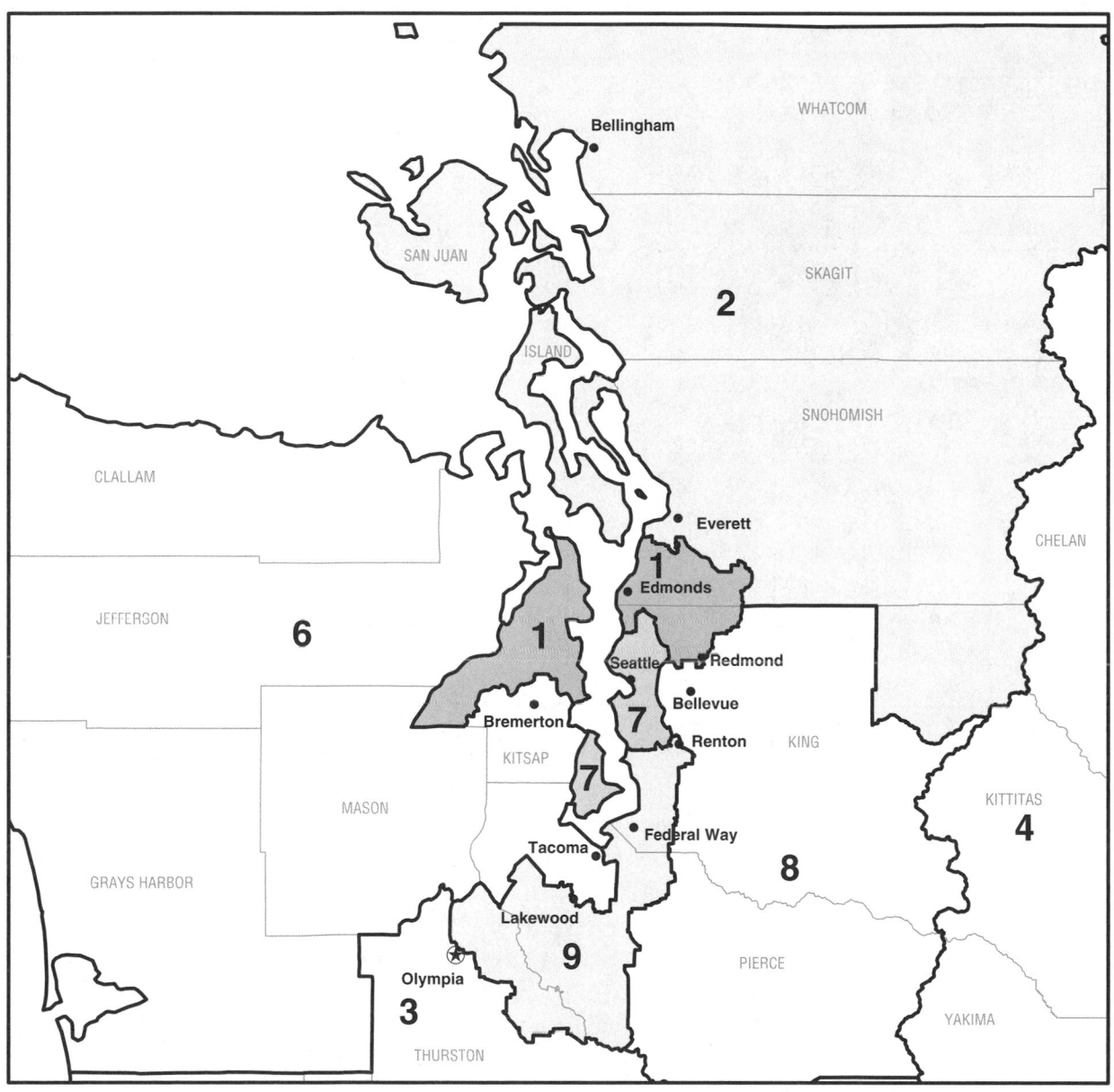

# WASHINGTON

## PRESIDENT 2004

| 2000 Census Population | County | Total Vote | Republican | Democratic | Other | Rep.-Dem. Plurality | | Percentage | | | |
|---|---|---|---|---|---|---|---|---|---|---|---|
| | | | | | | | | Total Vote | | Major Vote | |
| | | | | | | | | Rep. | Dem. | Rep. | Dem. |
| 16,428 | ADAMS | 5,127 | 3,751 | 1,315 | 61 | 2,436 | R | 73.2% | 25.6% | 74.0% | 26.0% |
| 20,551 | ASOTIN | 8,786 | 5,320 | 3,319 | 147 | 2,001 | R | 60.6% | 37.8% | 61.6% | 38.4% |
| 142,475 | BENTON | 66,886 | 44,350 | 21,549 | 987 | 22,801 | R | 66.3% | 32.2% | 67.3% | 32.7% |
| 66,616 | CHELAN | 29,396 | 18,482 | 10,471 | 443 | 8,011 | R | 62.9% | 35.6% | 63.8% | 36.2% |
| 64,525 | CLALLAM | 36,766 | 18,871 | 17,049 | 846 | 1,822 | R | 51.3% | 46.4% | 52.5% | 47.5% |
| 345,238 | CLARK | 170,439 | 88,646 | 79,538 | 2,255 | 9,108 | R | 52.0% | 46.7% | 52.7% | 47.3% |
| 4,064 | COLUMBIA | 2,107 | 1,470 | 605 | 32 | 865 | R | 69.8% | 28.7% | 70.8% | 29.2% |
| 92,948 | COWLITZ | 42,473 | 20,217 | 21,589 | 667 | 1,372 | D | 47.6% | 50.8% | 48.4% | 51.6% |
| 32,603 | DOUGLAS | 13,372 | 8,900 | 4,306 | 166 | 4,594 | R | 66.6% | 32.2% | 67.4% | 32.6% |
| 7,260 | FERRY | 3,341 | 2,019 | 1,201 | 121 | 818 | R | 60.4% | 35.9% | 62.7% | 37.3% |
| 49,347 | FRANKLIN | 16,159 | 10,757 | 5,188 | 214 | 5,569 | R | 66.6% | 32.1% | 67.5% | 32.5% |
| 2,397 | GARFIELD | 1,320 | 935 | 365 | 20 | 570 | R | 70.8% | 27.7% | 71.9% | 28.1% |
| 74,698 | GRANT | 25,995 | 17,799 | 7,779 | 417 | 10,020 | R | 68.5% | 29.9% | 69.6% | 30.4% |
| 67,194 | GRAYS HARBOR | 27,953 | 12,871 | 14,583 | 499 | 1,712 | D | 46.0% | 52.2% | 46.9% | 53.1% |
| 71,558 | ISLAND | 38,559 | 19,754 | 18,216 | 589 | 1,538 | R | 51.2% | 47.2% | 52.0% | 48.0% |
| 25,953 | JEFFERSON | 18,616 | 6,650 | 11,610 | 356 | 4,960 | D | 35.7% | 62.4% | 36.4% | 63.6% |
| 1,737,034 | KING | 893,534 | 301,043 | 580,378 | 12,113 | 279,335 | D | 33.7% | 65.0% | 34.2% | 65.8% |
| 231,969 | KITSAP | 118,453 | 55,608 | 60,796 | 2,049 | 5,188 | D | 46.9% | 51.3% | 47.8% | 52.2% |
| 33,362 | KITTITAS | 16,084 | 9,052 | 6,731 | 301 | 2,321 | R | 56.3% | 41.8% | 57.4% | 42.6% |
| 19,161 | KLICKITAT | 9,237 | 5,016 | 4,036 | 185 | 980 | R | 54.3% | 43.7% | 55.4% | 44.6% |
| 68,600 | LEWIS | 32,428 | 21,042 | 10,726 | 660 | 10,316 | R | 64.9% | 33.1% | 66.2% | 33.8% |
| 10,184 | LINCOLN | 5,811 | 4,015 | 1,706 | 90 | 2,309 | R | 69.1% | 29.4% | 70.2% | 29.8% |
| 49,405 | MASON | 25,394 | 11,987 | 12,894 | 513 | 907 | D | 47.2% | 50.8% | 48.2% | 51.8% |
| 39,564 | OKANOGAN | 16,342 | 9,636 | 6,309 | 397 | 3,327 | R | 59.0% | 38.6% | 60.4% | 39.6% |
| 20,984 | PACIFIC | 10,431 | 4,634 | 5,570 | 227 | 936 | D | 44.4% | 53.4% | 45.4% | 54.6% |
| 11,732 | PEND OREILLE | 6,198 | 3,693 | 2,310 | 195 | 1,383 | R | 59.6% | 37.3% | 61.5% | 38.5% |
| 700,820 | PIERCE | 313,331 | 150,783 | 158,231 | 4,317 | 7,448 | D | 48.1% | 50.5% | 48.8% | 51.2% |
| 14,077 | SAN JUAN | 10,088 | 3,290 | 6,589 | 209 | 3,299 | D | 32.6% | 65.3% | 33.3% | 66.7% |
| 102,979 | SKAGIT | 52,230 | 26,139 | 25,131 | 960 | 1,008 | R | 50.0% | 48.1% | 51.0% | 49.0% |
| 9,872 | SKAMANIA | 5,159 | 2,695 | 2,374 | 90 | 321 | R | 52.2% | 46.0% | 53.2% | 46.8% |
| 606,024 | SNOHOMISH | 294,997 | 134,317 | 156,468 | 4,212 | 22,151 | D | 45.5% | 53.0% | 46.2% | 53.8% |
| 417,939 | SPOKANE | 202,587 | 111,606 | 87,490 | 3,491 | 24,116 | R | 55.1% | 43.2% | 56.1% | 43.9% |
| 40,066 | STEVENS | 20,340 | 13,015 | 6,822 | 503 | 6,193 | R | 64.0% | 33.5% | 65.6% | 34.4% |
| 207,355 | THURSTON | 112,789 | 47,992 | 62,650 | 2,147 | 14,658 | D | 42.6% | 55.5% | 43.4% | 56.6% |
| 3,824 | WAHKIAKUM | 2,235 | 1,171 | 1,021 | 43 | 150 | R | 52.4% | 45.7% | 53.4% | 46.6% |
| 55,180 | WALLA WALLA | 22,925 | 14,323 | 8,257 | 345 | 6,066 | R | 62.5% | 36.0% | 63.4% | 36.6% |
| 166,814 | WHATCOM | 90,394 | 40,296 | 48,268 | 1,830 | 7,972 | D | 44.6% | 53.4% | 45.5% | 54.5% |
| 40,740 | WHITMAN | 18,012 | 9,397 | 8,287 | 328 | 1,110 | R | 52.2% | 46.0% | 53.1% | 46.9% |
| 222,581 | YAKIMA | 72,790 | 43,352 | 28,474 | 964 | 14,878 | R | 59.6% | 39.1% | 60.4% | 39.6% |
| 5,894,121 | TOTAL | 2,859,084 | 1,304,894 | 1,510,201 | 43,989 | 205,307 | D | 45.6% | 52.8% | 46.4% | 53.6% |

# WASHINGTON

## GOVERNOR 2004

| 2000 Census Population | County | Total Vote | Republican | Democratic | Other | Rep.-Dem. Plurality | | Percentage | | | |
|---|---|---|---|---|---|---|---|---|---|---|---|
| | | | | | | | | Total Vote | | Major Vote | |
| | | | | | | | | Rep. | Dem. | Rep. | Dem. |
| 16,428 | ADAMS | 5,091 | 3,481 | 1,529 | 81 | 1,952 | R | 68.4% | 30.0% | 69.5% | 30.5% |
| 20,551 | ASOTIN | 8,637 | 4,914 | 3,530 | 193 | 1,384 | R | 56.9% | 40.9% | 58.2% | 41.8% |
| 142,475 | BENTON | 65,847 | 44,895 | 19,834 | 1,118 | 25,061 | R | 68.2% | 30.1% | 69.4% | 30.6% |
| 66,616 | CHELAN | 29,038 | 18,438 | 10,077 | 523 | 8,361 | R | 63.5% | 34.7% | 64.7% | 35.3% |
| 64,525 | CLALLAM | 35,986 | 18,836 | 16,230 | 920 | 2,606 | R | 52.3% | 45.1% | 53.7% | 46.3% |
| 345,238 | CLARK | 162,875 | 85,924 | 72,828 | 4,123 | 13,096 | R | 52.8% | 44.7% | 54.1% | 45.9% |
| 4,064 | COLUMBIA | 2,079 | 1,371 | 671 | 37 | 700 | R | 65.9% | 32.3% | 67.1% | 32.9% |
| 92,948 | COWLITZ | 41,343 | 20,045 | 20,204 | 1,094 | 159 | D | 48.5% | 48.9% | 49.8% | 50.2% |
| 32,603 | DOUGLAS | 13,246 | 8,667 | 4,360 | 219 | 4,307 | R | 65.4% | 32.9% | 66.5% | 33.5% |
| 7,260 | FERRY | 3,296 | 1,900 | 1,278 | 118 | 622 | R | 57.6% | 38.8% | 59.8% | 40.2% |
| 49,347 | FRANKLIN | 15,838 | 10,634 | 4,977 | 227 | 5,657 | R | 67.1% | 31.4% | 68.1% | 31.9% |
| 2,397 | GARFIELD | 1,293 | 840 | 428 | 25 | 412 | R | 65.0% | 33.1% | 66.2% | 33.8% |
| 74,698 | GRANT | 25,787 | 17,431 | 7,821 | 535 | 9,610 | R | 67.6% | 30.3% | 69.0% | 31.0% |
| 67,194 | GRAYS HARBOR | 27,761 | 13,457 | 13,729 | 575 | 272 | D | 48.5% | 49.5% | 49.5% | 50.5% |
| 71,558 | ISLAND | 37,709 | 20,000 | 16,895 | 814 | 3,105 | R | 53.0% | 44.8% | 54.2% | 45.8% |
| 25,953 | JEFFERSON | 18,411 | 7,295 | 10,650 | 466 | 3,355 | D | 39.6% | 57.8% | 40.7% | 59.3% |
| 1,737,034 | KING | 876,452 | 351,306 | 506,194 | 18,952 | 154,888 | D | 40.1% | 57.8% | 41.0% | 59.0% |
| 231,969 | KITSAP | 117,108 | 57,775 | 56,236 | 3,097 | 1,539 | R | 49.3% | 48.0% | 50.7% | 49.3% |
| 33,362 | KITTITAS | 15,969 | 9,567 | 6,125 | 277 | 3,442 | R | 59.9% | 38.4% | 61.0% | 39.0% |
| 19,161 | KLICKITAT | 8,951 | 4,767 | 3,919 | 265 | 848 | R | 53.3% | 43.8% | 54.9% | 45.1% |
| 68,600 | LEWIS | 31,855 | 20,851 | 10,247 | 757 | 10,604 | R | 65.5% | 32.2% | 67.0% | 33.0% |
| 10,184 | LINCOLN | 5,636 | 3,686 | 1,850 | 100 | 1,836 | R | 65.4% | 32.8% | 66.6% | 33.4% |
| 49,405 | MASON | 24,996 | 12,519 | 11,797 | 680 | 722 | R | 50.1% | 47.2% | 51.5% | 48.5% |
| 39,564 | OKANOGAN | 16,035 | 9,460 | 6,107 | 468 | 3,353 | R | 59.0% | 38.1% | 60.8% | 39.2% |
| 20,984 | PACIFIC | 10,236 | 4,730 | 5,210 | 296 | 480 | D | 46.2% | 50.9% | 47.6% | 52.4% |
| 11,732 | PEND OREILLE | 6,114 | 3,368 | 2,567 | 179 | 801 | R | 55.1% | 42.0% | 56.7% | 43.3% |
| 700,820 | PIERCE | 310,591 | 157,905 | 145,431 | 7,255 | 12,474 | R | 50.8% | 46.8% | 52.1% | 47.9% |
| 14,077 | SAN JUAN | 9,852 | 3,660 | 5,872 | 320 | 2,212 | D | 37.1% | 59.6% | 38.4% | 61.6% |
| 102,979 | SKAGIT | 51,733 | 27,219 | 23,250 | 1,264 | 3,969 | R | 52.6% | 44.9% | 53.9% | 46.1% |
| 9,872 | SKAMANIA | 4,936 | 2,525 | 2,233 | 178 | 292 | R | 51.2% | 45.2% | 53.1% | 46.9% |
| 606,024 | SNOHOMISH | 291,678 | 145,628 | 139,189 | 6,861 | 6,439 | R | 49.9% | 47.7% | 51.1% | 48.9% |
| 417,939 | SPOKANE | 200,046 | 105,584 | 90,581 | 3,881 | 15,003 | R | 52.8% | 45.3% | 53.8% | 46.2% |
| 40,066 | STEVENS | 19,853 | 12,295 | 6,992 | 566 | 5,303 | R | 61.9% | 35.2% | 63.7% | 36.3% |
| 207,355 | THURSTON | 110,971 | 49,426 | 58,970 | 2,575 | 9,544 | D | 44.5% | 53.1% | 45.6% | 54.4% |
| 3,824 | WAHKIAKUM | 2,153 | 1,099 | 993 | 61 | 106 | R | 51.0% | 46.1% | 52.5% | 47.5% |
| 55,180 | WALLA WALLA | 22,676 | 14,290 | 8,008 | 378 | 6,282 | R | 63.0% | 35.3% | 64.1% | 35.9% |
| 166,814 | WHATCOM | 88,251 | 42,000 | 44,072 | 2,179 | 2,072 | D | 47.6% | 49.9% | 48.8% | 51.2% |
| 40,740 | WHITMAN | 17,544 | 9,365 | 7,722 | 457 | 1,643 | R | 53.4% | 44.0% | 54.8% | 45.2% |
| 222,581 | YAKIMA | 72,185 | 46,079 | 24,755 | 1,351 | 21,324 | R | 63.8% | 34.3% | 65.1% | 34.9% |
| 5,894,121 | TOTAL | 2,810,058 | 1,373,232 | 1,373,361 | 63,465 | 129 | D | 48.9% | 48.9% | 50.0% | 50.0% |

# WASHINGTON

## SENATOR 2004

| 2000 Census Population | County | Total Vote | Republican | Democratic | Other | Rep.-Dem. Plurality | | Percentage | | | |
|---|---|---|---|---|---|---|---|---|---|---|---|
| | | | | | | | | Total Vote | | Major Vote | |
| | | | | | | | | Rep. | Dem. | Rep. | Dem. |
| 16,428 | ADAMS | 5,061 | 3,362 | 1,607 | 92 | 1,755 | R | 66.4% | 31.8% | 67.7% | 32.3% |
| 20,551 | ASOTIN | 8,673 | 4,985 | 3,511 | 177 | 1,474 | R | 57.5% | 40.5% | 58.7% | 41.3% |
| 142,475 | BENTON | 65,983 | 38,690 | 25,863 | 1,430 | 12,827 | R | 58.6% | 39.2% | 59.9% | 40.1% |
| 66,616 | CHELAN | 28,742 | 16,874 | 11,307 | 561 | 5,567 | R | 58.7% | 39.3% | 59.9% | 40.1% |
| 64,525 | CLALLAM | 36,082 | 17,298 | 17,817 | 967 | 519 | D | 47.9% | 49.4% | 49.3% | 50.7% |
| 345,238 | CLARK | 165,883 | 81,888 | 80,134 | 3,861 | 1,754 | R | 49.4% | 48.3% | 50.5% | 49.5% |
| 4,064 | COLUMBIA | 2,104 | 1,318 | 741 | 45 | 577 | R | 62.6% | 35.2% | 64.0% | 36.0% |
| 92,948 | COWLITZ | 41,772 | 18,301 | 22,535 | 936 | 4,234 | D | 43.8% | 53.9% | 44.8% | 55.2% |
| 32,603 | DOUGLAS | 13,251 | 8,128 | 4,893 | 230 | 3,235 | R | 61.3% | 36.9% | 62.4% | 37.6% |
| 7,260 | FERRY | 3,312 | 1,847 | 1,362 | 103 | 485 | R | 55.8% | 41.1% | 57.6% | 42.4% |
| 49,347 | FRANKLIN | 15,963 | 9,495 | 6,215 | 253 | 3,280 | R | 59.5% | 38.9% | 60.4% | 39.6% |
| 2,397 | GARFIELD | 1,306 | 872 | 417 | 17 | 455 | R | 66.8% | 31.9% | 67.6% | 32.4% |
| 74,698 | GRANT | 25,724 | 16,091 | 9,015 | 618 | 7,076 | R | 62.6% | 35.0% | 64.1% | 35.9% |
| 67,194 | GRAYS HARBOR | 27,607 | 11,220 | 15,830 | 557 | 4,610 | D | 40.6% | 57.3% | 41.5% | 58.5% |
| 71,558 | ISLAND | 37,920 | 17,969 | 19,181 | 770 | 1,212 | D | 47.4% | 50.6% | 48.4% | 51.6% |
| 25,953 | JEFFERSON | 18,459 | 6,415 | 11,573 | 471 | 5,158 | D | 34.8% | 62.7% | 35.7% | 64.3% |
| 1,737,034 | KING | 879,655 | 287,456 | 573,506 | 18,693 | 286,050 | D | 32.7% | 65.2% | 33.4% | 66.6% |
| 231,969 | KITSAP | 117,232 | 50,574 | 63,684 | 2,974 | 13,110 | D | 43.1% | 54.3% | 44.3% | 55.7% |
| 33,362 | KITTITAS | 15,926 | 8,367 | 7,182 | 377 | 1,185 | R | 52.5% | 45.1% | 53.8% | 46.2% |
| 19,161 | KLICKITAT | 9,021 | 4,609 | 4,184 | 228 | 425 | R | 51.1% | 46.4% | 52.4% | 47.6% |
| 68,600 | LEWIS | 31,887 | 19,474 | 11,583 | 830 | 7,891 | R | 61.1% | 36.3% | 62.7% | 37.3% |
| 10,184 | LINCOLN | 5,767 | 3,703 | 1,956 | 108 | 1,747 | R | 64.2% | 33.9% | 65.4% | 34.6% |
| 49,405 | MASON | 25,050 | 10,998 | 13,349 | 703 | 2,351 | D | 43.9% | 53.3% | 45.2% | 54.8% |
| 39,564 | OKANOGAN | 16,068 | 8,931 | 6,616 | 521 | 2,315 | R | 55.6% | 41.2% | 57.4% | 42.6% |
| 20,984 | PACIFIC | 10,270 | 4,149 | 5,850 | 271 | 1,701 | D | 40.4% | 57.0% | 41.5% | 58.5% |
| 11,732 | PEND OREILLE | 6,134 | 3,241 | 2,703 | 190 | 538 | R | 52.8% | 44.1% | 54.5% | 45.5% |
| 700,820 | PIERCE | 310,127 | 136,084 | 167,428 | 6,615 | 31,344 | D | 43.9% | 54.0% | 44.8% | 55.2% |
| 14,077 | SAN JUAN | 9,919 | 3,164 | 6,376 | 379 | 3,212 | D | 31.9% | 64.3% | 33.2% | 66.8% |
| 102,979 | SKAGIT | 51,707 | 24,364 | 26,162 | 1,181 | 1,798 | D | 47.1% | 50.6% | 48.2% | 51.8% |
| 9,872 | SKAMANIA | 5,024 | 2,314 | 2,550 | 160 | 236 | D | 46.1% | 50.8% | 47.6% | 52.4% |
| 606,024 | SNOHOMISH | 292,003 | 124,986 | 160,402 | 6,615 | 35,416 | D | 42.8% | 54.9% | 43.8% | 56.2% |
| 417,939 | SPOKANE | 200,610 | 101,511 | 94,446 | 4,653 | 7,065 | R | 50.6% | 47.1% | 51.8% | 48.2% |
| 40,066 | STEVENS | 20,104 | 11,804 | 7,706 | 594 | 4,098 | R | 58.7% | 38.3% | 60.5% | 39.5% |
| 207,355 | THURSTON | 110,889 | 44,417 | 63,364 | 3,108 | 18,947 | D | 40.1% | 57.1% | 41.2% | 58.8% |
| 3,824 | WAHKIAKUM | 2,167 | 1,018 | 1,086 | 63 | 68 | D | 47.0% | 50.1% | 48.4% | 51.6% |
| 55,180 | WALLA WALLA | 22,669 | 12,243 | 9,972 | 454 | 2,271 | R | 54.0% | 44.0% | 55.1% | 44.9% |
| 166,814 | WHATCOM | 88,694 | 38,036 | 48,078 | 2,580 | 10,042 | D | 42.9% | 54.2% | 44.2% | 55.8% |
| 40,740 | WHITMAN | 17,721 | 9,073 | 8,152 | 496 | 921 | R | 51.2% | 46.0% | 52.7% | 47.3% |
| 222,581 | YAKIMA | 72,165 | 39,315 | 31,372 | 1,478 | 7,943 | R | 54.5% | 43.5% | 55.6% | 44.4% |
| 5,894,121 | TOTAL | 2,818,651 | 1,204,584 | 1,549,708 | 64,359 | 345,124 | D | 42.7% | 55.0% | 43.7% | 56.3% |

# WASHINGTON

## HOUSE OF REPRESENTATIVES

| CD | Year | Total Vote | Republican Vote | Republican Candidate | Democratic Vote | Democratic Candidate | Other Vote | Rep.-Dem. Plurality | Total Vote Rep. | Total Vote Dem. | Major Vote Rep. | Major Vote Dem. |
|---|---|---|---|---|---|---|---|---|---|---|---|---|
| 1 | 2004 | 327,769 | 117,850 | Eastwood, Randy | 204,121 | Inslee, Jay* | 5,798 | 86,271 D | 36.0% | 62.3% | 36.6% | 63.4% |
| 1 | 2002 | 205,034 | 84,696 | Marine, Joe | 114,087 | Inslee, Jay* | 6,251 | 29,391 D | 41.3% | 55.6% | 42.6% | 57.4% |
| 2 | 2004 | 316,682 | 106,333 | Sinclair, Suzanne | 202,383 | Larsen, Rick* | 7,966 | 96,050 D | 33.6% | 63.9% | 34.4% | 65.6% |
| 2 | 2002 | 202,150 | 92,528 | Smith, Norma | 101,219 | Larsen, Rick* | 8,403 | 8,691 D | 45.8% | 50.1% | 47.8% | 52.2% |
| 3 | 2004 | 312,653 | 119,027 | Crowson, Thomas A. | 193,626 | Baird, Brian* | | 74,599 D | 38.1% | 61.9% | 38.1% | 61.9% |
| 3 | 2002 | 193,329 | 74,065 | Zarelli, Joseph | 119,264 | Baird, Brian* | | 45,199 D | 38.3% | 61.7% | 38.3% | 61.7% |
| 4 | 2004 | 247,113 | 154,627 | Hastings, Doc* | 92,486 | Matheson, Sandy | | 62,141 R | 62.6% | 37.4% | 62.6% | 37.4% |
| 4 | 2002 | 161,829 | 108,257 | Hastings, Doc* | 53,572 | Mason, Craig | | 54,685 R | 66.9% | 33.1% | 66.9% | 33.1% |
| 5 | 2004 | 300,933 | 179,600 | McMorris, Cathy | 121,333 | Barbieri, Don | | 58,267 R | 59.7% | 40.3% | 59.7% | 40.3% |
| 5 | 2002 | 202,282 | 126,757 | Nethercutt, George* | 65,146 | Haggin, Bart | 10,379 | 61,611 R | 62.7% | 32.2% | 66.1% | 33.9% |
| 6 | 2004 | 294,147 | 91,228 | Cloud, Doug | 202,919 | Dicks, Norm* | | 111,691 D | 31.0% | 69.0% | 31.0% | 69.0% |
| 6 | 2002 | 196,444 | 61,584 | Lawrence, Bob | 126,116 | Dicks, Norm* | 8,744 | 64,532 D | 31.3% | 64.2% | 32.8% | 67.2% |
| 7 | 2004 | 337,528 | 65,226 | Cassady, Carol | 272,302 | McDermott, Jim* | | 207,076 D | 19.3% | 80.7% | 19.3% | 80.7% |
| 7 | 2002 | 211,003 | 46,256 | Cassady, Carol | 156,300 | McDermott, Jim* | 8,447 | 110,044 D | 21.9% | 74.1% | 22.8% | 77.2% |
| 8 | 2004 | 336,499 | 173,298 | Reichert, Dave | 157,148 | Ross, Dave | 6,053 | 16,150 R | 51.5% | 46.7% | 52.4% | 47.6% |
| 8 | 2002 | 203,335 | 121,633 | Dunn, Jennifer* | 75,931 | Behrens-Benedict, Heidi | 5,771 | 45,702 R | 59.8% | 37.3% | 61.6% | 38.4% |
| 9 | 2004 | 256,671 | 88,304 | Lord, Paul J. | 162,433 | Smith, Adam* | 5,934 | 74,129 D | 34.4% | 63.3% | 35.2% | 64.8% |
| 9 | 2002 | 163,710 | 63,146 | Casada, Sarah | 95,805 | Smith, Adam* | 4,759 | 32,659 D | 38.6% | 58.5% | 39.7% | 60.3% |
| Total | 2004 | 2,729,995 | 1,095,493 | | 1,608,751 | | 25,751 | 513,258 D | 40.1% | 58.9% | 40.5% | 59.5% |
| Total | 2002 | 1,739,116 | 778,922 | | 907,440 | | 52,754 | 128,518 D | 44.8% | 52.2% | 46.2% | 53.8% |

An asterisk (*) denotes incumbent.

# WASHINGTON

## GENERAL AND PRIMARY ELECTIONS

## 2004 GENERAL ELECTIONS

**President**   Other vote was 23,283 Independent (Ralph Nader); 11,955 Libertarian (Michael Badnarik); 3,922 Constitution (Michael Peroutka); 2,974 Green (David Cobb); 1,077 Workers World (John Parker); 547 Socialist Workers (James Harris); 231 Socialist Equality (Bill Van Auken).

**Governor**   Other vote was 63,465 Libertarian (Ruth Bennett).

**Senator**   Other vote was 34,055 Libertarian (J. Mills); 30,304 Green (Mark B. Wilson).

**House**   Other vote was:

CD 1   5,798 Libertarian (Charles Moore).
CD 2   7,966 Libertarian (Bruce Guthrie).
CD 3
CD 4
CD 5
CD 6
CD 7
CD 8   6,053 Libertarian (Spencer Garrett).
CD 9   5,934 Green (Robert F. Losey).

# WASHINGTON

## GENERAL AND PRIMARY ELECTIONS

## 2004 PRIMARY ELECTIONS

| | | | |
|---|---|---|---|
| **Primary** | September 14, 2004 | **Registration** (as of Sept. 14, 2004) | 3,279,205   No Party Registration |

**Primary Type**   Open—Registered voters could participate in the primary of their choice, but were limited to the ballot of one party.

Note:   An asterisk (*) denotes incumbent.

| | REPUBLICAN PRIMARIES | | | DEMOCRATIC PRIMARIES | | |
|---|---|---|---|---|---|---|
| Governor | Dino Rossi | 444,337 | 85.1% | Christine Gregoire | 504,018 | 65.6% |
| | Bill Meyer | 44,448 | 8.5% | Ron Sims | 228,306 | 29.7% |
| | John W. Aiken Jr. | 33,104 | 6.3% | Mike the Mover | 15,118 | 2.0% |
| | | | | Don Hansler | 8,636 | 1.1% |
| | | | | Scott Headland | 6,983 | 0.9% |
| | | | | Eugen Buculei | 5,005 | 0.7% |
| | TOTAL | 521,889 | | TOTAL | 768,066 | |
| Senator | George Nethercutt | 432,748 | 82.9% | Patty Murray* | 709,407 | 92.2% |
| | Reed Davis | 36,147 | 6.9% | Warren E. Hanson | 46,490 | 6.0% |
| | Brad Klippert | 29,870 | 5.7% | Mohammad H. Said | 13,527 | 1.8% |
| | Chuck Jackson | 10,033 | 1.9% | | | |
| | Gordon Allen Pross | 8,315 | 1.6% | | | |
| | William Edward Chovil | 4,981 | 1.0% | | | |
| | TOTAL | 522,094 | | TOTAL | 769,514 | |
| Congressional District 1 | Randy Eastwood | 50,050 | 100.0% | Jay Inslee* | 89,168 | 100.0% |
| Congressional District 2 | Suzanne Sinclair | 21,519 | 40.9% | Rick Larsen* | 77,962 | 100.0% |
| | Larry Klepinger | 19,568 | 37.2% | | | |
| | Glenn E. Coggeshell III | 11,523 | 21.9% | | | |
| | TOTAL | 52,610 | | | | |
| Congressional District 3 | Thomas A. Crowson | 30,877 | 67.6% | Brian Baird* | 61,110 | 85.3% |
| | Dawn Courtney | 14,769 | 32.4% | Cheryl A. Crist | 10,518 | 14.7% |
| | TOTAL | 45,646 | | TOTAL | 71,628 | |
| Congressional District 4 | Doc Hastings* | 65,213 | 100.0% | Sandy Matheson | 22,933 | 62.8% |
| | | | | Craig Mason | 7,418 | 20.3% |
| | | | | Richard K. Wright | 6,191 | 16.9% |
| | | | | TOTAL | 36,542 | |
| Congressional District 5 | Cathy McMorris | 42,948 | 49.7% | Don Barbieri | 56,199 | 100.0% |
| | Larry Sheahan | 23,593 | 27.3% | | | |
| | Shaun Cross | 19,878 | 23.0% | | | |
| | TOTAL | 86,419 | | | | |
| Congressional District 6 | Doug Cloud | 43,653 | 100.0% | Norm Dicks* | 82,331 | 100.0% |
| Congressional District 7 | Carol Cassady | 19,962 | 100.0% | Jim McDermott* | 124,779 | 100.0% |
| Congressional District 8 | Dave Reichert | 31,088 | 43.0% | Dave Ross | 39,347 | 48.4% |
| | Diane Tebelius | 16,468 | 22.8% | Alex Alben | 24,903 | 30.7% |
| | Luke Esser | 16,309 | 22.6% | Heidi Behrens-Benedict | 16,992 | 20.9% |
| | Conrad Lee | 8,350 | 11.6% | | | |
| | TOTAL | 72,215 | | TOTAL | 81,242 | |
| Congressional District 9 | Paul J. Lord | 20,829 | 53.4% | Adam Smith* | 65,185 | 100.0% |
| | C. Mark Greene | 18,183 | 46.6% | | | |
| | TOTAL | 39,012 | | | | |

# WEST VIRGINIA

## GOVERNOR
Joe Manchin III (D). Elected 2004 to a four-year term.

## SENATORS (2 Democrats)
Robert C. Byrd (D). Reelected 2000 to a six-year term. Previously elected 1994, 1988, 1982, 1976, 1970, 1964, 1958.

John D. Rockefeller IV (D). Reelected 2002 to a six-year term. Previously elected 1996, 1990, 1984.

## REPRESENTATIVES (2 Democrats, 1 Republican)
1. Alan B. Mollohan (D)    2. Shelley Moore Capito (R)    3. Nick J. Rahall II (D)

## POSTWAR VOTE FOR PRESIDENT

| | | Republican | | Democratic | | Other | | Percentage | | | |
| | Total | | | | | | | Total Vote | | Major Vote | |
| Year | Vote | Vote | Candidate | Vote | Candidate | Vote | Plurality | Rep. | Dem. | Rep. | Dem. |
|---|---|---|---|---|---|---|---|---|---|---|---|
| 2004 | 755,887 | 423,778 | Bush, George W. | 326,541 | Kerry, John | 5,568 | 97,237 R | 56.1% | 43.2% | 56.5% | 43.5% |
| 2000** | 648,124 | 336,475 | Bush, George W. | 295,497 | Gore, Al | 16,152 | 40,978 R | 51.9% | 45.6% | 53.2% | 46.8% |
| 1996** | 636,459 | 233,946 | Dole, Bob | 327,812 | Clinton, Bill | 74,701 | 93,866 D | 36.8% | 51.5% | 41.6% | 58.4% |
| 1992** | 683,762 | 241,974 | Bush, George | 331,001 | Clinton, Bill | 110,787 | 89,027 D | 35.4% | 48.4% | 42.2% | 57.8% |
| 1988 | 653,311 | 310,065 | Bush, George | 341,016 | Dukakis, Michael S. | 2,230 | 30,951 D | 47.5% | 52.2% | 47.6% | 52.4% |
| 1984 | 735,742 | 405,483 | Reagan, Ronald | 328,125 | Mondale, Walter F. | 2,134 | 77,358 R | 55.1% | 44.6% | 55.3% | 44.7% |
| 1980** | 737,715 | 334,206 | Reagan, Ronald | 367,462 | Carter, Jimmy | 36,047 | 33,256 D | 45.3% | 49.8% | 47.6% | 52.4% |
| 1976 | 750,964 | 314,760 | Ford, Gerald R. | 435,914 | Carter, Jimmy | 290 | 121,154 D | 41.9% | 58.0% | 41.9% | 58.1% |
| 1972 | 762,399 | 484,964 | Nixon, Richard M. | 277,435 | McGovern, George S. | | 207,529 R | 63.6% | 36.4% | 63.6% | 36.4% |
| 1968** | 754,206 | 307,555 | Nixon, Richard M. | 374,091 | Humphrey, Hubert H. | 72,560 | 66,536 D | 40.8% | 49.6% | 45.1% | 54.9% |
| 1964 | 792,040 | 253,953 | Goldwater, Barry M. | 538,087 | Johnson, Lyndon B. | | 284,134 D | 32.1% | 67.9% | 32.1% | 67.9% |
| 1960 | 837,781 | 395,995 | Nixon, Richard M. | 441,786 | Kennedy, John F. | | 45,791 D | 47.3% | 52.7% | 47.3% | 52.7% |
| 1956 | 830,831 | 449,297 | Eisenhower, Dwight D. | 381,534 | Stevenson, Adlai E. | | 67,763 R | 54.1% | 45.9% | 54.1% | 45.9% |
| 1952 | 873,548 | 419,970 | Eisenhower, Dwight D. | 453,578 | Stevenson, Adlai E. | | 33,608 D | 48.1% | 51.9% | 48.1% | 51.9% |
| 1948 | 748,750 | 316,251 | Dewey, Thomas E. | 429,188 | Truman, Harry S. | 3,311 | 112,937 D | 42.2% | 57.3% | 42.4% | 57.6% |

In past elections, the other vote included: 2000 - 10,680 Green (Ralph Nader); 1996 - 71,639 Reform (Ross Perot); 1992 - 108,829 Independent (Perot); 1980 - 31,691 Independent (John Anderson); 1968 - 72,560 American Independent (George Wallace).

## POSTWAR VOTE FOR GOVERNOR

| | | Republican | | Democratic | | Other | Rep.-Dem. | Percentage | | | |
| | Total | | | | | | | Total Vote | | Major Vote | |
| Year | Vote | Vote | Candidate | Vote | Candidate | Vote | Plurality | Rep. | Dem. | Rep. | Dem. |
|---|---|---|---|---|---|---|---|---|---|---|---|
| 2004 | 744,433 | 253,131 | Warner, Monty | 472,758 | Manchin, Joe III | 18,544 | 219,627 D | 34.0% | 63.5% | 34.9% | 65.1% |
| 2000 | 648,047 | 305,926 | Underwood, Cecil H. | 324,822 | Wise, Bob | 17,299 | 18,896 D | 47.2% | 50.1% | 48.5% | 51.5% |
| 1996 | 628,559 | 324,518 | Underwood, Cecil H. | 287,870 | Pritt, Charlotte | 16,171 | 36,648 R | 51.6% | 45.8% | 53.0% | 47.0% |
| 1992 | 657,193 | 240,390 | Benedict, Cleveland K. | 368,302 | Caperton, Gaston | 48,501 | 127,912 D | 36.6% | 56.0% | 39.5% | 60.5% |
| 1988 | 649,593 | 267,172 | Moore, Arch A. | 382,421 | Caperton, Gaston | | 115,249 D | 41.1% | 58.9% | 41.1% | 58.9% |
| 1984 | 741,502 | 394,937 | Moore, Arch A. | 346,565 | See, Clyde M. | | 48,372 R | 53.3% | 46.7% | 53.3% | 46.7% |
| 1980 | 742,150 | 337,240 | Moore, Arch A. | 401,863 | Rockefeller, John D. IV | 3,047 | 64,623 D | 45.4% | 54.1% | 45.6% | 54.4% |
| 1976 | 749,270 | 253,420 | Underwood, Cecil H. | 495,661 | Rockefeller, John D. IV | 189 | 242,241 D | 33.8% | 66.2% | 33.8% | 66.2% |
| 1972 | 774,279 | 423,817 | Moore, Arch A. | 350,462 | Rockefeller, John D. IV | | 73,355 R | 54.7% | 45.3% | 54.7% | 45.3% |
| 1968 | 743,845 | 378,315 | Moore, Arch A. | 365,530 | Sprouse, James M. | | 12,785 R | 50.9% | 49.1% | 50.9% | 49.1% |
| 1964 | 788,582 | 355,559 | Underwood, Cecil H. | 433,023 | Smith, Hulett C. | | 77,464 D | 45.1% | 54.9% | 45.1% | 54.9% |
| 1960 | 827,420 | 380,665 | Neely, Harold E. | 446,755 | Barron, W. W. | | 66,090 D | 46.0% | 54.0% | 46.0% | 54.0% |
| 1956 | 817,623 | 440,502 | Underwood, Cecil H. | 377,121 | Mollohan, Robert H. | | 63,381 R | 53.9% | 46.1% | 53.9% | 46.1% |
| 1952 | 882,527 | 427,629 | Holt, Rush D. | 454,898 | Marland, William C. | | 27,269 D | 48.5% | 51.5% | 48.5% | 51.5% |
| 1948 | 768,061 | 329,309 | Boreman, Herbert | 438,752 | Patteson, Okey L. | | 109,443 D | 42.9% | 57.1% | 42.9% | 57.1% |

# WEST VIRGINIA

## POSTWAR VOTE FOR SENATOR

| Year | Total Vote | Republican | | Democratic | | Other Vote | Rep.-Dem. Plurality | Percentage | | | |
|---|---|---|---|---|---|---|---|---|---|---|---|
| | | Vote | Candidate | Vote | Candidate | | | Total Vote | | Major Vote | |
| | | | | | | | | Rep. | Dem. | Rep. | Dem. |
| 2002 | 436,183 | 160,902 | Wolfe, Jay | 275,281 | Rockefeller, John D. IV | | 114,379 D | 36.9% | 63.1% | 36.9% | 63.1% |
| 2000 | 603,477 | 121,635 | Gallaher, David T. | 469,215 | Byrd, Robert C. | 12,627 | 347,580 D | 20.2% | 77.8% | 20.6% | 79.4% |
| 1996 | 595,614 | 139,088 | Burks, Betty A. | 456,526 | Rockefeller, John D. IV | | 317,438 D | 23.4% | 76.6% | 23.4% | 76.6% |
| 1994 | 420,936 | 130,441 | Klos, Stan | 290,495 | Byrd, Robert C. | | 160,054 D | 31.0% | 69.0% | 31.0% | 69.0% |
| 1990 | 404,305 | 128,071 | Yoder, John | 276,234 | Rockefeller, John D. IV | | 148,163 D | 31.7% | 68.3% | 31.7% | 68.3% |
| 1988 | 634,547 | 223,564 | Wolfe, M. Jay | 410,983 | Byrd, Robert C. | | 187,419 D | 35.2% | 64.8% | 35.2% | 64.8% |
| 1984 | 722,212 | 344,680 | Raese, John R. | 374,233 | Rockefeller, John D. IV | 3,299 | 29,553 D | 47.7% | 51.8% | 47.9% | 52.1% |
| 1982 | 565,314 | 173,910 | Benedict, Cleveland K. | 387,170 | Byrd, Robert C. | 4,234 | 213,260 D | 30.8% | 68.5% | 31.0% | 69.0% |
| 1978 | 493,351 | 244,317 | Moore, Arch A. | 249,034 | Randolph, Jennings | | 4,717 D | 49.5% | 50.5% | 49.5% | 50.5% |
| 1976 | 566,790 | | — | 566,423 | Byrd, Robert C. | 367 | 566,423 D | | 99.9% | | 100.0% |
| 1972 | 731,841 | 245,531 | Leonard, Louise | 486,310 | Randolph, Jennings | | 240,779 D | 33.5% | 66.5% | 33.5% | 66.5% |
| 1970 | 445,623 | 99,658 | Dodson, Elmer H. | 345,965 | Byrd, Robert C. | | 246,307 D | 22.4% | 77.6% | 22.4% | 77.6% |
| 1966 | 491,216 | 198,891 | Love, Francis J. | 292,325 | Randolph, Jennings | | 93,434 D | 40.5% | 59.5% | 40.5% | 59.5% |
| 1964 | 761,087 | 246,072 | Benedict, Cooper P. | 515,015 | Byrd, Robert C. | | 268,943 D | 32.3% | 67.7% | 32.3% | 67.7% |
| 1960 | 828,292 | 369,935 | Underwood, Cecil H. | 458,355 | Randolph, Jennings | 2 | 88,420 D | 44.7% | 55.3% | 44.7% | 55.3% |
| 1958 | 644,917 | 263,172 | Revercomb, Chapman | 381,745 | Byrd, Robert C. | | 118,573 D | 40.8% | 59.2% | 40.8% | 59.2% |
| 1958S | 630,677 | 256,510 | Hoblitzell, John D. | 374,167 | Randolph, Jennings | | 117,657 D | 40.7% | 59.3% | 40.7% | 59.3% |
| 1956S | 805,174 | 432,123 | Revercomb, Chapman | 373,051 | Marland, William C. | | 59,072 R | 53.7% | 46.3% | 53.7% | 46.3% |
| 1954 | 593,329 | 268,066 | Sweeney, Tom | 325,263 | Neely, Matthew M. | | 57,197 D | 45.2% | 54.8% | 45.2% | 54.8% |
| 1952 | 876,573 | 406,554 | Revercomb, Chapman | 470,019 | Kilgore, Harley M. | | 63,465 D | 46.4% | 53.6% | 46.4% | 53.6% |
| 1948 | 763,888 | 328,534 | Revercomb, Chapman | 435,354 | Neely, Matthew M. | | 106,820 D | 43.0% | 57.0% | 43.0% | 57.0% |
| 1946 | 542,768 | 269,617 | Sweeney, Tom | 273,151 | Kilgore, Harley M. | | 3,534 D | 49.7% | 50.3% | 49.7% | 50.3% |

One of the 1958 elections and the 1956 election were for short terms to fill vacancies.

# WEST VIRGINIA

Congressional districts first established for elections held in 2002
3 members

# WEST VIRGINIA

## PRESIDENT 2004

| 2000 Census Population | County | Total Vote | Republican | Democratic | Other | Rep.-Dem. Plurality | | Percentage | | | |
|---|---|---|---|---|---|---|---|---|---|---|---|
| | | | | | | | | Total Vote | | Major Vote | |
| | | | | | | | | Rep. | Dem. | Rep. | Dem. |
| 15,557 | BARBOUR | 6,655 | 4,004 | 2,610 | 41 | 1,394 | R | 60.2% | 39.2% | 60.5% | 39.5% |
| 75,905 | BERKELEY | 33,785 | 21,293 | 12,244 | 248 | 9,049 | R | 63.0% | 36.2% | 63.5% | 36.5% |
| 25,535 | BOONE | 10,198 | 4,207 | 5,933 | 58 | 1,726 | D | 41.3% | 58.2% | 41.5% | 58.5% |
| 14,702 | BRAXTON | 6,051 | 2,986 | 3,035 | 30 | 49 | D | 49.3% | 50.2% | 49.6% | 50.4% |
| 25,447 | BROOKE | 10,773 | 5,189 | 5,493 | 91 | 304 | D | 48.2% | 51.0% | 48.6% | 51.4% |
| 96,784 | CABELL | 37,950 | 21,035 | 16,583 | 332 | 4,452 | R | 55.4% | 43.7% | 55.9% | 44.1% |
| 7,582 | CALHOUN | 2,889 | 1,588 | 1,266 | 35 | 322 | R | 55.0% | 43.8% | 55.6% | 44.4% |
| 10,330 | CLAY | 4,072 | 2,198 | 1,835 | 39 | 363 | R | 54.0% | 45.1% | 54.5% | 45.5% |
| 7,403 | DODDRIDGE | 3,179 | 2,362 | 800 | 17 | 1,562 | R | 74.3% | 25.2% | 74.7% | 25.3% |
| 47,579 | FAYETTE | 16,967 | 7,881 | 8,971 | 115 | 1,090 | D | 46.4% | 52.9% | 46.8% | 53.2% |
| 7,160 | GILMER | 2,852 | 1,665 | 1,159 | 28 | 506 | R | 58.4% | 40.6% | 59.0% | 41.0% |
| 11,299 | GRANT | 5,047 | 4,063 | 963 | 21 | 3,100 | R | 80.5% | 19.1% | 80.8% | 19.2% |
| 34,453 | GREENBRIER | 14,553 | 8,358 | 6,084 | 111 | 2,274 | R | 57.4% | 41.8% | 57.9% | 42.1% |
| 20,203 | HAMPSHIRE | 7,996 | 5,489 | 2,455 | 52 | 3,034 | R | 68.6% | 30.7% | 69.1% | 30.9% |
| 32,667 | HANCOCK | 14,321 | 7,298 | 6,906 | 117 | 392 | R | 51.0% | 48.2% | 51.4% | 48.6% |
| 12,669 | HARDY | 5,276 | 3,635 | 1,617 | 24 | 2,018 | R | 68.9% | 30.6% | 69.2% | 30.8% |
| 68,652 | HARRISON | 30,588 | 17,111 | 13,238 | 239 | 3,873 | R | 55.9% | 43.3% | 56.4% | 43.6% |
| 28,000 | JACKSON | 13,158 | 7,686 | 5,384 | 88 | 2,302 | R | 58.4% | 40.9% | 58.8% | 41.2% |
| 42,190 | JEFFERSON | 19,993 | 10,539 | 9,301 | 153 | 1,238 | R | 52.7% | 46.5% | 53.1% | 46.9% |
| 200,073 | KANAWHA | 87,928 | 44,430 | 43,010 | 488 | 1,420 | R | 50.5% | 48.9% | 50.8% | 49.2% |
| 16,919 | LEWIS | 6,999 | 4,445 | 2,475 | 79 | 1,970 | R | 63.5% | 35.4% | 64.2% | 35.8% |
| 22,108 | LINCOLN | 8,312 | 4,102 | 4,048 | 162 | 54 | R | 49.4% | 48.7% | 50.3% | 49.7% |
| 37,710 | LOGAN | 14,987 | 7,047 | 7,877 | 63 | 830 | D | 47.0% | 52.6% | 47.2% | 52.8% |
| 27,329 | MCDOWELL | 7,299 | 2,762 | 4,501 | 36 | 1,739 | D | 37.8% | 61.7% | 38.0% | 62.0% |
| 56,598 | MARION | 25,194 | 12,150 | 12,771 | 273 | 621 | D | 48.2% | 50.7% | 48.8% | 51.2% |
| 35,519 | MARSHALL | 15,072 | 8,516 | 6,435 | 121 | 2,081 | R | 56.5% | 42.7% | 57.0% | 43.0% |
| 25,957 | MASON | 11,990 | 6,487 | 5,408 | 95 | 1,079 | R | 54.1% | 45.1% | 54.5% | 45.5% |
| 62,980 | MERCER | 22,379 | 13,057 | 9,178 | 144 | 3,879 | R | 58.3% | 41.0% | 58.7% | 41.3% |
| 27,078 | MINERAL | 11,461 | 7,854 | 3,518 | 89 | 4,336 | R | 68.5% | 30.7% | 69.1% | 30.9% |
| 28,253 | MINGO | 10,655 | 4,612 | 5,983 | 60 | 1,371 | D | 43.3% | 56.2% | 43.5% | 56.5% |
| 81,866 | MONONGALIA | 34,306 | 17,670 | 16,313 | 323 | 1,357 | R | 51.5% | 47.6% | 52.0% | 48.0% |
| 14,583 | MONROE | 5,951 | 3,590 | 2,311 | 50 | 1,279 | R | 60.3% | 38.8% | 60.8% | 39.2% |
| 14,943 | MORGAN | 6,847 | 4,511 | 2,272 | 64 | 2,239 | R | 65.9% | 33.2% | 66.5% | 33.5% |
| 26,562 | NICHOLAS | 10,351 | 5,485 | 4,788 | 78 | 697 | R | 53.0% | 46.3% | 53.4% | 46.6% |
| 47,427 | OHIO | 20,392 | 11,694 | 8,543 | 155 | 3,151 | R | 57.3% | 41.9% | 57.8% | 42.2% |
| 8,196 | PENDLETON | 3,544 | 2,146 | 1,381 | 17 | 765 | R | 60.6% | 39.0% | 60.8% | 39.2% |
| 7,514 | PLEASANTS | 3,435 | 2,061 | 1,349 | 25 | 712 | R | 60.0% | 39.3% | 60.4% | 39.6% |
| 9,131 | POCAHONTAS | 3,918 | 2,295 | 1,573 | 50 | 722 | R | 58.6% | 40.1% | 59.3% | 40.7% |
| 29,334 | PRESTON | 11,929 | 7,855 | 3,963 | 111 | 3,892 | R | 65.8% | 33.2% | 66.5% | 33.5% |
| 51,589 | PUTNAM | 25,151 | 15,716 | 9,301 | 134 | 6,415 | R | 62.5% | 37.0% | 62.8% | 37.2% |
| 79,220 | RALEIGH | 30,525 | 18,519 | 11,815 | 191 | 6,704 | R | 60.7% | 38.7% | 61.1% | 38.9% |
| 28,262 | RANDOLPH | 11,490 | 6,512 | 4,892 | 86 | 1,620 | R | 56.7% | 42.6% | 57.1% | 42.9% |
| 10,343 | RITCHIE | 4,196 | 3,086 | 1,070 | 40 | 2,016 | R | 73.5% | 25.5% | 74.3% | 25.7% |
| 15,446 | ROANE | 6,100 | 3,440 | 2,612 | 48 | 828 | R | 56.4% | 42.8% | 56.8% | 43.2% |
| 12,999 | SUMMERS | 5,524 | 2,978 | 2,504 | 42 | 474 | R | 53.9% | 45.3% | 54.3% | 45.7% |
| 16,089 | TAYLOR | 6,551 | 3,893 | 2,617 | 41 | 1,276 | R | 59.4% | 39.9% | 59.8% | 40.2% |
| 7,321 | TUCKER | 3,600 | 2,179 | 1,400 | 21 | 779 | R | 60.5% | 38.9% | 60.9% | 39.1% |
| 9,592 | TYLER | 4,245 | 2,798 | 1,401 | 46 | 1,397 | R | 65.9% | 33.0% | 66.6% | 33.4% |
| 23,404 | UPSHUR | 9,293 | 6,191 | 3,034 | 68 | 3,157 | R | 66.6% | 32.6% | 67.1% | 32.9% |
| 42,903 | WAYNE | 18,609 | 10,070 | 8,411 | 128 | 1,659 | R | 54.1% | 45.2% | 54.5% | 45.5% |
| 9,719 | WEBSTER | 3,714 | 1,724 | 1,965 | 25 | 241 | D | 46.4% | 52.9% | 46.7% | 53.3% |
| 17,693 | WETZEL | 7,038 | 3,656 | 3,330 | 52 | 326 | R | 51.9% | 47.3% | 52.3% | 47.7% |
| 5,873 | WIRT | 2,654 | 1,727 | 896 | 31 | 831 | R | 65.1% | 33.8% | 65.8% | 34.2% |
| 87,986 | WOOD | 39,227 | 24,948 | 14,025 | 254 | 10,923 | R | 63.6% | 35.8% | 64.0% | 36.0% |
| 25,708 | WYOMING | 8,718 | 4,985 | 3,694 | 39 | 1,291 | R | 57.2% | 42.4% | 57.4% | 42.6% |
| 1,808,344 | TOTAL | 755,887 | 423,778 | 326,541 | 5,568 | 97,237 | R | 56.1% | 43.2% | 56.5% | 43.5% |

# WEST VIRGINIA

## GOVERNOR 2004

| 2000 Census Population | County | Total Vote | Republican | Democratic | Other | Rep.-Dem. Plurality | | Percentage | | | |
|---|---|---|---|---|---|---|---|---|---|---|---|
| | | | | | | | | Total Vote | | Major Vote | |
| | | | | | | | | Rep. | Dem. | Rep. | Dem. |
| 15,557 | BARBOUR | 6,601 | 2,002 | 4,516 | 83 | 2,514 | D | 30.3% | 68.4% | 30.7% | 69.3% |
| 75,905 | BERKELEY | 33,308 | 16,630 | 16,044 | 634 | 586 | R | 49.9% | 48.2% | 50.9% | 49.1% |
| 25,535 | BOONE | 10,200 | 1,934 | 8,070 | 196 | 6,136 | D | 19.0% | 79.1% | 19.3% | 80.7% |
| 14,702 | BRAXTON | 5,870 | 1,376 | 4,404 | 90 | 3,028 | D | 23.4% | 75.0% | 23.8% | 76.2% |
| 25,447 | BROOKE | 10,752 | 2,961 | 7,591 | 200 | 4,630 | D | 27.5% | 70.6% | 28.1% | 71.9% |
| 96,784 | CABELL | 37,497 | 13,829 | 22,589 | 1,079 | 8,760 | D | 36.9% | 60.2% | 38.0% | 62.0% |
| 7,582 | CALHOUN | 2,886 | 799 | 1,957 | 130 | 1,158 | D | 27.7% | 67.8% | 29.0% | 71.0% |
| 10,330 | CLAY | 4,059 | 1,008 | 2,932 | 119 | 1,924 | D | 24.8% | 72.2% | 25.6% | 74.4% |
| 7,403 | DODDRIDGE | 3,177 | 1,603 | 1,492 | 82 | 111 | R | 50.5% | 47.0% | 51.8% | 48.2% |
| 47,579 | FAYETTE | 16,895 | 4,979 | 11,448 | 468 | 6,469 | D | 29.5% | 67.8% | 30.3% | 69.7% |
| 7,160 | GILMER | 2,826 | 739 | 1,975 | 112 | 1,236 | D | 26.2% | 69.9% | 27.2% | 72.8% |
| 11,299 | GRANT | 4,605 | 2,421 | 2,127 | 57 | 294 | R | 52.6% | 46.2% | 53.2% | 46.8% |
| 34,453 | GREENBRIER | 14,396 | 5,439 | 8,461 | 496 | 3,022 | D | 37.8% | 58.8% | 39.1% | 60.9% |
| 20,203 | HAMPSHIRE | 7,764 | 3,323 | 4,241 | 200 | 918 | D | 42.8% | 54.6% | 43.9% | 56.1% |
| 32,667 | HANCOCK | 12,895 | 4,115 | 8,586 | 194 | 4,471 | D | 31.9% | 66.6% | 32.4% | 67.6% |
| 12,669 | HARDY | 4,913 | 1,895 | 2,907 | 111 | 1,012 | D | 38.6% | 59.2% | 39.5% | 60.5% |
| 68,652 | HARRISON | 30,437 | 9,373 | 20,365 | 699 | 10,992 | D | 30.8% | 66.9% | 31.5% | 68.5% |
| 28,000 | JACKSON | 13,106 | 4,426 | 8,374 | 306 | 3,948 | D | 33.8% | 63.9% | 34.6% | 65.4% |
| 42,190 | JEFFERSON | 19,533 | 8,295 | 10,561 | 677 | 2,266 | D | 42.5% | 54.1% | 44.0% | 56.0% |
| 200,073 | KANAWHA | 86,590 | 28,817 | 54,620 | 3,153 | 25,803 | D | 33.3% | 63.1% | 34.5% | 65.5% |
| 16,919 | LEWIS | 7,020 | 2,041 | 4,806 | 173 | 2,765 | D | 29.1% | 68.5% | 29.8% | 70.2% |
| 22,108 | LINCOLN | 8,214 | 2,364 | 5,590 | 260 | 3,226 | D | 28.8% | 68.1% | 29.7% | 70.3% |
| 37,710 | LOGAN | 14,367 | 3,592 | 10,505 | 270 | 6,913 | D | 25.0% | 73.1% | 25.5% | 74.5% |
| 27,329 | MCDOWELL | 7,228 | 1,320 | 5,731 | 177 | 4,411 | D | 18.3% | 79.3% | 18.7% | 81.3% |
| 56,598 | MARION | 24,924 | 6,496 | 17,911 | 517 | 11,415 | D | 26.1% | 71.9% | 26.6% | 73.4% |
| 35,519 | MARSHALL | 15,053 | 4,535 | 10,256 | 262 | 5,721 | D | 30.1% | 68.1% | 30.7% | 69.3% |
| 25,957 | MASON | 11,930 | 3,159 | 8,504 | 267 | 5,345 | D | 26.5% | 71.3% | 27.1% | 72.9% |
| 62,980 | MERCER | 22,343 | 7,980 | 13,997 | 366 | 6,017 | D | 35.7% | 62.6% | 36.3% | 63.7% |
| 27,078 | MINERAL | 11,255 | 4,840 | 6,206 | 209 | 1,366 | D | 43.0% | 55.1% | 43.8% | 56.2% |
| 28,253 | MINGO | 10,604 | 1,734 | 8,730 | 140 | 6,996 | D | 16.4% | 82.3% | 16.6% | 83.4% |
| 81,866 | MONONGALIA | 33,561 | 11,220 | 20,512 | 1,829 | 9,292 | D | 33.4% | 61.1% | 35.4% | 64.6% |
| 14,583 | MONROE | 5,901 | 2,357 | 3,425 | 119 | 1,068 | D | 39.9% | 58.0% | 40.8% | 59.2% |
| 14,943 | MORGAN | 6,476 | 3,117 | 3,209 | 150 | 92 | D | 48.1% | 49.6% | 49.3% | 50.7% |
| 26,562 | NICHOLAS | 10,303 | 2,909 | 7,153 | 241 | 4,244 | D | 28.2% | 69.4% | 28.9% | 71.1% |
| 47,427 | OHIO | 20,067 | 6,263 | 13,470 | 334 | 7,207 | D | 31.2% | 67.1% | 31.7% | 68.3% |
| 8,196 | PENDLETON | 3,349 | 1,246 | 2,081 | 22 | 835 | D | 37.2% | 62.1% | 37.5% | 62.5% |
| 7,514 | PLEASANTS | 3,370 | 927 | 2,416 | 27 | 1,489 | D | 27.5% | 71.7% | 27.7% | 72.3% |
| 9,131 | POCAHONTAS | 3,855 | 1,329 | 2,344 | 182 | 1,015 | D | 34.5% | 60.8% | 36.2% | 63.8% |
| 29,334 | PRESTON | 11,869 | 5,610 | 5,889 | 370 | 279 | D | 47.3% | 49.6% | 48.8% | 51.2% |
| 51,589 | PUTNAM | 24,921 | 9,998 | 14,373 | 550 | 4,375 | D | 40.1% | 57.7% | 41.0% | 59.0% |
| 79,220 | RALEIGH | 30,329 | 12,359 | 17,363 | 607 | 5,004 | D | 40.7% | 57.2% | 41.6% | 58.4% |
| 28,262 | RANDOLPH | 11,446 | 3,160 | 7,952 | 334 | 4,792 | D | 27.6% | 69.5% | 28.4% | 71.6% |
| 10,343 | RITCHIE | 4,143 | 1,724 | 2,322 | 97 | 598 | D | 41.6% | 56.0% | 42.6% | 57.4% |
| 15,446 | ROANE | 6,108 | 2,039 | 3,874 | 195 | 1,835 | D | 33.4% | 63.4% | 34.5% | 65.5% |
| 12,999 | SUMMERS | 5,477 | 1,925 | 3,385 | 167 | 1,460 | D | 35.1% | 61.8% | 36.3% | 63.7% |
| 16,089 | TAYLOR | 6,498 | 1,975 | 4,451 | 72 | 2,476 | D | 30.4% | 68.5% | 30.7% | 69.3% |
| 7,321 | TUCKER | 3,565 | 1,083 | 2,361 | 121 | 1,278 | D | 30.4% | 66.2% | 31.4% | 68.6% |
| 9,592 | TYLER | 4,232 | 1,705 | 2,447 | 80 | 742 | D | 40.3% | 57.8% | 41.1% | 58.9% |
| 23,404 | UPSHUR | 9,288 | 3,130 | 5,992 | 166 | 2,862 | D | 33.7% | 64.5% | 34.3% | 65.7% |
| 42,903 | WAYNE | 17,618 | 5,903 | 11,479 | 236 | 5,576 | D | 33.5% | 65.2% | 34.0% | 66.0% |
| 9,719 | WEBSTER | 3,726 | 779 | 2,848 | 99 | 2,069 | D | 20.9% | 76.4% | 21.5% | 78.5% |
| 17,693 | WETZEL | 7,060 | 1,752 | 5,228 | 80 | 3,476 | D | 24.8% | 74.1% | 25.1% | 74.9% |
| 5,873 | WIRT | 2,585 | 787 | 1,765 | 33 | 978 | D | 30.4% | 68.3% | 30.8% | 69.2% |
| 87,986 | WOOD | 38,909 | 13,383 | 24,904 | 622 | 11,521 | D | 34.4% | 64.0% | 35.0% | 65.0% |
| 25,708 | WYOMING | 8,529 | 2,426 | 6,019 | 84 | 3,593 | D | 28.4% | 70.6% | 28.7% | 71.3% |
| 1,808,344 | TOTAL | 744,433 | 253,131 | 472,758 | 18,544 | 219,627 | D | 34.0% | 63.5% | 34.9% | 65.1% |

# WEST VIRGINIA

## HOUSE OF REPRESENTATIVES

| CD | Year | Total Vote | Republican Vote | Candidate | Democratic Vote | Candidate | Other Vote | Rep.-Dem. Plurality | Percentage Total Vote Rep. | Dem. | Major Vote Rep. | Dem. |
|----|------|-----------|-----------------|-----------|-----------------|-----------|------------|---------------------|---------|------|------|------|
| 1 | 2004 | 245,779 | 79,196 | Parks, Alan Lee | 166,583 | Mollohan, Alan B.* | | 87,387 D | 32.2% | 67.8% | 32.2% | 67.8% |
| 1 | 2002 | 111,261 | | | 110,941 | Mollohan, Alan B.* | 320 | 110,941 D | | 99.7% | | 100.0% |
| 2 | 2004 | 257,025 | 147,676 | Capito, Shelley Moore* | 106,131 | Wells, Erik | 3,218 | 41,545 R | 57.5% | 41.3% | 58.2% | 41.8% |
| 2 | 2002 | 163,676 | 98,276 | Capito, Shelley Moore* | 65,400 | Humphreys, Jim | | 32,876 R | 60.0% | 40.0% | 60.0% | 40.0% |
| 3 | 2004 | 218,852 | 76,170 | Snuffer, Rick | 142,682 | Rahall, Nick J. II* | | 66,512 D | 34.8% | 65.2% | 34.8% | 65.2% |
| 3 | 2002 | 125,012 | 37,229 | Chapman, Paul E. | 87,783 | Rahall, Nick J. II* | | 50,554 D | 29.8% | 70.2% | 29.8% | 70.2% |
| Total | 2004 | 721,656 | 303,042 | | 415,396 | | 3,218 | 112,354 D | 42.0% | 57.6% | 42.2% | 57.8% |
| Total | 2002 | 399,949 | 135,505 | | 264,124 | | 320 | 128,619 D | 33.9% | 66.0% | 33.9% | 66.1% |

An asterisk (*) denotes incumbent.

# WEST VIRGINIA

## GENERAL AND PRIMARY ELECTIONS

## 2004 GENERAL ELECTIONS

**President**  Other vote was 4,063 Independent (Ralph Nader); 1,405 Libertarian (Michael Badnarik); 82 write-in (Michael Peroutka); 13 write-in (John Kennedy); 5 write-in (David Cobb).

**Governor**  Other vote was 18,430 Mountain (Jesse Johnson); 114 write-in (Simon McClure).

**House**  Other vote was:

CD 1
CD 2    3,218 Mountain (Julian Martin).
CD 3

## 2004 PRIMARY ELECTIONS

**Primary**  May 11, 2004

**Registration** (as of May 11, 2004)

| | |
|---|---|
| Republican | 321,586 |
| Democratic | 655,646 |
| Mountain | 459 |
| Other Parties | 12,318 |
| No Party | 113,255 |
| TOTAL | 1,103,264 |

**Primary Type**  Only registered Democrats could vote in the Democratic primary. Registered Republicans and those with no party registration could vote in the Republican primary.

# WEST VIRGINIA

## GENERAL AND PRIMARY ELECTIONS

Note: An asterisk (*) denotes incumbent.

| | REPUBLICAN PRIMARIES | | | DEMOCRATIC PRIMARIES | | |
|---|---|---|---|---|---|---|
| **President** | George W. Bush* | 111,109 | 100.0% | John Kerry | 175,065 | 69.2% |
| | | | | John Edwards | 33,950 | 13.4% |
| | | | | Joseph I. Lieberman | 13,881 | 5.5% |
| | | | | Howard Dean | 10,576 | 4.2% |
| | | | | Wesley Clark | 9,170 | 3.6% |
| | | | | Dennis J. Kucinich | 6,114 | 2.4% |
| | | | | Lyndon H. LaRouche Jr. | 4,083 | 1.6% |
| | | | | TOTAL | 252,839 | |
| **Governor** | Monty Warner | 26,041 | 22.9% | Joe Manchin III | 149,362 | 52.7% |
| | Dan R. Moore | 22,748 | 20.0% | Lloyd Jackson | 77,052 | 27.2% |
| | Rob Capehart | 19,694 | 17.3% | Jim Lees | 40,161 | 14.2% |
| | Richard Robb | 11,824 | 10.4% | Lacy Wright Jr. | 4,963 | 1.8% |
| | Douglas E. McKinney | 10,476 | 9.2% | Jerry Baker | 3,009 | 1.1% |
| | Larry V. Faircloth | 9,123 | 8.0% | James A. Baughman | 2,999 | 1.1% |
| | Joseph "Joey" Oliverio | 7,687 | 6.8% | Phillip "Icky" Frye | 2,892 | 1.0% |
| | James D. Radcliff Jr. | 3,013 | 2.6% | Louis "Lou" Davis | 2,824 | 1.0% |
| | Charles G. "Bud" Railey | 2,345 | 2.1% | | | |
| | Carroll B. Bowden Sr. | 925 | 0.8% | | | |
| | TOTAL | 113,876 | | TOTAL | 283,262 | |
| **Congressional District 1** | Alan Lee Parks | 33,157 | 100.0% | Alan B. Mollohan* | 73,207 | 100.0% |
| **Congressional District 2** | Shelley Moore Capito* | 40,985 | 100.0% | Erik Wells | 35,265 | 53.6% |
| | | | | Christopher M. Turman IV | 18,912 | 28.8% |
| | | | | Howard Swint | 11,581 | 17.6% |
| | | | | TOTAL | 65,758 | |
| **Congressional District 3** | Rick Snuffer | 12,152 | 58.5% | Nick J. Rahall II* | 78,001 | 100.0% |
| | Gary M. "Marty" Gearheart | 8,631 | 41.5% | | | |
| | TOTAL | 20,783 | | | | |

# WISCONSIN

## GOVERNOR
James E. Doyle (D). Elected 2002 to a four-year term.

## SENATORS (2 Democrats)
Russell D. Feingold (D). Reelected 2004 to a six-year term. Previously elected 1998, 1992.

Herb Kohl (D). Reelected 2000 to a six-year term. Previously elected 1994, 1988.

## REPRESENTATIVES (4 Democrats, 4 Republicans)
1. Paul D. Ryan (R)
2. Tammy Baldwin (D)
3. Ron Kind (D)
4. Gwen Moore (D)
5. F. James Sensenbrenner Jr. (R)
6. Tom Petri (R)
7. David R. Obey (D)
8. Mark Green (R)

## POSTWAR VOTE FOR PRESIDENT

| Year | Total Vote | Republican Vote | Republican Candidate | Democratic Vote | Democratic Candidate | Other Vote | Plurality | Total Vote Rep. | Total Vote Dem. | Major Vote Rep. | Major Vote Dem. |
|------|-----------|-----------------|----------------------|-----------------|----------------------|------------|-----------|------|------|------|------|
| 2004 | 2,997,007 | 1,478,120 | Bush, George W. | 1,489,504 | Kerry, John | 29,383 | 11,384 D | 49.3% | 49.7% | 49.8% | 50.2% |
| 2000** | 2,598,607 | 1,237,279 | Bush, George W. | 1,242,987 | Gore, Al | 118,341 | 5,708 D | 47.6% | 47.8% | 49.9% | 50.1% |
| 1996** | 2,196,169 | 845,029 | Dole, Bob | 1,071,971 | Clinton, Bill | 279,169 | 226,942 D | 38.5% | 48.8% | 44.1% | 55.9% |
| 1992** | 2,531,114 | 930,855 | Bush, George | 1,041,066 | Clinton, Bill | 559,193 | 110,211 D | 36.8% | 41.1% | 47.2% | 52.8% |
| 1988 | 2,191,608 | 1,047,499 | Bush, George | 1,126,794 | Dukakis, Michael S. | 17,315 | 79,295 D | 47.8% | 51.4% | 48.2% | 51.8% |
| 1984 | 2,211,689 | 1,198,584 | Reagan, Ronald | 995,740 | Mondale, Walter F. | 17,365 | 202,844 R | 54.2% | 45.0% | 54.6% | 45.4% |
| 1980** | 2,273,221 | 1,088,845 | Reagan, Ronald | 981,584 | Carter, Jimmy | 202,792 | 107,261 R | 47.9% | 43.2% | 52.6% | 47.4% |
| 1976 | 2,104,175 | 1,004,987 | Ford, Gerald R. | 1,040,232 | Carter, Jimmy | 58,956 | 35,245 D | 47.8% | 49.4% | 49.1% | 50.9% |
| 1972 | 1,852,890 | 989,430 | Nixon, Richard M. | 810,174 | McGovern, George S. | 53,286 | 179,256 R | 53.4% | 43.7% | 55.0% | 45.0% |
| 1968** | 1,691,538 | 809,997 | Nixon, Richard M. | 748,804 | Humphrey, Hubert H. | 132,737 | 61,193 R | 47.9% | 44.3% | 52.0% | 48.0% |
| 1964 | 1,691,815 | 638,495 | Goldwater, Barry M. | 1,050,424 | Johnson, Lyndon B. | 2,896 | 411,929 D | 37.7% | 62.1% | 37.8% | 62.2% |
| 1960 | 1,729,082 | 895,175 | Nixon, Richard M. | 830,805 | Kennedy, John F. | 3,102 | 64,370 R | 51.8% | 48.0% | 51.9% | 48.1% |
| 1956 | 1,550,558 | 954,844 | Eisenhower, Dwight D. | 586,768 | Stevenson, Adlai E. | 8,946 | 368,076 R | 61.6% | 37.8% | 61.9% | 38.1% |
| 1952 | 1,607,370 | 979,744 | Eisenhower, Dwight D. | 622,175 | Stevenson, Adlai E. | 5,451 | 357,569 R | 61.0% | 38.7% | 61.2% | 38.8% |
| 1948 | 1,276,800 | 590,959 | Dewey, Thomas E. | 647,310 | Truman, Harry S. | 38,531 | 56,351 D | 46.3% | 50.7% | 47.7% | 52.3% |

In past elections, the other vote included: 2000 - 94,070 Green (Ralph Nader); 1996 - 227,339 Reform (Ross Perot); 1992 - 544,479 Independent (Perot); 1980 - 160,657 Independent (John Anderson); 1968 - 127,835 American Independent (George Wallace).

# WISCONSIN

## POSTWAR VOTE FOR GOVERNOR

| Year | Total Vote | Republican Vote | Republican Candidate | Democratic Vote | Democratic Candidate | Other Vote | Rep.-Dem. Plurality | Total Vote Rep. | Total Vote Dem. | Major Vote Rep. | Major Vote Dem. |
|---|---|---|---|---|---|---|---|---|---|---|---|
| 2002** | 1,775,349 | 734,779 | McCallum, Scott | 800,515 | Doyle, James E. | 240,055 | 65,736 D | 41.4% | 45.1% | 47.9% | 52.1% |
| 1998 | 1,756,014 | 1,047,716 | Thompson, Tommy G. | 679,553 | Garvey, Edward R. | 28,745 | 368,163 R | 59.7% | 38.7% | 60.7% | 39.3% |
| 1994 | 1,563,835 | 1,051,326 | Thompson, Tommy G. | 482,850 | Chvala, Chuck | 29,659 | 568,476 R | 67.2% | 30.9% | 68.5% | 31.5% |
| 1990 | 1,379,727 | 802,321 | Thompson, Tommy G. | 576,280 | Loftus, Thomas | 1,126 | 226,041 R | 58.2% | 41.8% | 58.2% | 41.8% |
| 1986 | 1,526,960 | 805,090 | Thompson, Tommy G. | 705,578 | Earl, Anthony S. | 16,292 | 99,512 R | 52.7% | 46.2% | 53.3% | 46.7% |
| 1982 | 1,580,344 | 662,838 | Kohler, Terry J. | 896,812 | Earl, Anthony S. | 20,694 | 233,974 D | 41.9% | 56.7% | 42.5% | 57.5% |
| 1978 | 1,500,996 | 816,056 | Dreyfus, Lee S. | 673,813 | Schreiber, Martin J. | 11,127 | 142,243 R | 54.4% | 44.9% | 54.8% | 45.2% |
| 1974 | 1,181,976 | 497,195 | Dyke, William D. | 628,639 | Lucey, Patrick J. | 56,142 | 131,444 D | 42.1% | 53.2% | 44.2% | 55.8% |
| 1970** | 1,343,160 | 602,617 | Olson, Jack B. | 728,403 | Lucey, Patrick J. | 12,140 | 125,786 D | 44.9% | 54.2% | 45.3% | 54.7% |
| 1968 | 1,689,738 | 893,463 | Knowles, Warren P. | 791,100 | LaFollette, Bronson C. | 5,175 | 102,363 R | 52.9% | 46.8% | 53.0% | 47.0% |
| 1966 | 1,170,173 | 626,041 | Knowles, Warren P. | 539,258 | Lucey, Patrick J. | 4,874 | 86,783 R | 53.5% | 46.1% | 53.7% | 46.3% |
| 1964 | 1,694,887 | 856,779 | Knowles, Warren P. | 837,901 | Reynolds, John W. | 207 | 18,878 R | 50.6% | 49.4% | 50.6% | 49.4% |
| 1962 | 1,265,900 | 625,536 | Kuehn, Philip G. | 637,491 | Reynolds, John W. | 2,873 | 11,955 D | 49.4% | 50.4% | 49.5% | 50.5% |
| 1960 | 1,728,009 | 837,123 | Kuehn, Philip G. | 890,868 | Nelson, Gaylord A. | 18 | 53,745 D | 48.4% | 51.6% | 48.4% | 51.6% |
| 1958 | 1,202,219 | 556,391 | Thomson, Vernon W. | 644,296 | Nelson, Gaylord A. | 1,532 | 87,905 D | 46.3% | 53.6% | 46.3% | 53.7% |
| 1956 | 1,557,788 | 808,273 | Thomson, Vernon W. | 749,421 | Proxmire, William | 94 | 58,852 R | 51.9% | 48.1% | 51.9% | 48.1% |
| 1954 | 1,158,666 | 596,158 | Kohler, Walter J. | 560,747 | Proxmire, William | 1,761 | 35,411 R | 51.5% | 48.4% | 51.5% | 48.5% |
| 1952 | 1,615,214 | 1,009,171 | Kohler, Walter J. | 601,844 | Proxmire, William | 4,199 | 407,327 R | 62.5% | 37.3% | 62.6% | 37.4% |
| 1950 | 1,138,148 | 605,649 | Kohler, Walter J. | 525,319 | Thompson, Carl W. | 7,180 | 80,330 R | 53.2% | 46.2% | 53.6% | 46.4% |
| 1948 | 1,266,139 | 684,839 | Rennebohm, Oscar | 558,497 | Thompson, Carl W. | 22,803 | 126,342 R | 54.1% | 44.1% | 55.1% | 44.9% |
| 1946 | 1,040,444 | 621,970 | Goodland, Walter | 406,499 | Hoan, Daniel W. | 11,975 | 215,471 R | 59.8% | 39.1% | 60.5% | 39.5% |

In 2002 Ed Thompson, the Libertarian Party candidate, received 185,455 votes (10.4 percent of the total vote). The term of office of Wisconsin's governor was increased from two to four years effective with the 1970 election.

## POSTWAR VOTE FOR SENATOR

| Year | Total Vote | Republican Vote | Republican Candidate | Democratic Vote | Democratic Candidate | Other Vote | Rep.-Dem. Plurality | Total Vote Rep. | Total Vote Dem. | Major Vote Rep. | Major Vote Dem. |
|---|---|---|---|---|---|---|---|---|---|---|---|
| 2004 | 2,949,743 | 1,301,183 | Michels, Tim | 1,632,697 | Feingold, Russell D. | 15,863 | 331,514 D | 44.1% | 55.4% | 44.4% | 55.6% |
| 2000 | 2,540,083 | 940,744 | Gillespie, John | 1,563,238 | Kohl, Herb | 36,101 | 622,494 D | 37.0% | 61.5% | 37.6% | 62.4% |
| 1998 | 1,760,836 | 852,272 | Neumann, Mark W. | 890,059 | Feingold, Russell D. | 18,505 | 37,787 D | 48.4% | 50.5% | 48.9% | 51.1% |
| 1994 | 1,565,628 | 636,989 | Welch, Robert T. | 912,662 | Kohl, Herb | 15,977 | 175,673 D | 40.7% | 58.3% | 41.1% | 58.9% |
| 1992 | 2,455,124 | 1,129,599 | Kasten, Robert W. | 1,290,662 | Feingold, Russell D. | 34,863 | 161,063 D | 46.0% | 52.6% | 46.7% | 53.3% |
| 1988 | 2,168,190 | 1,030,440 | Engeleiter, Susan | 1,128,625 | Kohl, Herb | 9,125 | 98,185 D | 47.5% | 52.1% | 47.7% | 52.3% |
| 1986 | 1,483,174 | 754,573 | Kasten, Robert W. | 702,963 | Garvey, Edward R. | 25,638 | 51,610 R | 50.9% | 47.4% | 51.8% | 48.2% |
| 1982 | 1,544,981 | 527,355 | McCallum, Scott | 983,311 | Proxmire, William | 34,315 | 455,956 D | 34.1% | 63.6% | 34.9% | 65.1% |
| 1980 | 2,204,202 | 1,106,311 | Kasten, Robert W. | 1,065,487 | Nelson, Gaylord A. | 32,404 | 40,824 R | 50.2% | 48.3% | 50.9% | 49.1% |
| 1976 | 1,935,183 | 521,902 | York, Stanley | 1,396,970 | Proxmire, William | 16,311 | 875,068 D | 27.0% | 72.2% | 27.2% | 72.8% |
| 1974 | 1,199,495 | 429,327 | Petri, Tom | 740,700 | Nelson, Gaylord A. | 29,468 | 311,373 D | 35.8% | 61.8% | 36.7% | 63.3% |
| 1970 | 1,338,967 | 381,297 | Erickson, John E. | 948,445 | Proxmire, William | 9,225 | 567,148 D | 28.5% | 70.8% | 28.7% | 71.3% |
| 1968 | 1,654,861 | 633,910 | Leonard, Jerris | 1,020,931 | Nelson, Gaylord A. | 20 | 387,021 D | 38.3% | 61.7% | 38.3% | 61.7% |
| 1964 | 1,673,776 | 780,116 | Renk, Wilbur N. | 892,013 | Proxmire, William | 1,647 | 111,897 D | 46.6% | 53.3% | 46.7% | 53.3% |
| 1962 | 1,260,168 | 594,846 | Wiley, Alexander | 662,342 | Nelson, Gaylord A. | 2,980 | 67,496 D | 47.2% | 52.6% | 47.3% | 52.7% |
| 1958 | 1,194,678 | 510,398 | Steinle, Roland J. | 682,440 | Proxmire, William | 1,840 | 172,042 D | 42.7% | 57.1% | 42.8% | 57.2% |
| 1957S | 772,620 | 312,931 | Kohler, Walter J. | 435,985 | Proxmire, William | 23,704 | 123,054 D | 40.5% | 56.4% | 41.8% | 58.2% |
| 1956 | 1,523,356 | 892,473 | Wiley, Alexander | 627,903 | Maier, Henry W. | 2,980 | 264,570 R | 58.6% | 41.2% | 58.7% | 41.3% |
| 1952 | 1,605,228 | 870,444 | McCarthy, Joseph R. | 731,402 | Fairchild, Thomas E. | 3,382 | 139,042 R | 54.2% | 45.6% | 54.3% | 45.7% |
| 1950 | 1,116,135 | 595,283 | Wiley, Alexander | 515,539 | Fairchild, Thomas E. | 5,313 | 79,744 R | 53.3% | 46.2% | 53.6% | 46.4% |
| 1946 | 1,014,594 | 620,430 | McCarthy, Joseph R. | 378,772 | McMurray, Howard J. | 15,392 | 241,658 R | 61.2% | 37.3% | 62.1% | 37.9% |

The 1957 election was for a short term to fill a vacancy.

466

# WISCONSIN

Congressional districts first established for elections held in 2002
8 members

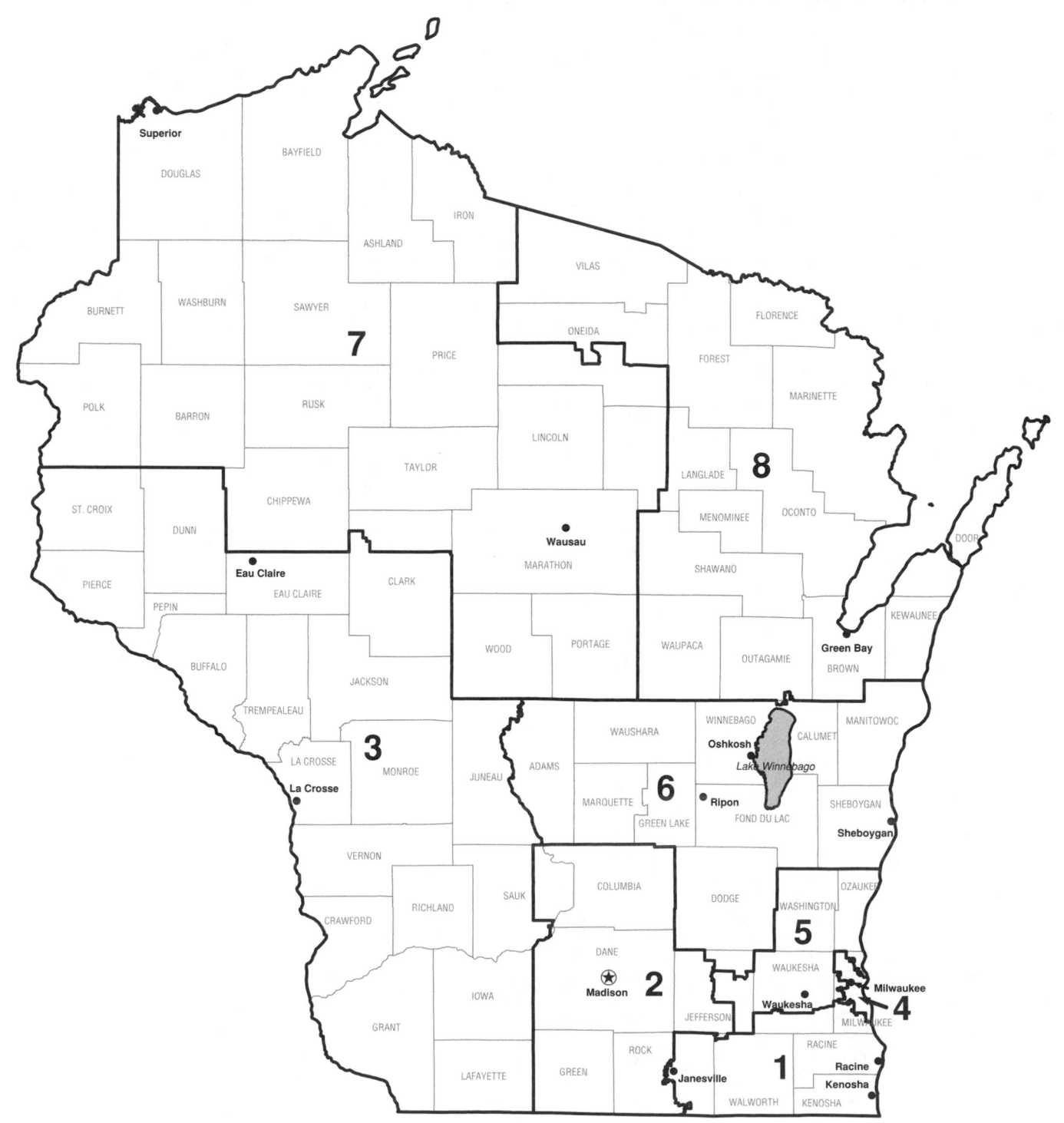

# WISCONSIN

## PRESIDENT 2004

| 2000 Census Population | County | Total Vote | Republican | Democratic | Other | Rep.-Dem. Plurality | Percentage Total Vote Rep. | Dem. | Major Vote Rep. | Dem. |
|---|---|---|---|---|---|---|---|---|---|---|
| 18,643 | ADAMS | 10,456 | 4,890 | 5,447 | 119 | 557 D | 46.8% | 52.1% | 47.3% | 52.7% |
| 16,866 | ASHLAND | 9,199 | 3,313 | 5,805 | 81 | 2,492 D | 36.0% | 63.1% | 36.3% | 63.7% |
| 44,963 | BARRON | 23,937 | 12,030 | 11,696 | 211 | 334 R | 50.3% | 48.9% | 50.7% | 49.3% |
| 15,013 | BAYFIELD | 9,699 | 3,754 | 5,845 | 100 | 2,091 D | 38.7% | 60.3% | 39.1% | 60.9% |
| 226,778 | BROWN | 123,294 | 67,173 | 54,935 | 1,186 | 12,238 R | 54.5% | 44.6% | 55.0% | 45.0% |
| 13,804 | BUFFALO | 7,591 | 3,502 | 3,998 | 91 | 496 D | 46.1% | 52.7% | 46.7% | 53.3% |
| 15,674 | BURNETT | 9,321 | 4,743 | 4,499 | 79 | 244 R | 50.9% | 48.3% | 51.3% | 48.7% |
| 40,631 | CALUMET | 25,276 | 14,721 | 10,290 | 265 | 4,431 R | 58.2% | 40.7% | 58.9% | 41.1% |
| 55,195 | CHIPPEWA | 30,524 | 15,450 | 14,751 | 323 | 699 R | 50.6% | 48.3% | 51.2% | 48.8% |
| 33,557 | CLARK | 15,125 | 7,966 | 6,966 | 193 | 1,000 R | 52.7% | 46.1% | 53.3% | 46.7% |
| 52,468 | COLUMBIA | 29,555 | 14,956 | 14,300 | 299 | 656 R | 50.6% | 48.4% | 51.1% | 48.9% |
| 17,243 | CRAWFORD | 8,459 | 3,680 | 4,656 | 123 | 976 D | 43.5% | 55.0% | 44.1% | 55.9% |
| 426,526 | DANE | 274,249 | 90,369 | 181,052 | 2,828 | 90,683 D | 33.0% | 66.0% | 33.3% | 66.7% |
| 85,897 | DODGE | 44,336 | 27,201 | 16,690 | 445 | 10,511 R | 61.4% | 37.6% | 62.0% | 38.0% |
| 27,961 | DOOR | 17,491 | 8,910 | 8,367 | 214 | 543 R | 50.9% | 47.8% | 51.6% | 48.4% |
| 43,287 | DOUGLAS | 25,187 | 8,448 | 16,537 | 202 | 8,089 D | 33.5% | 65.7% | 33.8% | 66.2% |
| 39,858 | DUNN | 23,172 | 10,879 | 12,039 | 254 | 1,160 D | 46.9% | 52.0% | 47.5% | 52.5% |
| 93,142 | EAU CLAIRE | 55,437 | 24,653 | 30,068 | 716 | 5,415 D | 44.5% | 54.2% | 45.1% | 54.9% |
| 5,088 | FLORENCE | 2,724 | 1,703 | 993 | 28 | 710 R | 62.5% | 36.5% | 63.2% | 36.8% |
| 97,296 | FOND DU LAC | 53,036 | 33,291 | 19,216 | 529 | 14,075 R | 62.8% | 36.2% | 63.4% | 36.6% |
| 10,024 | FOREST | 5,153 | 2,608 | 2,509 | 36 | 99 R | 50.6% | 48.7% | 51.0% | 49.0% |
| 49,597 | GRANT | 25,264 | 12,208 | 12,864 | 192 | 656 D | 48.3% | 50.9% | 48.7% | 51.3% |
| 33,647 | GREEN | 18,248 | 8,497 | 9,575 | 176 | 1,078 D | 46.6% | 52.5% | 47.0% | 53.0% |
| 19,105 | GREEN LAKE | 10,178 | 6,472 | 3,605 | 101 | 2,867 R | 63.6% | 35.4% | 64.2% | 35.8% |
| 22,780 | IOWA | 12,542 | 5,348 | 7,122 | 72 | 1,774 D | 42.6% | 56.8% | 42.9% | 57.1% |
| 6,861 | IRON | 3,879 | 1,884 | 1,956 | 39 | 72 D | 48.6% | 50.4% | 49.1% | 50.9% |
| 19,100 | JACKSON | 9,726 | 4,387 | 5,249 | 90 | 862 D | 45.1% | 54.0% | 45.5% | 54.5% |
| 74,021 | JEFFERSON | 42,115 | 23,776 | 17,925 | 414 | 5,851 R | 56.5% | 42.6% | 57.0% | 43.0% |
| 24,316 | JUNEAU | 12,379 | 6,473 | 5,734 | 172 | 739 R | 52.3% | 46.3% | 53.0% | 47.0% |
| 149,577 | KENOSHA | 76,428 | 35,587 | 40,107 | 734 | 4,520 D | 46.6% | 52.5% | 47.0% | 53.0% |
| 20,187 | KEWAUNEE | 11,273 | 5,970 | 5,175 | 128 | 795 R | 53.0% | 45.9% | 53.6% | 46.4% |
| 107,120 | LA CROSSE | 62,136 | 28,289 | 33,170 | 677 | 4,881 D | 45.5% | 53.4% | 46.0% | 54.0% |
| 16,137 | LAFAYETTE | 8,388 | 3,929 | 4,402 | 57 | 473 D | 46.8% | 52.5% | 47.2% | 52.8% |
| 20,740 | LANGLADE | 11,074 | 6,235 | 4,751 | 88 | 1,484 R | 56.3% | 42.9% | 56.8% | 43.2% |
| 29,641 | LINCOLN | 15,700 | 8,024 | 7,484 | 192 | 540 R | 51.1% | 47.7% | 51.7% | 48.3% |
| 82,887 | MANITOWOC | 44,160 | 23,027 | 20,652 | 481 | 2,375 R | 52.1% | 46.8% | 52.7% | 47.3% |
| 125,834 | MARATHON | 68,059 | 36,394 | 30,899 | 766 | 5,495 R | 53.5% | 45.4% | 54.1% | 45.9% |
| 43,384 | MARINETTE | 22,270 | 11,866 | 10,190 | 214 | 1,676 R | 53.3% | 45.8% | 53.8% | 46.2% |
| 15,832 | MARQUETTE | 8,477 | 4,604 | 3,785 | 88 | 819 R | 54.3% | 44.7% | 54.9% | 45.1% |
| 4,562 | MENOMINEE | 1,710 | 288 | 1,412 | 10 | 1,124 D | 16.8% | 82.6% | 16.9% | 83.1% |
| 940,164 | MILWAUKEE | 482,236 | 180,287 | 297,653 | 4,296 | 117,366 D | 37.4% | 61.7% | 37.7% | 62.3% |
| 40,899 | MONROE | 19,554 | 10,375 | 8,973 | 206 | 1,402 R | 53.1% | 45.9% | 53.6% | 46.4% |
| 35,634 | OCONTO | 19,794 | 11,043 | 8,534 | 217 | 2,509 R | 55.8% | 43.1% | 56.4% | 43.6% |
| 36,776 | ONEIDA | 22,039 | 11,351 | 10,464 | 224 | 887 R | 51.5% | 47.5% | 52.0% | 48.0% |
| 160,971 | OUTAGAMIE | 90,050 | 48,903 | 40,169 | 978 | 8,734 R | 54.3% | 44.6% | 54.9% | 45.1% |
| 82,317 | OZAUKEE | 53,032 | 34,904 | 17,714 | 414 | 17,190 R | 65.8% | 33.4% | 66.3% | 33.7% |
| 7,213 | PEPIN | 4,066 | 1,853 | 2,181 | 32 | 328 D | 45.6% | 53.6% | 45.9% | 54.1% |
| 36,804 | PIERCE | 21,876 | 10,437 | 11,176 | 263 | 739 D | 47.7% | 51.1% | 48.3% | 51.7% |
| 41,319 | POLK | 23,503 | 12,095 | 11,173 | 235 | 922 R | 51.5% | 47.5% | 52.0% | 48.0% |
| 67,182 | PORTAGE | 38,961 | 16,546 | 21,861 | 554 | 5,315 D | 42.5% | 56.1% | 43.1% | 56.9% |
| 15,822 | PRICE | 8,763 | 4,312 | 4,349 | 102 | 37 D | 49.2% | 49.6% | 49.8% | 50.2% |
| 188,831 | RACINE | 101,569 | 52,456 | 48,229 | 884 | 4,227 R | 51.6% | 47.5% | 52.1% | 47.9% |
| 17,924 | RICHLAND | 9,420 | 4,836 | 4,501 | 83 | 335 R | 51.3% | 47.8% | 51.8% | 48.2% |
| 152,307 | ROCK | 80,479 | 33,151 | 46,598 | 730 | 13,447 D | 41.2% | 57.9% | 41.6% | 58.4% |
| 15,347 | RUSK | 7,927 | 3,985 | 3,820 | 122 | 165 R | 50.3% | 48.2% | 51.1% | 48.9% |
| 63,155 | ST. CROIX | 41,835 | 22,679 | 18,784 | 372 | 3,895 R | 54.2% | 44.9% | 54.7% | 45.3% |
| 55,225 | SAUK | 30,417 | 14,415 | 15,708 | 294 | 1,293 D | 47.4% | 51.6% | 47.9% | 52.1% |
| 16,196 | SAWYER | 9,453 | 4,951 | 4,411 | 91 | 540 R | 52.4% | 46.7% | 52.9% | 47.1% |
| 40,664 | SHAWANO | 20,999 | 12,150 | 8,657 | 192 | 3,493 R | 57.9% | 41.2% | 58.4% | 41.6% |
| 112,646 | SHEBOYGAN | 62,625 | 34,458 | 27,608 | 559 | 6,850 R | 55.0% | 44.1% | 55.5% | 44.5% |

# WISCONSIN

## PRESIDENT 2004

| 2000 Census Population | County | Total Vote | Republican | Democratic | Other | Rep.-Dem. Plurality | Percentage | | | |
|---|---|---|---|---|---|---|---|---|---|---|
| | | | | | | | Total Vote | | Major Vote | |
| | | | | | | | Rep. | Dem. | Rep. | Dem. |
| 19,680 | TAYLOR | 9,543 | 5,582 | 3,829 | 132 | 1,753 R | 58.5% | 40.1% | 59.3% | 40.7% |
| 27,010 | TREMPEALEAU | 14,062 | 5,878 | 8,075 | 109 | 2,197 D | 41.8% | 57.4% | 42.1% | 57.9% |
| 28,056 | VERNON | 14,845 | 6,774 | 7,924 | 147 | 1,150 D | 45.6% | 53.4% | 46.1% | 53.9% |
| 21,033 | VILAS | 14,002 | 8,155 | 5,713 | 134 | 2,442 R | 58.2% | 40.8% | 58.8% | 41.2% |
| 93,759 | WALWORTH | 48,446 | 28,754 | 19,177 | 515 | 9,577 R | 59.4% | 39.6% | 60.0% | 40.0% |
| 16,036 | WASHBURN | 9,567 | 4,762 | 4,705 | 100 | 57 R | 49.8% | 49.2% | 50.3% | 49.7% |
| 117,493 | WASHINGTON | 72,467 | 50,641 | 21,234 | 592 | 29,407 R | 69.9% | 29.3% | 70.5% | 29.5% |
| 360,767 | WAUKESHA | 230,363 | 154,926 | 73,626 | 1,811 | 81,300 R | 67.3% | 32.0% | 67.8% | 32.2% |
| 51,731 | WAUPACA | 26,974 | 15,941 | 10,792 | 241 | 5,149 R | 59.1% | 40.0% | 59.6% | 40.4% |
| 23,154 | WAUSHARA | 12,246 | 6,888 | 5,257 | 101 | 1,631 R | 56.2% | 42.9% | 56.7% | 43.3% |
| 156,763 | WINNEBAGO | 88,596 | 46,542 | 40,943 | 1,111 | 5,599 R | 52.5% | 46.2% | 53.2% | 46.8% |
| 75,555 | WOOD | 40,071 | 20,592 | 18,950 | 529 | 1,642 R | 51.4% | 47.3% | 52.1% | 47.9% |
| 5,363,675 | TOTAL | 2,997,007 | 1,478,120 | 1,489,504 | 29,383 | 11,384 D | 49.3% | 49.7% | 49.8% | 50.2% |

# WISCONSIN

## SENATOR 2004

| 2000 Census Population | County | Total Vote | Republican | Democratic | Other | Rep.-Dem. Plurality | Percentage | | | |
|---|---|---|---|---|---|---|---|---|---|---|
| | | | | | | | Total Vote | | Major Vote | |
| | | | | | | | Rep. | Dem. | Rep. | Dem. |
| 18,643 | ADAMS | 10,350 | 4,505 | 5,765 | 80 | 1,260 D | 43.5% | 55.7% | 43.9% | 56.1% |
| 16,866 | ASHLAND | 8,612 | 2,726 | 5,852 | 34 | 3,126 D | 31.7% | 68.0% | 31.8% | 68.2% |
| 44,963 | BARRON | 23,056 | 10,612 | 12,361 | 83 | 1,749 D | 46.0% | 53.6% | 46.2% | 53.8% |
| 15,013 | BAYFIELD | 9,409 | 3,039 | 6,331 | 39 | 3,292 D | 32.3% | 67.3% | 32.4% | 67.6% |
| 226,778 | BROWN | 121,495 | 58,534 | 62,387 | 574 | 3,853 D | 48.2% | 51.3% | 48.4% | 51.6% |
| 13,804 | BUFFALO | 7,355 | 3,144 | 4,190 | 21 | 1,046 D | 42.7% | 57.0% | 42.9% | 57.1% |
| 15,674 | BURNETT | 8,972 | 4,115 | 4,815 | 42 | 700 D | 45.9% | 53.7% | 46.1% | 53.9% |
| 40,631 | CALUMET | 24,989 | 13,275 | 11,590 | 124 | 1,685 R | 53.1% | 46.4% | 53.4% | 46.6% |
| 55,195 | CHIPPEWA | 30,184 | 13,412 | 16,585 | 187 | 3,173 D | 44.4% | 54.9% | 44.7% | 55.3% |
| 33,557 | CLARK | 15,047 | 6,982 | 7,979 | 86 | 997 D | 46.4% | 53.0% | 46.7% | 53.3% |
| 52,468 | COLUMBIA | 29,359 | 13,249 | 15,893 | 217 | 2,644 D | 45.1% | 54.1% | 45.5% | 54.5% |
| 17,243 | CRAWFORD | 8,279 | 3,319 | 4,938 | 22 | 1,619 D | 40.1% | 59.6% | 40.2% | 59.8% |
| 426,526 | DANE | 271,462 | 74,787 | 194,999 | 1,676 | 120,212 D | 27.5% | 71.8% | 27.7% | 72.3% |
| 85,897 | DODGE | 44,005 | 25,731 | 18,019 | 255 | 7,712 R | 58.5% | 40.9% | 58.8% | 41.2% |
| 27,961 | DOOR | 17,318 | 8,075 | 9,146 | 97 | 1,071 D | 46.6% | 52.8% | 46.9% | 53.1% |
| 43,287 | DOUGLAS | 24,743 | 6,748 | 17,814 | 181 | 11,066 D | 27.3% | 72.0% | 27.5% | 72.5% |
| 39,858 | DUNN | 22,594 | 9,373 | 13,029 | 192 | 3,656 D | 41.5% | 57.7% | 41.8% | 58.2% |
| 93,142 | EAU CLAIRE | 54,724 | 21,192 | 33,188 | 344 | 11,996 D | 38.7% | 60.6% | 39.0% | 61.0% |
| 5,088 | FLORENCE | 2,622 | 1,430 | 1,183 | 9 | 247 R | 54.5% | 45.1% | 54.7% | 45.3% |
| 97,296 | FOND DU LAC | 52,586 | 30,853 | 21,515 | 218 | 9,338 R | 58.7% | 40.9% | 58.9% | 41.1% |
| 10,024 | FOREST | 4,930 | 2,092 | 2,828 | 10 | 736 D | 42.4% | 57.4% | 42.5% | 57.5% |
| 49,597 | GRANT | 24,409 | 11,577 | 12,762 | 70 | 1,185 D | 47.4% | 52.3% | 47.6% | 52.4% |
| 33,647 | GREEN | 18,073 | 7,002 | 10,966 | 105 | 3,964 D | 38.7% | 60.7% | 39.0% | 61.0% |
| 19,105 | GREEN LAKE | 10,083 | 5,989 | 4,042 | 52 | 1,947 R | 59.4% | 40.1% | 59.7% | 40.3% |
| 22,780 | IOWA | 12,495 | 4,948 | 7,530 | 17 | 2,582 D | 39.6% | 60.3% | 39.7% | 60.3% |
| 6,861 | IRON | 3,681 | 1,508 | 2,166 | 7 | 658 D | 41.0% | 58.8% | 41.0% | 59.0% |
| 19,100 | JACKSON | 9,460 | 3,826 | 5,617 | 17 | 1,791 D | 40.4% | 59.4% | 40.5% | 59.5% |
| 74,021 | JEFFERSON | 41,626 | 21,725 | 19,684 | 217 | 2,041 R | 52.2% | 47.3% | 52.5% | 47.5% |
| 24,316 | JUNEAU | 11,918 | 5,850 | 5,980 | 88 | 130 D | 49.1% | 50.2% | 49.5% | 50.5% |
| 149,577 | KENOSHA | 73,826 | 29,547 | 43,741 | 538 | 14,194 D | 40.0% | 59.2% | 40.3% | 59.7% |
| 20,187 | KEWAUNEE | 11,218 | 5,393 | 5,781 | 44 | 388 D | 48.1% | 51.5% | 48.3% | 51.7% |
| 107,120 | LA CROSSE | 61,430 | 24,249 | 36,797 | 384 | 12,548 D | 39.5% | 59.9% | 39.7% | 60.3% |
| 16,137 | LAFAYETTE | 8,218 | 3,521 | 4,679 | 18 | 1,158 D | 42.8% | 56.9% | 42.9% | 57.1% |
| 20,740 | LANGLADE | 10,871 | 5,272 | 5,562 | 37 | 290 D | 48.5% | 51.2% | 48.7% | 51.3% |
| 29,641 | LINCOLN | 15,566 | 6,601 | 8,877 | 88 | 2,276 D | 42.4% | 57.0% | 42.6% | 57.4% |

---

469

# WISCONSIN

## SENATOR 2004

| 2000 Census Population | County | Total Vote | Republican | Democratic | Other | Rep.-Dem. Plurality | | Total Vote Rep. | Total Vote Dem. | Major Vote Rep. | Major Vote Dem. |
|---|---|---|---|---|---|---|---|---|---|---|---|
| 82,887 | MANITOWOC | 43,380 | 21,392 | 21,788 | 200 | 396 | D | 49.3% | 50.2% | 49.5% | 50.5% |
| 125,834 | MARATHON | 67,738 | 30,254 | 37,153 | 331 | 6,899 | D | 44.7% | 54.8% | 44.9% | 55.1% |
| 43,384 | MARINETTE | 21,825 | 10,896 | 10,855 | 74 | 41 | R | 49.9% | 49.7% | 50.1% | 49.9% |
| 15,832 | MARQUETTE | 8,203 | 4,217 | 3,952 | 34 | 265 | R | 51.4% | 48.2% | 51.6% | 48.4% |
| 4,562 | MENOMINEE | 1,638 | 298 | 1,332 | 8 | 1,034 | D | 18.2% | 81.3% | 18.3% | 81.7% |
| 940,164 | MILWAUKEE | 472,980 | 157,576 | 312,914 | 2,490 | 155,338 | D | 33.3% | 66.2% | 33.5% | 66.5% |
| 40,899 | MONROE | 19,239 | 9,314 | 9,808 | 117 | 494 | D | 48.4% | 51.0% | 48.7% | 51.3% |
| 35,634 | OCONTO | 19,562 | 10,036 | 9,439 | 87 | 597 | R | 51.3% | 48.3% | 51.5% | 48.5% |
| 36,776 | ONEIDA | 21,807 | 9,638 | 12,079 | 90 | 2,441 | D | 44.2% | 55.4% | 44.4% | 55.6% |
| 160,971 | OUTAGAMIE | 88,714 | 42,808 | 45,395 | 511 | 2,587 | D | 48.3% | 51.2% | 48.5% | 51.5% |
| 82,317 | OZAUKEE | 52,580 | 31,620 | 20,744 | 216 | 10,876 | R | 60.1% | 39.5% | 60.4% | 39.6% |
| 7,213 | PEPIN | 3,930 | 1,619 | 2,298 | 13 | 679 | D | 41.2% | 58.5% | 41.3% | 58.7% |
| 36,804 | PIERCE | 21,030 | 8,931 | 11,914 | 185 | 2,983 | D | 42.5% | 56.7% | 42.8% | 57.2% |
| 41,319 | POLK | 22,078 | 10,265 | 11,660 | 153 | 1,395 | D | 46.5% | 52.8% | 46.8% | 53.2% |
| 67,182 | PORTAGE | 38,354 | 14,528 | 23,590 | 236 | 9,062 | D | 37.9% | 61.5% | 38.1% | 61.9% |
| 15,822 | PRICE | 8,548 | 3,683 | 4,835 | 30 | 1,152 | D | 43.1% | 56.6% | 43.2% | 56.8% |
| 188,831 | RACINE | 100,447 | 45,182 | 54,775 | 490 | 9,593 | D | 45.0% | 54.5% | 45.2% | 54.8% |
| 17,924 | RICHLAND | 9,230 | 4,468 | 4,739 | 23 | 271 | D | 48.4% | 51.3% | 48.5% | 51.5% |
| 152,307 | ROCK | 79,538 | 27,699 | 51,336 | 503 | 23,637 | D | 34.8% | 64.5% | 35.0% | 65.0% |
| 15,347 | RUSK | 7,809 | 3,337 | 4,415 | 57 | 1,078 | D | 42.7% | 56.5% | 43.0% | 57.0% |
| 63,155 | ST. CROIX | 40,566 | 19,555 | 20,415 | 596 | 860 | D | 48.2% | 50.3% | 48.9% | 51.1% |
| 55,225 | SAUK | 30,100 | 12,967 | 16,925 | 208 | 3,958 | D | 43.1% | 56.2% | 43.4% | 56.6% |
| 16,196 | SAWYER | 9,136 | 4,510 | 4,588 | 38 | 78 | D | 49.4% | 50.2% | 49.6% | 50.4% |
| 40,664 | SHAWANO | 20,401 | 10,936 | 9,397 | 68 | 1,539 | R | 53.6% | 46.1% | 53.8% | 46.2% |
| 112,646 | SHEBOYGAN | 62,095 | 31,572 | 30,245 | 278 | 1,327 | R | 50.8% | 48.7% | 51.1% | 48.9% |
| 19,680 | TAYLOR | 9,447 | 4,587 | 4,807 | 53 | 220 | D | 48.6% | 50.9% | 48.8% | 51.2% |
| 27,010 | TREMPEALEAU | 13,811 | 5,396 | 8,370 | 45 | 2,974 | D | 39.1% | 60.6% | 39.2% | 60.8% |
| 28,056 | VERNON | 14,486 | 5,856 | 8,597 | 33 | 2,741 | D | 40.4% | 59.3% | 40.5% | 59.5% |
| 21,033 | VILAS | 13,822 | 7,000 | 6,758 | 64 | 242 | R | 50.6% | 48.9% | 50.9% | 49.1% |
| 93,759 | WALWORTH | 47,790 | 25,235 | 22,210 | 345 | 3,025 | R | 52.8% | 46.5% | 53.2% | 46.8% |
| 16,036 | WASHBURN | 9,275 | 4,235 | 5,000 | 40 | 765 | D | 45.7% | 53.9% | 45.9% | 54.1% |
| 117,493 | WASHINGTON | 71,780 | 46,404 | 25,124 | 252 | 21,280 | R | 64.6% | 35.0% | 64.9% | 35.1% |
| 360,767 | WAUKESHA | 227,650 | 139,979 | 86,775 | 896 | 53,204 | R | 61.5% | 38.1% | 61.7% | 38.3% |
| 51,731 | WAUPACA | 26,538 | 14,750 | 11,694 | 94 | 3,056 | R | 55.6% | 44.1% | 55.8% | 44.2% |
| 23,154 | WAUSHARA | 11,888 | 6,176 | 5,657 | 55 | 519 | R | 52.0% | 47.6% | 52.2% | 47.8% |
| 156,763 | WINNEBAGO | 87,654 | 41,544 | 45,537 | 573 | 3,993 | D | 47.4% | 52.0% | 47.7% | 52.3% |
| 75,555 | WOOD | 39,709 | 18,519 | 20,986 | 204 | 2,467 | D | 46.6% | 52.8% | 46.9% | 53.1% |
| 5,363,675 | TOTAL | 2,949,743 | 1,301,183 | 1,632,697 | 15,863 | 331,514 | D | 44.1% | 55.4% | 44.4% | 55.6% |

# WISCONSIN

## HOUSE OF REPRESENTATIVES

| CD | Year | Total Vote | Republican Vote | Republican Candidate | Democratic Vote | Democratic Candidate | Other Vote | Rep.-Dem. Plurality | | Total Vote Rep. | Total Vote Dem. | Major Vote Rep. | Major Vote Dem. |
|---|---|---|---|---|---|---|---|---|---|---|---|---|---|
| 1 | 2004 | 356,976 | 233,372 | Ryan, Paul D.* | 116,250 | Thomas, Jeffrey Chapman | 7,354 | 117,122 | R | 65.4% | 32.6% | 66.7% | 33.3% |
| 1 | 2002 | 208,613 | 140,176 | Ryan, Paul D.* | 63,895 | Thomas, Jeffrey Chapman | 4,542 | 76,281 | R | 67.2% | 30.6% | 68.7% | 31.3% |
| 2 | 2004 | 397,724 | 145,810 | Magnum, Dave | 251,637 | Baldwin, Tammy* | 277 | 105,827 | D | 36.7% | 63.3% | 36.7% | 63.3% |
| 2 | 2002 | 247,410 | 83,694 | Greer, Ron | 163,313 | Baldwin, Tammy* | 403 | 79,619 | D | 33.8% | 66.0% | 33.9% | 66.1% |
| 3 | 2004 | 363,008 | 157,866 | Schultz, Dale W. | 204,856 | Kind, Ron* | 286 | 46,990 | D | 43.5% | 56.4% | 43.5% | 56.5% |
| 3 | 2002 | 208,581 | 69,955 | Arndt, Bill | 131,038 | Kind, Ron* | 7,588 | 61,083 | D | 33.5% | 62.8% | 34.8% | 65.2% |
| 4 | 2004 | 305,142 | 85,928 | Boyle, Gerald H. | 212,382 | Moore, Gwen | 6,832 | 126,454 | D | 28.2% | 69.6% | 28.8% | 71.2% |
| 4 | 2002 | 141,367 | | | 122,031 | Kleczka, Gerald D.* | 19,336 | 122,031 | D | | 86.3% | | 100.0% |

# WISCONSIN

## HOUSE OF REPRESENTATIVES

| | | Total | Republican | | Democratic | | Other | Rep.-Dem. | Percentage | | | |
| | | | | | | | | | Total Vote | | Major Vote | |
| CD | Year | Vote | Vote | Candidate | Vote | Candidate | Vote | Plurality | Rep. | Dem. | Rep. | Dem. |
|---|---|---|---|---|---|---|---|---|---|---|---|---|
| 5 | 2004 | 407,291 | 271,153 | Sensenbrenner, F. James Jr.* | 129,384 | Kennedy, Bryan | 6,754 | 141,769 R | 66.6% | 31.8% | 67.7% | 32.3% |
| 5 | 2002 | 222,012 | 191,224 | Sensenbrenner, F. James Jr.* | | | 30,788 | 191,224 R | 86.1% | | 100.0% | |
| | | | | | | | | | | | | |
| 6 | 2004 | 355,995 | 238,620 | Petri, Tom* | 107,209 | Hall, Jef | 10,166 | 131,411 R | 67.0% | 30.1% | 69.0% | 31.0% |
| 6 | 2002 | 171,161 | 169,834 | Petri, Tom* | | | 1,327 | 169,834 R | 99.2% | | 100.0% | |
| | | | | | | | | | | | | |
| 7 | 2004 | 281,752 | | | 241,306 | Obey, David R.* | 40,446 | 241,306 D | | 85.6% | | 100.0% |
| 7 | 2002 | 227,955 | 81,518 | Rothbauer, Joe | 146,364 | Obey, David R.* | 73 | 64,846 D | 35.8% | 64.2% | 35.8% | 64.2% |
| | | | | | | | | | | | | |
| 8 | 2004 | 353,725 | 248,070 | Green, Mark* | 105,513 | Le Clair, Dottie | 142 | 142,557 R | 70.1% | 29.8% | 70.2% | 29.8% |
| 8 | 2002 | 210,447 | 152,745 | Green, Mark* | 50,284 | Becker, Andrew M. | 7,418 | 102,461 R | 72.6% | 23.9% | 75.2% | 24.8% |
| | | | | | | | | | | | | |
| Total | 2004 | 2,821,613 | 1,380,819 | | 1,368,537 | | 72,257 | 12,282 R | 48.9% | 48.5% | 50.2% | 49.8% |
| Total | 2002 | 1,637,546 | 889,146 | | 676,925 | | 71,475 | 212,221 R | 54.3% | 41.3% | 56.8% | 43.2% |

An asterisk (*) denotes incumbent.

# WISCONSIN

## GENERAL AND PRIMARY ELECTIONS

## 2004 GENERAL ELECTIONS

**President**    Other vote was 16,390 Independent (Ralph Nader); 6,464 Libertarian (Michael Badnarik); 2,661 Wisconsin Green (David Cobb); 471 Independent (Walter F. Brown); 411 Independent (James Harris); 2,986 write-in.

**Senator**    Other vote was 8,367 Libertarian (Arif Khan); 6,662 Independent (Eugene Hem); 834 write-in.

**House**    Other vote was:

CD 1    4,252 Independent (Norman Aulabaugh); 2,936 Libertarian (Don Bernau); 166 write-in.
CD 2    277 write-in.
CD 3    286 write-in.
CD 4    3,733 Independent (Tim Johnson); 1,861 Independent (Robert R. Raymond); 897 Constitution (Colin Hudson); 341 write-in.
CD 5    6,549 Libertarian (Tim Peterson); 205 write-in.
CD 6    10,018 Wisconsin Green (Carol Ann Rittenhouse); 148 write-in.
CD 7    26,518 Wisconsin Green (Mike Miles); 12,841 Constitution (Larry Oftedahl); 1,087 write-in.
CD 8    142 write-in.

## 2004 PRIMARY ELECTIONS

**Primary**    February 17, 2004 (President)    No Statewide Registration
September 14, 2004 (Congress)

**Primary Type**    Open—Eligible citizens of voting age could participate in the primary of their choice.

# WISCONSIN

## GENERAL AND PRIMARY ELECTIONS

Note: An asterisk (*) denotes incumbent.

| | REPUBLICAN PRIMARIES | | | DEMOCRATIC PRIMARIES | | |
|---|---|---|---|---|---|---|
| **President** | George W. Bush* | 158,933 | 99.1% | John Kerry | 328,358 | 39.6% |
| | Uninstructed Delegation | 1,184 | 0.7% | John Edwards | 284,163 | 34.3% |
| | Write-in | 311 | 0.2% | Howard Dean | 150,845 | 18.2% |
| | | | | Dennis J. Kucinich | 27,353 | 3.3% |
| | | | | Al Sharpton | 14,701 | 1.8% |
| | | | | Wesley Clark | 12,713 | 1.5% |
| | | | | Joseph I. Lieberman | 3,929 | 0.5% |
| | | | | Lyndon H. LaRouche Jr. | 1,637 | 0.2% |
| | | | | Carol Moseley Braun | 1,590 | 0.2% |
| | | | | Richard A. Gephardt | 1,263 | 0.2% |
| | | | | Uninstructed Delegation | 1,146 | 0.1% |
| | | | | Write-in | 666 | 0.1% |
| | TOTAL | 160,428 | | TOTAL | 828,364 | |
| **Senator** | Tim Michels | 183,654 | 42.4% | Russell D. Feingold* | 251,915 | 99.7% |
| | Russ Darrow | 130,088 | 30.1% | Write-in | 862 | 0.3% |
| | Bob Welch | 99,971 | 23.1% | | | |
| | Robert Gerald Lorge | 18,809 | 4.3% | | | |
| | Write-in | 350 | 0.1% | | | |
| | TOTAL | 432,872 | | TOTAL | 252,777 | |
| **Congressional District 1** | Paul D. Ryan* | 39,935 | 99.8% | Jeffrey Chapman Thomas | 13,923 | 58.2% |
| | Write-in | 94 | 0.2% | Chet Bell | 9,966 | 41.6% |
| | | | | Write-in | 50 | 0.2% |
| | TOTAL | 40,029 | | TOTAL | 23,939 | |
| **Congressional District 2** | Dave Magnum | 26,974 | 61.3% | Tammy Baldwin* | 35,904 | 99.9% |
| | Ron Greer | 16,964 | 38.6% | Write-in | 53 | 0.1% |
| | Write-in | 38 | 0.1% | | | |
| | TOTAL | 43,976 | | TOTAL | 35,957 | |
| **Congressional District 3** | Dale W. Schultz | 38,230 | 99.8% | Ron Kind* | 29,464 | 99.7% |
| | Write-in | 92 | 0.2% | Write-in | 76 | 0.3% |
| | TOTAL | 38,322 | | TOTAL | 29,540 | |
| **Congressional District 4** | Gerald H. Boyle | 11,720 | 52.7% | Gwen Moore | 48,858 | 64.2% |
| | Corey Hoze | 10,490 | 47.1% | Matt Flynn | 19,377 | 25.5% |
| | Write-in | 44 | 0.2% | Tim Carpenter | 7,801 | 10.3% |
| | | | | Write-in | 67 | 0.1% |
| | TOTAL | 22,254 | | TOTAL | 76,103 | |
| **Congressional District 5** | F. James Sensenbrenner Jr.* | 76,179 | 99.6% | Bryan Kennedy | 17,750 | 72.6% |
| | Write-in | 328 | 0.4% | Gary Kohlenberg | 6,664 | 27.3% |
| | | | | Write-in | 39 | 0.2% |
| | TOTAL | 76,507 | | TOTAL | 24,453 | |
| **Congressional District 6** | Tom Petri* | 52,459 | 99.7% | Jef Hall | 13,754 | 99.8% |
| | Write-in | 160 | 0.3% | Write-In | 29 | 0.2% |
| | TOTAL | 52,619 | | TOTAL | 13,783 | |
| **Congressional District 7** | *No Republican candidate filed for the primary. There were 1,610 write-in votes.* | | | David R. Obey* | 29,390 | 99.9% |
| | | | | Write-in | 42 | 0.1% |
| | | | | TOTAL | 29,432 | |
| **Congressional District 8** | Mark Green* | 52,503 | 99.7% | Dottie Le Clair | 11,479 | 99.8% |
| | Write-in | 140 | 0.3% | Write-in | 25 | 0.2% |
| | TOTAL | 52,643 | | TOTAL | 11,504 | |

# WYOMING

## GOVERNOR
Dave Freudenthal (D). Elected 2002 to a four-year term.

## SENATORS (2 Republicans)
Michael B. Enzi (R). Reelected 2002 to a six-year term. Previously elected 1996.

Craig Thomas (R). Elected 2000 to a six-year term. Previously elected 1994.

## REPRESENTATIVE (1 Republican)
At Large. Barbara Cubin (R)

## POSTWAR VOTE FOR PRESIDENT

| Year | Total Vote | Republican Vote | Candidate | Democratic Vote | Candidate | Other Vote | Plurality | Rep. | Dem. | Rep. | Dem. |
|------|-----------|------|-----------|------|-----------|------|-----------|------|------|------|------|
| | | | | | | | | Total Vote | | Major Vote | |
| 2004 | 243,428 | 167,629 | Bush, George W. | 70,776 | Kerry, John | 5,023 | 96,853 R | 68.9% | 29.1% | 70.3% | 29.7% |
| 2000** | 218,351 | 147,947 | Bush, George W. | 60,481 | Gore, Al | 9,923 | 87,466 R | 67.8% | 27.7% | 71.0% | 29.0% |
| 1996** | 211,571 | 105,388 | Dole, Bob | 77,934 | Clinton, Bill | 28,249 | 27,454 R | 49.8% | 36.8% | 57.5% | 42.5% |
| 1992** | 200,598 | 79,347 | Bush, George | 68,160 | Clinton, Bill | 53,091 | 11,187 R | 39.6% | 34.0% | 53.8% | 46.2% |
| 1988 | 176,551 | 106,867 | Bush, George | 67,113 | Dukakis, Michael S. | 2,571 | 39,754 R | 60.5% | 38.0% | 61.4% | 38.6% |
| 1984 | 188,968 | 133,241 | Reagan, Ronald | 53,370 | Mondale, Walter F. | 2,357 | 79,871 R | 70.5% | 28.2% | 71.4% | 28.6% |
| 1980** | 176,713 | 110,700 | Reagan, Ronald | 49,427 | Carter, Jimmy | 16,586 | 61,273 R | 62.6% | 28.0% | 69.1% | 30.9% |
| 1976 | 156,343 | 92,717 | Ford, Gerald R. | 62,239 | Carter, Jimmy | 1,387 | 30,478 R | 59.3% | 39.8% | 59.8% | 40.2% |
| 1972 | 145,570 | 100,464 | Nixon, Richard M. | 44,358 | McGovern, George S. | 748 | 56,106 R | 69.0% | 30.5% | 69.4% | 30.6% |
| 1968** | 127,205 | 70,927 | Nixon, Richard M. | 45,173 | Humphrey, Hubert H. | 11,105 | 25,754 R | 55.8% | 35.5% | 61.1% | 38.9% |
| 1964 | 142,716 | 61,998 | Goldwater, Barry M. | 80,718 | Johnson, Lyndon B. | | 18,720 D | 43.4% | 56.6% | 43.4% | 56.6% |
| 1960 | 140,782 | 77,451 | Nixon, Richard M. | 63,331 | Kennedy, John F. | | 14,120 R | 55.0% | 45.0% | 55.0% | 45.0% |
| 1956 | 124,127 | 74,573 | Eisenhower, Dwight D. | 49,554 | Stevenson, Adlai E. | | 25,019 R | 60.1% | 39.9% | 60.1% | 39.9% |
| 1952 | 129,253 | 81,049 | Eisenhower, Dwight D. | 47,934 | Stevenson, Adlai E. | 270 | 33,115 R | 62.7% | 37.1% | 62.8% | 37.2% |
| 1948 | 101,425 | 47,947 | Dewey, Thomas E. | 52,354 | Truman, Harry S. | 1,124 | 4,407 D | 47.3% | 51.6% | 47.8% | 52.2% |

In past elections, the other vote included: 2000 - 4,625 Green (Ralph Nader); 1996 - 25,928 Reform (Ross Perot); 1992 - 51,263 Independent (Perot); 1980 - 12,072 Independent (John Anderson); 1968 - 11,105 American Independent (George Wallace).

## POSTWAR VOTE FOR GOVERNOR

| Year | Total Vote | Republican Vote | Candidate | Democratic Vote | Candidate | Other Vote | Rep.-Dem. Plurality | Rep. | Dem. | Rep. | Dem. |
|------|-----------|------|-----------|------|-----------|------|-----------|------|------|------|------|
| | | | | | | | | Total Vote | | Major Vote | |
| 2002 | 185,459 | 88,873 | Bebout, Eli | 92,662 | Freudenthal, Dave | 3,924 | 3,789 D | 47.9% | 50.0% | 49.0% | 51.0% |
| 1998 | 174,888 | 97,235 | Geringer, Jim | 70,754 | Vinich, John P. | 6,899 | 26,481 R | 55.6% | 40.5% | 57.9% | 42.1% |
| 1994 | 200,990 | 118,016 | Geringer, Jim | 80,747 | Karpan, Kathy | 2,227 | 37,269 R | 58.7% | 40.2% | 59.4% | 40.6% |
| 1990 | 160,109 | 55,471 | Mead, Mary | 104,638 | Sullivan, Mike | | 49,167 D | 34.6% | 65.4% | 34.6% | 65.4% |
| 1986 | 164,720 | 75,841 | Simpson, Peter | 88,879 | Sullivan, Mike | | 13,038 D | 46.0% | 54.0% | 46.0% | 54.0% |
| 1982 | 168,555 | 62,128 | Morton, Warren A. | 106,427 | Herschler, Ed | | 44,299 D | 36.9% | 63.1% | 36.9% | 63.1% |
| 1978 | 137,567 | 67,595 | Ostlund, John C. | 69,972 | Herschler, Ed | | 2,377 D | 49.1% | 50.9% | 49.1% | 50.9% |
| 1974 | 128,386 | 56,645 | Jones, Dick | 71,741 | Herschler, Ed | | 15,096 D | 44.1% | 55.9% | 44.1% | 55.9% |
| 1970 | 118,257 | 74,249 | Hathaway, Stan | 44,008 | Rooney, John J. | | 30,241 R | 62.8% | 37.2% | 62.8% | 37.2% |
| 1966 | 120,873 | 65,624 | Hathaway, Stan | 55,249 | Wilkerson, Ernest | | 10,375 R | 54.3% | 45.7% | 54.3% | 45.7% |
| 1962 | 119,268 | 64,970 | Hansen, Clifford P. | 54,298 | Gage, Jack R. | | 10,672 R | 54.5% | 45.5% | 54.5% | 45.5% |
| 1958 | 112,537 | 52,488 | Simpson, Milward L. | 55,070 | Hickey, J. J. | 4,979 | 2,582 D | 46.6% | 48.9% | 48.8% | 51.2% |
| 1954 | 111,438 | 56,275 | Simpson, Milward L. | 55,163 | Jack, William | | 1,112 R | 50.5% | 49.5% | 50.5% | 49.5% |
| 1950 | 96,959 | 54,441 | Barrett, Frank A. | 42,518 | McIntyre, John J. | | 11,923 R | 56.1% | 43.9% | 56.1% | 43.9% |
| 1946 | 81,353 | 38,333 | Wright, Earl | 43,020 | Hunt, Lester C. | | 4,687 D | 47.1% | 52.9% | 47.1% | 52.9% |

# WYOMING

## POSTWAR VOTE FOR SENATOR

| Year | Total Vote | Republican Vote | Republican Candidate | Democratic Vote | Democratic Candidate | Other Vote | Rep.-Dem. Plurality | Total Vote Rep. | Total Vote Dem. | Major Vote Rep. | Major Vote Dem. |
|---|---|---|---|---|---|---|---|---|---|---|---|
| 2002 | 183,280 | 133,710 | Enzi, Michael B. | 49,570 | Corcoran, Joyce Jansa | | 84,140 R | 73.0% | 27.0% | 73.0% | 27.0% |
| 2000 | 213,659 | 157,622 | Thomas, Craig | 47,087 | Logan, Mel | 8,950 | 110,535 R | 73.8% | 22.0% | 77.0% | 23.0% |
| 1996 | 211,077 | 114,116 | Enzi, Michael B. | 89,103 | Karpan, Kathy | 7,858 | 25,013 R | 54.1% | 42.2% | 56.2% | 43.8% |
| 1994 | 201,710 | 118,754 | Thomas, Craig | 79,287 | Sullivan, Mike | 3,669 | 39,467 R | 58.9% | 39.3% | 60.0% | 40.0% |
| 1990 | 157,632 | 100,784 | Simpson, Alan K. | 56,848 | Helling, Kathy | | 43,936 R | 63.9% | 36.1% | 63.9% | 36.1% |
| 1988 | 180,964 | 91,143 | Wallop, Malcolm | 89,821 | Vinich, John P. | | 1,322 R | 50.4% | 49.6% | 50.4% | 49.6% |
| 1984 | 186,898 | 146,373 | Simpson, Alan K. | 40,525 | Ryan, Victor A. | | 105,848 R | 78.3% | 21.7% | 78.3% | 21.7% |
| 1982 | 167,191 | 94,725 | Wallop, Malcolm | 72,466 | McDaniel, Rodger | | 22,259 R | 56.7% | 43.3% | 56.7% | 43.3% |
| 1978 | 133,364 | 82,908 | Simpson, Alan K. | 50,456 | Whitaker, Raymond B. | | 32,452 R | 62.2% | 37.8% | 62.2% | 37.8% |
| 1976 | 155,368 | 84,810 | Wallop, Malcolm | 70,558 | McGee, Gale | | 14,252 R | 54.6% | 45.4% | 54.6% | 45.4% |
| 1972 | 142,067 | 101,314 | Hansen, Clifford P. | 40,753 | Vinich, Mike | | 60,561 R | 71.3% | 28.7% | 71.3% | 28.7% |
| 1970 | 120,486 | 53,279 | Wold, John S. | 67,207 | McGee, Gale | | 13,928 D | 44.2% | 55.8% | 44.2% | 55.8% |
| 1966 | 122,689 | 63,548 | Hansen, Clifford P. | 59,141 | Roncalio, Teno | | 4,407 R | 51.8% | 48.2% | 51.8% | 48.2% |
| 1964 | 141,670 | 65,185 | Wold, John S. | 76,485 | McGee, Gale | | 11,300 D | 46.0% | 54.0% | 46.0% | 54.0% |
| 1962S | 119,372 | 69,043 | Simpson, Milward L. | 50,329 | Hickey, J. J. | | 18,714 R | 57.8% | 42.2% | 57.8% | 42.2% |
| 1960 | 138,550 | 78,103 | Thomson, E. Keith | 60,447 | Whitaker, Ray | | 17,656 R | 56.4% | 43.6% | 56.4% | 43.6% |
| 1958 | 114,157 | 56,122 | Barrett, Frank A. | 58,035 | McGee, Gale | | 1,913 D | 49.2% | 50.8% | 49.2% | 50.8% |
| 1954 | 112,252 | 54,407 | Harrison, William H. | 57,845 | O'Mahoney, Joseph C. | | 3,438 D | 48.5% | 51.5% | 48.5% | 51.5% |
| 1952 | 130,097 | 67,176 | Barrett, Frank A. | 62,921 | O'Mahoney, Joseph C. | | 4,255 R | 51.6% | 48.4% | 51.6% | 48.4% |
| 1948 | 101,480 | 43,527 | Robertson, Edward V. | 57,953 | Hunt, Lester C. | | 14,426 D | 42.9% | 57.1% | 42.9% | 57.1% |
| 1946 | 81,557 | 35,714 | Henderson, Harry B. | 45,843 | O'Mahoney, Joseph C. | | 10,129 D | 43.8% | 56.2% | 43.8% | 56.2% |

The 1962 election was for a short term to fill a vacancy.

# WYOMING

One member At Large

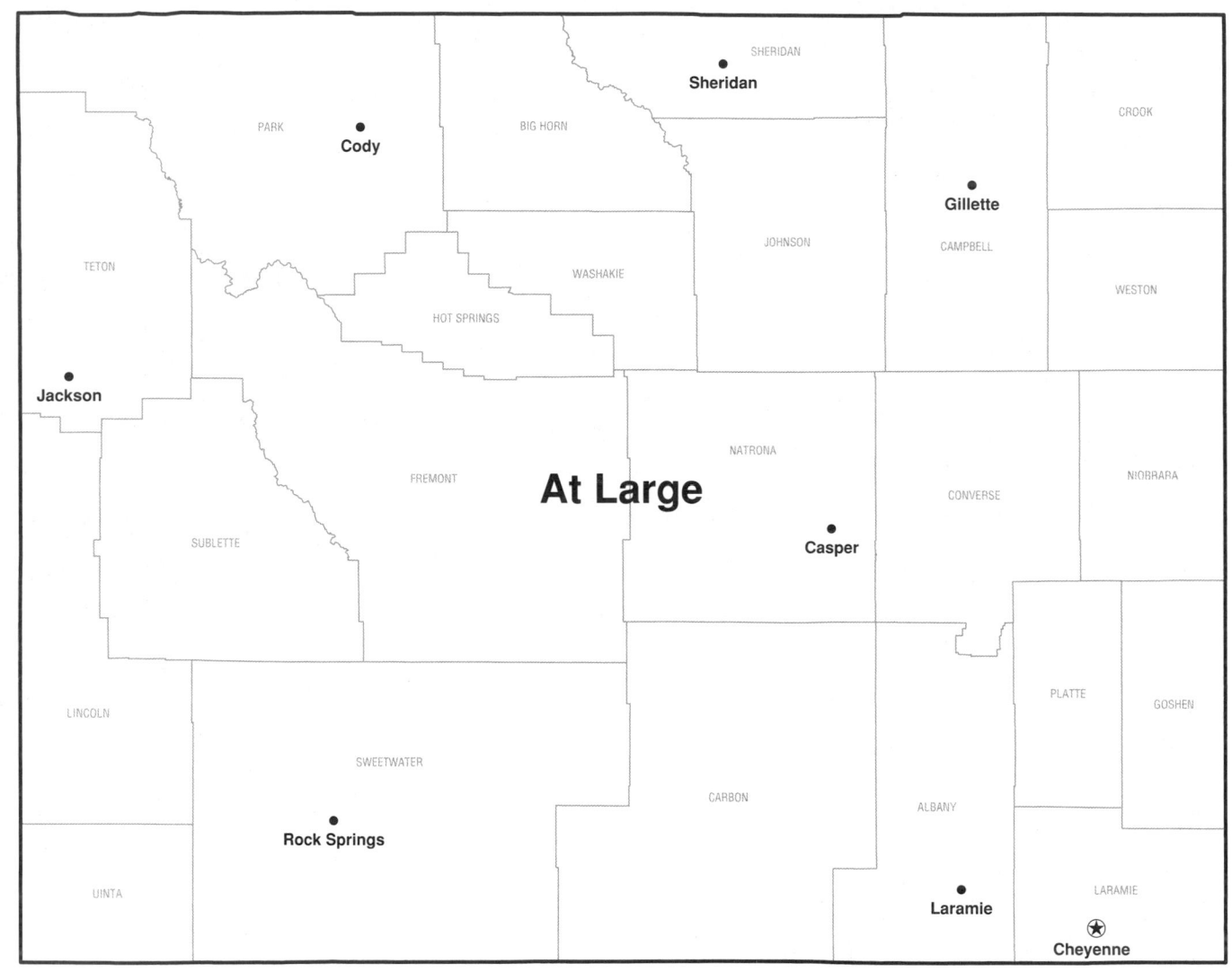

# WYOMING

## PRESIDENT 2004

| 2000 Census Population | County | Total Vote | Republican | Democratic | Other | Rep.-Dem. Plurality | Total Vote Rep. | Total Vote Dem. | Major Vote Rep. | Major Vote Dem. |
|---|---|---|---|---|---|---|---|---|---|---|
| 32,014 | ALBANY | 16,624 | 9,006 | 7,117 | 501 | 1,889 R | 54.2% | 42.8% | 55.9% | 44.1% |
| 11,461 | BIG HORN | 5,283 | 4,232 | 960 | 91 | 3,272 R | 80.1% | 18.2% | 81.5% | 18.5% |
| 33,698 | CAMPBELL | 15,099 | 12,415 | 2,464 | 220 | 9,951 R | 82.2% | 16.3% | 83.4% | 16.6% |
| 15,639 | CARBON | 7,077 | 4,758 | 2,158 | 161 | 2,600 R | 67.2% | 30.5% | 68.8% | 31.2% |
| 12,052 | CONVERSE | 5,725 | 4,447 | 1,184 | 94 | 3,263 R | 77.7% | 20.7% | 79.0% | 21.0% |
| 5,887 | CROOK | 3,396 | 2,836 | 501 | 59 | 2,335 R | 83.5% | 14.8% | 85.0% | 15.0% |
| 35,804 | FREMONT | 17,096 | 11,429 | 5,338 | 329 | 6,091 R | 66.9% | 31.2% | 68.2% | 31.8% |
| 12,538 | GOSHEN | 5,779 | 4,114 | 1,566 | 99 | 2,548 R | 71.2% | 27.1% | 72.4% | 27.6% |
| 4,882 | HOT SPRINGS | 2,480 | 1,812 | 623 | 45 | 1,189 R | 73.1% | 25.1% | 74.4% | 25.6% |
| 7,075 | JOHNSON | 3,991 | 3,231 | 676 | 84 | 2,555 R | 81.0% | 16.9% | 82.7% | 17.3% |
| 81,607 | LARAMIE | 39,879 | 25,951 | 13,171 | 757 | 12,780 R | 65.1% | 33.0% | 66.3% | 33.7% |
| 14,573 | LINCOLN | 7,914 | 6,423 | 1,364 | 127 | 5,059 R | 81.2% | 17.2% | 82.5% | 17.5% |
| 66,533 | NATRONA | 32,068 | 21,512 | 9,863 | 693 | 11,649 R | 67.1% | 30.8% | 68.6% | 31.4% |
| 2,407 | NIOBRARA | 1,314 | 1,064 | 230 | 20 | 834 R | 81.0% | 17.5% | 82.2% | 17.8% |
| 25,786 | PARK | 14,231 | 10,917 | 3,007 | 307 | 7,910 R | 76.7% | 21.1% | 78.4% | 21.6% |
| 8,807 | PLATTE | 4,574 | 3,149 | 1,328 | 97 | 1,821 R | 68.8% | 29.0% | 70.3% | 29.7% |
| 26,560 | SHERIDAN | 14,029 | 9,689 | 4,066 | 274 | 5,623 R | 69.1% | 29.0% | 70.4% | 29.6% |
| 5,920 | SUBLETTE | 3,651 | 2,847 | 730 | 74 | 2,117 R | 78.0% | 20.0% | 79.6% | 20.4% |
| 37,613 | SWEETWATER | 16,272 | 10,653 | 5,208 | 411 | 5,445 R | 65.5% | 32.0% | 67.2% | 32.8% |
| 18,251 | TETON | 11,359 | 5,124 | 5,972 | 263 | 848 D | 45.1% | 52.6% | 46.2% | 53.8% |
| 19,742 | UINTA | 8,081 | 6,081 | 1,815 | 185 | 4,266 R | 75.3% | 22.5% | 77.0% | 23.0% |
| 8,289 | WASHAKIE | 4,114 | 3,200 | 855 | 59 | 2,345 R | 77.8% | 20.8% | 78.9% | 21.1% |
| 6,644 | WESTON | 3,392 | 2,739 | 580 | 73 | 2,159 R | 80.7% | 17.1% | 82.5% | 17.5% |
| 493,782 | TOTAL | 243,428 | 167,629 | 70,776 | 5,023 | 96,853 R | 68.9% | 29.1% | 70.3% | 29.7% |

# WYOMING

## HOUSE OF REPRESENTATIVES

| CD | Year | Total Vote | Republican Vote | Republican Candidate | Democratic Vote | Democratic Candidate | Other Vote | Rep.-Dem. Plurality | Total Vote Rep. | Total Vote Dem. | Major Vote Rep. | Major Vote Dem. |
|---|---|---|---|---|---|---|---|---|---|---|---|---|
| AL | 2004 | 239,034 | 132,107 | Cubin, Barbara* | 99,989 | Ladd, Ted | 6,938 | 32,118 R | 55.3% | 41.8% | 56.9% | 43.1% |
| AL | 2002 | 182,152 | 110,229 | Cubin, Barbara* | 65,961 | Akin, Ron | 5,962 | 44,268 R | 60.5% | 36.2% | 62.6% | 37.4% |
| AL | 2000 | 212,312 | 141,848 | Cubin, Barbara* | 60,638 | Green, Michael Allen | 9,826 | 81,210 R | 66.8% | 28.6% | 70.1% | 29.9% |
| AL | 1998 | 174,219 | 100,687 | Cubin, Barbara* | 67,399 | Farris, Scott | 6,133 | 33,288 R | 57.8% | 38.7% | 59.9% | 40.1% |
| AL | 1996 | 209,983 | 116,004 | Cubin, Barbara* | 85,724 | Maxfield, Pete | 8,255 | 30,280 R | 55.2% | 40.8% | 57.5% | 42.5% |
| AL | 1994 | 196,197 | 104,426 | Cubin, Barbara | 81,022 | Schuster, Bob | 10,749 | 23,404 R | 53.2% | 41.3% | 56.3% | 43.7% |
| AL | 1992 | 196,977 | 113,882 | Thomas, Craig* | 77,418 | Herschler, Jon | 5,677 | 36,464 R | 57.8% | 39.3% | 59.5% | 40.5% |
| AL | 1990 | 158,055 | 87,078 | Thomas, Craig* | 70,977 | Maxfield, Pete | | 16,101 R | 55.1% | 44.9% | 55.1% | 44.9% |
| AL | 1988 | 177,651 | 118,350 | Cheney, Richard* | 56,527 | Sharratt, Bryan | 2,774 | 61,823 R | 66.6% | 31.8% | 67.7% | 32.3% |
| AL | 1986 | 159,787 | 111,007 | Cheney, Richard* | 48,780 | Gilmore, Rick | | 62,227 R | 69.5% | 30.5% | 69.5% | 30.5% |
| AL | 1984 | 187,904 | 138,234 | Cheney, Richard* | 45,857 | McFadden, Hugh B. | 3,813 | 92,377 R | 73.6% | 24.4% | 75.1% | 24.9% |
| AL | 1982 | 159,277 | 113,236 | Cheney, Richard* | 46,041 | Hommel, Theodore H. | | 67,195 R | 71.1% | 28.9% | 71.1% | 28.9% |
| AL | 1980 | 169,699 | 116,361 | Cheney, Richard* | 53,338 | Rogers, Jim | | 63,023 R | 68.6% | 31.4% | 68.6% | 31.4% |
| AL | 1978 | 129,377 | 75,855 | Cheney, Richard | 53,522 | Bagley, Bill | | 22,333 R | 58.6% | 41.4% | 58.6% | 41.4% |
| AL | 1976 | 151,868 | 66,147 | Hart, Larry | 85,721 | Roncalio, Teno* | | 19,574 D | 43.6% | 56.4% | 43.6% | 56.4% |
| AL | 1974 | 126,933 | 57,499 | Strook, Tom | 69,434 | Roncalio, Teno* | | 11,935 D | 45.3% | 54.7% | 45.3% | 54.7% |
| AL | 1972 | 146,299 | 70,667 | Kidd, William | 75,632 | Roncalio, Teno* | | 4,965 D | 48.3% | 51.7% | 48.3% | 51.7% |
| AL | 1970 | 116,304 | 57,848 | Roberts, Harry | 58,456 | Roncalio, Teno | | 608 D | 49.7% | 50.3% | 49.7% | 50.3% |
| AL | 1968 | 123,313 | 77,363 | Wold, John S. | 45,950 | Linford, Velma | | 31,413 R | 62.7% | 37.3% | 62.7% | 37.3% |
| AL | 1966 | 119,426 | 62,984 | Harrison, William H.* | 56,442 | Christian, Al | | 6,542 R | 52.7% | 47.3% | 52.7% | 47.3% |
| AL | 1964 | 139,175 | 68,482 | Harrison, William H.* | 70,693 | Roncalio, Teno | | 2,211 D | 49.2% | 50.8% | 49.2% | 50.8% |
| AL | 1962 | 116,474 | 71,489 | Harrison, William H.* | 44,985 | Mankus, Louis A. | | 26,504 R | 61.4% | 38.6% | 61.4% | 38.6% |
| AL | 1960 | 134,331 | 70,241 | Harrison, William H. | 64,090 | Armstong, H.T. | | 6,151 R | 52.3% | 47.7% | 52.3% | 47.7% |
| AL | 1958 | 111,780 | 59,894 | Thomson, E. Keith* | 51,886 | Whitaker, Ray | | 8,008 R | 53.6% | 46.4% | 53.6% | 46.4% |

# WYOMING

## HOUSE OF REPRESENTATIVES

| | | Total | Republican | | Democratic | | Other | Rep.-Dem. | Percentage | | | |
|---|---|---|---|---|---|---|---|---|---|---|---|---|
| | | | | | | | | | Total Vote | | Major Vote | |
| CD | Year | Vote | Vote | Candidate | Vote | Candidate | Vote | Plurality | Rep. | Dem. | Rep. | Dem. |
| AL | 1956 | 120,128 | 69,903 | Thomson, E. Keith* | 50,225 | O'Callaghan, Jerry | | 19,678 R | 58.2% | 41.8% | 58.2% | 41.8% |
| AL | 1954 | 108,771 | 61,111 | Thomson, E. Keith | 47,660 | Tully, Sam | | 13,451 R | 56.2% | 43.8% | 56.2% | 43.8% |
| AL | 1952 | 126,720 | 76,161 | Harrison, William H.* | 50,559 | Rose, Robert R. | | 25,602 R | 60.1% | 39.9% | 60.1% | 39.9% |
| AL | 1950 | 93,348 | 50,865 | Harrison, William H. | 42,483 | Clark, John B. | | 8,382 R | 54.5% | 45.5% | 54.5% | 45.5% |
| AL | 1948 | 97,464 | 50,218 | Barrett, Frank A.* | 47,246 | Flannery, L. G. | | 2,972 R | 51.5% | 48.5% | 51.5% | 48.5% |
| AL | 1946 | 79,438 | 44,482 | Barrett, Frank A.* | 34,956 | McIntyre, John J. | | 9,526 R | 56.0% | 44.0% | 56.0% | 44.0% |

An asterisk (*) denotes incumbent.

# WYOMING

## GENERAL AND PRIMARY ELECTIONS

## 2004 GENERAL ELECTIONS

**President**  Other vote was 2,741 Independent (Ralph Nader); 1,171 Libertarian (Michael Badnarik); 631 Independent (Michael Peroutka); 480 write-in.

**House**  Other vote was:

At Large  6,581 Libertarian (Lewis Stock); 357 write-in.

## 2004 PRIMARY ELECTIONS

**Primary**  August 17, 2004

| Registration (as of Aug. 6, 2004) | | |
|---|---|---|
| Republican | 133,044 |
| Democratic | 59,265 |
| Libertarian | 276 |
| Natural Law | 20 |
| Wyoming Reform | 6 |
| Other | 22,763 |
| TOTAL | 215,374 |

## 2004 PRIMARY ELECTIONS

**Primary Type**  Only registered Democrats and Republicans could vote in their party's primary, although on primary day any new voter could register with the party of their choice and any previously registered voter could participate in another party's primary by changing their registration to that party.

Note:  An asterisk (*) denotes incumbent.

| | REPUBLICAN PRIMARIES | | | DEMOCRATIC PRIMARIES | | |
|---|---|---|---|---|---|---|
| House | Barbara Cubin* | 45,433 | 55.0% | Ted Ladd | 14,716 | 47.8% |
| At Large | Bruce S. Asay | 20,332 | 24.6% | John L. Henley | 13,208 | 42.9% |
| | Cale Case | 13,104 | 15.9% | Al Hamburg | 2,845 | 9.2% |
| | Marvin "Trip" Applequist | 2,352 | 2.8% | | | |
| | James "Jim" Altebaumer | 1,374 | 1.7% | | | |
| | TOTAL | 82,595 | | TOTAL | 30,769 | |

# DISTRICT OF COLUMBIA

## DELEGATE

Eleanor Holmes Norton (D). Reelected 2004 to a two-year term. Previously elected 2002, 2000, 1998, 1996, 1994, 1992, 1990.

## POSTWAR VOTE FOR PRESIDENT

| Year | Total Vote | Republican Vote | Republican Candidate | Democratic Vote | Democratic Candidate | Other Vote | Plurality | Percentage Total Vote Rep. | Percentage Total Vote Dem. | Percentage Major Vote Rep. | Percentage Major Vote Dem. |
|------|-----------|-----------------|----------------------|-----------------|----------------------|-----------|-----------|------|------|------|------|
| 2004 | 227,586 | 21,256 | Bush, George W. | 202,970 | Kerry, John | 3,360 | 181,714 D | 9.3% | 89.2% | 9.5% | 90.5% |
| 2000** | 201,894 | 18,073 | Bush, George W. | 171,923 | Gore, Al | 11,898 | 153,850 D | 9.0% | 85.2% | 9.5% | 90.5% |
| 1996** | 185,726 | 17,339 | Dole, Bob | 158,220 | Clinton, Bill | 10,167 | 140,881 D | 9.3% | 85.2% | 9.9% | 90.1% |
| 1992** | 227,572 | 20,698 | Bush, George | 192,619 | Clinton, Bill | 14,255 | 171,921 D | 9.1% | 84.6% | 9.7% | 90.3% |
| 1988 | 192,877 | 27,590 | Bush, George | 159,407 | Dukakis, Michael S. | 5,880 | 131,817 D | 14.3% | 82.6% | 14.8% | 85.2% |
| 1984 | 211,288 | 29,009 | Reagan, Ronald | 180,408 | Mondale, Walter F. | 1,871 | 151,399 D | 13.7% | 85.4% | 13.9% | 86.1% |
| 1980** | 175,237 | 23,545 | Reagan, Ronald | 131,113 | Carter, Jimmy | 20,579 | 107,568 D | 13.4% | 74.8% | 15.2% | 84.8% |
| 1976 | 168,830 | 27,873 | Ford, Gerald R. | 137,818 | Carter, Jimmy | 3,139 | 109,945 D | 16.5% | 81.6% | 16.8% | 83.2% |
| 1972 | 163,421 | 35,226 | Nixon, Richard M. | 127,627 | McGovern, George S. | 568 | 92,401 D | 21.6% | 78.1% | 21.6% | 78.4% |
| 1968 | 170,578 | 31,012 | Nixon, Richard M. | 139,566 | Humphrey, Hubert H. | | 108,554 D | 18.2% | 81.8% | 18.2% | 81.8% |
| 1964** | 198,597 | 28,801 | Goldwater, Barry M. | 169,796 | Johnson, Lyndon B. | | 140,995 D | 14.5% | 85.5% | 14.5% | 85.5% |

In past elections, the other vote included: 2000 - 10,576 Green (Ralph Nader); 1996 - 3,611 Reform (Ross Perot); 1992 - 9,681 Independent (Perot); 1980 - 16,337 Independent (John Anderson). Under the 23rd Amendment to the Constitution, the District of Columbia became entitled to choose Electors beginning with the 1964 election.

## POSTWAR VOTE FOR DELEGATE

| Year | Total Vote | Republican Vote | Republican Candidate | Democratic Vote | Democratic Candidate | Other Vote | Rep.-Dem. Plurality | Percentage Total Vote Rep. | Percentage Total Vote Dem. | Percentage Major Vote Rep. | Percentage Major Vote Dem. |
|------|-----------|-----------------|----------------------|-----------------|----------------------|-----------|---------------------|------|------|------|------|
| 2004 | 221,213 | 18,296 | Monroe, Michael Andrew | 202,027 | Norton, Eleanor Holmes | 890 | 183,731 D | 8.3% | 91.3% | 8.3% | 91.7% |
| 2002 | 128,233 | | — | 119,268 | Norton, Eleanor Holmes | 8,965 | 119,268 D | | 93.0% | | 100.0% |
| 2000 | 175,631 | 10,258 | Wolterbeek, Edward | 158,824 | Norton, Eleanor Holmes | 6,549 | 148,566 D | 5.8% | 90.4% | 6.1% | 93.9% |
| 1998 | 136,359 | 8,610 | Wolterbeek, Edward | 122,228 | Norton, Eleanor Holmes | 5,221 | 113,618 D | 6.3% | 89.6% | 6.6% | 93.4% |
| 1996 | 149,998 | 11,306 | Simonds, Sprague | 134,996 | Norton, Eleanor Holmes | 3,696 | 123,690 D | 7.5% | 90.0% | 7.7% | 92.3% |
| 1994 | 173,664 | 13,828 | Saltz, Donald | 154,988 | Norton, Eleanor Holmes | 4,848 | 141,160 D | 8.0% | 89.2% | 8.2% | 91.8% |
| 1992 | 196,754 | 20,108 | Emerson, Susan | 166,808 | Norton, Eleanor Holmes | 9,838 | 146,700 D | 10.2% | 84.8% | 10.8% | 89.2% |
| 1990 | 159,627 | 41,999 | Singleton, Harry M. | 98,442 | Norton, Eleanor Holmes | 19,186 | 56,443 D | 26.3% | 61.7% | 29.9% | 70.1% |
| 1988 | 170,933 | 22,936 | Reed, William | 121,817 | Fauntroy, Walter E. | 26,180 | 98,881 D | 13.4% | 71.3% | 15.8% | 84.2% |
| 1986 | 126,855 | 17,643 | King, Mary L. H. | 101,604 | Fauntroy, Walter F. | 7,608 | 83,961 D | 13.9% | 80.1% | 14.8% | 85.2% |
| 1984** | 161,771 | | — | 154,583 | Fauntroy, Walter E. | 7,188 | 154,583 D | | 95.6% | | 100.0% |
| 1982 | 112,543 | 17,242 | West, John | 93,422 | Fauntroy, Walter E. | 1,879 | 76,180 D | 15.3% | 83.0% | 15.6% | 84.4% |
| 1980 | 151,046 | 21,245 | Roehr, Robert J. | 112,339 | Fauntroy, Walter E. | 17,462 | 91,094 D | 14.1% | 74.4% | 15.9% | 84.1% |
| 1978 | 96,306 | 11,677 | Champion, Jackson R. | 76,557 | Fauntroy, Walter E. | 8,072 | 64,880 D | 12.1% | 79.5% | 13.2% | 86.8% |
| 1976 | 159,790 | 21,699 | Hall, Daniel L. | 123,464 | Fauntroy, Walter E. | 14,627 | 101,765 D | 13.6% | 77.3% | 14.9% | 85.1% |
| 1974 | 104,014 | 9,166 | Phillips, William R. | 66,337 | Fauntroy, Walter E. | 28,511 | 57,171 D | 8.8% | 63.8% | 12.1% | 87.9% |
| 1972 | 159,612 | 39,487 | Chin-Lee, William | 95,300 | Fauntroy, Walter E. | 24,825 | 55,813 D | 24.7% | 59.7% | 29.3% | 70.7% |
| 1971S | 116,635 | 29,249 | Nevius, John A. | 68,166 | Fauntroy, Walter E. | 19,220 | 38,917 D | 25.1% | 58.4% | 30.0% | 70.0% |

In 1984 the Democratic candidate was also the nominee of the Republican and Statehood parties. The 1971 election was held in March for a short term to the end of the 92nd Congress.

# DISTRICT OF COLUMBIA

# DISTRICT OF COLUMBIA

## PRESIDENT 2004

| 2000 Census Population | Ward | Total Vote | Republican | Democratic | Other | Rep.-Dem. Plurality | Percentage | | | |
|---|---|---|---|---|---|---|---|---|---|---|
| | | | | | | | Total Vote | | Major Vote | |
| | | | | | | | Rep. | Dem. | Rep. | Dem. |
| 73,364 | Ward 1 | 26,096 | 1,751 | 23,727 | 618 | 21,976 D | 6.7% | 90.9% | 6.9% | 93.1% |
| 68,869 | Ward 2 | 24,933 | 3,713 | 20,691 | 529 | 16,978 D | 14.9% | 83.0% | 15.2% | 84.8% |
| 73,718 | Ward 3 | 35,993 | 6,953 | 28,358 | 682 | 21,405 D | 19.3% | 78.8% | 19.7% | 80.3% |
| 74,092 | Ward 4 | 32,849 | 2,156 | 30,341 | 352 | 28,185 D | 6.6% | 92.4% | 6.6% | 93.4% |
| 72,527 | Ward 5 | 29,177 | 1,520 | 27,348 | 309 | 25,828 D | 5.2% | 93.7% | 5.3% | 94.7% |
| 68,035 | Ward 6 | 29,531 | 3,339 | 25,654 | 538 | 22,315 D | 11.3% | 86.9% | 11.5% | 88.5% |
| 70,540 | Ward 7 | 27,112 | 1,006 | 25,914 | 192 | 24,908 D | 3.7% | 95.6% | 3.7% | 96.3% |
| 70,914 | Ward 8 | 20,683 | 689 | 19,872 | 122 | 19,183 D | 3.3% | 96.1% | 3.4% | 96.6% |
| | Federal Ballots | 1,212 | 129 | 1,065 | 18 | 936 D | 10.6% | 87.9% | 10.8% | 89.2% |
| 572,059 | TOTAL | 227,586 | 21,256 | 202,970 | 3,360 | 181,714 D | 9.3% | 89.2% | 9.5% | 90.5% |

Note: Federal ballots were for president only, were basically cast as absentee votes, and were not attributed to any particular ward.

# DISTRICT OF COLUMBIA

## GENERAL ELECTIONS

## 2004 GENERAL ELECTIONS

**President**  Other vote was 1,485 Independent (Ralph Nader); 737 D.C. Statehood Green (David Cobb); 502 Libertarian (Michael Badnarik); 130 Socialist Workers (James Harris); 506 write-in.

**Delegate**  Other vote was 890 write-in.